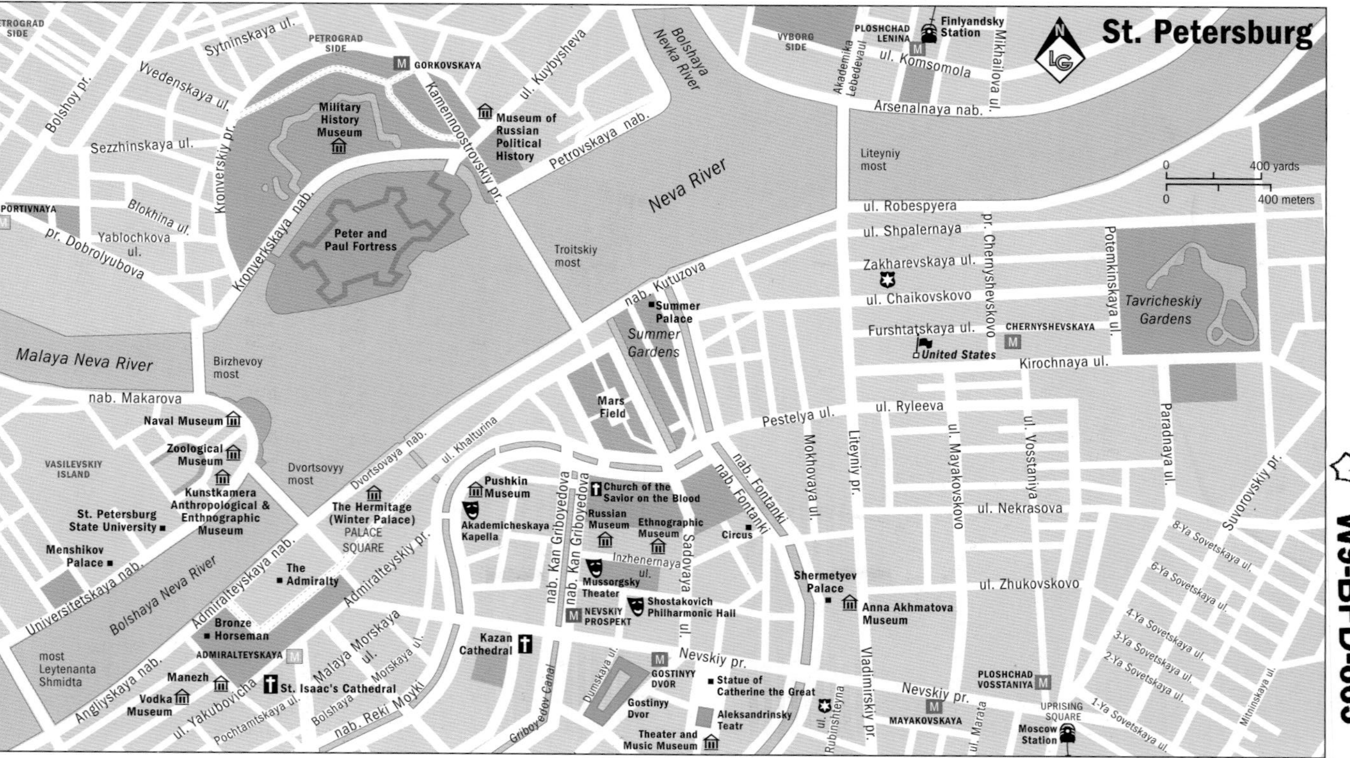
St. Petersburg
LG
N
0
400 yards
0
400 meters
PETROGRAD SIDE
Sytninskaya ul.
PETROGRAD SIDE
GORKOVSKAYA
Bolshoy pr.
Vvedenskaya ul.
ul. Kuybysheva
Bolshaya Nevka River
VYBORG SIDE
PLOSHCHAD LENINA
Finlyandsky Station
Akademika Lebedevaul
ul. Komsomola
Mikhailova ul.
Arsenalnaya nab.
Military History Museum
Kamennoostrovskiy pr.
Museum of Russian Political History
Petrovskaya nab.
Sezzhinskaya ul.
Kronverskiy pr.
Neva River
Liteyniy most
SPORTIVNAYA
Blokhina ul.
Yablochkova ul.
pr. Dobrolyubova
Kronverkskaya nab.
Peter and Paul Fortress
Troitskiy most
ul. Robespyera
ul. Shpalernaya
Zakharevskaya ul.
ul. Chaikovskovo
Furshtatskaya ul.
United States
pr. Chernyshevskovo
CHERNYSHEVSKAYA
Potemkinskaya ul.
Tavricheskiy Gardens
Kirochnaya ul.
Malaya Neva River
Birzhevoy most
nab. Kutuzova
Summer Palace
Summer Gardens
nab. Makarova
Naval Museum
Mars Field
Pestelya ul.
ul. Ryleeva
Paradnaya ul.
Zoological Museum
Dvortsovyy most
Dvortsovaya nab.
ul. Khalturina
VASILEVSKIY ISLAND
Kunstkamera Anthropological & Enthnographic Museum
The Hermitage (Winter Palace)
PALACE SQUARE
Pushkin Museum
Akademicheskaya Kapella
nab. Kan Griboyedova
nab. Kan Griboyedova
Church of the Savior on the Blood
Russian Museum
Ethnographic Museum
Inzhenernaya ul.
Sadovaya ul.
nab. Fontanki
nab. Fontanki
Circus
Mokhovaya ul.
Liteyniy pr.
ul. Mayakovskovo
ul. Vosstaniya
ul. Nekrasova
Suvorovskiy pr.
St. Petersburg State University
Menshikov Palace
Universitetskaya nab.
Bolshaya Neva River
Admiralteyskaya nab.
The Admiralty
Admiralteyskiy pr.
Mussorgsky Theater
Shostakovich Philharmonic Hall
NEVSKIY PROSPEKT
Shermetyev Palace
Anna Akhmatova Museum
ul. Zhukovskovo
8-Ya Sovetskaya ul.
6-Ya Sovetskaya ul.
4-Ya Sovetskaya ul.
3-Ya Sovetskaya ul.
2-Ya Sovetskaya ul.
1-Ya Sovetskaya ul.
Mitninskaya ul.
Bronze Horseman
ADMIRALTEYSKAYA
most Leytenanta Shmidta
Angliyskaya nab.
Manezh
Vodka Museum
ul. Yakubovicha
St. Isaac's Cathedral
Malaya Morskaya ul.
Bolshaya Morskaya ul.
Pochtamtskaya ul.
nab. Reki Moyki
Kazan Cathedral
Griboyedov Canal
Dumskaya ul.
Nevskiy pr.
GOSTINYY DVOR
Gostinyy Dvor
Statue of Catherine the Great
Aleksandrinsky Teatr
Theater and Music Museum
ul. Rubinshteyna
Vladimirskiy pr.
Nevskiy pr.
MAYAKOVSKAYA
ul. Marata
PLOSHCHAD VOSSTANIYA
UPRISING SQUARE
Moscow Station

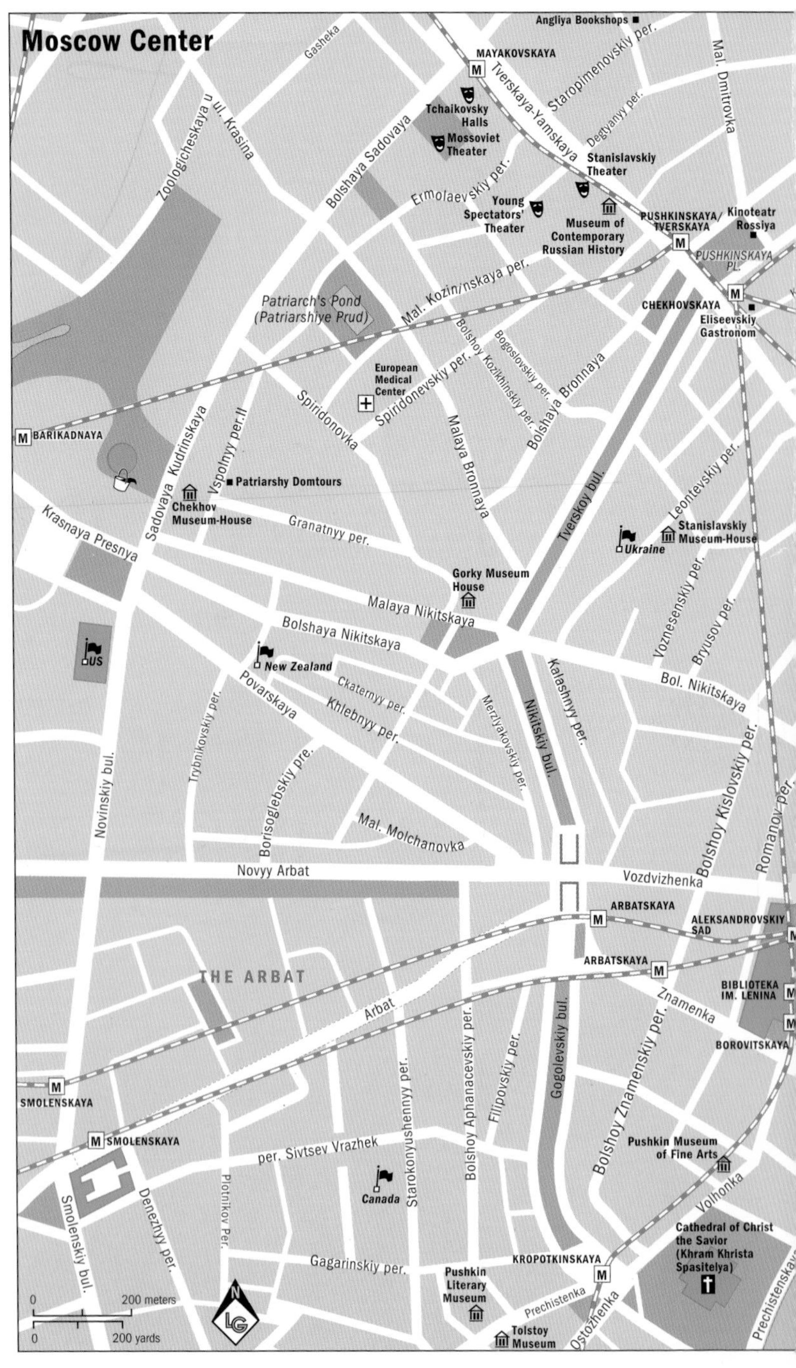
Moscow Center
Angliya Bookshops
MAYAKOVSKAYA
Tverskaya-Yamskaya
Staropimenovskiy per.
Mal. Dmitrovka
Degtyanyy per.
Gasheka
Tchaikovsky Halls
Mossoviet Theater
Stanislavskiy Theater
Zoologicheskaya u
ul. Krasina
Bolshaya Sadovaya
Ermolaevskiy per.
Young Spectators' Theater
Museum of Contemporary Russian History
PUSHKINSKAYA/ TVERSKAYA
Kinoteatr Rossiya
PUSHKINSKAYA PL.
Patriarch's Pond (Patriarshiye Prud)
Mal. Kozininskaya per.
CHEKHOVSKAYA
Eliseevskiy Gastronom
Bolshoy Kozikhinskiy per.
Bogoslovskiy per.
European Medical Center
Spiridonevskiy per.
Bolshaya Bronnaya
Spiridonovka
Malaya Bronnaya
BARIKADNAYA
Sadovaya Kudrinskaya
Vspolnyy per.
Patriarshy Domtours
Chekhov Museum-House
Granatnyy per.
Tverskoy bul.
Leontevskiy per.
Stanislavskiy Museum-House
Ukraine
Krasnaya Presnya
Gorky Museum House
Malaya Nikitskaya
Bolshaya Nikitskaya
US
New Zealand
Voznesenskiy per.
Bryusov per.
Kalashnyy per.
Bol. Nikitskaya
Povarskaya
Ckaternyy per.
Khlebnyy per.
Merzlyakovskiy per.
Nikitskiy bul.
Trybnikovskiy per.
Borisoglebskiy pre.
Novinskiy bul.
Mal. Molchanovka
Bolshoy Kislovskiy per.
Romanov per.
Novyy Arbat
Vozdvizhenka
ARBATSKAYA
ALEKSANDROVSKIY SAD
THE ARBAT
ARBATSKAYA
BIBLIOTEKA IM. LENINA
Znamenka
Arbat
BOROVITSKAYA
Bolshoy Aphanacevskiy per.
Filipovskiy per.
Gogolevskiy bul.
Bolshoy Znamenskiy per.
SMOLENSKAYA
Starokonyushennyy per.
SMOLENSKAYA
per. Sivtsev Vrazhek
Pushkin Museum of Fine Arts
Volhonka
Canada
Plotnikov Per.
Smolenskiy bul.
Denezhyy per.
Cathedral of Christ the Savior (Khram Khrista Spasitelya)
Gagarinskiy per.
KROPOTKINSKAYA
Pushkin Literary Museum
Prechistenka
Ostozhenka
Prechistenka
Tolstoy Museum
0
200 meters
0
200 yards
N
LG

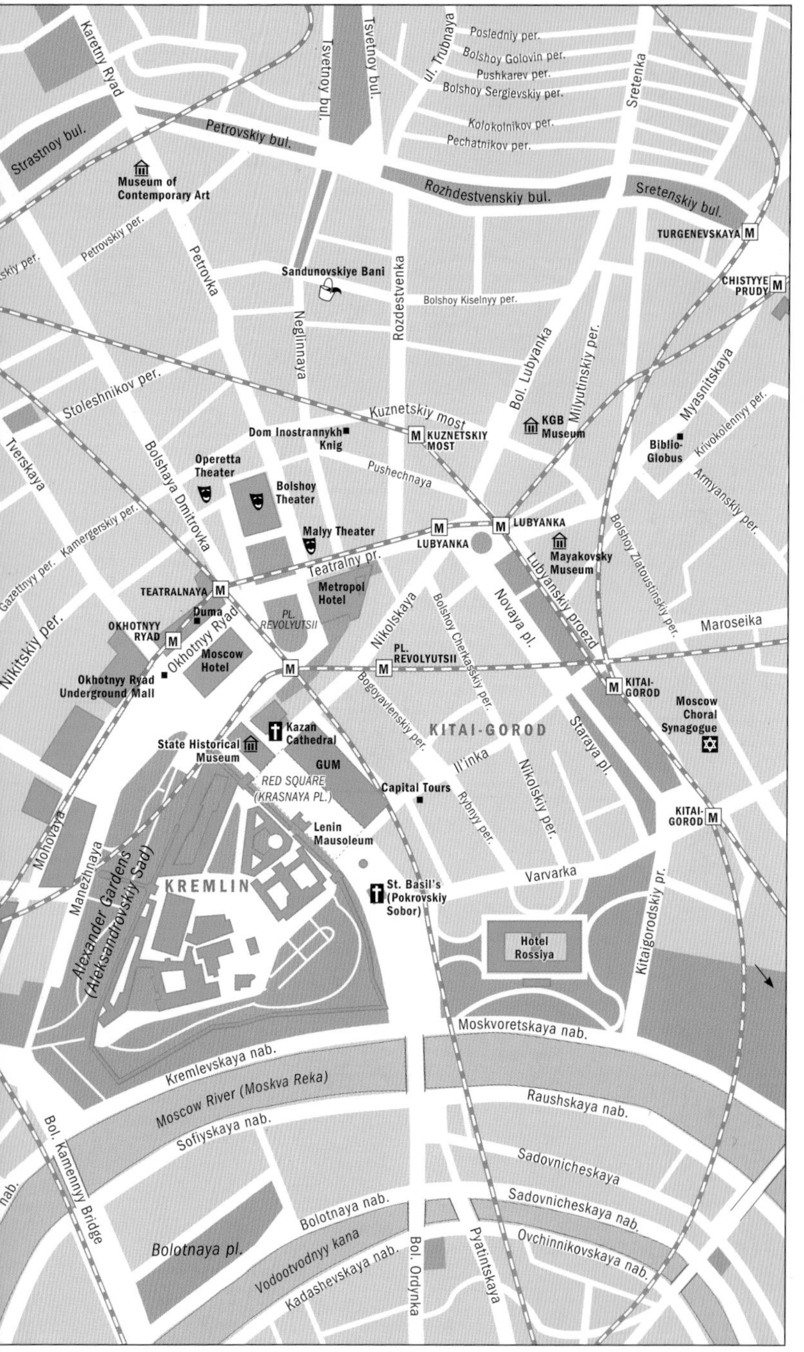

Karetny Ryad
Tsvetnoy bul.
Tsvetnoy bul.
ul. Trubnaya
Posledniy per.
Bolshoy Golovin per.
Pushkarev per.
Bolshoy Sergievskiy per.
Sretenka
Strastnoy bul.
Petrovskiy bul.
Kolokolnikov per.
Pechatnikov per.
Museum of Contemporary Art
Rozhdestvenskiy bul.
Sretenskiy bul.
TURGENEVSKAYA M
Petrovskiy per.
Petrovka
Sandunovskiye Bani
Rozdestvenka
CHISTYYE PRUDY M
Bolshoy Kiselnyy per.
Neglinnaya
Bol. Lubyanka
Milyutinskiy per.
Myasnitskaya
Stoleshnikov per.
Kuznetskiy most
KGB Museum
Krivokolennyy per.
Dom Inostrannykh Knig
M KUZNETSKIY MOST
Biblio-Globus
Tverskaya
Bolshaya Dmitrovka
Operetta Theater
Pushechnaya
Bolshoy Theater
Armyanskiy per.
Kamergerskiy per.
Malyy Theater
M
M LUBYANKA
LUBYANKA
Mayakovsky Museum
Bolshoy Zlatoustinskiy per.
Gazetnyy per.
Teatralny pr.
TEATRALNAYA M
Metropol Hotel
Lubyanskiy proezd
Novaya pl.
Nikitskiy per.
Duma
OKHOTNYY RYAD M
Okhotny Ryad
PL. REVOLYUTSII
Nikolskaya
Bolshoy Cherkasskiy per.
Maroseika
Moscow Hotel
PL. REVOLYUTSII
M
M
Okhotnyy Ryad Underground Mall
M KITAI-GOROD
Bogoyavlenskiy per.
Moscow Choral Synagogue
KITAI-GOROD
Staraya pl.
Kazan Cathedral
State Historical Museum
GUM
Il'inka
RED SQUARE (KRASNAYA PL.)
Capital Tours
Nikolskiy per.
KITAI-GOROD M
Rybnyy per.
Mohovaya
Lenin Mausoleum
Manezhnaya
Alexander Gardens (Aleksandrovskiy Sad)
KREMLIN
Varvarka
Kitaigorodskiy pr.
St. Basil's (Pokrovskiy Sobor)
Hotel Rossiya
Moskvoretskaya nab.
Kremlevskaya nab.
Moscow River (Moskva Reka)
Raushskaya nab.
Sofiyskaya nab.
Bol. Kamennyy Bridge
Sadovnicheskaya
nab.
Sadovnicheskaya nab.
Bolotnaya nab.
Ovchinnikovskaya nab.
Bolotnaya pl.
Vodootvodnyy kana
Kadashevskaya nab.
Bol. Ordynka
Pyatintskaya

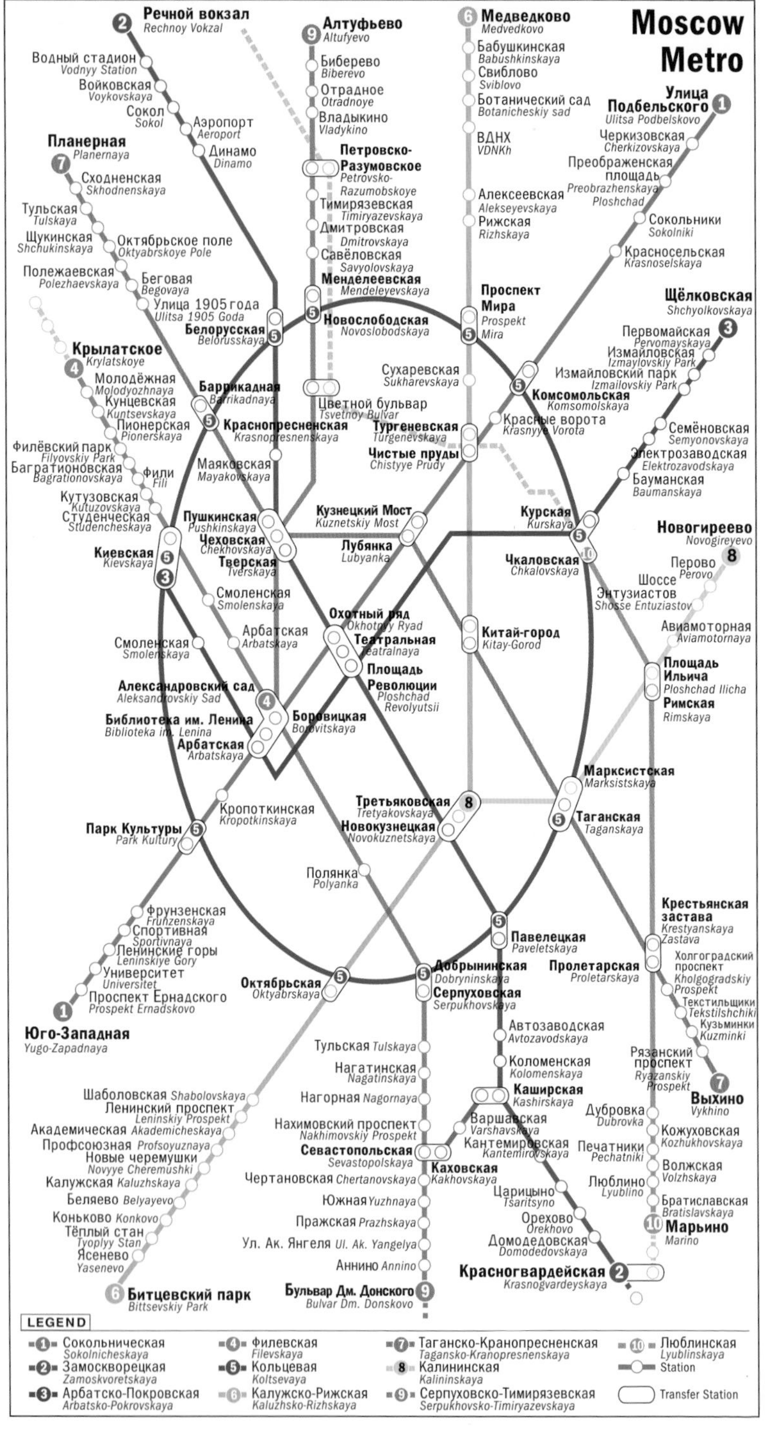

Moscow Metro
Речной вокзал
Rechnoy Vokzal
Водный стадион
Vodnyy Station
Войковская
Voykovskaya
Сокол
Sokol
Аэропорт
Aeroport
Динамо
Dinamo
Алтуфьево
Altufyevo
Бибирево
Biberevo
Отрадное
Otradnoye
Владыкино
Vladykino
Петровско-Разумовское
Petrovsko-Razumobskoye
Тимирязевская
Timiryazevskaya
Дмитровская
Dmitrovskaya
Савёловская
Savyolovskaya
Менделеевская
Mendeleyevskaya
Новослободская
Novoslobodskaya
Медведково
Medvedkovo
Бабушкинская
Babushkinskaya
Свиблово
Sviblovo
Ботанический сад
Botanicheskiy sad
ВДНХ
VDNKh
Алексеевская
Alekseyevskaya
Рижская
Rizhskaya
Проспект Мира
Prospekt Mira
Улица Подбельского
Ulitsa Podbelskovo
Черкизовская
Cherkizovskaya
Преображенская площадь
Preobrazhenskaya Ploshchad
Сокольники
Sokolniki
Красносельская
Krasnoselskaya
Щёлковская
Shchyolkovskaya
Первомайская
Pervomayskaya
Измайловская
Izmaylovskiy Park
Измайловский парк
Izmailovskiy Park
Комсомольская
Komsomolskaya
Красные ворота
Krasnyye Vorota
Семёновская
Semyonovskaya
Электрозаводская
Elektrozavodskaya
Бауманская
Baumanskaya
Курская
Kurskaya
Чкаловская
Chkalovskaya
Новогиреево
Novogireyevo
Перово
Perovo
Шоссе Энтузиастов
Shosse Entuziastov
Авиамоторная
Aviamotornaya
Площадь Ильича
Ploshchad Ilicha
Римская
Rimskaya
Марксистская
Marksistskaya
Таганская
Taganskaya
Планерная
Planernaya
Сходненская
Skhodnenskaya
Тульская
Tulskaya
Щукинская
Shchukinskaya
Октябрьское поле
Oktyabrskoye Pole
Полежаевская
Polezhaevskaya
Беговая
Begovaya
Улица 1905 года
Ulitsa 1905 Goda
Белорусская
Belorusskaya
Крылатское
Krylatskoye
Молодёжная
Molodyozhnaya
Кунцевская
Kuntsevskaya
Пионерская
Pionerskaya
Филёвский парк
Filyovskiy Park
Багратионовская
Bagrationovskaya
Фили
Fili
Кутузовская
Kutuzovskaya
Студенческая
Studencheskaya
Киевская
Kievskaya
Баррикадная
Barrikadnaya
Краснопресненская
Krasnopresnenskaya
Маяковская
Mayakovskaya
Сухаревская
Sukharevskaya
Цветной бульвар
Tsvetnoy Bulvar
Тургеневская
Turgenevskaya
Чистые пруды
Chistyye Prudy
Пушкинская
Pushkinskaya
Чеховская
Chekhovskaya
Тверская
Tverskaya
Кузнецкий Мост
Kuznetskiy Most
Лубянка
Lubyanka
Смоленская
Smolenskaya
Арбатская
Arbatskaya
Охотный ряд
Okhotnyy Ryad
Театральная
Teatralnaya
Площадь Революции
Ploshchad Revolyutsii
Китай-город
Kitay-Gorod
Смоленская
Smolenskaya
Александровский сад
Aleksandrovskiy Sad
Библиотека им. Ленина
Biblioteka im. Lenina
Арбатская
Arbatskaya
Боровицкая
Borovitskaya
Кропоткинская
Kropotkinskaya
Парк Культуры
Park Kultury
Третьяковская
Tretyakovskaya
Новокузнецкая
Novokuznetskaya
Полянка
Polyanka
Фрунзенская
Frunzenskaya
Спортивная
Sportivnaya
Ленинские горы
Leninskiye Gory
Университет
Universitet
Проспект Ернадского
Prospekt Ernadskovo
Юго-Западная
Yugo-Zapadnaya
Октябрьская
Oktyabrskaya
Добрынинская
Dobryninskaya
Серпуховская
Serpukhovskaya
Павелецкая
Paveletskaya
Пролетарская
Proletarskaya
Крестьянская застава
Krestyanskaya Zastava
Холгоградский проспект
Kholgogradskiy Prospekt
Текстильщики
Tekstilshchiki
Кузьминки
Kuzminkii
Рязанский проспект
Ryazanskiy Prospekt
Выхино
Vykhino
Автозаводская
Avtozavodskaya
Коломенская
Kolomenskaya
Каширская
Kashirskaya
Варшавская
Varshavskaya
Каховская
Kakhovskaya
Кантемировская
Kantemirovskaya
Царицыно
Tsaritsyno
Орехово
Orekhovo
Домодедовская
Domodedovskaya
Красногвардейская
Krasnogvardeyskaya
Дубровка
Dubrovka
Кожуховская
Kozhukhovskaya
Печатники
Pechatniki
Волжская
Volzhskaya
Люблино
Lyublino
Братиславская
Bratislavskaya
Марьино
Marino
Тульская Tulskaya
Нагатинская
Nagatinskaya
Нагорная Nagornaya
Нахимовский проспект
Nakhimovskiy Prospekt
Севастопольская
Sevastopolskaya
Чертановская Chertanovskaya
Южная Yuzhnaya
Пражская Prazhskaya
Ул. Ак. Янгеля Ul. Ak. Yangelya
Аннино Annino
Бульвар Дм. Донского
Bulvar Dm. Donskovo
Шаболовская Shabolovskaya
Ленинский проспект
Leninskiy Prospekt
Академическая Akademicheskaya
Профсоюзная Profsoyuznaya
Новые черемушки
Novyye Cheremushki
Калужская Kaluzhskaya
Беляево Belyayevo
Коньково Konkovo
Тёплый стан
Tyoplyy Stan
Ясенево
Yasenevo
Битцевский парк
Bittsevskiy Park
LEGEND
Сокольническая
Sokolnicheskaya
Замоскворецкая
Zamoskvoretskaya
Арбатско-Покровская
Arbatsko-Pokrovskaya
Филевская
Filevskaya
Кольцевая
Koltsevaya
Калужско-Рижская
Kalinhsko-Rizhskaya
Таганско-Кранопресненская
Tagansko-Kranopresnenskaya
Калининская
Kalininskaya
Серпуховско-Тимирязевская
Serpukhovsko-Timiryazevskaya
Люблинская
Lyublinskaya
Station
Transfer Station

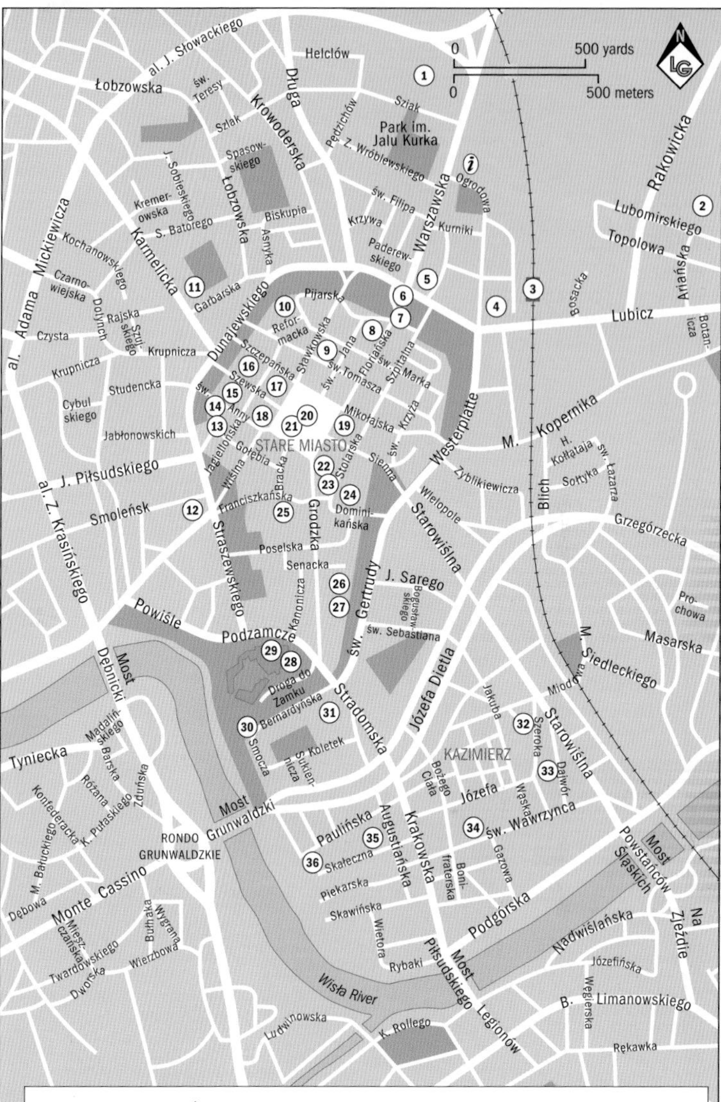

Central Kraków

Akademia Ekonomiczna, **2**
Almatur Office, **22**
Barbican, **6**
Bernardine Church, **31**
Bus Station, **4**
Carmelite Church, **11**
Cartoon Gallery, **9**
Collegium Maius, **14**
Corpus Christi Church, **34**
Czartoryski Art Museum, **8**
Dominican Church, **24**
Dragon Statue, **30**
Filharmonia, **12**
Franciscan Church, **25**
Grunwald Memorial, **5**
History Museum of Kraków, **17**
Jewish Cemetery, **32**
Jewish Museum, **33**
Kraków Główny Station, **3**
Monastery of the Reformed Franciscans, **10**
Pauline Church, **36**
Police Station, **18**
Politechnika Krakowska, **1**
St. Andrew's Church, **27**
St. Anne's Church, **15**
St. Catherine's Church, **35**
St. Florian's Gate, **7**
St. Mary's Church, **19**
St. Peter and Paul Church, **26**
Stary Teatr (Old Theater), **16**
Sukiennice (Cloth Hall), **20**
Town Hall, **21**
United States Embassy, **23**
University Museum, **13**
Wawel Castle, **28**
Wawel Cathedral, **29**

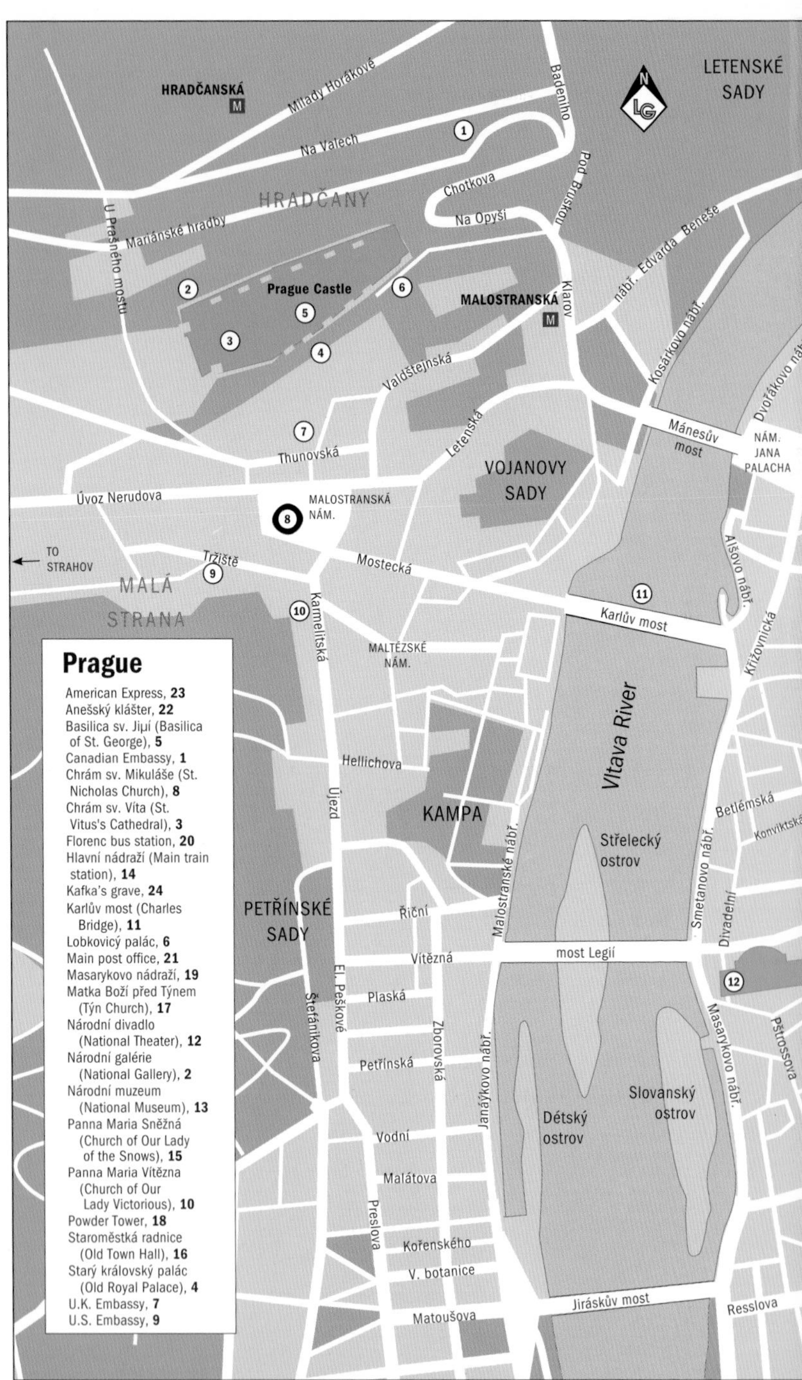

Prague

American Express, **23**
Anešský klášter, **22**
Basilica sv. Jiųí (Basilica of St. George), **5**
Canadian Embassy, **1**
Chrám sv. Mikuláše (St. Nicholas Church), **8**
Chrám sv. Víta (St. Vitus's Cathedral), **3**
Florenc bus station, **20**
Hlavní nádraží (Main train station), **14**
Kafka's grave, **24**
Karlův most (Charles Bridge), **11**
Lobkovicý palác, **6**
Main post office, **21**
Masarykovo nádraží, **19**
Matka Boží před Týnem (Týn Church), **17**
Národní divadlo (National Theater), **12**
Národní galérie (National Gallery), **2**
Národní muzeum (National Museum), **13**
Panna Maria Sněžná (Church of Our Lady of the Snows), **15**
Panna Maria Vítězna (Church of Our Lady Victorious), **10**
Powder Tower, **18**
Staroměstká radnice (Old Town Hall), **16**
Starý královský palác (Old Royal Palace), **4**
U.K. Embassy, **7**
U.S. Embassy, **9**

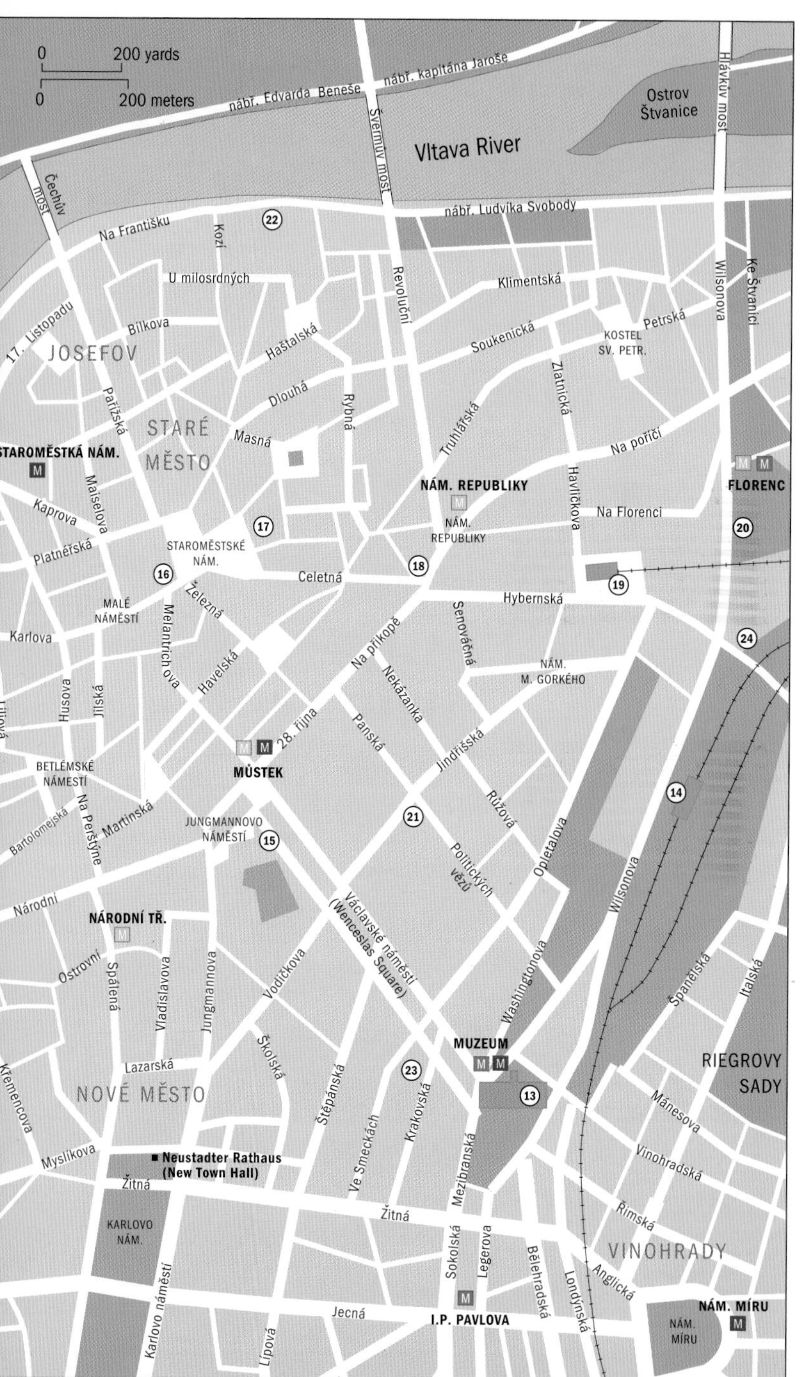

0 200 yards
0 200 meters
Vltava River
Ostrov Štvanice
nábř. Edvarda Beneše
nábř. kapitána Jaroše
nábř. Ludvíka Svobody
Čechův most
Švermův most
Hlávkův most
JOSEFOV
STARÉ MĚSTO
NOVÉ MĚSTO
VINOHRADY
RIEGROVY SADY
STAROMĚSTKÁ NÁM.
STAROMĚSTSKÉ NÁM.
MALÉ NÁMĚSTÍ
BETLÉMSKÉ NÁMESTÍ
JUNGMANNOVO NÁMĚSTÍ
NÁM. REPUBLIKY
FLORENC
KOSTEL SV. PETR.
NÁM. M. GORKÉHO
MŮSTEK
NÁRODNÍ TŘ.
MUZEUM
Neustadter Rathaus (New Town Hall)
KARLOVO NÁM.
I.P. PAVLOVA
NÁM. MÍRU
Václavské náměstí (Wenceslas Square)
Na Františku
Kozí
U milosrdných
Bílkova
17. Listopadu
Haštalská
Dlouhá
Masná
Rybná
Revoluční
Klimentská
Soukenická
Petrská
Wilsonova
Ke Štvanici
Zlatnická
Truhlářská
Na poříčí
Havlíčkova
Na Florenci
Pařížská
Maiselova
Kaprova
Platnéřská
Karlova
Celetná
Hybernská
Železná
Melantrichova
Havelská
Na příkopě
Senovážná
Nekázanka
Panská
28. října
Jindřišská
Husova
Jilská
Liliová
Bartolomějská
Na Perštýne
Martinská
Růžová
Politických vězňů
Opletalova
Národní
Ostrovní
Spálená
Vladislavova
Jungmannova
Vodičkova
Školská
Štěpánská
Ve Smečkách
Krakovská
Washingtonova
Španělská
Italská
Mánesova
Vinohradská
Římská
Anglická
Lazarská
Křemencova
Myslíkova
Žitná
Mezibranská
Sokolská
Legerova
Bělehradská
Londýnská
Karlovo náměstí
Lípová
Jecná
13
14
15
16
17
18
19
20
21
22
23
24

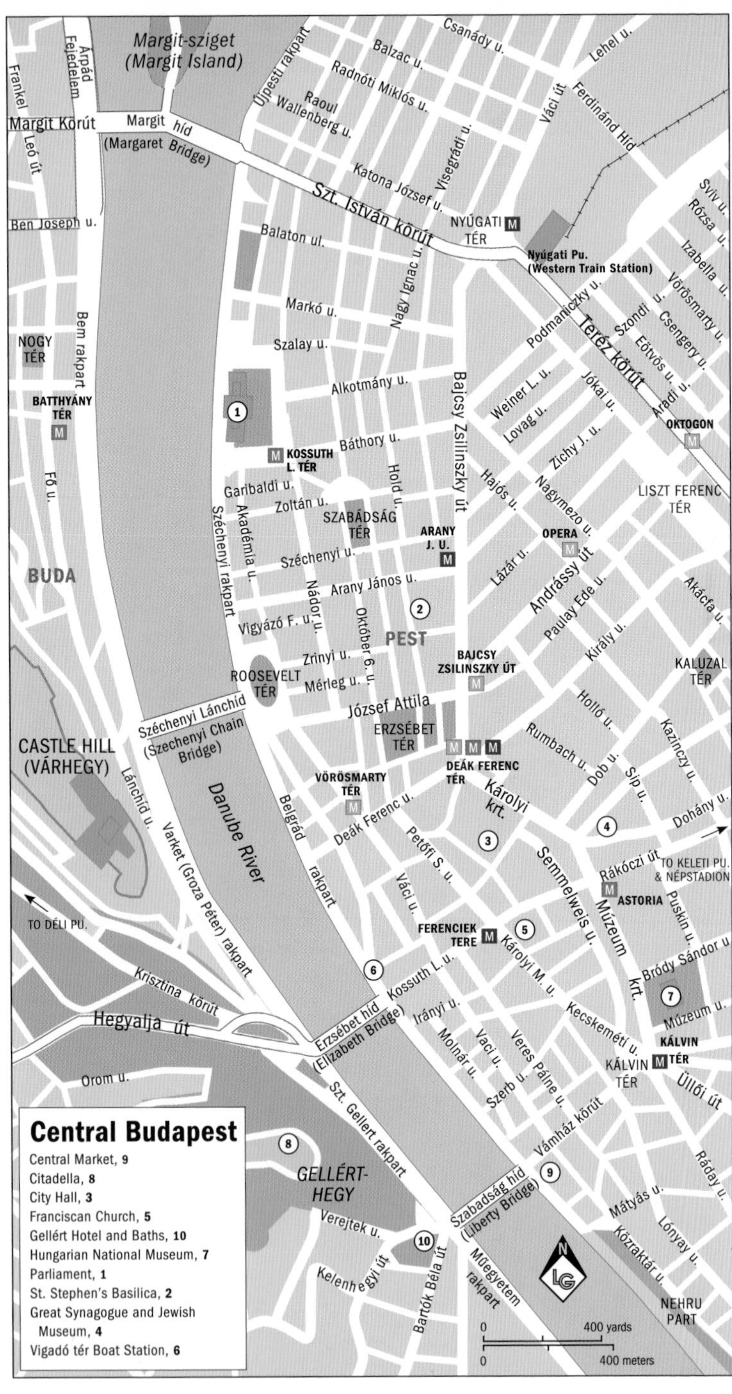

Central Budapest
Central Market, 9
Citadella, 8
City Hall, 3
Franciscan Church, 5
Gellért Hotel and Baths, 10
Hungarian National Museum, 7
Parliament, 1
St. Stephen's Basilica, 2
Great Synagogue and Jewish Museum, 4
Vigadó tér Boat Station, 6
Margit-sziget (Margit Island)
Margit híd (Margaret Bridge)
Szt. István körút
NYÚGATI TÉR
Nyúgati Pu. (Western Train Station)
Teréz körút
BATTHYÁNY TÉR
KOSSUTH L. TÉR
SZABADSÁG TÉR
ARANY J. U.
OPERA
OKTOGON
LISZT FERENC TÉR
BUDA
PEST
ROOSEVELT TÉR
BAJCSY ZSILINSZKY ÚT
KALUZAL TÉR
Széchenyi Lánchíd (Szechenyi Chain Bridge)
CASTLE HILL (VÁRHEGY)
ERZSÉBET TÉR
DEÁK FERENC TÉR
VÖRÖSMARTY TÉR
Danube River
TO KELETI PU. & NÉPSTADION
ASTORIA
TO DÉLI PU.
FERENCIEK TERE
Erzsébet híd (Elizabeth Bridge)
KÁLVIN TÉR
GELLÉRT-HEGY
Szabadság híd (Liberty Bridge)
NEHRU PART
400 yards
400 meters

LET'S GO

■ PAGES PACKED WITH ESSENTIAL INFORMATION

"Value-packed, unbeatable, accurate, and comprehensive."

—The Los Angeles Times

"The guides are aimed not only at young budget travelers but at the independent traveler; a sort of streetwise cookbook for traveling alone."

—The New York Times

"Unbeatable; good sight-seeing advice; up-to-date info on restaurants, hotels, and inns; a commitment to money-saving travel; and a wry style that brightens nearly every page."

—The Washington Post

■ THE BEST TRAVEL BARGAINS IN YOUR BUDGET

"All the dirt, dirt cheap."

—People

"Let's Go follows the creed that you don't have to toss your life's savings to the wind to travel—unless you want to."

—The Salt Lake Tribune

■ REAL ADVICE FOR REAL EXPERIENCES

"The writers seem to have experienced every rooster-packed bus and lunar-surfaced mattress about which they write."

—The New York Times

"[Let's Go's] devoted updaters really walk the walk (and thumb the ride, and trek the trail). Learn how to fish, haggle, find work—anywhere."

—Food & Wine

"A world-wise traveling companion—always ready with friendly advice and helpful hints, all sprinkled with a bit of wit."

—The Philadelphia Inquirer

■ A GUIDE WITH A SPIRIT AND A SOCIAL CONSCIENCE

"Lighthearted and sophisticated, informative and fun to read. [Let's Go] helps the novice traveler navigate like a knowledgeable old hand."

—Atlanta Journal-Constitution

"The serious mission at the book's core reveals itself in exhortations to respect the culture and the environment—and, if possible, to visit as a volunteer, a student, or a teacher rather than a tourist."

—San Francisco Chronicle

LET'S GO PUBLICATIONS

TRAVEL GUIDES

Australia 9th edition
Austria & Switzerland 12th edition
Brazil 1st edition
Britain 2008
California 10th edition
Central America 9th edition
Chile 2nd edition
China 5th edition
Costa Rica 3rd edition
Eastern Europe 13th edition
Ecuador 1st edition
Egypt 2nd edition
Europe 2008
France 2008
Germany 13th edition
Greece 9th edition
Hawaii 4th edition
India & Nepal 8th edition
Ireland 13th edition
Israel 4th edition
Italy 2008
Japan 1st edition
Mexico 22nd edition
New Zealand 8th edition
Peru 1st edition
Puerto Rico 3rd edition
Southeast Asia 9th edition
Spain & Portugal 2008
Thailand 3rd edition
USA 24th edition
Vietnam 2nd edition
Western Europe 2008

ROADTRIP GUIDE

Roadtripping USA 2nd edition

ADVENTURE GUIDES

Alaska 1st edition
Pacific Northwest 1st edition
Southwest USA 3rd edition

CITY GUIDES

Amsterdam 5th edition
Barcelona 3rd edition
Boston 4th edition
London 16th edition
New York City 16th edition
Paris 14th edition
Rome 12th edition
San Francisco 4th edition
Washington, D.C. 13th edition

POCKET CITY GUIDES

Amsterdam
Berlin
Boston
Chicago
London
New York City
Paris
San Francisco
Venice
Washington, D.C.

LET'S GO

EASTERN EUROPE

Ingrid Gustafson Editor

Rebecca Anders Associate Editor
Paul Franz Associate Editor
Jake Segal Associate Editor

Researcher-Writers

Christine Barron **Alina Mogilyanskaya**
Maciej Godlewski **Anna Shabalov**
Vanda Gyuris **Pio Szamel**
Lara Markstein **Alison Tarwater**
Peter Tilton

Andrea Tsurumi Map Editor
Calina Ciobanu Managing Editor

St. Martin's Press New York

HELPING LET'S GO. If you want to share your discoveries, suggestions, or corrections, please drop us a line. We read every piece of correspondence, whether a postcard, a 10-page email, or a coconut. **Address mail to:**

Let's Go: Eastern Europe
67 Mount Auburn St.
Cambridge, MA 02138
USA

Visit Let's Go at **http://www.letsgo.com,** or send email to:

feedback@letsgo.com
Subject: "Let's Go: Eastern Europe"

In addition to the invaluable travel advice our readers share with us, many are kind enough to offer their services as researchers or editors. Unfortunately, our charter enables us to employ only currently enrolled Harvard students.

Distributed outside the USA and Canada by Macmillan.

ISBN-13: 978-0-312-37446-4
ISBN-10: 0-312-37446-1
Thirteenth edition
10 9 8 7 6 5 4 3 2 1

Let's Go: Eastern Europe is written by Let's Go Publications, 67 Mount Auburn St., Cambridge, MA 02138, USA.

ADVERTISING DISCLAIMER. All advertisements appearing in Let's Go publications are sold by an independent agency not affiliated with the editorial production of the guides. Advertisers are never given preferential treatment, and the guides are researched, written, and published independent of advertising. Advertisements do not imply endorsement of products or services by Let's Go, and Let's Go does not vouch for the accuracy of information provided in advertisements.

If you are interested in purchasing advertising space in a Let's Go publication, contact: Let's Go Advertising Sales, 67 Mount Auburn St., Cambridge, MA 02138, USA.

HOW TO USE THIS BOOK

Dobryy den, adventurous reader. Call me **Let's Go: Eastern Europe.** This year, our intrepid and indefatigable team of researchers and editors went to new lengths to bring you the best that this sprawling, culturally rich, and rapidly changing region has to offer. While working tirelessly to expand our coverage of the quirky Baltics, the stunning Dalmatian and Black Sea coasts, rugged Ukraine, and bold, gigantic Russia, we added a new section on chaotic, must-see İstanbul. But have no fear—the coverage of powerhouses Prague, Budapest, Kraków, Moscow, and St. Petersburg has never been stronger. It's a good thing too, because there's hardly been a better time to go. Along the way, *Let's Go: Eastern Europe* will be your best travel buddy, your wise mentor, your pillow. And below, we tell you how to use it.

COVERING THE BASICS. The first chapter, **Discover Eastern Europe** (p. 1), contains highlights of the region, complete with **suggested itineraries.** The **Essentials** (p. 11) section contains practical information on planning a budget, making reservations, and other useful tips for traveling in Eastern Europe. For study abroad, volunteer, and work opportunities, **Beyond Tourism** (p. 52) has what you need. If you haven't yet mastered the 13 major Eastern European languages spoken in the countries covered in this book (or if gesticulating wildly and speaking loudly isn't working), look to the **Appendix** (p. 790) for key words and useful phrases—and a pronunciation guide for the inscrutable Cyrillic alphabet.

COVERAGE LAYOUT. *Let's Go: Eastern Europe* is divided by country, listed alphabetically from Bulgaria to Ukraine. Each chapter begins with a detailed introduction to the country's practical travel information, history, and culture. The country's capital immediately follows. Thereafter, the chapter is divided into regions, headlined by major cities and followed by smaller cities and hubs. Each of our chapters is jam-packed with hidden deals, tip boxes, detailed maps, and sidebar **features,** which provide in-depth looks at local traditions, politics, legends, and news. The book's final two chapters are meant to ease a traveler's sojourn into and around Eastern Europe: **Access Points** provides practical information on traveling through oh-so-complicated Moldova and Belarus, while **Gateway Cities** covers the key jump-off points of Berlin, Munich, Vienna, and Venice.

TRANSPORTATION INFO. For making connections between destinations, information is generally listed under both the arrival and departure cities. Parentheticals usually provide the trip duration followed by the frequency, then the price. For more general information on travel, consult the **Essentials** (p. 11) section.

PRICE DIVERSITY. Our researchers list establishments in order of value from best to worst, with absolute favorites denoted by the *Let's Go* thumbs-up (). Since the cheapest price does not always mean the best value, we have incorporated a system of price ranges for food and accommodations; see p. XVI.

A NOTE TO OUR READERS. The information for this book was gathered by *Let's Go* researchers from May through August of 2007. Each listing is based on one researcher's opinion, formed during his or her visit at a particular time. Those traveling at other times may have different experiences since prices, dates, hours, and conditions are always subject to change. You are urged to check the facts presented in this book beforehand to avoid inconvenience and surprises.

RESEARCHER-WRITERS

Christine Barron *Estonia, Latvia, and Lithuania*

Unfazed by long distances, hostile tourist offices, and sleeping quarters that would scare a Spartan, this lean, mean biking machine still managed to turn in uncompromising copy, improving our coverage of Asian and vegetarian cuisine, blazing a trail through the wilds of island Estonia, and keeping all our listings up to snuff. *Labai dėkui*, Christine!

Maciej Godlewski *Slovakia and Southern Poland*

Maciej traveled the southern Poland and Slovakia route in record time. In his native Poland, he exhaustively explored Kraków, from its laundromats to its infamous dragon's den and managed to find the Bledowska Desert that had eluded so many. Across the border, the recent grad was able to cobble together Polish-Slovak to communicate with the locals. Maciej impressed us with his meticulous descriptions, insightful questions, and general koolness.

Vanda Gyuris *Hungary*

Fiercely dedicated to the country, Vanda expertly traversed her native Hungary. In the process, she greatly improved our coverage of Budapest nightlife, contributed a fantastic new write-up of Miskolc, and constantly supplied her grateful editors with insider info. Vanda's infectious enthusiasm for Hungary's sights, nature, and *lángos* leapt off the page, as did her relentlessly positive outlook and descriptions of her intense experiences.

Lara Markstein *Croatia and Slovenia*

Combining an enterprising spirit with a strong sense of tradition, this courageous kiwi entertained the office with her off-beat marginalia as she weathered hunger, heatstroke, and the nudist hordes of Croatia and Slovenia. Whether trekking over limestone cliffs, hiking through cobblestone streets, or taking in the fresh sea air of beautiful Dubrovnik, Lara always maintained her poise, capturing it all in copy as limpid as the blue waters of the Adriatic.

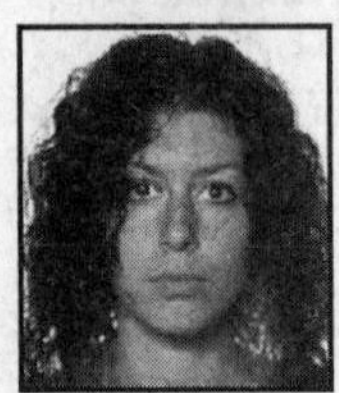

Alina Mogilyanskaya *Belarus and Russia*

For every shove Russia gave her, Alina shoved back twice as hard. Although she faced bureaucratic nightmares and "did not see" a certain surprise in a canal, Alina still managed to thrill her editors by verifying absolutely every fact along her route. After combing St. Petersburg for the best alternative bars and restaurants, Alina headed to the Russian countryside, where she produced new coverage that was at once thorough, honest, and edgy.

Anna Shabalov *Bulgaria and Romania*

Anna braved the bureaucratic wilderness of Romania and Bulgaria with unshakable determination and pluck, facing transportation hassles and 20km hikes uncomplainingly. She added exciting cities and towns on the Black Sea coast, completely revamped the coverage of Sofia, and improved every listing she touched, from national parks and monasteries to tiny towns and communist remnants.

RESEARCHER-WRITERS

Pio Szamel *Poland*

Returning to his native Poland, this adoptive Coloradan came to the Wild East with a Westerner's taste for adventure and the outdoors. With his keen insights and eye for detail, he thoroughly updated and improved our coverage, added many new listings, and, despite his penchant for Sartre, tried to convince us that Hel isn't other people. Team EEUR salutes you, Pio!

Alison Tarwater *Turkey and Ukraine*

Alison is tough. She rocked cities and mountains, bathtub vodka and streetcorner borscht, and mafia bars and transportation that "sketch" doesn't even begin to describe. Alison owned her route. She added pages of brilliant coverage in the West before skirting the Transnistrian border to the beaches of the Crimea and the behemoth that is İstanbul. "The best part," she maintains, "is that it's perfectly normal in Ukraine to walk around eating a popsicle."

Peter Tilton *Czech Republic*

After having traveled Spain for six weeks, Peter was no stranger to life on the road. He said *Ahoj* to the Czech Republic—and then blazed on through. Somewhere between getting his Nalgene filled with beer by the obliging tourguides at the Budvar factory, investigating new towns, and keeping us laughing with his weekly phonecalls and hilarious marginalia, Peter effortlessly picked up the Let's Go style. And our Czech coverage is all the better for it.

CONTRIBUTING WRITERS

Lauren Caruso — *Associate Editor:* Let's Go: Europe

Vinnie Chiappini — *Editor,* Let's Go: Italy

Emily Cunningham — *Venice*

Brianna Goodale — *Associate Editor:* Let's Go: Europe

David Paltiel — *Munich, Vienna*

Inés Pacheco — *Editor:* Let's Go: Europe

Jane Yager — *Berlin*

Hannah Brooks-Motl is a writer and teacher who lives and works in Prague, where she has not yet found herself. She is a graduate of Macalester College. Her favorite Czech beer is Staropramen; her favorite Czech food is the dumpling.

ACKNOWLEDGMENTS

TEAM EASTERN EUROPE THANKS: The tireless, wonderful Belle of Brașov, Calina; our fearless, communism-repellant RWs; Andrea, for mapping our souls; Western Europe, for late-night laughs and absurdly large boxes of food; Belarus; Prod, for ; lifesaving translators and last-minute editors; history; Stevie, Boney M, and Rasputin. Screw MS.
INGRID THANKS: Rebecca, for wit and impersonations; Paul, for pandemonium and musical education; Jake, for unflagging enthusiasm and humor—even if I didn't always get it; Calina, for superhuman kindness and work ethic; my parents, aunt, and uncle, for my sanity; Europod, my friends, et al, for letting me know that insanity is a viable alternative.
REBECCA THANKS: Team Eastern Europe: Paul, Jake, Ingrid, and Calina, for making work not feel like it; the rest of my summer support system: first and foremost, the fam; the rest of Let's Go; all of the erstwhile apartment gang, including its honorary members, and my amazing "Bline" friends.
PAUL THANKS: Rebecca, Jake, Ingrid, Calina, and the Let's Go gang; my family and friends in T.O. and elsewhere; my roommate Jeff and everyone in Cambridge; all who helped with translations and expertise, especially Marc Greenberg and Masa, Maciej, Laura, and Eric. Thanks to Antonija for all. Forgive what slipped through the cracks.
JAKE THANKS: Ingrid, for allowing my shenanigans; Rebecca, for hilarious sarcasm and ; Paul, for music with slamming lockers; Calina, for EEUR ownage; Cec, for ; Alison, for absurd dedication and KY; Andrea, because mapliness is next to godliness; Vicki, for fixing our lives; Silvia, sensei; Julie, ed past; my boy Tupac, for inspiration; A-town what.
CALINA THANKS: Ingrid, for running a tight ship, with coffee and class; Rebecca, for the quirkiness; Paul, for musical expertise; Jake, for well-timed high-fives; most of all, Mom, Dad, and Cosmi.
ANDREA THANKS: The EEUR editors & RWs, Mapland, Sam, Margaret, Phil, and Alexander.

CONTENTS

Eastern Europe: Chapter Divisions
FINLAND
Lake Ladoga
Vyborg
St. Petersburg
SWEDEN
Narva
Tallinn
Novgorod
Petrozavodsk
Estonia
pp. 225-261
Russia
pp. 552-616
Pskov
Gulf of Riga
Latvia
pp. 344-371
Rīga
Moscow
Baltic Sea
Klaipėda
Lithuania
pp. 372-410
Smolensk
Kaunas
Vilnius
Gdańsk
Belarus
pp. 758-761
Poland
pp. 411-503
Poznań
Warsaw
Chernyhiv
Łódź
Wrocław
Lublin
Kyiv
Prague
Kraków
Czech Republic
pp. 154-224
Lviv
Ukraine
pp. 702-757
Český Krumlov
Ivano-Frankivsk
Slovakia
pp. 617-656
Kirovohrad
Bratislava
AUSTRIA
Budapest
Moldova
pp. 762-764
Cluj-Napoca
Slovenia
pp. 657-683
Szombathely
Hungary
pp. 262-343
Odessa
Romania
pp. 504-551
Pécs
Ljubljana
Timişoara
Zagreb
Tulcea
Croatia
pp. 95-153
Bucharest
Constanţa
BOSNIA AND HERZEGOVINA
Split
SERBIA AND MONTENEGRO
Mangalia
Black Sea
Pleven
Adriatic Sea
Bulgaria
pp. 64-94
Sofia
Plovdiv
ITALY
MACEDONIA
ALBANIA
Turkey
pp. 684-701
GREECE
Aegean Sea
TURKEY

NORWAY
Dal R.
FINLAND
Vyborg
Lake
Ladoga
Helsinki
Oslo
Åland
Island
St. Petersburg
Lake
Vanern
Stockholm
Narva
Tallinn
Novgorod
Hiiumaa
Haapsalu
Lake
Peipsi
ESTONIA
Tartu
Lake
Vattern
Saaremaa
Pärnu
Kuressaare
Viljandi
Pskov
Kattegat
Gulf of
Riga
Cēsis
Otepää
Göteborg
Sigulda
Alborg
Ventspils
SWEDEN
Gotland
Island
Kuldīga
Rīga
Öland
Jūrmala
LATVIA
Liepája
Jelgava
Copenhagen
Palanga
Malmö
Baltic Sea
LITHUANIA
Polatsk
Smolensk
DENMARK
Klaipėda
Nida
Neman
Kaunas
Kaliningrad
RUSSIA
Vilnius
Minsk
Sopot
Druskininkai
Miedzyzdroje
Gdańsk
Mahileu
Olsztyn
Mazurian
Lakes
Hrodna
GERMANY
Szczecin
BELARUS
Białystok
Zhlobin
Homel
Berlin
Baranavichy
Toruń
Warta R.
Vistula R.
Luninets
Pripyat R.
Poznań
Oder R.
POLAND
Warsaw
Brest
Łódź
Leipzig
Kovel
Sarny
Chernobyl
Dresden
Wrocław
Lublin
Korosten
Czestochowa
Kyiv
Rovno
Prague
Kraków
Przemyśl
Karlovy Vary
UKRAINE
Plzeň
CZECH REP.
CARPATHIAN MOUNTAINS
Lviv
Olomouc
Zakopane
Bug
Český Krumlóv
Brno
Žilina
Poprad
Ivano-Frankivsk
SLOVAK REP.
Uzhhorod
Munich
Banská Bystrica
Košice
Balta
Inn R.
Mukacheve
Prut
Vienna
Bratislava
Tisza R.
Salzburg
Eger
MOLDOVA
Budapest
Satu Mare
AUSTRIA
Győr
Suceava
Sopron
Debrecen
Chişinău
ALPS
Graz
HUNGARY
Cluj-Napoca
Iaşi
Lake
Balaton
Oradea
Danube R.
Bacau
SLOVENIA
Drava R.
Szeged
ROMANIA
Ljubljana
Pécs
Arad
Sighişoara
Venice
Trieste
Sibiu
Zagreb
Timişoara
Novi Sad
Tulcea
Sava R.
Braşov
Pula
Rijeka
Buzău
BOSNIA AND
HERZEGOVINA
Belgrade
Tirgu Jiu
Bucharest
Constanţa
CROATIA
Morava R.
Craiova
Danube R.
Zenica
Sarajevo
Zadar
Lom
Ruse
Split
Vidin
Veliko Turnovo
BALKAN MTS.
Mostar
SERBIA AND
MONTENEGRO
Niš
Varna
Adriatic
Sea
Nessebar
BULGARIA
Kotor
Peć
Sofia
Burgas
Dubrovnik
Cetinje
Rome
Stara
Zagora
Budva
Plovdiv
Malko
Turnovo
Skopje
Istanbul
ITALY
Kurdzhali
Tirana
F.Y.R.
MACEDONIA
Durrës
Bitola
GREECE
Sea of
Marmara
Ohrid
Naples
ALBANIA
Thessaloniki
Korçë

Eastern Europe
0 200 kilometers
0 200 miles
NORTH RUSSIAN PLAIN
Vologda
Yaroslavl
Volga R.
Suzdal
Nizhnyy Novgorod
Kazan
Vladimir
RUSSIA
Simbirsk
Tolyatti
Samara
Moscow
Ryazan
Tula
Penza
Volsk
Saratov
Bryansk
Voronezh
Povorino
KAZAKHSTAN
Kursk
Konotop
Volgograd
Volga R.
CASPIAN DEPRESSION
Kharkiv
Donets R.
Don R.
Dniper R.
Dnipropetrovsk
Smila
Luhansk
Astrakhan
Donetsk
Kirovohrad
Krivy Rih
Zaporizhya
Rostov-na-Donu
Azov
Mariupol
Caspian Sea
Mykolayiv
Sea of Azov
Primorsko Akhtarsk
Stavropol
Odessa
Dzhankoy
Kerch
Yekaterinodar
Groznyy
Crimea
Yevpatoriya
Feodosiya
Simferopol
Sevastopol
Yalta
Tuapse
Sochi
CAUCASUS MOUNTAINS
GEORGIA
Tbilisi
Black Sea
Batumi
ARMENIA
Yerevan
Sinop
TURKEY
AZERBAIJAN
Kizilirmak
Ankara
Bursa

NORWAY
Oslo
FINLAND
Helsinki
Lake Ladoga
Vyborg
St. Petersburg
Aland Island
Stockholm
Narva
Tallinn
Novgorod
SWEDEN
Hiiumaa
ESTONIA
Saaremaa
Pärnu
Tartu
Kuressaare
Gulf of Rīga
Kattegat
Göteborg
Otepää
Pskov
Alborg
Gotland Island
Ventspils
Rīga
Öland
Liepaja
Jelgava
LATVIA
Copenhagen
Malmö
Baltic Sea
LITHUANIA
Polatsk
Smolensk
DENMARK
Kaunas
Kaliningrad
Vilnius
Maladechna
Minsk
Mahileu
Gdynia
Gdańsk
Olsztyn
Hrodna
GERMANY
Szczecin
BELARUS
Białystok
Berlin
Baranavichy
Zhlobin
Toruń
Homel
Poznań
Warsaw
Luninets
Brest
POLAND
Łódź
Leipzig
Kovel
Sarny
Chernobyl
Dresden
Wrocław
Lublin
Lutsk
Korosten
Kyiv
Rovno
Prague
Karlovy Vary
Kraków
Olomouc
Plzeň
Przemyśl
Lviv
CZECH REP.
Brno
Český Krumlov
SLOVAK REP.
Munich
Vienna
Uzhhorod
Ivano-Frankivsk
Balta
Salzburg
Bratislava
MOLDOVA
Budapest
Satu Mare
AUSTRIA
Chişinău
HUNGARY
Cluj-Napoca
Iaşi
Graz
Oradea
Bacău
ROMANIA
SLOVENIA
Ljubljana
Szeged
Sighişoara
Pécs
Venice
Trieste
Zagreb
Tulcea
Timişoara
Braşov
Novi Sad
Buzău
Pula
Rijeka
Belgrade
CROATIA
BOSNIA AND HERZEGOVINA
Bucharest
Zenica
Constanţa
Zadar
Sarajevo
Craiova
Ruse
Split
SERBIA AND MONTENEGRO
Varna
Mostar
Niš
Adriatic Sea
BULGARIA
Peć
Burgas
Sofia
Dubrovnik
Podgorica
Stara Zagora
Malko Turnovo
Rome
Bar
Skopje
Plovdiv
Shkodër
ITALY
Tirana
F.Y.R. MACEDONIA
Istanbul
Durrës
Sea of Marmara
GREECE
Naples
ALBANIA
Thessaloniki
Bursa
Korcë

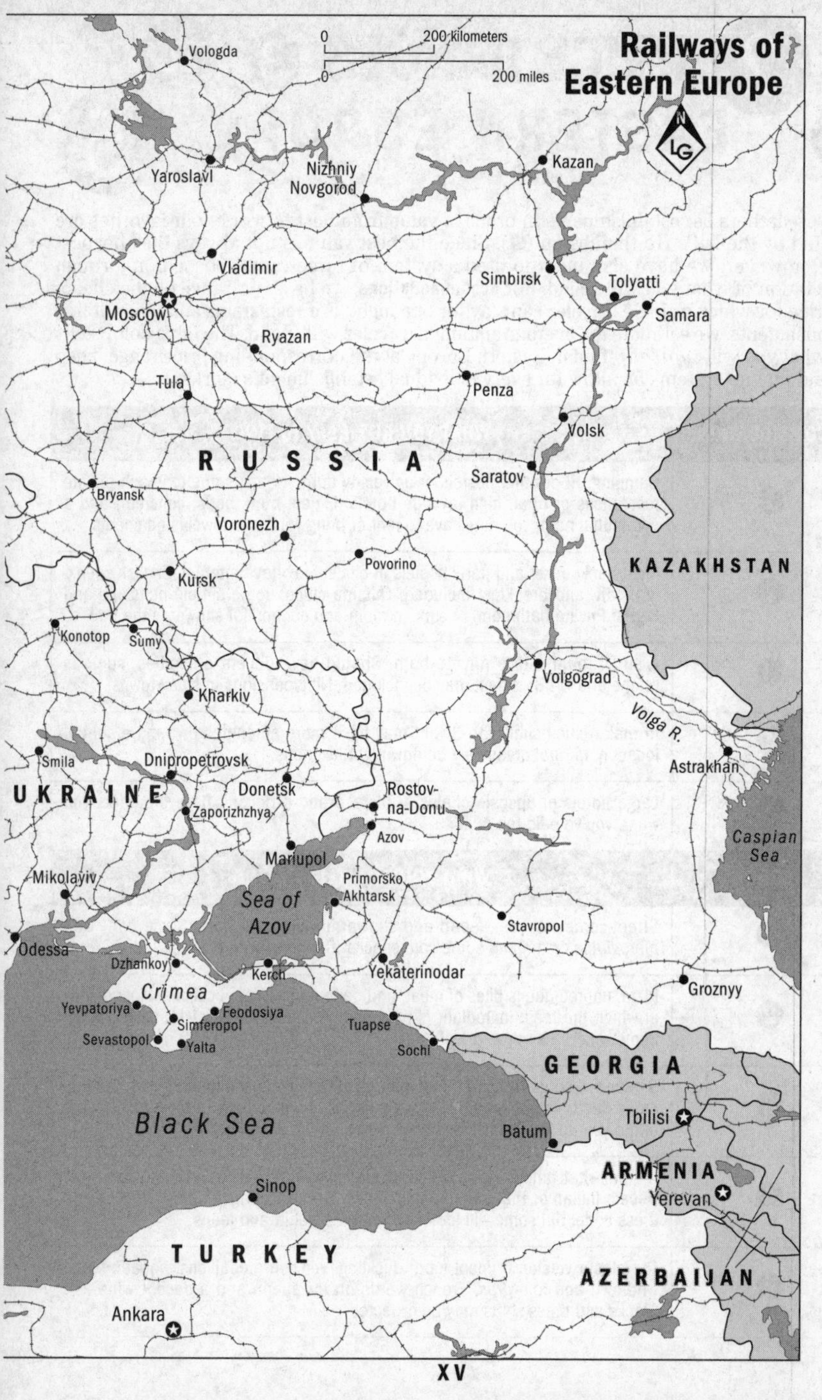

Railways of Eastern Europe
0
200 kilometers
0
200 miles
N
LG
Vologda
Yaroslavl
Nizhniy Novgorod
Kazan
Vladimir
Simbirsk
Tolyatti
Samara
Moscow
Ryazan
Penza
Tula
Volsk
RUSSIA
Saratov
Bryansk
Voronezh
Povorino
KAZAKHSTAN
Kursk
Konotop
Sumy
Volgograd
Kharkiv
Volga R.
Smila
Dnipropetrovsk
Astrakhan
UKRAINE
Donetsk
Rostov-na-Donu
Zaporizhzhya
Azov
Caspian Sea
Mariupol
Mikolayiv
Primorsko Akhtarsk
Sea of Azov
Stavropol
Odessa
Dzhankoy
Kerch
Yekaterinodar
Crimea
Groznyy
Yevpatoriya
Feodosiya
Simferopol
Tuapse
Sevastopol
Yalta
Sochi
GEORGIA
Black Sea
Tbilisi
Batum
ARMENIA
Sinop
Yerevan
TURKEY
AZERBAIJAN
Ankara

PRICE RANGES 1 2 3 4 5 EASTERN EUROPE

Our researchers list establishments in order of value from best to worst; our favorites are denoted by the Let's Go thumbs-up (☒). Since the best value is not always the cheapest price, however, we have also incorporated a system of price ranges, based on a rough expectation of what you will spend. For **accommodations,** we base our range on the cheapest price for which a single traveler can stay for one night. For **restaurants** and other dining establishments, we estimate the average amount a traveler will spend. The table below tells you what you will *typically* find in Eastern Europe at the corresponding price range; keep in mind that no system can allow for every individual establishment's quirks.

ACCOMMODATIONS	WHAT YOU'RE *LIKELY* TO FIND
1	Camping; HI or other hostels or university dorm rooms; some rooms in private residences or rural, highway-side hotels. Expect bunk beds, concrete, and a communal bath; you may have to rent or bring your own towels and sheets.
2	Most backpacker and party hostels in cities. May have Internet, English-speaking staff, and breakfast included. Outside cities, some simple pensions and B&Bs. Private bathroom, or sink, in room and communal shower in the hall.
3	A small room with a private bath. Should have decent amenities, such as phone and TV. Breakfast may be included. Nice pensions in small towns.
4	In major cities similar to 3, but may have more amenities or a more central location. In rural areas may be downright luxurious.
5	Large hotels or upscale chains. If it's a 5 and it doesn't have the perks you want, you've paid too much.
FOOD	**WHAT YOU'RE *LIKELY* TO FIND**
1	Street-corner stands, kebab and shawarma and milk bars. Some *bliny* and *pierogi.* Ice cream and some cafe snacks. Cafeteria-style offerings.
2	Pizza, unpretentious piles of meat, and deep-fried regional cuisine. Most dishes in which the main ingredient is potatoes. Pancakes, *naleśniki*, and breakfast items. Likely a sit-down meal.
3	Seafood, wild game, and meaty entrees. Many medieval-themed and hunting-lodge-decor establishments. A wine list. A cheeseburger in Moscow. Tip will bump you up a few smackers because you will have a waiter.
4	A somewhat fancy restaurant. Upscale vegetarian entrees. Attentive service. Decent Indian or Thai food in major cities. Few restaurants in this range have a dress code, but some will look down upon a T-shirt and jeans.
5	The all-out version of local food: duckling, venison medallions, aquatic birds, wildfowl, and *foie gras.* French words on the menu and a decent wine list. Slacks and dress shirts may be expected.

DISCOVER EASTERN EUROPE

The term "Eastern Europe" is a largely political and arbitrary designation: Prague is located farther west than Vienna, and Greece is separated from the "West" by hundreds of miles of the "East." Considering this fact, it seems unsurprising that many countries that once lived on the same Bloc now have little in common and, in some cases, little to do with each other. While many Eastern European states have made concerted efforts to integrate themselves into the global (or at least Western) community in the last two decades, behemoth Russia remains somewhat unpredictable and isolated from her neighbors. Perhaps all that can be said of the region as a whole is that the countries here are changing—and that the resulting aura of uncertainty, potential, and adventure makes the area a haven for budget travelers. Untouristed cities, pristine national parks, empty hostel beds, and cheap beer abound. Bratislava, Budapest, and St. Petersburg will charm even the most jaded backpacker, while the jagged peaks of the Tatras and the dazzling beaches of the Dalmatian Coast are sure to stagger any nature lover.

Eastern European bureaucracies can be infuriating and, in some cases, amenities that Westerners take for granted may be hard to find. Should the absurdity of the post-Soviet world ever get you down, take comfort in knowing that for every stoic border guard and badgering *babushka*, there are countless locals willing to give you a bed, a shot of homemade liquor, and a ride to the next town. No, Eastern Europe's not easy, but with flexibility, patience, and resilience, you can have an incredible journey through one of the most geographically varied, historically rich, and culturally dynamic areas of the world.

WHEN TO GO

Summer is Eastern Europe's high season. What this means, however, varies for each country and region. Budapest, Kraków, and Prague swarm with backpackers, while "high season" in the countryside simply means that hotels might actually have guests staying in them. Along the Adriatic, Baltic, and Black Sea coasts, tourists flock to the beach from June to September. In the Tatras, Julian Alps, and Transylvanian Alps, there is both a summer high season for hiking (July-Aug.) and a winter high season for skiing (Nov.-Mar.). In low season, you'll often be the only tourist in town. Although securing accommodations will be easier in low season, high season brings with it an entire subculture of young backpackers. Major national holidays are listed in the introduction to each country. Festivals are detailed in city listings where appropriate; major festivals in each country are summarized on p. 5.

WHAT TO DO

Like a tracksuit-clad mafioso on a Moscow street corner, Eastern Europe has what you need, from heavily backpacked cities to undiscovered terrain.

IN HIGH SPIRITS

Let's cut to the chase, if not the chaser: a lot of people come to Eastern Europe to party, and for good reason. The alcohol is potent and cheap, and the nightlife famously vibrant. Just don't let it keep you in bed all the next day; Eastern Europe also offers a spectacular range of architectural achievements that leave even the most hungover traveler enthralled. From Romans to Roma and Muslims to Magyars, the many peoples who have inhabited Eastern Europe have left some extraordinary relics and ruins for the modern-day traveler to marvel at.

GOD IS GOOD	GOOD GOD, I'M DRUNK
AYA SOFIA (İSTANBUL, TUR). The "Divine Wisdom" of Byzantine emperor Justinian's masterful cathedral-turned-mosque is truly inspiring—especially the gigantic dome (p. 698).	**ŁÓDŹ KALISKA (ŁÓDŹ, POL).** "Bar" hardly describes this rambling, eclectic funhouse, which shares its name with the influential Łódź art collective that designed it (p. 474).
BONE CHAPEL OF KUTNÁ HORA (CZR). After the Plague left the village's graveyard with a surplus of corpses, a monk, and later an artist, decided to do a little decorating (p. 193).	**MAAILM (TARTU, EST).** Its decor fueled by old magazines, pillows, and swings, this pub is just like your wacky best friend's attic—except it serves amazing milkshakes (p. 259).
WOODEN ARTICULATED CHURCH (KEŽMAROK, SLK). Swedish sailors helped build the porthole windows of this Reformation church, constructed in the shape of a Greek cross (p. 646).	**PROPAGANDA (MOSCOW, RUS).** New and old and white Russians get mixed up in this hip expat-friendly hot spot, where tasty dinners give way to a thumping dance party come midnight (p. 581).
CATHEDRAL OF CHRIST THE SAVIOR (MOSCOW, RUS). This reconstruction of St. Basil's—originally commissioned by Alexander I and torn down by Stalin—is unforgettable (p. 575).	**SULTANAHMET (İSTANBUL, TUR).** Bar hoppers in Sultanahmet's crowded street scene get wrecked by *balyoz* ("the wrecking ball")—a local specialty made from *rakı*, whiskey, vodka, and gin (p. 701).
ST. NICHOLAS ORTHODOX CATHEDRAL (LIEPĀJA, LAT). Set amid a sea of Soviet housing complexes, this gold-gilded church has survived the test of time, despite its lack of supporting columns (p. 366).	**EASTWEST COCKTAIL AND DANCE BAR (DUBROVNIK, CRO).** With its private Dalmatian beach location and spectacular views, East-West's motto, "Welcome to Heaven" rings true, especially after a few drinks (p. 152).
CAVE MONASTERY (KYIV, UKR). Candles light the way past stalagmites and the mummified remains of monks in one of Orthodox Christianity's most revered sites (p. 721).	**METELKOVA MESTO (LJUBLJANA, SLV).** Get lost among art-punks and graffiti at the best club/hostel/art collective complex ever to be housed inside a former Soviet military barracks (p. 668).
WIELICZKA SALT MINES (KRAKÓW, POL). An awe-inspiring church carved entirely out of salt is buried 200m underground in the center of Blessed Kinga (p. 448).	**PUB 13 (ALBA IULIA, ROM).** Built into the medieval citadel wall, this hot number packs in an international crowd that lines the incredibly long bar and lounges on an outdoor terrace (p. 537).
METROPOLITAN CATHEDRAL (TIMIȘOARA, ROM). Thirteen green-and-gold spires cap this regal orthodox church, whose eerie beauty comes out during nightly vespers (p. 539).	**NOWOWIEJSKIEGO STREET (POZNAŃ, POL).** At night, students transform this thoroughfare of cafes into a raging bar and club scene; check out club W Starym Kinie (p. 479).
ST. ISAAC'S CATHEDRAL (ST. PETERSBURG, RUS). The 100kg of pure gold that coats its Italian dome (which housed a museum of atheism under the Soviets) is visible for miles (p. 599).	**SOPOT, POL.** This beach town near Gdańsk plays home to Eastern Europe's own slice of Ibiza, a Baltic club paradise legendary for its hedonistic nightlife (p. 495).
PANNONHALMA ABBEY (GYŐR, HUN). This 1000-year-old monastery contains one of the largest libraries in the country (p. 319).	**ZÖLD PARDON AND RIO (BUDAPEST, HUN).** Sweaty summer crowds gyrate to fresh rock and house at these Danube-side hot spots (p. 289).

OUTDOORS

Ditch the crowds of Prague and head for the Eastern European wilderness. From the sand dunes of Lithuania to the jagged peaks of Slovenia, the region's rough edges are a thrill-seeker's Eden. The Tatras, Julian Alps, and Carpathians offer Olympic-quality skiing, heart-stopping hang-gliding and hiking, and spectacular views from lightly trodden hiking trails. The beaches of Eastern Europe come in every variety: sandy, wide, and windswept beside the Baltic in Estonia, Latvia, Lithuania, and Poland; rocky, colorful, and teeming with cafes along the sun-drenched Adriatic in Croatia and Slovenia; and wild and spectacular on the intensely blue (yes, blue) Black Sea Coast. Bicyclists can traverse the Estonian islands, the shores of Hungary's Lake Balaton, and trails along Poland's glassy Mazury Lakes.

BY LAND	BY SEA
MT. HOVERLA (CARPATHIAN NATIONAL PARK, UKR). Ukraine's tallest peak offers great skiing, hiking, and mushroom hunting to satisfy any aspiring Slavic woodsperson (p. 737).	**MIĘDZYZDROJE (WOLIN ISLAND, POL).** This Baltic island has more glacial lakes, sweeping sea bluffs, old forts, hiking, cycling, and bison than you've ever seen in one place (p. 485).
FĂGĂRAŞ MOUNTAINS (SIBIU, ROM). Wildflower meadows, cloud-shrouded summits, dramatic drops, and superb views of Wallachian plains and Transylvanian hills have earned the Făgăraş renown among Romanian hikers (p. 532).	**BRAĆ AND HVAR (DALMATIAN COAST, CRO).** These islands delight both chic beachgoers and ocean adventurers with their breathtaking scenery, white pebble beaches, and nightlife as thrilling as the water sports (p. 139, p. 142).
DOBŠINSKÁ ICE CAVES (SLOVENSKY RAJ, SLK). An awe-inspiring 110,000 cubic meters of beautifully frozen water got its start during the last Ice Age (p. 645).	**BLED, SLV.** Slovenia's only island, in the middle of Lake Bled and ringed by the Julian Alps, is achingly beautiful—for a challenge, swim there from the lakeshore (p. 670).
PAKLENICA NATIONAL PARK (CRO). The cliffs and valleys of this beautiful national park, covered by a carpet of pine forests, unique geological formations of limestone karsts, and pristine mountain lakes, are awesome (p. 133).	**DRIFTING DUNES OF PARNIDIS (NIDA, LIT).** Settlers have lived in this section of the Curonian Spit since the late 14th century, but their villages have been buried by shifting dunes on multiple occasions (p. 409).
ČESKÝ RÁJ (CZR). The region's dramatic landscape, with its sandstone monoliths jutting up from rolling hills, is enhanced by surrounding, untouristed base towns like Jičín (p. 220).	**YALTA, UKR.** Take a walk on the wild side of post-Soviet life in this lavish seaside city, where daytrips lead to a big botanical garden and an even bigger winery (p. 748).
MALÁ FATRAS AND SLOVENSKÝ RAJ (SLK). Avoid the overcrowded High Tatras and head to Slovakia's best hiking, replete with alpine meadows, steep ravines, and peaks (p. 634, p. 644).	**PLITVICE LAKES NATIONAL PARK (CRO).** Endless forested hills, 16 lakes, and hundreds of waterfalls make this heavenly refuge one of Croatia's most spectacular places to wander (p. 114).
ŠKOCJANSKE AND POSTOJNA CAVES (LJUBLJANA, SLV). Mind-blowing tours of these massive and stunning caverns offer visitors a window into the country's *other* underground scene (p. 669).	**ESTONIAN ISLANDS.** Sail to Hiiumaa, where Soviet neglect encouraged a wealth of wildlife, or cross to the small island of Kassari and explore the Sääretirp sandbar (p. 246).
BIAŁOWIEŻA PRIMEVAL FOREST (POL). Europe's only old-growth forest is still populated by 12,000 species, including bison and vole (p. 502).	**LAKE BALATON (BALATONFÜRED, HUN).** The best of Hungary's natural bounty and a thriving resort surround the country's largest lake (p. 308).
BADACSONY (HUN). Among the four resort towns at the base of the nearby volcanic mountain near Balatonfüred, Badacsony offers the best views, the best treks, and the best wine cellars (p. 311).	**İSTANBUL, TUR TO ODESSA, UKR.** Ferries traverse the former route of the Vikings—in reverse—across the sparkling blue waters of the Black Sea to the beaches and resorts of the Crimea (p. 691).

LITERARY GLORY

Eastern Europe has been home to a legion of moody, brilliant, and venerable writers. Some, like playwright-turned-president Václav Havel of the Czech Republic, garner enough fame to be elected as political leaders. Others, like Anton Chekhov, play post-mortem hosts to the hordes of tourists who flock to their former homes and graves. But Eastern European literary glory does not captivate only Eastern Europeans: the fall of the Berlin Wall saw throngs of Anglophone aspiring-Kafkas flooding eastward to create the expat Prague and Budapest cafe culture of the 1990s. Whether you're looking to trace the journey of Dostoevsky's Raskolnikov across St. Petersburg or write the next *War and Peace*, Eastern Europe has enough fog-draped bridges, white nights, and haunted landscapes to inspire any reader or would-be author.

WRITER'S BLOC	SO YOU WANT TO BE AN EXPAT
ANTON CHEKHOV'S HOUSE. See the desk in Yalta, UKR, where Chekhov wrote *The Cherry Orchard* and *Three Sisters*, and witness first-hand the regional habit of making pilgrimage sites of the homes of great writers (p. 751).	**KRAKÓW, POL.** Take a seat in a Rynek-side cafe with all the tourists—or score a cheap apartment in Kazimierz, the 600-year-old Jewish quarter of Kraków, now home to a colorful scene of artists, expats, and assorted local eccentrics (p. 437).
ELIE WIESEL. Visit the childhood residence of this Holocaust survivor and Nobel Laureate in Sighetu Marmației, ROM, the cultural center of Romania's most traditional region (p. 540).	**MOSCOW, RUS.** Brood on historic streets to your heart's content. If you need some comfort food, there's always the burgers and shakes at Starlite Diner (p. 571).
MOSCOW LITERARY MUSEUMS. Get to know Moscow's literary legacy at the city's museums devoted to renowned writers like Anton Chekhov, Fyodor Dostoevsky, Alexander Pushkin, and Leo Tolstoy (p. 579).	**BRAȘOV, ROM.** Play the ski bum in Brașov, or go all Goth and hang out around Bran Castle, the inspiration for modern takes on the vampire myth. If you go with the latter, *Let's Go* recommends stocking up on garlic and turtlenecks (p. 524).
ADAM MICKIEWICZ. Follow the path of the great Romantic poet from the Vilnius, LIT, Mickiewicz Museum all the way to the Warsaw, POL, Mickiewicz Museum (p. 389, p. 435).	**WARSAW, POL.** So concrete, so imposing, so mid-90s Berlin: what fodder for your novel! Not to mention the opportunities to drink your money away on Warsaw's awesome nightlife (p. 420).
SZOMBATHELY'S LEOPOLD BLOOM. Celebrate Bloomsday in Szombathely, HUN, where the Hungarian origins of James Joyce's character are grounds for a festival every June 16 (p. 322).	**TALLINN, EST.** A beautiful but unintimidating staff serves cheap and delicious coffee to a mostly local crowd in Kafe Kohvicum, a cozy, candle-lit basement cafe (p. 236).
TARAS SHEVCHENKO. Ukraine's favorite poet is everywhere in Kyiv—he has the requisite monument and museum, as well as a university, a popular street, and a park named in his honor (p. 710).	**İSTANBUL, TUR.** Cheap rooms in Sultanahmet overlooking the Grand Bazaar are perfect places to brood on the frailty of empire and the commodification of world culture (p. 695).
FRANZ KAFKA. Have an existential crisis at the Franz Kafka Museum in Prague, the city in which everyone's favorite angst-meister was born and raised (p. 187).	**ST. PETERSBURG, RUS.** The sleek decor and old-library motif of Cafe Zoom draw the city's artists and literati, who enjoy good food and frequent readings and performances (p. 595).
VÁCLEV HAVEL. Stay in his cell in Prague's Pension Unitis Art Prison Hostel and get inside the mind of the region's most famous living playwright, dissident, and Velvet revolutionary (p. 173).	**VILNIUS, LIT.** This city boasts a small but thriving expat scene entirely worthy of the quirky, oddball sensibilities of Lithuania. Just brace yourself for winter (p. 379).
GRASS'S GENIUS. Stop by Gdańsk, POL, to see the landscape that once inspired Günter Grass's beautifully crafted, Nobel Prize-winning epic *The Tin Drum* (p. 487).	**KYIV, UKR.** Settle in Kyiv to see first-hand the struggle to improve a democracy. Get a job at the English-language Kyiv Post, and chat with your coworkers over pints at The Drum (p. 723).
PUSHKIN THE ENVELOPE. See the statue in St. Petersburg, RUS, that inspired Pushkin's poem "The Bronze Horseman." Check out Dostoevsky's grave while you're in town (p. 601).	**DUBROVNIK, CRO.** If walled cities are your thing, you should definitely consider setting up shop in lovely Dubrovnik. We hear it's the new Prague (p. 146).

FESTIVALS!

	APRIL - JUNE	JULY - AUGUST	SEPTEMBER - MARCH
BULGARIA	**International Music Festival** June, Varna (p. 88)	**Sofia Music Week** June, Sofia (p. 71) **International Jazz Festival** Aug., Varna (p. 88)	**Love is Folly Film Festival** Aug.-Sept., Varna (p. 88) **International Jazz Festival** Oct., Sofia (p. 71)
CROATIA	**Cest is d'Best** June, Zagreb (p. 103) **Eurokaz Theater Festival** June, Zagreb (p. 103) **Int'l Children's Festival** June-July, Šibenik	**International Folklore Fest** July, Zagreb (p. 103) **Biker Days Festival** July, Pula (p. 114) **Split Summer Festival** July-Aug., Split (p. 133)	**Marco Polo Festival** Aug.-Sept., Korčula (p. 144) **International Puppet Fest** Sept., Zagreb (p. 103) **International Jazz Days** Oct., Zagreb (p. 103)
CZECH REPUBLIC	**Prague Spring Festival** May-June (p. 163) **Prague Fringe Festival** June (p. 163)	**International Film Festival** July, Karlovy Vary (p. 198) **International Music Fest** July-Aug., Český Krumlov (p. 205)	**International Organ Fest** Sept., Olomouc (p. 216) **Jazz Goes to Town** Oct., Hradec Králové (p. 220)
ESTONIA	**Country Dance Festival** June, Pärnu (p. 242) **Grillfest** June, Tallinn (p. 232) **Jaanipäev** June, Tallinn (p. 232)	**Beersummer** July, Tallinn (p. 232) **Watergate** July, Pärnu (p. 242)	**White Lady Days** Aug., Haapsalu (p. 245) **Dark Nights Film Festival** Dec., Tallinn (p. 232) **Student Jazz Festival** Feb., Tallinn (p. 232)
HUNGARY	**Bloomsday Festival** June, Szombathely (p. 322) **Danube Festival** June, Budapest (p. 270) **Sopron Festival Weeks** June-July (p. 319)	**Golden Shell Folklore** July, Siófok (p. 305) **Szeged Open Air Festival** July-Aug. (p. 335) **Sziget Rock Festival** Aug., Budapest (p. 270)	**Éger Vintage Days** Sept. (p. 292) **Festival of Wine Songs** Sept., Pécs (p. 326) **Jazz Days** Sept., Debrecen (p. 331)
LATVIA	**Midsummer's Eve** June (p. 351)	**Rīgas Ritmi Music Festival** July, Rīga (p. 351)	**Chamber Choir Festival** Sept., Rīga (p. 351)
LITHUANIA	**Vilniaus Festivalis** May, Vilnius (p. 379) **Pažaislis Music Festival** May-Sept., Kaunas (p. 392)	**Thomas Mann Festival** July, Nida (p. 409) **Night Serenades** Aug., Palanga (p. 406)	**SIRENOS Theater Festival** Sept.-Oct., Vilnius (p. 379) **Vilnius Jazz Festival** Sept.-Oct., Vilnius (p. 379)
POLAND	**Int'l Short Film Festival** May, Kraków (**p. 437**) **Wianki** June, Kraków (p. 437)	**Street Theater Festival** July, Kraków (p. 437) **Highlander Folklore** Aug., Zakopane (p. 456)	**Jazz Festival** Mar., Poznań (p. 475)
ROMANIA	**Int'l Theater Festival** June, Sibiu (p. 530)	**Medieval Festival** July, Sighişoara (p. 528)	**Int'l Chamber Music Fest.** Sept., Braşov (p. 524)
RUSSIA	**Music Spring** Apr., St. Petersburg (p. 587)	**White Nights Festival** June, St. Petersburg (p. 587)	**Maslyanitsa** Feb. (p. 562)
SLOVAKIA	**International Festival of Ghosts and Spirits** May, Bojnice (p. 634)	**Festival of Marian Devotion** July, Levoča (p. 647)	**Bratislava Music Festival** Sept.-Oct. (p. 623) **Jazz Days** Oct., Bratislava (p. 623)
SLOVENIA	**International Wine Fair** Apr., Ljubljana (p. 662) **Break 22 Festival** June, Ljubljana (p. 662)	**Bled Days** July (p. 670)	**International Film Festival** Nov., Ljubljana (p. 662) **Kurent Carnival** Feb., Ptuj (p. 682)
TURKEY	**Şeker Bayramı** Sept. 30-Oct. 2, 2008; Sept. 19-22, 2009	**Kurban Bayramı** Dec. 8-11, 2008; Nov. 17-20, 2009	**Apricot Festival** July, Malatya
UKRAINE	**Lviv City Days** May (p. 725) **Kyiv Days** End of May (p. 710)	**Local Sheep Cheese Festival** Sept., Uzhhorod (p. 732)	**Golden Lion Theater Festival** Sept., in even-numbered years, Lviv (p. 725)

SUGGESTED ITINERARIES

NEW SCHOOL (3 WEEKS)

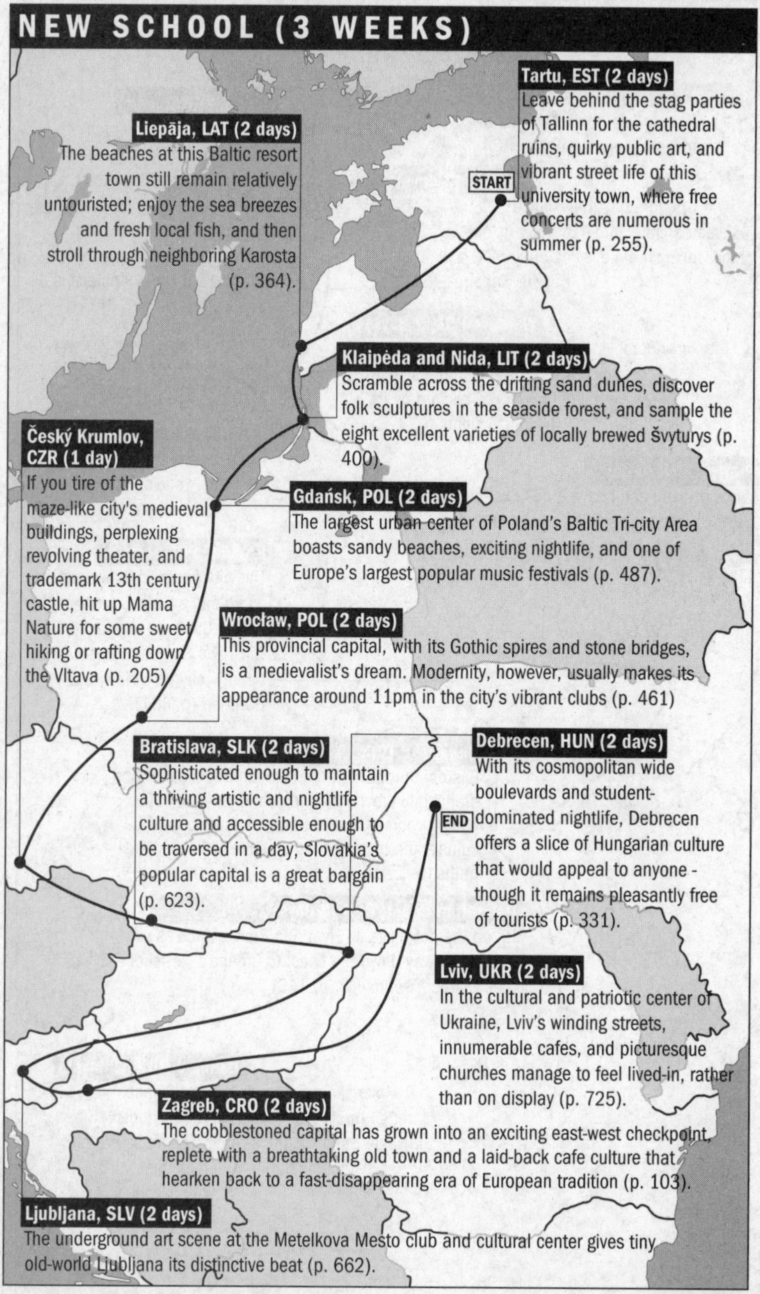

START

Tartu, EST (2 days)
Leave behind the stag parties of Tallinn for the cathedral ruins, quirky public art, and vibrant street life of this university town, where free concerts are numerous in summer (p. 255).

Liepāja, LAT (2 days)
The beaches at this Baltic resort town still remain relatively untouristed; enjoy the sea breezes and fresh local fish, and then stroll through neighboring Karosta (p. 364).

Klaipėda and Nida, LIT (2 days)
Scramble across the drifting sand dunes, discover folk sculptures in the seaside forest, and sample the eight excellent varieties of locally brewed Švyturys (p. 400).

Gdańsk, POL (2 days)
The largest urban center of Poland's Baltic Tri-city Area boasts sandy beaches, exciting nightlife, and one of Europe's largest popular music festivals (p. 487).

Wrocław, POL (2 days)
This provincial capital, with its Gothic spires and stone bridges, is a medievalist's dream. Modernity, however, usually makes its appearance around 11pm in the city's vibrant clubs (p. 461)

Český Krumlov, CZR (1 day)
If you tire of the maze-like city's medieval buildings, perplexing revolving theater, and trademark 13th century castle, hit up Mama Nature for some sweet hiking or rafting down the Vltava (p. 205).

Bratislava, SLK (2 days)
Sophisticated enough to maintain a thriving artistic and nightlife culture and accessible enough to be traversed in a day, Slovakia's popular capital is a great bargain (p. 623).

Ljubljana, SLV (2 days)
The underground art scene at the Metelkova Mesto club and cultural center gives tiny old-world Ljubljana its distinctive beat (p. 662).

Zagreb, CRO (2 days)
The cobblestoned capital has grown into an exciting east-west checkpoint, replete with a breathtaking old town and a laid-back cafe culture that hearken back to a fast-disappearing era of European tradition (p. 103).

Lviv, UKR (2 days)
In the cultural and patriotic center of Ukraine, Lviv's winding streets, innumerable cafes, and picturesque churches manage to feel lived-in, rather than on display (p. 725).

Debrecen, HUN (2 days)
With its cosmopolitan wide boulevards and student-dominated nightlife, Debrecen offers a slice of Hungarian culture that would appeal to anyone - though it remains pleasantly free of tourists (p. 331).

END

OLD SCHOOL (4 WEEKS)

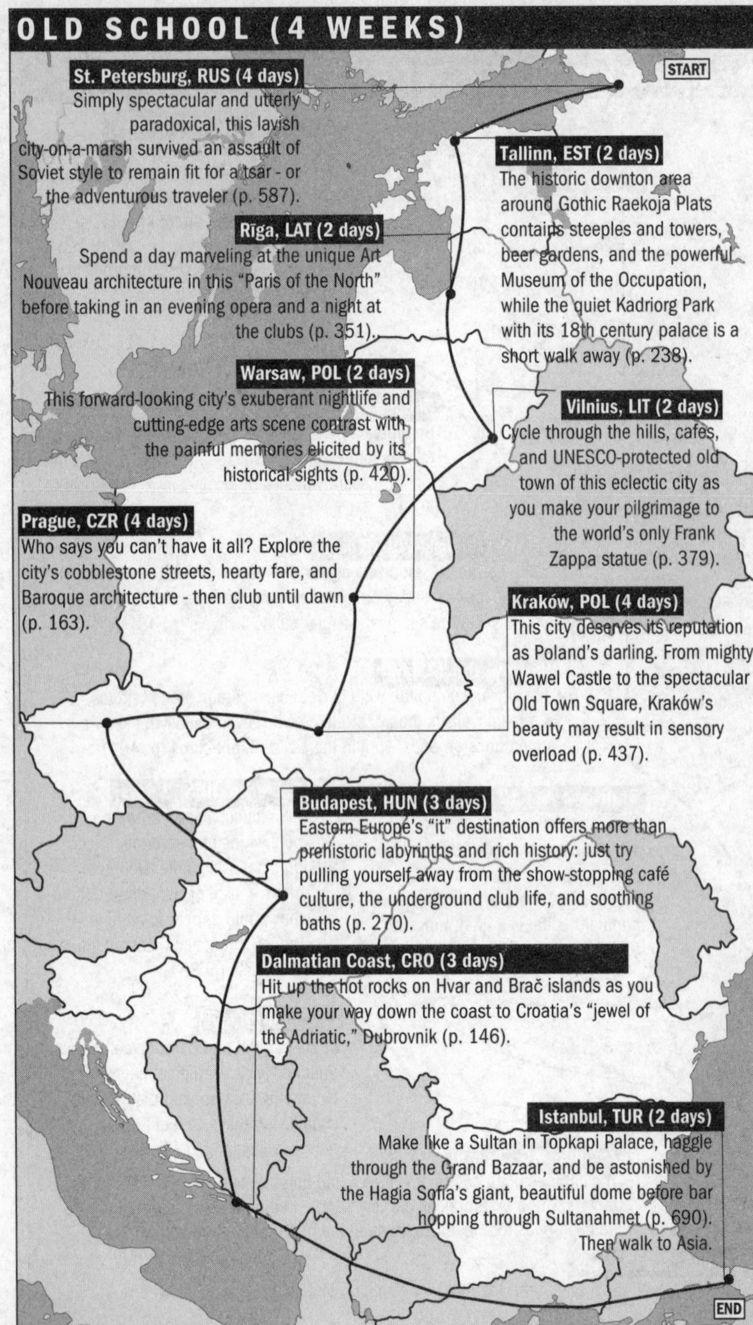

START
St. Petersburg, RUS (4 days)
Simply spectacular and utterly paradoxical, this lavish city-on-a-marsh survived an assault of Soviet style to remain fit for a tsar - or the adventurous traveler (p. 587).
Tallinn, EST (2 days)
The historic downton area around Gothic Raekoja Plats contains steeples and towers, beer gardens, and the powerful Museum of the Occupation, while the quiet Kadriorg Park with its 18th century palace is a short walk away (p. 238).
Rīga, LAT (2 days)
Spend a day marveling at the unique Art Nouveau architecture in this "Paris of the North" before taking in an evening opera and a night at the clubs (p. 351).
Warsaw, POL (2 days)
This forward-looking city's exuberant nightlife and cutting-edge arts scene contrast with the painful memories elicited by its historical sights (p. 420).
Vilnius, LIT (2 days)
Cycle through the hills, cafes, and UNESCO-protected old town of this eclectic city as you make your pilgrimage to the world's only Frank Zappa statue (p. 379).
Prague, CZR (4 days)
Who says you can't have it all? Explore the city's cobblestone streets, hearty fare, and Baroque architecture - then club until dawn (p. 163).
Kraków, POL (4 days)
This city deserves its reputation as Poland's darling. From mighty Wawel Castle to the spectacular Old Town Square, Kraków's beauty may result in sensory overload (p. 437).
Budapest, HUN (3 days)
Eastern Europe's "it" destination offers more than prehistoric labyrinths and rich history: just try pulling yourself away from the show-stopping café culture, the underground club life, and soothing baths (p. 270).
Dalmatian Coast, CRO (3 days)
Hit up the hot rocks on Hvar and Brač islands as you make your way down the coast to Croatia's "jewel of the Adriatic," Dubrovnik (p. 146).
Istanbul, TUR (2 days)
Make like a Sultan in Topkapi Palace, haggle through the Grand Bazaar, and be astonished by the Hagia Sofia's giant, beautiful dome before bar hopping through Sultanahmet (p. 690).
Then walk to Asia.
END

MOTHER RUSSIA (3 WEEKS)

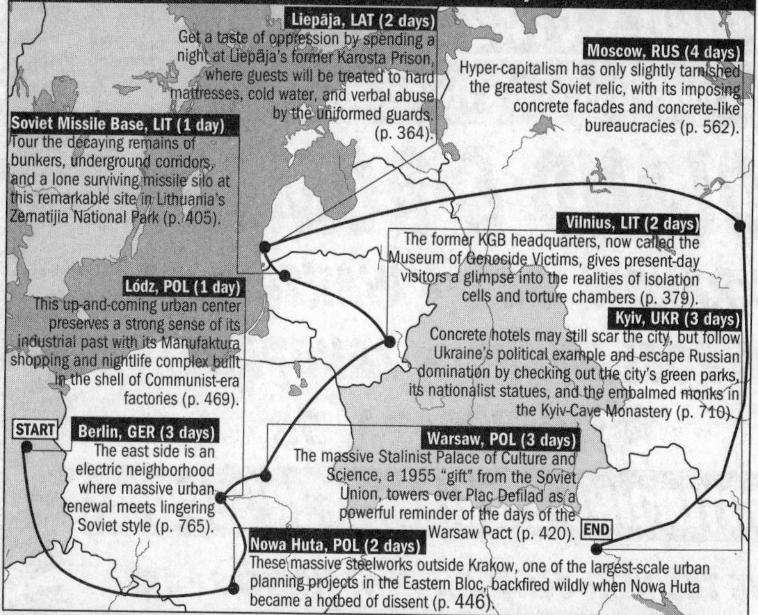

START

Berlin, GER (3 days) The east side is an electric neighborhood where massive urban renewal meets lingering Soviet style (p. 765).

Lódz, POL (1 day) This up-and-coming urban center preserves a strong sense of its industrial past with its Manufaktura shopping and nightlife complex built in the shell of Communist-era factories (p. 469).

Soviet Missile Base, LIT (1 day) Tour the decaying remains of bunkers, underground corridors, and a lone surviving missile silo at this remarkable site in Lithuania's Zematijia National Park (p. 405).

Liepāja, LAT (2 days) Get a taste of oppression by spending a night at Liepāja's former Karosta Prison, where guests will be treated to hard mattresses, cold water, and verbal abuse by the uniformed guards. (p. 364).

Moscow, RUS (4 days) Hyper-capitalism has only slightly tarnished the greatest Soviet relic, with its imposing concrete facades and concrete-like bureaucracies (p. 562).

Vilnius, LIT (2 days) The former KGB headquarters, now called the Museum of Genocide Victims, gives present-day visitors a glimpse into the realities of isolation cells and torture chambers (p. 379).

Kyiv, UKR (3 days) Concrete hotels may still scar the city, but follow Ukraine's political example and escape Russian domination by checking out the city's green parks, its nationalist statues, and the embalmed monks in the Kyiv-Cave Monastery (p. 710).

Warsaw, POL (3 days) The massive Stalinist Palace of Culture and Science, a 1955 "gift" from the Soviet Union, towers over Plac Defilad as a powerful reminder of the days of the Warsaw Pact (p. 420).

Nowa Huta, POL (2 days) These massive steelworks outside Krakow, one of the largest-scale urban planning projects in the Eastern Bloc, backfired wildly when Nowa Huta became a hotbed of dissent (p. 446).

END

MOTHER NATURE (2 WEEKS)

Tatras Mts., SLK/POL (2 days) The Tatras region is unbeatable for its gorgeous scenery, which includes underground waterfalls, rugged trails, and breathtaking vistas (p. 638).

Mt. Hoverla, UKR (1 day) Lounge in saunas, go mushroom picking, and absorb Hutsul folk culture around Ukraine's highest peak (p. 737).

Eger, HUN (1 day) Even the legendary, violent Turkish invasion could not destroy this city's wonderful ranges of deep green hills and its warm, relaxed atmosphere (p. 292).

Translyvania, ROM (1 day) The thickly forested slopes of the Carpathian Mountains shelter numerous hikers and skiers, as well as legendary villages and castles (p. 524).

Lake Balaton, HUN (2 days) The best place to lounge on a beautiful shoreline in landlocked Hungary, Lake Balaton, Central Europe's largest lake, neighbors the Tihany Peninsula nature preserve, as well as numerous spa towns (p. 304).

Bled, SLV (1 day) The crags of the Julian Alps rise above a subalpine lake cradling Slovenia's only island, home to a well-preserved 13th-century castle (p. 670).

END

Black Sea Coast, BUL/ROM (2 days) Surrounded by the stunning vista of Nessebar Bay, wander through countless ruins before heading north to soak up the sun and party on the beaches of multicultural Varna (p. 88) and Constanța (p. 547).

START

Paklenica National Park, CRO (2 days The stunning rock formations, caves, and lakes combine to make this nature preserve and rock-climbing center one of Croatia's most beautiful sights (p. 133).

Veliko Turnovo, BUL (2 days) In Bulgaria's most beautiful city, scramble over the ruins of a Roman citadel and explore surrounding hill towns and monasteries (p. 82).

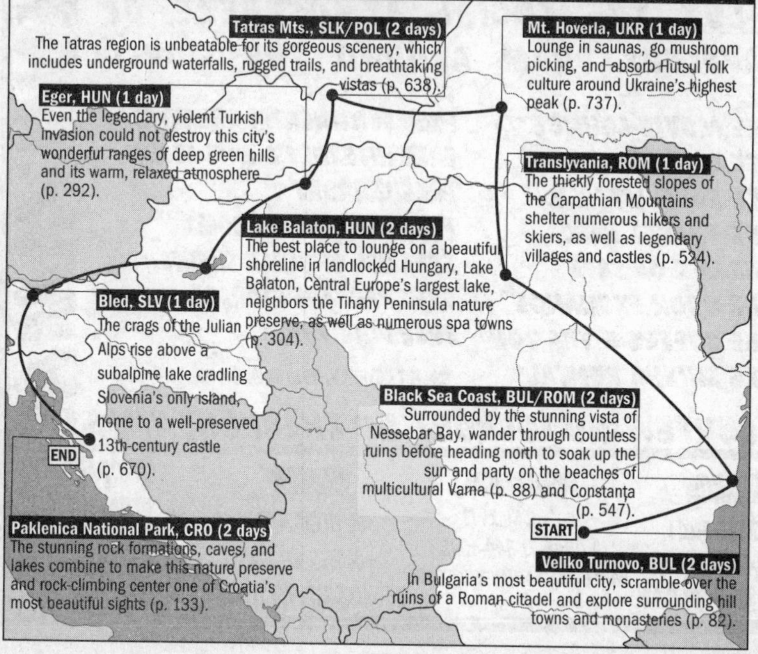

ESSENTIALS

PLANNING YOUR TRIP

ENTRANCE REQUIREMENTS.

Passport (p. 11). Required for citizens of Australia, Canada, Ireland, New Zealand, the UK, and the US to enter all countries in Eastern Europe.

Visa (p. 12). Required of all foreign citizens entering Russia, Belarus, and Turkey, of citizens of Australia and New Zealand entering Ukraine and Moldova, and of some foreigners entering other countries in Eastern Europe. Consult your destination's **Entrance Requirements** section for more information.

Letter of Invitation (p. 13). Required of all foreign citizens entering Belarus not seeking a transit visa, of all foreign citizens entering Russia, and of all citizens of Australia and New Zealand entering Moldova and Ukraine.

Inoculations (p. 25). Recommended up-to-date on DTaP (diphtheria, tetanus, and pertussis), Hepatitis A, Hepatitis B, MMR (measles, mumps, and rubella), polio booster, rabies, and typhoid.

Work Permit (p. 13). Required of foreigners planning to work in Eastern Europe.

EMBASSIES AND CONSULATES

Eastern European embassies and consulates abroad are listed in the **Documents and Formalities: Embassies and Consulates** section at the beginning of each chapter. Australian, Canadian, Irish, New Zealand, UK, and US embassies and consulates in Eastern European countries are listed in the **Practical Information** sections for the capitals of each country.

DOCUMENTS AND FORMALITIES

PASSPORTS

REQUIREMENTS

Citizens of Australia, Canada, Ireland, New Zealand, the UK, and the US need valid passports to enter any country in Eastern Europe, as well as to re-enter their home countries. Many Eastern European countries will not allow entrance if the holder's passport expires within six months; returning home with an expired passport is illegal and may result in a fine.

NEW PASSPORTS

Citizens of Australia, Canada, Ireland, New Zealand, the UK, and the US can apply for a passport at any passport office or at selected post offices and courts of law. Citizens of these countries may also download passport applications from the official website of their country's government or passport office. Any new passport or renewal applications must be filed well in advance of the departure date, though most passport offices offer rush services for a very steep fee. Note, however, that "rushed" passports may still take up to two weeks to arrive.

PASSPORT MAINTENANCE

ONE EUROPE. European unity has come a long way since 1958, when the European Economic Community (EEC) was created to promote European solidarity and cooperation. Since then, the EEC has become the European Union (EU), a mighty political, legal, and economic institution. On May 1, 2004, ten South, Central, and Eastern European countries–Cyprus, the **Czech Republic, Estonia, Hungary, Latvia, Lithuania,** Malta, **Poland, Slovakia,** and **Slovenia**–were admitted to the EU, joining 15 other member states: Austria, Belgium, Denmark, Finland, France, Germany, Greece, Ireland, Italy, Luxembourg, the Netherlands, Portugal, Spain, Sweden, and the UK. On January 1, 2007, **Romania** and **Bulgaria** also joined the EU, bringing the total number of EU countries to 27.

What does this have to do with the average non-EU tourist? The EU's policy of **freedom of movement** means that border controls between the first 15 member states (minus Ireland and the UK, but plus Norway and Iceland) have been abolished, and visa policies harmonized. Under this treaty, formally known as the **Schengen Agreement,** you're still required to carry a passport (or government-issued ID card for EU citizens) when crossing an internal border, but once you've been admitted into one country, you're free to travel to other participating states. The 10 member states that joined the EU in 2004 are anticipated to implement the policy in December of 2007 at the earliest; many estimate, however, that 2008 is more likely. **Bulgaria** hopes to implement the Agreement by 2009.

For other important consequences of the EU for travelers, see **European Customs** and **EU customs regulations** (p. 14).

Photocopy the page of your passport with your photo, as well as your visas, traveler's check serial numbers, and any other important documents. Carry one set of copies in a safe place, apart from the originals, and leave another set at home. Consulates also recommend that you carry an expired passport or an official copy of your birth certificate in a part of your baggage separate from other documents.

If you lose your passport, immediately notify the local police and the nearest embassy or consulate of your home government. To expedite its replacement, you must show ID and proof of citizenship; it also helps to know all information previously recorded in the passport. In some cases, a replacement may take weeks to process, and it may be valid only for a limited time. Any visas stamped in your old passport will be irretrievably lost. In an emergency, ask for immediate temporary traveling papers that will permit you to re-enter your home country.

VISAS, INVITATIONS, AND WORK PERMITS

VISAS

Citizens of **Australia, Canada, Ireland, New Zealand,** the **UK,** and the **US** need a visa in addition to a valid passport for entrance into **Russia, Belarus,** and **Turkey;** citizens of Australia and New Zealand need a visa for entrance into Moldova and Ukraine. Eastern European entrance requirements change frequently; always double-check with the nearest embassy or consulate of your destination for up-to-date info.

As soon as Bulgaria, the Czech Republic, Estonia, Hungary, Latvia, Lithuania, Slovakia, and Slovenia formally implement the **Schengen Agreement** (most likely in 2008 or 2009), citizens of Australia, Canada, New Zealand, and the US will not need a visa for stays of up to 90 days, though this three-month period begins upon entry into any of the countries that belong to the EU's **freedom of movement** zone. For more information, see **One Europe,** above. Entering **all Eastern European countries** to study requires a special visa. For more information, see **Beyond Tourism** (p. 52).

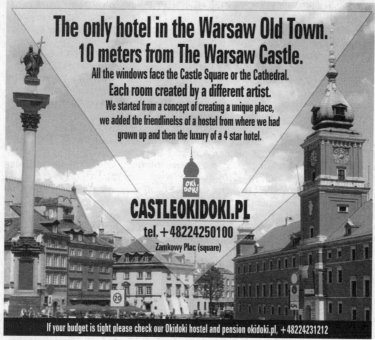

INVITATIONS

In their respective visa applications—excluding those for transit visas—Russia and Belarus require an invitation from a sponsoring individual or organization. A similar letter is required from citizens of Australia and New Zealand seeking a visa to Moldova or Ukraine. Specialized travel agencies and hotels can arrange invitations for those without private sponsors. Many travel agencies and online visa services will take care of visa processing (including letters of invitation). For agencies that specialize in visa acquisition and for additional information, see the **Visa and Entry Information** section at the beginning of each country chapter.

WORK PERMITS

Admission as a visitor does not include the right to work, which is authorized only by a work permit. For more information, see the **Beyond Tourism** chapter (p. 60).

IDENTIFICATION

When you travel, always carry at least two forms of identification on your person, including a photo ID; a passport and a driver's license is usually an adequate combination. Never carry all of your IDs together; split them up in case of theft or loss, and keep photocopies of all of them in your luggage and at home.

STUDENT, TEACHER, AND YOUTH IDENTIFICATION

The **International Student Identity Card (ISIC),** the most widely accepted form of student ID, provides discounts on some sights, accommodations, food, and transportation; access to a 24hr. emergency helpline; and insurance benefits for US cardholders (see **Insurance,** p. 25). Get discounts on bungee jumping in Bulgaria, bus services in Croatia, and language classes in Poland. (Visit www.myisic.com/

myisic/discountfinder/home.aspx to search for discounts in your country of destination.) Applicants must be full-time secondary or post-secondary school students at least 12 years of age. Because of the proliferation of fake ISICs, some services (particularly airlines) require additional proof of student identity.

The **International Teacher Identity Card (ITIC)** offers teachers the same insurance coverage as the ISIC and similar but limited discounts. To qualify for the card, teachers must be currently employed and have worked a minimum of 18hr. per week for at least one school year. For travelers who are under 26 years old but are not students, the **International Youth Travel Card (IYTC)** also offers many of the same benefits as the ISIC.

Each of these identity cards costs US$22. ISICs, ITICs, and IYTCs are valid for one year from the date of issue. To learn more about ISICs, ITICs, and IYTCs, try www.myisic.com. Many student travel agencies (p. 31) issue the cards; for a list of issuing agencies or more information, see the **International Student Travel Confederation (ISTC)** website (www.istc.org).

The **International Student Exchange Card (ISE Card)** is a similar identification card available to students, faculty, and youths aged 12 to 26. The card provides discounts, medical benefits, access to a 24hr. emergency helpline, and the ability to purchase student airfares. An ISE Card costs US$25; call ☎800-255-8000 (in North America) or ☎480-951-1177 (from all other continents) for more info, or visit www.isecard.com. The ISE Card does not cover Estonia, Moldova, or Ukraine.

CUSTOMS

Upon entering any country in Eastern Europe, you must declare certain items from abroad and pay a duty on the value of those articles if they exceed the allowance established by that country's customs service. Note that goods and gifts purchased at **duty-free** shops abroad are not exempt from duty or sales tax; "duty-free" merely means that you need not pay a tax in the country of purchase. Duty-free allowances were abolished for travel between EU member states on June 30, 1999, but still exist for those arriving from outside the EU. Upon returning home, you must likewise declare all articles acquired abroad and pay a duty on the value of the articles in excess of your home country's allowance. In order to expedite your return, make a list of any valuables brought from home and register them with customs before traveling abroad, and keep receipts for all goods acquired abroad.

CUSTOMS IN THE EU. As well as freedom of movement of people within the EU (see p. 12), travelers in the 15 original EU member countries (Austria, Belgium, Denmark, Finland, France, Germany, Greece, Ireland, Italy, Luxembourg, the Netherlands, Portugal, Spain, Sweden, and the UK) and—in 2008 or 2009—the newest member countries (**Bulgaria,** Cyprus, the **Czech Republic, Estonia, Hungary, Latvia, Lithuania,** Malta, **Poland, Slovakia,** and **Slovenia**) can also take advantage of the freedom of movement of goods. This means that there are no customs controls at internal EU borders (i.e., you can take the blue customs channel at the airport), and travelers are free to transport whatever legal substances they like as long as it is for their own personal (non-commercial) use—up to 800 cigarettes, 10L of spirits, 90L of wine (including up to 60L of sparkling wine), and 110L of beer. Duty-free allowances were abolished on June 30, 1999 for travel between the original 15 EU member states; this now also applies to Cyprus and Malta. However, travelers between the EU and the rest of the world still get a duty-free allowance when passing through customs.

MONEY

CURRENCY AND EXCHANGE

A chart at the beginning of each country chapter lists the August 2007 exchange rates between local currency and Australian dollars (AUS$), Canadian dollars (CDN$), New Zealand dollars (NZ$), British pounds (UK£), US dollars (US$), and EU euro (EUR€). Check the currency converter on financial websites such as www.xe.com for the latest exchange rates. As a general rule, it's cheaper to convert money abroad than at home. Still, it's wise to bring enough foreign currency to last the first 24 to 72 hours of a trip.

When changing money, go only to banks or exchange offices that have at most a 5% margin between their buy and sell prices. Since you lose money with every transaction, **convert large sums** (unless the currency is depreciating rapidly), but no more than you'll need within that one country, since it may be difficult or impossible to change it back. Some countries, such as the Czech Republic, Russia, and the Slovak Republic, may require transaction receipts to reconvert local currency. Of foreign currencies, US$ and EUR€ are the most widely—and at times the only—foreign currencies accepted for exchange.

If you use **traveler's checks** or bills, carry some in small denominations (the equivalent of US$50 or less) for times when you are forced to exchange money at disadvantageous rates, but bring a range of denominations since charges may be levied per check cashed. All travelers should also consider carrying some US dollars (about US$50 worth), which are sometimes preferred by local tellers.

PINS AND ATMS. To use a cash or credit card to withdraw money from a cash machine (ATM) in Europe, you must have a four-digit **Personal Identification Number (PIN).** If your PIN is longer than four digits, ask your bank whether you can just use the first four, or whether you'll need a new one. **Credit cards** don't usually come with PINs, so if you intend to hit up ATMs in Europe with a credit card to get cash advances, call your credit card company before leaving to request one. Travelers with alphabetic, rather than numerical, PINs may also be thrown off by the lack of letters on European cash machines. The following are the corresponding numbers to use: 1=QZ; 2=ABC; 3=DEF; 4=GHI; 5=JKL; 6=MNO; 7=PRS; 8=TUV; and 9=WXY. Note that if you mistakenly punch the wrong code into the machine three times, it will swallow your card for good.

On the whole, however, avoid using Western money at other venues: some establishments post prices in US$ or EUR€ due to high inflation and will insist that they don't accept anything else. Such prices, however, are generally more expensive than those in the local currency.

TRAVELER'S CHECKS

Traveler's checks are one of the safest means of carrying funds. American Express and Visa are the most recognized brands. Many banks and agencies sell them for a small commission. Check issuers provide refunds if the checks are lost or stolen, and many provide additional services, such as toll-free refund hotlines abroad, emergency message services, and stolen credit card assistance. It is best to get checks in either US$ or EUR€. They are readily accepted in Prague, Budapest, and similar urban centers, but unfortunately it is often difficult—if not impossible—to cash these checks in rural areas or anywhere in Russia.

American Express: Checks available with commission at select banks, at all American Express offices, and online (www.americanexpress.com; US residents only). American Express cardholders can also purchase checks by phone (☎800-721-9768). Checks available in Australian, British, Canadian, European, and US currencies, among others. American Express also offers the Travelers Cheque Card, a prepaid, reloadable card. Cheques for Two can be signed by either of two people traveling together. For purchase locations or more information, contact AmEx's service centers: in Australia ☎61 29 27 18 66, in New Zealand 64 93 67 45 67, in the UK 44 12 73 69 69 33, in the US and Canada 800-221-7282; elsewhere, call the US collect at 336-393-1111.

Travelex: Thomas Cook MasterCard and Interpayment Visa traveler's checks available. Travelex/Thomas Cook offices cash checks commission-free but are less common in Eastern Europe than American Express. For information about Thomas Cook MasterCard in Canada and the US, call ☎800-223-7373, in the UK 08 00 62 21 01; elsewhere call the UK collect at +441 733 318 950. For information about Interpayment Visa in the US and Canada ☎800-732-1322, in the UK 800 515 884; elsewhere, call the UK collect at +441 733 318 949. For more information, visit www.travelex.com.

Visa: Checks available (generally with commission) at banks worldwide. For the location of the nearest office, call the Visa Travelers Cheque Global Refund and Assistance Center: in the UK ☎08 00 89 50 78, in the US 800-227-6811; elsewhere, call the UK collect at ☎44 20 79 37 80 91. Checks available in British, Canadian, European and US currencies, among others. Visa also offers TravelMoney, a prepaid debit card that can be reloaded online or by phone. For more information on Visa travel services, see http://usa.visa.com/personal/using_visa/travel_with_visa.html.

ESSENTIALS

CREDIT, DEBIT, AND ATM CARDS

Where they are accepted, **credit cards** often offer superior exchange rates—up to 5% better than the retail rate used by banks and other currency exchange establishments. Credit cards may also offer services such as insurance or emergency help and are sometimes required to reserve hotel rooms or rental cars. **MasterCard (a.k.a. EuroCard in Europe; MC)** and **Visa (a.k.a. Carte Bleue; V)** are the most common; **American Express (AmEx)** cards work at some ATMs and major airports.

The use of **ATM cards** is relatively widespread in Eastern Europe, particularly in urban locations. Depending on the system that your home bank uses, you can most likely access your personal bank account from abroad; be sure to contact your bank before leaving. ATMs get the same wholesale exchange rate as credit cards, but there is often a limit on the amount of money you can withdraw per day (usually around US$500). There is typically also a surcharge of US$1-5 per withdrawal. While ATMs are generally easy to come by, particularly in cities, carry a bit of extra cash if traveling in rural regions.

A **debit card** can be used wherever its associated credit card company (usually MC or V) is accepted, but the money is withdrawn directly from the holder's checking account. Debit cards often also function as ATM cards and can be used to withdraw cash from associated banks and ATMs throughout Eastern Europe.

The two major international money networks are **MasterCard/Maestro/Cirrus** (for ATM locations ☎800-424-7787 or www.mastercard.com) and **Visa/PLUS** (for ATM locations ☎800-843-7587 or www.visa.com). Most ATMs charge a transaction fee that is paid to the bank that owns the ATM.

Identity theft is on the rise, especially in Belarus, Bulgaria, Moldova, Romania and Russia. This theft occurs in a variety of ways: some countries have established fake ATMs, minus the cash box, to steal the cardholder's information. Credit-card fraud is always a risk, especially in the former USSR Bloc, so travelers should be wary when they use their cards. Debit cards are less risky since they often have a daily limit, but beware: unlike credit cards, the funds are directly taken from the account and there is no recourse in the event of theft.

TOP 10 WAYS TO SAVE MONEY IN EASTERN EUROPE

Let's face it: one of the main reasons you're going to Eastern Europe is because it's inexpensive. But as any survivor of Soviet economic planning can tell you, there are always ways to get things a bit more cheaply.

1. Buy food (and maybe your tracksuits and DVDs, too) at **open-air markets.**
2. Avoid any establishment with **English words** in its name or on a sign or menu outside.
3. Find free **Internet access** in libraries and tourist offices, where you can avoid the chain-smoking teens playing CounterStrike.
4. Take **private microbuses** between cities; they're often cheaper and more comfortable than trains or buses.
5. Be on the lookout for days when you can get into **sights** and **museums** for free.
6. Buy dirt-cheap, quality **beer** and **vodka** at the grocery store.
7. If you take a **cab,** always have someone who speaks the local language call ahead for you so you won't be ripped off.
8. Talk to the **locals.** They know where the good deals are.
9. If you're bound for a major tourist city, go in **winter**—prices will be much lower in the snow.
10. In major cities, make your base on the **outskirts** of town, where accommodations and restaurants tend to be cheaper.

GETTING MONEY FROM HOME

If you run out of money while traveling, the easiest and cheapest solution is to have someone back home make a deposit to your bank account. Barring that, consider one of the following options.

WIRING MONEY

It is possible to arrange a **bank transfer,** which means asking a bank back home to **wire money** to a bank abroad. This is the cheapest way to transfer cash, but it's also the slowest, usually taking several days or more. Note that some banks may only release your funds in local currency, potentially sticking you with a poor exchange rate. Money transfer services like **Western Union** are faster than bank transfers, but also much pricier. Western Union has many locations worldwide. To find one, visit www.westernunion.com, or call in Australia ☎800 173 833, in Canada and the US 800-325-6000, in the UK 800 833 833. For large bank chains in specific countries, refer to the front of each country section. Money transfer services are also available to **American Express** cardholders and at select **Thomas Cook** offices.

US STATE DEPARTMENT (US CITIZENS ONLY)

In emergencies only, the US State Department will forward money within hours to the nearest consular office, which will then disburse it according to instructions for a US$30 fee. To use this service, you must contact the Overseas Citizens Service division of the US State Department (☎202-647-5225, toll-free 888-407-4747).

COSTS

The cost of your trip will vary considerably, depending on where you go, how you travel, and where you stay. The most significant expense will probably be your round-trip **airfare,** which can be much more expensive than a ticket to Western Europe (see **Getting to Eastern Europe: By Plane,** p. 30).

STAYING ON A BUDGET

Eastern Europe is the budget traveler's paradise. The accommodations, local restaurants, and transportation services in Eastern Europe charge a fraction of their Western counterparts. Often the difference of a couple US$ or EUR€ in price means an improvement by leaps and bounds in quality. Generally, a bare-bones day in Eastern Europe (camping or sleeping in hostels/guesthouses, buying food at supermarkets) will cost about US$30; a slightly more comfortable day (sleeping in hostels/guesthouses and the occasional budget hotel, eating one meal a day at a restaurant, going out at night) will run about

US$40-50. But even these ranges vary throughout the region: expect to spend US$10-15 more per day in Croatia, Slovenia, and Estonia, and US$5 less in Lithuania, Ukraine, and Slovakia. Also, don't forget to factor in emergency reserve funds (at least US$200) when planning how much money you'll need.

TIPS FOR SAVING MONEY

Some simple ways to save include seeking out opportunities for free entertainment, splitting accommodation and food costs with trustworthy fellow travelers, and buying food in supermarkets rather than eating out. Bring a **sleepsack** (p. 19) to save on linens charges in European hostels, and do your **laundry** in the sink. Some museums offer free admission on certain days of the month. If you are eligible, consider getting an ISIC or an IYTC (p. 13); sights and museums may offer reduced admission to students and youths. For getting around quickly, bikes are the most economical option. Drinking at bars and clubs quickly becomes expensive. It's cheaper to buy alcohol at a supermarket and imbibe before going out. That said, don't go overboard. Though staying within your budget is important, don't do so at the expense of your health or a great travel experience.

TIPPING AND BARGAINING

For information on tipping, bargaining, and taxes, refer to the **Customs and Etiquette** section before each country.

PACKING

Pack lightly: Lay out only what you absolutely need, then take half the clothes and twice the money. The Travelite FAQ (www.travelite.org) is a good resource for tips on traveling light. The online **Universal Packing List** (http://upl.codeq.info) will generate a customized list of suggested items based on your trip length, the expected climate, your planned activities, and other factors. If you plan to do a lot of hiking, also consult **The Great Outdoors,** p. 45.

Luggage: If you're covering most of your itinerary by foot, a sturdy **frame backpack** is unbeatable. (For the basics on buying a pack, see p. 46.) Toting a **suitcase** or **trunk** is fine if you plan to live in one or two cities and explore from there, but not a great idea if you move around frequently. In addition to your main piece of luggage, a **daypack** (a small backpack or courier bag) is useful.

Clothing: The **climate** of Eastern Europe is highly variable from region to region, so be prepared for all kinds of weather. No matter when you're traveling, it's a good idea to bring a warm jacket or wool sweater, a rain jacket (Gore-Tex® is both waterproof and breathable), sturdy shoes or hiking boots, and thick socks. Flip-flops or waterproof sandals are must-haves for grubby hostel showers, and extra socks are always a good idea. You may also want one outfit for going out, and maybe a nicer pair of shoes. Women should bring a **head covering** for mosque and monastery visits.

Sleepsack: Some hostels require that you either provide your own linens or rent sheets from them. Save cash by making your own sleepsack: fold a full-size sheet in half the long way, then sew it closed along the long side and one of the short sides.

Converters and adapters: Throughout Eastern Europe, electricity is 220 or 230V AC, enough to fry any 110V appliance. **Americans** and **Canadians** should buy an adapter (which changes the shape of the plug) and a converter (which changes the voltage; US$20). Don't make the mistake of using only an adapter (unless appliance instructions explicitly state otherwise). **Australians, Brits, Irish,** and **New Zealanders** (who use 230V at home) won't need a converter, but they will need a set of adapters to use anything electrical. Check out **kropla.com/electric.htm** for more info.

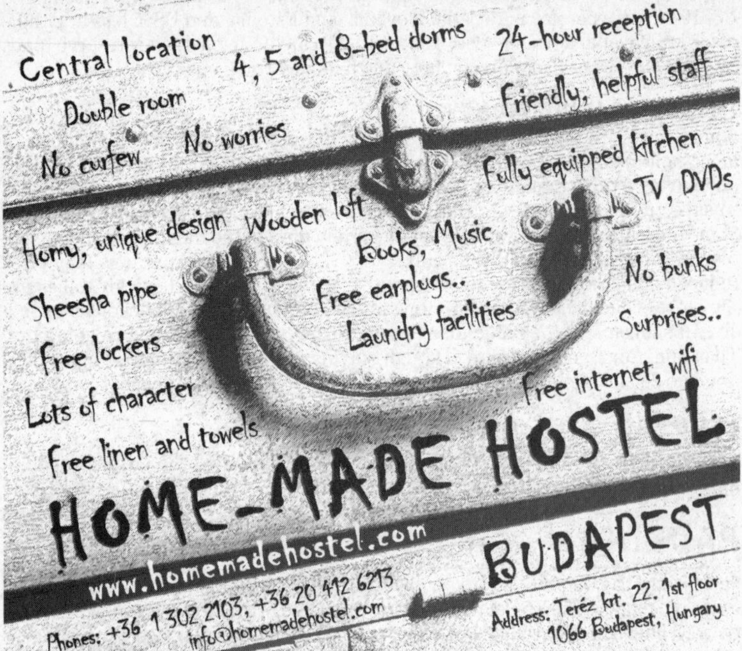

Toiletries: Condoms, deodorant, razors, tampons, and toothbrushes are often available, but it may be difficult to find your preferred brand; bring extras. Contact lenses are likely to be expensive and difficult to find, so bring enough extra pairs and solution for your entire trip. Also bring your glasses and a copy of your prescription in case you need emergency replacements. If you use heat-disinfection, either switch temporarily to a chemical disinfection system (check first to make sure it's safe with your brand of lenses), or buy a converter to 220/240V.

First-Aid Kit: For a basic first-aid kit, pack bandages, a pain reliever, antibiotic cream, a thermometer, a multifunction pocketknife, tweezers, moleskin, decongestant, motion-sickness remedy, diarrhea or upset-stomach medication (Pepto Bismol® or Imodium®), an antihistamine, sunscreen, insect repellent, burn ointment, and a syringe for emergencies (get an explanatory letter from your doctor).

Other useful items: For safety purposes, you should bring a money belt and small padlock. Basic **outdoors equipment** (plastic water bottle, compass, waterproof matches, sunglasses, hat) may also prove useful. A needle and thread can come in handy. Also consider bringing electrical tape for patching tears. If you're looking to cut costs and want to do laundry by hand, bring detergent, a small rubber ball to stop up the sink, and string for a makeshift clothes line. **Other things** you're liable to forget: an umbrella, an alarm clock, safety pins, rubber bands, a flashlight, earplugs, and garbage bags.

Important Documents: Don't forget your passport, traveler's checks, ATM and/or credit cards, adequate ID, and photocopies of all of the aforementioned in case these documents are lost or stolen (p. 11). Also remember any of the following that might apply to you: a hosteling membership card (p. 42); driver's license (p. 13); travel insurance forms (p. 25); ISIC (p. 13); and/or rail or bus pass (p. 35).

SAFETY AND HEALTH

GENERAL ADVICE

Your country's embassy abroad (p. 11) is usually your best resource when things go wrong; registering with that embassy upon arrival in the country is often a good idea. The government offices listed in the Travel Advisories box (p. 22) can provide information on the services they offer in case of emergencies abroad.

LOCAL LAWS AND POLICE

Laws in Eastern Europe naturally vary from country to country. Particularly in Russia, however, travelers may encounter strict and seemingly random laws, arbitrarily enforced by police who can legally stop foreigners at any time and demand to see identification. "Fines" in such circumstances are common. Travelers should inform themselves about the legal system of the country they are visiting.

DRUGS AND ALCOHOL

Throughout Eastern Europe, recreational drugs—including marijuana—are illegal, and often carry a much heavier jail sentence than in the West. For more specific information on the drug laws of Eastern European countries, consult the website at the US State Department's Bureau for International Narcotics and Law Enforcement Affairs (www.state.gov/g/inl/). If you carry **prescription drugs** while you travel, bring a copy of the prescriptions themselves and a note from a doctor. The legal drinking age in most Eastern European countries is 18. In most Eastern European countries, drunk driving carries strict penalties.

SPECIFIC CONCERNS

PETTY CRIME AND SCAMS

Unfortunately, one common problem encountered by visitors to Eastern Europe is the multitude of scams devised by clever locals. Throughout Eastern Europe there have been many reported cases of drugging combined with robbery and sometimes assault. The risk of drugging is highest in nightclubs and bars, or in scams in which a local invites or pressures an unsuspecting traveler to "have a drink" with him or her. Travelers should never leave their drinks unattended under any circumstances, and should be wary of accepting drinks from strangers. There is also a risk of robbery, drugging, or both on night trains and buses. Visitors to Eastern Europe should try to avoid traveling at night.

Another common scam in bars and nightclubs involves a local woman inviting a traveler to buy her drinks, which end up costing exorbitant prices; the proprietors of the establishment (in cahoots with the scam artist) may then use force to ensure that the bill is paid. Travelers should therefore always check the prices of drinks before ordering. Credit card fraud is common throughout Eastern Europe. Travelers who have lost credit cards or fear that the security of their accounts has been compromised should contact their credit card companies immediately.

In general, visitors to Eastern Europe should avoid circumstances in which they can be isolated and rendered defenseless. Accordingly, travelers should never enter a taxicab containing anyone in addition to the driver and should never split a cab ride with strangers. While traveling by train, it may be preferable to travel in cheaper "cattle-car" type seating arrangements; the large number of witnesses makes such carriages safer than seating in individual compartments. Travelers should avoid riding on night buses or trains, where the risk of robbery or assault is particularly high. Let's Go discourages hitchhiking and picking up hitchhikers, which is dangerous and also illegal in many Eastern European countries.

RACISM AND HATE CRIME

Incidents of racist hate crimes are rare; in most countries of Eastern Europe, especially outside of urban centers, minorities may experience stares, but likely little discrimination. There has, however, been an increase in recent years of racially-motivated attacks in Russia. Travelers most at risk are those of African, East Asian, and South Asian descent, or anyone perceived to be Roma or Sinti.

TERRORISM

As a result of the September 11, 2001 attacks on the US, airports throughout the world have heightened security. Terrorist acts are rare in Eastern Europe, and potentially violent situations are confined to the volatile regions of Russia. Terrorism in Russia has been blamed on **Chechen separatists,** a largely Muslim ethnic group in the Russian Caucasus region. The box on **travel advisories** below lists offices to contact and webpages to visit to get the most updated list of your home country's government's advisories about travel.

TRAVEL ADVISORIES. The following government offices provide travel information and advisories by telephone, by fax, or via the web:

Australian Department of Foreign Affairs and Trade: ☎61 26 26 11 111; www.dfat.gov.au.

Canadian Department of Foreign Affairs and International Trade (DFAIT): ☎800-267-8376; www.dfait-maeci.gc.ca. Call for their free booklet, *Bon Voyage...But.*

New Zealand Ministry of Foreign Affairs: ☎044 398 000; www.mfat.govt.nz.

United Kingdom Foreign and Commonwealth Office: ☎02 07 00 81 500; www.fco.gov.uk.

US Department of State: ☎888-407-4747; http://travel.state.gov. Visit the website for the booklet *A Safe Trip Abroad.*

PERSONAL SAFETY

EXPLORING AND TRAVELING

To avoid unwanted attention, try to blend in as much as possible. Respecting local customs (in many cases, dressing more conservatively than you would at home) may placate would-be hecklers. For women in Eastern Europe, skirts may be more appropriate than shorts and, for both men and women, it may be best to avoid baggy jeans, sneakers, and sandals, as well as flashy, brightly colored clothing. Backpacks also make one stand out as a tourist; courier or **shoulder bags** are less likely to draw attention, though in countries such as the Czech Republic, they are considered too effeminate for men. Check maps in shops and restaurants rather than on the street, which will signal that you are a tourist. If you are traveling alone, be sure someone at home knows your itinerary, and never tell anyone you meet that you're by yourself. When walking at night, stick to busy, well-lit streets. If you ever feel uncomfortable, leave the area as quickly and directly as you can.

As much as you may be tempted, do not "explore" in eastern Croatia: the countryside is littered with **landmines** and **unexploded ordnance (UXO).** While de-mining is underway, it will be years before all the mines are removed. UXOs are not a danger on paved roads or in major cities. Road shoulders and abandoned buildings are particularly likely to harbor UXOs. Travelers to these regions should consult the Croatian Mine Action Center website at www.hcr.hr for detailed information.

There is no sure-fire way to avoid all the threatening situations you might encounter while traveling, but a good **self-defense course** will give you concrete ways to react to unwanted advances. **Prepare** (☎800-442-7273, 212-255-0505; www.prepareinc.com) and **Model Mugging** (☎614-221-2811; www.modelmugging.org) can refer you to local self-defense courses in Australia, Canada, Switzerland, and the US. Most programs are designed for women, although programs for men and children are available as well. Visit the website of **Impact** (☎800-345-5425; www.impactpersonalsafety.com) for a list of local chapters.

If you are planning on using a **car,** learn local driving signals. Study route maps before you hit the road, and if you plan on spending a lot of time driving, consider bringing spare parts. For long drives in desolate areas, invest in a cellular phone and a roadside assistance program (see p. 36). Park your vehicle in a garage or well-traveled area, and use a steering wheel locking device in larger cities. **Sleeping in your car** is the most dangerous way to get your rest, and it's also illegal in many countries. For info on the perils of **hitchhiking,** see p. 38.

POSSESSIONS AND VALUABLES

Never leave your belongings unattended; crime occurs in even the most safe-looking hostel or hotel. Bring your own padlock for hostel lockers, and don't ever store valuables in a locker. Be particularly careful on **buses** and **trains;** horror stories abound about determined thieves who wait for travelers to fall asleep. Carry your bag or purse in front of you where you can see it. When traveling with others, sleep in alternate shifts. When alone, use good judgment in selecting a train compartment: never stay in an empty one, and use a lock to secure your pack to the luggage rack. Use extra caution if traveling at night or on overnight trains. Try to sleep on top bunks with your luggage stored above you (if not in bed with you), and keep important documents and other valuables on you at all times.

There are a few steps you can take to minimize the financial risk associated with traveling. First, **bring as little with you as possible.** Second, buy a few combination **padlocks** to secure your belongings either in your pack or in a hostel or train station locker. Third, **carry as little cash as possible.** Keep your traveler's checks and ATM/credit cards in a **money belt**—not a "fanny pack"—along with your passport and ID cards. Fourth, **keep a small cash reserve separate from your primary stash.** This should be about US$50 (US$ or euro are best) sewn into or stored in the depths of your pack, along with your traveler's check numbers and photocopies of your passport, your birth certificate, and other important documents.

In large cities **con artists** often work in groups and may involve children. Beware of certain classics: sob stories that require money, rolls of bills "found" on the street, mustard spilled (or saliva spit) onto your shoulder to distract you while they snatch your bag. **Never let your passport and your bags out of your sight.** Hostel workers will sometimes stand at bus and train station arrival points to try to recruit tired and disoriented travelers to their hostel; never believe strangers who tell you that theirs is the only hostel open. Beware of **pickpockets** in city crowds, especially on public transportation.

If you will be traveling with electronic devices, such as a laptop computer, check whether your homeowner's insurance covers loss, theft, or damage when you travel. If not, you might consider purchasing a separate insurance policy. **Safeware** (☎800-800-1492; www.safeware.com) specializes in covering computers and charges $90 for 90-day international travel coverage up to $4000.

PRE-DEPARTURE HEALTH

In your **passport**, write the names of any people you wish to be contacted in case of a medical emergency, and list any allergies or medical conditions. Matching a prescription to a foreign equivalent is not always easy, safe, or possible, especially since generic drugs manufactured in Eastern Europe may not be sold under the same names as their Western equivalents. Accordingly, if you take prescription drugs, consider carrying up-to-date prescriptions or a statement from your doctor stating the medication's trade name, manufacturer, chemical name, and dosage. Be sure to keep all medication with you in your carry-on luggage. For tips on packing a **first-aid kit** and other health essentials, see p. 20. Travelers curious about the safety of generic drugs can consult the database of the website of the US Department of Health and Human Services' Center for Drug Evaluation and Research (http://www.fda.gov/cder/ob/default.htm) to find ratings by the US Food and Drug Administration. (All drugs are rated either "A," equivalent to the brand-name original, or "B," not demonstrated to be equivalent to the brand-name original.)

IMMUNIZATIONS AND PRECAUTIONS

Travelers to Eastern Europe over two years old should make sure that the following vaccines are up to date: DTaP or Td (for diphtheria, tetanus, and pertussis); Hib (for *Haemophilus influenzae* B); HepA (for Hepatitis A); HepB (for Hepatitis B); IPV (for polio); MMR (for measles, mumps, and rubella); and typhoid. Adults traveling to Russia or Ukraine should consider getting an additional dose of **polio** vaccine if they have not already had one during their adult years. The viral infection tick-borne encephalitis occurs principally in Central Europe and the Baltics; consider getting a vaccination if you intend to visit wooded areas. Bulgaria requires documentation verifying that you are **HIV negative** in order to issue visas for periods longer than one month to study or work in the country. Belarus, Russia, and Ukraine require documentation of HIV negative to issue visas longer than 90 days. Hungary requires HIV testing for persons staying longer than one year; US test results are not accepted. Lithuania and Slovakia require HIV-negative documentation for those seeking a residency permit; Slovakia does not accept US test results. A **rabies** vaccine is recommended on account of the packs of stray dogs that roam the streets of Eastern Europe, especially in Latvia. For recommendations on immunizations, consult the CDC (p. 26) in the US or the equivalent in your home country. For recommendations on immunizations and prophylaxis, consult the Centers for Disease Control and Prevention (CDC; see below) in the US or the equivalent in your home country, and check with a doctor for guidance.

INSURANCE

Travel insurance covers four basic areas: medical/health problems, property loss, trip cancellation/interruption, and emergency evacuation. Though regular insurance policies may well extend to travel-related accidents, you may consider purchasing separate travel insurance if the cost of potential trip cancellation, interruption, or emergency medical evacuation is greater than you can absorb. Prices for travel insurance purchased separately generally run about US$50 per week for full coverage, while trip cancellation/interruption may be purchased separately at a rate of US$3-5 per day depending on length of stay.

Medical insurance (especially university policies) often covers costs incurred abroad; check with your provider. **US Medicare** does not cover foreign travel. **Canadian** provincial health insurance plans increasingly do not cover foreign travel; check with the provincial Ministry of Health or Health Plan Headquarters for details. **Homeowners' insurance** (or your family's coverage) often covers foreign theft or loss of documents (passport, plane ticket, railpass, etc.) up to US$500.

ISIC and **ITIC** (see p. 13) provide basic insurance benefits to US cardholders, including US$100 per day of in-hospital sickness for up to 100 days and US$10,000 of accident-related medical reimbursement (see www.isicus.com for details). Cardholders have access to a toll-free 24hr. helpline for medical, legal, and financial emergencies overseas. **American Express** (☎800-338-1670) grants most cardholders collision and theft car rental insurance on rentals made with the card.

STA (p. 31) offers a range of **insurance plans** that can supplement your basic coverage. Other private insurance providers in the US and Canada include: CSA Travel Protection (☎800-873-9855; www.csatravelprotection.com/comfort) and Travel Guard (☎800-826-4919; www.travelguard.com). Columbus Direct (☎08 70 03 39 988; www.columbusdirect.co.uk) operates in the UK, and AFTA (☎02 92 64 32 99; www.afta.com.au) in Australia.

USEFUL ORGANIZATIONS AND PUBLICATIONS

The American **Centers for Disease Control and Prevention** (**CDC;** ☎877-FYI-TRIP; www.cdc.gov/travel) maintains an international travelers' hotline and an informative website. Consult the appropriate government agency of your home country for consular information sheets on health, entry requirements, and other issues for various countries (see the listings in the box on **Travel Advisories,** p. 22). For quick information on health and other travel warnings, call the **Overseas Citizens Services** (M-F 8am-8pm from US ☎888-407-4747, from overseas 202-501-4444), or contact a passport agency, embassy, or consulate abroad. For information on medical evacuation services and travel insurance firms, see the US government's website at http://travel.state.gov/travel/abroad_health.html or the **British Foreign and Commonwealth Office** (www.fco.gov.uk). For general health information, contact the **American Red Cross** (☎202-303-4498; www.redcross.org).

STAYING HEALTHY

Common sense is the simplest prescription for good health while you travel.

ONCE IN EASTERN EUROPE

ENVIRONMENTAL HAZARDS

Heat exhaustion and dehydration: Visitors who will be spending their time outdoors in sunny areas (e.g. hiking in the nature preserves of Croatia) are at risk of heat exhaustion. Heat exhaustion leads to nausea, excessive thirst, headaches, and dizziness. Avoid it by drinking plenty of fluids, eating salty foods (e.g., crackers), abstaining from dehydrating beverages (e.g., alcohol and caffeinated beverages), and wearing sunscreen. Continuous heat stress can eventually lead to heatstroke, characterized by a rising temperature, severe headache, delirium and cessation of sweating. Victims should be cooled off with wet towels and taken to a doctor.

Sunburn: Always wear sunscreen (SPF 30 or higher) when spending large amounts of time outdoors. If you get sunburned, drink more fluids than usual and apply an aloe-based lotion. Severe sunburns can lead to sun poisoning, a condition that can cause fever, chills, nausea, and vomiting. Sun poisoning should always be treated by a doctor.

Hypothermia and frostbite: Travelers spending much of their time outdoors in cold regions of Russia, the Baltics, or other Eastern European countries may be at risk of hypothermia or frostbite. A rapid drop in body temperature is the clearest sign of overexposure to cold. Victims may also shiver, feel exhausted, have poor coordination or slurred speech, hallucinate, or suffer amnesia. **Do not let hypothermia victims fall asleep.** To avoid hypothermia, keep dry, wear layers, and stay out of the wind. When the temperature is below freezing, watch out for frostbite. If skin turns white or blue, waxy, and cold, do not rub the area. Drink warm beverages, stay dry, and slowly warm the area with dry fabric or steady body contact until a doctor can be found.

High Altitude: Travelers, such as hikers in the Tatras Mountains of Slovakia, who intend to visit sites at high altitudes should allow their bodies a couple of days to adjust to less oxygen before exerting themselves. Note that alcohol is more potent and UV rays are stronger at high elevations.

INSECT-BORNE DISEASES

Many diseases are transmitted by insects—mainly mosquitoes, fleas, ticks, and lice. Be aware of insects in wet or forested areas, especially while hiking and camping; wear long pants and long sleeves, tuck your pants into your socks, and use a mosquito net. Use insect repellents such as DEET and soak or spray your gear with permethrin (licensed in the US only for use on clothing).

Tick-borne Encephalitis: A viral infection of the central nervous system transmitted by tick bites or by unpasteurized dairy products. Occurs in wooded areas of Belarus, the Czech Republic, Estonia, Hungary, Latvia, Lithuania, Poland, Romania, Russia, Slovakia, and the Ukraine, as well as in the northern regions of Croatia and Slovenia. Vaccination recommended for those traveling in these areas for more than 3 weeks during warm weather months. Risk of contraction low when precautions are taken.

Lyme disease: A bacterial infection carried by ticks and marked by a circular bull's-eye rash of 2 in. or more. Later symptoms include fever, headache, fatigue, and aches and pains. Antibiotics are effective if administered early. Left untreated, Lyme can cause problems in joints, the heart, and the nervous system. If you find a tick attached to your skin, grasp the head with tweezers as close to your skin as possible and apply slow, steady traction. Removing a tick within 24hr. greatly reduces the risk of infection. Do not try to remove ticks with petroleum jelly, nail polish remover, or a hot match. Ticks usually inhabit moist, shaded environments and heavily wooded areas. If you are going to be hiking in these areas, wear long clothes and DEET.

FOOD- AND WATER-BORNE DISEASES

Prevention is the best cure: be sure that your food is properly cooked and the water you drink is clean. Unfortunately, in areas such as Romania, some cities and regions in Russia (such as St. Petersburg), Turkey, and Ukraine, the water is not safe. Peel fruits and vegetables before eating them and avoid tap water (including ice cubes and anything washed in tap water, like salad). Watch out for food from markets or street vendors that may have been cooked in unhygienic conditions. Other culprits are raw shellfish, unpasteurized milk, and sauces containing raw eggs. Buy imported bottled water, or purify your own water by bringing it to a rolling boil or treating it with **iodine tablets;** note, however, that some parasites, such as *giardia*, have exteriors that resist iodine treatment, so boiling is more reliable. Always wash your hands before eating or bring a quick-drying purifying liquid hand cleaner. Food- and water-borne diseases are the primary illnesses that affect travelers to Eastern Europe.

Cholera: An intestinal disease caused by bacteria in contaminated food. Symptoms include diarrhea, dehydration, vomiting, and muscle cramps. See a doctor immediately; if left untreated, cholera can be lethal within hours. Antibiotics are available, but the most important treatment is rehydration. No vaccine is available in the US.

Hepatitis A: A viral infection of the liver acquired through contaminated water or shellfish from contaminated water. Symptoms include fatigue, fever, loss of appetite, nausea, dark urine, jaundice, vomiting, aches and pains, and light stools. The risk is highest in rural areas and the countryside, but it is also present in urban areas. Ask your doctor about the Hepatitis A vaccine or an injection of immune globulin.

Giardiasis: Transmitted through parasites and acquired by drinking untreated water from streams or lakes. Symptoms include diarrhea, cramps, bloating, fatigue, weight loss, and nausea. If untreated, it can lead to severe dehydration. Giardiasis occurs worldwide.

Typhoid fever: Caused by salmonella bacteria; common in villages and rural areas in the developing regions of Eastern Europe. While mostly transmitted through contaminated food and water, it may also be acquired by direct contact with another person. Early symptoms include high fever, headaches, fatigue, appetite loss, constipation, and a rash on the abdomen or chest. Antibiotics can treat typhoid, but a vaccination (70-90% effective) is recommended.

OTHER INFECTIOUS DISEASES

The following diseases exist in every part of the world. Travelers should know how to recognize them and what to do if they suspect they have been infected.

Diphtheria: The 1990s saw a massive diphtheria outbreak in the former Soviet Union, and travelers to this area are still at risk for this highly infectious disease. Early symptoms, including severe sore throat, swollen lymph nodes, and fever, can lead to paralysis, heart failure, and death. Be up-to-date on diphtheria vaccinations before traveling.

Hepatitis B: A viral infection of the liver transmitted via blood or other bodily fluids. Symptoms, which may not surface until years after infection, include jaundice, appetite loss, fever, and joint pain. It is transmitted through unprotected sex and unclean needles. A 3-shot vaccination sequence is recommended for sexually-active travelers and anyone planning to seek medical treatment abroad; it must begin 6 months before traveling.

Rabies: Transmitted through the saliva of infected animals; fatal if untreated. By the time symptoms (thirst and muscle spasms) appear, the disease is in its terminal stage. If you are bitten, wash the wound, seek immediate medical care, and try to have the animal located. A rabies vaccine, which consists of 3 shots given over a 21-day period, is available and recommended for developing world travel, but is only semi-effective.

Tuberculosis: Tuberculosis (TB) is on the rise throughout Eastern Europe. Symptoms include fever, persistent cough, and bloody phlegm. TB is usually transmitted by breathing air in an enclosed area with an infected person. If untreated, the disease is fatal. It usually responds to antibiotics. If you think you are infected, tell your doctor you have been to Eastern Europe recently, as the recent return of TB indicates a drug-resistant strain that requires special treatment.

AIDS and HIV: For detailed information on Acquired Immune Deficiency Syndrome (AIDS) in Eastern Europe, call the 24hr. National AIDS Hotline at ☎800-342-2437. Note that some Eastern European countries (see **Immunizations and Precautions,** p. 25) screen incoming travelers for AIDS, primarily those planning extended visits for work or study, and denies entrance to those who test HIV-positive. Contact the consulate of your planned destination for information. The risk of contracting HIV/AIDS in Eastern Europe is rapidly on the rise.

Sexually Transmitted Infections (STIs): Gonorrhea, chlamydia, genital warts, syphilis, herpes, HPV, and other STIs are easier to catch than HIV and can be just as serious. Though condoms may protect you from some STIs, oral or even tactile contact can lead to transmission. If you think you may have contracted an STI, see a doctor immediately. STIs are extremely common in most regions of Eastern Europe.

OTHER HEALTH CONCERNS

MEDICAL CARE ON THE ROAD

The quality and availability of medical assistance varies greatly throughout Eastern Europe. In Westernized cities, like Prague and Budapest, foreigners can typically visit English-speaking medical centers or hospitals, where the care tends to be better than elsewhere in the region. In rural areas and the more impoverished regions of countries such as Russia and Romania, adequate and English-speaking health facilities may be impossible to find. In the event of an emergency, go to your embassy for recommendations. Tourist offices also sometimes have the names of local doctors who speak English. Private hospitals will generally have better facilities than the state-operated hospitals. For more specific information, see the **Safety and Health** section of the chapter for your destination country.

If you are concerned about obtaining medical assistance while traveling, you may wish to employ special support services. The *MedPass* from **GlobalCare, Inc.**, 6875 Shiloh Rd. East, Alpharetta, GA 30005, USA (☎800-860-1111; www.globalcare.net), provides 24hr. international medical assistance, support, and medical evacuation resources. The **International Association for Medical Assistance to Travelers** (**IAMAT**; US ☎716-754-4883, Canada 519-836-0102; www.iamat.org) has free membership, lists English-speaking doctors worldwide, and offers detailed info on immunization requirements and sanitation. If your regular **insurance** policy does not cover travel abroad, you may wish to purchase additional coverage (see p. 25).

Those with medical conditions (such as diabetes, allergies to antibiotics, epilepsy, or heart conditions) may want to obtain a **MedicAlert** membership (US$40 per year), which includes among other things a stainless steel ID tag and a 24hr. collect-call number. Contact the MedicAlert Foundation International, 2323 Colorado Ave., Turlock, CA 95382, USA (☎888-633-4298, outside US 209-668-3333; www.medicalert.org).

WOMEN'S HEALTH

Women traveling in unsanitary conditions are vulnerable to **urinary tract (including bladder and kidney) infections.** Over-the-counter medications can sometimes alleviate symptoms, but if they persist, see a doctor. **Vaginal yeast infections** may flare up in hot and humid climates. Wearing loosely fitting trousers or a skirt and cotton underwear will help, as will over-the-counter remedies like Monistat or Gynelotrimin. Bring supplies from home if you are prone to infection, as they may be difficult to find on the road. **Tampons, pads,** and **contraceptive devices** are widely available, though your favorite brand may not be stocked—bring extras of anything you can't live without. **Abortion** is legal for any reason in most Eastern European countries, except for Poland, which permits it only to save the life of the mother, or to preserve her physical or mental health.

GETTING TO EASTERN EUROPE

BY PLANE

When it comes to airfare, a little effort can save you a bundle. Courier fares are the cheapest for those whose plans are flexible enough to deal with the restrictions. Tickets sold by consolidators and standby seating are also good deals, but last-minute specials, airfare wars, and charter flights often beat these fares. The key is to hunt around, be flexible, and ask about discounts. Students, seniors, and those under 26 should never pay full price for a ticket.

AIRFARES

Airfares to Eastern Europe peak roughly between mid-June and early September (high season); holidays are also expensive. The cheapest times to travel are November through mid-December and mid-January through March. Midweek (M-Th, especially in the mornings), round-trip flights run US$40-100 cheaper than weekend flights, but they are generally more crowded and less likely to permit frequent-flier upgrades. Not fixing a return date ("open return") or arriving in and departing from different cities ("open-jaw") can be pricier than round-trip flights. Patching one-way flights together is the most expensive way to travel. For those willing to make the extra effort, the least expensive route is often to fly into London and connect to one of the many discounted flights that carriers such as **EasyJet** (www.easyjet.com) and **RyanAir** (www.ryanair.com) make to Eastern Europe.

If your destination is only one stop on a more extensive globe-hop, consider a round-the-world (RTW) ticket. Tickets usually include at least five stops and are valid for about a year; prices range US$1200-5000. Try **Northwest Airlines/KLM** (☎800-225-2525; www.nwa.com) or **Star Alliance,** a consortium of 16 airlines including United Airlines (www.staralliance.com).

Fares for round-trip flights to the larger, more touristed cities (Budapest, Prague, Warsaw) from the US or Canadian east coast can usually be found, with some work, for US$800-1000 in high season; from the UK, UK£100-180; from Australia, AUS$3000-4000; from New Zealand, NZ$3000-3500. From the US, tickets to mid-range cities, including Bucharest, Moscow, St. Petersburg, and Sofia generally cost about US$300 more, while Bratislava, Kyiv, Zagreb and the Baltic capitals can cost US$1000-1500/UK£400-600/AUS$4000-5000/NZ$5000-7000. Prices drop US$200-500 the rest of the year. For Eastern European-based flights, there are a number of new discount airlines, including **SkyEurope** (www.skyeurope.com), which have cheap fares to the major cities and some hubs in Western Europe.

BUDGET AND STUDENT TRAVEL AGENCIES

While knowledgeable agents specializing in flights to **Eastern Europe** can make your life easy and help you save, they may not spend the time to find you the lowest possible fare—they get paid on commission. Travelers holding **ISICs** and **IYTCs** (see p. 13) qualify for big discounts from student travel agencies. Most flights from budget agencies are on major airlines, but in peak season some may sell seats on less reliable chartered aircraft.

STA Travel, 5900 Wilshire Blvd., Ste. 900, Los Angeles, CA 90036, USA (24hr. reservations and info ☎800-781-4040; www.statravel.com). A student and youth travel organization with over 150 offices worldwide (check their website for a listing of all their offices), including US offices in Boston, Chicago, Los Angeles, New York, Seattle, San Francisco, and Washington, D.C. Ticket booking, travel insurance, railpasses, and more. Walk-in offices are located throughout Australia (☎03 92 07 59 00), New Zealand (☎093 099 723), and the UK (☎08 70 16 30 026).

Travel CUTS (Canadian Universities Travel Services Limited), 187 College St., Toronto, ON M5T 1P7, Canada (☎888-592-2887; www.travelcuts.com). Offices across Canada and the US including Los Angeles, New York, Seattle, and San Francisco.

USIT, 19-21 Aston Quay, Dublin 2, Ireland (☎016 021 904; www.usit.ie), Ireland's leading student/budget travel agency has 20 offices throughout Northern Ireland and the Republic of Ireland. Offers programs to work, study, and volunteer worldwide.

COMMERCIAL AIRLINES

The commercial airlines' lowest regular offer is the **APEX** (Advance Purchase Excursion) fare, which provides confirmed reservations and allows "open-jaw" tickets. Generally, reservations must be made seven to 21 days ahead of departure, with seven- to 14-day minimum-stay and up to 90-day maximum-stay restrictions. These fares carry hefty cancellation and change penalties (and fees rise in summer). Book peak-season APEX fares early. Use **Expedia** (www.expedia.com) or **Travelocity** (www.travelocity.com) to get an idea of the lowest published fares, then use the resources outlined here to try to beat those fares. Low-season fares should be much cheaper than the **high-season** (mid-June to early-Sept.) ones listed here.

TRAVELING FROM NORTH AMERICA

Air France: France ☎33 82 03 20 820, US and Canada 800-237-2747; www.airfrance.com. Covers much of Eastern Europe via Western Europe.

Austrian Airways: UK ☎44 87 01 24 26 25, US and Canada 800-843-0002; www.aua.com. Connects to many Eastern European cities via Vienna.

Delta Air Lines: US and Canada ☎800-221-1212, UK 08 45 60 00 950; www.delta.com. A reliable US carrier serving Eastern Europe.

Finnair: US ☎800-950-5000, Canada 800-461-8651; www.finnair.com. Cheap round-trip tickets from San Francisco, New York, and Toronto to Helsinki; connections throughout Europe.

Lufthansa: Canada ☎800-563-5954, US 800-399-5838; www.lufthansa.com. Has a wide variety of routes covering most of Eastern Europe.

TRAVELING FROM IRELAND AND THE UK

The **Air Travel Advisory Bureau** in London (☎02 07 63 72 444; www.atab.com) gives referrals to agencies and consolidators that offer discounted airfares from the UK.

Aer Lingus: Ireland ☎08 18 36 50 00, UK 08 70 87 65 000; www.aerlingus.ie. Return tickets from Dublin, Cork, and Shannon to Amsterdam, Bologna, Brussels, Copenhagen, Düsseldorf, Frankfurt, Lisbon, Madrid, Málaga, Milan, Munich, Nice, Paris, Rome, Vienna, and Zürich.

British Airways: UK ☎87 08 50 98 50, Canada and US 800-247-9297; www.britishairways.com. Flies into most large cities in Eastern Europe.

SAS: UK ☎087 060 727 727, US and Canada 800-221-2350; www.scandinavian.net. Reliably connects to Baltic cities.

TRAVELING FROM AUSTRALIA AND NEW ZEALAND

Air New Zealand: ☎800 737 000; www.airnewzealand.com. Reasonable fares from Auckland to London and special sales at much lower prices.

Lufthansa: Australia ☎13 00 65 57 27, New Zealand 08 00 94 52 20; www.lufthansa.com. Offers reliable flights that connect to a number of cities throughout Eastern Europe.

Qantas: Australia ☎13 13 13, New Zealand 08 00 80 87 67; www.qantas.com. Flies from Australia and New Zealand to London, where connecting flights are easy to find.

STANDBY FLIGHTS

Traveling standby requires considerable flexibility in travel dates. Companies dealing in standby flights sell vouchers rather than tickets, along with the promise to get you to your destination (or near your destination) within a certain window of time (typically 1-5 days). You call in before your specific window of time to hear your flight options and the probability that you will be able to board each flight. You can then decide which flights you want to try to catch, show up at the appropriate airport at the appropriate time, present your voucher, and board if space is available. Vouchers can usually be bought for both one-way and round-trip travel. You may receive a monetary refund only if every available flight within your date range is full; if you opt not to take an available (but perhaps less convenient) flight, you can only get credit toward future travel. Read agreements with any company offering standby flights with care, as tricky fine print can leave you in the lurch. To check on a company's service record in the US, contact the Better Business Bureau (☎703-276-0100; www.bbb.org). It is difficult to receive refunds, and vouchers will not be honored when an airline fails to receive payment in time.

TICKET CONSOLIDATORS

Ticket consolidators, or **"bucket shops,"** buy unsold tickets in bulk from commercial airlines and sell them at discounted rates. The best place to look is in the Sunday travel section of any major newspaper (such as *The New York Times*), where many bucket shops place tiny ads. Call quickly, as availability is extremely limited. Not all bucket shops are reliable, so insist on a receipt that gives full details of restrictions, refunds, and tickets, and pay by credit card (in spite of the 2-5% fee) so you can stop payment if you never receive your tickets. For more info, see www.travel-library.com/air-travel/consolidators.html.

TRAVELING FROM CANADA AND THE US

Some consolidators worth trying are **Rebel** (☎800-732-3588; www.rebeltours.com), **Cheap Tickets** (www.cheaptickets.com), **Flights.com** (www.flights.com), and **TravelHUB** (www.travelhub.com). Let's Go does not endorse these agencies. As always, be cautious, and research companies before you hand over credit card numbers.

BY TRAIN

Flying into a Western European city and then taking a train to Eastern Europe is often the cheapest option. Many travelers fly into Milan to connect by train to the Balkans; Munich or Berlin to reach Poland, the Baltics, and Ukraine; and Vienna for the short train ride to the Czech Republic, Hungary, and Slovakia. Check out **transit visa** requirements if you plan on passing through other Eastern European countries en route to your final destination; pay particular attention if there is a chance your train could travel through Belarus or Moldova. Those touring the EU on their way to or from Eastern Europe might consider a **Eurail Pass,** but should keep in mind that it is **not valid in Eastern Europe,** with the exception of Hungary and Romania. Trains in Eastern Europe are generally a reliable means of travel, as trains run both within countries and across national borders. Rail infrastructure is slightly weaker, however, in areas of the Balkans and certain areas of Bulgaria and Romania. Dubrovnik, Croatia is not connected by rail.

NIGHT TRAINS. Try to avoid night trains, especially on lines that connect Warsaw or Kraków with Prague, Budapest, or Berlin. Theft is rampant on these trains, and staying awake or traveling with a friend sometimes is no help: many travelers have reported scams in which groups of thieves board the night train and pass canisters of sleeping gas beneath the doors of train compartments. Travelers pass out, then wake to discover that they have been robbed.

BY BOAT

Ferries in the **North** and **Baltic Seas** are reliable and comfortable. Those in the **Black Sea** are less predictable, and traveling between the coasts of Bulgaria, Romania, Ukraine, and Russia is no easy task. Those content with deck passage rarely need to book ahead but should check in a few hours early. **Polferries** (☎913 22 61 40; www.polferries.pl), in Poland, go from Świnoujście, Poland to **Rønne, DEN** (6hr.),

Copenhagen, DEN (9hr.) and **Ystad, SWE** (7hr.) and from Gdańsk, Poland to **Nynäshamn, SWE** (7hr.). **Silja Line** (US ☎800-533-3755; www.silja.com) leaves Helsinki, FIN (2hr., early Apr. to late Dec.) and Stockholm, SWE (16hr., year-round) for **Tallinn, EST**; it also goes from Stockholm, SWE to **Rīga, LAT** (16hr., year-round).

GETTING AROUND EASTERN EUROPE

Fares are either **single** (one-way) or **return** (round-trip). "Period returns" require you to return within a specific time frame; "day return" means you must return on the same day. Unless stated otherwise, *Let's Go* always lists single fares. Round-trip fares in Eastern Europe are usually less than double the one-way fare.

BY PLANE

AIRLINE SAFETY. The airlines of the former Soviet Republics do not always meet safety standards, especially for internal flights. When flying within Eastern Europe, it's often safest to spend the few extra rubles and book a seat on a Western airline rather than a domestic carrier. When a foreign carrier is not an option, the *Official Airline Guide* (www.oag.com) and many travel agencies can tell you the type and age of aircraft on a particular route. The **International Airline Passengers Association** (US ☎800-821-4272, UK 02 08 68 16 555; www.iapa.com) provides region-specific safety information. The American **Federal Aviation Administration** (☎866-835-5322; www.faa.gov) reviews the airline authorities for countries whose airlines enter the US.

Flying across Eastern Europe on regularly scheduled flights can devour your budget, but if you're short on time (or flush with cash) you might consider it. Student travel agencies sell cheap tickets, and budget fares are often available in the spring and summer on popular routes. Consult budget travel agents and local newspapers for more info. A number of European airlines offer discount coupon packets. Most are available only as tack-ons for transatlantic passengers, but some are stand-alone offers. Most must be purchased before departure. **SkyEurope** is a new discount airline specifically serving Eastern Europe, with cheap fares between most major cities (☎248 504 850; www.skyeurope.com). **Europe by Air** (☎888-387-2479; www.europebyair.com) offers a *FlightPass* (US$99 per flight) that allows you to country-hop between over 150 European cities. **SAS** (☎800-221-2350; www.scandinavian.net) sells one-way coupons for travel within the Baltics and greater Europe. Most are available only to transatlantic SAS passengers, but some **United** and **Lufthansa** passengers also qualify (US$65-225).

BY BUS OR TRAIN

Second-class seating on Eastern European trains is pleasant, and compartments, which fit two to six, are great places to meet fellow travelers. Trains, however, are not always safe, especially at night. For safety tips, see **Safety and Health,** p. 21. For long trips, make sure you are on the correct car, as trains sometimes split at crossroads. Destinations listed in parentheses on Eastern European train schedules require a train switch, usually at the town listed immediately before the parenthesis. When traveling through Eastern Europe by train, you can either buy a **rail pass,** which allows you unlimited travel within a particular region for a given period of time, or rely on buying individual **point-to-point tickets** as you go, which is generally a much better value. When it comes to rail passes, check out **Eurail** (with service to Bulgaria,

Croatia, the Czech Republic, Hungary, Poland, Romania and Slovenia) and **European East Pass** (EastRail; with service to the Czech Republic, Hungary, Poland, and Slovakia). Almost all countries give students or youths (under 26) discounts on domestic rail tickets, and many sell a student or youth card that provides 20-50% off all fares.

Some Eastern European countries require **transit visas** for all travelers passing through the country by train; for example, trains from Central Europe must pass through Belarus to reach the Baltics or Russia. Be aware that some domestic trains in Ukraine pass through Moldova, which requires a transit visa. To avoid getting detained in Minsk, Chişinău, or elsewhere, have your paperwork in order or ensure that your route works around countries with transit visas. If in doubt, always ask at ticket counters which countries your route traverses, as this info will not always be provided. For more information, consult the **Visa and Entry Information** section of each country.

Many train stations have different counters for domestic and international tickets, seat reservations, and information—check before lining up. Seat reservations (usually US$3-10) are only required on select trains (usually major international lines), but you are not guaranteed a seat without one. Reservations are available on major trains as much as two months in advance, and Europeans often reserve far ahead of time. The Moscow-St. Petersburg train is famous for selling out weeks in advance during the summer.

All over Eastern Europe, buses reach rural areas inaccessible by train. In addition, long-distance bus networks may be more extensive, efficient, and sometimes more comfortable than train services. In the Balkans, air-conditioned buses run by private companies are a godsend. **Contiki Holidays,** 801 E. Katella Ave., 3rd fl., Anaheim, CA 92805, USA (☎866-266-8454; www.contiki.com) offers a variety of European vacation packages designed exclusively for 18- to 35-year-olds. For an average cost of US$65 per day, tours include accommodations, transportation, guided sightseeing, and some meals. **Eurolines,** 4 Cardiff Rd., Luton, Bedfordshire, L41 1PP, UK (☎990 143 219; www.eurolines.com), is Europe's largest coach operator, offering passes (UK£113-299) for unlimited 15-, 30-, or 60-day travel between 500 destinations in 25 countries, including many spots in Eastern Europe and Russia. It has offices in most countries in Eastern Europe; see website for details.

READING AND RESOURCES ON TRAIN TRAVEL.

Info on rail travel and railpasses: www.raileurope.com.

Point-to-point fares and schedules: www.raileurope.com/us/rail/fares_schedules/index.htm. Allows you to calculate whether buying a railpass will save you money.

European Railway Server: www.railfaneurope.net. Links to rail servers throughout Europe.

BY CAR

Public transportation is generally the best way to get around in Eastern Europe. Travelers unfamiliar with the region and its roads will likely find catching a bus or train more efficient than driving. Because car rental prices in Eastern Europe can be among the highest on the continent and gas (petrol, especially unleaded) is not always readily available, travel by bus, train, and sometimes even by plane, can be a cheaper alternative to hitting the road. Roads are often poorly maintained, and roadside assistance rarely exists, contributing to some of the highest driving fatality rates in the world. In recent years, a network of limited access highways has been expanding in Eastern Europe, such as an expressway linking Budapest to Vienna. Generally, conditions worsen the farther east you travel. As driving gains popularity in Central Europe, however, support services for drivers have been on the rise in countries like the Czech Republic, Hungary, and Poland. If you choose to strike off on your own, know the laws of the countries in which you'll be driving and read up on local road conditions. For a primer on European road signs and conventions, visit www.travlang.com/signs. The **Association for Safe International Road Travel (ASIRT),** 11769 Gainsborough Rd., Potomac, MD 20854, USA (☎301-983-5252; www.asirt.org), provides specific information about road conditions.

RENTAL AGENCIES

You can generally make reservations before you leave by calling major international offices in your home country. However, sometimes the price and availability information they give doesn't jive with what the local offices will tell you. Try checking with both numbers to make sure you get the best price and the most accurate information possible. Local desk numbers are included in town listings; for home-country numbers, call your toll-free directory.

To rent a car from most establishments, you need to be at least 21 years old. Some agencies require renters to be 25, and occasionally charge those aged 21-24 an additional insurance fee. Small local operations occasionally rent to people under 21, but be sure to ask about the insurance coverage and deductible, and always check the fine print. Most international rental agencies, such as Avis, Hertz, and Europcar, have rental cars in Eastern Europe. Another useful resource for finding car rentals is **Auto Europe,** 39 Commercial St., Portland, ME 04112, USA (☎888-223-5555; www.autoeurope.com).

COSTS AND INSURANCE

Many rental packages offer unlimited kilometers, while others offer a limited number of kilometers per day with a surcharge per kilometer after that. Expect to pay more for larger cars and for 4WD. It is often difficult to find an automatic 4WD. Be sure to ask whether the price includes **insurance** against theft and collision. Remember that if you are driving a conventional rental vehicle on an **unpaved road** in a rental car, you are almost never covered by insurance; ask about this before leaving the rental agency. Be aware that cars rented on an **American Express** or **Visa/MasterCard Gold** or **Platinum** credit card might *not* carry the automatic insurance that they would in some other countries; check with your credit card company. Insurance plans from rental companies almost always come with an **excess** for conventional vehicles; the excess is higher for younger drivers and for 4WD. This means that the insurance bought from the rental company only applies to damages over the excess; damages up to that amount must be covered by your existing insurance plan. Some rental companies require you to buy a **Collision Damage Waiver (CDW),** which will waive the excess in the case of a collision. **Loss Damage Waivers (LDWs)** do the same in the case of theft or vandalism.

National chains often allow one-way rentals (picking up in one city and dropping off in another). There is usually a minimum hire period and sometimes an extra drop-off charge of up to several hundred dollars.

DRIVING PERMITS AND CAR INSURANCE

INTERNATIONAL DRIVING PERMIT (IDP)

If you plan to drive a car while in Eastern Europe, you should have an International Driving Permit (IDP), though certain countries allow travelers to drive with a valid American, British, or Canadian license for a limited number of months. For specific info, consult the **Entrance Requirements** section of each country. It is useful to have one anyway, in case you're in an accident or stranded in a small town where the police do not speak English. Information on the IDP is printed in 10 languages, including German and Russian. Your IDP, valid for one year, must be issued in your own country before you depart. An application for an IDP usually requires one or two photos, a current local license, an additional form of identification, and a fee. To apply, contact your home country's automobile association. Be vigilant when purchasing an IDP online or anywhere other than your home automobile association. Many vendors sell permits of questionable legitimacy.

CAR INSURANCE

Most credit cards cover standard insurance. If you rent, lease, or borrow a car, you will need a **Green Card,** or **International Insurance Certificate,** to certify that you have liability insurance and that it applies abroad. Green cards can be obtained at car rental agencies, car dealers (for those leasing cars), some travel agents, and some border crossings. Rental agencies may require you to purchase theft insurance in countries that they consider to have a high risk of auto theft.

DRIVING PRECAUTIONS. When traveling in the summer or in the desert, bring substantial amounts of water (a suggested 5L of **water** per person per day) for drinking and for the radiator. For long drives to unpopulated areas, register with police before beginning the trek and again upon arrival at the destination. Check with the local automobile club for details. When traveling for long distances, make sure tires are in good repair and have enough air, and get good maps. A **compass** and a **car manual** can also be very useful. You should always carry a **spare tire** and **jack, jumper cables, extra oil, flares,** a **flashlight,** and **heavy blankets** (in case your car breaks down at night or in the winter). If you don't know how to **change a tire,** learn before heading out, especially if you are planning on traveling in deserted areas. Blowouts on dirt roads are very common. If your car breaks down, **stay in your vehicle;** if you wander off, there's less likelihood trackers will find you.

BY BICYCLE

Although bringing your own bike isn't worth the cost of transportation in most of Eastern Europe, cycling is one of the best ways to explore the region and get off the beaten path, literally. In many countries, especially the Baltic countries, Poland, and Slovenia, **renting** a bike will allow you to see much more of the natural scenery. For more information, consult the **Practical Information** section of the city or town in which you will be traveling.

BY THUMB

Let's Go never recommends hitchhiking as a safe means of transportation, and none of the information presented here is intended to do so.

Hitchhiking involves serious risks, including theft, assault, sexual harassment, and unsafe driving. For women traveling alone (or even in pairs), hitching is just too dangerous. If you do decide to hitchhike, consider where you are. Hitching remains relatively common in Eastern Europe, though Westerners are a definite target for theft. In Russia, the Baltics, Poland, and some other Eastern European countries, hitchhiking can be akin to hailing a taxi, and drivers will likely expect to be paid a sum at least equivalent to a bus ticket to your destination.

KEEPING IN TOUCH

The ease of communication varies widely from country to country. In Central European countries, such as Hungary, Poland, and the Czech Republic, postal and telephone systems are as reliable and efficient as in the US and Western Europe. Even the Russian mail system now offers relatively speedy delivery to the West. However, in Bulgaria and Ukraine—particularly outside the capital cities—postal services are less predictable and should not be depended upon. Phone cards can also be problematic throughout the region: double-check with your phone card carrier before departure in order to ensure that their service will allow you to call home. Keeping in touch can be troublesome, inefficient, and downright mind-boggling. For country-specific information, read **Essentials: Keeping in Touch** in each country chapter.

BY EMAIL AND INTERNET

Every major city in Eastern Europe has some sort of Internet access. While it may be more difficult to find in smaller towns and the rural countryside, Internet access is often available in public libraries and tourist offices. Rates are reasonable; 1hr. costs US$1-3 on average, though rates fluctuate from country to country.

Though in some places it's possible to forge a remote link with your home server, in most cases this is a much slower (and thus more expensive) option than taking advantage of free web-based email accounts (e.g., www.hotmail.com; www.yahoo.com; and www.gmail.com). Bringing a laptop can be a liability, and in some countries it may be considered offensive to use one in public. Internet cafes and free Internet terminals at public libraries or universities are listed in the **Practical Information** sections of major cities. For lists of additional cybercafes in Eastern Europe, check out www.cybercafes.com or www.netcafeguide.com.

WARY WI-FI. Wireless hot spots make Internet access possible in public and remote places. Unfortunately, they also pose **security risks.** Hot spots are public, open networks that use unencrypted, unsecured connections. They are susceptible to hacks and "packet sniffing"–ways of stealing passwords and other private information. To prevent problems, disable ad hoc mode, turn off file sharing, turn off network discovery, encrypt your e-mail, turn on your firewall, beware of phony networks, and watch for over-the-shoulder creeps. Ask the establishment whose wireless you're using for the name of the network so you know you're on the right one. If you are in the vicinity and do not plan to access the Internet, turn off your wireless adapter completely.

BY TELEPHONE

CALLING HOME FROM EASTERN EUROPE

A **calling card** is probably cheapest and your best bet. Calls are either billed collect or to your account. To obtain a calling card from your national telecommunications service before leaving home, contact the appropriate company listed below. Be forewarned that not all calling card companies offer service in every Eastern European country. To call home with a calling card, contact the local operator for your service provider by dialing the access numbers listed in the **Essentials: Keeping in Touch** section at the beginning of each country chapter and on the inside of the back cover. Not all of these numbers are toll-free; in many countries, phones will require coin deposit or a card to call the operator. Where available, locally purchased **prepaid phone cards** can be used for direct international calls, but they are still less cost-efficient than calling cards purchased through the service providers listed below. **In-room hotel calls** invariably include an arbitrary and sky-high surcharge and will sometimes charge you for the call even if you use a calling card. You can usually make **direct international calls** from pay phones, but if you aren't using a calling card you may need to drop your coins as quickly as your words.

PLACING INTERNATIONAL CALLS. The international dialing prefixes and country codes of Eastern European nations are listed at the beginning of each country chapter and on the inside of the back cover. To call Eastern Europe from home or to call home from Eastern Europe, dial:

1. The **international dialing prefix.** To dial out of Eastern Europe, use the international dialing prefixes listed at the beginning of each chapter and on the inside of the back cover; **Australia,** 0011; **Canada** or the **US,** 011; the **Republic of Ireland, New Zealand,** or the **UK,** 00. The international dialing prefix for each country in Eastern Europe can be found in the Facts and Figures table of every Essentials chapter.
2. The **country code** of the country you want to call. To call **Australia,** dial 61; **Canada** or the **US,** 1; the **Republic of Ireland,** 353; **New Zealand,** 64; the **UK,** 44; for Eastern European nations, codes are listed at the beginning of each country chapter and on the inside of the back cover.
3. The **city/area code.** *Let's Go* lists the city/area codes for cities and towns in Eastern Europe opposite the city or town name, next to a ☎. Omit initial digits in parentheses (e.g., (0)12 for Kraków) when calling from abroad.
4. The **local number.**

Placing a **collect call** through an international operator is even more expensive but may be necessary in case of emergency. You can place collect calls through the service providers listed below even if you don't have one of their phone cards. To reach an English-speaking operator, you must dial the phone company access number for the country you're in.

COMPANY	TO OBTAIN A CARD:
AT&T (US)	☎800-364-9292 or www.att.com
Canada Direct	☎800-561-8868 or www.infocanadadirect.com
MCI (US)	☎800-40-00-00 or http://consumer.mci.com
New Zealand Direct	☎0800 000 000 or www.telecom.co.nz
Telstra Australia	☎13 22 00 or www.telstra.com

CALLING WITHIN EASTERN EUROPE

The simplest way to call within the region is to use a coin-operated phone or to use **prepaid phone cards,** which are slowly phasing out coins in most Eastern European countries. Rates tend to be highest in the morning, lower in the evening, and lowest on Sunday and late at night.

CELLULAR PHONES

The international standard for cell phones is **Global System for Mobile Communication (GSM).** To make and receive calls in Eastern Europe you will need a **GSM-compatible phone** and a **SIM (Subscriber Identity Module) card,** a country-specific, thumbnail-sized chip that gives you a local phone number and plugs you into the local network. Many SIM cards are **prepaid,** meaning that they come with calling time included and you don't need to sign up for a monthly service plan. Incoming calls are frequently free. When you use up the prepaid time, you can buy additional cards or vouchers (usually available at convenience stores) to get more. For more information on GSM phones, check out www.telestial.com, www.orange.co.uk, www.roadpost.com, or www.planetomni.com. Companies like **Cellular Abroad** (www.cellularabroad.com) rent cell phones that work in a variety of destinations around the world, providing a simpler option than picking up a phone in-country.

GSM PHONES. Just having a GSM phone doesn't mean you're necessarily good to go when you travel abroad. The majority of GSM phones sold in the United States operate on a different **frequency** (1900) than international phones (900/1800) and will not work abroad. Tri-band phones work on all three frequencies (900/1800/1900) and will operate through most of the world. As well, some GSM phones are **SIM-locked** and will only accept SIM cards from a single carrier. You'll need a **SIM-unlocked** phone to use a SIM card from a local carrier when you travel.

TIME DIFFERENCES

A map with Eastern European time zones is on the inside back cover of this book—Vancouver, CAN and San Francisco, USA are GMT -8; New York, USA is GMT -5; Sydney, AUS is GMT +10; and Auckland, NZ is GMT +12. All Eastern European countries observe Daylight Saving Time.

BY MAIL

SENDING MAIL FROM EASTERN EUROPE

Airmail is the best way to send mail home from Eastern Europe. Write *"par avion"* or "airmail" in the language of the country you are visiting (in Cyrillic if applicable) on the front. Surface mail is by far the cheapest and slowest way to send mail. It takes one to three months to cross the Atlantic and two to four to cross the Pacific—good for items you won't need to see for a while, such as souvenirs or other articles that are weighing down your pack.

SENDING MAIL TO EASTERN EUROPE

Mark envelopes "airmail," *"par avion,"* or airmail in the language of the country that you are visiting. If regular airmail is too slow, **Federal Express** (Australia ☎ 13 26 10, Canada and US 800-463-3339, New Zealand 08 00 73 33 39, UK 08 00 12 38 00; www.fedex.com) offers three-day service to most of Eastern Europe. For a country-by-country guide to what can and can't be sent to each country, consult the US Postal Service at http://pe.usps.gov/text/Imm/Immctry.html, which also tells you how mail is likely to be treated upon arrival in each country. There are several ways to arrange pickup of letters sent to you by friends and relatives while you are in Eastern Europe. Mail can be sent to Eastern Europe through **Poste Restante** (the international phrase for General Delivery) to almost any city or town with a post office. While *Poste Restante* is reliable in most countries, it is far less likely to reach its intended recipient in less developed nations. Addressing conventions for *Poste Restante* vary by country; *Let's Go* gives instructions in the **Essentials: Keeping in Touch** section at the beginning of each country's chapter. As a rule, it is best to use the **largest post office** in the area, as mail may be sent there regardless of what is written on the envelope. When picking up your mail, bring a passport for identification. American Express travel offices will act as a mail service for cardholders if contacted in advance. Under this free **Client Letter Service,** they will hold mail for up to 30 days and forward it upon request. Some offices offer these services to non-cardholders (especially those who have purchased AmEx Travelers Cheques), but you must call ahead.

ACCOMMODATIONS

HOSTELS

Many hostels are laid out dorm-style, often with large single-sex rooms and bunk beds, although private rooms that sleep two to four are becoming more common. They sometimes have kitchens and utensils for common use, bike or moped rentals, storage areas, transportation to airports, breakfast and other meals, laundry facilities, and Internet access. There can be drawbacks: some hostels close during certain daytime "lockout" hours, have a curfew, don't accept reservations, or impose a maximum stay. In Eastern Europe, a bed in any sort of hostel will usually cost you US$10-15. Hostels, however, tend to be more expensive in Russia and in the well-touristed capitals of Eastern Europe, such as Prague or Budapest, and will typically run at least US$20. Hostels are practically non-existent in Belarus.

A HOSTELER'S BILL OF RIGHTS. There are certain standard features that we do not include in our hostel listings. Unless we state otherwise, you can expect that every hostel has no lockout, no curfew, free hot showers, some system of secure luggage storage, and no key deposit.

HOSTELLING INTERNATIONAL

Joining the youth hostel association in your own country (listed below) automatically grants you membership privileges in **Hostelling International (HI)**, a federation of national hosteling associations. Non-HI members may be allowed to stay in some hostels, but will have to pay extra to do so. HI hostels are scattered irregularly throughout Eastern Europe, but, if you will be spending time in the more touristed areas of Croatia, Hungary, and Poland, an HI card is a worthwhile investment. Hostels in Croatia, the Czech Republic, Hungary, Latvia, Lithuania, Poland, Romania, Russia, Slovakia, and Slovenia accept reservations via HI's umbrella organization's website (www.hihostels.com). Other comprehensive hosteling websites include www.hostels.com, www.hostelworld.com, and www.hostelplanet.com.

A new membership benefit is the FreeNites program, which allows hostelers to gain points toward free rooms. Most student travel agencies (see p. 31) sell HI cards, as do all of the national hosteling organizations listed below. All prices listed below are valid for **one-year memberships** unless otherwise noted.

ESSENTIALS

Australian Youth Hostels Association (AYHA), 422 Kent St., Sydney, NSW 200 (☎02 92 61 11 11; www.yha.com.au). AUS$52, under 18 AUS$19.

Hostelling International-Canada (HI-C), 205 Catherine St. Ste. 400, Ottawa, ON K2P 1C3 (☎613-237-7884; www.hihostels.ca). CDN$35, under 18 free.

An Óige (Irish Youth Hostel Association), 61 Mountjoy St., Dublin 7 (☎830 4555; www.irelandyha.org). EUR€20, under 18 EUR€10.

Hostelling International Northern Ireland (HINI), 22-32 Donegall Rd., Belfast BT12 5JN (☎02 89 03 24 733; www.hini.org.uk). UK£15, under 25 UK£10.

Youth Hostels Association of New Zealand Inc. (YHANZ), Level 1, 166 Moorhouse Ave., P.O. Box 436, Christchurch (☎800 278 299 (NZ only) or 033 799 970; www.yha.org.nz). NZ$40, under 18 free.

Scottish Youth Hostels Association (SYHA), 7 Glebe Cres., Stirling FK8 2JA (☎01 78 68 91 400; www.syha.org.uk). UK£8, under 18 £4.

Youth Hostels Association (England and Wales), Trevelyan House, Dimple Rd., Matlock, Derbyshire DE4 3YH (☎08 70 77 08 868; www.yha.org.uk). UK£16, under 26 UK£10.

Hostelling International-USA, 8401 Colesville Rd., Ste. 600, Silver Spring, MD 20910 (☎301-495-1240; www.hiayh.org). US$28, under 18 free.

BOOKING HOSTELS ONLINE. One of the easiest ways to ensure you've got a bed for the night is by reserving online. Click to the **Hostelworld** booking engine through **www.letsgo.com,** and you'll have access to bargain accommodations from Argentina to Zimbabwe with no added commission.

OTHER TYPES OF ACCOMMODATIONS

HOTELS, GUESTHOUSES, AND PENSIONS

Hotel singles in Eastern Europe cost about US$20-35 per night, doubles $30-60. You'll typically share a hall bathroom; a private bathroom will cost extra, as may hot showers. Smaller **guesthouses** and **pensions** are often cheaper and, after hostels, are the most common budget accommodation in Eastern Europe.

UNIVERSITY DORMS

Many colleges and universities open their residence halls to travelers when school is not in session; some do so even during term-time. Getting a room may take a couple of phone calls and require advanced planning, but rates tend to be low and many offer free local calls and Internet access.

PRIVATE ROOMS

An increasingly popular option in rural locations and in the larger cities of certain Eastern European countries (Bulgaria, Croatia, Russia, and Ukraine) is to rent a room in a private home. Although it may seem dangerous, going home with an old woman from the train station or knocking on doors advertising private rooms (often marked by *Zimmer frei*, *sobe*, etc.) is legitimate, generally reliable, and often even cheaper than staying in a hostel. Make sure to get the price in writing and always inspect a room before agreeing on a price.

HOME EXCHANGES

Home exchange offers the traveler various types of homes (houses, apartments, condominiums, villas), plus the opportunity to live like a native and cut down on lodging fees. For more info, contact HomeExchange.com Inc., P.O. Box 787, Hermosa Beach, CA 90254, USA (☎310 798 3864, toll free 800-877-8723; www.homeexchange.com), which has listings from **Bulgaria, Croatia, the Czech Republic, Estonia, Hungary, Latvia, Lithuania, Poland, Romania, Russia, Turkey,** and **Ukraine.**

LONG-TERM ACCOMMODATIONS

Travelers planning to stay in Europe for extended periods of time may find it most cost-efficient to rent an **apartment.** Generally, for stays shorter than three months, it is more feasible to **sublet** than lease your own apartment. It may also be possible to arrange to sublet rooms from university students on summer break. It is far easier to find an apartment once you have arrived at your destination than to attempt to use the Internet from home, though www.craigslist.org can be helpful for major cities. By staying in a hostel for your first week or so, you can make local contacts and, more importantly, check out your new digs before you commit.

CAMPING

Eastern Europe offers many opportunities for hiking, biking, mountain climbing, camping, trekking, and spelunking. Camping is one of the most authentic ways to experience the vacation culture of the region, as Eastern Europeans tend to spend their own vacations exploring the outdoors. There is very little English-language literature on outdoor opportunities and adventures available in the region. Untraveled as the Eastern European wilderness is, however, it's surprisingly difficult to truly rough it. In most countries, camping within the boundaries of national parks is either illegal or heavily restricted; many areas require a camping permit. Check with the local tourist office or locals before setting up camp in an area that's not explicitly designated for camping. Regulations vary: in Russia, for example, camping is extremely restricted, whereas Bulgaria allows campers almost anywhere. Alternatively, you can often stay in a **chata** located within a park; these huts offer dorm-style rooms for US$5-10, running water (not always hot), and some sort of mess hall. **Organized campgrounds** that offer tent space and bungalows are often situated around the borders of parks. All campgrounds have running water; some offer restaurants and other facilities. Tent sites range from US$3-10 per person with a flat tent fee of US$5-10. Bungalow fees are usually US$5-10. For more information on outdoor activities in Eastern Europe, see **The Great Outdoors,** below.

THE GREAT OUTDOORS

The **Great Outdoor Recreation Pages** (www.gorp.com) provides excellent general information for travelers planning on camping or spending time in the outdoors.

LEAVE NO TRACE. *Let's Go* encourages travelers to embrace the "Leave No Trace" ethic, minimizing their impact on natural environments and protecting them for future generations. Trekkers and wilderness enthusiasts should set up camp on durable surfaces, use cookstoves instead of campfires, bury human waste away from water supplies, bag trash and carry it out with them, and respect wildlife and natural objects. For more detailed information, contact the **Leave No Trace Center for Outdoor Ethics,** P.O. Box 997, Boulder, CO 80306 (☎800-332-4100 or 303-442-8222; www.lnt.org).

USEFUL RESOURCES

A variety of publishing companies offers hiking guidebooks to meet the educational needs of novice or expert. For information about camping, hiking, and biking, write or call the publishers listed below to receive a free catalog. Travelers planning to camp extensively in Eastern Europe might consider buying an **International Camping Carnet.** Similar to a hostel membership card, it's required at some campgrounds and provides discounts at many others. It's available in North America from the **Family Campers and RVers Association** (www.fcrv.org); in the UK from **the Caravan Club;** Australians, Irish, and New Zealanders can obtain one from their national automobile associations.

Automobile Association, Contact Centre, Lambert House, Stockport Rd., Cheadle, SK8 2DY, UK (☎08 70 60 00 371; www.theaa.co.uk). Publishes *Caravan and Camping: Europe* (UK£9). They also offer European road atlases.

The Mountaineers Books, 1001 SW Klickitat Way, #201, Seattle, WA 98134, USA (☎800-553-4453; www.mountaineersbooks.org). Over 600 titles on hiking, biking, mountaineering, natural history, and conservation.

WILDERNESS SAFETY

Staying **warm, dry,** and **well hydrated** is key to a happy and safe wilderness experience. For any hike, prepare yourself for an emergency by packing a first-aid kit, a reflector, a whistle, high-energy food, extra water, raingear, a hat, mittens, and extra socks. For warmth, wear wool or insulating synthetic materials designed for the outdoors. Cotton is a bad choice as it dries painfully slowly. Check **weather forecasts** often and pay attention to the skies when hiking, as weather patterns can change suddenly. Always let someone—a friend, a park ranger, or a local hiking organization—know when and where you are going. See **Safety and Health,** p. 21, for information on outdoor medical concerns. In Croatia there is a risk of **landmines** still buried in parks and the wilderness. To minimize the danger, stay on the beaten path and purchase a local **landmine map.**

CAMPING AND HIKING EQUIPMENT

WHAT TO BUY

Good camping equipment is both sturdy and light. North American suppliers tend to offer the most competitive prices.

Sleeping Bags: Most sleeping bags are rated by season; "summer" means 30-40°F (around 0°C) at night; "four-season" or "winter" often means below 0°F (-17°C). Bags are made of **down** (warm and light, but expensive, and miserable when wet) or of **synthetic** material (heavy, durable, and warm when wet). Prices range US$50-250 for a summer synthetic to US$200-300 for a good down winter bag. **Sleeping bag pads** include foam pads (US$10-30), air mattresses (US$15-50), and self-inflating mats (US$30-120). Bring a **stuff sack** to store your bag and keep it dry.

Tents: The best tents are free-standing (with their own frames and suspension systems), set up quickly, and only require staking in high winds. Low-profile dome tents are the best all-around. Worthy 2-person tents start at US$100, 4-person tents start at US$160. Make sure your tent has a rain fly and seal its seams with waterproofer. Other useful accessories include a **battery-operated lantern,** a plastic **groundcloth,** and a nylon **tarp.**

Backpacks: Internal-frame packs mold well to your back, keep a lower center of gravity, and flex adequately to allow you to hike difficult trails, while **external-frame packs** are more comfortable for long hikes over even terrain, as they carry weight higher and distribute it more evenly. Make sure your pack has a strong, padded hip-belt to transfer weight to your legs. There are models designed specifically for women. Any serious backpacking requires a pack of at least 4000 cu. in. (16,000cc), plus 500 cu. in. for sleeping bags in internal-frame packs. Sturdy backpacks cost anywhere from US$125-420—your pack is an area where it doesn't pay to economize. On your hunt for the perfect pack, fill up prospective models with something heavy, strap it on correctly, and walk around the store to get a sense of how the model distributes weight. Either buy a **rain cover** (US$10-20) or store all of your belongings in plastic bags inside your pack.

Boots: Be sure to wear hiking boots with good **ankle support.** They should fit snugly and comfortably over 1-2 pairs of **wool socks** and a pair of thin **liner socks.** Break in boots over several weeks before you go to spare yourself blisters.

Other Necessities: Synthetic layers, like those made of polypropylene or polyester, and a pile jacket will keep you warm even when wet. A **space blanket** (US$5-15) will help you to retain body heat and doubles as a groundcloth. Plastic **water bottles** are vital; look for shatter- and leak-resistant models. Carry **water-purification tablets** for when you can't boil water. Although most campgrounds provide campfire sites, you may want to bring a small **metal grate** or **grill.** For those places (including virtually every organized campground in

Europe) that forbid fires or the gathering of firewood, you'll need a **camp stove** (the classic Coleman starts at US$50) and a propane-filled **fuel bottle** to operate it. Also bring a **first-aid kit, pocketknife, insect repellent,** and **waterproof matches** or a **lighter.**

WHERE TO BUY IT

The mail-order and online companies listed below offer lower prices than many retail stores, but a visit to a local camping or outdoors store will give you a good sense of the look and weight of certain items before you buy.

Cotswold Outdoor, Unit 11 Kemble Business Park, Crudwell, Malmesbury Wiltshire, SN16 9SH, UK (☎08 70 44 27 755; www.cotswoldoutdoor.com).

Discount Camping, 833 Main North Rd., Pooraka, South Australia 5095, Australia (☎61 88 26 23 399; www.discountcamping.com.au).

Recreational Equipment, Inc. (REI), Sumner, WA 98352, USA (US and Canada ☎800-426-4840, elsewhere 253-891-2500; www.rei.com).

CAMPERS AND RVS

Renting an RV costs more than tenting or hosteling but less than staying in hotels while renting a car (see **Rental Cars,** p. 36). The convenience of bringing along your own bedroom, bathroom, and kitchen makes RVing an attractive option, especially for older travelers and families with children. Rates vary widely by region, season (July and Aug. are usually the most expensive months), and type of RV. Rental prices for a standard RV tend to be around US$800 per week. RV rentals in Eastern Europe are few and far apart; your best bet for rentals is in the Baltic countries and in Croatia. Consider starting and ending your trip in Germany, where RV rentals are usually cheaper.

ORGANIZED ADVENTURE TRIPS

Organized adventure tours offer another way of exploring the wild. Activities include hiking, biking, skiing, canoeing, kayaking, rafting, climbing, photo safaris, and archaeological digs. Tourism bureaus often can suggest parks, trails, and outfitters. Organizations that specialize in camping and outdoor equipment like REI (see above) also are good sources for information. Also try **Specialty Travel Index,** P.O. Box 458, San Anselmo, CA 94979, USA (US ☎888-624-4030, elsewhere 415-455-1643; www.specialtytravel.com).

SPECIFIC CONCERNS

SUSTAINABLE TRAVEL

As the number of travelers on the road continues to rise, the detrimental effect they can have on natural environments becomes an increasing concern. With this in mind, Let's Go promotes the philosophy of **sustainable travel.** Through a sensitivity to issues of ecology and sustainability, today's travelers can be a powerful force in preserving and restoring the places they visit.

Ecotourism, a rising trend in sustainable travel, focuses on the conservation of natural habitats and using them to build up the economy without exploitation or overdevelopment. Travelers can make a difference by doing advance research and by supporting organizations and establishments that pay attention to their impact on their natural surroundings and strive to be environmentally friendly.

ECOTOURISM RESOURCES. For more information on environmentally responsible tourism, contact one of the organizations below:

Conservation International, 2011 Crystal Dr., Ste. 500, Arlington, VA 22202, USA (www.conservation.org).

Green Globe, Green Globe vof. Verbenalaan 1, 2111 ZL Aerdenhout, The Netherlands (☎31 23 54 40 306; www.greenglobe.com)

International Ecotourism Society, 733 15th St., NW, Washington, D.C. 20005, USA (☎202-347-9203; www.ecotourism.org).

United Nations Environment Program (**UNEP;** ☎33 14 43 71 441; www.uneptie.org/pc/tourism).

The **environment** in Eastern Europe is particularly fragile, with air pollution a looming issue. To that end, consider taking public transportation in lieu of cabs or cars. The **Regional and Environmental Center for Central and Eastern Europe's** website (www.rec.org/REC/Databases/Databases.htm) contains helpful information.

RESPONSIBLE TRAVEL

The impact of tourist money on the destinations you visit should not be underestimated. The choices you make during your trip can have potent effects on local communities—for better or for worse. Travelers who care about the destinations and environments they explore should become aware of the social and cultural implications of the choices they make when they travel. Simple decisions such as buying local products instead of globally available products, paying a fair price for products or services, and attempting to say a few words in the local language can have a strong, positive effect on the community.

Community-based tourism aims to channel tourist money into the local economy by emphasizing tours and cultural programs that are run by members of the host community and that often benefit disadvantaged groups. This type of tourism also benefits the tourists themselves, as these tours often take them beyond the traditional tours of the region. An excellent resource for general information on community-based travel is *The Ethical Travel Guide* (UK£13), a project of **Tourism Concern** (☎+44 020 7133 3330; www.tourismconcern.org.uk).

TRAVELING ALONE

There are many benefits to traveling alone, including independence and greater interaction with locals. On the other hand, solo travelers are more vulnerable targets of harassment. If you are traveling alone, look confident, and be especially careful in deserted or very crowded areas. Stay away from areas that are poorly lit. If questioned, never say that you are traveling alone. Maintain regular contact with someone home who knows your itinerary, and always research your destination before traveling. For more tips, pick up *Traveling Solo* by Eleanor Berman (Globe Pequot Press, US$18), visit www.travelaloneandloveit.com, or subscribe to **Connecting: Solo Travel Network,** 689 Park Rd., Unit 6, Gibsons, BC V0N 1V7, Canada (☎800-557-1757; www.cstn.org; membership US$30-48).

WOMEN TRAVELERS

Women traveling on their own inevitably face some additional safety concerns, especially because solo female travelers are still a relatively new phenomenon in much of Eastern Europe. That said, it's easy to be adventurous without taking undue risks. If you are concerned, consider staying in hostels that offer single-sex rooms or single rooms that lock from the inside. Stick to centrally located accommodations and avoid solitary late-night treks or Metro rides.

Hitchhiking is never safe for lone women, or even for two women traveling together. Choose train compartments occupied by women or couples; ask the conductor to put together a women-only compartment if there isn't one. Look as if you know where you're going and approach older women or couples for directions if you're lost or uncomfortable. Generally, the less you look like a tourist, the better off you'll be. Dress conservatively, especially in rural areas. Wearing the clothes that are fashionable among local women will cut down on stares, and a *babushka*-style kerchief discourages even the most tenacious of catcallers. Wearing a conspicuous wedding band sometimes helps to prevent unwanted advances.

Your best answer to verbal harassment is no answer at all; feigning deafness, sitting motionless, and staring straight ahead at nothing in particular will usually do the trick. The extremely persistent can sometimes be dissuaded by a firm, loud, and very public "Go away!" in the appropriate language. Don't hesitate to seek out a police officer or a passerby if you are being harassed. If need be, turn to an older woman for help; her stern rebukes should usually embarrass the most persistent harassers into silence. Memorize the emergency numbers in places you visit, and consider carrying a whistle on your keychain. A self-defense course will both prepare you for a potential attack and raise your level of awareness of your surroundings (see **Personal Safety**, p. 22). Also be sure you are aware of the specific health risks that women face when traveling (see p. 30).

GLBT TRAVELERS

Although legal in most Eastern European countries, homosexuality is strongly stigmatized in much of the former Soviet Union. Public displays of homosexuality give local authorities an excuse to be troublesome. Within some major cities, gay nightclubs and social centers are hidden and frequently change location, though in cities such as Prague and Budapest, gay nightlife is becoming more mainstream. Be aware that GLBT rights are a particularly charged issue in Catholic Poland. For coverage of the current legal and social climate in each country, consult the website of the **International Lesbian and Gay Association** (www.ilga.org). Word of mouth is often a great source for finding the latest hot spots. Listed below are contact organizations, mail-order bookstores, and publishers that offer materials addressing some specific concerns. **Out and About** (www.planetout.com) offers a newsletter addressing travel concerns and a comprehensive site addressing gay travel concerns. The online newspaper **365gay.com** also has a travel section (www.365gay.com/travel/travelchannel.htm).

Gay's the Word, 66 Marchmont St., London WC1N 1AB, UK (☎20 72 78 76 54; www.gaystheword.co.uk). The largest gay and lesbian bookshop in the UK, with both fiction and non-fiction titles. Mail-order service available.

Giovanni's Room, 1145 Pine St., Philadelphia, PA 19107, USA (☎215-923-2960; www.queerbooks.com). An international lesbian and gay bookstore with mail-order service (carries many of the publications listed below).

International Lesbian and Gay Association (ILGA), Ave. des Villas 34 1060, Brussels, Belgium (☎32 25 02 24 71; www.ilga.org). Provides political information, such as homosexuality laws of individual countries.

TRAVELERS WITH DISABILITIES

Unfortunately, Eastern Europe is largely inaccessible to disabled travelers. Ramps and other amenities are all but nonexistent in most countries. Contact your destination's consulate or tourist office for information, arrange transportation early,

ADDITIONAL RESOURCES: GLBT TRAVEL.

Spartacus 2005-2006: International Gay Guide. Bruno Gmunder Verlag (US$33).

Damron Accommodations Guide, Damron City Guide, and *Damron Women's Traveller.* Damron Travel Guides (US$11-19). For info, call ☎800-462-6654 or visit www.damron.com.

The Gay Vacation Guide: The Best Trips and How to Plan Them, by Mark Chesnut. Kensington Books (US$15).

and inform airlines and hotels when making reservations; some time may be needed to prepare special accommodations. **Guide-dog owners** should inquire as to the specific quarantine policies of each destination.

USEFUL ORGANIZATIONS

Accessible Journeys, 35 West Sellers Ave., Ridley Park, PA 19078, USA (☎800-846-4537; www.disabilitytravel.com). Designs tours for wheelchair-users and slow walkers.

Flying Wheels Travel, 143 W. Bridge St., P.O. Box 382, Owatonna, MN 55060, USA (☎507-451-5005; www.flyingwheelstravel.com). Escorted trips to Europe.

MINORITY TRAVELERS

Minority travelers, especially those of African or Asian descent, will generally meet with more curiosity than hostility, especially outside big cities. Yet travelers with darker skin of any nationality may experience some prejudice, particularly in the Balkans, where ethnic tensions run high, and in Moscow and St. Petersburg, where they may encounter police harassment. In both of these Russian cities, violent crimes against those of African descent are on the rise. Anti-Muslim sentiment lingers in the Balkans from the conflicts that plagued the region throughout the 1990s. **Roma** (gypsies) also encounter substantial hostility in Eastern Europe. The number of **skinheads** is on the rise in Eastern Europe, and minority travelers, especially those of African and Jewish descent, should regard them with caution. **Anti-semitism** is still a problem in many countries, including Lithuania, Poland, Romania, and the former Soviet Union. Minority travelers should check with tourist bureaus to determine in advance unsafe areas of town. The Soros Foundation's Open Society Institute works to promote human rights and reform; their website may be especially useful for women and Roma. (Available at **www.soros.org/initiatives;** click on Central/Eastern Europe).

DIETARY CONCERNS

Vegetarian and **kosher** dining is often a challenge in Eastern Europe, although vegetarian restaurants are on the rise in Central Europe. Most of the national cuisines tend to be heavy in meat, particularly pork. **Markets** are often a good bet for fresh vegetables, fruit, cheese, and bread. The **North American Vegetarian Society,** P.O. Box 72, Dolgeville, NY 13329, USA (☎518-568-7970; www.navs-online.org), offers information and publications for vegetarian travelers. There are many resources on the web; try **www.happycow.net,** or **www.vegeats.com/restaurants/europe** for a directory of vegetarian-friendly dining at your destination. Travelers who keep kosher should beware of restaurants labeled "Jewish," many of which are not actually kosher. For information on kosher restaurants, contact synagogues in larger cities. A good resource is the *Jewish Travel Guide,* by Michael Zaidner (Vallentine Mitchell; US$18). Travelers looking for halal restaurants may find www.zabihah.com a useful resource.

OTHER RESOURCES

Let's Go tries to cover all aspects of budget travel, but we can't put *everything* in our guides. Listed below are books and websites that can serve as jumping-off points for your own research.

USEFUL PUBLICATIONS

Central Europe Profiled, Barry Turner ed. St. Martin's Press, 2000 (US$18). A breakdown of the culture, politics, and economy of each country in Eastern Europe.

On Foot to the Golden Horn, by Jason Goodwin. Picador, 2000 (US$11). Join this fellow backpacker on a journey from Poland to Turkey.

INTERNET RESOURCES

Listed here are some regional and travel-related sites to start off your surfing; other relevant websites are listed throughout the book. Because website turnover is high, use search engines (e.g., www.google.com) to strike out on your own.

WWW.LETSGO.COM. Our website features extensive content from our guides; a community forum where travelers can connect with each other, ask questions or advice, and share stories and tips; and expanded resources to help you plan your trip. Visit us to browse by destination and find information about ordering our titles.

Backpacker's Ultimate Guide: www.bugeurope.com. Tips on packing, transportation, and where to go. Also tons of country-specific travel information.

BootsnAll.com: www.bootsnall.com. Numerous resources for independent travelers, from planning your trip to reporting on it when you get back.

How to See the World: www.artoftravel.com. A compendium of great travel tips, from cheap flights to self-defense to interacting with local culture.

Travel Intelligence: www.travelintelligence.net. A large collection of travel writing by distinguished travel writers.

Travel Library: www.travel-library.com. A fantastic set of links for general information and personal travelogues.

INFORMATION ON EASTERN EUROPE

CIA World Factbook: www.odci.gov/cia/publications/factbook/index.html. Tons of vital statistics on Eastern Europe's geography, government, economy, and people.

Foreign Language for Travelers: www.travlang.com. Provides free online translating dictionaries and lists of phrases in various European languages, including Czech, Hungarian, Polish, and Turkish.

Geographia: www.geographia.com. Highlights, culture, and people of Eastern European countries.

PlanetRider: www.planetrider.com. A subjective list of links to the "best" websites covering the culture and tourist attractions of several Eastern European countries, including the Czech Republic, Hungary, and Russia.

BEYOND TOURISM

A PHILOSOPHY FOR TRAVELERS

HIGHLIGHTS OF BEYOND TOURISM IN EASTERN EUROPE

TEACH ENGLISH to orphans in rural Russia (p. 55).

LEARN music and theater arts in Vilnius, Lithuania (p. 59).

RESCUE endangered Eurasian griffons in the wilderness of Croatia (p. 57).

WORK on an organic farm in rural Estonia (p. 53).

As a tourist, you are always a foreigner. While hostel-hopping and sightseeing can be great fun, you may want to consider going *beyond* tourism. Experiencing a foreign place through studying, volunteering, or working can help reduce that touristy stranger-in-a-strange-land feeling. Furthermore, travelers can make a positive impact on the natural and cultural environments they visit. With this Beyond Tourism chapter, Let's Go hopes to promote a better understanding of Eastern Europe and to provide suggestions for those who want to get more than a photo album out of their travels. The "Giving Back" sidebar features (p. 125, p. 178, and p. 502) also highlight regional Beyond Tourism opportunities.

One of the most common Beyond Tourism activities in Eastern Europe is **volunteerism,** with both local and international organizations, either on a short-term basis or as the main focus of an extended trip. As a **volunteer** in Eastern Europe, one can participate in projects ranging from teaching English to orphans in rural Russia to protecting the habitats of Eurasian griffon vultures in Croatia. Later in this chapter, we recommend organizations that can help you find the opportunities that best suit your interests.

Throughout Eastern Europe, there are many opportunities for **studying** in a new environment, whether through enrolling as an exchange student at Russia's oldest university in Moscow, taking language classes on the edge of the Black Sea in Odessa, Ukraine, or getting hands-on filmmaking experience in Prague, Czech Republic.

Although the economic situation in most Eastern European countries means jobs for foreigners are not plentiful, for those willing to look there are still many opportunities to **work,** whether long-term as a teacher or intern, or short-term in a service industry, making just enough cash to cover the next leg of the journey.

VOLUNTEERING

Volunteering can be a deeply fulfilling experience, especially when combined with the thrill of traveling in a new place. For those looking to make a difference, Eastern Europe, with its stunning natural beauty, diverse populations, and history of political unrest, poses unique and important challenges. Researching a program before committing is your best bet to find the volunteer opportunity that is right for you. If you can, talk to people who have participated in the program, and find out what you're getting into, as living and working conditions vary greatly from one organization to another.

Travelers interested in volunteering in Eastern Europe can do so on either a short-term or long-term basis. For short-term volunteers, the most common option

WHY PAY MONEY TO VOLUNTEER? Many volunteers are surprised to learn that some organizations require large fees or "donations." While this may seem ridiculous at first glance, such fees often keep the organization afloat, in addition to covering airfare, room, board, and administrative expenses for the volunteers. (Other organizations must rely on private donations and government subsidies.) If you're concerned about how a program spends its fees, request an annual report or finance account. A reputable organization won't refuse to inform you of how volunteer money is spent. Pay-to-volunteer programs might be a good idea for young travelers who are looking for more support and structure (such as pre-arranged transportation and housing), or anyone who would rather not deal with the uncertainty implicit in creating a volunteer experience from scratch.

is a work camp, which for a moderate fee will offer a place to live and work on projects including farming, environmental protection, childcare, or construction.

Those looking for longer, more intensive volunteer opportunities usually choose to go through a parent organization that takes care of logistical details and often provides a group environment and support system for a fee. There are two main types of organizations—religious and non-sectarian—although there are rarely restrictions on participation for either.

In either case, prospective participants may find it useful to explore the General Resources below, the more specific entries later on in this chapter, or the literature listed at the end, in order to find the right volunteer opportunity.

GENERAL RESOURCES

Action Without Borders (www.idealist.org). An extensive Internet bulletin board listing over 46,000 volunteer organizations and with a versatile search engine.

Coordinating Committee for International Voluntary Service, UNESCO House, 31 r. François Bonvin, 75732 Paris Cedex 15, France (☎33 14 56 84 936; www.unesco.org/ccivs). This umbrella organization links over 140 NGOs worldwide. The "Members" section on the website includes a list of volunteer branches throughout Central and Eastern Europe with contact information.

Gençtur Turizm ve Seyahat Ac. Ltd., İstiklal Cad. 212, Aznavur Pasajı, Kat: 5, Galatasaray, İstanbul 80080 (☎21 22 44 62 30; www.genctur.com). A tourism and travel agency that sets up various workshops, nannying jobs, volunteer camps, and year-round study tours in Turkey.

GoAbroad.com (www.goabroad.com) maintains an extensive directory of study, work, and volunteer opportunities around the globe.

Transitions Abroad, P.O. Box 745, Bennington, VT 05201, USA (☎1-802-442-4827; www.transitionsabroad.com). This preeminent "beyond tourism" magazine also publishes a number of books and hosts an extensive list of online resources including opportunities to volunteer, work, or study abroad.

Working Abroad, P.O. Box 454, Flat 1, Brighton, East Sussex BN1 3ZS, UK (www.workingabroad.com). An online network of voluntary and professional work organizations. For a US$57 fee, they provide a personalized listing of overseas opportunities based on one's capabilities and interests.

World Wide Opportunities on Organic Farms (WWOOF), Main Office, P.O. Box 2675, Lewes BN7 1RB, UK (www.wwoof.org). Arranges volunteer work on organic and eco-conscious farms around the world. Branches in the **Czech Republic, Estonia,** and **Slovenia.**

BALKAN REBUILDING

Armed conflict in the Balkans—from the devastating war in Croatia and Bosnia in the early 90s to the 1999 conflict in Kosovo—has left deep scars and open wounds throughout the region. Genocide and military intervention by the international community left 300,000 dead and millions more displaced, and did massive damage to the region's infrastructure and economy. While most of the initial ethnic tensions have quieted down, disagreements between ethnic Albanians and Serbs still threaten to destabilize Kosovo, which is currently a province of Serbia but is governed by the United Nations. A variety of organizations continue to pick up the pieces by assisting refugees, helping children, and repairing the landscape.

Balkan Sunflowers, Youth, Culture and Sports Hall #114, Luan Haradinaj Street, Pristina, Kosovo (☎38 10 38 26 299; www.balkansunflowers.org). Programs in **Kosovo, Macedonia,** and **Albania.** Minimum volunteering period 6 months. Volunteers often work with children.

Coalition for Work With Psychotrauma and Peace, M. Drzica 12, 32000 Vukovar, Croatia (☎38 53 24 50 991; www.cwwpp.org). Work in education and health care related to long-term conflict stress in Croatia.

United Nations High Commission for Refugees (UNHCR), Case Postale 2500, CH-1211 Genève 2 Dépôt, Switzerland (☎41 22 73 98 111; www.unhcr.org). Provides opportunities to work or serve as an intern helping refugees worldwide.

YOUTH AND HEALTH OUTREACH

ChildAid to Russia and the Republics (ARRC), P.O. Box 200, Bromley, Kent BR1 1QF, UK (☎44 02 08 46 06 046). Christian-based humanitarian organization with projects focused on helping children in **Russia** and **Ukraine.**

Cadip, 111-1271 Howe Street, Vancouver, British Columbia V6Z 1R3, Canada (☎1-604-628-7400; www.cadip.org). Runs work camps of young volunteers who assist with orphan childcare in **Bulgaria.** Minimum program and membership fee US$270. Travel costs not included.

Cross-Cultural Solutions, 2 Clinton Pl., New Rochelle, NY 10801, USA (☎1-800-380-4777; crossculturalsolutions.org). 1- to 12-week education and social service placements in **Russia** and many other countries. Applicants under 18 need to fill out a special Minor Application Form. From US$2489.

Doctors Without Borders, 333 7th Ave., 2nd fl., New York, NY 10001, USA (☎1-212-679-6800; www.doctorswithoutborders.org/volunteer). Medical and non-medical volunteer assignments wherever there is need.

Downside Up, 15 Ozerkovsky per., Moscow 115184, Russia (☎/fax 01 17 95 10 079; www.downsideup.org). Bike 250km through the **Moscow** region in late Aug. to raise money for this organization that benefits Russian children with Down syndrome.

Global Volunteer Network (www.volunteer.org.nz). Volunteer opportunities helping children in **Romania** and **Russia.** From US$700 for 6 weeks in Romania; US$729 for 2 weeks in Russia; US$350 application fee.

UNICEF (United Nations Children's Fund), Regional Office for CEE/CIS, Palais des Nations, CH-1211 Geneva 10, Switzerland (☎41 22 90 95 433; www.unicef.org/ceecis). UN organization, with offices throughout Eastern Europe. Accepts volunteers for teaching and healthcare projects. Undergraduate degree and work experience required.

COMMUNITY DEVELOPMENT

Brethren Volunteer Service, 1451 Dundee Ave., Elgin, IL 60120, USA (☎1-800-323-8039, ext. 410; www.brethrenvolunteerservice.org). Christian organization places volunteers with civic and environmental groups in **Slovakia.**

European Roma Rights Center, H-1386 Budapest 62, P.O. Box 906/93, Hungary (fax 36 14 13 22 01; www.errc.org). Provides internship opportunities in human rights advocacy in **Hungary** lasting between 3 weeks and 6 months. Click on the link labeled "Human Rights Training" for more details.

Habitat for Humanity International, 121 Habitat St., Americus, GA 31709, USA (☎1-229-924-6935, ext. 2551; www.habitat.org). Volunteers build houses in over 83 countries, including **Bulgaria, Hungary, Poland, Romania,** and **Slovakia.** From 2 weeks to 3 years. Volunteers must pay for all living costs and airfare.

Peace Corps, Office of Volunteer Recruitment and Selection, 1111 20th St., NW, Washington, D.C. 20526, USA (☎1-800-424-8580; www.peacecorps.gov). Sends volunteers to developing nations, including **Bulgaria, Romania,** and **Ukraine.** Focus on business, education, or environmental issues. Must be a US citizen age 18+ willing to make a 2-year commitment. By application. Bachelor's degree usually required.

Service Civil International Voluntary Service (SCI-IVS), SCI USA, 5474 Walnut Level Rd., Crozet, VA 22932, USA (☎1-206-350-6585; www.sci-ivs.org). Placement in work camps throughout Eastern and Central Europe. 18+. US$195 for 2-3 weeks (depending on program); travel costs not included. Opportunities for longer stays of several months.

Volunteers for Peace, 1034 Tiffany Rd., Belmont., VT 05730, USA (☎1-802-259-2759; www.vfp.org). Arranges placement in work camps throughout Eastern Europe and **Turkey.** Membership required for registration. Annual *International Workcamp Directory* US$30. 2-3 week programs average US$250.

LITERACY AND CULTURAL EXCHANGE

Bridges for Education (☎1-716-839-0180; www.bridges4edu.org). Runs month-long programs at "peace camps" in several Eastern European countries including **Bulgaria, the Baltics,** and **Romania.** 3 weeks of teaching English and North American culture and 1 week of group travel. US$950 tax-deductible donation required. For more information contact Ms. Margaret Dodge, 8912 Garlinghouse Rd., Naples, NY 14512, USA.

Global Volunteers, 375 E. Little Canada Rd., St. Paul, MN 55117, USA (☎1-800-487-1074; www.globalvolunteers.org). Short-term volunteer opportunities (1-3 weeks) in **Hungary, Poland,** and **Romania.** Programs focus on teaching and aiding children. Program fees US$2100-2500; airfare not included.

Jewish Volunteer Corps, American Jewish World Service, 45 W. 36th St., New York, NY 10018, USA (☎1-800-889-7146). Places volunteers at summer camps and Jewish community centers in **Russia** and **Ukraine.**

Kitezh Children's Community (http://atschool.eduweb.co.uk/ecoliza/files/kitezh.html). Teach English to **Russian** orphans in a rural setting. Young people taking a "gap year" between high school and college are especially common as volunteers. Stays at Kitezh usually last 2 months or more.

Learning Enterprises, 2227 20th St. #304, NW, Washington, D.C. 20009, USA (☎1-202-309-3453; www.learningenterprises.org). 6-week summer programs place first-time English teachers in rural **Croatia, Hungary, Romania,** and **Slovakia,** with the option to switch countries half-way. No-fee program includes orientation and room and board with a host family, but volunteers must pay for airfare and expenses.

WorldTeach, 79 JFK St., Cambridge, MA 02138, USA (☎1-800-483-2240; www.worldteach.org). Spend 2 months living with a family in **Poland** and teaching English to high-school students. US$3990.

CONSERVATION AND PRESERVATION

Auschwitz Jewish Center, Auschwitz Jewish Center Foundation, 36 Battery Place, New York, NY 10280, USA (☎1-212-575-1050; www.ajcf.org). Offers fully paid 6-week

expat fun

teaching english as a foreign language in prague

In the 1990s, people began comparing Prague to the Paris of the 1920s. Both were allegedly fueled by the same sort of boozy, poetic energy that expats find so irresistable. By the time I graduated college, I knew that life held something grander—like the image of Prague.

Don't want to go to grad school? Tired of the service industry? The burgeoning Teaching English as a Foreign Language (TEFL) field may be for you. English teachers in Prague are a scruffy lot. We are tourists with permanent addresses, but if you want to immerse yourself in a culture, to learn the language and meet locals, Prague is probably not the best place to do it.

The good news is that jobs are plentiful, and getting started at TEFL is a simple, if costly, affair. Dozens of schools offer the four week, 120hr. training course. Such schools mushroom and disappear overnight, so research is recommended. The training experience is a bit like summer camp: often isolated on the outskirts of Prague, students participate in mock-lessons meant to teach methodology, but which more often resemble elementary school with their emphases on maps and games. Training also provides a mini social scene. The people I did my TEFL course with became my roommates and my first few friends here.

Once the strange initiation rites of TEFL are done, the apartment found and paid for through the nose, then the job hunt begins. Language schools are rampant in Prague, though "school" is a bit of a misnomer since they are actually more like agencies in the business of hooking up clients with teachers. The schools develop reputations: one hires good-looking American girls for its male clients, another buries its teachers in paperwork and pays poorly. There are distinct benefits to working for these schools, which provide textbooks and other teaching materials. Still, teachers see only a fraction of what students pay for their services. Do-it-yourself teaching—which depends on posting fliers and holding classes in coffeeshops—is popular but harder to do.

I was so broke that I took the first job I could find. I had come to Prague with the misconception that life here was dirt cheap. Essential items like food, beer, and cigarettes are still inexpensive, but rent, clothing, books, and movies cost about what they would in the US. It took about four months to build up a full schedule of three- to four classes a day, and by then I was already exhausted from constantly having to offer peppy praise and soft correction. I have become a stunning conversationalist, however, and can engage you for hours on the topic of your weekend plans. If nothing else, teaching English has forced me out of the narcissistic I developed in college. I'll return to the states broke, but also well armed and ready for small talk.

"If nothing else, teaching English has forced me out of the narcissistic shell I developed in college."

Hannah Brooks-Motl is a graduate of Macalester College. Though she has yet to "find" herself there, she lives and works in Prague. Her favorite Czech beer is Staropramen; *her favorite Czech food is the dumpling.*

programs for college graduates and graduate students in Oswiecim, **Poland.** Focuses on cultural exchange and the study of pre-war Jewish life in Poland, with visits to the Auschwitz-Birkenau State Museum and other sites.

Archaeological Institute of America, 656 Beacon St., Boston, MA 02215, USA (☎1-617-353-9361; www.archaeological.org). The *Archaeological Fieldwork Opportunities Bulletin,* available on the website, lists field sites throughout Europe including **Bulgaria, Poland, Romania, Russia,** and **Ukraine.** Print edition, with additional info, US$20.

The British Trust for Conservation Volunteers (BTCV), 163 Balby Rd., Balby, Doncaster DN4 ORH, UK (☎44 01 30 25 72 224; http://www2.btcv.org.uk), works in concert with the **Slovak Wildlife Society** (www.slovakwildlife.org) to give volunteers the opportunity to assist in monitoring bear and wolf populations in the Tatras Mountains of **Slovakia.**

Earthwatch, 3 Clocktower Pl., Ste. 100, P.O. Box 75, Maynard, MA 01754, USA (☎1-800-776-0188 or 1-978-461-0081; www.earthwatch.org). Arranges 1-3 week programs in the **Czech Republic, Estonia, Poland, Romania,** and **Russia** to promote conservation of natural resources. Programs average US$2000.

Eco-Centre Caput Insulae-Beli, Beli 4, 51559 Beli, Cres Island, Croatia (☎/fax 38 55 18 40 525; www.caput-insulae.com), protects the natural, cultural, and historical heritage of Cres Island, **Croatia.** Volunteers pay for room, board, and airfare. Bring 3 friends and get 1 free week of accommodations. 2-week minimum volunteer period.

EcoVolunteer (☎31 74 25 08 250; www.ecovolunteer.org). Offers wildlife conservation programs with animals ranging from Croatian vultures to Polish beavers. Programs in **Bulgaria, Croatia, Poland,** and **Russia.**

Green Balkans, 160 Shesti Septemvri Blvd., Plovdiv 4000, Bulgaria (☎35 93 26 26 977; www.greenbalkans.org). The largest conservation agency in **Bulgaria** offers volunteers the opportunity to perform office or field work in a variety of locations.

INEX–Association of Voluntary Service, Senovážné nám. 24, 116 47 Praha 1, Czech Republic (☎420 234 621 527; www.inexsda.cz/eng). Ecological and historical preservation efforts, as well as construction projects, in the **Czech Republic.**

Tahoe-Baikal Institute, P.O. Box 13587, South Lake Tahoe, CA 96151, USA (☎1-530-542-5599; www.tahoebaikal.org). Environmental exchange (typically 10 weeks). College students and young professionals spend 5 weeks at Lake Tahoe, CA and 5 weeks at Lake Baikal, **Russia.** AmeriCorps workers can receive a stipend with this program.

STUDYING

VISA INFORMATION. In most Eastern European countries, studying requires a special **student visa.** Applying for such a visa usually requires proof of admission to a university or program in your country of destination. Contact your local consulate or embassy. For additional visa information, see **Essentials** (p. 12) or consult the **Consulates and Embassies** section at the beginning of each country chapter.

Study-abroad programs range from basic language and culture courses to college-level classes. In order to choose a program that best fits your needs, research thoroughly to determine costs and duration, as well as what kind of students participate in the program and what sort of accommodations are provided.

In programs that have large groups of students who speak the same language, there is a trade-off. You may feel more comfortable in the community, but you will not have the same opportunity to practice a foreign language or to befriend other international students. For accommodations, dorm life provides a better opportunity to mingle with fellow students, but there is less of a chance to experience the local scene. If you live with a family, there is a potential to build lifelong friendships with natives and to experience day-to-day life in more depth, but conditions can vary greatly from family to family.

UNIVERSITIES

Foreign-study programs have multiplied rapidly in Eastern Europe. Most undergraduates enroll in programs sponsored by universities in their home countries, and many university study-abroad offices can provide advice and information. Those who are relatively fluent in an Eastern European language may find it cheaper to enroll directly in a university abroad, although getting college credit may be more difficult. You can search **www.studyabroad.com** for various semester-abroad programs that meet your criteria, including your desired location and focus of study. The following is a list of organizations that can help place students in university programs abroad, or have their own branch in Eastern Europe.

AMERICAN PROGRAMS

American Field Service (AFS), 71 W. 23rd St., 17th fl., New York, NY 10010, USA (☎1-212-807-8686; www.afs.org), with branches in over 50 countries. Offers summer-, semester-, and year-long homestay exchange programs in the **Czech Republic, Hungary, Latvia, Russia,** and **Slovakia** for high school students and graduating seniors. Community service programs also offered for young adults 18+. Teaching programs available for current and retired teachers. Financial aid available.

American Institute for Foreign Study (AIFS), River Plaza, 9 W. Broad St., Stamford, CT 06902, USA (☎1-800-727-2437; www.aifsabroad.com). Organizes programs for study in universities in the **Czech Republic, Hungary,** and **Russia.** Financial aid and scholarships available. US$95 application fee.

Association for International Practical Training (AIPT), 10400 Little Patuxent Pkwy., Ste. 250, Columbia, MD 21044, USA (☎1-410-997-2200; www.aipt.org). Runs 8- to 12-week and year-long programs in Eastern Europe for students ages 18-30 who have completed 2 years of technical study, as well as year-long programs for qualified professionals under 35. Scholarships available. Application fee US$75.

Council on International Educational Exchange (CIEE), 7 Custom House St., 3rd fl., Portland, ME 04101, USA (☎1-800-407-8839; www.ciee.org). Work, volunteer, and academic programs in the **Czech Republic, Hungary, Poland,** and **Russia.**

International Association for the Exchange of Students for Technical Experience (IAESTE), 10400 Little Patuxent Pkwy., Ste. 250, Columbia, MD 21044, USA (☎1-410-997-3068; www.iaeste.org). Offers 8- to 12-week internships in a variety of Eastern European countries for college students who have completed 2 years of technical study.

NYU Study Abroad, 7 East 12th Street, 6th fl., New York, NY 10003, USA (☎1-212-998-4433; www.nyu.edu/studyabroad). Offers a semester or year of liberal arts undergraduate study at the NYU Center in **Prague,** near Charles University.

NYU, Tisch School of the Arts, 721 Broadway, 12th fl., New York, NY 10003, USA (☎1-212-998-1500; www.specialprograms.tisch.nyu.edu). Spend time in **Prague** studying filmmaking and directing a film, or take film and acting classes in **St. Petersburg.**

School for International Training, College Semester Abroad, Admissions, Kipling Rd., P.O. Box 676, Brattleboro, VT 05302, USA (☎1-800-257-7751; www.sit.edu). Semester-long programs in the **Balkans,** the **Czech Republic, Poland,** and **Russia.** Must have completed at least 1 year of college with a minimum 2.5 cumulative GPA. Program costs average US$16,000. Financial aid available. Also runs the **Experiment in International Living** (☎1-800-345-2929; www.usexperiment.org), 5-week summer programs (US$5300) that offer high school students cross-cultural homestays, community service, ecological adventure, and language training in **Poland.**

The School of Russian and Asian Studies, 175 E. 74th, Ste. 21B, New York, NY 10021, USA (☎1-800-557-8774; www.sras.org). Provides study-abroad opportunities at language schools and in degree programs at universities in **Russia.** Also arranges work, internship and volunteer programs throughout Russia.

University Study Abroad Consortium, USAC/323, Reno, NV 89557, USA (☎1-775-784-6569; www.usac.unr.edu). Offers a program for the study of Czech language and culture in **Prague** for the duration of a summer, semester, or year. From US$3480.

Youth for Understanding USA (YFU), 6400 Goldsboro Rd., Ste. 100, Bethesda, MD 20817, USA (☎1-866-493-8872 or 1-240-235-2100; www.yfu.org). Places US high school students for a year, semester, or summer in various Eastern European countries, including **Bulgaria, Estonia, Hungary, Latvia, Lithuania, Poland, Romania, Russia, Slovakia,** and **Ukraine.** US$75 application fee plus $500 enrollment deposit.

EASTERN EUROPEAN PROGRAMS

American University in Bulgaria, Blagoevgrad 2700, Bulgaria (☎35 97 38 88 218; www.aubg.bg). University in **Bulgaria** based on the American liberal arts model.

Central European University, Nador u. 9, Budapest 1051, Hungary (☎36 13 27 30 09; www.ceu.hu). Affiliated with the Open Society Institute-Budapest. Offers international students the opportunity to take graduate-level courses in **Budapest.** Tuition US$9395 per semester, not including personal expenses. Financial aid available.

Charles University, Vratislavova 10/29, 128 00 Praha 2, Czech Republic (www.ujop.cuni.cz). Central Europe's oldest university offers courses in **Czech** culture, language, and history for durations ranging from 6 weeks to 10 months. Tuition from US$585 for a 6-week stay.

Jagiellonian University, Centre for European Studies, ul. Garbarska 7a, 31-131 Kraków, Poland (☎48 12 42 96 207; www.ces.uj.edu.pl). University founded in 1364 offers undergraduates summer- and semester-long programs in Central European studies and Polish language. Semester tuition US$5000. Scholarships available.

Liden & Denz Language Centre, Transportny per. 11, 5th fl., 191119 St. Petersburg, Russia (☎78 12 33 40 788; www.lidenz.ch). Another location at Grusinski per. 3-181, ground fl., 123056 Moscow, Russia. Russian language classes and cultural excursions in **Moscow** and **St. Petersburg.**

Lithuanian Academy of Theater and Music, Gedimino pr. 42, LT-01110 Vilnius, Lithuania (☎37 05 21 24 96; www.lmta.lt). Classes in music, art, and theater in **Lithuania.** Offers some music and multimedia arts classes in English.

Lomonosov Moscow State University, A-812a, Main Building, Moscow State University, Leninskie Gory, Moscow 119992-GSP-2, Russia (☎74 95 93 91 502; www.ied.msu.ru). **Russia's** oldest university welcomes international students.

Odessa Language Center (☎380 482 345 058; www.studyrus.com). Spend a year or a summer in **Ukraine** learning Russian and taking courses on history and culture.

University of Bucharest, 36-46, M. Kogălniceanu Bd., Sector 5, 70709 Bucharest, Romania (☎40 21 30 77 300; www.unibuc.ro). Accepts international students for study in **Romania.**

University of West Bohemia, Univerzitní 8, 306 14 Plzeň, Czech Republic (☎420 377 631 111; www.zcu.cz). An international university centrally located in a student-friendly **Czech** brewery city.

LANGUAGE SCHOOLS

Language schools are often independently run organizations or divisions of foreign universities; they rarely offer college credit. Language schools are a good alternative to university study if you desire a deeper focus on the language or a slightly less rigorous course load.

American Councils for International Education, 1776 Massachusetts Ave., Ste. 700, NW, Washington, D.C. 20036, USA (☎1-202-833-7522; www.actr.org). Summer-, semester-, and year-long college-level Russian programs across the former USSR.

Eurocentres, Seestr. 247, CH-8038 Zürich, Switzerland (☎41 14 85 50 40; fax 481 6124; www.eurocentres.com), offers 2- to 12-week Russian-language programs in **Moscow** and **St. Petersburg.** Prices range from US$800-7000, depending on the program.

Languages Abroad, 413 Ontario St., Toronto, ON M5A 2V9, Canada (☎1-800-219-9924 or 1-416-925-2112; www.languagesabroad.com), has 2- to 4-week language programs (US$1600-3000) in **Croatia,** the **Czech Republic, Hungary, Poland,** and **Russia,** as well as volunteer and internship opportunities (18+), and language programs for corporate executives (26+) and young multilinguals (10+).

WORKING

As with volunteering, work opportunities tend to fall into two categories. Some travelers want long-term jobs that allow them to integrate into a community, while others seek out short-term jobs to finance the next leg of their travels. In Eastern Europe, travelers looking for short-term work should consult classified sections in local English-language publications, available in most capital cities (see below). Service industries are common sources of short-term employment for foreigners. Teaching (see below, p. 61) is a common form of long-term employment abroad. When considering work, travelers should remember that jobs in Eastern Europe are scarce, even for locals, and payment is usually low.

LOCAL CLASSIFIEDS

Bulgaria: The Sofia Echo (www.sofiaecho.com).

Czech Republic: The Prague Post (www.praguepost.com).

Estonia, Latvia, and Lithuania: The Baltic Times (www.baltictimes.com).

Hungary: The Budapest Sun (www.budapestsun.com).

Poland: The Warsaw Voice (www.warsawvoice.pl).

Romania: Nine O'Clock (www.nineoclock.ro).

Russia: The Russia Journal (www.russiajournal.com).

Slovakia: The Slovak Spectator (www.slovakspectator.sk).

Ukraine: The Kyiv Post (www.kyivpost.com).

CUTTING THROUGH THE RED TAPE: VISAS AND PERMITS. Though working in Eastern Europe is rewarding, it requires jumping through an exhausting set of bureaucratic hoops. Already suffering from rampant unemployment, most countries make it very difficult for foreigners to work, requiring a work permit as well as a visa or a permit for temporary residency. In some countries, a special visa, often called a "visa with work permit," is required in addition to (not as a replacement for) a work permit. These visas are issued from the nearest consulate or embassy (see the **Embassies and Consulates** section of each country chapter). Applying for one will require you to present your work permit, which must be issued directly from the Labor Bureau of the country in question. Given these complications, making contact with prospective employers within the country is a good way to expedite permits or arrange work-for-accommodation swaps. US students and young adults may also wish to make use of a service such as the Council on International Educational Exchange (www.ciee.org), which will help applicants find work in their chosen country.

LONG-TERM WORK

If you're planning on spending a substantial amount of time (more than three months) working in Eastern Europe, search for a job well in advance. International placement agencies are often the easiest way to find employment abroad, especially for those interested in **teaching** English. Although they are often only available to college students, **internships** are a good way to segue into working abroad. Be wary of advertisements for companies claiming to be able get you a job abroad for a fee—the same listings are often available online or in newspapers. **Transitions Abroad** (www.transitionsabroad.com) offers an updated online listing of teaching and other work opportunities.

TEACHING ENGLISH

Teaching jobs abroad are rarely well-paid, although some elite private American schools offer competitive salaries. Volunteering as a teacher in lieu of getting paid is a popular option, but even then, teachers often receive some sort of a daily stipend to help with living expenses. That said, even if salaries may seem low by Western standards, the low cost of living in many Eastern European countries may render them more livable. In almost all cases, you must have at least a bachelor's degree to be a full-fledged teacher, although college undergraduates can often get summer positions teaching or tutoring.

Many schools require teachers to have a **Teaching English as a Foreign Language** (TEFL) certificate. You may still be able to find a teaching job without certification, but certified teachers often find higher-paying jobs. Native English speakers working in private schools are often hired for English-immersion classrooms where the local native language is not spoken. Those volunteering or teaching in public schools are more likely to be working in both English and the local language. Placement agencies or university fellowship programs are the best resources for finding teaching jobs. The following organizations are helpful in placing teachers in Eastern Europe:

Central European Teaching Program, 3800 NE 72nd Ave., Portland, OR 97213, USA (☎1-503-287-4977; www.ticon.net/~cetp). Places English teachers in state schools in Hungary and Romania for one semester (US$1700) or a full school year (US$2250).

Czech Academic Information Agency, Dům Zahraničních Služeb, Senovážné nám. 26, P.O. Box 8, 110 06 Praha 06, Czech Republic (☎420 224 229 698; www.dzs.cz/scripts/detail.asp?id=599). Helps prospective English teachers find posts in state primary and secondary schools in small Czech towns.

International Schools Services (ISS), 15 Roszel Rd., P.O. Box 5910, Princeton, NJ 08543, USA (☎1-609-452-0990; www.iss.edu). Hires teachers for more than 200 overseas schools, many in Eastern Europe. Candidates should have experience with teaching or international affairs. Bachelor's degree and 2-year commitment required.

Office of Overseas Schools, US Department of State, Room H328, SA-1, Washington, D.C. 20522, USA (☎1-202-261-8200; www.state.gov/m/a/os). Keeps comprehensive lists of schools abroad and agencies that place Americans as teachers.

Petro-Teach, Westpost, P.O. Box 109, Lappeenranta 53101, Finland (www.petroteach.com). Places teachers from abroad in schools in **St. Petersburg,** Russia, for a semester or a full academic year. US$3000-5000.

INTERNSHIPS

Internships, usually for college students, are a good way to segue into working abroad, although they are often unpaid or poorly paid. **Internships International,** 1612 Oberlin Rd., Raleigh, NC 27608, USA, offers unpaid internships and connections to language schools in cities around the world, including Budapest, Hungary. A fee of US$1100 guarantees placement in an internship. (June-Dec. ☎1-207-443-3019, Jan.-May 1-919-832-1575; www.internshipsinternational.org.)

AU PAIR WORK

Au pairs are typically women (although sometimes men), aged 18-27, who work as live-in nannies, caring for children and doing light housework in foreign countries in exchange for room, board, and a small spending allowance or stipend. One perk of the job is that it allows you an intimate view into life in a foreign country without the high expenses of traveling. Drawbacks, however, can include mediocre pay and long hours. Payment varies widely with placement, and much of the au pair experience depends on the family for which you'll be working. The agencies below are a good starting point for looking for this form of employment.

AuPairConnect, Max Global, Inc., 8370 W. Cheyenne Ave. #76, Las Vegas, NV 89129, USA (www.aupairconnect.com). Finds work in a variety of Eastern European countries.

Svezhy Veter, 426000 Izhevsk, P.O. Box 2040, Russia (☎73 41 24 50 037; www.sv-agency.udm.ru/sv/aupair.htm). Finds au pair placements in **Russia.**

SHORT-TERM WORK

Traveling for long periods of time can be hard on finances; therefore, many travelers try their hand at odd jobs for a few weeks at a time to help pay for another month or two of touring around. Working in a hostel or restaurant and teaching English are the most common forms of employment among travelers to Eastern Europe. Opportunities tend to be more abundant in larger cities, but so do prospective workers, creating increased competition. Word-of-mouth is often the best resource when seeking a job; ask other backpackers and friendly hostel or restaurant owners for tips on an appropriate opportunity. Another popular option is to work several hours a day at a hostel or on a farm in exchange for free or discounted room or board. Due to high turnover in the tourism industry, many places are eager for help, even if it is only temporary.

FURTHER READING ON BEYOND TOURISM.

Alternatives to the Peace Corps: A Guide of Global Volunteer Opportunities, by Paul Backhurst. Food First Books, 2005 (US$12).

The Back Door Guide to Short-Term Job Adventures: Internships, Summer Jobs, Seasonal Work, Volunteer Vacations, and Transitions Abroad, by Michael Landes. Ten Speed Press, 2005 (US$22).

Green Volunteers: The World Guide to Voluntary Work in Nature Conservation, ed. Fabio Ausenda. Universe, 2007 (US$15).

How to Get a Job in Europe, by Cheryl Matherly and Robert Sanborn. Planning Communications, 2003 (US$23).

How to Live Your Dream of Volunteering Overseas, by Joseph Collins, Stefano DeZerega, and Zahara Heckscher. Penguin Books, 2002 (US$20).

International Job Finder: Where the Jobs Are Worldwide, by Daniel Lauber and Kraig Rice. Planning Communications, 2002 (US$20).

Volunteer Vacations: Short-Term Adventures That Will Benefit You and Others, by Doug Cutchins, Anne Geissinger, and Bill McMillon. Chicago Review Press, 2006 (US$18).

Work Abroad: The Complete Guide to Finding a Job Overseas, by Clayton Hubbs. Transitions Abroad Publishing, 2002 (US$16).

Work Your Way Around the World, by Susan Griffith. Vacation-Work Publications, 2007 (US$22).

BULGARIA (БЪЛГАРИЯ)

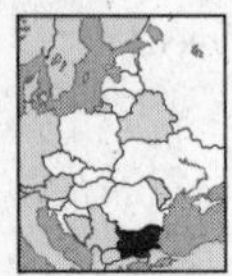

From the pine-covered slopes of the Rila, Pirin, and Rodopi Mountains to the beaches of the Black Sea, Bulgaria is blessed with a countryside rich in natural resources and steeped in ancient traditions. The history of the Bulgarian people, however, is not as serene as the landscape: crumbling Greco-Thracian ruins and Soviet-style high-rises attest to centuries of turmoil and political struggle. Though Bulgaria's flagging economy and dual-pricing system for foreigners can dampen the mood, travelers willing to make the trek to the beautiful Black Sea Coast, cosmopolitan Sofia, and picturesque villages will be greatly rewarded. And until the country adopts a more western economic and cultural bent, you can bet that Bulgaria will remain happily free of crowds.

DISCOVER BULGARIA: SUGGESTED ITINERARIES

THREE DAYS. Two days are probably enough to take in **Sofia's** (p. 71) museums, cathedrals, and cafes. Going to the **Rila Monastery** (1 day; p. 81) is often easier said than done, but the gorgeous atmosphere and environs are worth it.

ONE WEEK. After two days in historic, sun-drenched **Varna** (p. 88), bus to **Veliko Turnovo** (2 days; p. 82) for its Roman ruins, before heading to the **Rila Monastery** (1 day; p. 81). End in cosmopolitan, vibrant **Sofia** (2 days).

FACTS AND FIGURES

Official Name: Republic of Bulgaria.

Capital: Sofia.

Major Cities: Plodiv, Varna, Burgas.

Population: 7,323,000.

Time Zone: GMT + 2, in summer GMT + 3

Land Area: 110,550 sq. km.

Official Language: Bulgarian.

Religions: Bulgarian Orthodox (83%), Muslim (12%).

International Ranking on IQ Tests: 2.

Expected Sunflower Exports in 2007: 900,000 tons.

ESSENTIALS

WHEN TO GO

Bulgaria's temperate climate makes it easy to catch good weather. Spring (Apr.-May) is pleasant and has a bevy of festivals and events. Summer (June-Sept.) isn't too hot, making it perfect for hiking and beachgoing—just expect crowds on the Black Sea Coast and at campgrounds. Skiing is good from December until April.

DOCUMENTS AND FORMALITIES

EMBASSIES AND CONSULATES. Foreign embassies and consulates to Bulgaria are in Sofia (p. 71). Bulgarian embassies abroad include: **Australia,** 33 Cultoa Circuit, O'Malley, Canberra, ACT 2600 (☎62 86 97 11; www.bulgaria.org.au); **Canada,** 325 Stewart St., Ottawa, ON K1N 6K5 (☎613-789-3215; www.bgembassy.ca); **Ireland,** 22 Burlington Rd., Dublin 4 (☎16 60 32 93; www.bulgaria.bg/europe/dublin); **UK,** 186-188 Queensgate, London SW7 5HL (☎20 75 84 94 00; www.bulgaria.embassyhomepage.com); **US,** 1621 22nd St., NW, Washington, D.C. 20008 (☎202-387-0174; www.bulgaria-embassy.org).

ENTRANCE REQUIREMENTS.

Passport: Required for all travelers; must be valid for 6 months after end of stay.

Visa: Not required for citizens of Australia, Canada, Ireland, New Zealand, the UK, and the US for stays of up to 90 days.

Letter of Invitation: Not required.

Inoculations: Recommended up-to-date on DTaP (diphtheria, tetanus, and pertussis), Hepatitis A, Hepatitis B, MMR (measles, mumps, and rubella), rabies, polio booster, and typhoid.

Work Permit: Required of all foreigners planning to work in Bulgaria.

International Driving Permit: Required of all those planning to drive in Bulgaria.

VISA AND ENTRY INFORMATION. Citizens of Australia, Canada, Ireland, New Zealand, the UK, and the US do not need a **visa** for stays of up to 90 days within a six month period. Passports are required and must be valid for six months beyond the date of departure; proof of medical insurance is also required. Travelers should consult the Bulgarian embassy in their country of origin to apply for a long-term visa. The process typically takes two to four weeks. For US citizens, a single-entry visa costs US$60, a multiple-entry visa costs US$145, and both entail an additional US$25 processing fee. Such visas must be obtained before arrival; it is not possible to apply for a visa within Bulgaria. Upon entering the country, all tourists must declare the purpose of their trip and the address at which they intend to stay. If staying in a private residence, **register your visa** with police within 48 hours of entering Bulgaria; hotels and hostels will do this for you. Keep the registration with your passport, and make sure you re-register every time you change accommodations. A Bulgarian **border crossing** can take several hours, as there are three different checkpoints: passport control, customs, and police. The border crossing into Turkey is particularly difficult. Try to enter from Romania at Ruse or Durankulac.

TOURIST SERVICES

Tourist offices and local travel agencies—when they can be found—are generally knowledgeable and good at reserving private rooms. The most common foreign languages spoken by staff are English, German, and Russian. In smaller cities, tourist agencies are either privately owned or nonexistent. Big hotels offer a good alternative; they often have an English-speaking receptionist and **maps.**

MONEY

LEVA (LV)		
	AUS$1 = 1.16LV	1LV = AUS$0.87
	CDN$1 = 1.36LV	1LV = CDN$0.73
	EUR€1 = 1.96LV	1LV = EUR€0.51
	NZ$1 = 1.01LV	1LV = NZ$0.99
	UK£1 = 2.87LV	1LV = UK£0.35
	US$1 = 1.45LV	1LV = US$0.69

The Bulgarian unit of currency is the **lev** (lv), plural leva. Banknotes are issued in amounts of 1, 2, 5, 10, 20, and 50; coins come in amounts of 1, 2, 5, 10, 20, and 50 **stotinki** (singular stotinka; 1 lev=100 stotinki). Bulgaria does not plan to adopt the euro until at least 2010. US dollars and euro are sometimes accepted. The government is still struggling to control **inflation,** which has increased in recent years to around 6.5%. Private banks and exchange bureaus change money, but bank rates are more reliable. The four largest **banks** are Bulbank, Biochim, Hebros, and DSK. It is illegal to exchange currency on the street. **Traveler's checks** can only be cashed at banks. Many banks also give Visa **cash advances.** Typically, **ATMs** give the best exchange rates. They are common throughout Bulgaria and usually accept MasterCard, Visa, Plus, and Cirrus. As identity theft rings sometimes target ATMs, however, travelers should use machines located inside banks and check for evidence of tampering. **Credit cards** are rarely accepted, especially in the countryside. Beware officially sanctioned **tourist overcharging;** some museums and theaters will charge foreigners double or more.

BULGARIA

HEALTH AND SAFETY

EMERGENCY	Ambulance: ☎150. Fire: ☎160. Police: ☎166.

While basic **medical supplies** are available in Bulgarian hospitals, specialized treatment is not. Emergency care is better in Sofia than in the rest of the country, but it's best to avoid hospitals entirely. Although travelers are required to carry proof of insurance, most doctors expect cash payment. In case of extreme emergency, air evacuation costs about US$50,000.

The sign "Apteka" denotes a **pharmacy.** There is typically a night-duty pharmacy in larger towns. *Analgin* is headache medicine; *analgin chinin* is for colds and flu; *sitoplasty* are bandages. Tampons are widely available. Foreign brands of condoms *(prezervatifs)* are safer than the domestic brands. Public **bathrooms** ("Ж" for women, "M" for men) are often holes in the ground; pack toilet paper and hand sanitizer and expect to pay 0.05-0.20lv. Don't buy bottles of **alcohol** from street vendors, and be careful with homemade liquor. Also be wary of accepting drinks of any sort from friends met "by chance" on the street; some travelers have been poisoned or drugged and then robbed after accepting such offers.

Petty **street crime,** especially pickpocketing and purse snatching, is reasonably common in Bulgaria. Also be wary of people posing as government officials; ask them to show ID and, if necessary, to escort you to a police station. Before buying drinks for strangers, always ask to see a menu to verify the price and then clarify exactly what you want. The price might otherwise prove astronomical; some travelers report that bartenders will use force to assure payment of bills as high as several thousand dollars. Nightclubs in large cities are often associated with organized crime; avoid fights. It's generally safe for **women** to travel alone, but it's always safer to have at least one travel companion. Women should wear skirts and blouses to avoid unwanted attention, as Bulgarian women tend to dress quite formally. Visitors with physical **disabilities** will confront many challenges in Bulgaria.

Darker-skinned travelers may be mistaken for **Roma** (gypsies), the target of Bulgarian **racial discrimination.** While hate crimes are rare, those of foreign ethnicities may receive stares. Acceptance of homosexuality is slow in coming; it is prudent to avoid public displays of affection. For more information about gay and lesbian clubs and resources, check out www.queer_bulgaria.org or www.bulgayria.com.

TRANSPORTATION

BY PLANE. All flights to Sofia (SOF) connect through Western European cities. Though tickets to the capital may run over US$1500 during the summer months, budget airline **WizzAir** offers cheap flights from London, Paris, and Frankfurt through Budapest, HUN (☎029 603 888; www.wizzair.com). Travelers might also fly into a nearby hub—Athens, İstanbul, or Bucharest—and take a bus to Sofia.

BY TRAIN. Bulgarian trains run to Greece, Hungary, Romania, and Turkey and are the best form of transportation in the north. **Rila** is the main international train company; find international timetables at www.bdz-rila.com. Neither the **Eurail Pass** nor the **Eastpass** is accepted in Bulgaria. The train system is comprehensive but slow, crowded, and smoke-filled. Purse-slashing, pickpocketing, and theft have been reported in more crowded lines. Buy tickets at the Ticket Center *(Bileti Tsentur)* in stations. There are three types of trains: express *(ekspres)*, fast *(burz)*, and slow *(putnicheski)*. Avoid *putnicheski* at all costs—they stop at anything that looks inhabited, even if only by goats. Arrive well in advance if you want a seat. Station markings are irregular and often only in Cyrillic; know when you're reaching your destination, bring a map, and ask for help. First class *(purva klasa)* is identical to second *(vtora klasa)*, and not worth the extra money.

BY BUS. Buses are often faster and more comfortable than trains, though they are less frequent and less comfortable. Buses head north from Ruse to İstanbul, Turkey, and to Greece from Blagoevgrad. For long distances, **Group Travel** and **Etap** have modern buses with A/C and bathrooms. Some buses have set departure times; others leave when full.

BY FERRY, BY TAXI, AND BY CAR. Ferries from Varna make trips to İstanbul, Turkey and Odessa, Ukraine. Yellow **taxis** are everywhere in cities. Refuse to pay in dollars and insist on a ride *sus apparata* (with meter); ask the distance and price per kilometer. Don't try to bargain. Some taxi drivers rig the meters to charge more. Tipping taxi drivers usually means rounding up to the nearest lev or half-lev. Some Black Sea towns can only be reached by car. Renting is usually €15-60 cheaper from a local agency than the a larger company. Driving in Bulgaria is dangerous; roads in disrepair, aggressive driving habits, and a high number of old-model cars contribute to a high fatality rate. Rocks and landslides pose a threat in mountainous areas. Those driving in Bulgaria should be aware that a police officer cannot enforce fines on the spot, but only issue tickets.

BY BIKE AND BY THUMB. **Motoroads** (www.motoroads.com) and travel agencies offer bike tours. Stay alert when bicycling in urban areas, as Bulgarian drivers disregard traffic signals. Although **hitchhiking** is rare in Bulgaria, it is often free. While those who hitchhike say it is generally safe, Let's Go does not recommend it.

KEEPING IN TOUCH

EMAIL AND INTERNET. **Internet cafes** can be found throughout urban centers, cost approximately 1-3lv per hr., and are often open 24hr.

TELEPHONE. Making international **telephone** calls from Bulgaria can be a challenge. Pay phones are ludicrously expensive; opt for phone offices instead. If you

PHONE CODES	**Country code:** 359. **International dialing prefix:** 00. From outside Bulgaria, dial international dialing prefix (see inside back cover) + 359 + city code + local number. Within Bulgaria, dial city code + local number for intercity calls and simply the local number for calls within a city.

must make an **international call** from a pay phone with a card, purchase the 400 unit, 22lv card. Units run out quickly on international calls, so talk fast or have multiple cards ready. There are two brands: **BulFon** (orange) and **Mobika** (blue), which work only at telephones of the same brand; BulFon is more prevalent. To **call collect,** dial ☎01 23 for an international operator. The Bulgarian phrase for collect call is *obazhdane na smetka na abonata.* For **local calls,** pay phones do not accept coins, so it's best to buy a phone card (see above). You can also call from the post office, where a clerk assigns you a booth, a meter records your bill, and you pay when finished. International access codes include: **AT&T Direct** (☎800 0010); **British Telecom Payphones** (☎800 99 44); **Canada Direct** (☎800 1359; service not available from payphones); **MCI** (☎800 0001); and **Sprint** (☎800 1010).

MAIL. "Въздушна поща" on letters indicates **airmail.** Sending a letter or postcard abroad costs 1.40lv; a Bulgarian return address is required. Packages must be unwrapped for inspection. Mail can be received through **Poste Restante,** though the service is unreliable. Address envelope as follows: first name, LAST NAME, POSTE RESTANTE, писма до поискване централна поща, post office address (optional), city, Postal Code, България (Bulgaria).

BULGARIA

ACCOMMODATIONS AND CAMPING

BULGARIA	❶	❷	❸	❹	❺
ACCOMMODATIONS	under 25lv	25-35lv	36-49lv	50-70lv	over 70lv

Bulgarian **hotels** are classed on a star system and licensed by the Government Committee on Tourism; rooms in one-star hotels are nearly identical to rooms in two- and three-star hotels, but have no private baths. All accommodations provide sheets and towels. Expect to pay US$25-35. Beware that foreigners are often charged double of what locals pay. **Hostels** can be found in most major cities and run US$10-18 per bed. For a complete list of hostels in Bulgaria, see www.hostels.com/en/bg.html. **Private rooms,** which can be found in any small town, are cheap (US$6-12) and usually have all the amenities of a good hotel. Outside major towns, most **campgrounds** provide spartan bungalows and tent space. Call ahead in summer to reserve bungalows.

FOOD AND DRINK

BULGARIA	❶	❷	❸	❹	❺
FOOD	under 5lv	5-9lv	10-14lv	15-18lv	over 18lv

Kiosks sell *kebabcheta* (sausage burgers), sandwiches, pizzas, and *banitsa sus sirene* (feta-cheese-filled pastries). *Kavarma,* meat with onions, spices, and egg is slightly more expensive than *skara* (grills). **Vegetarians** should request *jadene bez meso* (JA-de-ne bez meh-SO) for meals without meat. **Kosher** diners would be wise to order vegetarian meals, as pork often works itself into main dishes. Bulgaria is known for its cheese and yogurt. *Ayran* (yogurt with water and ice) and *boza* (similar to beer, but sweet and thicker) are popular drinks that complement breakfast. Melnik produces famous red **wine,** while the northeast is known for its excellent white wines. On the Black Sea Coast, *Albenu* is a good sparkling wine. Bulgarians begin meals with *rakiya* (grape or plum brandy). Good Bulgarian **beers** include Kamenitza and Zagorka. The drinking age is 18.

LIFE AND TIMES

HISTORY

BATTLES OF THE BULG. Bulgaria was officially declared a separate state in the seventh century AD, making it the third oldest country in Europe. Between 852 and 927, emperor **Boris I** and his son **Simeon I** integrated the Bulgars and Slavs under a common language (Old Church Slavonic) and religion (Christianity). The **First Bulgarian Empire** did not last long, however; it was conquered by Byzantium in 1018. A revolt led by the brothers Ivan and Peter Asen of Tarnovo established the **Second Bulgarian Empire** in 1185, which extended from the Black Sea to the Adriatic. In 1396, the Turks conquered the remains of a Bulgaria weakened by internal upheaval, wars with the Serbian and Hungarian kingdoms, and Mongol attacks.

REVOLUTIONARY RUMBLINGS. For the next 500 years, Bulgaria suffered under the **"Turkish yoke."** During this period of repression, bandits known as **heiducs** kept the spirit of resistance alive. The **National Revival,** a period of Bulgarian cultural and educational awakening, was triggered in the 1760s when a monk from Athon named **Paisiy Hilendarski** wrote a history of Bulgaria. The movement grew political when leaders **Lyuben Karavelov** and **Vasil Levski** created the Bulgarian Secret Central Committee. In 1886, the revolutionaries planned the **April Uprising,** which was so brutally suppressed that the Turkish reprisals became known in Europe as the **Bulgarian Horrors.** A conference of European leaders convened after the uprising and proposed reforms, which Turkey rejected. Russia declared war in response.

PUSHING BOUNDARIES. The **Russo-Turkish War** (1877-78) ended with the **Treaty of San Stefano** and the expansion of Bulgaria's boundaries from the Danube to the Aegean and to the Black Sea. Austria-Hungary and Britain, however, were dissatisfied with such a large Slavic state in the Russian sphere of influence. Another pan-European conference in 1878, the **Congress of Berlin,** overturned San Stefano to create a smaller state under the influence of the Ottoman empire. Although the new state began on an egalitarian note, resentment over its borders lingered and in-fighting kept tensions high. Eventually, border disputes erupted during the **First** and **Second Balkan Wars** in 1912 and 1913.

THE WORLD WARS. These brief wars resulted in a further loss of territory for Bulgaria, which then abandoned its initial neutrality in WWI and sided with the Central Powers in the hope of recovering its losses. Though Bulgaria was neutral at the start of

BULGARIA TOP 10

1. Best pilgrimage: the climb through **Ivan Rilski's cave** at Rila Monastery, a journey symbolizing rebirth (p. 82).

2. Best place to launch a crusade: Veliko Turnovo's massive **Tsarevets,** the perfect medieval fortress (p. 84).

3. Best place to get a tan: Varna's stunning beach and cosmopolitan boulevards, frequented by the rich and the beautiful (p. 88).

4. Best communist throwback: Sofia's **National History Museum,** housed in an imposing concrete communist summer palace (p. 77).

5. Best culture: *bacillus bulgaricus,* a bacterium used in the production of yogurt and named for Bulgaria, where yogurt was likely first developed.

6. Best place to get cultured: Plovdiv's **Roman Amphitheater,** which still hosts theatrical events 2000 years later (p. 87).

7. Best buzz: Bulgaria's world-renowned wines, or the potent local brandy, *rakiya* (p. 68).

8. Best place to be an outlaw: the mountains above Plovdiv, which sheltered political dissidents for 500 years of Turkish rule (p. 85).

9. Best dance party: the traditional *Nestinari* **fire dance,** which has locals in the mountains south of Burgas treading over hot coals (p. 80).

10. Best graffiti: the scribblings of 18th-century pastors among the 11th-century murals of Sofia's UNESCO-protected **Boyana Church** (p. 76).

WWII, a lust for Greek territories caused Boris III (1894-1943) to join the Axis Powers in 1941, and in 1944 the Soviet Union declared war on Bulgaria. Three years later, the Communist Party completed its takeover of the country.

GROWING PAINS. Bulgaria saw nationalization under **Georgi Dimitrov** in the late 1940s, isolationism under **Vulko Chervenkov** in the 1950s, and rapid industrialization and alignment with the Soviet Union under **Todor Zhivkov** from 1962-89. With sociologist **Zhelyu Zhelev** as president and poet **Blaga Dimitrova** as vice-president in the 90s, the government embraced openness and ended repression of ethnic Turks. Economic troubles, however, led to soaring inflation; the situation stabilized only when Prime Minister **Ivan Kostov** rose to power in 1997.

TODAY

Kostov's government fell out of favor amid ever-increasing accusations of corruption and complaints concerning the slow pace of reforms. A surprising candidate won the prime ministry in 2001: **Simeon II,** the former child-king who had been deposed in 1946. Economic progress has continued, and Bulgaria was accepted into NATO in 2004. Although the country did join the EU in January 2007, the government still must address widespread corruption in order to avoid losing much-needed international aid. In 2005, **Sergei Stanishev** was elected prime minister.

PEOPLE AND CULTURE

DEMOGRAPHICS. The country is overwhelmingly Bulgarian, with Turks and Roma together representing 14.1% of the population. An additional 2% consists mostly of Tatars, Macedonians, and Circassians. With respect to religion, Bulgarians are 83% Bulgarian Orthodox, with a Muslim minority of 12%.

LANGUAGE. Bulgarian is a South Slavic language written in the Cyrillic alphabet. Though a few words are borrowed from Turkish and Greek, most are similar to Russian. English is most commonly spoken by young people in cities and tourist areas. Russian is often understood and is spoken by virtually everyone over the age of 35. The Bulgarian alphabet is much the same as Russian (see **Cyrillic alphabet,** p. 790), except that "щ" is pronounced "sht" and "ъ" is "u" (like the "u" in bug). For a phrasebook and glossary, see **Appendix: Bulgarian,** p. 791.

YES AND NO. Bulgarians shake their heads from side to side to indicate "yes" and up and down to indicate "no," the exact opposite of Brits and Yanks. For the uncoordinated, it's easier to just hold your head still and say *da* or *neh*.

CUSTOMS AND ETIQUETTE. Making the **"V" sign** signifies showing support for the opposition party; don't do it. Do not address new acquaintances—except for children and young people—by their first names. Avoid mentioning Bulgaria's relationship to Turkey. Always shake hands when introduced. If invited to a home, it is a good idea to bring a **gift** of flowers, candy, or wine. Don't bring calla lilies or gladioli, as they are only used for weddings or funerals. Bulgarians rarely wear shorts. When visiting churches, visitors must cover their shoulders and knees. Seat yourself at **restaurants** and ask for the *smetka* (сметка; bill) when you're done. It is customary to share tables in restaurants. When toasting make sure to look the person in the eye and call *Nazdrave!* (Наздраве!; cheers!) loudly. While dining, rest your wrists on the table; do not put one hand in your lap. **Tipping** is not obligatory, but give 10% for good service and in Sofia, where waitstaff expect it.

THE ARTS

LITERATURE. Following the arrival of Church Slavonic, Bulgarian literature entered a **Golden Age** that threatened to rival the literary dominance of **Constantinople.** Conquest by the Byzantines, however, halted progress. Following a resurgence in the 13th and 14th centuries, literary culture again went into hibernation during 500 years of Ottoman rule. Then, in 1762, **Paisiy Hilendarski's** romanticized *Istoria slavyanobulgarska* (Slavo-Bulgarian History) sowed the seeds of the National Revival. Realists **L. Karavelov** and **V. Drumev** wrote some of the first important Bulgarian fiction, **Khristo Botev** composed passionately nationalistic poetry, and journalists **Petko Slaveykov** and **Georgi Rakovski** revived Bulgarian folklore. In the early 20th century, Bulgarian poets, such as symbolist **Peyo Yavorov,** experimented with poetic form. Arguably Bulgaria's most important 20th-century poet, **Elisaveta Bagryana** skillfully fused the new and the traditional in her love poems.

MUSIC. Bulgarian **folk music** belongs to the Balkan tradition. Music differs according to region but is usually played on local variants of Turkish instruments, and accompanied by distinctive chain dances. Bulgarian **women's choirs** are one of the region's unique features; singers produce polyphonic, drone-like tones. Bulgarian **pop music** often draws on folk influences; cross-dressing male vocalist **Azis** is a leading exponent of **chalga,** which fuses traditional Bulgarian folk with Turkish and Arabic influences. Tourists are just as likely, however, to hear Western pop hits in Bulgarian establishments as regional music.

THE VISUAL ARTS. Like Bulgarian literature, the **visual arts** were hampered by Ottoman rule, but rebounded during the National Revival. Through the 20th century, most artists depicted Bulgarian life from a realist perspective. Particularly notable are the paintings of **Vladimir Dimitrov** and the graphic art of **Tsanko Lavrenov.**

HOLIDAYS AND FESTIVALS

Holidays: New Year's Day (Jan. 1); Baba Marta Spring Festival (Mar. 1); Liberation Day (Mar. 3); Orthodox Easter (Apr. 27, 2008; Apr. 19, 2009); Labor Day (May 1); St. George's Day (May 6); Education and Culture Day/Day of Slavic Heritage (St. Cyril and Methodius Day; May 24); Festival of the Roses (Kazanluk; June 5); Day of Union (Sept. 6); Independence Day (Sept. 22); Christmas Holiday (Dec. 24-26).

Festivals: On Christmas, groups of carolers go from house to house performing *koledouvane* (caroling), while holding oak sticks called *koledarkas.* On New Year's, a group of *sourvakari* wish their neighbors well while holding decorated cornel rods called *sourvachka. Baba Marta* (Spring Festival) celebrates spring with gifts of *martenitzas*, a fertility charm made from small red-and-white tassels formed to look like a boy or a girl. The Festival of Roses is celebrated in Kazanlŭk and Karlovo on the first Sunday in June.

SOFIA (СОФИЯ) ☎(0)2

Far from the concrete Soviet grayscape you might expect, Sofia (pop. 1,100,000) is a city of magnificent domed cathedrals and grand old buildings, all set against the backdrop of nearby Mt. Vitosha. Although the city lacks the old-world feel of Prague or Vienna—when Sofia was made Bulgaria's capital in 1879, it was a muddy village of 12,000 residents—it is remarkably diverse. Skateboarders listen to American rock music in front of the Soviet Army monument, while worshippers pass each other near the central square on their way to a synagogue, mosque, or cathedral. Sofia is a manifestation of the Bulgarian mentality, both very aware of its diverse and complex past, and moving quickly, if a bit unsurely, to join the West.

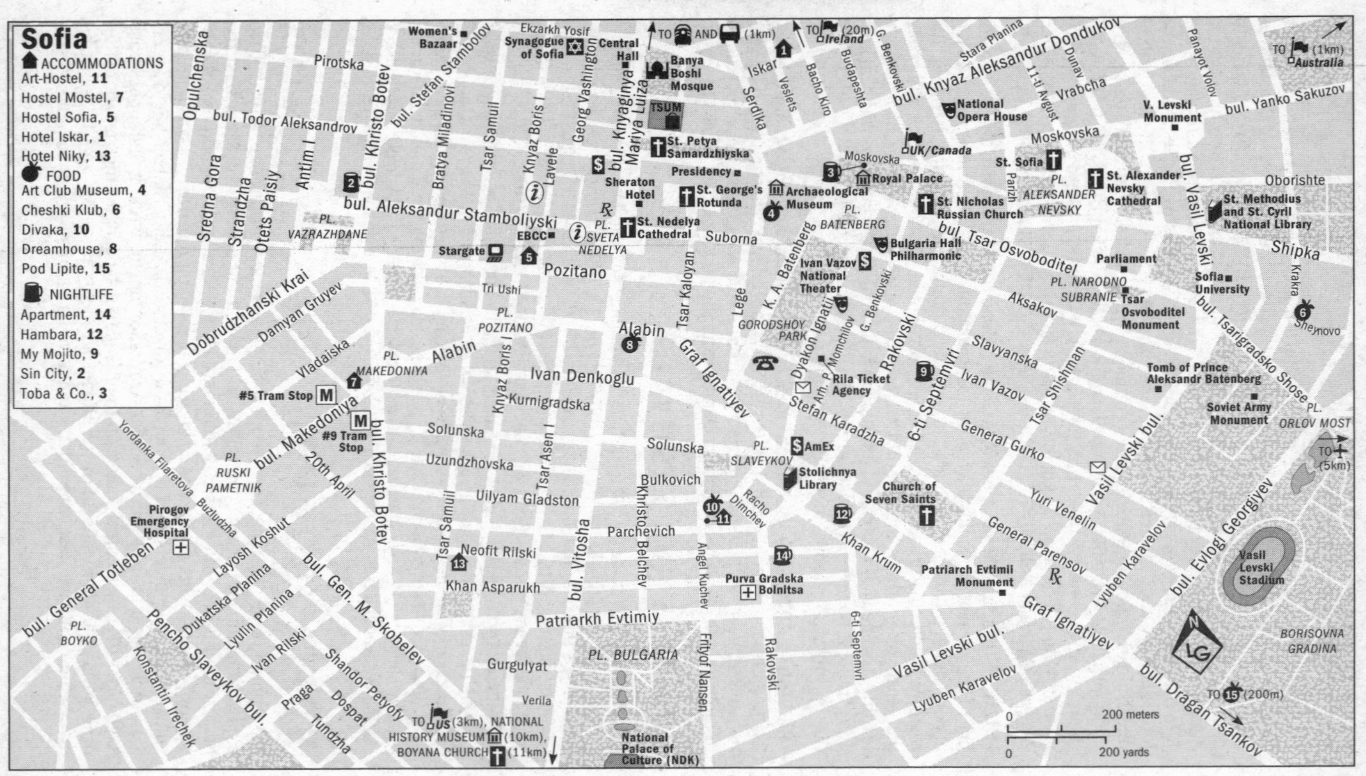
Sofia
ACCOMMODATIONS
Art-Hostel, 11
Hostel Mostel, 7
Hostel Sofia, 5
Hotel Iskar, 1
Hotel Niky, 13
FOOD
Art Club Museum, 4
Cheshki Klub, 6
Divaka, 10
Dreamhouse, 8
Pod Lipite, 15
NIGHTLIFE
Apartment, 14
Hambara, 12
My Mojito, 9
Sin City, 2
Toba & Co., 3
bul. Vasil Levski
bul. Tsar Osvoboditel
bul. Knyaz Aleksandur Dondukov
bul. Aleksandur Stamboliyski
bul. Khristo Botev
bul. Vitosha
bul. Evlogi Georgiyev
bul. Dragan Tsankov
bul. Gen. M. Skobelev
bul. Makedoniya
bul. Tsarigradsko Shose
bul. General Totleben
bul. Yanko Sakuzov
bul. Todor Aleksandrov
bul. Stefan Stambolov
bul. Knyaginya Mariya Luiza
Graf Ignatiyev
Patriarkh Evtimiy
Pencho Slaveykov bul.
Vasil Levski bul.
St. Alexander Nevsky Cathedral
St. Methodius and St. Cyril National Library
Sofia University
Parliament
Tsar Osvoboditel Monument
V. Levski Monument
National Opera House
St. Sofia
St. Nicholas Russian Church
Royal Palace
Archaeological Museum
Bulgaria Hall Philharmonic
Ivan Vazov National Theater
St. George's Rotunda
Presidency
St. Petya Samardzhiyska
St. Nedelya Cathedral
Sheraton Hotel
Central Hall
Banya Boshi Mosque
TSUM
Synagogue of Sofia
Women's Bazaar
Stargate
EBCC
Rila Ticket Agency
AmEx
Stolichnya Library
Church of Seven Saints
Patriarch Evtimii Monument
Purva Gradska Bolnitsa
Pirogov Emergency Hospital
Tomb of Prince Aleksandr Batenberg
Soviet Army Monument
Vasil Levski Stadium
Borisovna Gradina
National Palace of Culture (NDK)
PL. BULGARIA
#5 Tram Stop
#9 Tram Stop
TO AND (1km)
TO Ireland (20m)
UK/Canada
TO Australia (1km)
TO (5km)
TO 15 (200m)
TO US (3km), NATIONAL HISTORY MUSEUM (10km), BOYANA CHURCH (11km)
200 meters
200 yards

TRANSPORTATION

Flights: Airport Sofia (☎937 2211; www.sofia-airport.bg) is a 5km hike from the center, so you're better off taking public transportation into the city. Bus #84 is to the right as you exit international arrivals. Buy tickets (0.70lv) at kiosks with "Билети" (bileti) signs. The bus runs from the airport to Eagle Bridge (Орлов Мост; Orlov Most), near Sofia University, a 10min. walk from the city center. Minibus #30 (in front of international arrivals exit; 1lv) runs between the airport and pl. Sv. Nedelya (Св. Неделя), the city center, along bul. Tsar Osvoboditel (Цар Освободител). The minibus has no predetermined stops; to ride, flag it down and request a stop. If you take a taxi, make sure to go with **OK Supertrans** (☎973 2121); others will overcharge you. They have a desk inside the terminal and a stand outside. Fare should run about 5-10lv to the center.

Trains: Tsentralna Gara (Централна Гара; Central Train Station), Knyaginya Mariya Luiza (Княгиня Мария Луиза; ☎931 1111), a 1.6km walk north from pl. Sveta Nedelya past department store TSUM (ЦУМ) and a mosque. Trams #1 and 7 run between pl. Sveta Nedelya and the station; #9 and 12 head down Khristo Botev (Христо Ботев) and bul. Vitosha (Витоша). Ticket counter for Varna and Northern Bulgaria are on the 1st fl.; the one to Burgas and Southern Bulgaria is in the basement. To: **Burgas** (6 per day, 16lv); **Plovdiv** (14 per day, 6.70lv); **Ruse** (4 per day, 15lv); **Varna** (6 per day, 19lv); **Veliko Turnovo** (6 per day, 12lv). Trip lengths and prices depend on type of train (Пътнически, *putnicheski*, slow; Бързэ, *bure*, fast; Експрес, *ekspres*, express). Train schedules vary with season. International tickets available at the **Rila Travel Bureau** (☎932 3346; open daily 7am-11pm) desk on the 1st fl., to the left of the main entrance. **Branch** at Gurko 5 (Гурко), off pl. Sveta Nedelya (☎987 0777; open M-F 7am-7:30pm, Sa 7am-6:30pm). Destinations include: **Athens, GCE** via **Thessaloniki, GCE** (2 per day; 25lv to Thessaloniki, where you must purchase a separate ticket for Athens); **Bucharest, ROM** (2 per day, 36lv); **Budapest, HUN** via Bucharest (1 per day, 105lv, sleeper car only), and **Istanbul, TUR** (1 per day, 52lv, sleeping car only).

Buses: Private buses leave from either the **Central Bus Station** (Централна Автогара; Tsentralna Avtogara; ☎090 021 000; www.centralbusstation-sofia.com), Mariya Luiza 100 (Мария Луиза), down the street from the train station; or the parking lot across from the train station, which is called the **Trafik-Market** (☎981 2979). Though a bit pricier than trains, private buses are often faster and more comfortable. Several international bus companies are across from the entrance to the train station, while buses to destinations within Bulgaria are more likely to leave from the bus station.

Public Transportation: Trams, trolleys, and **buses** cost 0.70lv per ride, 6lv for 10 rides, day pass 3lv, month pass 37lv. Buy tickets from the driver (single rides only; 0.10lv extra) or at kiosks with "билети" (bileti) signs in the window; exact change only. Punch the tickets in the machines on board to avoid a 5lv fine. If you put your backpack on a seat, you may be required to buy a 2nd ticket, or pay a 7lv fine for an "unticketed passenger." This policy is observed much more stringently on routes to and from the airport. All transportation runs daily 5:30am-11pm; after 9pm, service becomes less frequent.

Taxis: Some travelers relate horror stories about local taxi companies, but **OK Supertrans** (ОК Супертранс; ☎973 2121) remains a reliable option. Always make sure the company's name and phone number are on the side of the car. Additionally, insist that the driver turn on the meter or agree on a fare ahead of time. Many drivers don't speak English, so learn to pronounce Bulgarian names for destinations. 0.50-0.60lv per km; slightly more expensive 10pm-6am.

ORIENTATION AND PRACTICAL INFORMATION

Sv. Nedelya Church is the locus of the city center, **ploshtad Sveta Nedelya** (Света Неделя), which is flanked by the Sheraton Hotel and the Presidency building. **Bulevard Knyaginya Mariya Luiza** (Княгиня Мария Луиза) connects pl. Sveta Nedelya to the train station. Trams #1 and 7 run from the train station through pl. Sveta Nedelya to **bulevard Vitosha** (Витоша), one of the main shopping and nightlife thoroughfares. Bul. Vitosha links pl. Sveta Nedelya to **ploshtad Bulgaria** and the huge, concrete **Natsionalen Dvorets na Kulturata** (Национален Дворец на Културата; NDK, National Palace of Culture). Historic **bulevard Tsar Osvoboditel** (Цар Освободител; Tsar the Liberator) runs by the Presidency building on the north, starting at **ploshtad Nezavisimost** (Независимост). Follow the yellow brick road, Bul. Tsar Osvoboditel (Цар Освободител), to the former **Royal Palace,** the **Parliament** building, and **Sofia University;** along it are some of the city's hottest spots for dancing and drinking. The free *Insider's Guide* and *In Your Pocket Sofia* (available at the Sheraton Hotel and at tourist centers) are indispensible to English speakers. *The Program* (Програмата; Programata; www.programata.bg) is a weekly city guide. The print version is in Bulgarian and can be found in tourist offices, hotels, museums, and cafes; look online for the English version. **Maps** are available for free in the lobby of the Sheraton Hotel and for 2lv at the open-air book market at Slaveykov Sq. (Славейков) on Graf Ignatiyev (Граф Игнатиев).

TOURIST, FINANCIAL, AND LOCAL SERVICES

BULGARIA

Tourist Offices: Tourist Information Center, pl. Sveta Nedelya 1 (☎933 5826; www.bulgariatravel.org), next to Happy Bar and Grill. The English-speaking staff answers questions about Sofia and Bulgaria and hands out free maps and English-language publications about Sofia. Open M-F 9am-6pm. **Odysseia-In/Zig Zag Holidays,** bul. Stamboliyski 20-B (Стамболийски; ☎980 5102; www.zigzagbg.com). Knowledgeable staff arrange tour packages, including homestays in Bulgarian villages, tours of Sofia, trips to Rila Monastery, and varied outdoor activities. Consultation 5lv per session; individualized tours from €30; commission on accommodations booking 10%. Open in high season daily 8:30am-7:30pm; in low season M-F 8:30am-7:30pm. MC/V.

Embassies: Australia, Trakiya 37 (Тракия; ☎946 1334). Consulate only. **Canada,** Moskovska 9 (Московска; ☎969 9710; consular@canada-bg.org). **Ireland,** Bacho Kiro 26-28 (Бачо Киро; ☎985 3425; info@embassyofireland.org). Citizens of **New Zealand** should contact the UK embassy. **UK,** Moskovska 9 (☎933 9222; www.britishembassy.bg). Open M-Th 9am-noon and 2-4pm, F 9am-noon. **US,** Kozyak 16 (Козяк; ☎937 5100; www.usembassy.bg). Open M-F 9am-noon and 2-4pm.

Currency Exchange: Bulbank (Булбанк), pl. Sv. Nedelya 7 (☎923 2111; www.unicreditbulbank.com), exchanges currency and cashes **traveler's checks** for 1.5% commission. 24hr. **ATM** outside. Open M-F 8am-6pm.

Luggage Storage: Downstairs at the central train station. 2lv per piece. Claim bags 30min. before departure. Open daily 6am-11pm.

Library: Stolichnya Biblioteka (Столичня Библиотека), Slaveykov 4 (Славейков; ☎980 6688, ext. 530), has an English section. Library cards 4lv for a year membership. Open M-Tu and Th-F 8:30am-7:45pm, W 2-7:45pm, Sa 9am-2:45pm.

Cultural Center: Euro-Bulgarian Cultural Centre (EBCC; Евро-Бьлгарски Културен Центьр; Evro-Bulgarski Kulturen Tsentr), bul. Stamboliyski 17 (Стамболийски; ☎988 0084; www.eubcc.bg). Knowledgeable, English-speaking staff provides info about cultural activities in Sofia. Check out the Arts Cinema (3-6 movies per day; 4-5lv), and the bookstore Khelikon (Хеликон; ☎488 4029; open daily 9am-8pm; MC/V), which has English selections. Provides **Internet** (1.20lv per hr.; open M-F 9am-9pm, Sa-Su 11am-7pm), scanning, and photocopies. Hours vary.

GLBT Resources: BulGAYria, www.gay.bg, has nightlife, accommodations, and restaurants listings in Sofia. Within the city, contact one of the two Bulgarian gay advocacy associations. **BGO Gemini,** Vasil Levski 3 (Васил Левски), 1st fl, apt. 7 (☎987 6872; www.bgogemini.org). **Queer Bulgaria,** Lavele 8, 2nd fl. (Лавеле; ☎980 1979).

EMERGENCY AND COMMUNICATIONS

24hr. Pharmacies: Apteka Sv. Nedelya (Аптека Св. Неделя), pl. Sv. Nedelya 5 (☎950 5026; www.apteka.bg), on bul. Stamboliyski. MC/V. **Apteka Vasil Levski** (Аптека Васил Левски), bul. Vasil Levski 70 (☎986 1755), around the corner from Popa (the statue at the east end of Patriarkh Evtimiy; Патриарх Евтимий). MC/V.

Medical Services: State-owned hospitals offer foreigners free 24hr. emergency aid, but the staff may not speak English, and many facilities are not up to Western standards. **Pirogov Emergency Hospital** (Пирогов), bul. Gen. Totleben 21 (Ген. Тотлебен; ☎515 31), across from Hotel Rodina. Take trolley #5 or 19 from the center. The **International Medical Center,** Gogol 28 (☎944 9326; www.imc-sofia.com), provides out-patient services and has a full English-, French-, and Russian-speaking staff. Open M-F 8:30am-8pm, Sa 9am-3pm. MC/V.

Telephones: Telephone Center, General Gurko 4 (Гурко; ☎980 1010). Go right out of the post office on Vasil Levski (Васил Левски) and then left on Gurko; it's a large white building 1 block down. Offers telephone and fax services. To make a call, go to windows 2 or 3; staff will assign you a booth. Local calls 0.09lv, international calls from 0.36lv per min. **Internet** 0.80lv per hr., 1.40lv per 2hr., 2lv per 3hr. Fast connections.

Internet: Available at the Euro-Bulgarian Cultural Center and Telephone Center (see above). **Stargate,** Pozitano 20 (Позитано), near Hostel Sofia. 1.20lv per hr. Open 24hr. Cash only.

Post Office: General Gurko 6 (Гурко; ☎949 6446; www.bgpost.bg). From bul. Vitosha (Витоша), turn on Alabin (Алабин) and walk east. The street becomes Gen. Gurko; the post office is the large white building past the telephone office. International mailing at windows #6-8 in the 2nd hall. **Poste Restante** at window #12 in the 2nd hall; look for the signs in English. International money transfers at window #4 in the 1st hall. Open M-Sa 7am-8:30pm, Su 8am-1pm. **Postal Code:** 1000.

BULGARIA

ACCOMMODATIONS

Big hotels are rarely worth the exorbitant prices—smaller, privately owned hotels or hostels are better alternatives. If the hostels are full, private rooms are also good options (available through Odysseia-In; see **Tourist Office,** p. 74).

Hostel Sofia, Pozitano 16, 3rd fl. (Позитано; ☎989 8582; www.hostelsofia.com). Absurdly comfortable feather pillows and home-cooked Bulgarian breakfasts make this one of the best hostels in town. Sociable, yet still reasonably quiet. Shared kitchen, a balcony, and a small living room with cable TV. Laundry 5lv. Free Internet. Reception 24hr. Flexible check-out. 8-11 bed dorms €10 for 1st and 2nd nights, €9 thereafter. 10% discount Nov.-May. Cash only. ❶

Art-Hostel, Angel Kunchev 21A (Ангел Кънчев; ☎987 0545; www.art-hostel.com). Both a hostel and a bohemian artists' gathering place. Draws a lively, international crowd that stays up late at the bar or the garden. Kitchen, bar, free Internet, and tea room. 2 shared baths. Breakfast included. Laundry 5lv. Reception 24hr. 6- to 10-bed dorms June-Aug. €10 for 1st to 3rd nights, €9 thereafter; Sept.-May €8/7. Cash only. ❶

Hostel Mostel, Makedoniya 2A (Македония; ☎922 3296; www.hostelmostel.com). In a restored 19th-century house, this hostel is bright, clean, and new, with a large common room, cable TV, and English-speaking staff. Tons of free amenities are included: breakfast, 1 beer per day, Internet, kitchen access, luggage storage, a bowl of pasta, and a map of Sofia. Free pickup from train and bus stations. Daytrips 30lv per person for groups of 3 or more. Laundry €2. Check-out noon. Reserve ahead. 8- to 10- bed dorms June-Aug. 20lv for 1st to 2nd nights, 18lv thereafter; Sept.-May 18/16lv. Cash only. ❶

Hotel Iskar, Iskar 11b (Искар; ☎986 6750; www.hoteliskar.com). Newly furnished rooms decorated in cheerful color schemes in a refurbished old building. Restaurant and bar downstairs. English spoken. Breakfast 4lv. Check-out noon. Doubles with detached private bath 40-45lv, with private bath in room 53lv. Cash only. ❷

Hotel Niky, Neofit Rilski 16 (Неофит Рилски; ☎952 3058; www.hotel-niky.com). Turn east off Vitosha onto Neofit Rilski; Niky is in the 3rd block on the left. Modern, spacious, and comfortable rooms in the center of Sofia. Restaurant downstairs. English spoken. Free Internet. Doubles €40; apartments €65-105. MC/V. ❸

FOOD

From fast food to Bulgarian classics, low-priced meals are easy to find. Over 100 shops and a fast-food court fill **Central Hall** (Хали; Khali), bul. Mariya Luiza 25 (Мария Луиза)—a modern, three-floor cross between a shopping mall and an open-air market. (☎917 6106. Open daily 7am-midnight.) The **Women's Bazaar,** just down Ekzarkh Yosif (Екзарх Йосиф) past the synagogue, is a more traditional **open-air market.** (Open daily dawn-dusk.)

Divaka (Дивака), William Gladstone 54 (Уилям Гладстон; ☎989 9543). Turn east from bul. Vitosha (Витоша). So popular you might have to share a table with strangers. The dining room calls to mind a greenhouse, despite minimalist rough white walls and unpolished wood decor. English menu. Vegetarian options. Beer from 1.10lv. Traditional entrees 3-12lv. Call ahead for reservations. Open 24hr. Cash only. ❷

Pod Lipite (Подъ Липите), Elin Pelin 1 (Елин Пелин; ☎866 5053). Walk down Graf Ignatiyev (Граф Игнатиев), which becomes bul. Dragan Tsankov (Драган Цанков) when it hits the park; continue for a long time. Pod Lipite serves authentic Bulgarian cuisine in a recreated old tavern with stone walls. English menu. Beer from 1.10lv. Wine from 19lv per bottle. Entrees 3.30-17lv. Vegetarian options. Terrace seating. Call ahead for reservations. Open daily noon-1am. Cash only. ❷

Cheshki Club (Ческий Клуб), Krakra 15 (Кракра; ☎944 1383), in the yard of the Czech Club. A no-frills dining experience, with outdoor seating at simple wooden tables and a menu of Czech specialties and Bulgarian favorites at amazing prices. No English menu. Beer from 1lv. Entrees 1.50-8.80lv. Open M-F noon-10:30pm. Cash only. ❶

Art Club Museum, Suborna 2 (Съборна; ☎980 6664). This lively and sophisticated cafe, hidden behind the Archaeological Museum, serves light international fare to a young business crowd in a dark-wood interior; outdoor seating is dotted with Roman statues and tableaus. English menu. Salads 5-9lv. Entrees 4-19lv. Open 24hr. MC/V. ❷

Dreamhouse, Alabin 50A, 1st fl. (Алабин; ☎980 8163; www.dreamhouse-bg.com). Go east on Alabin from Vitosha and enter the shopping center at Alabin 50. Go through the white door to your left and up the stairs. This purely vegetarian restaurant is fittingly outfitted with bright green walls and bamboo accents. The menu changes daily, with a choice of 3 entrees. Entrees under 4lv. Open 11am-11pm. AmEx. ❶

SIGHTS

BOYANA CHURCH (БОЯНСКА ЦЪРКВА; BOYANSKA TSURKVA). In the woods of the Boyana suburb, this UNESCO World Heritage site boasts some of the most striking religious artwork in the country. The tiny red-brick church houses two layers of religious murals painted by unknown medieval masters. The older layer, which depicts the 80 murals of St. Nicholas, dates back to the 11th century; the newer, to the 13th century. Ask the curator to show you where pastors scribbled their names on the murals in the 17th and 18th centuries. The church is in a little park with such a striking sense of tranquility that Queen Eleanor broke royal protocol and asked to be buried on the grounds. *(☎959 0939. Take bus #64 from Khladilnika (Хладилника), or a taxi from the center for 4-5lv. Open daily Nov.-Mar. 9am-5:30pm; Apr.-Oct. 9:30am-6pm. 10lv, students 5lv; free M after 3pm. Tour in English 5lv. English pamphlet 5lv. Combined ticket with the National History Museum 12lv.)*

BULGARIA

NATIONAL HISTORY MUSEUM. Opulent residence of former Bulgarian dictator Todor Zhivkov, the fortress-like Natural History Museum, (Национален Исторически Музей; Natsionalen Istoricheski Muzey) is communist architecture at its most imposing. In a sprawling park at the base of Vitosha Mountain, the museum in this concrete-and-glass behemoth traces the evolution of Bulgarian culture from prehistoric times to the present. It is home to impressive archaeological finds, including Greek and Thracian gold, and a large collection of medieval church art. An exhibit on the top floor now pays homage to the roles of minority ethnicities and religions in Bulgarian life. *(Residence Boyana, Palace 1. Take minibus #21, trolley #2, or bus #63 or 111 from the center, or tram #5 from Makedonya to Boyana. Even then, it's about a 15min. walk; taxis 5lv. ☎955 4280; www.historymuseum.org. Open daily Nov.-Mar. 9am-5:30pm, Apr.-Oct. 9:30am-6pm. English captions. 10lv, students 5lv. Combined ticket with Boyana Church 12lv. Tours in English 10lv. Photo 10lv. Cash only.)*

ST. ALEXANDER NEVSKY CATHEDRAL. The huge gold- and green-domed Byzantine-style St. Alexander Nevsky Cathedral (Св. Александър Невски; Sv. Aleksandur Nevski) dominates the Sofia skyline. Erected from 1904 to 1912 in memory of the 200,000 Russians who died in the 1877-78 Russo-Turkish War, the cathedral is named after the patron saint of the tsar-liberator. Housing over 400 frescoes by Russian and Bulgarian artists, it is the grandest edifice in all of Sofia. In a separate entrance to the left of the church, the **crypt** contains the National Art Gallery's spectacular array of painted icons and religious artifacts from the past 1500 years. The adjacent square has become a marketplace for religious, WWII, and Soviet souvenirs. *(In the center of pl. Aleksandur Nevski. Open daily 7am-7pm; crypt open Tu-Su 10am-6pm. English captions. Cathedral free. Crypt 4lv, students 2lv. Guided tours of the crypt for 5 or more people 25lv, for fewer 20lv.)*

ST. NICHOLAS RUSSIAN CHURCH (СВ. НИКОЛАЙ; SV. NIKOLAI). Named for the patron saint of marriage, fish, and sailors, this 1913 church was built to appease a Russian diplomat unwilling to worship in Bulgarian churches. Richly hued patterns, elegant domes, and exquisite ornamentation make this one of Bulgaria's finest churches. Surrounded by birch trees, the church is crowned by a glittering green and gold tent roof that is at once beautiful and blinding at sunset. In the crypt, the Russian Orthodox come to write prayers to place with the remains of Patriarch Serafim. *(On bul. Tsar Osvoboditel near pl. Sveta Nedelya. Open daily 7:45am-6:30pm. Liturgy W 9am and 5pm, Th 9am, F 9am, Sa 9am and 5:30pm, Su 9:30am. Free.)*

SYNAGOGUE OF SOFIA (СОФИЙСКА СИНАГОГА; SOFIYSKA SINAGOGA). Built upon a foundation of Jewish gravestones, Sofia's only synagogue opened in 1909 as the largest Sephardic synagogue in the Balkans, and one of the largest in Europe. It boasts a star-spangled dome, marble columns, and the largest chandelier in Bulgaria. Recent renovations repaired damage done by a stray Allied bomb from WWII, which miraculously didn't explode. A museum upstairs outlines the history of Jews in Bulgaria, chronicling their role in Bulgarian history through ancient tablets, religious and personal artifacts, photographs, and written records. *(On the corner of Ekzarkh Yosif (Екзарх Йосиф) and George Washington (Георг Вашингтон), at Ekzarkh Yosif 16. ☎983 5085; www.sophiasynagogue.com. Open daily 8:30am-4pm. Services M-F and Su 8am, Sa 8 and 10am. Museum open M-F 8:30am-12:30pm and 1-3:30pm. English captions. Museum 2lv, students 1lv. Synagogue 2/1lv; price includes English pamphlet.)*

BANYA BOSHI MOSQUE (БАНЯ БОШИ). Constructed in 1576 during the Ottoman occupation, this mosque escaped the fate suffered by the 26 mosques in Sofia that were shut down or destroyed during the communist era. The mosque's name derives from the old Turkish bath upon which it is built. The red brick building with minaret still intact has a sumptuous interior of red and blue floral tiled walls and a ceiling inscribed with golden calligraphy. *(Across from Central Hall, on Mariya*

Luiza (Мария Луиза). Open daily 3:30am-11:30pm. Entrance is free, but tourists are allowed to enter only when prayer is not underway. Shoe removal required at door. Females must wear mosque-provided robe with hood to cover knees, shoulders, and head.)

NATIONAL ART GALLERY. Displaying Bulgaria's most prized traditional and contemporary art in a palatial setting, the National Gallery (Национална Художествена Галерия; Natsionalna Khudozhestvena Galeriya) showcases an array of exhibits, predominantly paintings from the 19th and 20th centuries, beginning with the National Revival movement. *(In the Royal Palace on bul. Tsar Osvoboditel. ☎980 0093. Open W and F-Su 10am-6pm, Tu and Th 10am-7pm. English captions. 4lv, students 2lv. Guided tours in English for groups of 5 or more 20lv, for fewer 15lv.)*

ST. GEORGE'S ROTUNDA (СВ. ГЕОРГИ; SV. GEORGI). This fourth-century red-brick rotunda, tucked away behind the Presidency and the Sheraton, is Sofia's oldest preserved building. The rotunda, built on ruins of Roman baths, was originally a site of ancient cult worship, but was made a baptistery following the AD 313 edict permitting the practice of Christianity. The interior of the dome is adorned in 11th- to 14th-century murals, which were covered by the Ottomans, but have now been restored and decorate the functioning church, which holds daily liturgies in Old Church Slavonic. *(Enter the courtyard from bul. Tsar Osvoboditel or Suborna (Съборна). Open June-Aug. daily 8am-7pm. Services daily 9am. Some English captions. Free.)*

BULGARIA

NATIONAL ARCHAEOLOGICAL MUSEUM. The National Archaeological Museum (Национален Археологически Музей; Natsionalen Arkheologicheski Musey), housed in an old mosque, expounds upon the selection of artifacts displayed in the National History Museum, with a much less sparkling, but more thorough and varied selection of tombstones, sarcophagi, statues, mosaics, weapons, pottery, jewelry, and icons. *(Suborna 2 (Съборна), behind the Presidency building. ☎988 2406; http://aim.sofianet.net. Open May-Oct. 10am-6pm; Nov.-Apr. 10am-5pm. English captions. 10lv, students 2lv; Nov.-Apr. last Su of the month free. English lecture 20lv. Cash Only.)*

NATIONAL PALACE OF CULTURE. This monolith of black glass and white paneling was erected by the Communist government in 1981 to celebrate the country's 1300th birthday. It dominates the surrounding square, which is filled with a jumble of both communist statues and newer anti-communist memorials. The Palace of Culture (Национален Дворец на Културата; Natsionalen Dvorets na Kulturata) houses a number of restaurants, cinemas (screening both local and recent American movies), and concert halls. Its 12 halls host everything from conferences to chamber music to rock concerts. *(From pl. Sv. Nedelya, take bul. Vitosha to bul. Patriarkh Evtimiy (Патриарх Евтимий) and enter the park. The Palace is at Pl. Bulgaria 1. ☎916 6369; www.ndk.bg. Ticket office open M-Sa 9am-7pm. Cinema downstairs ☎951 5101; tickets 4-10lv.)*

CHURCH OF SEVEN SAINTS (ЦЪРКВА СВЕТИ СЕДМОЧИСЛЕНИЦИ; TSURKVA SVETI SEDMOCHISLENITSI). This many-domed, red building, originally a mosque, was erected in 1528 at the request of Sultan Süleyman the Great and earned the name "Black Mosque" for its dark granite composition. Although it was turned into a church in 1903, the square floor plan gives the the building an odd shape for an Orthodox church. The church honors Saints Cyril and Methodius, along with their 5 disciples—hence seven saints—for creating the Cyrillic alphabet; frescoes detail the creation of the alphabet and the conversion of the Slavs to Christianity. *(On Graf Ignatiyev (Граф Игнатиев). Open daily 7:30am-6:30pm. Some English captions.)*

ST. SOFIA CHURCH (СВ. СОФИЯ; SV. SOFIYA). Dating back to the sixth century, this is the oldest Eastern Orthodox church in Sofia; the city, in fact, took the church's name in the 14th century. The stern red brick exterior gives way to a similarly understated interior. During the 19th century, when the church was being used as Sofia's main mosque, a series of earthquakes repeatedly destroyed the minarets. Amazingly, the fifth-century floor mosaic survived. The crypt, under restoration, contains tombs that date from the second century. *(On pl. Alexandur Nevski. Open daily 7am-7pm. Some English captions. Free.)*

ENTERTAINMENT

To get the latest events and nightlife listings, buy the English-language newspaper, the *Sofia Echo* (2.40lv), from a kiosk. For more info, consult the Cyrillic guide **"Program"** (Програмата), or check its English version online at www.programata.bg. Sofia's weeklong **Beer Fest** takes place in late summer. Each night, different bands play traditional music, as well as pop and jazz. The event takes place in Alexander Batemberg Square, which also houses the three-week stint of performances called **Opera in the Square.** The **International Jazz Festival** comes to Sofia the second week of October. Catch the traditional **Sofia Music Week** festival during the first week of June. Theatres abound in the city and range from musical theater to tiny experimental venues. Many theaters take a summer break in July or August.

National Opera and Ballet (Национална Опера и Балет; Natsionalna Opera i Balet), Vrabcha 1 (Врабча; ☎987 1366; www.operasofia.com). Venue of the Bulgarian National Ballet and Opera companies. Hosts international companies. Box office open M-F 9:30am-6:30pm, Sa-Su 10:30am-6pm. Closed July-Aug. 6-30lv. Cash only.

Ivan Vazov National Theatre (Иван Вазов Народен Театър; Ivan Vazov Naroden Teatur), Dyakon Ignatii 5 (Дякон Игнатий; ☎811 9219; www.nationaltheatre.bg). Sofia's chief theater, staging both traditional and modern productions. Box office open M-F 9:30am-7pm, Sa 11am-7pm, Su 11am-3pm. Closed July-Aug. Tickets 5-15lv. Cash only.

Bulgaria Hall (Зала България; Zala Bulgariya), Aksakov 1 (Аксаков; ☎987 7656). Home to the world-class Bulgarian Philharmonic. Box office open M-F 10:30am-1pm and 3-6pm. Tickets 5-15lv. Cash only.

BULGARIA

NIGHTLIFE

Nightlife centers on **bulevard Vitosha** (Витоша) and Sofia University at the intersection of **Vasil Levski** (Васил Левски) and **Tsar Osvoboditel** (Цар Освободител).

Apartment, Neofit Rilski 68 (Неофит Рилски; ☎08 86 65 50 93; www.apartment.org). A chill hangout that achieves the practically impossible: artsiness that is effortless. Comfortable couches and armchairs fill 19th-century rooms. DJ table open to enterprising guests. Foreign films most nights at 10:30pm. Free Wi-Fi. Fresh squeezed juice 3lv. Beer from 1.50lv. No cover. Open daily noon-2am. Cash only.

Hambara, 6-ti Septemvri 22 (6-ти Септември). In a wooden building behind Zion Restaurant. Candlelight and rough-hewn wooden chairs combine with smooth jazz to provide the backdrop for this mellow and slightly eerie 2-level student den. Beer 3lv. W and Sa live music. Open 8pm-4am. Cash only.

My Mojito, Ivan Vazov 12 (Иван Вазов; ☎08 89 52 90 01). A young crowd flocks to My Mojito, composed of 2 rooms with warm red walls and hip decor. Relaxed during the evening and hopping to loud techno beats at night. Th Retro Party. Beer from 3lv. Mixed drinks from 4.80lv. Cover F-Sa men 5lv. Open daily 9pm-5am. Cash only.

Toba & Co, 6 Moskovska (Московска; ☎989 4696). Behind the Royal Palace, in the courtyard. Party like a tsar in the garden and back room of the former Bulgarian monarch's residence. The city's sophisticated young elite sip cocktails at snow-white outdoor tables and in the red-lit bar room, while Euro-techno plays in the background. Beer from 1.80lv. Open daily 8:30pm-6am. Cash only.

Sin City, Khristo Botev 61 (Христо Ботев; ☎810 8888), at the intersection with Stamboliyski (Стамболийски). For a small cover charge, you get 3 parties in one at this new entertainment complex. There's a bar and lounge in addition to 2 dance floors, one featuring hip hop and techno music, and the other blasting Balkan folk pop. Cover 5lv. Beer from 3lv. Mixed drinks from 8lv. Open 9pm-7am. MC/V.

DAYTRIP FROM SOFIA

VITOSHA NATIONAL PARK (ПРИРОДЕН ПАРК ВИТОША)

Take tram #9 from the intersection of Khristo Botev (Христо Ботев) and Makedonya (the stop is on the right side of Botev just past the intersection) to Khladilnika Station (Хладилника), the last stop. From there, take bus #122 to the Simeonovo lift, which goes to Khizha Aleko (Хижа Алеко), or bus #93 to the Dragalevtsi lift, which goes to Bai Krustjo and Goli Vrkh stations. It's best to visit Sa or Su, when the lifts are guaranteed to be open and reliably running. Lifts run less frequently Th-F in the summer, and are closed M-W. Without the lifts, the park is inaccessible to all but the most dedicated climbers. Buses run infrequently, so taking a taxi (7-10lv) is generally faster.

Although it lies just next to Sofia, Vitosha National Park mutes the din of the neighboring metropolis. The park shelters a monastery, a river, and a waterfall, but **Mount Vitosha,** rising 2290m to its peak, Cherni Vrukh (Черни Връх), dominates this natural sanctuary. Trails to the peak rise from Aleko hut (Хижа Алеко; Khizha Aleko), and there's winter skiing and snowboarding on Vitosha's scenic slopes. (Winter sport supplies can be rented at the Aleko hut station.) The most direct, difficult path to the summit starts at the Dragalevtsi lift station by the #93 bus station; you can get a head start by riding up the **Dragalevtsi chairlift** (open June-Aug. Th-F 8:30am-6:30pm, Sa-Su 8:30am-7pm; ski season F-Sa 8:30am-dusk) to either the lower Bai Krustjo station (10min.; 1.50lv) or the higher Goli Vrkh station (25min.; 2.50lv). The **Simeonovo gondola lift** (open June-Aug. F 8:30am-6:30pm, Sa-Su 8:30am-7pm; ski season 8:30am-dusk) can be taken up to several stations, although most ride to Aleko, the last station (20min.; 3.50lv). From there, ask the lift attendants to point you to the summit trail. The park also offers a variety of easier and shorter hikes. A 30min. trail connects the Aleko Hut and the Bai Krustjo station and offers stunning views of Sofia's expanse. Trek the 20min. along the paved road from the #93 bus stop to Dragalevtsi chairlift to reach the **Dragalevtsi Monastery.** Built in 1328, destroyed shortly thereafter, and rebuilt again in the 15th century, the monastery is famous for sheltering national hero Ivan Vazov during the Bulgarian resistance to Turkish rule in the 1870s. This tiny plaster and red-brick church is bare inside except for hanging icons, but it's worth the trip for the nuns' bright white towering residence. (Monastery open in summer 8am-6pm; in winter 8am-5pm. Free). Another short but challenging hike is to the 40m high **Boyana Waterfall,** accessible from Boyana Church. Once there, ask the staff to direct you to the trail that runs from behind the church.

Pick up English maps and brochures from the **Information Center,** near the Dragalevtsi chairlift, 200m back down the paved road taken by bus #93, past Restaurant Vodenitsata. Trails and points of interest are not always well marked, so it's worth stopping. (Природозащитен Информационен Център "Витоша." ☎967 3140; www.vitoshacentre.org. Open daily 9am-5pm.) Paths are dotted with well-marked **campsites** and shelters; several sites are at the immediate top of the chairlift, including the Aleko hut. Alternatively, beds are available in the huts maintained by the park administration. Prices differ depending on the hut, but typically range from 15 to 40lv. (Contact **Sofia Regional Environmental Inspectorate** to reserve. ☎955 5440; riew-sofia@riew-sofia.government.bg.) If exhausted after a long day of hiking, try **Restaurant Vodenitsata** (Ђоденицата) ❸, by the Dragolevtsi chairlift, set next to a picturesque, rushing mountain stream. The restaurant provides a taste of Bulgarian folk culture and the traditional *nestinari* dance, in a complex of stone houses decorated with national handicrafts. (☎967 1058; www.vodenitzata.com. Entrees 3.90-30lv. Open daily noon-midnight. MC/V.)

RILA MONASTERY

☎(0)7054

Rila Monastery (Рилски Манастир) was built in the 10th century. The founder, Ivan Rilski, was set on returning to true religious practice, and so secluded himself far in the Rila Mountains. This seclusion allowed the monastery to shelter the arts of icon painting and manuscript copying during the Byzantine and Ottoman occupations; it remained a refuge for Bulgarian culture during five centuries of foreign rule. Today, its spectacularly colorful murals make it the most artistically significant monastery in Bulgaria, and the church's bright yellow and red walls, surrounded by the pure white of the monks' quarters, make it a colorful oasis in its mountainous and wooded surroundings.

TRANSPORTATION AND PRACTICAL INFORMATION. Take **tram** #5 from pl. Sveta Nedelya to Ovcha Kupel Station (Овча Къпел) to make one of the two daily buses to Rila Town (2hr., 6:25am and 10:20am, 5lv). From there, you can hop on a **bus** to the monastery (30min.; 7:40am, 12:50, 3:30pm; 1.50lv). Buses back to Rila Town from the monastery run at 8:20am, 2:10, and 5pm. Buses from Rila to Sofia depart at 6:20am, 3, and 3:30pm. The 3pm bus starts at the monastery, going through town, and continues on to Sofia. Alternatively, many hostels and private tourism agencies in Sofia run daytrips to Rila, a faster but more expensive option. If you'd like to spend more than 1½hr. at the monastery and plan on using public transportation, staying the night is recommended. There is an **ATM** on the storefront opposite the bus station in Rila Town. Blue Mobika **telephones** are by the shops behind the monastery; phone cards are available in the souvenir shop.

ACCOMMODATIONS AND FOOD. **Hotel Rilets** (Хотел Рилец) ❷, down the road from the monastery, is aging but retains some of its past glory. Low prices, a beautiful dining room, and private baths make up for small beds and old furnishings. From the rear of the monastery, follow the leftmost road to the intersection; turn right and follow the signs. (☎70 54 21 06. Reception daily 8am-midnight. Singles 26lv; doubles 45lv. Cash only.) Inquire at room #170 in the monastery about staying in a heated **monastic cell** ❶, but be prepared for bare rooms and no shower. (☎22 08. Monastery doors close at 9pm during summer and 7pm during winter; ring the bell if you're out later than that. Reception daily 2-5pm and 6pm-late. Cells 20lv.) **Camping Bor** ❶ is tucked away at the base of the mountains with clean but bare campsites and bungalows. Walk down the leftmost road behind the monastery and take a right across the bridge at the triangular intersection, then take a left and follow the signs. (☎72 25 64. Reception 8am-midnight. 2-bed bugalows €10 per person, €5 per tent, €1 per car.) Behind the monastery are several cafes and a mini-mart. Try the monks' homemade bread (1lv) at **Restaurant Rila** ❷, a *mekhani* (механи; Bulgarian folk restaurant) right across from the back entrance of the monastery, with a beautiful view of the mountains. (☎048 890 418. Entrees 3-13lv. Open daily 9am-10pm. Cash only.)

SIGHTS. The original 10th-century **monastery** was destroyed. Today's monastery was built between 1834 and 1837, save for a 14th century brick tower. The fortress-like outer walls of the monastery contrast with the multicolor brilliance of the central church inside. The monastery's vibrant murals were painted by brothers Dimitar and Zahari Zograf—"Zograf" actually means "mural painter." The 1200 frescoes on the central chapel form a brilliantly colored outdoor art display. Inside, the iconostasis is one of the largest and most ornate in Bulgaria. The church is also the final resting place of both the heart of Bulgaria's last tsar, Boris III, and the remains of St. Ivan Rilski; pilgrims flock to kiss his bones when his coffin is opened. (Monastery open daily in high season 6am-6pm; in low season 8am-6pm. Backpacks, cameras, shorts, and sleeveless shirts not permitted. Free.) The

museum in the far right corner of the monastery displays centuries-old weapons, embroidery, illuminated texts, and icons. The exhibit includes a **wooden cross** that took 12 years to carve and left its creator, the monk Rafail, blind. (Open daily 8:15am-4pm. No English captions. 8lv, students 4lv. English tour 20lv. Cash only.)

HIKING. Maps and hiking routes through **Rila National Park** are posted on signs at the monastery, but these can be a bit difficult to carry. Instead, look in the **Manastirski Padarutsi** (Манастирски Падаръци) shop, just outside the monastery's back entry, for a Cyrillic/English map of the paths (7lv). Incredible views of the hilly terrain—particularly at **Seventh Lake** (Седемте Езера; Sedemte Ezera) and **Malovitsa** (Мальовица)—and welcoming huts (Хижы; khizhy) await in the park. (Singles 5-10lv.) Follow the **yellow markings** to the **Khizha Sedemte Ezera** (Хижа Седемте Езера; Seventh Lake Hut; 6½hr.), passing through a region of beautiful lakes and wetlands. The **blue** trail leads to **Khizha Malovitsa** (Мальовица; 7hr.), past many fast-rushing mountain streams and springs. The **red trail** runs along a mountain ridge to the highest hut in the Balkans, **Ivan Vazov** (Иван Вазов; 6hr.).

A short hike (1hr.) to the **cave** where Holy Ivan, the builder of Rila Monastery, lived and prayed for years, is not to be missed. To reach it, walk down the topmost road running out from behind the monastery. After the triangular intersection, head left up the path through the field. Follow the "гроб" signs (grob; grave), which point the way to the church, St. Luke, where Ivan was originally buried. Behind the church is the entrance to the cave; according to local legend, passing through will **purify your soul.** Enter at the bottom and crawl through the dark winding passages (a flashlight or lighter is helpful here). Emerge at the top for a symbolic rebirth—unless, of course, you have sinned too much, in which case, the story goes, rocks will fall on you. Next, continue uphill 40m to the spring and cleanse yourself in the cold mountain spring near the shrine to St. Ivan. After such a ritual purification, you're now ready to enter the chapel guilt-free.

BULGARIA

VELIKO TURNOVO (ВЕЛИКО ТЪРНОВО) ☎(062)

Perched on the slopes above the Yantra River, 5000-year-old Veliko Turnovo (Veh-LEEK-oh TURN-oh-voh; pop. 73,100) was Bulgaria's capital from 1185 to 1393, and was home to the nation's greatest kings—Petur, Asen I, Kaloyan, and Asen II. Tapping into its glorious legacy, revolutionaries wrote Bulgaria's first constitution here in 1879. Today, Turnovo is filled with testaments to its noble past, none more breathtaking than the enormous hilltop fortress Tsarevets, former home to tsars, which still keeps watch over the town's sparkling river and winding streets.

TRANSPORTATION. The **train station** is south of town and across the river; it's a hike from the center, so your best bet is a taxi (4lv) or city bus #4, 5, or 13 (0.50lv). Trains to some destinations depart from the nearby **Gorna Oryakhovitsa** (Горна Оряховица) train station. Bus #10 runs to Gorna from the main square; it's timed to meet trains (1.40lv). **Trains** run to: Burgas (6hr., 7 per day, 11lv); Sofia (5hr., 8 per day, 14lv); Varna (4-5hr., 5 per day, 12lv); Bucharest, ROM (6hr., 2 per day, 35lv); Budapest, HUN (22hr., 1 per day, 123lv; sleeping car only); İstanbul, TUR (10hr., 1 per day, 50lv; sleeping car only); Thessaloniki, GCE (12hr., 1 per day, 42lv). Train tickets are sold at the station and at **Rila,** Kaloyan 2a (Калоян), directly behind the tourist bureau, off the main square. (☎62 21 30. English spoken. Open daily 7:30am-noon, 12:30pm-6pm. Cash only.) The west bus station, **Avtogara Zapad** (Автогара Запад; ☎64 09 08.), Nikola Gabrovski 74 (Никола Габровски), is 5 stops from the center on bus #10 (0.50lv), heading right when facing the post office. Buses and minibuses connect Veliko Turnovo with Gorna and run from the intersection of Nikola Gabrovski and Bulgaria to Gorna's train station (20min., every 30min., 1.50lv). **Etap,** a private daily bus service to most major cities, including Varna (10 per day, 40lv) and Sofia (12 per day, 40lv), is located in Hotel Etur, Aleksandur Stamboliyski 1. (☎63 05 64. Open 24hr.) Rent a **bike** at Gorgona Rent-a-Bike, Zelenka 2 (Зеленка). Walk upstairs to the right of the municipal building on the main square and veer to the right at the top. (☎60 14 00. Open M-F 10am-1pm and 2-7pm, Sa 10am-2pm. Mountain bikes 12lv per day.)

ORIENTATION AND PRACTICAL INFORMATION. Veliko Turnovo is spread along a loop of the Yantra River, with its central square, **ploshtad Maika Bulgariya** (Майка България), located on the outside bank. Through the center, the main drag follows the river east, changing its name as it goes: it begins as **bulevard Vasil Levski** (Васил Левски), becomes **Nezavisimost** (Независимост), and turns into **Stefan Stambolov** (Стефан Стамболов), **V. Dzhandzhiyata** (В. Джанджията), **Nikola Pikolo** (Никола Пиколо), and **Mitropolska** (Митрополска) as it reaches the ruins of **Tsarevets Krepost** (Царевец Крепост). The other key street, **Khristo Botev** (Христо Ботев), intersects Nezavisimost at pl. Mayka Bulgaria. With your back to the train station, go uphill along the river to the left for 10min. and then cross the bridge, which leads to **Aleksandur Stamboliyski** (Александър Стамболийски). Turn right on Khristo Botev (Христо Ботев). You can also take almost any bus (0.50lv, timed to meet trains) from the station.

The **tourist office,** Khristo Botev 5 (Христо Ботев), is in the main square, pl. Mayka Bulgaria. (☎62 21 48; www.velikoturnovo.info. English spoken. Open M-F 9am-noon and 1-6pm. Maps 2-3lv.) **Luggage storage** is at the train station. Luggage must be claimed at least 30min. prior to departure. (2.50lv per day. Open 24hr.) A **pharmacy,** Tsentur Apteka (Центур Аптека), is at Vasil Levski 3. (Васил Левски; ☎60 34 07. Open daily 8am-8pm. Cash only.) The **telephone office** shares a building with the post office. (Open M-F 8am-7pm, Sa 10am-4pm. Cash only.) **Navigator Internet Club** (Навигатор), Nezavisimost 3 (Независимост), along the main street and downstairs in the shopping center, is open 24hr. (☎67 02 88. 1am-10pm 0.79lv per hr., 10pm-11am 0.49lv per hr. Cash only.) The **post office,** Khristo Botev 1, is on the main square. (☎61 22 85. Open M-F 7am-10pm, Sa-Su 8am-9pm). **Poste Restante** is out the door and to the right, down the stairs between the main building and the next. (Open M-F 7am-6pm, Sa 7am-3pm.) **Postal Code:** 5000.

ACCOMMODATIONS AND FOOD. Rooms in Veliko Turnovo are plentiful, and if you wear a backpack for more than five seconds in public, you'll be approached by locals offering **private rooms** (10-20lv), which can also be arranged through the tourist bureau. **Hiker's Hostel ❶,** Rezervoarska 91 (Резервоарска), hidden in the corner of the Samovodene Market in the Old Town, serves enormous complimentary breakfasts and has free Internet. The helpful and laid-back staff offers free pickup and daytrips to various locations. With your back to the post office, head right on Nezavisimost, which becomes Stambolov. Veer left on Rakovski (Раковски), the uphill cobblestone street that splits from the main road. Go straight at the small square on Rakovski, and take the smaller uphill street to the left. (☎889 691 661; www.hikers-hostel.org. English spoken. Dorms 20lv. Cash only.) Another hostel in town, **Nomads Hostel ❶,** Gurko 27 (Гурко), has airy rooms, a comfortable common area, and a balcony with a view of the river valley. Walking down Stambolov (Стамболов), take a sharp right on Gurko; the hostel is on the right. (☎60 30 92; www.nomadshostel.com. English spoken. Free Internet and pickup service. 15lv; mixed dorms 20lv; doubles 25lv. Cash only.)

A large **open-air market** sells fresh fruit and vegetables daily from dawn to dusk at the corner of Bulgaria and Nikola Gabrovski (Никола Габровски), and there's a *mekhana* (механа; tavern) on just about every balcony overlooking the river. **Shtastlivetsa Pasta and Pizza** (Щтастлевица) **❷,** Stambolov 79 (Стамболов), is next door to the Trapezitsa Hotel. Calling this a pizza parlor is an understate-

BULGARIA

ment—you could spend an hour reading the two separate menus of seemingly infinite Bulgarian, Italian, Turkish, Roma, and other dishes. (☎60 06 56. English Menu. Entrees 4-25lv. Open daily 11am-1am. MC.) Dark woodwork, exposed stone walls, and a view of an old church create an elegant atmosphere at **The Architect's Club ❷**, Dzhandzhiyata 14 (Джанджията). A large selection of local wines and *rakiya* (ракия) complement traditional dishes. (☎62 14 51. English menu. Entrees 3.50-12lv. Beer and *rakiya* from 1.20lv. Open noon-midnight. Cash only.)

SIGHTS. The ruins of ancient **Tsarevets** (Царевец) still dominate the skyline of Veliko Turnovo. Much of the citadel was destroyed by Turks in 1393, but long stretches of the outer wall and several inner towers still stand. Nikola Pikolo (Никола Пиколо) leads to the gates and *kasa*. (Каса. Open 8am-7pm. 4lv, students 2lv. Tours in English 10lv.) At the pinnacle of the hill stands the beautiful and aptly named **Church of the Ascension** (Църква Възнесениегосподне; Tsurkva Vuzneseniyegospodne), restored in 1981 for Bulgaria's 1300th anniversary. The murals inside are shockingly modern and depict ghostly kings and saints in black, red, and gray hues. (Open hours same as for fortress. Free.) Back in town, the **National Revival Museum** (Музей на Възраждането и Учредително Събрание; Muzey na Vuzrazhdaneto i Uchreditelno Cubraniye) exhibits items from the National Revival movement, including the first Bulgarian Parliament chamber and the first Bulgarian constitution. From the center, follow Nezavisimost until it becomes Nikola Pikolo (Никола Пиколо), then veer right on Ivan Vazov (Иван Вазов). (☎62 98 21. Open M and W-Su 9am-6pm. Limited English captions. 4lv, students 2lv. Cash only.) Two other museums flank the main building; downstairs to the left is the **Archaeological Museum** (Археологически Музей; Arkheologicheski Muzey), in the same building as the library. Ring the bell if the door is locked. Although the museum has a variety of exhibits, its main draw is a stunning medieval collection, which includes chain mail, gold filigree rings, and weapons. (Open Tu-Su 8am-6pm. Some English captions. 4lv, students 2lv. Photo 3lv. Cash only.)

BULGARIA

ENTERTAINMENT AND NIGHTLIFE. On summer evenings there's often a **sound-and-light show** above Tsarevets Hill—huge projectors light the ruins for an unforgettable sight. (Show starts 9:45-10pm.) There is no set schedule for the show; it goes off whenever enough tourists scrape together 450lv. During the summer this happens several times a week. Individual travelers can join a group for 15lv; ask at the tourist bureau for details. If a hard day of medieval tourism has left you in want of more modern pleasures, try the clubs that line the main street. It's Halloween every night at **Scream Club**, on Nezavisimost (Независимост), a bar done up in blood-red pleather sofas. The fun starts, of course, at the witching hour. (☎897 938 266. Beer from 0.60lv. Open daily midnight-5am.) If a casual drink is more your thing, head to **Pepy's Bar**, Slaveykov Pl. 1 (Славейков), just off Nezavisimost. Pleasant seating outside gives way to dark wood, comfortable couches, and photographs inside, making this bar popular with the locals. (☎60 30 41. Beer 1.20-2lv. Mixed drinks 2-7lv. Open noon-late. Cash only.)

SOUTHERN MOUNTAINS

The thickly forested mountains of Rila, Pirin, and Rodopi sheltered Bulgaria's cultural and political dissidents during 500 years of Turkish rule. Local monks preserved their culture in secret by copying manuscripts in remote monasteries, while other dissidents, like the *haiduc* outlaws, took an activist approach, using mountain hideouts to launch attacks against unwanted visitors. Today, the mountains still cradle traditional Bulgarian culture both in monasteries and in rural villages, surrounded by some of the best hiking and scenery in Bulgaria.

PLOVDIV (ПЛОВДИВ) ☎(0)32

Long ago, Plovdiv (pop. 350,000) was a Thracian settlement and an important city in the Roman empire. Traces of its former glory remain, including the ruins of theaters, temples, and palaces, including one of the best-preserved amphitheaters in the world. The Old Town is graced with National Revival houses and 19th-century churches, and when the sun goes down, some rolicking nightlife.

TRANSPORTATION. The main train station is on bul. Khristo Botev. (Христо Ђотев; ☎63 27 20. Open daily 7:30am-7:30pm.) **Trains** run to: Burgas (5hr., 4 per day, 11lv) via Karlovo; Sofia (2½-3hr., 15 per day, 6.70lv); and Varna (6-7hr., 3 per day, 14lv). Most trains from Sofia to Burgas or İstanbul, Turkey stop in Plovdiv. **Rila station,** bul. Khristo Botev 31a, sells international train tickets. (☎64 31 20. Open M-F 8am-7:30pm, Sa 8am-2pm. Cash only.) There are 3 main bus stations in Plovdiv; each serves different destinations. The Yug (South) and Rodolpi stations are within walking distance from the center. Take a city bus or taxi (2lv) to the Sever (north) station. **Yug** (Юг; South; ☎62 69 37), bul. Khristo Botev 47, across from the train station, is the main station. **Buses** service southern Bulgaria and go to: Sofia (2hr., 1 per hr., 10lv) and Varna (4hr., 2 per day, 18lv). Private companies send buses to international destinations, including İstanbul, TUR (4 per day; 35lv, students 30lv). **Sever station** (Север; North; ☎95 37 05) is at the intersection of Dimitur Stambolov (Димитьр Стамболов) and Pobeda (Победа). Bul. Ruski (Руски) becomes Pobeda across the river. Take bus #12 from the intersection of Gladston (Гладстон) and Ruski. (Ticket counter open 6am-8pm.) Buses go to Koprivshtitsa (2hr., 1 per day, 6lv). **Rodopi** (Родопи; ☎69 76 07), behind the train station through the underpass, services the Rodopi Mountains.

ORIENTATION AND PRACTICAL INFORMATION. Although the center is clearly defined, Plovdiv's streets are poorly marked; an up-to-date **map** is essential. Street vendors sell good Cyrillic maps (2.50lv) in addition to less-detailed maps with street names transliterated into the Roman alphabet (2lv). Running past the train station, the east-west thoroughfare **bulevard Khristo Botev** (Христо Ђотев) marks the town's southern edge. With your back to the train station, turn right on Khristo Botev to get to **bulevard Ruski** (Руски); a left turn on Ruski takes you across the river and to Sever bus station. Khristo Botev also intersects with **bulevard Tsar Boris III Obedinitel** (Цар Ђорис III Обединител), which runs to the **Maritsa River** (Марица), at the northern end of **Stariya Grad** (Стария Град; Old Town). The pedestrian way **Knyaz Aleksandr** (Княз Александр) connects to the central square. In the middle of town, bul. Tsar Boris III Obedinitel runs along the eastern side of **ploshtad Tsentralen** (Централен). To get to the center from the train station, take bus #2, 20, or 26 (0.40lv) or cross under bul. Khristo Botev and take **Ivan Vazov** (Иван Вазов). The municipal **tourist information center** is at pl. Tsentralen 1. (☎65 67 94; tic@plovdiv.bg. Open 9am-7pm.) **Luggage storage** is in the train station. (1lv per bag. Open 24hr.) **Telephones** for international calls are in the **post office** building on pl. Tsentralen. (☎65 73 20. Open daily 6am-11pm.) **Internet** cafe **Speed,** Knyaz Aleksandr 12 (Княз Александр), on the left before the mosque, has new computers. (1lv per hr., 2lv per 3hr. Open 24hr.) The **post office,** on pl. Tsentralen, has **Poste Restante** in the room to the left of the entrance across from the park. (Open M-Sa 7am-7pm, Su 7-11am.) **Postal Code:** 4000.

ACCOMMODATIONS AND FOOD. In Plovdiv, higher prices don't always mean higher quality. Prices uniformly triple, however, during trade fairs (the first weeks of May and the end of Sept.). Reserve ahead in July and August, as budget hotels are often full. The clean and bright **Queen Mary Elizabeth Guesthouse ❶,** Gustav Vaigand 7 (Густаф Вайганд), rolls out the red carpet for weary guests. Walking down Ruski from the train station, turn right on Gustav Vaigand. It's on the right side, 100m down; ring the bell. (☎62 93 06; www.qm-b-and-b.com. English

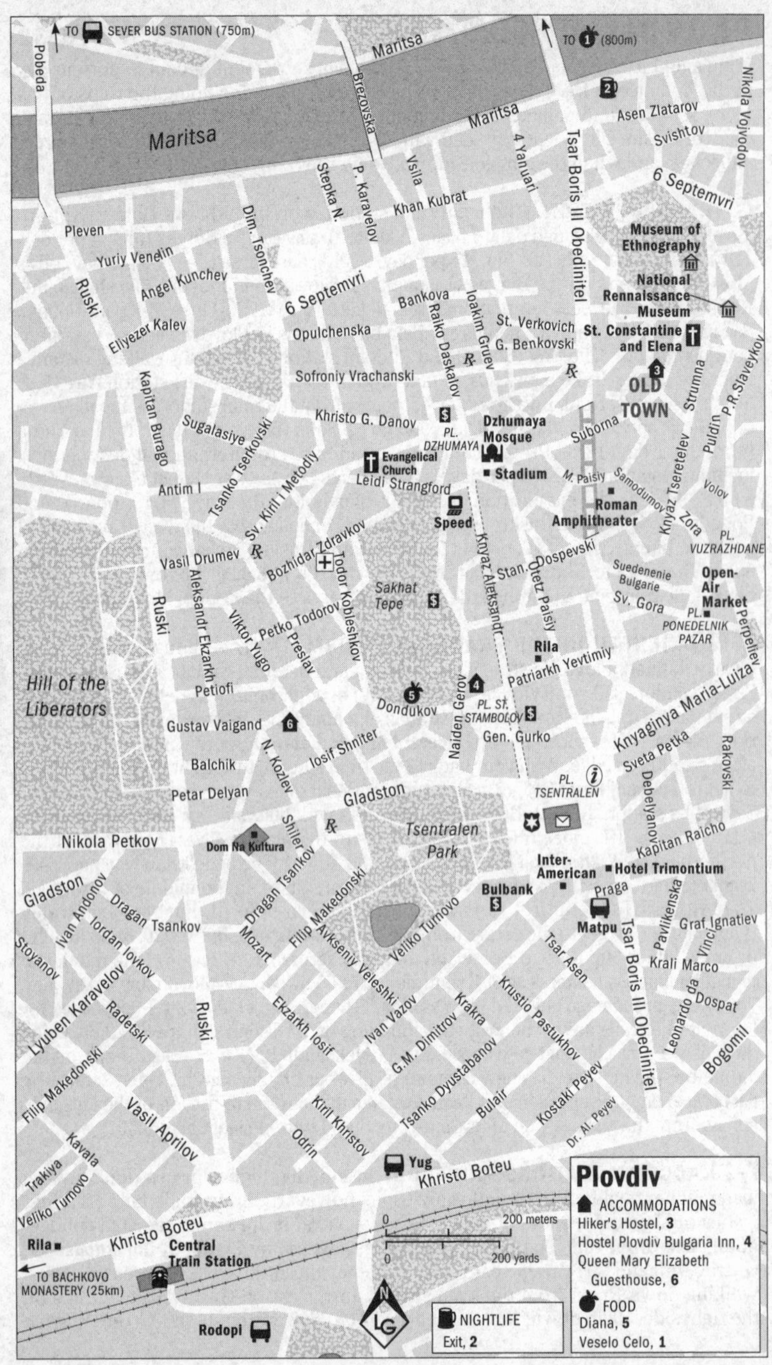

Plovdiv
ACCOMMODATIONS
Hiker's Hostel, 3
Hostel Plovdiv Bulgaria Inn, 4
Queen Mary Elizabeth Guesthouse, 6
FOOD
Diana, 5
Veselo Celo, 1
NIGHTLIFE
Exit, 2
0 200 meters
0 200 yards
TO SEVER BUS STATION (750m)
TO 1 (800m)
TO BACHKOVO MONASTERY (25km)
Maritsa
Pobeda
Brezovska
Asen Zlatarov
Nikola Vojvodov
Svishtov
Tsar Boris III Obedinitel
4 Yanuari
Vsila
P. Karavelov
Stepka N.
Khan Kubrat
6 Septemvri
Pleven
Yuriy Venelin
Dim. Tsonchev
Angel Kunchev
Ruski
Eliyezer Kalev
Bankova
Raiko Daskalov
Ioakim Gruev
St. Verkovich
G. Benkovski
Opulchenska
Sofroniy Vrachanski
Kapitan Burago
Museum of Ethnography
National Rennaissance Museum
St. Constantine and Elena
OLD TOWN
Strumna
P.R.Slaveykov
Khristo G. Danov
PL. DZHUMAYA
Dzhumaya Mosque
Sugalasiye
Tsanko Tserkovski
Sv. Kiril i Metodiy
Evangelical Church
Leidi Strangford
Stadium
Suborna
M. Paisiy
Samodumov
Roman Amphitheater
Knyaz Tseretelev
Puldin
Volov
Zora
PL. VUZRAZHDANE
Antim I
Speed
Vasil Drumev
Bozhidar Zdravkov
Todor Kobleshkov
Knyaz Aleksandr
Otetz Paisiy
Stan. Dospevski
Suedenenie Bulgarie
Sv. Gora
Open-Air Market
PL. PONEDELNIK PAZAR
Perpeliev
Aleksandr Ekzarkh
Viktor Yugo
Petko Todorov
Preslav
Sakhat Tepe
Rila
Patriarkh Yevtimiy
Hill of the Liberators
Petiofi
Dondukov
Naiden Gerov
PL. ST. STAMBOLOV
Knyaginya Maria-Luiza
Gustav Vaigand
Gen. Gurko
Iosif Shniter
Sveta Petka
Rakovski
Balchik
N. Kozlev
Debelyanov
Petar Delyan
Gladston
PL. TSENTRALEN
Nikola Petkov
Dom Na Kultura
Shiler
Tsentralen Park
Kapitan Raicho
Inter-American
Hotel Trimontium
Bulbank
Praga
Matpu
Dragan Tsankov
Filip Makedonski
Ivan Andonov
Iordan Iovkov
Mozart
Avkseniy Veleshki
Veliko Tumovo
Tsar Asen
Graf Ignatiev
Pavlikenska
Vinci
Krali Marco
Stoyanov
Lyuben Karavelov
Radetski
Ekzarkh Iosif
Ivan Vazov
G.M. Dimitrov
Krakra
Krustio Pastukhov
Leonardo da
Dospat
Bogomil
Tsanko Dyustabanov
Bulair
Kostaki Peyev
Dr. Al. Peyev
Kiril Khristov
Odrin
Vasil Aprilov
Kavala
Trakiya
Yug
Khristo Boteu
Central Train Station
Rodopi

spoken. Laundry 2lv per kg. Reception 24hr. 2- to 4-bed rooms 15lv. Cash only.) The social **Hiker's Hostel ❶,** Suborna 59 (Съборна), has a great location in Plovdiv's historic Old Town. Walking north on Knyaz Aleksandr (Княз Александр), turn right at Dzhimaya (Джимая) onto Suborna. It's a 5min. walk uphill, on the left. Perks include free Internet access, pickup service, and large breakfasts. (☎885 194 553; www.hikers-hostel.org. Laundry 4lv. Daytrips from 15lv. Dorms 20lv. Cash only.) **Hostel Plovdiv Bulgaria Inn ❶,** Naiden Gerov 13 (Найден Геров), just off Knyaz Aleksandr, offers cheap, clean, and centrally located accommodations, with the added perks of a bar, a book exchange, and satellite TV. (☎63 84 67; www.pbihostel.com. Reception 24hr. Dorms 20lv. Cash only.)

The **open-air market,** in pl. Ponedelnik Pazar (Понеделник Пазар) just northeast of pl. Tsentralen (Централен), sells all sorts of fruits and vegetables. (Open daily dawn-dusk.) Popular cafes line the pedestrian street Knyaz Aleksandr (Княз Александр). Though a bit far from the center, **Veselo Selo** (Весело Село) ❸, Dunav 53 (Дунав), is well worth the trip. Extremely popular with the locals, this traditional restaurant serves enormous portions, specializing in appetizer sampler plates (10-20lv) that literally can take up the whole table. Almost every night at 9:30 or 10pm, a group performs hour-long song-and-dance routines to Bulgarian folk music. Take Bus #1 from Pl. Tsentralen to the first stop on Dunav, then backtrack down the street past Obedinitel. (☎95 51 18. Open 10am-2am. Cash only.) **Diana** (Даяна) ❷, Dondukov 3 (Дондуков), at the base of Plovdiv's central hill, specializes in Bulgarian grill. Go all-out with the giant "Sword of the Tsar" (14lv), served straight off the sword. (☎62 30 27. English menu. Vegetarian options. Entrees 2.50-16lv. Open daily 24hr. Cash only.)

SIGHTS. Most of Plovdiv's treasures are on Stariya Grad's **Trimontium** (three hills). Begin or end a long day of sightseeing with a stroll up the **Hill of the Liberators** for a wonderful view of the city. The hill itself is topped with a massive monument depicting a young Soviet soldier standing at attention, and a smaller monument to Russian Tsar Alexander II, who fought the Russo-Turkish War in the 1870s in order to achieve Bulgarian Independence. A second-century **Roman Amphitheater** (Античен Театър; Antichen Teatur), one of the best preserved in the world, looms over the city; over 20 rows of seats and two floors of the stage backdrop remain. To reach the amphitheater, turn right off Knyaz Aleksandr (Княз Александр) on Suborna (Съборна) and then right up the steps along Mitropolit Paisiy. Continue uphill to another small set of steps next to the music academy. At the top, walk past the cafes to the theater. (Open daily 9am-7pm. 3lv.) An **ancient stadium** (Античен Стадион; Antichen Stadion), which once seated 30,000 spectators, now consists of just the poorly preserved bottom 10-15 rows. The public may view, but not enter, the ruins. An unfortunate bit of city planning has allowed a garish glass-and-metal cafe (now closed) to be built literally on top of the stadium. Follow Knyaz Alexander to its end; the stadium is underneath pl. Dzhumaya (Джумая). Built in the fourth century, the **Church of St. Constantine and Elena,** on Suborna (Съборна), is embellished with murals and icons dating from an artful 1832 renovation. The church now resembles National Revival period houses and has elaborate woodwork inside to match. (☎62 45 78. Open daily 9am-6pm. Free.)

ENTERTAINMENT AND NIGHTLIFE. The amphitheater serves as a popular performing arts venue, hosting the **Festival of the Arts** and the **Opera Festival** in June. Summer night operas in the lit amphitheatre are not to be missed. Most festival tickets are available at the opera box office on the ground floor of the Inter-American building, pl. Tsentralen 1 (Централен). Tickets are also sometimes sold at tables in the square and on the main pedestrian street. (☎62 55 53; www.ofd-plovdiv.org. Box office open 10am-6pm. Tickets 8-20lv. Cash only.) If a wild party full of scantily clad revelers is more up your alley, head to **Exit,** Maritsa 122 (Марица), where hardcore European clubbing and Bulgarian tradition unite—somewhat.

CHEAP SEATS. Although tickets to operas in Plovdiv's amphitheater are relatively inexpensive (8-20lv), it's possible to see the performance for free. Above the amphitheatre, several viewing platforms were built so tourists could view the ruins; luckily, the stage is also completely visible from them. Conveniently, the platforms are located immediately to the left of the ampitheater's entrance. Be aware, however, that this is a popular trick among locals; arrive early to grab a spot to sit–or be willing to stand for 2 hours.

The club plays *Chalga* (Bulgarian folk-pop) and sports trendy flashing lights and leather couches. (☎26 70 70. Frequent visiting DJs and live performances on weekends. Cover 5lv. Open daily 7:30pm-late. Cash only.)

BLACK SEA (ЧЕРНО МОРЕ)

Bulgaria's most popular destination for foreigners and natives alike, the Black Sea coast is covered with centuries-old fishing villages, secluded bays, energetic seaside towns, and mammoth resorts.

VARNA (ВАРНА) ☎(0)52

By 600 BC, Varna (pop. 360,000) was already the thriving Greek town of Odessos, later becoming even more important after its transfer into Roman hands. Both cultures left indelible marks, but none is more evident than the immense Roman thermal baths and the Old Town, still known as the "Greek Quarter." Today, Varna has it all; this cosmopolitan hub—the fastest-growing city in Bulgaria—caters to virtually any tourist. The city is perfect for relaxing on the beach, visiting museums, or hitting the town for shopping, strolling, and clubbing.

Black Sea Coast of Bulgaria

TRANSPORTATION. The **train station,** Gara Varna (Гара Варна) near the commercial harbor, runs trains to: Plovdiv (6½hr., 2 per day, 14lv); Ruse (3-4hr., 2 per day, 8lv); Shumen (2½hr., 3 per day, 5lv); Sofia (9-11hr., 6 per day, 19lv); Veliko Turnovo (4hr., 3-4 per day, 11lv). **Rila,** a private international travel company at Preslav 13, sells tickets to Budapest, HUN (25hr., Su 9:50pm, 155lv) and İstanbul, TUR (12hr., 1 per day, with bed 79lv) via Stara Zagora. (☎63 23 47; www.bdz-rila.com. Open M-F 8am-7:30pm, Sa 8am-3:30pm. Cash only.) To reach the **bus station,** Vladislav Varenchik (Владислав Варенчик), take city bus #1, 22, 40, or 41 from either the train station or the side of the cathedral opposite the post office, or walk 30min. on Preslav from pl.

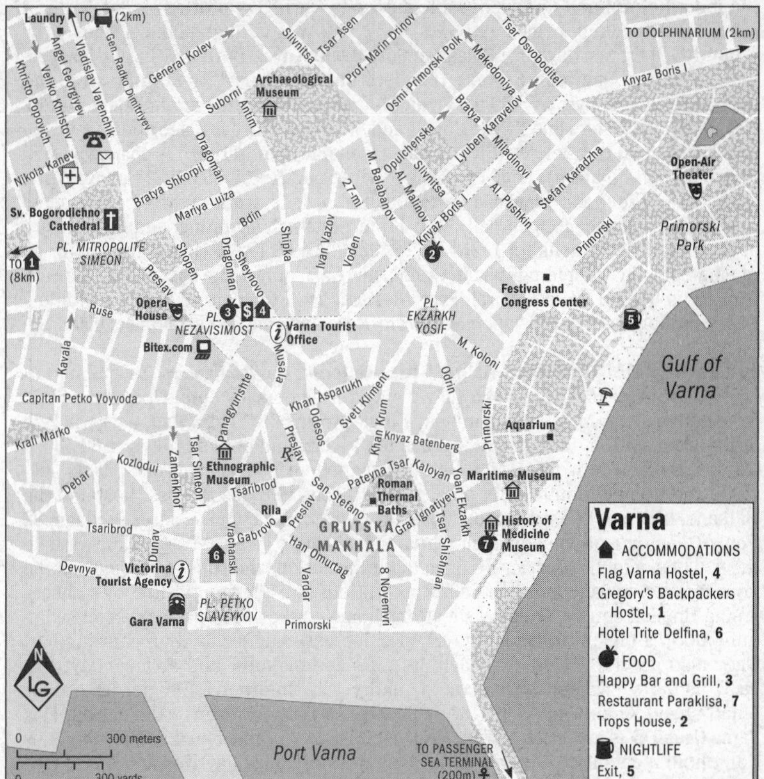

Nezavisimost (Независимост) to Varenchik. **Buses** run to Burgas (2hr., 3 per day, 8lv), and **private buses** leave for Sofia from the bus station (6hr., 15 per day, 20-25lv). **Minibuses** depart from the private station **Mladost** (Младост). Cross the busy street in front of the station and start walking left; take the first right onto Ul. Cherkazki (Черказки) and the station is down the street. Minibuses run to: Balchik (40min., 1 per hr. 6:30am-7:30pm, 4lv) and Burgas (2hr., 1 per hr. 7am-6pm., 8lv). City **buses** cost 0.60lv; pay on board. **Taxis** are plentiful in the city, but not all companies are reputable; **Lasiya** (Лacия) is generally a good choice, but always agree on a price before the trip.

ORIENTATION AND PRACTICAL INFORMATION. All major sights are within a 30min. walk of one another. To get to the central **ploshtad Nezavisimost** (Независимост) from the train station, take **Tsar Simeon I** (Цар Симеон I). **Preslav** (Преслав) heads from pl. Nezavisimost to the Sv. Bogorodichno Cathedral. Varna's main pedestrian artery, **bulevard Knyaz Boris I** (Княз Ђорис Ш), starts at pl. Nezavisimost, and **Slivnitsa** (Сливнитса) connects it to the sea garden's main entrance. The beach can be reached from Knyaz Boris I by taking any street downhill and walking through the sea garden, or from the train station by going right on **Primorski** (Приморски).

The city **tourist office** is on Knyaz Boris I, near the Moussala Palace Hotel. (☎65 45 18. Open daily 9am-6pm.) Alternatively, **Sea Shadow Travel** boasts Patrick, one of the most helpful and knowledgeable guides in Varna, who offers individualized tours for affordable prices. (☎08 87 36 47 11; www.guide-bg.com. Prices vary; around €10-20 per daytrip.) **Bulgarian Post Bank,** Knyaz Boris I 3, in pl. Nezavisimost, cashes **American Express Travelers Cheques** for 1.2% commission and exchanges currency. (☎68 69 03. Open M-F 8:30am-5pm.) Several **ATMs** are in pl. Nesavisimost; others line Knyaz Boris I and Slivnitsa. Store **luggage** at the train station, by the end of track #8. (3lv per bag. Open daily 6am-11pm.) A **pharmacy,** Mak Pharma (Мак Фарма), is at Preslav 35 (Преслав). (☎65 55 34. M-Sa 9am-7pm. Cash only.) Enter the **telephone office,** bul. Suborni 42, from the right of the main post office entrance. (Open daily 7am-11pm.) **Internet,** scanning, and printing are at **Bitex.com,** Ul. Zamenkhof 1, 3rd fl. (Заменхоф; ☎63 17 65. 1lv per hr., 2lv for all of 9am-2pm, 3lv for midnight-8am. Open 24hr. Cash only.) The **post office,** bul. Suborni 42, is behind the cathedral. **Poste Restante** is in the central room at window #12. (Съборни; ☎614 666. Open M-Sa 7am-7pm. Cash only.) **Postal Code:** 9000.

ACCOMMODATIONS AND FOOD. **Victorina Tourist Agency,** Tsar Simeon I 36, books **private rooms.** (☎60 35 41; www.victorina.borsabg.com. Open June-Sept. 8:30am-8pm; Apr.-May M-F 10am-6pm. Singles from 30lv.) **Astra Tour,** near track #6 at the train station, finds private rooms for 16-24lv and books hotels. (☎60 58 61; astratur@yahoo.com. Open May-Oct. daily 6am-9pm.) Locals approach backpackers at the train station to offer lodging for 10-15lv. Perhaps the best hostel in the Balkans, **Gregory's Backpackers Hostel ❶,** is in Zvezditsa (Звездица) village, 82 Fenix (Феникс), about 8km from Varna. Call ahead to arrange free pickup, or take the #36 bus, which stops across from the train station, and runs every hour on the hour from town 6am-9pm (with a few exceptions late afternoon). Run by a cheery young English couple, Gregory's features home-cooked breakfasts, a small swimming pool, a big TV with plenty of DVDs, leather couches, and an amazing bar. They also provide free daily beach dropoffs and pickups, and arrange daytrips. (☎37 99 09; www.hostelvarna.com. Laundry 12lv. Internet 1.40lv per hr. Call or email ahead. Open Apr.-Oct. Dorms 20lv. Cash only.) Closer to the action, **Flag Varna Hostel ❶** is just a step off Pl. Nezavisimost, at 25 Opalchenska. The amenities don't hold a candle to Gregory's, but Flag does organize daytrips and offers free laundry, clean beds, and lockers. (☎64 88 77; flagvarna@yahoo.com. Dorms 20lv. Cash only.) **Hotel Trite Delfina** (Трите Делфина; Three Dolphins) **❸,** Gabrovo 27, boasts well-kept, spacious rooms close to the train station and beach, with cable TV and private baths. (☎60 09 11. Breakfast included. Reception 24hr. Check-out noon. Call 3-4 days ahead. Singles 42lv; doubles 51lv.)

Bulevard Knyaz Boris I and **Slivnitsa** are swarming with cafes and kiosks. Many beachside restaurants serve fresh seafood. For an elegant dining experience, head to **Restaurant Paraklisa** (Параклиса) **❸,** Primorski 47 (Приморски), a traditional Bulgarian restaurant with a convent-like atmosphere ("Paraklisa" means "in the chapel") and terrific food. The chef permits half- and even quarter-orders, perfect for the indecisive eater. (☎61 18 30; www.monahini.com. English menu with vegetarian options. Beer from 1lv. Entrees 3-26lv. Open daily 11am-midnight. MC/V.) **Trops House** (Тропс Къща) **❶,** at bul. Knyaz Boris I 48, dishes up the cheapest Bulgarian cafeteria grub in town. (Entrees 1-5lv. Open daily 8:30am-10pm.) **Kushata** (Къшата) **❷,** 8 Noyemvri 7 (Ноември), also serves traditional Bulgarian fare, like *pletena nadenitsa*, a giant braided sausage (4.80lv), on a terrace decorated with local handicrafts. (☎60 59 09. No English menu. Beer from 1.10lv. Entrees 4-16lv. Open daily 10am-midnight. Cash only.)

SIGHTS. The **Archaeological Museum** (Археологически Музей; Arkheologicheski Muzey), in the park on Mariya Luiza 41 (Мария Луиза), traces the region's history from the Stone Age, with a dazzling array of artifacts from the first recorded civilization in Europe and the world's oldest discovered golden treasures. (☎68 10 30; www.amvarna.com. Open high season Tu-Su 10am-6pm; low season Tu-Sa 10am-5pm. English captions. 8lv, students 2lv. English tours 20lv, booklet 6lv.) The **Roman Thermal Baths** (Римски Терми; Rimski Termi), the largest ancient complex in Bulgaria, stand on 13 San Stefano in the old quarter, **Grutska Makhala** (Гръцка Махала), and have walls, arches, and the remains of the plumbing system still intact. (☎60 00 59. Open high season Tu-Su 10am-5pm; low season Tu-Sa 10am-5pm. 4lv, students 2lv. Cash only.) In pl. Metropolite Simeon, the **Sv. Bogorodichno Cathedral** is the second-largest Bulgarian Orthodox church in the country. While the exterior of stone and dull gold domes isn't spectacular, the interior, which took 50 years to complete, is breathtaking. The colorful murals blend ancient Orthodox style with modern technique, incorporating realism to a degree unusual for an Orthodox church. (☎61 30 05. Open daily 7am-7pm. Free.) The **Ethnographic Museum** (Етнографски Музей; Etnografski Muzey), Panagyurishte 22, features displays depicting Varna's seafaring past. The top floor is recreated as an upper-class house from the Bulgarian National Revival in the 19th century. (☎63 05 88. Open in high season Tu-Su 10am-5pm; in low season Tu-Sa. Some English captions. 4lv, students 2lv.) The **Maritime Museum** (Военно-Морски Музей; Voyenno-Morski Muzey), at Primorski 22 (Приморски), at the southern edge of the sea garden, highlights the history of naval enterprise in Varna through old uniforms, photographs, navigational devices, diving suits, and a variety of other artifacts. The museum's courtyard serves as a graveyard for decommissioned ships and weapons, ranging from a submarine to a full helicopter. (☎63 20 18. Open daily 10am-6pm. 2lv, students 1lv. Cash only.)

NIGHTLIFE AND FESTIVALS. The **beach,** lined with bars and restaurants, stretches north from the train station and is separated from bul. Primorski (Приморски) by the seaside gardens. In summer, a long strip of discos and bars rocks the beach. Hardcore partying and dancing doesn't really get going until past midnight and often lasts until sunrise. Crowds pack the outdoor disco **Exit,** a two-level, three-bar, raucous beach party. Take Slivnitsa (Сливнитса) to its end at the sea garden, proceed down the steps, and head left. (Beer 2-3.50lv. Mixed drinks 1.20-5lv. Open daily 10pm-4am.)

Hidden among the fountains and trees in the seaside gardens, at the corner of bul. Tsar Osvoboditel (Цар Освободител) and bul. Primorski (Приморски), is a vine-covered **open-air theater,** home of the biannual **International Ballet Festival** (May-Oct.). Buy tickets at the Festival and Congress Center (see below). As the theater is under repair as of summer 2007, its shows will be transferred to the pink **Opera House,** on pl. Nezavisimost, which has weekly performances and sells theater tickets. (Opera ☎22 33 88, theater ☎60 07 99; opera www.operavarna.bg. Open M-F 10am-1pm and 2-6pm. Theater closed July-Aug. Tickets 10-15lv.) In late August, Varna holds an **International Jazz Festival.** (☎65 91 67; www.vsjf.com.) The international music festival **Varna Summer** (Варненско Лято; Varnensko Lyato; www.varnasummerfest.org) runs from the last week of June through the last week of July; ticket prices vary and are available at the Opera House. The **Festival and Congress Center,** on 2 Slivnitsa (Сливнитса), has cafes, Internet, and a cinema. (☎60 84 45. Center box office open daily 10am-9pm. 1 movie per day. 5lv. Cash only.) From late August to early September, the international **Love is Folly** film festival takes place at the complex.

BURGAS (БУРГАС) ☎(0)56

Burgas (BOOR-gahs; pop. 205,000), Bulgaria's fourth largest city, is a calm seaside town much like Varna, but less crowded and with less to do. Vacationers stroll leisurely along the many pedestrian streets and sit in the shaded Seaside Park (Приморски Парк; Primorski Park), full of Soviet monuments and modern sculpture.

Although Burgas lacks budget accommodations and the excitement of Varna, it is a great jumping-off point for Bulgaria's less-touristed beaches; its beach, the city's main attraction, boasts the best windsurfing on the coast.

TRANSPORTATION. The **train station,** Gara Burgas (Гара Бургас), send **trains** to Sofia (8hr., 7 per day., 19lv) via Plovdiv (7hr., 3 per day, 14lv). Buses, although more expensive, are the fastest way to travel from Burgas. The **bus station,** Avtogara Yug (Автогара Юг), runs **buses** to: Ruse (5hr., 5 per day, 22lv); Shumen (3hr., 3 per day, 13lv); Sofia (5hr., 11 per day, 22lv); Varna (2hr., every 30min. 7am-7pm, 8lv). Buses also depart from Avtogara Yug for closer destinations along the coast, including Nessebar (50min., every 40min. 6:20am-10:30pm, 4lv). Private companies send buses to many cities in Bulgaria, including Sofia, Plovdiv, and Veliko Turnovo, and to international locations like İstanbul, TUR. Inquire about times and prices at their offices and in the city's main hotels, including Hotel Bulgaria. **Taxis** are common throughout the city and should run about 0.59lv per km.

ORIENTATION AND PRACTICAL INFORMATION. The train and bus stations are conveniently located side by side on Bul. Bulair (Булайр), which runs to the right of the stations and then curves left at the Seaside Park to become Bul. Demokratsiya (Демократсиа). Burgas centers around two main pedestrian streets: **Ulitsa Aleksandrovska** (Александровска) runs north from the train station towards Troykata Pl. (Тройката), while **Ulitsa Bogoridi** (Богориди) branches off to the right from Aleksandrovska at Hotel Bulgaria.

Dimant Travel Agency, Ul. Tsar Simeon I 15 (Цар Симион), just off Bogoridi, provides info and **maps** and books accommodations in both private rooms and hotels. Prices start at 10lv per night for a room with shared bath in a city apartment. (☎84 07 79. Open daily 9am-5pm. Cash only.) Raiffeisen **Bank** (Райфайзен), Ul. Alexandrovska 115 (Александровска), cashes **traveler's checks** for a 1% commission (€5 min.), and has a **24hr. ATM.** (☎87 59 23. Open M-F 8:30am-7pm.) **Luggage storage** is in the bus station, in the room marked Гардероб. (Open daily 6am-9pm. 2lv.) **Apteka Aptiya** (Аптека Аптия), a **pharmacy,** is on Pl. Troikata (Тройката). (☎80 01 93. Open M-F 9am-8:30pm, Sa-Su 10am-8pm. Cash only.) **Internet** is on Knyaz Boris (Княз Борис), just off Troikata Pl. (1.20lv per hr. Open 24hr. Cash only.) The **post office,** Tsar Peter 2 (Цар Петр), has **Western Union** and **Poste Restante** services. (☎85 11 13. Open M-F 7:30am-8pm, Sa 8am-noon and 1-6pm, Su 8am-1pm. Cash only.) **Postal Code**: 8000.

ACCOMMODATIONS AND FOOD. There are no hostels in Burgas. By far, the best deal in town is to stay in a private room, which can be arranged by Dimant Travel Agency (see above), or a number of agencies at the bus and train stations. **Hotel Cosmos** (Космос) ❷, Ul. Stambolov 2 (Стамболов), is popular with both tourists and businesspeople. This highrise offers decently sized rooms with private baths, and has a bar and two restaurants on its property. A solid 20min. walk from the center, the hotel's location makes it affordable. From the train station, walk down Aleksandrovska (Александровска), veer right on Ul. Bogoridi (Богориди), and take a left on Stambolov. (☎81 34 00. Check-out noon. Singles 29lv; doubles 37lv. Cash only.) A better-located option is **Hotel Elite** ❷, Ul. Morska 35 (Морска), just a step off of Bogoridi and only a 5min. walk from the beach. The rooms offer new bathrooms and balconies. (☎84 57 80. Doubles 45lv. MC/V.) Restaurants line Aleksandrovska and Bogoridi, but most are indistinguishable pizza places and grills. For something different, try **Watermill** (Воденица; Vodenitsa) ❷, on the beach's northern end, which specializes in sizzling plates of meats and vegetables. The wooden architecture includes a working watermill. (☎08 97 98 83 34. Entrees 5-20lv. Open daily 10am-late. Cash only.) For cheap eats, head to **Katmaniya** (Катмания) ❶, across Bogoridi from Hotel Bulgaria. Try *katmi*, the Bulgarian variation on the crepe or pancake. (Entrees 1-4lv. Open 24hr. Cash only.)

BULGARIA

SIGHTS AND ENTERTAINMENT. The main church of the city, **Sts. Cyril and Methodius Church,** Ul. Vuzrozhdeniye (Възрождение), features an ornate interior of marble columns, frescoes of foreboding religious figures, and a carved wooden iconostasis. (Open 7am-7pm. Free.) The small **Archaeological Museum** (Археологически Музей; Arkheologicheski Muzey), Bogoridi 21 (Богориди), traces the region's rich history of Greek and Roman settlement. (☎84 35 41. Open M-F 10am-7pm, Sa 10am-6pm. 2lv, students 1lv. Cash only.) The **Ethnographical Museum** (Етнографски Музей; Etnografski Muzey), Slavyanska 69 (Славянска), explains the traditions of residents from the Burgas area. The exhibits on fire-dancing and mid-summer fortune telling are particularly fascinating. (☎84 25 87. Open M-F 10am-7pm, Sa 10am-6pm. 2lv, students 1lv. Cash only.)

Burgas' popular **beach** runs along the city's eastern edge parallel to Demokratsiya (Демократсиа). The **Burgas Opera,** Okhridski 2 (Охридски), has musical and theater performances. (☎84 07 89. Box office open 10am-6pm. Tickets 5-10lv. Cash only.) Multiple nightclubs blast techno for the young masses in both the Seaside Park and on the beach, but if flashing lights and scantily clad teens aren't your thing, head for **Party Club Live,** at Bogoridi 36 (Богориди). Don't be fooled by the name; this "club" is actually a cool bar with walls of exposed stone downstairs and outdoor seating upstairs. Youth gather here for drinks and the live rock and jam bands that perform on weekends in the summer. (☎08 98 63 51 27. Open daily 5pm-4am. Beer from 1.50lv. Cash only.)

NESSEBAR (НЕСЕБЪР) ☎(0)55

Ancient Nessebar (Neh-SEH-bahr; pop. 10,200), formerly Mesembria, a Thracian village, is now a tiny, secluded peninsular town surrounded by the gorgeous vista of Nessebar Bay. Travelers flock to this small town to wander the narrow, winding streets and explore the countless church ruins, but even the influx of souvenir stands and touristy cafes can't mask Nessebar's historic and tranquil beauty. Conveniently, Nessebar's best sights are also free. While the beach has been listed among the most beautiful in Bulgaria, the city is also well-known for its many **church ruins,** almost all of which can be explored without charge. The ubiquitous churches share a common architectural pattern: they are built of plaster and terracotta brick, with frequent arch motifs and ceramic decor in the walls. The almost entirely intact **Church of Christ Pantokrator,** which stands in the main square, is a spectacular example of this 14th-century style. The remains of the **Old Metropolitan Church,** on Metropolitska (Митролитска), are the largest in town; the church served as the seat of the Metropolit until it fell into disuse. The ruins of **Basilica "Virgin Merciful Eleusa,"** on Kraibrezhna (Крайбрежна), are particularly romantic. All that remains of this seventh-century church standing at the top of the hill overlooking Nessebar Bay is a part of an old tower and the church floor. To gain insight into the city's even earlier history, head to the **Archaeological Museum** (Археологически Музей; Arkheologicheski Muzey), Mesambriya 2a, to the right as soon as you enter the Old Town. The museum proudly chronicles the town's ancient importance as a Thracian settlement all the way through its Greek, Roman, and Byzantine periods. (☎44 60 12. Open M-F 9am-7pm, Sa-Su 9am-1pm, 1:30-6pm. English captions. 4lv, students 2lv. Photo 4lv. Cash only.)

Budget travelers can book a **private room** through **Messemvria Holidays** (see above.) Hotels and guesthouses abound in town, but while they are quite reasonably priced in low season, prices jump significantly in July and August. **St. George House ❸,** Ul. Salada 10 (Салада), offers large, brightly decorated rooms with new private baths and balconies overlooking church ruins and Nessebar Bay. (☎44 40 45; www.gsk.5u.com. Check-out noon. July-Aug. doubles 80lv; May-June and Sept. doubles 50lv. Cash only.) Nessebar teems with every international food imaginable, from curry to schnitzel to Yorkshire pudding. If you didn't travel to Bulgaria to eat specialties from home, try **Kapitanska Sreshta** (Капитанская Среща) ❸, Мена 22 (Мена). Set in a 19th-century National Revival house, this restaurant specializes in seafood, which is served on a terrace overlooking the sea. (☎44 21 24. Entrees 7-30lv. Open daily noon-late. Cash only.) **Restaurant Emona** (Емона) ❷, tucked away at the very end of Mesembriya, serves traditional food, including extensive vegetarian dishes, on a green and shady terrace overlooking the sea. (☎44 20 22. Entrees 4-20lv. Open daily 11am-midnight. MC/V.)

Buses leave from the entrance to the Old Town for seaside destinations, including Burgas (50min., every 40min. 6:20am-10:30pm, 4lv) and Varna (1½hr., 7 per day, 20lv). A **travel agency,** Messemvria Holidays, is at Ul. Ribarska 1 (Рибарска), just off the main square. The staff speak limited English but book hotels and private accommodations (from 18lv). They also offer a variety of day tours, including fishing and boat trips to historic inland cities, for about 60lv per person. (☎888 806 413; www.messemvria.com. Open daily high season 10am-9pm; low season 11am-4pm. Cash only.) A city **tourist information office,** Mesembriya 20 (Месембрия), sells maps for 2lv. (www.visitnessebar.org. Open M-F 10am-6pm. Cash only.) **Bank Biochim,** Ul. Mesembriya 19, **changes currency** and has a **24hr. ATM.** (☎42 19 22; www.biochim.com.) **Internet** can be found in the **White House Hotel,** just off the main square, behind the post office. (4lv per hr. Open daily noon-midnight. Cash only.) The **post office,** Mesembriya 10, has **telephones** inside. (Open M-F 8am-9pm. Cash only.) **Postal Code:** 8231.

CROATIA (HRVATSKA)

With attractions ranging from the sun-drenched beaches and cliffs around Dubrovnik to the dense forests around Plitvice, Croatia's wonders never cease. And, like so many treasures, Croatia has been fought over many times, often finding itself in the middle of dangerous political divides and deadly ethnic tensions. It was only after the devastating 1991-95 ethnic war that Croatia achieved full independence for the first time in 800 years. That said, while some marked-off areas still contain landmines, the biggest threats currently facing travelers to Croatia are the ever-rising prices and tides of tourists who clog the ferryways. Still, this friendly, fun-loving, and upbeat country demands to be seen at any cost.

DISCOVER CROATIA: SUGGESTED ITINERARIES

THREE DAYS. Spend a day poking around the bizarre architecture of **Split** (p. 133) before ferrying down the coast to the beach paradise of either **Hvar** or **Brač** islands (1 day; p. 139). Then make your way to former war-zone—and what some consider Eastern Europe's most beautiful city—**Dubrovnik** (1 day; p. 146).

ONE WEEK. Enjoy the East-meets-West feel of **Zagreb** (1 day; p. 103) and head to **Zadar** (1 day; p. 128), with a few hours' stop in gorgeous **Paklenica National Park** (p. 133). Next, ferry to tree-lined **Korčula** (1 day; p. 144) before **Hvar** and **Brač** (2 days). End your journey in **Dubrovnik** (2 days).

FACTS AND FIGURES

Official Name: Republic of Croatia.
Capital: Zagreb.
Major Cities: Dubrovnik, Split.
Population: 4,493,000.
Time Zone: GMT + 1, in summer GMT + 2.
Language: Croatian.
Religions: Roman Catholic (88%).
Population Growth Rate: -0.035%.

CROATIA

ESSENTIALS

WHEN TO GO

Croatia's best weather lasts from May to September, and crowds typically show up along the Adriatic coast in July and August. If you go in late August or September, you'll find fewer crowds, lower prices, and an abundance of fruits such as figs and grapes. Late autumn is wine season. While April and October may be too cool for camping, the weather is usually nice along the coast, and private rooms are plentiful and inexpensive. You can swim in the sea from mid-June to late September.

DOCUMENTS AND FORMALITIES

EMBASSIES AND CONSULATES. Foreign embassies in Croatia are in Zagreb (p. 103). Croatian embassies abroad include: **Australia,** 14 Jindalee Crescent, O'Malley ACT 2606, Canberra (☎262 866 988; croemb@dynamite.com.au); **Canada,** 229 Chapel St., Ottawa, ON K1N 7Y6 (☎613-562-7820; www.croatiaemb.net); **Ireland,** Adelaide Chambers, Peter St., Dublin 8 (☎014 767 181; croatianembassy@eircom.net); **New Zealand,** 291 Lincoln Rd., Henderson (☎98 36 55 81; cro-consulate@xtra.co.nz), mail to: P.O. Box 83-200, Edmonton, Auckland; **UK,** 21 Conway St., London W1P 5HL

ENTRANCE REQUIREMENTS.

Passport: Required for all travelers.

Visa: Not required for stays of under 90 days for citizens of Australia, Canada, the EU, Ireland, New Zealand, the UK and the US.

Letter of Invitation: Not required for citizens of Australia, Canada, the EU, Ireland, New Zealand, the UK, and the US.

Inoculations: Recommended up-to-date on DTaP (diphtheria, tetanus, and pertussis), Hepatitis A, Hepatitis B, MMR (measles, mumps, and rubella), polio booster, rabies, and typhoid.

Work Permit: Required for all foreigners planning to work in Croatia.

International Driving Permit: Required for all those planning to drive in Croatia.

(☎02 07 38 72 022; http://croatia.embassyhomepage.com); **US,** 2343 Massachusetts Ave., NW, Washington, D.C. 20008 (☎202-588-5899; http://www.croatiaemb.org).

VISA AND ENTRY INFORMATION. Citizens of the EU, Australia, Canada, New Zealand, the UK, and the US do not need a visa for stays of up to 90 days. Visas cost US$26 (single-entry), US$33 (double-entry), and US$52 (multiple-entry). Apply for a visa at your nearest Croatian embassy or consulate at least one month before planned arrival. All visitors must register with the police within 48hr. of arrival—

hotels, campsites, and accommodation agencies should automatically register you, but those staying with friends or in private rooms must do so themselves to avoid fines or expulsion. To register, go to room 103 on the second floor of the central police station at Petrinjska 30, Zagreb. (☎456 3623, after hours 456 3111. Bring your passport and use form #14. Open M-F 8am-4pm.) Police may check foreigners' passports at any time and place. The easiest way of entering or exiting Croatia is by bus or train between Zagreb and a neighboring capital.

TOURIST SERVICES

Even the smallest towns have a branch of the excellent and resourceful **state-run tourist board** *(turistička zajednica)*. The staff speaks English and hands out **free maps** and booklets. Private agencies *(turistička/putnička agencija)*, such as the ubiquitous **Atlas,** handle private accommodations. Local outfits are cheaper.

MONEY

KUNA (KN)		
	AUS$1 = 4.44KN	1KN = AUS$0.23
	CDN$1 = 5.07KN	1KN = CDN$0.20
	EUR€1 = 7.39KN	1KN = EUR€0.14
	NZ$1 = 3.89KN	1KN = NZ$0.26
	UK£1 = 10.94KN	1KN = UK£0.09
	US$1 = 5.91KN	1KN = US$0.17

The Croatian unit of currency is the **kuna** (kn), which is divided into 100 lipa. Inflation hovers around 2.6%, so prices should stay relatively constant in the near future. Croatia became an official candidate for European Union membership in 2004, with admission projected for the end of the decade; travelers may occasionally find prices listed in euro (€), especially in heavily-touristed areas like the Istrian Peninsula. Most tourist offices, hostels, and transportation stations **exchange currency** and **traveler's checks;** banks have the best rates. Some establishments charge a 1.5% commission to exchange traveler's checks. Most banks give MasterCard and Visa cash advances, and **credit cards** (especially American Express, MasterCard, and Visa) are widely accepted. Common banks include Zagrebačka Banka, Privredna Banka, and Splitska Banka. **ATMs** are everywhere.

HEALTH AND SAFETY

EMERGENCY	**Ambulance:** ☎94. **Fire:** ☎93 **Police:** ☎92. **General Emergency:** ☎112.

Medical facilities in Croatia include public hospitals, clinics, private medical practitioners, and pharmacies. Due to disparities in funding, private clinics and pharmacies tend to be better supplied. Both public and private facilities may demand cash payment for services, and most do not usually accept credit cards. **Pharmacies** *(apoteka)* sell Western products, including tampons, sanitary napkins *(sanitami ulosci)*, and condoms *(prezervativ)*. UK citizens receive free medical care with a valid passport. Tap water is chlorinated; though relatively safe, it may cause mild abdominal discomfort. **Bottled water** is readily available. Croatia's **crime** rate is relatively low, but travelers should beware of pickpockets on crowded buses and trains. Travel to the former conflict areas of **Slavonia** and **Krajina** remains dangerous due to **unexploded landmines,** which are not expected to be cleared until at least 2010. In 2005, a tourist was injured by a mine on the island of Vis, which inspectors had previously declared safe. If you choose to visit these or other regions, do not stray from known safe areas, and consult the Croatian Mine Action Center website at www.hcr.hr for detailed information. **Women** should go out in public with a companion to ward off unwanted attention. Although hate crimes in Croatia are rare, **minority** travelers may experience stares. **Disabled travelers** should contact Savez Organizacija Invalida Hrvatske (☎ 14 82 93 94), in Zagreb. Although **homosexuality** is slowly becoming accepted, discretion is recommended.

TRANSPORTATION

BY PLANE. Croatia Airlines flies to and from many cities, including Frankfurt, London, Paris, Zagreb, Dubrovnik, and Split. Rijeka, Zadar, and Pula also have tiny international airports. Book in advance for a cheap seat or consider buying a flight pass from Europe by Air (www.europebyair.com), which will let you fly anywhere in Europe for US$99 or $129 per leg.

BY TRAIN. Trains are slow everywhere and nonexistent south of Split; they are, however, often cheaper than buses. Trains (www.hznet.hr) run to Zagreb from Budapest, HUN; Ljubljana, SLO; Venice, ITA; and Vienna, AUS, and continue on to other Croatian destinations. **Eurail** (www.eurail.com) offers unlimited travel passes for between four and ten days in Austria/Croatia/Slovenia and Hungary/Croatia/Slovenia. *Odlazak* means departures, while *dolazak* signifies arrivals.

BY BUS. Buses run faster and farther than trains at comparable or slightly higher prices and are the easiest way to get to many destinations, especially those south of Split. Major companies include Croatiabus (www.croatiabus.hr), Autotrans Croatia (www.autotrans.hr), and Austobusni Promet Varaždin (www.ap.hr). The website of the main bus terminal in Zagreb (Austobusni Kolodvor Zagreb; www.akz.hr) provides info on timetables, although unfortunately not in English.

BY CAR AND BY TAXI. Anyone over the age of 18 can rent a **car** in larger cities, but parking and gas are expensive. Rural roads are in bad condition, and those traveling through the Krajina region and other conflict areas should be cautious of off-road landmines. **Taxis** are reliable and run on meter.

BY BOAT. The Jadrolinija ferry company (www.jadrolinija.hr) sails the Rijeka-Split-Dubrovnik route, stopping at islands on the way. Ferries also go to Ancona, Italy from Split and Zadar, and to Bari, Italy from Split and Dubrovnik. Though slower than buses and trains, ferries are more comfortable. A basic ticket only grants a place on the deck. Cheap beds sell out fast, so buy tickets in advance.

BY BIKE AND BY THUMB. Moped and **bike rentals** are an option in resort or urban areas. **Hitchhiking** is relatively uncommon and is not recommended by Let's Go.

KEEPING IN TOUCH

PHONE CODES	**Country code:** 385. **International dialing prefix:** 00. From outside Croatia, dial international dialing prefix (see inside back cover) + 385 + city code + local number. Within Croatia, dial city code + number, or simply the number for local calls.

EMAIL AND INTERNET. Most towns, no matter how small, have at least one **Internet** cafe. Connections on the islands are slower and less reliable than those on the mainland. Internet usage typically costs 20kn per hour.

TELEPHONE. Post offices usually have **public phones;** pay after you talk. All phones on the street require a country-specific phone card *(telekarta)*, sold at newsstands and post offices for 15-100kn. A Global Card allows calls for as low as 0.99kn per minute and provides the best international rates. For the **international operator,** dial ☎901. Croatia has two **cell phone** networks: T-Mobile and VIP. If you bring or buy a phone compatible with the GSM 900/1800 network, SIM cards are widely available. Pressing the "L" button will cause the phone instructions to switch into English.

MAIL. The Croatian Postal Service is reliable. Mail from the US arrives within a week. A postcard or letter to the US typically costs 3.50kn. *Avionski* and *zrakoplovom* both mean "airmail." Mail addressed to **Poste Restante** will be held for up to 30 days at the receiving post office. Address envelopes: first name LAST NAME, POSTE RESTANTE, post office address, Postal Code, city, CROATIA.

ACCOMMODATIONS AND CAMPING

CROATIA	❶	❷	❸	❹	❺
ACCOMMODATIONS	under 150kn	151-250kn	251-350kn	351-450kn	over 450kn

For info on Croatia's youth hostels (in Krk, Pula, Punat, Šibenik, Veli Losinj, Zadar, and Zagreb), contact the **Croatian Youth Hostel Association,** Savska 5/1, 10000 Zagreb (☎14 82 92 94; www.hfhs.hr/home.php?lang=en). **Hotels** in Croatia can be expensive. If you opt for a hotel, call a few days ahead, especially in the summer along the coast. Those looking to stay in either hostels or hotels in the July-August tourist season should book early, as rooms fill up quickly. Apart from hostels, **private rooms** are the major budget option for accommodations. Look for *sobe* signs, especially near transportation stations. English is rarely spoken by room owners. All accommodations are subject to a tourist tax of 5-10kn (one reason the police require foreigners to register). Croatia is also one of the top **camping** destinations in Europe—33% of travelers stay in campgrounds. Facilities are usually comfortable, and prices are among the cheapest along the Mediterranean. Camping outside of designated areas is illegal. For more info, contact the **Croatian Camping Union,** 8 Marta 1, P.O. Box 143, HR-52440 Poreč (☎52 45 13 24; www.camping.hr).

FOOD AND DRINK

CROATIA	❶	❷	❸	❹	❺
FOOD	under 30kn	31-60kn	61-90kn	91-150kn	over 150kn

Croatian cuisine is defined by the country's varied geography. In Croatia in and to the east of Zagreb, heavy meals featuring meat and creamy sauces dominate. Popular dishes are *burek*, a layered pie made with meat or cheese, and the spicy Slavonian *kulen*, considered one of the world's best **sausages.** On the coast, textures and flavors change with the presence of **seafood** and Italian influence. Don't miss out on *lignje* (squid) or *Dalmatinski pršut* (Dalmatian smoked ham). The **oysters** from Ston Bay have received a number of awards at international competitions. If your budget does not allow for such treats, *slane sardele* (salted sardines) are a tasty substitute. **Vegetarian** and **kosher** eating are difficult in Croatia, but not impossible. In both cases, pizza and bakeries are safe and ubiquitous options. Price is usually the best indicator of quality for **wines.** Mix red wine with tap water to get the popular *bevanda*, and white wine with carbonated water to get *gemišt*. *Šljivovica* is a hard-hitting plum brandy found in many small towns. Karlovačko and Ožujsko are the two most popular beers.

LIFE AND TIMES

HISTORY

DALMATIANS 101. Today's Croatia has its roots in the Roman province of Dalmatia, with its capital at Salona, near what is now Split (p. 133). The Slavic ancestors of Croatia's present inhabitants settled the region in the 6th and 7th centuries, partly expelling and partly assimilating the indigenous Illyrian population. Over the next two centuries, the Croats slowly accepted Catholicism. In the 9th century, an independent Croatian state was consolidated by King Tomislav (910-928), who earned papal recognition for his country. Pope Gregory crowned King Zvonimir in 1076, solidifying Croatia's ties with Catholic Europe.

UNDER THE HUNGARIAN YOKE. In 1102, the Croatian Kingdom entered into a dynastic union with Hungary. Croatia was soon stripped of all independence and effectively disappeared for 800 years. Following Hungary's defeat by the Ottomans in 1526, the **Austrian Habsburgs** took over what remained of Croatia and turned it into a buffer zone against Ottoman aggression. Orthodox Christians from the Ottoman-controlled area migrated to the region, establishing the presence of the Serbian minority in Croatia. The Croats, led by **Josip Jelačić,** attempted to please their Austrian rulers by remaining loyal to the empire when Hungary revolted in 1848, but their later demands for self-government fell on deaf ears.

BITTERSWEET UNION. After Croat troops fought alongside the Germans and Austro-Hungarians during WWI, Croatia declared **independence** from a defeated Austria-Hungary on December 1, 1918. It then announced its incorporation into the **Kingdom of the Serbs, Croats, and Slovenes** under the Serbian **King Alexander.** To the dismay of the Croats, Alexander eventually declared a dictatorship and, on January 6, 1929, renamed the kingdom **Yugoslavia.** In 1934, Alexander was killed by Croat nationalists from the **Ustaše** (Insurgents), a terrorist organization demanding Croatian independence.

CROATIA

TITO'S REIGN. The Ustaše finally achieved Croatia's "independence" in 1941 in the form of a fascist puppet state. Seeking to eliminate the country's Jewish and Serbian populations, the ruthless regime killed more than 350,000 people in massacres and concentration camps. Though the government supported the Axis powers during **WWII,** the majority of Croats joined the communist-led **Partisan** resistance early in the war. The Partisans, led by **Josip Brož Tito,** demanded the creation of a federal Yugoslav state. In 1945, as communist regimes took power across Eastern Europe, the **Socialist Federal Republic of Yugoslavia** declared its independence. Though Yugoslavia broke from Moscow in 1948, it retained communism and suppressed civil rights and the ambitions of Croat nationalists. Student leaders of a 1971 independence movement were imprisoned, but their struggle eventually led to the ratification of a new constitution in 1974.

A COSTLY FREEDOM. The rotating presidency established upon Tito's death was unable to curb the tide of nationalism. In April 1990, Croat nationalist **Franjo Tudjman** was elected President of Croatia, and on June 25, 1991, Croatia declared **independence.** Tensions between Croats and the Serbian minority escalated rapidly. The Serb-controlled **Yugoslav National Army** invaded Croatia, driving out hundreds of thousands of Croats from Eastern Slavonia and shelling Vukovar, Zadar, and Dubrovnik. Meanwhile, the Serbian minority declared its own independent republic, **Serbian Krajina,** around Knin in central Croatia. Not until the destruction of Dubrovnik did the international political community realize that Croatia was occupied. In January 1992, the European Community recognized Croatia's independence, and a UN military force arrived to quell further fighting and ethnic cleansing. In May 1995, Croatia seized Krajina, expelling over 150,000 Serbs. The Croatian leadership then made claims on Bosnia and Herzegovina, sent troops, and massacred Bosnian Serbs and Muslims. The 1995 **Dayton Peace Accords,** negotiated by American Richard Holbrooke, established a cease-fire in Bosnia and Herzegovina and stabilized the disputed areas of Croatia.

TODAY

GOVERNMENT. Croatia is a **parliamentary democracy** with power shared between the **Sabor** (parliament), whose deputies are elected for four years, and the **president,** who is elected by popular vote for a five-year term. During his tenure as president from 1991 until his death in December 1999, Franjo Tudjman and his nationalist **Croatian Democratic Union** (Hrvatska Demokraticka Zajednica; HDZ) established Croatia as a sovereign state, but HDZ's corruption, abuse of power, and censorship also isolated the country from the West. The current decade has seen power shared between the left and the right, beginning with the 2000 transfer of parliamentary control to a leftist coalition and presidential victory of pro-Western **Stipe Mesić** of the Croatian People's Party (HNS). Although the 2003 elections reinstalled the HDZ as the dominant party in parliament under Prime Minister **Ivo Sanader,** Mesić was narrowly re-elected to the presidency in 2005.

CURRENT EVENTS. As it emerges from a period of widespread **unemployment** after the Balkan War and the 1999 Kosovo crisis that disrupted its tourist industry, Croatia has focused on improving its legal system, rebuilding infrastructure, and cultivating closer ties with the EU. Accession, which is expected by the end of the decade, may be facilitated by the 2005 capture of General **Ante Gotovina,** who now faces charges at the Hague for war crimes against ethnic Serbs. Despite these allegations, Gotovina is still viewed by many Croats as a national hero, and Prime Minister Sanader has recently pledged governmental financial support for all Croatian nationals on trial in the Hague.

PEOPLE AND CULTURE

DEMOGRAPHICS. An overwhelming 89.6% of Croatia's inhabitants are ethnic **Croats.** The country retains a significant **Serbian** minority (4.5%) despite an exodus at the end of the war in 1995. Tensions between Serbs and Croats still run high, but outbreaks of violence are now rare. Each community remains relatively closed to the other, and the Serbian population suffers from stigmatization and unemployment. Croatia's **Bosniak** minority (0.5%) also suffers discrimination, but to a much milder extent than the Serbian population. Nearly all of the ethnically Croat population is **Roman Catholic.** Serbs remaining in the country belong to the **Serbian Orthodox Church,** while the Bosniak minority practices **Islam.**

LANGUAGE. Croats speak **Croatian,** a South Slavic language written in the Latin alphabet. The language has fairly recently become differentiated from Serbo-Croatian. Only a few expressions differ from Serbian, but be careful not to use the Serbian ones in Croatia—you'll make few friends. **German** and **Italian** are common second languages among adults. Most Croatians under 30 speak some **English.** For a phrasebook and glossary, see **Appendix: Croatian,** p. 792.

CUSTOMS AND ETIQUETTE. If you wear **shorts** and **sandals,** you'll stick out as a tourist in the cities but will blend in along the coast. Though southern Croatia tends to be beach-oriented, remember that this land of skin and shorts is also devoutly Catholic. In cathedrals, wear long pants or skirts and closed-toed shoes. Croats have few qualms about **drinking** and **smoking,** but abstain in buses, trains, and other marked areas. Maintain eye contact when clinking glasses or face seven years of bad luck. **Tipping** is not expected, although it is appropriate to round up when paying; in some cases, the establishment will do it for you—check your change. Fancy restaurants often add a hefty service charge. **Bargaining** is reserved for informal transactions, such as hiring a boat for a day or renting a private room directly from an owner. Posted prices should usually be followed.

THE ARTS

LITERATURE. Croatian texts first emerged during the 9th century, but for the next 600 years, literature consisted almost entirely of translations from other European languages. Because Dubrovnik was the only independent part of Croatia after 1102, it produced literature that had a lasting impact on Croatian culture. But after the city's devastation by an earthquake in 1667, the nexus of Croatian literature shifted north. The 16th-century dramatist **Martin Držić** and the 17th-century poet **Ivan Gundulić** turned to Italy for literary models. During Austrian and Hungarian repressions of the Croatian language in the 19th century, **Ljudevit Gaj** led the movement to reform and codify the Croatian vernacular. **August Šenoa,** Croatia's dominant 19th-century literary figure, played a key part in the formation of a literary public. Croatian prose sparkled in the late 20th century. **Dubravka Ugrešić's** personal, reflective novels, which discuss nostalgia and the revision of history, have become instant bestsellers. The novelist **Slavenka Drakulić** is popular abroad.

MUSIC. Croatia has a vibrant music scene featuring folk and contemporary styles, as well as unique hybrids of the two, such as the **Turbo-Folk** genre, which gained popularity in the 1990s and drew controversy for its nationalistic and sexualized content. Pop singers like **Mišo Kovač** and rock groups like **Prljavo Kazalište** have enjoyed longstanding popularity. Current performers include Tony Cetinski in the pop genre, rapper Edo Maajka, and surf-rockers The Bambi Molesters.

THE VISUAL ARTS. Characterized by the rejection of conventional and "civilized" depictions, **native art** presides as the most popular painting style. This movement, begun by **Krsto Hegedušić** (1901-71), is highly influenced by folk traditions. It eliminates perspective and uses only vivid colors. Croatia's most famous modern sculptor and architect, **Ivan Meštrović,** has achieved fame outside Croatia. His wooden religious sculptures can be seen in London's Tate Gallery and New York City's Metropolitan Museum of Art, as well as in squares throughout his homeland. **Vinko Bresan** is Croatia's most prominent contemporary filmmaker.

HOLIDAYS AND FESTIVALS

Holidays: New Year's Day (Jan. 1); Epiphany (Jan. 6); Easter Sunday and Easter Monday (March 23-4, 2008; April 12-3, 2009); May Day (May 1); Anti-Fascist Struggle Day (June 22); National Thanksgiving Day (Aug. 5); Assumption (Aug. 15); Independence Day (Oct. 8); All Saints' Day (Nov. 5); Christmas (Dec. 25-26).

Festivals: In June, Zagreb holds the catch-all festival Cest Is D'Best ("The Streets are the Best"). An easygoing philosophy keeps revelers on city streets out all night (p. 110). Open-air concerts and theatrical performances make the Dubrovnik Summer Festival (*Dubrovački Ljetni;* from early July to late Aug.) the event of the summer in that city (p. 152). During the same period, a similar festival showcasing music and theater takes over Split. From July to Aug., Korčula (p. 144) unsheathes the Festival of Sword Dances *(Festival Viteških Igara)* with performances of the *Moreška, Moštra,* and *Kumpanija* sword dances all over the island. Zagreb's International Puppet Festival (late Aug. to early Sept.) draws children and adults alike.

ZAGREB ☎(0)1

Too often treated as little more than a stop-over en route to the Adriatic coast, Croatia's largest city nonetheless provides a perfect introduction to the country as a whole. In the Old City center, smartly-dressed Zagrebčani outnumber visitors as both enjoy the sights and smells of outdoor cafes, flower markets, and fresh fruit stands. With its welcoming, English-speaking inhabitants, growing economy, impressive cultural offerings, and unspoiled surroundings, Zagreb is an attractive blend of East and West.

INTERCITY TRANSPORTATION

Flights: Pleso (☎626 5222; www.zagreb-airport.hr), about 30min. from the city center. **Airport lost and found** ☎456 2229. **Information** ☎456 2222. Croatia Airlines runs

GETTING IN. When you first arrive in Zagreb, your best bet is to take cash out at an ATM in the airport as they have no commission and better rates than currency exchange kiosks. If you need to make international phone calls to let loved ones know you've arrived, call from the post office in the airport, as it offers better rates than phone cards and is very user-friendly—just call from the telephone booth and pay at the counter when you're done.

buses (☎633 1982; www.plesoprijevoz.hr) between the main bus station and the airport (daily every 30min. 5:30am-7:30pm, 30kn). **Taxis** to the city, which can be found behind the Croatia Airlines office, start their meters at a hefty 25kn and cost 150-250kn. **Croatia Airlines,** Zrinjevac 17 (toll-free ☎08 00 77 77, reservations 627 7777 or 487 2727; www.croatiaairlines.hr) offers flights to and from most cities in Europe. Flying to Zagreb from overseas might prove cheaper if connecting in London (going eastbound) or Vienna (going westbound) to a European budget airline, train, or bus. Domestic destinations include **Dubrovnik** (1hr., 3-7 per day), **Split** (45min., 4-7 per day), and **Zadar** (40min., M-F and Su 2-3 per day). Sometimes, the plane is cheaper than the bus. International flights to the Balkan region include **Sarajevo, BOS** and **Skopje, MAC.** Also inquire here to book flights on other airlines. Open M-F 8am-8pm, Sa 9am-noon.

Trains: Glavni Kolodvor (Main Station), Trg Kralja Tomislava 12 (☎060 333 444, international info 378 2583; www.hznet.hr). From the bus station, take tram #2, 6, or 8 to the 3rd stop ("Glavni Kolodvor"). Buses are generally considered better for domestic travel as they offer more flexibility in routes and departure times; trains, however, often provide cheaper rates, especially for the following destinations: **Ljubljana** (2hr.; 8 per day; 100kn, round-trip 130kn); **Rijeka** (4-6hr., 3 per day, 102kn); **Split** (6-9hr., 5 per day, 152kn); **Budapest, HUN** (7¼hr., 3 per day, 224kn); **Venice, ITA** (6hr., 1 per day, 320kn); **Vienna, AUT** (6½hr., 2 per day, 355kn); **Zürich, SWI** (14hr., 1 per day, 647kn). There are no trains to **Dubrovnik.** AmEx/MC/V.

Buses: For travel within Croatia, buses are often more efficient than trains. **Autobusni Kolodvor** (Bus Station), Držićeva bb (☎060 313 333, information and reservations from abroad 611 2789; www.akz.hr, click on "Vozni red"). Buy tickets on either side of the ticket area. Luggage storage in the **garderoba** up the staircase to the right of the main hall (1.20kn per hr). Restrooms (3kn) upstairs in the waiting lounge. To: **Dubrovnik** (11hr., 9 per day, 190-230kn); **Plitvice** (2½hr., 15 per day, 65-83kn); **Pula** (4½hr., 15 per day, 139-192kn); **Rijeka** (3½hr., 15 per day, 130kn); **Split** (7-9hr., 1 per hr., 155kn); **Varaždin** (1¾hr., 1 per hr., 66kn); **Frankfurt, GER** (15hr., 1 per day, 685kn); **Ljubljana, SLV** (2½hr., 1 per day, 100kn); **Vienna, AUT** (8hr., 2 per day, 250kn). Large backpacks 7kn extra.

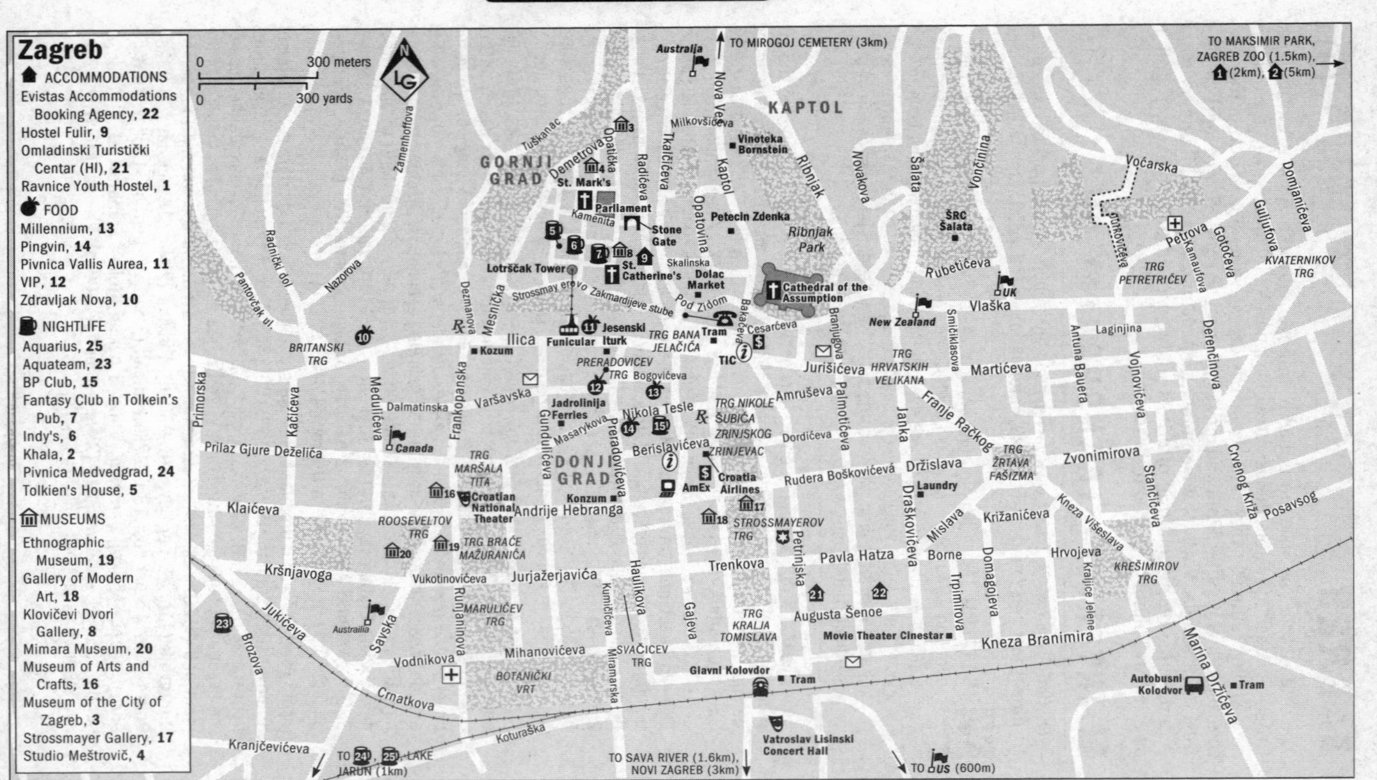
Zagreb
ACCOMMODATIONS
Evistas Accommodations Booking Agency, 22
Hostel Fulir, 9
Omladinski Turistički Centar (HI), 21
Ravnice Youth Hostel, 1
FOOD
Millennium, 13
Pingvin, 14
Pivnica Vallis Aurea, 11
VIP, 12
Zdravljak Nova, 10
NIGHTLIFE
Aquarius, 25
Aquateam, 23
BP Club, 15
Fantasy Club in Tolkein's Pub, 7
Indy's, 6
Khala, 2
Pivnica Medvedgrad, 24
Tolkien's House, 5
MUSEUMS
Ethnographic Museum, 19
Gallery of Modern Art, 18
Klovičevi Dvori Gallery, 8
Mimara Museum, 20
Museum of Arts and Crafts, 16
Museum of the City of Zagreb, 3
Strossmayer Gallery, 17
Studio Meštrovič, 4
300 meters
300 yards
TO MIROGOJ CEMETERY (3km)
TO MAKSIMIR PARK, ZAGREB ZOO (1.5km), 1 (2km), 2 (5km)
TO SAVA RIVER (1.6km), NOVI ZAGREB (3km)
TO US (600m)
TO 24, 25 LAKE JARUN (1km)
KAPTOL
GORNJI GRAD
DONJI GRAD
Cathedral of the Assumption
Ribnjak Park
TRG BANA JELAČIĆA
TIC
Dolac Market
Stone Gate
St. Mark's
Parliament
St. Catherine's
Lotrščak Tower
Funicular
Jesenski Iturk
Glavni Kolodvor
Autobusni Kolodvor
Vatroslav Lisinski Concert Hall
Croatian National Theater
Movie Theater Cinestar
Laundry
Croatia Airlines
AmEx
Jadrolinija Ferries
Konzum
Kozum
Petecin Zdenka
Vinoteka Bornstein
ŠRC Šalata
Australija
Canada
New Zealand
UK
Tram
Ilica
Vlaška
Jurišićeva
Martićeva
Savska
Marina Držićeva
Kneza Branimira
Zvonimirova
Franje Račkog
Petrinjska
Praška
Trenkova
Pavla Hatza
Augusta Šenoe
Andrije Hebranga
Klaićeva
Frankopanska
Medulićeva
Primorska

Ferries: Jadrolinija, Masarykova 24 (☎481 5216; www.jadrolinija.hr), in the Marko Polo Travel Agency. Reserves tickets for travel along the Dalmatian coast to **Dubrovnik, Rijeka, Split, Zadar,** and the islands, and to **Ancona** and **Bari, ITA.** Ferries are the best way to move along the coast. Open M-F 9am-5pm, Sa 9am-1pm.

ORIENTATION

Unlike the city's sprawling outskirts, the center of Zagreb, bounded by Mount Medvednica and the Sava River, is easily walkable. To the north, historic **Gornji Grad** (Upper Town) is composed of the **Kaptol** and **Gradec** hills, once warring towns and the focus of the city's historic sites and churches. The central **Donji Grad** (Lower Town), home to most museums, squares and parks, spreads south of these ancient sites before reaching the train station. Beyond the station lies the **Sava River,** which separates these neighborhoods from the modern residential area **Novi Zagreb** (New Zagreb). Both Gornji and Donji Grad are bustling centers of activity, but the winding streets of Gornji Grad, often open to pedestrians only, tend to be more peaceful. Most shopping is located around the city's central square, **Trg bana Josipa Jelačića,** and on **Ilica,** the commercial artery that runs westward through the square. With your back to the bus station, walk left up Avenija Marina Držića and turn left on Branimirova. Follow the parks opposite the train station into the city center or catch tram #6 towards Črnomerac, which goes to the main square.

LOCAL TRANSPORTATION

Trams: The **Zagreb Electric Tram** is the best way to cruise around town (☎365 1555; www.zet.hr). Organized by number (1-17), trams are often sweltering in the summer and packed year-round, but cover the entire city. Buy tickets at any newsstand (6.50kn) or from the driver (8kn). Day pass 18kn. Punch them in boxes near the doors—an unpunched ticket is as good as no ticket. Fine for riding ticketless is 150kn. Night trams are not reliable, although supposedly run every 30min. 11:45pm-4am; tickets cost 20% more. Get a tram route map at the TIC (see **Tourist and Financial Services,** p. 105).

Buses: Ozaljska 105 (☎660 0446). Beyond the city center, buses pick up where the trams stop. All the same rules and fares apply as for trams.

Taxis: (☎660 0671; www.radio-taksi-zagreb.hr). On Gajeva south of Teslina, at the corner of Trg Jelačića and Bakačeva, and in front of major hotels and the bus and train stations. Cabs are common at night. 25kn base, 7kn per km, luggage 5kn; waiting charge 80kn; prices rise 20% 10pm-5am, Su, and holidays.

PRACTICAL INFORMATION

TOURIST AND FINANCIAL SERVICES

Tourist Office: Tourist Information Center (TIC), Trg Jelačića 11 (☎481 4051; www.zagreb-touristinfo.hr). The friendly, resourceful staff will supply you with **free maps** and pamphlets. Ask for the invaluable and free *Zagreb Info A-Z* and *Zagreb in Your Pocket* pamphlets for updated listings. Also request the free publication *Events and Performances,* a monthly list of cultural offerings. You can also buy a **Zagreb Card** (☎481 4052; www.zagrebcard.fivestars.hr; 60kn for 24hr., 90kn for 72hr.), which covers all bus and tram rides and gives discounts in restaurants and museums. Open in high season M-F 8:30am-9pm, Su 9am-5pm; in low season M-F 8:30am-8pm.

Embassies and Consulates: Australia, Centar Kaptol, Nova Ves 11, 3rd fl. (☎489 1200, emergency 098 414 729; www.auembassy.hr). Open M-F 9:30-11am. **Canada,** Prilaz Gjure Deželića 4 (☎488 1200; www.international.gc.ca/canada-europa/croatia). Open M-F 10am-noon, 1-3pm. **New Zealand,** Vlaška 50a (☎461 2060). Open M-F 11am-2pm. **UK,** Lučića 4 (☎600 9100; www.britishembassy.gov.uk/croatia). Open M-Th 8:30am-5pm, F 8:30am-2pm. **US,** Thomas Jefferson 2 (☎661 2200; www.usembassy.hr). Open M-F 8am-4:30pm.

Currency Exchange: You'll get better rates by going directly to ATMs, and you won't have to pay the standard 1.5% commission fee. *Mjenjačnica* (exchange counters) and **Zagrebačka Banka** are everywhere. The main branch is at Trg Jelačića 10 (☎610 4000; www.zaba.hr) and cashes **traveler's checks** for a 1.5% commission. Open M-F 7:30am-7pm, Sa 7:30am-noon. **ATMs** *(bankomat)* are at the bus and train stations and all over the city center. Locals usually pay cash for everything.

LOCAL SERVICES

Luggage Storage: At the train station. 10kn per day. At the bus station, 2nd fl. 1.20kn per hr., 2.30kn for bags over 15kg. Both open 24hr.

English-Language Bookstore: Algoritam, Gajeva 1 (☎481 8672; www.algoritam.hr), next to Hotel Dubrovnik. Carries international newspapers, magazines, and music on the ground floor. The basement has Croatian phrasebooks, English fiction, and travel guides. Open M-F 8:30am-9pm, Sa 8:30am-3pm. AmEx/MC/V.

Photography Services: Foto Plus, Praška 2 (☎481 8420), right off the main square. Print photographs from a digital camera for 2kn per picture. Copy your memory card to a CD for 10kn. Open M-F 8am-7pm, Sa-Su 8am-4pm. AmEx/MC/V.

Laundromat: Predom, Draškovićeva 31 (☎461 2990). No English spoken. 2-day service 2-30kn per item; next-day 50% more. Open M-F 7am-7pm, Sa 8am-noon. Cheaper rates can be found at **Self Service Laundry Lahor,** Stupnička 16 or Horvaćanska c. 27 (☎606 1483). Open M-F 8am-10pm.

CROATIA

EMERGENCY AND COMMUNICATIONS

Police: Department for Foreign Visitors, Petrinjska 30 (☎456 3127, after hours 456 3311), room #103 on the 2nd fl. of the central police station. If you are not staying in a hotel or hostel, you will need to **officially register** your arrival with the police within 24hr. of your arrival, although this is sometimes not enforced. Bring your passport and use form #14. Open M-F 8am-4pm.

Pharmacy: 24hr. pharmacy at Trg Jelačića 3 (☎48 6198) and Ilica 301 (☎375 0321). AmEx/D/MC. Two centrally located *ljekarnas* (pharmacies) are on the corners of Petrinjska and Boškovićeva, and Teslina and Masarykova.

Medical Services: Hospital REBRO, Kišpatićeva 12 (☎238 8888). Open 24hr.

Telephones: Be aware that payphones take only prepaid cards, not coins. Buy a **phone card** (*telekarta,* 15-100kn; Voicecom has good rates on international calls) from any news kiosk, or call from at the **post office** and pay afterward (6kn per min.).

WHERE IT'S @. Can't find that all-important @ key on any keyboard in Croatia? Never fear–it's Ctrl-Alt-V.

Internet: The *Zagreb Info A-Z* pamphlet lists several Internet cafes. **Ch@rlie's,** Gajeva 4a (☎488 0233), through the courtyard and on the right, has great connections, printing, and scanning. English spoken. Also offers coffees and drinks. 16kn per hr. Open M-Sa 8am-10pm, Su 11am-9pm.

Post Office: Post offices are widespread. Look for the yellow "Poste" sign. Next to the train station is Branimirova 4 (☎498 1300). From Branimirova, turn left up the stairs. **Poste Restante** on 2nd fl. at desk #3. Desk #1 **exchanges currency** and cashes **traveler's checks** for a 1.5% commission. Open 24hr. The Central Post Office is at Jurišićeva 4 (☎481 1090). Open M-F 7am-9pm, Sa 7:30am-2pm. General info on the Croatian postal service: www.posta.hr. **Postal Code:** 10000.

ACCOMMODATIONS

Cheap accommodations are scarce in Zagreb, and budget travelers are becoming more common. When hostels are full, try a **private room** *(sobe)* through **Evistas,** Augusta Šenoe #28; buzz for entry. This friendly travel agency can register you and reserve beds in private rooms or hotels, even at the height of festival season. (☎483 9554; www.travel-tourist.com/obj2496_hr.htm. Open M-F 9am-1:30pm and 3-8pm, Sa 9:30am-5pm. Singles 185-230kn; doubles 264-314kn; triples 345kn; apartments 390-750kn. Min. 2-day stay for apartments. 20% more for 1 night only; 30% more during festivals; under 26 10% off. Tax 7kn.)

Ravnice Youth Hostel, 1. Ravnice 38d (☎233 2325; www.ravnice-youth-hostel.hr). Tram #11 or 12 from Trg Jelačića, #4 from the train station, or #7 from the bus station to Dubrava or Dubec. The unmarked Ravnice stop is 2 stops past football stadium "Dinamo"; look for a white sign marked "hostel." Rooms in this friendly, family-run hostel are clean, with brightly colored tie-dyed curtains and hardwood floors. English spoken. Laundry 40kn. Internet 16kn per hr. Bike rental 8kn per hr., 60kn per day. Reception daily 9am-10pm. Check-out noon. Dorms 125kn. Cash only. ❶

Omladinski Turistički Centar (HI), Petrinjska 77 (☎484 1261; www.hfhs.hr). With your back to the train station, walk right on Branimirova; Petrinjska will be on your left. Omladinski is one of the cheapest sleeping options in Zagreb. The location, a short stroll from the train station, is phenomenal. Free luggage storage. Free Internet 6am-10pm. Reception 24hr. Check-in 2pm-1am. Check-out 9am. 6-bed dorms 83kn; singles 158kn, with bath 218kn; doubles 211/286kn. ❶

Hostel Fulir, Radiceva 3a (☎483 0882; www.fulir-hostel.com). The name says it all for Fulir, Croatian slang for "pimp." This hostel, in a neighborhood packed with bars, is perfect for partygoers. The owners have been known to take their guests on explorations of Zagreb's vibrant nightlife. Kitchen access. Free Internet. Dorms 145kn. MC/V. ❶

FOOD

Zagrebčani adore meat, and restaurant menus reflect their carnivorous tastes, offering local specialities like *čevapčići* (beef or pork meatballs with distinctive Croatian spices) and the ubiquitous *prsut* (smoked ham). For cheap eats, try a *pekarna* (bakery) or a fresh fruit market; stalls selling *burek*, a heavy meat- or cheese-filled pastry, also line the streets. The largest open-air market, **Dolac,** is behind Trg Jelačića in Gornji Grad, along Pod Zidom. (Open M-Sa 6am-3pm, Su 6am-1pm.) There is a **Konzum** grocery store at the corner of Preradovićeva and Hebrangova. (Open M-F 7am-8pm, Sa 7am-3pm. AmEx/MC/V.)

VIP, Preradovicev Trg 5 (☎152 8696), on the western side of the square. Look for the "KinoZagreb" sign and the red umbrellas. This modern restaurant offers tasty, inexpensive Italian fare alongside great people-watching in the middle of the flower market. Sandwiches 15kn. Pizza 25-32kn. Pasta and lasagna 25-40kn. Internet 15kn per hr. ❶

Millennium, Bogovićeva 7 (☎481 0850), between Trg. b Jelaića and Trg. Preradovicev. This stylish ice-cream place offers *sladoled* (ice cream) whipped into artful clouds of sugary bliss that taste as good as they look. Despite a fancy, white-leather interior and gourmet flavors, a scoop is only 5kn. Open daily 9am-11pm. Cash only. ❶

Pingvin (Penguin), Teslina 7. Right next to BP Club, this courtyard sandwich shop is a local favorite. Grilled sandwich and drink combos (16-23kn) come served in a wicker basket, or to go. Open M-Sa 24hr., Su 5am-noon. Cash only. ❶

Pivnica Vallis Aurea (Golden Valley), Tomičeva 4 (☎483 1305). From the bottom of the funicular, walk down the hill toward Ilica; the restaurant is on the left. This local favorite offers large portions of traditional Croatian meat dishes with a hint of Hungarian spices. Paintings of a past Zagreb adorn the bare brick walls. English menu. Entrees 30-65kn. Open M-Sa 9am-11pm. AmEx/MC/V. ❷

SIGHTS

The best way to explore Zagreb is by foot. A short walk up any of the streets behind Trg Jelačića, the main city square, leads to the compact cobblestone Upper Town. To explore the more commercial Lower Town, start at Trg Jelačića and head south along Gajeva, a thrumming center of sidewalk cafes, with street performances in the summer. Strolling down Masarykova will bring you to the monumental Croatian National Theater, adorned with sculptures by the renowned Ivan Meštrovič. Farther south, peaceful parks and stately buildings mark the museum center, which leads to the Botanic Gardens. If all that walking tires you out, hop on the **funicular,** an entertaining but peculiarly inefficient way of getting up the short hill. Walk down Ilica from Trg Jelačića; the funicular is on the right. (Open daily 6:30am-9pm. 3kn, with Zagreb Card free.) The free and informative *Zagreb: City Walks*, available at the TIC, has additional sightseeing routes.

CATHEDRAL OF THE ASSUMPTION (KATEDRALA MARIJINA UZNESENJA). Known simply as "the Cathedral," this church has graced Zagreb since the late 11th century. There seems to be no end in sight for the additions and renovations that began centuries ago following sieges by the Tatars; the iconic neo-Gothic bell towers were added in 1902. The gilded interior is decked out in a range of deep colors with ornate mosaic-trimmed pillars and gold candelabras. *(Kaptol 1. Open daily 10am-5pm. Services M-Sa 7, 8, 9am; Su 7, 8, 9, 10, 11:30am. Free.)*

CROATIA

ST. MARK'S CHURCH (CRKVA SV. MARKA). The red-and-white checkered tiles on St. Mark's roof, which might help orient those lost in Gornji Grad, surround the colorful coat of arms of Croatia, Dalmatia, and Slavonia on the left side and that of Zagreb on the right. The entrance to the church is on the left (west) side, which leads you to an interior with gold ceilings and dark, newly restored frescoes. Meštrovič sculptures join their Gothic counterparts in this elegant building. A series of natural disasters has meant that little remains of the original 14th-century church. *(From the top of the funicular, turn right and then left onto Cirilometodska; the church is straight ahead. Enter to the left. Open daily 7am-1:30pm and 5:30-7pm. Free.)*

LOTRŠČAK TOWER (KULA LOTRŠČAK). Part of the original city wall, this 13th-century white tower offers a great panoramic view of Zagreb. Originally built as a fortification, the tower transformed when the danger of Turk attacks subsided, becoming a fireman's surveillance lookout, a city alarm tower, a warehouse, and a wine cellar. The cannon near the top of the tower has been fired at noon every day since 1877. *(At the corner of Strossmayerovo and Dverce, at the top of the funicular. Open May-Sept. daily 11am-8pm. 10kn, students 5kn.)*

ST. CATHERINE'S CHURCH (CRKVA SV. KATRINSKI). Built by the Jesuits between 1620 and 1632, St. Catherine's simple white exterior does nothing to prepare you for the elaborate Baroque interior. Decorated with gifts from Croatian nobles and designed by Italian master Anton Joseph Quadrio, the pink interior, covered in intricate white swirls and curlicues, contrasts with the six black-and-gold shrines lining the sides. *(Katarinin trg bb. From the top of the funicular, the 1st church on your right. Open M-F and Su 7am-11pm, Sa 7am-6:30pm. Services M-F 6pm, Sa 6:30pm, Su 11am. Free.)*

MIROGOJ CEMETERY. Cypress trees, wide avenues, and endless rows of elaborate gravestones comprise this serene park, whose majestic entrance is framed by 12 cream-colored and lime green towers. The cemetery, which is still in use, is the resting ground for an array of notable Croatians: mafiosos, writers, the first president of Croatia, and even one of the stars of Croatia's soccer team Dinamo, who was buried in 2004. A walk in this park is well worth the time, but be respectful—you will find many Croats mourning and honoring their loved ones. *(Take the #106 "Mirogoj" bus from Kaptol in front of the cathedral; 8min., every 15min. Open M-F 6am-8pm, Su 7:30am-6pm. Free. No cameras.)*

RIBNJAK PARK. Spacious, tree-covered Ribnjak Park offers the chance for a peaceful walk without leaving the city. *(Behind the Cathedral. From Trg Jelačića, turn down Jurišićeva, then right on Palmotićeva. The entrance is on the left.)*

MAKSIMIR PARK AND THE ZAGREB ZOO. Covered in meadows, lakes, and tall oaks, the 18 hectares of Maksimir Park make it one of the largest parks in southeast Europe—so big, in fact, that hundreds of animals reside comfortably in the **Zagreb Zoo** within the park's borders. If the seal or piranha shows, rhinos, elephants, hippos, birds, and pumas aren't your thing, take a stroll or a bike ride on the shaded paths between the huge trees, and pass by the white swans in the willow-lined lake. *(From Trg Jelačića, take tram #11 or 12 to Dubrava or Dubec. Get off across the street from the stadium. Continue walking down the road; the park entrance is on the left. Park open daily sunrise to sunset. Free. ☎230 2199; www.zoo.hr. Zoo open daily 9am-8pm; ticket office closes 5pm. 20kn, under seven 10kn. M is family day, all 10kn.)*

STONE GATE (KAMENITA VRATA). Once one of the four gateways into the city, the Stone Gate was reconstructed in 1731 after a fire burnt everything save a wooden figure of Madonna. It now houses an altar to the Virgin Mary and wooden pews. This open-air place of worship stuns with its many candles lighting the shadows of the fortress walls. *(Kamenita bb, east down Kamenita from St Mark's.)*

MUSEUMS

While you may not find many famous masterpieces in Zagreb, exceptional collections and exhibits will still occupy art-lovers for days, particularly as Zagreb is home to the New Tendencies art style. For listings of events, consult the monthly *Zagreb: Events and Performances*, free at the TIC (see **Tourist and Financial Services**, p. 105). Trams #12, 13, 14, and 17 reach the Museum of Arts and Crafts, the Mimara, and the Ethnographic Museum.

ETHNOGRAPHIC MUSEUM (ETHNOGRAFSKI MUZEJ). Displaying artifacts from Croatian voyages to Africa, Asia, and South America in the 19th and 20th centuries, this museum also offers a look at Croatia's traditional culture, with rotating exhibits focusing on diverse regions of the country. It includes an eclectic mix of traditional costumes and etchings of local architecture. *(Mažuranicev trg 14, across the street from the Mimara. ☎482 6220; www.etnografski-muzej.hr. Open Tu-Th 10am-6pm, F-Su 10am-1pm. English captions. 15kn, students and over 60 10kn; Th free. Cash only.)*

STUDIO MEŠTROVIČ. This was the former home and studio of the most celebrated Croatian sculptor, Ivan Meštrovič, who was responsible for many of the buildings and statues in Zagreb, including the reliefs in St. Mark's and the statues in front of the Art Pavilion, Strossmayer trg, and the National Theater. His work has been recognized worldwide, and he was the first Croatian artist given a one-man exhibition at the Metropolitan Museum in New York City. While his figures, with their contorted bodies and evocative expressions, are themselves arresting, the three floors and garden housing his work are not without their own surprises, such as a series of American Indian works. *(Mletačka 8, just behind St. Mark's Church. ☎485 1123. Open Tu-F 10am-6pm, Sa-Su 10am-2pm. 20 kn, students 10kn. Cash only.)*

KLOVIČEVI DVORI GALLERY (GALERIJA KLOVICEVI DVORI). Behind the wooden front doors of this former 17th-century monastery is housed the most impressive collection of modern art in Zagreb. Check the listings to find out what is being displayed during your visit, but no matter what it is, with four ample floors, there is sure to be plenty to stimulate both political and aesthetic interests. After visiting the gallery, enjoy a coffee (7kn) in the elegant courtyard. *(Jesuitski trg 4, to the left of St. Catherine's. ☎485 1926. Open Tu-Su 11am-7pm. 20kn, students 10kn. Cash only.)*

MUSEUM OF ARTS AND CRAFTS (MUZEJ ZA UMJETNOST I OBRT). Featuring delicate porcelain teacups and saucers, intricate woodwork, tapestries, wrought-iron pieces, and graphic art, exhibits offer visitors a glimpse into the opulent lives of the Croatian aristocracy. *(Trg Maršala Tita 10. ☎488 2111; www.muo.hr. Open M 1-7pm; Tu, W, and F-Su 10am-7pm; Th 10am-10pm. 20kn, students 10kn. Cash only.)*

GALLERY OF MODERN ART (MODERNA GALERIJA). This attractive gallery features rotating exhibitions of Croatia's best artists. With a collection of 9500 paintings, sculptures, watercolors, drawings, and prints, as well as a new permanent collection of Croatian modern art spanning the past 200 years, this gallery is a great way to explore the country's budding modern art scene. *(Hebrangova 1, across from the Strossmayer Gallery. ☎492 2368. Open Tu-F 10am-6pm, Sa-Su 10am-1pm. Prices vary by exhibition. Cash only.)*

MIMARA MUSEUM (MUZEJ MIMARA). A former grammar school, this monumental museum features a collection ranging from prehistoric Egyptian art to a handful of lesser-known works by famed European masters, including Raphael, Velasquez, Renoir, Manet, Rubens, and Rembrandt. *(Rooseveltov trg 5. ☎482 8100. Open Tu-W and F-Sa 10am-5pm, Th 10am-7pm, Su 10am-2pm. 40kn, students 30kn. Cash only.)*

STROSSMAYER GALLERY (STROSSMAYER GALERIJA STARIH MAJSTORA). Founded by Bishop Josip Juraj Strossmayer in 1884, the permanent collection includes paintings from the Flemish, Dutch, French, and Italian schools from the Renaissance through Baroque periods, featuring in particular Bruegel and Carpeaux. *(Zrinjskog trg 11. Go up 2 flights in the beautiful Croatian Academy of Arts and Sciences. ☎489 5111 or 489 5115; www.mdc.hr/strossmayer. Open Tu 10am-1pm and 5-7pm, W-Su 10am-1pm. 10kn, students 5kn. Cash only.)*

MUSEUM OF THE CITY OF ZAGREB (MUZEJ GRADA ZAGREBA). An interactive museum, complete with theme music and multilingual captions, traces the city's— and the nation's—history and culture from pre-Roman times to the present. *(Opaticka 20. ☎485 1361; www.mdc.hr/mgz. Open T-W, F 10am-6pm, Th 10am-10pm, Sa-Su 10am-2pm. 20kn, students 10kn.)*

ENTERTAINMENT AND FESTIVALS

With its fifteen theaters, numerous music stages, and varied open-air festivals, Zagreb makes a strong claim to being the cultural center of Croatia. The latest schedules can be found in the monthly *Zagreb: Events and Performances*, free at the TIC. **Vatroslav Lisinski Concert Hall**, Trg Stjepana Radića 4, two blocks behind the train station, is home to the Zagreb Philharmonic and visiting orchestras and artists. (☎612 1166; www.lisinski.hr. Box office open M-F 9am-8pm, Sa 9am-2pm. Tickets 50-100kn for local performers, 100-300kn for foreign performers. Student discounts available.) The **Croatian National Theater** (Hrvatsko Narodno Kazalište), Trg Maršala Tita 15 (☎482 8532; www.hnk.hr), produces dramas, ballets, and operas. From April to October, the **Arts Pavilion** in Zrinjevac Park holds weekly Promenade Concerts and varied performances from tango to jazz. The largest and most popular cinemas are **Cinestar**, Branimirova 29 (☎468

6600; www.blitz-cinestar.hr), in the Branimirova Shopping Center, and **Broadway 5,** Nova Ves 11 (☎466 7686; www.broadway-kina.com), in the Centar Kaptol.

At **Jarun Lake,** "Theater on the Water" plays throughout the summer. In the beginning of June, the streets burst with performances for the annual Zagreb street festival **Cest is d'Best** ("The Streets are the Best") and the **Eurokaz Avant-Garde Theaters Festival.** The **Sports and Recreation Center** hosts **Jarunfest,** a series of musical theater, ensemble, and operetta performances in late June and early July. In mid- to late July, Zagreb holds the **International Folklore Festival,** the premier gathering of European folk dancers and singing groups. Each year kicks off with a **blues festival** in January. The huge **International Puppet Festival** occurs in early September, and late October sees Zagreb's **International Jazz Days.** Every year, mid-December is filled with the colorful **Christmas Fair.** For up-to-date, detailed info and schedules, check out www.zagreb-touristinfo.hr.

NIGHTLIFE

The colorful and lively outdoor **cafes** lining **Tkalčićeva,** in Gornji Grad, attract young people from all over the city; most are indistinguishable from each other but pleasant. Many **discos** are open all week, except in the beginning of August, when the entire city goes on holiday. The best nightlife is at **Lake Jarun,** which is a bit difficult to reach but worth the trip.

Aquarius, Aleja Mira bb (☎364 0231; www.aquarius.hr), on Lake Jarun. Take tram #17 from the center and get off on Srednjaci, the 3rd stop after Studenski dom "S. Radić." At the church, cross the street; it's the last building on the boardwalk (15min.). This popular lakeside cafe and nightclub is worth the trek. Boogie inside or out to house and techno beats, or take a late-night dip in the lake. Drinks 15-45kn. Cover 30kn. Cafe open daily 9am-9pm; club Tu-Su 10pm-4am. Cash only.

Khala, Nova Ves 17 (☎486 0647), up the street from the cathedral in the Kaptol Center/ Broadway 5 movie complex. Handmade paper menus and low tables give Khala a hip, intellectual vibe. Drinks from 14kn. Open M-Th 8am-1am, F-Su 8am-4am. Cash only.

Pivnica Medvedgrad, Savska 56 (☎617 7119). Tram #13, 14, or 17 from Trg Jelačića to the corner of Avenija Vukovar and Savska. A local favorite, with the cheapest beer in town. This microbrewery's homemade beer (18kn per 1L) attracts all types. Try the whole-grain bread and *čevapčici* (small sausages served with raw onion; 22kn), or snack on *perec* (soft pretzels; 2kn). Open M-Sa 10am-midnight, Su noon-midnight.

BP Club, Teslina 7 (☎481 4444; www.bpclub.hr), on the right side of the courtyard, down the yellow stairs. The classic Zagreb venue for jazz, blues, and trance. Live music Sept.-Apr. Open daily 10pm-2am.

Tolkien's House, Vsanicanijeva 8, next door to Indy's. Indulge your questionable hobbit fetish at this quirky Irish pub, festooned with memorabilia from J.R.R. Tolkien's books. Even if you aren't part of the Fellowship of the Ring, you'll still enjoy the Irish music and Guinness (27kn). Drinks 13-32kn. Open M-Sa 9am-11pm, Su 10am-11pm.

Fantasy Club in Tolkien's Pub, Katarinin trg 3. A sister establishment to **Tolkien's House,** Fantasy Club is down the street. Budweiser special: the more you drink, the cheaper it gets. Open M-Sa 8am-midnight.

Indy's, Vranicanijeva 6 (☎485 2053). From St. Mark's, go down Cirilometodska and right on Vranicanijeva. Enjoy a creatively named Martian Sex Monster (30kn) or a Test Tube Baby (20kn) in the private, salmon-colored interior. Open daily 9am-11pm.

Aquateam, Brozova 8a (☎533 7757; www.gay.hr). This cross between a bar and a Finnish sauna caters in particular to GLBT travelers. Open daily 3-11pm.

DAYTRIPS FROM ZAGREB

On the crests of Zagreb's surrounding hilltops are the 56 mysterious **castles** of Hrvatsko Zagorje (the region north of Zagreb), formerly owned and constructed by warring Croatian nobles. Most now lie in various states of disrepair. Trakoščan is in the best shape and is the most popular. Consult *Zagreb and Surroundings*, available at the TIC in Zagreb (see **Tourist and Financial Services,** p. 105).

TRAKOŠČAN

From the Zagreb bus station, take a bus to Varaždin (1¾hr., 20 per day, 68kn), and change to a local bus (1¾hr., 1 per hr., 35kn). Leave early in order to make the connection. The last bus back from Trakoščan to Varaždin leaves M-F around 9pm, Sa-Su around 5pm. ☎42 79 62 81; www.trakoscan.hr. Open daily Apr.-Oct. 9am-6pm; Nov.-Mar. 9am-4pm. 20kn, students 10kn. English booklet 20kn.

The white walls of Trakoščan rise high above the surrounding forests and rolling hills. Built as a defense tower in the 13th century, it passed in 1584 to the Drašković nobility, who enlarged and refurbished it, retaining the castle until WWII. Today, stately family portraits, elaborate tapestries, Rococo furniture, mounted antlers, and collections of firearms and armor from the 15th to 19th centuries are on display in the preserved interior. The castle evokes a fairytale world: knights' armor is mixed in with the surreal paintings of Julijana Erdödy, the first woman in Croatia to achieve the title of academic painter. Leave time to wander around the quiet lake and hike through the oak and hornbeam hills. The restaurant at the bottom of the hill is expensive, so bring a sandwich.

PLITVICE LAKES NATIONAL PARK

Buses run from Zagreb (2½hr., 1 per hr., 70kn) and Zadar (2½hr., 6-7 per day, 72kn). Ask the bus driver to let you off at one of the park entrances. Be aware when you return that full buses may not pick you up, so weekends might not be the best time to visit the Park. Also note that bus times are highly irregular and may not correspond to the official schedule. Tourist centers at each of the 3 park entrances sell tickets and offer maps and a guide. Most buses stop near tourist center #2. To get to the tourist center, walk toward the pedestrian overpass. Head up the stairs and follow the path on the left downhill. Tourist office in Zagreb ☎461 3586, reservation office 75 10 14; www.np-plitvicka-jezera.hr. Park open daily 8am-7pm. Apr.-Oct. 110kn, students 55kn; Nov.-Mar. 70/40kn. Tour guide 700kn, 4hr. minimum. MC/V.

Plitvice Lakes National Park lies in the Krajina region, where Croatia's bloody war for independence began. Throughout the conflict (1991-95), the Serbians holding the area planted **landmines** in the ground. There are still landmines in the surrounding area. Under no circumstances should you leave the road or the marked paths. It's worth visiting the natural wonder of the Plitvice lakes; just be cautious about where you walk.

Though a bit of a trip from either Zagreb or Zadar, Plitvice Lakes National Park (Nacionalni Park Plitcicka Jezera) is worth the transportation hassle. Some 30,000 hectares of forested hills, dotted with 16 electric blue lakes and hundreds of waterfalls, make this pocket of paradise one of Croatia's most spectacular sights. Plitvice was added to the UNESCO World Heritage list in 1979 for the unique evolution of its lakes and waterfalls, which formed through the interaction of water and petrified vegetation. A system of wooden pathways hovers just above the iridescent blue surface of the lakes and winds around the many waterfalls.

Two bus routes (every 20min.) help you get around the park, while a boat runs on the largest of the lakes (every 30min.). Though most tourists circulate around the four lower lakes (Donja Jezera) to snap pictures of Plitvice's famous 78m waterfall, **Veliki Slap** (trail F, 2-3hr.), the true adventurer explores the hidden falls of the 12 upper lakes, **Gornja Jezera** (4hr.). If you find yourself awestruck by the beauty and can't bring yourself to leave, the private accommodation service across from tourist center #2 will find you a room. (Open daily noon-9pm. Singles 150kn; doubles 220-300kn.)

VARAŽDIN

The bus and train stations are only 1km apart. Both stations exchange money and sell local and international tickets. Open M-Sa 8am-8:30pm, Su 1-8:30pm. From the train station, walk straight along Kolodvorska, which becomes Augusta Cesarca. Passing the Patačić-Puttar Palace, go left up Janko Draskovića, then onto Gundulića, the main commercial street that leads to the town's main square, Kralja Tomislava. Along Pavlinska is the impressive County Hall as well as the Rococo Patačić Palace and the main churches. The monumental Romanesque-Gothic town hall lies farther up, just beyond the square.

Situated at the crossroads between Central Europe and the Adriatic, the former Croatian capital of Varaždin (pop. 43,000) is an architectural beauty filled with numerous artists' workshops. The **Miljenko Stančić Collection** is possibly the town's most original and exciting exhibition, a phenomenal collection of work from this icon of the Croatian art scene, whose dreamily introspective paintings explore his memories of childhood and experience of the city he called "my model and my scale." (☎52 42 31 13 12. Open Tu-Su 10am-1pm and 5-8pm.)

The architectural distinctiveness of the town's Gothic 13th-century fortress outshines the **City Museum,** Strossmera 7, that it houses. Eight furnished rooms complement the displays on the history of the city's guilds and prominent citizens. (☎05 24 26 58 755; www.mdc.hr/varazdin. Open Apr.-Sept. Tu-Su 10am-6pm; Oct.-Mar. Tu-F 10am-5pm, Sa-Su 10am-1pm. 20kn, students 12kn.) The unusual and elaborate **Entomological Collection,** Franjevački Trg 6, displays thousands of insect species. The rare stag beetle and Great Speckled Blue butterfly are only two of the many highlights. (☎052 210 474. Open mid-May to mid-Sept. Tu-F 10am-3pm, Sa-Su 10am-1pm. 20kn, students 12kn.) The impressive Baroque **Cathedral,** Pavlinska 5 (☎052 210 688), was built in the 17th century as a Jesuit church. Perhaps even more beautiful is the **Franciscan Church of St. John the Baptist,** Franjevački Trg 4, whose 18th-century frescoes are stunning amidst the Gothic architecture.

Over 200,000 tourists descend on the town at the end of August for the vibrant festival of **Špancirfest** (www.spancirfest.com), which hosts international musicians, actors and entertainers. The city is also home to the well-known **Baroque Evenings** in September and October. Within its opulent churches and architecturally rich Old Town, both Croatian and international orchestras and ensembles play classical pieces. For more information, contact the **Concert Office.** (☎052 212 907; www.koncertni-ured.hr. Tickets 10-100kn.) In May, the town hosts the **International Festival of Traditional Jazz.** During the summer don't miss the displays of traditional skills at the Saturday **Trades and Crafts** fairs.

The coats of arms of leading Varaždin families hang on the walls beside old swords and flags at **Zlatna Guska ❷,** Habdelića 4, a knight's stone dining hall. The restaurant serves up medieval meals with names like "Daggers of the Count of Bandenbury." Vegetarian options are available. (☎052 213 393. Entrees 38-70kn.) For a more relaxed meal, try **Park ❶,** Habdelić 6, which specializes in dishes on the spit, and appropriately enough, overlooks a park. (☎052 211 499. Entrees 25-55kn. Open 8am-11pm.) The affordable, cafeteria-style **Raj Club ❶,** Gundulića 11, draws locals with traditional dishes like goulash for 15-25kn. (Open M-Sa 9am-11pm.)

The **tourist office,** Ivana Padovca 3, provides free maps and helpful info. (☎052 210 987; www.tourism-varazdin.hr. Open daily Mar.-Sept. 8am-6pm; Oct.-Feb. 8am-4pm.) **Zagrebaćka Banka,** Kapucinski Trg 5, is across from the bus station. There are also **ATMs** in town. **Internet** access is available at **Caffe Bar Aquamarin,** Gajeva 1, a funky wooden cafe. (☎31 18 68. 7.50kn per 30min. Open M-Th 7am-midnight, F 7am-1am, Sa 7am-2pm, Su 9am-midnight.) The **post office** is at Trg Sloboda 9. (Open M-Sa 7am-9pm, Su 9am-noon.) **Postal Code:** 42000.

ISTRIA

The Istrian Peninsula lies on the northern part of the Adriatic Coast, where the Mediterranean laps at the feet of the Alps. Thanks to the influence of its larger neighbor, the region has a strong Italian flavor. Today the mosaics of Poreč, the ruins of Roman Pula, the unspoiled architecture of 19th-century Rovinj, and the clear waters of the Adriatic give Istria an air of pristine beauty.

PULA ☎(0)52

At the threshold of Pula's old center, a billboard welcomes visitors to Croatia's "3000-year-old town." Pula's Roman amphitheater, an entertainment stage since ancient times, has featured everything from gladiatorial combat to rock concerts. Despite the crowds of tourists, Pula (pop. 65,000) remains a laid-back destination where travelers can relax on the rocky coast, mingle in outdoor cafes, and take in the vibrant local culture.

TRANSPORTATION

Trains: Kolodvorska 5 (☎54 17 83). Ticket window open daily 8:10am-3:40pm. To: **Rijeka** (2½hr., 3 per day, 53kn); **Zagreb** (7hr., 3 per day, 148kn); and **Ljubljana, SLV** (7½hr., 2 per day, 127kn).

Buses: Trg Istarske Brigade bb (☎50 29 97), off Ulica 43 Istarske Divizije. Ticket office open M-Sa 4:30am-8:30pm; tickets can also be purchased on board. To: **Dubrovnik** (15hr., 1 per day, 477kn); **Poreč** (1½hr., 8-14 per day, 43kn); **Rijeka** (2½hr., 14-21 per day, 78kn); **Rovinj** (1hr., 12-23 per day, 29kn); **Šibenik** (9hr., 1 per day, 273kn); **Split** (10hr., 1 per day, 331kn); **Zagreb** (5-6hr., 15 per day, 148kn); **Koper, SLV** (3¼hr., 1 per day, 100kn); **Milan, ITA** (8½hr., in summer 1 per day, €100); **Trieste, ITA** (3hr., 5 per day, 88-112kn); **Venice, ITA** (6hr., 1 per day, 170kn).

Ferries: Jadrolinija Jadroagent, Riva 14 (☎21 04 31). Open M-F 8am-4pm, Sa-Su 11am-4pm. To: **Zadar** (8hr., 5 per week, 123kn) and **Venice, ITA** (6hr., 2 per week, 365kn).

Public Transportation: Local **buses** depart from the bus station, and most stop on Giardini (M-Sa every 20min., Su 1 per hr.; run until 10:30pm). Purchase tickets on board (11kn).

Taxis: (☎22 32 28). Opposite the bus station. 23kn base, 7kn per km; 3kn per bag. A cheaper option is **Citycab** (☎09 11 11 10 52). 30-50kn anywhere within greater Pula.

CROATIA

ORIENTATION AND PRACTICAL INFORMATION

Sergijevaca, Pula's main street, circles around the central hill in **Stari Grad** (Old Town) and turns into **Kandlerova** after the **Forum. Castropola,** a parallel street higher up, also circles the hilltop. To get to Sergijevaca from the **train station,** walk on Kolodvorska for 5min., keeping the sea to your right. Turn right onto **Istarska** at the **amphitheater.** Follow Istarska through its name change to **Giardini.** After the park, a right through the tall **Arch of the Sergians** (Slavoluk Sergijevaca) leads to Sergijevaca, which runs to the Forum and the waterfront. To get there from the **bus station,** turn left onto Ulica 43 Istarske Divizije, veer left at the roundabout onto Flavijevska, and left at the amphitheater onto Istarska.

Tourist Office: Tourism Office Pula, Forum 3 (☎21 29 87; www.pulainfo.hr). English-speaking staff provides city **maps** and info on accommodations, events, and entertainment, as well as ferry and bus schedules. Open M-Sa 8am-midnight, Su 10am-6pm.

Currency Exchange and Banks: Zagrebačka Banka (☎38 54 57), at the corner of Giardini and Flanatička. Exchanges cash for no commission and cashes **traveler's checks** for

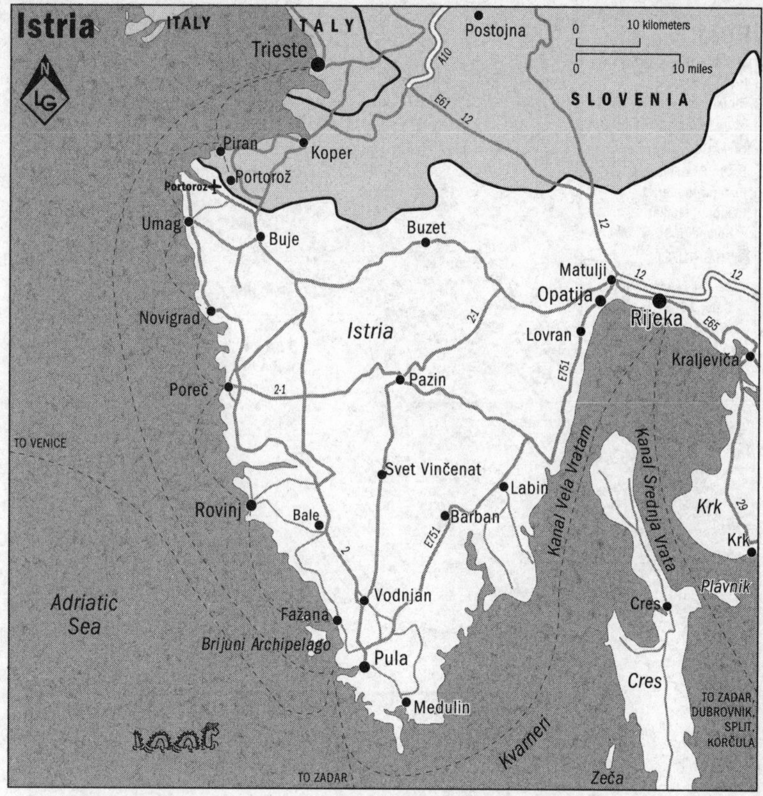

1.5% commission. Open M-F 7:30am-7pm, Sa 8am-noon. A currency exchange machine is outside **Raiffeisen Bank,** 43 Istarske Divizije, next to the bus station. **Banka Sonic,** Sergijevaca 16, exchanges cash for no commission and has **Western Union** services. Open M-F 8am-6pm, Sa 8am-noon. **ATMs** are common in the city center.

Luggage Storage: In the bus station. 1.20kn per hr., over 15kg 2.20kn per hr. Open M-F 4:30-9:30am, 10am-6pm, and 6:30pm-midnight; Su 5am-midnight.

English-Language Bookstore: Algoritam, Prolaz Kodkazalista 1 (☎39 39 87), off Sergijevaca toward the post office. Stocks recent fiction and travel guides. Open M-F 8am-8pm.

Police: Trg Republike 2 (☎53 21 11).

24hr. Pharmacy: Ljekarna Centar, Giardini 15 (☎22 25 44). From 9pm until 7am, use the side window on Giardini instead of the main entrance. AmEx/MC/V.

Hospital: Clinical Hospital Center, Zagrebačka 34 (☎21 44 33). Open 24hr.

Internet: MMC Luka, Istarska 30, a block from the amphitheater. Fast connections in a hip bar. 20kn per 30min. Open M-Sa 8am-midnight. **Enigma,** Kandlerova 19 (☎38 26 15), also serves drinks and food. 10kn for 20min. Open daily June-Sept. 10am-midnight; Oct.-May 10am-2pm and 5-8pm.

Post Office: Danteov trg 4 (☎21 59 55). Go left for mail and right for **Poste Restante** and telephones. Open M-F 7am-10pm, Sa 7am-2pm, Su 8am-noon. **Postal Code:** 52100.

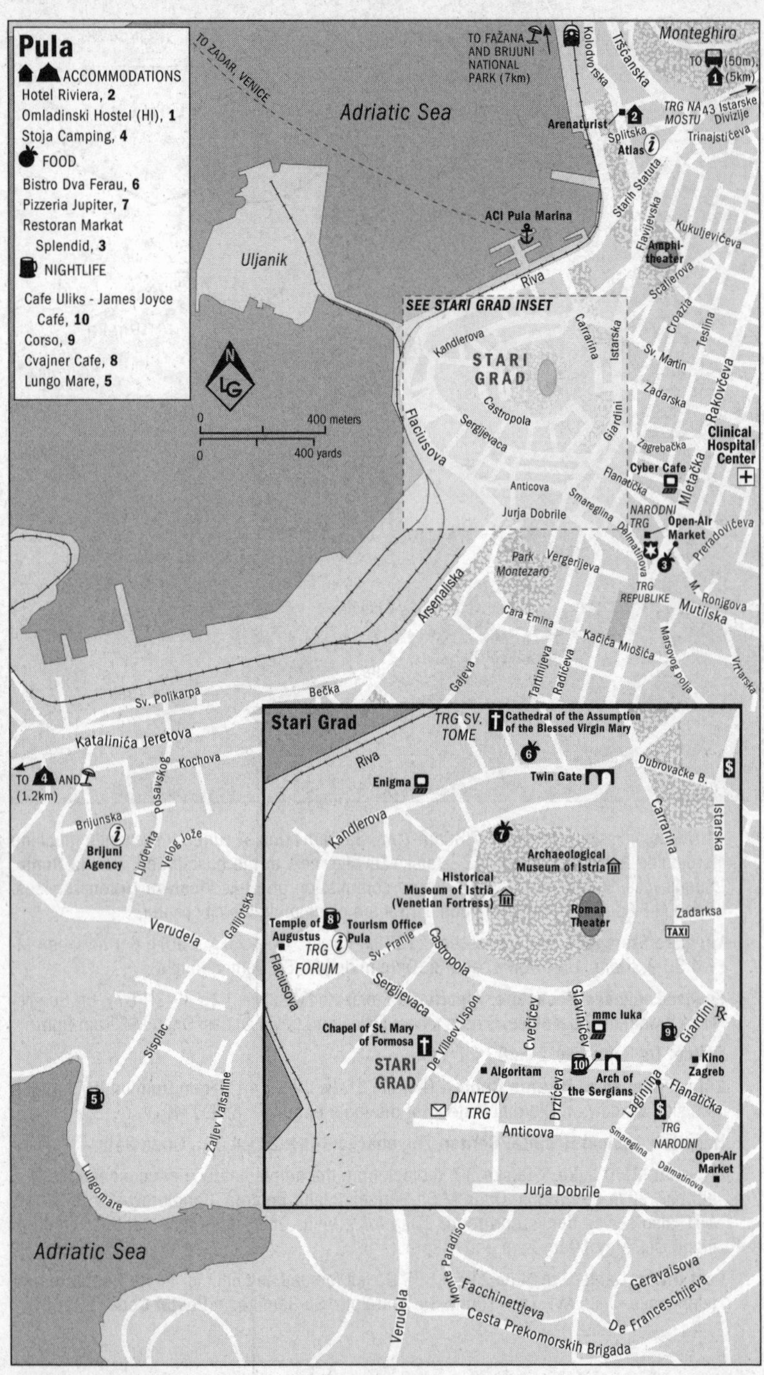

Pula
ACCOMMODATIONS
Hotel Riviera, 2
Omladinski Hostel (HI), 1
Stoja Camping, 4
FOOD
Bistro Dva Ferau, 6
Pizzeria Jupiter, 7
Restoran Markat Splendid, 3
NIGHTLIFE
Cafe Uliks - James Joyce Café, 10
Corso, 9
Cvajner Cafe, 8
Lungo Mare, 5
TO ZADAR, VENICE
Adriatic Sea
TO FAŽANA AND BRIJUNI NATIONAL PARK (7km)
Monteghiro
TO (50m), (5km)
Arenaturist
Atlas
ACI Pula Marina
Uljanik
Amphitheater
SEE STARI GRAD INSET
STARI GRAD
Clinical Hospital Center
Cyber Cafe
NARODNI TRG
Open-Air Market
Park Montezaro
TRG REPUBLIKE
400 meters
400 yards
TO 4 AND (1.2km)
Brijuni Agency
Stari Grad
TRG SV. TOME
Cathedral of the Assumption of the Blessed Virgin Mary
Enigma
Twin Gate
Archaeological Museum of Istria
Historical Museum of Istria (Venetian Fortress)
Roman Theater
Temple of Augustus
Tourism Office Pula
TRG FORUM
TAXI
Chapel of St. Mary of Formosa
mmc luka
Kino Zagreb
Algoritam
Arch of the Sergians
DANTEOV TRG
Adriatic Sea

CROATIA

ACCOMMODATIONS AND CAMPING

Private accommodations are the most convenient choice in Pula. Several agencies help visitors locate private rooms, but the tourist office can help find the best deals. The friendly, helpful, and English-speaking staff at **Arenaturist,** Splitska 1, inside Hotel Riviera, arranges accommodations throughout Pula with no registration fee. (☎52 94 00; www.arenaturist.hr. Open in high season M-Sa 8am-8pm, Su 8am-1pm; low season M-Sa 8am-8pm. Rooms from €31 to 83.)

Omladinski Hostel (HI), Zaljev Valsaline 4 (☎39 11 33; www.hfhs.hr). From the bus station, catch bus #2 or 3 toward "Veruda" at the far end of the station, platform #8. Get off at the Villa Idola stop, follow the HI signs, and go downhill. Though a trek from the city center, this HI hostel is a budget beacon, frequented by families, teenage tour groups, and backpackers. Private cove, diving school, bar, trampolines, shared showers. Simple breakfast included. Internet access. Reception daily 8am-10pm. Reserve ahead. Dorms July-Aug. 110kn; Sept. and June 84kn; Oct. and May 89kn; Nov. and Apr. 84kn. Camping July-Aug. 75kn; Sept.-June 50kn. Four-person private homes with bathrooms also available. 10kn HI discount. Registration 10kn. Tax 4.50-7kn. ❶

Stoja Camping (☎38 71 44). From Giardini, take bus #1 toward Stoja to the end. Within walking distance of town (3km, 20min.), Stoja is loved by families and backpackers alike, who delight in the surrounding beaches and thick pine forests. Showers, bathroom, sports facilities, restaurant, and grocery. €3-14 per person. Electricity €2.50. Mobile homes for up to 5 people are also now available at €35-110 depending on the season. A/C €5 extra. ❶

Hotel Riviera, Splitska 1 (☎21 11 66), across the park from the amphitheater by the waterfront. This refurbished 67-room Habsburg-era hotel offers large beds, private bathrooms, and televisions, and, in some rooms, panoramic waterfront views. Breakfast included. Singles Feb.-May and Sept.-Dec. 226kn; May-Sept. 263kn; mid-Aug. 299kn. Doubles also available. ❷

FOOD

Fresh fish, meat, and cheese are available in the **market** building. (Fish market open M-Sa 7am-1:30pm, Su 7am-noon. Meat and cheese markets open M-Sa 7-noon, Su 7am-2pm.) **Puljanka** grocery store has several branches throughout the town, including one at Sergijevaca 4. (Open M-F 6am-8pm, Sa 8am-1:30pm, Su 7am-noon.) Buffets and fast-food restaurants line **Sergijevaca.** There is an open-air fruit and vegetable **market** at Trg Narodni, off Flanatička. (Open daily 6am-2pm.)

Pizzeria Jupiter, Castropola 42 (☎21 43 33). Walk behind the bus station along Carrarina, past the Archaeological Museum. Curve to the left up the ramp; it's on the left. Praised by Pulians young and old, this is the perfect spot for a bite before amphitheater concerts. Log benches hidden in warm yellow alcoves create a welcoming atmosphere. Pizza 20-39kn. Open M-F 9am-11pm, Sa-Su 1-11pm. AmEx. ❶

Restoran Markat Splendid, Trg Privoga Svibvija 5 (☎22 32 84), across from the far side of the market building at Narodni Trg. A Croatian version of the school lunch-lady fills trays with inexpensive delights in this cafeteria-style eatery. Soups, salads, and entrees 6-30kn. Open M-F 9:30am-9pm, Sa-Su 9:30am-4pm. Cash only. ❶

Bistro Dva Ferau, Kandlerova 32 (☎22 33 65). Walk along Kandlerova from the amphitheater, just before the cathedral. Dva Ferau stands out among the interchangeable eateries lining this street with its maritime theme: dark wooden booths rest below hanging nets and wooden anchors. Prices are reasonable (25-45kn), but those looking to indulge might want to splurge on the fish platters for two (150-230kn), often accompanied by a bottle of wine. ❷

SIGHTS

AMPHITHEATER. Completed in the first century AD during the reign of Roman Emperor Vespasian, this towering limestone arena was used for gladiatorial combat until sport killing was outlawed four centuries later. Today, it provides the perfect venue for entertainment of a different sort: concerts, from opera to heavy metal, and film. While the tangle of grass and clusters of boulders are not awe-inspiring, the view of the ocean is superb. An underground system of passages, constructed for drainage purposes, now houses a **museum** of Istrian history, with a focus on the role of olive oil in Pula's development. *(From the bus station, take a left on 43 Istarske Divizije and another on Flavijevska, which becomes Istarska. Open daily in high season 8am-9pm; in low season 8:30am-4:30pm. 30kn, students 15kn. English booklet 30kn.)*

THE AMPHITHEATER FOR FREE. Visiting Pula's must-see amphitheater needn't set you back US$40. Climb the hill to the left of the amphitheater, place yourself in sight of the stage, and you may be able to see the entire show for free, from not much farther away than some of the best seats in the house. Since the sound quality surpasses the view, the arrangement is better for concerts than for ballet or dance performances. Go early to get good seats.

ARCH OF THE SERGIANS (SLAVOLUK OBITELJI SERGII). The sturdy stone arch was built in 29 BC for three local members of the Sergii family, one of whom commanded a Roman battalion at the battle of Actium between Mark Antony and Octavian. It is now a gateway to Sergijevaca, Pula's main street. Don't miss the intricate reliefs of grapes and battles that adorn the outer walls. *(From the amphitheater, follow Istarska left as it turns into Giardini. The arch is on the right.)*

THE FORUM. The Forum, at the end of Sergijevaca, was the central gathering place for political, religious, and economic activities in Roman days. Today, the original cobblestones lie buried safely 1.2m beneath the ground and the square is used primarily for cafe lounging and gazing at the nearby Temple of Augustus.

TEMPLE OF AUGUSTUS (AUGUSTOV HRAM). This remarkably preserved temple was constructed between 2 BC and AD 14 and dedicated to Roman Emperor Augustus. Until the early Middle Ages, two similar temples stood nearby; the larger was destroyed, but the rear wall of the smaller Temple of Diana survived and now serves as the facade of Pula's City Hall, the town's administrative center since 1296. The Temple of Augustus houses a small **museum** with pieces of Roman statues and sculptures from the first and second centuries AD. *(At the Forum. ☎21 86 89. Open M-F 9:30am-1:30pm and 4-9pm, Sa-Su 9:30am-1:30pm. 10kn, students 5kn.)*

OTHER SIGHTS. Up the hill from Castropola, the **Venetian Fortress** (Kaštel) has guarded Pula since Roman times, but in 2002 it became the **Historical Museum of Istria** (Povjesni Musej Istre), a small maritime and military history exhibit. Although collections are limited, the view from the citadel summit is spectacular. *(Open daily in summer 8am-8pm; in winter 9am-5pm. 20kn.)* On the nearby hilltop stand the remains of a **Roman Theater** (Malo Rimsko Kazaliste). Farther down is the **Twin Gate** (Dvojna vrata). The **Archaeological Museum of Istria** (Arheološki Muzej Istre), up the hill from the Twin Gate, offers an overview of Istrian history, emphasizing Roman stone artifacts from the second century BC to the sixth century AD. *(Carrarina 3. ☎21 86 09. Open May-Sept. M-F 9am-8pm, Su 10am-3pm; Oct.-Apr. M-F 9am-2pm. 20kn, students 10kn. English guidebook 30kn.)* Near the waterfront, off Trg Sv. Tome, the **Cathedral of the Assumption of the Blessed Virgin Mary** (called simply "Katedrala" by locals), dating from the fourth century AD, retains stunning floor mosaics.

CROATIA

FESTIVALS AND BEACHES

Amphitheater shows are the highlight of a trip to Pula. Tickets (150-800kn) are available at the theater from the booking agency, **Lira Intersound** (☎21 78 01; open M-F 8am-3pm), or from tourist agencies. The popular **Biker Days Festival** takes place during the first week of August. (Tickets 150kn.) Past exhibitions at this chrome-and-leather celebration have included female mud wrestling. Movie buffs can enjoy the **Pula Film Festival** (www.pulafilmfestival.com), which occurs in mid-July. The **International Accordion School** hits town in the second half of July, offering a series of concerts and classes. During the first week of August, the annual **Festival "Monte Paradiso"** turns an old army barracks into a stage and mosh pit with a range of punk-rock musical events. Pula is lined with private coves and **beaches.** To find the perfect spot, take bus #1 to Stoja Campground. Facing the sea, walk left down the coastline, where rock shelves run from the campground to the hostel. A pleasant pebble beach curves in front of the hostel, which rents **paddleboats** (40kn per hr.). For less crowded beaches, head to the neighboring town of **Fazana.**

NIGHTLIFE

Lungo Mare, Gortanova Uvala bb (☎39 10 84). Take bus #2 or 7 from Giardini, get off at Verud, go right on Verudela to Hotel Pula, and go down to the sea. A relaxed outdoor cafe by day and a raging club by night. Blasting music in its own cove, this is a favorite among young Pulian clubbers. *Favorit* 25kn per 1L. Open daily 10am-4am.

Corso, Giardini 3 (☎53 51 47). Occupying a prime people-watching spot in Stari Grad, this chic cafe/bar is often filled with trendy young Pulians sipping *bijela kava* (latte; 9kn) by day and mixed drinks (40kn) by night. Open daily 8am-midnight.

Cafe Uliks, Trg Portarata 1 (☎21 91 58). If the statue outside does not tip you off, the James and Nora Joyce cocktails certainly will: this tourist-infested cafe was the site where the author taught a century ago. Otherwise a fairly standard Irish pub, although the plush red cushioned seats and shining dark wooden tables make for a relaxing atmosphere. Wine from 7kn a glass. Open daily 8am-midnight.

POREČ ☎(0)52

A stone's throw from Slovenia and Italy, Poreč sits on a tiny peninsula jutting into the azure Adriatic. The town is distinguished by its Gothic and Romanesque houses, unique 6th-century Byzantine mosaics, Roman ruins, and, unfortunately, throngs of tourists. Nevertheless, this foreign influx gives the town an internationally festive flair, and Poreč proves a fun stop for island-hopping down the coast.

TRANSPORTATION AND PRACTICAL INFORMATION. There is no train station for Poreč. The **bus station,** K. Hoguesa 2 (☎43 21 53; MC), sends buses to: Pula (1hr., 8 per day, 40kn); Rijeka (2hr., 5 per day, 70kn); Rovinj (1hr., 6 per day, 32kn); Zagreb (6hr., 4 per day, 200kn); Koper, SLV (30min., 3 per day, 65kn); Portoroz, SLO (1½hr., 1per day, 65kn); and Trieste, ITA (2hr., 3 per day, 65kn). Buses take cash only.

Poreč is easy to navigate. The marina is situated behind and downhill from the bus station, while the town center is just behind and to the right of the station, through the park. Walking towards the town center you will see a sign (an "I" with an arrow pointed left) for the tourist office. Follow the sign and go up pedestrian Milanovića, which will curve left and then right, to reach the main square, **Trg Slobode** (a 5min. walk). The main pedestrian walkway, **Decumanus,** begins at Trg Slobode and runs through **Stari Grad** (Old Town), which is lined with shops, cafes, and restaurants. The **tourist office,** Zagrebačka 9, is up the road and to the right from Trg Slobode and should be your first stop for free maps, accommodation info, and bus schedules. (☎45 12 93; www.istra.com/porec. Open May-Oct. M-Sa 8am 9pm, Su 9am-1pm.) **Zagrebačka Banka,** Obala M. Tita bb, by the sea, exchanges cash for no commission, cashes **traveler's checks** for 1.5% commission, and provides **Western Union** services. (☎45 11 66. Open M-F 7:30am-7pm, Sa 8am-2pm.) There is a MasterCard **ATM** and a **currency exchange** machine outside. Other MasterCard and Visa ATMs are available throughout Stari Grad. **Luggage storage** is available at the bus station. (10kn. Open daily 5-9am, 9:30am-5:30pm, and 6-9pm.) A **pharmacy** is at Trg Slobode 13. (☎43 23 62. Open daily July-Aug. 7:30am-10pm; Sept.-June M-Sa 7:30am-8pm.) The tourist office has one computer with free Internet access (10min. limit), but be prepared to wait. There are also connections at **Cybermac,** M. Grahalića 1. From Trg Svobode, head up Zagrebačka and turn left before the tourist office, then right. (☎42 70 75. 25kn per 30min., 42kn per hr. Open M-Sa 8am-midnight, Su 10am-midnight.) Alternatively, walk along the marina in the direction of Stari Grad to **Atelier P,** Obala M. Tita 3a, a bar that also offers Internet access. (35kn per hr. Open M-Sa 8am-2am, Su noon-2am.)The **post office,** Trg Svobode 1, is opposite the pink church with the yellow facade. (☎43 18 08. Open Sept.-June M-F 7:30am-7pm, Sa 7:30am-noon.) **Postal Code:** 52440.

ACCOMMODATIONS AND CAMPING. Accommodations in Poreč are abundant but expensive, particularly if you're staying fewer than three nights. Many travel agencies book private rooms. The tourist office can also recommend or book rooms. **Eurotours ❷,** Nikole Tesle 12, has decent rates and a huge stock of rooms in locations ranging from the city center to the hinterlands of Poreč. (☎45 15 11; eurotours@pu.hinet.hr. Open daily June-Aug. 7:30am-10pm; Sept.-May 8am-2pm and 5-9pm. Doubles 270-443kn; apartments 194-280kn. 30% more for stays under 3 nights. Registration fee 15kn.) **Hotel Poreč ❺,** R. Končara 1, has simple, functional rooms with TVs, fridges, and phones. A bar, restaurant, and casino are at the hotel. (☎45 18 11; www.hotelporec.com. For stays over 3 nights singles 313kn; doubles 262kn. For stays under 3 nights 375/290kn. AmEx/MC/V.)

The following **campgrounds** offer a range of services (grocery stores, restaurants, laundromats, Wi-Fi) and are accessible by the same bus from the station (25min.; 5 per day 6:15am-9:20pm to Lanterna, 7:30am-10:30pm back to Poreč; 20kn). **Lanterna Camp ❶** is 13km to the north and has 3km of stunning beach, with moorings available. (☎40 45 00. Open Apr.-Oct. €3.85-6.60 per person; €6.60-12.25 for tent, car, and electricity. **Plava Laguna ❶** runs three other campgrounds. (Low season ☎41 01 01; www.plavalaguna.hr. Open Mar.-Oct. Camping €3.80-7; car, tent and electricity €7.90-13.20.) **Zelena Laguna ❶** and **Bijela Uvala ❶** offer recreation activities on sandy beaches and lie close to nightclub hot spots. (Zelena ☎41 07 00, Bijela Uvala 41 05 51. Open Mar.-Oct.)

FOOD. **Konzum ❶** supermarket is at Zagrebačka 2, next to the church at Trg Slobode. (☎45 24 29. Open daily 7am-10pm.) **Ulixes ❷,** Decumanus 2, peaceful and away from the main tourist strip, offers a daily selection of fresh meat and seafood. White porticos and stylish Roman artifacts line the stone walls. Log benches allow you to sit beside flowering vines on the terrace. (☎45 11 32. Entrees 60-110kn. Open daily noon-3pm and 6pm-midnight.) **Gostionica Istra ❷,** Milanovića 30, by the bus station, serves delicious fish, meat, and pasta dishes. (☎43 46 36. Entrees 25-80kn. Open daily noon-10pm. AmEx/D/MC/V.) Perched atop the stone defense tower, **Caffe Torne Rotunda,** Narodni Trg 3, provides a postcard-perfect view of Poreč's tiled rooftops and bright ocean. Enjoy the military regalia of cannons and armory that await you. (Macchiato 16kn. Open daily 10am-1am.) **Bistro Karaka ❶,** next to Istra, is a lively restaurant offering standard Italian fare. Some travelers report bringing their friends and receiving a meal on the house, or free drinks for all. (Pizza 30-50kn. Open noon-3pm and 6-11pm.)

SIGHTS. From Trg Slobode, walk down to the **Pentagonal Tower** (Peterokunta Kula), built in 1447 as a city gate. Continuing down Decumanus, turn right on Sv. Eleuterija to find the 6th-century **St. Euphrasius's Basilica** (Eufrazijeva Bazilika), which was placed on UNESCO's World Heritage list in 1997 for its preserved **mosaics.** Across from the basilica entrance stands the octagonal baptistry and **bell tower,** which has a view of the tiled roofs of Poreč. (Open daily 7:30am-7pm. Services M-Sa 7:30am and 7pm; Su 7:30, 11am and 7pm. Basilica free. Bell tower 10kn.) To the right of the basilica entrance, the **museum,** housed in the ancient bishop's palace, displays fragments of the intricate floor mosaics from the original chapel floor, as well as statues and paintings from the early to medieval Christian period. (☎09 15 21 78 62. Open daily 10am-6pm. 10kn.) Upon returning to Decumanus, walk across the street to the **Regional Museum,** the oldest museum in Istria, founded in 1884. Fragments of Roman mosaics are on display alongside an array of Baroque furniture and paintings that chart Poreč's history. Continue down Decumanus through Trg Marator and toward the right to the pile of stones and columns on the left side that was once the Roman **Temple of Neptune,** constructed around the first century AD. A stroll left along Obala m. Tita, next to the ocean, brings you to the **Round Tower,** a 15th-century defensive structure.

BEACHES AND ENTERTAINMENT. Beaches in Poreč are steep and rocky but offer convenient tanning shelves cut into the shoreline. The best sites near town are south of the marina. Hop on the passing **mini-train** (every 35min. 9am-11pm, 15kn), or face the sea on Obala m. Tita, turn left, and head along the coast for about 10min. to reach the **Brulo** resort, which offers **waterslides** (10kn per hr.), **tennis** (50kn), and **minigolf** (10kn) to non-guests. Another 5min. walk takes you to the outdoor playground of the **Blue Lagoon** (Plava Laguna) resort, and 10min. more gets you to the **Green Lagoon** (Zelena Laguna). Or, take a bus straight to the latter (10min., 7 per day, 9kn). To escape the crowds, continue past the Green Lagoon toward the marina (30min.). A ferry leaves from the marina for the quieter **Saint Nicholas Island** (Sveti Nikola), just across the harbor (every 30min. 6:45am-midnight, round-trip 20kn.), where you can find a secluded rock shelf. To see more of the coast, rent a **bike** from **Ivona,** Prvomajska 2, a block from the tour-

THE LOCAL STORY

UNTYING THE CRAVAT

Although one might expect the necktie to have originated in fashion-conscious Italy or France, the word cravat (from *hrvat,* or "croat" in Croatian) hints at its true roots. According to legend, a Croatian woman once tied a scarf around her lover's neck as a token of her devotion; the historical record tells of a similar emblem worn by Croatian mercenaries during the Thirty Years' War.

Recently, Croatia has launched a campaign to use its cravat heritage to establish ties with the rest of the world. In 1990, the nonprofit organization Academia Cravatica was born, solely responsible for promoting what the group's founder Marijan Busic calls "Croatia's contribution to global culture." Their endeavors include tying an 808m long red "mega-tie" around the Pula Arena in 2003, as well as the recent traveling art exhibit, "The Challenge of the Tie," which addresses the neckwear's ambiguous purpose through the work of Croatian and international artists. The organization has brought "tie art" and Croatian culture to regions as diverse as the Baltics, Egypt, and South Africa.

Even if the invention of the necktie seems an obscure claim to fame, there are some who think otherwise: as British historian Norman Davies observes, "those who deny the influence of Europe's smaller nations should remember that the Croats have us all by our necks."

ist office across Trg J. Rakovca. Ask for a free **bike map.** (☎43 40 46. 20kn per hr., 35kn per 2hr., 80kn per day. ID or passport required. Open M-Sa 8am-1pm and 4-7pm, Su 8am-1pm.) Two trails run through more than 50km of olive groves, forests, vineyards, and medieval villages. Named beaches have hotel complexes and discos, invariably frequented by (mostly German) tourists of all ages. **Plava,** near the Plava Laguna, is one of the better international centers with European and Croatian bands. (Open Apr.-Sept. W-Sa 10pm-4am.) To dance with a young and more local crowd, walk 10min. south on the beach past the marina to the open-air **Colonia Iulia Parentium,** where you'll hear anything from pop to acid jazz to ska. (☎51 89 41. Open daily Apr.-Sept. 9pm-4am.) **Mango Mambo,** Trg Marafor 10, the coolest of a cluster of bars and cafes at the end of Decumanus, stays lively all week long with cocktails (32kn) like the "rubber duck" and the "slippery surprise." (Open daily 6pm-4am.)

ROVINJ ☎(0)52

Once Istria's central fishing settlement and a fortress for the Venetian Navy, this summer vacation-spot of the Austro-Hungarian emperors offers modern-day travelers a vision of unspoiled beauty. Boasting a natural, spa-like atmosphere, an elegant cobblestoned marina, and unpretentious attitude, Rovinj (ro-VEEN; pop. 14,000), provides a quiet, picturesque escape, its unique Baroque and neo-classical buildings spilling down to the crisp waters below.

TRANSPORTATION. Rovinj sends **buses** to Poreč (1hr., 7-10 per day, 32kn); Pula (¾hr.; 20 per day 4:40am-7pm, M-Sa also 11:30pm; 29kn); Rijeka (3½hr., 7 per day, 102kn); Zagreb (5-6hr., 9 per day, 165kn); Ljubljana, SLV (5hr., in high season 1 per day, 146kn); Trieste, ITA (2½hr., 2-3 per day, 81kn). The tourist office (see below) has **free maps** for suggested bike routes 22-60km long. Rent bikes at **Bike Planet,** Trg na Lokvi 3, across the street from the bus station. (☎81 11 61. 15kn per hr., 70kn per day. Open M-Sa 8:30am-12:30pm and 5-8pm.) **Globtours,** Rismondo 2, off the main square on the waterfront, also rents bikes. (15kn per hr., 40kn per ½-day, 60kn per day.)

ORIENTATION AND PRACTICAL INFORMATION. Turn left out of the bus station and walk down **Nazora** toward the marina or up **Karera** to **Stari Grad** (Old Town). Alternately, turn right out of the bus station on **Carera** to get to the main square. The main tourist office is just past the main square, away from the marina. Street signs and numbers in Rovinj are often difficult to find or nonexistent, but the town is small enough that you won't stay lost for long.

The **tourist office** nearest to the bus station is just around the corner toward the ocean; it's the yellow-orange building on the corner at Nello Quarantotto bb. The friendly, English-speaking staff will cash **traveler's checks** and **exchange money** for no commission. (☎81 16 59. **Internet** access 5kn per 10min. Bike rental 20kn per hr., 20kn per ½-day, 70kn per day. Open daily 9am-7pm.) **Zagrebačka Banka,** Carera 21, right next to the main square, Trg m. Tita, will cash traveler's checks for a 1.5% fee (20kn min.) and exchange money for no commission. (☎81 11 88. Open M-F 7:30am-8pm, Sa 8am-2pm.) **ATMs** are located in the town center near Stari Grad. For **luggage storage,** ask for the *garderoba* at the ticket counter of the bus station on M. Benussi. (☎81 14 53. 10kn, over 30kg 15kn. Open 6:30am-8:30pm.) The **Hospital** is located at M Benussi bb. (☎81 30 04). With your back to the bus station, turn right on M. Benussi to get to **Gradska Ljekarna,** M. Benussi bb, a **pharmacy.** (☎81 35 89. Open M-F 7:30am-9pm, Sa 8am-4pm, Su 9am-noon. AmEx/MC/V.) **A-Mar,** Carera 26, down the street from the bus station, has 10 computers with fast connections. (☎84 12 11. 18kn per 30min. MC/V.) **Poste Restante** and **telephones** are available at the **post office,** M. Benussi 4, 30m uphill and to the right of the bus station. (☎81 33 11. Open M-F 7:30am-7:30pm, Sa 7:30am-2pm.) **Postal Code:** 52210.

ACCOMMODATIONS AND FOOD. As usual, the best bet for budget accommodations is to search for a **private room.** Across the street from the bus station, **Futura,** M Benussi 2, arranges affordable and pristine rooms in and around the city and organizes tours in the region. (☎81 72 81; www.futura-travel.hr. Open M-F 8:30am-6pm, Sa 9am-2pm. Doubles from 150kn, including registration and tax.) Nearby, **Natale,** Carducci 4, offers similar accommodation services. Call ahead in the summer. (☎81 33 65; www.rovinj.com. Open July-Aug. M-Sa 7:30am-9:30pm, Su 8am-9:30pm; Sept.-June M-Sa 7:30am-8pm, Su 8am-noon. Singles €14-18; doubles €20-26; apartments €32-57.) For solo travelers, **Globtours ❷,** Rismondo 2 (☎81 15 66) is a good option. They also organize excursions and bike rentals. (Open daily Sept.-June 9am-9pm; July-Aug. 9am-11pm. Doubles 180-260kn.) **Hotel Monte Mulini ❷,** A. Smareglia bb, above a pebbly beach, offers rooms with private bathrooms; many have balconies. After renovations (slated to finish in June 2008) the hotel promises to be a five-star attraction, with corresponding prices. Facing the sea at the end of Nazora, walk to the left past the marina and go up the steps on your left. (☎81 15 12; mulini@jadran.tdr.hr. Breakfast and dinner included. Singles €22-40; doubles €34-70.) **Camping Polari ❶,** 2.5km east of town has a supermarket, several bars, and a new pool. Take one of the frequent buses (6min., 9kn) from the bus station. (☎80 15 01; fax 81 13 95. July-Aug. 100kn per person; June 85kn per person.)

Buy groceries at **Trg na Lokvi bb,** between the bus station and the sea. (Open M-Sa 6:30am-8pm, Su 7am-noon. AmEx/DC/MC/V.) Find fruit, vegetables, cheese, and delicious homemade liquor at the **open-air market** on Trg Valdibora. (Open daily 7am-9pm.) Hot spot **Veli Jože ❸,** Svetog Križa 3, at the end of the marina past the tourist office, serves excellent Istrian seafood amid funky maritime artifacts, including netting, shells, wooden anchors, and a primitive deep-sea diving suit. Prices vary by season, but you can usually get first-rate fish for 250kn per kilo and meals for about 35-70kn. (☎81 63 37. Open daily noon-2am. AmEx/MC/V.) For a great bargain and a filling meal in the perfect waterfront location, head across the street to **Stella di Mare ❷,** S. Croche 4, which has a terrace overlooking the ocean. (Huge pizzas and pastas 30-45kn. Seafood 45-120kn. Open daily 10am-11pm. AmEx/MC/V.) For a change from the waterfront, head to **Neptun ❷,** J. Rakovca 10, a rustic sidewalk restaurant serving tasty Italian fare. (☎81 60 86. Entrees 34-150kn. Open 8am-midnight. AmEx/DC/MC/V.)

SIGHTS. Although Rovinj has been surrounded by walls since the 7th century, only three of the original seven gates—**St. Benedict's, Holy Cross,** and the **Portico**—survive today. When entering Stari Grad, you'll probably walk through the **Balbijer Arch** (Balbijer luk), just off Trg Maršala Tita. Look out for the Turkish head on the outside and the Venetian head on the inside, a testament to the region's turbulent past. Narrow streets lead uphill to the 18th-century **St. Euphemia's Church** (Crkva Sv. Eufemije), built when Rovinj was a fortress under the Venetian Navy. During Roman Emperor Diocletian's reign, Euphemia and other Christians were imprisoned and tortured for refusing to deny their faith. The 15-year-old martyr survived the torture wheel, but not the pack of lions. Amazingly, the beasts left her body intact, and her fellow Christians encapsulated it in a **sarcophagus.** The vessel made its way to Constantinople but disappeared in 800—only to float mysteriously back to Rovinj later that year. Today, Euphemia is the patron saint of Rovinj, and her sarcophagus, behind the right altar, is often visited by locals, particularly on St. Euphemia's Day (Sept. 16). The stairs up to the **bell tower** (61m) lead visitors to a majestic view of the city and sea, well worth the price. In summer, the lawn outside hosts classical music performances. (Open M-Sa 10am-2pm and 4-6pm, Su 4-6pm. Services Su 10:30am and 7pm. Church free. Tower 10kn.)

The worthwhile **City Museum of Rovinj,** Trg Maršala Tita 11, offers changing displays of local modern art and archaeological exhibits. (Open in high season Tu-Sa 9am-noon and 7-10pm; in low season 9am-1pm. 15kn.) Boats anchored in the harbor take passengers to the 22 nearby **islands** (90kn) or to the serene **Lim Fjord** (150kn), a flooded canyon that separates Rovinj from Poreč and is touted as the highlight of the region. (Buy tickets at the tourist office or from boat owners. Prices and departure times vary by boat.) The winding cobbled streets of **Grisia** are lined with modern art galleries.

BEACHES AND ENTERTAINMENT. For the best beaches in the area, take a ferry to **Red Island** (Crveni Otok; 15min., 17 per day, 30kn), where nude sunbathing is permitted. On the mainland, reach natural rock shelves by walking left past the marina for 30min. and cutting through **Golden Cape** (Zlatni Rt). Ferries from the marina also go to beaches on **Katarina Island** (Sv. Katarina; 7min., 1 per hr. 5:45am-midnight, 10kn). For three days in the last week of August, Rovinj looks to the sky for **Rovinjska noć** (Rovinj Night), its famous annual night of fireworks. On the second Sunday of August, international artists come to display their work at the traditional open-air art festival, **Grisia,** held on the street of the same name. **Kanfanar** (July 25th), a folk festival dedicated to St. Jacob, features traditional Istrian music played on *mih* (bagpipes) and the *roženice* (flute), as well as a healthy spread of regional cuisine—wine, cheese, and the region's famous olive oil.

At night, Rovinj's cafe culture springs to life. Most of the action takes place along the marina or in **Valentino Bar,** via Santa Croce 28 (☎83 06 83). Here, to the sounds of smooth jazz, tourists watch the sunset or sunrise from cushions spread out on rocks above the sea. Recline in wicker chairs or on Indonesian wood benches with international trendsetters at **Zanzibar,** next to the tourist office on the marina, where international trendsters lounge in wicker chairs or on Indonesian wood benches. (Mixed drinks 30-50kn. Open daily 8am-1am.) **Bar Sax Cafe,** Ribarski Prolaz 4, in an alley off the marina, hosts lively patrons inside and out. Old film posters adorn walls painted in the cubist style in this smooth establishment. (Favorit 14kn per 0.5L. Mixed drinks 35-45kn. Open daily 8am-1am.) Much of the young Istrian club scene congregates at **Monvi,** Luda Adamovica, south of the marina by the resorts. This huge complex boasts three clubs, a Mexican restaurant, and an amphitheater that has hosted such international acts as Basement Jaxx. At times a little mall-like, the Center does offer an array of evening options. (☎54 51 17; www.monvicenter.com. Open 11pm-4am.)

GULF OF KVARNER

Blessed with long summers and gentle sea breezes, the islands just off the coast of mainland Croatia attract visitors with their pristine Adriatic beauty and the lack of crowds that fill up their Istrian and Southern Dalmatian neighbors.

RIJEKA ☎(0)51

A sprawling port town that serves primarily as a gateway to the Gulf Islands, Rijeka (ree-YEH-kah) has historical sites that make it a great urban stopover.

TRANSPORTATION AND PRACTICAL INFORMATION. The **train station** is located at Kralja Tomislava 1. (☎21 33 33. Info desk open daily 8:30am-3:30pm.) Trains run to: Split (7hr., 2 per day, 183kn) via Ogulin; Zagreb (3½hr., 4 per day, 102-117kn); Berlin, GER (11¾hr., 3 per day, 1001kn); Budapest, HUN (9hr., 2 per day, 326kn) via Zagreb; Ljubljana, SLV (2½hr., 4 per day, 83kn); Vienna, AUT (9hr., 1 per day, 450kn) via Zagreb. The **bus station,** Žabica 1, is down Krešimirova, to the right of the train station. (☎21 38 21. Open daily 5:30am-9pm.) Buses run to: Dubrovnik (12hr., 4 per day, 427kn); Krk Town (1½hr., 13 per day, 48kn); Pula (2½hr., 1 per hr., 91kn); Split (8hr., 12 per day, 236kn); Zagreb (2½hr., 1 per hr., 140kn); Ljubljana, SLV (3hr., 1 per day, 100kn); Trieste, ITA (2hr., 5 per day, 60kn). For **ferry tickets,** face the sea from the bus station and go left to **Jadrolinija,** Riva 16.

(☎21 14 44. Open M and W-F 7am-8pm, Tu and Sa 7am-6pm.) **Ferries** run to: Dubrovnik (18-24hr., June-Sept. M and F 8pm, 233kn); Hvar (12½hr.; M, W, F, and Su 8pm; 187kn); Korčula (15-18hr., 4 per week, 210kn); and Split (12hr., 4 per week, 169kn). Prices drop September-June. A catamaran (30kn) also runs to Cres at Mali Losinj in the summer at 5pm. There are several **taxi** companies in Rijeka, including **Auto-Taxi Rijeka** (☎33 28 93; 40kn per 5km, 7kn per km thereafter, 20% nighttime surcharge) and **Kvarner Taxi** (☎30 13 01; 30kn per 5km, 50kn per 10km, 70kn per 15km.) Buy tickets for **local buses** from kiosks (round-trip 14-32kn) or from the driver (10kn).

Easy to navigate, the pedestrian-only Korzo, lined with cafes and restaurants, is the life of Rijeka. To reach Korzo from the train station, turn right on Krešlimirova, passing the bus station until you reach the beginning of Jadranski Trg. Free **maps** are available at the **tourist office,** Korzo 33. From the stations, turn right onto Trpimirova, cross the street, and continue right down the Korzo. (☎33 58 82; www.tz-rijeka.hr. Open mid-June to mid-Sept. M-Sa 8am-8pm, Su 8am-2pm; mid-Sept. to mid-June M-Sa 8am-8pm.) The train station has a **bank,** which **exchanges currency,** cashes **traveler's checks** for no commission, and has an **ATM.** (☎21 33 18. Open M-Sa 8am-8pm, Su 8am-12:30pm.) **Luggage storage** is available at the train station (15kn per day; open 9am-11am, 11:30am-6:30pm, and 7-9pm) and in the bus station (9-12kn; open daily 5:30am-10:30pm). Emergency health care is available 24hr. at **Hitna medicinska pomoć,** Branka Blečića bb (☎67 29 92). **Internet** access can be found at **Erste Club,** Korzo 22, a terraced cafe on the main city strip. (☎32 00 72; www.ersteclub.com. Open M-F 8am-8pm, Sa 9am-1pm.) For better prices and Wi-Fi, head to **Inter Club Cont,** Kačića Miošića 1, by the cake shop, which offers a full bar along with fast connections. (☎37 16 30; www.cont.hr. 5kn per 15min., 8kn per 30min., 15kn per hr. Open 7am-10pm.) During the summer, the Korzo becomes an Internet hot spot—check with the **tourist information center** for the exact dates. The main **post office** is at Korzo 13. (Open M-Sa 7am-9pm.)

ACCOMMODATIONS AND FOOD. Accommodations in Rijeka's center can be expensive. If you wish to be in the heart of the town, your best bet is to knock on doors bearing *sobe* signs, as no agency officially finds accommodations. **Omladinski Youth Hostel ❶,** Šetalište XIII, divizije 23, is one of the cheapest options around, boasting immaculate linoleum-floored rooms, sparkling facilities, and an English-speaking staff. Although the hostel is only a 25min. walk from the city center, the #2 bus goes there; get off at the fourth stop. (☎40 64 20; www.hfhs.hr. Simple breakfast included. Luggage storage 5kn per day. Internet 5kn per hr.

DEFENDING THE DOLPHINS

Human tourists aren't the only ones who flock to the Adriatic waters off Veli Losinj; in recent years, a large pod of around 120 bottlenose dolphins have become permanent residents. Fortunately, you won't find the Losinj harbors teeming with tour boats offering travelers a chance to swim with these sleek creatures. Instead, **Blue World,** a marine research and conservation organization, has established itself in the port and has made protecting the dolphins' natural habitat its primary mission.

Cooperating with local excursion companies to avoid interference with ongoing research, Blue World's workers have been given unique dolphin-studying opportunities, which are in turn open to anyone who wishes to join a minimum 12-day volunteer course in Rovenska Bay.

Volunteers help with collecting and logging data as well as doing preliminary analysis. When the weather prevents researchers from taking to the waters, volunteers can listen to lectures by experts in marine biology.

For those who wish to aid Blue World but cannot volunteer for the minimum period, the organization accepts donations as part of its adopt-a-dolphin program. All funds go directly toward the organization's non-profit activties. Check out the website www.blueworld.com for more details.

Dorms 130-203kn; doubles 155-228kn; singles 235-308kn. Non-members 10kn extra.) **Prenoćište Rijeka ❷**, 1. Maja 34/1, is close to the train and bus stations and offers reasonable rates. With your back to the train station, turn right on Krešimirova and left on Alessandra Manzonia. As you continue up the hill for 5min., the road becomes 1. Maja. Look for a small white sign on the right. (☎55 12 46; www.zug.hr. Reception 24hr. Singles 200kn, with bath 280kn; doubles 270/550kn. AmEx/MC.)

A large **supermarket** is in the building next to the hostel and to the right of the train station. (Open daily 6am-10pm.) A smaller version at the bus station is open 24 hr. **Viktorija ❶**, Manzoni 1a, on the left as you head to the Prenoćište Rijeka from the train station, serves a good selection of grilled specialties (29-85kn) and pizza in an historic Baroque building. (☎33 74 16. Open M-Sa 7am-11pm, Su noon-11pm.) At **Cont ❶**, Šetalište A, Kačić Miošića 1, in the Hotel Continental, indulge your sweet tooth with homemade goods on the terrace. (☎37 21 54; www.cont.hr. Pastries and cakes 8-13kn. Open 7am-10pm.) A self-service, cafeteria style establishment, **Ri ❷**, Riva 6, provides filling local specialties like *jota* (sauerkraut soup). (☎31 10 26. Entrees 20-60kn. Open M-Sa 8am-10pm, Su 10am-10pm.)

SIGHTS. Numerous museums and galleries dot Rijeka, but the highlight of the city is its architecture, with a series of palaces lining the streets. The **Trsat** fortress, a remnant of Illyrian times, is worth visiting for the harbor view alone. Climb the 16th-century stairs leading up to the fort on the traditional pilgrim route, or catch bus #1 or 1a. The complex includes the church where Pope John Paul II was a pilgrim; **St. Mary of Trsat,** a Frankopan masterpiece housing a valuable art collection (open by appointment only); a Franciscan monastery; and peaceful landscaped gardens. (☎21 77 14. Entry 15kn. Open Apr.-Nov. Tu-Su 9am-11pm; Dec.-Mar Tu-Su 9am-3pm.) Across from the bus station, the ornate neo-gothic **Capuchin Church,** Kapusinske Stube 5 (☎33 52 33), is decorated with angelic frescoes and provides great views of the harbor. Given the importance of seafaring to the town, the museum to visit is undoubtedly the **Maritime and History Museum of the Croatian Litto,** Muzejskitrg 1., whose extensive collections of artifacts detail the lifestyle of the Kvarner region. The highlight, however, is the opulent palace furniture and the statue park with its series of grotesque faces—false accusers of citizen Adamić. (☎21 35 78; www.ppmhp.hr. Entry 10kn. Open Tu-F 9am-8pm, Sa 9am-1pm.)

NIGHTLIFE AND FESTIVALS. Croatians from across the country take to Rijeka's streets in elaborate and inventive masks during **February Carnival;** accommodations can be scarce during the celebration. In July, the **Summer Nights Festival** is popular among locals for its concerts and theatrical performances. **Indigo,** Stara vrata 3, Koblerov Trg, seems like a bordello of pop art. Electronica rules after 11pm when the restaurant turns into a bar. (☎31 51 74. Open M-Th 8am-midnight, F-Sa 8am-4am.) The namesake of **Palach,** Kružna ulica 6, Jan Palach, was a Czech student who protested the 1968 Soviet invasion by setting himself on fire. Accordingly, the bar and dance hall is dedicated to the student counter-culture scene, with a series of industrial-style rooms housing art exhibitions or tables for drinking. (www.mmc.hr. Open M-F 9am-11pm, Sa 5pm-1am, Su 5pm-11am.) Along the waterfront, the **Opium Buddha Bar,** Riva 12a, offers zen with style. Always trendy, the beautiful patrons are almost as impressive as the 7ft. golden Buddha and live 6ft. iguana. (☎33 63 97. Open M-W 7am-3am, Th-Su 7am-5am.)

KRK ISLAND ☎(0)51

Croatia's largest island is only a short ride across the bridge that connects it to the mainland. The white stone mountains that rise right out of the clear, blue water are especially stunning in the town of Baška towards its southern end. But while Baška reels in the tourists, Krk Town remains more peaceful.

KRK TOWN

Krk Town (pop. 5500) is a perfect stop for exploring cobblestone alleys and lounging in mellow bars as you begin island-hopping down the coast.

TRANSPORTATION AND PRACTICAL INFORMATION. The bus station (☎22 11 11) is at Šetalište Sv. Bernardina 1. **Buses** run from Rijeka to Krk Town (1½hr., 10-16 per day, 50kn), and most continue to Baška (40min., 5-9 per day, 24kn). **Jadrolinija** operates a **ferry** between Baška and Lopar on the northern tip of Rab Island (1hr.; June-Aug. 5 per day; 31kn, car 140kn, bike 30kn). To get to **Stari Grad** and its main square, Vela placa, from the bus station, walk to your right (keeping the sea on your right). The tourist and travel agency **Autotrans,** Šetalište Sv. Bernardina 3, is a few doors down. The helpful, English-speaking staff finds private accommodations, **exchanges currency,** and cashes **traveler's checks** for no commission. **Bike rentals** are also available. (☎22 26 61. 11kn per hr., 90kn per day. Open M-Sa 9am-9pm, Su 9am-1:30pm.) **Erste Bank,** Trg b. Josipa Jelačića 4, up and left of Vela pl., offers **Western Union** services and has a MasterCard and Visa **ATM.** (Open M-F 8am-8pm, Sa 8am-noon.) There's a **pharmacy** at Vela pl. 3. (☎22 11 33. Open M-F 7:30am-8pm, Sa 7am-noon and 6-8pm, Su 9-11am. AmEx/MC/V.) **Enigma Internet Cafe,** Šetalište Sv. Bernardina bb, is on the second floor of the building across the street from the bus station. (☎22 23 00. 15kn per hr. Open M-F 8am-1:30pm and 5:30-9pm. Cash only.) The harbor around Krk is a Wi-Fi hot spot. The **post office,** Trg b. Josipa Jelačića bb, offers **Western Union** services, gives MasterCard **cash advances,** and has **phones** inside and outside. (☎22 11 25. Open M-F 7am-8pm, Sa 7am-2pm.) **Postal Code:** 51500.

ACCOMMODATIONS AND FOOD. **Autotrans** (see above) books private rooms. (July-Aug. singles 100-150kn; doubles 180-240kn. Sept.-June 70-110/140-200kn. Tourist tax 4.50-7.50kn. Stays under 4 days 30-50% more. Registration 10kn.) *Sobe* signs line **Slavka Nikoliča** and **Plavnička,** but before you climb the hill, be forewarned that many owners deal only with agencies. The tree-covered **Autocamp Ježevac ❶,** Plavnička bb, is a 5min. walk from the bus station in the opposite direction from Stari Grad. The reception is through the gates, past the campers, and at the end of the road. (☎22 10 81; jezevac@zlatni-otok.hr. Mar. 23-May 31 and Sept. 1-Oct. 15 26kn per person, 17kn per tent; July-Aug. 36/24kn; June 33/22.50kn.) In the opposite direction is **Naturist Camp Politin ❶,** Narodnog Preparodna bb, with a magnificent beach just past the hotel complexes. (☎22 13 51; www.krkonline.com. Open Apr.-Sept. 42kn per person, 54kn per site.)

There is a **supermarket,** Šetalište Sv. Bernardina bb, across the street from the bus station. (☎85 82 02. Open M-Sa 7am-9pm, Su 7am-1:30pm. AmEx/MC/V.) Popular seaside restaurant **Galeb ❷,** Obala hrvatske mornarice bb, serves delicious Adriatic standards, including fabulous *pureći odrezak* (turkey with rice, curry, and pineapple; 70kn) to an international crowd. (Meat entrees 35-80kn. Vegetarian dishes 30-40kn. Open daily 9am-midnight.) **Konoba Šime ❷,** A. Mahnića 1, is another good option. Tucked into the city wall, this restaurant serves Adriatic cuisine on its large terrace. (☎22 20 42. Entrees 45-75 kn.)

SIGHTS AND ENTERTAINMENT. The town's main attractions are the city walls and fort dating from the first century BC. The **Kaštel,** with its round tower and quadratic courtroom from the 12th century, and the Romanesque **Cathedral** with its gothic **bell tower,** give shape to the Krk skyline. Otherwise, the main focus is on the surrounding waters rather than the town itself. **Fun Diving Krk,** Brace Juras 3, leads underwater expeditions throughout the year to exotic red coral and sunken Greek vessels. (☎/fax 22 25 63; www.fun-diving.com. Beginners: 1 dive €45, 2 dives €79; everything included. Experienced divers: full day with 2 dives €39, with full equipment €59. Snorkeling €13. All are available 9am-4pm at the

Island of Plavnik, 45min. away by boat. Lunch is sold onboard. Cash only.) Less-populated, cleaner beaches are near Autocamp Ježevac (see above).

Šoto Baterije, a self-dubbed "chill out lounge," is a laid-back, self-service bar right on the rocks. It's near the church at the top of Stari Grad, past the smooth white stone square. (Open daily 8pm-1am. Cash only.) **Casa del Padrone,** Šetalište Sv. Bernardina bb, with a maritime-themed terrace, is right on the waterfront as you head away from the bus station, past the stands, before the row of restaurants. (☎22 21 28. Cash only.) At night, the club **Jungle,** S. Radića, just up from Vela Placa, with its wicker lounge chairs and mixed-drinks menu, is the place to be. (Open 10pm-late. Cash only.)

DALMATIAN COAST

The Dalmatian Coast, home to over 1000 islands (only 66 of which are inhabited), presents a seascape of unfathomable beauty against a dramatic backdrop of sun-drenched mountains. Deep blue waters wash endless stretches of rocky beach, and even during the busiest travel seasons, many parts of the coast remain the perfect refuge from the bustle of urban Europe.

ZADAR ☎(0)23

Zadar (za-DAR; pop. 77,000), the administrative center of northern Dalmatia, hides its many scars well. Allied attacks destroyed Zadar during WWII, and the recent war (1991-1995) shattered much of what had been rebuilt. But the local residents have restored their homes yet again and the city now stands beautifully rejuvenated, with a series of white stone buildings running down to the brink of the indigo sea. Even ancient Roman ruins are pressed into service as public benches. With the extraordinary Kornati Islands only a boat ride away, Zadar's varied offerings make it the quintessential Dalmatian city.

CROATIA

TRANSPORTATION

Trains: Ante Starčevića 4 (☎21 25 55). Info office open M-F 7:30am-3:30pm and 6:30-9:30pm. To **Zagreb** via **Knin** (5-7hr.; 2 per day; 200kn, direct 150kn).

Buses: Ante Starčevića 1 (☎21 10 35, info 21 15 55). More reliable than trains. To: **Dubrovnik** (8hr., 8 per day, 157-220kn); **Rijeka** (4½hr., 12 per day, 125-159kn); **Split** (3hr., 2 per hr., 88-107kn); **Zagreb** (5hr., 2 per hr., 102-127kn); **Trieste, ITA** (7hr., 2 per day, 166kn).

Ferries: Ferries run May 25-June 26 and Sept. 16-Oct. 2 and depart from Liburnska Obala, 5min. up from the pedestrian bridge. **Jadrolinija** (☎25 48 00) has ferry info and sells tickets. Open M-F 6am-9pm, Sa 5:30am-midnight, Su 7am-9pm. To: **Dubrovnik** (16hr., 2 per week, 157kn); **Korčula** (12hr., 2 per week, 119kn); **Rijeka** (7hr., 2 per week, 97kn); **Split** (6hr., 2 per week, 97kn); **Ancona, ITA** (6hr., 4-7 per week, 306kn).

Public Transportation: Schedules for buses (M-Sa every 15-20min., Su and holidays 1 per hr. 5am-11:20pm; ☎21 15 55) are posted at the main bus station and at most stops. Station names are rarely posted at each stop; ask for help. Buy tickets from the driver (8kn) or any kiosk (round-trip 13kn) and validate on board.

ORIENTATION AND PRACTICAL INFORMATION

Most of the city's businesses and sights are scattered along **Široka,** the main street in **Stari Grad** (Old Town). The bus and train stations are at Ante Starčevića 1. To get to Široka, with your back to the main entrance, go through the pedestrian underpass and continue straight until you hit **Zrinsko-Frankopanska.** Follow this street (and the signs to the "Centar") all the way to the water, then walk along the left

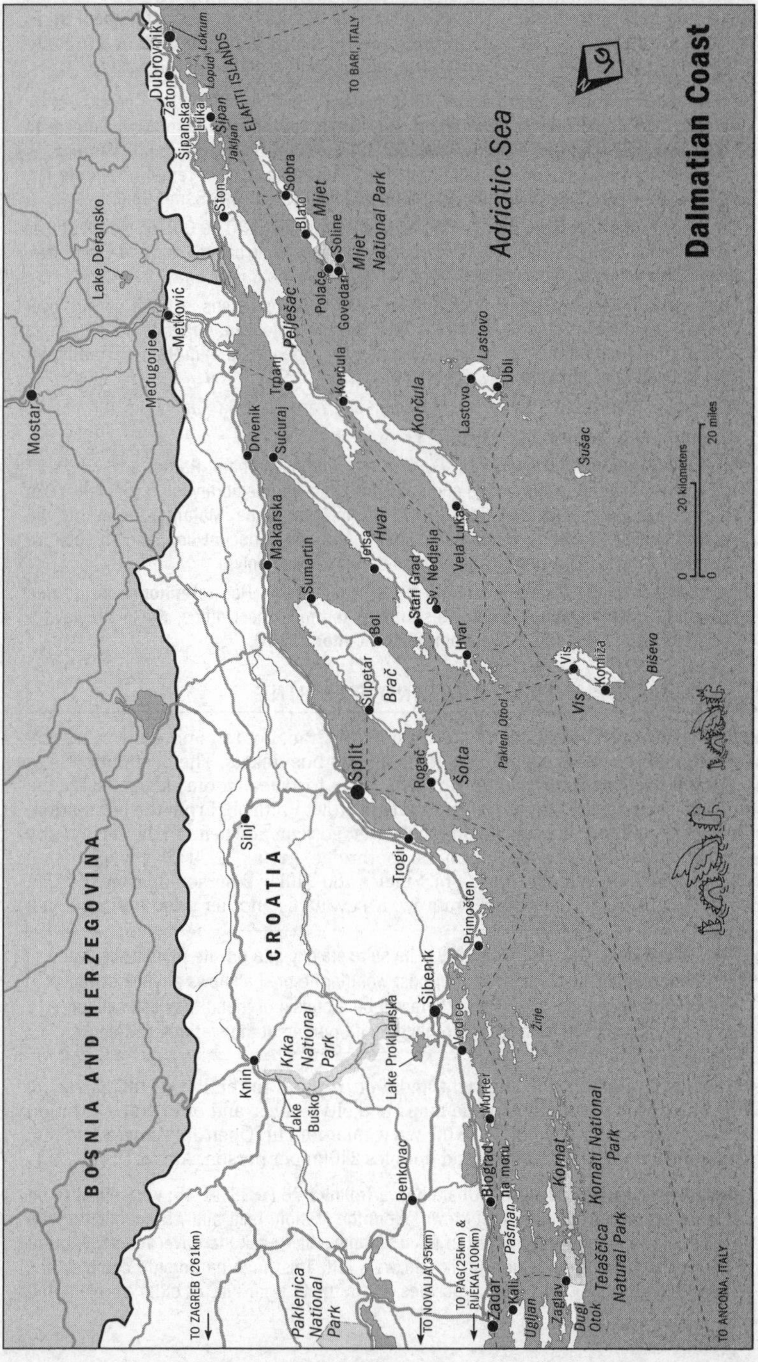

Dalmatian Coast

Adriatic Sea

BOSNIA AND HERZEGOVINA

CROATIA

Mostar
Lake Deransko
Međugorje
Metković
Dubrovnik
Lokrum
Lopud
Zaton
Šipanska Luka
Šipan
Jakljan
ELAFITI ISLANDS
TO BARI, ITALY
Ston
Sobra
Blato
Mljet
Soline
Polače
Govedari
Mljet National Park
Pelješac
Trpanj
Korčula
Lastovo
Ubli
Drvenik
Sućuraj
Sušac
Makarska
Jelsa
Hvar
Vela Luka
Sumartin
Stari Grad
Sv. Nedjelja
Bol
Supetar
Brač
Vis
Komiža
Biševo
Pakleni Otoci
Split
Rogač
Šolta
Sinj
Trogir
Primošten
Šibenik
Vodice
Žirje
Knin
Krka National Park
Lake Prokljanska
Lake Buško
Murter
Benkovac
Biograd na moru
Kornat
Kornati National Park
Pašman
Telašćica Natural Park
Zaglav
Dugi Otok
Ugljan
Kali
Zadar
Paklenica National Park
TO ZAGREB (261km)
TO NOVALJA (35km)
TO PAG (25km) & RIJEKA (100km)
TO ANCONA, ITALY

0 — 20 kilometers
0 — 20 miles

CROATIA

side of the harbor to the first gate of Stari Grad. Široka branches off **Narodni trg** to the right after you pass through the gate. Alternatively, hop on bus #2 or 4 to Poluotok. Facing the water, head right to the main gate opposite the footbridge.

Tourist Office: Tourist Board Zadar, Ilije Smiljanića 5. The Information Center is at M. Klaića 2 (☎31 61 66; www.tzzadar.hr). Go straight on the road from the main gate to the far corner of Narodni trg. Free **maps** and an info booklet on Zadar. **Ventura,** V. Desnice 18 (☎33 70 66), in Borik, offers a reasonable scooter rental (70kn per hr., 240kn per day). Open daily June-Aug. 8am-midnight; Sept.-May 8am-10pm.

Currency Exchange: Hypo Alpe-Adria-Bank, Barakovića 4 (☎20 09 00), on the left side as you enter the main gate of Stari Grad. Exchanges currency for no commission and cashes **traveler's checks** for 1.5% commission. Open M-F 8am-8pm, Sa 8am-noon.

Luggage Storage: At the bus station; follow the *garderoba* signs. 1.20kn per hr.; over 15kg 2.20kn per hr. Open daily 6am-10pm. **Bagul Garderoba,** opposite the Jadrolinija office on the waterfront. 5kn per hr., 15kn per day. Open M-Sa 7am-9pm, Su 5-9pm. At the train station. 15kn per day. Open 24hr.

Pharmacy: Barakovića 2 (☎21 33 74). Open M-F 7am-9pm, Sa 8am-noon.

Hospital: Bože Peričića 5 (☎31 56 77).

Internet: Gradska Knjižnica Zadar (Zadar City Library), Stjepana Radića 116 (☎31 57 72). Cross the pedestrian bridge and continue 2 blocks; the library is on your left. 10kn per hr.; 10kn min. Open M-F 8am-7pm, Sa 8am-1pm. **Acme,** Matafara 2a, next to the Forum and St. Donat's church, has 7 computers and a decent connection. Look for signs off Siroka. 10kn per 30min. Open 9am-9pm. Cash only.

Post Office: Nikole Matafara 1 (☎25 05 06), off Široka. Has **telephones** inside and gives MC **cash advances. Poste Restante** at the main post office, Kralja Držislava 1 (☎31 60 23). Open M-Sa 7am-9pm. **Postal Code:** 23000.

ACCOMMODATIONS AND CAMPING

Zadar has a youth hostel, but it's far from Stari Grad, not too impressive, and you may ultimately end up spending a good deal on bus tickets. The best option is to find a **private room** in the center of town. Look for *sobe* (room) signs, or try the **Aquarius Travel Agency,** inside the main gate at Nova Vrata bb. From the bus station, take bus #2 or 4 to Poluotok. Facing the water, go right and head to the second city entrance on your right across from the footbridge. (☎/fax 21 29 19; www.juresko-aquarius.com. Open daily 7am-10pm. Singles 180-240kn; 2-person apartments 250-300kn. Tax 5.50-7kn.) **Miatours,** Vrata Sv. Krševana, is another good option. You'll

MAKING CONNECTIONS. If you're staying in a private room while island hopping, make sure to ask your host whether he or she knows anyone at your future destinations. It's likely there will be a cousin or friend they can call for you—saving you from having to haggle with people at the stations and docks.

see a Jadrolinija booth to the right and a *garderoba* to the left of the entrance. They book private rooms, provide maps and city guides, and offer transportation to the islands. (☎25 44 00 or 25 43 00; www.miatours.hr. Open July-Aug. 8am-8pm; Sept.-June 8am-2:30pm. Singles and doubles 240kn per person. AmEx/DC/MC/V.)

Omladinski Hostel Zadar (HI), Obala Kneza Trpimira 76 (☎33 11 45; www.hfhs.hr), on the waterfront at the outskirts of town. From the station, take bus #5 heading to Puntamika (15min., 6kn) or bus #8 to Diklo (20min., 6kn); ask the driver to let you off at the 1st stop after Autocamp Borik and walk left. This huge harborside complex has dorm rooms, a bar, and sports facilities and attracts a mixture of older travelers and children's camp excursions. Simple breakfast included. Internet 5kn per 10min. Reception 8am-10pm. Check-out 10am. Call ahead. July 1-Aug. 29 114kn. Prices drop in low season. Tourist tax 5.50-7.50kn. 12kn member discount. ❶

Omladinski Hostel, Obala kneza Branimira 10a (☎22 48 40; djacki-dom@zd.htnet.hr). Across the footbridge from town, you couldn't ask for a better budget location. 3-bed dorms 103kn. ❶

Autocamp Borik, Gustavo Matoša bb (☎33 20 74; fax 33 20 65), on the beach. Follow directions to Hostel Zadar and look for large signs on the right. Ample, clean sites, but the trees don't quite block the road noise. July-Aug. 52.50kn per person, 60kn per tent, 75kn per car. Tax 7.50kn. May-June and Sept. 37.50/45/52/50/5.50kn. ❶

FOOD

The **Konzum** supermarket has several branches, including Široka 10 and J. Štrossmayerova 6. (Both open M-Sa 7am-9pm, Su 7am-8pm.) A **market** on Zlatarska, below Narodni trg and past the cinema, sells produce, meat, cheese, and bread; it also doubles as a densely packed flea market. (Open daily 6am-2pm.) Don't forget to pick up a bottle of the Zadar's regional specialty, a maraschino liqueur.

Trattoria Canzona, Stomorica 8 (☎21 20 81). Right in the middle of the young hangout spot and always packed. Try the warm-cold salad (lettuce and tomatoes covered in sauteed mushrooms, baby shrimp, and onions; 45kn). Entrees 45-70kn. Open 10am-11pm. Cash only. ❷

Restaurant Dva Ribara (Two Fishermen), Blaža Jurjeva 1 (☎21 34 45), off Plemića Borelli. A local favorite. In addition to the ubiquitous Croatian standards, this legendary duo offers leafy salads, vegetarian plates (40-50kn), and a colorful array of pizzas (30-50kn). Open daily 10:30am-midnight. AmEx/V. ❷

Foša, Kralja Dmitra Zvonimira 2 (☎31 44 21). Named after the inlet upon which it sits outside the city walls, Foša grills up sizable portions of fresh fish (45-160kn) and meat (55-75kn) on a wide patio overlooking the bay. The atmosphere is romantic after sundown. Open M-Sa 11am-midnight, Su 5pm-midnight. ❷

Zalogajnica Ljepotica, Obala Kneza Branimira 4b (☎31 12 88). While it isn't in the center, Zalogajnica has excellent views of the marina, making the simple, flavorful meals even more of a steal. Entrees from 25kn. ❶

CROATIA

SIGHTS

SEA ORGAN. The coolest sight in Zadar is a sound. The city's distinctive Sea Organ, said to be the first of its kind, was built in 2005 by architect Nikola Bašić, in consultation with other Croatian experts in hydraulics and organ making and tuning. Rushing seawater causes pipes beneath this 70m long stairway to play notes at random. The resulting music sounds something like a whale choir might.

FORUM. The most storied area in Zadar is the ancient Forum, a wide-open square ornamented with heaped stone relics, located on Široka, in the center of the peninsula. In the evenings, watch out for kids driving around a section of the ruins in rented mini play-cars. Built in Byzantine style in the early ninth century, **St. Donat's Church** (Crkva Sv. Donata) sits atop the ruins of an ancient Roman temple; the ruins are still visible from inside. Today, the building is one of only three circular Catholic churches in the world. Though no longer a place of worship, it is still used for the occasional high school graduation. *(Open daily 9am-2pm and 4-8pm. 5kn.)*

ST. MARY'S CHURCH (CRKVA SV. MARIJA). Across the square and toward the water from St. Donat's, St. Mary's is a more traditional place of worship, housing the fabulous **Permanent Exhibition of Religious Art** (Stalna Izložba Crkvene Umjetnosti). Its gold and silver busts, reliquaries, and crosses are regarded as some of Croatia's most precious artifacts. Don't miss the gold and silver reliquary of Zadar's patron Saint Simon, said to be the largest in Europe. Shrewd nuns keep a close watch over visitors. *(Trg Opatice Čike 1. ☎21 15 45. Buy tickets to the left of the church. Open M-Sa 10am-1pm and 6-8pm, Su 10am-1pm. 20kn, students 10kn.)*

ARCHEOLOGICAL MUSEUM (ARHEOŠLOKI MUZEJ). This museum, next to St. Mary's, documents the epochal history of Zadar with aerial photographs of towns and archaeological sites, beautiful medieval stonework, and innumerable shards of prehistoric pottery. The captions are in Croatian. *(☎25 05 16. Open M-Sa 9am-1pm and 5-7pm. 10kn, students 5kn.)*

NATIONAL MUSEUM (NARODNI MUZEJ ZADAR). The National Museum offers an accessible and entertaining view of the city's history. Scale models of Zadar chronicle its development through the centuries. Local works of art from the 15th and 16th centuries accompany superbly crafted 17th- and 18th-century furniture. The same ticket provides access to the **Art Gallery,** which is filled with changing exhibits of Croatian painters. *(From St. Mary's, follow the same street to the other side of the peninsula away from the water; the museum is on the right. ☎25 18 51. Open M-Tu and Th-F 9am-noon, W 6-9pm, Sa-Su 9am-1pm. 10kn, students 5kn.)*

OTHER SIGHTS. Enter the city through the Renaissance **city gate,** which still bears the Venetian lion. Only a street back at Trg bunara 5 are the **five wells,** which supplied Zadar with water until 1838. The **Franciscan Church and Monastery,** Zadarskog mira 1358 (☎25 04 68), dating back to 1280, is the oldest Gothic church in Dalmatia and displays artwork from the Renaissance. *(Open daily 7:30am-noon and 4.30-6pm.)*

CROATIA

ENTERTAINMENT AND NIGHTLIFE

Kino Pobjeda, on Jurja Dalmatinca just off Narodni trg, shows mainstream English-language movies with Croatian subtitles in an enormous theater. (Open daily 6:30-11pm. 15-25kn. Later screenings are more expensive.) **Swimming** can be found at the coastal promenade of Kralja Dmitra Zvonimira, bordered on one side by a pine-filled park. Otherwise, the nearby tourist centers **Borik** and **Puntamika** have pebble beaches aplenty, as well as concrete sunbathing walkways. For a sandy seaside landscape, catch a ferry to one of the many nearby islands. **Dugi Otok,** one of the closest, is a favorite with the locals. Zadar hosts classical and medieval concerts in St. Donat's Cathedral from early July to mid-August. Ask the tourist office for details. The concurrent **Zadar Dreams** festival sees the parks and streets of the city turned into stages for quirky theatrical performances. If possible, try to arrive for the city's **Night of the Full Moon,** which celebrates the town's ancient customs and culinary specialties on the quayside by moonlight. The youth scene is centered around the sidewalk cafes along **Varoška** and **Stomorica,** just off of Špire Brusine.

Maya Pub, Liburnska Obala 6 (☎25 17 16), is one of Zadar's more unique nightlife options. A looming statue of Shiva watches over patrons as they relax to electro music when there isn't a local act on stage. Open 7am-2am. Cash only.

The Garden, Bedemi zadarskih pobuna bb (☎36 47 39; www.thegardenzadar.com), owned by a former UB40 drummer, attracts a relaxed daytime crowd of board-game players and espresso drinkers. At night, it draws locals and foreigners with its blasting reggae, ambient, and funk. International DJs are often featured. Lounge on white sofas or mattresses on the wooden deck overlooking the marina. Beer 11-20kn per 0.33L. Mixed drinks 28-45kn. Open 11am-1am. Cash only.

Arsenal, Trg Tri Bunara 1 (☎25 05 37; www.arsenalzadar.com), is a former 18th-century warehouse that now hosts local musical acts. Mixed drinks 25-35kn. Open daily 7am-3am.

Caffe Bar Forum, on Široka at the Forum, has comfortable chairs and outdoor seating overlooking the ruins. It's perfect for a casual sunset drink. Karlovačko 13kn per 0.33L. Wine from 10kn. Open daily 7:30am-midnight.

DAYTRIP FROM ZADAR

PAKLENICA NATIONAL PARK

To reach Paklenica, take the Rijeka-Zadar bus. You will find the park entrance at Hotel Alan, and the Southern gorge entrance, which is perfect for exploring Mala Paklenica, at Seline. Facing Hotel Alan, walk to your right 300m to the sign that leads to the entrance.

The 400m cliffs of Paklenica make the national park a favorite among climbers, but hikers and nature lovers will also enjoy the park's brooks, shaded pine forests, and chalky karst mountains. The park's wildlife includes peregrine falcons, sparrowhawks, more than 80 species of butterfly. The **park office** provides a free map with the entrance fee. Serious hikers should shell out for the more detailed maps that range from 15 to 25kn. (☎36 92 02; www.paklenica.hr. Open Apr.-Oct. M-F 8am-3pm. 30kn, 60kn per 3 days, 90kn per 5 days.) **Mala** and **Vela Paklenica** are popular cliffs to climb, while underground explorers prefer the half-submerged caves, the largest of which, **Manića Paklenica,** runs for 200m inside the mountain range. Along the road to the actual park is a set of tunnels once used by Jugoslav President Josip Broz Tito for emergency refuge. Ask at the park office for opening hours. Two hiking routes (both 6hr. round-trip) lead up the 712m summit of Anića Kuk, an isolated mountain that provides views worth the difficult descent. Another hike (6hr. round-trip) goes to the beautiful cave Manita Peć before climbing 866m to Vidakov Kuk. The cave must be visited with a guide and is open only three times a week; contact the park office for info. The trail is difficult, crossing scree-covered slopes and rocky outcroppings. For a wide view of the islands, try **Velika Golić,** a 1285m peak farther up from Manita Peć. Passing through limestone ridges and bordered by drystone walls, the walk itself is a hard but rewarding 4-5hr. ascent.

CROATIA

SPLIT ☎(0)21

Metropolitan Split (pop. 300,000) is by no means a typical Dalmatian town. Croatia's second-largest city, it is more a cultural center than a beach resort, boasting a wider variety of activities and nightlife than any of its neighbors. Stari Grad, wedged between a high mountain range and a palm-lined waterfront, is framed by the luxurious palace where Roman emperor Diocletian spent his summers. In the seventh century, the local Illyrian population fled to the palace to escape marauding Slavs, built a town, and incorporated the walls and arches of the palace into their houses and public squares. The result is a UNESCO-protected city with some of Europe's most puzzling and interesting architecture.

TRANSPORTATION

Flights: Split Airport (☎20 35 06; fax 20 35 07) sends planes to domestic and international destinations. A bus (25min., 30kn) runs between the airport and the waterfront near the catamaran dock, Gat. Sv. Nikole, 1½hr. before each departure. **Croatia Airlines,** Obala hrvatskog narodnog preporoda 9 (☎36 29 97), flies through Split Airport. Airport open M-F 8am-8pm, Sa 9am-noon.

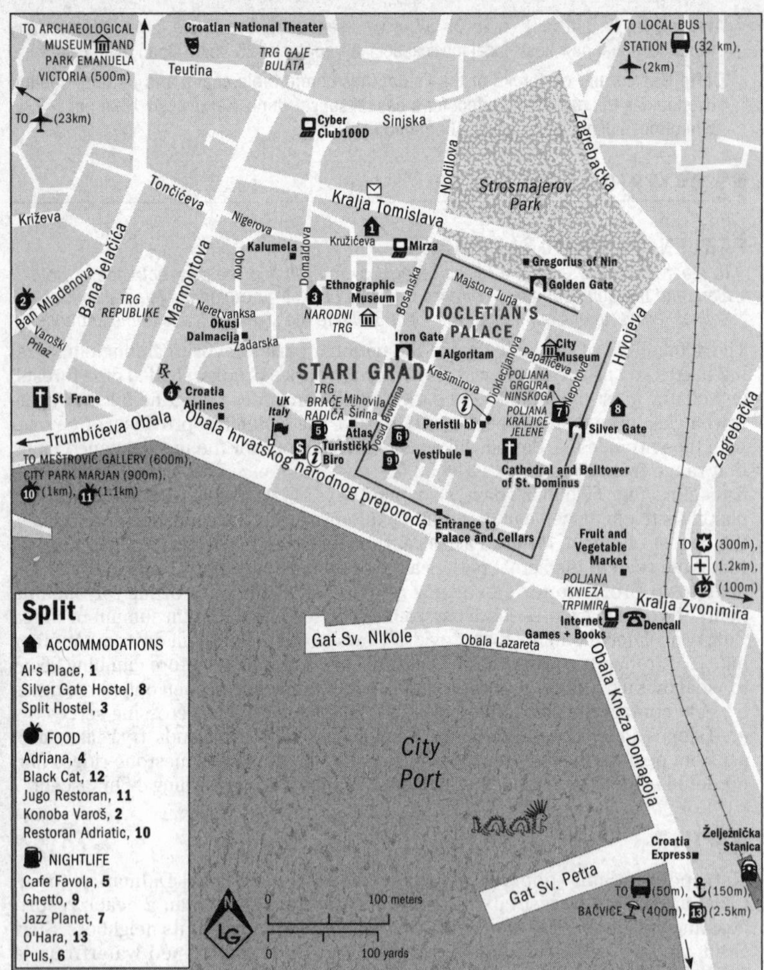

Trains: Obala Kneza Domagoja 8 (☎33 85 25, info 33 34 44). Trains do not run south of Split. Ticket office open daily 6:10am-10:20pm. To: **Rijeka** (12hr., 2 per day, 183kn) via **Oguli; Zadar** (6½hr., 1 per day, 82kn) via **Knin; Zagreb** (5-8hr., 5 per day, 158kn); **Budapest, HUN** (16hr., 1 per day, 370kn); **Ljubljana, SLV** (12hr., 2 per week, 237kn).

Buses: Obala Kneza Domagoja 12 (☎33 84 83, schedule info 060 327 327). Domestic tickets sold inside at the main counter, international tickets *(međunarodni karte)* in the small office to the right. Open daily 5am-11pm. To: **Dubrovnik** (4½hr., 19 per day, 89-122kn); **Rijeka** (7hr., 13 per day, 220kn); **Zadar** (3½hr., 2 per hr., 97kn); **Zagreb** (5½hr., 2 per hr., 140kn); **Ljubljana, SLV** (11hr., 1 per day, 260kn). Buses to **Trogir** (30min., 3 per hr., 19kn) leave from the **local bus station** on Domovinskog rata.

Ferries: Obala Lazareta (☎33 83 33; fax 33 82 22; www.jadrolinija.hr). To: **Dubrovnik** (8hr., 2 per week, 115kn); **Korčula** (6hr., 2 per week, 55kn); **Rijeka** (10½hr., 2 per week, 169kn); **Ancona, ITA** (10hr., 4 per week, 329kn); **Bari, ITA** (25hr., 3 per week, 329kn).

Public Transportation: Buses run all night but are few and far between after midnight. Buy tickets (8kn) from the driver and punch them on board.

Taxis: Many wait in front of Diocletian's Palace on Obala hrvatskog narodnog preporoda and at the bus station and ferry terminal. Base 18kn, 9kn per km. **Radio Taxi** (☎970; www.970-radiotaxisplit.com.hr).

ORIENTATION AND PRACTICAL INFORMATION

The train and bus stations lie on **Obala Kneza Domagoja** across from Gat Sv. Petra, where the ferries arrive. With your back to the stations, follow Obala Kneza Domagoja, often referred to as **Riva,** to the right along the water until it runs into **Obala hrvatskog narodnog preporoda,** which runs roughly east to west. Behind this boulevard, opposite the water, lies **Stari Grad** (Old Town), centered on the main square, **Narodni trg,** and packed inside the walls of **Diocletian's Palace** (Dioklecijanova Palača). To reach Stari Grad from the local bus station, go right on Domovinskog Rata, which becomes Livanjska and then Zagrebačka. Go right on Kralja Zvonimira at the end of Zagrebačka and follow it to the harbor.

Tourist Offices: Turistički Biro, Obala hrvatskog narodnog preporoda 12 (☎/fax 34 71 00), sells **maps** for 15-30kn. Open M-Sa 8am-9pm, Su 9am-1pm. The **Tourist Information Center (TIC),** Peristil bb (☎34 56 06; www.visitsplit.com), beside the cathedral, hands out free, detailed maps of Stari Grad and brochures. Both sell the **Splitcard** (60kn, free if you stay in a city-registered hotel for 3 nights or more; valid for 72hr.), which is good for freebies and discounts at museums, theaters, hotels, and restaurants.

Consulates: UK, Obala hrvatskog narodnog preporoda 10 (☎34 60 07, emergencies 09 14 55 53 26), above Zagrebačka Bank, shares a building with **Italy.** Open M-F 9am-1pm.

Currency Exchange: Splitska Banka, Obala hrvatskog narodnog preporoda 10 (☎34 74 23). Exchanges currency for no commission and cashes **traveler's checks** for 2% commission. **Western Union** available. Open M-F 8am-8pm, Sa 8am-noon.

American Express: Atlas Travel Agency, Trg Braće Radić 6 (☎34 30 55). Open M-Sa 8am-8pm, Su 8am-noon and 6-9pm.

Luggage Storage: At the bus station kiosk marked *Garderoba.* 20kn per day. Open daily 6am-10pm. Also at the train station, Obala Kneza Domagoja 6. 20kn per day. Open daily 6am-11pm.

English-Language Bookstore: Algoritam, Bajamotijeva 2. Decent selection of English–language novels and nonfiction. Books 50-150kn. Open M-F 8am-8:30pm, Sa 8am-1pm. AmEx/MC/V.

Police: Trg Hrvatske Bratske Zajednice 9 (☎30 71 11). From Stari Grad, take Kralja Zvonimira and bear right onto Pojišanka; the station is on the right.

Pharmacy: Marmontova 2 (☎34 57 38). Open M-F 7am-8pm, Sa 7am-1pm. MC/V. 24hr. pharmacies **Dobri,** Gundulićeva 52 (☎34 80 74), and **Lučac,** Pupačićeva 4 (☎53 31 88).

Hospital: Klinička Bolnica Split, Spinčiceva 1 (☎55 61 11). From Stari Grad, follow Kralja Zvonimira until it runs into Poljička. Turn right onto Pt. Iza Nove Bolnice; the hospital is on the right. Cash only.

Internet: Cyber Club 100D, Sinjska 2/4 (☎34 81 10), around the corner from the main post office, has 9 computers with fast connections and Wi-Fi. Cold and hot drinks 2-8kn. 20kn per hr.; 15min. minimum. Memory card reader and CD-burning 15kn. Open M-Sa 9am-10pm, Su 4-10pm. Cash only.

Post Office: The main branch is at Kralja Tomislava 9 (☎36 14 21). Mail services through the main doors; **telephones** and **fax** through the doors to the left. Also **exchanges currency** for 1.5% commission. Open M-F 7:30am-9pm, Sa 7am-1pm. **Poste Restante** at Hercegovačka 1 (☎38 33 65). Take Zagrebačka from Stari Grad to

Domovinskog Rata and go left on Pt. Stinica (20min.). Take a right onto Hercegovačka. Open M-Sa 7am-8pm. Buses #5, 9, 10, and 13 run here from the market; ask the driver where to get off. More convenient is the location on the waterfront near the bus and train stations at Obala Domagoja 3 (☎38 34 74). **Telephones** are on the left. **Western Union** services and **currency exchange** for 1.5% commission. Open daily 7:30am-9pm. **Postal Code:** 21000.

ACCOMMODATIONS

Split has bounced back from the war with a reinvigorated tourist industry, and hotels and hostels are becoming more common. Private accommodations still tend to be the best budget option, and the quality of rooms is generally high. **Daluma Travel Agency,** Obala Kneza Domagoja 1, near the bus and train stations, can help find **private rooms.** (☎33 84 84; www.daluma.hr. Open M-F 7am-9pm, Sa 8am-2pm. Singles 230kn, with bath 255kn; doubles 380kn.) If affordability is a priority, consider staying with people who advertise at the bus station and ferry landing. Bargaining should get you a room for at least 100kn less than the agencies are offering. It is advisable to take a look at any room before striking a deal—rooms are of varying quality. Moreover, Split is a sprawling city, and particularly low prices may indicate long bus rides into town.

Al's Place, Kruziceva 10 (☎09 89 18 29 23; www.hostelsplit.com.), feels more like a cozy pension than a hostel. British Al, an expert on Split, organizes group dinners, nights out on the town, and excursions to go horseback riding. Book early, as the 12 beds fill up fast. Some double bedrooms available in summer. Check-in 2-8pm. Dorms June-Aug. 120kn; Sept.-May 100kn. Cash only. ❶

Split Hostel, Narodni Trg 8 (☎34 27 87; www.splithostel.com). The catchphrase "booze and snooze" says it all about this centrally located, party-themed establishment. Dorms 120-150kn. ❶

Silver Gate Hostel, Hrvojeva 6 (☎32 28 57; www.silvergatehsotel.com), offers views of Diocletian's Palace from every room and a staff devoted to seeking out the best nightlife in Split. Dorms 120-150kn. ❶

CROATIA

FOOD

There are small **supermarkets** inside the Jadrolinija complex across from the bus station (open M-Sa 6am-9pm, Su 7am-9pm) and at Svačićeva 4 (open daily 7am-10pm). If you're in Stari Grad and don't feel like shelling out for a restaurant meal, go to **Okusi Dalmaciju,** Dobrić 14, the market just off of Trg Brače Radić. With your back toward the water, head left through the square and down the street parallel to the waterfront—it will be on your right. (☎34 31 85. Open M-Sa 6:30am-9pm, Su 7am-1pm. AmEx/MC/V.) There's also an organic market and bakery, **Kalumela,** Domaldova 7, near the northern edge of Stari Grad, between the northwest corner of Narodni Trg and Kralja Tomislava. It offers soy, tofu, and rice products as well as baked goods. (☎34 81 32. Open 8am-9pm. AmEx/MC/V.) The **food court ❶,** Obala Kneza Domagoja 1, between Stari Grad and the stations, has fast food and fresh sandwiches. (8-15kn. Open daily 8am-midnight.)

Black Cat (☎49 02 84). On the corner of Petrova and Šegvića. From the station, walk toward the city and turn right up Kralja Zvonimirova, then right again down Petrova. This vine-trellised bistro is an affordable and welcome respite from risotto and pizza, serving excellent international cuisine from Thai to Mexican to Indian. The relaxed service also means you can linger over your cocktail in the air-conditioned salon. Entrees 30-60kn. Open 8am-midnight. ❷

Jugo Restoran, Uvala Baluni bb (☎37 89 00). Facing the water on Obala hrvatskog narodnog preporoda, walk right along the waterfront (10min.) to Branimirova Obala. Veer right at the fork near the marina; go left on the 1st street after the fork and head through the park; it's on the left. This modern restaurant, boasting one of the best views in Split, seduces beautiful people with excellent seafood, brick-oven pizza, and homemade Slavonian sausage. Entrees 30-200kn. Open daily 11am-midnight. AmEx/MC/V. ❷

Restoran Adriatic, Uvala baluni bb (☎39 85 60). Just before the crop of trees at the end of the marina. Only slightly more expensive than the average tourist eatery, elegant Adriatic offers a stellar seaside view and impressive cuisine. Try the *piletina okko* (grilled chicken with ham, eggs and cheese; 60kn) or pasta with shrimp in bean soup, an old fisherman's recipe (55kn). With the changing wind, it's best to sit inside during lunch and outside during dinner. Cover 12kn. AmEx/MC/V. ❷

Konoba Varoš, Ban Mladenova 7 (☎39 61 38). Facing the water on Obala hrvatskog narodnog preporoda, head right on Varoški Prilaz and then left on Ban Mladenova. A true Dalmatian feast, prepared and served in a den adorned with fishing nets and wine racks. Try the spaghetti with mushrooms (35kn), or something different like steamed octopus (75kn), ostrich steak (80kn), or bread-crumbed frogs (260kn per kg). Open M-F 9am-midnight, Sa-Su noon-midnight. AmEx/MC/V. ❷

SIGHTS

DIOCLETIAN'S PALACE (DIOKLECIJANOVA PALAČA). The eastern half of Split's Stari Grad occupies the one-time fortress and summer residence of the Roman Emperor Diocletian. Adorned with Italian and Greek marble, as well as Egyptian sphinxes, this colossal stone palace, built between AD 395 and 410, is an overwhelming emblem of the city. With its ancient walls peeking out between palm fronds, it is easy to imagine that the palace has seen its fair share of empires—and refugees. Having first protected Roman royalty, it later served as a sanctuary for Galla Placidia, daughter of Byzantine Emperor Theodosius, and her son Valentinius III, when they were busy dodging the blades of usurpers. In the seventh century, local residents used the fortress for protection from Slavic raids, and they later built their city within its walls. More than a time capsule, the palace today serves as a living historical tableau, as *sobe* signs hanging from the stones and coffee drinkers lounging upon its shiny steps attest. *(Across from the taxis on Obala hrvatskog narodnog preporoda. Go right and down into the cool, dark corridor.)*

CELLARS. The city's haunting cellars are located near the entrance to the palace. Nearly two millennia ago, the dark stone passages served as the floor for the emperor's apartments. The central hall runs from Obala hrvatskog narodnog preporoda to the Peristyle and holds booths that sell local crafts. The hall on the left houses an interactive station that gives a wealth of history about the palace and city while entertaining visitors with Renaissance music. Some archaeological finds are displayed in hallways to the left of the entrance. The airier right side is used as a gallery that houses rotating exhibits by local artists, authors, and filmmakers. Every year the palace grows as more rooms (some right under local residences) are excavated. *(Cellars open M-F 9am-9pm, Sa-Su 10am-6pm. 8kn.)*

CATHEDRAL. The cathedral on the right side of the Peristyle is one of architecture's great ironies: it's one of the oldest Catholic cathedrals in the world but was originally the mausoleum of Diocletian, who was known for his violent persecution of Christians. The octagonal cathedral is home to a plethora of wooden and stone sculptures, friezes, and paintings from a medieval Croatian master. While appreciating this elaborate place of worship is worth the ticket price in itself, entry to the cathedral **treasury,** upstairs and to the right, is also included. Displays include 15th-century ecclesiastical garments, delicate 13th-century books, and many silver busts and goblets. Construction began on the adjoining **Bell tower of St. Domnius** (Zvonik Sv. Duje) in the 13th century and took 300 years to complete. The view from the top of its 186 steps is spectacular. *(Cathedral and tower open daily 8:30am-8pm. Cathedral and treasury 10kn. Tower 5kn.)*

OTHER SIGHTS IN STARI GRAD. Stari Grad is framed on its eastern side by the **Silver Gate** (Srebrna Vrata), which leads to the main open-air market. Outside the northern **Golden Gate** (Zlatna Vrata) stands Ivan Meštrović's portrayal of **Gregorius of Nin** (Grgur Ninski), the 10th-century Slavic champion of commoners. The western **Iron Gate** (Željezna Vrata) leads to Narodni trg. Medieval architecture dominates this side of town, where many of the houses are crumbling with age and occasionally drop their stones. **Park Emanuela Victoria,** off Zrinsko-Frankopanska en route to the Archaeological Museum, is a great locale for a daytime stroll. Another nice park with a great view of the ocean and surrounding islands is **Sustipan,** located right at the end of the marina—just look for the trees at the end of the peninsula facing the bus and train stations. A cemetery until WWII, this quiet and peaceful park is perfect for a picnic or a nap while waiting for your ferry, bus, or train out of Split. (Open daily 6am-11pm.)

MUSEUMS

CROATIA

MEŠTROVIĆ GALLERY (GALERIJA IVANA MEŠTROVICA). This gallery has a comprehensive collection of works by famed Croatian sculptor **Ivan Meštrović** (see **The Visual Arts,** p. 102), and tremendous views of the ocean. The entrance fee includes the **gallery,** housed in a stately villa that the artist built for himself, and the 17th-century **Kaštelet,** decorated with wood carvings of New Testament scenes. While all of Meštrović's works are dazzlingly intricate, his marble Roman Pietà (ground floor) and agonized Job (1st fl.) are particularly impressive. *(Šetaliste Ivana Meštrovica 46. A 25min. walk along the waterfront, or take bus #12 from the stop across from Trg Franje Tuđmana. ☎34 08 00 or 34 08 01; www.mdc.hr/mestrovic. Open May-Sept. Tu-Sa 9am-9pm; Oct.-Apr. Tu-Sa 9am-4pm, Su 9am-6pm. 20kn, students 10kn. English booklet 20kn.)*

ARCHAEOLOGICAL MUSEUM (ARHEOLOŠKI MUZEJ). One of the oldest museums in Croatia, this institution makes shards of pottery interesting. The beautiful garden is filled with an impressive hodge-podge of Roman statuary and finds from Solana, a nearby ancient town. *(Zrinsko-Frankopanska 25. From the waterfront, follow Marmontova to Trg Gaje Bulata, turn left on Teutina, and take the 1st right. ☎31 87 21. Open M-Sa 9am-2pm and 4-8pm. English captions. 10kn, students 5kn.)*

CITY MUSEUM (MUZEJ GRADA SPLITA). Despite housing a minimal selection of artifacts, this museum tells the history of Split in detail. Set beside a scenic stone courtyard, the 15th-century building was designed by **Dalmatinac,** architect of Šibenik's Cathedral. The 17th-century weapons and 14th-century documents housed in this museum only have Croatian captions, but rooms have multilingual panels. *(Papalićeva 1. From the Golden Gate, enter Stari Grad and turn left on Papalićeva. ☎34 49 17; www.mgst.net. Open Tu-F 9am-4pm, Sa-Su 10am-1pm. 10kn, students 5kn.)*

ETHNOGRAPHIC MUSEUM (ETNOGRAFSKI MUZEJ). This museum displays artifacts from Croatia's past domestic and ceremonial life. Reassembled city wells, fisherman's boats, and traditional costumes are some of the more interesting exhibits. Captions are in Croatian. *(Severova 1. ☎34 41 08; www.et-mu-st.com. Open M-F 9am-2pm and 5-8pm, Sa 10am-1pm. 10kn, students 5kn.)*

BEACHES AND ENTERTAINMENT

The rocky cliffs, wide green hills, and pebbly beaches on the western end of Split's peninsula make up 100-year-old **City Park Marjan,** a great expanse for walking or jogging through forests, by crumbling chapels, and over the 126m hill. From Obala hrvatskog narodnog preporoda, face the water and head right (15min.). Paths are indicated on the map; you can find your own way, but watch for signs marking trails that lead to private lands. The closest beach to downtown Split is crowded **Bačvice,** a favorite among nocturnal skinny-dippers. Bačvice is also the starting point of a strip of popular bars along the waterfront. **Kašjuni Cove,** by City Park Marjan, is a lot less crowded.

There are many cinemas throughout the city, including **Central,** Trg Gaja Bulata bb (☎34 38 13); **Tesla,** Kralja Tomislava 5 (☎34 46 33); and **Kinoteka,** Dioclecijanova 7 (☎36 12 55). In early May, Split honors its patron saint, St. Domnius, with festivities in Stari Grad, which include Dalmatian *klapa* singers, folk dancing, and a lot of bingo. From mid-July to mid-August, Split hosts an annual **Summer Festival.** The region's best artists and international guests perform ballets, operas, plays, and classical concerts in the town's churches and ruins. (Info and ticket reservations ☎36 30 14. Tickets 754-215kn.)

NIGHTLIFE

Bačvice is where all the clubs are—tons of bars and clubs sit side by side and play all types of music in a two-story complex. Head away from Stari Grad, past the bus and train stations, and continue left along the water (after crossing the bridge over the train tracks) and down the hill; just follow the crowds and the noise. In Stari Grad, the popular bars for young people are just off **Trg Brače Radič.** Head toward the Slavija Hotel and continue up the stairs to find bar after bar of local hipsters.

Ghetto, Dosud 10 (☎348 79), at the top of stairs, off Brače Radič. The eccentric decor at this colorful club features a neon shag carpet, bean bags, and suggestive muraled walls, making it the venue of choice for the hip arts crowd. The cool open courtyard, with its bubbling fountain, is a welcome respite from Split's summer heat. DJs spin funk and lounge music. Open daily 10am-1am. Cash only.

O'Hara Music Club, Uvala Zenta 3 (☎51 94 92). Follow the waterfront past Tropic Club Equador for 20min. 2 floors of raging techno. Cover 30kn. Open Th-Su 11pm-late.

Cafe Favola, Trg Braće Radić 1. (☎34 48 48). A chic, laid-back bar that lures both locals and tourists with views of one of the city's quietest and most beautiful squares. Prošek 10kn. Open daily 7am-midnight.

Jazz Planet, Grgura Ninskoga 3 (☎34 76 99). Hidden on a tiny but lively square opposite the City Museum, Jazz Planet has low, comfortable chairs outside, and Picasso-esque paintings, sizzling jazz, and plentiful beer inside. Guinness 25kn per 0.5L. Open M-Th and Su 8am-midnight, F-Sa 8am-2am.

Puls, Buvinina 1, just off Trg Braće Radić. This party bar is both well known and well loved, as the crowds spilling out into the streets attest. Puls caters to 2 distinct and important niche markets: young disco dancers upstairs, serious drinkers and smokers downstairs. Open daily 10am-1am.

BRAČ ISLAND: BOL ☎(0)21

Central Dalmatia's largest island, Brač (brach) is an ocean-lover's paradise. It has more to offer than just its location, however: the churches, galleries, nightlife, and water sports in the tourist haven of Bol (pop. 1500), situated under the ancient

CROATIA

stronghold of Koštilo Hill, will keep loungers and adventurers occupied for days. Most visitors come here for Zlatni Rat (Golden Horn), a sleepy, picturesque peninsula with a smooth white pebble beach just a short walk from the town center. Elsewhere on the island, sights include bougainvillea-entwined balconies, olive groves, and stone houses that dot the stunning landscape.

TRANSPORTATION. The **ferry** from Split docks at Supetar (1hr., July-Aug. 12-16 per day, 25kn). From there, take a **bus** to Bol (1hr., 9 per day, 24kn). The last bus back to the ferry leaves at 7pm in high summer; the last ferry to Split leaves at 10:15pm (June-Aug.) or 8:30pm (Sept.-May). A bus also departs to and from Zagreb (8¾hr., 1 per day, 185kn). The **bus station** is a 7min. walk away from the ferry dock at Supetar. Alternatively, a **catamaran** runs to Bol from Split. (☎63 56 38. 40min. M-Sa leaves Bol 6:30am, Split 4pm; Su 7:30am and 4pm. 22kn. Buy tickets on board.)

ORIENTATION AND PRACTICAL INFORMATION. The streets of Bol cluster around a waterfront of many names. At the bus stop and marina, the waterfront is called **Obala Vladimira Nazora.** Left of the bus station (facing the water) it becomes **Riva,** then **Frane Radića,** then **Porat bolskih pomorca.** To the right it's **Put Zlatnog Rata.** Facing the sea on the far side of the small marina, walk 5min. to the left of the bus station to reach the **tourist office,** Porat bolskih pomorca bb. The staff dispenses a free Bol guide and a large selection of free **maps,** although the number of useful English materials is limited. (☎63 56 38; www.bol.hr. Open M-Sa 8:30am-2pm and 5-9pm, Su 9am-1pm.) **Adria Tours,** Obala Vladimira Nazora 28, to the right of the bus station facing the water, **rents scooters** (200kn per day) and **cars** (500kn per day, unlimited km). The staff also books rooms and organizes excursions (70-190kn) to nearby islands. There's a **pharmacy** and **medical clinic** at Porat bolskih pomorca bb. (☎63 59 87. Open M-Sa 7:30am-9pm, Su 8am-noon.) **M@3X,** on Rudina, a few doors down from Aqvarius, has fast and cheap **Internet** access. (www.orca-sport.com/caffe. 25kn for 1st hr., 20kn per hr. thereafter. Open daily 9:30am-11:30pm.) **Info-Graf,** uz. Pjacu bb. also offers Internet access at 30kn per hr. (☎71 88 77; www.info-graf.com). The **post office,** Uz Pjacu 5, has **telephones** outside. (☎63 56 78. Open M-Sa 7:30am-9pm.) **Postal Code:** 21420.

CROATIA

ACCOMMODATIONS AND FOOD. If the locals are all at the beach, leaving no one at the ferry dock or bus station to offer you a room, **Adria Tours** (see above) can help. (☎63 59 66; www.adria-bol.hr. Open daily 8am-9pm. July-Aug. 60-115kn per person; singles 105-170kn. Tax 10kn. 20% surcharge for stays under 4 nights.) Note that finding a single room can be very difficult in Brač; call ahead or you may have to splurge on a double. Adria Tours offers special deals on local hotel rooms from €75. There are five **campgrounds** around Bol; the largest is **Kito ❶,** Bračka bb, on the main road into town. (☎63 55 51; kamp_kito@inet.hr. Open May-Sept. 60kn per person, including tent and tax.)

Konzum, Riva bb (☎71 83 00), located right on the waterfront, tucked into the corner of Uz Pjacu, has a good selection and reasonable prices. An open-air **market** sells fresh produce to the right of Konzum on Riva. **Konoba Gušt ❷,** Frane Radića 14, offers shaded respite among hanging fishing gear, quirky photographs, and local diners and serves an array of fresh seafood. (☎63 59 11. Entrees 40-150kn. Open daily noon-2am.) Drawing flocks of locals and tourists to its hearty portions and perfect terrace view, **Taverna Riva ❸,** Trg Brace Radica 5, serves savory fish and meat, including grilled tuna (75kn), alongside traditional Croatian pastas and risottos. (☎63 52 36; www.riva-bol.com. Entrees 42-160kn. Cover 10kn. Open daily 11am-3pm and 6-11pm. AmEx/MC/V.) **Pizzeria**

Topolino ❶, Riva 2, on the waterfront in the town center, has tasty pizza and pasta (42-65kn), traditional Croatian meat dishes (55-75kn), and an impressive selection of salads from 35kn. (☎63 57 67. Open daily 8am-2am.) For a quick and tasty grilled sandwich, try **Mancini ❶**, Rudina 26, located right across from and slightly to the left of the bus station on the waterfront. (Drinks 12-20kn. Sandwiches 15-25kn. Burgers 25kn. Open 11am-4am. Cash only.)

SIGHTS AND ENTERTAINMENT. Bol's most important sight is the 1475 **Dominican Monastery**, located on the eastern tip of the town. Facing the water, walk left for 15min. beyond the tourist office. Look out for the extravagant ceiling paintings in the Church of Our Lady of Mercy, as well as the pavement of tombstones, often in Galgolitic script. The highlight of the monastery, however, is Tintoretto's altar painting of the **Madonna with Child.** Apparently concerned they'd need a refund, the monks kept the masterpiece's invoice, which is on display in the **museum,** among other artifacts of local history. (☎77 80 02. Museum and monastery open daily 10am-noon and 5-7pm. 10kn. Dress appropriately.) The **Dešković Gallery,** on Porat bolskih pomorca, behind the pharmacy, exhibits contemporary Croatian art in a small, 17th-century Baroque mansion. (Open daily 5-10pm. 5kn.) For exceptional views of the island, walk for 2hr. up **Vidova Gora,** the 778m mountain framing Bol.

More art comes to town during **Bol Cultural Summer** (Bolsko Kulturno Ljeto), which runs throughout July and August and features a variety of classical and folk music concerts. (Tickets free-20kn.) The **Bol Fair** and **Procession of Our Lady's Statue** in August are also events not to be missed by those who want to gain insight into this island's culture. The English-speaking staff at **Big Blue Sport,** Podan Glavice 2, on the way to Zlatni rat, organizes water sports. Back on land, they also offer beach volleyball and rent **bikes.** (☎098 635 614; www.big-blue-sport.hr. Beach volleyball 50kn per hr. Bikes 15kn per hr., 70kn per day. Open M-Sa 9:30am-noon and 5:30-10pm, Su 10am-noon and 5:30-10pm.) If you need speed, **waterskiing** (200kn, with lesson 300kn), **windsurfing** (8hr. course 890kn; rentals 360kn per day, 280kn per ½-day), and **banana boat rides** (50kn per person, 3-person min.) are organized by **Nautic Center Bol.** (☎63 53 67; www.nautic-center-bol.com. Walk-ins welcome. Open 9am-6pm.) **Boat rentals** are available through Adria Tours (see above) and on the waterfront past the bus station. The **outdoor cinema,** opposite the bus station, has nightly showings, weather permitting. (Shows 8:30-11pm. Tickets 15-18kn.)

NIGHTLIFE. Bol's awe-inspiring natural beauty shines even brighter once the sun goes down. Soak in the calm sea under the clear starry sky near one of the small piers along **Put Zlatnog Rata,** or head to the center of town for a surprisingly lively night scene. **Varadero,** at the base of Hotel Kaštil, has the hippest terrace in town, complete with wicker couches, tiki torches, and ambient house. It's the perfect place to start the morning with a frothy cappuccino (9kn) or cap off the night with a delicious cocktail. (Mixed drinks 35-50kn. Open daily 9am-1am.) To get out of Stari Grad, go to **Bolero,** Put Zlatnog Rata bb or Promenada bb, located just past Big Blue Sports if you're heading away from Stari Grad. (Open 8am-2am. Cash only.) Join a friendly crowd of vacationing Croatian youths and a live DJ at **Aquarius,** which starts at Rudina 26 and spills over across the street to an outdoor terrace on Radića 8, overlooking the beach. (☎63 58 03. Open May-Sept. daily 9am-1am; Oct.-Apr. M-Th and Su 9am-11pm, F-Sa 9am-midnight. Cash only.) **Faces Club,** Bračke ceste, is owned by Croatian football icon Igor Štimac, who makes sure that an array of international DJs pump out the beats over this open air dance club. (☎63 54 10. Open in summer 9pm-late.)

HVAR ISLAND ☎(0)21

This narrow, 88km long island affords breathtaking views of the mainland mountains from its high, rugged, and lavender-covered hills. Home to the first tourist association in Europe, Hvar (pop. 4,000) has proved a favorite summer getaway for chic urbanites and yacht-bound high rollers. Fortunately, the nearby Pakleni Otoci (Hellish Islands) provide enough beach for everyone. Many resort hotels actually guarantee the weather—if the temperature dips too low or it rains long enough, rooms are on the house.

TRANSPORTATION. **Ferries** make the trip from Split to Hvar's Stari Grad (Old Town; 2hr.; June 21-Sept. 9 M-Th 3 per day, F-Su 5 per day; 38kn, with car 216kn). From there, **buses** scheduled around the ferry take passengers to Hvar Town (25min., 7 per day, 17kn). Alternatively, head straight from Split to Hvar Town: there's a fast **catamaran** in the morning (1 hr., 1 per day, 32kn) in addition to a regular ferry (2hr., 2 per day, 32kn). Check times online at www.krilo.hr. A **bus** runs to Hvar Town from Jelsa (40min.; M-Sa 6 per day, Su 5 per day; 19kn), from which **taxi boats** run every morning at 9am to Bol on Brač Island (40-50kn). To reach the **bus station,** walk through Trg Sv. Stjepana from the marina and then left of the church; the station is on your left. **Jadrolinija,** Riva bb, on the left tip of the waterfront, sells ferry tickets. (☎74 11 32. Open M-Sa 5:30am-1pm and 3-8pm; Su 8-9am, noon-1pm, and 3-4pm. Hours vary.) **Pelegrini Tours,** Riva bb, located next to the post office, runs a catamaran between Hvar and Komiža during the summer (1½hr., 1 per week, round-trip 160kn). Pelegrini also **rents cars** (513kn per day), **scooters,** and **boats** in the summer. (☎74 27 43; pelegrini@inet.hr. Open daily 7am-1pm and 5-9pm.)

ORIENTATION AND PRACTICAL INFORMATION. Hvar Town has virtually no street names and even fewer signs. The main square, **Trg Sveti Stjepana,** directly below the bus station by the waterfront, is the one place graced with a name. Facing the sea from the main square, take a left along the waterfront to reach the **tourist office, bank,** and **ferry terminal;** a right leads to the major hotels and beaches. The tourist office, **Turistička Zajednica,** Trg Sv. Stjepana 16, is on the corner of the main square closest to the water. The staff provides bus schedules and detailed **maps** of the island's beaches, hiking, and biking trails (20kn), as well as a guidebook to the city's sights and services for 50kn. (☎74 10 59; www.tzhvar.hr. Open in high season M-Sa 8am-1pm and 5-9pm, Su 9am-noon; in low season M-Sa 8am-2pm.) **Splitska Banka,** Riva 4, offers **Western Union** services, **exchanges currency** for no commission, and cashes **traveler's checks** for 1% commission. (Open M-F 8am-2:30pm and 6-8pm, Sa 8am-noon.) There's an **ATM** outside the bank and an American Express and MasterCard ATM across the harbor in front of **Privredna Banka Zagreb,** Riva bb. **Store luggage** at the bus station (*garderoba;* 10kn per hr., 60kn per 12-24hr.), which also has **restrooms** (3kn), **showers** (20kn), and a **laundromat** (wash 50kn per 30min., dry 15kn; detergent 5kn). A well-stocked **pharmacy** is in Trg Sv. Stjepana. (☎74 10 02. Open M-F 8am-9pm, Sa 8am-1pm and 6-9pm, Su 9am-noon. AmEx/MC/V.) **Internet Club Luka Rent,** at Riva bb, has Internet access and offers a variety of rentals. (☎74 29 46; www.lukarent.com. Internet 30kn per hr. Bikes 20kn per hr., 100kn per day. Scooters 90/250-300kn. Boats 300-1700kn per day, 6-person max. AmEx/MC/V.) Alternatively, there's **Cima,** Dolac bb. From the bus station, veer left away from Trg Sv. Stjepana, cross the street, and look for a blue sign with dolphins. (☎71 87 52. 30kn per hr. Open daily 9am-2pm and 5-11pm.) The **post office** is on Riva just past Splitska Banka, and has **phones, Western Union** services, and **Poste Restante.** (☎74 24 13. Open M-Sa 7:30am-9pm.) **Postal Code:** 21450.

ACCOMMODATIONS AND FOOD. As in other Croatian resort towns, the only budget accommodations are **private rooms,** and even these are expensive. **Pelegrini Tours,** located next to the post office, can make arrangements. (Doubles July 31-Aug. 28 269-360kn; July 3-31 and Aug. 28-Sept. 11 277kn; May-July 3 and Sept. 12-Oct. 2 219kn; in low season 146kn. Tax and registration 4.50-7kn. 30% surcharge for stays under 3 nights.) Friendly **Luka Visković ❶,** Lućica bb, has a three-story house with doubles, some with private baths, and a shared kitchen, located just minutes from Hvar Town. If you call ahead of time, he may even come pick you up at Stari Grad from the ferry dock; if he's booked, he might help you find somewhere else to stay. (☎74 21 18, mobile 09 17 34 72 30. Aug. 150-200kn per person; July 100-120kn. Cash only.) The **Green Lizard Hostel ❶,** Lučića bb, offers spotless dorms, as well as private doubles for reasonable rates. (☎74 25 60; www.greenlizard.hr. July-Aug dorms 135-150kn. Reserve ahead.) **Camping Vira ❶** is run by the Sunčani hotel group and has excellent facilities right on the beach, bordered by pine groves. (☎74 18 03. 66kn per adult, 100kn per site.)

A small **open-air market** between the bus station and the main square sells primarily fruits and vegetables. (Open daily 7am-8pm.) There's also a large **Konzum** supermarket at Dolac bb, next to the open-air market and bus station, which stocks anything you'll need. (☎77 82 30. Open daily 7am-10pm. AmEx/MC/V.) Overpriced pizza and pasta restaurants line the waterfront and the square. For a cheaper, better meal, head one block up the steps leading from the main square to the fortress to visit **Luna ❷.** On the gorgeous rooftop terrace, you'll dine on excellent fish, poultry, and meat standards. Try the fettucine with salmon (59kn) for a flavorful treat. (☎74 86 95. Entrees 50-120kn. Cover 8kn. Open daily noon-3pm and 6pm-midnight). For a splurge, **Macondo ❹,** one street above Luna, transforms a marble alleyway into a seafood connoisseur's dream. Elegant ambience and gourmet fish dishes (70-250kn), such as lobster risotto (150kn), keep this upscale bistro packed. Meat dishes start at 80kn. (☎74 28 50. Open daily noon-2pm and 6pm-midnight).

SIGHTS. The stairs to the right of the square (as you face the sea) lead to a 13th-century **Venetian fortress,** with amazing views of the town and surrounding islands. Although Turkish attacks weakened the fortress, the lightning bolt that struck the gunpowder room proved even more devastating. Inside, the fortress is completely empty, save for a few cannons, a cafe, and a tiny **marine archaeological collection** (hidroarheološka zbirka) displaying Greek and Byzantine relics from shipwrecked boats. (Open daily 8am-10pm. 15kn.) Stop by the **Last Supper Collection** in the **Franciscan monastery,** down Riva, past the ferry terminal, which includes another famous *Last Supper*, an oil-painting by Matteo Ignoli. Exquisite 15th- and 16th-century artwork is featured inside the Church. Outside, a peaceful courtyard contains a 300-year-old cypress tree. (☎74 11 23. Open M-Sa 10am-noon and 5-6pm. 15kn, students 10kn.) The **Gallery Arsenal,** up the stairs next to the tourist office, is worth a look. It features rotating exhibits by local artists, as well as a Renaissance theater. (☎74 10 09. Open daily 10am-noon and 8-11pm. 10kn.) The **Cathedral of St. Stjepan** that towers over the square is open twice daily for mass.

NIGHTLIFE AND FESTIVALS. The most crowded bars line the waterfront. For something smaller and more intimate, head to **Caffe Bar Jazz,** Burak bb, on a side street uphill from Splitska Banka. The bar's funky footstools, technicolor interior, inexpensive drinks, and local flavor help revive the sun-weary psyche for a nocturnal second wind. (Vodka and juice 15kn. Open daily 8pm-2am.) **Konoba Katarina,** Groda bb, on the steps to the fortress, offers delicious homemade sweet and dry wines in a wood-paneled cellar. Samples abound, and the decadent dessert wine *prosek* is so good you might be tempted to take a bottle home. (Wine 35-

70kn. Open daily 10am-1pm and 6pm-midnight.) **Zimmer Frei,** on Groda, is a no-nonsense bar, usually filled with serious drinkers taking advantage of the excellent 40-60kn mixed drinks. Just off the main square, white-cushioned seats line the street (☎59 61 82). At the end of Riva past the Jadrolinija office, **Carpe Diem** hosts live DJs playing from inside the Roman stone walls and boasts the best outdoor terrace on the waterfront. Always busy with hip and hot twenty-somethings, this bar is the place to be in Hvar. Jumpstart a vigorous day of sunbathing with a delicious cappuccino (25kn) or fruit smoothie. (Beer 25-30kn. Mixed drinks 55-75kn. Open daily 9am-2am.) Walk all the way around to the opposite side of the marina and up the garden path on your right to get to the local disco **Veneranda,** which has dancing indoors and outdoors around a big fountain. (Open daily 10pm-5am.) Earlier in the evenings, this same space functions as an **open-air cinema.** Look for posters advertising what's playing. (Tickets 15-20kn.)

Watch out for upcoming tennis champions at the **Sunčani Hvar Tennis Open** for women in April. During the **Days of Theater** in the last two weeks of May, Hvar celebrates the stage above the Arsenal in one of Europe's oldest **community theaters,** dating from 1612. The Franciscan monastery and the theater host outdoor drama performances during the **Hvar Summer Festival.** (Mid-June to early Oct. Performances 30-50kn.) For 10 days each September, the monastery hosts the **Shakespeare Days Festival,** which includes performances and workshops dedicated to the Bard. Inquire at the tourist office (see above) for more info.

BEACHES AND ISLANDS. To enjoy some of the Adriatic's clearest waters, you'll have to brave loud, crowded **beaches.** Quieter beaches, as well as terraced-rock sunbathing and swimming areas, are a 20min. walk to the left down the waterfront. Alternatively, head to **Jevolim, Ždrilca,** and **Palmižana,** known collectively as the **Hellish Islands** (Pakleni Otoci). The last is home to **Palmižana beach,** which has waterside restaurants, rocks for tanning, sparse sand, and an area frequented by nude bathers at the far tip of the cove. **Taxi boats** run between the islands (every 30min. 10am-6:30pm, round-trip 20-40kn).

KORČULA ISLAND ☎(0)20

Korčula (KOHR-choo-lah) got its name from the Greek words *kerkyra melaina* (black woods) because of the dark macchia thickets and woods that cover the island. Korčula Town (pop. 4000) faces the stunning mountains of the Croatian mainland, just a short ferry trip away. A healthy crop of tourists has made it significantly more developed than its neighbors Vis and Mljet, while weekly sword dances in the summer, a superb music scene, and friendly locals combine to create one of the most exciting atmospheres along the coast.

TRANSPORTATION. Korčula is one of the few islands served by buses (which board a ferry to the island). The **bus station** is at Porat bb. (☎71 12 16. Ticket window open M-Sa 6:30-9am, 9:30am-4pm, and 4:30-7pm; Su 2-7pm.) **Buses** run to: Dubrovnik (3½hr., 2 per day, 77kn); Split (5hr., 1 per day, 90kn); Zagreb (11-13hr., 1 per day, 209kn) via Knin or Zadar; Sarajevo, BOS (6½hr., 4 per wk., 145kn). For **ferry info** and tickets, check the **Jadrolinija** office, 20m toward Stari Grad (Old Town) from the ferry landing. (☎71 54 10. Open M-F 5:30am-7pm, Sa-Su 7:30am-7:30pm.) **Ferries** run from Korčula Town to Dubrovnik (3½hr., 5 per wk., 79kn), Hvar (3hr., 1-2 per day, 79kn), and Split (5hr., 1 per day, 97kn). Ferries arrive in **Korčula Town** or in **Vela Luka** on the opposite side of the island. A bus meets ferries for the latter and transports you to Korčula Town (1hr.; 5 per day; 30kn, plus 10kn for each bag stored). The most convenient option is to go directly to Korčula Town, either from Split or Dubrovnik, as the buses from Vela Luka are often overcrowded. **Marko Polo** also runs a **catamaran** that goes directly from Korčula Town to Hvar and Split (2 or 3hr., respectively; 6am; 55kn.) For a **taxi,** call ☎71 54 52.

ORIENTATION AND PRACTICAL INFORMATION. The town is situated beside the sea on the end of the island. **Stari Grad** (Old Town) was built on a small oval peninsula, and its streets are arranged in a herringbone pattern. Outside the city walls, medieval, Baroque, and modern houses blend together, tapering off into hotels farther down the coastline. Street addresses are rare, but the town is small and easily navigable. The **tourist office, Turistička Zajednica,** Obala Dr. Franje Tudjmana 6, is on the opposite side of the peninsula from the bus and ferry terminals. To get there, face the water and walk left, following the main street as it curves away from the marina and passing the Jadrolinija office along the way. When you reach the water on the other side, head right along the water toward the peninsula to Hotel Korčula; the office is just before the hotel in a glass building. (Open M-Sa 8am-3pm and 4-8pm, Su 9am-1pm.) **Splitska Banka,** in front of the stairs to Stari Grad, **exchanges currency** for no commission, cashes **traveler's checks** for 2% commission, gives **cash advances,** and offers **Western Union** services. (☎71 10 52. Open M-F 8am-4pm, Sa 8am-noon.) There is a 24hr. MasterCard and Visa **ATM** outside Splitska Banka and another around the corner toward Stari Grad. The **pharmacy,** Trg Kralja Tomislava bb, is at the foot of the Stari Grad stairs. (☎71 10 57. Open M-F 7am-8pm, Sa 7am-noon and 6-8pm, Su 9-11am. AmEx/MC/V.) For fast Internet access, a good choice is **Tino Computers,** Pr. Tri Sulara 9, before Stari Grad, on a little street heading away from the marina. (☎71 60 93. 25kn per hr.; 10kn min. Open daily 9am-midnight.) **Rent-a-Đir,** next door to Marko Polo, rents **cars** (296kn per day; €100 deposit), **scooters** (185-250kn per day; 50kn deposit), and **boats.** (☎71 19

MARKO! POLO! Wondering why Marko Polo's name is dropped so much here? While evidence is sketchy at best, locals believe the explorer was born in Korčula, pointing to records showing that the shipbuilding Polo family settled in the area in the 13th century. Whatever you believe, you can visit the remains of what is alleged to be Marko Polo's house, near the Town Museum (see **Sights**), and appreciate the festival Korčula throws in his honor in early July.

08. 10-person boat 520-1850kn per day; boat license required. Open daily 9am-8pm.) The **post office** is just to the right of the pharmacy (facing the stairs) at Trg Kralja Tomislava. It has **Poste Restante, telephones,** and **currency exchange** for 1.5% commission. (☎71 11 32. Open M-Sa 7:30am-9pm.) **Postal Code:** 20260.

ACCOMMODATIONS AND FOOD. Korčula Town's only hostel, **The Korčula Backpacker ❶,** Hrvatske Bratske Zajednice 6, provides a great seaside location and a very social atmosphere. Manager Zlatko, a young South-African-born Croatian, provides a wealth of info on the area. Book ahead or look out for someone in a cowboy hat and holding a sign at the bus station. (☎09 89 97 63 53; www.thekorculabackpacker.blogspot.com. 4-, 6-, or 10-bed dorms 90kn.) If you're seeking peace and quiet, **Marko Polo ❷,** Biline 5, on the waterfront where the ferries dock, will arrange private accommodation for you. (☎71 54 00; www.korcula.com. Open daily 8am-9pm. July 12-Aug. 23 singles 188kn; doubles 263kn; triples 330kn. May 17-July 11 and Aug. 24-Sept. 30 150/210/285kn. Oct.-May 16 105/150/210kn. 30% more for stays under 3 nights.) Or, look for *sobe* signs uphill from the bus station, away from Stari Grad, or on the road to Hotel Park (see below). While not exactly budget, **Hotel Park ❺,** Šetalište, F. Kršinića 102, offers simple, functional rooms near the beach, some with balconies and marina views. From the bus station, walk away from Stari Grad along the waterfront and follow the signs. (☎72 62 86; marketing@htp-korcula.hr. Breakfast included. July and Aug. singles

532-628kn; doubles 760-912kn. Sept. and June 319-395/608-760kn. Jan. and May 319-395/456-608kn.) Camping is available farther out at **Autocamp Kalac ❶**, with a sandy beach and nice views of the mainland across the water. A bus (10min., 1 per hr., 13kn) runs to the camp from the station. (☎71 11 82. Reception 7am-10pm. 40kn per person, 35kn per tent. Tourist tax 7.5kn.)

The frugal should try **Konzum** supermarket (open M-Sa 6:30am-9pm, Su 7am-9pm), by the bus station and next to Marko Polo, and the open-air **produce market** to the right of the Stari Grad stairs (open daily 6am-9pm). **Fresh ❶** is a wrap and smoothie stand right next to the bus station. (☎09 18 96 75 09. Smoothies 20kn. Sangria 25kn per bucket. Wraps 20-25kn. Open daily 8am-2am. Cash only.) At **Adio Mare ❷**, Marko Polo bb, next to Marko Polo's house, local specialties like *korčulanska pasticada* (beef stewed in vegetables and plum sauce with dumplings; 70kn) or *Ražnjic Adio Mare* (mixed meats skewered with apples, onions, and bacon; 60kn) draw crowds. (☎71 12 53. Entrees 40-80kn. Open M-Sa 5:30pm-midnight, Su 6pm-midnight.) Restaurants in Korčula are expensive and tourist-driven. There is a string of nearly identical *konoba* overlooking the bay down the road from Gaudi (see **Entertainment and Nightlife,** below). They serve the usual assortment of seafood and pasta, but you'll pay for the view.

SIGHTS. Korčula's grandest tribute to its patron, **St. Mark's Cathedral** (Katedrala Sv. Marka), sits at the highest point of the Stari Grad peninsula. Although planning began in the 14th century, inspired by the founding of the Korčula Bishopric, construction wasn't completed until 1525. The Gothic-Renaissance cathedral is complemented by the older **bell tower.** (Open daily 9am-9pm. Services M-Sa 6:30pm; Su 7, 9:30am, and 6:30pm. Dress appropriately.) The **Abbey Treasury of St. Mark** (Opatska Riznica Sv. Marka), next to the cathedral, houses a large collection of 12th-century manuscripts, Renaissance and Baroque drawings, religious robes, and coins. (Open M-Sa 9am-10pm. 15kn.) The **Town Museum** (Gradski Muzej) is opposite the treasury in the Renaissance Gabrielis Palace and displays nearly five millennia of Korčula's culture, including everything from 5000-year-old knives to a 19th-century wedding dress. (Open M-Sa 10am-9pm. 10kn, students 5kn.)

CROATIA

NIGHTLIFE AND FESTIVALS. The most popular bar these days is thatched-roof **Dos Locos,** Šet. F. Kršinića 14, located right next to the bus station. For a club-like vibe, try **Gaudi.** The cafe outside has gorgeous views, but the real action happens inside the stone cocoon of sound and colored lights behind it. Go up the ramp to the right of the steps that lead to Stari Grad (toward the cannon) and it will be on your left. (Beer 12-18kn. Nightclub open daily 11pm-4am.)

Carnival celebrations, including weekly masked balls *(maškare)*, are held from Epiphany to Ash Wednesday (Free). The beginning of July is dedicated to the **Marco Polo Festival.** Events include folk entertainment and a grand reconstruction of a famous 1298 naval battle in the Pelješac channel.

DUBROVNIK ☎(0)20

The poet Byron considered Dubrovnik (du-BROV-nik; pop. 43,770) "the pearl of the Adriatic" and George Bernard Shaw called it "Paradise on Earth." A stroll along the sun-kissed white marble of the vibrant Old Town soon reveals why. Although ravaged by war with Serbia in 1991 and 1992, Dubrovnik appears miraculously scarless; only close inspection reveals the occasional bullet hole. For centuries, the azure waters, golden sunsets, and Italian marble of this Adriatic gem have enchanted visitors, who are now beginning to return in force.

TRANSPORTATION

Flights: Dubrovnik Airport Ćilipi (DBV; ☎77 33 77) serves national and European destinations. A bus (30kn) to the airport from the main station leaves 1½hr. before each flight. **Croatia Airlines,** Brsalje 9 (☎41 37 76 or 41 37 77), just outside the Stari Grad Pile. Open M-F 8am-4pm, Sa 9am-noon.

Buses: Pt. Republike 19 (☎35 70 88). To get to Stari Grad, keep your back to the bus station and turn left onto Ante Starčevića. Follow this road uphill to the Pile Gate (25min.). Local buses running to Stari Grad make several stops along Ante Starčevića before reaching Pile. To: **Rijeka** (12hr., 4 per day, 415kn); **Split** (4½hr., 1 per hr., 132kn.; **Zadar** (8hr., 8 per day, 240kn); **Zagreb** (11hr., 8 per day, 234kn); **Frankfurt, GER** (27hr., 2 per week, 800kn); **Trieste, ITA** (15hr., 1 per day, 370kn).

Ferries: Jadrolinija, Obala S. Radića 40 (☎41 80 00; www.jadrolinija.tel.hr/jadrolinija). Open M-Tu and Th 8am-8pm, W and F 8am-8pm and 9-11pm, Sa 8am-2pm and 7-8pm, Su 8-10am and 7-8:30pm. The ferry terminal is opposite the Jadrolinija office. When facing away from the bus station, go left; when the road forks, bear right (5min.). To: **Korčula** (4hr.; M, W, Sa 8:30am; Th, Su 10am; 79kn; daytrips are possible with the Nona Ana on T and Th at 10:45am returning at 3:50pm); **Rijeka** (22hr., 2 per week, 233kn); **Split** (8hr., 4 per day, 115kn); **Bari, ITA** (9hr., 5 per week, 97kn).

Public Transportation: (☎35 70 20). All **buses** except #5, 7, and 8 go to Stari Grad's Pile Gate. Tickets 8kn at kiosks, 10kn from the driver. Exact change required except on buses #1a and 1b. The driver checks everyone's ticket upon boarding.

Taxis: Radio Taxi Dubrovnik (from bus station ☎35 70 44, from Pile Gate 42 43 43). 25kn base, 8kn per km. 50kn from the bus station to Stari Grad. 200kn to the airport.

ORIENTATION AND PRACTICAL INFORMATION

The walled **Stari Grad** (Old Town) is the city's cultural, historical, and commercial center. Its main street, called both **Placa** and **Stradun,** runs from the **Pile Gate,** the official entrance to Stari Grad, to the **Old Port** at the opposite tip of the peninsula. Outside the city walls, the main traffic arteries, **Put Republike** and **Ante Starčevića,** sandwich the **bus station** from the front and rear, respectively, merge into Ante Starčevića, and end at the Pile Gate. The new **ferry terminal** in Gruž is a 15min. bus ride from Stari Grad; with your back to the ferry dock, walk left 50m along Gruška obala to the bus stop and take bus #1a, 1b, or 3 to the last stop. To the west of Stari Grad, two hilly peninsulas—**Babin Kuk** and **Lapad**—are home to modern settlements, sand beaches, and a number of tourist-ridden hotels.

Do not explore the beautiful bare mountains rising above Dubrovnik–these peaks may still harbor concealed **landmines.**

Tourist Office: Turistički Informativni Centar (TIC), Placa bb (☎42 63 54; fax 42 63 55), next to the fountain at the head of Placa. Arranges private rooms, **exchanges currency** for 2% commission, and gives out free **maps** of the city. Open daily June-Aug. 9am-8pm; Sept.-May 9am-7pm.

Budget Travel: Atlas, Cira Carica 3 (☎08 00 44 22 22; www.atlas-croatia.com). The friendly, English-speaking staff arranges accommodations, sells plane and ferry tickets (ask about student and under-26 discounts), **exchanges currency** for 1% commission, and sells **American Express Traveler's Cheques.** Organizes expensive but convenient tours to: **Elafiti Islands** (2 per wk., 300kn); **Mljet National Park** (3 per wk., 450kn); **Neretva River Delta** (2 per wk., 440kn with lunch). Branches at Sv. Đurđa 1 (☎44 25 74), near the Pile Gate, and at Gruška Obala (☎41 80 01), near the ferry terminal. All open June-Aug. M-Sa 8am-9pm, Su 8am-10am and 5-9pm; Sept.-May M-Sa 8am-8pm, Su 8am-1pm. AmEx/DC/MC/V.

Currency Exchange: OTP Banka, Placa 16 (☎062 201 316; fax 32 10 19). This centrally located bank exchanges currency for no commission, cashes **traveler's checks** for 1.5% commission, and offers **Western Union** services. **ATM** located outside. Open M-F 8am-10pm, Sa 8am-noon. Branch at Pt. Republike 9 (☎35 63 33), next to the bus station. Open M-F 8am-10pm, Sa 8am-noon.

Luggage Storage: At the bus station kiosk marked *Garderoba.* 15kn per day. Open daily 4:50am-10:30pm.

English-Language Bookstore: Algoritam, Placa 8, on the main walkway in Stari Grad. Open M-Sa 9am-11pm, Su 10am-1pm. AmEx/DC/MC/V.

Internet: Dubrovnik is full of Internet cafes. There are 3 outside the main gate of Stari Grad. Inside the gate are others, and Lapad also has several. Most charge 5-10kn per 15min. **Hugo Internet and Call Center,** Prijeko 13 (☎32 20 69), is convenient and has ADSL connections, CD burning, scanning, printing, and a call center. (5kn for 15min.; calls 1.83kn per min. to the USA, 1.95kn per min. to Australia).

Post Office: Široka 8 (☎32 34 27), in Stari Grad. Has public **telephones** and **Western Union** services. Open M-F 7:30am-9pm, Sa 10am-5pm. **Postal Code:** 20108.

ACCOMMODATIONS AND CAMPING

Dubrovnik offers accommodations in the city center, by the beach in Lapad, and near the ferry terminal. Due to lingering damage from the war and the subsequent refugee situation, however, the city's hotel scene leaves something to be desired—establishments tend to be either exorbitantly expensive or somewhat run-down. Consequently, **private rooms** or **apartments** tend to be the most comfortable and least expensive option. Arrange one through the TIC, or through **Atlas** (singles €15-20 slightly out of town). For far cheaper rooms, enter into the bargaining fray with the locals holding *sobe* signs at the bus and ferry terminals.

Apartmani Burum, Dubravkina 16 (☎43 54 67), in Babin Kuk on the hill above Lapad. Take bus #6 to Babin Kuk and get off 2 stops past the Lapad post office. Cross the street and go uphill on Mostarska; turn left at Dubravkina. Some rooms have balconies and private baths. Social atmosphere, with beaches nearby. The owner's brother-in-law, Nikola, will drive you to Burum if you make arrangements ahead of time; call ☎09 15 64 39 29. Common kitchen. Dorms 100-125kn; doubles and triples 200-300kn. ❶

Begović Boarding House, Primorska 17 (☎43 51 91). From the bus station, take bus #6 toward Dubrava; ask the driver to let you off at Post Office Lapad. Facing the pedestrian walkway, turn right at the intersection, go left at the fork, and take the 1st right on Primorska. Go uphill and turn left at the fork; Begović will be on the left at the very end. Call ahead and the owner, Sado, will pick you up at the bus or ferry terminal. A cozy villa with 10 spacious doubles, kitchens, TVs, and a terrace shaded by fig trees. Social atmosphere. Triples 80-100kn per person; doubles 110-120kn per person. ❶

Hotel Zagreb, Šetalište Kralja Zvonimira 27 (☎43 89 30; www.hotels-sumratin.com). Follow directions to Post Office Lapad (see above). Walk through the 1st intersection and turn left onto the pedestrian walkway Šetalište Kralja Zvonimira; the hotel is on the left, near the beach and an array of cafes. Veranda and clean rooms with hardwood floors, bath, TV, A/C, and phone. Breakfast included. Reception 24hr. Singles 400-660kn; doubles 1400-2120kn. Tourist tax 5.50-7kn. AmEx/DC/MC/V. ❹

Autocamp Solitudo, Vatroslava Lisinskog 17, Babin Kuk (☎44 86 86; sales.department@babinkuk.com), 5km from Stari Grad. From the bus station, take bus #6 toward Dubrava and ask the driver to let you off at Autocamp. Follow the signs downhill. Clean bathrooms, small grocery store, cafe, laundry facilities, and access to a long and uncrowded beach. Open Apr.-Nov. Reception 7am-10pm. 49kn per person, 70kn per tent or car. AmEx/MC/V. ❶

FOOD

Though food is reasonably priced in Dubrovnik, drinks can be costly. **Prijeko,** the first street parallel to Placa on the left when coming from Pile Gate, is lined with *konobi* (taverns), which cater almost exclusively to tourists. The **open-air market,** on Gundulićeva Poljana, sits behind St. Blasius's Church. (Open daily 7am-8pm.) **Konzum,** facing the market, offers groceries at very low prices by Stari Grad standards. (Open daily 7am-8pm. AmEx/MC/V.) Another location, with the same hours, is outside the Stari Grad gate, Marijana Čavića 1a. If you're staying in Lapad, check out **Kerum** supermarket, Kralja Tomislava 7, which has a wider selection. With your back to Post Office Lapad, turn left toward the white shopping center; Kerum is on the ground floor, at the back. (Open M-Sa 7am-10pm, Su 8am-9pm.)

Lokanda Peskarija, Ribarnica bb (☎32 47 50). From the bell tower at the end of Placa, turn right on Pred Dvorom, and take the 1st left out of the city walls. This charming out-

CROATIA

door cafe, tucked behind the Old Port, offers the freshest, least expensive seafood in Stari Grad, making it a local favorite. Seafood 35-50kn. Open daily 8am-3am. ❷

Konoba Atlantic, Kardinala Stepinca 42 (☎09 81 85 96 25). Take bus #6 to Post Office Lapad and go straight on the walkway; take a right on the staircase before Hotel Kompas, which takes you to Kardinala Stopinga. This tiny, family-run restaurant above the beach is worth the walk. Homemade bread, some of the best pasta in Croatia (49-260kn), and a wide range of seafood (48-120kn). Open daily 11am-11pm. ❷

Kamenica, Gundulićeva poljana 8 (☎32 36 82). Located under large umbrellas, Kamenice specializes in shellfish (38kn) and other aquatic delicacies. For breakfast, try a fluffy omelette (20-30kn). Open daily 7am-11pm. ❶

Express-restaurant, Slačićeva 8. For the cheapest restaurant meal in Dubrovnik head to this self service canteen, where pre-cooked meals won't break the bank. Entrees 28kn. Open daily 11am-5pm. ❶

Chihauhau Cantina Mexicana, Hvarska 6 (☎42 44 45), offers welcome respite from pasta and pizza. Serving up tapas and an impressive array of salads, Chihauhau is a hit among the younger Dubrovnik residents. Entrees 40kn. ❷

SIGHTS

The sun-drenched beachfront Stari Grad (Old Town) is packed with churches, museums, palaces, and fortresses—every turn yields a new sight. The most popular are those along the broad Placa.

CITY WALLS. Providing stunning views of orange-tiled roofs set against the sapphire blue backdrop of the Adriatic, a climb atop the city walls (Gradske zidine) is the highlight of any trip to Dubrovnik. Originally constructed in the 8th century, the thick limestone connects fanciful towers, fortresses, and gates. The fortifications took their present form in the 13th century when the newly independent city of Ragusa needed stronger defenses against potential Turkish attacks. Once you've seen the sunset from the top of the walls, you may want to stay in the city forever. *(Entrances to walls are through the Pile Gate on the left and at the Old Port. Open daily May-Oct. 9am-7pm; Nov.-Apr. 10am-3pm. 50kn, children 20kn. Audio tour 40kn; recommended as there are no captions.)*

CROATIA

FRANCISCAN MONASTERY AND PHARMACEUTICAL MUSEUM. Masterly stonework encases this 14th-century monastery (Franjevački Samostan). The cloister was built in 1360 by famous architect Mihoje Brajkov. The southern portal that opens on the Placa includes a Pietà relief by the Petrović brothers, the only relic from the original church. No two capitals of the colonnade are the same. Take a stroll into the gardens and check out the glass-encased shell holes, reminders of the city's war-torn past. The monastery also houses the oldest working pharmacy in Europe, established in 1317. The small museum displays elegant medicinal containers, historical tools, icons, and gold and silver jewelry. *(Placa 2, on the left side of Placa, just inside Pile Gate next to the entrance to the city walls. ☎42 63 45. Open daily 9am-6pm. 20kn, children 12.50kn. Appropriate dress required for those visiting the chapel.)*

CATHEDRAL OF THE ASSUMPTION OF THE VIRGIN MARY. This Baroque cathedral (Riznica Katedrale) was built after the Romanesque original was destroyed in the 1667 earthquake. In 1981, the foundations of a 7th-century Byzantine cathedral were found beneath the cathedral floor, necessitating considerable revision of Dubrovnik's history. The cathedral **treasury** houses religious relics collected by Richard the Lionheart, Roman refugees, and a few centuries of fishermen. Crusaders in the 12th century brought back a silver casket from Jerusalem that contains an ancient garment said to have been worn by Jesus. *(Kneza Damjana Jude 1. From Pile Gate, follow Placa to the Bell Tower and turn right on Poljana Marina Držića. Cathedral open daily 6:30am-8pm. Treasury open daily 8am-8pm. 10kn.)*

ORTHODOX CHURCH AND MUSEUM OF ICONS. Around 2000 Serbs live in Dubrovnik—only a third of the prewar population. The museum (Pravoslavna Crkva i Muzej Ikona) houses a variety of 15th- to 19th-century icons gathered by local families. *(Od Puča 8. From Pile Gate, walk 100m down Placa and turn right onto Široka, the widest side street. Turn left down Od Puča. Church open daily 8am-noon and 5-7pm. Museum open M-Sa 9am-2pm. 10kn.)*

MOSQUE. This former apartment of Dubrovnik's first Imam (installed in 1934) is a rich cultural center for the city's 5000 Muslims. The beautifully carpeted room upstairs is divided in two: one half contains an Islamic school for children, and the other is used for prayer. A small anteroom serves as a social center for the Bosnian community. Tourists are welcome in the mosque if they take off their shoes and dress appropriately. *(Miha Pracata 3. From Pile Gate, walk down Placa and take the 8th street on the right. The mosque is marked by a small sign on the left side of the street. Open daily 10am-1pm and 8-9pm.)*

SEPHARDIC SYNAGOGUE. Round off your tour with a visit to the second oldest Sephardic synagogue in Europe (the oldest is in Prague), which is home to a Jewish community that now numbers fewer than 50. Most of Dubrovnik's Jewish archives were lost during the Nazi occupation, but a number of families (Jewish, Catholic, and others) risked their lives to hide many of the synagogue's possessions in their own homes. *(Žudioska 5. From the Bell Tower, walk toward Pile Gate and take the 3rd right onto Žudioska. Open May-Oct. M-F 9am-8pm. Museum 15kn.)*

WAR PHOTO LTD. MUSEUM. Catering more to local patrons than tourists, War Photo Ltd. is a gallery featuring temporary exhibits by internationally renowned photographers, with a small space devoted to the Balkan conflict. The high standard of the artwork displayed makes sense given that the proprietor, Wade Goddard, was once a war photographer himself. *(Antuninska 6, from Pile Gate the 4th street on your left. ☎32 21 66; www.warphotoltd.com. Open June-Aug. daily 9am-9pm; Sept.-May Tu-Sa 10am-4pm, Su 10am-2pm. 25kn.)*

RECTOR'S PALACE. This Venetian Gothic seat of the former government of Ragusa and Dubrovnik is now a large complex housing several period rooms as well as portraits of leading statesmen. Since there are English captions, the audio tour might prove most informative. Be on the lookout for clocks set to 5:45pm, the time at which Napoleon's troops entered the city walls in 1806. *(Open daily 9am-6pm. 35kn, students 15kn. Audio tour 30kn.)*

BEACHES

One of the most beautiful beaches in Dubrovnik lies just beyond the city walls. From the **bell tower,** turn left onto Svetog Dominika, bear right after the footbridge, and continue along Frana Supila. Descend the stairs next to the post office to discover a pristine pebble **beach** with spectacular views of Lokrum Island. Although privately owned, it is free and open to the public. The best beach in the area is on the nearby island of Lopud and has sand, not stones. (See **Daytrips,** p. 152).

Alternatively, for sand, palms, and crowds, hop on bus #6 toward Dubrava and ask to get off at Post Office Lapad. Go through the intersection to the pedestrian boulevard and follow the bikinis. You can also continue on the path to the beach below Hotel Bellevue. Walk along Starčevića (10min.), then take a left after the hotel. Another option is the nearby island of **Lokrum,** which features a **nude beach** and 10m high cliff jumping. Ferries run daily from the Old Port (20min., 9am and every 30min. 10am-8pm, round-trip 35kn). To get to the nude beach, follow the main path from the ferry stop that traces the perimeter of the island; veer left at the restaurant and follow the "FKK" signs. For those who prefer to stay clothed, there is a smaller beach adjacent to the boat dock, as well as a small **nature preserve,** complete with gum trees and cacti. A fort built in 1806 by the French affords incredible views of Dubrovnik.

FESTIVALS AND NIGHTLIFE

The **Dubrovnik Summer Festival** (Dubrovački Ljetni Festival; mid-July to mid-Aug.) transforms the city into a cultural mecca and lively party scene. (☎32 34 00; www.dubrovnik-festival.hr.) Cinema **Sloboda,** Luža bb. (☎32 14 25), is centrally located. Young hipsters and cafe loungers flock to **Stari Grad.** An older crowd congregates in **Šetalište Kralja Zvonimira,** near Begović Boarding House (see **Accommodations,** p. 149), a hot spot for cafes, bars, and evening strolls by the nearby sea.

EastWest Cocktail and Dance Bar, Frana Supila 4 (☎41 22 20; www.ew-dubrovnik.com). On a private beach with spectacular ocean views, this lounge includes a bar with plush white couches and a sand "living room." Those craving complete relaxation can recline on one of the decadent beachside canopy beds. Beer 12-30kn. Mixed drinks 33-78kn. Open daily 10pm-4am. Restaurant open daily noon-midnight.

Buža, Crijevićeva 9. From the open air market, walk upstairs toward the monastery. Veer left and follow the signs along Od Margarite for "Cool Drinks and the Most Beautiful View." Hidden beneath the city walls, this terrace bar is romantic yet laid-back—the perfect spot for taking a dip in the Adriatic followed by conversation under the stars. Beer 17-22kn. Open 9am-late.

Club Roxy, B. Josipa Jelačića 11. Only a short stumble from the HI hostel, the Roxy's hanging motorcycles and hot-rod paraphernalia beckon a relaxed local crowd looking to avoid the downtown crunch. Coffee 6kn. Domestic draft 15kn per 0.5L. Guinness 18kn per 0.33L. Open daily 8am-late.

Latino Club Fuego, Pile Brsalje 11, right outside Pile Gate. Because this is the only place open until 4am, many party-goers end up here dancing to techno and pop. Cover 30kn; 1 drink included.

CROATIA

DAYTRIPS FROM DUBROVNIK

LOPUD ISLAND

A ferry (50min., June-Aug. 8 per day, round-trip 120kn) runs to Lopud and the Elafiti Islands. Run by Nova International, look for the Nova boat and purchase tickets 30min. before departure, or at Nova Dubrovnik, Sv. Križa 3 (☎31 35 99; www.nova-dubrovnik.hr). The sand beach, Sunj, is on the opposite side of the island from the village. Facing the water at the dock, turn left and walk 8min. Take a left on the concrete walkway between the palm tree park and the wall, where you'll see a sign for Konoba Barbara. Head uphill and bear right at the fork. After about 15min. you'll see steps that lead down through a dirt trail to the beach.

Less than 1hr. from Dubrovnik, the island of Lopud has one of the best beaches on the Adriatic. The tiny village, dotted with white buildings, chapels, and parks, stretches along the island's waterfront *(obala)*. **Dordič Mayneri** remains among the most beautiful parks in Croatia. Signs from Kavana Dubrava on the waterfront point to the **museum,** the meeting place for **tours** (Th 9am) of the church, museum, and monastery. A 15min. stroll along the waterfront leads to a gazebo with a breathtaking view of the white cliffs and the dark-blue sea. A short walk in the other direction brings you to an abandoned **monastery.** Though it is slated for reconstruction and development, its current semi-ruined state makes for wonderful exploration. Be careful: many of the floors have collapsed. The Plaža Šunj **beach,** treasured by locals, has sand—a rare characteristic on the Dalmatian Coast. Numerous hotels and restaurants on the island make it possible to stay for longer periods of time, but it is far more cost effective to use Dubrovnik as a base.

MLJET NATIONAL PARK

*Nona Ana, Obala S. Radića 26 (☎41 90 44), behind the Jadrolinija office, runs ferries to the park. The ferry (1½hr., June-Sept. 1 per day, round-trip 120kn) leaves in the morning, stops in Pomena, and returns in the evening. In winter, the Jadrolinija ferry drops passengers on the eastern side of the island in Sobra (2hr., 2 per day, 38kn). The bus meets the ferry in Sobra and travels to its western end, Pomena (1hr., 28kn). Park entrances are in Polače and Pomena. ☎74 40 58; www.np-mljet.hr. 90kn admission ticket includes boat and minivan rides in the park. Atlas (**see p. 148**) and other travel agencies offer 1-day excursions to the park. Private rooms (75-100kn) are available in Sobra or Pomena; inquire at the cafe or look for signs.*

The legendary land where Odysseus spent seven years mesmerized, Mljet is captivating enough to lure tourists to its shores as well. Mljet's relative isolation and small population make it an ideal location for a national park, especially since locals are willing to forego the monetary rewards of tourism for tranquility, relying instead on their wine and olive industry to survive. The saltwater **Large** and **Small Lakes** (Veliko and Malo Jezero), created by the rising sea level 10,000 years ago, are the most unique formations on the island. Every 6hr., the direction of flow between the lakes changes with the tides, so the water is constantly cleansed. In the center of Veliko Jezero sits the **Island of St. Maria** (Sv. Marija), home to a beautiful, white-stone **Benedictine monastery,** built in the 12th century and abandoned 700 years later when Napoleon conquered the area. Today, it houses a restaurant and a church.

If you have time, **Polače** is worth a stop for its **Roman ruins** and **Christian basilica,** once part of the second-largest Roman city in Croatia. Unfortunately, most of the city is now underwater. Get off at Polače (which also has a tourist office), walk 2km to Pristanište to the park's info center, and jump on the boat to St. Maria (5min., 1 per hr.). To return, take the boat to Mali Most (2min.) and walk another 3km to Pomena. Alternatively, a minivan run by park management may give you a ride, or you can catch one of the Atlas-operated buses.

CZECH REPUBLIC (ČESKÁ REPUBLIKA)

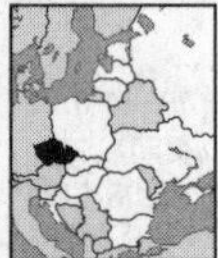

From the days of the Holy Roman Empire to reign of the USSR, the Czech people have stood at a crossroads of international affairs. Unlike many of their neighbors, however, the citizens of this small, landlocked country have rarely resisted as armies marched across their borders, often choosing to protest with words instead of weapons. As a result, Czech towns and cities are among the best-preserved and most beautiful in Europe. Today, the Czechs face a different kind of invasion, as enamored tourists sweep in to savor the magnificent capital, the baroque architecture, and some of the world's best beer.

DISCOVER THE CZECH REPUBLIC: SUGGESTED ITINERARIES

THREE DAYS. Dedicate your time to an exploration of the country's capital, **Prague** (p. 164). Stroll across the **Charles Bridge** (p. 179) to see **Prague Castle** (p. 184), leave the beaten-path to explore areas like **Josefov** (p. 182), the gorgeous neighborhood of **Troja** (p. 186), and the **Petřín Hill and Gardens** (p. 183)

ONE WEEK. Keep exploring **Prague** (5 days); there's plenty more to see. Visit the **Mucha Museum** (p. 187) and go to the **theater** (p. 188) for Czech-style entertainment. Take a daytrip to **Terezín,** a former concentration camp (p. 192). For a break from big city life, head to **Český Krumlov** (2 days; p. 205) for hiking, biking, and another ancient castle.

BEST OF CZECH REPUBLIC, THREE WEEKS. Begin with one week in **Prague,** including daytrips to **Terezín** and the delightfully creepy **Kutná Hora** chapel (p. 193). Take in the soothing waters at Karlovy Vary for two days (p. 198) before a one-day stopover in Plzeň to tour the Pilsner Brewery en-route to **Český Krumlov** (3 days). Spend 2 days in the intellectual and business hub of **Brno** (p. 211). Nearby **Olomouc** (p. 216), a less touristy version of Prague, is easily a 3-day stop. Wrap things up in **Hrádec Králové** (3 days; p. 220), basing your wilderness exploration out of lovely **Jičín** (p. 223) and making sure to visit **Litomyšl's** gorgeous castle (p. 223).

FACTS AND FIGURES

Official Name: Czech Republic.

Capital: Prague.

Major Cities: Brno, Olomouc, Plzeň.

Population: 10,229,000.

Time Zone: GMT + 1, in summer GMT + 2.

Language: Czech.

Religions: Atheist (49%), Roman Catholic (27%), Protestant (2%).

Beer Consumption Per Capita: 161 liters per year (largest in the world).

ESSENTIALS

WHEN TO GO

The Czech Republic is the most touristed country in Eastern Europe, and Prague in particular is overrun. To beat the crowds, you may want to avoid the high season (June-Aug.), though the weather is most pleasant then. A good compromise is to go in late spring or early fall.

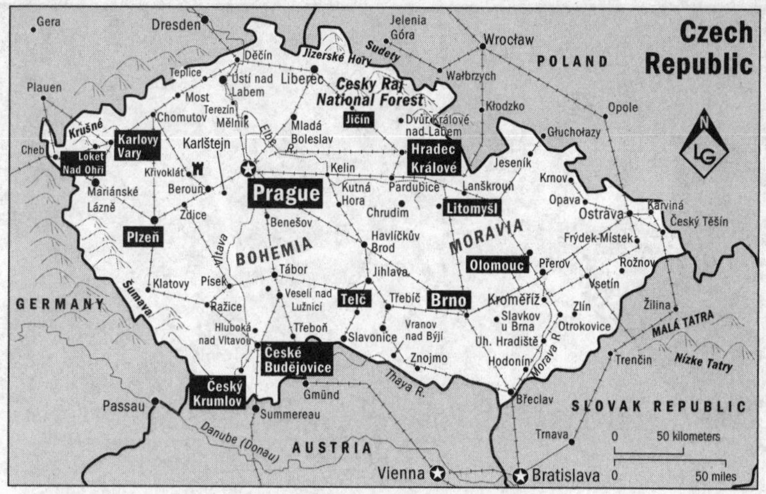

DOCUMENTS AND FORMALITIES

ENTRANCE REQUIREMENTS.

Passport: Required for all travelers. Must be valid for 90 days after end of stay.

Visa: Not required for stays over 90 days for citizens of Australia, Canada, Ireland, New Zealand, and the U.S. Citizens of the UK may remain in the country for up to 180 days without a visa.

Letter of Invitation: Not required for citizens of Australia, Canada, Ireland, New Zealand, the UK, and the US.

Inoculations: Recommended up-to-date on DTap (Diphtheria, tetanus, and pertussis) Hepatitis A, Hepatitis B, MMR (measles, mumps and rubella), polio booster, rabies, and typhoid.

Work Permit: Required for all foreigners planning to work in the Czech Republic.

International Driving Permit: Required for foreigners. For EU citizens, a national driver's license is sufficient.

EMBASSIES AND CONSULATES. Foreign embassies to the Czech Republic are in Prague (p. 163). Czech consulates and embassies abroad include: **Australia,** 8 Culgoa Circuit, O'Malley, Canberra, ACT 2606 (☎02 62 90 13 86; www.mzv.cz/canberra); **Canada,** 251 Cooper St., Ottawa, ON K2P 0G2 (☎613-562-3875; www.embassy.mzv.cz/Ottawa); **Ireland,** 57 Northumberland Rd., Ballsbridge, Dublin 4 (☎016 681 135; www.embassy.msz.cz/Dublin); **New Zealand,** Level 3, BMW Mini Centre, 11-15 Great South Road and corner of Margot Street, Newmarket, Auckland. (☎9 522 8736; auckland@honorary.mvz.cz); **UK,** 6-30 Kensington Palace Gardens, Kensington, London W8 4QY (☎020 72 43 11 15; www.mzv.cz/london); **US,** 3900 Spring of Freedom St., NW, Washington, D.C. 20008 (☎202-274-9100; www.mzv.cz/washington).

VISA AND ENTRY INFORMATION. Citizens of Australia, Canada, New Zealand and the US do not need a visa for stays of up to 90 days; UK citizens do not need visas for stays of up to 180 days. Visas for extended stays are available at those countries' embassies or consulates. One cannot obtain a Czech visa at the border. Processing takes 14 days when visa is submitted by mail, 7 when submitted in person.

Open all year • 24 hour reception
No curfew, no lockout
Private rooms of varying sizes
Spacious dorm rooms
Free WIFI internet
Internet terminals • Library
Casual cellar bar • Living room
Extensive information about Prague
Comfy, relaxed kitchen sitting room
Backyard garden with BBQ
Board games • Security lockers
Luggage storage • Laundry service
Tickets for public transportation
International payphone
Chapel / Reading room
SIR TOBY'S
PRAGUE
www.sirtobys.com
Where true
travellers meet...
Dělnická 24, 170 00 Praha 7 • Czech Republic • Phone: (+420) 246 032 610 • www.sirtobys.com

TOURIST SERVICES

Municipal **tourist offices** in major cities provide info on sights and events, distribute lists of hostels and hotels, and often book rooms. **Tourist Infomration Centrum** is state-run. Be aware, however, that in Prague these offices are often crowded and may be staffed by disgruntled employees. **CKM,** a national student tourist agency, books hostel beds and issues ISICs and HI cards. Most bookstores sell a national hiking map collection, *Soubor turistických map*, with an English key.

MONEY

KORUNY (Kč)		
	AUS$1 = 16.34Kč	10Kč = AUS$0.61
	CDN$1 = 19.33Kč	10Kč = CDN$0.52
	EUR€1 = 27.33Kč	10Kč = EUR€0.36
	NZ$1 = 14.26Kč	10Kč = NZ$0.70
	UK£1 = 40.74Kč	10Kč = UK£0.25
	US$1 = 20.56Kč	10Kč = US$0.49

The Czech unit of currency is the **koruna** (Kč; crown), plural koruny. The government postponed its slated 2009 conversion to the euro and 2012 has been suggested as the earliest date. **Inflation** is around 2%. The Czech Republic's inflation rate is quite stable. Banks offer good exchange rates; **Komerční banka** is a common bank chain. **ATMs** are everywhere—look for *Bankomat* signs—and offer the best exchange rates. **Traveler's checks** can be exchanged almost everywhere, though rarely without commission. MasterCard and Visa are accepted at most establishments. Bargaining is usually acceptable, especially in heavily touristed areas, though less so in formal indoor shops.

HEALTH AND SAFETY

EMERGENCY	**Ambulance:** ☎155. **Fire:** ☎150. **Police:** ☎158. **General Emergency** ☎112

Medical facilities in the Czech Republic are of high quality, especially in Prague, and sometimes employ English-speaking doctors. They often require cash payment, but some may accept credit cards. Travelers are urged to check with their insurance companies to see if they will cover emergency medical expenses. **Pharmacies** are *Lekarna*, and the most common chain is Droxi; they and supermarkets carry international brands of *náplast* (bandages), *tampóny* (tampons), and *kondomy* (condoms). For prescription drugs and aspirin, look for pharmacies marked with a green cross. The Czech Republic has quite a low level of violent crime, but **petty crime** has increased with the influx of tourism, it is especially common in big cities, on public transportation, and near sites known to be touristy, such as main squares in Prague. Tourists should be alert and avoid carrying large bags. **Women** traveling alone should not experience many problems in the Czech Republic, but should exercise caution while riding public transportation, especially after dark. Hate crimes are rare in the Czech Republic, but **minorities** might experience some discrimination. This is especially true for travelers with darker skin, Jews, and Roma. Travelers with **disabilities** might encounter trouble with the Czech Republic's accessibility, but there is a strong movement to make Prague's transportation system more wheelchair-friendly. Gay nightlife is taking off in Prague, and the country recently legalized registered partnerships for same-sex couples. Though tolerance is increasing, **GLBT travelers** are advised to avoid public displays of affection, especially outside Prague.

TRANSPORTATION

BY PLANE. Most major European carriers, including **Air Canada, Air France, American Airlines, British Airways, CSA, Delta, KLM, Lufthansa,** and **SAS** fly into Prague. Direct flights are quite expensive; travelers might consider flying to a Western European capital and taking a train or discount airline into Prague.

BY TRAIN. The easiest and cheapest way to travel between cities in the Czech Republic is by **train. Eastrail** is accepted in the Czech Republic, but **Eurail** is not. The fastest international trains are *EuroCity* and *InterCity* (*expresní*; marked in blue on schedules). *Rychlík* trains are fast domestic trains (*zrychlený vlak*; marked in red on schedules). Avoid slow *osobni* trains, marked in white. *Odjezdy* (departures) are printed on yellow posters, *příjezdy* (arrivals) on white. Seat reservations (*mistenka,* 10Kč) are recommended on express and international trains and for first-class seating.

BY BUS. Czech **buses** are often quicker and cheaper than trains in the countryside. **CSAD** runs national and interntational bus lines (www.ticketsbti.csad.cz), and many European companies operate international service. Consult the timetables or buy a bus schedule (25Kč) from kiosks.

BY CAR AND BY TAXI. Roads are generally well-kept, but side-roads can be dangerous, and the number of fatal car accidents is increasing in the Czech Republic. **Roadside assistance** is usually available. To drive in the Czech Republic, an **International Driver's Permit** is required. **Taxis** are a safe way to travel, though many overcharge you. Negotiate the fare beforehand and make sure the meter is running during the ride. Phoning a taxi service is generally more affordable than flagging down a cab on the street.

BY BIKE AND BY THUMB. Biking is not particularly common in the Czech Republic. Renting bikes is possible, but sometimes expensive and difficult. Although common in the Czech Republic, Let's Go does not recommend **hitchhiking.**

KEEPING IN TOUCH

PHONE CODES	**Country code:** 420. **International dialing prefix:** 00. From outside the Czech Republic, dial international dialing prefix (see inside back cover) + 420 + city code + local number. Within the Czech Republic, simply dial the local number.

EMAIL AND INTERNET. Internet access is readily available throughout the Czech Republic. Internet cafes offer fast connections for 1-2Kč per minute; the local keyboard can be tricky, but there should be options to change to the English setting.

TELEPHONE. Card-operated phones (175Kč per 50 units; 320Kč per 100 units) are simpler to use and easier to find than coin phones. You can purchase phone cards *(telefonní karta)* at most *Tábaks* and *Trafika* (convenience stores). To make domestic calls, dial the entire number. City codes no longer exist in the Czech Republic, and dialing zero is not necessary. To make an international call to the Czech Republic, dial the country code followed by the entire phone number. Calls run 8Kč per minute to Australia, Canada, the UK, or the US; and 12Kč per minute to New Zealand. Dial ☎1181 for English info, 0800 12 34 56 for the international operator. International access codes include: **AT&T** (☎00 800 222 55288); **British Telecom** (☎00 420); **Canada Direct** (☎800 001 115); **MCI** (☎800 001 112); **Sprint** (☎800 001 187); and **Telstra Australia** (☎800 001 161).

MAIL. The postal system is reliable and efficient, though finding English-speaking postal employees can be a challenge. A postcard to the US costs 12Kč, to Europe

9Kč. To send airmail, stress that you want your package to go on a plane *(letecky)*. Go to the customs office to send packages heavier than 2kg abroad. Poste Restante is generally available. Address envelopes as follows: first name, LAST NAME, POSTE RESTANTE, Postal Code, city, country.

ACCOMMODATIONS AND CAMPING

CZECH REPUBLIC	❶	❷	❸	❹	❺
ACCOMMODATIONS	under 320Kč	320-500Kč	501-800Kč	801-1200Kč	over 1200Kč

Hostels and **university dorms** are the cheapest options in July and August; two- to four-bed dorms cost 250-500Kč. Hostels are clean and safe throughout the country, though they are often rare in areas with few students. **Pensions** in small towns are approximately equivalent. **Hotels** (from 1000Kč) tend to be more luxurious and expensive. From June to September, reserve at least a week ahead in Prague, Český Krumlov, and Brno. **Private homes** are not nearly as popular (or as cheap) as in the rest of Eastern Europe. Scan train stations for *Zimmer frei* signs. As quality varies, don't pay in advance. There are many **campgrounds** scattered throughout the country; most, however, are open only from mid-May to September.

FOOD AND DRINK

CZECH REPUBLIC	❶	❷	❸	❹	❺
FOOD	under 80Kč	80-110Kč	111-150Kč	151-200Kč	over 200Kč

Loving Czech cuisine starts with learning to pronounce *knedlíky* (KNED-lee-kee). These thick, wheat- or potato-based loaves of dough, feebly known in English as dumplings, are a staple. Meat, however, lies at the heart of almost all main dishes. If you're in a hurry, grab *párky* (frankfurters) or *sýr* (cheese) at a food stand. **Vegetarian** restaurants serving *bez masa* (meatless) specialties are uncommon outside Prague; traditional restaurants serve few options beyond *smaženy sýr* (fried cheese) and *saláty* (salads), and even these may contain meat products. Eating **kosher** is feasible, but beware—pork may sneak into many dishes. *Jablkový závin* (apple strudel) and *ovocné knedlíky* (fruit dumplings) are favorite sweets, but the most beloved is *koláč*—a tart filled with poppy seeds or sweet cheese. Moravian **wines** are of high quality. They're typically found at a *vinárna* (wine bar) that also serves a variety of spirits, including *slivovice* (plum brandy) and *becherovka* (herbal bitter), the **national drink.** World-class local brews like *Plzeňský Prazdroj* (Pilsner Urquell), Budvar, and *Krušovice* dominate the drinking scene. Daring travelers might sometimes sample **absinth,** an exotic, anise-flavored beverage illegal in the US.

LIFE AND TIMES

HISTORY

AND SO IT BEGINS. According to legend, **Father Čech** climbed Říp Mountain near present-day Prague and ordered the surrounding land settled. Textbooks, however, trace civilization back to the first-century arrival of the Celtic Boii. By the sixth century, Slavs had settled in the region, and by the 10th century, the Czechs were united under the **Přemyslid Dynasty. Wenceslas** (Václav), legendary patron saint and king of Bohemia, was one of the dynasty's earliest rulers. In 1114, the Holy Roman Empire invited the Czech kings to join.

PEACE THROWN OUT THE WINDOW. The reign of Holy Roman Emperor **Charles (Karel) IV** (1346-1378) was a golden era of Czech culture. His achievements included the promotion of Prague to an archbishopric and the 1348 founding of Charles University, the first university in Central Europe. Unfortunately, Charles' eldest legitimate son, Václav, was unable to attain the golden heights of his father. During his reign, proto-Protestant **Jan Hus** was burned at the stake for his protests against the corruption of the Catholic church. In response to the execution, the **Hussite movement** organized the **First Defenestration of Prague** in 1419—protestors threw members of the city council from a window of the Council House. Years of fighting followed. Two centuries later, the **Second Defenestration of Prague** set off the **Thirty Years' War** (1618-48). This time the victims survived, saved by a pile of manure. The Protestants' eventual defeat was sealed after an early, harsh blow in the Battle of White Mountain in November 1620. Their loss led to the absorption of Czech territory into the Austrian Empire and three centuries of oppression.

CHECKMATE. The nationalism that engulfed Europe during the 19th century invigorated the Bohemian peoples. The sentiment was crushed, however, in the imperial backlash that followed the 1848 revolutions. While WWI did little to increase harmony among the nationalities of the Habsburg Empire, mutual discontent united the Czechs and Slovaks. In the postwar confusion, **Edvard Beneš** and **Tomáš G. Masaryk** convinced the victorious Allies to legitimize a new state that united Bohemia, Moravia, and Slovakia into Czechoslovakia. This First Republic enjoyed remarkable economic prosperity but was torn apart when Hitler exploited the Allies' appeasement policy. The infamous 1938 **Munich Agreement** handed the Sudetenland to Germany. The following year, Hitler annexed the entire country.

UN-CRUSHED VELVET. Following the Allied liberation, the Communists won the 1946 elections, seizing permanent power in 1948. In 1968, Communist Party Secretary **Alexander Dubček** sought to reform the country's nationalized economy and ease political oppression during the **Prague Spring,** but the Soviets invaded immediately and deposed him. **Gustáv Husák** became Communist Party Secretary in 1969, ushering in 20 years of repression: he denounced the Prague Spring, consolidated power, and bestowed the title of President upon himself in 1975. Czech intellectuals protested his human rights violations with the nonviolent **Charter 77** movement. Its leaders were persecuted and imprisoned but still fostered increasing levels of dissidence. Communism's demise in Hungary and Poland and the fall of the Berlin Wall in 1989 opened the way for Czechoslovakia's **Velvet Revolution,** named for the nearly bloodless transition to a multi-party state system. The Communist regime's violent suppression of a peaceful demonstration outraged the nation, which retaliated with a strike. Within days the Communists resigned, and **Václav Havel,** a long-imprisoned playwright and the leader of both the Charter 77 and the Velvet Revolution, became president in December 1989. Slovak pleas for independence grew stronger and, after much debate, the Czech and Slovak Republics parted ways on January 1, 1993.

TODAY

The Czech Republic has enjoyed a post-Communist status as one of the most stable and prosperous countries in Eastern Europe. Playwright and former dissident **Václav Havel,** re-elected to the presidency in 1998 by the margin of a single vote in Parliament, remained the country's official head of state until the 2003 presidential election. Havel was succeded by **Václav Klaus,** co-founder of the Civic Democratic Party (ODS) and former Prime Minister. Klaus now enjoys a soaring popularity rating. In 2004, the Social Democrat Stanislav Gross suceeded **Vladimir Spindla** as prime minister, becoming the youngest Prime Minister in Europe at the age of 34. Allegations of misconduct led to his resignation less than a year later, however, and **Jíri Paroubek** soon replaced him as the leader of the troubled party. This challenge proved daunting and Paroubek resigned in August of 2006 after an inconclusive lower-house election. His replacement, **Mirek Toplánek,** implemented a center-right coalition that gained the confidence of the Chamber of Deputies in 2007, but has been under scrutiny recently for financial scandals that occurred during his tenure on the board of an engineering company.

The Czech Republic joined **NATO** in March 1999 and was admitted to the **EU** in May 2004. Klaus, who refers to himself as a Eurorealist, has often criticized the EU's centralization and what he views as their illiberal tendencies.

PEOPLE AND CULTURE

LANGUAGE. Czech is a West Slavic language, closely related to Slovak and Polish. English is widely understood among young people, and German can be useful, especially in South Bohemia. In eastern regions, you're more likely to encounter Polish. Russian was taught to all school children under communism, but use your *"privet"* carefully, as the language is not always welcome. For a phrasebook and glossary, see **Appendix: Czech,** p. 794.

DEMOGRAPHICS. The Czech Republic is comprised of 95% Czechs and 3% Slovaks. Other ethnic minorities include Germans, Roma, and a growing population of Vietnamese.

CUSTOMS AND ETIQUETTE. Firmly established customs govern wining and dining. When beer is served, wait until all raise the common *"na zdraví"* (to your health) toast before drinking, and always look into the eyes of the person with whom you are toasting. Similarly, before biting into a saucy *knedlík*, wish everyone *"dobrou chut"* (to your health). As a rule, foreigners should tip restaurants and taxis at a rate of around 10%.

THE ARTS

LITERATURE. Writers in the Czech Republic have long held a privileged position as important social and political commentators. From the first Czechoslovak president, **T.G. Masaryk,** to the recently retired **Václav Havel,** literary figures have also come to occupy positions of great power. The Habsburgs repressed Czech literature in the 18th century, but the 19th century saw a revival. In 1836, **Karel Hynek Mácha** penned his celebrated epic *May (Máj)*. The 1858 founding of the literary journal *Máj*, named after Mácha's poem, marked the beginning of the **National Revival.** One of its brightest stars, **Bozena Němcová,** introduced the novel to modern Czech literature with *Granny* (*Babička;* 1855). **Jaroslav Hašek's** satire, *The Good Soldier Švejk* (*Osudy dobrého vojáka Svejka za svetové války;* 1920-1923), became a classic commentary on life under Habsburg rule. **Franz Kafka's** experiences as a German-speaking Jew in his native Prague pervade his work. After Kafka, **Jaroslav Seifert** and **Vítězslav Nezval** produced image-rich works of poetry. In 1984, Seifert became the first Czech writer to receive a Nobel Prize.

The Czech literary tradition remains strong today. The country's best-known contemporary writer is **Milan Kundera,** whose philosophical novel *The Unbearable Lightness of Being*, set against the backdrop of Communist Prague, met with international acclaim. Former president **Havel** is a well-known playwright with several revered dramas to his name.

MUSIC. The 19th-century National Revival brought out the best in Czech music. The nation's most celebrated composers, **Antonín Dvořák, Leoš Janáček,** and **Bedřich**

Smetana, are renowned for transforming Czech folk tunes into symphonies and operas. Dvořák's *Symphony No. 9, From the New World,* combining Czech folk tradition with melodies gathered during the composer's trip to America, is probably the most famous Czech masterpiece. Among Czechs, however, Smetana's symphonic poem *My Country (Má vlast)* remains more popular. Currently, **jazz** and **bluegrass** music have gained popularity, and many American pop hits are sung over in Czech. **Support Lesbiens** is a popular band with **New Age** and **rock** features.

THE VISUAL ARTS. Marie Čerminová Toyen, a Surrealist born in Prague, immigrated to Paris in the 1920s to work with André Breton. One of the most important Czech artists of the 20th century, **Alfons Mucha** also worked in Paris and helped develop **Art Nouveau. Josef Čapek** was a Cubist and cartoonist best known for his satirical depiction of Hitler's ascent to power. While few Czech architects have become household names, the country itself is rife with architectural treasures. Both **Český Krumlov** and **Kutná Hora** have been declared protected cultural monuments by UNESCO for their medieval buildings and winding streets. The capital hosts the annual **Art Prague** each May, a modern art exhibition that expands each year as interest in art increases.

FILM. The Czech Republic has been successful in the film world. In 1967, director **Jiří Menzel's** *Closely Watched Trains (Ostre sledované vlaky)* won the Academy Award for Best Foreign Film. Director **Milo Forman** immigrated to the US in 1968 and exploded onto the film scene with the acclaimed *One Flew Over the Cuckoo's Nest* (1975). His 1984 film *Amadeus* won eight Oscars. Film has become increasingly popular in the Czech Republic, and **Karlovy Vary** hosts a major film festival. In 1997, **Jan Svěrák's** *Kolya* received an Oscar for Best Foreign Language Film.

HOLIDAYS AND FESTIVALS

Holidays: New Year's Day (Jan. 1); Easter Holiday (Mar. 24, 2008; Apr. 13, 2009); May Day/Labor Day (May 1); Liberation Day (May 8); Saints Cyril and Methodius Day (July 5); Jan Hus Day (July 6); St. Wenceslas Day (Sept. 28); Independence Day (Oct. 28); Struggle for Freedom and Democracy Day (Nov. 17); Christmas (Dec. 24-26).

Festivals: Classical musicians and world-class orchestras descend on Prague (p. 163) for the Spring Festival held from mid-May to early June. In June, the Five-Petaled Rose Festival, a boisterous medieval festival in Český Krumlov (p. 205), features music, dance, and a jousting tournament. Masopust, the Moravian version of Mardi Gras, is celebrated in villages across the Czech Republic from Epiphany to Ash Wednesday (Jan.-Mar.). Revelers dressed in animal masks feast, dance, and sing until Lent begins.

PRAGUE (PRAHA)

King of Bohemia and Holy Roman Emperor Charles IV refashioned Prague (pop. 1,200,000) into a city of soaring cathedrals and lavish palaces in the 14th century. A maze of shady alleys lends the city a dark, ethereal atmosphere, which continues to captivate writers, artists, and tourists alike. That magic has been well tested in recent years. Since the lifting of the Iron Curtain, hordes of outsiders have flooded the capital. In summer, most locals leave for the countryside and the foreigner-to-resident ratio soars above nine-to-one; but walk a few blocks from any of the major sights and you'll be lost in the labyrinthine cobblestone alleys. And even in the hyper-touristed Staré Město (Old Town), Prague's Charles Bridge—packed so tightly in summer that the only way off is to jump—is still breathtaking at sunrise, eerie in a fog, and stunning after a fresh snowfall.

INTERCITY TRANSPORTATION

Flights: Ruzyně Airport (☎220 111 111), 20km northwest of the city. Bus #119 runs between the airport and Metro A: Dejvická (5am-midnight; 12Kč, 6Kč per bag). Buy tickets in kiosks or machines before boarding. An **airport bus** run by **Cedaz** (☎220 114 296; 20-45min., every 30min. 5:30am-9:30pm) stops outside Metro stations at nám. Republiky (120Kč) and Dejvická (90Kč). **Taxis** to and from Ruzyně are expensive but may be the only option at night. Try to settle on a price before (700-900Kč). Airlines include: **Air France,** Václavské nám. 57 (☎221 662 662); **British Airways,** Ruzyně Airport (☎239 000 299); **Czech Airlines (ČSA),** V Celnici 5 (☎239 104 111); **Delta,** Národní třída 32 (☎224 947 332); **KLM,** Na Příkopě 21 (☎233 090 933); **Lufthansa,** Ruzyně Airport (☎220 114 456); **Swissair,** Ruzyně Airport (☎008 227 230).

Trains: (☎221 111 122, international info 224 615 249; www.vlak.cz). English spoken on international info line and attempted at station info offices. Prague has 4 main terminals. **Hlavní nádraží** (☎224 615 786; Metro C: Hlavní nádraží) and **Nádraží Holešovice** (☎224 624 632; Metro C: Nádraží Holešovice) are the largest and cover most international service. Domestic trains leave from **Masarykovo nádraží** (☎840 112 113, 221 111 122; Metro B: nám. Republiky), and from **Smíchovské nádraží** (☎972 226 150; Metro B: Smíchovské nádraží). International trains run to: **Berlin, GER** (5hr., 6 per day, 1400Kč); **Bratislava, SLK** (4½-5½hr., 6 per day, 600Kč); **Budapest, HUN** (7-9hr., 5 per day, 1400Kč); **Kraków, POL** (7-8hr., 3 per day, 900Kč); **Moscow, RUS** (31hr., 1 per day, 3000Kč); **Munich, GER** (7hr., 3 per day, 1650Kč); **Vienna, AUT** (4½hr., 7 per day, 1000Kč); **Warsaw, POL** (9½hr., 2 per day, 1290Kč). If you arrive into **Hlavní nádraží** at night, take the path straight out of the station to Opletalova instead of cutting through the park. The area is poorly lit and a common sleeping ground for vagrants.

Buses: (☎900 149 044; www.vlak-bus.cz). The state-run **ČSAD** (☎257 319 016) has several bus terminals. The biggest is **Florenc,** Křižíkova 4 (☎900 149 044). Metro B or C: Florenc. Info office open daily 6am-9pm. Buy tickets in advance. Direct buses to: **Berlin, GER** (7hr., 2 per day, 900Kč); **Budapest, HUN** (7½hr., 3 per day, 1600Kč); **Paris, FRA** (15hr., 2 per day, 2200Kč); **Sofia, BUL** (24hr., 2 per day, 1600Kč); **Vienna, AUT** (5hr., 1 per day, 600Kč). 10% ISIC discount. The **Tourbus** office (☎224 218 680; www.eurolines.cz), on the main fl. of the terminal, sells tickets for **Eurolines** and airport buses. Open M-F 7am-7pm, Sa 8am-7pm, Su 9am-7pm.

ORIENTATION

Shouldering the river **Vltava,** greater Prague is a mess of suburbs and maze-like streets. Fortunately, nearly everything of interest to travelers lies within the compact downtown. The Vltava runs south to north through central Prague before curving east, separating **Staré Město** (Old Town) and **Nové Město** (New Town) from **Malá Strana** (Lesser Side). On the right bank of the river, Staré Město's **Staroměstské náměstí** (Old Town Square) is Prague's focal point. From the square, the elegant **Pařížská ulice** (Paris Street) leads north into **Josefov,** the old Jewish quarter. Just south of Staré Město, the more modern **Nové Město** houses **Václavské náměstí** (Wenceslas Square), the administrative and commercial core of the city. To the west of Staroměstské nám., the picturesque **Karlův most** (Charles Bridge) spans the Vltava, connecting Staré Město with **Malostranské náměstí** (Lesser Town Square). **Pražský Hrad** (Prague Castle) overlooks Malostranské nám. from **Hradčany** hill. Prague's **train station, Hlavní nádrazí,** and **Florenc bus station** are northeast of Václavské nám. All train and bus terminals are on or near the **Metro** system. To get to Staroměstské nám., take Metro A line to Staroměstská and follow Kaprova away from the river. Kiosks and bookstores sell an indexed *plán města* (map), essential for newcomers to the city.

LOCAL TRANSPORTATION

Public Transportation: Prague's **Metro, tram,** and **bus** services are excellent and all share the same ticket system. 8Kč tickets are good for one 15min. ride or 4 stops on the Metro. 12Kč ticket valid for 1hr. of bus, tram, and Metro travel, with unlimited connections in the same direction. Large bags and baby carriages 6Kč. Validate tickets in machines above the escalators to avoid 900Kč fines (500Kč if paid on the spot) issued by plainclothes inspectors who roam the transport lines. Buy tickets at newsstands, *tabák* kiosks, machines in stations, or DP (*Dopravní podnik;* transport authority) kiosks. DP offices (☎296 191 817; open daily 7am-9pm), near the Jungmannovo nám. exit of the Můstek Metro stop, sell **multiday passes** valid for the entire network (1-day 80Kč, 3-day 220Kč, 1-week 280Kč, 15-day 320Kč). The 3 **Metro** lines run daily 5am-midnight: A is green on maps, B is yellow, and C is red. **Night trams** #51-58 and **buses** #502-514 and 601 run after the last Metro and cover the same areas as day trams and buses (every 30min. 12:30-4:30am); look for dark blue signs with white letters at bus stops. For the most up-to-date information, contact DP (☎296 191 817; www.dpp.cz).

CZECH TRANSPORT. On newer buses and trams, the doors don't open unless you press the button on the handbar next to the door. When you're on the train, press the button *before* you arrive at your stop, as buses might continue on to the next stop if nobody has done so—however far away that is.

Taxis: City Taxi (☎257 257 257) or **AAA** (☎140 14). 30Kč base, 22Kč per km, 4Kč per min. waiting. You can hail a cab anywhere on the street, but call ahead or have a local call for you to avoid getting ripped off. To sidestep the frequent taxi scams, always ask for a receipt *("Prosím, dejte mi paragon")* with distance traveled and price paid. If the driver doesn't comply, you aren't obligated to pay. Many drivers speak some English.

Car Rental: Hertz, at the airport (☎233 326 714; www.hertz.cz/en). Cars from 1880Kč per day for the 1st 5 days with unlimited mileage. Must have a 1-year-old driver's license and major credit card. 21+. Open daily 8am-10pm. Branch at Karlovo nám. 28 (☎222 231 010). Open daily 8am-10pm.

Bike Rental: Praha Bike, Dlouhá 24 (☎732 388 880; www.prahabike.cz). Bikes delivered to your hotel. Bike rental includes helmet, lock, luggage storage, and map. Bike rentals 200Kč per 2hr., 500Kč per 8hr., 550Kč per 10hr.; 2hr. min. 10% ISIC discount. 2hr. city

CZECH THE SCHEDULE

Catching intercity transport in the Czech Republic is a tricky endeavor. Czech bus and train stations are littered with posted schedules, each a maze of numbers, hammers, sickles, and circles that bear a closer resemblance to target practice than an intelligible course from point A to point B.

The clearest Czech train and bus schedules are on the Internet, at www.vlak.cz, which has recently been translated into English. But in case you arrive at the station without having done any online research, here's a rough guide to deciphering the hieroglyphics you'll encounter on the schedule: crossed mallets indicate services that operate only on weekdays. The number 6 indicates Saturday service. A "K" or an "L" accompanied by a number corresponds to notes at the bottom of the schedule which detail periods of time during which the bus does not run as scheduled. Also, check the arrival time at your destination: if you see a vertical or zig-zagged line running through it, this means that the service is express and passes through but does not stop at that destination. With this code cracked, you can breathe a sigh of relief, knowing you really will get to Litomyšl, even though you're on a bus labeled "Libec."

—Lauren Rivera

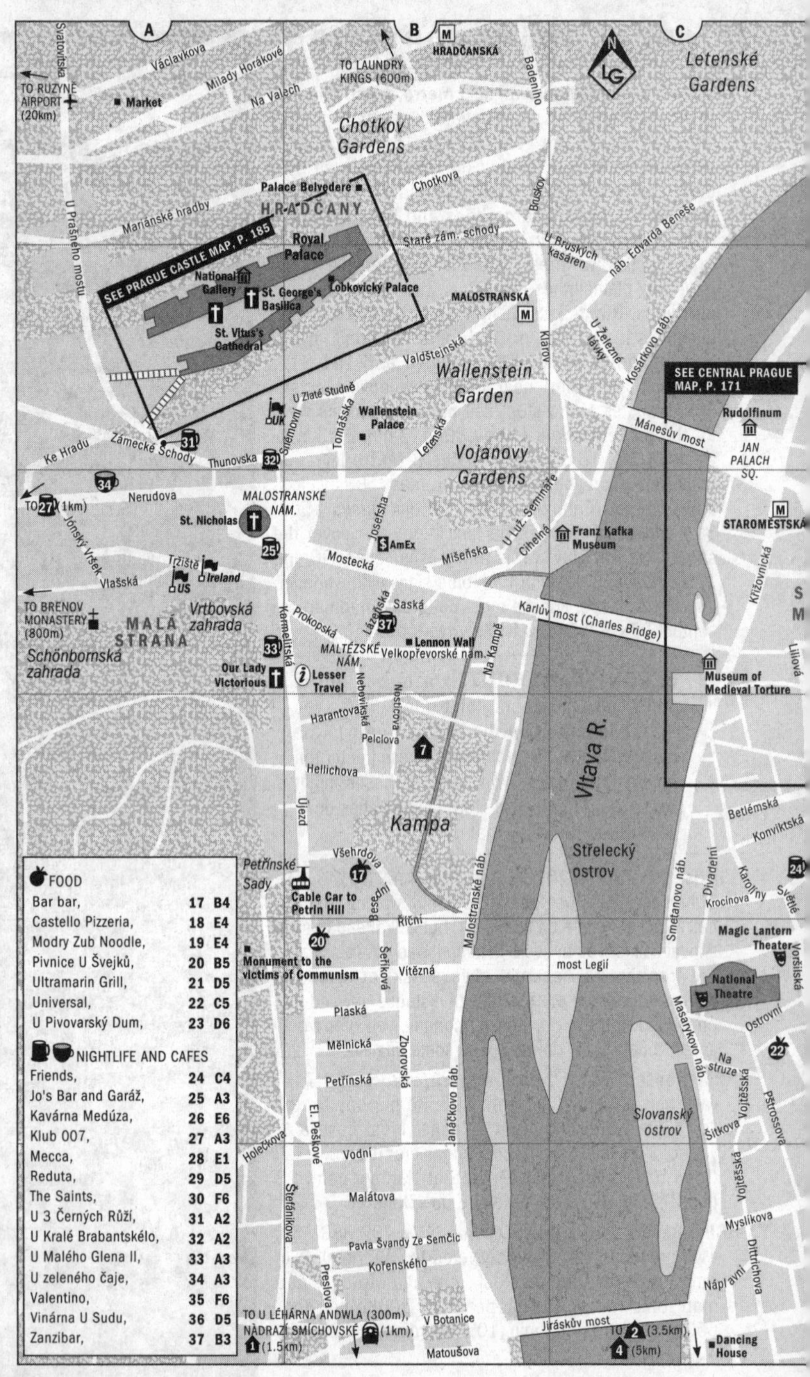

A
B
C
TO LAUNDRY KINGS (600m)
HRADČANSKÁ
Letenské Gardens
TO RUZYNĚ AIRPORT (20km)
Market
Svatovítská
Václavkova
Milady Horákové
Na Valech
Badeniho
Chotkov Gardens
Chotkova
Palace Belvedere
HRADČANY
Mariánské hradby
U Prašného mostu
SEE PRAGUE CASTLE MAP, P. 185
Royal Palace
National Gallery
St. George's Basilica
Lobkovický Palace
St. Vitus's Cathedral
Staré zám. schody
Bruskov
U Bruských kasáren
náb. Edvarda Beneše
MALOSTRANSKÁ
Klárov
U Železné lávky
Kosárkovo náb.
Valdštejnská
Wallenstein Garden
SEE CENTRAL PRAGUE MAP, P. 171
Rudolfinum
U Zlaté Studně
Sněmovní
Tomášská
Wallenstein Palace
Letenská
UK
Mánesův most
JAN PALACH SQ.
Ke Hradu
Zámecké Schody
Thunovska
Vojanovy Gardens
TO 27 (1km)
Nerudova
MALOSTRANSKÉ NÁM.
St. Nicholas
Josefská
AmEx
U Luž. Semináře
Cihelná
Franz Kafka Museum
STAROMĚSTSKÁ
Jánský Vršek
Tržiště
Ireland
US
Vlašská
Mostecká
Míšeňská
Křižovnická
TO BRENOV MONASTERY (800m)
MALÁ STRANA
Vrtbovská zahrada
Karmelitská
Prokopská
Lázeňská
Saská
Karlův most (Charles Bridge)
Schönbornská zahrada
MALTÉZSKÉ NÁM.
Lennon Wall
Velkopřevorské nám.
Na Kampě
Our Lady Victorious
Lesser Travel
Museum of Medieval Torture
Liliová
Nebovidská
Nosticova
Harantova
Pelclova
Vltava R.
Hellichova
Újezd
Kampa
Betlémská
Konviktská
Všehrdova
Petřínské Sady
Cable Car to Petrin Hill
Besední
Střelecký ostrov
Malostranské nábř.
Smetanovo náb.
Divadelní
Karolíny Světlé
Krocínova
Říční
Magic Lantern Theater
Monument to the victims of Communism
Šeříková
Vítězná
most Legií
Voršilská
National Theatre
Plaská
Ostrovní
Masarykovo náb.
Mělnická
Zborovská
Na struze
Petřínská
Janáčkovo náb.
Vojtěšská
Pštrossova
Slovanský ostrov
Šítkova
Holečkova
El. Peškové
Vodní
Malátova
Myslíkova
Štefánikova
Pavla Švandy Ze Semčic
Dittrichova
Preslova
Kořenského
Náplavní
TO U LÉHÁRNA ANDWLA (300m), NÁDRAŽÍ SMÍCHOVSKÉ (1km), 1 (1.5km)
V Botanice
Jiráskův most
TO 2 (3.5km), 4 (5km)
Dancing House
Matoušova
FOOD
Bar bar, 17 B4
Castello Pizzeria, 18 E4
Modry Zub Noodle, 19 E4
Pivnice U Švejků, 20 B5
Ultramarin Grill, 21 D5
Universal, 22 C5
U Pivovarský Dum, 23 D6
NIGHTLIFE AND CAFES
Friends, 24 C4
Jo's Bar and Garáž, 25 A3
Kavárna Medúza, 26 E6
Klub 007, 27 A3
Mecca, 28 E1
Reduta, 29 D5
The Saints, 30 F6
U 3 Černých Růží, 31 A2
U Kralé Brabantskélo, 32 A2
U Malého Glena II, 33 A3
U zeleného čaje, 34 A3
Valentino, 35 F6
Vinárna U Sudu, 36 D5
Zanzibar, 37 B3

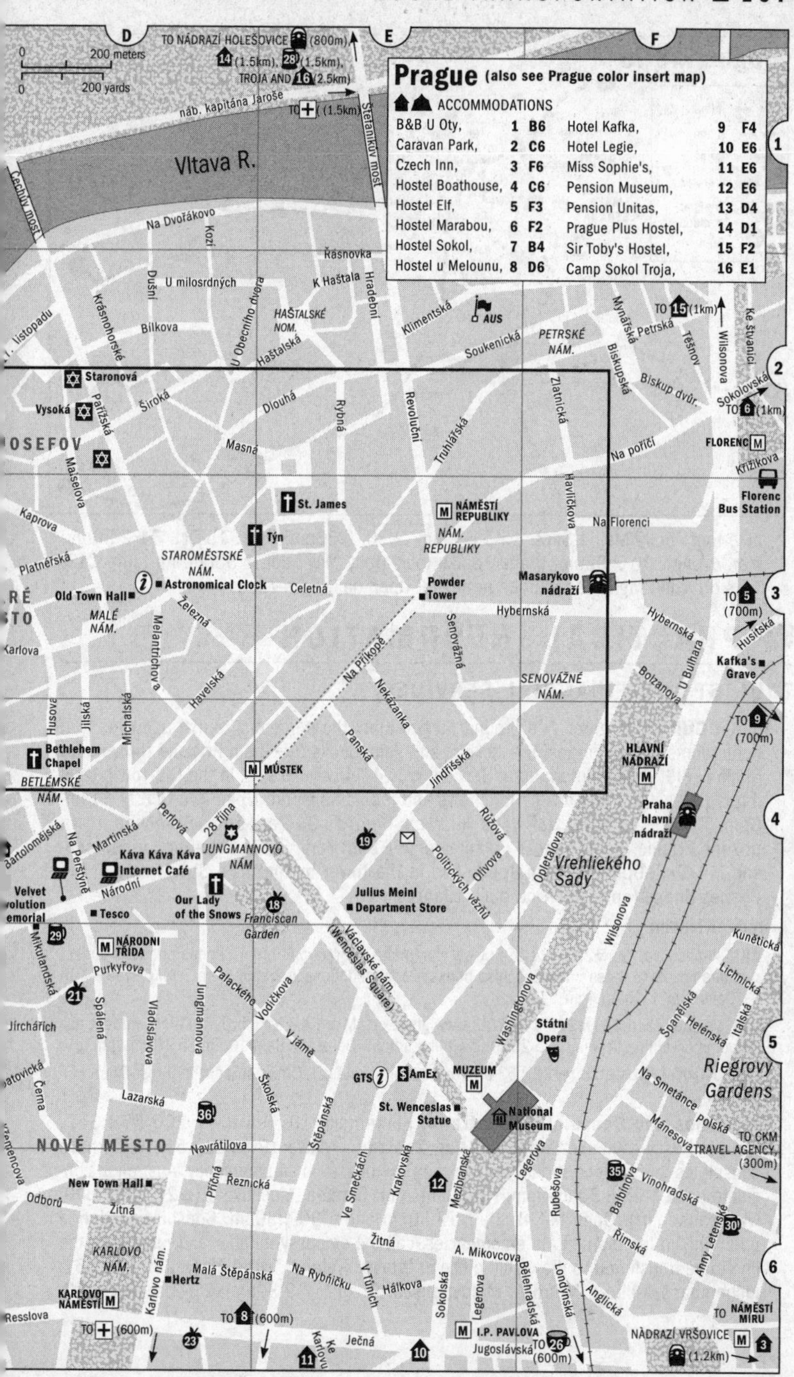
Prague (also see Prague color insert map)
ACCOMMODATIONS
B&B U Oty, 1 B6
Caravan Park, 2 C6
Czech Inn, 3 F6
Hostel Boathouse, 4 C6
Hostel Elf, 5 F3
Hostel Marabou, 6 F2
Hostel Sokol, 7 B4
Hostel u Melounu, 8 D6
Hotel Kafka, 9 F4
Hotel Legie, 10 E6
Miss Sophie's, 11 E6
Pension Museum, 12 E6
Pension Unitas, 13 D4
Prague Plus Hostel, 14 D1
Sir Toby's Hostel, 15 F2
Camp Sokol Troja, 16 E1
200 meters
200 yards
TO NÁDRAŽÍ HOLEŠOVICE (800m)
(1.5km), (1.5km),
TROJA AND (2.5km)
TO (1.5km)
Vltava R.
náb. kapitána Jaroše
Štefánikův most
Čechův most
Na Dvořákovo
Kozí
Řásnovka
Dušní
U milosrdných
K Haštala
Hradební
Klimentská
AUS
HAŠTALSKÉ NOM.
Haštalská
U Obecního dvora
Bílkova
Krásnohorské
17. listopadu
Soukenická
PETRSKÉ NÁM.
Petrská
Mlynářská
Těšnov
Wilsonova
Ke štvanici
TO (1km)
Biskupská
Biskup dvůr
Sokolovská
TO (1km)
Staronová
Vysoká
Pařížská
Široká
Dlouhá
Rybná
Revoluční
Zlatnická
JOSEFOV
Masná
Truhlářská
Na poříčí
FLORENC
Křižíkova
Florenc Bus Station
Maiselova
St. James
NÁMĚSTÍ REPUBLIKY
NÁM. REPUBLIKY
Havlíčkova
Na Florenci
Kaprova
Týn
STAROMĚSTSKÉ NÁM.
Platnéřská
Astronomical Clock
Old Town Hall
Celetná
Powder Tower
Masarykovo nádraží
TO (700m)
MALÉ NÁM.
Železná
Hybernská
Husitská
Karlova
Melantrichova
Senovážná
Kafka's Grave
Na Příkopě
Nekázanka
Bolzanova
U Bulhara
Havelská
SENOVÁŽNÉ NÁM.
TO (700m)
Husova
Jilská
Michalská
Panská
Jindřišská
HLAVNÍ NÁDRAŽÍ
Bethlehem Chapel
BETLÉMSKÉ NÁM.
MŮSTEK
Praha hlavní nádraží
Perlová
28 října
Růžová
Bartolomějská
Martinská
Na Perštýně
JUNGMANNOVO NÁM.
Káva Káva Káva
Internet Café
Politických vězňů
Olivova
Opletalova
Vrchlického Sady
Velvet Revolution Memorial
Národní
Our Lady of the Snows
Julius Meinl Department Store
Tesco
Franciscan Garden
Wilsonova
Mikulandská
NÁRODNÍ TŘÍDA
Václavské nám. (Wenceslas Square)
Kunětická
Purkyňova
Lichnická
Palackého
Vodičkova
Washingtonova
Jircháříh
Spálená
Vladislavova
Jungmannova
V jámě
Státní Opera
Španělská
Helénská
Italská
Riegrovy Gardens
GTS
AmEx
MUZEUM
Na Smetánce
Lazarská
Školská
St. Wenceslas Statue
National Museum
Polská
Mánesova
TO CKM TRAVEL AGENCY (300m)
NOVÉ MĚSTO
Navrátilova
Štěpánská
Ve Smečkách
Krakovská
Legerova
Rubešova
Balbínova
Vinohradská
New Town Hall
Příčná
Řeznická
Mezibranská
Odborů
Žitná
Anny Letenské
Římská
KARLOVO NÁM.
Karlovo nám.
Malá Štěpánská
Na Rybníčku
V Tůních
A. Mikovcova
Bělehradská
Londýnská
Anglická
Hertz
Hálkova
Sokolská
KARLOVO NÁMĚSTÍ
Resslova
TO (600m)
TO (600m)
Ke Karlovu
Ječná
I.P. PAVLOVA
Jugoslávská
TO (600m)
TO NÁMĚSTÍ MÍRU
NÁDRAŽÍ VRŠOVICE
(1.2km)

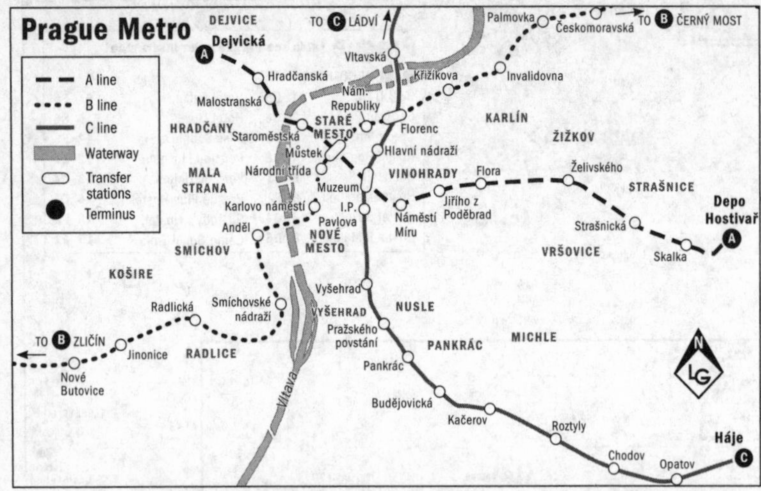

bike tours daily May 1-Sept. 15 11:30am, 2:30, 5:30pm; Sept. 15-Oct. 31 2:30pm; Mar. 14-Apr. 30 2:30pm. Prague parks tours daily May-Sept. 5:30pm. All tours €13. Trips outside Prague can also be arranged. Open daily 9am-7pm.

PRACTICAL INFORMATION

TOURIST AND FINANCIAL SERVICES

Tourist Office: The green "i"s around Prague mark the numerous tourist agencies that book rooms and sell maps, bus tickets, and guidebooks. The main **Pražská Informační Služba** (**PIS;** Prague Information Service; ☎124 44; www.pis.cz) in the Old Town, sells maps (30-199Kč) and tickets for shows and public transport. Open Apr.-Oct. M 11am-6pm, Tu-Su 9am-6pm; Nov.-Mar. M 11am-5pm, Tu-Su 9am-5pm. Branches at Na příkopě 20 and Hlavní nádraží (in summer M-F 9am-7pm, Sa-Su 9am-5pm; in low season M-F 9am-6pm, Sa 9am-3pm), and in the tower by the Malá Strana side of the Charles Bridge (open Apr.-Oct. daily 10am-6pm).

Budget Travel:

CKM, Mánesova 77 (☎222 721 595; www.ckm-praha.cz). Metro A: Jiřího z Poděbrad. Sells budget airline tickets to those under 26. Also books accommodations in Prague from 300Kč. Open M-Th 10am-6pm, F 10am-4pm.

GTS, Ve smečkách 27 (☎222 119 700; www.gtsint.cz). Metro A or C: Muzeum. Offers student discounts on airline tickets (225-2500Kč within Europe). Open M-F 8am-10pm, Sa 10am-4pm.

Lesser Travel, Trziste 13 (☎257 534 130; www.airtickets.cz). Offers student airfares. Open M-F 10am-5pm.

Embassies and Consulates: Australia, Klimentská 10, 6th fl. (☎296 578 350; www.embassy.gov.au/cz.html) and **New Zealand,** Dykova 19 (☎222 514 672) have consulates, but citizens should contact the UK embassy in an emergency. Australian consulate open M-Th 8:30am-5pm, F 8:30am-2pm. **Canada,** Muchova 6 (☎272 101 800; www.canada.cz). Open M-F 8:30am-12:30pm and 1:30-4:30pm. Consular section is open only in the morning. In emergencies, call the embassy number and remain on the line to be transferred to the watch office in Ottawa. **Ireland,** Tržiště 13 (☎257 530 061; irishembassy@iol.cz). Metro A: Malostranská. Open M-F 9:30am-12:30pm and 2:30-

4:30pm. **UK,** Thunovská 14 (☎257 402 111; consular and visa info prague@fco.gov.uk, other info info@britain.cz). Metro A: Malostranská. Open M-Th 9am-noon. **US,** Tržiště 15 (☎257 530 663, after-hours emergency 257 022 000; www.usembassy.cz). Metro A: Malostranská. Open M-F 8am-4:30pm. Consular section open M-F 8:30-11:30am.

The different lengths of telephone numbers, ranging from 4 to 9 digits, can be confusing. Prague updates its phone system incessantly. The city modified all numbers in 2002, adding a 2 before most land lines and removing the 0 for mobile numbers. Updated numbers have 9 digits; if a number has fewer than 9, it either is an information or emergency line or is missing a city area code. The city area code is the first three digits of a number, usually a 2 followed by a number between 10 and 35. The numbers listed here reflect the most recent changes, but call the city's telephone info line for any updates (☎141 11).

Currency Exchange: Exchange counters are everywhere and rates vary wildly. Don't bother with the expensive hotels, and never change money on the streets. **Chequepoints** are plentiful and stay open until about 11pm, but sometimes charge suspicious commissions, so do the math. **Komerční banka,** Na příkopě 33 (☎222 432 111; fax 224 243 018), buys notes and checks for 2% commission. Open M-W 9am-6pm, Th-F 9am-5pm. Branch at Staroměstské nám. 24. Open M-F 9am-5pm. **E Banka,** Václavské nám. 43 (☎222 115 222; www.ebanka.cz). Open M-F 8am-7pm.

ATMs: Though you can't throw a rock without hitting a currency exchange, ATMs are surprisingly scarce, and are most often found attached to banks. A **24hr. Citibank** is at Rytířska 24, near Wenceslas Square.

American Express: Václavské nám. 56 (☎222 800 224). Metro A or C: Muzeum. AmEx **ATM** outside. **Western Union** available. MC/V **cash advances** (3% commission). Open daily 9am-7pm. Branches at Mostecká 12 (☎257 313 638; open daily 9:30am-7:30pm), Celetná 17 (☎222 481 205; open daily 8:30am-7:15pm), and Staroměstské nám. 5 (☎224 818 388; open daily 9am-7:30pm).

LOCAL SERVICES

Luggage Storage: Lockers in train and bus stations take two 5Kč coins. Fine for forgotten lock code 30Kč. For storage over 24hr., use the luggage offices to the left in the basement of Hlavní nádraží. 20Kč per day, bags over 15kg 40Kč. Fine for forgotten lock code 30Kč. Open 6-11am, 11:30am-5:30pm, 6pm-5:30am.

English-Language Bookstores:

The Globe Bookstore, Pštrossova 6 (☎224 934 203; www.globebookstore.cz). Metro B: Národní třída. Exit Metro left on Spálená, make the 1st right on Ostrovní, then the 3rd left on Pštrossova. A haven for English speakers, this social center disguised as a bookstore and coffeehouse sells a wide variety of new and used books and periodicals, and offers **Internet** (1.50Kč per min.). Its cafe serves fruit smoothies (55-70Kč) and brunch. Open daily 9:30am-midnight.

Anagram Bookshop, Týn 4 (☎224 805 137; www.anagram.cz). Metro A: Staroměstská. Behind Týn Church, a short way down Týn. Anagram stocks a wide selection of literary fiction, philosophy, political theory, art books, and literary guides to Prague. The proprietor has a wealth of knowledge about the literary and political history of Prague. Trade-ins are available for store credit. Open M-Sa 10am-10pm, Su 10am-6pm. MC/V.

Big Ben Bookshop, Malá Štupartská 5 (☎224 826 565; www.bigbenbookshop.com). Stocks a good selection of classics and bestsellers. Metro A: Staroměstská. Open M-F 9am-6:30pm, Sa 10am-5pm, Su noon-5pm. MC/V.

Laundromat: Laundry Kings, Dejvická 16 (☎233 343 743; www.laundry.czweb.org). Metro A: Hradčanská. Trams #1, 8, 18, 25, 26. Exit Metro to Dejvická, cross the street, and turn left. Travelers flock here at night to watch CNN and pick each other up. Bulletin board for apartment-seekers, English teachers, and "friends." Internet 55Kč per 30min. Wash 40Kc per 8 min., dry 90Kč, more for heavier materials; detergent 10-20Kč. Open M-F 6am-10pm, Sa-Su 8am-10pm. Last wash 9:30pm. **Laundromat/Internet Cafe,** Korunní 14 (☎222 510 180; www.volny.cz/laundromat). Metro A: nám. Míru. Trams #10, 16, 22, 23. English spoken. Internet 30Kč per 15min. Wash and dry 70Kč each; detergent 75Kč. Open daily 8am-8pm.

Central Prague (also see Prague color map)

ACCOMMODATIONS
Hostel Týn, **12**
Hotel King George, **21**
Old Prague Hostel, **4**
Traveller's Hostel Dlouhá, **1**
Traveller's Hostel Husova 3, **20**
U Lilie, **17**

FOOD
Cafe Bambus, **3**
Country Life, **18**
Klub architektů, **22**
Lehká Hlava, **23**
U Řozvarilů, **5**
Yami Sushi, **8**

NIGHTLIFE
Bombay Cocktail Bar, **9**
Karlovy Lázně, **16**
Kozička, **6**
Le Chateau, **14**
M1 Lounge, **7**
Repete, **15**
Roxy, **2**

CAFES
Bohemia Bagel, **10**
Cafe Ebel, **13, 19**
Cajevna Sivna, **11**

EMERGENCY AND COMMUNICATIONS

24hr. Pharmacy: U Lékárna Anděla, Štefánikova 6 (☎257 320 918 or 257 324 686; after-hours 257 320 194; lekandela@volny.cz). Metro B: Anděl. With your back to the Anděl Metro station, turn left and follow Nádražní, which becomes Štefánikova. Open M-F 7am-9pm, Sa-Su 8am-9pm. After-hours service M-F 9pm-7am and from Sa 1pm to M 7am. For after-hours service, press button marked *Pohotovost,* left of the main door.

Medical Services: Na Homolce (Hospital for Foreigners), Roentgenova 2 (☎257 271 111, reception for foreigners 257 272 146; www.homolka.cz). Bus #167 runs to the hospital from Na Knižecí (Metro B: Anděl). Open 24hr. **Canadian Medical Center,** Veleslavínská 1 (☎235 360 133, after-hours 724 300 301; www.cmc.praha.cz). Most major payment plans accepted. Open M, W, F 8am-6pm; Tu and Th 8am-8pm.

Telephones: Virtually everywhere. Card phones are the most common and convenient. Phone cards are sold at kiosks, post offices, and some exchange establishments for 200Kč and 300Kč. Coins also accepted (local calls from 4Kč per min.).

Internet: Internet access is everywhere in Prague; however, it is also more expensive than in the rest of the Czech Republic. Access is available in libraries, hostels, cafes, bars, and even laundromats. **Národní třída** is home to several lab-like cyber cafes.

Bohemia Bagel, Masná 2 (☎224 812 560; www.bohemiabagel.cz). Metro A: Staroměstská. Internet kiosks 2Kč per min. Open daily 7am-midnight.

Káva Káva Káva, Národní třída 37 (☎253 142 68; www.kava-coffee.cz). Metro B: Národní třída. Across the street from Tesco, to the right and through the arch on the left. Classic European coffeehouse: patrons sit out front around marbletop tables, or people-watch through giant glass windows. Espresso from 45Kč. Milkshakes 40Kč. Internet downstairs 2.50Kč per min. until 6pm, 2Kč per min. thereafter; 20Kč minimum. Another branch is located at Lidická 42. Open M-F 7am-10pm, Sa-Su 9am-10pm. AmEx/MC/V.

Professional PC Arena G8, Národní třída 25 (☎777 571 537, 605 732 966). Metro B: Národní třída. Across from Tesco, inside the Pasáž paláce Metro. Past KFC, follow the sign that says "Laser Game" downstairs, through the arcade. Internet 1Kč per min. Open 24hr.

Post Office: Jindřišská 14 (☎221 131 445). Metro A or B: Můstek. **Poste Restante** available. Take a number from the kiosk in the main hallway and wait to be called. Internet 1Kč per min. Tellers close 7pm. Open daily 2am-midnight. **Postal Code:** 11000.

ACCOMMODATIONS

While hotel prices are rising exponentially, hostel prices have stabilized around 400-600Kč. Small, family-run hostels are cheaper than the large hostels in the center of town. Reserve rooms in advance, and at least a month ahead in June, July, and August. Many hostels have 24hr. reception and require check-in after 2pm and check-out by 10am. Though less common than in other parts of Eastern Europe, affordable rooms are being rented out by a growing number of Prague residents.

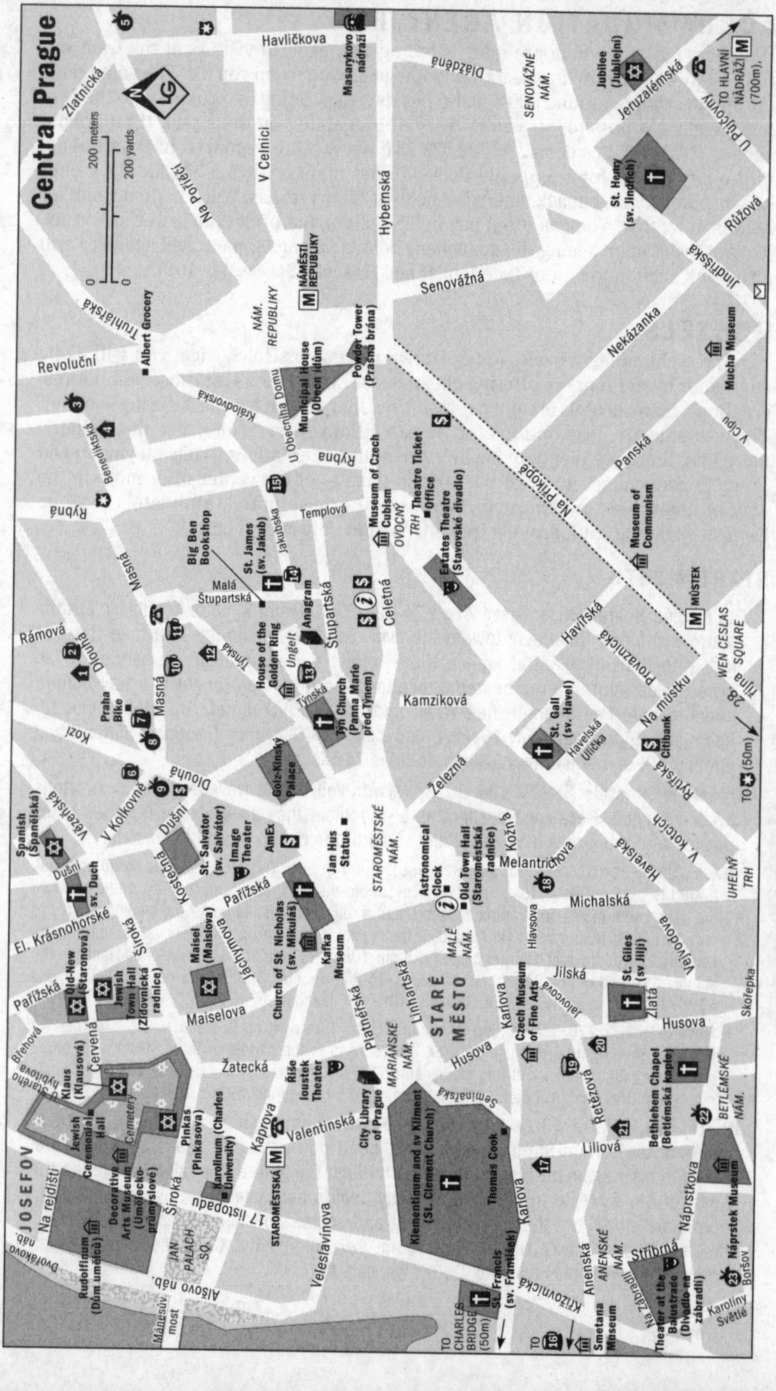
Central Prague
200 meters
200 yards
JOSEFOV
STARÉ MĚSTO
Zlatnická
Na Poříčí
Havlíčkova
Masarykovo nádraží
V Celnici
Hybernská
Dlážděná
SENOVÁŽNÉ NÁM.
Jubilee (Jubilejní)
Jeruzalémská
TO HLAVNÍ NÁDRAŽÍ (700m)
U Půjčovny
St. Henry (sv. Jindřich)
Růžová
Jindřišská
Senovážná
Truhlářská
Albert Grocery
Revoluční
NÁM. REPUBLIKY
NÁMĚSTÍ REPUBLIKY
Municipal House (Obecní dům)
Powder Tower (Prašná brána)
U Obecního Domu
Králodvorská
Benediktská
Rybná
Big Ben Bookshop
St. James (sv. Jakub)
Jakubská
Templová
Museum of Czech Cubism
Theatre Ticket Office
Estates Theatre (Stavovské divadlo)
OVOCNÝ TRH
Na Příkopě
Nekázanka
Mucha Museum
Panská
V Cípu
Museum of Communism
MŮSTEK
WEN CESLAS SQUARE
28. října
Rámová
Dlouhá
Masná
Malá Štupartská
Štupartská
Týnská
House of the Golden Ring
Ungelt
Anagram
Celetná
Kamzíková
Havířská
Provaznická
Na můstku
Týn Church (Panna Marie před Týnem)
Praha Bike
Kozí
Goltz-Kinský Palace
St. Gall (sv. Havel)
Havelská Ulička
Citibank
Železná
Rytířská
TO (50m)
Spanish (Španělská)
Vězeňská
V Kolkovně
Dušní
St. Salvator (sv. Salvátor)
Image Theater
AmEx
Jan Hus Statue
STAROMĚSTSKÉ NÁM.
Astronomical Clock
Old Town Hall (Staroměstská radnice)
Kožná
Melantrichova
V. kotcích
Havelská
UHELNÝ TRH
sv. Duch
Kostečná
Pařížská
El. Krásnohorské
Široká
Church of St. Nicholas (sv. Mikuláš)
Kafka Museum
MALÉ NÁM.
Michalská
Hlavsova
Vejvodova
Old-New (Staronová)
Jewish Town Hall (Židovnická radnice)
Maisel (Maiselova)
Jáchymova
Maiselova
Linhartská
Platnéřská
Jilská
St. Giles (sv Jiljí)
Jalovcova
Zlatá
Husova
Skořepka
Břehová
Červená
Klaus (Klausová)
U Starého hřbitova
Jewish Ceremonial Hall
Cemetery
Žatecká
Říše Ioustek Theater
MARIÁNSKÉ NÁM.
Czech Museum of Fine Arts
Karlova
Řetězová
Bethlehem Chapel (Betlémská kaple)
BETLÉMSKÉ NÁM.
Pinkas (Pinkasova)
Kaprova
Valentinská
City Library of Prague
Klementinum and sv Kliment (St. Clement Church)
Seminářská
Thomas Cook
Liliová
Decorative Arts Museum (Umělecko-průmyslové)
Karolinum (Charles University)
STAROMĚSTSKÁ
Na rejdišti
17 listopadu
Rudolfinum (Dům umělců)
Dvořákovo nábř.
JAN PALACH SQ.
Alšovo nábř.
Mánesův most
Veleslavínova
St. Francis (sv. František)
TO CHARLES BRIDGE (50m)
Křižovnická
Smetana Museum
Anenská
ANENSKÉ NÁM.
Náprstkova
Náprstek Museum
Stříbrná
Na Zábradlí
Theater at the Balustrade (Divadlo na zábradlí)
Karolíny Světlé
Boršov
1
2
3
4
5
6
7
8
9
10
11
12
13
14
15
16
17
18
19
20
21
22
23

ACCOMMODATION AGENCIES

Hawkers, most of whom are mere hired agents, besiege visitors at the train station. Many offer legitimate deals, but some just want to rip you off. The going rates for **apartments** are around 600-1200Kč per day, depending on proximity to the center; haggling is possible. If you're wary of bargaining on the street, try a private agency. **RENTeGO,** Lesnicka 7 (☎224 323 734; www.rentego.com) rents apartments in the city center for 1-8 people (€50-175 per night). Staying outside the center can be convenient, but ask where the nearest Metro stop is. When in doubt, ask for details in writing. You can often pay in US dollars, but prices are lower in koruny. Always insist upon seeing the apartment before paying. Some travel agencies will also book accommodations (see **Tourist and Financial Services,** p. 168).

HOSTELS

If you're schlepping a backpack in Hlavní nádraží or Holešovice, you will likely encounter hostel runners offering cheap beds. Easy options for those without reservations, many hostels are university dorms that take in travelers during summer. These rooms are easy options for those without reservations. For more than a mere bed, there are plenty of smaller, friendlier alternatives. While staying in Old Town is convenient, many of the hostels outside of the center offer more in the way of amenities and character. Unless otherwise noted, all hostels have an English-speaking staff, provide free linens, and only accept cash.

STARÉ MĚSTO

Old Prague Hostel, Benediktská 2 (☎224 829 058). Metro B: nam. Republiky. Exit the Metro and follow Revoluční toward the river. Turn left on Dlouhá and take the first left onto Benediktská. Old Prague Hostel offers a lively atmosphere headed by an experienced staff in an unbeatable location. The dorms are bright and tidy. Added perks include free Internet, free Wi-Fi, and on-site DVD rental. Breakfast included. Reception 24hr. Check out 10am. 8-bed dorms 440Kč; 6-bed dorms 475Kč; 5-bed dorms 530Kč; 4-bed dorms 560Kč; doubles 710Kč. ❷

Travellers' Hostels (☎224 826 6623; www.travellers.cz). Travellers' has 5 locations around Prague. Because Travellers' is a franchise, they have all the facilities backpackers want, but they may be lacking some of the charm of smaller hostels.

Dlouhá 33 (☎224 826 662; fax 224 826 665). Metro B: nám. Republiky. Exit the Metro and walk toward Hotel City Center, following Revoluční toward the river. Go left on Dlouhá; the hostel is on the right. Large rooms, unbeatable location, and a terrace bar make up for the peeling paint. The only Travellers' Hostel open year-round, it has social dorms and private renovated apartments. Laundry 150Kč. Internet 1Kč per min. Check-out 10am. Reserve at least a week in advance in the summer. 10-bed dorms 380Kč; 6-bed dorms 450Kč; doubles 650Kč, with bath 750Kč; singles 1120/1300Kč; apartments 2400-3500Kč. 40Kč ISIC discount. AmEx/D/MC/V. ❷

Husova 3 (☎222 220 078). Metro B: Národní třída. Turn right on Spálená, which becomes Na Perštýně, then right on Husova. Smaller, quieter, and in the middle of Staré Město, with bright rooms, gingham sheets, and remarkably soft pillows. Courtyard picnic area. Satellite TV. Check-out 10am. Breakfast included. Open July-Aug. 4- to 5-bed dorms 450Kč; doubles 620Kč. ❷

Hostel Týn, Týnská 19 (☎224 828 519; www.hostel-tyn.web2001.cz). Metro A: Staroměstská. From Staroměstské nám., head down Dlouhá, bear right on Masná, and turn right again on Týnská. Hostel is through the gate to the right. Located in the heart of Staré Město, Hostel Týn skillfully avoids both overcrowding and boredom: dorms are small, but the crowd is young and social. Soft beds. Clean, orderly facilities. Lockers in rooms. No common room. Reception 24hr. Check-out 10am. 5-bed dorms 400Kč; doubles 1100Kč. 200Kč deposit. ❷

NOVÉ MĚSTO

Czech Inn, Francouzská 76 (☎267 267 600; www.czech-inn.com). Metro A: nám. Míru. From the Metro, take tram #4, 22, or 23 to Krymská and walk uphill. Arguably the best hostel in Prague, the Czech Inn strikes the perfect balance between stylish and social. The spacious, high ceilinged bedrooms have the softest beds in town, and the designer bathrooms are a sight to be seen. The bar downstairs is full until the wee hours. Breakfast 120Kč. Internet 50Kč per hr. Wheelchair accesible. Reception 24hr. Check-in 3pm. Check-out 11am. Reserve 2 weeks ahead. Dorms 390-450Kč; singles 1200Kč; doubles 1400Kč. Private room prices increase 200Kč on weekends. AmEx/MC/V. ❷

Hostel u Melounu (At the Watermelon), Ke Karlovu 7/457 (☎224 918 322; www.hostelumelounu.cz). Metro C: IP Pavlova. With your back to the Metro, turn left on Sokolská, make an immediate right on Na Bojišti, and turn left at the street's end on Ke Karlovu. Hostel u Melounu provides a welcome respite from the often impersonal hostels of downtown Prague. Located in a former hospital, it has soft beds, clean bathrooms, free Wi-Fi, and a large garden. Breakfast included. Internet 2Kč per min. Check-out 10am. Dorms 390Kč; singles 750Kč; doubles 1000Kč. 30Kč ISIC discount. AmEx/MC/V. ❷

Miss Sophie's, Melounová 3 (☎296 303 532; www.missophies.com). Metro C: IP Pavlova. Take 1st left from subway platform, then follow Katerinská and take the 1st right onto Melounová. A brick cellar lounge, artistically spare dorm decor, and bathrooms replete with rain showers make Miss Sophie's a hostel you could show off to your parents; the only downside is a shortage of bathrooms. Free Internet. Wheelchair accessible. Reception 24hr. Check-in 3pm. Check-out 10am. In high season dorms 400-490Kč; singles 1590Kč; doubles 1790Kč; triples 2100Kč; apartments 1990-3390Kč. In low season 300/1200/1500/1700/1400-1900Kč. AmEx/MC/V. ❷

Pension Unitas Art Prison Hostel/Cloister Inn, Bartolomějská 9 (☎224 221 802; www.unitas.cz). Metro B: Národní třída. With Tesco on your right, cross Národní and continue down Na Perštýně. Turn left on Bartolomějská. Once home to a Communist jail, the "pink prison" today offers clean, pleasant dorms. The bright decor makes it hard to imagine what Václav Havel's cell looked like when he was incarcerated here. The more spacious Cloister Inn is upstairs in the former offices of the secret police. Reception 24hr. Check-out 10am. Reserve ahead. Apr.-Oct. Dorms 440Kč; singles 1350Kč; doubles 1700Kč; triples 2100Kč; quads 2360Kč. Nov.-Mar. 350/890/980/1380/1700Kč. 7th night free. MC/V. Hostel ❷

MALÁ STRANA AND VINOHRADY

Hostel Sokol, Nosticova 2 (☎257 007 397; www.sokol.edu). Metro A: Malostranská. From the Metro, take tram #12 or 22 to Hellichova; or, from Malostranské nám., walk down Karmelitská about 300m. Take a left on Hellichova, then the last left on Nosticova, and watch for signs. Sokol is at the far end of a small park, past the restaurant on your left. Reception on 3rd fl. Meticulously maintained and functional rooms at excellent prices. Roof terrace and kitchens upstairs. Includes special discount at neighboring Bohemia Bagel. Reception 24hr. Check-out 10am. Reserve ahead. June-Sept. 16-bed dorms 350Kč; doubles 900Kč. Oct.-May 300/700Kč. ❷

Hostel Elf, Husitská 11 (☎222 540 963; www.hostelelf.com). Metro B: Florenc. Take bus #207 to U Památníku. Upstairs through the wooden gate, next to the orange wall surrounded by swooshy paint. Elf has a highly social atmosphere, bright colors, and a multitude of services. Comfy leather couches in the living room and a gardened terrace are perfect for late-night gatherings. No alcohol in dorms. Transport to airport 450Kč. Breakfast included. 100Kč deposit for sheets in dorms. Laundry 200Kč. Free Internet. 9-bed dorms 340Kč; singles 800Kč, with baths 1000Kč; doubles 900/1200Kč. ❷

OUTSIDE THE CENTER

Hostel Boathouse, Lodnická 1 (☎241 770 051; www.aa.cz/boathouse). Take tram #3, 17, or 52 from Karlovo nam. south toward Sídliště. Get off at Černý Kůň (20min.), go down the ramp from the tram, turn left toward the Vltava, and follow the yellow hostel signs. The matron of the house, Věra, has one of the most highly praised staffs in all of Europe, making up for the stuffy rooms in summer. The walls are covered in letters of thanks from former guests. Boathouse serves meals (hot dinner 120Kč) in its lively dining room and offers board games, Internet (1Kč per min.), satellite TV, and laundry (150Kč). Breakfast included. Call ahead; if they're full, Věra might let you sleep in the hall. Email reservations preferred. 3- to 5-bed dorms above a working boathouse 420Kč; 8-bed dorm 390Kč. ❷

Hostel Marabou, Konevova 55 (☎222 581 182; www.hostelmarabou.com). Metro B: Florenc; take bus #133 or #207 3 stops to Cerninova. Bright red walls and a knowledgeable staff define Marabou. Foosball and pool available in the intimate lounge, the scene of many late-night gatherings. Comfy beds. Free breakfast and Internet. 24hr. reception. Apr.-Oct. dorms 320-350Kč; singles 800Kč, with bath 1050Kč; doubles 960/1360Kč. Nov.-Mar. 220-320/750/950/900/1300Kč. ❶

Sir Toby's Hostel, Dělnická 24 (☎283 870 635; www.sirtobys.com). Metro A: Vltavická. From the station, take any of the trams headed to your left. Get off at Dělnická. Tram deposits you on Komunardů. Keep walking in the direction of the tram and turn left on Dělnická. Sir Toby's occupies a renovated Art Nouveau building in a neighborhood of shops and pubs. Breakfast 90Kč. Laundry 150Kč. Internet 50Kč per hr. Dorms 350-420Kč; singles 1000Kč; doubles 2900Kč. ❷

Prague Plus Hostel, Přívozní 1 (☎ 220 510 046; www.plusprague.com). From Metro C Nádraží Holešovice take tram #5, 12 or 15 one stop to Ortenovo nam. Walk toward Hotel Alta and turn left at the intersection. The hostel is 100m on the left. Offers many amenities including an indoor pool, free Internet, and bathrooms in every room. Many groups travel here, making it slightly more difficult for the solo backpacker to socialize. Ladies, check into the "Plus Girls" zone where rooms come with large vanities and a free cosmetic bag of goodies. A lively industrial-chic bar and restaurant out back have pool and foosball. Breakfast included. Reception 24hr. Check-out 11am. 8-bed dorms €15; 6-bed dorms €17; 4-bed dorms €19. "Plus Girls" dorms €16/18/20. ❷

HOTELS AND PENSIONS

As tourists colonize Prague, hotels are upgrading their services—and their prices. Budget hotels are now near extinction. Call several months ahead to book a room for the summer and confirm by fax with a credit card. For something out of the ordinary, try the admirably renovated prison cells at the Cloister Inn (see above).

STARÉ MĚSTO

Hotel King George (Dům U Krále Jiřího), Liliová 10 (☎222 220 925; www.hotelkinggeorge.cz). Metro A: Staroměstská. Exit at nám. Jana Palacha. Facing the river, turn left and walk down Křižovnická until you reach a tunnel, then turn left onto Karlova. Liliová, the 1st right, is easily missed. Enter through the restaurant. King George's rooms have TVs, minibars, couches, private baths, and luxurious furniture. Buffet breakfast included, as well as a 10% discount on food and drink at the restaurant. Safes 60Kč per night. Reception daily 7am-11pm. Mar.-Oct. singles 2250Kč; doubles 3550Kč; triples 4950Kč; apartments 3550-7500Kč. Prices fall by 500-900Kč Nov.-Feb. ❺

U Lilie, Liliová 15 (☎222 220 432; www.pensionulilie.cz). Metro A: Staroměstská. Follow the directions to Dům U Krále Jiřího. U Lilie boasts a lovely courtyard, as well as satellite TV, telephone, and minibar in every room. Great location near Staromestke nam. Breakfast included. Reception daily 10am-11pm. Singles 2000Kč; doubles 3050Kč, with bath 3500Kč. Cash only. ❺

NOVÉ MĚSTO

Pension Museum, Mezibranská 15 (☎296 325 186; www.pension-museum.cz). Metro C: Muzeum. From the Metro, go right on Mezibranská and walk uphill. It's on the right. This modern B&B near Wenceslas Sq. is worth the splurge. Beautiful courtyard leads to elegant rooms with TVs and spacious baths. Welcoming staff. Decadent breakfast buffet included. Reserve 1-2 months in advance. Apr.-Dec. singles 2460Kč; doubles 2920Kč; apartments 3000-6000Kč. Jan.-Mar. 1580/1970/2000-5000Kč. AmEx/MC/V. ❺

Hotel Legie, Sokolská 33 (☎224 266 231, reservations 224 266 240; www.legie.cz). Metro C: IP Pavlova. From the Metro, turn left on Ječná; hotel is across the street. The nondescript facade of this high-rise hotel hides sparkling modern rooms with private showers, phone, and cable TV; some afford great views of Prague Castle. Breakfast included. Reception 24hr. Jan. and Apr.-Oct. singles 2750Kč; doubles 3300Kč; triples 4300Kč. Feb. and Nov.-Dec. 1800/2300/3100Kč. AmEx/MC/V. ❺

OUTSIDE THE CENTER

Hotel Kafka, Cimburkova 24 (☎222 781 333, reservations 224 225 769), in Žižkov near the TV tower. From Metro C: Hlavní nádraží, take tram #5 toward Harfa, #9 toward Spojovací, or #26 toward Nádraží Hostivař; get off at Husinecká. Head uphill on Seifertova 3 blocks and go left on Cimburkova. Spotless, comfortable hotel located in a residential neighborhood. Phone and TV in every room. Breakfast included. Apr.-Oct. singles 1700Kč; doubles 2300Kč; triples 3200Kč; quads 3500Kč. Nov.-Mar. 1000/1300/1700/2200Kč. MC/V with 5% fee. ❺

B&B U Oty (Ota's House), Radlická 188 (☎257 215 323; www.bbuoty.cz). Metro B: Radlická. Exit the Metro up the stairs to the left, go right past Bistro Kavos on Radlická, and walk 400m. Although it's far from the city center, U Oty offers spacious, well-furnished rooms at an affordable price. Best for groups of 2 or more due to the walk to and from the Metro station along a poorly lit highway. Kitchen. Breakfast included. Laundry free after 3 nights. Reserve ahead. Singles 700Kč; doubles 770Kč; triples 990Kč; quads 1300Kč. 100Kč extra if staying only 1 night. ❸

CAMPING

Campsites have taken over both the outskirts and the centrally located Vltava Islands and are becoming a more popular option as accommodation-prices rise. Reserve bungalows in advance. Tents are generally available without prior notice. Tourist offices sell a guide (20Kč) to campsites near the city.

Camp Sokol Troja, Trojská 171a (☎/fax 233 542 908; www.camp-sokol.troja.cz/en). From Metro C: Nádraží Holešovice, take bus #112 to Kazanka, the 4th stop. Prague's self-proclaimed largest campground, and a unique camping experience: pitch a tent in this grassy lot and admire the houses of a wealthy Prague neighborhood. Sparkling bathrooms. At least 4 similar establishments line the same road. July-Aug. 120Kč per person, 90-150Kč per tent. Oct.-June 70-100Kč per tent. Private rooms available. July-Aug. singles 380Kč; doubles 660Kč. Oct.-June 350/600Kč. ❶

Caravan Park, Císařská louka 599 (☎02 54 09 25), on the Císařská louka peninsula. Metro B: Smíchovské nádraží, then any of the 300-numbered buses to Lihovar. Go left on the shaded path as you head to the river (1km). Or, take a 15min. ferry; they depart every hour on the hour until about 10pm from the landing, 1 block from Smíchovské nádraží (10Kč). Small, tranquil campground on the banks of the Vltava. Clean facilities, friendly staff, and convenient cafe make up for the rather long journey. Currency exchange on premises. 95Kč per person, 90-140Kč per tent. Local tax 15Kč per person; national tax 5%. Students exempt from local tax. ❶

FOOD

The nearer you are to the center, the more you'll pay. In less-touristed areas away from Old Town and Wenceslas squares, you can have pork, cabbage, dumplings, and a beer for 125Kč. Always bring cash and check the bill, as you'll pay for everything, including ketchup and bread. For lunch, *hotová jídla* (prepared meals) are cheapest. For fresher alternatives, head to the daily market at the intersection of Havelská and Melantrichova in Staré Město.

STARÉ MĚSTO RESTAURANTS

Klub architektů, Betlémské nám. 52A (☎224 401 214). Metro B: Národní třída. Take Spálená until it becomes Na Perštýně, then turn left on Betlémské nám. Walk through the gate immediately on your right and descend underground. Klub architektů is a magnificent hybrid of first class and budget. Enjoy intimate lighting and a cellar setting. Features dishes with Asian influences, including chicken cooked with pineapple (185Kč). Non-smoking section. Beer from 39Kč. Entrees 90-350Kč. Open daily 11:30am-midnight. Kitchen closes 11pm. Reservations recommended. AmEx/MC/V. ❸

Lehká Hlava (Clear Head), Boršov 2 (☎222 220 665; www.lehkahlava.cz). Metro A: Staroměstská. Follow Křízovnická south past the Charles Bridge, bear left onto Karoliny Světle, and turn left onto Boršov. Tucked into a quiet alley, Lehká Hlava cooks up vegetarian and vegan cuisine that even devout carnivores will enjoy. Try the eggplant-and-cheese quesadilla with fresh guacamole (110Kč) and wash it down with fresh, mint-infused lemonade (50Kč). Entrees 80-160Kč. Open M-F 11:30am-11:30pm, Sa-Su noon-11:30pm. Kitchen closes 2:30-5pm. Only cold food after 10pm. Cash only. ❷

Yami Restaurant, Masná 3 (☎222 312 756). Metro A: Staroměstská. Follow directions to Bohemia Bagel (see p. 178). Offering some of the best—and most reasonably priced—sushi in Prague, Yami dishes up a wide variety of Japanese dishes in a zen-like dining room. The courtyard out back holds four coveted tables hidden behind a bamboo screen, where diners devour Yami's creative fusion rolls (8pc. 196-320Kč). Sushi 55-320Kč. Entrees 120-260Kč. Open daily noon-11pm. MC/V. ❸

Country Life, Melantrichova 15 (☎224 213 366; www.countrylife.cz). Metro A: Staroměstská. Follow directions to U Špirků (see below). After days of dumplings and fried cheese, Country Life's salad bar is the perfect antidote. Pick up a plate and head to Country Life's 3 buffets (hot, cold, salad bar); you'll pay 23Kč per 100g for whatever fits on your plate. Soups 20Kč. Health food store next door sells organic products. Open M-Th 9am-8pm, F 9am-6pm, Su 11am-8pm. Cash only. ❷

Cafe Bambus, Benediktská 12 (☎224 828 110; www.bambus.cz). Metro B: nám. Republiky. Follow directions to Hostel Dlouhá 33 (see **Accommodations,** p. 170) and take a left on Benediktská. Step out of the tourist jungle into this African oasis where masks, statuettes, and crocodiles adorn the walls. Sweet and savory Czech pancakes 55-75Kč. Asian and international cuisine 55-228Kč. Open M-Th 10am-1am, F 10am-2am, Sa 11am-2am, Su 11am-11pm. ❷

OUTDOOR DINING. If you're dying to eat a meal in the pricey Old Town Square, consider your seating choices carefully: some restaurants charge up to 60% more for outside dining than inside. Don't try to act surprised when the bill comes—it won't work.

NOVÉ MĚSTO RESTAURANTS

Universal, V jirchářích 6 (☎224 934 416). Metro B: Národní třída. Cross the tram tracks and follow Ostrovní, then take a left on Opatovická and head right around the church to

CZECH REPUBLIC

V jircháŕích. A fusion of Mediterranean, French, and Asian flavors, Universal offers huge, fresh salads (119-170Kč) in a bright dining room. Imaginative pasta, and meat entrees (115-329Kč) go brilliantly with a glass or two of Moravian wine (small carafe 50Kč, large carafe 100Kč). Save room for the delicious desserts (45-90Kč). Scrumptious Su brunch buffet 135Kč. Open M-Sa 11:30am-1am, Su 11am-midnight. ❸

Castello Pizzeria & Restaurant, Václavsté nam. 20 (☎224 228 388; www.castello.cz). Metro B: Mustek. Right in the thick of the tourist district, Castello's basement dining room is a welcome retreat. The intimate space is a perfect setting for digging into filling portions of pasta, pizza, and salads (65-185Kč). The professional waitstaff keep things running smoothly. Try the fettucine alfredo with prosciutto (145Kč). Service charge included. Open daily 11am-11pm. MC/V. ❷

Pivovarský Dům, Ječná 15 (☎296 216 666; www.gastroinfo.cz/pivodum). The two enormous copper vats in the corner of this neighborhood joint aren't just for show; Pivovarský Dům actually brews its own unfiltered, unpasteurized brews. Locals and tourists alike cram into the bright dining room. Try washing down any of the traditional Czech dishes with the restaurant's sour cherry lager (35Kč), or ask the helpful waitstaff which goes best with your entree. Entrees 115-230Kč. Open daily 11am-11pm. ❸

Modry Zub Noodle Bar, Jindinska 5 (☎222 212 622). Step out of the chaos of Wenceslas Square and into the sleek surroundings of this pan-Asian eatery. Modry Zub dishes up a surprising range of tasty noodle dishes (110-145Kč) in its two dining rooms. Pull up a stool to the counter of the cool-blue back room, or see and be seen in the fiery red front room facing the street. Food also available for take-away. English menu. Open M-F 10am-midnight, Sa 11am-midnight, Su 11am-11pm. ❷

Ultramarin Grill, Ostrovni 32 (☎224 932 249; www.ultramarin.cz). Metro B: Národní třída. With your back to the Metro, turn left and immediately right; Ultramarin will be on the left. This classy bar and restaurant, complete with an open grill and occasional liv music, provides a chic alternative to the more touristed options in Staré Město. Though the chef specializes in steak, duck, and lamb (100-165Kč), a variety of more familiar dishes, like a delicious take on Buffalo Wings, make Ultramarin a haven for those seeking comfort food. Krušovice on tap. Open daily 10am-11pm. AmEx/MC/V. ❸

U Řozvarilů, Na Poříčì 26. Metro B: nám. Republiky. Exit the station on Na Poříčì and take a sharp right around the church. Quality dining doesn't come cheaper—Czech regulars gorge themselves on traditional meals like meat with cream sauce (50Kč) and potato dumplings (13-15Kč). The stainless-steel decor of this cafeteria-style establishment may feel sterile, but the jovial company and hearty food are perfect antidotes. Open M-F 7:30am-8:30pm, Sa 8am-6pm, Su 10am-6pm. AmEx/MC/V. ❶

MALÁ STRANA RESTAURANTS

Bar bar, Všehrdova 17 (☎257 313 246). Metro A: Malostranská. Follow the tram tracks from the Metro station down Letenská, through Malostranské nám., and down Karmelitská. Take the left on Všehrdova after the museum. The diverse selection of meats, cheeses, and veggie dishes (45-135Kč), as well as delicious sweet and savory Czech-style filled pancakes (48-89Kč), will please every palate. Funky atmosphere for whiskey (from 65Kč) and jazz. Set lunch menu (daily noon-4pm) €4. Open M-Th and Su noon-midnight, F-Sa noon-2am. MC/V. ❶

Pivnice U Švejků, Újezd 22 (☎257 313 244; www.usvejku.cz). Metro A: Malostranská. From the Metro, head down Klárov and right on Letenská. Bear left through Malostranské nám. and follow Karmelitská until it becomes Újezd. Converted to a restaurant in 1993, this former inn dates back to 1618. After a few beers (or a massive 1L brew), try to dance with the accordionist (plays after 7pm). Few vegetarian options. Entrees 108-148Kč. Open daily 11am-midnight. AmEx/DC/MC/V. ❷

ROMA ADVOCACY

The Czech population is fairly homogenous and, on the surface, unmarred by major racial turmoil. Yet, a significant portion of the population belongs to the darker-skinned Roma population. Roma face rampant racial discrimination in the Czech Republic, suffer from high rates of unemployment and poverty, and are victims of violent crimes at a higher rate than lighter skinned people or Czechs. The Czech Republic has received criticism from members of the EU as well as other international observers for their poor treatment of Roma, and several organizations have cropped up in the country to rectify years of wrongdoing.

One such organization is **People In Need,** which has been working in the country since 1999. The program focuses on social integration, and provides free services like help obtaining employment, legal assistance in filing discrimination cases and tutoring programs. They operate out of some fourteen different points within the country, including the city of Prague.

The organization accepts English speaking interns year round. Those interested in volunteering should contact Sarah Mackenzie (sarah.mackenzie@peopleinneed.cz). For more information, see their website at www.clovekvtisni.cz.

SUPERMARKETS

The basements of most Czech department stores have food halls and supermarkets. *Potraviny* (delis) and vegetable stands can be found on most street corners.

Tesco, Národní třída 26 (☎222 003 111; www.tesco-shop.cz). Next to Metro B: Národní třída. Sprawling supermarket carrying a wide variety of fruits and familiar brands. Several produce stands in the coutyard outside. Open M-F 7am-10pm, Sa 8am-8pm, Su 9am-8pm. AmEx/MC/V.

Albert (☎221 229 311), at the corner of Revoluční and nám. Republiky, in front of the Kotva department store. Metro B: nám. Republiky. 2-fl. supermarket with fresh cheese and deli counters. Open M-Sa 7am-9pm, Su 8am-9pm.

CAFES

Prague's population, once firmly loyal to coffee, has expanded its horizons in recent years. Tea is all the rage, and tea houses are popping up everywhere, often doubling as bars, nightclubs, and hookah joints. Java junkies shouldn't fret: there are also numerous quality coffeehouses. If you desire email and fiction with your coffee, rather than just sugar, head to the **Globe Bookstore** (p. 169).

Bohemia Bagel, Masna 2 (☎224 812 560; www.bohemiabagel.cz). Metro A: Staroměstská. An expatriate favorite, Bohemia Bagel dishes up a giant, American-style breakfast of pancakes, eggs, bacon, and hashbrowns (The Charles IV; 160Kč), as well as a bottomless cup of coffee (45Kč). For lunch try any of the tasty bagel sandwiches. Background music runs the gamut from James Brown to Europop to DJ Optik. Small selection of English periodicals. Courtyard out back. Entrees 125-185Kč. Open M-F 7am-midnight, Sa-Su 8am-midnight. Branch at Újezd 16. Open daily 9am-midnight. ❸

Čajovna Sivna, Masna 8 (☎222 315 983). Metro A: Staroměstská. Step out of Eastern Europe and into the Middle East at this laid-back tea shop. A wide selection of teas is complemented by an equally wide selection of flavored tobacco (60-120Kč). Retreat here for a hazy afternoon of relaxation. Open daily noon-midnight. ❷

Cafe Ebel, Řetězová 9 (☎603 441 434). Metro A or B: Staroměstská. Ebel offers Prague rarities: freshly ground beans and cups to go. In addition to excellent coffee, Ebel's main branch offers a great continental breakfast (165Kč). Single espresso 40Kč, double 50Kč. Open M-F 8am-8pm, Sa-Su 8:30am-8pm. AmEx/MC/V. Branches: Týn 2 (open daily 9am-10pm); Kaprova 11 (open M-F 8am-8pm, Sa-Su 8:30am-8pm). ❷

Kavárna Medúza, Belgická 17 (☎222 515 107). Metro A: nám. Míru. Head down Rumunská, and turn left at Belgická. During the day, locals read or chat quietly, but at night the space fills, and then overfills, with impeccably dressed hipsters. Excellent espresso and "Czech traditional pancakes" (*staročeská pelačincky sladké;* thin pancakes with plum jam, cinnamon, whipped cream, and ice cream; 48Kč). Entrees 44-200Kč. Open M-F 11am-1am, Sa-Su noon-1am. ❷

U zeleného čaje, Nerudova 19 (☎225 730 027). Metro A: Malostranská. Follow Letenská to Malostranské nám. Stay right of the church and go down Nerudova. This shop at the foot of Prague Castle takes tea to new heights. Choose from over 60 varieties of fragrant tea. To add a little kick, try an alcoholic tea drink like the Boiling Communist or the Grandmother's Caress (35Kč). Sandwiches 30-70Kč. Open daily 11am-10pm. ❶

SIGHTS

One of the only major Central European cities unscathed by WWII, Prague is a combination of labyrinthine alleys and Baroque buildings. To find respite from the throngs of tourists, head beyond Staroměstské nám., the Charles Bridge, and Václavské nám. to nám. Miru, Vinohrady, and the southern part of Nové Město. To see a Prague not entirely made of crystal and tacky souvenir shops, visit a suburb like Troja, head north of Staré Město, or explore any of the city's beautiful gardens. Best traveled by foot, central Prague—Staré Město, Nové Město, Malá Strana, and Hradřany—is compact enough to be traversed in one day, but don't leave without strolling through the synagogues of Josefov, exploring the heights of Vyšehrad, or meandering through the streets of Malá Strana. The true magic of the city is in ancient, eminently walkable, streets.

STARÉ MĚSTO

Settled in the 10th century, Staré Město (Old Town) is a maze of narrow streets and alleys. Eight magnificent towers enclose **Old Town Square** (Staroměstské nám.) in the heart of Staré Město. The vast stone plaza fills with blacksmiths, painters, carriages, and ice-cream vendors in summer. Navigating the square can be a difficult undertaking at midday. But as soon as the sun sets, the labyrinth of narrow roads and alleys comes alive with a younger crowd seeking midnight revelry at Staré Město's jazz clubs and bars.

LITTLE GREEN MEN. Crossing Prague's streets provides an interesting puzzle for foreigners. There are stoplights with designated crossing areas for pedestrians, but the lights seem eternally stuck on the "don't walk" signal, a red man standing still. Prague's crossings seem intended for sprinters instead of ordinary folk, and drivers aren't happy when forced to stop. So instead of jay-walking, join the crowd on the street corner and begin your wait for that elusive little green man.

CHARLES BRIDGE (KARLŮV MOST). This Baroque footbridge has become one of Prague's most treasured landmarks. Charles IV built the 520m bridge to replace the wooden Judith Bridge, the only bridge crossing the Vltava, which washed away in a 1342 flood. Defense towers border the bridge on each side; the shorter Malostranská mostecká věž (Malá Strana Bridge Tower) dates from the 12th century, while the taller Staroměstská mostecká věž (Old Town Bridge Tower) was erected in the 15th century. According to legend, St. Jan Nepomuk was tied in goatskin and thrown into the river from this bridge for concealing the extramarital secrets of his queen from a suspicious King Wenceslas IV. A halo of five gold stars appeared as Jan plunged into the water. The right-hand rail, from which Jan was tossed, is now marked with a cross and five stars between the fifth and sixth statues. Marked by the hordes of tourists straining to touch the plaque at its base, statue of Jan stands midway across the bridge. Legend has it that those who touch the plaque will return to Prague again. The oldest statue, dating back to 1657, is the Crucifix, towards the Staré Město side. *(The best way to reach Charles Bridge is on foot. Metro stops A: Malostranská on the Malá Strana side and A: Staroměstská on the Staré Město side.)*

OLD TOWN HALL (STAROMĚSTSKÉ RADNICE). Next to the grassy knoll in Old Town Square, Old Town Hall is a multi-faceted building composed of several different architectural styles. Originally constructed in 1338, the Hall was partly demolished in WWII; the original pink facade juts out from the tower. Old Town Hall has long been a witness to violence—crosses in front mark the spot where 27 Protestant leaders were executed on June 21, 1621 for staging a rebellion against the Catholic Habsburgs. Now the main office of Prague Information Services occupies the first floor. On the second floor, one of the locations of the City Gallery of Prague hosts short-term exhibits of contemporary Czech art. The entrance to the tower is on the third floor, where you can take in an aerial view of Staroměstké nám. Outside, throngs of crowds watch on the hour as the astronomical clock, built in 1490 by master craftsman Hanuš, chime as skeletal Death empties his hourglass and an anticlimactic procession of apostles marches by. The clock's operation stops for the night at 9pm. *(Metro A: Staroměstská; Metro A or B: Můstek. In Staroměstské nám. Open in summer M 10am-7pm, Tu-F 9am-7pm, Sa-Su 9am-6pm. Exhibition hall 20Kč, students 10Kč. Clock tower open daily 10am-6pm; enter through 3rd fl. of Old Town Hall. 60Kč, students 40Kč. Tours of the interior available on the hr.; 60Kč, students 40Kč.)*

JAN HUS STATUE. Burned at the stake in 1415 for his diatribes against the Catholic Church's quest for power and its practice of selling indulgences, Jan Hus now stands as a symbol of Czech nationalism. In this massive Expressionistic tableau, impassioned figures writhe in the background while Jan stands stoically apart. The statue was restored in summer 2007 and is expected to be unveiled in early fall. *(In the center of Staroměstské nám.)*

TÝN CHURCH (CHRÁM MATKY BOŽÍ PŘED TÝNEM). Across from Old Town Hall, the spires of the Gothic Týn Church rise above a mass of baroque homes, reassuring many a lost tourist wandering the alleys of Staré Město. The Týn only recently opened its sanctuary to tourists, who are still restricted to the very back of the church. Despite the limited access, the high Gothic interior makes it worth a visit. The famous astronomer Tycho Brahe is buried in the church's hallowed halls. *(In Staroměstské nám.; enter through the tunnel to the left of Cafe Italia. Open M-F 9am-noon and 1-2pm. Mass W-F 6pm; Sa 8am; Su 11am and 9pm. July-Aug. also 12:30pm. Free.)*

ST. JAMES'S CHURCH (KOSTEL SV. JAKUBA). Barely a surface in the Baroque St. James's Church remains un-figured, un-marbleized, or unpainted. Keep your hands to yourself, though: legend has it that 500 years ago a thief tried to pilfer a gem from the Virgin Mary of Suffering, whereupon the figure sprang to life and yanked off his arm. *(Metro B: Staroměstská. On Malá Štupartská, off Staroměstské nám. behind Týn Church. Open M-Sa 10am-noon and 2–3:45pm. Mass Su 8, 9, 10:30am.)*

MUNICIPAL HOUSE AND POWDER TOWER (PRAŠNÁ BRÁNA, OBECNÍ DŮM). The juxtaposition of styles represented by the Gothic Powder Tower and the Municipal House provides a fitting entrance to Staré Město. Built on the former site of the royal court, the Municipal House was designed and built by Czech representatives of the Art Nouveau movement. Inside, Neoclassical figures support archways and light fixtures while metal sculptures imitate trees and flowers, providing the perfect backdrop for the daily classical orchestral performances. *(Nám. Republiky 5. Metro B: nám. Republiky. www.obecni-dum.cz. Open only by tour, available at var-*

ious times 10am-6pm. 150Kč. Concerts M-F evening. Tickets 50-1200Kč. Box office ☎ 222 002 101 open M-F 10am-6pm and 1 hr. before concerts. Next door, the Gothic **Powder Tower** is the ugly stepsister to Prague's predominantly pastel-colored architecture. One of the last remnants of the city walls that once protected Staré Město, the Powder Tower was rendered obsolete by the construction of Nové Město beyond its borders. Today, you can still climb the winding tower to appreciate the expansive views from its topmost lookout. *(Metro B: nám. Republiky. Open daily July-Aug. 10am-10pm; Sept.-Oct. and Apr.-June 10am-6pm. Last entry 5:30pm. 50Kč, students 40Kč.)*

JAN PALACH SQUARE (NÁMĚSTÍ JANA PALACHA). Downriver from the Charles Bridge, Jan Palach Sq. offers a peaceful view of the Vltava. Originally called Red Army Sq., the square now honors the student who set himself on fire on Václavské nám. in 1969 to protest the Soviet invasion. Near the river banks is the Rudolfinum, a concert hall that hosts the annual classical music festival **Pražské jaro** (Prague Spring). Across the tram tracks from the Rudolfinum, the main building of the Faculty of Arts of Charles University (Filozofická fakulta Univerzity Karlovy) shelters a statue of Palach. *(Metro A: Staroměstská. Just off the Metro exit on Kĺižovnická.)*

NOVÉ MĚSTO

Nové Město (New Town) has become Prague's commercial core. The New Town is hardly new, however: Charles IV established the area back in 1348. Today, the monumental facade of the National Museum and the serenity of Mary of the Snows and the Franciscan Gardens contrast the consumer chaos of Wenceslas Square.

WENCESLAS SQUARE (VÁCLAVSKÉ NÁMĚSTÍ). More a boulevard than a square, Wenceslas Square owes its name to the statue of 10th-century Czech ruler and patron St. Wenceslas (Václav) that stands in front of the National Museum. At his feet in solemn prayer kneel smaller statues of the country's other patron saints: St. Ludmila, St. Agnes, St. Prokop, and St. Adalbert (Vojtěch). The sculptor, Josef Václav Myslbek took 25 years to complete the statue. The inscription under St. Wenceslas reads, "Do not let us and our descendants perish." The boulevard has become sufficatingly commercial in recent years, but the view of the statue from the Můstek stop remains hypnotic at full moon. *(Metro A or B: Můstek serves the bottom of the square; Metro A or C: Muzeum serves the top of the square.)*

FRANCISCAN GARDEN (FRANTIŠKÁNSKÁ ZAHRADA). Amazingly, the Franciscans have maintained this bastion of serenity in the heart of Prague's commercial district. The rose garden provides a perfect respite from Wenceslas Sq. *(Metro A or B: Můstek. Enter through the arch to the left of the intersection of Jungmannova and Národní, behind the Jungmannova statue. Open daily mid-Apr. to mid-Sept. 7am-10pm; Sept. 15-Oct. 14 7am-8pm; Oct. 15-Apr. 14 8am-7pm. Free.)*

CHURCH OF OUR LADY OF THE SNOWS (KOSTEL PANNY MARIE SNĚŽNÉ). Founded by Charles IV in 1347, Our Lady of the Snows was meant to surpass St. Vitus's as the largest church in Prague. The Gothic walls are, indeed, taller than those of any other house of worship, but there wasn't enough in the coffers to complete the building. The result: extraordinarily high ceilings in a church of strikingly short length. The church is frequented by locals praying during the day, so use your indoor voice. *(Metro A or B: Můstek. From the bottom of Wenceslas Sq., turn left on Jungmannovo nám.; the entrance is behind the statue.)*

THE DANCING HOUSE (TANČÍCÍ DŮM). Built by American architect Frank Gehry, of Guggenheim-Bilbao fame, in cooperation with Slovenian architect Vladimir Milunic, the building—known as "Fred and Ginger" to Western visitors and the "Dancing House" to Czechs—is a controversial landmark. Many residents protested its construction, arguing that such modern architecture had no place in Prague. Its nicknames derive from the building's undulating glass wall and cone and cube, which evoke a dancing couple. *(Metro B: Karlovo nám. Exit to Karlovo nám. and head down Resslova toward the river. It's at the corner of Resslova and Rašínovo nábřeží.)*

VELVET REVOLUTION MEMORIAL. Under Národní's arcades stands a memorial to the hundreds of Czech citizens beaten in a 1989 protest against the Communist Regime. In this same place 50 years earlier, police attacked a march organized by students to mourn the Nazi execution of nine Czech students. The simple yet moving plaque depicts a wall of hands, and visitors place flowers in their fingers in remembrance. The inscription—*Máme holé ruce* (Our hands are empty)—was the protesters' cry as they were beaten by the police. At the nearby **Magic Lantern Theater,** Národní 4, Revolutionary leader Havel once plotted to overthrow the old regime. *(Metro B: Národní třída. Exit the Metro and head down Spálená; go left on Národní. The memorial is in the arcade across from the Black Theater.)*

JOSEFOV

Prague's historic Jewish neighborhood and the oldest Jewish settlement in Central Europe, Josefov is north of Staroměstské nám., along Maiselova and several side streets. In reaction to the Pope's 1179 decree that all Christians avoid contact with Jews, Prague's citizens constructed a 4m wall surrounding the area. The gates were opened in 1784, but the walls didn't come down until 1848, when the city's Jews were granted limited civil rights. The closed neighborhood bred fantastical legends, many of which surrounded the famed **Rabbi Loew ben Bezalel** (1512-1609), who was said to have created the golem—a creature made from mud that came to life to protect Prague's Jews. In an attempt to turn Prague into a small Paris (evident in today's Pařížská), devoid of all less desirable neighborhoods, the whole quarter—save the synagogues—was demolished in the 19th century. When the Nazis rose to power, most of Prague's Jews were deported to Terezín (see **Terezín,** p. 192) and the death camps. Ironically, Hitler's decision to create a "museum of an extinct race" led to the preservation of Josefov's old Jewish cemetery and synagogues. *(Metro A: Staroměstská. From the Metro, walk down Maiselova, which is parallel to Kaprova. ☎222 325 172; www.jewishmuseum.cz. Synagogues and museum open M-F and Su Apr.-Oct. 9am-6pm, Nov.-Mar. 9am-4:30pm; box office closes 30min. earlier. Closed Jewish holidays. Admission to all synagogues except Staronová Synagogue 290Kč, students 190Kč. Staronová Synagogue 200/140Kč. Admission to all sites 470/310Kč. Buy tickets at any of the synagogues. A head covering is required for men at most sites;* kippahs *provided free of charge.)*

PINKAS SYNAGOGUE (PINKASOVA SYNAGOGA). At the time of the Nazi takeover, 118,310 Jews lived in the Prague ghetto, many of them refugees from the conquered provinces. A few fled before further Nazi persecution, but about 92,000 remained. Of these, 80,000 were deported to meet their deaths in Terezín or other concentration camps. Today, all of their names cover the walls of Pinkas Synagogue, overwhelming the otherwise bare rooms. Upstairs, drawings made by children imprisoned at Terezín, as well as various relics from daily life there, give faces to a few of the names. *(On Široká, between Žatecká and Listopadu 17.)*

OLD JEWISH CEMETERY (STARÝ ŽIDOVSKÝ HŘBITOV). The Old Jewish Cemetery stretches between the Pinkas Synagogue and the Ceremonial Hall, its small expanse filled entirely with the aged, cracked, and broken stone markers of thousands of graves. Between the 14th and 18th centuries, the graves were dug in layers. Over time, the earth settled and those from the bottom fought to the surface, pushing other stones aside and creating an indistinguishable jumble of stones. Rabbi Loew is buried by the wall opposite the entrance. His grave can be recognized by the pebbles and coins placed atop it. *(At the corner of Široká and Žatecká.)*

SPANISH SYNAGOGUE (ŠPANĚLSKÁ SYNAGOGA). The Spanish Synagogue gets its name from its Byzantine-Moorish, or "Spanish Moorish," style. The most visually stunning of the synagogues, the interior is a complex of domes. This was the first synagogue to adopt the 1830s Reform movement. On display is a post-Enlightenment history of Czech Jews. *(On the corner of Široká and Dušní.)*

MAISEL SYNAGOGUE (MAISELOVA SYNAGOGA). This synagogue displays treasures from the extensive collections of the Jewish Museum, which were returned to the city's Jewish community in 1994 after being confiscated by the communist government in its effort to promote secularization. Its exhibits provide an excellent history of the Jews in Bohemia and Moravia, and especially in Prague's ghetto. *(Maiselova, between Široká and Jáchymova.)*

OLD-NEW SYNAGOGUE (STARONOVÁ SYNAGOGA). The oldest operating synagogue in Europe and the earliest Gothic structure in Prague, the tiny Old-New Synagogue is still the religious center of Prague's Jewish community. Originally called the "New" synagogue when it was built, it later became the Old-New synagogue when other synagogues were built. Behind the iron gates fly the tattered remnants of the Star of David flag flown by the congregation in 1357, when Charles IV first allowed them to display their own emblem. Prague's Jews were the first to adopt the Star of David as their official symbol. *(On the corner of Maiselova and Pařížská. Entrance fee not included in price of museum ticket. Open in summer M-Th and Su 9:30am-6pm, F 9:30am-5pm. Services F and Sa at 8pm reserved for practicing members of the Jewish community. 200Kč, students 140Kč.)*

MALÁ STRANA

The hangout of criminals and counter-revolutionaries for much of the 20th century, the cobblestone streets of Malá Strana have recently become the most prized real estate on the Vltava. Urbanites dream of flats overlooking St. Nicholas's Cathedral, while affluent foreigners sip beer in the former hangout of Jaroslav Hašek and his bumbling soldier Švejk. In the 15th century, the Austrian nobility built great churches and palaces here. Now carefully restored, Malá Strana is home to some of Prague's most impressive architecture.

PETŘÍN HILL AND GARDENS (PETŘÍNSKÉ SADY). Petřín Gardens, on the hill beside Malá Strana, provide a tranquil retreat from Prague's urban bustle and offer spectacular views of the city. Although the climb to the garden's peak is steep, the beauty of its forested footpaths is worth the trek. For a more relaxed ascent, take the funicular to the top from just above the intersection of Vítězná and Újezd. *(Look for Lanovka Dráha signs. Daily every 10-15min. 9am-11pm. 20Kč.)* At the summit, lush rose gardens, a small Eiffel-esque Tower *(open daily 10am-10pm; 50Kč, students 40Kč)*, the city's observatory, and the Church of St. Lawrence await. *(☎257 315 272. Open daily 10am-9:30pm. 50Kč, students 40Kč.)* Just east of the park, **Strahov Stadium,** the world's largest, covers the space of 10 soccer fields. Under the Communist regime, the stadium was commonly used for "Spartakiádas," where large groups of athletes would perform choreographed gymnastic to show off the success of the regime.

WALLENSTEIN GARDEN (VALDŠTEJNSKÁ ZAHRADA). This tranquil, meticulously maintained, 17th-century garden is enclosed by old buildings. General Albrecht Wallenstein, owner of the famous Prague palace of the same name and hero of Schiller's grim plays (the *Wallenstein* cycle), held parties here among classical bronze statues. When the works were plundered by Swedish troops in the waning hours of the Thirty Years' War, Wallenstein replaced the original casts with duplicates. Frescoes inside the arcaded patio depict episodes from Virgil's *Aeneid*. *(Letenská 10. Metro A: Malostranská. Exit the Metro and turn right on Letenská. The garden will be on the right. Open Apr.-Oct. daily 10am-6pm. Free.)*

ST. NICHOLAS'S CATHEDRAL (CHRÁM SV. MIKULÁŠE). The towering dome of St. Nicholas's Cathedral is one of Prague's most discernible landmarks. St. Nicholas's is the definition of Baroque, claustrophobically full of paintings and statuary. Climb the stairs to the left of the Altar of the Virgin Mary (itself left of the main altar), and the lofty perspective will reveal that much of the Cathedral's marble is actually painted, demonstrating how hard the muralists worked to paint details that people on the ground would never see. Unfortunately you will also see the handiwork of hundreds of tourists clever enough to carve their names in the banister. Props to you, Paco. Concerts are held each night in the early evening. Those seeking a bigger challenge can climb to the top of the church's belfry. *(Metro A: Malostranská. Follow Letenská from the Metro to Malostranské nám. ☎257 534 215. Open daily 8:30am-4:45pm; last entrance 4:45pm. 50Kč, students 25Kč. Entrance to pray 8:30am-9am, free. Tower 40/30Kč. Concerts 390/290Kč.)*

CHURCH OF OUR LADY VICTORIOUS (KOSTEL PANNY MARIE VÍTWZNÉ). The Church of Our Lady Victorious is an odd mix of tourist destination and pilgrimage site. The church itself is plain in comparison to the nearby St. Nicholas. Inside, however, the church contains the famous polished-wax statue of the **Infant Jesus of Prague,** which many believe can perform miracles for the faithful. According to legend, the statue arrived in Prague in the arms of a 16th-century Spanish noblewoman who married into Bohemian royalty; the plague bypassed the city shortly thereafter. In 1628, the Carmelite abbey gained custody of the statue and allowed pilgrims to pray to it. In the back of church, a small museum displays some of the vestments given to the Infant Jesus over the centuries. *(Metro A: Malostranská. Follow Letecká through Malostranské nám. and continue on Karmelitská. ☎257 533 646. Open daily 8:30am-7pm. Museum open M-Sa 9:30am-5:30pm, Su 1-6pm. No admittance during mass. Mass in 5 languages. English-speaking mass for Catholics Su noon. No talking. Free.)*

MEMORIAL TO THE VICTIMS OF COMMUNISM. Contructed by the government in 2002, the memorial is powerful in its simplicity. A set of concrete steps move up the hill, each with a sculpture created by Olbram Zoubek of an increasingly abstract man. *(Metro A: Malostranská. In Petrin Gardens near the funicular.)*

PRAGUE CASTLE (PRAŽSKÝ HRAD)

Take tram #22 or 23 from the center, get off at "Pražský Hrad," and go down U Prašného Mostu past the Royal Gardens and into the Second Courtyard. Or, hike up picturesque Nerudova street. ☎224 373 368; www.hrad.cz. Open daily Apr.-Oct. 9am-5pm; Nov.-Mar. 9am-4pm. Castle grounds open Apr.-Oct. 5am-midnight; Nov.-Mar. 9am-midnight. Ticket office opposite St. Vitus's Cathedral, inside the castle walls, at the info center. Tickets provide you with access to 5 different routes. Route A gets you into everything; 350Kč, students 175Kč. Tickets are valid for 2 successive days. Grounds free.

Prague Castle has been the seat of the Bohemian government since it was built over 1000 years ago. After the declaration of independent Czechoslovakia in 1918, first President Tomáš Masaryk invited Slovenian architect Josip Plečnik to rebuild his new residence, which had suffered from centuries of Habsburg neglect. Plečnik not only restored the castle's buildings and redesigned its gardens, but added fountains, columns, and embellishments. Arrive on the hour to catch the changing of the guard, daily from 5am-midnight.

HRADČANY SQUARE AND FIRST CASTLE COURTYARD. Outside the Castle gates at Hradčany Sq. lies the **Šternberg Palace,** home to the National Gallery's collection of European Old Masters, including works by Rembrandt, El Greco, Goya, and Rubens. *(☎230 090 570. Open Tu-Su 10am-6pm. 150Kč, students 70Kč.)* The Baroque **Matthias Gate** (Matyášská brána), inside the First Castle Courtyard, is the castle's official entrance. Plečnik designed the two spear-like wooden flagpoles next to it.

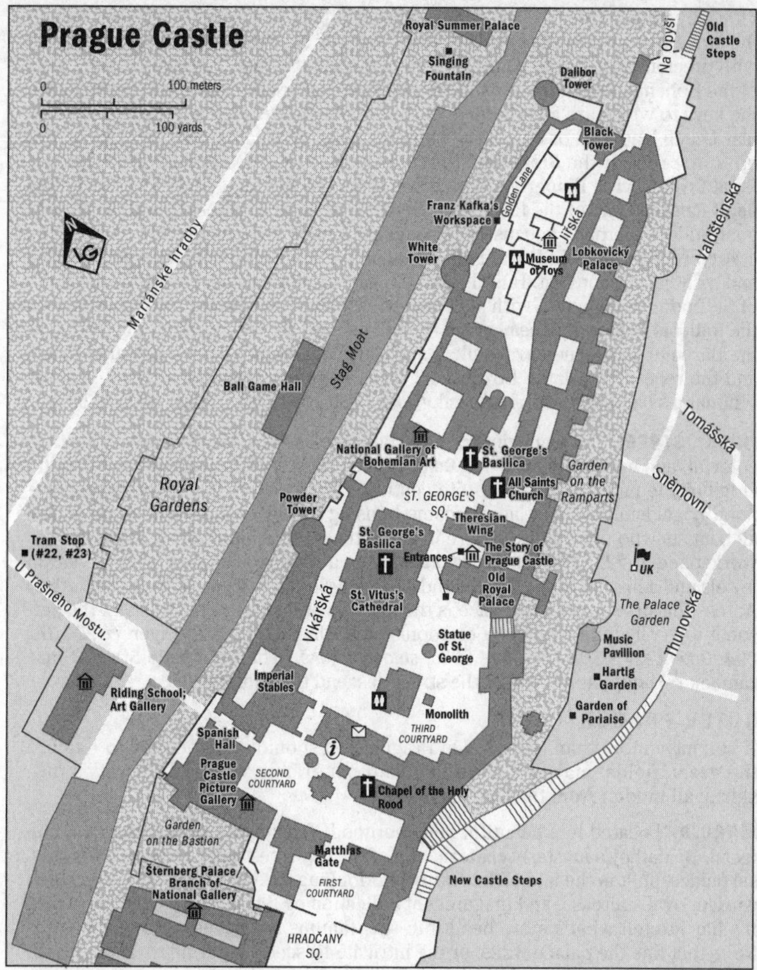

SECOND CASTLE COURTYARD, ROYAL GARDEN (KRÁLOVSKÁ ZAHRADA). After passing through Matthias Gate, turn left in the Second Castle Courtyard for access to the lush Royal Garden. Opened to the public after years as a private paradise for only the highest Communist officials, the serene and expansive Royal Garden offers a respite in the midst of one of the city's most popular tourist attractions. Past the tulip beds, the trickling **Singing Fountain** spouts its watery, harp-like tune before the **Royal Summer Palace.** Place your head under the fountain to hear the chiming water. *(Royal Garden open 24hr. Apr.-Oct.)*

THIRD CASTLE COURTYARD. In the Third Castle Courtyard stands Prague Castle's centerpiece, the colossal **St. Vitus's Cathedral**, which was completed in 1929 after some 600 years of construction. Right of the high altar stands the silver **tomb** of **St. Jan Nepomuk**. A statue of an angel holds a silvered tongue believed to have belonged to Jan, whose tongue was reputedly severed after he was thrown into the

Vltava by King Charles IV (see **Charles Bridge,** p. 179). It remains on display, though the story was proven false in 1961. The walls of **St. Wenceslas's Chapel** are lined with precious stones and paintings telling the saint's story. The real crown jewels of the Bohemian kings are kept in an adjoining inaccesible room with seven locks, the keys to which are kept in the hands of seven different living religious and secular Czech leaders. For one of the city's best views, scale the 287 steps that spiral up to the roof of the **Great South Tower.** Alternatively, head underground to the **Royal Crypt** to visit Emperor Charles IV's tomb. To the right of St. Vitus's, the **Old Royal Palace** is one of the few Czech castles that allows visitors to wander largely unattended—perhaps because its rooms are almost completely bare. Across the courtyard from the Old Royal Palace stands the Romanesque **St. George's Basilica** and its adjacent convent. Built in AD 921, the elegant basilica enshrines the tomb of St. Ludmila, complete with skeleton on display. The convent next door houses the **National Gallery of Bohemian Art,** which displays art ranging from the Gothic to the Baroque. In the medieval galleries, Master Theodorik's ecclesiastical portraits and the relief from Matka Boží před Týnem stand out; upstairs, Michael Leopold Willmann's paintings warrant a visit. *(Open Tu-Su 10am-6pm. 100Kč, students 50Kč.)*

JIŘSKÁ STREET. Jiřská begins to the right of the basilica. Halfway down, the tiny, colorful, and extremely crowded **Golden Lane** (Zlatá ulička) heads off to the right. Originally founded in the early 16th century, it was used to house tradespeople—notably goldsmiths—and later became housing for the castle's artillerymen. The alchemists who once worked here inspired the street's name. **Franz Kafka** had his workspace at #22. The **Lobkovický Palace** has a replica of Bohemia's coronation jewels and a history of the Czech lands. *(Open Tu-Su 9am-4:30pm. 40Kč, students 20Kč.)* Across the street from the Palace is the **Museum of Toys** (Muzeum hraček), the personal toy collection owned by cartoonist and filmmaker Ivan Steiger. *(☎224 372 294. Open daily 9:30am-5:30pm. 50Kč, students 30Kč.)* The **Old Castle Steps** (Staré zámecké schody) at the end of the street descend to Malostranská.

OUTER PRAGUE

If you have more than two days in Prague, you should take the time to explore the green fields, majestic churches, and panoramic vistas of the city's outskirts, all hidden from the touring hordes.

TROJA. Located in a beautiful neighborhood, Troja is the site of French architect J. B. Mathey's masterly **château,** one of the city's best-kept secrets. The colossal palace, built in the late 17th century overlooking the Vltava, includes a terraced garden, oval staircase, and magnificent collection of 19th-century Czech artwork. It's hard to tell what's more beautiful—the famous landscapes and moving portraits that line the palace walls, or the intricate frescoes featuring royal, mythical, and religious figures that adorn the ceilings. Don't miss Prague's answer to the Sistine Chapel, the **Main Hall,** with its 30 ft. walls covered from floor to ceiling in magnificent frescoes. *(Metro C: Nádraží Holešovice, take bus #112 to Zoologická Zahrada. Open Apr.-Oct. Tu-Su 10am-6pm; Nov.-Mar. Sa-Su 10am-5pm. 100Kč, students 50Kč.)* If you fancy wilder pursuits, venture next door to the **Prague Zoo.** *(Open daily 9am-7pm. Apr.-Sept. 80Kč, students 50Kč; Oct.-Mar. 50/30Kč.)*

BŘEVNOV MONASTERY. The oldest monastery in Bohemia was founded in AD 993 by King Boleslav II and St. Adalbert, who were both guided by a divine dream to build a monastery atop a bubbling stream. **St. Margaret's Church** (Bazilika sv. Markéty), a Benedictine chapel, awaits you inside. The monastery's green bell tower and red roof were the only parts of the original Romanesque structure that were spared when the Dientzenhofers, Prague's leading father-and-son architects, redesigned the complex in a High Baroque style. A beautiful stream leads to a small pond to the right of the church. Guided tours (in Czech only) are essential, as they allow you to access the monks' quarters and the crypt. *(Metro A: Malostranská. Take a 15min. ride uphill on tram #22 to Břevnovský klášter. Facing uphill, cross the road to the right. Entrance is on the left, under the monk statue. Church open only for mass: M-Sa 7am, 6pm; Su 7:30, 9am, 6pm. Tours Sa-Su 10am, 2, 4pm. 50Kč, students 30Kč.)*

MUSEUMS

Prague's exceptional art museums are some of the few impressive spots in Prague not yet swamped by tourists. There are new treasures to discover, variations on old themes, and styles you won't find elsewhere.

MUCHA MUSEUM. This is the only collection devoted entirely to the work of Alfons Mucha, the Czech Republic's most celebrated artist, who gained his fame in Paris for his poster series of "la divine Sarah." It was through this series—devoted to Sarah Bernhardt, Paris's most famous actress—that Mucha pioneered the Art Nouveau movement. Be sure to see the collection of Czech and Parisian posters, including the famous *Gismonda*, which revolutionized poster design, as well as Mucha's panel paintings. Don't miss the excellent documentary video of Mucha's life towards the end of the exhibit. *(Panská 7. Metro A or B: Můstek. Head up Václavské nám. toward the St. Wenceslas statue. Hang a left on Jindřišská and turn left again on Panská. ☎221 451 333; www.mucha.cz. Open daily 10am-6pm. 120Kč, students 60Kč.)*

FRANZ KAFKA MUSEUM. This museum provides an excellent in-depth look into the life of Franz Kafka, from his troubled relationship with his father to his numerous love affairs, all documented through his own letters and journal entries. The museum ends in a fittingly creepy endless maze of file cabinets with an eternally ringing telephone representing the bureaucracy that troubled Kafka so greatly. *(Cilhená 2b. Metro A Malostranská. Go down toward Klárov toward the river. Turn right onto U. Luzické Semináré and bear left on Cilhená. ☎221 451 333; www.kafkamuseum.cz. Open daily 10am-6pm. 120Kč, students 60Kč. Buy ½-price tickets at the Mucha Museum.)*

CITY GALLERY PRAGUE (GALERIE HLAVNÍHO MĚSTA PRAHY). The City Gallery of Prague has seven locations throughout the city and its suburbs, four of which house permanent collections; three have rotating exhibitions. The **House of the Golden Ring** is one of only two permanent collections in Prague proper, with an especially massive collection of 19th- and 20th-century Czech art. The four floors of winding corridors lead through Czech contributions to all the major 20th century art movements. *(Týnská 6. Metro A: Staroměstská. Behind and to the left of Týn Church in Old Town Sq., through a small door. ☎222 327 677; www.citygalleryprague.cz. Open Tu-Su 10am-6pm. Top 3 floors 60Kč, students 30Kč; entire museum 70Kč; 1st Tu of each month free.)*

MUSEUM OF CZECH CUBISM. The Museum of Czech Cubism follows the cubist movement that Czech artists embraced and transformed in the beginning of the 20th century. Located in the **House of the Black Madonna,** the building alone is worth the trip. The museum houses three floors of works, from elaborate paintings to pieces of furniture by some of the country's best-known cubists. Browse the books in the gift shop before touring the museum to gather some background info. *(Ovocný trh 19. Metro B: nám. Republiky. Follow Celetná towards Staroměstské nam. Museum is on the left. ☎224 211 746; www.ngprague.cz. Open Tu-Su 10am-6pm. 100Kč, students 50Kč/30Kč after 4pm.)*

MUSEUM OF COMMUNISM. Nowhere will you find more propaganda, busts of Stalin, and pitchforks. Located behind a McDonald's and on the same floor as a casino, this museum takes you through the dream, reality, and nightmare of Soviet occupation. The exhibit culminates with a powerful documentary about the Czech struggle for independence that led up to the Velvet Revolution. *(Na Příkopě 10. Metro A: Můstek. Exit the Metro and turn right on Na Příkopě; enter through Casino. ☎224 212 966; www.museumofcommunism.com. Open daily 9am-9pm. 180Kč, students 140Kč.)*

CZECH MUSEUM OF FINE ARTS (ČESKÉ MUZEUM VÝTVARNÝCH UMWNÍ). The Czech Museum of Fine Arts, occupying three buildings in Prague's Staré Město, puts on focused exhibitions derived from its extensive collections of works by Czech artists. The first two floors are devoted to a history of Czech Cubism, while the downstairs gallery exhibits the works of other European Modernists. *(Husova 19-21. Metro A: Staroměstská. Follow Karlova down from Charles Bridge. Turn right on Husova. ☎222 220 218. Open Tu-Su 10am-6pm. 50Kč, students 20Kč.)*

MONUMENT TO NATIONAL LITERATURE (PAMÁTNÍK NÁRODNÍHO PÍSEMNICTVÍ). Part of the Strahov Monastery, the star attraction here is the **Strahov Library,** with its magnificent **Theological and Philosophical Halls.** *(Strahovské nádvoří 1. From Metro A: Hradčanská, take tram #25 toward Bílá Hora to Malovanka. Turn around, follow the tram tracks, then turn right on Strahovská through an arch, into the park. The museum is inside the monastery on the left. ☎220 516 671. Open daily 9am-noon and 1-5pm. 70Kč, students 50Kč.)*

ENTERTAINMENT

THEATER

It is hard to overstate the role of theater in Czech culture, and on any given night, world-class performances of all genres are staged in town. For a list of concerts and performances, consult *The Prague Post*, *The Pill*, *Threshold*, or *Do města-Downtown* (the latter three are distributed for free at cafes and restaurants). Most performances begin at 7pm; unsold tickets are sometimes available at a discount 30min. before curtain. The majority of Prague's theaters close in July and August, but the selection is extensive during the rest of the year. The **Prague Fringe Festival** each June features all things avant-garde, including dancers, comedians, and everyone's favorite, mimes. (☎224 935 183; www.prague-fringe.cz.)

National Theatre (Národní divadlo), Národní třída 2/4. Metro B: Národní třída. The National Theatre, opened in 1883, was Prague's 1st venue for performances in the Czech language and an important symbol of national pride. Fittingly, the building fuses classical architecture with images from Czech mythology. Also oversees the **Estates Theatre** and the **Kolowrat Theatre.** Tickets for all 3 theaters are available at the box office in Kolowrat Palace at Ovocný trh 6, next to the Estates Theatre, or at Národní třida 2-4 (☎224 901 448, reservations 901 487; www.narodni-divadlo.cz). Open daily Sept.-June 10am-6pm, and 45min. before curtain. Formal dress required. Tickets 30-1000Kč. Discounted tickets announced as they become available.

State Opera (Státní opera), Wilsonova 4 (info ☎296 117 111, box office 224 227 266; www.opera.cz/en). Metro A or C: Muzeum. This gorgeous neo-Rococo building is now home to the Prague State Opera, as part of the National Theatre. Box office open M-F 10am-5:30pm, Sa-Su 10am-noon, 1-5:30pm, and 1hr. before each show.

Theatre Image Black Light Theatre, Pařížská 4 (☎222 314 448; www.imagetheatre.cz). Every performance at Theatre Image is silent, conveying its message through dance techniques and black light. Shows daily 8pm. Box office open daily 9am-8pm.

Laterna Magika, Národní třída 4 (☎224 931 482; www.laterna.cz). Also delivering silent performances, the acclaimed Laterna Magika began in 1958 at the world exposition in Brussels. Box office open M-Sa 10am-8pm. Tickets 700Kč, students 560Kč.

Marionette Theater (Říše loutek), Žatecká 1 (☎224 819 322; www.mozart.cz). Metro A: Staroměstská, trams #17 and 18, or bus #207. On the corner of Žatecká and Mariánské nám. The world's oldest marionette theater is a cultural staple of the Czech Republic. The current show, a version of Mozart's *Don Giovanni* performed entirely by puppets, has been running since 1991. The humorous, amazingly lifelike marionettes include a drunken Mozart who interacts with the audience during interludes. Performances M-Tu and Th-Su 8pm. Tickets available at the box office on Žatecká 1, the secondary box office at Celetná 13, and the tourist office in the Old Town Hall. Box office open June-Oct. daily 10am-8pm. 490Kč, students 390Kč.

MUSIC

The **Prague Spring Festival** (www.festival.cz) showcases of talent from across the globe. The festival opens with Smetana's "Má Vlast" ("My Country") and closes with Beethoven's 9th symphony. Tickets are available at the Prague Spring box office in the Rudolfinum, Hellichova 18. (☎257 312 547; www.ticketpro.cz. Open M-F 10am-6pm.) It's hard to walk down Staroměstké nám. without having a flyer (or 20) thrust into your hand advertising orchestral concerts in nearby churches and halls. The ticket costs vary; concerts in the churches tend to be cheaper (10-15Kč) than those sold by private agencies. The beautiful rooms in which they are held, such as Municipal Hall's Art Nouveau Smetana Hall, are as much of a draw as the music itself. Shows are usually at 5pm and 8pm.

FILM

Prague has its share of theaters showing big-budget American blockbusters. Even more common, however, are small cinemas showing art-house and independent films from all around the world. The **Kino Perštýn,** Na Perštýné 6 (☎221 668 432), shows one or two recent films daily. International films are shown with Czech subtitles and Czech films with English subtitles. Call ahead for reservations. **KinoSvétozor Arthouse,** Vodičkova 41 (☎224 946 824; www.kinosvetozor.cz), has two screens, the *velký* (big) and the *malý* (small), with a total of eight screenings per day. Recent American hits are on the menu, but so are all sorts of international classics. (1st show 11am, last 9:15pm. Bar and box office open daily at 10:30am. Tickets 100Kč unless otherwise noted.)

NIGHTLIFE

A good way to experience Prague at night is to wander, taking in all the city's nightlife has to offer. Authentic pub experiences are often restricted to the suburbs and outlying Metro stops. You may have to look a bit harder for them, but a few Czech pubs remain scattered throughout Staré Město and Malá Strana. Prague's clubbing scene is developing fast and there are plenty of dance clubs pumping out techno. Guys heading to clubs should wear leather shoes—many clubs don't allow patrons in wearing sandals or sneakers. Even more popular among Czechs are the city's many jazz and rock clubs, which host excellent local and international acts. Whichever way you indulge in Prague nightlife, swig a few pints of *pivo*, grab some 4am snacks, and forgo the night bus for the morning Metro.

BEER HALLS AND WINE CELLARS

Vinárna U Sudu, Vodičkova 10 (☎222 232 207). Metro A: Můstek. Cross Václavské nám. to Vodičkova and follow it as it curves left. Undiscovered by tourists, this Moravian wine bar looks plain from its 1st fl. entrance, but beneath the facade sprawls a labyrinth of cavernous cellars, where the carafes of smooth red wine (125Kč) go down frighteningly fast as the hours fly by. Open M-Th 8pm-3am, F-Sa 8pm-4am, Su 8pm-2am.

U Kralé Brabantskélo, Thunovská 15 (☎724 007 265). Metro A: Malostranská. Go downhill on Letenská. Turn right at the square onto Tomášká and left onto Thunovská. Somewhat kitschy, but very fun. This pub, founded in 1475, still serves up pints of beer in its cavernous interior amidst much revelry. Occasional fire-dancing by the staff makes for an exciting diversion. Beer from 28Kč. Wine from 45Kč. Open daily 11am-2am.

THE REAL DEAL. Many bars in Prague now display prominent NO STAG PARTIES signs in their windows. Why, you ask? Well, stag parties tend to sing so loud it chases away business, tear up bars, perpetrate most of Prague's few violent crimes, and behave at the age of 45 in a way most people wouldn't behave in their teens. The stag party is not a wide-ranging creature, however, and it lumbers about almost entirely within the area between Staroměstské nám. and the Charles Bridge. Intrigued? Horrified? To join in–or avoid–the raucous destruction, here are some places to go, or to stay the hell away from: **George and Dragon,** Staroměstské nám., named after England, mothership of most stags; **O'Caffrey's,** next to George and Dragon, for when you want that Irish pub atmosphere–in order to destroy it with your mates; **U Fleků,** the saddest casualty: the oldest beer hall in Prague is often full of stag parties. In general, any establishment that prints its name in English somewhere on its facade is likely to be a den of stag. You stand warned.

BARS

Kozička, Kozí 1 (☎224 818 308; www.kozicka.cz). Metro A: Staroměstská. Take Dlouhá from the square's northeast corner, bear left on Kozí. The giant cellar bar is always packed until closing–you'll know why after your first *Krušovice* (30Kč). Great if you're looking for a Czechmate. Open M-F noon-4am, Sa 6pm-4am, Su 6pm-3am. MC/V.

Le Chateau, Jakubská 2 (☎222 316 328). From Metro B: nám. Republiky, walk through the Powder Tower to Celetná, then take a right on Templová. On the corner of Templová and Jakubská. Seductive red walls and youthful clientele keep this place overflowing until dawn. Open M-Th noon-3am, F noon-6am, Sa 4pm-6am, Su 4pm-2am.

Bombay Cocktail Bar, Dlouhá 11 (☎222 324 040). Metro A: Staroměstská. Flat screen TVs show last season's runway shows at this chic watering hole. The crowd is young, well heeled, and social. Exhaustive cocktail list, but few draft beers. Nightly DJ. Sex on the Beach 135Kč. Open M-W and Su 5pm-4am, Th 5pm-5am, Fr-Sa 5pm-6am.

Zanzibar, Lázenská 6 (☎312 246 876). Metro A: Malostranská. From the square, head down Mostecká toward the Charles Bridge, turn right on Lázeňská, and left on Saská. The tastiest, priciest, and most exotic mixed drinks this side of the Vltava (80-190č). Cuban cigars 30-170Kč. Open daily 5pm-3am.

Repete, Rybna 17 (☎224 814 062). Metro A: Staroměstská. An intimate, cavern-like bar filled with locals downing tasty, inexpensive drinks. A small dance club downstairs will hold you over, but the drink menu is the main draw here. Anyone care to try "sperm" (90Kč)? Open M-Th 3pm-2:30am, F-Sa 4pm-3:30am, Su 5pm-1:30am.

U 3 Černých Ruží, Zámecká 5. Metro A: Malostranská. Take tram #12, 22, or 23 to Malostranské nám and turn right, then left on Zámecká. At the foot of the New Castle Steps. A small, quirky, dimly lit bar that pours endless pints at low prices (Budvar 22Kč) for a thirsty local crowd. If you can still stand after sitting in one of the not-so-comfy armchairs, end the night with a moonlit walk to the castle. Open daily 11am-midnight.

Jo's Bar and Garáž, Malostranské nám. 7. Metro A: Malostranská. If you can't bear the idea that the people at the next table might not speak English, Jo's Bar is the perfect spot for you, offering foosball, darts, card games, and a packed dance floor downstairs. Some of Prague's best DJs spin acid jazz, techno, house, and dance. Offers a good selection of American bar food (70-180Kč). Beer 40Kč. Long Island iced tea 115Kč. Open daily 11am-2am. AmEx/MC/V.

CLUBS AND DISCOS

Radost FX, Bělehradská 120 (☎224 254 776; www.radostfx.cz). Metro C: IP Pavlova. Although heavily touristed, Radost remains the gem of Prague nightlife, playing only the hippest techno, jungle, and house music from internationally renowned DJs. The spa-

A SPOONFUL OF SUGAR. Those who have journeyed to the Czech Republic hoping to imbibe absinthe, the elusive "green fairy" outlawed in the US, may be disappointed to find that the Czech version lacks many of its former hallucinogenic qualities. Hence, this version is known simply as "absinth," without an "e." Fear not, however, the Bohemia version contains more than enough firepower to fuel a hazy night–but make sure to drink it the correct way. First, take a spoonful of sugar and dip it in the absinth. Then, light the sugar on fire until it caramelizes and the flames extinguishes itself; be sure not to let the absinth catch fire. As soon as the sugar extinguishes, stir it into the absinth, add 1 part water, and it may be the greatest night you'll never remember.

cious, chill-out room is perfect for taking a break from the dance floor and watching the throngs of trendy clubbers strut their stuff. Creative drinks (Frozen Sex with an Alien 140Kč) will expand your clubbing horizons. Also serves brunch (see **Nové Město Restaurants,** p. 176). Cover 100-250Kč. Open M-Sa 10pm-5am.

Roxy, Dlouhá 33 (☎224 826 296; www.roxy.cz). Metro B: nám. Republiky. Walk up Revoluční to the river; go left on Dlouhá. Hip locals and informed tourists come to this converted theater for the experimental DJs and theme nights. Often full until breakfast. Beer 30Kč. Cover Tu and Th-Sa 100-350Kč. Open M-Tu and Th-Sa 9pm-late.

Mecca, U Průhonu 3 (☎283 870 522; www.mecca.cz). Metro C: Nádraží Holešovice. The place for Prague's beautiful celebrities to pass the night, Mecca offers a packed house filled with locals and foreigners. Industrial-chic decoration. House music, with some techno thrown in. Dress to impress. Live DJs every night. Open 9pm-late.

M1 Lounge, Masná 1 (☎227 195 235; m1lounge.com). For those seeking respite from drunken American teens, M1 is strictly 21+. The cozy, low ceilinged room is lined with benches, creating an intimate yet happening atmosphere. Music rotates with the party schedule. Open Su-Th 7pm-4am; F 7pm-5am; Sa 7pm-10am.

Karlovy Lázně, Novotného Lávka 1 (☎222 220 502). The teenagers and 20-somethings in line at the door stare eagerly at televisions broadcasting from inside this pulsing 4-story complex. Different, equally sweaty rooms play R&B, techno, oldies, and pop music. Often overrun by stag parties. Cover 120Kč; 50Kč before 10pm and after 4am. Open daily 9pm-5am.

Klub 007, Chaloupeckého 7 (☎257 211 439; www.klub007strahov.cz). Metro A: Dejvicka. From Dejvicka take bus #217 to Stadion Strahov and walk uphill on Chaloupeckého for 450m. A favorite of local students, this club is more for music-appreciation than dancing. Hard core, punk, and reggae alternate nights. Open M-Sa 7pm-2am.

JAZZ CLUBS

U staré paní (The Old Lady's Place), Michalská 9 (☎603 551 680; www.jazzlounge.cz). Metro A or B: Můstek. Walk down Na můstku at the end of Václavské nám., through its name changes to Melantrichova. Turn left on Havelská and right on Michalská. High, plush stools, small black tables and a metal bar face the stage, where on any given night you can take in the products of the Czechs' love for jazz. Some of the best music in the city. Pilsner Urquell 45Kč. Mixed drinks 115-145Kč. Performances every night at 9pm. Cover M-Th and Su 150Kč, F-Sa 200Kč. Open daily 7pm-2am. AmEx/MC/V.

Ungelt, Týn 2 (☎224 895 748; www.jazzblues.cz). Metro A or B: Staroměstská. From Old Town Square, follow Týnska and take a right on Týn. A passage in the unassuming bar upstairs leads down into the vaults of this UNESCO-protected building. There waits a small, low-lit room with stone walls and polished wood tables where people chat animatedly. Musicians provide background with lots of solos and lots of electric bass. Menu of absinthe mixed drinks includes the Hemingway (absinthe, sparkling wine and ice; 90Kč). Beer 38Kč. Live concerts daily 9pm-midnight; cover 200Kč, students 150Kč, or listen from the pub for free. Open daily 8pm-midnight.

Reduta, Národní 20 (☎224 933 487; www.redutajazzclub.cz). Metro A: Národní třída. Exit on Spálená, take a left on Národní, and go through the facade of the Louvre cafe. This venue is an old haunt of Presidents Clinton and Havel. Distinguished from the street only by a small neon sign, descend into this cavernous smoke-filled joint to enjoy classic jazz in an appreciative atmosphere. Cover 200Kč. Open daily 9pm-midnight.

U Malého Glena II, Karmelitská 23 (☎257 531 717; www.malyglen.cz). In the basement of U Malého Glena, there's a bar and a small stage with a handful of tables. And on M nights, Stan the Man and his Bohemian Blues Band play English songs under low lights. Other nights there's salsa, or jazz; always, a packed house. Bernard Beer 35Kč per 0.5L. Cover 100-150Kč. Shows start at 9:30pm, except F and Sa, when they start at 10pm. Open daily 8pm-2am. Call ahead for weekend tables. AmEx/MC/V.

GLBT PRAGUE

Prague's gay and lesbian scene is developing fast: transvestite shows, stripteases, discos, bars, cafes, restaurants, and hotels aimed at gay and lesbian travelers can be easily found. At any of the places listed below, you can pick up a copy of Amigo (90Kč; www.amigo.cz), the most thorough English guide to gay life in Prague. They also carry *Gayčko* (60Kč), a glossy magazine mostly in Czech. Check out www.praguegayguide.net or www.praguesaints.cz.

The Saints, Polská 32 (☎222 250 041; www.praguesaints.cz; www.saintsbar.cz). Metro A: Jiřího z Poděbrad. On Vinohradská, head away from the giant clock. Take a right on Slavikova and then the 2nd left on Polská. The Saints is an advocacy group that introduces GLBT visitors to Prague and organizes the local community; they also run a small, comfortable club. With plush couches, small tables, and free Wi-Fi, the welcoming underground club draws a mixed crowd of Czech and foreign men, and the occasional woman. Beer from 22Kč. Open M-Th 1pm-2am, F and Sa 5pm-4am, Su 1pm-1am.

Friends, Bartolomejská 11 (☎224 236 272; www.friends-prague.cz). Metro B: Narodní třída. Exit on Spálená, turn right, and cross Narodní třída, heading down Na Perštýně. Turn left on Bartolomejská. The only GLBT dance club in Staré Město, Friends has a rotating schedule of parties and theme nights. The tapestried interior attracts young locals early in the week, with more tourists on the weekends. Women and straight customers are welcome but uncommon. Beer from 20Kč. Open daily 6pm-5am. No cover.

Valentino, Vinohradská ul. 40 (☎222 513 491; www.club-valentino.cz). Metro A or C: Muzeum. The Czech Republic's largest gay club draws an equally large crowd to its 4 bars, 3 stories, and 2 dance floors. House music dominates the packed and sweaty dance floors, although the rotating DJs spice it up. Chill out downstairs or at the outside tables. No cover. Open daily 11am-late.

DAYTRIPS FROM PRAGUE

TEREZÍN (THERESIENSTADT)

Buses from Florenc (1hr., 16 per day, 61Kč). Exit at the Terezín stop by the tourist office. You can also catch a train from Hlavní Masarykovo to the station 2km from town. Ask for directions, as there are no street signs or signposts. Trains are more reliable on weekends. The museum 500m right of the bus stop sells tickets to Terezín's sights. ☎416 782 576; www.pamatnik-terezin.cz. Open daily Apr.-Oct. 8am-6pm; Nov.-Mar 8am-4:30pm. Museum, barracks, and fortress 180Kč; students 160Kč. Crematorium and graveyard open Apr.-Oct. M-F and Su 10am-5pm; Nov.-Mar. 10am-4pm. Free.

The fortress town of Terezín (Theresienstadt) was built in the 1780s by Austrian Emperor Josef II to safeguard his empire's northern frontier. In 1940, Hitler's Gestapo set up a prison in the Small Fortress, and in 1941 the town became a concentration camp. By 1942, the entire prewar civilian population had been evacuated, and the town became a waystation for over 140,000 Jews awaiting transfer farther east. Terezín was one of Hitler's most successful propaganda ploys. The camp was intended to paint a false portrait of ghetto life for Red Cross delegations, so sparkling clean bathrooms and sleeping facilities were created purely for show. The large park that dominates the town square was built to create an illusion of aesthetic and athletic opportunities for residents, yet, except for publicity stunts, Jews were not allowed to enter it. Nazi films described the area as a "self-governed" settlement, where Jews were allowed to educate their children, partake of arts and recreation, and live a "fulfilling" life. In reality, overcrowding, malnourishment, and death chambers killed over 30,000 people in the camp. Since the war, Terezín has been repopulated, but the streets still radiate an eerie aura. The tourist office, nám. ČSA 179, is near the bus stop and provides maps and accommodations. *(☎416 782 616; www.terezin.cz. Open M-Th 8am-5pm, F 8am-1:30pm, Su 9am-3pm.)*

TOWN AND CEMETERY. To walk the quiet streets of Terezín is to confront its ghosts. Every building here was used to house and monitor Jews during the war. The former school has been converted into a **museum** of life in the camp, displaying documents that place Terezín in the wider context of WWII. The museum's most moving exhibits are dedicated to the rich art that emerged among the Jews in response to the horrors of persecution—the second floor features original paintings, music, theater, and poetry by children and adults imprisoned in Terezín. East of the marketplace, the **Magdeburg Barracks** document the lives of Jews within their prison walls. Outside the walls lie Terezín's **Cemetery and Crematorium,** where Nazis disposed of the remains of the executed.

SMALL FORTRESS. The Small Fortress sits across the river, much of it left bare and untouched for visitors to explore. Permanent exhibitions chart the town's development from 1780 to 1939, as well as the story of the fortress during WWII when it was used as a labor camp. Above the entrance hangs the ironic epitaph of the Nazi concentration camps: *"Arbeit macht frei"* ("Work shall set you free"). The true horror of this phrase is revealed in the dim, underground passage to the excavation site, where prisoners were buried after being literally worked to death. Liberators uncovered mass graves after the war and transferred many of the bodies to the breathtaking memorial cemetery. *(Open daily Apr.-Oct. 8am-6pm; Nov.-Mar. 8am-4:30pm. Closed Dec. 24-26 and Jan. 1. 160Kč, students 130Kč.)*

KUTNÁ HORA

Trains run from Hlavní nádraží (1hr., 1 per hr., round-trip 120Kč). A 1km. walk from the train station. From the train station, turn right, then left, and left again on the highway. After 500m, turn right at the church. The ossuary is at the end of the road. Open daily Apr.-Sept. 8am-6pm; Oct. 9am-noon and 1-5pm; Nov.-Mar. 9am-noon and 1-4pm. 35Kč, students 20Kč. Camera 30Kč, video 60Kč.

Kutná Hora, a small, picturesque village 1hr. from Prague, is both famous and infamous for its ossuary, a chapel filled with artistic and religious creations made entirely from parts of human skeletons. The village was originally formed around silver mines; its morbid side only came out when the plague and a superstition about the holiness of the village's graveyard combined to leave the cemetery overflowing with corpses. The Cistercian Order built a chapel in order to house the extra remains, and in a fit of whim (or possibly insanity), one monk began designing flowers from pelvises and crania. He never finished the ossuary, but the artist František Rint eventually completed the project in 1870, decorating the chapel from floor to ceiling with the bones of over 40,000 people. In town the **Church of Saint Barbara,** completed in 1905 after over 500 years of halting construction, is a sight to behold. Note the four statues situated high up in the rafters representing the four Christian values of justice, bravery, caution, and temperance.

KARLŠTEJN

Trains from Hlavní nádraží (55min., 4 per day, 50Kč). Head right from the station and take the 1st left over the Berounka River. Turn right after the bridge, take a left onto the sidewalk that splits off from the road, and walk through the village (25min., steeply uphill). ☎311 681 617; www.hradkarlstejn.cz. Open Tu-Su July and Aug. 9am-6pm; Sept. and May-June 9am-5pm; Oct. and Apr. 9am-4pm; Jan.-Mar. 9am-3pm. Closed May-Sept. noon-12:30pm; Oct.-Apr noon-1pm. Mandatory tours in English: 7-8 per day, hours vary; 220Kč; children 150Kč, groups must reserve in advance. Chapel tours July-Oct. by reservation only; adults 300Kč, children 150Kč. ☎274 008 154, email rezervace@stc.npu.cz. No pictures. MC/V.

The famous tourist attraction of Karlštejn is a walled and turreted fortress built by Emperor Charles IV in the 14th century on a mountain peak, overlooking the surrounding countryside. The tours capitalize on Karlštejn's status as a major tourist attraction, however, by offering rather basic tours of the unfurnished fortess. Though the **Chapel of the Holy Cross** houses the castle's most precious jewels and holy relics, it is not part of the standard tour and must be viewed separately.

Back in Karlštejn, you can take a coach ride through town by standing anywhere and paying 100Kč when the coach shows up. The surrounding countryside is part of the Bohemian karst region, the only place in the world where the karst ash tree can be found. It is also home to over 1380 butterfly species. Enjoy the splendor, but be careful: trails are not always clearly marked.

WEST BOHEMIA

West Bohemia is an oasis bursting at the seams with healing waters of all sorts. Over the centuries, emperors and intellectuals alike soaked in the waters of Karlovy Vary (*Carlsbad* in German). Today, tourists still flock to the town's bubbling springs and wander through its colonnades, but they come seeking beer, including one of the world's finest brews, Pilsner Urquell.

PLZEŇ ☎377

Plzeň (PUHL-zen-yeh; pop. 175,000) was once notorious for pollution, and Czechs might accordingly advise you to skip it. But travelers quick to pass by Plzeň are missing out, as recent efforts have left its beautiful architecture and gardens looking clean and new. It is the city's world-famous beer and not architecture, however, that lures many to Plzeň. The Pilsner Brewery, the Brewery Museum, and the countless beer halls make Plzeň a beer-lover's utopia.

TRANSPORTATION

Trains: ☎32 20 79, on Širková between Americká and Koterovská. Domestic tickets on the 1st level; international tickets on the 2nd. To **Český Krumlov** (3hr., 3 per day, 140-200Kč) via **České Budějovice** and **Prague** (1¾hr., 14 per day, 140Kč). Open M-F 3:15am-2am, Sa 2:45am-2am, Su 3:30am-12:30am.

Buses: Husova 58 (☎23 72 37). Many Euroline buses pass through en route to **Prague** (2hr., 16 per day, 70-90Kč) from **France, Germany, the Netherlands,** and **Switzerland.** To **Karlovy Vary** (1¼hr., 16 per day, 70-80Kč). Open M-F and Su 5am-10:30pm, Sa 5am-8pm.

Public Transportation: Trams run until 11:45pm; after that, **night trams,** labeled with an N followed by the number of the tram, take over with service every hr. Get tickets (12Kč, backpacks 4Kč) from any *tabák* or from machines at the tram stops, and punch them on board by pressing hard on the orange box. Machines require exact change.

Fine for riding without ticket 200-1000Kč. Tram #1 goes from the train and bus stations, nám. Republiky. Tram #4 runs north-south along Sady Pětatřicátníků.

Taxis: Radio Taxi (☎377 377). Taxis frequent the stations and nám. Republiky.

ORIENTATION AND PRACTICAL INFORMATION

Most of the city's sights surround **Náměstí Republiky,** the main square. From the train station, turn right on Sirková and enter the pedestrian underpass. When you emerge from the Americká exit, continue down Sirková (300m). Turn left on **Pražská,** then right at the fork to reach the center. From the bus station, turn left on Husova. After the street becomes Smetanovy sady, turn left on Bedřicha Smetany and follow it to nám Republiky (15min.).

Tourist Office: Městské Informační Středisko (MIS), nám. Republiky 41 (☎035 330; www.icpilsen.cz). Offers free **maps,** books rooms, and sells OSKAR phone cards. Some English spoken. Internet 5Kč up to 5min., 20Kč for 6-15min., 40Kč for 16-30min., 2Kč per min. thereafter. Open daily 9am-7pm.

Budget Travel: GTS Int, Pražská 12 (☎32 86 21; www.gtsint.cz). Arranges plane and train tickets. Open M-F 8am-5pm.

Currency Exchange: Plzeňská Banka, nám. Republiky 16 (☎235 354), cashes **traveler's checks** for 2% commission. Open M-F 8:30am-4:30pm. A 24hr. **currency exchange** machine is located in **ČSOB,** Americká 60, near the train station. MC/V **ATMs** are scattered throughout nám. Republiky.

Luggage Storage: On the 1st fl. of the train station. 15Kč per day, bags over 15kg 30Kč per day. Lost ticket charge 30Kč. Lockers 30Kč per day (24hr. limit). Open daily 7-11:15am and 11:35am-7pm.

Pharmacy: Lékárna U Bílého Jenorožce, nám. Republiky (☎24 07 88 or 53 32 59), near the corner of Prešovská and Bedřicha Smetany. Open M and W-Th 7am-6pm, Tu and F 7am-8pm, Sa 8am-noon.

Internet: Internet Kavárna Aréna, Františkánská 10 (☎22 04 02), has flat screens, fast connections, and a comfortable atmosphere. Ring bell to enter. 0.90Kč per min. Open M-F 9am-10pm, Sa-Su 10am-10pm.

Post Office: Solní 20 (☎21 15 43). **Poste Restante** available at all windows. Open M-F 9am-7pm, Sa 8am-1pm, Su 8am-noon. **Postal Code:** 30101.

ACCOMMODATIONS

There aren't many budget accommodations in Plzeň, as the tourist industry caters mainly to older German travelers. **MIS** (p. 195) books **private rooms** (from 179Kč; 10-15min. walk from main square). **Pensions** range from 300 to 900Kč.

Hotel Slovan, Smetanovy sady 1 (☎22 72 56; www.hotelslovan.pilsen.cz), at the corner of Jungmannova and Smetanovy sady. Despite an atmosphere of decaying grandeur, the hotels' rooms are appointed with functional furnishings and heavenly beds. Decent English. Reception 24hr. Budget rooms with shared bathrooms: singles 620Kč; doubles 900Kč. Luxury rooms with private bathrooms and breakfast: singles 1450Kč; doubles 2100Kč. AmEx/D/MC/V. ❸

Pension U Salzmannů, Pražská 8 (☎23 58 55; www.usalzmannu.cz). Attached to a well-known restaurant of the same name, this pension boasts an unbeatable location and reasonable prices. The rooms and bathrooms are spotless, but are very few in number, especially at the lower end of the price range: book at least a week in advance. Budget singles with shared baths from 550Kč; doubles from 700Kč. Rooms with private bath from 1350Kč. Luxury suites 1900Kč. Cash only. ❸

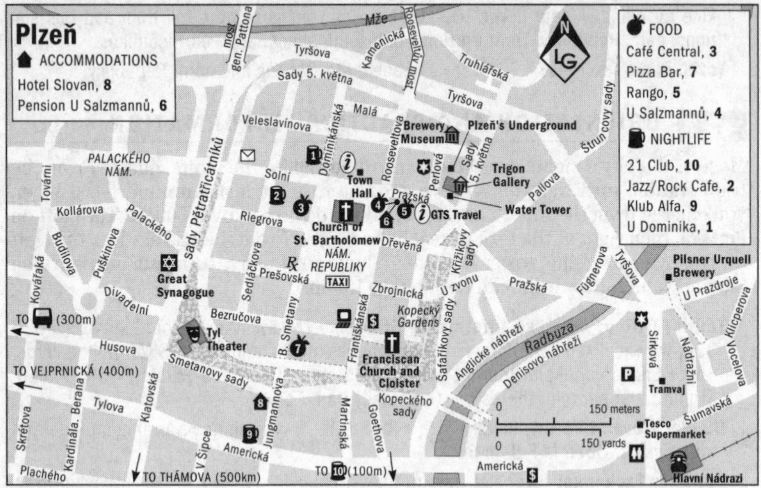

FOOD

Every meal in Plzeň should include a glass of Pilsner Urquell, a smooth, golden beer, or its dark, stronger brother, Purkmistr. If you can't decide, have a Rezané, a Czech black-and-tan, which mixes the two varieties. For groceries, try **Potraviny Nuen,** nám. Republiky 30 (open M-F 7am-7pm, Sa 7am-noon), or **Tesco,** Sirková 47. (Open M-W 7am-7pm, Th-F 7am-8pm, Sa-Su 8am-6pm. AmEx/MC/V.)

U Salzmannů Restaurace, Pražská 8 (☎23 58 55). Just when you think you've had enough of beer halls, U Salzmannů re-justifies their existence. Established in 1637, the restaurant specializes in the old Czech standbys. The goulash (Plzeňsky Guláš; 129Kč) is enormous and sure to satiate even the most ravenous of travelers. Giant Pilsner Urquell 25Kč. Open M-Th and Sa-Su 11am-11pm, F 11am-midnight. MC/V. ❷

Cafe Central, nám. Republiky 33 (☎042 377 226 059). Located within the hotel of the same name, Cafe Central's sleek stainless steel chairs and bright interior are a welcome change from the smoky beer halls of the rest of the city. Fresh salads and sandwiches dominate the menu and the expresso is excellent. Open daily 9am-10pm. Cash only. ❶

Rango, Pražská 10 (☎329 969). Elegant Rango, with its stucco walls, stained glass, and candlelit tables, is one of the few restaurants in Plzeň that does not pledge allegiance to a particular beer. The *risotto con di frutti del mar* is fantastic (shellfish risotto; 150Kč). Open M-F 11am-11pm, Sa-Su noon-11pm. Entrees 100-150Kč. MC/V. ❸

Pizza Bar, B. Smetany 15 (☎337 330 888). The name might not be too creative, but the pizza is. Huge, crispy pies come covered with every topping from spicy salami to fresh pineapple. The courtyard tables, well-stocked, social bar, and latest American radio hits playing in the background make Pizza Bar a relaxing place to pass the evening. Pizzas 50-110Kč. Salads 40-95Kč. Cash only. ❶

SIGHTS

GREAT SYNAGOGUE (VELKÁ SYNAGOGA V PLZŇI). Long ago, leaders of the Jewish community in Plzeň determined that the plans for the synagogue too closely resembled a church, and ordered that the spires be lowered and that "Oriental" elements be introduced. It still vaguely resembles an exotic church, with its Moorish-style, onion-domed towers. Inside, the high, arched ceilings recall the best of high neo-Renaissance architecture, and the building plays host to a series of classical concerts each year. Post-Holocaust, regular services resumed in 1998, in the "Winter Synagogue" at the rear of the building. The synagogue also rotates small exhibitions of work by Jewish artists. *(From the southern end of nám. Republiky, go down Prešovská to Sady Pětatřicátníků and turn left; the synagogue is on the right. Concert info at www.synagogaconcerts.cz. Open Apr.-Sept. M-F and Su 10am-6pm; Oct. M-F and Su 10am-5pm; Nov. M-F and Su 10am-4pm. Closed for Jewish Holidays. 50Kč, students 30Kč.)*

PILSNER URQUELL BREWERY. In 1842, the over 30 independent brewers practicing their trade in Plzeň's beer cellars united to form the Pilsner Urquell Burghers' Brewery, hoping to create the best beer in the world. The result of that union was the legendary **Pilsner Urquell.** Walking through the huge gate and spotting the famous Prazdroj sign behind the billowing smoke, it's hard not to feel like you've entered beer heaven—or the Disneyworld of Beer. Knowledgeable guides explain the brewing process and lead visitors to the fermentation cellars for samples straight from the barrel. The cellars are chilly; bring a sweater. *(From nám. Republiky, follow Pražská east over the Radbuza River, where it becomes U Prazdroje; cross the street and take the pedestrian overpass. ☎06 28 88; www.beerworld.cz. 1¼hr. tours daily 12:30, 2, occasionally 4pm. Call ahead. 140Kč, students 70Kč. In large groups, every 21st person is free.)*

REPUBLIC SQUARE (NÁMĚSTÍ REPUBLIKY). Imperial dwellings loom over this marketplace, but none overshadow the **Cathedral of St. Bartholomew** (Katedrále sv. Bartoloměje), the country's tallest belfry. Inside, Gothic statues and altars lead to the stunning 14th-century statue Plzeňská Madona. Visitors can climb the 291 steps to the tower's observation deck for a dazzling view. *(Tours Apr.-Dec. W-Su 10am-4pm. Tower open daily 10am-6pm. 30Kč, students 20Kč.)* Head back into the square to see Plzeň's Renaissance town hall, topped by a golden clock. *(Nám. Republiky 39.)*

WATER TOWER COMPLEX. Head down Pražská from the square to reach the **water tower** (vodárenská véž), Pražká 19, which once stored the crystal-clear water necessary for fine beer. A 40min. tour of the tower and **Plzeň's underground** (Plzeňské podzemí) winds through the town's early beer cellars. *(Perlová 4. ☎22 52 14. Open June-Sept. Tu-Su 9am-5pm; Apr.-May and Oct.-Nov. W-Su 9am-5pm. Tours 30-40min.; last tour leaves 4:20pm. 50Kč, students 35Kč.)* Next door, the **Trigon Gallery** features works by recent and contemporary artists, with a free gallery of items for sale downstairs. *(Pražská 19. ☎377 328 621. Open M-F 8am-5pm. 10Kč, students 5Kč.)*

OTHER SIGHTS. The sprawling **Brewery Museum** (Pivovanské Muzeum) displays all things beer-related, from medieval taps to a coaster collection. Learn about the history of brewing through miniature brewing plants, reconstructed malt houses, chemical laboratories, and simulated pub environments. *(Veleslavínova 6. From the square, go down Pražská and turn left on Perlová, which ends at Veleslavínova. ☎377 235 574; fax 377 224 955. Open daily Apr.-Sept. 10am-6pm; Jan.-Mar. 10am-4pm. Free English brochure. 120Kč, students with ISIC 60Kč.)* The iron gate of the **Franciscan Church and Cloister** (Františkánský kostel a klášter) leads to a quiet garden with statues and ice cream vendors. Inside, the highlight is the 15th-century **Chapel of St. Barbara,** decorated with brilliant frescoes. *(Enter at Františkánská 11, south of nám. Republiky. Open M and W 9-11:45am and 2-5pm, Tu and Th-F 9-11:45am. 30Kč, students 15Kč.)* At the edge of Staré Město, stroll through the **Kopecký gardens** (Kopeckého sady) to the sound of performing brass brands. *(Františkánská runs into the park south of nám. Republiky.)*

NIGHTLIFE

Thanks to students from the University of West Bohemia, Plzeň has a great number of bars and late-night clubs. In **náměstí Republiky** and along **Smetanovy sady,** things heat up around 10:30pm.

21 Club, Prokopova 21 (☎22 08 60). Going south from nám. Republiky, turn left on Americká. At the McDonald's on the corner, turn right on Prokopova. The club is on the left. Downstairs, in a darkened cellar, actual Czechs actually dance—with abandon—to rock and roll with techno beats. Upstairs, purple lights swirl over the figured wood of one bar, while Renaissance- and Rococo-style paintings and figurines populate the second. Foosball and gambling in the back. A favorite of students looking for a wild night out. Open M-F 11am-3am, Sa 1pm-3am, Su 3-11pm. Cash only.

Jazz/Rock Cafe, Sedláčkova 18 (www.jazzrockcafe.cz). From the square, go down Solní and take the first left on Sedláčkova. Staying true to the Czech fascination with all things rock and roll, images of Aerosmith, Led Zeppelin, and Lou Reed cover the walls. Beer from 35Kč. The bar hosts regional bands for late night jam sessions regularly. Check website for shows. Open M-F 10am-4am, Sa 6pm-4am, Su 4pm-2am. Cash only.

Klub Alfa (☎606 842 526), at the intersection of Americká and Jungmannova. Stained-glass windows of saints overlook Alfa, which fills up after all but the most hard-core partiers have called it a night. In the basement, the rock club fills patrons up with death metal and liquor (Jim Beam 47Kč). Upstairs, the locals dance the night away in a gigantic ballroom. Open M-Th and Su 7:30pm-5am, F-Sa 7:30pm-6am. Cash only.

U Dominika, Dominikánská 3 (☎22 32 26), off nám. Republiky. Even during the middle of the day, hordes of people congregate in Dominika's large, open space just to sit, drink, and converse amid the leafy decor that makes the bar feel like a constant garden party. Stage in the back for rock and jazz shows. Open M-Th 10:30am-12:30am, F 10:30am-1am, Sa 11:30am-1am, Su 11:30am-midnight. Cash only.

KARLOVY VARY ☎353

From the bus station, Karlovy Vary (Kar-LOH-vee VAR-ee; pop. 60,000) doesn't look like much, but a stroll into the spa district reveals why Johann Sebastian Bach, Peter the Great, Sigmund Freud, and even Karl Marx frequented salons here. The town hosts mostly older, wealthy Germans and Russians seeking the springs' therapeutic powers, but many of Karlovy Vary's luxuries can be enjoyed for free.

TRANSPORTATION. The train station (☎91 31 45) is northwest of the center and has few connections. Trains run to Prague via Chomutov (5-6hr., 4-5 per day, 280Kč) and Berlin, GER (6-8hr., 1 per day, 1300Kč). Buses are more convenient. The bus station (☎50 45 16), on Západní, is closer to town; **buses** go to Plzeň (1¾hr., 10 per day, 80Kč) and Prague (2½hr., 10 per day, 120Kč). Buy tickets on board. **Local buses** pass through the main city stop on **Varšavská** (10Kč at the tabák, 15Kč on board) and run 4am-10pm. **Night buses** are infrequent. **Taxis** line the main bus stop (Varšavská) and the street in front of the train station. **Centrum Taxi,** Zeyerova 9 (☎22 32 36), has 24hr. service.

ORIENTATION AND PRACTICAL INFORMATION. Karlovy Vary is located at the confluence of two rivers. The commercial district lies below the **Ohře River,** and **T.G. Masaryka** leads to the **Teplá River.** The spa district, called **Kolonáda** (Colonnade), begins at **Hotel Thermal,** from which **Mlýnská nábreží** winds through the town's hot springs, changing its name to **Lázeňská, Tržiště,** and **Stará Louka** before ending at the **Grandhotel Pupp.** To reach the spa district from the train station, take bus #11 or 13 to the last stop. From there, it's 15min. downhill on foot. Cross the street and go right on Nákladní. Take the first left and cross **Ostrovský most** at the highway. Follow the Teplá to T.G. Masaryka, which leads to Hotel Thermal. To get to the center from the **bus station,** turn left and take the left fork of the pedestrian underpass, toward Lázně. Turn right at the next fork, following the sign for the supermarket, and go straight up the stairs to reach **T.G. Masaryka,** which runs parallel to **Dr. Davida Bechera,** the other main street.

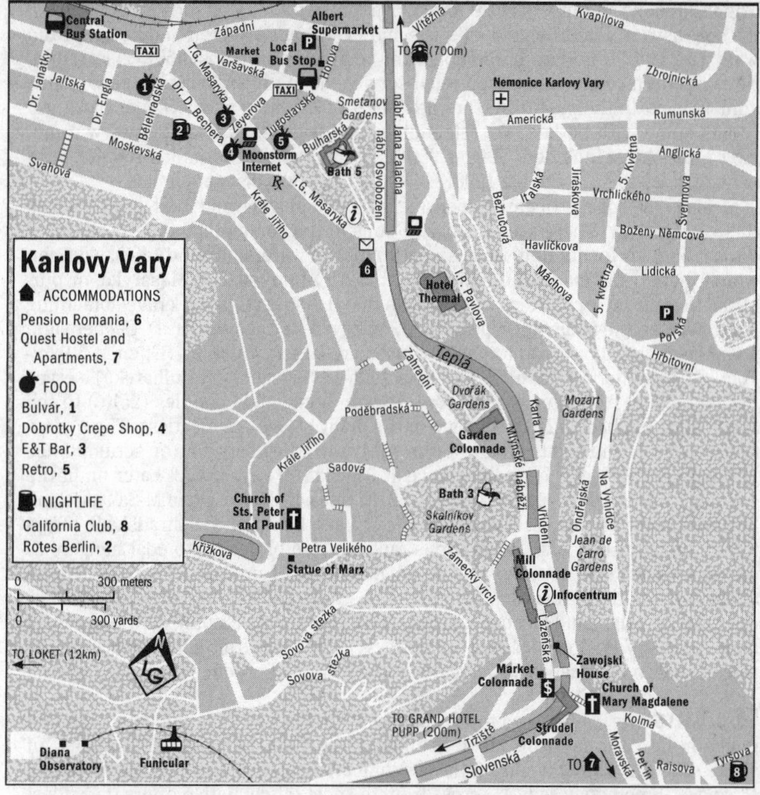

Pick up **maps** (110Kč), theater tickets (200-900Kč), and *Promenada* (15Kč), a monthly booklet with event schedules, at the **Infocentrum tourist office,** Lázeňská 1, which also **exchanges currency** for no commission. (☎353 224 097; www.karlovy-vary.cz. Open Jan.-Oct. M-F 8am-6pm, Sa-Su 10am-4pm; Nov.-Dec. M-F 7am-5pm.) **Komerční banka,** Tržištê 11, exchanges **traveler's checks** for 2% commission and has an **ATM** outside. (☎22 22 05. Open M-F 9am-noon and 1-5pm.) **Luggage storage** is at the train station. (15Kč per day, bags over 15kg 30Kč. Lockers 510Kč.) **Centralni Lékárna,** Dr. D. Bechera 3, is a **pharmacy.** (☎23 08 86. Open M-F 8am-6pm, Sa 8am-noon.) The **hospital,** Bezrucová 19 (☎11 51 11), is northwest of the spa district. Surf the Internet at the **Infocentrum** or at **Moonstorm,** T. G. Masaryka 31. (☎353 232 041. Internet 1Kč per min. Open M-F 9am-6pm, Sa 9am-noon.) The **post office,** T.G. Masaryka 1, offers **Western Union** and **Poste Restante** services. (☎16 11 07. Open M-F 7:30am-7pm, Sa 8am-1pm, Su 8am-noon.) **Postal Code:** 36001.

ACCOMMODATIONS AND FOOD. Budget accommodations are hard to come by in Karlovy Vary. During festival time in July, most rooms are booked four to five months in advance. **Infocentrum** books rooms (from 400Kč). Private agencies can also help you out. **City Info** is at the kiosk at T.G. Masaryka 9. (☎22 33 51). Open daily 10am-6pm. Singles in pensions from 630Kč; hotel doubles from 950Kč.) A quick bus ride out of the spa district will save you quite a few crowns. **Quest Hostel and Apartments ❷,** Moravská 42, offers apartments with bright kitchens and bunks with orange bedspreads. Although located 5min. from the spa district, a nearby grocery store and lively bar downstairs make up for the walk. (☎23 90 71. Bed in shared apartment including breakfast 450Kč.) For luxurious, modern rooms and exceptional service, head to **Pension Romania ❹**, Zahradní 49, next to the post office on the corner of Zahradní and T.G. Masaryka. All rooms come with baths, TVs, telephones, and fridges. (☎22 28 22; www.romania.cz. Breakfast included. Singles 950Kč, students 715Kč; doubles 1580Kč, with view of river 1680Kč; triples 1900Kč. Oct.-Mar. 15-30% discount.)

Meals in the spa district are expensive, but the ambience and food may be worth the extra money. There are cheaper options in the commercial district. Karlovy Vary is known for its delicious, sweet *oplatky* (wafers; around 6Kč). You can watch them being made at the kiosk next to City Info, on T.G. Masaryka, or purchase them from any of the vendors who line the streets. If you crave something even sweeter, the **Dobrotky Crepe Shop ❶**, on Zeyerova between Dr. D. Bechera and T.G. Masaryka, allows you to design your own dessert for 35Kč. (Open M-F 9am-7pm, Sa 10am-noon.) **Retro ❸**, T.G. Masaryka 18 (entrance on Bulharská), serves dishes ranging from chicken *consomme* with homemade noodles (25Kč) to the "maxi steak on beer" (279Kč). Some of the many salads are meatless. The restaurant becomes a hip nightspot as the sun goes down. Regulars dine on scrumptious, hearty Czech fare at the lovely terrace at **E&T Bar ❷**, Zeyerova 3. Later on in the evening, the beer flows freely. (☎22 60 22. Entrees 40-210Kč. Open M-Sa 9am-2am, Su 10am-2am.) The funkiest cafe in Karlovy Vary, **Bulvár ❹**, Bélehradská 9, offers international dishes amid decorations ranging from birdcages to coat hangers to oxcarts. (☎585 199. Entrees 40-300Kč. Open daily 11am-2am.) There is also an **Albert** supermarket, Horova 1, behind the bus stop. Look for the *Městská trznice* (city market) sign, and be sure to bring a 5Kč coin for a shopping cart. (Open M-F 6am-7pm, Sa 7am-5pm, Su 9am-5pm. MC/V.) For fresh fruit and vegetables, the row of stalls on **Varnšavská** provides a good selection of produce fresh off the farm.

SIGHTS. As in every spa town, sightseeing in Karlovy Vary involves self-indulgence in its various forms. Just strolling along Mlýnské nábř. offers plenty of sights. The **spa district** begins with the manicured gardens of the Victorian **Bath 5** (Lázně 5), Smetanovy sady 1, across from the post office. Bath 5 offers the widest selection and most affordable treatments in town. Among these delights are thermal baths (355Kč), underwater massages (360-600Kč), paraffin hand treatments (255Kč), and the mysterious mouth irrigation (200Kč). More arcane procedures include iodine baths (390Kč) and "lymph drainage by hand" (600Kč); these are available, however, only with a doctor's prescription or a solemn declaration of illness. (☎22 25 36; www.spa5.cz. Pool and sauna open M-F 8am-9pm, Sa 8am-6pm, Su 10am-6pm. 90Kč. Treatments M-F 7am-3pm; select treatments Sa 7am-noon. Reserve 1-2 days in advance. MC/V.) After crossing the bridge on T.G. Masaryka, turn right, and continue along the river. The path crosses back over the Teplá and leads through the **Dvořák Gardens** to the Victorian **Garden Colonnade.** Here, you can sip the supposedly curative waters of the **Snake Spring** from a serpent's mouth. During the summer, the Colonnade also hosts free outdoor **concerts.** (Daily 2-3:30pm). **Bath 3,** at Mlýnské nábř. 5, offers massages as well as other, more exotic treatments. (☎22 56 41; www.lazneIII.cz. Treatments daily 7-11:30am and noon-3pm. Pool and sauna open M, W, and F 7am-2:30pm for women; Tu, Th and Sa 7am-noon for men. 150Kč. Full body massage 550Kč. Moor Mineral Bath 420Kč.) Next door, the Greek-inspired **Mill Colonnade** shelters five separate springs with water that tastes less pungent than that of its neighbors. Farther along, the former **market** appears by the white **Market Colonnade,** with two more springs. The modernist **Strudel Colonnade,** a massive iron-and-glass building, looms next door. Inside, springs flow like faucets next to clothing stores and souvenir shops; the impressive **Strudel Spring** spouts 30L of water per second at 72°C. (Open daily 6am-7pm.)

At the end of Stará Louka is **Grandhotel Pupp,** founded in 1774 by Johann Georg Pupp. From the right side of the hotel, follow the walkway Mariánská to the funicular, which leads to the **Diana Observatory** and a great view of the city and surrounding forest. (Funicular runs 4 per hr. June-Sept. 9:15am-6:45pm; Oct. and Apr.-May 9:15am-5:45pm; Feb.-Mar. and Nov.-Dec. 9:15am-4:15pm. 50Kč, round-trip 70Kč. Tower open daily 9am-7pm. Free.) To return to town, either take the funicular back down or walk through the wooded paths of Petra Velikého, ending at a statue of **Karl Marx** that commerates Marx's visits to the bourgeois spa between 1874 and 1876. Ironically, the statue stands at the border of one of the most expensive parts of town. Around the corner on Krále Jiřího, the domes of the 19th-century, Russian Orthodox **Church of Saints Peter and Paul** can be seen over the treetops.

ENTERTAINMENT AND NIGHTLIFE. *Promenáda* (15Kč), a brochure available at the tourist office, lists the month's concerts and performances and includes info for Karlovy Vary's **International Film Festival,** held in July, which screens independent films from all over the globe. A pass to see five films per day is sold inside **Hotel Thermal,** the festival's center. Tickets go quickly; get to the box office early. Kiosks lining Mlýnské nábř also sells tickets. Otherwise, remainders can be purchased 1hr. before each showing.

Like its restaurants, Karlovy Vary's nightlife is geared toward older tourists. Though clubs are sparse, expensive cafes abound. Both **E&T** and **Retro** host rotating parties—check the flyers outside. **Rotes Berlin,** Jaltská 7, off D. Bechera, seems to attract every young person in Karlovy Vary to its seductive red interior. (☎23 37 92. Beer from 15Kč. Mixed drinks 35-70Kč. Live DJs most nights. Open M-F noon-2am, Sa-Su 3pm-2am.) It's a steep hike up Kolmá from behind the Church of Mary Magdalene to **California Club,** Tyrsova 2, but the late hours and hot dancing make it worth the trek. (☎173 222 087. Beer from 15Kč. Open daily 1pm-5am.)

DAYTRIP FROM KARLOVY VARY: LOKET

Although it lacks the glamor of its neighbor, weary travelers may find Loket's sumptuous budget accommodations and the nearby Svatošske Skálly Nature Preserve even more curative than Karlovy Vary's waters. Loket, Czech for "elbow," is cradled on three sides by Ohřē River; the town dates back to the 12th century. Its sights—most notably the castle and Baroque church—can be seen in a day, but Loket's bargain rooms make it worth spending a night. From the tourist office go 15m towards the center, then turn left and follow the signs to Loket's **castle,** which also dates back to the 12th century; it was used as a prison, however, up through the mid-20th century. Visitors can climb to the top of its tower for a remarkable view of the surrounding valley. (Open daily Apr.-Oct. 9am-4:30pm; Nov.-Mar. 9am-3:30pm. Tours 90Kč, students 60Kč. With text 80/45Kč. Photography 20Kč.) The town's original Gothic church burned down in 1725, and on its surviving foundation a baroque masterpiece was built. The **Church of St. Wenceslas** contains a magnificently carved altar and frescoes. (Open M-Sa 9am-5pm. Free.) Deep within the Svatošske Skálly Nature Preserve are the **Svatošske Skálly** (Svatošske Rocks). This unusual cluster of soaring stone columns in a secluded valley is breathtaking. Legend has it that the rocks were a wedding procession that was turned to stone.

Loket's slew of pensions offers fairly luxurious rooms for a fraction of the standard Karlovy Vary price. One standout is **Penzion Jan Hála ❸,** TGM 115. Festively painted walls, sparkling tiled bathrooms, and TVs round out the spacious rooms. (☎352 684 440. Single 400Kč; doubles 750Kč.) The Czech meals served by its handful of restaurants are also noteworthy. **Švjek Restaurace ❸,** T.G.M. 134, serves up heaping portions of traditional fare. (☎252 331 401. English menu.

Entrees 60-200Kč. Pilsner Urquell 30Kč. Open daily 10am-11pm. Cash only). For a truly memorable meal, hoof it or bike the 7km path leading to **Svatošske Skálly,** and dine at **Lesní Restaurace Svatošske Skálly ❺,** where the breathtaking location overlooking the valley's steep rock pillars more than justifies the cost. (☎353 332 595. Entrees 125-400Kč. Open daily 11am-10pm. Cash only.)

Loket can be reached by **bus** from Karlovy Vary (11 per day; 20Kč). To get to the center from the bus, cross the street and follow the bridge over the river until you reach **Trída TGMA,** the town's center. The **Tourist Infocentrum,** TGM 12, has a friendly English-speaking staff that can provide you with **maps** (40-60Kč), book accomodations, and give information about the Svatošske Skállyy Nature Preserve. **Internet** access is available for 5Kč per 15min. (☎352 684 123; infoloket@volny.cz. Open daily 10:30am-12:30pm and 1-6pm.) A **Bankomat ATM** is located at 107 TCM. A **Pharmacy, Lekárna,** 95 TCM, is nearby. (☎352 684 037. Open M-F 8am-noon and 1pm-4:30pm.) The **post office,** 99 TCM, provides **Western Union** services. (Open M-F 8-11am and 1-6pm, Sa 8-10am.)

SOUTH BOHEMIA

Truly a rustic Eden, South Bohemia's hills make the region a favorite among Czech cyclists and hikers, who flock to the countryside to traipse through castles, observe wildlife in virgin forests, and guzzle Budvar from the source.

ČESKÉ BUDĚJOVICE ☎38

České Budějovice (CHES-kay BOO-dyeh-yoh-vee-tseh; pop. 97,000), deep in the heart of the Bohemian countryside, is a great base for exploring the surrounding region. It lacks the old-world charm of Český Krumlov but boasts a beautiful town square and a relative absence of tourists. Home to the great Budvar brewery, the city houses a multitude of pubs in which beer flows freely—quite helpful, since it may take a stein before you can pronounce the town's name.

CZECH REPUBLIC

TRANSPORTATION. The **train station** is at Nadražní 12. (☎785 4490. Info office open daily 6:30am-6:30pm. Ticket booths open daily 3:45am-midnight.) **Trains** run to: Brno (4½hr., 5 per day, 274Kč); Český Krumlov (50min., 9 per day, 46Kč); Plzeň (2hr., 9 per day, 162Kč); Prague (2½hr., 13 per day, 204Kč); Milan, ITA (2330Kč); Munich, GER (1494Kč); Rome, ITA (3201Kč). **Buses** run from Žizkova, around the bend from the train station. (☎635 4444. Info office open M-F 5:30-10:15am and 10:45am-6:30pm, Sa 8am-noon, Su 8-11:30am.) Destinations include: Brno (4½hr., 6 per day, 220 Kč); Český Krumlov (50min., 22 per day, 28Kč); Plzeň (2¾hr., 1 per day, 110-140Kč); Prague (2½hr., 10 per day, 120-144Kč), Milan, ITA (14hr., 2 per wk., 2100Kč); Munich, GER (4½hr., 4 per week, 1000Kč). Explore České Budějovice by **bus** and **trolley** (info ☎635 8 116). Buy tickets (10Kč per 1 bus, 12Kč per transfer) at the tourist office, kiosks, *tabáky*, or machines by bus stands. Punch them on board. Buses run only on the major roads that encircle the city center (Na Sadech, Lidická tř., Rudolfovská tř., Husova tř.). You get 20min. per ticket; those who try to cheat the system are frequently caught by undercover officers and face stiff faces. For a **taxi,** call **Taxi-Budějovice** (☎800 141 516).

ORIENTATION AND PRACTICAL INFORMATION. Staré Mêsto (Old Town) centers on the gigantic **náměsti Přemysla Otakara II.** From the train station, turn right on **Nadražní** and hang a left at the first crosswalk on the pedestrian **Lannova třída.** This stretch of road, which becomes **Kanovnická** after the canal, meets the northeast corner of nám. Otakara II. The **bus station** is on **Žižkova.** To get to the center from the bus station, turn left on Žižkova and then right on **Jeronýmova.** Go left on Lannova třída, which leads to the center.

The **Turistické Informační Centrum (TIC)** is at nám. Otakara II 2. (☎680 1413; www.c-budejovice.cz. English spoken. Open M-F 8:30am-6pm, Sa 8:30am-5pm, Su 10am-noon and 12:30-4pm.) **CTS Travel Services,** nám. Otakara II 38, cashes **traveler's checks** for a 0.8% commission. (☎636 0543. Open M-F 8:45am-12:15pm and 12:45-4:45pm.) MasterCard and Visa **ATMs** line nám. Otakara II. **Luggage storage** is along the right wall of the train station. (12Kč per day, bags over 15kg 25Kč per day. Lockers 12Kč per day. Be sure to set the combination on the inside of the locker door before you shut it. Open daily 4:45-10:55am and 11:25am-8pm.) **Omikron,** nám. Otakara II 25, has a small selection of English-language books, maps, and newspapers. (☎077 46 68 34 57. Open M-F 8am-6pm, Sa 8am-noon.) Other services include: **emergency** ☎787 890; a **pharmacy** at nám. Otakara II 26 (☎635 3063; open M-F 8am-6pm); and a **hospital,** B. Nemcove 54 (☎787 1111). **Na Půdě Internetovy Klub,** Krajinská 28, has flat-screen computers and fast connections. (☎731 3529; www.napude.cz. 15Kč per 15min. Open daily 9am-10pm. MC/V.) **3D-Arena,** 48 Lannova třída, also houses a number of fast computers with even faster connections. (☎72 53 48 00. 1Kč per min or 200Kč per 4½hr. Open daily 9am-9pm.) The **post office,** nám. Senovázné 1, is the large pink-and-yellow building to the south, on Lannova as it enters Staré Mêsto. **Poste Restante** available at windows #12 and 13. (☎773 4122. Open M-F 7am-7pm, Sa 8am-noon.) The store in the post office sells international calling cards. **Postal Code:** 37001.

ACCOMMODATIONS. Hostels are scarce in České Budějovice, but smaller, more personal pensions are plentiful. To get to the **AT Penzion ❸,** Dukelská 15, head right on Dr. Stejskala from nám. Otakara II. Turn left at the first intersection and follow Široká, veering right on Dukelská. Go straight, well beyond the yellow museum on your left. Private baths, well-furnished rooms, and friendly English-speaking family management make this residential pension worth the extra crowns. (☎/fax 635 1598. Breakfast 50Kč. Book in advance during summer. Singles 500Kč; doubles 800Kč. Cash only.) If AT Penzion is full, visit **Alton Hotýlek ❸,** Na Nábřeží 14, an equally attractive lodging operated by the same family. To reach it, continue down Dukelská until you reach Havickova. Turn right, then left at the river, following the path until you reach the pension. (☎602 421 004; www.altonhotylek.cz. Breakfast 100Kč. Singles 650Kč; Doubles 750Kč. Cash only.)

FOOD. The main streets of nám. Otakara II and their offshoots house numerous restaurants. It's very easy to find a table on a terrace, a giant glass of

BREW HA-HA

Befuddled tourists visiting the Czech factory of the allegedly all American Budweiser aren't alone in their confusion. In fact, they've stumbled upon one of the world's longest standing legal battles who has the right to use the Budweiser name on their product.

The American version, first bottled under the name in 1876 reminded its brewer, Adolphus Busch, of the lagers from his German homeland; he therefore gave his beer a distinctly German name. While the Czech version received the name in 1895, the beer had been brewed in Budějovice since the 14th century. Initially, the identically titled beers did not compete with one another. But the increasing popularity of both products has led to heated court battles across the globe. The Czech version, banned in the US by a 1939 agreement has won out in much of the rest of the world. In Germany, Budweiser Budvar has rights to the name and Anheuser-Busch must sell its products under a different name In the UK, both companies have been permitted to hawk their products under the Budweiser name, leading to quite a bit of confusion. Needless to say, while in the Czech Republic, there is nary an American Budweiser in the land-and asking for it will no endear you to Czechs.

world-renowned beer, and a plate heaped with inexpensive but filling Czech cuisine. Vegetarian and non-native cuisines can be found in the streets and alleyways off the main square. The grocery store **Ovoce a Zelenina Nedorost,** Dr. Stejskala 8, off nám. Otakara II, has a remarkably wide selection of fresh fruits and vegetables, as well as a bakery. (☎635 6048. Open M-F 7:30am-6pm, Sat 7am-noon.) **Albert Supermarket,** 56 Lannova třída, near the McDonald's, offers a more complete selection of dry goods. (Open M-F 7:30am-7pm, Sa. 7:30am-1:30pm. MC/V.) **Zeleninovy Bar** ❶ (Vegetable Bar), nám. Otakara II 2, is through the tunnel next to the pharmacy, behind a courtyard. This tiny, cafeteria-style restaurant is a great budget option and a haven for health-food lovers and vegetarians. (☎72 16 11 83. Open M-F 8am-6pm. Cash only.) **Pranenka Cukrovinky ❶,** 4 Lannova třída, offers a mouthwatering selection of fresh-baked pastries (9.50-20Kč) and ice cream (7Kč). It also carries a wide range of wine and liquor. (Open M-F 9am-5:30pm, Sa 8am-1pm. Cash only.) At **Restaurace Kněžská ❷,** Kněžská 1, locals chat with the bartender at unadorned tables. "Jagersteak" (sirloin, cream, champignons; 249Kč), is a pricey treat. Excellent margherita pizza (50Kč) and garlic soup (25Kč) are cheaper options. (☎635 8829. Entrees 25-249Kč. Open M-Th 10am-11pm, F 10am-midnight, Sa 11am-midnight. Cash only.) When you're sick of eating like a backpacker, head to **Restaurace u Královské at the Hotel Malý Pivovar ❸,** Karla IV 8-10. Just off nám. Otakara II, Hotel Malý Pivovar's lobby, the restauarant serves classy cuisine that won't break the bank; the menu also contains a huge wine list. (☎636 0471. Entrees 35-200Kč. Dress code. Open daily 7-10am, 11am-2pm, and 6-11pm. Cash only.)

SIGHTS. Budvar Brewery, Karoliny Světlé 4, is a must. Multilingual guides are remarkably knowledgeable about Budvar's brewing process. Bring a water bottle; the women doling out at the tasting station will be more than happy to fill it for you. (Take bus #2 toward Nemcance from anywhere on Na Sadech. Get off at the Budvar stop. ☎770 5341; www.budvar.cz. English tours M-F at 2:00pm. Call ahead to join a group touring 9am-4pm. Tasting tours in Czech 60Kč, students 30Kč; in English 100/50Kč. AmEx/V.) Surrounded by colorful Renaissance and Baroque architecture, **náměsti Otakara II** encompasses over one hectare of cobblestone. The early 18th-century Baroque **town hall** rises a full story above the square's other buildings. The ornate 1726 **Samson's Fountain** stands in the center of the square, making it a great orientation point. Samson's right eye looks across the square to the 72m **Black Tower**, at the intersection of Hroznová and Černé véze. The balcony offers panoramic views of České Budějovice and environs, including Brno, nám. Otakara II, and the scenic cooling towers of the nearby nuclear power plant. Four maps on the parapet describe the view. Visitors should exercise caution as the low ceilings can prove to be a little tricky. (☎635 2508. Open daily 10am-6pm; last climb 5:45pm. The climb up is free, but the balcony is 20Kč.) The tower once served as a belfry for the neighboring 17th-century Baroque **Cathedral of St. Nicholas.** Choral and orchestral concerts now make use of the cathedral's acoustics; check the posted schedules. (Open daily 7am-6pm.) České Budějovice's other famous place of worship is the **Cloister Church of the Sacrifice of the Virgin Mary** located in historic nám. Piaristické. The cobbled square and small courtyard garden offer a respite from the more touristed main square. (☎731 1263. Open M-Th 2-6pm, Su 9:30-11:30am. 10Kč.) **The Museum of Motorcycles** (Jihočeské Motocyklové Muzeum) stands next door to the Panny Marie complex. The more than 100 bikes on display provide a thorough history of motorcycle production, from the early 20th century to the present. The collection of WWII-era bikes is particularly impressive. (☎723 247 104. Open Tu-Su 10am-6pm. 40Kč, students 20Kč.)

NIGHTLIFE. České Budějovice is more of a pubbing than a clubbing town. The restaurants that line the cobblestone streets of the town center serve beer late into the night, but the hidden pubs on the upper floors of the buildings overlooking **náměsti Otakara II** are the best places to taste local brews. Watch for signs on the street or sidewalk that point to the action. **Club B-26,** Sokolská 61, facing the nám on the third floor, is the happening place for both locals and travelers. Enjoy a Cuba Libre (50Kč) out on the terrace, or pull up a barstool to watch one of the flat-screen televisions on the walls. (☎741 5022. Open M-Th 3pm-midnight, F 3pm-2am, Sa 5pm-2am.) From the nám. go down Radniční, then through the small covered alley on the left of the fork. Cross the river and turn right through the small park to get to **K2,** Sokolský ostrov 1, next to Plavecký Stadion. This could be a dance/rock club anywhere in the world if it weren't for the Soviet-era car inexplicably parked in the back of the room. (☎70 65 48 91. Th Oldies, F Rock Night, Sa concerts and DJs. Cover 30-60Kč. Open M-Tu and Th-Sa 9pm-3am. Cash only.) Posters around town also advertise summertime open-air **concerts** around the lakes, including the **Emmy Destinn International Music Festival** in late August and the **Kytaravy Festival Na Dvanacti Strunach** (Guitar Music Festival) in late June. Call the TIC for tickets.

BIKING AT NIGHT. Public transport shuts down early in smaller Czech towns, but if you've rented a bike, think twice before riding it back at night. Czechs seriously regulate biking: you must have a red rear light, flashing white front light, and wheel reflectors. More importantly, biking under the influence is prohibited, and those found guilty of doing so can be fined up to 15,000Kč.

ČESKÝ KRUMLOV ☎38

This once-hidden gem of the Czech Republic has been discovered—some might say besieged—by tourists seeking refuge from Prague's hectic pace and overcrowded streets. Český Krumlov (CHES-kee KRUM-loff) won't disappoint those who take the time to explore its medieval streets, raft down the meandering Vltava, and admire the enormous 13th-century castle, gorgeously lit at night. This UNESCO-protected town has countryside charm and beautiful surrounding hills. Apart from hiking, horseback riding, and kayaking, the town lures visitors with its affordable accommodations and burgeoning nightlife.

TRANSPORTATION

Trains: Nádrazní 31 (☎755 1111), 2km uphill from the center. Trains go to: České Budějovice (1hr., 8 per day, 46Kč) and Prague (2½hr., 5 per day, 224Kč). A bus runs from the station to the center of town (5Kč). The train station in **Linz, AUT** offers international connections to **Bratislava, SLK; Budapest HUN; Munich GER;** and **Salzburg** and **Vienna AUT.** Lobo runs a bus to the station 3x daily. (☎071 3153. www.shuttlelobo.cz. Daily at 9, 11am, and 2pm; 1½hr.)

Buses: Kaplická 439 (☎380 715 415). Buses run to **České Budějovice** (30min.; M-F 26 per day, Sa-Su 14 per day; 28Kč) and **Prague** (3hr.; M-F 5 per day, Sa-Su 6 per day; 130-145Kč). **Taxis:** call **Krumlov Taxi** (☎380 712 712) or catch one in nám. Svornosti.

ORIENTATION AND PRACTICAL INFORMATION

The curves of the **Vltava River** cradle the central square, **náměstí Svornosti.** The main **bus station** is on **Kaplická,** east of the square. To reach the square from the bus station, take the path behind the terminal to the right of stops #20-25. Go downhill from the intersection with Kaplická. At the light, cross the highway and go straight on **Horní,** which leads into the square. If you get off the bus at the **Špičák** stop north of town, it's an easy downhill walk to the center. From Špičák, take the overpass, walk through **Budějovice Gate,** and follow **Latrán** past the castle and over the Vltava. It becomes **Radniční** as it enters Staré Město and leads to nám. Svornosti.

Tourist Office: nám. Svornosti 2 (☎071 1183; www.ckrumlov.cz/infocentrum). Books accommodations, sells trail **maps** (25-140Kč), and rents audio tours (1hr. 100Kč, students 80Kč; 2hr. 150/100Kč; 3hr. 180/120Kč; each additional hr. 30/20Kč; 500Kč deposit). Also arranges passenger transport (car and minibus) to: Budapest, HUN, Linz, Munich, GER, Prague, Salzburg, AUT and Vienna, AUT. DHL services. Bus and train listings are on the wall across from the front desk. Internet access 5Kč per min., min. 10Kč. Open M-Sa 9am-1pm and 2-7pm.

Currency Exchange: Oberbank, Panská 22 (☎071 2221), cashes **traveler's checks** for 0.75% commission (100Kč minimum). Exchanges cash for 1.5% commission (min. 30Kč.) Open M, W, and F 8:30am-5pm; Tu and Th 8:30am-4pm. There is a 24hr. MC/V **ATM** on the left side of Horní, just before nám. Svornosti. Another is on the right side of Latrán and Radniční, just outside the square.

Luggage Storage: At the train station, across from the ticket booths. 15Kč per day, bags over 15kg 20Kč per day. Open daily 6:15am-7:15pm. The tourist information center will also store bags for 10Kč per day.

English-Language Bookstore: Shakespeare and Sons (Shakespeare á Synové), Soukenická 44 (☎271 740 839; www.shakes.cz). An excellent selection of new and used books in English from 30Kč. Also carries a good selection of German, French, and Spanish works. Open daily 11am-7pm.

Laundromat: Lobo, Latrán 73 (☎071 3153; www.pensionlobo.cz), part of the Lobo Pension. Wash 100Kč, dry 10Kč per 10min.; detergent and fabric softener included. Open M-F 9am-noon and 1-4pm, Sa 9-11am.

Emergency: ☎158 or 0 717 646.

Pharmacy: nám. Svornosti 16 (☎071 1787). Open M-F 8am-noon and 1-4pm.

Hospital: Horní Braná, Hřbitovní 424 (☎037 8396), behind the bus station.

Telephones: Card-operated phones are located in the nám., around the corner from the post office on Pivovarská and near Krumlov House. Buy cards inside or at local *tábaky*.

Internet: At the **tourist offices** at nám. Svornosti (DIAC) and at the castle. No chairs at nám. Svornosti location. **Internet Café,** Zámek 57 (☎0 712 219), in the same building as the castle tourist office. 1Kč per min. Open daily 9am-8pm. **VLTAVA,** Kájovská 62. Enter at the left side, toward Café Retro. 1Kč per min. Open M-F 9am-5pm.

Post Office: Latrán 193 (☎071 6610). **Poste Restante** at window #2 on the right. Open M-F 7am-6pm, Sa 8am-noon. **Postal Code:** 38101.

ACCOMMODATIONS

Krumlov's stellar hostels offer the best deals in town. They fill up fast in summer, so make reservations at least four days in advance. Small **pensions** offer a relaxed atmosphere; look for *Zimmer frei* signs on Parkán, or contact the tourist office.

Krumlov House, Rooseveltova 68 (☎071 1935, mobile 72 82 87 19; www.krumlovhostel.com). From nám. Svornosti, turn left on Rooseveltova and follow the signs. Founded, owned, and operated by backpackers, this hostel is highly communal and cost-effective. Spacious dorms and clean bathrooms. English-speaking staff arranges everything from massages to horseback riding. Free inner tubes in summer and skates in winter. Laundry in summer 150Kč per 5kg. Book a week in advance during high season (Apr. 1-Oct. 31). High season 6-bed dorms 300Kč; doubles 400, with bath 450Kč. Low season 250/350/400Kč. 7th night free. MC/V. ❶

Accomodation Ubytování, Zámecké Schody 12 (☎712 335; www.ubytovani-kozakova.cz). As you pass through the first courtyard on your way to the castle, turn down the alley on the left. Halfway down the stairs, Ubytovani offers spotless, bright rooms equipped with private baths, satellite television, and minibars. An unbeatable location,

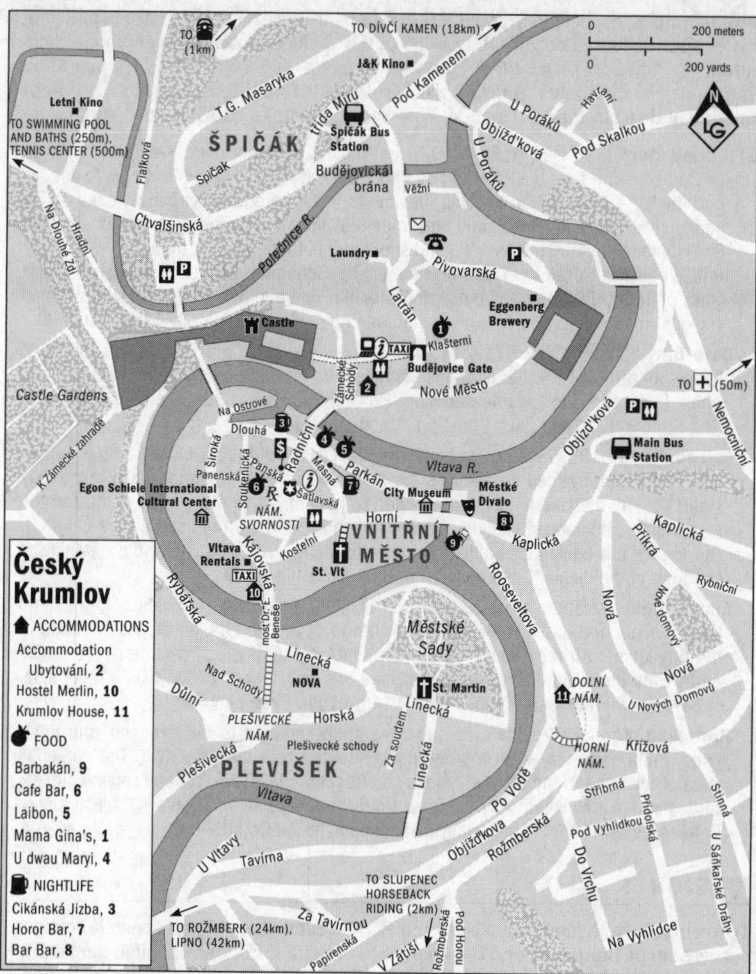

steps from the castle and only a short walk from the nam., seals the deal. Apr.1-Oct. 31 singles 600Kč; doubles 900Kč; Nov. 1-Mar. 31 500/800Kč. Cash only. ❸

Hostel Merlin, Kájovská 59 (☎602 432 747; www.hostelmerlin.com). From nám. Svornosti, go left on Kájovská. Merlin is on the right before the bridge. Private and relaxing hostel. Free coffee 24hr. Balcony and backyard. Free inner tubes in summer and free skates in winter. 10% off raft, canoe and kayak rentals at VLTAVA. Free Internet 8am-8pm (30min. limit). Reception daily 11am-8pm. Check-out 10am. Book well in advance. One bed in shared room 250Kč; doubles 500Kč, with bath 660Kč. Cash only. ❶

FOOD

While many restaurants pander to tourists, a few serve quality, distinctive fare. Český Krumlov is home to the oldest cuisine in Bohemia, so medieval-style food is everywhere. There is also an ever-increasing presence of international and vegetarian options, especially in Staré Město. There are several grocery stores in Krumlov proper: **Jednota Potraviny,** Latrán 55 (☎047 2830; open M-F 7am-6pm, Sa 8am-noon, Su 9am-2pm), and **NOVA Potraviny,** Linecká 49. (☎607 915 911; open M-Sa 7am-7pm, Su 7am-5pm). **Zdravá Výziva,** Trída Míru 135, offers a good selection of organic and vegan foods. (Open M, W, F 9am-5:30pm; Tu and Th 9am-4:30pm.)

U dwau Maryi (Two Marys), Parkán 104 (☎071 7228). From nám. Svornosti, turn right on Radniční and take the 2nd right on Parkán. U dawu Maryi labors to be as faithful as possible to old Bohemian cooking, basing its flavor palette on cabbage, eggs, fruits, honey, legumes, milk, millet, and mushrooms. Waitstaff in period dress speak excellent English, laugh among themselves, and shout orders to the kitchen through a hole in the wall. Vegetarian options. Wash down your Old Bohemian Feast (140-175Kč) with a glass of mead (50Kč) on the patio alongside the waters of the Vltava. Delicious "rolled cookies" made with raisins, brown sugar, and nuts 20Kč. Open daily 11am-11pm. ❷

Cafe Bar, Pánska 17 (☎071 2785). This quiet, modern Cafe Bar just off the nám. boasts an atmosphere that is at once familial and hip. Jazz music in the back terrace, which is excellent for people-watching. Excellent espresso. 39Kč gets you the filling "Big Sandwich." Open daily 9pm-9pm. Cash only. ❶

Laibon, Parkán 105. Vegetarians wandering the Czech lands can rejoice: though Laibon has the customary fried cheese, it's the more complex delights that make this eatery stand out. Try the *Labyrint Chuti* (Labyrinth of Tastes), a sampler platter of most of the restaurant's specialties, including lentil-, hummus-, and carrot-based dishes (149Kč). The terrace out back goes all the way down to the river; sit and enjoy your meal in the shadows of the castle. Open daily 10am-10pm. Cash only. ❷

Mama Ginas, Klašterní Ulíce 52 (☎337 717 181), from nam. turn right onto Klašterní Ulíce. Locals and in-the-know tourists gather to devour the Italian dishes prepared in the tiny kitchen. If they aren't full, grab a seat on one of the streetside picnic tables and try the Pizza Giardiniera with mozzarella and artichokes (120Kč). On a quiet side-street near the monastery. Open daily 11am-11pm. Cash only. ❷

Barbakán, Kaplická 26, halfway down the stairs heading to the river, on your right. Long, multi-party tables on a stone patio situated high over the river. The gorgeous vista of foliage and the town will make you forget the less-than-speedy service. Adventurous eaters may want to try the River Trout—head and all—with butter. English menu. Entrees run 85-195Kč. Open daily 11am-midnight. AmEx/MC/V. ❸

SIGHTS

Towering above Krumlov since the 1200s, the **Castle** *(Zamek)* has been home to a succession of Bohemian and Bavarian noble families. Follow Radniční across the river to the castle's main entrance on Latrán. As you follow the crowds up the hill from the nám., note the gigantic stone bears in the moat as you cross the bridge. The first stone courtyard you enter includes the TIC, an Internet cafe, bathrooms, the Lapidarium, the dungeon, and an art gallery *(sloupova sín)*. The second courtyard, off a ramp after the moat, includes the castle's box office, the information center, the **Castle Tower** (Zámecká Vez), and a second art gallery (Máselnice). Route of the Castle tours I and II begin in the third courtyard, which is smaller and surrounded by tourist covered benches. The fourth courtyard houses the Baroque **Castle Theater** (Zámecké Divadlo), a registered UNESCO World Heritage site. Fifth and last are the also-Baroque **Castle Gardens** *(Zámecká Zahrada)*, followed by Krumlov's **Revolving Theater.** (*Otáčivé Hlediště.* Garden open daily June-Aug. 8am-7pm; Sept. and May 8am-6pm; Oct. and Apr. 8am-5pm. Free.)

Routes of the Castle I and II each last an hour. **Route I** covers the castle chapel, its Baroque rooms, and Eggenberg Hall, in which stands a giant gilded coach that was used exactly once, to deliver gifts to the pope. The tour concludes amid the festive excess of the frescoed **Masquerade Hall,** where concerts are still held. **Route II** moves through the Schwarzenbergs' portrait gallery and showcases their 19th-century suites. Both tours depart from the third stone courtyard. Tickets are sold at the **box office** in the second courtyard. (☎070 4721. Open daily June-Aug. 8:45am-5pm; Sept.-Oct. and Apr.-May 8:45am-4pm; last tour 1hr. before closing. Tour in Czech 100Kč, students 50Kč; in English 160/80Kč. MC/V.) Tours of the **Castle Theater** are approximately 40min, and English-language tours are recommended. (Open daily May-Oct. 10-11am and 1-4pm. Tour in Czech 100Kč, students 50Kč; in English 180/90Kč. All tours incur a 10% service fee for reservations, and a 100% service fee for tours scheduled outside of regular hours.) Make your way up the **Castle Tower** for an eyeful of medieval and Renaissance architecture, cradled among the hills and dales surrounding Krumlov. (Open daily June-Aug. 9am-5:30pm; Sept.-Oct. and Apr.-May 9am-4:30pm. 35Kč, students and children 20Kč.) Down from the heights and into the depths, the **Labyrinth of Castle Cellars** has been transformed into a gallery of ceramic art. Most pieces are for sale. Ambient music wafts through the chilly rooms. (Open daily 10am-5pm. 50Kč.)

Across the bridge from the castle, the **Egon Schiele Art Center** (Egon Schiele Art Centrum), Široká 70-72, highlights the work of the Austrian painter Egon Schiele (1890-1918), who set up shop in Krumlov in 1911. The citizens ran him out of town, however, when he started painting burghers' daughters and local prostitutes in the nude. Although the Schiele exhibit only takes up about half of one of the floors of the Art Center, biographical information and artifacts make this a stellar tribute. The rest of the museum is devoted to his Expressionist contemporaries. (☎070 4011; www.schieleartcentrum.cz. Open daily 10am-6pm. 120Kč, students 70 Kč.)

ENTERTAINMENT AND FESTIVALS

The **Revolving Theater** (Otáčivé Hlediště), in the castle garden, hosts opera, ballet, Shakespeare, and classic comedies for the summer season of the South Bohemian Theater Company. (Reservations ☎635 6643; www.otacivehlediste.cz. The tourist office lists showings and sells tickets. Performances June-Sept. Tu-Su 8:30-9:30pm. Box office open Tu-Su 1-7pm. Tickets 224-390Kč. For a 30% discount, purchase remainders 1hr. before showtime outside the main entrance to the castle gardens.) **Kino J&K,** Highway 159 next to the Špičák bus stop, shows reasonably recent Hollywood films. (☎071 1892. Tickets 40-70Kč.) The same company runs the town's summer **open-air cinema,** the **Letni Kino.** Heading north on Latrán, take a left on Chvalšinská. Continue to a sign for Na Ziméku on the right, with a parking lot behind. The Letni Kino is back and to the left in the parking lot. (☎071 1892. Open July-Aug. Shows 9:30pm. 74Kč.)

For **The Celebrations of the Five-Petalled Rose,** during the third weekend of every June, the citizens of Český Krumlov don tights and doublets to party like it's 1588. The festival commemorates the reconciliation between brothers who were kings of two of the five city-states controlled by their family in the late 16th century. Throughout the event, the streets overflow with people, food, theater, music, dancing, and beer. Specific festivities include a medieval feast, a fireworks show, and the Tournament of the Roses, during which contestants prove their mettle in feats of strength, including jousting. On the final day, the champion of the Tournament enters the Revolving Theater to play chess against an actor depicting the king, using human "pieces"; the king always wins. Reserve accommodations a couple of weeks early. Admission is free for those wearing tights, armor, or poofy dresses. (Book tickets through the TIC or Unios Tourist Service, Zámek 57, ☎380 725 110 or 380 725 119; tourist.service@unios.cz. Info available at www.ckrumlov.cz/slavnosti. 3 days 200Kč; F 100Kč, Sa 150Kč, Su free; disabled guests free.)

Krumlov hosts several world-class music festivals. The **Chamber Music Festival** in the castle (☎721 470 558; hpelzova@wo.cz) runs for 10 days starting in late June. The **Early Music Festival** (☎0 711 681 or 724 045 727; www.earlymusic.cz) occurs in early July and lasts a week and a half, overlapping with the six-week-long **International Music Festival Český Krumlov.** (☎241 445 404 www.czechmusicfestival.com.)

NIGHTLIFE

Party animals enjoy the city's full array of bars and cafes, many of which line Rybářská. The city is fairly quiet during the week, but the fun picks up early Friday evening and lasts all weekend. The backpacking crowd tends to gather at the Travellers Hostel bar, where the drinks are the cheapest (Pilsner 23Kč).

Cikánská Jizba (Gypsy Bar), Dlouhá 31 (☎071 7585), left off Radniční. Sketches of ordinary people line one wall, with gypsy *objets d'art* framing a crucifix on another. On weekends, locals and tourists jam the place to listen to gypsy bands and drink beer that starts at 18Kč. On weeknights, the bartender sits and drinks with the locals. Live music some nights; check for flyers outside during the day. Jack Daniels 45Kč. Open M-Th 11am-10pm, F-Sa 11am-midnight. Cash only.

Horor Bar, Masná 129 (☎728 682 724). With a giant metal cross hanging over the bar, red-draped tables, candelabras, and a broken grand piano, Horor Bar is perhaps the goth-est place on earth. Skeletons hanging from the ceiling look down on a mixed crowd of locals and travelers, old and young. Despite all this, the bar, built in the bottom of an old Protestant church, is low-key and perfect for quiet conversation. Pilsner Urquell 40Kč. Open daily 6pm-late. Cash only.

Bar Bar, Kaplická 3 (☎777 100 432). Bar Bar is about as much of a dive bar as one can reasonably hope to find within the ancient walls of Český Krumlov. A stone patio winds behind the building; inside, tropical murals zest up the walls. Alterna-rock on the jukebox. Foosball in the corner. Bernard beer is on tap, and liquors are well stocked. Open daily 8pm-late. Cash only.

OUTDOOR ACTIVITIES

Český Krumlov is a paradise for the outdoorsy. The town lies at the southern border of the 212 sq. km **Chko Blanský Les Protected Landscape Area,** which contains a monastery, **Zlatá Koruna,** as well as the ruins of the Schwarzenbergs' summer mansion, **Dívčí Kámeru.** South of town lie the Šumava foothills, which run along the Austrian border; the **Cistercian monastery** at **Vyšši Brod;** and the **castle** at **Rozmberk.**

BIKING. At least four major biking trails run through Český Krumlov, forming wandering and often mountainous routes to all the above-mentioned sites, as well as to numerous small towns and villages. Biking maps of the region are available at the **Tourist Information Center** shop for around 70Kč. **Bikes** can be rented at **VLTAVA,** Kajovská 62. Some hostels, including Hostel Merlin (see p. 207), have special discounts with the agency. Bicyclists are advised to keep their bikes locked in even the smallest towns. (☎0 711 988; www.ckvltava.cz. Bike rental 320Kč for first day, 300Kč for second day. Open daily 9am-5pm.)

KAYAKING/CANOEING/RAFTING/INNERTUBING. Throughout the summer, a steady stream of canoes and inner tubes fills Krumlov's river. Many hostels provide free innertubes; for kayaks, canoes, and rafts, VLTAVA provides numerous package trips that range in distance (5-35km) and in time (1-8hr.). The route from Vetrni to Krumlov is the shortest (kayaks 330Kč, canoes 500Kč, rafts 700Kč). From Vyšši Brod back to Krumlov is the longest (kayaks 650Kč, canoes 930Kč, rafts 1500Kč). Contact VLTAVA for the full list of trips. Boats, paddles, waterproof bag, life jackets, maps, and transport to and from Český Krumlov are all available.

HORSEBACK RIDING. To reach **Slupenec Horseback Riding Club** (Jezdecký klub Slupenec), located at Slupenec 1, go to the end of Rooseveltova, where it intersects the highway; another intersection with Křížová is on the right, and a sign indicates the distance (2km) to Slupenec. Turn left onto Křížová, then take an immediate right onto Rozmberska. Continue on Rozmberska to Slupenec. Trips last from an hour (250Kč) to several days (from 2500Kč, depending on size of group and duration). Longer trips include refreshments and take you high into the hills above Český Krumlov. (☎/fax 0 711 052; www.jk-slupenec.cz. English and German spoken. Horses available Tu-Su 9am-6pm. Call ahead.)

SWIMMING. An indoor swimming pool *(plavecký bazén)*, Fialková 225, is north, near the Letni Kino. Follow Latrán north, go left onto Chvalšinská, then right on Fialková. (☎711 702. Adult 1½hr. swim 30Kč, any longer swim 40Kč; students 30Kč. Open Tu 7-10:30am, 2:30-4pm, 6-11pm; W 7-8am, 10am-5pm, 6-10pm; Th 7-8am and 1:30-4pm; F 7-10:30am, 12:30-5pm, 6-10pm; Sa 1-9:30pm; Su 1-9pm.)

TENNIS. The Tenis Centrum Český Krumlov, Chvalšinská 247, across the swimming pool, has three indoor grass courts and eight outdoor clay courts for hourly rental. Rackets and lessons available. (☎/fax 071 1418; tenis@tenis-centrum.cz. In high season, courts 8am-3pm 370Kč, 3-9pm 450Kč, 9pm-midnight 290Kč. In low season, courts 300Kč. Racket rentals 80Kč. Open daily 8am-midnight.)

MORAVIA

Winemaking Moravia, home of the country's finest folk music and two leading universities, is also the birthplace of a number of Eastern European notables, including Czechoslovakia's first president, Tomáš G. Masaryk; psychoanalyst Sigmund Freud; and chemist Johann Gregor Mendel, avatar of modern genetics. Best of all, tourists have yet to overwhelm Brno's cosmopolitan vigor or disrupt Olomouc's cobblestoned charm. Outside the city, the low hills of the South Moravian countryside cradle the architectural pearls of Telč.

BRNO ☎(0)5

The Czech Republic's second-largest city, Brno (berh-NO; pop. 388,900) has been an international marketplace since the 13th century. Today, emissaries of global corporations compete for space and sales among local produce stands. The result is a dynamic, spirited, and relatively untouristed city, where historic churches soften the bustle of the streets.

TRANSPORTATION

Trains: Nádražní (☎541 171 111). To: **Prague** (3-4hr., 23 per day, 130-160Kč); **Bratislava, SLK** (2hr., 8 per day, 250Kč); **Budapest, HUN** (4hr., 6 per day, 945Kč); **Vienna, AUT** (1½hr., 5 per day, 536Kč): **Krakow, POL** (6hr, 1 per day, 450Kč).

Buses: (☎543 217 733). On the corner of Zvonařka and Plotní. To: **Prague** (2½hr.; several per day; 140Kč) and **Vienna, AUT** (2½hr.; 8 per day; 400Kč).

Public Transportation: Tram, trolley, and **bus** tickets at a *tábak* or any kiosk. 10min. costs 8Kč; 40min. 13Kč; 24hr. pass 50Kč. Luggage requires an extra ticket; 10min. 4Kč; 40min. 6Kč. Fine for riding ticketless 400-800Kč; ticket checks are common. Bus routes #90 and above run all night; trams and all other buses run daily 5am-11pm.

Taxis: Impulse Taxi (☎542 216 666). Taxis line Starobrněnská and Husova.

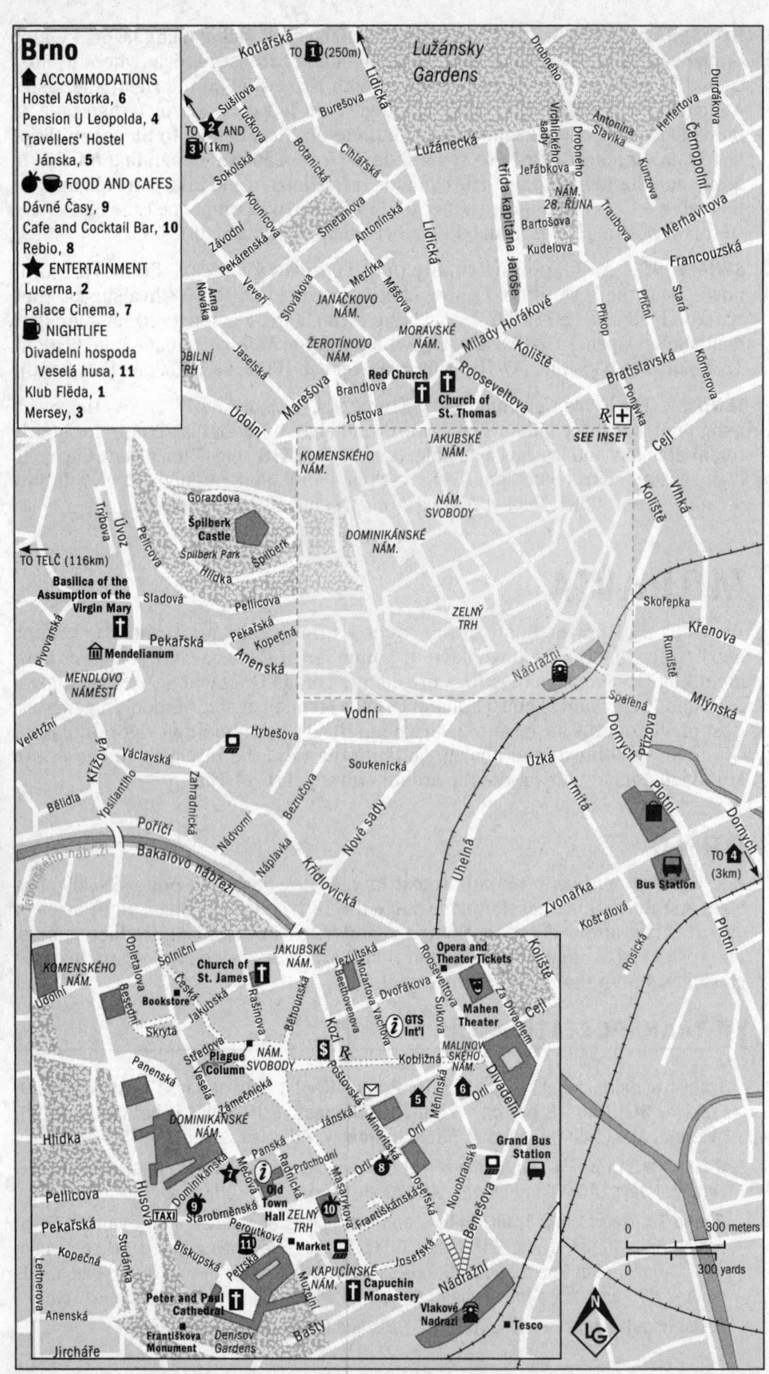
Brno
ACCOMMODATIONS
Hostel Astorka, 6
Pension U Leopolda, 4
Travellers' Hostel Jánska, 5
FOOD AND CAFES
Dávné Časy, 9
Cafe and Cocktail Bar, 10
Rebio, 8
ENTERTAINMENT
Lucerna, 2
Palace Cinema, 7
NIGHTLIFE
Divadelní hospoda Veselá husa, 11
Klub Flěda, 1
Mersey, 3
TO 1 (250m)
TO 2 AND 3 (1km)
Lužánsky Gardens
TO TELČ (116km)
TO 4 (3km)
Red Church
Church of St. Thomas
SEE INSET
Špilberk Castle
Špilberk Park
Basilica of the Assumption of the Virgin Mary
Mendelianum
MENDLOVO NÁMĚSTÍ
JANÁČKOVO NÁM.
ŽEROTÍNOVO NÁM.
MORAVSKÉ NÁM.
KOMENSKÉHO NÁM.
JAKUBSKÉ NÁM.
NÁM. SVOBODY
DOMINIKÁNSKÉ NÁM.
ZELNÝ TRH
NÁM. 28. ŘÍJNA
Bus Station
Church of St. James
Bookstore
Plague Column
Opera and Theater Tickets
Mahen Theater
GTS Int'l
Old Town Hall
Market
KAPUCÍNSKÉ NÁM.
Capuchin Monastery
Peter and Paul Cathedral
Františkova Monument
Denisov Gardens
Grand Bus Station
Vlakové Nadrazí
Tesco
TAXI
0 300 meters
0 300 yards

ORIENTATION AND PRACTICAL INFORMATION

Everything in central Brno is accessible by foot. Its main streets radiate from **náměstí Svobody** (Freedom Square). From the **train station** entrance, cross the tram lines on **Nádražní,** turn left, walk 15m, and then turn right on **Masarykova,** which leads to nám. Svobody. From the **bus station,** facing the main schedule board, ascend the stairs at the leftmost corner of the station. Go straight on the pedestrian overpass and through the shopping mall. After exiting the mall, pass **Tesco** and take the pedestrian underpass to the train station. When you resurface, with your back to the train station, go left on Nádražní; Masarykova is on the right.

Tourist Office: Kulturní a informační centrum města Brna, Radnická 8 (☎542 211 090), in the town hall. From nám. Svobody, go down Masarykova, turn right on Průchodní, and then right on Radnická. Free **maps** of city center with self-guided tours. Maps of the whole city 29-79Kč. English spoken. Open M-F 8am-6pm, Sa-Su 9am-5pm.

Budget Travel: GTS International, Vachova 4 (☎844 140 140 or 257 187 100). ISIC 250Kč. Arranges discount air and train travel. English spoken. Open M-F 9am-6pm, Sa 9am-noon.

Currency Exchange: Komerční banka, Kobližná 3 (☎521 271 11), just off nám. Svobody. Gives V **cash advances,** cashes **traveler's checks** for 2% commission (100Kč min.), on the 2nd fl., and has an AmEx/MC/V **ATM.** Open M-F 8am-5pm.

Luggage Storage: At the train station. 20Kč per 15kg bag per day, 30Kč per 15-20kg bag, 25Kč per 25kg bag, 35Kč plus 9Kč per 5kg thereafter. Lockers 10Kč per day. Open 24hr.

English-Language Bookstore: Barvič á Novotný, Česká 13 (☎542 215 040; www.barvic-novotny.cz). Wide fiction selection. Open M-Sa 8am-7pm, Su 10am-1pm. MC/V.

Laundromat: Kavarna Pradelna, Hybešova 45. Take tram #1 or 2 from the train station to "Hybešova"; it's 25m ahead on the left. Wash 60Kč, dry 40Kč. Detergent 35Kč. Offers the best **Internet** rates in town. M-F 30Kč per hr., Sa-Su 20Kč per hr. Open M-F 10am-1am, Sa 2pm-1am, Su 2-11pm. Internet is also available at **Veřejny Internet Center,** Masarykova 24, through the courtyard, which has free Internet access. Open daily 9am-noon and 12:30-5pm. **Postal Code:** 60100.

Pharmacy: Kobližná 7 (☎542 212 110). Open M-F 7am-10pm, Sa 8am-1pm. AmEx/MC/V. **Lékárna Koliště,** Koliště 49 (☎545 424 811). Open 24hr. MC/V.

Hospital: Urazova Nemocnice, Ponávka 6 (☎532 260 111). From nám. Svobody, take Kobližná to Malinovského nám. Continue on Malinovského nám. to Celi (300m) and take a left on Ponávka. There are 10 hospitals in the Brno area. The main one is the **Fakultní Nemocnice,** Vihlavská 100 (☎547 791 111).

Post Office: Poštovská 3/5 (☎542 153 622). **Poste Restante** at corner entrance. Open M-F 7am-7pm, Sa 8am-noon. **Postal Code:** 601 00.

ACCOMMODATIONS

Brno's hotel scene is geared toward business suits, so it's no great surprise that one of the city's budget hotels was recently replaced by the "Moulin Rouge Erotic Night Club Disco." Though rare, budget options are available, especially in the summer. Student dormitories, transformed into hostels from July to September, are the best deal in town. During the low season, the best option is to have the local tourist office arrange **private rooms** (from 500Kč).

Hotel Astorka, Novobranská 3 (☎542 510 370; astorka@jamu.cz). With your back to the train station, cross the tram tracks, turn right, and make an immediate left up a set of stairs. At the top, turn right on Novobranská and cross Orli. Centrally located, brand-new Astorka boasts clean, modern dorm-style rooms that come with a host of amenities. Reception on 3rd fl. Open July-Sept. Singles 520Kč; doubles 1040Kč; triples 1560Kč. Students 260/520/780Kč. AmEx/MC/V. ❸

Pension U Leopolda, Jeneweinova 49 (☎545 233 036; fax 545 233 949). Take tram #12 or bus #A12 to the last stop, Komárov. Take a left behind the *tábak* huts on Studnicni. At the end of Studnicni, turn right on Jeneweinova. Quite a trek from the center (15min. by public transport), this suburban pension is nonetheless the most affordable of its kind. It offers small, beautifully furnished rooms with TV and private baths. Ground floor houses an intimate restaurant with a cozy fireplace. Check-out 11am. Singles 610Kč, with breakfast 690Kč; doubles 820/980Kč; triples 1100/1350Kč. ❸

Travellers' Hostel Jánska, Jánska 22 (☎542 213 573; www.travellers.cz). Head up Masarykova from the train station and take a right on Jánska. Brand-new hostel located in the town center. While this installment of the Travellers' chain hostel—a school during the year—is central and well staffed, it is also lacking in comfort or personality. The hostel offers rows of rusty metal beds with rock-hard mattresses. No common room. Free Internet. Breakfast included. Reception 24hr. Open July-Aug. 15-bed dorms 290Kč. MC/V. ❶

 FOOD

Pizza and kebab joints, and coffee bars are everywhere. The fruit and vegetable **market** is on Zelný trh. (Open M-F 9am-5pm.) **Tesco,** Dornych 4, behind the train station, has groceries. (☎543 543 111. Grocery section open M-F 6am-10pm.)

Rebio, Orlí 26. (☎542 211 130.) For a delicious break from pork, beer, and kraut, head over to Rebio's organic, cafeteria-style dining room. Delicious entrees make use of local produce. Entrees 18.90Kč per 100g. Open M-F 8am-7pm, Sa 10am-3pm. Cash only. ❶

Dávné Časy, Starobrněská 20 (☎544 215 292), up Starobrněnská from Zelný trh. As the Czech inscription at the door reads, forget your problems and visit the world of medieval feasts and knights. Menu has "Dishes from nations that have never known hunger," including a few selections "with no meat (or just a little)." Coveted outside tables on a quiet side street near the cathedral. Excellent chicken with mustard sauce 115Kč. Salads 59-69Kč. Entrees 69-400Kč. Open daily 11am-11pm. AmEx/MC/V. ❹

Cafe and Cocktail Bar, Masarykova 8/10 (☎542 221 880). A hangout for Brno's young fashionistas, this chic cafe serves up a touch of New York, along with some phenomenal breakfasts of omelettes and toasted baguette sandwiches (53-100Kč), creative pasta and fresh fish entrees (113-216Kč), and massive salads (90-147Kč). Cover 20Kč. Open M-Th 8am-10pm, F 8am-11pm, Sa 9am-11pm, Su 10am-8pm. MC/V. ❷

 SIGHTS

PETER AND PAUL CATHEDRAL. Brno was allegedly saved from the Swedish siege of 1645 by the guile of its citizens: the attacking general promised to retreat if his army didn't capture the city by noon, so when the townsfolk learned of his plan, the bells struck noon one hour early and the Swedes slunk away. The bells have been striking noon at 11am ever since. Although the Swedes burnt the cathedral (Biskupská katedrála sv. Petra a Pavla) as they retreated, some of it was left intact, and the remains of the earliest Romanesque church on Petrov are still visible in the current cathedral's crypt. *(On Petrov Hill. Climb Petrska from Zelný trh. Cathedral open M-Sa 8:15am-6:15pm; Su 7am-6pm. Chapel, tower, and crypt open M-Sa 11am-6pm, Su 1-6pm. Cathedral and chapel free. Tower 25Kč, students 20Kč. Crypt 25/10Kč.)*

ŠPILBERK CASTLE (HRAD ŠPILBERK). Once home to Czech kings and a mighty Habsburg fortress, Špilberk served as a prison for convicted criminals and revolutionaries in the 18th and 19th centuries. The gruesome torture methods employed here earned the castle a reputation for being the cruelest prison in Habsburg Europe. During WWII, the Nazis kept prisoners here. The corridors now contain extensive galleries detailing the prison's history and the art, architecture, and social history of Brno. For a taste of prison life, trek through the moat's tomb-like encasements, where the most dangerous criminals were imprisoned. The memorial to those who lost their lives here, in the final cell of the prison museum, is particularly moving. *(Take Zámečnická from nám. Svobody through Dominikánské nám. and go right on Panenská. Cross Husova and follow the path uphill. ☎542 123 611; muzeum.brno@spilberk.cz. Open May-Sept. Tu-Su 9am-6pm; Oct. and Apr. Tu-Su 9am-5pm; Nov.-Mar. W-Su 9am-5pm. Call ahead to reserve a tour in English. Full admittance to all exhibits 100Kč, students 45Kč. Castle tower 20/10Kč.)*

CAPUCHIN MONASTERY CRYPT (HROBKA KAPUCÍNSKÉHO KLÁŠTERA). If bones and bodies catch your fancy, you'll love this morbid resting place. The monks at this crypt developed an innovative burial method in which a series of air ducts allowed bodies to dry out naturally. As a result, the crypt preserved more than 100 18th-century monks and nobles. The displayed results now enlighten the living: the crypt opens with the Latin inscription, "Remember death!" and ends with the dead monks' dark reminder: "What you are, we were. What we are, you will be." *(Left of Masarykova from the train station. ☎542 221 207. Open May-Sept. M-Sa 9am-noon and 2-4:30pm, Su 9am-noon. English brochures 40Kč, students 20Kč.)*

AROUND MENDEL SQUARE (MENDLOVO NÁMĚSTÍ). In the heart of Old Brno sits the beautiful Gothic **Basilica of the Assumption of the Virgin Mary.** *(From Špilberk, walk downhill on Pelicova and take the stairs to Sladová. Go left on Úvoz to Mendlovo nám. Open Tu, Th-F, and Su 5:45-7:15pm.)* The Augustinian monastery next door was home to **Johann Gregor Mendel,** father of modern genetics. The newly renovated and expanded **Mendelianum,** Mendlovo nám. 1a, features slide shows, audio presentations, and exhibits documenting the his life and experiments. After watching the interactive **video** on how Mendel's pea plants led him to the theory of inherited genotypes, you can explore the garden that houses the foundation of his greenhouse and a recreated version of his pea garden. The barley grown is used by the brewery next door where, by tasting the beer, you can fully appreciate Mendel's work. *(☎543 424 043; www.mendel-museum.org. Open May-Oct. Tu-Su 10am-6pm; Nov.-Apr. W-Su 10am-4pm. 80Kč. Abbey open for viewing at 10am; 60Kč. Tours of the monastery M-F 10am and 3pm, Sa-Su 10am and 6pm; 60Kč.)*

ENTERTAINMENT AND NIGHTLIFE

The Old Town Hall hosts frequent summer **concerts;** buy tickets (100-600Kč) at the tourist office (p. 213). **Theater** and **opera** tickets available at Dvořákova 11. (☎542 321 285. Open M-F July-Aug. 8am-noon and 12:45-3pm; Sept.-June 8am-noon and 1-4:30pm.) **Cinemas** playing Western and Czech flicks abound (80-140Kč). **Palace Cinema,** Mecova 2, features American blockbusters and mainstream Czech films. (☎543 560 111; www.palacecinemas.cz. 145Kč, students 115Kč. M special 99Kč.) **Lucerna,** Minská 19, shows British and American independent films, as well as Czech originals. (☎605 282 438 or 549 247 070. Showtimes 5-8:30pm.) Look for posters advertising **techno raves,** Brno's hottest summer entertainment. While it's surprisingly easier to find a beer hall than a wine cellar in the heart of wine-producing Moravia, there is an occasional *vinárna* (bottles 80-150Kč).

Divadelní hospoda Veselá husa (Merry Goose Theatrical Pub), Zelný trh 9 (☎542 211 630), just behind the theater. This pub's hip, young crowd gathers after experimental performances in the attached Merry Goose Theater. Performances start between 7:30 and 8pm and last 1-3hr. Pilsner 23Kč. Open M-F 11am-1am, Sa-Su 3pm-1am.

Klub Flëda, Stefánikova 24 (www.fleda.cz). Flëda, Brno's biggest nightclub, hosts packed houses for concerts and live DJs. Check website for details on the rotating schedule of parties. Take tram #26 up Štefánikova to Hrncirska; Flěda is on the right. (Open daily 2pm-midnight.) The free guide Metropolis lists upcoming events.

Mersey, Minská 15 (☎541 240 623; www.mersey.cz). Take tram #3 or 11 from Česká to Tábor and continue down Minská. This rock club-disco-pub hosts live bands and DJs playing funk, disco, and rock. Check website for schedule. Easygoing, hip atmosphere. Large crowds gather for theme events, like James Bond nights. Beer 25Kč. Internet access 30Kč per hr. Cover F-Sa 30Kč. Open Tu-W 8pm-2am, Th-Sa 8pm-4am.

OLOMOUC ☎585

Today, Olomouc (OH-lo-mohts; pop. 103,400) is an echo of what Prague was before it became engulfed by tourists. The historic capital of Northern Moravia, Olomouc embodies the best aspects of the Czech Republic. By day, locals enjoy the Baroque architecture and cobblestone paths of the rebuilt town center. By night, inexpensive restaurants dish out delicious Czech favorites and students from the local university keep the clubs thumping until dawn.

TRANSPORTATION. The train station is at Jeremenkova 23 (☎78 54 90). **Trains** run to Brno (1½hr., 7-8 per day, 120Kč) and Prague (3½hr., 19 per day, 294Kč). The bus station, Rolsberská 66 (☎31 38 48), has an info office open M-F 6am-6pm, Sa-Su 6am-2pm. **Buses** run to Brno (1½hr., 10 per day, 75-85Kč) and Prague (4½hr., 3 per day, 310Kč). Olomouc's public transportation is easily accessible. Buy tickets (8-10Kč) for the **trams** and **buses** at kiosks by the station and machines at each stop. **Taxis** congregate in front of the train station and at the intersection of Riegrova and Národních hridinů. **Eurotaxi** (☎603 449 541) is a reliable company.

ORIENTATION AND PRACTICAL INFORMATION. Olomouc's **Staré Město** (Old Town) forms a triangle, in the center of which is the enormous **Horní náměstí** (Upper Square). Behind the **radnice** (town hall), **Dolní náměstí** (Lower Square) connects with Horní nám. **Masarykova třída** leads west from the train and bus stations to the town center, though not before changing its name to **1. máje** and then **Denišova.** Trams or buses marked "X" shuttle between the **train station** and the center (5 stops, 6Kč per ticket). Get off at Koruna, in front of the **Prior** department store, then follow **28. října** to Horní nám. Trams #1-6 also stop just outside the center. Get off at **náměstí Hridinů** and follow **Riegrova** to the center. From the **bus station,** just beyond the train station, take the pedestrian passageway beneath Jeremenkova to reach trams #4 and 5, which run to the center.

The **tourist office,** Horní nám., in the *radnice,* offers free **maps** of the town center, helpful self-guided tours, and detailed city maps (49-59Kč). The English-speaking staff also books hotels, hostels, and private rooms. (☎51 33 85; www.olomoucko.cz. Open daily Mar.-Nov. 9am-7pm; Dec.-Feb. 9am-5pm.) **Komerční banka,** Svobody 14 (☎550 91 11) and Denišova 47 (☎585 509 169), cashes commonly used **traveler's checks** for 1% commission and gives MC **cash advances** for 2% commission; the Denišova branch gives AmEx/MC cash advances for 2% commission. (Svobody branch open M-F 8am-7pm.) **Luggage storage** is available at the train station. (20Kč per day per piece under 15kg, 30Kč per piece over 15kg. Lockers 5Kč. Open daily 1:45-6:15am, 6:30-10:30am, 11:30am-6:15pm, and 6:30pm-1am.) **Pharmacy Lékárna** is on the corner of Ostružnická and Horní nám., behind the *radnice.* (Open M-F 7am-6pm, Sa 8am-noon.) For medical services, go to the **Fakultni Nemocnice Hospital,** IP Pavlova 6, southwest of the center off Albertova. (☎85 11 11; fax 41 38 41. English spoken.) For fast, cheap Internet access, visit **Internet u Dominika,** Slovenská 12. (☎777 181 857. 1Kč per min. 2nd hr. free. Open

M-F 9am-9pm, Sa-Su 10am-9pm.) The **post office** is on Horní nám. 27. (**Western Union** services. Open M-F 8am-7pm, Sa-Su 8am-noon.) **Postal Code:** 77127.

ACCOMMODATIONS AND FOOD. The cheapest beds (from 230Kč) pop up in summer when **Palacký University dorms ❶** open to tourists; most are opposite the Botanical Gardens, on the other side of 17 Listopadu, a 15min. walk from the center. The tourist office has info on arranging these accommodations and **private rooms** (from 360Kč). **Poet's Corner Hostel ❶,** Sokolská 1, is located near the center. From the train or bus station, take trams #4-7 to nám. Hridinů and walk 2 blocks, continuing in the same direction to Sokolská. From Horní nám., walk down 28. října 2 blocks; go left on Sokolská. This apartment feels more like a home than a hostel. Bright rooms and soft beds make it hard to leave, but the friendly staff provides enough great insider info to encourage exploring. ☎777 570 730; www.hostelolomouc.com. Laundry 100Kč. Bike rental 100Kč per day. Dorms 300Kč; doubles 800Kč; triples 1000Kč.) Also located near the center, on a quiet street, is **Pension na Hradbách ❸,** Hrnčířská 3. From Horní nám., head down Školní, go straight along Purkrabská, and turn right on Hrnčířská. A small, homey pension; back rooms overlook the old city walls. Call ahead. (☎23 32 43; nahradback@quick.cz. Singles with private bath and TV 650Kč; doubles 900Kč; triples 600-1200Kč.) Another good option is **Penzion Best ❷,** Na Strelnici 48; take tram #1 or 4-7 to nám. Hridinů, then bus #17, 18, or 22 to Na Strelnici. Continue in the same direction until the hotel appears on your right. Though a little out of the way, all of Best's rooms have comfortable furnishings, bathrooms, and TVs. (☎/fax 23 14 50. Breakfast 40Kč. Singles 500Kč; doubles 750Kč. MC/V.)

Numerous restaurants line both **Horní náměstí** and **Dolní náměstí,** serving various types of fare for 50-150Kč. Grab groceries at **Supermarket Delvita,** 8. května 24, in the basement of Prior, at the corner of 28. října. (☎53 51 35. Open M-F 7am-8pm, Sa 7am-2pm.) **Hanácká Hospoda ❷,** Dolní nám. 38, is always packed with locals, and serves up the very best of Czech food at bargain prices. (☎777 721 171. English menu. Entrees 33-222Kč. Open daily 10am-midnight. AmEx/MC/V.) Less Czech, but still delicious, is **Cafe Caesar ❷,** Horní nám., in the *radnice.* Named after Julius Caesar, the supposed founder of Olomouc, this terraced Italian restaurant serves dishes that could have fed his armies. (☎685 229 287. Entrees, including garlicky pizzas and pastas 52-170Kč. Open M-Sa 9am-1am, Su 9am-midnight. AmEx/MC/V.) For a creative dining experience, try **Čajovna Dřevená Panenka** (Wooden Doll Teahouse) **❶,** Hrnčířská 12., across the street from Pension na Hradbách (see above). Smoke one of several flavored tobaccos (75Kč), sip one of over 70 varieties of tea (35-65Kč), or enjoy freshly made couscous (50Kč), all in the peaceful, incense-filled atmosphere of a labyrinthe, multi-story teahouse. Menu limited to salads and sandwiches. (☎23 38 58. Open M-F 11am-11pm, Sa-Su 3-11pm.) Another, more casual option is **Café 87 ❶,** Denisova 47. Owner Vera runs a remarkable cafe, with Internet access in back (1Kč per min.). Relax with a cup of java (20Kč) and a delicious slice of chocolate pie (35Kč) or enjoy quiches and sandwiches from 25Kč. (☎20 25 93. Open M-F 6:30am-10pm, Sa-Su 8am-10pm.)

SIGHTS. The massive 1378 **radnice** *(town hall)* and its spired clock tower dominate the town center; the tourist office arranges trips to the top. (Daily 11am, 3pm. 15Kč.) An **astronomical clock** is set in the town hall's north side. In 1955, communist clockmakers replaced the mechanical saints with archetypes of "the people." Since then, the masses strike daily at noon with their hammers and sickles. The 35m black-and-gold **Trinity Column** (Sloup Nejsvětější Trojice), a UNESCO World Heritage Site, is the tallest Baroque sculpture in the country, covered with dozens of elaborate golden figures. One of Europe's largest Baroque organs plays every Sunday in the **Church of St. Maurice** (Chram sv. Mořice), 28. října, and also stars in Olomouc's **International Organ Festival** each September.

Returning to Horní nám., take Mahlerova to the intimate **Jan Sarkander Chapel** (Kaple sv. Jana Sarkandra). Its intricate frescoes honors a Catholic priest tortured to death by Protestants in 1620 after he refused to divulge a confessor's secret. (Open daily 10am-noon and 1-5pm. Free.) On Mahlerova, turn left on Univerzitní, and then right on Denišova. The **Museum of National History and Arts** (Vlastivědné Muzeum), nám. Republiky 5, tells the history of the astrological clock and displays 16th- to 19th-century timepieces. There is a zoological exhibit on the first floor. (☎51 51 11; www.vmo.cz. Open Apr.-Sept. M-Tu and Su 9am-6pm; Oct.-Mar. M-W and Su 10am-5pm. 40Kč, students 20Kč.)

From nám. Republiky, continue away from the center on 1. máje and then climb Dómská, on the left, to reach Václavské nám. Let the spires of **St. Wenceslas Cathedral** (Metropolitní Kostel sv. Václava), reminiscent of Paris's Notre Dame, lead the way. The church interior is in excellent condition, having been renovated virtually every century since it was damaged by a 1265 fire. Its wall designs are quite impressive, as is the crypt containing the gold-encased skull of Olomouc's protectress saint. (www.ado.cz/dom. Cathedral open W 9am-4pm, Tu and Th-Sa 9am-5pm, Su 11am-5pm. Free. Crypt open Tu and Th-Sa 9am-2pm, W 9am-4pm, Su 11am-5pm. 40Kč, students 20Kč. Donations requested.) Next door to the cathedral, the walls of the wondrous **Přemyslid Palace** (Přemyslovský palác) are covered in 15th- and 16th- century frescoes. The recently opened **Archdiocese Museum** inside displays the treasures of the Olomouc diocese. (☎23 09 15. Open Apr.-Sept. Tu-Su 10am-6pm. 50Kč, students 25Kč; W and Su free.) Continue away from the center on 1. máje and go right on Kosinova to reach the path that runs through **Bezrucovy sady,** the city park. Stroll through the forested paths and take a left past the statues. Go over the footbridge and along the tennis courts to reach the **Botanical Garden.** The highlight of the manicured grounds is the rosarium, which blossoms in summer. (Bezrucovy sady open dawn-dusk. Free. Botanical gardens open Tu-Su May-Sept. 9:30am-6pm; Apr. 9:30am-4pm. 20Kč, students 15Kč.)

NIGHTLIFE. Exit Discoteque, Holická 8, is the Czech Republic's largest outdoor club. From Horní nám., walk to Dolní nám., then follow Kateřinská 400m to 17 Listopadu. Turn left, then take a right on Wittgensteinova; follow it across the bridge (200m). The club is on the right. The loud techno and spotlights emanating from the building draw clubbers like moths to a flame, and with eight bars, you'll never wait for a drink. The terraces are perfect for sipping a cocktail while watching clubbers on the dance floor below. Those older than 25 may feel rather out of place. (☎23 05 73. Cover 50-60Kč. Open June-Sept. F-Sa 9pm-5am.) Those seeking a drunken workout should head to **9A Bar and Boulder,** Premyscorcu 9A, which tempts its lively patrons to scale its rock climbing wall in the back. Probably better to stop earlier in the night, before that *pivo* affects your coordination. (Open M-F 3pm-late, Sa-Su 5pm-late.) Another student favorite, **Vertigo,** Universitni 6, pours cheap beer in a perenially lively—and smoky—cavern. (☎777 059 150. Tequila 25Kč. Open M-Th 1pm-2am, F-Su 4pm-2am.) Closer to town is **Barumba,** Mlýnská 4, which churns out techno and beer. Follow Pavelčákova out of Horní nám.; go left on Mlýnská. (☎20 84 25. Beer 24Kč. Cover 30-60Kč for men, women free. Open M-Th 7pm-3am, F-Sa 9pm-6am. MC/V.) For a unique experience, check out **Vinárna Letka,** Legionářská 6, an old Soviet airplane converted into a bar. The decor is tacky, the crowd touristy, and the beer warm, but the opportunity to pretend the Cold War never ended is not to be missed. (Open M-Th 9pm-6am, F-Sa 9pm-7am.)

TELČ

☎(0)66

The Italian aura of tiny Telč (TELCH; pop. 6000) stems from a 1546 trip made to Genoa, Italy by the town's ruler, **Zachariáš of Hradec.** He was so enamored of Renaissance style that he brought back a battalion of Italian artists and craftsmen to spruce up his humble Moravian castle and town. With a cobblestone footbridge and a square flanked by arcades of peach-painted gables, it is easy to see why UNESCO named the gingerbread village a World Heritage site.

The highlight of Telč's many attractions is its breathtaking **castle,** a monument from the town's glory days as a water fortress. Arguably the most magnificent castle in the country, the stone building, complete with courtyard garden and lily pond, houses an amazingly well-kept interior filled with original pieces. There are two options for viewing the castle, both 45min. Tour A goes through the Renaissance hallways, past tapestries and exotic hunting trophies, through the old chapel, and beneath extravagant ceilings. Tour B leads through the rooms decorated in the 18th and 19th centuries, untouched since the Czech state seized control of the castle in 1945. (☎567 243 821, box office 567 243 943; www.zamek-telc.cz. Open Tu-Su May-Aug. 9am-noon and 1-5pm; Sept.-Oct. and Apr. 9am-noon and 1-4pm. 80Kč, students 40Kč. English tours: Tours A and B 140Kč.) In the courtyard, a **museum** displays examples of Telč's folklore. (Same hours as castle. 20Kč, students 15Kč.) The **gallery** is a memorial to artist **Jan Zrzavý** (1890-1977), who trained as a neo-Impressionist, dabbled in Cubism, and produced religious paintings. (Open Tu-F and Su 9am-noon and 1-4pm, Sa 9am-1pm. 30Kč, students 15Kč.) Beside the castle grounds stands the town's 14th-century **tower.** The climb to the top offers a stunning view of Telč. (☎604 985 3398. Open June-Aug. Tu-Sa 10-11:30am and 12:30-6pm, Su 1-6pm; Sept. and May Sa-Su 1-5pm. 20Kč, students 15Kč.) There's a lovely, quiet **park** at the castle's edge, where the stone walls meet the river. (Open daily dawn-dusk. Free.)

While Telč has a curiously large number of hostels and pensions, the central ones fill quickly in July and August, and there aren't many budget accommodations. **Campgrounds ❶** outside of town are available through the tourist office (see above; 80-100Kč), but you can get a **private room** with bath for 350Kč. Reserve rooms a week ahead in summer. **Hostel Pantof ❶,** nám. Zachariáše Hradce 42, offers a few comfortable beds in a spacious, historic building. (☎776 887 466; www.pantof.com. 6-bed dorms 100Kč; doubles 400Kč.) **Privát U Šeniglu ❹,** nám. Zachariáše Hradce 11, offers well-kept rooms with private baths, skylights, and some views of the square. (☎567 243 406. Doubles 300Kč.) **Šenk pod vez i ❷,** Palackého 116/11, serves cheap Czech food. Salads are also fresh and tasty. A long stone terrace out back overlooks the town moat. (☎567 243 889. Salads 39-45Kč. Entrees 54-222Kč. Open daily 11am-10pm; bar open daily 8pm-5am.) The grocery store, **Horacké Potraviny,** is at nám. Zachariáše Hradce 65. (Open M-F 7am-6pm, Sa 7am-noon.)

The **bus station** (☎567 302 477), which provides the only viable means of intercity transport, is on Slavíčkova, a 5min. walk from the main square. Buses run to Prague (3hr., 7 per day, 100Kč) and Brno (2hr., 8 per day, 88Kč). **Taxis** line the main square (☎602 517 775.) The town center forms a peninsula jutting into two conjoining rivers, with **náměstí Zachariáše Hradce,** the oblong main square, in the middle. To reach it from the bus station, follow the walkway and turn right on Tyršova, then left on Masarykovo. Enter the square through the archway on the right. The **tourist office,** nám. Zachariáše Hradce 10, in the town hall, sells **maps** and has **Internet** and accommodations listings. (☎567 112 407; www.telc-etc.cz. Open M-F 8am-6pm, Sa-Su 10am-6pm.) Across the street, **Česká Spořitelna,** nám. Zachariáše Hradce 62, exchanges **traveler's checks** and has an **ATM.** (Open M and W-Th 9am-12:30pm and 1:30-5pm, Tu and F 9am-12:30pm.) There are two **pharmacies** on Masarykovoa. **Lékárna U sv Anny** is at Masarykova 65. (☎567 213 622; lektelc@volny.cz. Open M-F 7:15am-5pm, Sa 8:30-11am. MC/V.) **Lékárna Telč** is at

Masarykova 66 (☎567 213 579. Open M-F 7:30am-5pm, Sa 8-11am. MC/V.) The **post office** is down the street at Tyršova 294. (☎567 243 212. **Western Union** and **Poste Restante.** Open M-F 8-11am and 1-6pm, Sa 8-10am.) **Postal Code:** 588 56.

EAST BOHEMIA

From the fertile lowlands of the Elbe to the mountain ranges that shape the border with Poland, East Bohemia is the Czech capital of outdoor activities. During Habsburg rule, the Czech language was kept alive among the people of East Bohemia. Consequently, within these villages, many 19th-century Czech intellectuals and nationalists were born. Today, Hradec Králové, the region's administrative and cultural center, combines well-preserved medieval buildings with an urban pace, while the forests of Český Ráj offer an unspoiled wilderness too often overlooked.

HRADEC KRÁLOVÉ ☎49

At the confluence of the Elbe and the Orlice Rivers, Hradec Králové (HRA-dets KRAH-lo-veh; pop. 95,000), literally "Queens' Castle," once served as a depository for royal widows whose Catholicism forbade them to remarry. Now it's a youthful university town, full of Art Nouveau buildings and thriving nightlife. Cyclists rule the city's boulevards and many bike paths. The town also plays host to cultural events, festivals, and outdoor activities through the year.

TRANSPORTATION. The train station is at Riegrovo nám. 914. (☎553 75 55. Open daily 3am-11:30pm; info center open daily 6am-7pm.) **Trains** go to Prague (2hr., 1 per hr. 5am-8pm, 222Kč). **Buses** run from the train station to Prague (2hr., 1 per hr., 72-80Kč). Buy tickets on board. **Public bus** tickets (8-12Kč) are sold at kiosks and at the station. Validate your ticket in the red boxes by placing the ticket in the top and pulling the black lever toward you. **Sprint Taxis** (☎551 5151) are in front of the train station.

ORIENTATION AND PRACTICAL INFORMATION. Separated by the **Labe** (Elbe) River, Hradec Králové feels like two separate towns. On the west side, the pedestrian-only **Čelakovského** is a favorite local drag along the shop-infested **Nové Město** (New Town). The east side is home to the churches and cafes of **Staré Město** (Old Town). The **train** and **bus stations** are next to each other, on the edge of Nové Město away from the river. To get to **Velké náměstí** (Great Square) from the stations, take a right on Puskinova and then a left on **Gočárova třída.** Follow Gočárova through Nové Město to the river, cross the bridge, and continue for one block. When you hit **Červenej armády,** head left and turn right on **V kopečku,** which leads to Velké nám. Buses #1, 5, 6, 11, and 16 go from Hlavní Nadraží to the Adalbertinum stop, just outside the city center.

The English-speaking staff at **Information Center,** Gočárova třída 1225, arranges accommodations and sells tickets to events in town. They also provide **maps** (free-70Kč), information on trails in the region, and info on town festivals. (☎553 4485; www.ic-hk.cz. Open June-Aug. M-F 8am-6pm, Sa 10am-4pm; Sept.-May M-F 8am-6pm.) Another tourist office sits in Staré Město at Velké náměstí 152. (☎495 534 482. Open June-Sept. M-F 8am-4pm. Sa-Su 9am-3pm; Oct.-May M-F 8am-4pm.) **Komerční Banka,** Čelakovského 642, at Masarykovo nám., charges 2% commission on **currency exchange** and has an **ATM** inside. (☎581 5550. Open M-F 8:30am-5pm.)

The train station has **luggage storage.** (10Kč, bags 15kg and up 20Kč. Lockers 10Kč. Open 24hr.; breaks 10:45-11:15am, 1:25-1:40pm, and 6:30-7pm.) The **police station** is at Dlouhá 211/10 (☎551 5284). The **pharmacy, Centrální lékárna,** is across from Komerční Banka (☎551 1614; open M-F 7am-6pm, Sa 8am-noon); and the **hospital** is on Sokolská 534, south of Staré Město (☎583 1111). Internet access is availible at the tourist office (45Kč per hr.), as well as at **Gamesbar,** Ak. Heyrovského 1178, down the street from Hotelový Dům. (☎608 979 088; www.gamesbar.cz. 40Kč per hr. Open M-F noon-midnight, Sa-Su 5pm-midnight.) The **post office,** Riegrovo nám. 915, is next to the train station. Get a ticket from the machine in the waiting area. Send packages at window #6. (☎554 0733. **Western Union.** Card **telephones** in front; buy cards inside. Open M-F 7am-7pm, Sa 7am-1pm, Su 8am-noon.) **Postal Code:** 50002.

ACCOMMODATIONS AND FOOD. You won't find truly budget accommodations in the center of Staré Město. Inexpensive options are plentiful around the university, however, just a short walk south of the center. The best deal near the center is at **Hotelový Dům ❶,** Ak. Heyrovského 1177, a 10min. walk from Staré Město right in the middle of the university campus. From the train station, take bus # 1, 9, 21, or 28 to Heyrovského, cross Sokolská, and take the first right on Heyrovského. Clean, bright rooms have fridges and desks. (☎551 1175; www.hotelovydum.cz. Reception 24hr. Check-out 9am. Dorms 210Kč; doubles 310Kč.) Farther outside the center is **Hotel Garni ❷,** Na Kotli 1147. All its hotel rooms have baths, TVs and fridges. In summer, Garni offers more basic hostel-style accommodations. Take bus #1, 9, or 28 from the station; Hotel Garni is to the right of the bus stop. (☎576 3600. Breakfast included. Reception 24hr. Dorms 450Kč; singles 690Kč; doubles 1260Kč. Hostel beds July 15-Sept. 15 250Kč. 80-200Kč discount for HI members.) In a great location sandwiched between the cathedral and the town square, **Penzion Pod Věží ❹,** Velké nám. 165, offers massive, luxurious rooms equipped with TVs, phones, private baths, and minibars. Rooms facing the front have views of Velké nám. (☎551 4932; www.pod-vezi.cz. Breakfast included. Singles 1155Kč; doubles 1680Kč. 10% discount on cash payments. AmEx/MC/V.)

Almost all of Staré Město's many pubs and restaurants serve traditional Czech fare. One of the better ones can be found in the upscale setting of **U Rytíře ❸,** Velké nám. 144/145. (☎603 464 389. Entrees 95-200Kč. Open M-Th 8:30am-11pm, F 8:30am-2am, Sa 10am-2am, Su noon-11pm.) For a lighter meal, **Atlanta ❸,** Švehlova 504, offers an excellent selection of salads (80-130Kč), in addition to more substantial dishes. Its sprawling patio dominates Masarykovo nám. (☎551 5431. Entrees 90-300Kč. Open M-Th 8am-midnight, F 8am-1am, Sa 9am-1am, Su 10am-11pm. MC/V.) There's a huge **Tesco** supermarket on nám. 28. října 1610. (Buses #1, 3, 7, 10, 12, 13. ☎507 2111. Open M-F 7am-8pm, Sa 7am-7pm, Su 8am-6pm.)

SIGHTS. Most sights in Hradec Králové are on **Velké náměstí,** the center of Staré Město. Here, the 1307 **Church of the Holy Spirit** attests to the town's royal past with priceless items, like a 1406 tin baptismal font (one of the oldest in Bohemia) and tower bells affectionately named Eagle and Beggar. The church underwent resorations in 2007. (Open M-Sa 10-11am and 2:30-3:30pm, Su 2-3:30pm. Free.) Climb up the 71m **White Tower** beside the church to see a giant bell and a view of the town. You may feel your inner Klappermeister stirring, but the bell ringing is reserved for eight burly men who have been assigned to perform the honor on special occasions only. (Open daily 9am-noon and 1-5pm. 40Kč, students 20Kč.) In the middle of the square at #139, the excellent **Gallery of Modern Art** showcases 20th-century Czech painting and sculpture. The floors take you through Czech perspectives on Impressionism, Cubism, Expressionism, and more recent trends. A highlight is the first floor's collection of František Bílek's wood sculptures. (☎551 48 93. Open Tu-Su 9am-noon and 1-6pm. Permanent collection 25Kč, students 10Kč; exhibitions 15/5Kč.) Walk across the square from the museum to the Baroque **Church of the Assumption of the Virgin Mary** (Kostel Nanebevzetí Panny Marie), constructed by Jesuits between 1654 and 1666. Prussian soldiers destroyed its interior in 1792, but it was later renovated. (Hours vary. 20Kč, students 10Kč.)

ENTERTAINMENT AND NIGHTLIFE. In late October, Hradec Králové's largest festival, **Jazz Goes to Town** (www.jazzgoestotown.com), hosts musicians from all over the world at the **Aldis Center,** Eliščino náb. 357 (☎505 21 11), and various pubs. You can buy tickets at the tourist office. For more information, call ☎541 1140. The **Theater Festival of European Regions** (www.klicperovodivadlo.cz) is held in late June. Classic and modern plays are performed daily all over town by professional groups from the Czech Republic and nearby regions. Schedules and tickets available at the tourist office (☎551 4876). **Kino Sirak,** Orlické nábreži, shows American blockbusters and foreign films outdoors during the summer. (☎495 513 297; www.adalbertinium.cz/letnikino. Shows at 9:30pm; days vary.) Head to **Vojtěch Kulhanek,** Karla IV 662, to rent a bike (200Kč per day). The tourist office can provide info about trails. (☎495 220 411; www.vojtechkulhanek.cz.)

Hradec Králové's nightlife is hopping, especially in the summer months, and bars line the main squares. At night, students flock to **Hogo Fogo Bar,** 19 Eliščino náb., a relaxing pub. (☎551 5592. Beer 18Kč. Open M-Th 3pm-1am, F 3pm-3am, Sa 4pm-3am, Su 4pm-1am.) For a livelier setting try **Paradise Cocktail Bar,** Velké nám. 158/159, with tables scattered on the square and an extensive drink menu. Daquiris 58-69Kč. (☎604 253 551. Open M-Th 9am-midnight; F 9am-2am, Sa 6pm-2am.)

LITOMYŠL ☎461

Litomyšl (LIT-ohm-ee-shil; pop. 10,200) is home to a magnificent château and wonderful architecture. The town is easily covered in a day and is a perfect respite from the crowds of the country's better-known cities.

TRANSPORTATION AND PRACTICAL INFORMATION. The train station, Nádražni 510 (☎61 22 03), is inconvenient, and most trains require a connection. **Trains** go to Hradec Králové (2hr., 6-8 per day, 88Kč). **Buses** run from Mařákova 1078 (☎61 33 52) to Hrádec Kralové (1hr., 12 per day, 52Kč). There aren't many taxis in town, so call ahead for **Taxi Dańsa** (☎602 411 844).Litomyšl's tiny center is dominated by the banana-shaped **Smetanovo náměstí** (Smetana Sq.). A series of small, uphill paths lead to the château and gardens that make up the town's cultural core. Almost everything of interest is either on the main square or on one of its side streets. To reach the center from the bus station, turn left on Mařákova and follow it over the river to Tyršova. Turn left and then bear left again at Braunerovo nám. to get to Smetanovo nám.

The **tourist office,** Smetanovo nám. 72, provides free **maps** of the town center, has accommodations listings, and sells phone cards. (☎61 21 61; www.litomysl.cz. English spoken. Open M-F 9am-7pm, Sa-Su 9am-3pm.) **Komerční banka,** Smetanovo nám. 31, cashes **traveler's checks** for 2% commission and has an **ATM** outside. (Open M-F 8:30am-4:30pm.) Other services include: a **pharmacy,** Lékárna U anděla Strážce, Smetanovo nám. (open M-F 7:30am-5:30pm, Sa 8am-noon); a **hospital,** J.E. Purkyně 652 (☎65 51 11), south of the center, off Mařákova; **Internet** at the tourist office (speedy connections 1Kč per min.); and the **post office,** Smetanovo nám. 15 (☎65 43 72; open M-F 8am-6pm, Sa 8am-noon). **Postal Code:** 57001.

ACCOMMODATIONS AND FOOD. While Litomyšl does not have much of a hostel scene, it also does not have sky-high hotels prices. Strictly budget travelers will have to venture about 10min. from the town center. Inquire about camping, the cheapest option (from 50Kč), at the tourist office. For something more central, try **Pension Kraus ❷,** Havlíčkova 444. From the main square, walk to the end farthest from the train and bus stations and continue down Havlíčkova; it's on the right. This beautiful pension provides spacious rooms with soft beds, private bathrooms, satellite TV, and a garden. Book one week ahead for singles. (☎61 48

23; www.pension-kraus.cz. Breakfast buffet 100Kč. Singles 500Kč; doubles 800Kč. AmEx/MC/V.) Outside the center, the **Pedagogical School ❷,** Strakovská 1071, provides basic rooms in a university boarding house, with comfortable beds, shared baths, and kitchenettes. From the bus station, turn left on Mařákova and then right on Strakovská, the highway. Continue for 600m; the school is on the right. (☎65 46 12; novotna@vospspgs.lit.cz. Open June-Sept. Doubles 400Kč; triples 600Kč.)

Litomyšl's restaurant selection isn't huge, but its portions of mainly Czech food are, and prices are low. Most restaurants are scattered along the main square and the uphill paths to the château. Arrive early, as many restaurants close down earlier than their stated hours. Overlooking a cobbled square in the shadow of the château, **Restaurace Pod Klásterem ❷,** B. Nemcove 158, is always packed with locals enjoying massive platters of grilled meats and pastas served by attentive staff. The lovely, geranium-filled terrace is the perfect place to indulge in a delicious ice cream sundae. (☎602 712 703. Entrees 90-160Kč. Open M-Th 11am-11pm, F-Sa 11am-1am, Su 11am-10pm.) **Supermarket Kubik** at Smetanovo nám. 72, carries groceries. (Open daily 7am-8pm. MC/V.)

SIGHTS AND ENTERTAINMENT. The town's highlight is the magnificent UNESCO-protected **château,** which overlooks the center from its hilltop perch. Built between 1568 and 1581 by Vratislav of Perštejn, the château was intended to relieve the homesickness of the supreme chancellor's wife, the Spaniard Marie Manrique de Lara, who desperately missed the Renaissance architecture of her home country. Tours wind through the château's salons and parlors, but the main attraction is the 1797 wooden **theater.** To get there from the square, ascend Váchalova, take a right, and hang a quick left up the covered stairs. (☎461 615 067. Open May-Aug. Tu-Su 9am-noon and 1-5pm; Sept. Tu-Su 9am-noon and 1-4pm; Oct. and Apr. Sa-Su 9am-noon and 1-5pm. Tour 1 covers the theater and state rooms; Tour 2 starts in the chapel and travels through the many banquet rooms. Both tours last 50min. Tours in Czech 80Kč, students 40Kč; in English 160Kč. Free English info.)

Visitors can also stroll through the castle brewery, birthplace of "Bartered Bride" composer **Bedřich Smetana.** While the exhibit is tiny, seeing Smetana's cradle while his compositions play in the background is a must for any music lover. (Same hours as château. 20Kč, students 10Kč.) The surrounding **castle gardens** make a lovely break after a tour. (Open M-Sa 5am-10pm, Su 8am-8pm. Free.) Opposite the château, locals lounge among the garden statues of **Klášterní Zahrady.** (Open daily 8am-11pm. Free.) Two blocks away, on Terezy Novákové 75, lies the **Portmoneum House.** Its interior was vibrantly decorated by experimental painter **Josef Váchal** in the 1920s. (☎61 20 20. Ring the bell to enter. Open May-Sept. Tu-Su 9am-noon and 1-5pm. 60Kč, students 30Kč.) During the last weeks of June, the château courtyard houses the **Smetana Opera Festival.** (Check www.litomysl.cz for dates, as well as info on other local festivities. ☎616 070. Tickets 80-1200Kč.)

CZECH REPUBLIC

JIČÍN

Located in the southeastern part of Cesky Ráj, Jičín (yit-cheen; pop. 16,400) is one of the better access points to the park. With its bustling town center and beautiful Baroque architecture, Jičín offers an excellent home base for hikers, bikers, and outdoor enthusiasts in general. The sandstone pillars and gorges of **Prachovské skály** (Prachovské rocks) offer climbs and hikes with stunning views. Highlights include the **Pelíšek** rock pond and the ruins of the 14th-century **Pařez** castle. A network of **trails** cross the 588 acres of the park; green, blue, and yellow signs guide hikers to sights, while triangles indicate scenic vistas. Red signs mark the "Golden Trail," which connects Prachovské skály to **Hrubá Skála** (Rough Rock), a rock town surrounding a castle. From the castle, the trail leads up to the remains of **Valdštejnský Hrad** (Wallenstein Castle). The red and blue trails are open to cyclists, but only the blue trail is suited for biking. Buses go to Prachovské skály and other spots in Český Ráj. Buses can be unpredictable; you can also walk along a 6km trail beginning at Motel Rumcajs, Konwva 331.

Camping in the woods is heavily restricted in Ceský Ráj, and the few campsites don't allow a fire. Instead, opt for one of the campsites near Jičín or settle into a homey *privat*. The tourist information center provides details on the ever-changing campsites, most of which charge 30-60Kč per person plus tent. A more luxurious option is **Privat Sedličky 59 ❶,** Sedličky 59, which offers immaculate rooms with private bath and kitchenettes. (☎723 674 425; stech@email.cz. Singles 320Kč; doubles 400Kč). To get there from the center follow Revolučni for 2km or take a bus from the station to Sedličky (5min., 5Kč). Jičín offers a fair number of restaurants, many of which line Valdštejnovo nam. and its offshoots. For a delicious lunch in a surprisingly stylish atmosphere, head to **Restaurant U Mata Je ❶,** Nerudova 46, which dishes up Czech classics as well as lighter lunch options. (☎493 532 641. Entrees 45-120Kč. Open daily 11am-5pm.) When night falls, head to Bowling Bar, Zizkovo nam. 3, inside the Hotel Pariz. With a stocked bar, bowling, foosball, pool, and a dance floor, there's something for everyone. (☎602 544 975. Open daily 3pm-late. Bowling 220Kč per game.)

Buses run from Jičín to Prague's Florenc. (1½hr., 8 per day except Su, 86Kč.) **Trains** run from Hradec Králové to Jičín (1½ hr., 4 per day, 80Kč.) For a taxi, call **Taxi Nonstop** (☎603 245 593 or 775 245 593). The town centers on the splendid **Valdštejnovo naměstí,** distinguishable from the surrounding areas by the soaring gothic tower of **Valdická Gate.** To get there from the bus and train stations, follow the signs up the hill to Husova, turn left, and follow Husova into the center. The extremely helpful **tourist office,** Valdštejnovo nam. 1, provides maps (5-90Kč), books accommodations, and can recommend hiking and biking trips throughout the region (☎493 534 390; www.jicin.org. Open M-F 9am-5pm, Sa and Su 9am-noon.) A bank, **CSOB,** Husova 393, **exchanges currency** for a 2% commission and has an **ATM** outside. (☎493 544 111. Open M and W 9am-5pm, Tu and Th-F 9am-6pm.) A pharmacy, **Dr. Max,** is inside the Kaufland supermarket. (☎493 520 263; Open daily 8am-8pm.) **Internet** is available at the tourist office. (5Kč per 10min.) The **post office** is located at Safarikova 142. (Open M-F 7am-5pm.)

ESTONIA (EESTI)

Eager to sever its Soviet bonds, Estonia has been quick to revive its historical and cultural ties to its Nordic neighbors, while Finnish tourism and investment help to revitalize the nation. The wealth that has reinvigorated Tallinn, however, belies the poverty that still predominates outside of Estonia's big cities, as well as the discontent of its ethnically Russian minority, uneasy with Estonia's increasingly European leanings. Still, having overcome successive centuries of domination by the Danes, Swedes, and Russians, most Estonians are now proud to take their place as members of modern Europe.

DISCOVER ESTONIA: SUGGESTED ITINERARIES

THREE DAYS. If you're arriving in **Tallinn** (p. 232), spend a day exploring the streets and sights of the Old Town—don't miss the enthralling **Museum of Occupations.** Take another day to go beyond the walls of the Old City and see the **Maarjamäe** branch of the Estonian History Museum before catching some afternoon rays at **Pirita Beach.** If you have a car, spend your last day in the beautiful **Lahemaa Nature Preserve** (p. 241); if you're traveling by bus, relax in the seaside town of **Haapsalu** (p. 245).

ONE WEEK. Get out of Tallinn, seriously! Going beyond the capital city will be a welcome relief for your wallet. If arriving from the south, spend 2 days enjoying the unique sights and sounds of **Tartu** (p. 255) before moving west to **Pärnu** (p. 242), on the coast. After a day, head out to the island of **Saaremaa** (2 days; p. 246), where you can bike around and take in the unspoiled beauty of the region. Then catch a bus to **Tallinn** (2 days), where you can see the churches and towers of the historic Old Town.

FACTS AND FIGURES

Official Name: Republic of Estonia.

Capital: Tallinn (pop. 409,516).

Major Cities: Pärnu, Tartu.

Population: 1,316,000

Time Zone: GMT +2, in summer GMT +3.

Language: Estonian.

Religions: Evangelical Lutheran (65%), Russian and Estonian Orthodox (19%), Baptist (15%).

Words with many vowels: töööööbik (nightingale, workaholic); hauaööõudused (horrors of the night in the grave).

ESTONIA

ESSENTIALS

WHEN TO GO

The best time to visit is in late spring (Apr.-May) and summer (June to early Sept.). Temperatures reach 30°C (86°F) in July and August. Although winters can be cold, with limited daylight hours, Estonia offers an abundance of skiing and skating. Beware, however, that the warm summer weather draws in the tourist crowds, which overrun Tallinn and the beaches.

DOCUMENTS AND FORMALITIES

EMBASSIES AND CONSULATES. Foreign embassies to Estonia are in **Tallinn** (p. 232). Estonia's embassies and consulates abroad include: **Australia,** 86 Louisa Rd., Birchgrove, NSW 2041 (☎298 107 468; eestikon@ozemail.com.au); **Canada,** 260 Dal-

ENTRANCE REQUIREMENTS.

Passport: Required for all travelers.
Visa: Not required for citizens of EU countries, Australia, Canada, New Zealand, the US, and assorted other countries for stays under 90 days.
Letter of Invitation: Not required.
Inoculations: Recommended up-to-date on DTaP (diphtheria, tetanus, and pertussis), Hepatitis A, Hepatitis B, MMR (measles, mumps, and rubella), polio booster, tick-borne encephalitis, and typhoid.
Work Permit: Required of all those planning to work in Estonia.
International Driving Permit: Required of all those planning to drive.

housie St., Ste. 210, Ottawa, ON K1N 7E4 (☎613 789 4222; www.estemb.ca); **UK,** 16 Hyde Park Gate, London SW7 5DG (☎020 75 89 34 28; www.estonia.gov.uk); **US,** 2131 Massachusetts Ave., NW, Washington, 20008 (☎202 588 0101; www.estemb.org).

TOURIST SERVICES

Offices of the **Estonian Tourist Board,** marked with a small white "i" on a green background, are present in most towns and sell maps and offer helpful advice about accommodations and other services. They keep extended hours during the summer months, except on the national holidays of June 23-24 and August 20, when they are open from 10am to 3pm.

MONEY

KROONI (EEK)		
	AUS$1 = 9.95EEK	1EEK = AUS$0.10
	CDN$1 = 10.79EEK	1EEK = CDN$0.09
	EUR€1 = 15.64EEK	1EEK = EUR€0.06
	NZ$1 = 9.03EEK	1EEK = NZ$0.11
	UK£1 = 23.25EEK	1EEK = UK£0.04
	US$1 = 11.31EEK	1EEK = US$0.09

At the time of publication, the Estonian unit of currency is the **kroon** (EEK), plural krooni, which is divided into 100 **senti.** Since its 2004 accession to the EU, however, Estonia has followed the path of economic integration and intends to switch to the **euro** on January 1, 2008. Currently, the best foreign currencies to bring to Estonia are the euro and US dollar; travelers should stay attuned to economic developments. Annual inflation averages 4.1%, although this has been decreasing over the last decade. Common banks in Estonia are **Hansabank,** which offers the most services, including **Western Union** transfers, exchanging **currency** and **traveler's checks.** Hansabank also generally offers the best rates. **SEB Banks** are also very common. **ATMs** are available everywhere and offer acceptable exchange rates. Many restaurants and shops accept **MasterCard** and **Visa. Tipping** is becoming more common; 10% is expected in restaurants. **Bargaining** is appropriate only at outdoor markets; written prices should generally be treated as fixed. Discounts are typically extended to student travelers with proper ID.

HEALTH AND SAFETY

EMERGENCY	**Ambulance and General Emergency:** ☎112. **Fire:** ☎112. **Police:** ☎110.

Medical services for foreigners are few and far between and usually require cash payments. Foreign insurance policies are likely to be accepted in major cities. English-speaking doctors can be found fairly easily on the mainland and in major cities on the Islands. There are two kinds of **pharmacies** (both called *apteek*). Some only stock prescription medication, but most are well-equipped Scandinavian chains that stock just about everything else. The Estonian word for condom is *kondoom*; the word for tampon is *tampoon*. Public **toilets** *(tasuline)*, marked by "N" or a triangle pointing up for women and "M" or a triangle pointing down for men, usually cost 5-10EEK and include a very limited supply of toilet paper. While Tallinn's tap water is generally safe to drink, **bottled water** is safer and is necessary in the rest of the country. The **crime** rate is low, though pickpocketing is common in Talllin's Old Town, especially along crowded Viru street. **Women** should not have a problem traveling alone, though it is wise to dress conservatively. **Minorities** in Estonia are rare; they receive stares but generally experience little discrimination. Travelers with **disabilities** may experience some inconveniences, particularly in historical sites, although the situation is improving with modern construction. In planning their trip, disabled travelers should consult the Estonian Chamber of Disabled People (www.epikoda.ee) and http://liikumisvabadus.invainfo.ee, which provides detailed information on the accessibility of establishments in Tallinn and other cities. **Homosexuality** is generally treated with curiosity rather than suspicion, but same-sex displays of affection are typically kept private.

TRANSPORTATION

BY PLANE. Several international airlines offer flights to Tallinn, the site of Estonia's major international airport; try **SAS** or **AirBaltic.** For flights from Europe, consider the budget airlines **easyJet** and **Fly Nordic.** Some travelers find it easier to fly into the larger international airport in **Riga, Latvia,** from which some regions in southern Estonia can be reached as or more easily than from Tallinn itself.

BY TRAIN. Trains in Estonia are mainly used for hauling freight, not passengers. Major domestic passenger lines include **Edeleraudtee** (http://www.edel.ee; English site offers little information), which provides service on the Tallinn-Viljandi-Pärnu, Tallinn-Tartu, Tallinn-Narva, Tartu-Valga and Tartu-Orava lines, and **Elektriraudtee,** which serves the area of Tallinn. International trains connect Tallinn to St. Petersburg and Moscow, Russia. Eurail passes are not accepted in Estonia.

BY BUS. Euroline buses are generally the cheapest way to reach the Baltics. Domestically, buses are much cheaper and more efficient than trains, though service can be infrequent between non-major cities. Although buses on the islands can be frustrating, it is possible to ride from the mainland to island towns (via ferry) for less than the price of a typical ferry ride. During the school year (Sept. to late June), students receive half-price bus tickets. Internationally, buses can be slow, as clearing the border may take hours.

BY CAR AND BY TAXI. If crossing into Estonia by car, be sure to avoid the less-than-scenic routes through Kalingrad or Belarus. Although **road conditions** in Estonia are steadily improving, the availability of **roadside assistance** remains poor. Your best bet (as voted 6 years in a row by the Estonian Association of Travel Agents) for renting a car inside Estonia is with Avis (www.avis.ee/?lang=en), located on the ground floor at the Tallinn airport (☎605 82 22; open Mon-Sun 8:45am-6pm); renters must be 23 years old and present a valid driver's license from their country of origin. The driving age in Estonia is 18. **Taxis** are a safe means of transportation, though drivers may try to part fools from their money; non-fools should watch the meter, or agree on the price in advance for longer routes.

BY BOAT. If you are traveling from Russia or another Baltic state, you may consider taking a **ferry,** but expect more red tape when crossing the border. The Silja Line serves the entire Baltic Sea region (www.tallinksilja.com/en/). Ferries also connect with **Finland, Sweden,** and **Germany**

BY BIKE AND BY THUMB. Bicycling is popular in Estonia's scenic countryside, but be careful of aggressive motorists. CityBike (www.citybike.ee) is the major bike rental company. Tallinn cycling maps can be found at www.tallinn.ee, listed under "Maps." Hitchhiking is fairly common in Estonia, and travelers should stick out their thumb. Let's Go does not recommend hitchhiking.

KEEPING IN TOUCH

PHONE CODES	**Country code:** 372. **International dialing prefix:** 011. From outside Estonia, dial international dialing prefix (see inside back cover) + country code + 7-digit local number. Within Estonia, simply dial the local number.

EMAIL AND INTERNET. Although **Internet** cafes are not as common as you might expect, Wi-Fi access widespread. Free Wi-Fi is available throughout Tallinn and in many locations across the country; check **www.wifi.ee** for more info or look for the wifi.ee sign. Internet access in cafes usually costs about 25EEK per hour.

TELEPHONE. Public **telephones,** which are very common at bus stations and shopping malls, require magnetic cards, available at any kiosk. These come in 20, 50, 100 EKK denominations. International calls are expensive, usually costing around US$0.80 per minute. **Tele 2** cards offer the best rates. International access codes include: **AT&T** (☎0 800 12 001), **Canada Direct** (☎0 800 12 011), and **MCI** (☎0 800 12 122). If you bring a GSM mobile phone, SIM cards offer a convenient and sometimes cheap way to keep in touch. Tallinn, unlike other Estonian cities, has no city code; to call Tallinn from outside Estonia, dial Estonia's country code (372) and then the number. To call any city besides Tallinn from outside the country, dial the country code, the city code, and then the number. The 0 listed in parentheses before each city code need only be dialed when placing calls within Estonia. SIM cards are easy to find and cost around US$1.

MAIL. Estonia's state-run **postal system** is reliable, and mail from Estonia generally arrives in the US or Canada within 5-9 days. Most postal workers speak good

English. Mail can be received general delivery through **Poste Restante** to Tallinn, Pärnu and Tartu. Address envelopes as follows: First name, LAST NAME, POSTE RESTANTE, post office address, Postal Code, city, ESTONIA.

ACCOMMODATIONS AND CAMPING

ESTONIA	❶	❷	❸	❹	❺
ACCOMMODATIONS	under 200EEK	201-300EEK	301-400EEK	401-500EEK	over 500EEK

Each tourist office has accommodations listings for its town and can often arrange a bed for visitors. There is little distinction between **hotels, hostels,** and **guesthouses;** some upscale hotels still have hall toilets and showers. The word *võõrastemaja* (guesthouse) in a place's name usually implies that it's less expensive. Many hotels provide laundry services for an extra charge. Some hostels are part of larger hotels, so be sure to ask for the cheaper rooms. **Homestays** are common and inexpensive. For info on HI hostels around Estonia, contact the **Estonian Youth Hostel Association,** Narva Mantee 16-25, 10121 Tallinn (☎372 646 1455; www.balticHostels.net). Camping is the best way to experience Estonia's islands and their unique selection of fauna and flora; doing so outside of designated areas, however, is illegal and a threat to wildlife. Farm stays provide a great peek into local life. For more info visit Rural Tourism (www.maaturism.ee), or search for a variety of accommodations at www.visitestonia.com.

FOOD AND DRINK

ESTONIA	❶	❷	❸	❹	❺
FOOD	under 50EEK	50-80EEK	81-100EEK	101-140EEK	over 140EEK

Most cheap Estonian food is fried and doused with **sour cream.** Local specialties include *schnitzel* (breaded, fried pork fillet), *seljanka* (meat stew), *pelmenid* (dumplings), and smoked fish. Bread is usually dark and dense; a loaf of *Hiiumaa leib* easily weighs a kilo. Pancakes with cheese curd and berries are a common, delicious dessert. The national beer *Saku* and the darker *Saku Tume* are acquired tastes; local beer, like Kuressaare's *Saaremaa*, is of inconsistent quality. *Värska*, a brand of carbonated mineral water, is particularly salty. It is hard to keep a vegetarian or kosher diet in Estonia; buying your own groceries may be your best bet.

LIFE AND TIMES

HISTORY

THOR, BJÖRN, ET AL. Estonia has struggled for centuries to gain independence and retain its identity. Ninth-century **Vikings** were the first to impose themselves on the Finno-Ugric people who inhabited the area that is now Estonia. In 1219, King Valdemar II of **Denmark** conquered northern Estonia. Shortly thereafter, Livonia, now Estonia and Latvia, fell to German knights of the **Teutonic Order,** who purchased the rest of Estonia in 1346.

FOREIGN KINGS. German domination continued until the emergence of Russian **Tsar Ivan IV** (the Terrible), who, in the **Livonian War** of 1558-83, crushed many of the tiny feudal states that had developed in the region. In an attempt to oust Ivan, the defeated states looked for foreign aid: northern Estonia capitulated to Sweden in 1561, while Livonia joined the Polish-Lithuanian Commonwealth. During the **Swedish Interlude** (1629-1710), when the entire country came under Swedish control, **Tartu University** (p. 258) and other Estonian-language schools were established.

YOU GOT SERFED. The 1721 **Peace of Nystad** concluded the Great Northern War, handing the Baltics to Peter the Great. Russian rule reinforced the power of the nobility, and the serfs lost all rights until Estonian serfdom was finally abolished by **Tsar Alexander I** in 1819, 45 years earlier than in Russia. The attempts of reactionary **Tsar Alexander III** (1881-1894) to Russify Estonia prompted a nationalistic backlash led by **Konstantin Päts,** who would later become president. The backlash peaked in a bid for independence during the Russian Revolution of 1905.

BETWEEN ESTONIA AND A HARD PLACE. At the start of **WWI,** Estonians were caught in a tough spot. Most of the Estonian-German population sympathized with Prussia, but had to fight in the Russian army. The **1917 Russian Revolution** spurred Estonian nationalism, but by the time the state declared **independence** in 1918, it was already under German occupation. After WWI, the country prospered until the **Depression** of the 1930s, which allowed extreme right-wing parties to gain public support, leading President Päts to proclaim a state of emergency and institute repressive measures. Päts's tenure was cut short by the Soviets, who occupied Estonia in 1940 under the **Nazi-Soviet Non-Aggression Pact.** The Soviets deported Päts and arrested, exiled, or killed many other Estonian leaders. In 1941, **Hitler** reneged on the pact, annexing Estonia and stationing German troops there until 1944. When the Red Army returned, thousands of Estonians fled; many more died trying to escape as Estonia became part of the **USSR.**

THE IRON CURTAIN DROPS. In the 1950s, Estonia saw extreme repression and Russification under **Soviet rule,** when internal purges removed the few native Estonians left in the ruling elite. It was not until *glasnost* and *perestroika* in the 1980s that Estonians won enough freedom to establish a political renaissance. In 1988, the **Popular Front** emerged in opposition to the Communist government, pushing a resolution on independence through the Estonian legislature. Nationalists won a legislative majority in the 1990 elections and successfully declared independence.

ESTONIA'S RISING STAR. The 1992 general election, Estonia's first after declaring independence, saw the rejection of the government of **Edgar Savisaar,** who had founded the Popular Front in the twilight of Soviet rule. Savisaar's regime was replaced by a coalition of parties committed to radical economic reform, a trend that has continued to the present. The government has managed to privatize most industries, lower trade barriers, and add a balanced budget amendment to its constitution. This success has made the country the darling of Western investors.

TODAY

Estonia is a **parliamentary democracy** with a much weaker presidency than most other post-Soviet states. **Prime Minister Andrus Ansip,** who was elected in April 2005, currently presides over the **Riigikogu** (Parliament) with a coalition party of pro-business **Res Publica,** the **Center Party,** and the center-right **Reform Party.** Under the second Estonian President Arnold Rüütel, elected in September 2001, the state made **NATO** and **EU** accession its top priorities, joining both organizations in 2004. Current **President Toomas Hendrik Ilves,** of the Social Democratic Party, elected in 2006, has continued policies of integration with Western Europe. A major source of friction in post-independence Estonia has been with **Russia,** beginning with attempts by the Estonian government in the early 1990s to deny citizenship to those unable to speak Estonian. Tensions were pushed near the breaking point in the spring of 2007, when the relocation of a **Soviet War Memorial** from downtown Tallinn prompted rioting by Estonia's Russian minority. Shortly thereafter, computer service across Estonia was nearly brought to a standstill by a flood of foreign data, in what Estonia alleges was a "cyberattack" perpetrated by the Russian government or its sympathizers.

PEOPLE AND CULTURE

LANGUAGE. Estonian is a Finno-Ugric language, closely related to Finnish. Knowledge of English is widespread among Estonians, especially those of the younger generations. Many also know Finnish or Swedish, but German is more common among the older set and in resort towns. Russian was once mandatory, but Estonians in secluded areas are likely to have forgotten much of it since few Russians live there. For a phrasebook and glossary, see **Appendix: Estonian,** p. 796.

DEMOGRAPHICS. About 67% of Estonia's inhabitants are ethnically **Estonian.** The significant **Russian** minority comprises almost 25% of the population, while **Ukrainian** (2.1%), **Belarusian** (1.3%), and **Finnish** (0.9%) minorities are also present. Estonia is a predominantly Christian country: most Estonians are members of the **Evangelical Lutheran** church, and the country has significant **Russian Orthodox** and **Estonian Orthodox** minorities.

CUSTOMS AND ETIQUETTE. Expect to be bought a drink if you talk with someone for a while; repay the favor in kind. If you're invited to a meal in someone's home, bring a **gift** for the hostess (an odd number of flowers is customary). **Handshaking** is a form of greeting. **Shops** sometimes close between noon and 3pm.

THE ARTS

LITERATURE. The oldest book in Estonian is the **Wanradt-Koell Lutheran Catechism** (1535), but local literature didn't flower until the Estophile period (1750-1840) centuries later. The most notable publication of this period was **Anton Thor Helle's** 1739 translation of the Bible. Folklore provided the basis for **Friedrich Reinhold Kreutzwald's** *Kalevipoeg* (1857-61), an epic that became the rallying point of Estonian national rebirth in the Romantic period. Toward the end of the century, the neo-Romantic nationalist **Noor-Eesti** (Young Estonia) movement appeared, led by the poet **Gustav Suits** and the writer **Friedebert Tuglas. Anton Tammsaare's** *Truth and Justice* (*Tõde ja õigus;* 1926-33), is essential to the Estonian canon, and he has been praised as Estonia's foremost writer. The strictures of the official Soviet style of **Socialist Realism** sent many authors abroad or into temporary exile in Siberia, but under Khrushchev's government in the early 1960s, Modernism arose via the work of **Artur Alliksaar, Lydia Koidula,** and **Juhan Viidng.** Frequent Nobel nominee **Jaan Kross** managed to criticize the realities of Soviet life despite USSR censors in *The Tsar's Madman* (1978). In the same year, **Aimée Beekman** addressed the plight of women in *The Possibility of Choice.* In the last decade, several Estonian writers have been nominated for the Nobel Prize. Among them are poet and essayist **Jaan Kapinski** and novelist **Emil Tode,** whose 1993 *Border State (Piiririik)* was internationally acclaimed as a great postmodern text. **Aarne Ruben** has attracted the public's attention with *The Volta Works Whistles Mournfully* (*Volta annab Kaeblikku vilet;* 2001). The most popular Estonian writer today is **Andrus Kivirähk,** best known for his humorous *Memoirs of Ivan Orav (Ivan Orava mälestused).*

MUSIC. Popular contemporary Estonian **composers** include **Arvo Pärt,** known for *Tabula rasa* (1977) and *St. James's Passion* (1992), pieces reminiscent of medieval compositions; **Veljo Tormis,** who revived the **runic,** an ancient chanting-style of choral singing; and **Alo Mattisen,** whose pop-rock songs became pro-independence anthems. Conductors and musical groups from around the world are drawn to Pärnu, the so-called "summer capital" of Estonia.

THE VISUAL ARTS. The first Estonian art school was founded at **Tartu University** (p. 258) in 1803. Nationally conscious Estonian art emerged at the close of the 19th century with sculptor **August Weizenberg** and painters **Johann Köler** and **Amandus Adamson.** The Neo-Impressionist paintings of **Konrad Mägi** and the landscapes of **Nikolai Triik** moved toward abstraction at the end of the 19th century, while the later painting of the 1920s and 1930s was heavily influenced by European trends, including Cubism and the principles of the German *Bauhaus* movement.

FILM. Beginning in 1908 with newsreel footage of Swedish King Gustav IV's visit to Tallinn, Estonian film has had a long and diverse history. The period of Soviet domination saw the production of feature films that glorified the reigning ideology. Post-independence cinema has seen the rise of documentary cinema, as well as sweeping historical films like *Nimed marmortahvlil* (2002), which focus on themes of national identity.

HOLIDAYS AND FESTIVALS

Holidays: New Year's Day (Jan. 1); Independence Day (Feb. 24); Good Friday (Mar. 21, 2008; Apr. 10, 2009); Easter Sunday (Mar. 23, 2008; April 12, 2009); Labor Day (May 1); Pentecost (May 11, 2008; May 31, 2009); Victory Day (June 23); Jaanipäev (June 23-24); Restoration of Independence (Aug. 20); Christmas (Dec. 25); Boxing Day (Dec. 26).

Festivals: As of 2005, Jaanipäev (St. John's Day) is celebrated across the Baltic states every June 23-24. Tallinn's Beersummer (see Entertainment and Festivals, p. 240), held in early July, is the kind of celebration its name leads you to expect. The same city hosts the Dark Nights Film Festival in December, featuring student and animation subfestivals in addition to showcasing international films. Pärnu's mid-June Estonian Country Dance Festival culminates in a line dance the length of a city street. An updated list of Estonia's cultural events is at www.kultuuriinfo.ee.

TALLINN

Crisp sea air gusts over the medieval buildings and glorious spires of Tallinn (TAH-lin; pop. 370,800), the self-proclaimed "Heart of Northern Europe." Unfortunately, invading tourists and vendors in "historical dress" often give the cobblestone streets of the Old Town a theme-park feel. Visitors who venture beyond the compact center, however, will be delighted by quirky cafes, lush parks, and the seaside promenade.

TRANSPORTATION

INTERCITY TRANSPORTATION

Flights: Tallinn Airport, Lennujaama 2 (☎605 8888, 24hr. info 605 8887; www.tallinn-airport.ee). Bus #2 runs between the airport and the intersection of Gonsiori and Laikmaa, 300m southeast of the Old Town. Airlines include: **Estonian Air,** Lennujaama tee 1 (☎640 1101; www.estonian-air.ee); **Finnair,** Roosikrantsi 2 (☎611 0950; www.finnair.ee); **LOT,** Tallinn Airport (☎605 85 53; lot@lot.ee); **SAS,** Rävala pst. 2 (☎666 3030; www.scandinavian.net). **Copterline,** Mere pst. 20, at the port side of the Linnahall arena (☎610 1818; www.copterline.com) runs a **helicopter** service to **Helsinki, FIN** (18min., 1 per hr. 8:30am-9:30pm, €59-220). Open daily 9am-7pm.

Trains: Toompuiestee 35 (☎615 6851; www.evr.ee). Book ahead for international routes, or buy your tickets upstairs 45min. before departure. Buy domestic tickets on the 1st fl. or on board. International ticket windows open daily 9am-10pm; domestic 6am-10pm. Take trams #1 or 2 three stops to Mere pst., on the northeast edge of Old Town. To: **Pärnu** (3hr., 2 per day, 60EEK); **Tartu** (2-3hr., 5 per day, 85-125EEK); **Moscow, RUS** (14½hr., 1 per day, 568-1951EEK); **Saint Petersburg, RUS** (10hr., 1 per day on even days, 310-517EEK).

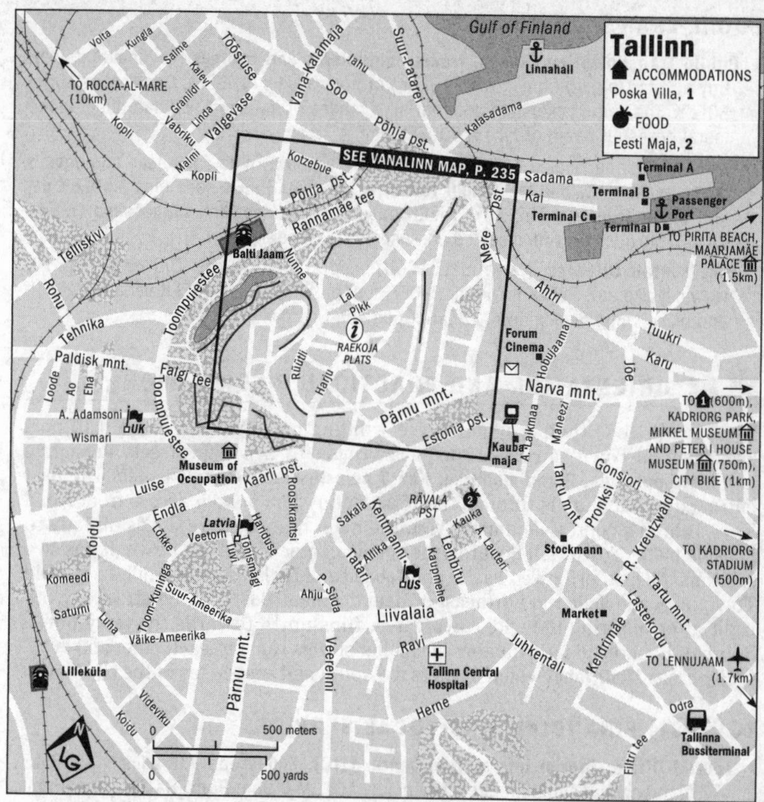

Buses: "Bussijaam" Lastekodu 46 (☎680 0900), 1.5km southeast of Vanalinn. To reach the southern edge of the Old Town, walk 1 block over to Tartu mtn. and take tram #2 or 4 four stops. Or, take bus #17, 23, or 23A from the stop next to platform 1 four stops to Vabaduse valjak, southeast of the Old Town. Open daily 6:30am-11:30pm; ticket office 6:30am-9:15pm. International schedules www.eurolines.ee, domestic schedules www.bussireisid.ee. To: **Haapsalu** (1½-2½hr., 1-2 per hr., 85-90EEK); **Pärnu** (2½hr., 2 per hr., 95-125EEK); **Tartu** (2½-3hr., 2-3 per hr., 120-150EEK); **Berlin, GER** (27hr., 1 per day, 1314EEK); **Kaliningrad, RUS** (15hr., 1 per day, 370EEK); **Rīga, LAT** (5-6hr., 9 per day, 200-250EEK); **Saint Petersburg, RUS** (8-10½hr., 6 per day, 190-270EEK); **Vilnius, LIT** (10½hr., 4 per day, 415-430EEK); 10% ISIC discount.

Ferries: (☎631 8550), at the end of Sadama. Boats, hydrofoils, and catamarans cross to **Helsinki, FIN. Eckerö Line,** Terminal B (☎631 8606; www.eckeroline.ee). 3½hr., 2 per day, 310EEK. MC/V. **Viking,** car ferry, Terminal A (☎666 3966; www.vikingline.ee). 3hr., 2 per day; Su-Th 295-495EEK. MC/V. **Nordic Jet Line,** Terminal C (☎613 7000; www.njl.info). 1½hr., 7 per day, 420-720EEK. MC/V. **Silja Line,** Terminal D (☎611 6661; www.silja.ee). 1½hr.; 7 per day; 360-705EEK, students 310-655EEK. MC/V. **Tallink,** Terminals A and D (☎640 9808; www.tallink.ee). 3¼hr., 3 per day, 315-345EEK. Express ferries 1½hr.; 16 per day; 470-770EEK, ask for student discount. MC/V. **LindaLine Express,** Linnahall passenger terminal (☎699 9333; www.lindaliini.ee). 1½hr., 420EEK. **Mainedd** travel agency, Raekoja plats 18 (☎644 4744; mainedd@datanet.ee), books ferry tickets with no commission. Open M-F 9:30am-5:30pm. MC/V.

LOCAL TRANSPORTATION

Public Transportation: Buses, trams, minibuses, and **trolleys** run 6am-midnight. Buy tickets *(talong)* from kiosks (10EEK) or from drivers (15EEK). Booklets of 10 for 80EEK. The same tickets are good for all 4 modes of transport. Validate them in the metal boxes on board or face a 600EEK fine.

Taxi: Price per km should be posted on your taxi window. Try to call ahead and order a car to avoid a "waiting fee." **Klubi Takso** (☎142 00). 35EEK base plus 7.50EEK per km. **Silver Takso** (☎152 22). 35EEK base, 7.50EEK per km. **Linnatakso** (☎644 2442), provides taxis for disabled passengers. 7EEK per km.

Bike rental: CityBike, Narva mnt. 120b, inside Comfort Hotel Oru (☎511 1819; www.citybike.ee). 35EEK for 1st hr., 30EEK per hr. thereafter; 206EEK per day. Dropoff and pickup anywhere in town, 23EEK. Open Apr.-Oct. daily 10am-8pm.

ORIENTATION AND PRACTICAL INFORMATION

Even locals lose their way along the winding medieval streets of Tallinn's **Vanalinn** (Old Town), an egg-shaped maze ringed by five main streets: **Rannamäe tee, Mere puiestee, Pärnu maantee, Kaarli puiestee,** and **Toompuies tee.** The best entrance to Vanalinn is through the 15th-century **Viru ärarad,** across from Hotel Viru, Tallinn's central landmark. **Viru,** the main thoroughfare, leads directly to **Raekoja plats** (Town Hall Square), the scenic center of the Old Town. It has two sections: **All-linn,** or Lower Town, and **Toompea,** a rocky, fortified hill. In the Old Town, **Pikk** and **Vene** run northeast of Raekoja plats. **Uus,** the first street on your right after entering the Old Town gates, runs north towards the ferry ports. South of Raekoja plats, a number of smaller streets run into each other and eventually cross **Muurivahe,** which borders the south and east edges of the Old Town.

TOURIST, FINANCIAL, AND LOCAL SERVICES

Tourist Office: Tourist Information Center (TIC), Kullassepa 4/Niguliste 2 (☎645 7777; www.tourism.tallinn.ee). Open July-Aug. M-F 9am-8pm, Sa-Su 10am-6pm; May-June M-F 9am-7pm, Sa-Su 10am-5pm; Sept. M-F 9am-6pm, Sa-Su 10am-5pm; Oct.-Apr. M-F 9am-5pm, Sa 10am-3pm. Branch at Sadama 25, in Ferry Terminal A (☎/fax 631 8321). Open daily 8am-4:30pm.

Embassies: For a complete list, check www.vm.ee. **Canada,** Toom-kooli 13 (☎627 33 11; tallinn@canada.ee). Open M, W, F 9am-noon. **Russia,** Pikk 19 (☎646 4175; www.estonia.mid.ru), visas around back on Lai. Open M-F 9am-5pm. **UK,** Wismari 6 (☎667 4700; www.britishembassy.ee). Open M-F 10am-noon and 2-4:30pm. **US,** Kentmanni 20 (☎668 8100, emergency 509 2129; www.usemb.ee). Open M-F 9am-noon and 2-5pm.

Currency Exchange: Located throughout the city, though banks have better rates than hotels and private exchange bureaus. Try **Eesti Uhispank,** Pärnu mnt. 12. Open M-F 9am-6pm, Sa 10am-3pm. **ATMs** are located throughout the city.

American Express: Suur-Karja 15 (☎626 6211; www.estravel.ee). Books hotels and tours; sells airline, ferry, and rail tickets; and provides visa services. Open June-Aug. M-F 9am-6pm, Sa 10am-5pm; Sept.-May M-F 9am-6pm, Sa 10am-3pm.

Luggage Storage: At the bus station. 10EEK per day. Open daily 6:30am-11:30pm. At the train station. 15-30EEK per day. Open daily 8am-8pm.

English-Language Bookstore: Apollo Raamatumaja, Viru 23 (☎654 8485; www.apollo.ee), stocks an impressive selection of guides, bestsellers, and classics. Open M-F 10am-8pm, Sa 10am-6pm, Su 11am-4pm. MC/V.

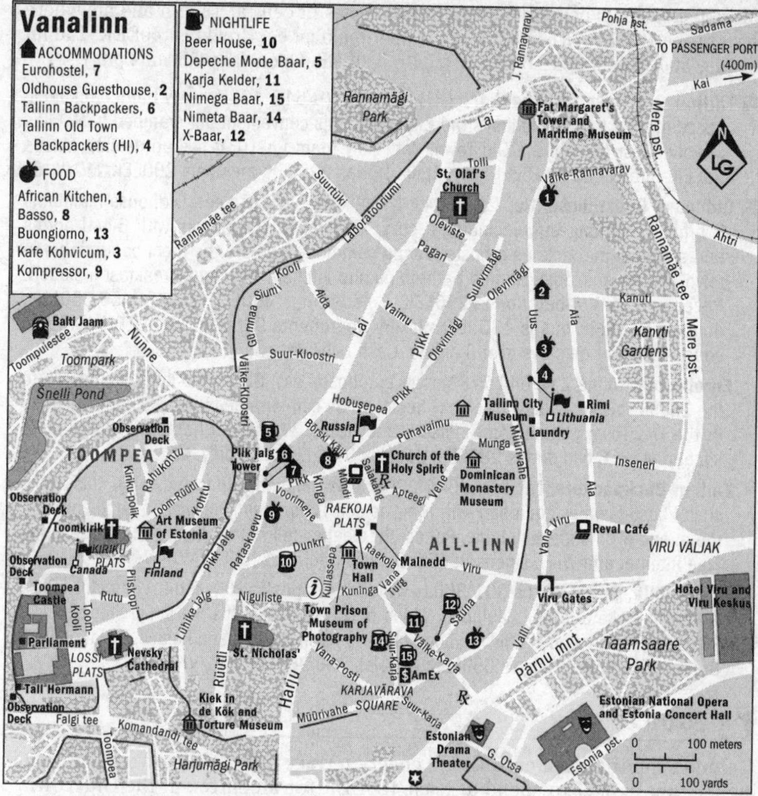

Laundromat: Kati Koduabi, Uus 9 (☎631 4566). Look for the blue sign with washing symbols. 24hr. service 25EEK per kg. Open M-F 9am-6pm, Sa 10am-4pm. Cash only.

EMERGENCY AND COMMUNICATIONS

Pharmacies: Tõnismae Apteek, Tõniamagi 5 (☎644 2282). Open 24hr.

Medical Services: Tallinn Central Hospital, Ravi 18 (☎697 3002, 24hr. info 620 7015). **Tallinn First Aid Hotline** (☎697 1145).

Internet: Reval Cafe, Aia 3 (☎827 1229), entrance on Vana-viru. 25EEK per hr. Open M-Su 10am-11pm. **Central Library,** Estonia pst. 8, 2nd fl. (☎683 0900). Free if you reserve in advance. Open M-F 11am-7pm, Sa 10am-5pm.

Post Office: Narva mnt. 1 (☎661 6616), opposite Hotel Viru. **Poste Restante** in basement. Open M-F 7:30am-8pm, Sa 8am-6pm, Su 9am-3pm. **Postal Code:** 10101.

ACCOMMODATIONS

In summer, Tallinn's hostels get filled up, and landing lodgings in the Old Town is expensive and difficult. If you haven't booked in advance, start knocking on doors early in the day to find a bed that someone else might have cancelled. **Rasastra,**

ESTONIA

Mere pst. 4, finds beautiful, clean **private rooms** in central Tallinn and anywhere else in the Baltics. (☎661 6291; www.bedbreakfast.ee. Breakfast 50EEK. Tallinn singles 300EEK; doubles 500EEK; triples 650EEK. Open daily 9:30am-6pm.)

Tallinn Old Town Backpackers (HI), Uus 14 (☎517 1337; www.balticbackpackers.com). Just north of Tallinn's Old City gates, this convenient but cramped hostel has the cheapest beds in the Old Town. With only room for 10, it fills up quickly. Linens 25EEK. Internet access 5EEK per 15min. Dorms 225EEK, members 200EEK. MC/V. ❷

Oldhouse Guesthouse, Uus 22 (☎641 1464; www.oldhouse.ee). Oldhouse maintains 3 properties along Uus, including a cozy, Asian-style guesthouse with 6-bed dorms and a school that acts as a hostel during summer. Beds are the most comfortable in town. Pianos available. Shared bathrooms and kitchen. Delicious breakfast included. Reception 24hr. 8-bed dorms 250EEK; 6-bed dorms 290EEK; singles 450-550EEK; doubles 650EEK; quads 1300EEK; luxury apartments 950-1900EEK. 10% ISIC discount; discount on stays over 3 nights. Cash only. ❹

Eurohostel, Nunne 2 (☎644 7788; www.eurohostel.ee). Buzz to be let in, and go up to the 2nd fl. This small, slightly smoky hostel offers comfortable bunks. Its prime location in the Old Town means some noise is inevitable. Whimsical baths. Fully equipped kitchen. 4- to 6-bed dorms 280EEK; doubles 580EEK. Cash only. ❷

Tallinn Backpackers, Lai 10 (☎644 0298; www.tallinnbackpackers.com). This lively, social hostel comes equipped with a big-screen TV for nightly movies, a large common room, and even a foosball table. Perfect for meeting fellow travellers. Kitchen available. Free Internet and Wi-Fi. Linens 25EEK. 8-person dorms 225EEK. MC/V. ❷

Poska Villa, Poska 15 (☎601 3601; www.hot.ee/poskavilla). From Vanalinn, follow Gonsiori; make a left on Laulupeo, which becomes Poska; it's the small green house. Pleasant B&B in a quiet neighborhood close to Kadriorg Park and Palace. Private baths. Breakfast included. Singles 650EEK; doubles 760-980EEK. MC/V. ❺

FOOD

Tallinn's international cuisine and cheery terrace cafes are growing in prominence, but expect to spend at least 120EEK for an entree in the Old Town. Vene St. and restaurants outside the Old City walls offer delicious meals at slightly more reasonable prices. A **Rimi** supermarket is at Aia 7. (☎644 3855. Open daily 8am-10pm.) A well-stocked **Stockmann** supermarket is on the corner of Liivalaia and Tartu. (☎63 39 59. Open M-F 9am-10pm, Sa-Su 9am-9pm.) The **market,** Keldrimäe 9, is on the right as you take Lastekodu toward the bus station, and hawks a classically Eastern European assortment of excellent produce, bread, and shiny clothes. (Open M-Sa 7am-5pm, Su 7am-4pm.) **Kolmjalg,** Pikk 3, sells a decent selection of food and is open 24hr.

Kompressor, Rataskaevu 3 (☎646 4210). Choose from incredible Estonian pancakes and giant portions of meat, fish, and veggie fillings (45-80EEK). If it's crowded, locals tend to share the large wooden tables with each other, so you might make some new friends. Open F-Sa noon-10pm, Su 11am-10pm. Cash only. ❶

Kafe Kohvicum, Aia 13/Uus 16 (☎520 1240). Look for an archway in the heavily graffitied wall on Aia; ring the bell if you're entering through Uus. To really get away from the hungry tourists, relax for an afternoon on velvet cushions in the Old Town's best-kept secret. Hidden in a courtyard, candlelit Kohvicum is an oasis of good coffee (20-30EEK), *gelato* (20EEK), and gourmet cakes (25EEK), served by charming baristas. The tiramisu is divine. Open daily 10am-11pm. Cash only. ❶

Eesti Maja, Lauteri 1 (☎645 5252), at the corner with Rävala pst. This dark cellar kitchen serves traditional Estonian favorites like blood pudding, sauerkraut stew, and—

for the adventurous diner with a strong stomach—*sült,* an Estonian meat jelly of pig hooves, thighs, and beef. Entrees 45-165EEK. Open daily 11am-11pm. MC/V. ❷

Buongiorno, Müürivahe 17 (☎53 91 08 46). Murals of Venice and haphazard old photographs adorn the walls of this authentic Italian cellar. The pasta is perfection, the menu will please vegetarians, and the bruschetta (30EEK) is delectable. Open daily 10am-midnight. Entrees 75-135EEK. Cash only. ❷

Basso, Pikk 13 (☎641 9312). Kick back for a lunchtime mixed drink at this classy jazz cafe. The delectable soups (40-60EEK) and pastas (55-80EEK) are a rare budget option for so elegant a setting. Live jazz Th at 9pm. Entrees 35-135EEK. Open M and Su 11am-midnight, Tu-Th 1pm-1am, F-Sa 11am-3am. MC/V. ❷

African Kitchen, Uus 34 (☎644 2555; www.africankitchen.ee). Soy, curry, fruit, and spice combine to make unique meals at this undiscovered hideout. Steal a spot in the cave-like interior, or head up to the rooftop terrace to enjoy hearty, fresh fare with a tropical African flare. Most entrees 95-130EEK; but beware of the pricey drink menu. Ample vegetarian options. Open M-Th and Su noon-1am, F-Sa noon-2am. MC/V. ❸

SIGHTS

Tallinn's sights are concentrated in the Old Town, a well-preserved and well-restored bundle of cobblestone streets, medieval towers, and sections of the original city wall. It's worth going beyond the walls, however, to see the excellent Maarjamäe branch of the History Museum, the quiet expanse of Kadriorg Park, or the sands of Pirita Beach—and to sidestep the summertime tourist stampedes.

TOOMPEA HILL (CASTLE SQUARE). The **Castle Square** (Lossi plats), a cobblestoned hilltop shaded by trees, is home to Tallinn's most impressive sights. **Alexander Nevskiy Cathedral,** the Russian Orthodox cathedral whose majestic spires dominate Toompea Hill, was named for the 13th-century Russian warrior who conquered much of Estonia. The builders insisted the church be built on his grave, resulting in constant structural problems over the years. Duck inside for a quick glimpse of its beautifully ornate interior. *(Open daily 8am-8pm. Services 9am, 6pm. Free.)* **Toompea Castle,** the present seat of the Estonian **Parliament** (Riigikogu), also faces the square, but is closed to visitors. Directly behind it, a fluttering Estonian flag tops **Tall Hermann** (Pikk Hermann), Tallinn's tallest tower and most impressive medieval fortification. Follow Toom-Kooli north one block to get to the **Dome Church** (Toomkirik), Toom-Kooli 6, whose 13th-century spire towers over Toompea. As you walk in, you'll step over the tomb of the slatternly Johann Thume, who asked to be buried at the church's entrance, hoping that the steps of pious worshippers would wash away his carnal sins. Over 300 barons are buried just inches below the floor; their intricately carved, wooden family crests line the walls of the church. *(☎644 4140. Open Tu-Su 9am-5pm.)* To get to **Kiek in de Kök,** a 1483 tower, walk on Toompea away from Lossi plats and turn left on Komandandi tee. Its name, which means "peep in the kitchen," comes from the views its windows provide of neighboring houses. Inside the tower, the **tower museum** consists of three stories of contemporary art and a haunting **torture exhibit.** *(☎644 6686. Open Tu-Su Mar.-Oct. 10:30am-6pm; Nov.-Feb. 11am-5pm. 25EEK, students 15EEK.)* Follow Toompea south just beyond the Old Town to reach **Saint Charles's Church** (Kaarli Kirik), Toompuiestee 4, at the intersection with Kaarli pst. The highlight of the 19th-century limestone behemoth is Johann Köler's *Come to Me* mural, which the master finished in just 10 days. The largest organ in Estonia can be seen near the exit. *(☎611 9100. Open M-F 10am-2pm. Services Su 10am. Donations requested.)*

LOWER TOWN (ALL-LINN). Tallinn's 14th-century **town hall** is the oldest in Europe, and contains several rooms decorated in classic medieval style. The hall features a **tower** with one of the world's tallest toilets (77m), built so that guards could relieve themselves without descending the winding, narrow steps. *(Raekoja plats. ☎645 7900. Ask for booklet with English translations of captions. Open July-Aug. M-Sa 10am-4pm. 35EEK. Tower open mid-May to Aug. daily 11am-6pm. 25EEK, students 15EEK.)* The other dominant feature of the All-linn skyline is the 123.7m tower of **Saint Olaf's Church.** As you climb up, tread carefully to avoid the fate of the architect, who fell from the tower to his death. Also beware of lightning: a bolt struck the tower in 1820, knocking off nearly 20m and reducing it to its present height. The top offers a great view of the Old Town—so great that the KGB used it as an observation post. *(Lai 50. ☎641 2241; www.oleviste.ee. Open Apr.-Oct. daily 10am-4pm. Services M and F 6:30pm; Su 10am, noon. Church free. Tower 30EEK, students 15EEK.)* On the south side of the Old Town is **Saint Nicholas Church** (Niguliste Kirkko), Niguliste 3. The Soviets destroyed the original 13th-century Gothic building when they bombed Tallinn in 1944, but restored it years later so it could house part of the Art Museum of Estonia collection. *(☎631 4327. Open W-Su 10am-5pm. Last entry 4:30pm. 35EEK, students 20EEK. Organ concerts Sa-Su 4-4:30pm.)* The **Church of the Holy Spirit,** at the corner of Pikk and Pühavaimu, is notable for its intricate 17th-century exterior clock and its former minister, Jakob Koell, who wrote the first book in Estonian in 1525. It's worth a peek inside for the beautifully carved wooden interior and Baroque pews. *(☎646 4430. Open M-Sa May-Sept. 10am-4pm; Oct.-Apr. 10am-2pm. Services in English Su 3pm. 10EEK, students 5EEK.)*

KADRIORG. Quiet paths, beautifully landscaped gardens, and fountains adorn Kadriorg Park. Its jewel, **Kadriorg Palace,** was designed by Niccolo Michetti, the architect of Peterhof in St. Petersburg, as a summer palace for Tsar Peter the Great. *(Weizenbergi 37. ☎606 6400. Open May-Sept. Tu-Su 10am-5pm; Oct.-Apr. W-Su 10am-5pm. 45EEK, students 35EEK.)* Its collection of 17th-century Dutch and Flemish art includes two works by Pieter Brueghel the Younger. The only Rembrandts in the Baltics are at the nearby **Mikkel Museum;** they include a 1621 self-portrait by the Dutch master. *(Weizenbergi 28. ☎601 3430; www.ekm.ee. Open W-Su 11am-6pm. 25EEK, students 10EEK. Joint ticket with Kadriorg Palace 55/30EEK.)* Cross the flower garden to admire the outside of the President's Palace, a pink building. Beyond the palace is the small cottage which houses the **Peter I (The Great) House Museum** (Peeter I Majamuuseum). Peter stayed in this simple home before the palace was completed, and today it houses his original furnishings, as well as an imprint of his extremely large hand. *(Mäekalda 2, near the New Building of the Art Museum of Estonia. ☎601 3136; www.linnamuuseum.ee/peeter1maja. Open mid-May to Sept. W-Su 10:30am-5:30pm. 15EEK, students 10EEK.)* To reach Kadriorg Park from the Old Town, follow Narva mnt. and veer right on Weizenbergi when it splits from Narva mnt. Trams #1 and 3 also run to Kadriorg. *(Flower garden open daily May-Aug. 9am-10pm; Sept.-Oct. 9am-9pm. Free.)* Behind the park is the Song Festival Grounds, where 20% of the country's citizens gathered in 1989 to sing the then-banned national anthem.

ROCCA-AL-MARE. This peninsula, 10km west of central Tallinn, includes a popular **Zoo** (Loomaaed), Paldiski mnt. 145, which boasts one of the most impressive collections of exotic animals in the Baltics; it's best known for housing the endangered Bactrian red deer and wild yak. *(Take trolley #6 from Kaarli pst., at the edge of the Old Town, to the Zoo stop. The zoo is just across the street. ☎694 3300; www.tallinnzoo.ee. Open daily 9am-7pm. Elephant house open Tu-Sa 9am-8pm. 90EEK.)* The peninsula's main attraction is the **Estonian Open Air Museum,** a refurbished, theme-park-esque area with 68 buildings transplanted from the countryside, including the 1699 **Sutlepa Chapel.** *(The Open Air Museum is a 15min. walk from the zoo; cross the shopping center parking lot and turn left on Vabaõhumuuseumi tee, which leads to the museum. ☎654 9100. Museum and chapel open May-Oct. daily 10am-6pm. Park and restaurant open daily May-Sept. 10am-8pm; Nov.-Apr. 10am-5pm; Oct. 10am-4pm 90EEK; last Tu of each month free. Tours in English Sa-Su noon. Bikes 35EEK per hr., 65EEK per 2hr.)*

MUSEUMS

MUSEUM OF OCCUPATION AND OF THE FIGHT FOR FREEDOM. This eye-opening multimedia collection documents Estonia's time under Soviet and German rule, breaking the 20th century into seven distinct periods of development and decline. Artifacts, including telephone booths, household goods, a hairdresser's chair, and a piece of a spacecraft, accompany high-tech displays and informative documentary videos dubbed in English. Testaments to Soviet-era heroes have been moved to the basement, where massive memorials and sculptures sit next to the bathrooms. *(Toompea 8. ☎668 0250; www.okupatsioon.ee. Open Tu-Su 11am-6pm. 10EEK, students 5EEK.)*

ART MUSEUM OF ESTONIA (EESTI KUNSTIMUUSEUM). Art and architecture lovers will enjoy the stunning, cutting-edge modern building and extensive collections. The excellent art gallery houses remarkable cityscapes of early 18th-century Tallinn, provocative early 20th-century avant-garde works, and rotating contemporary exhibitions. Much of the collection is also distributed in exhibits throughout the city; see the website for details. *(Main branch, Rumu, Weizengergi 34/Valge 1. ☎644 1478; www.ekm.ee. Open May-Sept. Tu-Su 11am-6pm; Oct.-Apr. W-Su 11am-6pm. Last entry 5:30pm. Contemporary art 30EEK, permanent exhibition 55EEK, combined ticket 75EEK. family ticket 150EEK. Free admission Feb. 21, Mar. 29, May 18, June 1 and 28, Sept. 27, Dec. 27.)*

ESTONIAN HISTORY MUSEUM (EESTI AJALOOMUUSEUM). Soviet archaeologists in the early 1950s tried to dispel the notion that Danes and Germans founded medieval Tallinn. Now, the museum's **Great Guild** branch restores Scandinavian warriors and Teutonic Knights to prominence. *(Pikk 17. ☎641 1630; www.eam.ee. Open M-Tu and Th-Su 10am-6pm. 10EEK, students 8EEK; last Sa of the month free.)* Those in a hurry should head straight to where the Great Guild leaves off, the **Maarjamäe Loss** branch. This restored palace east of the city documents 20th- and 21st-century Estonia, with exhibitions on Estonia's independence and jarring photographs of Tallinn and Pärnu residents cheering the arrival of Nazi "liberators" in 1941. *(Pirita 56. From Kadriorg Park, follow Pirita along the bay 1km. ☎601 4599. Open W-Su 11am-6pm. 10EEK, students 8EEK; last Sa of month free.)*

TALLINN CITY MUSEUM (TALLINNA LINNAMUUSEUM). Home to comprehensive displays of Tallin's history, this modern museum also has exhibits on Tallinn's historical characters, such as Old Thomas, the dutiful town watchman, and Johann von Uexkyll, the brutal serf-beating nobleman. *(Vene 17. ☎644 6553; www.linnamuuseum.ee. Open Mar.-Oct. M and W-Su 10:30am-5:30pm; Nov.-Feb. 11am-4:30pm. Captions in English and Estonian. Tours available in English. Museum 35EEK, students 25EEK.)*

DOMINICAN MONASTERY MUSEUM (DOMINIIKLASTE KLOOSTRI MUUSEUM). To enter, buy a copper coin (45EEK, students 30EEK), which you'll have to hammer into an amulet. Keep it, since it's a lifetime pass to this peaceful courtyard set apart from the Old Town bustle. Displays include the historic work of famous stonemasons dating as far back as the 13th century. *(Vene 16. ☎644 4606; www.kloostri.ee. Open May 15-Sept. 23 daily 10am-6pm; in winter by appointment only.)*

ESTONIAN MARITIME MUSEUM (MEREMUUSEUM). A massive metal diving suit greets you at the entrance to this museum, which chronicles Estonia's relationship with the vicious seas that surround the country. A refugee boat rowed from Hiiumaa to Sweden in 1944 is among the artifacts that illustrate the changing ways of sea transport throughout the centuries. *(In Fat Margaret's Tower, Pikk 30. ☎641 1408; www.meremuuseum.ee. Open W-Su 10am-6pm. 35EEK, students 15EEK.)*

ENTERTAINMENT AND FESTIVALS

Tallinn This Week, free at tourist offices, lists performances. The **Estonia Concert Hall** and the **Estonian National Opera** (Rahvusooper Estonia), both at Estonia pst. 4, are the primary venues for performances of opera, ballet, musicals, and chamber music. (Concert hall ☎614 7760; www.concert.ee. Box office open M-F noon-7pm, Sa noon-5pm, Su 1hr. before curtain. Tickets 60-400EEK. Opera ☎626 0260; www.opera.ee. Box office open daily noon-7pm. Tickets 60-570EEK.) The **Forum Cinema** at Coca-Cola Plaza, Hobujaama 5, shows Hollywood films in English. (Tickets for daytime showings 50-80EEK, for evening and weekend shows 115EEK.) There is a **beach** at Pirita (bus #1, 1a, 8, 34, or 38 from the post office). In early June, chefs from nearby countries face off during **Grillfest** (www.grillfest.ee). During **Old Town Days,** held the first weekend of June, the city hosts open-air concerts, fashion shows, singing, and skits. **Jaanipaev** (Midsummer's Day), June 23-24, is a pagan celebration featuring bonfires and barbecues. Celebrate the power of barley during **Beersummer** (www.ollesummer.ee), in early July. In late February, the **Student Jazz Festival** brings prodigies from all over northern Europe. In the middle of December, the international **Dark Nights Film Festival** (www.poff.ee) showcases cinematic talent.

NIGHTLIFE

Depeche Mode Baar, Nunne 4 (☎644 2350; www.edmfk.ee/dmbaar). For those who just can't get enough Depeche Mode, or for those who've had enough of Tallinn's rowdy tourists, the DM Baar and its funky clientele are paradise. The circular interior is outfitted with autographed posters, photographs, and album covers. A TV plays music videos and concert footage. Cheap beer (45EEK per 0.5L) and mixed drinks named after DM songs (40-80EEK) will convert even the non-fan. Open daily noon-4am. Cash only.

Karja Kelder, Väike-Karja 1 (☎644 1008). A warm, inviting cellar pub. Established in 1832 as a brewery, local favorite Karja Kelder claims to have the city's widest selection of beers, with over 40 on the menu. Beer 30-40EEK per 0.5L. Open M and Su 11am-1am, Tu-Th 11am-2am, F-Sa 11am-4am.

Beer House, Dunkri 5 (☎627 6520). The only on-site microbrewery in Tallinn features excellent inhouse varieties. The 1st fl. contains the vats where the brewing process takes place; upstairs is the disco. House beer 35-50EEK per 0.5L. Live music F-Sa 10pm. Open M-Tu and Su 10am-midnight, W-Th 10am-2am, F-Sa 10am-4am. MC/V.

Nimeta Baar (The Pub with No Name), Suur-Karja 4/6 (☎641 1515). The place to meet jolly, rugby-loving expats in a comfortable, laid-back setting. Beer 35EEK. Happy hour 6-7pm, 2-for-1 beers. Open M-Th and Su 11am-2am, F-Sa 11am-4am. MC/V.

Nimega Baar (The Pub with a Name), Suur-Karja 13 (☎620 9299). Crowds of local young people cram themselves onto Nimega's tiny dance floor. Disco-esque flashing lights take over after midnight. Beer 35EEK. Open M-Thu and Su 11am-2am, F-Sa 11am-4am. MC/V.

X-Baar, Sauna 1 (☎620 9266). With a rainbow flag spray-painted outside, X has a relaxed atmosphere, though the small dance floor remains active till late. Largely gay clientele consists of both men and women. Beer 35EEK. Open M-Th 2pm-1am, F-Sa 2pm-3am. MC/V.

COASTAL ESTONIA

East of Tallinn, vast Lahemaa National Park shelters pristine coastline, dense forests, and historic villages. To the west, popular summer location Pärnu and quiet Haapsalu offer beaches and mud baths, and are gateways to the Estonian Islands.

LAHEMAA NATIONAL PARK

Founded in 1971, Lahemaa was the USSR's first national park. Today, it's one of Europe's largest, protecting numerous animals and over 838 plant species. seventeenth-century **Palmse Manor** is among the best-restored estates in Lahemaa. The manor grounds include carefully manicured gardens, stables, a pond, and streams. The former servants' quarters now house a small **Old Cars Museum.** (Kodanik Kirsi Erahobiklubi; ☎326 8888. Manor open daily May-Sept. 10am-7pm; Oct.-Apr. 10am-3pm. Car museum open daily May-Aug. 10am-7pm; Sept. 10am-5pm. Manor 50EEK, family 100EEK. Car museum 25EEK.) The stacked **famine stones,** 1km past the tourist office, were piled up by serfs picking rocks from the fields in preparation for plowing. On the far side of the Puhkemajaad Neemetee, an overgrown path through the woods opens to a secluded beach where the **stone hill** is said to grant wishes to those who add a new rock to the pile. The dilapidated fishing huts on the cape are part of an **open-air museum.** (Open 24hr. Free.) As you continue around the cape and cross the river, white stripes on the trees mark a short trail through the forest and back to town. The harbor you will find is **Vergi,** connected to the cape by a land bridge 2.5km farther along the road. In early July, every other year, the **Vihula Folklore Festival** summons storytellers from around the world. The biannual **Lahemaa Bagpipe Music Festival** draws bagpipers from across Lahemaa.

Near Palmse, the best bet is the **Ojaäärse Hostel ❶,** which offers basic single rooms. From Viitna, take the road to Palmse and turn right about 500m before the Visitors Center. (☎324 4675. 275EEK.) Situated a scenic 8km hike from Võsu in the village of Käs mu, **Hostel Merekalda ❶,** Neeme tee 2, is a beautiful guesthouse on the water with spacious, clean rooms and a welcoming staff. (☎323 8451. Bicycle rental 100EEK per day, boat rental 30EEK per hr. Small wooden cottages for 2 with kitchen facilities, and shared baths without hot water 290EEK; doubles 590EEK.) In Viitna proper, the lakeside **campground ❶** is 400m past the bus stop, through the wooden arch on the right. Campsites and rooms in log cabins are available. (☎329 3651. Campsites 30EEK per person. Doubles 290EEK.) In the wilds of Palmse Mõis, **Park Hotel Restaurant ❷** has fresh salads for 30-50EEK and *schnitzel* for 82EEK. (☎322 3626. Open daily 11am-10pm.) The **tavern ❷** (☎325 8681) in Viitna, opposite the bus stop, has dishes for 70-130EEK.

As Lahemaa is very large and public transportation is infrequent, your best bet is to rent a car in Tallinn. The most convenient base for exploring the park is

CYBERWARS

On April 29th, 2007, the very same night that Tallinn erupted in violent protest over the removal of a bronze Soviet WWII memorial, a mysterious wave of data began to flow through Estonia's websites. This junk data, initially merely a small nuisance, increased dramatically in volume over several days, flooding key government and financial websites. In Estonia, where voting, banking, bill payment, and filing taxes are all conducted over the Internet, business came to a sudden halt. By the time the worst was over, Parliament had been without email for days, and several major banks were forced to shut down.

Estonian officials accused the Russian government of secretly orchestrating the attacks, and investigators found detailed instructions on how to send junk data to Estonian websites on Russian language forums and chat groups. The attack spiked dramatically on May 9th, or Victory Day, the Russian holiday that marks the Soviet Union's defeat of Nazi Germany and the start of their occupation of the Baltic countries. Nevertheless, the Internet's sheer scale and anonymity makes identifying the true identities of the hackers virtually impossible. Estonia's relationship with Russia is the most strained of the Baltic countries, and the political and social tensions only strengthened in the wake of 2007's first-ever large-scale cyber-attack.

Palmse, home to the **Lahemaa National Park Visitors Center,** which offers help with booking rooms, as well as free maps and brochures. Ask to see the interesting 15min. educational video about the park's history and attractions. (☎329 5555; info@lahemaa.ee. Open daily 9am-7pm. English; subtitles in German, Russian, French. Free.) From Tallinn, take the **Rakvere bus** to Viitna (1hr.; 2 per day; 15-45EEK, ISIC discount). From there, catch a bus to Palmse Mõis or walk the 7km road. Basic bus schedule at www.bussireisid.ee; call the Visitors Center for more info. As there are only two buses per day, visitors occasionally hitchhike from Viitna, though Let's Go does not recommend it. For direct access to the **coast** and the **Palmse Manor House,** inquire at the Tallinn station about buses to Võsu (3 per week). Rent **bikes** at the Park Hotel Restaurant (150EEK per day). **Postal Code:** 45202.

PÄRNU

In July and August, Estonians and cosmopolitan Europeans flock to the pristine beaches of Pärnu (PAER-noo; pop. 45,000), Estonia's summer capital. Music, theater, art, and film festivals throughout the summer ensure that there's no shortage of fun to be had in any weather. The city is also famous for its relaxing mud baths.

TRANSPORTATION. The **train station,** at Riia mnt. 116, is 3km east of the center, near the corner of Riia and Raja; take bus #15 or 40 to Raeküla Rdtj (10EEK). **Trains** run to Tallinn (3hr.; 2 per day; 60-80EEK, ISIC discount). Buses run from the bus station to: Haapsalu (2½hr., 6 per day, 160-190EEK); Kuressaare (3¼hr., 9 per day, 155EEK); Tallinn (2hr., 2 per hr., 100-110EEK); Tartu (2½hr., 1 per hr., 120-135EK); Rīga, LAT (3½hr., 6-8 per day, 180-200EEK). ISIC discounts are available for domestic fares. **Buses** are the best way to travel to Pärnu. The bus station, Ringi 3 (☎447 1002, Eurolines 442 7841; fax 444 1755), is located convienently in the center of town at the intersection of Pikk and Ringi. From the station, walk 350m down Pikk toward the center and turn left on Nikolai to reach the Tourist Information Center. **Pärnu Takso** (☎443 9222) and **E-Takso** (☎443 1111) **taxis** both charge 10EEK per km. **City Bike,** based in Rannahotel, delivers bicycles anywhere in Pärnu. (☎56 60 80 90; www.citybike.ee. 120EEK per ½-day., 150EEK per day.)

ORIENTATION AND PRACTICAL INFORMATION. The **River Pärnu** neatly bisects the city. The town center stretches from **Tallinn Gate** to the bus station on **Ringi.** The main street is **Rüütli.** A short walk down **Nikolai** and **Supeluse** from the center of town leads to the **mud baths** and **Ranna puiestee,** which runs parallel to the **beach.** Be sure not to confuse **Aia** and **Aisa.** From the bus station, follow Pikk towards the town center and hang a left on Nikolai to reach the **Tourist Info Center,** Rüütli 16. (☎447 3000; www.pärnu.ee. Open mid-May to mid-Sept M-F 9am-6pm, Sa 9am-5pm, Su 10am-3pm; mid-Sept. to mid-May M-F 9am-5pm.) When the Tourist Center is closed, head to the 24hr. reception desk at **Best Western Hotell Pärnu,** Rüütli 44 (☎447 8911; hotPärnu@pergohotels.ee). Rüütli is lined with 24hr. **ATMs. Cargobus,** along the bus station platforms, offers **luggage storage.** (10-30EEK per day per item, depending on weight. Open M-F 8am-7:30pm, Sa 8am-1pm and 1:45-5pm, Su 9am-1pm and 1:45-5pm.) **Pärnu Hospital** is at Ristiku 1. (☎447 3101; www.ph.ee.) **Keskraamatukogu** (Central Library), Akadeemia 3, a large white building set back from the street, has nine computers in a spacious reading room. Show your passport at the info desk for a pass. (☎445 5707; www.pkr.ee. Free. Open M-F 10am-6pm, Sa 10am-5pm.) **Rüütli Internetipunkt,** Rüütli 25 (entrance through the courtyard in the yellow building), has 13 fast connections. (☎315 52. 10EEK per 15min; 25EEK per hr. Open M-F 10am-9pm, Sa-Su 10am-6pm.) At the west end of Rüütli, the **post office,** Akadeemia 7, has **Poste Restante.** (☎447 1111; www.prn.ee/post. Open M-F 8am-6pm, Sa 9am-3pm.) **Postal Code:** 80010.

ACCOMMODATIONS AND FOOD. Rooms at hotels and guesthouses fill quickly. It's best to reserve as far in advance as possible, but even booking the day before can save you from being stranded upon arrival. The **TIC** books rooms for a 25EEK fee. **Tanni-Vakoma Majutusbüroo,** Hommiku 5, behind the bus station, rents **private rooms.** The office can be reached by phone year-round. (☎518 5319; tanni@online.ee. From 200EEK. Open May-Aug. M-F 10am-8pm, Sa 10am-3pm.) To get to **Hostel Lõuna ❷,** Lõuna 2, from the bus station, walk down Ringi; turn right on Rüütli. Go 500m, then turn left on Akadeemia. It's at the end of the street on the left. Located conveniently near the beach and the city center, Lõuna has comfortable rooms with clean shared baths and a large kitchen and common area. (☎443 0943; www.eliisabet.ee/hostel. Reception 24hr. Dorms 250-300EEK; doubles 500-900EEK; triples 750-900EEK.) **Tiia majutus ❷,** Nikolai 28, offers renovated private rooms with 19th-century fireplaces for budget prices. (☎511 7339; www.zone.ee/tiiamajutus. Singles 250EEK; doubles 500EEK.)

An indoor market *(turg)* on the corner of Sepa and Karja sells everything from antiques to baked goods. (Open M-F 7am-4:30pm, Su 7am-3pm.) **Kadri Kohvik ❶,** Nikolai 12, around the corner from the TIC, is a popular green-colored cafeteria for locals that serves filling fish and meat dishes. (☎442 9782. Entrees 30-70EEK. Open M-F 7:30am-9pm, Sa-Su 9am-5pm.) **Alex Maja ❷,** Kuninga 20, serves expertly prepared main courses in a chic basement location. The salmon pastry puff is excellent. (☎446 1866; www.alexmaja.ee. Entrees 60-110EEK. Open M-F noon-10pm, Sa-Su 10am-11pm. MC/V.) The **Jazz Cafe,** Ringi 11, offers delicious cakes, coffee, and free Wi-Fi in a sophisticated environment. Many evenings feature live piano jazz; ask at the counter for details. (☎442 7546. Open daily 9am-2am. MC/V.)

SIGHTS. The 18th-century **Elizabeth's Church** (Eliisabeth Kirik), Nikolai 22, was named after the Russian empress. J.H. Wulburn, the architect who planned its peacock-topped maroon spire in 1747, also designed the spire of St. Peter's Church in Rīga. (☎443 1381. Open M-Sa noon-6pm, Su 10am-1pm. Services Sa 8:30am, 6pm; Su 9am, 5pm.) Catherine the Great one-upped her predecessor with the Russian Orthodox **Catherine Church** (Ekateriina kirik), Vee 8, at the corner of Uus and Vee, a block north of Rüütli. The interior, which shimmers with ornate icons, is even more astonishing than the imposing silver-and-green spires. (☎444 3198. Open M-F 11am-6pm, Sa-Su 9am-6pm. Services Sa 8:30am, 6pm; Su 9am, 5pm.)

On the east end of pedestrian street **Kuninga,** at the corner with Ringi, is a **statue of Lydia Koidula** (1843-1885), the Estonian poet who wrote the famous anthem, "My Fatherland is My Beloved." At the opposite end of Kuninga stands the 17th-century **Tallinn Gate.** Stop by the funky, underground **Estonian Lithograph Center** (Eesti Litograafiakeskus), Kuninga 17, to see printmakers at work. (☎55 60 46 31; www.hot.ee/litokeskus. Hours vary.) Sculpture, painting, and experimental work fills the **Museum of New Art,** Esplanaadi 10, also referred to as the Museum of Modern Art or the **Chaplin Center,** in honor of the silent film star. Go around back to see an old Lenin statue sporting a new head with a glowing strobe light inside and missing his right hand. The **cafe** offers some of the cheapest sandwiches (10EEK) and pastries (5-6EEK) in town. (☎443 0772; www.chaplin.ee. Open daily 9am-9pm. 25EEK, students 15EEK.) The town's **beach** has swings, trampolines, and a waterslide (open June-Aug.). **Mudravilla,** Ranna pst. 1, by the beach, offers mud bath treatments (☎442 5525; www.mudaravila.ee. Head to toe 150EEK, localized therapy 100EEK. Medical examination 60EEK.)

NIGHTLIFE AND FESTIVALS. Head to the Swedish-owned **Veerev Olu** (The Rolling Beer), Uus 3a, in a courtyard behind the TIC. The owner is a fan of the Rolling Stones and brings in live rock and folk bands Saturdays 9:30pm-1am. (☎53 40 31 49. Beer 20EEK per 0.5L. Entrees 35-80EEK. Open M-Th and Su 11am-midnight,

F-Sa 11am-1am.) Try Saku (25-30EEK per 1L), Estonia's national brew, at **Tallinna Väravad,** Vana-Tallinna 1, atop the historic Tallinn Gate. If it's raining, you can sit inside the low-roofed tavern. (☎444 5073. Open daily 11am-11pm.) Pärnu's most famous disco is **Sunset Club,** Ranna pst. 3. By the beach, this stylish club offers chill-out couches and a busy dance floor. The room upstairs blares classic tunes for a slightly more mature crowd. (☎443 06 70. Cover varies; on weekends generally 100-120EEK. Open in summer M-Th and Su 10pm-4am, F-Sa 10pm-6am.)

The **Estonian Line Dance Festival** takes place in mid-June at Sassi Horse Farm, near Pärnu. It ends with a line dance that stretches the length of Rüütli (☎445 0070; www.estonianlinedance.com). The longest day of the year, June 21, kicks off festival season with beachside celebrations. In late May and early June, song takes over the city for the **International Opera Museum Festival** (www.xxiso.ee). The **Pärnu David Oistrakh Festival,** in late July, is one of Estonia's most prestigous classical music festivals, drawing international musicians and conductors. Most concerts take place at the town hall and Elizabeth Church (☎446 6540; www.oistfest.ee). The **International Film Festival,** in early July, screens amateur documentaries and anthropological films (☎443 0772; www.chaplin.ee). In mid-July, the **Watergate Festival,** popular throughout Estonia, brings every watersport imaginable to Pärnu. (☎449 1966; www.watergate.ee. 40-90EEK per day; entire festival including admission to Sunset Club 340EEK.) If you happen to be in Pärnu in early December, don't miss the **International Conference of Santa Clauses,** in which hundreds of Santas participate in Santa Olympics events across town.

DAYTRIP FROM PÄRNU: KIHNU ISLAND. The tiny rural island of **Kihnu** (pop. 540) offers a respite from the seaside antics of Pärnu. Still covered in dense woodlands and ringed by deserted beaches, the island was first settled in 1518 and has a mixed Swedish, Livonian, and Estonian heritage. Kihnu offers a glimpse of traditional Estonian ways of life: many women still wear traditional wool striped skirts, and most men work in the fishing industry. The **Kihnu Museum** (Kihnu Koduloomuuseum) is housed in a 16th-century church that served as a schoolhouse in the 1800s. Exhibits display photographs of island settlements from the mid-20th century, as well as anthropological artifacts relating to Kihnu's history. (☎446 9983. Open daily 10:30am-4pm. 15EEK, students 5EEK.) Across from the museum, a 16th-century church is locked behind an impressively elaborate iron-and-stone gate. Behind the church, hidden amongst the trees, is a **graveyard of crosses**, where the island's legendary hero, Kihnu Jõnn, is buried. At the southern tip of the island, a humble lighthouse built in 1864 keeps watch over Kihnu's quiet coast.

The **Rock City Guesthouse and Tavern ❸,** in Lemsi village, has rustic rooms and is one of the only accommodations on Kihnu Island. (☎446 9947 or 446 9956; www.kihnu.ee/rockcity. Doubles 385EEK; triples 570EEK; camping 25EEK per person.) For basic, homemade meals, try Liiva's **cafe ❶** in Kurase Center. (Entrees 30-60EEK. Open June-Aug. daily 10am-1am. Kitchen closes 10:30pm.) **Ferries** to the island run regularly during summer from Pärnu harbor, Kalda 2; follow Vee toward the river and turn left into the parking lot and harbor before the bridge. (Ferries run May 16-Oct. 2 M, Th-Sa 9am, 6:15pm, Su 6:15pm. Ferries from Kihnu return to Pärnu M, Th-Sa 6am, 3pm, Su 7pm. 2½hr.; 70EEK, bikes 25EEK.) **Munalaid Harbour,** 50km from Pärnu, also runs ferries. (☎443 1069. May 16-Oct. 2 M-Th 9am, 6pm, F 2, 6pm, Sa 9am, Su 3, 6pm. Ferries return from Kihnu M-F 7am, 4:15pm; Sa 7am; Su 2, 4:15pm. 50min.; 40EEK, bikes 15EEK.) Check the schedule for both routes at the Pärnu TIC beforehand, as times change frequently. Although the island is small enough to see on foot, bicycling is often more enjoyable. It's easiest to bring a bicycle from the mainland, but you can arrange to pick one up at the ferry port from Kihnurand (☎446 9924). The **tourist agency** organizes farmstays and camping on the island. After 2km, you will reach an intersection and signpost. Continue ahead to reach the **post office** (open M-F noon-3pm) and a tiny **grocery store.** (Open M-F 9:30am-9pm, Sa-Su 9:30am-6pm).

HAAPSALU

Haapsalu (HAHP-sah-lu; pop. 12,000) is the gateway to the Estonian Islands. Historically, its location was too strategic for its own good: the Soviets planted a military base there and cut the city off from the outside world. Today, it's a bright and lively seaside town, providing an invigorating getaway from the bustle of Tallinn.

TRANSPORTATION AND PRACTICAL INFORMATION. The bus station, Raudtee 2, has a 216m long platform. (☎473 4791. Ticket office open daily 5am-1pm and 2-7pm.) **Buses** go to Kärdla (3hr., 5 per day, 100-150EEK), Pärnu (2-3hr., 5 per day, 100-200EEK), and Tallinn (1½-2hr., 24 per day, 75-80EEK). ISIC discounts are available. Travelers can **store luggage** behind the ticket window (15EEK per day; closes briefly at noon). **Taxis** (☎473 3500) charge 10EEK per km. Rent **bikes** at **Rattad Vabatog,** Karja 22. (☎472 9846. 150EEK per day, 100EEK if bike is returned before 6pm. To reach the center from the bus station, walk down Jaama and turn left on Posti; you'll see a graveyard on your left. Open M-F 10am-6pm, Sa 10am-3pm.) At the **Tourist Information Center,** Posti 37, the extremely friendly staff books rooms for a 25EEK fee. (☎473 3248; www.haapsalu.ee. English spoken. Open mid-May to mid-Sept. 15 M-F 9am-6pm, Sa-Su 10am-3pm; mid-Sept. to mid-May M-F 9am-5pm.) A branch is outside the castle entrance. (Open daily 10am-6pm.) Free **Internet** access is at the **Lääne County Library,** Posti 3. (Open Tu-F 10am-7pm, Sa 10am-3pm.) Free Wi-Fi can be found at Müüriääre Cafe (see below) and throughout town. The **post office,** Nurme 2, is around the corner from the TIC. (☎472 0400. Open M-F 7:30am-6pm, Sa 9am-3pm.) **Postal Code:** 50901.

ACCOMMODATIONS AND FOOD. Take Lahe toward Bergfeldt, then turn right on Wiedemanni to reach **Sport Hostel ❶,** Wiedemanni 15, which offers plain private rooms with shared baths and a common kitchen. (☎472 5063 or 473 5140; haapsalu@spordibaasid.ee. Reception M-F noon-8pm. Reserve ahead. Rooms 200EEK. Cash only.) **Endla Hostel ❹,** Endla 5, is conveniently located on a residential street between the bus station and the Old Town. From the traffic circle on Jaama, take a left on Jüriöö, which runs into Endla. Clean, beach-themed rooms share a common kitchen and bathrooms. (☎473 7999. Reception daily 1-6pm.; call if arriving outside of those hours. Doubles 420EEK; triples 600EEK; quads 720EEK. Cash only.) **Lemmik,** Jaama 11, has an array of

THE LOCAL STORY

SPOT ON THE SPAS

The spas of Haapsalu were established during the Napoleonic Wars as a place for wounded Russian officials to recuperate; their dark clay mud continued to exert an influence upon rich Russian writers, politicians, and aristocrats for the remainder of the 19th century. Emperor Alexander II felt so healed after spending his time on the Baltic Coast that he regularly donated money to their upkeep, and it is said that Tchaikovsky may have composed while he relaxed in the steaming mud.

Today, visitors can kick back in the same salty waters as the famous writers, politicians, and musicians of the past. Particularly popular are baths made with local, homemade products such as honey and milk. For a romantic, rural spa experience, try **Padaste Manor,** on Muhu Island (☎454 8800). Luxuries like champagne milk crème baths, pumpkin-seed body wraps and sea salt massages start at around 500EEK per 20min. For the young and stylish, the **Georg Ots Spa,** Tosi 2 in Kureessaare is a Scandinavian spa that offers sea salt massages (1hr., 400EEK) and 100% organic cuisine in their restaurant (☎454 8800). Though you'll pay high prices in Tallinn, the **Pirita Top Spa** is a mere 10min. away from the city center and is perhaps the most luxurious of the Baltic Spas (☎639 8600).

groceries and household goods. (Open daily 8am-10pm.) **Müüriääre Kohvik ❸**, Karja 7, is a bright cafe filled with comfortable, well-worn couches. Feast on excellent French fare, such as the salmon and zucchini quiche (40EEK), while admiring the southern wall of the castle. (☎473 7527; www.muuriaare.ee. Free Wi-Fi. Entrees 40-90EEK. Open M-Th 10am-8pm, F-Su 10am-10pm. MC/V.) Down the street, the gourmet **Restoran Central ❹**, Karja 21, serves pork fillet with baked apples (121EEK) and other hearty medieval-style dishes. (☎473 5595; centraal@hot.ee. Entrees 60-150EEK. Open M-Th and Su noon-11pm, F-Sa noon-2am. MC/V.)

SIGHTS AND FESTIVALS. At the end of the bus station platform is the fantastic **Estonian Railway Museum,** which pays tribute to railway history with old conductor uniforms and equipment, vintage carriages, and photographs of Estonian train stations. (☎473 4574; www.jaam.ee. Open W-Su 10am-6pm. 15EEK, students 10EEK.) The crumbling 13th-century **Episcopal Castle** (Piiskopilinnus) in the center of town is said to be haunted by the ghost of the White Lady, who was once imprisoned in the castle; watch carefully during the full moon in February and August. The castle courtyards are free; inside you'll find a tiny **museum** and the impressive **Dome Church,** built in 1290. (☎473 7076. Open mid-May to mid-Sept. Tu-Su 10am-6pm. 15EEK, students 5EEK. In low season, call ☎473 5516 or email kk@haapsalu.ee to arrange a visit.) **White Lady Days** festivities in August include fencing tournaments and concerts. Early August brings the **Augustibluus Blues Festival,** Estonia's only blues festival (☎564 890 166; www.haapsalu.ee/augustibluus). Complementing this uniquely American musical form, the organizers of Augustibluus also display American cars at the **American Beauty Automobile Festival.** In mid-July, the **String Music Festival** (☎503 2468) spotlights Pyotr Tchaikovsky, who spent a summer in Haapsalu in 1867. The TIC has free pamphlets describing summer festivities, including locations and ticket prices.

NIGHTLIFE. Africa Beach, the most naturally beautiful of Haapsalu's coast, features serene views of Haapsalu Bay. The best swimming is on the western edge of town at **Paralepa Beach,** but between the tourists and the rocky shores, don't expect to find many comfortable places to tan. Cross the train tracks and follow the signs along the concrete path. You'll pass a skateboard park on your left; turn right at the fork to reach the shore. Dance until sunrise at **Africa,** Tallinna mnt. 1, in the shopping center, Haapsalu's main pub and club. Its restaurant is open daily 11am-midnight; the space next door is Haapsalu's best disco. (☎479 0507. Cover 100EEK. Mixed drinks 20-65EEK. Beer 22-33EEK per 0.33L. Entrees 30-80EEK. Open F-Sa 10pm-4am.) Enjoy satisfying junk food and karaoke at the popular underground **Posti 43,** Posti 43. (☎473 3347. Open daily 7am-3am.)

ESTONIAN ISLANDS

Many Estonians say the country's islands offer a glimpse of the way life used to be, with farms dotting their green and forested terrain. Afraid that the 1500 islands would become an escape route out of the USSR, the Soviets isolated the region, shielding it from outside influence. Today, the islands remain naturally beautiful, and rural life is punctuated by just a few large towns. The coastal areas are a top holiday spot for those looking to hike, bike, or merely relax in the countryside.

SAAREMAA

Meteorite craters, bubbling springs, rugged coasts, and formidable cliffs attest to the natural beauty of Saaremaa (SAH-reh-mah; pop. 38,760), Estonia's largest and most popular island. Come summer, Estonians from the mainland arrive in droves to party beachside and enjoy Saaremaa's pristine shores. The island's interior is mostly farmland and dense green woods. As distances are long and buses infrequent, the best way to get around the island is to rent a car in Kuressaare. Ambitious travelers can take in all the major sights by bike; be sure to bring rain gear. Though you'll log 100-150km of cycling each day, Saaremaa's terrain is mostly flat.

KURESSAARE

Kuressaare (KOO-rehs-sah-re; pop. 15,820), on Saaremaa's southern coast, is the island's largest town. The local accent and folklore distinguish it from the mainland, although tourists seem to outnumber locals during the summer months.

TRANSPORTATION. Flights depart from Tallinn to Kuressaare (45min., 1-2 per day, 245-455EEK). See www.avies.ee for info. **Buses** run from Tallinn via Haapsalu (4-6hr., 9-11 per day, 190-200EEK) and from Tartu via Pärnu (6hr., 3-5 per day, 180-194EEK). **Ferries** from the northern island of Hiiumaa depart from Sõru to Triigi, on Saaremaa. (Daily 8:15am, noon, 4, 8pm. 20EEK, students 10EEK, bikes 15EEK, cars 75EEK.) It's a 3km walk from Triigi to Leisi, where you can catch one of four buses daily to Kuressaare. Drivers are often happy to give you a ride; Let's Go does not recommend hitchhiking. Ferries from Saaremaa head to the mainland, making the short trip from Kuivastu to Virtsu almost hourly during the summer (30EEK, cars 45EEK, bikes 15EEK). If you're headed back to Tallinn, book your bus ticket one day in advance. If you're traveling by car and headed east to the mainland, you must reserve a spot on the ferry in advance by contacting **AS Saaremaa Laevakompanii** (☎452 4444; www.laevakompanii.ee); if you're traveling between the islands, contact the **Sõru booking office.** (☎469 5205. Open daily 8am-1pm and 4-7pm.) **Taxis** run from the town hall, the bus station, and Smuuli puiestee (☎533 33). The cheapest **car rental** rates are at **Metra,** Aia 25, behind the hospital. (☎453 9361; www.metra.ee. From 400EEK per day. Open daily 8am-6pm. MC/V.) Call at least one week in advance. Rent **bikes** from **Bivarix,** Tallinna 26. Call in advance, or show up early, as they sometimes sell out. Helmets (25EEK) are available upon request. (☎455 7118; bivarix@bivarix.ee. 150EEK for the 1st day, 125EEK per day thereafter. Open M-F 10am-6pm, Sa 10am-2pm. MC/V.)

ORIENTATION AND PRACTICAL INFORMATION. The town is centered on narrow **Raekoja plac** (Town Hall Square). The **Tourist Information Center (TIC),** Tallinna 2, inside the town hall, offers car rental advice, updated ferry and bus schedules, and free **maps.** Those planning to travel around the region should buy a detailed map (45 EEK) of Saaremaa. (☎453 3120; www.visitestonia.com. Open May to mid-Sept. M-F 9am-7pm, Sa 9am-5pm, Su 10am-3pm; mid-Sept. to mid-Apr. M-F 9am-5pm.) The island's website, www.saaremaa.ee, is invaluable for information about transportation, accommodations, local activities, and a brief history of the region. **Eesti Ühispank,** Kauba 2, **exchanges currency,** cashes **traveler's checks,** and gives MasterCard and Visa **cash advances.** (☎452 1500; fax 452 1533. Open M-Sa 9am-6pm, Su 9am-2pm.) In Kuressaare's center, 24hr. **ATMs** are easy to find. **Store luggage** outside the bus station. (10-15EEK per day. The TIC will store your bags for free. Open M-F 7:15am-2pm and 2:30-8pm, Sa 7:15am-2pm and 2:30-6pm.) Free **Internet** access and Wi-Fi is available at the **library,** Tallinna 8. Go upstairs and reserve a computer for a block of 1hr., or grab one of six terminals designated for 15min. use only. (Open July-Aug. M-F 11am-7pm; Sept.-June M-F 10am-7pm, Sa 10am-4pm.) The **post office,** Torni 1, is on the corner of Komandandi. (☎452 4080. Open M-F 8am-6pm, Sa 8:30am-3pm.) **Postal Code:** 93801 in the town center; different sections of town have difference postal codes.

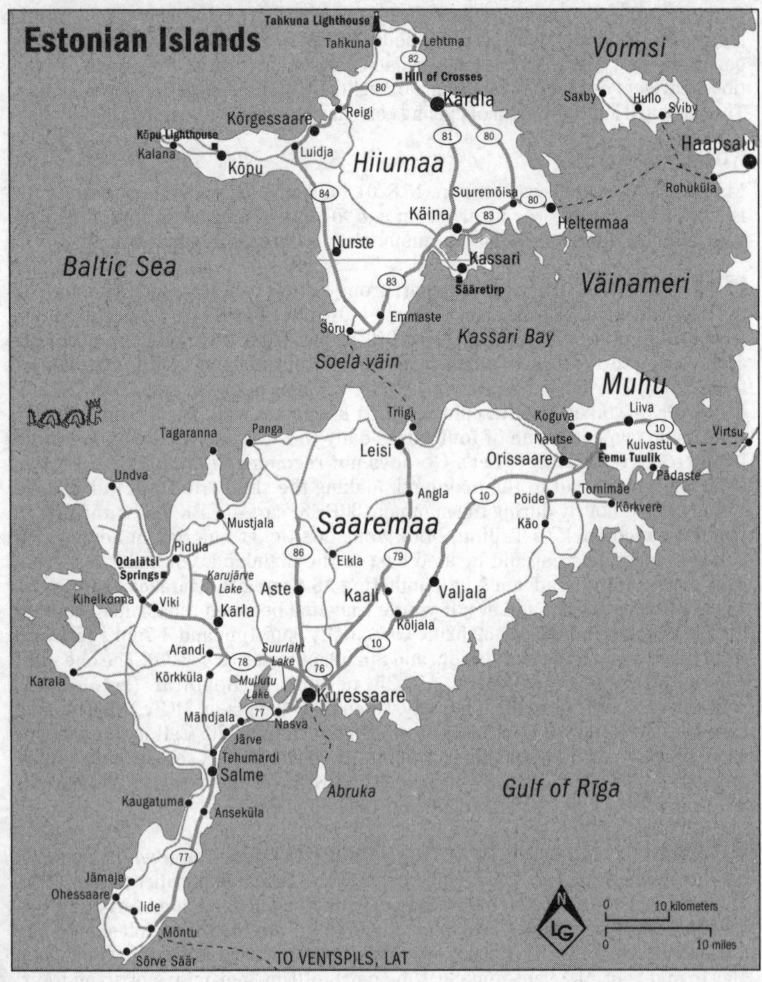

ACCOMMODATIONS AND FOOD. The staff at the **TIC** make same-day bookings at local B&Bs free of charge. Family-run **Transvaali 28 B&B ❷**, Transvaali 28, is a great deal. From the bus station, cross Pihtla tee and continue along Transvaali, a paved residential road, for three blocks. All three bright, cozy rooms (300-330EEK) include spotless private baths, TVs, and breakfast. (☎453 3334 or 525 3415; www.saaremaa.ee/transvaali28. Bargain down even farther on weekdays. Cash only.) From the station, follow Põhja past Tallinna, turn left on Hariduse, and turn right on Kingu to reach **SYG Hostel ❶**, Kingu 6. A dorm during the academic year, SYG offers clean, spacious rooms with Internet access, Wi-Fi, and fitness facilities. (☎455 4388. Breakfast 40EEK. Open June-Aug. Singles 255EEK; doubles 300-350EEK; quads 480-580EEK. 15% discount M-W and Su. MC/V.)

A small **market** is hidden among buildings between Kohtu and Torni, across from the TIC. Vegetables and homemade honey are sold at some tables, while handicrafts and knitted sweaters take up most of the space. (Open M-Sa 8am-3pm.) **Raekeskus,** Raekoja 10, just behind the TIC, is a huge shopping center with a supermarket. (Open daily 9am-10pm. MC/V.) **Pannkoogikohvik ❶,** Kohtu 1, serves hearty "hot pots" (41-61EEK) of rice, pasta, or potatoes, mixed with your choice of meat, fish, or vegetables. Huge and delicious thin-crust pizzas with unique toppings (30-72EEK) are also available. (☎453 3575. Open M-Th 8:15am-midnight, F-Sa 8:15am-2am, Su 9:15am-midnight. MC/V.) **John Bull Pub ❷,** Lossipark 4, across the moat from the castle, may be the only place that serves *Saku* (30EEK per 0.5L) in a school bus. Sit outside for a spectacular view of the castle and grounds. (☎453 9988. Open daily 11am-last customer.)

SIGHTS AND FESTIVALS. Follow Tallina and merge onto Lossi to reach the massive 13th-century **Bishopric Castle** (Piiskopilinnus). Legend has it that when the Bishop of Saare-Lääne served as judge at the castle, convicts were thrown to a pack of hungry lions. You can hear a recording of the lions' roar if you climb up the watchtower. The eclectic **Saaremaa Museum** inside the castle showcases a hodgepodge of medieval weaponry, stuffed swans, and local contemporary art. Visitors can skip to the most interesting part of the exhibit, a technologically enhanced history of the island and Estonia in the 20th century, next to the cafe. At the end of the exhibits, don't miss the stairs that lead to the cafe and defense gallery, where the castle roof opens onto a spectacular view of the town and coast. (☎455 6307. Open May-Aug. daily 10am-7pm. Last entry 6pm; Sept.-Apr. W-Su 11am-6pm. 50EEK, students 30EEK; with 2hr. audio tour in English, Estonian, Finnish, or Russian 60EEK. Cash only.) For a complete medieval experience, test your **archery** skills outside. (Archery daily 10am-5pm. 4 arrows 15EEK, 15min. 60EEK.) Inside the 1670 **town hall** *(raekoja)*, a gallery presents rotating exhibits of contemporary Estonian artwork, and the second floor has a 17th-century painted ceiling. The biblical painting was found in a house in Kuressaare after WWII. (☎443 3266. Open Tu-F 10am-5pm, Sa 10am-3pm.) Kuressaare's popular, tiny **beach** is directly behind the castle.

On weekends in July, there's **live music** in the park around the castle. (Brass band Sa, orchestra Su. Shows 6pm.) In late July, **Õlletoober,** a beer festival, peps up Leisi, on the northern coast of Saaremaa, while an **Opera Festival** takes over Kuressaare. At the end of June and beginning of July is the **Saaremaa Waltz Festival,** which features Finnish-style dancing and a deluge of tourists from Helsinki.

WEST SAAREMAA

Follow Rte. 78 from Kuressaare 30km toward **Kihelkonna** to reach the **Mikhli Farm Museum,** a well preserved example of the typical Estonian farm. You can climb inside a working windmill, which spins only on very gusty days. If you're lucky, the blacksmith will teach you how to make horseshoes. (☎454 6613. Open daily May-Sept. 10am-6pm. 25EEK, students 15EEK.) One kilometer down the road, hang a left at the signpost to reach the 13th-century **Kihelkonna Church.** Although there's a sign indicating that visitors can't enter the late 19th-century tower 100m away from the church, an attendant may let you climb to the top as long as you pledge not to ring the bell. (☎454 6558. Open daily 10am-5pm.) Backtrack along Rte. 102, crossing Rte. 78, and continue 8km along a bumpy dirt path to reach **Pidula Fish Farm** (Pidula Veskitiigi Forellipüük) ❶, where the pond is swarming with trout. Cast a line, reel in your catch, and pay 120EEK per kilogram. They'll gut (5EEK), salt (15EEK), and grill (40EEK) for you as well. If you don't feel like getting fish scales on you, choose instead from their selection of fresh catch (60-120EEK). You can also **rent your own island** ❷, in the center of the pond, where there's a one-room cabin. (☎454 6513; www.pidulakalakasvatus.ee. No running water. Reserve weeks in advance. 350EEK per night.) It's another 7km to Rte. 101, where you'll hang a left toward **Mustjala.** The town **church,** 2km down the road, is a popular concert venue; events are posted on the door. Next door is a grocer, **Mustjala Kauplus.** (Open daily 9am-8pm. MC/V.) Just down the hill is a small local art gallery and cafe, **Musta Jala Galerii.** Stop in for tea or coffee (15EEK) and home-baked pie (7-8EEK per slice). The road becomes unpaved; continue toward **Ninase** for 6km, where a **windmill** decorated as a peasant greets you. Head straight to the fishing village of **Tagaranna,** which offers views of the jagged **Panga cliffs** on your right. This infamous 16th-century child sacrifice site has been immortalized on the back of the 100EEK note. From Tagaranna, it's 40km back to Kuressaare.

SOUTHWEST SAAREMAA

Fifty kilometers from Kuressaare down the narrow **Sõrve Peninsula,** Southwest Saaremaa's southernmost tip affords glimpses of Latvia, which lies 25km south across the Baltic. **Sõrve,** the last stronghold of the Germans in Estonia, was the scene of numerous gruesome battles against the Soviets in WWII. At the tip is the **Sõrve lighthouse,** built in the 1960s. Three kilometers down the Sääare-Kaugatuma road is the turnoff to **Stebel's Battery,** where the Soviets built towering defense complexes that were later blown apart by the German forces and filled with water. Today, an **observation tower** lets you take in the remains. At the 4km mark, a concrete obelisk stands where Stebel's command center one stood.

Riding out of Kuressaare, you'll pass a string of sandy **beaches** 8-12km out of town; you won't find a private place to bathe in the sun, however, as locals line the shores on summer weekends. At Tehumardi, 17km from Kuressaare, a giant concrete sword and rows of **memorials** mark the location of a 1944 WWII battle. Your last chance to stock up on bottled water and snacks is 4km farther at **Salme Kauplus** (open daily 8am-10pm), which has a 24hr. MasterCard and Visa **ATM** outside. After another 15km, the road is paved only sporadically. Campsites are available throughout the peninsula. Ask at the TIC for more info before leaving Kuressaare.

MUHU

You can reach Muhu Island from the mainland via the **Virtsu-Kuivastu ferry** route (30min.; 1 per hr., on the hr.; 35EEK, students 10EEK; cars 55-80EEK; bikes 15EEK); motorists should reserve a spot with the Kuressaare booking office in advance (☎452 4444). All buses running from Kuressaare to Tallinn or Pärnu stop in Liiva, even if it's not on the bus schedule (2 per hr., 40-80EEK). There are no bike rental agencies on Muhu—you have to rent either on the mainland or on Saaremaa. It's an ambitious but manageable 55km ride from Kuressaare to Väikese Väine Tamm, the 1896 causeway that connects Saaremaa to Muhu. After you cross, watch for **Eeme Tuulik,** an ancient windmill built on the site of an old emu farm. (Open W-Su 10am-6pm. 10EEK, students 5EEK.) Buy **fresh bread** (25-30EEK) made from locally ground flour. Past the windmill, go left toward Nautse; in 700m, you'll reach the quirky **Laasu Ostrich Farm,** where you can buy a giant egg (300EEK), which can only be cracked open with a drill or hatchet. The friendly owners, Helena and Elmet, provide information in English. (☎452 8148; www.jaanalind.ee. Open in the summer 10am-6pm; call for appointments in the winter.) About 1km down the dirt path, turn left on the paved road to Koguva (4km), a well-preserved 19th-century fishing village and open-air museum. (☎452 8148. Open daily in summer 10am-6pm; in winter 10am-5pm. No English captions.)

Bed and breakfasts line the roads of Muhu; look for the standard blue sign with a bed on it. **Vanatoa Tunsmitalu** ❷ offers bright rooms in a stone longhouse with a shared bath and sauna. (Breakfast included. 300EEK per person; tent space with shower 40EEK.) The adjacent **restaurant** ❹ (☎488 84) serves *solyanka* (40EEK), a thick Russian soup, and oven-baked eel in tartar sauce (180EEK). There's **bus** service (2 per day) here from Kuressaare and Kuivastu; check the hotel reception for schedules. It's 6km back to Rte. 10, where you'll turn left toward Liiva; on your right after 5km, you'll see the white-walled 13th-century **Muhu Katariina Church.** Portions of the early-Gothic church's 13th-century murals are still visible through the layers of whitewash with which they were covered during the Reformation. (Open daily 10am-6pm.) Just down the road on your left, you'll find the well-stocked supermarket **Liiva Pood** (open daily 8am-10pm), with a 24hr. **ATM.** It's 65km back to Kuressaare; after 49km, you'll see a turn-off on the left to the Kaali meteorite **crater field** (Kaali meteroiidikraatrite rühm). The main crater, with a diameter of 110m, was created about 4000 years ago by a massive, 1000-ton meteor. A green pond now fills the impact mark. A **Visitors' Center** at the site also houses a geological museum with rock core samples from all over the island and a piece of iron meteorite that fell on Russia in 1947. (☎459 1184; www.kaali.kylastuskeskus.ee. Open May-Oct. daily 9am-8pm. 25EEK, students 10EEK.)

HIIUMAA

By restricting access to the island of Hiiumaa (HEE-you-ma; pop. 11,500) for 50 years, the Soviets unwittingly preserved many rare plant and animal species, as well as the island's traditional way of life. Hiiumaa remains the most forested county in Estonia and locals still speak of the ghosts, giants, and devils of legend.

More than two-thirds of all the plant species native to Estonia exist only on Hiiumaa. Due to this biodiversity, much of the island now belongs to the **West Estonian Islands Biosphere Reserve.** Hiking and camping are permitted and encouraged; just be sure to pick up info at the tourist office about off-limits regions. Motor vehicles are not allowed within 20m of the seashore, and campfires and smoking are prohibited in some areas due to dry conditions.

KÄRDLA

The Swedish settlers who stumbled upon this sleepy spot on Hiiumaa's north coast named it "Kärrdal," meaning "lovely valley" in Swedish. Home to many more creeks and trees than houses, Kärdla (pop. 4118) is hardly an urban center, but remains the capital of the island and a popular stop for tourists. Home to the only Information Center on Hiiumaa, Kardla is an important stop for bus schedules and information about the island.

TRANSPORTATION AND PRACTICAL INFORMATION. Tiit Reisid, the tourist agency at Kärdla's **bus station,** Sadama 13, will help you navigate Hiiumaa's horrendous public transit system. (☎463 2077; hiiumaa@tiitreisid.ee. Open M-F 7am-7pm; Sa-Su 7-9am, 11am-3pm, and 4-7pm.) From Kärla, **buses** run west to Kõrgessaare and Kõpu (2-3 per day; 14-26EEK) and south to Käina (3-4 per day, 16EEK). A **ferry** runs from Hiiumaa's southern town of Sõru to Triigi on Saaremaa (1hr.; 50EEK, students 20EEK; bikes 25EEK; cars 75EEK). Bus fare to Kärdla from Tallinn (4½hr., 110EEK) includes a **ferry ticket** from Rohükla (on the mainland) to Heltermaa, Hiiumaa's easternmost port. For a **taxi,** call ☎463 1447. Rent **bikes** from **Nõmme Puhkemaja,** Nõmme 30. (☎463 1338. 100EEK per day.) Arrive early or call the day before to reserve a bike at **Kerttu Sport,** Sadama 15, across the bridge past the bus station. (☎463 2130; fax 463 2076. 100EEK per day, 50EEK if returned before 6pm the day of rental. Open M-F 10am-6pm, Sa 10am-3pm.)

The island's **Tourist Information Center,** Hiiu 1, in **Keskväljak,** the main square, gives out free maps and sells the handy **Lighthouse Tour** guide (25EEK), available in English. (☎462 2232; www.hiiumaa.ee. Open May-Sept. M-F 9am-6pm, Sa-Su 10am-3pm; Oct.-Apr. M-F 10am-4pm.) **Eesti Ühispank,** Keskväljak 7, **exchanges currency,** cashes **traveler's checks,** and has an **ATM.** (☎463 2040. Open M-F 9am-4pm.) The **pharmacy, Keskväljaku Apteek,** Põllu 1, is just off the main square. (☎463 2137. Open M-F 9am-6pm, Sa 10am-2pm. MC/V.) The **cultural center,** Rookopli 18, has free **Internet** access but you must reserve in advance. (☎463 2182. Open M-F noon-6pm, Su 10am-1pm.) Free Wi-Fi is available in the town square. The **post office,** Keskväljak 3, is on the main square. (☎463 2013. Open M-F 8am-5:30pm, Sa 8:30am-1pm.) **Postal Code:** 92412.

ACCOMMODATIONS AND FOOD. Eesti Posti Hostel ❷, Posti 13, 5min. from the town center and close to the beach, has bare private rooms, clean shared baths, a fully equipped kitchen, and a common room. Follow Sadama over the stream from the bus station and turn right on Posti. (☎53 31 18 60. Call ahead. Rooms May-Sept. 255EEK; Oct.-Apr. 200EEK. Cash only.) If you're at the beach, try **Rannapaargu ❷,** Lubjaahja 3, a spacious dining room that offers drinks and full meals with splendid coastal views. (☎463 2053. Entrees 35-90EEK. Open M-Sa noon-11pm, Su noon-9pm. MC/V.) **Arteesia Kohvik ❶,** Keskväljak 5, is run by locals for locals. They serve up generous portions of meat and seafood. (☎463 2173. Entrees 30-85EEK. Open M-Th 9am-11pm, F-Sa 9am-midnight, Su 11am-10pm.) It's above the small grocer **Toidukauplus.** (Open daily 9am-11pm.) Toidukauplus and **Konsum,** Keskväljak 1 (open daily 9am-10pm; MC/V), stock the unskimmed Hiiumaa yogurt **Anno** (7.39EEK per 500g).

SIGHTS. Rannapark, at the end of Lubjaahju, is a rocky **beach** lined with benches and a 14-hole miniature golf course. (Open 10am-10pm. English descriptions. 10EEK, students 5EEK. Golf 20EEK.) Follow Rookopoli to the main crossroads to see a forlorn **memorial** to the Soviet soldiers who defeated the Germans in WWII. Nicknamed "Kivi Jüri" by the locals, it is jokingly referred to as the last Russian soldier remaining on Hiiumaa. Turn left toward Heltermaa and, after 3km, bear left toward the airport to reach **Paluküla Church.** Continue along the road until you reach a triangular intersection; the church is in the trees on your right. Built in 1820, it was a landmark for sailors—and later target practice for Soviet soldiers. You'll see hundreds of rusty bullet shells scattered on the ground. What you can't see is that the church is built on the rim of a Paleozoic meteorite crater. The crater was discovered in the early 1970s; a signpost in the church yard describes, in several languages, the unique geology of the area and maps the various impact craters on Hiiumaa. For a taste of the local culture, check the **TIC** for the dates of monthly **craft fairs,** which feature handmade trinkets and dance performances.

BIKING TO KÕPU. Densely wooded forests and small farming towns dot this scenic ride. It's 60km to see all the sights on the way to Kopu; start early in the day and take a good map. For a more relaxed pace, turn around at the Tahkuna Lighthouse (20km). Heading west out of Kärdla toward Kõrgessaare, you'll pass the spooky **Hill of Crosses** (Ristimägi) after about 6km, commemorating the Hiiumaa Swedes deported to Ukraine by Catherine the Great. About 2km past the Hill of Crosses, a right turn leads to the cast-iron **Tahkuna Lighthouse** (11km from the turn-off), built in Paris in 1874. The lighthouse consistently failed to warn ships about the coast's shallow waters, but no one seemed to mind, since salvaging loot and rescuing passengers was quite profitable. Just past the lighthouse is the **Tahkuna Labyrinth** (Tahkuna Kivilaburint), built by the Hiiumaa Royal Association of Temperate Bee-Lovers in 1997. On the way back to the main road, detour to the open air **Mihkli Farm Museum** off the lighthouse road, on a plot of land that's been cultivated since 1564. The bundle of eight farm buildings gained fame in 2001, when it hosted the reality television show *Farm*, in which contestants from all over the Baltics had to live in 200-year-old farm conditions. (☎463 2091. Open mid-May to mid-Sept. daily 10am-6pm. 10EEK, students 5EEK.) Go back to the main road and turn right, heading toward Kõrgessaare. Down 7km, you'll see the red roof of **Reigi Church,** built in 1802. After a few kilometers, turn right into Kõrgessaare, where you can take a break at excellent **Restoran Viinaköök ❸,** Sadama 2, in an old whiskey distillery. Lunch and dinner buffets (30-150EEK) feature hot meat and vegetarian entrees, as well as a fresh salad bar. (☎469 3337. Open daily noon-10pm. MC/V.) Continue 20km past Kõrgessaare to reach Western Hiiumaa's most impressive site, the **Kõpu Lighthouse,** built of six thousand tons of stone. Construction started in 1504, when island residents of the Hanseatic Merchants League became concerned that so many of their ships were getting lost in the Baltic Sea. The ticket office houses a **cafe** with **Internet** access (15EEK per 30min.). It hosts **concerts** every Friday in July at 9pm (tickets 50-100EEK). Climb the lighthouse's narrow staircase to see how far you've come. (Open daily 10am-8pm. 25EEK.)

KÄINA

Käina (pop. 2500), southwest of Suuremõisa, is Hiiumaa's second-most populous urban center. Sights in town are scarce, but it's an excellent base for exploring the island's southern tip. Head toward the coast and the island of Kassari to see the natural countryside and sapphire blue seas.

TRANSPORTATION AND PRACTICAL INFORMATION. Driving a car is the most reliable method of transport around the area. The main **bus stop** in town is located at Hiiu mnt. 11, next to the grocery store and a large map of the town. Infrequent buses (☎463 2077; fax 463 2065) run daily to Haapsalu and Sõru (M-F 7:25am and 4:45pm; Sa-Su 4:45pm), where a ferry connects to the port of Triigi, on Saaremaa. Local buses also go to Kärdla (25-30min., 5 per day, 16EEK). The morning bus from Käina (6:25am) makes a loop around Kassari. Rent **bikes** at your guesthouse or **Rattad Vaba Aeg,** Hiiu mnt. 13, the yellow house next to the bus station. (☎56 49 13 72. 100EEK per day. Open Su-M 10am-6pm, Tu-F 10am-5pm.) The **cultural center** has **tourist info** and free **Internet** access. (☎463 6231. From Ratted Vaga Aeg, walk straight 750m down Mäe. Open M-F 10am-5pm, Sa 10am-2pm.) **Hansapank** is on the first floor. (Open M-F 9am-5pm.) A 24hr. **ATM** is outside.

ACCOMMODATIONS AND FOOD. Though there are several hotels in Käina, the family-run bed & breakfasts that line the roads are both cheaper and cozier. Look for the standard blue accommodation sign with a bed on it. Directly opposite the bus stop when you arrive, **Tondilossi öömaja ❷,** Hiiu mnt. 11, is right in Käina's center and offers small, wood-paneled private rooms (250EEK) with shared baths. The central location is invaluable. (☎463 6337; kylvi.rannu@mail.ee. Break-

ESTONIA

fast included.) From Käina's center, head 2km toward Emmaste on Hiiu mnt. and hang a left toward Kassari. If arriving by bus, get off at the Luguse stop on the main road and follow the sign toward Kassari. After another 2km, you'll be at **Puulaiu Matkamaja ❶**, a certified Green Label accommodation, which is designed to minimize adverse consequences for the surrounding environment. The friendly, English-speaking owner offers beautiful beachside cabins and tent space. (☎463 6126 or 508 8610. Breakfast 50EEK. Bikes 100EEK per day. Boats 30EEK per hr. Call ahead. Cabins 130-200EEK per person. Tent space 25EEK per person.) With your back to the bus stop, follow Hiiu mnt. as it curves right and turns into Mae. Head 1km on Mae, past highway 83 to Lookese. **Karukoobas ❷**, Lookese 10, is a clean country home with private rooms and beautiful gardens. Included in your stay is a hearty breakfast, cooked by the friendly owners. (☎463 6495 or 511 1214. Rooms 250EEK per person. Cash only.) Three doors down, **Peedu ❷**, Lookese 4, has similar rooms and identical prices. (☎463 6495 or 513 9108. Breakfast included. Cash only.)

The family-run **Töidubaar ❶**, in a small wood cabin next to Tondilossi öömaja, serves hearty shares of meat and potatoes. It's the cheapest of the handful of restaurants in town. (Entrees 30-60EEK. Open M-F 11:30am-6pm, Sa 10am-6pm.) Hotel Liilia's popular **Restaurant Liilia ❸**, decorated with fishing nets and lanterns, offers upscale dishes such as beefsteak with juniper berries and gin sauce, fish dishes (90-130EEK), and breakfast options for 30-40EEK. (☎463 6146. Vegetarian options. Open daily 11am-11pm. MC/V.) The aptly named **Konsum**, Hiiu mnt. 9, is a well-stocked grocery store. (Open daily 9am-10pm. MC/V.)

SIGHTS. Turn right on Hiiu mnt. toward the **Rudulf Tobias House-Museum** (R. Tobiase Maja-Muuseum), Hiiu mnt. 33. The famous Estonian composer, who was born here in 1873, started writing music when he was six years old. Captions are in Estonian and Russian only, but if you're lucky the receptionist will give you an English tour. (☎463 6586. Open mid-May to mid-Sept. W-Su 10am-6pm. 15EEK, students 5EEK. Call in advance during winter.) To pay for his son's piano—which you can play in the museum—Tobias's father worked to build the organ at **Käina Church** on the other side of town. A German fighter plane turned the house of worship to a smoldering ruin in WWII; today, you can wander its dilapidated, roofless interior. To get to the church, follow Hiiu through Käina past Lillia.

BIKING TO SUUREMÕISA AND KASSARI. **Pühalepa Church,** in Suuremõisa, is the oldest on the island and contains the graves of the family of 19th century Baltic-German Count Ungern-Sternberg. The Count wanted to acquire the entire island, but his shipping business was cut short when he killed an employee and was banished to Siberia. Today, you can climb into the lofts and peer through the tall windows. From the church parking lot, take a right onto a gravel road to the mysterious **Contract Stones** (Põhilise leppe kivid). Some believe the stones were placed here in the sixth century to mark the grave of a Swedish king, while others think sailors stacked the boulders for good luck as a symbol of their devotion to God. From the stones, head back to the highway and take the next right onto an oak-lined alley. After about 200m is the **Suuremõisa Palace,** a beautiful 18th-century manor passed from generation to generation among the ruling families of the island. Call ahead for info about Night Tours, when you can visit the manor by candlelight to hear tales of ghosts haunting the halls. (☎469 4391. Open July-Aug. M-F noon-6pm, Sa-Su 10am-3pm; Sept.-June M-F 8am-4pm. 15EEK, students 5EEK.)

The ride to **Kassari** (kah-SAH-ree; pop. 286), a tiny village on its own island southeast of Käina, passes through fantastic forest scenery and along the beautiful blue Baltic coast. Roads from the east and the west feed into Kassari; a circular ride of 15km allows you to see all the sights in a relaxing afternoon bike ride.

Enter the loop from the west, where you'll first pass the small village of Orjaku. Climb the **bird observation tower** for spendid views of Käina Bay. When you reach Kassari, in the middle of the island, 7km from the turn-off, look for signs to the **Hiiumaa Museum,** whose succinct exhibit chronicles the geological and social history of the island, complete with meterorites found in the region. (☎469 7121. Open mid-May to mid-Sept. daily 10am-5:30pm. English captions. 15EEK, students 5EEK.) Backtrack to the main road, head straight, and veer right at the signpost, following the road to the most beautiful of the island's sights, **Säaretirp,** a 1.3m wide sandbar lined with strawberry and juniper bushes. Legend holds that this 3km peninsula is the remains of an ancient bridge between Hiiumaa and Saaremaa. Continue down the main road 4km to reach the turn-off for Kassari Church. Follow the signs 2km to reach a quiet, secluded stone structure, whose bells and interiors were looted during Soviet times. Back on the main road a mere 200m before you're back on Highway 83 to Käina, the **Vamela Wool Factory** has been passed down in the Vamela family for generations. The father Yuri can be seen working the gigantic steel looms, while his wife Tiiu gives informative English tours of the looms and spinning process. Refuel at the family's **cafe** right next door to the factory. (Open daily 10am-6pm. Coffee 15EEK. Sandwiches 9EEK.) Finally, turn left on the main road, Highway 83, and bike the 3km back to Käina.

INLAND ESTONIA

All roads inland from Tallinn lead to Tartu, the historic cultural and nationalistic heart of Estonia. The region's smaller towns, however, should not be overlooked. Visitors can immerse themselves in the mystical surroundings of Otepää or take a daytrip to Viljandi to explore the medieval castle that once protected the town.

TARTU

Tartu (pop. 110,000) bills itself as "the city of good thoughts," a fitting moniker for the intellectual capital of Estonia. Even in the summer, students fill the many bookstores and cozy coffee shops that line the streets. Tartu is home to a rich array of museums, a broad selection of performing arts events, and the top university in the country. Even as posh hotels spring up like mushrooms, it remains a down-to-earth college town, perfect for travelers on a budget.

TRANSPORTATION

Trains: Vaksali 6 (☎615 6851; www.edel.ee), at the intersection with Kuperjanovi, 1.5km from the city center. Although the station itself is closed, a few trains to **Tallinn** stop here (3hr., 3 per day, 85-100EEK). Buy your ticket from the conductor on board.

Buses: Intercity station (autobussijaam), Soola 2 (☎747 7227), on the corner of Riia and Turu, 300m southeast of Raekoja plats along Vabaduse. Info office open daily 8am-8pm. To: **Pärnu** (2½hr., 20 per day, 110EEK); **Tallinn** (2-3hr., 50 per day, 130-140EEK); and **Rīga, LAT** (5hr., 1 per day, 170-200EEK). 30-50% ISIC/ITIC discount on some routes. A complete bus schedule is available at **www.bussireisid.ee;** international connections schedule at www.eurolines.ee.

Public Transportation: Bus tickets 13EEK from kiosks, 15EEK on board. You can also purchase a 1hr. ticket (16EEK) or day pass (40EEK). Buses #5 and 6 go from the train station to Raekoja plats and the bus station. Bus #4 travels up and down Võru. Buses #2 and 22 travel away from the river on Riia; #6, 7, and 21 head toward it; #3, 8, and 11 go both ways. Bus routes converge at the Kaubamaja on Riia.

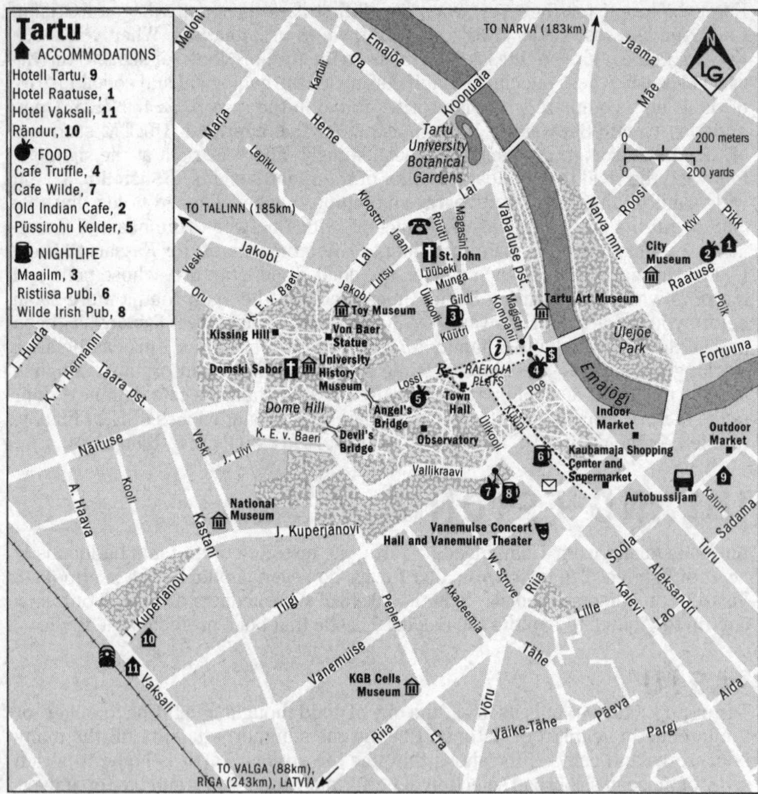

Taxis: Tartu taksopark (☎730 0200). 25EEK base, 12EEK per km. **Tax Tuo** (☎733 3666 or 513 3366). 25EEK base, 10 EEK per km. Be sure that the meter is running.

Bike Rental: Sportex, Raekoja plats 11 (☎740 1000), across from the TIC. 170EEK per day. Open M-F 10am-6pm, Sa 10am-4pm, Su 10am-3pm. MC/V.

PRACTICAL INFORMATION

Tourist Office: Raekoja plats 14 (☎44 21 11; www.tartu.ee). Arranges guides, rental cars, and **private rooms** for free (180EEK, outside Tartu 25EEK). It also sells copies of *Tartu in Your Pocket* (25EEK), and offers a **free map** of Tartu and free **Internet**. Open June-Aug. M-F 9am-6pm, Sa 10am-5pm, Su 10am-3pm; Sept.-May M-F 9am-5pm, Sa 10am-3pm.

Currency Exchange: Hansapank, Raekoja plats 20 (☎740 0740). Cashes **traveler's checks** (AmEx and Thomas Cook) offers **cash advances,** and exchanges **currency.** 24hr. **ATM** outside. Open M-F 9am-5pm, Sa 10am-2pm. Privately owned **Tavid,** Rüütli. 2 (☎37 27 30 11 70), offers the best exchange rates. **American Express: Estravel,** Vallikraavi 2 (☎44 03 00; www.estravel.ee). Open M-F 9am-6pm, Sa 10am-3pm.

Luggage Storage: Around the corner from the front door of the bus station. 6-20EEK per bag per day. Open daily 7:30am-9pm.

24hr. Pharmacy: Raekoja Apteek (☎43 35 28), around the side of the Town Hall building, facing Rüütli.

Internet: Free Internet at the **Tourist Info Center** (see above) and the **Tartu Public Library** (Tartu Linnaraamatukoga); go upstairs to the 2nd fl., through the door on your left, and continue down the hallway until you see a door marked "Internet." 1st hr. free, 10EEK per hr. thereafter. Open M-F 9am-7pm, Sa 10am-4pm; summer hours may vary. If you have your own laptop, use free Wi-Fi in the town square, **Wilde Irish Pub** (p. 259), or anywhere with the **wifi.ee** sign.

Post Office: Vanemuise 7 (☎741 0600; www.post.ee). Open M-F 9am-5pm, Sa 10am-3pm. **Postal Code:** 51003.

ACCOMMODATIONS

Hostel Raatuse, Raatuse 22 (☎740 9958; www.kyla.ee). These modern Tartu University dorms are more luxurious than many upscale hotels. 4 rooms share a shower and fully equipped kitchen; each suite has its own Internet connection and cable TV. Laundry 30EEK; bring your own detergent. Singles 300EEK; doubles 500EEK. MC/V. ❷

Hotell Tartu, Soola 3 (☎731 4300; www.tartuhotell.ee), across the street from the inter-city bus station. A blessing for late-night arrivals, this hotel provides spartan rooms with private baths, phones, and TVs. Breakfast included. Singles 600EEK; doubles 900EEK; triples 1100EEK. 15% ISIC discount; 10% off online bookings. ❺ Space is almost always available in the **youth rooms,** with wooden bunk and single beds, where it's unlikely you'll have roommates. 3-bed rooms 300EEK. ❷

Rändur, Kuperjanovi 66 (☎742 7190; www.zone.ee/randur), opposite the train station. Quality varies: the shared-bath single (350EEK) and double (500-600EEK) on the 1st fl. are nicer than the identically priced, older rooms upstairs. All rooms have TVs. Doubles with private bath 500EEK. Cash only. ❹

Hostel Vaksali, Vaksali 4 (☎509 3743; jaaktaru@hot.ee). Next to the train station. This shining new hostel has clean, cozy, rooms and a friendly staff. Shared bath. Singles 300EEK, doubles 500EEK. Cash only. ❷

FOOD

Kaubamaja supermarket is located at Riia 1, on the ground floor of the Kaubamaja shopping center (☎731 5100). Open M-Sa 9am-9pm, Su 9am-6pm. MC/V.) Near the river at the end of Soola, an **open-air market** sells fresh fruit and vegetables. (Open M-F 8am-5pm, Sa 8am-4pm, Su 8am-3pm.) The indoor *turg* (market), on the corner of Vabaduse and Vanemuise, sells cheap, fresh food, primarily meat and fish. (Open M-F 7:30am-5:30pm, Sa 7:30am-4pm, Su 7:30am-3pm.)

Püssirohu Kelder (Gunpowder Cellar), Lossi 28 (☎730 3555), in the park behind the town hall. Look for the 2 cannons outside. Catherine the Great ordered the construction of this former gunpowder vault to fortify Tartu. Drink from tankards at massive wooden tables, or steal off to the wine cellar for a more intimate experience. Live music (Tu-Sa around 9pm) often ends in tabletop dancing. Beer 30EEK per 0.5L. Open M-Th noon-2am, F-Sa noon-3am, Su 11am-midnight. MC/V. ❷

Cafe Wilde, Vallikraavi 4 (☎730 9764). Linger on the terrace with your tea (12EEK) and a good book–if you haven't brought one with you, check out the English titles at Wilde Bookstore next door. Old printing presses stand as reminders of the building's previous life as a publishing house. Sandwiches (30-45EEK), pancakes (25-35EEK), and desserts (25-50EEK) served. Open M-Sa 9am-7pm, Su 10am-6pm. MC/V. ❶

Old Indian Cafe, Raatuse 22 (☎37 25 05 67 77; www.oldindian.ee). Located right downstairs from Hostel Raatuse, this student hangout offers pool tables, a TV, and the accompanying enthusiastic football fans. The almond chicken with curry is excellent

(66EEK), as are the pancakes (20-30EEK), hot sandwiches (20-30EEK), and hot entrees (50-70EEK). Open M-F and Sa 10am-10pm, Su 9am-10pm. MC/V. ❶

Cafe Truffle, Raekoja plats 16 (☎742 8840; www.cafetruffle.ee). Feast on unique salads (35-60EEK), pastas (75EEK), and other entrees (70-110EEK) such as goat cheese ravioli with pesto. Then indulge in their decadent handmade truffles and desserts (20-52EEK). Open M-Th and Su 10am-10pm, F 10am-9pm, Sa 10am-10pm. MC/V. ❶

SIGHTS

TOWN HALL SQUARE (RAEKOJA PLATS). In front of the 1775 Dutch-style **town hall** stands a 1998 statue of students kissing in a fountain. The buildings on the south side of the Square were destroyed in WWII and rebuilt by the Soviets; look for the hammer and sickle still etched into their facades. Near the bridge, the **Tartu Art Museum** (Tartu Kunstimuuseum) hosts exhibits in a building that, like the student population, leans a little to the left. Of particular note is Peeter Allik's massive canvas *State Secret to Cheat the People*. Every summer, new work by the graduating classes of the Tartu Art School is featured on the first floor. *(Raekoja plats 18. ☎44 10 80. Open W-Su 11am-6pm. 25EEK, students 10EEK; F free. Call ahead for a tour; 100EEK.)*

TARTU UNIVERSITY MAIN BUILDING (TARTU ÜLIKOO). In 1632, the Swedish King Gustavus Adolfus II established the first university in Estonia (Academia Gustaviana) on this spot. It became Tartu University when Estonia achieved independence in 1919. The **main building** of the university, featured on the back of the 2EEK banknote, includes an **assembly hall** *(aula)* that hosted concerts conducted by Liszt and Schumann. Today the magnificent blue-and-white room still holds concerts. The **student lock-up** *(kartser)* in the attic was used until 1892 to detain students for offenses like late library books (2 days' confinement). Drawings and cartoons by detainees still line the walls of the small room. Tartu was the only university in the Russian empire allowed to have fraternities after the Great Northern War. It used the privilege well: in 1870, the **Estonian National Awakening** began here with the founding of the Estonian Student Association (Eesti Üliõpilaste Selts). The Association's members were so central to Estonia's struggle for independence that the nation's flag bears the frat's colors: blue, black, and white. *(Ülikooli 18. ☎37 53 84. Open M-F 11am-5pm. 10EEK, students 5EEK. Student lock-up 5EEK.)*

DOME HILL (TOOMEMÄGI). The hill's central site is the once-majestic 15th-century **Domski Sabor** (Dome Cathedral; a.k.a. Cathedral of St. Peter and Paul), which is now in ruins. Heed the sign: "Be cautious! The building is liable to fall down." An adjoining building houses the **Tartu University History Museum** (Museum Historicum Universitatis Tartuensis), featuring an array of intriguing displays, including old scientific instruments, a terrifying dentist's chair, and an account of student life over the centuries. A museum ticket also grants access to the steep staircases of the **Cathedral Towers** (15EEK)—the view is worth the climb. *(Lossi 25. ☎375 674; www.ut.ee/ream. Open W-Su 11am-5pm. 20EEK, students 10EEK. Some English captions. Tours in English or German 120EEK.)* **Kissing Hill** (Musumägi), once part of a prison tower, is the site of an ancient pagan sacrificial stone—where Tartu University students burn their lecture notes at the end of every year. Each April, the university choirs compete on the two bridges that lead to the east hump of Toomemägi. Women crowd onto the wooden **Angel's Bridge** (Inglisild), while men stand on the concrete **Devil's Bridge** (Kuradisild). Be sure to hold your breath for good luck when crossing. Cathedral Hill is also littered with **statues.** The seated figure of embryologist Karl Ernst von Baer might be recognizable from the 2EEK banknote. As per tradition, biology students douse the sculpture with champagne each year.

OTHER SIGHTS. Don't miss the **Estonian National Museum** (Eesti Rahva Muuseum), which charts the evolution of Estonian culture from the Stone Age to the Soviet era and features extensive collections of costumes and artifacts from Estonian folk and peasant culture. Among the USSR's stranger dictates were orders cracking down on the wearing of wedding rings and the cultivation of tomatoes and roses, which were considered "elements of the bourgeois past." *(Kuperjanovi 9. ☎742 1311. Open W-Su 11am-6pm. Permanent exhibit 12EEK, students 8EEK; with admission to temporary display 20/14EEK; F free.)* Let your inner child loose at the **Tartu Toy Museum** (Tartu Mänguasjamuuseum). Rooms crammed with 19th-century dolls, stuffed animals, miniature cars, and an impressive model railway set that would delight even an old curmudgeon. Make a stop at the board game table, where you can learn to play a number of different games (instructions in English and Estonian) or take a break upstairs in the massive **play room.** *(Lutsu 8. ☎736 1551, play room 736 1554; www.mm.ee. Facing the town hall, turn right on Rüütli and hang a left on Lutsu. Open W-Su 11am-6pm. Play room open W-Su 11am-4pm. 20EEK, students and children 15EEK. Play room 5EEK.)* The **KGB Cells Museum** (KGB Kongid muuseum) is housed in the Soviet spy agency's former South Estonian headquarters; besides viewing the tiny basement pens where prisoners were fed a meager 200g of bread per day, visitors can view an extensive exhibit on the deportations and resistance movements. *(Riia 15b. ☎746 1717; www.tartu.ee/linnamuuseum. Open Tu-Sa 11am-4pm. 5EEK, students 3EEK.)* The **Tartu City Museum** (Tartu Linnamuuseum) displays the most comprehensive history of the city in a gorgeous 18th-century manor house. Visitors can see the table on which the 1920 Peace Treaty of Tartu was signed with the USSR, granting Estonia what turned out to be a temporary independence. *(Narva mnt. 23. ☎46 19 11; www.tartu.ee/linnamuuseum. Open Tu-Su 11am-6pm. English captions. 20EEK, students 5EEK. Tours 120EEK.)*

ENTERTAINMENT AND NIGHTLIFE

For listings of cultural events in Tartu, go to www.kultuuriaken.tartu.ee or check out *Tartu in Your Pocket* (25EEK). The **Tourist Information Office** provides a detailed pamphlet with listings for summer theater, music, and art happenings in the city. The **Vanemuise Concert Hall** (Vanemuise Kontserdimaja), Vanemuise 6 (☎737 7530; www.vkm.ee), has classical concerts. The 1870 theater **Vanemuine,** Vanemuise 6 (☎744 0165; www.vanemuine.ee), holds theater performances and operas, including some in English. The **Plink-Plonk Independent Music Festival** (www.plinkplonk.ee) at the end of July features indie, metal, and hardcore music from both Estonian and international bands. The second week of February brings the **Tartu Marathon,** which features a 63km cross-country ski race and non-competitive 16 and 31km group jaunts (☎742 1644; tartumaraton@tartumaraton.ee). **Midsummer's Eve** festivities take over the city every June 23, when darkness falls for only about 4hr. A huge bonfire at the **Tartu Song Grounds** is traditional. And, during the **Hanseatic Days** (www.tartu.ee/hansa) at the end of June, when the Middle Ages return with craft fairs and folk dancing in Raekoja plats.

Maailm (World), Rüütli 12, with its walls plastered with newspaper and magazine clippings, velvet armchairs and swings to sit on, makes you feel as if you've stepped into a crazy art student's attic. Try one of Maailm's famous ice cream shakes (25EEK) for as long as it stays open. Beer is only 25EEK per 0.5L; but remember: you still have to make it down the stairs at the end of the night. Occasional special events. Open M-Sa noon-1am, Su noon-10pm. MC/V.

Wilde Irish Pub, Vallikraavi 4 (☎730 9764; www.wilde.ee). A bronze Oscar Wilde meets his Estonian counterpart Eduard Wilde (VIL-de) outside this dark pub, furnished with mahagony armchairs. Vegetarian options. Irish and Estonian dishes (69-170EEK). Guinness (50EEK per 0.5L). Tu karaoke, F-Sa live music 9pm. Open M-Tu noon-midnight, W-Th noon-1am, F-Sa noon-2am, Su 1pm-midnight. MC/V.

Ristiisa Pubi (Godfather Pub), Küüni 7 (☎730 3970; www.ristiisapubi.ee.), is down the street from Raekoja plats. Crowds mob the outdoor terrace on summer nights, but inside the brick building, you're part of a young, merry family. Extensive list of mixed drinks. Cuban cigars from 25EEK. 0.5L *Saku* 25EEK. Th 10pm live music. Open M-Tu and Su 11am-midnight, W-Th 11am-1am, F-Sa 11am-3am. MC/V.

DAYTRIP FROM TARTU

VILJANDI

Buses arrive from Tartu (1¼hr.; 20 per day; 40-70EEK; ISIC discount) and head back no later than 8:30pm (check the schedule at the station or Tourist Info Center). The Tourist Info Center, Vabaduse plats 6, gives out free maps, provides pamphlets with a walking tour, and has free Internet. ☎304 42; viljandi@visitestonia.com. Open mid-May to mid-Sept M-F 9am-6pm, Sa-Su 10am-3pm; mid-Sept to mid-May M-F 10am-5pm, Sa 10am-2pm. To get to the castle from the bus station, take a left on Tallinna and go through Vabaduse plats (the main square) toward the river. The road becomes Tasuja pst.; follow it to its end. The path just to your left leads to the castle. St. John's Church ☎330 00; vilijandi.jaani@eelk.ee. Open mid-May to mid-Sept. daily 10am-5pm; mid-Sept to mid-May M-F noon-1pm. Free. Museum ☎433 3316; www.muuseum.viljandimaa.ee. Open W-Su 10am-5pm. 20EEK.

Viljandi is an old-world diorama of rolling hills and medieval sights, all of which can be seen in a couple of hours. Resting below the town is a peaceful lake, perfect for a lengthy boat trip or relaxing on the shore. The imposing **Order's Castle** (Ordulinnuse varemed), constructed by the Knights of the Sword in the 13th century, was once one of the largest in the Baltics, spanning three hilltops connected by bridges. Although the castle is now in ruins, what is left offers a panorama of **Viljandi Lake** (Viljandi järv), the largest lake in the region, and provides the backdrop for a **Folk Music Festival** each summer. Around the back of the ruins is the red-and-white 1879 **suspension footbridge** *(rippsild)*, which leads to town. In the central castle park is the sparsely decorated 15th-century red-brick **St. John's Church** (Jaani kirik), Pikk 6. Its organ was shipped north to Poltsamaa when Soviet authorities converted the church into a granary in the mid-1950s. The replacement is used for concerts each Saturday at 2pm. In the center of town, the **Viljandi Museum,** Kindval Laidoneri plats 10, sports a collection of stuffed lynx and wolves, a small exhibition on Estonian medieval culture, and the first-ever model of an Ericsson phone, dating from 1892. The 158-step staircase leading to the **lake** passes the statue of a **runner.** The names of past winners of hilly Viljandi's annual 15km foot race are engraved on the nearby pillars.

OTEPÄÄ

Otepää (pop. 4800), Estonia's highest town, with an altitude of 152m, and self-proclaimed "winter capital," exerts a magnetic pull on snowboarders and cross-country skiers in winter. Come summertime, it's ideal for cyclists and hikers. **Pühajärve** (Holy Lake), a famous site for deep meditation, was blessed by the Dalai Lama in 1991. Follow Pühajärve tee south from the town center and go left after 1km onto Mae to reach Otepää's **Energy Column** (Energiasammas), a 4m high wooden pole at a site selected by psychics for its positive vibes. Head back to Pühajärve tee and continue another 2.5km to reach Pühajärve, where you can enjoy the beach or rent boats and other watercraft.

Downhill skiers head to **Vaike-Munamae Skiing and Snowboarding Centre** (☎521 4040; www.munakas.ee), 4km from the center of town. At a height of 70m and with a longest run of 500m, it might be the best skiing in the flat-as-a-pancake Baltics.

Take a **taxi** (about 40EEK from the bus station) to get there. (Open Oct.-Apr. M-F noon-8pm, Sa and holidays 10am-8pm, Su 10am-5pm. Ski rental M-F 250EEK per day, Sa-Su 70EEK per day. Snowboards 300/90EEK. Lift ticket 200/80EEK, free with rental.) **O'Boy Snowtubing Park,** off Valga Mountain, just south of the center, offers two lifts for snowtubing and sledding. (☎521 4040; www.snowtubing.ee. Open late Oct. to late Apr. M-F 50EEK per hr., Sa-Su 100EEK per hr., 250EEK per day.) The **TIC** offers a free guide to the region's skiing opportunities. Karupesa Hotel is right by the **Tehvandi Olympic Center,** where Estonia's national ski-jumping team trains; they'll make way for amateurs. Hiking trails that wind around the beautiful lakes. (☎766 9500; www.tehvandi.ee. Training session 50EEK per day, 200EEK per wk.) Beneath Karupesa. Skis and other equipment. Also check out **Fansport.** (☎05 07 75 37; www.fansport.ee. 225EEK per day; sleds 30EEK per day. Bikes 200EEK per day. Canoes 300EEK per day. Reserve in advance.) **Club Tartu Marathon** (☎742 1644; www.tartumaraton.ee.) has the area's longest cross-country track (63km), which opens to tourists in the second week of February. Rent **water-bikes, rowboats,** and **canoes** (100EEK per hr.) at the lake's **beach,** in a small hut near the pier. (☎765 5219. Open in summer daily 10am-7pm.)

Buses run from **Tartu** (1hr.; 15 per day; 30-45EEK, with ISIC 25EEK). The last bus from Otepää to Tartu leaves at 8:30pm on weekdays and at 9pm on weekends. The **tourist office,** Lipuväljak 13, next to the bus station, offers a small **guidebook** with **maps** (25EEK). The office has free guides to **hiking, biking, cross-country skiing,** and accommodations. (☎766 1200; otepaa@visitestonia.com. Open mid-May to mid-Sept. M-F 9am-6pm, Sa-Su 10am-3pm; mid-Sept. to mid-May M-F 9am-5pm, Sa 10am-3pm.) **Hansapank,** Lipuväljak 3, **exchanges currency,** cashes **traveler's checks** (Thomas Cook and American Express) for 1% commission. A MasterCard and Visa **ATM** is outside. (Open M-F 9am-5pm.) The **post office** is at Lipuväljak 24. (☎767 9385; otepaapost@hot.ee. Open M-F 9am-5pm, Sa 10am-3pm.) **Postal Code:** 67405.

HUNGARY (MAGYARORSZÁG)

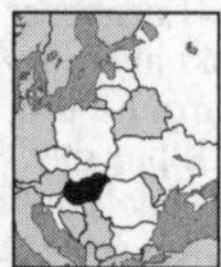

A country as singular as its language, Hungary has much more to offer than a profusion of wine, goulash, and thermal spas. Hip and vibrant Budapest remains Hungary's ever-ascending social, economic, and political capital. But beyond the big-city rush are towns lined with cobblestone streets and lush wine valleys nestled in Hungary's northern hills; luxurious beach resorts and expansive plains abound in the east. Though Hungary can be more expensive than some of its neighbors, you always get what you pay for.

DISCOVER HUNGARY: SUGGESTED ITINERARIES

THREE DAYS. Three days is hardly enough for the action-packed city of **Budapest** (p. 270). Spend a day at the churches, labyrinths, and museums of **Castle Hill** and an afternoon relaxing in the thermal waters of the **Széchényi Baths** before exploring the rest of the **City Park.** Get a lesson in Hungarian history on the **Parliament** tour before experiencing the country's more artistic side during an evening at the **Opera House.**

ONE WEEK. Spend four days in the thriving capital, taking in the sights and partaking in the vibrant, varied nightlife. Then, head up the Danube Bend by train or boat to experience the more rustic side of Hungary in **Szentendre** (1 day; p. 290), where cafes and cobblestone streets welcome tourists. The next day, explore the boulevards of **Eger** (p. 292) and sample the ample wines of the scenic **Valley of Beautiful Women** (p. 294). Take a daytrip from Eger to the fantastic, 200 million-year-old **Baradla Caves** on the Slovak-Hungarian border (p. 297).

BEST OF HUNGARY, THREE WEEKS. Begin in tiny **Tokaj,** renowned for its local wines (1 day; p. 301), before heading to **Eger** (2 days). Afterward, journey to lively **Debrecen,** home to Hungary's oldest university (2 days; p. 331). After spending four days in **Budapest,** visit the Danube Bend towns of **Szentendre** and **Visegrád** for a change of pace (2 days; p. 303). Then, head west to spend a day in **Sopron,** known for its combination of sophistication and old-world charm (p. 319). The next stop, **Lake Balaton** (p. 304), is Hungary's summertime pride: spend two days lounging on the beach and touring Festetics Palace in **Keszthely** (p. 313), then hike in the vineyards of **Badacsony** (p. 311). Continue along the lake to **Balatonfüred** (1 day; p. 308) and tour the Benedictine Abbey on the stunning **Tihany Peninsula** (1 day; p. 312). Cross the lake to the party town of **Siófok** (1 day; p. 305) before enjoying **Pécs** (2 days; p. 326). End in artsy **Szeged,** a small city with an easy-going, Mediterranean feel (2 days; p. 335).

FACTS AND FIGURES

Official Name: Hungary.

Capital: Budapest.

Major Cities: Debrecen, Miskolc, Szeged.

Population: 9,957,000.

Time Zone: GMT + 1, in summer GMT + 2.

Language: Hungarian.

Religions: Roman Catholic 52%, Calvinist 16%, unaffiliated 15%.

Newspaper circulation per capita: 471 per 1000 (#2 in the world).

ESSENTIALS

WHEN TO GO

Spring is the best time to visit Hungary, as flowers are in bloom throughout the countryside and the tourists haven't yet arrived in droves. July and August comprise Hungary's high season, which entails crowds, booked hostels, and sweltering summer weather; consider going before or after. Autumn is beautiful, with mild, cooler weather through October. Avoid going in January and February, as temperature average around freezing and many museums and tourists spots shut down or reduce their hours.

DOCUMENTS AND FORMALITIES

ENTRANCE REQUIREMENTS.

Passport: Required of all travelers.

Visa: Not required for stays of under 90 days for citizens of Australia, Canada, Ireland, New Zealand, the UK, and the US.

Letter of Invitation: Not required of citizens of Australia, Canada, Ireland, New Zealand, the UK, and the US.

Inoculations: Recommended up-to-date on DTaP (diphtheria, tetanus, and pertussis), Hepatitis A, Hepatitis B, MMR (measles, mumps, and rubella), polio booster, and typhoid.

Work Permit: Required of all foreigners planning to work in Hungary.

International Driving Permit: Required of all those planning to drive.

EMBASSIES AND CONSULATES. Foreign embassies to Hungary are in Budapest (see p. 274). Hungary's embassies and consulates abroad include: **Australia,** 17 Beale Crescent, Deakin, ACT 2600 (☎62 82 32 26; www.mata.com.au/~hungemb); **Canada,** 299 Waverley St., Ottawa, ON K2P 0V9 (☎613-230-2717; www.docuweb.ca/Hungary); **Ireland,** 2 Fitzwilliam Pl., Dublin 2 (☎661 2902; www.kum.hu/dublin); **New Zealand,** Consulate-General, 37 Abbott St., Wellington 6004 (☎973 7507; www.hungarianconsulate.co.nz); **UK,** 35 Eaton Pl., London SW1X 8BY (☎20 72 35 52 18; www.huemblon.org.uk); **US,** 3910 Shoemaker St., NW, Washington, D.C. 20008 (☎202-362-6730; www.hungaryembwas.org).

VISA AND ENTRY INFORMATION. Citizens of Australia, Canada, Ireland, New Zealand, and the US can visit Hungary without **visas** for up to 90 days; those from the UK can visit without a visa for up to 180 days. Consult your embassy for longer stays. Passports must be valid for six months after the end of the trip. There is no fee for crossing a Hungarian border. In general, border officials are efficient; plan on 30min. crossing time.

TOURIST SERVICES

TOURIST OFFICES. Tourinform has branches in most cities and is a useful first-stop **tourist service.** Tourinform doesn't make accommodation reservations but will find vacancies, especially in university dorms and private *panzió*. Agencies also stock maps and provide local information; employees generally speak English and German. Most **IBUSZ** offices throughout the country book private rooms, exchange money, and sell train tickets, but they are generally better at assisting in travel plans than at providing info. Pick up *Tourist Information: Hungary* and *Budapest in Your Pocket* and the monthly entertainment guide *Programme in Hungary* (all are free and in English). Local agencies may be staffed only by Hungarian and German speakers, but they are often very helpful and offer useful tips.

MONEY

FORINTS (FT)		
	AUS$1 = 155,96FT	1000FT = AUS$6.41
	CDN$1 = 173.71FT	1000FT = CDN$5.76
	EUR€1 = 250.43FT	1000FT = EUR€3.99
	NZ$1 = 138.24FT	1000FT = NZ$7.23
	UK£1 = 371.214FT	1000FT = UK£2.69
	US$1 = 182.99FT	1000FT = US$5.46

MONEY. The national currency is the **forint** (Ft). One forint is divided into 100 fillérs, which have disappeared almost entirely from circulation. Hungary has a **Value Added Tax (VAT)** rate of 20%. **Inflation** hovers at a relatively stable 3.5%. Currency exchange machines are slow but offer good rates, though banks like **OTP Bank** and **Raiffensen** offer the best exchange rates for **traveler's checks.** Never change money on the street, as it is illegal, and avoid extended-hour exchange offices, which have poor rates. Watch for scams: the maximum legal commission for cash-to-cash exchange is 1%. 24-hr. **ATMS** are common and are located next to most banks. Major **credit cards** are accepted in many hotels and restaurants in large cities, but they're very rarely accepted in the countryside. Standard business hours in Budapest are Monday through Thursday 9am-4pm, Friday 9am-1pm. Businesses generally close on holidays.

Service is not usually included in restaurant bills and while **tipping** is not mandatory, it's generally appropriate to do so at around a 10% rate. Tipping bartenders is not customary, but waiters often expect tips from tourists. Don't bother bargaining with cabbies, but make sure to set a price before getting in.

HEALTH AND SAFETY

EMERGENCY	**Ambulance:** ☎104 **Fire:** ☎105. **Police:** ☎107, in English ☎1 311 1666.

In Budapest, **medical assistance** is easy to obtain and fairly inexpensive, but may not always be up to western standards. In an emergency, especially outside Budapest, one might be sent to Germany or Vienna. Most hospitals have English-speaking doctors on staff. **Tourist insurance** is useful—and necessary—for many medical services. In the event of an emergency, however, even non-insured foreigners are entitled to free medical services. **Tap water** is usually clean, but the water in Tokaj is poorly purified. **Bottled water** can be purchased at most food stores. **Public bathrooms** (*férfi* for men, *női* for women) vary in cleanliness: pack soap, a towel, and 30Ft for the attendant. Carry **toilet paper,** as many hostels do not provide it and public restrooms provide only a single square. Many **pharmacies** *(gyógyszertár)* stock Western brands, tampons *(betet)*, and condoms *(ovszer)*. Most towns have pharmacies that list after-hours service availability.

Violent **crime** is rare. Tourists, however, are targets for petty theft and pick-pocketing that typically occurs on public transportation and in urban centers. Check prices before getting in taxis or ordering food or drinks; cab drivers and servers may attempt to overcharge unsuspecting tourists. In an emergency, your embassy will likely be more helpful than the **police. Women** traveling alone in Hungary should take the usual precautions. **Minorities** are generally accepted, though dark-skinned travelers may encounter prejudice. Travelers with **disabili-**

ties will find that Hungarians are friendly and used to assisting the disabled despite the complete lack of facilities. Though Hungary is known for being open-minded, **GLBT** travelers may face serious discrimination, especially outside Budapest. Public displays of affection are not widespread, even in the country's capital. For more information, visit www.gay.hu.

TRANSPORTATION

BY PLANE. Many international airlines fly to Budapest. The national airline, **Malév,** flies to Budapest's airport, **Esterhazy,** from London, New York and other major cities. Direct flights can be quite expensive, starting at around $1,500. Flying to another European hub and taking a connecting plane or train may be the cheapest option. Other European airlines that fly to Hungary include **Sky Europe** (www.skyeurope.com) and **WizzAir** (www.wizzair.com).

BY TRAIN. Budapest is connected by train to most European capitals. Several types of **Eurail passes** are valid in Hungary, including **Eastpass.** Check international and domestic schedules and fares at **www.elvira.hu.** *Személyvonat* trains have many local stops and are excruciatingly slow; *gyorsvonat* trains, listed in red on schedules, move much faster for the same price. Large towns are connected by blue express lines; these air-conditioned InterCity trains are the fastest. A *pótjegy* (seat reservation) is required on trains labeled "R," and violators face a hefty fine. A basic vocabulary can help you navigate the train system: *érkezés* (arrival), *indulás* (departure), *vágány* (track), and *állomás* or *pályaudvar* (station, abbreviated *pu*) are useful words. The *peron* (platform) is rarely indicated until the train approaches the station and will sometimes be announced in Hungarian; look closely out the window as you approach a station. Many stations are not marked; ask the conductor what time the train will arrive (or simply point to your watch and say the town's name). Train reservations cost around US$5, and are recommended during the summer and for night trains to get a sleeper compartment.

BY BUS AND BY FERRY. Buses tend to be efficient and well-priced, but generally not more so than trains. The major line is **Volanbusz,** a privately owned company. Purchase tickets on board, and arrive early for a seat. In larger cities, buy tickets at a kiosk, and punch them as you get on. Beware: plainclothes inspectors fine those caught without a ticket. A ferry runs down the Danube from Vienna and Bratislava to Budapest. For more info, contact **Utinform** (☎322 3600).

BY CAR AND BY TAXI. To **drive** in Hungary, carry your **International Driving Permit** and registration, and insurance papers. Car rental is available in most major cities but can be expensive. For 24hr. English assistance, contact the **Magyar Autóklub** (**MAK;** in Budapest, ☎345 1800). **Taxi** prices should not exceed the following: 6am-10pm base fare 200Ft per km, 60Ft per min. waiting; 10pm-6am 300/70Ft. Beware of taxi scams. Before getting in, check that the meter is working and ask how much the ride will cost. Taxis ordered by phone charge less than those hailed on the street.

BY BIKE AND BY THUMB. Biking terrain varies. The northeast is topographically varied; the south is flat. **Bike** rental is sometimes difficult to find; tourist bureaus should have information on where and how to rent. Biking can be dangerous because bicyclists do not have the right of way and drivers are not careful. Though it is fairly common in Hungary, Let's Go does not recommend **hitchhiking.**

KEEPING IN TOUCH

PHONE CODES	**Country code:** 36. **International dialing prefix:** 00. From outside Hungary, dial the international dialing prefix (see inside back cover) + 36 + city code + local number. Within Hungary, for intercity calls use the city code; simply dial the local number within the city.

EMAIL AND THE INTERNET. **Internet** is readily available in major cities. The Hungarian keyboard differs significantly from English-language keyboards. After logging on, click the "Hu" icon at the bottom right corner of the screen and switch the setting to "Angol" to shift to an English keyboard. Look for free Internet access at hostels. Most Internet cafes charge 500-600Ft per hour.

TELEPHONE. For **intercity calls,** wait for the tone and dial slowly; "06" goes before the phone code. **International calls** require red or blue phones. The blue phones tend to end calls after 3-9min. Phones often require *telefonkártya* (phone cards). The best for international calls is **Barangolo.** International calls cost around 9Ft. Make direct calls from Budapest's phone office. International phone cards are sold by 2000Ft, and national cards are 800Ft. A 20Ft coin is required to start most calls. International access numbers include: **AT&T Direct** (☎06 800 01111); **Australia Direct** (☎06 800 06111); **BT Direct** (☎0800 89 0036); **Canada Direct** (☎06 800 01211); **MCI WorldPhone** (☎06 800 01411); **NZ Direct** (☎06 800 06411); and **Sprint** (☎06 800 01877).

Mobile phones are common in Hungary, and service can be purchased from Pannon GSM, T-Mobile, or Vodafone, which have shops in Budapest. Dialing a mobile from a public or private phone anywhere in Hungary is treated as a long distance call, requiring the entire 11-digit number. To install a new SIM Card, switch the country code before you leave, as it takes two weeks.

MAIL. Hungarian mail is usually reliable; **airmail** *(légiposta)* takes one week to 10 days to the US and Europe. Mailing a letter costs about 36Ft domestically and 250Ft internationally.Those without permanent addresses can receive mail through **Poste Restante.** Use Global Priority mail, as it is reliable. Address envelopes: First name, LAST NAME, POSTE RESTANTE, Post office address, Postal Code, city, HUNGARY.

ACCOMMODATIONS AND CAMPING

HUNGARY	❶	❷	❸	❹	❺
ACCOMMODATIONS	under 2500Ft	2500-4000Ft	4000-7000Ft	7000-12,000Ft	over 12,000Ft

Tourism is developing rapidly, and rising prices make **hostels** attractive. Hostels are usually large enough to accommodate summer crowds. Many hostels can be booked through **Express** (in Budapest ☎266 3277), a student travel agency, or through local tourist offices. From June to August, many university dorms become hostels. These may be the cheapest options in smaller towns, as hostels are less common outside Budapest. Locations change annually; inquire at Tourinform and call ahead. **Guesthouses and pensions** *(panzió)* are more common than hotels in small towns. Singles are scarce, though some guesthouses have a singles rate for double rooms—it can be worth finding a roommate, as solo travelers must often pay for doubles. Check prices; agencies may try to rent you their most expensive rooms. **Private rooms** booked through tourist agencies are often cheap. Outside Budapest, the best offices are region-specific (e.g., Eger Tourist in Eger). They will often make advance reservations for your next stop. After staying a few nights, make arrangements with the owner to save your agency's 20-30% commission.

Over 300 **campgrounds** are sprinkled throughout Hungary. Most open from May to September and charge for unfilled spaces in their bungalows. For more information, consult *Camping Hungary*, a booklet available in most tourist offices, or contact Tourinform in Budapest (see **Tourist And Financial Services,** p. 273).

FOOD AND DRINK

HUNGARY	❶	❷	❸	❹	❺
FOOD	under 600Ft	600-1200Ft	1200-2000Ft	2000-3200Ft	over 3200Ft

Hungarian food is more flavorful than many of its Eastern European culinary counterparts, with many spicy meat dishes. **Paprika,** Hungary's chief agricultural export, colors most dishes red. In Hungarian restaurants *(vendéglő* or *étterem)*, *halászlé*, a spicy fish stew, is a traditional starter. Or, try *gyümölesleves*, a cold fruit soup with whipped cream. The Hungarian national dish is *bográcsgulyás*, a soup of beef, onions, green pepper, tomatoes, potatoes, dumplings, and plenty of paprika. *Borjúpaprikás* is veal with paprika and potato-dumpling pasta. For **Vegetarians** there is tasty *rántott sajt* (fried cheese) and *gombapörkölt* (mushroom stew). Delicious Hungarian fruits and vegetables abound in summer. Vegetarians should also look for *salata* (salad) and *sajt* (cheese), as these will be the only options in many small-town restaurants. Keeping kosher, on the other hand, is fairly difficult. Avoid American food like hot dogs which can cause food poisoning.

Hungary produces an array of fine **wines** (see **Wines of Tokaj,** p. 302). The northeastern towns of Eger and Tokaj produce famous red and white wines, respectively. *Sör* (Hungarian **beer**) ranges from first-rate to acceptable. Lighter beers include *Dreher Pils*, *Szalon Sör*, and licensed versions of *Steffl*, *Gold Fassl*, *Gösser*, and *Amstel*. Hungary also produces *pálinka*, which resembles brandy. Among the best-tasting are *barackpálinka* (an apricot schnapps) and *körtepálinka* (pear brandy). *Egessegedre* means "cheers." *Unicum*, advertised as the national drink, is an **herbal liqueur** containing over 40 herbs; it was once used by the Habsburgs to cure digestive ailments.

LIFE AND TIMES

HISTORY

THE MIGHTY MAGYARS. In the third century BC, **Celtic tribes** invaded what is now Hungary. They were followed by the **Romans,** who founded the provinces of Pannonia and Dacia, which they held until the fifth century AD. The **Magyars,** Central Asian warriors, arrived in 896, a century after Charlemagne defeated the previous residents, the Goths, Huns, and Turkish Avars. Led by **Prince Árpád,** the Magyars conquered the middle Danube. Árpád's descendant, **Stephen I,** became Hungary's first king on Christmas Day, 1000. Canonized as the nation's patron saint in 1083, Stephen is considered the founder of Hungary.

THOSE GOLDEN YEARS. As Hungarian warlords grew stronger, the nobles forced the king to sign the **Golden Bull** (1222), a charter that granted rights to the people and restricted monarchical power. Two decades later, a devastating Mongolian invasion swept through, killing over half a million people and effectively ending the Árpáds' reign. But as the 14th century progressed, Hungary entered a **Golden Age** of economic well-being and military prowess. King **Matthias Corvinus** (1458-1490) reigned during Hungary's renaissance while keeping conspiring nobles at bay. Corvinus also consolidated the administration, supported education, and cultivated a huge library at Buda. But these reforms were lost when the Turks conquered the Hungarians at Mohács in 1526.

EMPIRE FALLS. Conflict between the Holy Roman Empire, Protestants, and Ottomans plagued Hungary for the next 150 years, until the Austrian **Habsburgs** took over in the early 17th century. After a national reform movement in the 1700s, a push for independence began in 1848, led by young poet **Sándor Petőfi** and lawyer **Lajos Kossuth.** The movement convinced the **Diet** (Parliament) to pass reforms known as the **March Laws.** Kossuth's newly independent state resisted Austrian aggression for a year, but in 1849, Habsburg Emperor Franz Josef I regained Budapest with the support of Russia's Tsar Nicholas I. Nonetheless, the revolution, coupled with Austria's defeat in a war with Prussia, led Austria to grant Hungary significant powers under the **Compromise of 1867,** which created the dual monarchy of the **Austro-Hungarian Empire. Magyarization,** a set of Hungarian nationalist policies, provoked opposition among restless Croats, Romanians, Serbs, and Slovaks. These divisions erupted during WWI and resulted in the permanent dissolution of the Austro-Hungarian Empire. After the war, Hungary lost two-thirds of its territory to the Allies in the 1920 **Treaty of Trianon.**

APOCALYPSE NOW. As the empire collapsed, a democratic revolution emerged in 1918; in less than six months, it gave way to the communist **Hungarian Republic of Councils** under Bolshevik **Béla Kun.** Counter-revolutionary forces eventually took control and mercilessly punished those involved with the communist administration. Admiral **Miklós Horthy** settled in for 24 years of dictatorship just as brutal as that of Kun. A tentative alliance with Hitler in **WWII** led to Nazi occupation and the near-total destruction of Budapest during the two-month Soviet siege of 1945. Two-thirds of Hungary's **Jews,** whose pre-war population numbered close to one million, were murdered in the Holocaust. Nearly all survivors fled the country.

GET UP, STAND UP. In 1949 Hungary became a People's Republic under **Mátyás Rákosi.** Rákosi tied Hungary to the **USSR,** which used the country as a "workshop" for Soviet industry. Rákosi lost control in the violent **1956 Uprising** in Budapest, during which **Imre Nagy** declared a neutral government. Soviet troops crushed the revolt and executed Nagy and his supporters.

MAGYAR MODERNIZATION. Over the next three decades, **János Kádár** oversaw the partial opening of borders and a rising standard of living. Inflation halted progress in the 1980s, but democratic reformers in the Communist Party, seeking freedom and a proto-market economy, pushed Kádár aside in 1988. Hungary peacefully broke free of the Soviet orbit in 1989, and in 1990 power was transferred to the **Hungarian Democratic Forum** in free elections. As privatization began, slow progress, inflation, and unemployment eroded the Forum's popularity. Subsequent elections returned the Socialists to power.

TODAY

Hungary has come a long way since communism. Its government is led by a **president** who serves a five-year term in a largely ceremonial role. Chosen every four years, the powerful **National Assembly** elects the president, who appoints the **prime minister,** who in turn appoints the **cabinet ministers.** Four **parties** participate regularly in parliament: the Hungarian Democratic Forum, the Hungarian Civic Alliance, the Alliance of Free Democrats, and the Hungarian Socialist Party. In 1994, Hungary opened its borders to the West and regained economic and social stability. Today, wage problems and inflation are of diminishing gravity, and Hungary has managed to stem unemployment and stabilize GDP growth. The country is politically stable and entered the **European Union (EU)** on May 1, 2004.

Ferenc Mádl was president from 2000-2005. He was succeeded in 2005 by **Lászlo Sólyom,** a former judge known for his liberal decisions to eliminate capital punishment and strengthen domestic partnerships for homosexuals. In 2004, former Prime Minister **Péter Medgyessy,** sacked by his one-time Socialist allies for dismissals of his cabinet members, was replaced by socialist **Ferenc Gyurcsány,** the former sports minister. Gyurcsány's time in office sparked controversy when an audio-recording from a private meeting with his political party revealed him conceding that they had misled the public. Despite public outrage, Gyurcsány refused to resign, and won a parliamentary vote of confidence in 2006. Later that year, he was reelected to a second term as Prime Minister.

PEOPLE AND CULTURE

LANGUAGE. Hungarian, a Finno-Ugric language, is distantly related to Turkish, Estonian, and Finnish. After Hungarian and German, English is Hungary's third most commonly spoken language. Almost all young people know some English. "*Hello*" is often used as an informal greeting. Coincidentally, "*Szia!*" (sounds like "see ya!") is another greeting—friends will often cry, "Hello, see ya!" For a phrasebook and glossary, see Appendix: Hungarian, p. 796.

DEMOGRAPHICS. Hungary's population is 95% Magyar (ethnic Hungarian), with Roma, Germans, and Serbs constituting sizable minorities.

CUSTOMS AND ETIQUETTE. Rounding up the bill as a tip is standard for everyone from waiters to hairdressers. Check the bill; gratuity may be included. Foreigners should tip 15%. When the waiter brings the bill, pay immediately. Hand your tip to your server. At meals, **toasts** are common and should be returned; raise your glass and say, *egészségünkre* ("to our health"). **Bargaining** over open air market goods and taxi fare is appropriate. **Clothing** is westernized—jeans and T-shirts are the norm. In cities, women often dress in tight or revealing attire. Religious sites may require covered knees and shoulders.

THE ARTS

LITERATURE. The writers who lived through the Revolution of 1848 greatly impacted the country's literature. The Populist **Sándor Petőfi** fueled nationalistic rhetoric that drove the revolution, **Ferenc Kazinczy** was an early promoter of national literature in the Hungarian language, and **Mór Jókai's** nationalism and down-to-earth tone endeared him to 19th-century readers. Hungarian literature gained attention with the 1908 founding of the *Nyugat* (West) literary journal, and with the work of avant-garde poet and artist **Lajos Kassák,** who chronicled working-class life. **Attila József,** an influential poet, merged Freudian thought with Marxism. After WWII, communists forced Hungarian writers to adopt Socialist Realism, but the next generation developed individual styles more freely. In 2002, **Imre Kertész** won Hungary's first Nobel Prize in Literature for his work drawing on his experiences as a teen in Nazi concentration camps. Less concerned with historical issues than with the exploration of language, the work of **Péter Esterházy** marks a new movement in contemporary Hungarian literature.

MUSIC. Hungary has gained the most international acclaim for its **music.** The greatest piano virtuoso of his time, **Franz Liszt** (1811-1886) is the most prolific musician in Hungary's history. His contributions range from advancing piano composition technique to inventing the symphonic poem. Though Liszt spoke German, not Hungarian, his heritage shines through in his Hungarian Rhapsodies, 19 pieces based on Hungarian folk music. Similarly, **Béla Bartók** (1881-1945) was noted for his use of folk material to create music that expressed a strong sense of nationalism. His most famous works include string quartets and the *Concerto for Orchestra.* In recent years, **Roma** music has gained increasing popularity.

VISUAL AND PERFORMING ARTS. The growth of fine arts in Hungary was influenced by artistic evolution in the rest of Europe, yet Hungary managed to add its own character at each stage. Renaissance and medieval frescoes were the most widely-practiced art forms, and later gave birth to historical painting and portraiture. In the 20th century, **Lajos Kassák** and **László Moholy-Nagy** emerged as avant-garde painters, and **Miklós Jancsó** and **István Szabó** stood as pioneers in Hungarian **film.** Nature has been an increasing influence in the architectural arena. **Imre Makovecz's** pavilion at the Seville Expo won him international acclaim in 1992. Hungarian **folk dancing** is also a point of cultural and artistic pride. **Csárdás,** the national dance, includes a women's circle and men's boot-slapping dances. All begin with a slow section *(lassú)* and end in a fast section *(friss)*. Dancers don embroidered costumes and perform music in double time.

HOLIDAYS AND FESTIVALS

Holidays: New Year's Day (Jan. 1); National Day (Mar. 15); Easter Holiday (Mar. 24, 2008; Apr. 13, 2009); Labor Day (May 1); Pentecost (May 11, 2008; May 31, 2009); Constitution Day (St. Stephen's Day, Aug. 20); Republic Day (Oct. 23); All Saints' Day (Nov. 1); Christmas (Dec. 25-26).

Festivals: Central Europe's largest rock festival, Sziget Festival, hits Budapest for a week in late July or early August, featuring rollicking crowds and international superstar acts. Eger's fabulous World Festival of Wine Songs celebration kicks off in late September, bringing together boisterous choruses and world-famous vintage wines.

BUDAPEST ☎(06)1

A vibrant mix of medieval and modern, Budapest (pop. 1.9 million) offers spectacular views, Roman ruins and nightlife teeming with university students and backpackers. While other parts of Hungary seem uninterested in adopting a hectic pace of life, Budapest has seized upon cosmopolitan chic with a vengeance—without giving up such old-time charms as the Turkish thermal baths that bubble up from beneath the city. Unlike toyland Prague, energetic Budapest has a life independent of the growing crowds of tourists.

INTERCITY TRANSPORTATION

Flights: Ferihegy Airport, BUD (☎296 9696, departures 296 5882, arrivals 296 5052). **Malév** (Hungarian Airlines; reservations ☎235 3888). To the center, take **bus** #93 (20min., every 15min. 4:55am-11:20pm, 260Ft), then take M3 to Kőbánya-Kispest (15min. to Deák tér, in downtown Budapest). To catch this bus, turn right from Terminal A or left from B and find the "BKV Plusz Reptér Busz" sign. Purchase tickets from the kiosk in Terminal B or the machines outside Terminal A. Alternatively, take the **Airport Minibus** (☎296 8555) to hotels or hostels. Service is 2300Ft and runs 24hr.; call 1 day in advance for flights leaving Budapest.

Trains: For a complete listing of Hungarian rail schedules, go to www.elvira.hu. (☎40 49 49 49). The main stations–**Keleti pályaudvar, Nyugati pályaudvar,** and **Déli pályaudvar**–are also Metro stops. Most international trains arrive at and depart from Keleti pu. To: **Berlin, GER** (12-15hr.; 2 per day; 28,305Ft, reservation 765Ft); **Bucharest, ROM** (14hr., 5 per day, 19,482Ft); **Prague, CZR** (8hr., 4 per day, 11,700Ft); **Vienna, AUT** (3hr., 17 per day, 3315Ft); **Warsaw, POL** (11hr., 2 per day, 18,411Ft). The daily **Orient Express** stops on its way from **Paris, FRA** to **Istanbul, TUR.** Trains depart from Budapest to most major destinations in Hungary. Check www.elvira.hu for schedules and some prices or ask at the info booths in the stations. For **student discounts,** show your ISIC and tell the clerk "diák." On domestic trains an ISIC is technically invalid, but ask anyway.

International Ticket Offices: Keleti pu. Open daily 8am-7pm; info desk 24hr. Nyugati pu. Open M-Sa 5am-9pm.

MÁV Hungarian Railways, VI, Andrássy út 35 (☎461 5500; www.mav.hu). Branch offices at all train stations. Sells domestic and international tickets. Check the website for prices and ask about ISIC discounts. Open M-F Apr.-Sept. 9am-6pm; Oct.-Mar. 9am-5pm.

Carlson Wagonlit Travel, V, Dorottya u. 3 (☎483 3384), off Vörösmarty tér. Open M-Th 9am-12:45pm and 1:30-5pm, F 9am-12:45pm and 1:30-3:30pm. AmEx/MC/V.

Buses: The most common and fastest mode of transport between towns in Hungary is by bus. Bus schedules are at www.volanbusz.hu/english/index.php. Buses to international and some domestic destinations arrive at and depart from the **Népliget** station, X, Ulloi u. 131, (☎382 0888), near the Népliget Metro station. M3: Népliget. Ticket window open M-F 6am-9pm, Sa-Su 6am-4pm. To: **Berlin, GER** (14½hr., 6 per week, 17,010Ft); **Prague, CZR** (8hr., 6 per week, 9810Ft); **Vienna, AUT** (3-3½hr., 5 per day, 2950Ft). Catch buses to and from destinations east of Budapest at the **Népstadion** station, XIV, Hungária krt. 46-48 (☎252 4498). M2: Népstadion. Open M-F 6am-6pm, Sa-Su 6am-4pm. Buses to the Danube Bend and parts of the Uplands (☎329 1450) depart outside the **Árpád híd** Metro station on the M3 line. Cashier open 6am-8pm.

ORIENTATION

Budapest was once two entities, separated by the Danube: the pasture land of Pest and vineyards of Buda. In 1873, the two areas separated by the Danube River were unified by a Habsburg initiative. The modern capital preserves the character of each. On the west side, **Buda's** tree-lined streets wind through the cobblestone **Castle District** on the way to the hilltop citadel. On the east side, grid-like avenues, shopping boulevards, and the Parliament spread over the commercial center of **Pest.** Like most cities built around a river, Budapest is easily navigable using the Danube as reference point. Six main bridges tie the two sides together: at **Arpád híd** on the Pest side is the domestic bus station. **Margit híd** connects a major tram stop on the Buda side to **Jászai Mari tér** on the Pest side and lies at the south end of Margit Island. **Széchényi Lánc híd** connects **Roosevelt tér** to the **Várhegy** (Castle Hill) cable car. To the south, **Erzsébet híd** runs from near **Petőfi tér** to the St. Gellért monument at **Gellérthegy** (Gellért Hill). Farther along the **Danube, Szabadság híd** links

Fővám tér to the south end of Gellérthegy. Finally, **Petőfi híd** and **Lágymányosi híd,** farther south, also connect Buda with Pest. Budapest's tram and transportation hub is north of the Castle District at **Moszkva tér,** and the HÉV commuter railway, which heads north through **Óbuda** to **Szentendre,** starts at **Batthyány tér,** opposite Parliament, one Metro stop past the Danube in Buda. Budapest's **Metro** is the oldest in Continental Europe. Its three lines (orange M1, red M2, and blue M3) converge at **Deák tér.** Deák tér is at the center of Pest. Two blocks toward the river is **Vörösmarty tér.** The pedestrian shopping zone **Váci utca** is to the right, facing the statue of Mihály Vörösmarty. The zone ends at the central market, which is housed in a building with a multicolored tile roof. Addresses in Budapest begin with a Roman numeral representing one of the city's **23 districts.** Central Buda is I; central Pest is V. The middle two digits of Postal Codes indicate the district.

BUS TICKETS. Hungarian buses, whether between cities or simply in local public transportation, can be unfamiliar territory for travelers. On intercity buses, tickets are purchased from the driver rather than in advance. It's first come, first served, so people tend to jostle at the door to get a seat. On public transportation, tickets generally can be purchased in advance or from the driver. While it may seem easy just to jump on for the ride without paying, be careful: drivers often watch the rearview mirror closely, and the fines can be steep.

LOCAL TRANSPORTATION

Commuter Trains: The **HÉV commuter railway** station is across the river from Parliament, 1 Metro stop past the Danube in Buda at Batthyány tér. Trains head to **Szentendre** (45min., every 15min. 5am-9pm, 460Ft). Purchase tickets at the station for transport beyond city limits or face a hefty fine. On the list of stops, those within city limits are in a different color. Békásmegyer is the last stop within city limits. For travel within the city, a simple transportation ticket or pass will work.

Public Transportation: Budapest's public transport is inexpensive, convenient, and easy to navigate. The **Metro** and **trams** run every few minutes. 4:30am-11:30pm, and **buses** are generally on time (schedules posted at stops). Many buses run 24hr.

FINES. Riding ticketless means a 5000Ft fee if you can pay on the spot—much more if you need to pay by mail. Inspectors in red armbands prowl the **Deák tér** Metro stop in particular, and are especially likely to stop tourists. They often wait at the top of escalators. Punch a new ticket when switching lines. Inspectors also issue fines for losing the cover sheet to the 10-ticket packet.

Budapest Public Transport (BKV; ☎80 40 66 86; www.bkv.hu) has info in Hungarian. Open M-F 7am-3pm. **Tickets** (230Ft, 10 tickets 2050Ft, 20 tickets 3900Ft), sold in Metro stations, Trafik shops, and kiosks. Buses and trams use different tickets, both of which can also be purchased at machines at individual stops (160Ft, coins only). Punch them in orange boxes at Metro gates and on buses and trams. A ticket is valid for a single trip on only 1 Metro line; a *metrószakaszjegy* (180Ft) is valid for 3 Metro stops. Consider buying a **pass.** Day pass 1350Ft, 3-day 3100Ft, 1-week 3600Ft, 2-week 4800Ft, 1-month 7350Ft. Unlimited public transportation and other perks available with the Budapest Card; see **Tourist and Financial Services,** below. Monthly passes require a transport ID card (150Ft), so bring a photo. Budapest transport tickets are good on HÉV suburban trains within city limits. Otherwise, purchase separate HÉV tickets.

Night Transportation: The Metro shuts down around 11:30pm, but gates may lock at 10:30pm. All Metro stops post the times for the first and last trains by the tracks. Buses and trams stop running at 11pm. Buses with numbers ending in "É" run midnight-5am. Buses #7É and 78É follow the M2 route, #6É follows the 4/6 tram line, and bus #14É and 50É run the same route as M3.

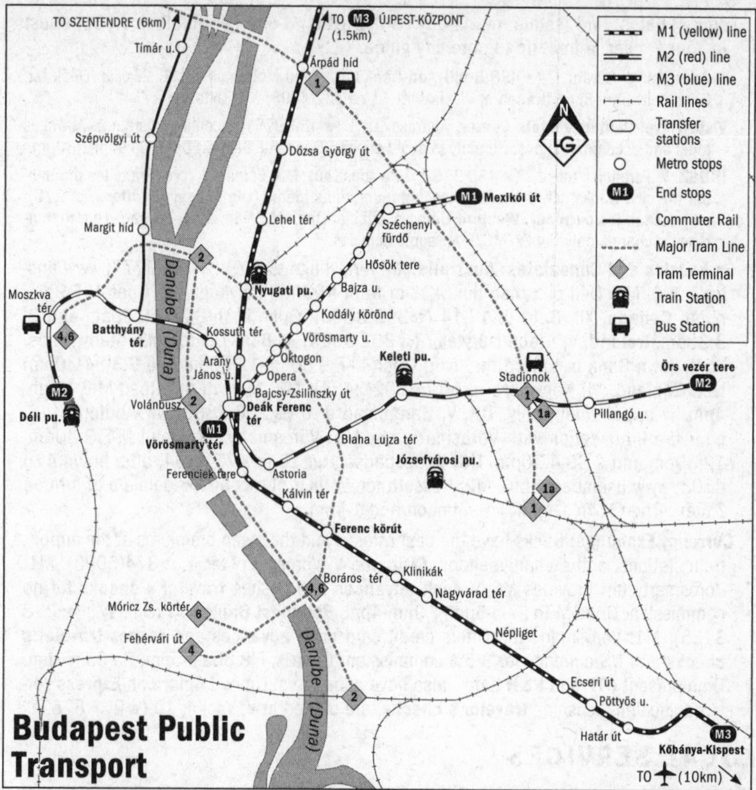

Budapest Public Transport

Taxis: The transport system in Budapest is efficient, so there's rarely a need for a taxi. Beware of scams; check for a yellow license plate and a running meter. Before getting in, ask how much the ride costs. Prices should not exceed: base fare 300Ft, 350Ft per km, 70Ft per min. waiting. **Budataxi** (☎222 4444). 150Ft per km by phone, 240Ft per km on the street. To the airport: 3500Ft from Pest and 4000Ft from Buda. **Főtaxi** (☎222 2222). 155Ft per km by phone and 250Ft per km on the street. To the airport: 4300Ft from Pest and 4800Ft from Buda. **6x6 Taxi** (☎466 6666), **City Taxi** (☎211 1111), **Rádió Taxi** (☎377 7777), and **Tele 5 Taxi** (☎355 5555) are also reliable.

Car Rental: There are several reliable rental agencies. Cars from US$50-60 per day. Credit card required. Few agencies rent to those under 21. **Avis,** V, Szervita tér 8 (☎318 4240; www.avis.hu). Open M-Sa 7am-6pm, Su 8am-noon. **Budget,** I, Krisztina krt. 41-43 (☎214 0420; www.budget.hu). Open M-F 8am-8pm, Sa-Su 8am-6pm. **Hertz,** Mednyánszky u. 13 (☎296 0997). Open daily 7am-7pm.

PRACTICAL INFORMATION

TOURIST AND FINANCIAL SERVICES

Tourist Offices: Tourist offices, Metro stations, and travel agencies sell the **Budapest Card** (Budapest Kártya). It includes unlimited public transport, entrance to most museums, reduced rates on car rental and the airport minibus, and discounts at shops, baths, and restaurants. 2-day card 6450Ft, 3-day 7950Ft. Pick up *Budapest in Your Pocket,* a free, up-to-date city guide.

Tourinform, V, Sütő u. 2 (☎438 8080), off Deák tér behind McDonald's. M1, 2, or 3: Deák tér. Open daily 8am-8pm. **Branch** at VI, Liszt tér 11 (☎322 4098) M1: Oktogon.

Vista Travel Center: Visitors Center, Andrássy út 1 (☎429 9751; incoming@vista.hu). Arranges tours and accommodations. Go early to avoid crowds. Open M-F 9am-6:30pm, Sa 9am-2:30pm.

IBUSZ, V, Ferenciek tere 10 (☎485 2767; www.ibusz.hu). M3: Ferenciek tere. Branches throughout the city. Books tickets and sightseeing tours; finds rooms (see **Accommodations,** p. 275); and **exchanges currency. Western Union** available. Open M-F 9am-5pm, Sa 9am-1pm for currency exchange only. AmEx/MC/V for some services.

Embassies and Consulates: Australia, XII, Királyhágó tér 8/9 (☎457 9777; www.australia.hu). M2: Déli pu., then bus #21 or tram #59 to Királyhágó tér. Open M-F 9am-noon. **Canada,** XII, Ganz u. 12-14 (☎392 3360). Open M-Th 8:30-10:30am and 2-3:30pm. **Ireland,** V, Szabadság tér 7 (☎302 9600), in Bank Center. M3: Arany János. Walk down Bank u. toward the river. Open M-F 9:30am-12:30pm and 2:30-4:30pm. **New Zealand,** VI, Nagymezo u. 50 (☎302 2484). M3: Nyugati pu. Open M-F 11am-4pm by appointment only. **UK,** V, Harmincad u. 6 (☎266 2888; www.britemb.hu), near the intersection with Vörösmarty tér. M1: Vörösmarty tér. Open M-F 9:30am-12:30pm and 2:30-4:30pm. **US,** V, Szabadság tér 12 (☎475 4164, after hours 475 4703; www.usembassy.hu). M2: Kossuth tér. Walk 2 blocks on Akadémia and turn on Zoltán. Open M-Th 1-4pm, F 9am-noon and 1-4pm.

Currency Exchange: Banks have the best rates; avoid the steep premiums at the airport, train stations, and exchange shops. **Citibank,** V, Vörösmarty tér 4 (☎374 5000). M1: Vörösmarty tér. Provides MC/V **cash advances** and cashes **traveler's checks** for no commission. Open M-Th 9am-5pm, F 9am-4pm. **Budapest Bank,** V, Váci u. 1/3 (☎328 3155). M1: Vörösmarty tér. Offers credit card **cash advances** and cashes **traveler's checks** into US currency for 3.5% commission. Open M-F 8:30am-5pm, Sa 9am-2pm. Omnipresent **OTP** and **K&H** banks also have good rates. Limited **American Express** services, including cashing **traveler's checks,** are offered at V, Váci u. 10 (☎267 6262).

LOCAL SERVICES

Luggage storage: Keleti pályaudvar, across from international cashier 300Ft per day, large bag 600Ft per day. **Nyugati pályaudvar,** in the waiting room near ticket windows. 300Ft per day, large bag 600Ft. Open 24hr. **Déli pályaudvar.** 150Ft per 6hr., 300Ft per day; large bag 300/600Ft. Lockers 200Ft per day. Open daily 3:30am-11:30pm.

English-Language Bookstores: Libri Könyvpalota, VII, Rákóczi u. 12 (☎267 4843). M2: Astoria. The best choice. A multilevel bookstore, it has 1 fl. of up-to-date English titles. Open M-F 10am-7:30pm, Sa 10am-3pm. MC/V. **Bestsellers Livres,** V, Október 6 u. 11 (☎312 1295; www.bestsellers.hu), off Arany János u. M1, 2, or 3: Deák tér or M3: Arany János. Open M-F 9am-6:30pm, Sa 10am-5pm, Su 10am-4pm.

GLBT Hotline: GayGuide.net Budapest (☎06 30 93 23 334; www.budapest.gayguide.net). Posts an online guide and runs a hotline (daily 4-8pm) with info and reservations at GLBT-friendly lodgings. See also **GLBT Budapest,** p. 290

THE REAL VÁCI U. If you're hoping to do some shopping along Váci u., be careful: Budapest has 2 streets named Váci u. that are far apart from each other–one is in district XIII, while the shopping boulevard is in district V.

EMERGENCY AND COMMUNICATIONS

Tourist Police: V, Sütő u. 2 (☎438 8080). M1, 2, or 3: Deák tér. Inside the Tourinform office. Tourists can report stolen and lost items and other police matters. Tourist Police often can't do much. Beware of people pretending to be Tourist Police who demand your passport. Open 24hr. In the event of an emergency, call the **police** at ☎107, in English ☎1 311 1666.

Pharmacies: II, Frankel Leó út 22 (☎212 4406). AmEx/MC/V. **VI,** Teréz krt. 41 (☎311 4439). Open M-F 8am-8pm, Sa 8am-2pm. **VII,** Rákóczi út 39 (☎314 3695). Open M-F 7:30am-9pm, Sa 7:30am-2pm; no after-hours service. **VIII,** Üllöi út 121 (☎215 3900). Look for a green-and-white *Apotheke, Gyógyszertár,* or *Pharmacie* sign in the window.

Medical Assistance: Ambulance (☎104). **Falck (SOS) KFT,** II, Kapy út 49/b (☎275 1535). Ambulance service US$120. **American Clinic,** I, Hattyú u. 14 (☎224 9090; www.americanclinics.com). Accepts walk-ins, but calling a day ahead is helpful. Open M 8:30am-7pm, Tu-W 10am-6pm, Th 11:30am-6pm, F 10am-6pm. You will be charged for the physician's time plus tests. Direct insurance billing available. 24hr. emergency ☎224 9090. The US embassy also maintains a list of English-speaking doctors.

Telephones: Domestic operator and info ☎198; international operator 190, info 199. Most phones use **phone cards,** available at kiosks and Metro stations. 50-unit card 800Ft, 120-unit card 1800Ft.

Internet: Cyber cafes litter the city, but access can be expensive and long waits are common. Internet is available at many hostels, where it is usually cheaper than at cafes. **Ami Internet Coffee,** V, Váci u. 40 (☎267 1644; www.amicoffee.hu). M3: Ferenciek tere. Lounge with drinks. 200Ft per 15min., 700Ft per hr. Open daily 9am-2am. Internet access also at **Libri Könyvpalota,** VII, Rákóczi út 12 (☎267 4843; www.libri.hu), and M2: Astoria. English-language bookstore. 250Ft per 30min., 400Ft per hr. Open M-F 10am-7:30pm, Sa 10am-3pm.

Post Office: V, Városház u. 18 (☎318 4811). **Poste Restante** (Postán Mar) in office around the right side of the building. Open M-F 8am-8pm, Sa 8am-2pm. Branches at Nyugati pu.; VI, Teréz krt. 105/107; Keleti pu.; VIII, Baross tér 11/c; and elsewhere. Open M-F 7am-8pm, Sa 8am-2pm. **Postal Code:** Depends on the district–Postal Codes are 1XX2, where XX is the district number (1052 for post office listed above).

ACCOMMODATIONS

Tourists fill the city in July and August; phone first or store luggage while looking for a bed. If you book a room, call again the night before to confirm: hostels have been known to "misplace" reservations. It's a chaotic scene at Keleti pu., as hostel representatives jostle each other for guests. Don't be drawn in by promises of rides or discounts: some hostel-hawkers stretch the truth and you may find yourself a bit surprised when the price comes with a few little "extras." Set the price of your stay before you tag along for the ride.

ACCOMMODATION AGENCIES

Private rooms ❷ (4000Ft-7000Ft; prices decrease with longer stays) are slightly more expensive than hostels, but offer what most hostels can't: peace, quiet, and private showers. Accommodation agencies are everywhere. For cheaper rooms, try to be there when the agency opens. Before accepting a room, make sure it is easily accessible by public transport. Most are cash only. **Best Hotel Service,** V, Sütö u. 2, in the courtyard, makes accommodation reservations; car rentals; and city tours. (M1, 2, or 3: Deák tér. ☎318 4848. Rooms from 6000Ft. Open daily 8am-8pm.) **IBUSZ,** V, Ferenciek tere 10, books fairly cheap rooms. (M3: Ferenciek tere. Doubles 5000-10,000Ft; triples 6500-12,000Ft. 1800Ft fee for stays of fewer than 4 nights.) IBUSZ also rents central Pest apartments with kitchen and bath. Reserve by email or fax. (☎485 2700; accommodation@ibusz.hu. 1-bedroom flat from 9000Ft; 2-bedroom from 14,000Ft. Open M-F 8:15am-5pm.) There is also a branch at VIII, Keleti pu. (☎342 9572. Open M-F 8am-6pm.)

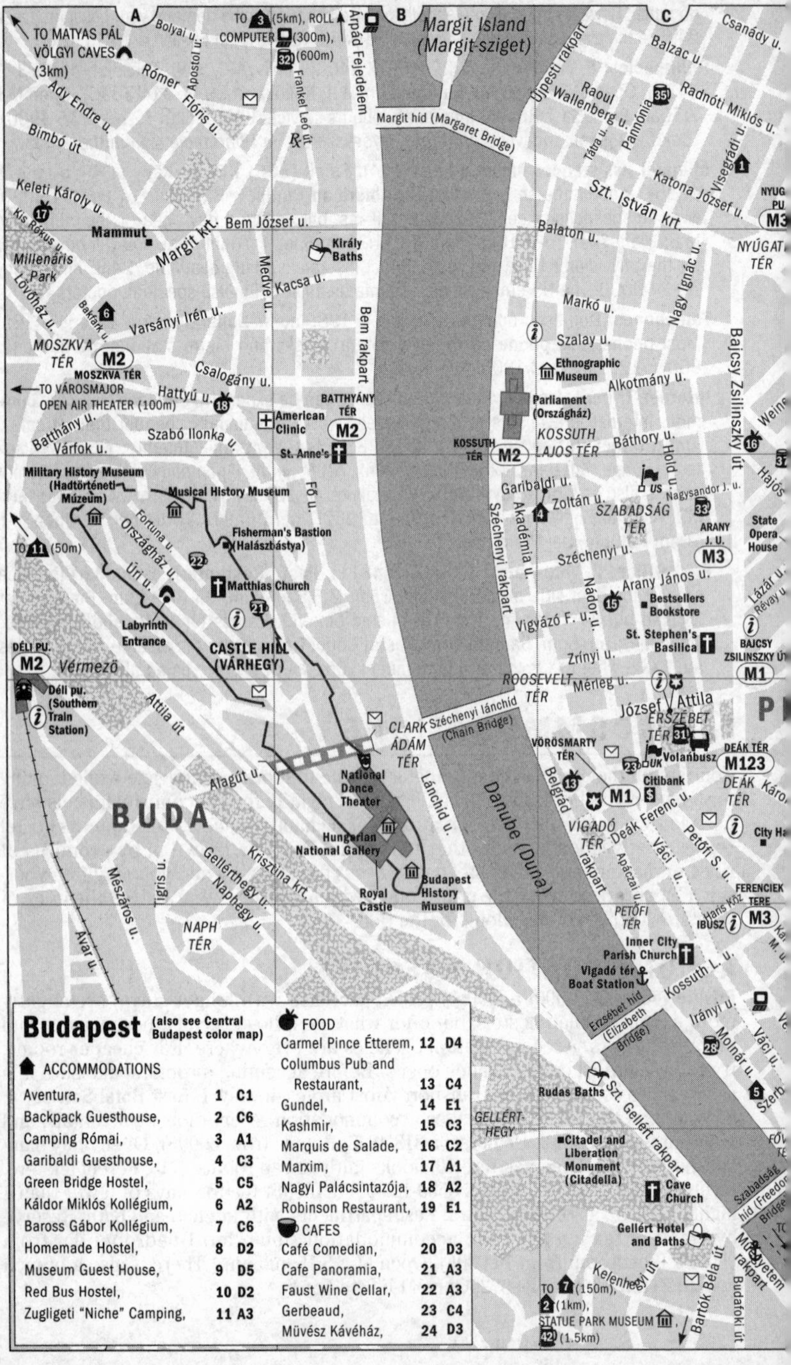

Budapest (also see Central Budapest color map)

ACCOMMODATIONS

Aventura,	1	C1
Backpack Guesthouse,	2	C6
Camping Római,	3	A1
Garibaldi Guesthouse,	4	C3
Green Bridge Hostel,	5	C5
Káldor Miklós Kollégium,	6	A2
Baross Gábor Kollégium,	7	C6
Homemade Hostel,	8	D2
Museum Guest House,	9	D5
Red Bus Hostel,	10	D2
Zugligeti "Niche" Camping,	11	A3

FOOD

Carmel Pince Étterem,	12	D4
Columbus Pub and Restaurant,	13	C4
Gundel,	14	E1
Kashmir,	15	C3
Marquis de Salade,	16	C2
Marxim,	17	A1
Nagyi Palácsintazója,	18	A2
Robinson Restaurant,	19	E1

CAFES

Café Comedian,	20	D3
Cafe Panoramia,	21	A3
Faust Wine Cellar,	22	A3
Gerbeaud,	23	C4
Müvész Kávéház,	24	D3

NIGHTLIFE		
A-38 Ship,	25	C6
B7 Klub,	26	D3
Café Eklektika,	27	D3
Capella,	28	C5
Club Seven,	29	E4
Crazy Café,	30	D2
Gödör Klub,	31	C4
Hajogyári Sziget,	32	B1
Le Cafe M,	33	C3
Morrison's Music Pub,	34	C3
Mosselen,	35	C1
Old Man's Music Pub,	36	E4
Piaf,	37	C3
Rio,	38	D6
Szimpla Kert,	39	D3
West Balkan,	40	E6
Zöid Pardon,	41	D6
Wigwam Rock Club,	42	C6

HOSTELS AND HOTELS

From wild hostels to hushed hotels, Budapest has accommodations to fit every preference. Many university dorms become hostels from late June to late August. The **Hungarian Youth Hostels Association,** which operates from Keleti pu., runs many hostels. Their staff wear Hostelling International T-shirts and will—along with legions of competitors—accost you as you get off the train. Many provide free transport, but set the price of your stay before you agree.

Backpack Guesthouse, XI, Takács Menyhért u. 33 (☎385 8946; www.backpacker.hu), 12min. from central Pest. From Keleti pu., take bus #7 or 7a toward Buda. Get off at Tétényi u., then backtrack and turn left to go under the bridge. Take another left on Hamzsabégi út and continue to the 3rd right. The 49E night bus runs here after trams stop. Creative designs animate the walls, a movie-stocked common room provides a sanctuary for free hookah smoking, and a slew of hammocks rest in an inner garden, making this neighborhood Buda hostel a hideaway from the traffic of the city. Yoga classes in the common room (1500Ft), goulash-cooking lessons, and skateboards for rent. Laundry 1500Ft. Free Internet. Reception 24hr. 7- to 11-bed dorms 3000Ft, 4- to 5-bed dorms 3500Ft; doubles 9000Ft; mattress in gazebo 2500Ft. MC/V. ❷

Homemade Hostel, III, Teréz krt. 22, 1st fl. (☎302 2103; www.homemadehostel.com). Follow the stairs to the right. True to its name, the decor is all recycled and reconstructed furniture. This relaxed Pest hostel is the backpacker's paradise: casual without being grungy, Homemade offers reasonable prices in a prime location. Kitchen stocked with tea, coffee, and breakfast foods. Laundry 1300Ft. Free Internet, maps and brochures. Reception 24hr. Reserve ahead. Dorms 4000Ft-4750Ft; private double 13,700Ft. Cash only. ❷

Aventura Hostel, XIII, Visegrádi u. 12 (☎703 102 003; www.aventurahostel.com), in Pest. M3: Nyugati tér. Tasteful interior design and clean bathrooms. Board provides special event and party listings for the best nightclubs in town, updated daily. Breakfast included. Laundry 1500Ft. Free Internet. Reception 24hr. Dorms 3500-4500Ft; private double 12,500Ft. Cash only. ❸

Museum Guest House, VIII, Mikszáth Kálmán tér 4, 1st fl. (☎318 9508; museumgh@freemail.c3.hu). M3: Kálvin tér. Take the left exit on Baross u.; at the fork, go left on Reviczky u. At the square, go to the right corner and ring buzzer 3 at gate #4. Conveniently located a few blocks from both the National Museum, the Museum Guest House manages to create a haven with its freshly painted rooms, and lofted beds. English spoken. Kitchen, luggage storage. Laundry 1200Ft. Free Internet. Reception 24hr. Check-out 11am. Reserve ahead. Dorms 3500Ft. Cash only. ❷

Red Bus Hostel, V, Semmelweis u. 14 (☎266 0136; www.redbusbudapest.hu). Newly renovated rooms on a beautiful, quiet street a few blocks from downtown Pest. A large common room provides a hangout for travelers. Kitchen and complimentary breakfast. Free luggage storage. Laundry 1300Ft. Internet 10Ft per min. Reception 24hr. Check-out 10am. Dorms 3600Ft; singles and doubles 9500Ft; triples 11,350Ft. V. ❷

Green Bridge Hostel, V, Molnár u. 22-24 (☎266 6922; greenbridge@freemail.hu), in Pest's central district. The unbeatable location, friendly staff, and free snacks earn rave reviews. Free Internet. Reception 24hr. Flexible check-out. Reserve ahead. Dorms 3750-4500Ft. Cash only.❷

Garibaldi Guesthouse, V, Garibaldi u. 5 (☎302 3456; garibaldiguest@hotmail.com). M2: Kossuth tér. Head away from Parliament along Nádor u. and take 1st right on Garibaldi u. The guesthouse is welcoming and comfortable, in a serene neighborhood only 1 block from the Parliament building in Pest. Spacious rooms with TVs, kitchenettes, and spotless baths. Owner has rooms throughout the city, including some near Astoria. Laundry. Singles 7000Ft; doubles 8000Ft; apartments 6000-10,000Ft per person. Prices decrease with longer stays, big groups, and low season. Cash only. ❸

SUMMER HOSTELS AND CAMPING

Many **university dorms** moonlight as hostels in July and August. Most are clustered around Móricz Zsigmond Körtér in District XI. All have kitchens, luggage storage, and common room TVs. Budapest's nearest **campgrounds** are a bit out of the way, but can be peaceful and scenic alternatives to the city.

Káldor Miklós Kollégium, II, Bakfark u. 1/3 (☎201 5807). M2: Moszkva tér. Walk along Margit krt. and take 1st right after Mammut. Although across the river from the action, these dorms are among the most comfortable in town, with lofted beds. Students get a heavy discount, making this an unbeatable Buda bargain. Check-out 10am. Open June 15-Aug. 28. 6-bed dorms 2500Ft per person. 10% HI discount. Cash only. ❶

Baross Gábor Kollégium, XI, Bartók Béla út 17 (☎463 4158). Take bus #7 or 7A across the river to Gellért. Ample natural light bathes this old building. Laundry service available. Check-out 9am. Open July to early Sept. Call between 8am-4pm at least one day ahead. Doubles 4500Ft, with private bath 5000Ft. Cash only. ❷

Zugligeti "Niche" Camping, XII, Zugligeti út 101 (☎/fax 200 8346; www.camping-niche.hu). Take bus #158 from above Moszkva tér to Laszállóhely, the last stop. Restaurant. Communal showers. 1400Ft per person, 990Ft per tent, 1400Ft per large tent, 1050Ft per car, 2550Ft per caravan. Cash only. ❶

Camping Római, III, Szentendrei út 189 (☎388 7167). M2: Batthyány tér. Take HÉV to Római fürdő; walk 100m toward the river. This campground offers a huge complex with swimming pool, shady park, and nearby grocery store and restaurants for those looking to get away from the buzz of the city. Laundry 800Ft. Campsites 4400Ft per person; bungalows 3000Ft per person; cars 4710Ft. Electricity included. Reserve far in advance as campsites fill up quickly in the summer. 3% tourist tax. 10% HI discount. ❷

HUNGARY?

For something cheap, explore the cafeterias beneath "Önkiszolgáló Étterem" signs (meals 300-500Ft) or seek out a neighborhood *kifőzés* (kiosk) or *vendéglő* (family-style restaurant). Corner markets stock the basics, and many have 24hr. windows. The king of them all, the **Grand Market Hall,** IX, Várház körút 1/3 on Fövam tér, built in 1897, boasts 10,000 sq. m of stalls. You'll find produce, baked goods, meat, and every souvenir imaginable. (M3: Kálvin tér. ☎217 6067. Open M 6am-5pm, Tu-F 6am-6pm, Sa 6am-2pm.) For ethnic restaurants, try the upper floors of **Mammut Plaza** (see **Entertainment,** p. 287), just outside the Moszkva tér Metro stop in Buda, or the **West End Plaza,** accessible from the Nyugati Metro stop in Pest.

Robinson Mediterranean-Style Restaurant and Cafe, XIV, Városliget tó (☎422 0222), sits on a lake in the scenic City Park, overlooking the castle. A deck-like patio and upstairs lounge provide a calm, open-air experience. Robinson dishes up enchanting Mediterranean fare. Try a salmon steak with asparagus sauce (3990Ft). Also serves local favorites like liver (2350Ft) and paprika veal (3800Ft). Vegetarian options available. Entrees 1800-3900Ft. Open daily noon-4pm and 6pm-midnight. MC/V. ❹

Marquis de Salade, VI, Hajós u. 43 (☎302 4086), at the corner of Bajcsy-Zsilinszky út, 2 blocks from the Metro. M3: Arany János. An elegant cellar restaurant with a huge menu of offerings from Azerbaijan and Russia, such as *jalancs dolma,* a vegetarian dish of veggies stuffed with rice. Portions are large and the appetizers can be as filling as an entree elsewhere. Entrees 1200Ft-3400Ft. Open daily noon-midnight. Cash only. ❸

Kashmir, V, Arany János u. 13 (☎354 1806; www.kashmiretterem.hu). This premier Indian restaurant offers lighter alternatives to Hungarian cuisine with its kashmiri specialties (saffron chicken, 1800Ft) and vegetarian options. Get comfortable on cushioned benches as Indian beats play softly in the background. Hungarian dishes are also available. English menu. M-F 11am-11pm, Sa-Su 5-11pm. Cash only. ❸

ROMAN AROUND BUDAPEST

he Romans occupied modern lay Transdanubia in the AD first entury, creating the provinces of 'annoia. Present-day Buda, then nown as Aquincum, served primarily as a civilian town, though a nilitary settlement lay nearby. Its nhabitants developed the area nto a sophisticated network of queducts and cultural centers, uilding a majestic villa that erved as a home for government fficials and regulators.

Extensive excavations in the 960s uncovered roughly one-hird of the Aquincum that flourshed in the second and third cen-uries. Among these ruins was an mphtheater that seated 7,000 or theatrical performances, animal duels, sporting events, and olitical rallies and conferences. lavish home, called the Hercules Villa for its nearly intact vall-painting depicting the mytho-ogical fight between Hercules nd the Centaur, was equipped vith an intricate floor-heating sys-em. The still-standing ruins of quincum and its numerous rchaeological artifacts can be een in Budapest today.

ake the HÉV going toward Szentenre and get off at the Aquincum top. Ruins open Tu-Su 9am-5pm. Museum of artifacts open 10am-pm. 900Ft, students 450Ft English our 2100Ft.

Carmel Pince Étterem, VII, Kazinczy út 31 (☎322 1834). In the old Jewish quarter near Dohány Synagogue. M2: Astoria. Serves generous portions of Jewish and Hungarian delicacies like matzah ball soup and heavy stews. Not kosher. Entrees 1800Ft-3900Ft. Live klezmer every Thursday at 7:30pm. Open Sept.-June daily noon-11pm; June-Aug. M-F and Su noon-11pm. AmEx/MC/V. ❹

Columbus Pub and Restaurant, V, Danube (☎266 9013), on the promenade near the Chain Bridge. If you haven't spent enough time with the beautiful Danube during your stay in Budapest, enjoy a meal on this moored ship. A great view of Castle Hill and the citadel go along with the fine selection of Hungarian cuisine, beer, and drinks. Entrees 1300-3500Ft. Open daily 11am-midnight. AmEx/MC/V. ❹

Marxim, II, Kis Rókus u. 23 (316 0231; www.marximpub.extra.hu). M2: Moszkva tér. Walk along Margit krt, then turn left after passing Mammut. Hip locals unite at this tongue-in-cheek, communist-themed pizzeria, painted with red stars and graffiti. Pizzas (650-1350Ft) are named in honor of Lenin and "Papa Marx" and come hot from the oven, "a la anarchy." Open M-Th noon-1am, F-Sa noon-2am, Su 6pm-1am. Cash only. ❷

Nagyi Palacsint ázója, II, Hattyú u. 16 (☎212 4866). The perfect stop after a day of heavy sightseeing on Castle Hill, or, better yet, after a night of even heavier drinking. This 24hr. joint dishes out both sweet (125Ft-185Ft) and savory crepes (230-330Ft) piled high with cheese, fruit, chocolate sauce, or anything else you could possibly desire. Chairs are squeezed in everywhere, even on the wall along the stairwell, in this tiny, mirror-covered restaurant. English menu. Cash only. ❶

Gundel, XIV, Állatkertu u. 2 (☎468 4040). One of Hungary's most famous restaurants, Gundel has served its cuisine to Queen Elizabeth II. 7-course meals (13,000-18,500Ft) astound guests, but if you just want to say you've been, opt for a sandwich (1000Ft) or a marzipan dessert (990Ft). The house speciality is goose liver (3590Ft). Su brunch buffet 11:30am-3pm (5800Ft). Open daily noon-4pm and 6:30pm-midnight. AmEx/MC/V. ❺

CAFES

The former haunts of writers, artists, and dissidents, Budapest's cafes boast rich histories. The current expat and yuppie cafes of choice are at **Ferenc Liszt tér** (M1: Oktogon), and often prove pricier than cafes in other neighborhoods. Each cafe has a large summer patio—come early to stake out a post for people-watching.

Muvész Kávéház, VI, Andrássy út 29 (☎352 1337). M1: Opera. Across from the Opera. Stop in for a cappuccino (350Ft) and a slice of flamboyantly decorated cake (250Ft-480Ft) before or after a show, and brew in intellectual conversation under the crystal chandeliers. Open daily 9am-11:45pm. Cash only. ❶

Cafe Comedian, VI. Nagymező u. 26. M1: Oktogon. Waiters in suspenders and funky hats give this centrally located cafe a light-hearted ambience, drawing an eclectic crowd of local artists and free spirits. Smoothies 690Ft. Beer 360Ft. Open M-F 8am-midnight, Sa-Su 2pm-midnight. Cash only. ❷

Gerbeaud, V, Vörösmarty tér 7 (☎429 9020; www.gerbeaud.hu). M1: Vörösmarty tér. Hungary's most famous cafe and dessert shop has served delicious, homemade layer cakes (680Ft) and ice cream (260Ft) since 1858, most recently to flocks of tourists. Large terrace sprawls over Vörösmarty tér. Go for the tradition of the place, but beware that sweets you get here are going to cost at least double the price of any other dessert shop in the city. Open daily 9am-9pm. AmEx/MC/V. ❸

Faust Wine Cellar, I, Hess András tér 1-3 (☎488 6873). Enter the Hilton on Castle Hill, head left, and descend into the 13th-century cellar. An overwhelming array of excellent Hungarian vintages served with cheese and salami at intimate candlelit tables. Wine 300-4500Ft per glass. Open daily 4-11pm. Cash only. ❷

Cafe Panorama, I, Szentháromság tér, behind the Castle Hill Church. If you're thirsty after climbing the hill, reward yourself with a coffee or beer (both from 360Ft) at this cafe, which boasts amazing views of the Danube and Pest. Open daily 10am-10pm. ❶

SIGHTS

In 1896, on the verge of its Golden Age and its 1000th birthday, Budapest constructed many of its most prominent sights. These works included **Heroes' Square** (Hősök tere), **Liberty Bridge** (Szabadság híd), **Vajdahunyad Castle** (Vajdahunyad vár), and continental Europe's first **Metro;** they have since been damaged by time, war, and communist occupation. Budapest is easily explored on your own, but for a guided exploration, consider **Absolute Walking and Biking Tours.** The basic tour (3½hr.; 4000Ft, students 3500Ft) meets daily April through October at 9:30am and 1:30pm, on the steps of the yellow church in Deák tér. Low season tours, September through May, leave at 10:30am from Deák tér. Choose from among tours that focus on everything from communism to pubbing. (30 211 8861; www.absolutetours.com. Specialized tours 3½-5½hr. 4000-7000Ft.) Boat tours leave from Vigadó tér piers 6-7. Danube Legend, which runs in the evening, costs 4200Ft. Duna Bella is a daytime boat (3800Ft). Biking tours are run through a company called **Yellow Zebra Bikes** and meets at Deák tér. daily July-Aug. 4, 11pm; Apr.-Oct. at 11pm. ☎266 8777, yellowzebrabikes.com. 5000Ft, students 4500Ft. Specialized tours 3½-5½hr. 4000-7000Ft.) Boat tours leave from Vigadó tér piers 6-7.

BUDAPEST FOR POCKET CHANGE. The eager sightseer in Budapest is in luck, as many of the permanent collections in the city's museums are free. After dropping your bags at **Backpack Guesthouse** (p. 278), check out the Hungarian impressionists at the **National Gallery** (p. 282), where admission is free. Next, hike up the nearby **Citadel** (p. 283) for the best view in the city. Cross the bridge for cheap grub at **Grand Market Hall** (p. 279), then walk back to **St. Stephen's Basilica** (p. 284) for a glimpse of its grandeur.

BUDA

Older and with less metropolitan bustle than Pest, Buda tumbles down from Castle and Gellért Hills on the east bank of the Danube and sprawls into Budapest's main residential areas. Rich in parks, lush hills, and spacious, suburban-style homes, Buda abounds with beautiful views of the city and great opportunities to get in touch with nature through hikes, biking, and climbing.

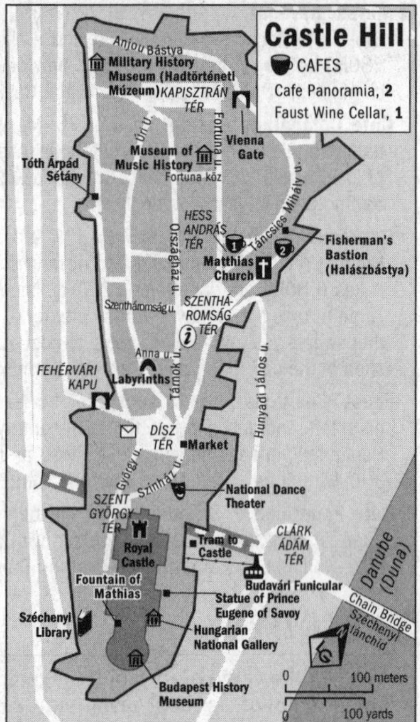

CASTLE HILL (VÁRHEGY)

M1, 2, or 3: Deák tér; then take bus #16. Alternatively, M2: Moszkva tér; then walk uphill on Várfok u. Or take an elevator (650 Ft up, 550Ft to return). Bécsi kapu marks castle entrance.

Towering above the Danube, the castle district has been razed and rebuilt three times over 800-year history, most recently in 1945 after its near total destruction at the hands of the Red Army. Today, its winding streets are cluttered with art galleries, souvenir shops, and cafes that afford views of the city.

MATTHIAS CHURCH (MÁTYÁS TEMPLOM). Rising from a multicolored roof, the oft-photographed Gothic tower of Matthias Church pierces the city sky. When Ottoman armies seized Buda in 1541, the church was converted into a mosque. In 1688, the Habsburgs defeated the Turks, sacked the city, and reconverted the building. Inside and out, the church's style is a combination of eastern and western influences. Climb the staircase to reach the Museum of Ecclesiastical Art, and walk to the royal oratory room that once seated the king during mass and now houses the St. Stephen's Crown of Hungary. *(I, Szentháromság tér 2. Open M-F 9am-5pm, Sa 9am-1:45pm, Su 1-5pm. High mass M-Sa 7, 8:30am, 6pm; Su and holidays also 7, 8:30, 10am, noon, 6pm. Church and museum 650Ft, students 450Ft.)*

CASTLE LABYRINTHS (BUDAVÁRI LABIRINTUS). These caves, which once housed prehistoric Neanderthals, later served as bomb refuges and military barricades. Created naturally by thermal springs that extend 1200m underground, this dark and damp expanse has been converted into a series of chambers that walks the line between museum and haunted house. Fantastical displays vary from cavern to cavern, with some holding statues and one memorable display centered on a fountain of red wine: you can taste it, if you don't mind the risk of spattering it on your clothes. For a creepier experience, go between 6 and 7:30pm, when they shut off the lights and hand out oil lamps. Children under 14 and people with heart conditions are advised not to participate in the spooky festivities. *(Úri u. 9. ☎212 0207; www.labirintus.com. Open daily 9:30am-7:30pm. 1500Ft, students 1200Ft.)*

ROYAL PALACE. Leveled at the end of WWII, the rebuilt palace with flowery inner courtyards and panoramic views of the city, houses several museums. (I. szent györgy tér 2. M1, 2 or 3: Deák Tér, then take bus #16 across the Danube to the top of Castle hill. ☎375 7533.) Wings B-D hold the Hungarian National Gallery (Magyar Nemzeti Galéria). The gallery displays Hungarian fine art organized chronologically from medieval and Renaissance periods to 20th-century fluid sculptures. *(☎375 7533. Open Tu-Su 10am-6pm. Permanent collections free. Temporary exhibits on the ground floor 800Ft, students 400Ft. English tour by appointment.)* Wing E houses the Budapest History Museum (Budapest Történeti Muzeúm), which traces the timeline of the area's development from Roman times through a collection of recently unearthed weapons and crafts. *(Open daily Apr.-Oct. 10am-6pm; Nov.-Mar. 10am-4pm. 1100Ft, students 550Ft. English captions. Audio tour available for 800ft in several languages.)*

OTHER SIGHTS IN BUDA

GELLÉRT HILL (GELLÉRT HEGY). In the 11th century, the Pope sent Bishop Gellért to the coronation of King Stephen, the first Christian ruler of Hungary, to convert the pagan Magyars to Christianity. Unconvinced, the Magyars revolted and hurled the bishop to his death from atop the hill that now bears his name. Completed in the 1930s by Hungarian pilgrims impressed after their visit to the French Lourdes, **St. Ivan's Cave Church** (Szikla Templom), on the south side of the hill, was barricaded with a concrete wall by the Soviets, and did not reopen until 1989. *(Mass daily 11am, 5:30, 8pm. Additional Su mass at 9:30am.)* Atop Gellért Hill, the **Liberation Monument** (Szabadság Szobor), a bronze statue of a woman raising a palm branch, commemorates the liberation of Budapest after WWII. The adjoining **Citadel** was in 1848. Inside, you'll find an exhibit about the hill's history as well as unobstructed views of the city, especially gorgeous at night. A short way from the Citadel, the **statue of St. Gellért** overlooks Erzsébet híd. *(XI. Tram #18 or 19, or bus #7, to Hotel Gellért. Follow Szabó Verjték u. to Jubileumi Park and continue on paths to the summit. Or, take bus #27, get off at Búsuló Juhász, and walk 5min. to the peak. Citadel 1200Ft.)*

MARGIT ISLAND (MARGIT-SZIGET). The garden pathways of Margit Island offer a refreshing break from the city heat. Off-limits to private cars, the island park is named after King Béla IV's daughter, whom he vowed to rear as a nun if the nation survived the 1241 Mongol invasion. When Hungary survived, Margit was confined to the island convent. These days, however, nuns have been replaced by children ready to run you down with pedal cars. **Palatinus Strandfürdő,** on Borsodi Beach, a huge water park equipped with slides and several pools, is consistent with the Hungarian summertime tradition of lounging poolside. *(Open M-F 10am-6pm, Sa-Su 9am-7pm weather permitting. 1800Ft, students 1620Ft with BudapestCard.)* You can rent **bikes, rollerskates, electric scooters** or **bike-trol-**

THE SANDWICH OF DEATH

The descent into the Matyas Caves, situated in the depths of the Buda Hills, is met by overwhelming darkness and absolute silence. The air is so cold—hovering at a chilly 10°C—that you would be able to see your breath as clearly as a bellowing chimney—that is, if you could see.

What brings travelers into the silent depths is the opportunity to partake in caving, the unforgettable experience of snaking through the underground labyrinthine caves. Yet what draws visitors to these particular caves is the "Sandwich of Death," the finale of the journey. Equipped only with a helmet and flashlight, spelunkers venture through the path that descends 220m to sea level and back up again, inching past heart-stopping 40m drops and squeezing through crevices barely large enough to fit your helmet. The climactic sandwich isn't quite as dangerous as it sounds—it's a 12m stomach-crawl through two slabs of limestone.

Caving is not for the claustrophobic. That said, the experience certainly isn't only for the rough-and-ready. Guides judge the skill level of their groups and choose the difficulty of the path accordingly.

Follow directions to the Pál-Völgyi Caves (p. 284). Call ahead (☎28 49 69) to reserve a spot and check tour times. 2100Ft.

leys, cars that you pedal with your feet. *(Bikes 450Ft per 30min. Rollerskates 880Ft per 30min. Electric scooter 990Ft per 30min. Bike-trolleys 1480Ft per 30min. Prices slightly lower at Margit híd, but selection is slimmer than at Bringóhintó, on the far side of the island.)* For the less active, **golf carts** allow easy transport across the island. *(2900Ft for 4 person car, 3900Ft for 6 person car per 30min.).* **Szabadtéri Szinpad,** the theater at the island's center, hosts concerts and plays throughout the summer, from *Jekyll and Hyde* to Irish dancing. *(M3: Nyugati pu. Take tram #4 or 6 or the HÉV from Batthyány tér to Margit híd. ☎340 4196; www.szabadter.hu. Ticket office open W-F 1pm-6pm, Sa 1-5pm, Su 1-4pm.)*

PÁL-VÖLGYI CAVES. Descend the 40m ladder for a tour (1hr.) of the caves, which were formed by the thermal springs that now supply the baths in the city. Wear warm clothing, as the caves are 10°C. For spelunking or a more challenging cave visit, see **The Sandwich of Death,** p. 283. *(Bus #86 from Batthyány tér to Kolosy tér; backtrack up the street and make the 1st right to get to the bus station. From there, catch bus #65 to the caves. ☎325 9505. Open Tu-Su 10am-4pm. Tours every hr. 1000Ft, students 750Ft. Tours also in Szemlőhegy Cave 1250/850Ft for a combination ticket for entry to both caves. English tours available, call for schedules.)*

PEST

Though downtown Pest dates to medieval times, it feels decidedly modern. Pest is Budapest's commercial and administrative center and holds many of the city's museums and architectural phenomena. Its streets, laid out on a grid in the 19th century, run past shops, cafes, restaurants, and Hungary's biggest corporations.

PARLIAMENT (ORSZÁGHÁZ). "The motherland does not have a house," Hungarian poet Mihály Vörösmarty lamented in 1846. In response to such nationalistic strivings, Budapest built a Parliament that looks more like a cathedral than a government building. The neo-Gothic building once required more electricity than the entire rest of the city for its massive 692-room structure. The gold-and-marble interior is stunning, and now houses the original St. Stephen crown. The informative tour leads through the enormous cupola room where statues of the nation's founding figures stand several meters tall. *(M2: Kossuth tér. ☎441 4000. Ticket office opens 8am. English tours M-F 10am, noon, 2, 2:30pm; Sa-Su 10am. Min. 5 people. Ask the guard to let you in, and purchase tickets at Gate X. Plan ahead so you don't miss the group as tours leave promptly. Entrance with mandatory tour 2300Ft, students 1150Ft; with EU passport free.)*

ST. STEPHEN'S BASILICA (SZ. ISTVÁN BAZILIKA). Although the city's largest church was seriously damaged in WWII, the red-and-green marble and gilded arches of its massive interior still attract tourists and worshippers. The 360° balcony of the Panorama Tower, Pest's highest vantage point, offers views of Gellért Hill and Pest. Through the church to the left is **St. Stephen's** mummified right hand, one of Hungary's most revered religious relics. *(V. M1, 2, or 3: Deák tér. Church open M-Sa May-Oct. 9am-5pm; Nov.-Apr. M-Sa 10am-4pm. Mass M-Sa 7, 8am, 6pm; Su 8:30, 10am (High Mass), noon, 6pm. Free. See the relic Apr.-Aug. M-Sa 9am-4:30pm, Su 1-4:30pm; Oct.-Mar. M-Sa 10am-4pm, Su 1-3:30pm. 300Ft, students 250Ft. Tower open daily June-Aug. 9:30am-6pm; Sept.-Oct. 10am-5:30pm; Apr.-May 10am-4:30pm. 500Ft, students 400Ft.)*

GREAT SYNAGOGUE (ZSINAGÓGA). The largest synagogue in Europe and the second largest in the world, the 1859 Great Synagogue was designed to hold 3000 congregants. Renovations begun in 1990 are nearly complete. Next to the synagogue is the last **ghetto** established in WWII. More than 80,000 Jews were imprisoned and 10,000 died in the final two months of the war. Today, the 2500 people whose bodies could be identified are buried here; the rest lie in a common grave in the Jewish Cemetery. In the garden sits the **Tree of Life,** an enormous metal tree honoring Holocaust victims. Each leaf bears the name of a Hungarian family whose members perished, and names can be added upon request. Next to it, four granite memorials honor "Righteous Gentiles," non-Jews who aided Jewish victims during the Holocaust. The English-speaking guides give excellent tours. *(VII. M2: Astoria. At the corner of Dohány u. and Wesselényi u. Open May-Oct. M-Th 10am-5pm, F 10am-2pm, Su 10am-2pm; Nov.-Apr. M-Th 10am-3pm, F and Su 10am-1pm. Services F 6pm. Admission often starts at 10:30am. Covered shoulders and head covering for men required. Tours M-Th 10:30am-3:30pm on the half-hour, F and Su 10:30, 11:30am, 12:30pm. Admission 1400Ft, students 750Ft; includes admission to the Jewish Museum, see p. 286. Tours 1900Ft, students 1600Ft.)*

ANDRÁSSY ÚT AND HEROES' SQUARE (HŐSÖK TERE). The elegant balconies and gated gardens of Hungary's grandest boulevard, laid out in 1872 and renovated after the 1989 communist turnover, preserve the splendor of Budapest's Golden Age. The most vivid reminder of this era is the gilt-and-marble interior of the Neo-Renaissance **Hungarian State Opera House** (Magyar Állami Operaház), adorned with magnificent frescoes. *(Andrássy út 22. M1: Opera. ☎332 8197. 1hr. English tours daily 3, 4pm. 2500Ft, students 1300Ft. 20% off with Budapest Card. See* ***Entertainment*** *p. 287 for show info.)* The **House of Terror** (see p. 286) lies on Andrássy út. The boulevard's most majestic stretch is near Heroes' Square, where the sweeping **Millennium Monument** (Millenniumi emlékmű) dominates the street. The structure, built for the city's millennial anniversary in 1896, commemorates prominent figures in Hungarian history. The seven horsemen at the base represent the Magyar tribes who settled the Carpathian Basin. Archangel Gabriel, atop the statue, offers the Hungarian crown to St. Stephen. On either side are the **Museum of Fine Arts** and the **Museum of Modern Art.** *(VI. Andrássy út runs along M1 from Bajcsy-Zsilnszky út to Hősök tere.)*

CITY PARK (VÁROSLIGET). The shaded paths of City Park are perfect for lazy strolls by the lake—or for visiting the small amusement park, permanent circus, and zoo. Vajdahunyad Castle sits in the center. Created for the millennium celebration, the castle's facade is a quirky pastiche of Hungarian architectural styles. The only part open to visitors is the **Magyar Agricultural Museum** (Magyar Mezogazdasagi Múzeum), which has exhibits on rural life. *(Open Tu-Su 10am-5pm. 600Ft, students 300Ft.)* Outside the castle broods the hooded statue of Anonymous, King Béla IV's scribe and the country's first historian, who recorded everything about medieval Hungary but his own name. Across the castle moat lies the Bridge of Love. Legend holds that if sweethearts kiss below the bridge, they'll marry within three years. Those already married can kiss to secure eternal love. Be sure to take a dunk in the **Széchényi baths** (p. 287) before leaving. *(XIV. M1: Széchényi Fürdő. Zoo ☎343 3710. Open May-Aug. M-Th 9am-6:30pm, F-Su 9am-7pm; Mar. and Oct. M-Th 9am-5pm, F-Su 9am-5:30pm; Apr. and Sept. M-Th 9am-5:30pm, F-Su 9am-6pm; Nov.-Jan. daily. 9am-4pm. 1700Ft, students 1200Ft. Park ☎363 8310. Open July-Aug. daily 10am-8pm; May-June M-F 11am-7pm, Sa-Su 10am-8pm. Weekdays 3100Ft, kids 2100Ft; weekends 3500Ft/2500Ft.*

MUSEUMS

MUSEUM OF APPLIED ARTS (IPARMŰVÉSZETI MÚZEUM). This collection of handcrafted pieces—including ceramics, furniture, metalwork, and Tiffany glass—deserves careful examination. Excellent temporary exhibits highlight specific crafts. Built for the 1896 millennium, the tiled Art Nouveau edifice is as intricate and important as the pieces within. *(IX. Üllői út 33-37. M3: Ferenc krt. ☎456 5100. Open Tu-Su 10am-6pm. Prices vary with changing exhibits, but usually around 1600Ft, students 800Ft. Tours also vary, usually 2300Ft/1150Ft. English pamphlet 100Ft.)*

HOUSE OF TERROR (TERROR HÁZA). The Museum's name, printed in giant block-lettering that extends into the sky, greets visitors to this former home of the Hungarian Nazi Party and, later, the Soviet secret police. The city's most high-tech museum, the

House of Terror uses videos and an audio tour (1200Ft) to explain its strikingly realistic exhibits. For further explanation, pick up summaries, available in each of the rooms, of the horrific history of German occupation and ensuing Communist regime. *(VI. Andrássy Út 60. M1: Vörösmarty u. ☎374 2600; www.terrorhaza.hu. Open Tu-F 10am-6pm, Sa-Su 10am-7:30pm. 1500Ft, students 750Ft.)*

LUDWIG MUSEUM (LUDVIG MÚZEUM). Relocated from the palace on Castle Hill to an industrial neighborhood on the outskirts of the city, the Ludwig Museum—LuMu, as it fancies itself—features the most recent incarnations of Hungarian painting and sculpture, in addition to a small collection of works by international favorites like Picasso and Warhol. Galleries with stark white walls create a dramatic effect; light flows through large windows overlooking the Danube. The museum is housed in the right wing of the Palace of Arts. *(IX. Komor Marcell u. 1. Take tram #4 or #6 to Boráros tér, then take the HEV commuter rail 1 stop to Lágymányosi híd. The stop is right in front of the museum. ☎555 3444; www.lumu.org.hu. Open Tu-Su 10am-8pm, last Sa of the month 10am-10pm. Temporary exhibit 1200Ft, students 600Ft.*

MUSEUM OF FINE ARTS (SZÉPŰVÉSZETI MÚZEUM). This striking building contains a roster of European painting's luminaries, from Giotto to Breugel to Monet. The museum also houses a collection of Roman ruins, Egyptian tombs and mummified alligators, and several Rodin sculptures. The structure that houses these masterpieces is a work of art in itself; resembling a dignified, worn temple from the outside, the entry hall opens onto a glorious marble atrium inside. *(XIV. M1 Hösök Tere. ☎496 7100. Open Tu-Su 10am-6pm, ticket booth until 5pm. 2400Ft, students 1200Ft. Thursday night specials, open 6pm-10pm. 2800/1500Ft. Call ahead to reserve tours for groups over 15 members.)*

NATIONAL MUSEUM (NEMZETI MÚZEUM). An exhaustive exhibition chronicles the history of Hungary, from the Neolithic Era through the 21st century. Exhibits have English captions and historical maps, and there are several film displays. The building is palatial, with a columned facade, marble staircases, and a tremendous domed roof. *(VIII. Múzeum krt. 14/16. M3: Kálvin tér. ☎338 2122; www.mng.hu. Open Tu-Su 10am-6pm. Permanent exhibit free, temporary 600Ft. Ticket booth open until 5:30pm.)*

JEWISH MUSEUM (ZSIDÓ MÚZEUM). Next to the synagogue, the small and beautiful Jewish Museum, birthplace of Zionist Theodor Herzl (1860-1904), displays religious artifacts from the 18th- and 19th-century heyday of Jewish Budapest. A permanent exhibit commemorates Hungarian Holocaust victims; the upper floor holds temporary exhibits. *(VII. See p. 284 for directions. Open May-Oct. M-Th 10am-5pm, F 10am-1pm, Su 10am-2pm; Nov.-Apr. M-F 10am-3pm, Sa 10am-1pm, Su 10am-1pm. Tours M-Th 10:30am-3:30pm every 30min., F and Su 10:30, 11:30am, 12:30pm. Museum 1400Ft, with ISIC 750Ft. Admission includes entrance to the Great Synagogue. Tours 1900Ft, students 1600Ft.)*

STATUE PARK MUSEUM (SZOBORPARK MÚZEUM). Encircled by a brick wall so that citizens avoid seeing the faces of their oppressors, this park houses an imposing collection of social realist statues gathered from Budapest's parks and squares after the collapse of Soviet rule. The indispensable English guidebook (1000Ft) explains the facts. *(XXII. On the corner of Balatoni út and Szabadkai út. Take express bus #7 from Keleti pu. to Étele tér, then take the yellow Volán bus from terminal #7 bound for Diósd 15min., every 15min., and get off at the Szoborpark stop. You must get a ticket from the ticket office at the bus station; BudapestCards and 2-week passes for intercity transportation are not acceptable. ☎424 7500; www.szoborpark.hu. Open daily 10am-dusk. 600Ft, students 400Ft.)*

MILLENÁRIS PARK. An endless-pool water fountain and trees growing from the the lake that lies at the center make Millennium Park a modernist marvel. The park houses three indoor theaters, an outdoor theater, and an outdoor projection screen broadcasting live sports. Occasional art shows take place, and the theaters host acts ranging from jazz performances to ballets to movie screenings. Call or visit the box office inside the theater for program listings. *(Féy u.20-22. M2: Moszkva tér. ☎336 4000; www.millenaris.hu. Park open daily 6am-midnight. Tickets 500-9500Ft.)*

ENTERTAINMENT

Budapest's cultural life flourishes in a series of performance events. For info and reservations for every imaginable event or venue, check out www.ticketpro.hu. In August, Óbudai Island hosts the week-long **Sziget Festival,** an open-air rock festival that draws major European and American acts. (☎372 0650; www.sziget.hu. Call for ticket prices.) Hungary's largest cultural festival, the **Budapest Spring Festival** (☎486 3311; late Mar.) showcases Hungary's premier musicians and actors. The **Danube Festival** in late June celebrates the building of the Chain Bridge. Highlights include traditional Hungarian folk dancing, contemporary dance acts and fireworks. Racing enthusiasts zoom to the suburb of Mogyoró in August for the **Formula 1 Hungarian Grand Prix** (☎317 2811; www.hungaroring.hu). Prices for most events are reasonable; check **Ticket Express Hungary,** Andrássy u. 18 (☎312 0000; www.tex.hu). Free guides available at tourist offices; hotels detail everything from festivals to art showings. The "Style" section of the English-language *Budapest Sun* (www.budapestsun.com; 300Ft) has 10-day listings and film reviews, while the plucky web guide *Pestiside* (www.pestiside.hu) lists nightlife and cultural offerings. **State Opera House** (Magyar Állami Operaház), VI, Andrássy út 22 (☎331 2550, box office 353 0170), located at the stop M1: Opera, is one of Europe's leading performance centers; it hosts operettas, ballets, and orchestra concerts. While some shows sell out a year ahead, many have seats available the day of the performance. (Box office open M-Sa 11am-7pm, Su 4-7pm. Closes at 5pm on non-performance days. Call for show schedules, or check the poster at the gates. Tickets 800-8700Ft.) **Westend City Center,** next to Nyugati Pu. on the city's west end, is Budapest's biggest shopping mall. (M3: Nyugati Pu. ☎238 7777. Open daily 8am-11pm.) The five levels of **Mammut,** in central Buda, are packed with boutiques. (M2: Moszkva tér. ☎345 8020. Open M-Sa 10am-9pm, Su 10am-6pm.)

LET IT RAIN. Always, always have a poncho with you traveling through Hungary, as 5-10 min. showers roll through constantly in the summer.

BATHS

Hot water bubbles in underground springs just beneath the surface of Budapest. For nearly 2000 years, the city has been channeling this natural treasure into its distinctive thermal baths, which are a must for visitors. Some baths have sections allocated for nude bathing, and most are separated by gender. Most are clean and enforce rules strictly. For more information, consult www.spasbudapest.com.

Széchényi, XIV, Állatkerti u. 11/14 (☎321 0310), in the center of City Park. M1: Széchényi fürdő. Statues and a fountain line one of the biggest, most luxurious bath complexes in Europe. Play on floating chessboards in the outdoor pool. Massages and spas are available at the 3 pools and 12 thermal baths. Open daily May-Sept. 6am-7pm; Oct.-Apr. M-F 6am-7pm, Sa-Su 6am-5pm. 2800Ft. 400Ft returned if you leave within 2hr., 200Ft within 3hr.; keep your original receipt. 15min. massage 2800Ft. Cash only.

Gellért, XI, Kelenhegyi út 2-6 (☎466 6166). Bus #7 or tram #47 or 49 to Hotel Gellért, at the base of Gellérthegy. Beautiful green-and-blue-tiled columns and massive wooden doors welcome visitors to a rooftop sundeck, a wave pool, and a la carte spa options, including mud baths and massages (from 2000Ft). Baths and pools open May-Sept.

daily 6am-7pm; Oct.-Apr. M-F 6am-7pm, Sa-Su 6am-5pm. Thermal bath and pool 3100Ft. Refunds based on time spent in the baths. 15min. massage 2500Ft. MC/V.

Király, I, Fő u. 84 (☎202 3688). M2: Batthány tér. Basic baths in a building featuring Turkish architecture. Almost 500 years old, these baths have remained authentic and have no swimming pools. Bathing here is a truly relaxing experience. Women only M, W, F 7am-6pm; men only Tu, Th, Sa 9am-8pm; ticket office closes 1hr. earlier. 1300Ft. 15min. massage in private room 2500Ft. Cash only.

 NIGHTLIFE

NIGHTLIFE SCAM. Following reports of cafes and bars overcharging tourists by obscene amounts, the US embassy has advised against certain establishments in the Váci u. area. In one scam, a woman approaches a foreign man and asks him to buy her a drink. When the bill arrives, accompanied by imposing thugs, the price of the drink turns out to be astronomical. Check prices before ordering at places you don't know well, and try to keep cash and credit cards concealed. For a current list of establishments about which complaints have been filed, check the list at www.usembassy.hu/conseng/announcements.html#advisory. If you suspect you have been the victim of a scam, call the police. Keep receipts to complain formally at the Consumer Bureau.

Whether you want to chill out in a jazz club, down a beer at a local pub, or dance the night away in an ear-splitting disco, Budapest has it all. Despite throbbing crowds in the clubs and pubs, the streets themselves are fairly empty. In summer, the scene moves to outdoor venues, the biggest of which are along the Danube, with plenty of great views and cheap drinks. Outdoor venues open from late April to mid-September. Ask Tourinform for entertainment guides. The Budapest *FUNZINE* is an invaluable resource for everything loud, funky, and cheap.

CLUBS

B7 Klub, VI, Nagymező u. 46-48 (☎633 6000; www.b7.hu). Hip hop with a smattering of electronic plays to an international crowd under the disco lights at this up-and-coming club. A small, translucent dance fl. hovers above the main one. Cover varies; usually free before midnight. Open M-Sa 5pm-5am. Cash only.

Szimpla Kert, VII, Kazinczy u. 14 (www.szimpla.hu). Graffiti designs on the walls, unique furniture, and colorful lighting give this garden/cafe/bar with movie screen and concert stage the most balanced and down-to-earth atmosphere in the city. Fresh crepes (100Ft) and a changing menu satisfy midnight cravings and the booze is plentiful and a bargain. Beer 250Ft. Open daily 10am-2am. Cash only.

West Balkan, VIII, Futó u. 46 (☎371 1807; www.west-balkan.com), in Pest. M3: Ferenc körút. 3 bars, indoor dance fl., and a whimsical outdoor garden keep Budapest's alternative scene grooving. Beer 450Ft. Open daily 4pm-4am.

Piaf, VI, Nagymező u. 25 (☎312 3823). A much-loved after-hours spot. Guests are admitted into the red velvet lounge after knocking on an inconspicuous door and meeting the approval of the club's matron. The party starts at 1am. Cover 800Ft; includes 1 beer. Open M-Th and Su 10pm-6am, F-Sa 10pm-7am. Cash only.

Club Seven, VII, Akácfa u. 7 (☎478 9030). M2: Blaha Lujza tér. Upscale, crowded local favorite plays funk, jazz, soul, or disco every night of the week. Cover Sa-Su men 2000Ft, women free. Open Sept.-May M-Th 6pm-5am, F-Sa-5pm-5am. Cash only.

A-38 Ship, XI (☎464 3940; www.a38.hu), anchored on the Buda side of the Danube, south of Petőfi Bridge. DJs spin on the decks of this revamped Ukrainian freighter. Check website for theme nights and schedule. Beer 300Ft. Cover varies. Restaurant open daily 11am-midnight. DJ nights open 11am-4am.

Gödör Klub, V, Erzsébet tér (☎202 013 868 www.godorklub.hu). The outdoor setting in the middle of Elizabeth Square makes you the center of attention at this nightclub that hosts nightly jazz and rock concerts and other special events beginning around 9pm. Check website for schedules. Beer 400Ft. Hard alcohol 300Ft. Open M-Sa 5pm-4am.

WigWam, XI, Fehérvári u. 202. (☎208 5569; www.wigwamrockclub.hu), via tram #47 Tram from Moricz Zsigmond. Crowded with young locals and adventure-seeking travelers, this club is host to rock-music-weekends, karaoke, erotic shows, singing competitions, and wild foam parties. Cover varies. Open daily 9pm-5am. Cash only.

PUBS

Old Man's Music Pub, VII, Akácfa u. 13 (☎322 7645; www.oldmans.hu). M2: Blaha Lujza tér. Popular with locals, expats, and tourists, this eclectic institution features live blues and jazz every night at 11pm—check the schedule and arrive early, because it gets very crowded very quickly. Relax in a booth in the pub area (open 3pm-3am) or hit the downstairs dance fl. (11pm-late). Open M-Sa 3pm-5am. Cash only.

Crazy Café, VI, Jókai u. 30 (☎302 4003). M3: Nyugati pu. The place to start a long night of drinking. With 30 kinds of whiskey (450-890Ft) and 17 kinds of vodka (590-690Ft), the scene at this vaguely jungle-themed basement bar has been known to get rowdy. Live DJ. Karaoke M-Tu and Su. Open M-Th 4pm-1am, F-Su 11am-1am. Cash only.

Mosselen, XIII Pannónia u. 14 (☎452 0535; www.mosselen.hu). One of the most popular pubs in the city, Mosselen is lined with huge windows that provide great street-side views. Specialty beers from 400Ft. Open daily 11am-2am. Cash only.

Morrison's Music Pub, XI Révay u. 25 (☎ 269 4060; www.morrisons.hu), next to the Opera. Popular among young locals, this place has a long list of events on its schedule: Karaoke, disco, drink specials, and parties every weekend. Beer 200-600Ft. Mixed drinks 300-1000Ft. Open M-Sa 7pm-5am.

SUMMER VENUES

Hajógyári Sziget (the location of the Sziget Festival), HEV towards Szentendre and get off at the Arpad Hid stop. By day, this island is known for its boat manufacturing. But at night, the venue offers something for every musical and alcoholic taste. Five different clubs, each with its own music and style, give partygoers the opportunity to mix it up all in one location. **Dokk Beach** (www.dokkbeach.hu), plays pop music along the water. Open F-Sa 10pm-5am. Nearby, on a huge boat, **Dokkoló** (www.dokkolo.co.hu), features ear-blasting techno music. Open Th-Su 10pm-5am. The trendiest of them all is **Bed Beach** (www.bedbeach.hu), with slick white leather couches. Open F-Sa 10pm-5am. At **Cafe Puerto** (www.cafepuerto.hu), Latin music complements some serious dancing. Open F-Sa 8pm-4am. The DJs at **Sláger Terasz** (www.cafepuerto.hu), above Cafe Puerto, emphasize whatever is hot and new in Hungarian pop. Open daily 8pm-4am.

Zöld Pardon, XI, on the Buda side of Petőfi Bridge. In a club that easily holds 1000, 3 large screens project surreal graphic designs. The music is hit-or-miss, but the chance to dance along the riverside is an undeniable hit. Live concerts every day by local bands. One of the many bars is elevated from the dance floor on a mock island. Snack bar. Beer 350-600Ft. Cover 100Ft. Open daily Apr.-Oct. 11am-5am. Cash only.

Rio, XI (☎302 972 158; www.rio.hu), on the Buda side of Petőfi Bridge. Budapest's young and raucous convene under the large white tents of Rio, where scenesters groove to hip hop and contemporary pop. Open daily 6pm-5am. AmEx/MC/V.

GLBT BUDAPEST

GLBT Budapest is beginning to appear in the mainstream. Still, it's safer to be discreet. If you run into problems or are looking for info, contact the **gay hotline** (☎06 30 93 23 334; budapest@gayguide.net), and take advantage of the knowledgeable staff. The website **www.budapest.gayguide.net** has up-to-date info on what's hot. **Na Végre** is a free monthly digest with English-language entertainment listings and is an invaluable source for festivals, events and GLBT venues throughout the city. It can be found at most of the establishments below, all of which are either gay or gay-friendly. **Omszki Lake** is a nude beach frequented by gay men. (Take the HÉV to Budakalász and walk 25min.) The Budapest **GLB Pride Festival** is the first weekend of July and hosts the popular **Rainbow Party** with a night full of concerts and special events that run from 10pm-5am; check *Na Végre* for details.

Capella, V, Belgrád rakpart 23 (☎318 6231; www.extra.hu/capellacafe). This very popular 3-level cafe along the Danube has reopened after renovations and has several dance rooms, each with different themes that match the varying music. Thoroughly entertaining drag shows every night. Attracts a mixed gay, lesbian, and straight crowd. Cover M-Th 500 Ft, F-Sa 1500Ft. Open W-Su 10am-5am. Cash only.

Café Eklektika, Nagymező u. 30 (☎266 1226). This centrally located, gay-friendly bar and cafe serves light meals and excellent wines. The jazz is as smooth as the interior, which has sleek leather chairs and a tiled marble floor. Open M-F noon-midnight, Sa-Su 5pm-midnight. Cash only.

Le Cafe M, V, Nagysándor József u. 3 (☎312 1436). M3: Arany János. A rainbow flag welcomes patrons to this laid-back bar, which attracts a primarily gay and lesbian clientele. Open M-F 4pm-4am, Sa-Su 6pm-4am.

DAYTRIPS FROM BUDAPEST

SZENTENDRE

HÉV runs from Batthyány tér (45min., every 20min., 480Ft). Buses run from the station by Árpád híd Metro station (30min., every 20-40min., 330Ft). Boats (☎484 4000) leave from pier below Vigadó tér (1½hr., 2 per day, 1800Ft). The train and bus stations are a 10min. walk from Fő tér, the main square. Descend the stairs past the end of the HÉV tracks, go through the underpass, and head up Kossuth út. At the fork in road, bear right on Dumtsa Jenő út. From the ferry station, turn left on Czóbel sétány and left on Dunakorzó u. In summer, a huge festival, usually June 24-Aug. 26, sweeps through town, with concerts, meat-grilling booths and other lively festivities, both in the town square and on the riverbank. Check www.szentendreprogram.hu for details. Usually runs from June 24-Aug. 26.

To glimpse Hungary's rural past without straying far from Budapest, head to relaxing Szentendre (sehn-TEHN-dreh), known for its cobblestone streets and masterful art. The streets are packed with tourists during summer, but the museums and art galleries remain manageable. Start your visit by climbing **Church Hill** (Templomdomb), above the town center in Fő tér, to visit the 13th-century **Parish Church of St. John** (Plébánia-templom), one of the few intact medieval churches in Hungary, for the best view in town. (Open Tu-Su 10am-4pm. Services Su 7am. Free.)

The **Czóbel Museum,** Templom tér 1, left of the church, displays the work of Béla Czóbel, Hungary's foremost post-Impressionist painter, including his "Venus of Szentendre." Admission includes access to the adjoining exhibit of works by the Szentendre Artists' Colony. (☎026 312 721. Open W-Su 10am-6pm. English captions. 500Ft, students 300Ft.) Szentendre's most popular museum, the **Kovács Margit Museum,** Vastagh György út 1, exhibits whimsical ceramic sculptures by the 20th-century Budapest artist Margit Kovács. (☎026 310 244, ext. 114; fax 310 790. Open mid-Mar.-Sept. M-Th 10am-5:30pm, F-Su 10am-7:30pm; Oct.-mid-Mar. daily 9am-5pm. 700Ft.) The **National Wine Museum** (Nemzeti Bormúzeum), Bogdányi u.

10, is a cellar exhibit of wines from Hungary's eight wine-making regions. A wine tasting (1900Ft) includes 10 samples, Hungarian appetizers, and an English tour of the exhibition. (☎026 317 054. Open daily 10am-10pm. Exhibit 200Ft.) Enjoy the edible exhibits of the **Szabó Marzipan Museum and Confectionery,** Dumtsa Jenő út 12. Watch the artists work, then look at creations including scenes from fairy tales, historical figures, and a white chocolate life-size statue of Michael Jackson. Indulge your sweet tooth downstairs at the gift shop or the adjacent cafe. (☎31 19 31. Open daily May-Sept. 9am-7pm; Oct.-Apr. 10am-6pm. 400Ft.)

The charming **Ilona Panzió ❸,** Rákóczi Ferenc út 11, rents rooms with private baths. (☎026 313 599. Breakfast included. Call ahead. Singles 5500Ft; doubles 7700Ft; triples 9000Ft.) **Pap-szigeti Camping ❷** is two kilometers north of the center along the main waterside road on its own island in the Danube, near a small, popular beach. (☎026 310 697. Call ahead. Open May-Oct. 15. Tent sites 3500Ft, which includes beach entry. 2-person caravan 4200Ft; additional person 1000Ft. Motel doubles 4500Ft. Pension doubles 5500Ft; triples 7500Ft.) **Nostalgia Cafe ❶,** Bogdányi u. 2, owned by opera singers, occasionally hosts outdoor concerts. Try the "Special Nostalgia Coffee" (500Ft), made with orange liqueur, chocolate bits, and whipped cream. (☎026 311 660. Pastries and coffee from 350Ft. Open daily 10am-8pm.) Get info and **maps** from **Tourinform,** Dumsta Jenő út 22. (☎02 64 38 80 80; www.szentendre.hu. Open Mar. 16-Nov. 2 M-W 9:30am-1pm and 1:30-6pm, Th-Su 9:30am-1pm and 1:30-7:30pm; Nov. 3-Mar. 15 M-F 9:30am-1pm and 1:30-4:30pm.)

ESZTERGOM

Trains run from Budapest (1½hr., 22 per day, 620Ft). Buses run from Szentendre (1½hr., 1 per hr., 490Ft) and Visegrád (45min., 1 per hr., 320Ft). Ferries (☎484 4000) run from Budapest (4hr., 3 per day, 1450Ft), Szentendre (2¾hr., 2 per day, 1100Ft), and Visegrád (1½hr., 2 per day, 750Ft). The train station is 15min. from town. Facing away from the station, go left on the main street. Follow the street around the bend to the left and turn right at Kis János Vezerezredes út. From the bus station, walk up Simor János u. toward the market.

One thousand years of religious history have made Esztergom (ess-TAYR-gahm) a major pilgrim and tourist destination. The birthplace of Saint-King Stephen and the site of the first Royal Court of Hungary, the town is also home to Hungary's largest cathedral, the **Basilica of Esztergom.** This neoclassical cathedral was built on the site of an 11th-century cathedral; to the nave's left, the red-marble **Bakócz Chapel,** is a Renaissance masterpiece, hundreds of years older than the cathedral. (Open daily Mar.-Oct. 6:30am-6pm; Nov.-Dec. 7am-4pm. Chapel free. English-language guidebook 100Ft.) The cathedral **treasury** houses icons, relics, and textiles spanning a millennium. A jeweled cross served as the **Coronation Oath Cross**, on which Hungary's rulers pledged their oaths until 1916. (Open Mar.-Oct. Tu-Su 9am-4:30pm; Nov.-Dec. Tu-F 9am-4:30pm, Sa-Su 10am-3:30pm. 450Ft, students 220Ft.) Ascend interminable staircases to the cathedral **cupola** (200Ft) for the best view of the Danube Bend. On clear days, you can see the Slovak Low Tatras. The **crypt** below the cathedral holds the remains of Hungary's archbishops. (Open Tu-Su 9am-4:45pm. 100Ft.) The **museum,** an architecture-lover's dream, surrounds the cathedral and was built atop the ruins of the **castle** where St. Stephen was born. It exhibits fragments of the 10th-century castle and allows you to peer through a glass floor to an excavation site. (☎033 415 986. Open Tu-Su 10am-4:45pm. English captions. Free.) The **Maria Valeria Bridge** spans the Danube from Esztergom to Slovakia. Reopened in 2001, the bridge is a major link between the two nations. **Csülök Csárda ❷,** Batthyány út 9, serves fine cuisine just below the basilica in a picnic-like setting. Try the mushroom soup (790Ft) or the catfish filet with garlic (1790Ft). (☎033 412 420. Vegetarian options available. Entrees 480-2690Ft. Open daily noon-10pm.) For info, visit **Grantours,** Széchényi tér 25, at the edge of Rákóczi tér, which also sells **maps.** (☎033 417 052; grantour@mail.holop.hu. Open July-Aug. M-F 8am-5pm, Sa 9am-noon; Sept.-June M-F 8am-4pm.)

SZÉKESFEHÉRVÁR

Trains run from Budapest (1hr., 21 per day, 820Ft). To get to the center from the train station, walk down Deák Ferenc u. Turn left on Budai út and then right on Varkörút. Buses also run from Budapest (1hr., 4 per day, 840Ft). From the bus station (☎31 10 57), on Piac tér, veer left of terminal #2 and take a right on Liszt Ferenc u., which becomes Városház tér.

Géza, St. Stephen's father, established Székesfehérvár in AD 972, making it Hungary's oldest town. Today, those traveling from Budapest to Balaton stop in this friendly city to visit the **Bory Castle** (Bory-vár) and to take a stroll down the town's cobblestoned promenade. Take bus #32 from the train station to Vágújhelyi u., cross the street, walk downhill, and turn left on Bory tér. Unique partly because it remains intact, this castle was built over the course of nearly 40 summers, beginning in the 1920s. Architect and sculptor Jenő Bory constructed this mansion by hand. The palace resembles a fairy-tale castle: it is endowed with whimsical towers, terraced gardens, crooked paths and winding staircases. The small museum displays Bory's sculptures as well as his and his wifes' paintings. Today Bory's grandson and family live in the castle and care for the museum. (☎022 305 570. Open daily 9am-5pm. 500Ft, students 250Ft.) In the center, the **King Saint Stephen Museum** (Szent István Király Múzeum), Fő u. 6, houses an archaeology exhibit that showcases Roman artifacts. (☎022 315 583. Open Apr. 29-Oct. 10am-4pm; Mar. 4-Apr. 28 10am-2pm. 500Ft, students 250Ft.) The **Budenz House: Ybl Collection** (Budenzház: Ybl Gyűjtemény), Arany János út 12, includes exquisite 18th- to 20th-century Hungarian art and furniture by Miklós Ybl, the designer of Budapest's State Opera House. (☎022 313 027. Open Tu-Su 10am-4pm. 500Ft, students 300Ft.) Pick up a guidebook and free **maps** at **Tourinform,** Városház tér 1. (☎022 537 261. Open May 15-Sept. 15 daily 9am-7pm; Sept. 16-May 14 M-F 9am-4pm.)

If you're spending the night in Székesfehérvár, check out **Szent Gellért Tanulmányi Ház** ❷, Mátyás Király krt 1, a 10min. walk from the city center. It offers rooms and cheaper dorms. (☎022 510 810; szentgellert@axelero.hu. Dorms 3500 for 1 person or 3000Ft per person for 2 or more people; singles 10,900Ft; doubles 13,400Ft; triples 20,400Ft. Tax 300Ft. AmEx/MC/V.) **Match** supermarket, Palotai u. 1-3, inside Alba Shopping Plaza by the bus station, sells the basics. (Open M-Sa 7am-9pm, Su 8am-6pm.) Straddling Fő u., **Korzó Söröző** ❸ serves Hungarian dishes like liver soup and goulash on one side, and beers and spirits on the other. (☎022 312 674. Entrees 1200-3200Ft. Open daily 10am-midnight.)

NORTHERN HUNGARY

Hungary's northern upland is dominated by a series of low mountain ranges running northeast from the Danube Bend along the Slovak border. The small, intimate mountain villages are steeped in local customs; Eger and Tokaj are home to world-famous wineries, while Bükk and Aggtelek National Parks beckon hikers with scenic trails and stunning caves.

EGER ☎(06)36

Once known for the Ottoman conquest of its castle in 1552, Eger (EGG-air; pop. 57,000) is now a comfortable escape for travelers, with its quiet square and pastel architecture. Although the town continues to pride itself on its rich history, hailing Captain István Dobó's victorious stand against the besieging Turks as a miracle, the region's real claim to fame is its homemade wines. Eger's spirited cellars in the Valley of Beautiful Women lure travelers from Budapest with the promise of the strengthening powers of *Egri Bikavér* (Bull's Blood) wine, a blended red made with the indigenous, spicy Kadarka grape.

TRANSPORTATION

Trains: Vasút u. (☎31 42 64). Trains go to: **Budapest** (2hr.; 21 per day, 4 direct; 1242Ft, Students 1150 Ft) and **Szeged** (4½hr., 12 per day, 3050Ft). Non-direct trains to Budapest via **Füzesabony.**

Buses: Barkóczy u. (☎51 77 77; www.agriavolan.hu). To: **Aggtelek** (3hr., 8:45am daily, 1330Ft); **Budapest** (2hr., 25-30 per day, 1360Ft); **Debrecen** (3hr., 10 per day, 1296Ft); **Szilvásvárad** (45min., 40 per day, 363Ft).

Taxis: City Taxi (☎55 55 55).

ORIENTATION AND PRACTICAL INFORMATION

The **train station** lies on the outskirts of town. To walk to **Dobó tér,** the main square and town center, from the train station (15min.), head straight and take a right on **Deák Ferenc utca,** keep to the right and when you see the Cathedral on the opposite side, cross the cross-walk and take a left on **Jókai utca.** To get to the center from the bus station, turn right on **Barkóczy utca.** from terminal #10 and right again about two blocks down at **Bródy utca.** Follow the stairs to the end of the street and turn right on **Széchényi utca.** which becomes Eszterházi tér; a left up **Érsek utca** leads to Dobó tér. Most sights are within a 10min. walk of the square.

Tourist Office: Tourinform, Bajcsy-Zsilinszky u. 9 (☎51 77 15; www.ekft.hu/eger), has **free maps,** event calendars, and a helpful English-speaking staff. One computer with Internet (200Ft per 30min.). Open June-Sept. M-F 9am-7pm, Sa-Su 10am-6pm; Oct.-May M-F 9am-5pm, Sa 9am-1pm.

Bank: OTP, Széchényi u. 2 (☎31 08 66), at the corner of Érsek u., just down the street from Tourinform. Gives AmEx/MC/V **cash advances** and cashes **AmEx Traveler's Cheques** for no commission. MC/V **ATM** outside. Open M 7:45am-6pm, Tu-Th 7:45am-5pm, F 7:45am-4pm; currency desk open M-Tu and Th 7:45am-2:45pm, W 7:45am-4:30pm, F 7:45am-noon.

Luggage Storage: Available at the bus station.

English-Language Bookstore: InMedio, next to the Széchényi u. post office, carries English-language periodicals. Open M-F 6am-6pm, Sa 6am-1pm, Su 6-11am.

Pharmacy: Rossmann (☎51 85 42), on the corner of Katona István Tér and Sándor Imre u., stocks international brands. Open M-F 8am-7pm, Sa 8am-1pm. AmEx/MC/V.

Hospital: Knézich Károly u. 1-3 (☎41 14 14). Open M-Th 7am-6pm, F 7am-4pm. Call for emergency service.

Internet Access: Available at **Tourinform** (see above). Also at **Bambi Eszpresszo,** Pyrter 3. Next door to Club Amazon under Eger Cathedral. Modern style with bar and outdoor patio seating, serves drinks (soft and alcoholic). 200Ft per 30min., 300Ft per 1 hr. M-Sa 10am-midnight, Su 4pm-12am.

Post Office: Széchényi u. 22 (☎41 16 72). Open M-F 8am-8pm, Sa 8am-1pm. **Poste Restante** available. **Telephones** outside. Public telephones also available outside the taxi service on Bajcsy-Zsilinszky u. **Postal Code:** 3300.

ACCOMMODATIONS

Accommodations are plentiful in Eger's center. Look for *Zimmer frei* or *szoba kiadó* signs outside the main square, particularly near the castle on Almagyar u. and Mekcsey István u. **Eger Tourist,** Bajcsy-Zsilinszky u. 9, arranges **private rooms.** (☎51 70 00; fax 51 02 70. Open M-F 9am-5pm. Rooms around 3000Ft.)

Lukács Vendégház, Bárány u. 10 (☎/fax 41 15 67), next to Eger Castle. The communal garden tables, living room, and kitchen create a friendly atmosphere for the young travelers that frequent this family-owned hostel. Follow Servita u. into the center of town. Singles 3000Ft; doubles 5000Ft. Cash only. ❷

Hotel Minaret, Knézich K. u. 4 (☎41 02 33; www.hotelminaret.hu), is centrally located. Named for the slender minaret across the street, this pricier option offers simple rooms with satellite TV, a restaurant, a massage center, and a courtyard swimming pool that hosts grill parties in the summer. Apr.-Oct. singles 10,600Ft; doubles 18,500Ft; triples 24,400Ft; quads 28,900Ft. Nov.-Mar. prices about 2000Ft lower. AmEx/MC/V. ❹

Youth Hostel and Dormitory (Ifjusági Szálás), Servita u. 25 (☎53 71 57). On the same side as the Church, a little way down the road. Teenagers crowd the downstairs and overflow onto the outdoor courtyard, lending this fun yet minimalist hostel a backpacker feel. Smallest room has two beds, largest has six. As many showers as there are beds. Reservations recommended. Bed 2100Ft; 310Ft foreigner fee. Cash only. ❶

FOOD

Piaccsarnok market runs along Katona I. tér, opposite the hospital. Go right on Árva Köz from Széchényi u.; the market is on the right. (Open June-Sept. M-F 6am-6pm, Sa 6am-1pm, Su 6-10am; Oct.-May M-F 6am-5pm, Sa 6am-1pm, Su 6-10am.) **Hossó ABC** supermarket is across the street. (Open M-F 6am-7pm, Sa 6am-1pm, Su 6am-11am. MC/V.)

Kulacs Csárda Panzió (☎/fax 31 13 75), in the Valley of Beautiful Women. Vines and ceramic dishes line the walls of this cavernous restaurant, which serves heaping portions of goulash, peasant sausage (*hurka, kolbász),* and other Hungarian classics. Live music draws young travelers and older couples on weekend getaways. English menu available. Entrees 950-2000Ft. Open daily noon-11pm. AmEx/MC/V. ❸

Dobos Cukrászda, Széchényi u. 6. (☎41 33 35) Offers tortes handmade daily and other *sutemény* (dessert; 170-350Ft), ice cream cones (130 Ft.), or special sundaes with added toppings (800Ft). Classic Hungarian edible marzipan figurines in a glass display make a great gift or after-dinner treat (280Ft). Open daily 9:30am-9pm. Cash only. ❶

Hotel Senátor-Váz Restaurant (☎32 04 66), just over the bridge near Dobó tér. The patio overlooking bustling Dobó tér and live music from the neighboring gazebo are pleasant accompaniments to traditional Hungarian dishes. Inside, enjoy the airy white stucco decor. English menu. Entrees 900-2200Ft. Open daily 10am-10pm. MC/V. ❸

Gyros, Széchényi u. 10 (☎41 37 81). Sit and enjoy gyros (450-950Ft) and roasts (850-1800Ft) on an outdoor patio surrounded by flower boxes. Seating also available inside. English menu. Vegetarian options. Open daily 9am-10pm. Cash only. ❷

SIGHTS

VALLEY OF BEAUTIFUL WOMEN (SZÉPASSZONY-VÖLGY). After museum exploring and castle hiking, treat yourself to the delicate tastes of Eger's wines in the 200 cellars comprising the Valley of Beautiful Women. While the origins of the name are uncertain (some locals claim it refers to the enhancement of a woman's appearance after a night of tippling), the valley's charms are not. Following WWII, low land prices allowed hundreds of wine cellars to sprout up on this volcanic hillside. Most are little more than a tunnel and a few tables and benches, but each has its own personality: some are hushed, family-run establishments with a small selection of home-grown grapes, while others burst with Hungarian and Roma sing-alongs. Subdued in the afternoon, the valley springs to life at night, when the cellars open their doors to host wine tasters and those who prefer to linger amidst

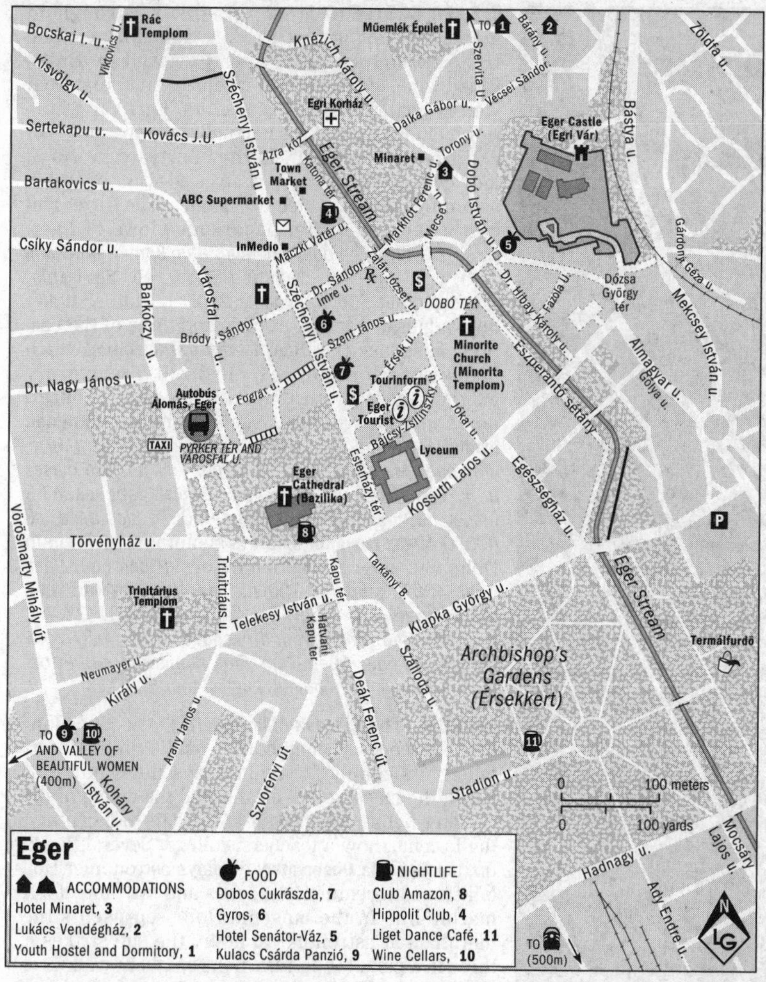

the music and the revelers. The cellars are all in a row, so it is easy to experience each different atmosphere and sample the wines. Most popular is *Bikavér* (Bull's Blood), imagined to hold incredible strengthening powers. There is even one called the Város Nyerö, or City Conquerer. *Egri Leányka* is Eger's fiery white wine most noted for its sweet, flower-like fragrance. After 10pm, some cellars become after-hours bars, with DJs or live music. For those who don't want to stumble to town, there are plenty of *Zimmer frei* signs and small hotels in the valley. *(Start out on Széchényi u. with Eger Cathedral on the right. Go right on Kossuth Lajos u. and continue until it dead ends into Vörösmarty u. Turn left and continue to Király u. Take a right and keep walking for several minutes on the curvy, ascending road (beware of the narrow sidewalk and oncoming cars). Some cellars open at 9am, but all remain quiet until nightfall. Closing times vary. July-Aug some open until midnight. Most samples free, some 50Ft per dl., 350Ft per 1L.)*

STAYIN' A-LAVA

A bustling town by day, Eger seems suspiciously quiet at night. That's because the real scene is underground—literally—as Eger continues to offer festive diversions in the form of clubs built into a series of lava tunnels.

Unknown to most visitors, an elaborate labyrinth lies below Eger, the carved remnants of the 120km bed of lava upon which the city was founded. Locals have converted three sections into nightclubs, invisible to the world above except for small, barely marked entrances.

One of the most popular is Club Amazon (☎ 30/596 3848), on Pyrter 3, alongside Kossuth L. u., under the Eger Cathedral, where youths dance the night away in the jungle-like disco. Guest DJs give the place a dynamic vibe. (Open W 10pm-5am. Cover Sa 10pm-5am 500Ft, every 2nd F 10pm-5am 800Ft.)

Another popular spot is the Liget Dance Cafe, Erksekkert, under Excalibur Restaurant in the Archbishop's Gardens. (☎427 7547. Cover 800Ft. Open F-Sa 10pm-5am. AmEx/MC/V; cash only for cover). Clearly marked by spotlights, the club draws a younger crowd. Hippolit Club and Restaurant, Katona ter 2, is classier and more subdued with a secluded, candlelit second-floor patio. (☎411 031. Open Tu-Th 9pm-3am, F-Sa 9pm-5am).

EGER CASTLE (EGRI VÁR). A military stronghold in the 16th century, Eger Castle gained fame when Dobó István, supposedly empowered by Bull's Blood wine, led Hungarian troops to an unexpected victory against Ottoman invaders. Egri Vár's interior includes barracks, catacombs, a crypt, and— of course—a wine cellar. In the courtyard, hosts in medieval costume teach visitors to walk on stilts, sword fight, or play medieval games. The tower and castle perimeter offer panoramic views of Eger. *(☎31 27 44. Open daily Apr.-Aug. 8am-8pm; Sept. 8am-7pm; Oct. and Mar. 8am-6pm; Nov.-Feb. 8am-5pm; Grounds ticket 500Ft, students 250Ft.)* Another ticket buys admission to the grounds and three of the castle's museums: the **Dobó István Vármúzeum,** which displays armor and weaponry and a temporary exhibit; a **gallery** with 16th- to 19th-century Hungarian landscapes and war scenes; and the **dungeon exhibition,** which features torture equipment. *(Museums open Mar.-Oct. Tu-Su 9am-5pm; ticket office closes at 4:20pm; Nov.-Feb. 10am-4pm. English captions. All 3 museums Tu-Su 1200Ft, students 600Ft, kids ages 3-6 400Ft)* A **wax museum** displays sculptures of Captain Dobó and other Hungarian heroes. *(Open daily 9am-6pm. 400Ft, students 300Ft.)* The 400-year-old **wine cellars** are also open for tastings. *(☎31 27 44; www.div.iif.hu. Underground passages open daily 9am-5pm. Open daily 10am-7pm. Free admission; 200Ft per tasting. Tour guide required. English tour 600Ft.)*

LYCEUM. The **Diocesan Library,** on the second floor of the Rococo Lyceum, houses handwritten Mozart music. Its ceiling fresco portrays the Council of Trent, the meeting that established the edicts of the Counter-Reformation. Built in the late 18th century, the Lyceum, now a teachers' college. Several flights up, the **Specula Observatory** displays astronomer Hell Miksa's 18th-century telescopes and instruments. A marble line in the museum floor represents the meridian: at astronomical noon, the sun strikes it through a pinhole aperture in the southern wall. Two floors up, a 1776 **"camera obscura,"** constructed of a mirror and lenses inside a small darkroom, projects a stunning live picture of the surrounding town onto a table. Nicknamed the "eye of Eger," it justifies the 302-step hike to the top. *(At the corner of Kossuth Lajos u. and Eszterházy tér. ☎ 32 52 11. Open Apr.-Sept. Tu-Su 9:30am-3:30pm; Oct.-Mar. Tu-F 9:30am-1pm, Sa-Su 9:30am-1:30pm. English captions. Library 500Ft, students 350Ft; museum and camera obscura 500Ft/350Ft.)*

EGER CATHEDRAL. The only Neoclassical building in Eger, the writing on this columns of this massive 1887 cathedral proclaims, "Come, let us adore Thee."

The soaring architecture, soft pastel hues, and stained-glass windows create a bright ambience. **Organ Concerts** (30min.) are held from May to mid-October. *(On Eszterházy tér just off Széchényi u. Concerts M-Sa 11:30am, Su 12:45pm. 500Ft, students 120Ft. Church entrance free when concerts are not in progress.)*

OTHER SIGHTS. Once the Ottomans' northernmost possession in Hungary, the **Minaret,** Knézich K. u., called Muslim villagers to prayer. Now, tourists climb the 97-step staircase that provides a panoramic view of the city. *(☎702 024 353. Open daily Mar.-Oct. 9:30am-6pm. 200Ft.)* Below the high-vault ceiling frescoes of the 1758 pink marble **Minorite Church** hang detailed sculptures and paintings of biblical scenes. *(In Dobó tér. ☎51 66 13. Open Apr.-Oct. Tu-Su 9am-6pm. Services Su 9am. Free. Organ Concerts May-Sept. Th 7-7:30pm.)* The 18th-century **Serbian Orthodox Church** (Rác Templom), on Vitkovics u. at the center's northern end, is host to interesting, though not widely famous, artwork and memorials. Follow Széchényi u. from the center for roughly 10min. and enter at #55. Go up the stairs on the right, then up the stairs through the tunnel, and request admittance at the green fence behind the temple. *(Open daily 10am-4pm. 320Ft.)*

ENTERTAINMENT AND NIGHTLIFE

While Eger's popular **bath complex (Termálfurdö)** offers a respite from the summer heat, the Turkish baths first garnered fame for the curative effects of their water. Fed by Artesian wells 3km away, the unique water is prescribed by local doctors as therapy for chronic diseases. Located on the outskirts of the Archbishop's gardens—which provide much-needed shade during the summer—the complex also contains swimming pools, waterslides, playgrounds, and a soccer field. From Dobó tér, take Jókai u. to Kossuth Lajos u. and continue on Egészségház u. Make a left on Klapka György u. and cross the stream, or from Deák Ferenc u. take a left on Stadion and walk through the garden past the waterfountain. (☎31 15 85. Open May-Aug. M-F 8:30am-6pm, Sa-Su 8am-6:30pm; Oct.-Apr. 9am-7pm daily. Ticket window closes at 6pm. 1050Ft, students 900Ft, seniors 450Ft.) While Eger may seem quiet by day, the town livens up at night. After drinking in the valley, check out one of the **underground discos** (see **Stayin' A-Lava,** p. 296). Eger hosts free music on **Small Dobó tér** nightly at 6pm. From late July to mid-August, the town celebrates its cultural heritage during the **Baroque Festival.** Nightly music and opera performances take place in and around the city. Buy tickets at the venue. A folk dance festival, **Eger Vintage Days,** takes place in early September. Tourinform (see **Orientation and Practical Information,** p. 293) provides festival schedules.

DAYTRIP FROM EGER: BARADLA CAVES

A bus leaves Eger daily at 8:45am and arrives in Aggtelek at 11:25am. Returning bus leaves at 3pm. Another bus leaves Miskolc at 9:15am, arrives in Aggtelek around 11am, and heads back from the same stop at 5pm. To get to the caves from the bus, cross the street and go down the path to the caves; the park entrance is on the right. (☎503 002; www.anp.hu.) 1hr. Hungarian tours daily 10am, noon, 1, 3pm; in high season also 5pm. 1900Ft, students 1100Ft.) Tours of the main branch of the cave arranged by Tourinform. (☎503 000.Call ahead.) Open daily Apr.-Sept. 8am-6pm; Oct.-Mar. 8am-4pm. If you choose to do the long hike, you will miss the return bus; plan to stay overnight.

On the Slovak-Hungarian border, **Aggtelek National Park** is home to more than 1000 caves, including the popular Baradla Cave. One-kilometer tours are led by knowledgeable guides, beginning in an ancient cave where skeletons from the Neolithic period were found. Concerts, violin competitions, and wedding ceremonies are held in the music hall throughout the year. Calendars of events are available at the Tourinform office. Tours range from 1hr. basic and "Bat Branch" tours (Daily high season 10am, noon, 1, 3, 5pm; low season 10am, noon, 1, 3pm; 4000Ft, students 2400Ft) to 5hr. guided hikes (6000/2400Ft). Arrange longer tours with **TourInform** (☎50 30 00). The temperature is 10°C year-round, so bring a jacket. The caves can be visited as a daytrip from Eger, but the return bus leaves fairly early. The **bus** leaves Eger daily at 8:45am and arrives in Aggtelek at 11:25am, returning from the stop across the street at 3pm. From the bus, cross the street and follow the path to the caves; the park entrance is on the right. **Baradla Hostel and Camping** is a few steps from the entrance to the caves, offering clean and convenient cottages. (☎48 503 005. 1900Ft, students 1600Ft. Camp sites 1100Ft, students 800Ft. 1000Ft per site fee. Cash only.) **Barlang Vendéglö,** adjacent to the hostel, serves a number of classic Hungarian dishes, as well as vegetarian salads, on an outdoor patio overlooking the playground in the park. (☎48 34 31 77. Entrees 750-2400Ft.)

MISKOLC ☎(06)36

A refreshingly friendly up-and-coming hub, Miskolc (mee-SHKOLTZ; pop 174,900) is the third largest city in Hungary, but has long been cast aside as an industrial town. While there is some truth to that reputation, downtown Miskolc, with its newly built Heroes Court and frequent outdoor concerts and festivals, provides a pleasant sanctuary from the smoggy outskirts. Miskolc's lack of tourists and proximity to scenic hills and wine cellars make it an ideal base for exploring the beautiful surrounding countryside.

TRANSPORTATION AND PRACTICAL INFORMATION. The easiest way to get to Miskolc is to take the bus to Búza Tér, which is a 10 minute walk into the center of town. **Volánbusz** (☎219 8080) is the company that operates out of Miskolc. Helpful information desk and bus schedules at the ticket window. For **train** transportation, look for schedules on www.elvira.hu or call MAV transportation services (☎25 74 95), as they change often. Trains go to Budapest (19 per day) and Szilvásvárad (6 per day; 2290Ft). To walk to **Széchényi István utca,** the main street and central location of Miskolc, from the bus station, head straight and cross the main road, **Király utca,** at the crosswalk, and walk to the left side of the mall. Continue going straight for a few minutes on Horváth Lajos until it becomes Palóczy László and take a left to Városház Tér via Széchényi István u. The **tourist office, Tourinform,** on Városház Tér 13, provides free maps, as well as helpful calendars of cultural events and tips for getting around the city. (☎35 04 25; miskolc@tourinform.hu.) The **bank,** OTP, Rákoczy u. 1, has a 24hr. **ATM.** (Open M 7am-5pm, Tu-F 7:45am-4pm.) In the event of an **emergency,** call ☎112. For medical care, **Rossmann,** located on Széchényi István u 11-13. across the street from the Raiffeisen Bank, stocks international brands. (Open M-F 8am-7pm, Sa 8am-2pm. AmEx/MC/V.) There is a **hospital, Megyei Kórház,** at 3526 Szent Péter Kapu. (☎51 52 00.) **Internet access** is available at **Chip Land,** 14 Rákóczi u. (280Ft per 30 min. Open M-F 9:30am-5pm, Sa 9am-noon. MC/V.) The **post office** is on Kazinczy u. 16, across the street from Heroes Court. (☎06 80 20 06 31. Open M-F 8am-7pm, Sa 8am-noon.)

ACCOMMODATIONS AND FOOD. Affordable accommodations convenient to the city's hub are hard to come by, but a few university dorms in outskirts serve as summer youth hostels. In the center, expect to pay at least 7000Ft for a single. **Leány Kollégium ❶,** an all-girls school during the year, opens its doors to travelers of both sexes during the summer months. A dining hall downstairs serves three meals a day (breakfast 450Ft, lunch 700Ft, dinner 550Ft) and is a communal space to meet other travelers. (☎50 83 59. Free Internet. 24hr. reception. Call ahead. Check-out noon. 4- or 6-bed dorms 1600Ft.) **Bolyai Kollégium ❶,** at Miskolc University, is a 15 min. bus ride from the center. Take bus #22 from the Centrum shopping mall (every 10 min.). The dorm provides spotless rooms with fridges and personal bathrooms. Summer-school students and travelers gather outside on the steps of the six-dorm buildings to chat and relax in the afternoon. (☎56 52 60; fax 56 51 24; uni-miskolc.hu. Reception 24hr. Check-out noon. Call ahead to reserve. Dorms 2840Ft. Cash only.) **Korona Panzió ❸,** Kis Avas u. 19-20, appeals to travelers who don't mind shelling out extra for a central location; the hostel also boasts its own Hungarian restaurant and TVs. (☎50 68 82. Reception 24hr. Check-out noon. Singles 7000Ft; doubles 10,000Ft; Triples 12,000Ft.)

Just off the bustling Széchényi István u. is the **Mona Lisa Café and Pub ❶,** Déryné u. 3. Hungarian artwork lines the walls of this cozy bar, which serves coffee as well as various alcoholic drinks. It also serves Hungarian fast food like *zsiros kenyér* (greasy bread) at 80Ft per slice. (Cocktail of the day 400Ft. Open daily 1pm-midnight.) **Hús Bolt ❷,** 18 Széchényi István u., serves Hungarian sausage old-school style—on a paper plate, eaten standing—in the local butcher shop. (☎067 02 39 49 20. M 8am-2pm, Tu-W 6:30am-5pm, Th-F 6:30am-6pm, Sa 6:30am-1pm.)

SIGHTS. The Miskolc downtown is a sight in itself. Starting from the **City Square** (Város Tér) check out the statue of 19th century politcal leader **Széchényi István,** known as "The Biggest Hungarian," and walk down Széchényi István u., where the summer months bring an influx of festivals and wine tastings, as well as tents that sell clothes and handmade souvenirs. To the left through Déryné u. is **Heroes Court,** host to frequent jazz concerts and numerous beer stands. Walk back through the alley on Déryné u. and cross the street to Uitz Béla u. Follow the stairs through the church and graveyard to the **Avasi Kilátó,** a TV lookout tower that gives a panoramic view of the city. The **Ottó Herman Museum,** Görgey Artúr u. 28, is just across the street from Népkert Park. Named for the famous Hungarian naturalist, the museum holds a large archaeological collection of remains from the Neolithic period, as well as a rock and mineral display from the Carpathian Basin. (☎56 01 70; www.hermuz.hu. Open Tu-Su 10am-4pm. 600Ft, students 300Ft.) To get to the **Diósgyor Castle,** Vár u. 24, take the 1 Bus from the Centrum mall to Diosgyor. Built in the 13th century, the castle provides a panoramic view of both the Bukk Moutains and Miskolc. A wax museum in the castle displays medieval scenes, and the adjacent recreational area has a pool, a park, and a volleyball court. Medieval stage at the center of the castle hosts concerts, history lessons and feudal-period plays throughout the summer. Check the website for a calendar of events. (☎53 33 55; www.diosgyorivar.com. Open daily May-Sept. 9am-5pm; Oct.-Apr. 9am-6pm. Castle 700Ft, students 350Ft; recreational park 600/400Ft.) Those craving more exotic wildlife than offered by the surrounding plains should visit the **Miskolc City Wildlife Park,** adjacent to the Bukk National Park. The park organizes its display of over 150 animal species, including bengal tigers and ostriches, by habitat region. Throughout the summer, nighttime tours take visitors on a moonlit journey through the animal kingdom. (☎33 21 21 www.miskolczoo.hu. Open Oct.-Mar. daily 9am-4pm; Mar.-Oct. M-F 9am-5pm. 700Ft, ages 3-18 500Ft.) To get to the incredible hot springs at **Cave Bath,** Miskolc-tapolca, Pazár István 1, take Bus #2 from Búza Tér to the last stop. The bath is just up the hill. The caves offers hydrotherapy and massage services, as well as a separate sauna park. Relax in the dimly lit corridors of the caves or swim outside through the huge circular opening that leads to a larger pool. (☎56 00 30; www.barlangfurdo.hu. Open daily Sept.-May 9am-6pm; June-Aug. 9am-7pm. Cave baths May-Aug. 2000Ft, students 1400Ft; Sept-Dec 1800Ft/1300Ft; night bathing 1400Ft.)

ENTERTAINMENT AND NIGHTLIFE. Theater has been an integral part of Miskolc culture ever since the city established Hungary's first stage in 1823. The **Miskolc National Theatre,** Széchényi István u. 23. has a June opera festival, held in various concert halls and outdoor courtyards. (☎51 67 35; www.mnsz.eu. Evening concerts 6000Ft. Specials during the afternoon with first-come, first-served seating for 500Ft.) The newly built **Hosok Tere,** across the post office on Kazinczy, just off Széchényi István u., is an open park that draws both tourists and locals looking for a laid-back evening. A large dance floor that doubles as a concert stage rests atop a water fountain, giving the illusion that the dancers are walking on water. The annual opera festival in mid-June offers beer and wine stands and live bands. The eclectic **Club Tsunami,** 3525 Kossuth Lajos u. 1, boasts a sizable selection of East Asian teas, as well as Hungarian wines, hard liquor, and beer. Patrons dance up a storm to Hungarian pop music and the occasional American hit on a large dance floor, or relax on communal plush couches and bean bags in secluded corners. (☎202 555 055. Drinks 200-650Ft. Open M-F 11am-10pm, Sa-Su 24 hr).

DAYTRIP FROM MISKOLC

SZILVÁSVÁRAD

Trains run from Eger (1hr., 7 per day, 326Ft) and Miskolc (2hr., 1 per day 1:05pm from Búza tér, 400Ft.). Buses are generally the most convenient transport; they go to Aggtelek (1¾hr., daily 9:20am, 744Ft) and Eger (45min., 1-2 per hr., 363Ft). The bus stops just outside the park entrance. The main street, Egri út, extends from the Szilvásvárad-Szalajkavölgy train station and bends sharply. Szalajka u. leads to the national park. Farther north, Egri út becomes Miskolci út. There's no tourist office, so get info and a basic map at the Eger Tourinform (p. 293) before heading out. The staff at Hegyi Camping provide a wealth of info about the area and sell maps. Hiking maps posted throughout the park. Free maps of the mountains are available at the bike shop, on Szalajka u., past the stop sign at the park entrance. (☎335 2695. Open M-W and Sa-Su 9am-6pm, Th-F 9am-1pm).

From leisurely biking in the Szalajka Valley to strenuous hikes through the mountains, Szilvásvárad's **Bükki National Park** offers a variety of outdoor opportunities. If you decide to stay, expect to pay at least 4000Ft at a vendégház (guesthouse) or *panzio*, or 6000Ft at a private home that gives out rooms. Look for **szoba kiadó** or *Zimmer frei* signs along Egri u. From the bus stop, walk up through the park's entrance, and consider taking the 15-min. open-air train ride that stops right above the waterfall (7 per day 9:25am-4:10pm; 350 Ft, students 250Ft). From the train-stop, hike upward to the cave where Hungarian naturalist Herman Ottó found remains from a prehistoric human group. The trek to the cave is a near 45-degree slope that takes about 10min. each way, but the result is a vast opening that leads to the cave dwellers' living space, now inhabited by a clan of bats. Walk back towards the trainstop, past the grassy clearing for picnicking and sunbathing near the **Fátyol Waterfall**. Hidden behind a curtain of alden-groves, the multi-step waterfall delicately drips down the Szalajka stream. The entrance to **Millennium Lookout Tower,** just a little ways down the trail from the waterfall, offers a spectacular view of the town and surrounding countryside. (250Ft, students 200Ft). The road that leads to the tower is 4km; horses and cars are allowed, but you can avoid the crowds by **renting a bike** (900Ft 1st hr., 200Ft per hr. thereafter), at Szalajka u., just past the stop sign at the park entrance. Pick up a tourist guide before hitting the trails. The shop can also arrange other outdoor activities (900Ft, children 800Ft) in the nearby trees at **Adventure Forest.** (☎380 443. Open Sa-Su 10am-7pm.)

The arena on Szalajka u., just off the park entrance, hosts weekend **horseshows** (800Ft). You can learn to drive a carriage, brandish a whip, or ride a steed (200Ft-400Ft). Hungarians from across the country, as well as occasional Slovakian guest competitors, flock in mid August to the three-day **Lipicai Festival.** Saturday night is host to a horseshow where riders display their skills for a massive audience (call Lipicai Stables or Hegyi Camping for info and event schedules).

Lipicai Stables, the stud farm for Szilvásvárad's famed Lipizzaner breed, is at the heart of the town's horse tradition. In addition to the stables, the farm displays a historic carriage-barn and offers rides. For a glimpse of the famous horses, head away from the park on Egri út, turn left on Fenyves u., and follow the signs to the farm. (☎355 155. Open daily 9:30am-noon and 2-4pm. 350Ft.)

After the parking ticketing booth on Szalajka u., is a row of stands that sell Hungarian fast-food—try a *palacsinata* (crepe) for 100Ft. For a scenic restaurant offering indoor and patio seating, visit **Csobogó Étterem ❷,** alongside a waterfall and miniature mill in an evergreen tree garden. (Entrees 700-2000Ft. Open daily noon-6pm.) To stock up on trail food, go to **Nagy ABC,** Egri út 6. (Open M-F 6am-6pm, Sa 6am-1pm, Su 8am-noon.) A small **bank** is to the left of the bus stop. (☎35 41 05. Open M-F 8am-noon and 12:30-4pm.) An **ATM** can be found at Nagy ABC.

TOKAJ ☎(06)47

Tokaj is to white wine what Eger is to red. Called home to "the wine of kings and the king of wines" by French King Louis XIV, Tokaj (tohk-OY; pop. 5100) has enjoyed an illustrious reputation since before the 12th century. Even Pope Pius I drank the famed white wine on his doctor's recommendation. Practically every other building is a wine cellar, and vineyards are visible in the lush hills above town. Housing is expensive, however, and Tokaj lacks a nightlife, so unless you are an avid outdoor adventurer planning on taking advantage of the nearby Kopasz mountains, you might consider visiting Tokaj as a daytrip.

TRANSPORTATION AND PRACTICAL INFORMATION. The train station, Baross G. u. 18 (☎352 020; www.elvira.hu), sends **trains** to Debrecen (2hr., 8 per day, 1350Ft) via Nyíregyháza, and Miskolc (1hr., 10 per day, 900Ft). **Buses** from the train station serve local towns. Check www.menetrendek.hu for bus schedules.

To get to the center of town, take a left from the train station entrance and follow the tracks, then turn left on **Bajcsy-Zsilinszky utca.** Bear left as the road forks by Tokaj Hotel. Bajcsy-Zsilinszky u. becomes **Rákóczi utca** after the Tisza bridge, then **Bethlen Gábor u.** after **Kossuth tér. Tourinform,** Serház u. 1, on the right side of Rákóczi u. as you walk into town, arranges accommodations and can set you up with a canoe or bike. (☎352 259; www.tokaj.hu, tokaj@tourinform.hu. Open daily M-W 10:30am-6pm, Th-Sa 9am-7pm, Su 9am-1pm.) **Exchange currency,** cash **traveler's checks,** and get MasterCard and Visa **cash advances** at **OTP,** Rákóczi u. 35. (☎352 523. Open M noon-4pm, Tu-F 7:45am-1:30pm.) A MasterCard and Visa **ATM** sits outside. **Paracelsus Pharmacy** (in a building labeled Gyógyszertár) is on Kossuth tér.; after hours, ring bell for emergencies. (☎35 20 52. Open M-F 8am-5pm, Sa-Su 8am-noon.) There is a **medical center,** labeled "Szakorvosi Rendelő," on Bethlen G. u. 4, with doctors available daily 8am-7pm. An **ambulance service** (☎104) can take you to the nearest hospital in Miskolc. **Internet Club,** Bajcsy-Zsilinszky 34, provides **Internet.** (☎353 137. Open M-Sa noon-9pm.) There are public **telephones** at the **post office** (Rákóczi u. 24) and all along Rákóczi as well as the train station. (☎353 647. Open M-F 8am-5pm, Sa 8am-noon.) **Postal Code:** 3910.

ACCOMMODATIONS AND FOOD. You can check for rooms at **Tourinform,** but look for *Zimmer frei* and *szoba kiadó* (rooms available) signs along Rákóczi u. and the little streets that branch off from the main road. (Singles 2000-3000Ft; doubles 4000-6000Ft.) **Angela Vendégház ❷,** on Zákó Köz 3, offers huge rooms with large private baths; also, a TV and patio that opens into a welcoming garden with small pond. (☎303 250 322. Breakfast included. Doubles 6000Ft.) At private homes, don't be afraid to bargain, but beware: your host may talk you into sampling—and buying—expensive homemade wine. For more rugged accommodations, cross the Tisza

WINES OF TOKAJ

The Tokaj region has a perfect climate to produce some of the world's finest wines. Its fertile land allows vines to grow especially deep and at a sloping angle; perhaps it's no coincidence that 25-million-year-old fossils found in the area suggest that it may have been the origin of the grape. Tokaj is known for its sweet white wines and has a unique system of measurement to determine its level of puttonyos, or sweetness.

Furmint is a basic dry white wine, with a fruity, aromatic character; it complements seafood and poultry.

Hárslevelu is made from a traditional thin-skinned grape. Served chilled, this dry, young, fresh wine enhances seafood entrees, and can also be enjoyed as an *aperitif.*

Aszuhe is the most famous of Tokaj's wines: a very sweet dessert wine. *Aszu* in Hungarian means that the grapes are not picked from the vine until they have reached their utmost level of ripeness, and posseses a heavy concentration of natural sugars.

Eszencia, which means "essence," is a true delicacy, and is made from the first juices of Aszu grapes and should be drunk on its own. .

The years 1972, '75, '79, '83, '88, '93, and '99 and 2000 are considered good vintages of Tokaj wines. It's best to try wines in order from the driest to sweetest; when dry wines follow sweet

and take the second left to reach **Vizisport Centrum Youth Hostel ❶,** which provides a campground and bungalows with a river view. (☎35 26 45. First night 1400Ft, additional nights 1200Ft.)

MaxiCoop supermarket is on Kossuth tér. (Open M-F 6am-6pm, Sa 6am-1pm, Su 7-11am.) **ABC Coop,** on Rákóczi u., is a little more expensive but offers more vegetarian foods. (Open M-F 6:30am-6:30pm, Sa 6:30am-1pm, Su 7-11am.) Nothing goes better with great wine than a spicy bowl of fish soup cooked in a traditional Hungarian bogrács, a large iron kettle that is hung above a fire pit. **Bonchidai Csárda ❸,** on Bajcsy Zsilinszki u. 21. (☎352 632) has a large deck overlooking the Tisza. Try the catfish soup. (Entrees 950-2750Ft. Open M-Su 10am-10pm.) **Taverna ❹,** is on Hősök tér, across the street from the Tisza bridge, and burrowed into the hill. This restaurant serves a carefully selected menu, including soups and entrees paired with Tokaj wines, in a sleek interior or a spacious terrace. (☎204 394 389. Meals 2500Ft-3000Ft. Open daily 11am-midnight.)

SIGHTS AND ENTERTAINMENT. Signs reading "Bor Pince" offer a wide range of wine-cellar experiences, from tiny, family-run underground tunnels to royal treatment at more commercial tourist attractions. Owners are generally pleased to let visitors sample their wares (about 1000Ft for 5 0.1L samples). Cellars on the main road are usually more touristy—on the side streets you'll find higher-quality wines and homier atmospheres. For an authentic wine-tasting experience, head to the 1.5km tunnel cellar of **Rákóczi Pince,** Kossuth tér 15. Tastings take place in the 500-year-old, 10°C underground hall, which has a small museum of winemaking implements, and where János Szapolyai was elected king of Hungary in 1526. Wine tastings and tours of the cellar and hall are arranged on the hour, but can be preempted by tour groups. Individual tours can be arranged at any time; English-speaking guides are available at no extra cost. (☎35 24 08; fax 35 27 41. Open 11am-7pm. 2100Ft for 1hr. tour and 6-glass tasting. Call ahead or email at rakoczip@t-online.hu for special events. AmEx/MC/V.) The 300-year-old **Tóth Family Cellar,** Óvár út 40, produces five exceptional whites. Take the small, upward-sloping side-street across from the Tokaj Hotel and keep left until you see their bold sign. Wait a few minutes after ringing the bell for one of the family members to and open the cellar door. (6-glass tasting 800Ft, 1L of Tokaji 6 *puttonyos* 4600Ft, 0.5L 3000F. Open daily 9am-7pm. See **Wines of Tokaj,** at left.)

If you've had enough to drink, venture to the **Tokaj Museum,** down Bethlen Gábor u. past the square, built in 1790. The stairs inside have original wood-paneling, and the rooms contain a wide collection of artifacts representing Tokaj's rich history and culture. (☎352 636. Open Tu-Su 10am-4pm. 400Ft, students 200Ft.) **Outdoor recreation** is almost as popular in Tokaj as wine. The steep vineyard slopes make for challenging climbs, and the languid Tisza and Bodrog are often filled with paddleboats. **Vízisport Centrum** (☎35 26 45) rents bikes (600Ft per day) and canoes (600Ft per person per day; 2-4 person canoes available.) To arrange horseback riding, call the local training school located on Apponyi u. 26. (☎702 241 061. Ask for owner Kudri László.) The best place to canoe is the Bodrog River. Paddle upstream, and you will be rewarded with a pleasant ride back to town. Tourinform (see p. 301) gives advice about **hikes.** While the red and blue trails are easy to follow, the green is steep and poorly marked. **Halihó Sörkert ❶**, at the end of the block directly after Toldi Fogadó is a hamburger joint by day and a popular hangout by night. Local youths sip drinks at outdoor picnic tables. Crowds begin to arrive around 8:30pm. (Burgers 260-500Ft. Open daily 6pm-midnight.) **Műhely Söröző,** Rákóczi u. 42, is an Irish pub that packs in students. It is also the place to go for hardcore karaoke; the pub arranges competitions and music-themed parties throughout the year. (Beer 300-500Ft. Pool 60Ft per game. Open daily 9am-11pm. MC/V.)

VISEGRÁD ☎(0)26

Once the seat of the royal court, Visegrád (VEE-sheh-grad) is now mere ruins. Turkish invaders destroyed the town in 1544, and it was only partly rebuilt when Germans resettled the region in the 18th century. Today, visitors wander the remains of the royal palace and castle and view the excavation exhibits inside. Although the town is an easy daytrip from Budapest, its beautiful mountain trails and spectacular views of the Danube entice hikers and bicyclists to stay longer.

TRANSPORTATION AND PRACTICAL INFORMATION. **Buses** depart from Budapest at Árpád híd, M3 (1½hr., 30 per day, 500Ft). There are four stops in Visegrád. Get off at the first stop for the citadel or Solomon's tower; stay on until the third stop to reach the town center. **Ferries** (3½hr., 2 per day, 1180Ft) from the Budapest pier, below Vigadó tér on the Buda side, stop in front of the town center. **Buses** stop along **Harangvirag utca,** which runs parallel to the river. The town's main road, **Fő út,** is a pedestrian street behind Harangvirag u. **Visegrád Tours,** Rév út 15, across the street from the river at the third bus stop, provides accommodations info and hiking maps. (☎39 81 60; fax 39 75 97. Bike rental 1700Ft per day. Open daily Apr.-Oct. 8am-6pm; Nov.-Mar. M-F 10am-4pm.) There's an **ATM** at Fő út. 34, and a **post office** across the street (open M-F 8am-4pm).

ACCOMMODATIONS AND FOOD. Visegrád's cheapest accommodations are **private rooms** outside the town center. Search for *Zimmer frei* signs on the south side of Fő út and on Nagy Lajos út. **Mátyás Tanya ❹**, Fő út 47, has sunny rooms in a comfortable guesthouse. (☎39 83 09. Breakfast included. Reserve ahead. Doubles 10,500Ft; triples 10,500-13,000Ft. Tax 300Ft. Cash only.) The rooms at the comparatively posh **Hotel Visegrád ❹,** Rév út 15, have balconies overlooking the castle and the Danube. (☎39 70 34; hotelvisegrad@visegradtours.hu. Breakfast included. Doubles 10,500Ft; triples 15,000Ft. Tax 300Ft. Cash only). The banks of the Danube provide a perfect picnic spot. Pick up supplies at **CBA Élelmiszer** supermarket, across from Visegrád Tours at the end of Rév út. (Open M 7am-6pm, Tu-F 7am-7pm, Sa 7am-3pm, Su 7am-1pm. AmEx/MC/V.) On weekends, **food stalls** lining Fő út sell gyros (600-1000Ft) and a variety of fried foods. For something more substantial, head to **Don Vito Pizzeria ❷**, Fő út 83, where waiters serve brick-oven pizza. (☎39 72 30. Pizza 300-1700Ft. Pasta 800-1300Ft. Live jazz Sa-Su 9pm. Open daily noon-midnight.) **Gulyás Csárda ❸**, Nagy Lajos út 4, prepares a variety of excellent Hungarian dishes; the smell of garlic carries out to its garden. (☎39 83 29. Menu in English. Entrees 1200-2300Ft. Open daily noon-10pm.)

SIGHTS. The **citadel** is Visegrád's main attraction. This former Roman outpost is the highest vantage point for miles and provides a sweeping panorama of the Danube bend. Heading north on Fő út, go right on Salamontorony u. and follow the path, which turns into a dirt trail past the tower. Named for a king imprisoned there in the 13th century, the Romanesque **Solomon's Tower** (Alsóvár Salamon Torony), on the path to the citadel, gives a view of the medieval district. In the foothills above Fő út are the ruins of King Matthias's **Royal Palace** (Királyi Palota), considered a myth until archaeologists unearthed its remains. Exhibits include a computerized reconstruction of the original palace. At the end of Salamontorony u., inside Solomon's Tower the **King Matthias Museum** exhibits artifacts from the ruins. (☎39 80 26. Palace open Tu-Su 9am-5pm. Museum open May-Oct. Tu-Su 9am-5pm. Free. 50min. English-language tours of palace and museum 9000Ft.) The palace grounds relive their glory days with jousting, parades, and music during the mid-July **Viségrád Palace Games.** (☎309 337 749; www.palotajatekok.hu. Prices vary: call or check website for info.) **Nyári Bobpálya** is a toboggan slide close to the citadel and Royal Palace. From the citadel, go left up Panorama út. (☎39 73 97. Open daily Apr.-Aug. 9am-6pm, Sept.-Oct. 10am-5pm; Nov.-Feb. 11am-4pm; Mar. 11am-5pm. 350Ft, children 300Ft). If you'd rather take a hike, pick up a **map** (400Ft) from Visegrád Tours (see p. 303)or the Solomon's Tower ticket office.

LAKE BALATON

Surrounded by the volcanic hills of Badacsony, the shaded parks of Balatonfüred, and the sandy beaches of Keszthely, Lake Balaton is one of Central Europe's most popular vacation spots. The lake became a playground for the European elite when the railroad linked the surrounding towns in the 1860s. Frequented by nature-lovers, family vacationers, and partygoers, Balaton attracts the young and the old, the rich and the budget-conscious, with incomparable vistas, beautiful weather, and boisterous nightlife. Teeming with fish, the lake is the source of the region's distinct cuisine, which is complemented by wines from the nearby hills.

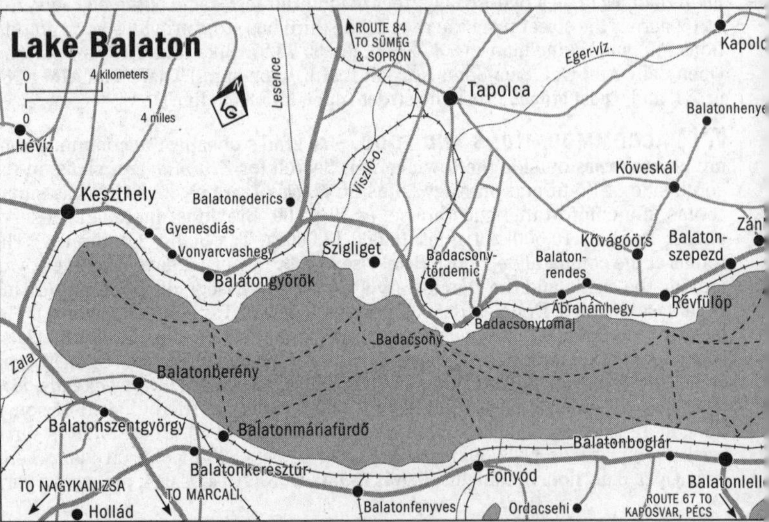

HUNGARY

Storms roll over Lake Balaton in less than 15min., raising dangerous whitecaps on the usually placid lake. Yellow lights on top of tall buildings at Siófok's harbor give **weather warnings.** If the light flashes once per 2 seconds, stay within 500m of shore; 1 flash per second means swimmers must return to shore. Don't worry too much about storms spoiling your vacation; most last fewer than 30min.

SIÓFOK ☎(06)84

There are more tourist offices per sq. km in Siófok (SHEE-o-foke, pop. 27,000) than in any other Hungarian city—its population more than quadruples in summer. The lake provides ample excuse for the bikinis, beer, and bacchanalia that rule this summer capital. Students, families, elderly people, and everyone in between come to Siófok to take in the sun and party along the shore.

TRANSPORTATION

Trains: Trains and buses stop at Siofok, or nearby the hostels at Szeplak Felso, and run to: **Budapest** (2½hr.; 20 per day; 1250Ft); **Keszthely** (3-5hr., 15 per day, 2100Ft); **Pécs** (4-8hr., 1 per day, 2220Ft). Siófok is a stop on the Budapest lines to: **Ljubljana, SLV; Split, CRO; Venice, ITA; Zagreb, CRO.**

Buses: To: **Budapest** (1½hr., 9 per day, 1480Ft) and **Pécs** (3hr., 4 per day, 255Ft).

Ferries: The quickest way to north Balaton is the hourly **MAHART ferry,** 10min. from the train station, in the Strand center. To: **Balatonfüred** (1hr.; 6-9 per day; 1180Ft, students 850Ft) and **Tihany** (1¼hr., 6-9 per day, 1180/850Ft).

ORIENTATION AND PRACTICAL INFORMATION

Siófok's great transport services to other parts of the lake make it an ideal base for exploring the region. The **train** and **bus stations** straddle **Kálmán Imre sétány,** near the center of town. The main street, **Fő út,** runs parallel to the tracks in front of the station. **FA Canal** connects the lake to the Danube and divides town. The eastern

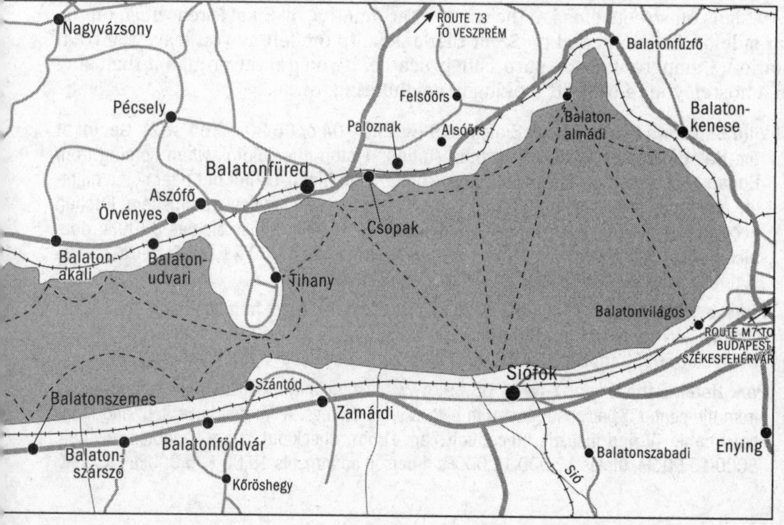

HUNGARY

Gold Coast (Arany-part), to the right as you face the water, is home to older, larger hotels, while the **Silver Coast** (Ezüst-part), to the left, has newer, slightly cheaper accommodations. Each is a 20-30min. walk from the city center, which sits between them. The Silver Coast has its own train station, **Balatonszéplak felső.**

Tourist Offices: Tourinform (☎31 53 55; www.siofok.com), Fő út at Szabadság tér, in water tower opposite the train station. English-speaking staff find rooms and offer free **maps.** Open June 15-Sept. 15 M-F 8am-8pm, Sa-Su 9am-6pm; Sept. 16-June 14 M-F 9am-4pm. **IBUSZ,** Fő út 176, 2nd fl. (☎510 720). Exchanges currency for no commission and books **private rooms.** Open M-F 8am-6pm, Sa 9am-1pm. AmEx/MC/V.

Currency Exchange: OTP, Szabadság tér 10 (☎31 04 55). Exchanges currency for no commission and cashes **traveler's checks.** A MC/V **ATM** is outside. Open M 7:45am-6pm, Tu-Th 7:45am-5pm, F 7:45am-4pm.

Luggage Storage: Available at the train station. Small bags 150Ft per 6hr., 300Ft per 24hr. Large bags 600/300Ft.

Emergency: Police, Sió u. 14. ☎31 07 00. **Coast Guard:** ☎310 990.

Pharmacy: Régi Pharmacy, Fő út 202 (☎31 00 41). Posts lists of pharmacies open late. Extra 200Ft per item after hours. Open M-F 8am-7pm, Sa 8am-2pm; Th ring bell for after-hours service. AmEx/MC/V.

Internet: Net Game Pont, Fő út 45 (☎77 66 70). 200Ft per 15min., 300Ft per 30min. Open daily 10am-10pm.

Post Office: Fő út 186 (☎31 02 10). **Poste Restante** available; go upstairs and left. Open M-F 8am-7pm, Sa 8am-noon. **Telephones** and **ATM** outside. **Postal Code:** 8600.

ACCOMMODATIONS

Because Balaton is frequented by rich Western tourists, particularly Germans, sojourns have become even more expensive than in Budapest. Several agencies offer **private rooms.** Your best bets are **Tourinform** (see above), which finds rooms and negotiates rates with hotels (doubles 6000-17,000Ft), and **IBUSZ** (doubles 7500Ft; tourist tax 300-340Ft per night; 30% surcharge for fewer than 4 nights). If you'd rather bargain on your own, knock on doors with *Panzió* and *Zimmer frei* signs on streets close to the water. Start hunting on **Erkel Ferenc utca,** on the far side of the canal, and on **Szent László utca,** to the left as you leave the train station. Campgrounds are surprisingly scarce. If you'd rather rough it than stay in a hostel, you're best off looking in neighboring towns.

Villa Benjamin Youth Hostel, Siófoki u. 9 (☎35 07 04 or 06 20 44 64 182). Get off at the Balatonszéplak felső bus or train station, 1 stop after Siófok when coming from Budapest. Located on the Silver Coast, 25min. from Siófok center but near some nightlife and food establishments. Dorm rooms have a beach-bungalow atmopshere. Kitchen access, free Internet and laundry. Garden singles 3000Ft, house singles 3500Ft; doubles 6000Ft; triples 9000Ft; 4- to 6-person apartments 14,000-21,000Ft; 8- to 10-person house 28,000-35,000Ft. 340Ft tax per night. ❷

Piroska, Petőfi sétány 14/a (☎314 251), just down the street from the main boardwalk. Simple, airy rooms with private baths in a big pink house with balconies. Call ahead. Doubles 5500Ft; triples 8000Ft. Reception 24hr. Check-out noon. Cash only. ❷

Park Hotel, Batthyány u. 7 (☎31 05 39; www.parkhotel.hu), near the main strand, 5min. from the center. Spacious rooms with high vaulted ceilings. All rooms have A/C, and many have cable TV and jacuzzis. Reception 7am-10pm. Check-out 10am. Doubles July-Aug. 8000-15,000Ft; triples 12,000-18,000Ft; 4-person apartments 15,000-35,000Ft. MC/V. ❸

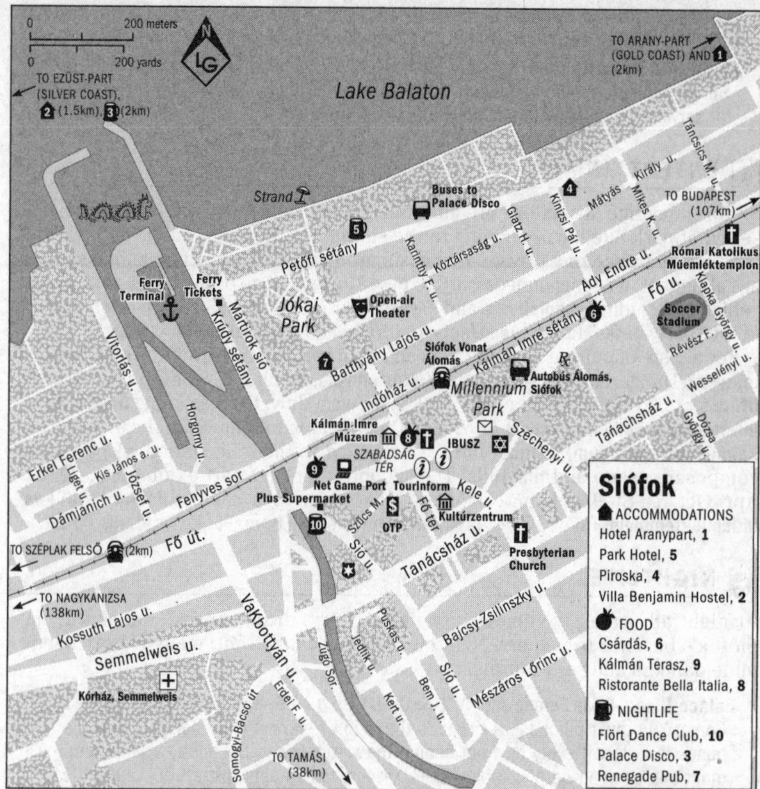

Hotel Aranypart, Beszédes J. sétány 82 (☎519 450; www.aranypart.hu). Take bus #2 from the city center to the front of the hotel. On the Gold Coast beach, with beautiful views. Spacious rooms with full baths. Restaurant, coffee shop, and safe in lobby. Sauna and tennis courts. Rooms have freezer, radio and TV. Breakfast included. Singles 12,500Ft; doubles 16,900Ft. Extra bed 6400Ft. Tourist tax 340Ft. MC/V. ❹

FOOD

In the Lake region, many restaurants serve a combination of Hungarian and Italian food. Grab supplies for the beach at **Plus Supermarket,** Fő út 156-160. (Open M-F 7am-8pm, Sa 7am-3pm. MC/V.) For those staying on the Silver Coast, **CBA Supermarket** is open daily 7am-10pm. The strand kiosks offer snack foods, including *lángos* (200-450Ft), hamburgers (400Ft), and pizza (450Ft).

Csárdás, Fő út 105 (☎31 06 42). Proximity to the lake makes Csárdás's tasty local dishes ideal for an after-beach meal. Romantic candlelit terrace. Live gypsy music Th-Sa 6pm. Entrees 660-2390Ft. Open daily 11:30am-10pm. AmEx/MC/V. ❸

Kálmán Terasz, Kálmán Imre sétány 13 (☎31 06 51), at the far end of Kálmán Imre sétány on the corner of Fő tér. Offers a variety of fish dishes and other local foods, on a covered patio. The real treat is the decadent sundae (black forest cup with rum-soaked cherries; 990Ft). Entrees 520-2890Ft. Open daily 10am-10pm. Cash only. ❸

Ristorante Bella Italia, Szabadság tér 1 (☎310 826). Red-brick columns hold up this Hungarian-Italian patio restaurant that dishes out enticing entrees with speed and stellar service. Open daily 9am-midnight. Pizza and pasta 630-2390Ft. Cash only. ❷

ENTERTAINMENT

Siófok's daytime attractions are entertaining, but none compare to the **strand,** a series of park-like lawns running to the shoreline. There are public and private sections; entrance to a private area costs around 500Ft, and since public spaces are abundant, it seems unnecessary to pay. Most sections of the beach rent water vehicles, including **paddleboats** and **kayaks** (500-700Ft per hr.). Youth often gather in the "party cafes" lining the streets, before heading out to beach parties.

For a taste of culture beyond the beach-bum variety, check out the nightly German and Hungarian operettas in the **Kultúrzentrum,** Fő tér 2. Tourinform (see **Tourist Offices,** p. 306) sells tickets (1200-7000Ft). In early July, the week-long **Golden Shell International Folklore Festival** (☎50 42 62) celebrates folk music and dancing. The **Kálmán Imre Múzeum,** Kálmán Imre sétány, next to the train station, displays the composer's piano and playbills. The second floor hosts art exhibitions. (Open Apr.-Oct. Tu-Su 9am-5pm; Nov.-Mar. Tu-Su 9am-4pm. 350Ft.) **Római Katolikus Műemléktemplom,** Fő út 57, holds organ concerts. (Sa 8pm; 950Ft, students 650Ft.)

NIGHTLIFE

At nightfall, excessive displays of debauchery, drunkenness, and skin from Siófok's beaches to its bars. Nightclubs line the lakefront; many feature semi-nude dancers and sexy murals.

Palace Disco, Deák Ferenc sétány 2 (☎06 84 35 12 95; www.palace.hu), on the Silver Coast. You must purchase a ticket to the club or show a club stamp to ride the free buses that depart every hr. from behind the watch tower. Spotlights visible from town mark this open-air party complex—bars, discos, restaurants (pizza 990-1290Ft), which houses an *"erotic galerie"* with dancers and is surrounded by a courtyard with another dance floor. Beer from 600Ft. Mixed drinks 980-1750Ft. Cover after 10pm. 1500-2500Ft. Disco open daily May to mid-Sept. 10pm-5am. Pizzeria open daily 11am-5am.

Renegade Pub, Petőfi sétány 3 (www.renegade-pub.com), in the center of the strand. This bar and dance club is full by 11pm. Feast your eyes on the beautiful people dancing on tables to the latest Europop hits. Enough beer (420-530Ft) and sweet and salty mixed drinks (980-1400Ft) to float you home. Open daily June-Aug. 8pm-4am.

Flört Dance Club, Sió u. 4 (☎06 20 333 3303; www.flort.hu). Follow the spotlights to this 2-story hotspot in the center of town. Admire yourself—and the young crowd shaking it to house music—on the mirrored walls. Beer 790-950Ft. Cover 2500Ft; Tourinform often has fliers for a 300Ft discount. Erotic and alcohol-themed nightly parties, check website for schedules. Open daily mid-June to late-Aug. 10pm-6am. Cash only.

BALATONFÜRED ☎(06)87

Across the lake from Siófok, Balatonfüred (BAL-a-ton-FEWR-ed; pop. 13,500) is its quieter counterpart. Sandy beaches, a central park with volcanic springs, and a convenient location near Tihany and Badacsony make this friendly town a haven for families and those looking for a mellow escape. Thanks to cheap yet central accommodations, it's easy to enjoy the bountiful outdoor activities and savor the fresh seafood that makes Balaton famous.

TRANSPORTATION

Trains: The **train station** is located on Horvath Mihaly, about a 15min. walk from Lake Balaton. To: **Badacsony** (55min., 2 per hr., 600Ft); **Budapest** (2½hr., 1 per hr., 2040Ft); **Győr** (4hr., 20 per day, 2540Ft); **Keszthely** (2hr., 12 per day, 1200Ft); **Pécs** (4-8hr., 13 per day, 3440Ft).

Buses: Located in front of the train station on Horvath Mihaly. Express buses *(gyorsjárat)* go to **Budapest** (1½hr., 5 per day, 2180Ft) and **Keszthely** (1½hr., 9 per day, 1020Ft).

Ferries: The quickest way to south Balaton is the hourly **MAHART ferry** (10min.), which leaves from the main pier. To: **Siófok** (1hr.; 6-9 per day; 1200Ft, students 800Ft) and **Tihany** (15min., 6-9 per day, 820/640Ft).

Bike rental is at **Rent-a-Bike,** across from Esterházy Strand on Deák Ferenc u. (☎48 06 71. Open daily 9am-7pm. 350Ft per hr., 2400Ft per day, 12,000Ft per week.)

ORIENTATION AND PRACTICAL INFORMATION

The **train** and **bus stations** are next to each other, 10min. from the town center. To get to town, take a left on Horváth Mihály u., then a right on Jókai Mór u., and walk toward the lake. Jókai Mór u. runs perpendicular to the water from the upper part of town to the ferry dock. To the right of the ferry dock, **Záconyi Ferenc utca** is home to the tourist office, many restaurants, and the central market. To the left, **Tagore sétány** leads through the town park and to the main *strand* (beach) and curves into **Aranyhíd sétány,** which leads to **Kisfaludy Strand.** In **Gyógy tér,** above the park, you can fill your water bottle with sulfuric-smelling **volcanic spring water** under the **Well House Pavilion.** The **Tourinform** office, the bank, and a large supermarket line **Petőfi Sándor utca,** which runs through the center.

Tourist Office: The **City Tourist Bureau,** to the left of the ferry dock on Záconyi Ferenc u., offers free info on maps and accommodations. Open July-Aug. M-Sa 9am-9pm, Su 9am-2pm. At **Tourinform,** Petőfi Sándor u. 68 (☎58 04 80; www.balatonfured.hu.), the English-speaking staff suggest **private rooms** and supply **free maps** and info. Open July-Aug. M-F 9am-7pm, Sa 9am-6pm, Su 9am-1pm; Sept.-June M-F 9am-4pm.

Currency Exchange: OTP, Petőfi Sándor u. 8 (☎58 10 70), **exchanges currency** for no commission and has **Western Union.** A MC/V **ATM** is outside. Open M 7:45am-5pm, Tu-F 7:45am-4pm.

Pharmacy: Krisztina Pharmacy, on Csokonal u., has 24hr. emergency service. Open M-F 8am-6pm. AmEx/MC/V.

Internet: Internet is expensive; the cheapest is at **NETov@abb Eszpresszó,** Horváth M. u. 3 (☎34 22 35.), 1 street past Petőfi Sándor u. when walking up Jókai Mór u. 10Ft per min.; min. 10min. Open M-F 8am-10pm, Sa-Su 10am-10pm.

Post office: Branch at Zsigmond u. Open M-F 8am-4pm. The main post office, Kossuth L. u. 19, with the entrance off Ady Endre u., is 20min. from the beach. Open M-F 8am-4pm, Sa 8am-noon. **Postal Code:** 8230.

ACCOMMODATIONS

Accommodations in Balatonfüred are mid-price range, but convenient and comfortable. Almost every house on **Petőfi Sándor utca** offers **private rooms,** starting at about 5000Ft; look for *Zimmer frei* signs. The **City Tourist Bureau** and **Tourinform** can tell you where to look, but you're on your own when it comes to bargaining. Facing the docks, follow the water to the right; after 15min. from the harbor turn right at the roundabout. Unlike the New York prison of the same name, **Sing-Sing**

❶, Fűrdő u. 32, boasts a genial staff and simple dorm rooms close to the water. (☎06 30 93 91 156. Dorms July-Aug. 2000Ft; Sept.-Oct. and May-June 1000Ft.) **Hotel Aranyhíd ❹,** Aranyhíd sétány 2, is near the main *strand*. Though the exterior masks its luxury, this beachside hotel boasts large apartments with kitchenettes, baths, phones, TVs, and balconies. Ask for a room overlooking the water—it's the same price. (☎34 20 58. July-Aug. singles 9800Ft; doubles 15,500Ft; triples 18,000Ft. Sept. and May-June, 8100/12,000/14,800Ft. Tax 340Ft.) **Camping Füred ❷,** Széchényi u. 24, is on the shore to the right of town when facing the water. At this spacious campsite, bungalows are pricey but small tents are reasonable. ☎58 02 41. Tents 510-5600Ft per person. Bungalows 1500-26,300Ft. Rates vary by season. MC/V.)

FOOD

The local diet is based largely on seafood from the lake. Stock up on food, snacks, and beach supplies at the **Silbergold ABC** supermarket, on Tagore sétány. (Open daily 8am-8pm.) Restaurants and cafes line the beach promenade. **Halászkert Étterem ❷,** Zákonyi u. 3, serves dozens of the region's famous fish dishes, including Balaton pike perch (1350Ft) and *halászlé* (900Ft), on a patio opposite the docks. (☎58 10 50. Entrees 750-2200Ft. Open daily 11am-10pm. Cash only.) **Brázay Kert ❶** is at the entrance to Brázay Strand on Aranyhíd sétány. Satiate your desire for hamburgers (350Ft), *lángos* (250-350), and pizza (990Ft) at wood tables overlooking a small pond and bridge. Afterwards, lounge on the private beach (350Ft, children 200Ft) behind the restaurant. (☎32 16 33. Open daily 10am-10pm.) Situated just off the harbor, **Borcsa Restaurant ❷,** next to the entrance to Esterházy Strand on Tagore sétány, offers a range of fish and game dishes. The two terraces and beautiful dining room are polished and sophisticated. (☎58 00 70. Many vegetarian options. Entrees 890-1980Ft. Open daily 11am-11pm. AmEx/MC/V.)

ENTERTAINMENT AND NIGHTLIFE

Balatonfüred is a city visited mainly for its *strands* (beaches) and water sports. The most popular destination is the main beach, **Eszterházy Strand,** on Tagore sétány. A walk through the park from the ferry dock reveals sandy beaches, a water park equipped with pools, slides and waterfalls (600Ft per 2hr.), swinging lounge chairs (599Ft), and paddleboats (1600Ft). If you leave the park and return, you'll have to pay the entrance fee again, so bring everything you will need during your visit. (Beach ☎34 38 17. Open 8:30am-7pm. Admission 550Ft. Safe 315Ft.) Should lazing about make you hungry, there are countless restaurants and a mini **ABC** supermarket close to the beach. **Kisfaludy Strand,** on Aranyhíd sétány next door, is host to the Fitt Diák program in the summer months. Established to encourage an active lifestyle, it hosts dancing and other activities free with beach entry. (☎34 29 16. Open 8:30am-7pm. 350Ft, children 220Ft.) Also popular is **Oszi Go-Kart,** at the corner of Munkácsy Mihály u. and Kosztolányi Dezső u. (☎309 898 843. Open daily 10am-8pm. 5min. 2000Ft.) There are **souvenir markets** on Jókai Mór u., off Petőfi Sándor u. (Open 9am-9pm.)

The tourist season kicks off with the **Sail Unfurling Ceremony** in mid-May. Sailing competitions are frequent during the summer. In early August, winemakers set up tents on Tagore sétány for **Balatonfüred Wine Weeks.** At night, folk-dancing ensembles perform; on the last day, there is a celebration complete with fireworks. Call Balatonfüred Tourinform (p. 306) for info and tickets.

While you won't find the same throngs of partygoers as in Siófok, the cafes and bars along the beach attract small crowds in the evening. On the downtown promenade, Blaha L. u. 7, try Kedves **Cukrászda ❶,** for an early night of drinks and sweets starting at 95ft. (☎87 34 32 29. Open 8am-8pm. Cash only.) If you're still not tired from a day at the beach, party until the morning at **Columbus Dance Club,** at Honvéd u. 3. A popular spot in the summer, this cabana with dance floor and cool terrace hosts several themed parties with guest DJs. (☎302 670 083; www.columbusclub.hu. Beer 350Ft. Open daily 10pm-5am.)

DAYTRIPS FROM BALATONFÜRED

BADACSONY AND BADACSONYTOMAJ

Trains run from Balatonfüred (55min., 2 per hr., 600Ft). You can also get to Badacsony by bus from Keszthely (1hr., 12-14 per day, 365Ft).

Though four resort towns lie at the foot of the volcanic Badacsony Mountain (Badacsonyhegy), **Badacsony** and **Badacsonytomaj** (BAHD-uh-chohn-TOH-mai) are the most popular and are about 2km apart. The towns' main draw's are the **wine cellars,** on the southern face of the hill, where you can sample a vintage or purchase it by the 1L plastic jug (from 500Ft). Unlike those in Eger and Tokaj, the local wine cellars sit beside the vineyards on the hill. Each offers a different variety of the region's popular *Olaszrizling* and *Kéknyelű* (Blue Stalk) wines. For a free "wine map" and brochures about the cellars, head to **Tourinform Badacsony,** Park u. 6 (☎43 10 46). A steep walk uphill yields views of Balaton and the vineyards, but can take 20-30min. The paved road ends at **Kisfaludy Ház ❸,** which serves Hungarian dishes and regional wines on a patio with a beautiful view of the lake. (☎43 10 16. Entrees 1090-3500Ft. Open daily 11am-11pm. Cash only.) Surrounded by vineyards, the cellar **Szent Orbán Borház ❸,** Kisfaludy S. u. 5, serves Hungarian oxtail soup (1700Ft) and other game dishes. Their homegrown vintages are also available for **tasting,** starting at 260Ft. (☎43 13 82. Entrees 1200-3700Ft. Open daily noon-10pm. MC/V.) Two more affordable cellars sit on cobblestone Hegyalja u., which is part of the yellow-cross hiking trail. (Samples from 55Ft.)

If the wine samples haven't done you in, head farther uphill to one of Badacsony's pleasantly shaded—but challenging—hikes. Pick up a hiking map from Tourinform (400Ft). A short trek on the red trail leads to **Rose Rock** (Rózsa-kő), where legend has it that any couple who sits facing away from the water will marry within a year. An hour's hike farther up the rocky stairs brings you to **Kisfaludy Lookout Tower** (Kisfaludy kilátó), which offers a gorgeous view of Lake Balaton. Walk right when facing the Rose Rock and follow the **Hegyteto trail.** The **stone gate** (kőkapu), a cliffside basalt formation, is farther along the trail. Badacsony's **beach** (open daily 9am-6pm; 350Ft) is small, and the lively **marketplace** around it creates a carnival atmosphere. **Egry Fogadó ❶,** Római út 1, in Badacsonytomaj, rents cheap rooms. If you'd rather not walk from Badacsony, you can get off at the town train station. (☎471 057. Call ahead for July and Aug. weekends. Rooms June 20-Aug. 20 2400Ft; Aug. 20-Oct. 15 and Apr. 15-June 19 1800Ft. Cash only.)

VESZPRÉM

Buses (☎42 38 15) run from Balatonfüred (30min., 18 per day, 190Ft). From the bus station, Jutasi u. 4, head straight across Budapest u. past the market hall and turn right on Kossuth u. Follow the signs to the Castle.

Known as the "City of Queens," Veszprém's regal air dates back to the 9th century, when it is said to have first been used as a Frankish fortress. Its romantic Castle District is known for preserved Baroque buildings and royal churches, cozy cafes along winding cobblestone roads, and hidden vistas with fantastic views of the valley below. The **Fire Tower,** left of the **Hero's Gate** entrance, was once used as a watch tower. Its balcony now offers visitors a bird's-eye view of town. (Open daily 10am-6pm. 300Ft, students 200Ft.) Stylized paintings of Jesus, saints, and famous kings are displayed along the pastel walls of the **Piarist Church,** Vár u. 12. (Open daily Mar.-Aug. 10am-6pm; Sept.-Oct. 10am-5pm. Free.) Farther down Var u., 10th-century **Saint Michael's Cathedral** is famous for its stained glass windows and royal artifacts, including a bone from the corpse of Gizella, Hungary's first queen. (Open daily Mar.-Aug. 10am-6pm; Sept.-Oct. 10am-5pm. Mass Sa 7pm; Su 9, 11:30am, and 7pm. Free.) The current **Archbishop's Palace,** Vár u. 16, has been the seat of the Archbishop of Veszprém since 1993. Beautiful frescoes adorn the dining hall, where windows reveal a panoramic view of the valley. (Open May-Oct. Tu-Su 10am-5pm. Groups only. Tours hourly. 800Ft, students 400Ft.) Across the street at Var. u. 35, the **Queen Gizella Museum** houses ecclesiastical relics such as a golden cloak that belonged to Bishop Albert Vetesi. (Open daily Mar.-Aug. 10am-6pm; Sept.-Oct. 10am-5pm. 400Ft, students 200Ft.) A short walk to the end of Var u. leads to a cliff with an expansive view of the valley. Statues of the first Hungarian royal couple, St. István I and Queen Gizella, rise above the town.

After seeing the sights, head down the hill to enjoy a variety of Italian dishes at **Elefant Étterem és Kávézo ❷,** Óváros tér 6, where colorful fish swim in the restaurant's tank. (☎334 1217. Salads 1150-1350Ft. Pizzas 950-1450Ft. Open M-Sa 9am-10pm, Su 10am-10pm. MC/V.) **Tourinform,** Vár u. 4, located under the entrance to Castle Hill, provides free **maps** and accommodations info.

TIHANY PENINSULA ☎(06)87

A possible daytrip from Balatonfüred and a terrific destination for simple hikes, the beautiful Tihany (TEE-hahn-yuh; pop. 1,500) Peninsula is known as the pearl of Balaton. It is heavily touristed, but Tihany retains historical weight and outdoorsy charm, making this area seem more mature than its hard-partying peers.

TRANSPORTATION AND PRACTICAL INFORMATION. Buses are the most convenient option, and run to Balatonfüred train station (20min., every 45min., 125Ft). The bus stops at Kossuth u., in front of the abbey. The **ferry** to Balatonfüred (15min.; every hour; 1020Ft, students 765Ft) docks at the harbor down the hill, 2km away. You'll have to walk or take the bus into town if arriving by **train**—the station is at the edge of the peninsula.

The main road, **Kossuth utca,** spans the peninsula and runs through town, just below the abbey. There are several bus stops on the peninsula. Get off at the first stop to hit the beach; otherwise, stay on until the bus stops in front of the abbey. The **red trail** runs beside the abbey stop; follow the red arrows. **Tourinform,** below the abbey, has **maps** of Tihany and of hiking trails. (☎43 88 04; tihany@tourinform.hu. Open June-Aug. M-F 9am-7pm, Sa-Su 9am-6pm; Sept. M-F 9am-5pm, Sa 9am-3pm; Oct. to mid-Apr. M-F 9am-3pm; mid-Apr. to May M-F 9am-4pm, Sa 9am-1pm;) **Rent-a-bike** is at Kossuth u. 32. (2600Ft per day. Open daily 10am-6pm.) There's a **pharmacy** at Kossuth u. 10 (☎44 84 80; open M-F 8am-noon and 1-6pm, Sa 8am-noon) and an **ATM** up the hill at Kossuth u. 12. The **post office,** Kossuth u. 37 (open M-F 8am-4pm), is adjacent to **Mini Market Élelmiszer,** which sells snacks and drinks. (Open daily 8am-8pm.) **Postal Code:** 8237.

ACCOMMODATIONS AND FOOD. To find accommodations, head down **Kossuth utca,** then make a left on **Kiss utca** and a right on **Csokonai utca.** This street consists of many houses that rent **private rooms,** marked by *Zimmer frei* signs. Most are reasonably priced (starting at 5000Ft) and have views of the valley and lake. **Kántas Pension ❸,** Csokonai u. 49, has good-sized doubles with balconies overlooking the valley. (☎44 80 72; kantaspension@axelero.hu. Breakfast included. Doubles 10,500Ft. AmEx/MC/V.) The food stalls around the beach and by the abbey will hold you over with fried fast food. If you'd rather sit down, try **Echo Restaurant ❸,** Visszhang u. 23, along the green and red hiking trails. This beautiful restaurant serves typical Hungarian dishes atop a cliff overlooking

Balaton. Ask for a spot on the roof for a great lakeview. (☎44 84 60. Entrees 1200-3500Ft. Open daily Mar.-Nov. 10am-10pm. MC/V.)

SIGHTS AND HIKING. The small but magnificent **Benedictine Abbey** (Bencés Apátság) presides over the hillside. Its pastel frescoes, intricate Baroque altars, and views of the lake draw over a million visitors each year. On the ceiling, images of angels watch the tourist crowds from on high. The church's foundation letter, scripted in 1055, is the oldest written document in the Hungarian language. A copy is on display inside the church, while the original is in the archives at the abbey in Pannonhalma (p. 319). The András I crypt (András kriptája) contains the remains of King András I, one of Hungary's earliest kings and the abbey's founder. To the right of the crypt, the **Tihany Museum,** an 18th-century former monastery, exhibits an odd combination of contemporary art, Roman archaeological finds, and monastic history, all on display in the subterranean lapidarium. (Abbey, crypt, and museum open daily Mar.-Oct. 9am-6pm. Mass M and Sa 7:30pm; Th 7:30am; Su 7:30, 10am, 7:30pm. Church, crypt, and museum combined 600Ft, students 300Ft; Su free.) **Echo Hill** rises to the left of the church. On a calm day, if you stand on Echo Hill's stone pedestal and shout, the yell will echo off the church wall. Follow the promenade behind the church and descend to the **beach,** where you can rent paddleboats (1500Ft per hr.) and play beach volleyball and lakeside ping-pong. (Open daily 9am-7pm. 350Ft.) If you'd rather soak up the sun, walk along the shore toward the mainland, where you can rent beach chairs (400Ft per hr.).

With beautiful clearings, winding mountain paths, and steep inclines, Tihany serves all levels with trekking opportunities. **Hiking** across the peninsula through hills, forests, farms, and marshes takes only an hour or two. For an even shorter hike, take the **red cross trail** around Belső-tó Lake and turn right on the **red line trail** on the opposite side. The path will take you to the summit of Kiserdő Tető (Top of Little Wood), from which you can see Belső-tó and Külső-tó, Tihany's other interior lake. The **green line trail,** which covers the eastern slope of Óvár, snakes past Barátlakások (the Hermits' Place), where you can escape flocks of tourists and see cells and a chapel hollowed out of the rocks by 11th-century Greek Orthodox ascetics. Pick up a free **hiking map** at Tourinform. If you'd rather traverse the paved roads, bikes are a leisurely way to explore the hillside.

KESZTHELY ☎(06)83

Sitting at the lake's west tip, Keszthely (KEST-hay) was once the toy town of the powerful Festetics family. Though their palace continues to be the main attraction, the city that sprung up around the gates has a charm of its own. Street cafes and souvenir shops dot the promenade, while the beach draws a crowd with its waterslide and rows of food stands. In nearby Hévíz, yet more swimmers relax in the healing waters of the thermal spring. Though the center of Keszthely has less of a resort feel than other Balaton towns, its streets are just as crowded.

TRANSPORTATION. The train station is on Kazinczy u. InterCity trains run to Budapest (3hr., 7 per day, 2780Ft plus 440Ft reservation fee), while slow **trains** *(személyvonat)* go to: Balatonfüred (2-3hr., 7 per day, 1200Ft); Pécs (3-5hr., 10 per day, 2780Ft); Siófok (1½-2hr., 19 per day, 1200Ft); Szombathely (3hr., 1 per day, 2040Ft). The bus terminal is next to the train station; **buses** are faster for local travel to Balatonfüred (1½hr., 9 per day, 1020Ft) and Pécs (4hr., 5 per day, 2320Ft). Some buses leave from the terminal, while others use stops at Fő tér or Georgikán u. Each departure is marked with an "F" or a "G" to indicate which stop it uses; check the schedule. From April to September, **boats** run to Badacsony (1¾hr.; 1-4 per day; 1300Ft, students 650Ft) from the end of the dock near the beach.

ORIENTATION AND PRACTICAL INFORMATION. The main street, **Kossuth Lajos utca,** runs parallel to the shore a ways inland, from **Festetics Palace** (Festetics Kastély) to the center at **Fő tér.** To reach the main square from the train station, walk up **Mártirok utca** to its end at Kossuth Lajos u. and turn right (10min.). The main **beach** *(strand)* is to the right as you exit the stations. If coming from the pier, head straight and follow **Erzsébet Királyné utca** to get to Fő tér.

Tourinform, Kossuth Lajos u. 28, off Fő tér, distributes free **maps** and info and finds rooms. (☎/fax 31 41 44. Open July-Aug. M-F 9am-8pm, Sa-Su 9am-6pm; Oct.-June M-F 9am-5pm, Sa 9am-1pm.) **OTP Bank,** at the corner of Kossuth L. u. and Helikon u., **exchanges currency** and cashes **traveler's checks** for no commission. There's a 24hr. MasterCard and Visa **ATM** and currency exchange machine outside. (Open M 7:45am-5pm, Tu-F 7:45am-4pm.) **Luggage storage** is at the train station. (150Ft per 6hr. Open 3:30am-11:30pm.) The **Ezüstsirály Patika pharmacy,** Sopron u. 2 in the hospital, posts a list of pharmacies with after-hours service. Walk through the palace gates on Kossuth L. u. and out the next set of gates; it's immediately on your left. (☎31 45 49. Open M-Th 7:30am-5pm, F 7:30am-7pm.) **Internet** access is available at **Mikro-net Internet Kávézó,** Nádor u. 13. Walking down Kossuth L. u. from the palace, take the first right. (☎31 40 09. 5Ft per min. Open daily 9am-9pm.) **Telephones** are outside the **post office,** Kossuth L. u. 48. (☎51 59 60. **Poste Restante** and **Western Union** available. Open M-F 8am-6pm, Sa 8am-noon.) **Postal Code:** 8360.

ACCOMMODATIONS AND FOOD. Most homes on the winding streets display *Zimmer frei* signs. Wander from Fő tér down Erzsébet Királyné u. and near Castrum Camping on **Ady Endre utca.** Head up Kossuth L. u. and turn right on Szalasztó u. before the palace entrance; Ady Endre is a few streets down on the right. Expect to pay 3000-4000Ft. **Szabó Lakás ❷,** Arany János 23, offers spacious rooms and a common room with a kitchen and cable TV, in the Szabó family's multi-story house, where the resident dogs roam. (☎31 25 04; jutka.szabo@axelero.hu. Rooms 3000Ft.) **Kiss-Máté Panzió ❸,** Katona J. u. 27, offers rooms near the castle with TVs and fridges, plus a large common kitchen, and access to a tennis court. (☎31 90 72. Singles 5000Ft; doubles 8000Ft; triples 12,000Ft; quads 16,000Ft.) Near the main market, **Castrum Camping ❶,** Móra F. u. 48, boasts large sites with full amenities: tennis courts, beach access, a restaurant, a swimming pool, and close proximity to the nightspots by the water. (☎31 21 20. 1000Ft per adult, 750Ft per child. July-Aug. 1000Ft per tent, with electricity 750Ft; Sept.-June 550Ft per tent. Tax 375Ft.)

There has been a **fruit and flower market** on Piac tér since medieval times and it still fills with persuasive sellers and gullible buyers every day of the week. Merchants start setting up around 6am and linger until 3pm (noon on Su). At its center, the supermarket **Match** sells everything you need. (Open M-F 6:30am-6:30pm, Sa 6:20am-2pm. MC/V.) Most restaurants around Fő tér and on Kossuth L. u. are overpriced, but there are reasonable options farther from the center. **Corso Restaurant ❸,** Erzsébet Királyné u. 23, closer to the *strand* in the Abbázia Club Hotel, draws on Balaton's fish stock to make its food and has great lunch deals for under 1000Ft. (☎31 25 96. Pizza from 850Ft. Entrees 950-3800Ft. Live music nightly from 6pm. Open M-Sa 7am-10pm. MC/V.) **Párizsi Udvar ❷,** Kastély u. 5, offers both Hungarian and Italian dishes ("pork cutlet a la countryman" 890Ft) in a casual outdoor setting en route to the palace. (☎31 12 02. Entrees 600-2400Ft. Open 11am-11pm. MC/V.) Stop by the cafe at the **Marcipán Muzeum,** Katona J. u. 19, for delectable pastries and candies and a look at the marzipan model of the palace. (☎31 93 22. Open June-Aug. daily 10am-6pm; Sept.-Dec. and Mar.-May Tu-Su 10am-6pm. Museum 160Ft, children 100Ft. Cakes 160-290Ft.)

SIGHTS AND ENTERTAINMENT. Keszthely's pride is the **Helikon Palace Museum** (Helikon Kastélymúzeum) in the **Festetics Palace.** From Fő tér, follow Kossuth L. u. past Tourinform. Built by one of the most powerful Austro-Hungarian families of the 18th century, the storybook Baroque palace is like a smaller version of Versailles without the crowds. Its fanciful architecture and lush gardens were once the backdrop for lavish literary events hosted by György Festetics (1755-1819); the name "Helikon" comes from Helicon Hill, the mythical Greek home of the nine muses. Of the 360 rooms, visitors may only enter those in the **central wing,** but if the mirrored halls and extravagantly furnished chambers aren't captivating enough, take a peak into the 90,000-volume, wood-paneled **Helikon Library,** just past the entrance, with its dramatic walls of books and hanging chandelier. The arms collection, with weapons spanning 1000 years, and the exhibit of the Festetics's elaborate porcelain pieces are also worth a look. To find out the details, rent an audio tour (500Ft) or pick up an English guidebook (700Ft). There are a few English translations. (Open Sept.-May Tu-Su 10am-5pm; June Tu-Su 9am-5pm; July-Aug. daily 9am-6pm. 1500Ft, students 850Ft.) Popular chamber music **concerts** are held frequently in the mirrored ballroom; reserve tickets two weeks ahead by calling the ticket office. (☎31 21 92. 1000-5500Ft.) In summer, the palace holds **candlelit tours** through the castle. (W and F-Sa 10pm. English tours upon request. Call the ticket office to reserve, or buy tickets at the door at 9pm. 2500Ft, students 1500Ft.) The 1896 mint-green tower of the **Church of Our Lady** on Fő tér conceals the original structure, which dates from 1386 and is a great example of Gothic architecture. Spectacular stained glass and 14th-century paintings adorn the sanctuary. (Open M-Sa 8am-7pm, Su 11am-7pm. Free.)

Keszthely boasts many sandy beaches, and families throng to the main *strand.* From the center, walk down Erzsébet u. as it curves right into Vörösmarty u. Cut through the park on the left and cross the train tracks on the other side. This arcade-lined strip along the shore offers volleyball nets, a giant slide, paddleboats, and kayaks. (Open daily 8:30am-7pm. 700Ft, children 500Ft; after 6:30pm free.)

DAYTRIPS FROM KESZTHELY

SÜMEG

Buses run from Hévíz (45min., 1 per hr., 370Ft) and Keszthely (1hr., 1 per hr., 510Ft). From the station, cross Petőfi Sándor u. to Kossuth L. u., the main street. To reach the castle, take a right on Vak Bottyán u. off Kossuth L. u. Bear right at Szent István tér and continue up the street. Turn left onto Városdal u. and walk until you see the path. From there, it's a 5min. walk to the castle. Easily combined with Hévíz as a daytrip.

Though only a little farther inland than its coast-hugging neighbors, Sümeg feels worlds away. This cobblestone town appeals more to families and schoolchildren eager to get a glimpse of the medieval era than to the hedonistic crowds that frequent most of Balaton's resorts. Trek up the stone path to visit the **castle** *(vár),* one of Hungary's largest and best-preserved strongholds. Built as a defense against the Mongols, the 13th-century fortress also resisted the Turks, standing until the Habsburg army burned it down in 1713. If the trek to the castle seems steep, ride up to the ticket counter in one of the vans waiting at the bottom of the hill; look for the "VárTaxi" emblem (350Ft). The atmosphere in the castle is kitschy, with magic shows, pony rides, archery ranges, and costumed characters performing with mandolin music. (☎87 35 25 98. Open daily May-Oct. 8am-8pm. 1200Ft, students 800Ft.) There's a **museum** inside, as well as the requisite **torture chamber,** but the wait may prove to be more torturous than the instruments themselves. As you leave the castle, stop at the tournament stadium at the bottom of the hill, where you can watch sword-fighting, archery, and a horseshow, followed by a meal in an old-fashioned tavern. (Shows M-Sa 6:30pm. 5000Ft, students 4000Ft; includes entrance to the castle and a meal at the restaurant.)

The **Church of the Ascension,** at the corner of Deák F. u. and Széchényi G. u., is a must-see. Follow Deák F. u. downhill from the intersection across from the OTP bank on Kossuth L. u. The church's mundane exterior conceals a frescoed marvel known to locals as the "Hungarian Sistine Chapel." While this comparison may be an exaggeration, Franz Anton Maulbertsch's 1757 Rococo masterpiece, which covers the ceilings and walls of the church, is highly impressive. Maulbertsch left his signature by painting himself—he's the one on the left side of the first fresco to the right as you enter the church. The platter of cheese he's holding is, curiously, a symbol of humility. (Open M-F 9am-noon and 1-6pm, Sa 10am-noon and 2-5pm, Su 2-5pm. Free.) **Ferences Templom,** on Szent István tér on the way up to the castle, is also a pleasant stop. Its frescoed ceiling, though not as famous, has vivid colors. (Open daily 7am-6pm. Free.) Across the street, **Scotti Udvarház ❷,** Szent István tér 1, serves pastas (990-1350Ft) and pizzas (580-1680Ft) in a courtyard with ivy overhangings. Ask to try some water from the spring shooting up in the middle of the restaurant. (☎87 35 09 97. Open daily 10am-midnight.)

HÉVÍZ

Buses leave from Keszthely's Fő tér (15min., every 30min., 200Ft) and from Sümeg (55min., every 1-2hr., 370Ft). A visit to Hévíz can be combined with a trip to Sümeg.

Eight kilometers outside Keszthely, Hévíz is home to the world's largest **thermal lake.** Surrounded by imposing pines, spotted with gigantic lilies, and concealed by a slight mist, the sulfurous and slightly radioactive water is rumored to have miraculous healing powers. In summer, the water is naturally heated to 35°C (90-95°F), and it moves quickly: the spring that fills this soothing lake pumps so fast that the water is replaced every 28hr. To bathe in these legendary waters, head to the **Fin-de-Siècle bathhouse,** Dr. Schülhof Vilmos sétány 1, across from the bus station. Look for the sign that reads "Tó Fürdő." Unique because of its natural setting, the house sits on stilts above the center of the scenic lake. Specialists recommend bath treatments for persistent aches or pains. Massages and pedicures are also available. (☎83 50 17 00; fax 54 01 44. Open daily in summer 8:30am-8pm; in winter 9am-4pm. 3hr. 1500Ft, 4hr. 1600Ft, 5hr. 1900Ft, whole day 2800Ft.) Grab a snack at one of the cafeterias or cafes in the park or dine at **MalomKerék Vendéglő ❸,** Kölcsey u. 4, on the opposite side of the bus station from the bath, which serves delicious dishes on log tables as pianists play in the background. (☎83 54 04 25; www.malomkerek.hu. English menu. Entrees 1090-1590Ft. Open daily 11am-10pm. Cash only.) If you plan to spend a few days cooling your heels in the hot healing waters, your best bet is a **private room** (start at 3000Ft). Spa hotels have sky-high prices, but *Zimmer frei* signs advertise cheaper lodgings all over town. Visegrád Tours rents bikes (1700Ft per day).

WESTERN TRANSDANUBIA

During the Cold War, authorities discouraged people from entering the pastoral region of Western Transdanubia, as they believed capitalist Austria and Tito's Yugoslavia were too close for comfort. Thus, a region that had always been a bit behind the times—electricity didn't arrive until 1950—fell even farther beyond modernity's reach. Today, the untouched rolling hills and stretches of farmland are perfect for summertime strolls, bicycle rides, and hikes, while holiday fairs light up town streets in winter.

GYŐR ☎(0)96

The streets of Győr (DYUR; pop. 130,000) wind peacefully around the city's many museums and seemingly untarnished 17th- and 18th-century architecture. With its thousand-year-old cathedral and the magisterial Archabbey of Pannonhalma nearby, Győr is a popular stopover for both religious pilgrims and tourists traveling from Budapest to Vienna. The city—home to the cookie manufacturer, Győri édesség—has a bit of an industrial feel, though its downtown promenade strikes a lighter note, playing host to several musical and historical festivals.

TRANSPORTATION AND PRACTICAL INFORMATION. The train station, Révai út 4-6 (domestic ☎31 16 13, international 52 33 66), is 3min. from the city center; turn right as you exit the station. Turn left before the underpass and cross the street to Baross Gábor út. **Trains** run to: Budapest (2½hr., 34 per day, 2040Ft); Sopron (1½hr., 10 per day, 1350Ft); and Vienna, AUT (2hr., 13 per day, 5250Ft). The bus station, Hunyadi út 9 (☎31 77 11), is connected to the train station at the end of the underpass. **Buses** run to Budapest (2½hr., 1 per hr., 2040Ft).

Tourinform (☎31 17 71) is at Árpád út 32. (Open June-Aug. M-F 8am-8pm, Sa-Su 9am-6pm.) **OTP Bank,** Teleki L. út 51, at the corner of Bajcsy-Zsilinszky út, has good **exchange** rates. (MC/V **ATM** and currency exchange. Open M 7:45am-6pm, Tu-Th 7:45am-5pm, F 7:45am-4pm.) The **Postabank** desk in the post office cashes American Express **Traveler's Cheques** for no commission. **Luggage storage** is at the train station. (300Ft per day. Open daily 3am-midnight.) A **pharmacy,** Aranyhajó Patika, can be found at Jedlik Á. út 16. A sign in the window lists pharmacies with emergency hours. (☎32 88 81. Open M-F 7am-6pm, Sa 7am-2pm.) For **medical services,** go to Vasvári P. u. 2. (☎418 244. Open M-F 8am-5pm.) For cheap **Internet access,** try the second floor of Darius Music Club on Czuszor G. u. 6. (186Ft per hr., 850Ft per 5hr. Open M-F 9am-9pm, Sa-Su 10am-9pm.) The **post office** is at Bajcsy-Zsilinszky út 46. (☎31 43 24. **Poste Restante** available. Open M-F 8am-6pm.) **Postal Code:** 9021.

ACCOMMODATIONS AND FOOD. Accommodations may overflow in summer, so it's smart to make reservations before arriving. **Tourinform** (p. 317) can help you find a *panzió* or hotel room. They also keep a list of **campsites.** **Katalin Kert ❹,** Sarkantyú köz 3, off Bécsi Kapu tér, is hidden in a quiet courtyard below the Chapter Hill. Its huge, modern rooms include TVs and showers. A restaurant downstairs has live music. (☎54 20 88; katalinkert@matavnet.hu. Breakfast included. Singles 7100Ft; doubles 9900Ft.) **Széchényi István Főiskola Egyetem ❶,** Hédevári út 3, is across the Moscow-Dune River. Follow Czuczor Gergely út, which runs parallel to Baross Gábor út, across the bridge. Hang a left on Káloczy tér and continue to the parking lot. The entrance is to the left, at K4; after 9pm, enter at K3. Modern buildings offer standard dorms with shared hall baths. (☎503 400. Reception 24hr. Check-out 9am. Open July-Aug. Dorms 1800Ft.)

Kaiser's Szupermarket sprawls on the corner of Arany János út and Aradi út. (Open M 7:30am-7pm, Tu-F 6:30am-7pm, Sa 6:30am-3pm.) For sublime baked goods, head to **Rárói Pékség ❶,** Teleki László u. 30. (Open daily 5am-8pm; after 7pm 50% off all goods.) **Tejivó ❶,** Kisfaludy u. 30, is a young, local hotspot to get good, fast, cheap food. Cozy wooden furniture picnic tables provide a perfect setting. (☎51 26 30. Entrees 180Ft-900Ft. Open M-F 8am-5pm, Sa 8am-1pm.) **Matróz Restaurant ❷,** is at Dunakapu tér 3, off Jedlik Ányos. This local favorite fries up mouthwatering fish, turkey, and pork dishes in two cozy wooden rooms near the river, with dwarf-sized wooden chairs rounding out the folksy atmosphere. (☎33 62 08. Entrees 500-1350Ft. Open M-Th and Su 9am-10pm, F-Sa 9am-11pm.)

SIGHTS. Head uphill on Czuczor Gergely út, parallel to Baross Gábor u., and then take a left at Gutenberg tér to reach **Chapter Hill** (Káptalandomb), the oldest sector of Győr. Overlooking the junction of three rivers—the Danube, the Rába, and the Rábca—the hill is covered in monuments that testify to Győr's rich history as a cultural crossroads. The striking 1731 **Ark of the Covenant statue** (Frigyláda Szobor) was bankrolled by the taxes that King Charles III levied on his impoverished mercenaries. The **Episcopal Cathedral** (Székesegyház), at the top of the hill, has been under frequent construction since 1030. Its exterior is now a medley of Romanesque, Gothic, and Neoclassical styles. Gilded cherubs perch above the heavenly frescoes that illuminate the Baroque interior. Seeking refuge from Oliver Cromwell's forces in the 1650s, a priest brought the miraculous **Weeping Madonna of Győr** to the Cathedral from Ireland. On St. Patrick's Day in 1697, the image reportedly wept blood and tears for the persecuted Irish Catholics. The painting is to the left of the main altar. (Open M-Sa 8am-noon and 2-6pm, Su 8am-noon and 3-6pm. Free.) In the alley directly behind the cathedral, the **Diocesan Library and Treasury** (Egyházmegyei Kincstár), Káptalandomb 26, displays 14th-century gold and silver religious artifacts and an extensive collection of old books, including a display of some illuminated manuscripts. (☎31 11 53. Open Tu-Su 10am-4pm. English captions. 700Ft, students 400Ft.)

The **Imre Patkó Collection** (Patkó Imre Gyűjtemény), Széchényi tér 4 (enter on Lajos u.), has two floors of expressionist and abstract works by modern Hungarian artists and one floor of 16th-century Asian and African works. The museum is housed in the **Iron Log House** (Vastuskós ház), a centuries-old former inn for traveling craftsmen. (☎31 05 88. Open Tu-Su 10am-6pm. Buy tickets in the Xántus János Museum next door. English info available. 500Ft, students 300Ft.) Down Kenyér Köz from Széchényi tér, the **Margit Kovács Museum** (Kovács Margit Gyűjtemény), Apáca út 1, displays the Győr artist's expressive ceramic sculptures and tiles. (☎32 67 39. Open Tu-Su Mar.-Oct. 10am-6pm; Nov.-Feb. 10am-5pm. 600Ft, students 300Ft; Su free.)

ENTERTAINMENT AND NIGHTLIFE. In summer, major forms of local entertainment involve splashing in the water or basking in the sun. Across the river, thermal springs supply a large **water park** *(fürdő)*, Cziráky tér 1. Sprawling over a beautiful complex at the crossing of two rivers, the park has a waterslide, two outdoor swimming pools, two thermal baths, and a spa. From Bécsi kapu tér, walk over the bridge to the island and take the first right. (Open M-Th 9am-8pm, F-Su 9am-9pm. 3hr. ticket 1400Ft, students 1000Ft, full day ticket 1800/1200Ft.) Győr also boasts **Győri Nyár,** a June-July festival of concerts, drama, and the city's famous ballet. Schedules are at Tourinform (see **Practical Information,** p. 317); buy tickets at the box office on Baross Gábor út. or at the venue. The **Győr National Theater** (Nemzeti Színház), Czuczor Gergely u. 7, has a line-up of opera, rock, musicals, and plays; buy tickets at the box office. (☎31 48 00; fax 326 999. Theater open July 15-Aug. 22 M-F 9am-1pm and 2-6pm. Tickets 2500-5500Ft.)

A variety of nightlife options and styles come into full swing as the sun sets. Sophisticates head to **Komédiás Biergarten,** Czuczor Gergely u. 30, which has a lively patio. (☎52 72 17. Beer 220-580Ft. Open M-Sa 11am-midnight.) For an after-hours drink or snack, try **Patio Belvárosi Kavéház,** Baross Gábor út 12, which serves drinks, along with gigantic ice cream sundaes. (☎31 00 96. Open 24hr.) For a change of pace, hit the dance floors at **Darius Music Club,** Czuszor u. 6, a popular local spot for its changing scene and music. "Latin Nights," with Salsa dancing, are a particular favorite. (☎309 360 878. Beer 450Ft. Open M-W 9am-10pm, Th 9am-2am, F-Sa 9am-4am. Cash only.)

DAYTRIP FROM GYŐR: ARCHABBEY OF PANNONHALMA. Visible from Győr on a clear day, the hilltop **Archabbey of Pannonhalma** (Pannonhalmi Főapátság) has seen a millennium of destruction and rebuilding since the Benedictine order established it in A.D. 996. Now a UNESCO World Heritage site, it is home to some of the most valuable ecclesiastical treasures and diverse architecture in the world. About 50 monks live in the abbey, which houses a 13th-century basilica, an opulent 360,000-volume library, a small gallery of icons, and one of the finest boys' schools in Hungary. Its treasures include a 1055 deed founding the Benedictine abbey in Tihany—the oldest document with Hungarian writing—and a charter from 1001, bearing St. Stephen's signature, which established the Archabbey of Pannonhalma. Unfortunately, these charters are in the archives and only reproductions are on display. There is also a famous **mosaic** of the Madonna created from naturally bright stones. Though the large library, where students still work, is now wired with electric lights, one of its most interesting features is the natural lighting provided by a series of large windows and mirrors. Most of the aging books remain behind protective grates, but some hand-painted manuscripts and early scientific texts sit open in display cases. You can hear **Gregorian chant** at the Sunday 10am mass and at frequent classical music concerts in the halls of the abbey. Required tours begin with a film on the monastic order at the recently built **TriCollis Tourist Office.** The office also arranges tours of the neighboring **winery,** which explain the process of winemaking and show off modern furnishings, concluding with a tasting in the cellar. For a bite to eat, stop at **Szent Marton Étterem ❸,** opposite the tourist center, for the usual meaty Hungarian dishes (1100-2700Ft) and a few healthier options, as well as local wine and a view of the abbey. *(Take the bus from platform #11; 35min., 1 per hr., 380Ft. Ask the driver if the bus is going to Pannonhalma vár. If so, get off at the huge gates. If not, the uphill walk from Pannonhalma takes 20min. From the bus stop, face the abbey, walk left, and turn right up the main road on the hill just after Borpince. The abbey can be visited only by guided tour. English tours June-Sept. daily 11:20am, 1:20, 3:30pm; Oct.-May Tu-Su 11:20am, 1:20pm. English tour 2400Ft, students 1500Ft. Winery tour including tasting 1600Ft. Tickets at TriCollis Tourist Office, Vár 1. ☎57 01 91; www.bences.hu. Leaving the abbey, take a left and head down the hill; the ticket office is on the right side. MC/V. Restaurant ☎47 07 93. Open daily 11am-5pm. AmEx/MC/V.)*

SOPRON ☎(0)99

At first glance, Sopron (SHO-pron; pop. 54,000) appears to have drifted from its traditions and cultural history. Lined with brand-name boutiques and mouth-watering dessert shops, it exudes efficiency and industry. But the city's alleyways reveal the older town. The winding cobblestone side streets of Inner Town are home to museums, monuments, churches, and 4th-century ruins from the Roman city Scarbantia. Many stop in Sopron en route to Vienna out of mere convenience, only to find themselves entranced by its charm.

TRANSPORTATION AND PRACTICAL INFORMATION. Trains run to: Budapest (3-4hr., 14 per day, 3390Ft); Győr (1½hr., 14 per day, 1350Ft); Szombathely (1¼hr., 14 per day, 1050Ft); Vienna, AUT (1-2hr., 1 per hr., 3800Ft). The bus station, Lackner Kristóf u. 9, sends **buses** to Budapest (4hr., 5 per day, 3010Ft) and Győr (2hr., 1 per hr., 1350Ft). Belváros (Inner Town), the historic center, is a 1km horseshoe bound by three main streets: **Ógabona tér, Várkerület utca,** and **Széchényi tér.** At the end farthest from the train station, museums and notable buildings line **Fő tér.** To get to the center from the train station, veer to the left following Mátyás Király ut., which leads to Széchényi tér and becomes Várkerület u. as it curves around the Inner Town. The bus station is 5min. from the center. Exit the station and turn right on Lackner Kristóf ut.; turn left at Ógabona tér to reach Várkerület near Fő tér and keep walking straight to reach Széchényi tér.

Tourinform is at Liszt Ferenc u. 1, off Széchényi tér. (☎33 88 92. Open M-F 9am-5pm, Sa-Su 9am-3pm.) **OTP,** Várkerület u. 96A, offers good **currency exchange** rates and cashes **traveler's checks.** (24hr. **ATM** outside. Open M 7:45am-6pm, Tu-Th 7:45am-5pm, F 7:45am-4pm.) **Store luggage** at the train station. (150Ft per 6hr. 300Ft per day.) There are five **pharmacies:** Deák tér 35, Magyar út 6, Mátyás király út 23, and 2 on Várkerület u. All lists emergency services; look for Gyógyszertár signs. **Medical services** are at Győri u. 15. (☎31 21 20. Open M-F 9am-5pm.) **Teaház,** Széchényi tér 16 (☎34 07 67), has **Internet** in a cool cafe setting that serves exotic teas for 500Ft. (Internet 450Ft per hr. Open M-F 9am-10pm, Sa-Su 10am-10pm.) The **post office** is at Széchényi tér 7/10, outside Belváros. **Telephones** are inside. (☎31 31 00. Open M-F 8am-7pm, Sa 8am-noon.) **Postal Code:** 9400.

ACCOMMODATIONS AND FOOD. Ciklámen Tourist, Ógabona tér 8, can set you up with a **private room.** (☎31 20 40. Singles from 5500Ft; doubles from 6000Ft. Open M-F 8am-4:30pm, Sa 8am-noon.) **Tourinform** (see **Orientation and Practical Information**) has a list of all the accommodations in the area and can check on room availability. **Bécsi Vendégház ❷,** Bécsi u. 35, offers rooms in a family house with a peaceful garden, just up the street from the bus station. Kitchen and personal TVs. (☎32 07 57; becsivendeghaz@freemail.hu. 24hr. reception. Check-out 10am. Singles 3500Ft; doubles 5500-6000Ft. Cash only.) **Ringhofer Vendégház ❸,** Balfi út 52, has large rooms with clean showers, TVs, and refrigerators, overseen by a wonderfully kind owner. From Széchényi tér, go down Várkerület u. Turn right on Ikva híd u. and right again on Balfi út. (☎32 50 22; ringhofer@freemail.hu. Breakfast 600Ft. Bike rental 1000Ft per day. Reception 24hr. Check-out 10am. Doubles 6000Ft; triples 8000Ft. Tax 330Ft. Cash only.) **ETI Sopron Hallgatói Otthon ❶,** Damjanich u. 9, just two blocks from the bus station, is a standard university dorm that offers cheap beds in an unbeatable location. (☎31 43 39. Open July-Aug. Dorms 2300Ft. Reserve ahead. Cash only.)

Coffeehouses are more common than restaurants on the streets of Sopron, but a walk around the city's main loop reveals a variety of tasty options. The large **Match** supermarket, at Várkerület u. 100/102, has dietary staples. (Open M-F 6:30am-7pm, Sa 6:30am-4pm. MC/V.) **Várkerület Restaurant ❸,** Várkerület u. 83, near Széchenyi tér, diversifies a traditional Hungarian menu with Asian wok items and vegetarian options. (☎31 92 86. Entrees 1200-3100Ft. Open M-Sa 9am-1am, Su 11am-1am. AmEx/MC/V.) Hunting-themed pictures line the walls of the elegant underground restaurant **Graben ❷,** Várkerület u. 8. Located just outside Fő tér, Graben adds even more meats to the Hungarian standards such as stewed stag. (☎34 02 56. Entrees 690-2490Ft. Open daily 8am-10pm. AmEx/MC/V.)

SIGHTS AND ENTERTAINMENT. Most of Sopron's sights are in the Inner City. The **fire tower** *(tuztorony)* was originally built from the remains of a town wall during Roman times and rebuilt after it was destroyed in a 1676 fire. During reconstruction, a balcony was added, from which guards could signal the position of fires with flags during the day and lanterns at night. Climb up the narrow spiral staircase to the balcony for a 360° view of the surrounding hills and the Inner City. (Open Tu-Su Apr. and Sept.-Oct. 10am-6pm; May-Aug. 10am-8pm. 700Ft, students 350Ft.) Originally the site of an ancient Roman bath, the **Fabricius House,** Fő tér 6, boasts a well-organized **archaeological museum,** with artifacts of the area's inhabitants dating from the Bronze Age. Jewelry, urns, pottery, and tombstones are among its holdings. Thorough English captions provide an account of the region's settlements. The underground **Roman Lapidarium** (Római

Kőtár) houses tombs and statues that date from Sopron's origins as the Roman colony of Scarbantia. Don't miss the museum exhibit showcasing regional 18th-century furniture, from inlaid writing tables to antique stoves. English info sheets are provided in each room. (Open Tu-Su 10am-6pm. Archaeological Museum and Lapidarium 700Ft, students 350Ft. Furniture exhibit 700/350Ft.) Built in the 13th century by a herder whose goats stumbled upon a cache of gold, the **Benedictine Church** (Bencés Templom) was the site of coronations for three monarchs. Since 1997, it has been under restoration to become a votive church to thank God for Hungary's liberation from communism. (Open daily 10am-5pm. Mass M-F 8am, Su 9:30am.) Just outside the church, the most prominent sight on Fő tér and one of Europe's first corkscrew column sculptures, is the **Trinity Column,** built to commemorate the Great Plague of 1695-1701. The **Old Synagogue,** Kőzépkori Ó-zsinagőga, Új út 22, is now a museum depicting the daily life of the local Jewish community before it was expelled from Sopron in 1526. Built around 1300, it has a stone Torah ark, women's prayer room, and ritual bath well. An English info sheet is provided. (Open May-Oct. Tu-Su 10am-6pm. 600Ft, students 300Ft.)

Sopron is a good base for outdoor enthusiasts. Bike trails begin just north of the center, leading to **Lake Fertő-Hanság National Park** (a UNESCO World Heritage site), and Fertőd, 30km away (p. 321). Bike maps are free at Tourinform (see **Transportion and Practical Information,** p. 320), which also lists **bike** rental shops (rentals about 2000Ft per day). During the **Sopron Festival Weeks** (late June to mid-July), the town hosts opera, ballet, and concerts. Some are set in the **Fertőrákos Quarry,** 10km away, reachable by hourly buses from the terminal. (Quarry 300Ft, students 150Ft. Concerts 4000-8000Ft.) Fertőrákos also plays host to **watersports** on the lake, such as waterskiing and sailing. Buy tickets for all events from the **Festival Bureau,** Liszt Ferenc u. 1, on Széchényi tér. (☎51 75 17. Open M-F 9am-5pm, Sa 9am-noon.)

Cézár Pince, Hátsókapu 2, is near Fő tér. You may never want to leave this classy bar, converted from a spacious 17th-century home. Sip a drink on the vine-draped patio, served by waitstaff in period garb. (☎31 13 37. Wine 650-1200Ft. Open M-Sa 11am-midnight, Su 1-11pm.) The multi-purpose **Old Boy's Pub,** Gyár u. 1, down the street from the bus station, has a dance floor, pub, and restaurant as well as a summer patio to enjoy drinks. Parties throughout the year and frequent guest DJs. (☎33 33 55; www.oldboyssopron.hu. Beer 250-650Ft. Mojitos 690Ft. Open M 10am-8pm, Tu-F 10am-10pm, Sa 9am-4am, Su 11am-9pm.)

DAYTRIP FROM SOPRON

FERTŐD

Buses leave from platform #11 in Sopron (45min., every 30-60min., 450Ft). Get off at the 3-way intersection in Fertöd. From the bus stop, walk in the direction the bus goes, along the forest, toward the castle. ☎53 76 40. Palace open Mar. 16-Sept. 30 Tu-Su 10am-6pm; Oct. 1-Mar. 15 F-Su 10am-4pm. Tours (1hr.) in summer 2 per hr.; low season variable; last tour 1hr. before closing. Call ahead to request a tour in English, or take an English info sheet along for a Hungarian tour. 1300Ft, students 750Ft. MC/V.

Twenty-seven kilometers east of Sopron, Fertőd (FER-tewd) is home to the pleasant **Esterházy Palace,** Joseph Haydn 2. Step through the wrought-iron gates into manicured gardens that lead to a bright yellow edifice. Prince Miklós Esterházy ordered its construction in 1766, to host his Bacchic feasts and operas. A small exhibit inside recounts the life of **Joseph Haydn,** who lived here for almost 30 years as Eszterházy's composer. **Concerts** of his work are held in the castle's small concert hall, where Haydn himself conducted, during the semi-annual **Haydn Festival,** in mid-July and during the first week of September. (Concerts 7pm. Reserve ahead. 6000-8000Ft.) On weekends throughout the year, less-expensive performances (2500Ft) are held. (Tickets ☎53 76 40. Open daily 10am-6pm.) **Gránátos Étterem ❸**, Joseph Haydn u. 1, just across the street, offers local dishes and desserts. (☎37 09 44. Entrees 990-2190Ft. Open daily 9am-10pm.)

Sarród, right next door to Fertőd, is part of **Fertő-Hanság National Park,** a UNESCO World Heritage site. Lake Fertő, in the park's center, is one of Europe's most diverse water habitats, while the surrounding swampland is home to over 200 species of birds. For preservation purposes, some parts of the park can be visited only with a certified guide, but bike and hiking trails are scattered throughout the park. Pick up a **map** from **Tourinform Fertőd,** Joseph Haydn 3, just behind the palace (☎55 76 20; www.ferto-hansag.hu; open Apr.-June Tu-F 10am-5pm, Sa 10am-4pm), or from **Park Information,** Sarród u. 4 (☎53 76 20). The trails begin 2km from the Palace; follow Sarród u., the street perpendicular to the bus stop. The paved bike path is popular and provides for leisurely adventures. Bike rental info is available at the Park Information office.

SZOMBATHELY ☎(06)94

Beneath the cover of its modern storefronts and Baroque buildings, Szombathely (SOM-baht-hay; pop. 80,000), a major crossroads between Transdanubia and Austria, hides 2000-year-old ruins of Roman Savaria. Its lively cafes and festivals give it a contemporary feel, making it a relaxing stop for travelers crossing the border or for those hoping to hike in the buzzing forests of Őrség National Park.

TRANSPORTATION AND PRACTICAL INFORMATION. The train station is located on Vasut utca. **Trains** (☎31 14 20; www.elvira.hu) run to: Budapest (3¾hr., 12 per day, 3535Ft; InterCity 2¾hr., 4935Ft); Győr (2hr., 19 per day, 1725Ft; InterCity 1¼hr., 10 per day, 2675); Keszthely (2½hr., 3 per day, 2040Ft) and Vienna, AUT (4hr., 17 per day, price varies). **Buses** (☎31 20 54; www.volanbusz.hu.) run to: Budapest (3½hr., 6 per day, 3230Ft); Győr (2½hr., 8 per day, 2040Ft); Keszthely (2½hr., 6 per day, 1350Ft); Sopron (2hr., 5 per day, 1200Ft).

Szombathely is formed from several interconnected squares, the largest of which is Fő tér, home to the main tourist offices. From the train station, turn left and then right on Széll Kálmán út. Continue to Mártírok tere. Turn left on Király **utca,** which ends in **Savaria tér.** The **bus station** sits on the opposite side of the center; turn left on the street with the gas station, parallel to the station and follow it into town (5min.). Cross Kiskar utca and then head straight to the pedestrian Belsikátor, which ends in Fő tér.

Tourinform, Kossuth Lajos u., on the edge of Fő tér, has a helpful staff, who offer **free maps** and book rooms. (☎51 44 51. Open M-F 9am-5pm.) **Savaria Tourist** provides info, books rooms, and gives out free **maps** at two locations: Király u. 1 (☎50 94 85), Mártírok tere 1 (☎51 14 35). All locations **exchange currency.** (Open M-F 8:30am-4:30pm, Sa 8am-noon.) **OTP Bank,** Fő tér 4, exchanges currency and has a MasterCard and Visa **ATM** outside. (Open M 7:45am-6pm, Tu-Th 7:45am-5pm, F 7:45am-4pm.) For **medical services,** go to **Markusovszky Hospital,** Markusovszky u. 3 (☎31 15 42). **Free Wi-Fi** anywhere in Fő tér. There is also **Internet** at **Szombathelyi Siker Könyvtár,** Ady tér 40, behind the bus station. (80Ft per 30min. Open M-F 9am-5pm.) The **post office,** Kossuth Lajos u. 18, has **Poste Restante.** (☎31 15 84. Open M-F 8am-6pm, Sa 8am-noon.) **Postal Code:** 9700.

ACCOMMODATIONS AND FOOD. To book a **private room,** visit **IBUSZ,** Fő tér 44. (☎314 141; i090@ibusz.hu. Open M-F 8am-5pm, Sa 9am-1pm. Singles from 5000Ft; doubles from 5200Ft.) **Berzsenyi Dániel Főiskola Pável Ágoston Kollégiuma ❶,** Ady tér 3/A, has clean dorms with antiquated decor in two buildings near the bus station. (☎31 35 91. Check-out 9am. Dorms 1500Ft.) **Hotel Liget ❸,** Szent István park 15, accessible by bus 2c or 2a from the train station, offers

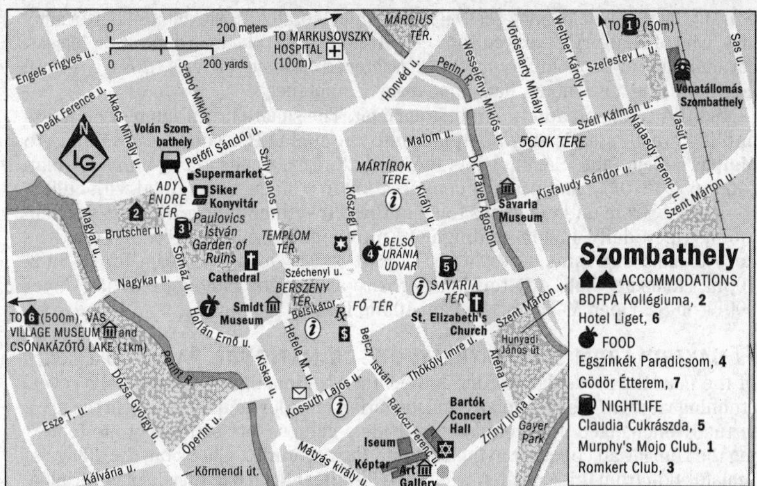

pleasant rooms in St. Stephen's Park, within easy reach of the city center and the Vas County Museum Village (see below). From the bus station, follow the directions for Vas Village but head to the left side of the park. (☎509 323; www.hotels.hu/liget_szombathely. Reception 24hr. Singles 8000Ft; doubles 9000-10,000Ft; triples 12,000-15,000Ft. MC/V.) Most restaurants line Fő tér's pedestrian walkway. **Match** supermarkets are at Fő tér 17 (open M-F 7am-7:30pm, Sa 7am-4pm; MC/V) and behind the bus station (open M-F 6am-7pm, Sa 7am-3pm; MC/V). **Égszínkék Paradicsom ❷** (Sky-blue Paradise), Fő tér 24 in the Belső Uránia udvar, serves heavenly pasta (870-1360Ft) by candlelight in its mural-covered dining room. Walk through the archway at Kőszegi u. 2, off Fő tér. (☎34 20 12. Open daily 11am-11pm.) **Gödör Étterem ❸,** Hollán Ernő 10/12, dishes up Hungarian specialties in a brick cellar. (☎510 078. Entrees 760-2690Ft. Open M-Th 11am-11pm, F-Sa 11am-midnight, Su 11am-3pm.)

SIGHTS AND ENTERTAINMENT. The outdoor **Vas County Museum Village** (Vasi Múzeum Falu) displays authentic 200-year-old farmhouses relocated from villages throughout the region, along with collections of pottery, kitchenware, and farming tools. From Ady tér, walk 10min. down Nagykar u., which becomes Gagarin u., cross Bartók Béla, the main street, then go up Árpád u. to the end. (☎31 10 04. Open Apr.-Nov. Tu-Su 9am-5pm. 600Ft, students 350Ft. English brochure 100Ft.) Szombathely is the proud site of Hungary's third-largest **cathedral,** built in 1797 in Baroque and Neoclassical styles. Red marble columns support a domed ceiling and gold-trimmed archways. The chapel to the right is the only portion of the original building that stands today. To the right of the cathedral, the **Paulovics István Garden of Ruins** (Paulovics Romkert), Templom tér 1, was once the center of the Roman colony of Savaria and now contains traces of 4th-century ruins. From Fő tér, go left on Széchényi út, right on Szily János út, and straight to Templom tér. (☎31 33 69. Open Mar.-Dec. 15 Tu-Su 9am-5pm. 460Ft, students 250Ft. English brochure 20Ft.) In the evening, laze on the banks of the beautiful lake Csonakázó-tó, or rent a boat and paddle on its waters (750-1600Ft per hr.). The **Savaria Historical Carnival,** held in Fő tér at the end of August, brings the city's medieval history to life with historical reenactments and an open-air market. The **Bartók Seminar and Festival,** in the middle of July, attracts musicians and music-lovers from around the world. The two-week **Spring Festival** in March celebrates music and the performing arts. One of Hungary's most curious celebrations takes place on June 16th: **Bloomsday,** in honor of Leopold Bloom, the character from James Joyce's *Ulysses*, whose ancestors, the novel notes, had come from Szombathely.

Nightlife in Szombathely centers on **Fő tér.** The square hosts summer concerts and ice cream stands stay open late into the night. The younger set flocks to **Murphy's Mojo Club,** Semmelweis Ignác út 28. Enjoy beer (210-740Ft), Serbian food (650-1370Ft), and friendly conversation in a dining room filled with collector's items, from antique lamps to an entire old automobile. (☎31 58 91. English menu. Open daily 4:30pm-midnight.) Enjoy a gooey pastry (160-480Ft) at the cozy **Claudia Cukrászda,** Savaria tér 1. (☎31 33 75. Open M-Sa 9am-10pm, Su 2-10pm.) **Romkert Club,** Ady tér, is a favorite among the dancing crowd. (Cover 900Ft on Sa. Open M-Th and Su 9am-10pm, F-Sa 11am-2am.)

DAYTRIP FROM SZOMBATHELY: ŐRSÉG NATIONAL PARK. Just south of the near the Slovenian border is the Őrség National Park. Hiking trails reveal stunning views of the Slovenian and Hungarian hillsides, and the towns in the area, virtually unchanged over centuries, provide a glimpse into settlement life following the Hungarian conquest in the 10th and 11th centuries. Check out the village of **Szalafő,** 4km from **Őriszentpéter,** where the **Pityerszer Rural Museum** displays original pastoral huts with thick hay roofs.(Open Apr-Oct. Tu-Su 10am-6pm. 400Ft, students 200Ft.) **Magyarszombatfa,** 7km south of Őriszentpéter, is known for its ceramics. In nearby **Pankasz,** check out the famous wooden belfry, and the wooden headstones in the cemetery. Local buses run among the towns; check schedules posted on the bus stops. The park, popular for its variety of plants and animals, is home to 500 species of **butterflies**—more than anywhere else in Hungary—and **rare birds** like the **black stork** and honey buzzard. For help locating wildlife, pick up an English guide from the park information building. If you have time, visit the **Árpádkori Műemlék Templom,** the small, 12th-century church 500m from the park info building. Guarded by the statue of King Stephen I, Hungary's first Christian king, it was a fortress during Turkish invasions. (Mass Su 8:30am.)

Buy camping supplies in the building labeled **Iparcikkek,** in the center of Őriszentpéter. (☎54 80 15. Open M-F 7:30am-noon and 1-4:30pm, Sa 7:30am-noon.) **Keserűszer Camping ❶,** 2km to the right on the road in front of the Park Information Office, is a convenient base for trail wandering. Contact the park Tourinform to reserve spaces at 840Ft per person. The entrance is on Őriszentpéter. Take the bus from Ady tér in Szombathely, (1½-2hr., 8 per day, 525Ft) and turn right out of the bus station. From the center, take a right on Városszer u. and walk 1km to the park information building. Here you'll find maps (680Ft) as well as hiking and camping advice. (Open M-Th 8am-noon and 1-4:30pm, F 8am-2pm, Sa 10am-5pm. Before leaving Szombathely, ask at Tourinform for the free "Camping in Hungary" map.) A **Coop** supermarket, also in the center, provides sustenance for the hike. (Open M-F 6am-5pm, Sa 6am-1pm, Su 7-11am.) Before heading into the hills, fill up on fried Hungarian food at **Centrum Étterem ❷,** located right across from the bus station. (Entrees 450-1200Ft. Open M-F 6am-10pm, Sa-Su 7am-10pm.)

KŐSZEG ☎(06)94

The town at the foot of the Kőszeg mountains is quiet, with more bikes than cars traversing the roads. Neverthless, Kőszeg charms visitors with beautiful churches, historical monuments, and country cottages. Just a mile from the Austrian border, the town was a defense against Austria's repeated attempts at expansion and became famous when it stopped the Turks in 1536 and deflected their march on Vienna. The castle, which withstood the siege, serves as a reminder of this unlikely victory, all the while offering lovely views of the Austrian countryside.

TRANSPORTATION AND PRACTICAL INFORMATION. The train station, krt 2 (☎36 00 53), is 1km south of town. Trains run to: Szombathely (30min., 15 per day, 300Ft). Várkör u. encircles the center of town. The two main squares, **Fő tér** and **Jurisics tér,** lie on the southern end, while the **castle** *(vár)* sits in the northern end. The bus station, Liszt Ferenc 16 (☎36 01 80), is a block from the town center. **Buses** run to Szombathely (30min., 8-10 per day, 190Ft) and Sopron (1¼hr., 10 per day, 1050Ft).

To get to the center from the bus station, go right out of the station onto **Kossuth Lajos utca,** which leads to Fő tér. From the train station, follow **Rákóczi Ferenc utca** to get to Fő tér.

Tourinform, Rajnis u. 7, just past the Town Hall through Hero's Gate, has **free maps** and helps find accommodations. (☎56 31 21. Open in summer M-F 8am-4pm, Sa 9am-1pm; in winter M-F 8am-4pm.) The **OTP bank,** Kossuth L. u. 8, has an **ATM** and a **currency exchange** machine. (Open M 7:45am-5pm, Tu-Th 7:45am-3pm, F 7:45am-12:30pm.) A **pharmacy** is at Kossuth L. u. 12. (☎56 30 78. Open M-F 8am-6pm, Sa 8am-2pm.) The **post office** is at Várkör u. 65. (☎36 00 94. Open M-F 8am-4pm, Sa 8am-11am.) **Postal Code:** 9732.

ACCOMMODATIONS AND FOOD. **Savaria Tourist,** Várkör u. 69, arranges **private rooms.** (☎56 30 48; tourist.koszeg@vivadsl.hu. Open M-F 8am-4pm, Sa 8am-noon. Singles from 4000Ft; doubles from 6000Ft.) Most restaurants in town have guest rooms upstairs, although the cheaper rooms generally lie off Várkör u. **Kóbor Macska Pension ❸,** Várkör u. 100, offers clean rooms with views of the belltower of St. Imre Church. (☎36 22 73; www.hotels.hu/kobor. Breakfast 600Ft, free with singles. Internet 150Ft per 30min. Reception 24hr. Singles 5500Ft; doubles 6300Ft; triples 8300Ft.) In the heart of town, **Hotel Arany Strucc ❸,** Várkör u. 124, provides luxurious, well-furnished rooms. For noise-sensitive travelers, it is worth noting that the bells of the nearby Church of Jesus's Heart toll every quarter-hour. (☎36 03 23; www.aranystucc.hu. Breakfast included. Reception 24hr. Singles 6000Ft; doubles 9100-10,100Ft; triples 12,300Ft.). Set up camp at **Gyöngyvirág Camping ❶,** Bajcsy-Zsilinszky u. 6, on the shore of peaceful Gyöngyös River. (☎36 04 54. Breakfast 700Ft. 750Ft per person, 500Ft per tent, 400Ft per car. 300Ft tax. Cash only.)

Pick up groceries at **Match** supermarket, Várkör u. 20 (Open M-F 6am-7pm, Sa 6am-4pm. MC/V.) **Pizzéria da Rocco ❷,** Várkör u. 55, bakes delicious pizzas in its wood oven. The castle is within view of the patio. If you prefer to eat indoors, relaxing jazz plays under the arched roof of the dining room. (☎36 37 45. Salads 550-850Ft. Pizza 450-1450Ft. Open M-Sa noon-midnight, Su noon-10pm. Cash only.) Revert to the Middle Ages in the time-warped ambience of **Bécsikapu Étterem ❸,** Rajnis u. 5, which serves game dishes fit for a king. (☎56 31 22. Entrees 890-2750Ft. Open daily 11am-10pm. Cash only.) The modern **Portré Restaurant ❷,** Fő tér 7, serves a variety of dishes and has vegetarian options. (☎46 57 22. Coffee 300-620Ft. Entrees 890-1790Ft. Open M-Sa 8am-10pm, Su 10am-8pm. Cash only.)

SIGHTS. The most imposing of Kőszeg's sights is **Jurisics Castle** *(Vár)*, constructed in Gothic style during the late 13th century. It was at this castle that 4000 people fought against the ultimately doomed Turkish siege of 1532. The last Turkish contingent left the outskirts of town at 11am on Aug. 30, 1532. The town church bells have since tolled daily at 11am as a reminder of that remarkable victory. The castle, now open to visitors, houses the **Jurisich Miklós Museum,** in memory of the man who led the Hungarian forces. The museum displays artifacts from the blockade and other historical documents important to the town, but the most interesting part is the long hallway connecting the rooms, where you'll find paintings of the town during various stages of its history. The views from the **belltower,** just beside the museum, offer a glimpse of the city and nearby hills. (☎36 02 40. Castle open Tu-Su 10am-5pm. 130Ft, students 90Ft. Museum 500/250 Ft.)

The 1894 **Church of Jesus's Heart** (Jézus Szíve Plébánia templom) dominates Fő tér. The colorfully patterned walls and columns complement the intricate stained-glass windows behind the altar. (Open daily 9am-6pm. Mass Su 10am. Free.) Branching off Fő tér, Városház u. leads onto Jurisics tér, which is ringed by monuments. To enter the square, you'll pass under **Heroes' Gate** (Hősi kapu), built on the 400th anniversary of the Turkish blockade. A highlight of Jurisics tér is the patriotically striped **Town Hall** *(Városház)*, Jurisics tér 8, which has served the town since the 15th century. The **Pharmacy Museum** *(Apotéka)*, Jurisics tér 11, in an elegant, 18th-century pharmacy, houses instruments and medicine from old pharmacies in the region. Check out the special collection of medicinal herbs on the second floor. (☎36 03 37. English info. Open Tu-Su 10am-5pm. 400Ft, with ISIC 250Ft.) The highlight of **St. James Church** (Szent Jakab templom), in the center of the square, is the beautiful Gothic wooden Madonna sculpture near the altar. (Open daily 9am-6pm. Free.) The more modest **St. Henry's Church** next door has an equally dramatic Gothic altar. (Open daily 9am-6pm. Free.) The **synagogue ruins** stand on the corner of Várkör u. and Gyöngyös u. Though you can't go past the gates, the Hebrew inscription over the main entrance is worth a look.

ENTERTAINMENT AND NIGHTLIFE. Kőszeg's serenity extends into the night. The scenic **Chernel Kert** (Chernel Park) offers shaded walks at the base of the tree-covered Kőszeg mountains. You can also begin hikes from here—pick up maps and info at **Tourinform** (see p. 325). To get to the park, follow Várkör u. past Fő tér, keeping the Church of Jesus's Heart to your left. Go left on Hunyadi u. and continue to the end of the road. For something more upbeat, join the locals at **Ciao Amico,** Rákoczi Ferenc u. 13, where you can enjoy pizza (520-1150Ft) and beer (210-320Ft) at the bar or try your luck in the adjoining casino and arcade. (☎34 99 52. Bar, arcade, and casino open 24hr. Pizzeria open daily 11am-11pm.) In mid-June, the town's biggest festival, the **Ost-West Fesztival,** features open-air performances of folk music and dance in the town's main squares and the castle courtyard. For exact dates and tickets (2000Ft, students 1500Ft), contact Tourinform.

SOUTHERN TRANSDANUBIA

Framed by the Danube to the west, the Dráva to the south, and Lake Balaton to the north, southern Transdanubia is known for its mild climate, rolling hills, and sunflower fields. Once the southernmost portion of Roman Pannonia, the region is filled with historical memorials and palaces, weathered castles, and ancient burial grounds. The people of southern Transdanubia are as diverse as the sights: the Bosnians, Croats, Germans, and Serbs who call the region home have influenced the cuisine and culture west of the Danube.

PÉCS ☎(06)72

Pécs (PAYCH; pop. 180,000), a vibrant city with a small-town feel, is the most popular destination in southern Hungary, as weekend busloads of tourists attest. Nestled at the base of the Mecsek Mountains, Pécs enjoys a warm climate and captivating architecture. Its monuments reveal a 2000-year-old legacy of Roman, Ottoman, and Habsburg occupation. The famous Zsolnay porcelain, produced in a factory just outside the city, adorns many of its buildings. Evenings bring out a more exuberant side of Pécs, as students pack local bars and clubs.

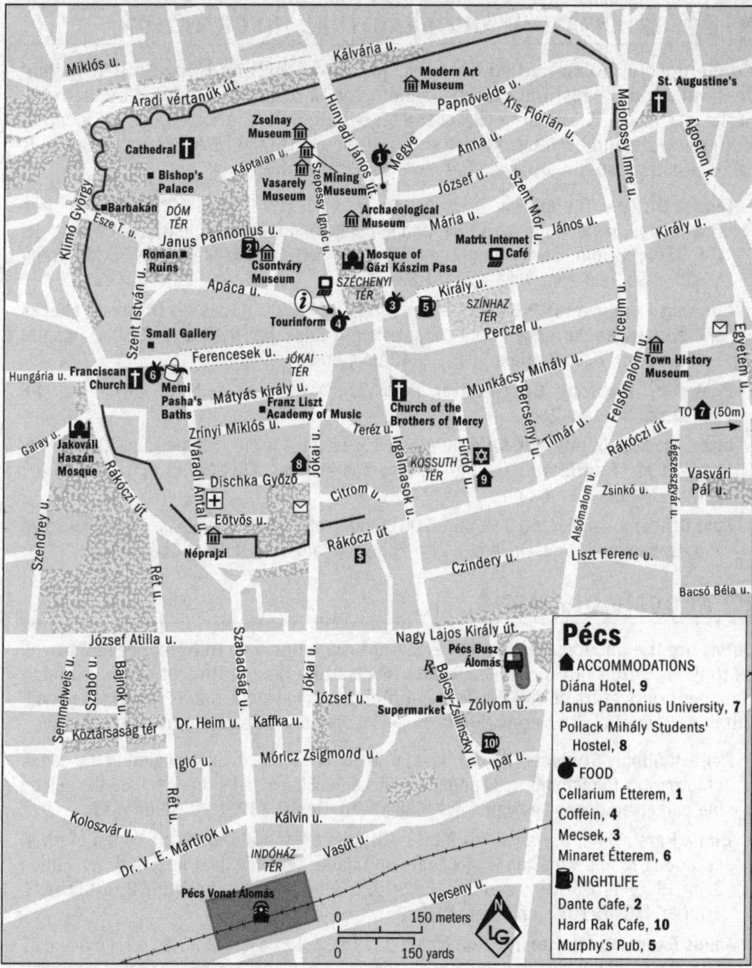

TRANSPORTATION

Trains: Take bus #30, 32, or 33 from the center or walk 15min. from Széchényi tér down Jókai u. To: **Budapest** (4½hr., 16 per day, 2220Ft). 4 trains leave daily for the **Lake Balaton** towns; get tickets at the MÁV office in the station (☎21 50 03 or ☎21 27 34; www.elvira.hu; open daily 5:30am-6:30pm) or at Jókai u. 4 (open M and F 9am-3:30pm, Tu-Th 9am-4:30pm).

Buses: ☎215 215; www.agria.hu. To **Budapest** (4½hr., 5 per day, 2450Ft), **Keszthely** (4hr., 6 per day, 2100Ft), and **Szeged** (4½hr., 7 per day, 2520Ft).

Public Transportation: Bus tickets cost 260Ft at kiosks and 270Ft on board.

Taxis: Volán and **Euro** are the reputable companies. Don't take other cabs, as they may scam you. Base 300Ft, 200Ft per km.

ORIENTATION AND PRACTICAL INFORMATION

Conveniently, north and south correspond to uphill and downhill. Tourists descend upon the historic **Belváros** (Inner City), a rectangle bounded by the ruins of the city walls. The center is **Széchényi tér,** where most tourist offices are located. Both the train and bus stations are south of the center, within walking distance. It takes less than 20min. to cross Belváros going downhill.

Tourist Offices: Tourinform, Széchényi tér 9 (☎51 12 32; fax 213 315), offers free small **maps,** large maps for 520Ft, phone cards, and stamps. Open June 16-Sept. 15 M-F 8am-5:30pm, Sa-Su 9am-2pm; Sept. 15-Oct. 16 and May-June 15 M-F 8am-5:30pm, Sa 9am-2pm; Nov.-Apr. M-F 8am-4pm.

Currency Exchange: OTP Bank, Rákóczi út 44 (☎50 29 00). Cashes **traveler's checks** and **exchanges currency** for no commission. A 24hr. MC/V **ATM** is outside. Open M 7:45am-6pm, Tu-Th 7:45am-5pm, F 7:45am-4pm.

Pharmacy: Mozsonyi Gyógyszertár, Bajcsy-Zsilinszky u. 6 (☎31 56 04). Open M-F 7am-7pm, Sa 7am-2pm.

Internet: Matrix Internet Café, Király u. 15. (☎21 44 87). 5Ft per min. Open daily 9am-11pm. **Tourinform** (see above) also has Internet. 25Ft for up to 15min. 100Ft per hr. Open M-F 9am-5pm.

Post Office: Jókai Mór u. 10 (☎50 60 00). 2nd fl. office has so many services there's an info desk to guide you. Open M-F 7am-7pm, Sa 8am-noon. **Postal Code:** 7621.

ACCOMMODATIONS

Dorms are the cheapest option in Pécs, but bring your own toilet paper and towel, as they are often not included. **Private rooms** are a decent budget option, though they generally start at 4000Ft. Pécs's efficient bus system makes cheaper rooms outside town almost as convenient. Reserve ahead in summer and on weekends.

Pollack Mihály Students' Hostel, Jókai u. 8 (☎315 846). Ideally located in the center of town, this former university dorm has kitchen facilities and a lounge. Ring the bell on the unmarked door when you arrive. Call ahead. Dorms 2300Ft. Cash only. ❶

Diána Hotel, Timár u. 4a (☎/fax 33 33 73), just off Kossuth tér in the center of town. Luxurious rooms with hardwood floors and cable TV. Breakfast included. Reception 24hr. Singles 9500Ft; doubles 13,500Ft; 4-person apartments 22,000Ft. A/C 1000Ft. MC/V; 10% surcharge. ❹

Janus Pannonius University, Universitas u. 2 (☎31 14 01 or 23 37 81). Take bus #21 from the main bus terminal to 48-as tér, or walk up the hill to Rákóczi út and turn right. The dorm is to the right, on the street behind McDonald's. Private baths. Reception 24hr. Check-out 9am. Call ahead. Open July-Sept. 3-bed dorms 1800Ft. Cash only. ❶

FOOD

Because of the town's steep incline, many of its restaurants, cafes, and bars lie underground in cellars. These vaults are attractions in themselves; most serve Hungarian dishes with an array of wines. Reservations are necessary at more popular restaurants on weekend nights, but a walk down **Király utca, Apáca utca,** or **Ferencesek utca** yields a variety of tasty options. **Interspar,** Bajcsy-Zsilinszky u. 11, downstairs inside Árkád Shopping Mall, has a wide variety of food, a salad bar, a deli, and a bakery. (Open M-Th and Sa 7am-9pm, F 7am-10pm, Su 8am-7pm.)

Minaret Étterem, Ferencesek u. 35 (☎31 13 38; www.minaretetterem.hu). This casual restaurant dishes out classic Hungarian recipes (gypsy roast; 1700Ft) in a lush, walled courtyard full of trees. The chiming of the bells from the Franciscan Church, which looms overhead, accompanies your meal, as well as live gypsy music on Friday and Saturday nights. Open daily noon-midnight. Cash only. ❹

Coffein, (☎20 52 24 40), Széchényi tér next to TourInform. The multi-level deck patio in front of this small cafe provides a great people-watching post. Enjoy the music playing in the background and a unique Italian-Hungarian sandwich. Entrees 690Ft-1590Ft. Speciality teas and coffees from 280Ft. Open daily 10am-midnight. Cash only. ❸

Mecsek, Hunyadi u. 20 (☎31 54 44), corner of Hunyadi and Király. Boasts an ample supply of cakes and pastries (159Ft-269Ft) and ice cream (130Ft). Stand at marble counters and enjoy a Hungarian chocolate cream cake, topped with caramel (279Ft). Open daily 9am-10pm. Cash only. ❶

Cellarium Étterem, Hunyadi u. 2 (☎314 453). Buried in a cellar at the bottom of a long stairway, this prison-themed restaurant will let you live out your fantasy of eating Hungarian fare while being served by waiters in inmate costumes. The menu promises that the house champagne is "equal with a good foreplay on a table (instead of a bed)." Entrees 950-4000Ft. Live Hungarian music on weekends. AmEx/MC/V. ❸

SIGHTS

ROMAN RUINS. Once a mass burial site for Roman Pécs (Sopianae), the fourth-century Christian mausoleum near the cathedral is the largest excavated burial ground in Hungary. Over 100 corpses have been uncovered from the area, and a chilling crypt with well-preserved Roman Christian paintings sits underneath the ruins. *(Across Janus Pannonius u. from the cathedral. Open Apr.-Oct. Tu-Su 10am-6pm; Nov.-Mar. 10am-4pm. 350Ft, students 200Ft. Photos 500Ft. See the first layer of ruins for free as you stand on glass flooring, left of the Cathedral.)*

MOSQUE OF GHAZI KASSIM PASHA (GÁZI KHASIM PASA DZSÁMIJA). Nicknamed the "Mosque Church," this green-domed building is a former Turkish mosque. Today, it serves as a Christian church, though it still retains some Turkish flavor. Verses from the Koran decorate the walls, and an ablution basin, where the faithful washed their feet before entering the mosque, now serves as a baptismal font. The largest Ottoman structure still standing in Hungary, the church intertwines Christian and Muslim traditions. *(Széchényi tér. ☎32 19 76. Open mid-Apr. to mid-Oct. M-Sa 10am-4pm, Su 12:30-4pm; mid-Oct. to mid-Apr. M-Sa 10am-noon. Mass Su 9:30, 10:30, and 11:30am. Admission free, but donations requested.)*

CATHEDRAL. Perched atop the Pécs hilltop, the fourth-century neo-Romanesque Cathedral and adjoining Bishop's Palace make the hill a perfect respite from the bustling city. Inside the cathedral, a small museum displays medieval stone carvings and intricate wall paintings, while the crypt that once housed the tomb of the first Bishop of Pécs is now a venue for music festivals. *(On Dóm tér. From Széchényi tér, walk left on Janus Pannonius u., take the 1st right, then go left on Káptalan to Dóm tér. ☎51 30 30. Cathedral open M-F 9am-5pm, Sa 9am-2pm, Su 1-5pm. Mass M-Sa 6pm; Su 8, 9:30, 11am and 6pm. 800Ft, students 400Ft.)*

SYNAGOGUE. The stunning 1869 synagogue has a painted ceiling and shelters an incredible replica of the Ark of the Covenant. Because the city's Jewish population now numbers a mere 140, however, services are no longer held here. The English pamphlet has detailed information on Jewish traditions and the devastating effect of WWII on the local Jewish community. *(On Kossuth tér. Walk downhill from Széchényi tér on Irgalmasok u. Open May-Sept. 10am-5pm. 350Ft, students 250Ft.)*

MUSEUMS

VASARELY MUSEUM. One of Hungary's most important 20th-century artists, Pécs native Viktor Vasarely (1908-97) is best known as the pioneer of Op-Art and geometric abstraction. The house in which he was born has been converted to a museum and now displays some of his most important paintings and sculptures, along with works by his contemporaries, among them Hans Arp, Frantisek Kupka, and François Morellet. *(Káptalan u. 5, across from Zsolnay. ☎32 48 22, ext. 21; www.vpm.hu. Open Apr.-Oct. Tu-Sa 10am-6pm, Su 10am-4pm. 600Ft, students 350Ft.)*

ZSOLNAY MUSEUM. A family workshop has handcrafted the famously colorful and intricate Zsolnay porcelain since the 1800s. The porcelain adorns many central Pécs buildings: the Zsolnay Well, Széchényi tér 1, sports a rare Eosin glaze; the windows of County Hall, Jókai u. 10, are framed by detailed tiles; and Pécs National Theater, Színáz tér, houses Zsolnay sculptures and reliefs. The museum itself showcases the Zsolnay's many wares, from delicate porcelain birdcages to iridescent glazed vases. *(Káptalan u. 4. Walk up Szepessy I. u. behind the Mosque Church and go left at Káptalan u. ☎32 48 22. Open Tu-Sa 10am-6pm, Su 10am-6pm. 750Ft, students with ISIC 450Ft. Photos 300Ft.)*

CSONTVÁRY MUSEUM. This museum displays the works of Tivadar Csontváry Kosztka (1853-1919), a local painter who won international acclaim. His mastery of luminous expressionism earned him the nickname "the Hungarian Van Gogh." The exhibit highlights Csontváry's interest in nature. *(Janus Pannonius u. 11. ☎31 05 44. Open Tu-Su 10am-6pm. 700Ft, students 400Ft.)*

MINING MUSEUM. The largest underground exhibit in Hungary, this labyrinth shares a courtyard with the Vasarely Museum. The museum (Mecseki Bányászati Múzeum) was designed to show what mines were really like, and explains—in Hungarian—the coal mining process that once drove Pécs's economy. The tunnels are a refreshing refuge from the summer heat. *(Káptalan u. 3. ☎32 48 22. www.kbm.hu. Open Tu-Su Apr.-Oct. 10am-6pm; Nov.-Mar. 10am-4pm. 500Ft, students 300Ft.)*

FESTIVALS AND NIGHTLIFE

The activities that fill the main square in summer range from theater performances to markets of handmade goods. September is the height of festival season in Pécs. Choir music mingles with wine at the mirthful **Festival of Wine Songs** late in the month. For info, contact Pécsi Férfikar Alapitvány (☎21 16 06). Other festivals include the **Gastronomic Pleasures of the Pécs Region,** the **Pécs City Festival,** and the **Mediterranean Autumn Festival.** Pécs offers lively **nightlife** that ranges from mellow coffee shops to raging clubs. Hit the crowded, colorful bars near **Széchényi tér,** especially on the first two blocks of Király u. Clubs are located close to the train station and pack in a vivacious crowd.

Dante Cafe, Janus Pannonius u. 11 (☎21 03 61; www.cafedante.hu), in the Csontváry Museum building and the courtyard behind it. Originally founded to finance the Pécs literary magazine Szép Literaturari Ajándék, Dante now packs in artists and local youth. Live jazz on summer weekends plays in the courtyard; a basement jazz club, **Alcafé,** opens in winter. Beer 340-450Ft. Open daily 10am-1am, later on weekends.

Hard Rak Cafe, Ipar u. 7 (☎50 25 57), 10min. from the main town. Turn left at the corner of Bajcsy-Zsilinszky u. The name refers to the music and the walls built from boulders, not the American restaurant chain. Local teens swarm the entrance of this cavernous club, which boasts a solid drink lineup (shots from 450Ft) and live musical acts. Live rock in summer F-Sa nights. Cover Th-Sa 800Ft. Open M-Sa 7pm-6am.

Murphy's Bar and Pub, Király u. 2 (☎579 7759). Serves light meals and snacks and a wide selection of alcoholic beverages on a patio in the center of the action. Jazz and rock music plays in the background, making this place a popular nightspot for locals and tourists. Try the fruit soup (550Ft). Beer 270Ft. Open 11am-midnight. Cash only.

DAYTRIPS FROM PÉCS: SZIGETVÁR

Buses run from Pécs (45min., 26 per day, 264Ft). The bus station is close to the town center. With the station behind you, follow the main road as it ears left toward the center. To reach the castle, turn left on József Attila u. at Kossuth tér and follow it until it opens into another square. Turn right on Vár u. and follow it to the castle entrance.

The castle in the quiet town of **Szigetvár** (see-GHET-vahr) is a major landmark and point of Hungarian pride. In 1566, **Zrinyí-Vár** marked the site of a Turkish siege in which Hungarian troops fended off the sultan's invasion for a month before finally sacrificing their lives as they stormed out of the fortress into battle. Today Szigetvár makes a pleasant daytrip from Pécs; it is easy to fill a day strolling within the castle walls. (Open Tu-Su 9am-5pm. 400Ft, students 250Ft.) More a fortress than a castle, it offers ample space for exploration. The centerpiece of the castle is the **Vár-Múzeum,** which incorporates part of the old foundations.

Pick up supplies for a scenic picnic inside the castle walls at **ABC Coop,** at the end of VárVárda u., off József Attila u. on the way to the castle. (Open M-F 6am-6pm, Sa 6am-noon, Su 7-11am.) For lunch, consider checking out the **open-air market,** to the left of the bus station, that has fresh fruits, veggies, and breads, as well as several varieties of fried foods. (Open M-Sa 6am-4pm, Su 6am-11am.)

THE GREAT PLAIN (NAGYALFÖLD)

Romanticized in tales of cowboys and bandits, the grasslands of Nagyalföld stretch southeast of Budapest, covering almost half of Hungary. This diverse region is home to arid Debrecen, fertile Szeged, and the vineyards of Kecskemét, which rise out of the flat soil like Nagyalföld's legendary mirages.

DEBRECEN ☎(06)52

Protected by the mythical phoenix and dubbed the festival capital of Hungary, Debrecen (DEH-bre-tsen; pop. 210,000) has miraculously survived over 30 devastating fires. Recent reconstructions have bestowed wide boulevards and lush parks upon the city; the largest, Nagyerdei Park, is called the "Great Forest." The ultra-modern city, one of Hungary's largest, is a center of education, religious and otherwise: Debrecen is the historical center of Hungarian Protestantism and is famed for its Reformed College, one of the country's oldest and largest universities. The student population fills the streets by day and takes to the pubs by night.

TRANSPORTATION

Trains: Petőfi tér. ☎31 67 77. To: **Budapest** (2½-3hr., 8-13 per day, 2192-2226Ft); **Eger** (3hr., 6 per day, 1142Ft) via **Füzesabony; Miskolc** (2½-3hr., 5 per day, 1338Ft); **Szeged** (3½hr., 7 per day, 2536Ft) via **Cegléd**. Visit www.elvira.hu for train schedules.

Buses: ☎41 39 99. At the intersection of Nyugati u. and Széchényi u. To: **Eger** (2½-3hr., 4 per day, 1690Ft); **Kecskemét** (5½hr., 1 per day, 2910Ft); **Miskolc** (2hr., 1-2 per hr.,

1210Ft); **Szeged** (4-5½hr., 4 per day, 2910Ft); **Tokaj** (2hr., 2 per day, 1090Ft). Check out www.menetrendek.hu for bus schedules.

Public Transportation: The best way to get around Debrecen: **Tram #1** runs from the train station through Kálvin tér, loops around the park past the university, and returns to Kálvin tér. Get off at Városháza for tourist offices and other necessities. Ticket checks are frequent and fines are severe (2000-5000Ft); buy tickets (160Ft) or day passes (550Ft) from the newspaper shop inside the train station, or tickets from the driver (240Ft). Prices change frequently. Once on board, validate your ticket in a red puncher.

Taxis: City Taxi (☎55 55 55). **Főnix Taxi** (☎44 44 44).

ORIENTATION AND PRACTICAL INFORMATION

Debrecen is a big city, but it has a small and easily navigable center 15min. from the train station. With your back to the station, head down **Petőfi tér,** which becomes **Piac utca,** a main street perpendicular to the station. Piac u. leads to **Kálvin tér** and runs parallel to it, where the huge, yellow **Nagytemplom** (Great Church) presides over the center. After Kálvin tér turns towards the university, Piac u. becomes Péterfia u., which runs north to **Nagyerdei Park** and **Kossuth Lajos University** (KLTE). Trams and buses run from the train station through Kálvin tér. to Nagyerdi Park; the info desk in the station lists schedules and prices. The bus station is 10min. from the center. From the station, go right on **Széchényi,** then left on Piac u., which opens onto Kálvin tér.

Tourist Office: Tourinform, Piac u. 20 (☎41 22 50; tourinform@ph.debrecen.hu), above Széchényi u., under the cream-colored building on the right side of Kálvin tér just after Kossuth u. Free **maps** and info on hostels, food, and daytrips. Open mid-June to mid-Sept. M-F 8am-8pm, Sa-Su 10am-6pm; mid.Sept to mid-June M-F 9am-5pm.

Currency Exchange: Several **Banks** line Piac u. **OTP,** Piac u. 16 (☎52 26 10), **exchanges currency,** gives MC **cash advances,** accepts most **traveler's checks,** and has a 24hr. MC/V **ATM.** Open M 7:45am-5pm, Tu-F 7:45am-4pm.

Luggage Storage: Available at the train station. 120Ft per 6hr., large bags 240Ft; 240/480Ft per day. After 10pm, luggage can be stored at the info desk, counter #9.

Pharmacy: Nap Patika, Hatvan u. 1 (☎41 31 15). Open M-F 8:30am-6pm, Sa 8am-1pm. AmEx/MC/V. **Arany Egyszarvú,** Kossuth u. 8 (☎53 07 07). Open M-F 8:30am-6pm. MC/V.

Medical Services: Emergency room (☎40 40 40, Free English Line ☎112), at **Főnix,** Lehel u. 22.

Internet: DataNet Cafe, Kossuth u. 8 (☎53 67 24; www.datanetcafe.hu) Also provides phones, fax, printing, scanning and copying services. Internet 8Ft per min. Open daily 8am-midnight.

Post Office: Hatvan u. 5-7 (☎41 21 11). Open M-F 7am-7pm, Sa 8am-1pm. **Postal Code:** 4025.

ACCOMMODATIONS

IBUSZ, on Széchényi u. near Piac u., arranges centrally located **private rooms.** (☎415 5155; fax 41 07 56. Doubles 5000Ft; triples 7000Ft. Open M-F 9am-5pm, Sa 8am-1pm. AmEx/MC/V.) The staff at **Tourinform** (see p. 332) can also arrange rooms. In July and August, many **university dorms** ❶ rent rooms (1300-2000Ft); ask at Tourinform, since many dorms book only school groups or traveling summer camps. During the summer, this is the cheapest option; during the rest of the year, most budget travelers stay in pensions. Reserve rooms early during festival season.

Stop Panzió, Batthány u. 18 (☎42 03 01; www.stop.at.tf). From Kossuth u., turn right on Batthány u. At the *Stop Panzió* sign, go down the left side of the building to the back to find the entrance. Near the center. Bright, well-furnished rooms with TV and private bath look out through lace curtains onto a courtyard. Breakfast 900Ft. Reception 24hr. Check-out 11am. Singles 6500Ft; doubles 7400Ft-9900Ft. Cash only. ❸

Kölcsey Kollégiuma, Blaháné u. 15 (☎50 27 80). From Kossuth u., go left on Újházi and right on Blaháné. The doubles can barely fit 2 beds side-by-side, and the baths are shared, but the dorm is cheap, well located and frequented by young travelers. Open June-Aug. Singles 1800Ft; doubles 3720Ft. 200Ft surcharge for a room with a TV. Tax 400Ft. Cash only. ❶

Centrum Panzió, Péterfia u. 37/a (☎41 61 93). Comfortable and air-conditioned. Large, well-decorated rooms feature marble-floored private baths and open into a flower garden with lounge chairs, swings, and a shower. Breakfast included. Singles 7500Ft; doubles 8000Ft; apartments 9500Ft-18,500Ft. Tax 200Ft per day. Cash only. ❹

FOOD

The **Match Supermarket** at the Debrecen Plaza, Péterfia u. 18, is well stocked with fresh fruits and vegetables. (Open M-F 7am-9pm, Sa 6am-9pm, Su 8am-8pm.) **Heliker,** across from McDonald's, on Piac u., offers a smaller selection of snacks. (Open M-F 6:30am-7:30pm, Sa 6:30am-2pm, Su 7-11am. MC/V.) There is an **open-air market** every day from 6am-3pm that sells fresh fruits and vegetables outside the Plaza. Bakeries also have stands that sell bread and breakfast goods.

Carpe Diem Tea & Cafe, Batthyány u. 8 (☎31 90 07; www.diem.hu). For an afternoon snack or a dose of caffeine, this tea house is the best bet in town. The only thing more exotic than the menu of international teas and coffees is the setting: red chiffon curtains conceal a side room for hookah-smoking, and world beats play in the background. Teas 500-800Ft. Open M-Th 9am-11pm, F-Sa 9am-midnight, Su 10am-10pm. Cash only. ❷

Csokonai Söröző, Kossuth u. 21 (☎41 08 02), in a posh, candle-lit cellar with brick walls. The food proves as delectable as the pictures on the menu suggest. At the end of your meal, the waiter offers a glass with four die, each marked with a "C" on one side; if you roll straight "C's," dinner is free. Entrees 580-1900Ft. M-F 40% off on entrees Noon-1pm. Open daily noon-11pm. MC/V. ❷

Lucullus Étterem, Piac u. 41 (☎ 41 85 13, luculluseu.com) Duck into the alleyway with the sign that reads "Belvárosi Udvarház." Eat like a king without paying the price–the downstairs cozy dining area has red, plushy throne-like chairs set around massive wooden tables. Éterrem offers Debrecen-style twists on traditional Hungarian meals. Most entrees under 2000Ft. Open daily 11am-11pm. MC. ❸

SIGHTS

REFORMÁTUS KOLLÉGIUM. Established in 1538 as a center for Protestant education, the Rerformátus has evolved into a Calvinist school with a museum on the first floor that traces the history of the Reformation and ecclesiastical arts in Hungary. Its Reformation roots are evident in its architecture, with simple, arched hallways surrounding a central courtyard. The highlight, however, is the 650,000-volume Library of the Reformed Church and College on the second floor. This collection includes books dating as far back as the 16th century. *(Kálvin tér 16, behind the church. ☎414 744. Open Tu-Sa 10am-4pm, Su 10am-1pm. 500Ft, students 150Ft. Tours of the school and museum available with prior booking. 3000Ft, English tour 4000Ft. 20min. organ concerts throughout the summer, contact tourinform for event schedules.)*

GREAT CHURCH. Hungary's largest Protestant church, built in 1836, dominates Kálvin tér. With a commanding yellow facade, white pillars, and twin spires, the Great Church, is the city's emblem, appearing in almost every pamphlet and postcard. The view over Debrecen is worth the trip up the bell tower. The organ plays every Friday at noon. *(☎412 694. Open Apr.-Oct. M-F 9am-4pm, Sa 9am-1pm, Su 10am-4pm; Nov.-Mar. M-F 10am-noon, Su 1-3pm. 300Ft, students 150Ft. Concerts 1hr. Free.)*

DÉRI MUSEUM. The Déri Museum boasts a diverse collection of Hungarian cultural artifacts ranging from fossils of prehistoric peoples to local tinware to gold-framed masterpieces. Perhaps most noteworthy are the paintings by famous Hungarian artist **Mihály Munkácsy** depicting Jesus's trial and crucifixion. You can spot the artist's self-portrait in Ecce Homo, next to the arch. Coming from Kálvin tér, steer left of the Great Church and turn left on to Múzeum u.; the museum is on the right. Walk up the stairs, past the four lounging Renaissance sculptures through the impressive wooden double-doors. *(☎41 75 77. Open Apr.-Oct. Tu-Su 10am-6pm; Nov.-Mar. Tu-Su 10am-4pm. Museum 580Ft, students 290Ft; special exhibits 300/150Ft. English guide 200Ft. No photography.)*

ENTERTAINMENT AND FESTIVALS

Many of the city's inhabitants congregate in **Nagyerdei Park,** next to the university, where families crowd the pond with paddleboats and walkways with strollers by the day and students pack the bars by night. (Paddleboats 900Ft per hr.; rowboats 850Ft per hr.) There is also a **zoo** and children's **amusement park,** both in the **Vidámpark** complex. (Info ☎514 100; fax 346 883. Zoo open M-F 9am-6pm. 300Ft, children 250Ft. Amusement park 200Ft; rides 100Ft each.) At the **municipal thermal bath,** you can soak in the steamy pools with elderly locals. (Thermal bath open daily 7am-8:30pm. 840Ft, children 660Ft. Sauna open daily Sept.-May 10am-10pm. 650Ft per 2hr. Swimming pool open M-F 7am-6:30pm. 350Ft, students 310Ft.)

The festival season officially runs from June to August. The end of June brings Hungarian bands to the **Vekeri-tó Rock Festival,** held at a park 10km from the city. Camp out, or take the free bus from Debrecen. In July of even-numbered years, the **Béla Bartók International Choral Competition** attracts choirs from around the world. The festival season culminates with the popular **Flower Carnival** parade, in which floats are made entirely of flowers, held August 15-20. Starting the second week of September, well-known musicians and bands come to town for **Jazz Days.**

NIGHTLIFE

Debrecen is dominated by its students, and staid sightseeing plays second fiddle to the youthful energy provided by the university. Locals prefer the bar scene to the club scene, so you may have a hard time finding frenetic dancing to techno-pop.

Bázis Bar-Cafe, in the center of town. Enter the Aranybika Hotel; it's in the left corner on the ground floor. A sophisticated alternative to the usual Western-themed bar. Dim lighting lends a romantic flair to the portrait-covered walls. Open Tu and F-Sa 10am-6am.

Belgian Beer Cafe, Piac u. 29 across from tourinform, provides a cool terrace. A diverse clientele matches the diverse menu offerings–try a Debrecen-style rolled turkey dish with braised vegetables (1590Ft). Several vegetarian options (990Ft-4000Ft). For a lighter gastronomic experience, sip a glass of Bikavér (230Ft). Open M-F 10am-12am, Sa-Su noon-midnight. MC/V.

Yes Jazz Bár, Kálvin tér 4 (☎ 309 659 497). Go right after the last building on the right side of Kálvin tér and enter through the Civis Étterem. The bar is at the upper end of the shopping area. Not the mellow jazz bar implied by its name, but rather a hotspot for a younger, teenage crowd to spend time at outside tables with rock music in the background. Gösser 300Ft, Heineken 320Ft. Open daily 5pm-4am.

Civis Gösser Söröző, Kálvin tér 8-12, (☎ 418 132), across the way from Yes Jazz Bar. Quieter than its neighbor, this bar attracts more of a 20- and 30-something crowd. Ecclectic style furniture provides a cozy upstairs hangout. Gösser and Tokaj wine 300Ft. Open M-Sa 10am-midnight, Su 4pm-midnight.

SZEGED ☎(06)62

The artistic capital of the Great Plain, Szeged (SEH-ged; pop. 166,000) has an easygoing charm that has prompted some to describe it as a Mediterranean town on the Tisza. After an 1879 flood practically wiped out the city, streets were laid out in orderly curves punctuated by large, stately squares. The result is the quiet, cosmopolitan atmosphere of a European seaside city. The colorful Art Nouveau buildings lining the streets reflect Szeged's festival culture and vibrant social scene.

TRANSPORTATION

Trains: Szeged pu. (☎42 18 21; www.elvira.hu), on Indóház tér on the west bank of the Tisza. International ticket office on 2nd fl. Open daily 6am-5:45pm. To: **Budapest**

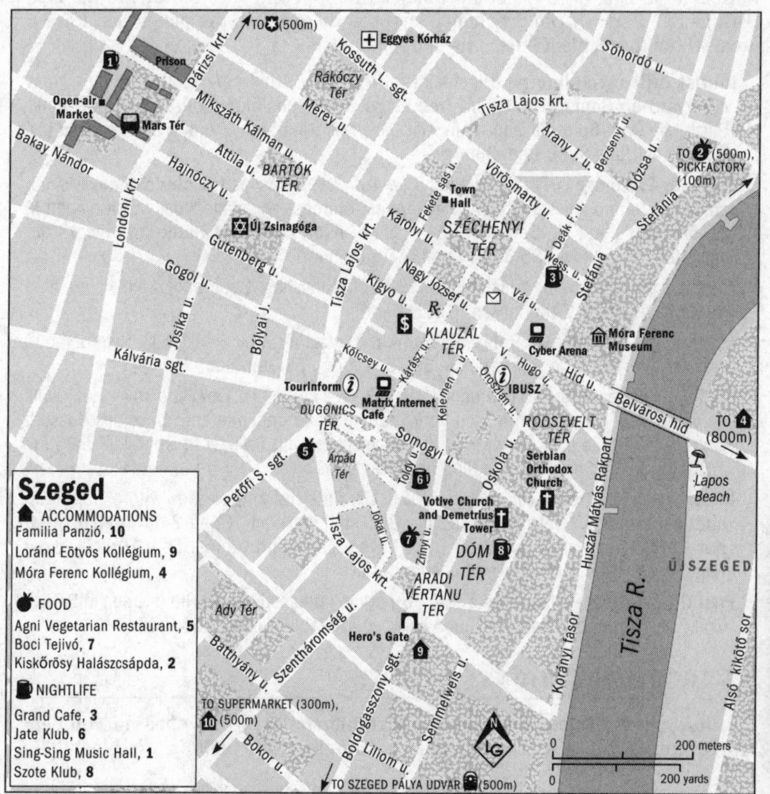

(2½hr.; 11 per day; 2076Ft, students 675Ft), **Debrecen** (3-4hr.; 9 per day; 2526Ft, students 821Ft) via **Cegléd** and **Kecskemét** (1¼hr., 11 per day, 838Ft).

Buses: (☎55 11 66), on Mars tér. From the station, cross the street at the lights and follow Mikszáth Kálmán u. toward the Tisza. This intersects Széchényi tér after becoming Károlyi u. To: **Budapest** (3½hr., 7 per day, 2170Ft); **Debrecen** (5¼hr., 3-6 per day, 2910Ft); **Eger** (5hr., 2 per day, 3020Ft); **Győr** (6hr., 2 per day, 3510Ft); **Kecskemét** (1¾hr., 9-10per day, 1090Ft); **Pécs** (4½hr., 7 per day, 2410Ft).

Public Transportation: Tram #1 connects the train station with Széchényi tér (4-5 stops). Otherwise, it's a 20min. walk. Tickets from kiosks 190Ft; from the driver 220Ft. Fine for riding without a ticket is a painful 2000Ft.

Taxis: ☎444 444, 490 490, or 480 480. 200Ft base, 200Ft per km; students approximately 150Ft per km with no base fare. Taxis are more reliable here than in other cities, but it is still best to clarify the price before getting in.

ORIENTATION AND PRACTICAL INFORMATION

Szeged is divided by the **Tisza River,** with the city center on the west bank. The east side is home to a large park, baths and residences of **Újszeged** (New Szeged). The downtown forms a semicircle against the river, bounded by **Tisza Lajos körút** and centered on **Széchényi tér,** the main square, which makes up one end of the busy Kárász utca; Dugonics tér compromises the opposite end. Parallel to **Híd utca** (Bridge St.) across from Széchényi, shops and cafes line the pedestrian Kárász utca, which forms **Klauzál tér** at its midpoint.

Tourist Office: Tourinform, Dugonics tér 2 (☎488 690; szeged@tourinform.hu), in a courtyard on Somogyi u. Offers **free maps** and accommodations info. Open June-Sept. M-F 9am-6pm, Sa 9am-1pm; Oct.-May M-F 9am-5pm. **Branch** at Széchényi tér. Open daily June-Sept. 9am-9pm.

Currency Exchange: OTP, Klauzál tér 5 (☎480 380). Cashes **traveler's checks** for no commission and gives MC/V **cash advances.** Currency exchange kiosk outside open M 7:45am-5pm, Tu-F 7:45am-4pm. 24hr. MC/V **ATM. Budapest Bank Ltd.,** across the way, Klauzál tér 4 (☎485 585). Open M-F 8am-5pm.

Luggage Storage: At the train station. 150-200Ft per bag. Open daily 4am-11pm. Also at the bus station. 24hr. lockers. 100Ft per 6hr.

Pharmacy: Kígyó Richter Referenciapatika, Klauzál tér 3 (☎54 71 74). Ring bell outside for after-hours service. Open M-Sa 7am-10pm, Su 7am-8pm. MC/V.

Medical Services: Kossuth Lajos sgt. 15/17 (☎47 43 74). From the Town Hall, walk across Széchényi tér, turn left on Vörösmarty u., and continue as it becomes Kossuth Lajos sgt. The medical center is at the intersection with Szilágyi u. Open M-F 5:30am-7:30pm, Sa 7:30am-7:30pm. Ring bell after hours.

Internet: Cyber Arena, Híd u. 1 (☎42 28 15). Internet and phones with cheap international rates. 6Ft per min; 840Ft per 8hr. midnight-8am. Open 24hr. **Matrix Internet Cafe,** Kárász u. 5 (☎42 38 30). Plays techno and trance. 6am-10pm 6Ft per min., 10pm-6am 3.60Ft per min. Open 24hr.

Post Office: Széchényi tér 1 (☎47 62 76), at the intersection with Híd u. Open M-F 8am-7pm, Sa 8am-noon. **Western Union** services available. **Postal Code:** 6720.

ACCOMMODATIONS

Tourinform (see **Orientation and Practical Information,** p. 336) has info on pensions, hotels, hostels, and campsites. (Singles 1100-9000Ft; doubles 3000-

12,000Ft; triples 4600-14,500Ft; quads 4600-15,000Ft.) Also provides helpful event schedules and free maps. **IBUSZ,** Oroszlán u. 3, arranges private rooms in flats. (☎/fax 471 177. Open M-F 9am-6pm, Sa 9am-1pm. 3000-3500Ft; additional 30% charge for stays fewer than 4 nights.) University dorms are generally the cheapest option, but are only available in July and August.

Loránd Eötvös Kollégium, Tisza Lajos krt. 103 (☎54 41 24; eotvos@petra.hos.u-szeged.hu). On your way out of town, the hostel is to the left of Hero's Gate. The entrance is hidden from the street, to the left of the restaurant. Cheap, centrally located dorms with mosquito-proof screens that come in handy in the humid summer weather. Pleasant and well lit. Laundry service included. Call ahead. Open July-Aug. Singles 1000Ft; doubles 2100Ft. ❶

Familia Panzió, Szentháromság u. 71 (☎44 11 22; www.familiapanzio.hu), near the train station. This clean and comfortable family-run pension is a 15min. walk from the center; buses and trams run by regularly. Breakfast 800Ft. Singles with bath 6000Ft; doubles 6000-9000Ft; triples 9000-12,000Ft; quads 10,000-13,000Ft. Cash only. ❸

Móra Ferenc Kollégium, Közép fasor 31-33 (☎ 544 101, www.mora.u-szeged.hu), in Uj Szeged, just across the New Bridge. Long hallways open onto single and double rooms; buzzes with backpackers and university students. Reserve ahead. Singles 1400Ft; doubles 2500-2800Ft. Cash only. Open July-August. ❶

FOOD

Not only is Szeged the paprika capital of Hungary, it is also home to the country's finest lunch meats, courtesy of the local Pick Salami Factory. Don't miss the *halászlé* (spicy soup made with fresh Tisza fish). Keep in mind that it is taboo to order water with your soup, as it dilutes the paprika flavor; wine and beer are better matches. The **CBA Supermarket,** Szentháromság u. 39, provides snacks. (Open M-Sa 6am-8pm, Su 7am-noon. MC/V.) The daily **open-air market,** with meat and fruits, is opposite the bus station on Mars tér.

Boci Tejivó, Zrinyi u. 2 (☎42 31 54; www.bocitejivo.hu), a block from Dóm tér. The best place in town for a quick bite. In an underground cellar, this cool cafe is a popular student sanctuary from the summertime heat. Try a raspberry crepe (99Ft) or *grizes tészta* (pasta with jam, 200Ft). Check online for occasional specials like free soup or free admission to the SZOTE Klub (see below). Open 24hr. Cash only. ❶

COOKING SCHOOLS

Every year since 1969, scores of people have migrated to the small town of Baja (Bah-yah) in early July for a one-day fish feast, called the Bajai Halászlé Fesztivál. Hungary's spicy fish soup has become a national delicacy—and Baja, located in southern Hungary, is the self-proclaimed "capital of fish soup."

Thousands of revelers come from all over the country to participate in the cookathon, tending their huge iron cauldrons for hours as music blasts from nearby speakers. Special touches vary from cook to cook, but the basic ingredients stay the same: loads of paprika, onions, and, of course, a medley of fresh fish.

A rival fish soup festival, also during the summer, exists in neighboring Szeged. Besides geography, however, the festivals are separated by an irreconcilable difference in opinion. Szegedians scoff at at the thin pasta added to Baja soups, arguing that the starchy substance soaks up much of the broth, leaving a thick, almost sauce-like consistency.

Both agree, however, on the dish's best alcoholic accompaniment: red wine. For more information on the festivals, as well as recipes and cooking tips, check out www.bajaihalaszle.hu or pick up a menu at any restaurant in Hungary with "Csárda" in the name (this means they serve the fish soup)—and have a taste for yourself.

Kiskőrösy Halászcsárda, Felső Tisza-part 336 (☎495 698). The best place for fresh Tisza fish and other traditional Hungarian dishes, right on the riverbank in a friendly, outdoor setting. Entrees 600Ft-1800Ft. Open 11am-midnight. Cash only. ❷

Agni Vegetarian Restaurant, Tisza Lajos krt. 76, just behind the Szeged Nagyáruház on Dugonics tér. (☎47 77 39, www.agnietterem.hu). One of the best vegetarian restaurants in Hungary, Agni draws an earthy crowd. Try the cheese and walnut balls (580Ft). Entrees 500Ft-750Ft. Open M-Sa 11am-9pm. Cash only. ❶

SIGHTS

NEW SYNAGOGUE (ÚJ ZSINAGÓGA). The synagogue, finished in 1903, is an awesome display of craftmanship and style, with Moorish altars, Romanesque columns, Gothic domes, and Baroque facades. The brilliant blue stained-glass cupola sheds light on the vestibule walls, which are lined with the names of the 3100 congregation members killed in Nazi death camps. Szeged's small Jewish community still worships here. *(Jósika u. 8. From Széchényi tér, walk away from the river on Híd u. past Bartók tér; turn left on Jósika. Synagogue is on the left. Open M-F and Su 10am-noon and 1-5pm. Closed to visitors on holy days, though worshippers are welcome at services. Men must wear hats. 300Ft, students 150Ft.)*

FEKETE HÁZ (BLACK MUSEUM). Ever-changing exhibits makes this small museum a dynamic companion to the classical Móra Ferenc Museum. Previous exhibits have included Dali and Munkácsy; call Tourinform or the museum itself for calendar of events. *(Somogyi u. 13, ☎42 58 72. Open Tu-Su 10am-5pm. 300Ft, students 150Ft.)*

MÓRA FERENC MUSEUM. Exhibits in this eclectic riverside museum detail Szeged's history and its love-hate relationship with the Tisza River, which both fueled its growth and, in 1879, destroyed the city with a flood. Fascinating displays feature everything from archaeological findings to modern city plans. The permanent exhibit "They Called Themselves Avars" includes among its artifacts two corpses (the "avars") buried in a double grave. *(Roosevelt tér 1/3. ☎54 90 40. Open July-Sept. Tu-Su 10am-6pm; Oct.-June 10am-5pm. 1000Ft, students with ISIC 500Ft.)*

VOTIVE CHURCH (FOGADALMI TEMPLOM). The dual clock towers of this unusual neo-Romanesque church pierce the skyline. At night, their lights can be seen from many kilometers away. The church houses a 9040-pipe organ that is used for occasional afternoon concerts. Inside you'll also find János Fadrusz's sculptural masterpiece, "Christ on the Cross." The 12th-century **Demetrius Tower** (Dömötör torony) is the oldest monument in Szeged and all that remains of the original church from before the Great Flood of 1879 that destroyed most of the city. On the walls surrounding the church, **National Pantheon** portrays Hungary's great political, literary, and artistic figures. *(Dóm tér. Open M-W and F-Sa 8am-5:30pm, Th noon-5:30pm, Su noon-5:30pm. Free guided tours daily 11am and 2pm; English tours available. Shoulders must be covered. 400Ft, students 250Ft; Su and after 5pm free. Tower open briefly M-F 11am and 3:30pm, Sa-Su 3:30pm. 600Ft, students 400Ft. Cash only.)*

OTHER SIGHTS. The yellow **Town Hall,** reshingled with red-and-green tiles after the devastating 1879 flood, overlooks grassy Széchényi tér. The building's inner courtyard is host to many concerts and operas throughout the summer. *(Contact Tourinform for schedules. Széchényi tér 10.)* The late-baroque style 1778 **Serbian Orthodox Church** (Szerb templom) holds impressive ground across the street from the dominating Votive Church. The iconostasis holds 80 paintings in interwoven gold frame, and reaches up to a ceiling covered by a starry fresco of God creating the Earth. *(Somogyi u. 3a. ☎32 52 78. Opened by request at the green door of the building opposite. 150Ft, students 100Ft.)* **Hero's Gate** (Hősök kapuja), actually a short tunnel, was erected in 1936 as a memorial to the soldiers who died in WWI. Two plaster soldiers guard the gate, while a mural of Jesus guiding soldiers during battle decorates the underside of the archway. *(Start at Dóm tér and head away from the center to reach the gate, in Aradi vértanúk tere.)*

ENTERTAINMENT

The **Szeged Open Air Festival** *(Szabadtéri Játékok)*, from early July to late August, is Hungary's largest outdoor performance event. International troupes perform dances, operas, and musicals in the courtyard at *Dóm tér*. Buy tickets (1500-12,000Ft) at Tourinform (see **Orientation and Practical Information,** p. 336) or the ticketing office at Kárász u. 9 (☎54 12 05, www.szegediszabadteri.hu). Other festivals fill the streets from spring to autumn. The mid-July **beer festival,** the **wine festival,** and the **jazz jamboree** are all popular. **Swimming pools** in New Szeged and **baths** in the downtown provide escapes from the summer heat. Most pools and baths are open daily and charge 300-600Ft. Or, try **Anna Thermal Bath,** renovated in 2006 and located centrally in the downtown for relaxation in natural mineral hot springs. Late-night hours draw many young locals. *(Tisza Lajos krt. 24. ☎42 57 21; www.szegedifurdok.hu. Open M-F 6am-8pm, Sa-Su 8am-8pm. 1400Ft, students 1150Ft; M, W, F 9pm-midnight, 950Ft. Cash only.)* Over the old bridge (Belvárosi Híd) from Szeged and to the-right is a small **beach** (strand) and swimming area. **Bike paths** line the streets, and you can **kayak** on the Tisza River. To rent equipment, contact **Vizisporttelep** at Felső-Tisza part 4 (☎42 55 74).

NIGHTLIFE

For a city of moderate size, Szeged has a lot of cosmopolitan know-how. Many of the restaurants and cafes that line the streets are transformed into popular nightspots after dark, just as the city's bars and clubs are beginning to open their doors.

JATE Klub, Toldy u. 2 (☎54 40 56; www.jateklub.hu). Orange walls and playful seating arrangements make for a relaxed daytime hangout that turns into a busy dance scene by night, frequented by Szeged's high school and university students. Sip a coke (200Ft) or an ice-cold beer (300Ft). Cover charge 600Ft on special occasions, usually entrance is free. Open M-F 10am-5am, Sa 10pm-6am. Cash only.

SZOTE Klub, Dóm Tér 13 (☎54 57 73; www.szoteklub.hu). Another hotspot for Szeged's young locals, and similar to the JATE Klub. One large room with dance floor and seating around the perimeter, this disco plays a variety of music and hosts several guest DJs. Cover 600Ft for special events. Open M-F 10am-6am, Sa 9pm-6am. Cash only.

Grand Cafe, Deák Ferenc u. 18, 3rd fl. (☎42 05 78), through an inconspicuous door. Start your night at this intimate cafe, which screens 3 art films each evening. Sip coffee or red wine (550Ft) as you watch a film, or relax to jazz in the coffee shop. Films daily 5, 7, and 9pm. Open Sept.-July M-F 3pm-midnight, Sa-Su 5pm-midnight. Cash only.

Sing-Sing Music Hall (www.sing.hu), on Mars tér, C Pavilion, on the street to the left as you face the bus station. DJ turns popular beats for a scantily clad, ready-to-rave crowd. 0.5L Amstel 500Ft. Cover around 500Ft. Open W-Sa 10pm-dawn. Cash only.

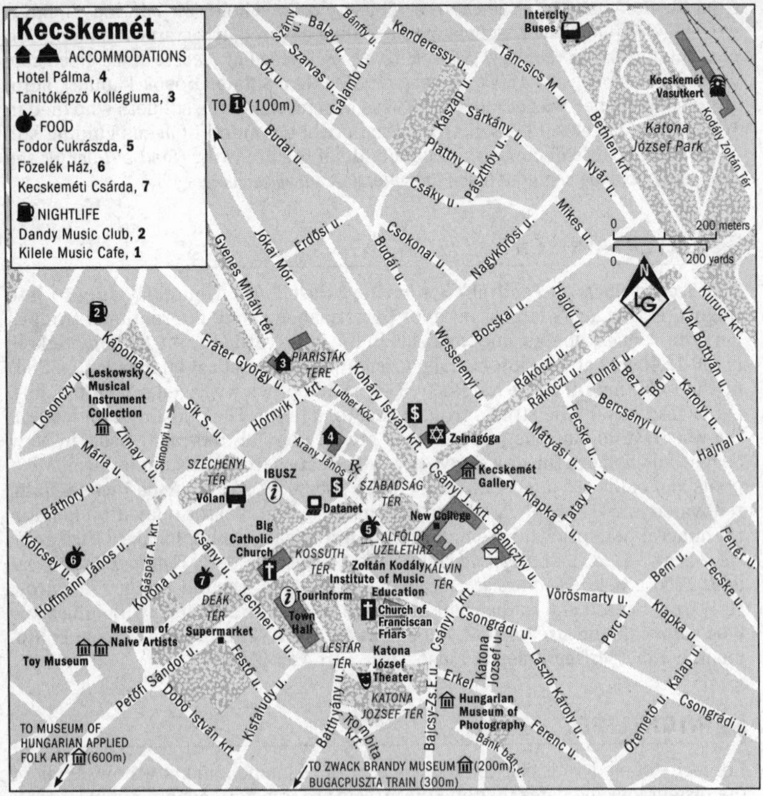

Kecskemét

ACCOMMODATIONS
Hotel Pálma, 4
Tanitóképzö Kollégiuma, 3

FOOD
Fodor Cukrászda, 5
Főzelék Ház, 6
Kecskeméti Csárda, 7

NIGHTLIFE
Dandy Music Club, 2
Kilele Music Cafe, 1

KECSKEMÉT ☎(06)76

Surrounded by vineyards, fruit groves, and vast *puszta* (plains), Kecskemét (KETCH-keh-mate; pop. 110,000) lures tourists with a lush central square, famous *barackpálinka* (apricot brandy), and the musical genius of native composer Zoltán Kodály (1882-1967). While it resembles other larger Hungarian towns, Kecskemét stands out for its many festivals and its proximity to Bugacpuszta, for which it serves as a convenient base.

TRANSPORTATION AND PRACTICAL INFORMATION. The train station is on Kodály Zoltán tér, at the end of Rákóczi út. Trains go to: Budapest (2hr.; 15 per day; 946Ft, InterCity 1276Ft); Pécs (5hr., 13 per day, 2888Ft) via Kiskunfélegyháza; Szeged (1¼hr., 14 per day, 888Ft). **Buses** run from the bus station, just around the corner from the train station on Kodály Zoltán tér, to: Budapest (1hr., many per day, 1323Ft), Pécs (5hr., 3 per day, 1992Ft) and Szeged (1¾hr., 12 per day, 1090Ft). The **Volán** bus terminal, for local routes, is a block from Kossuth tér; turn right from the terminal on Sík S. u. Timetables are posted at stops. Buses stop running around 10pm. Tickets are 132Ft from kiosks, 180Ft from drivers.

Most sights are within walking distance. The town surrounds a loosely connected string of squares. The largest, **Szabadság tér** (Liberty Square), is ringed by three squares, **Kossuth tér, Kálvin tér,** and **Széchényi tér.** To get to Szabadság from the train or bus station, go left, then right on Rákóczi út and continue for 10min. **Tourinform** is at Kossuth tér 1. (Open July-Aug. M-F 9am-6pm, Sa-Su 9am-1pm; Sept.-June M-F 8am-5pm). **OTP,** Szabadság tér 5, **exchanges currency** at good rates and cashes **traveler's checks** for no commission. (24hr. MC/V **ATM** outside. Open M 7:45am-5pm, Tu-F 7:45am-4pm.) For **Internet,** go to **DataNet,** Kossuth tér 6-7 in the shopping plaza. (5Ft per min. Open M-F 8am-10pm, Sa-Su 9am-10pm.) The **post office** is at Kálvin tér 10/12. (Open M-F 8am-7pm, Sa 8am-1pm.) **Postal Code:** 6000.

ACCOMMODATIONS AND FOOD. Dorm rooms and pensions are generally the best deals in town. **Hotel Pálma ❸,** Arany János u. 3 to the left of the church, in the heart of the city, has rooms with full baths and beachy decor. (☎321 045. Singles 5750Ft, 1st-class 7250Ft; doubles 8000/9500Ft; triples 9250/10,750Ft; quads 10,100Ft. Includes breakfast). **Tanitóképző Kollégiuma** (Teachers' College) **❶,** Piaristák tere 4, 5min. from Kossuth tér, rents good-sized singles, triples and quads on a per-person basis, but be prepared to brave curtainless showers. (☎48 69 77. Call 1-2 days ahead. Rooms 2500Ft per person.)

Kecskemét is famous for its apricot *barackpálinka* (brandy), distilled from apricot. **Főzélek Ház ❶,** Deák Tér 6, in the courtyard of Alföldi Üzeletház has delicious Hungarian food in an eclectic setting. Take your pea soup (210Ft) upstairs to the lounge area, or to the terrace. M-F 5:30pm-6pm ½-price entrees. Open daily 9am-11pm. Cash only. Try **Fodor Cukrászda ❶,** Szabadság tér 2, for dessert (100-450Ft) and ice cream. (Open M-F 9am-6:30pm, Sa-Su 9am-8:30pm). **Kecskeméti Csárda ❸** on Kölcsey u. 7, is the place to go for goulash and fresh, spicy fish soup (990Ft-3000Ft). A secluded courtyard with lush garden provides a hiding place from the noise of the downtown and summer heat. (Vegetarian options. Open M-Sa 11am-10pm, Su 11am-4pm. Cash only.)

SIGHTS AND MUSEUMS. The salmon-colored **Town Hall,** Kossuth tér 1, dominates the main square. (☎513 513. For a tour, register ahead at Tourinform. Tours M-Th 7:30am-4pm, F-Sa 7:30am-1:30pm. 300Ft.) Next door, the **Big Catholic Church,** the largest Baroque cathedral on the Great Plain, has marble columns and intricate ceiling frescoes. (Open daily 9am-noon and 3-6pm.) From the entrance on the right, climb the **tower** for a good view. (Open daily July-Aug. 10am-10pm; Sept.-June 10am-8pm. Groups only. 200Ft, students 100Ft.) At stalls in the square, vendors sell arts and souvenirs. The cupola-topped **Synagogue,** Rákóczi u. 2, is no longer used for worship, but boasts plaster-casts of 15 Michelangelo sculptures and, strangely enough, a ground-floor bar. (☎48 76 11. Open M-F 10am-4pm.) At the **Leskowsky Musical Instrument Collection,** Zimay u. 6/a, Albert Leskowsky offers a one-hour concert and lesson with various musical instruments drawn from the large collection. (☎48 36 16. Call ahead. 500Ft, students 300Ft.)

At the **Zwack Fruit Brandy Distillery and Exhibition,** Matkói u. 2, over 15 tons of apricots are turned into *barackpálinka* each day. Tour the bottling lines where the famous brandy is prepared. (☎487 711. Open M-F to groups of 10 or more, Sa-Su to groups of 20 or more. Individuals can call ahead or join a F 1pm group. 1350Ft.) The **Hungarian Museum of Photography** (Magyar Fotográfiai Múzeum), Katona tér 12, displays a poignant collection of 19th-century photographic portraits and lithographs. (☎483 221; www.fotomuzeum.hu. Open W-Su 10am-5pm. 200Ft, students 100Ft.) The **Museum of Applied Folk Art** (Népi Iparmüvészet Múzeuma), Serfözö u. 19, has an extensive collection of costumes, furniture,

A FESTIVAL A DAY

One of the joys of city-hopping in southern Hungary is that the festival scene is almost always in full swing in the summer. On my first day back on the road after a two-week stint in Budapest, I was expecting a mellow evening far from the hectic pace of city life. But as I wandered the streets in the town of Kecskemét, I quickly discovered that it was anything but quiet—a raucous rock band had taken thte stage in the main square, cranking out power ballads to a packed crowd. Everybody in town seemed to be out to nod along to the music and to down ice cream from the stands set up throughout the park.

When I arrived in Pécs two days later, the festival scene only picked up. I stumbled on the Pécs Weeks of Art and Gastronomy, a festival celebrating regional crafts and cuisine. The street was lined with stalls cooking up meals on the spot. At one, the smell of some unidentifiable meat wafted up from a smoky skillet; at the next, a crew of old women crafted cylinders out of dough before baking them over an open flame and coating them in a sugar glaze. *Kurtos*, I learned as I happily tasted the wares, was the name of this sweet pastry.

At the end of this tempting row of makeshift wine cellars and candy shops, the street widened into a square in front of the cathedral, where a huge crowd had

ceramics, whips, and wood and bone carvings. Follow Petőfí Sándor u. from the center, turn left on Maria krt., and then left again on Serfözö u. (☎/fax 327 203. Open Tu-Sa 10am-5pm. 200Ft, students 100Ft. English guide 50Ft.) Once a boarding house with a casino and ballroom, the **Kecskemét Gallery** (Kecskeméti Képtár), Rákóczi u. 1, features works by local artists. The colorful building is an attraction in itself. (☎480 776. Open Tu-Su 10am-5pm. 300Ft, students 150Ft.)

NIGHTLIFE AND FESTIVALS. The city is fairly quiet at night if there aren't performances in the main square, but **Dandy Music Club and Pool,** on Kápolna u. 3, boasts a disco, an adjoining building for intense rounds of pool (600Ft) and a swanky jazz club. (☎204 812 838. Open 1pm-midnight. Cash only. Beer and drinks 210Ft-360Ft.) An adult crowd relaxes to jazz in the basement of **Kilele Music Cafe,** Jókai u. 34. (☎41 88 13. Open M-F 5pm-1am, Sa 6pm-4am, Su 6pm-midnight.)

Festivals are held most weekends in Kecskemét. The **Kodaly Music Festival** remembers the composer through a series of concerts. The **Kecskemét Spring Festival** in March features music, theater, and literary readings. In late summer, regional food, music, and dance take over during the **Hírös Week Festival.** Shakespeare may lose a bit in translation, but the elegant stage at the **József Katona Theater** (Színház), Katona tér 5, lends grace to any script. (☎483 283; www.katonaj.hu. Box office open Sept.-June M-F 10am-7pm. Tickets from 1300Ft.)

DAYTRIP FROM KECSKEMÉT: BUGACPUSZTA. One of the last places to watch Hungarian Grey Cattle graze, Bugacpuszta (BOO-gahtc poo-stah) also serves as a forum for cowboys to showcase traditional herding skills and for horse-drawn carriages to pull eager visitors along dirt roads. Don't be fooled by the appearance of the cowboys, who may look less than macho in their flowing white linen pants and feathered hats. These plainsmen ride without saddles: they stand up on horses galloping at full speed, and sometimes hold brimming pints of wine steadily in hand as they ride. Bugacpuszta is the most touristed part of the **Kiskunság National Park** and the second largest *puszta* (plain) in Hungary. The 11am bus from Kecskemét is perfect, as it arrives in Bugac in time for visitors to visit the museum, see the stables, and grab a snack before the horse show. With admission, you can visit the **Shepherd's Museum,** which displays a teepee, musical instruments, and stuffed animals from the *puszta*. Then, head to the stables to see the pigs, sheep, and horses. Be sure to find a seat on the wooden benches for the horseshow. The 30min. performance is action-packed: cowboys round up wild horses and crack their whips in time. In an impressive trick, a cowboy stands with each foot on a different galloping horse and holds the reins of three others. Take your time getting back to the entrance: the next bus won't come until 4pm. Once there, consider **Bugaci Karikás Csárda ❸,** Nagybugac 135, which serves a range of traditional Hungarian dishes and offers overnight stays in a luxurious *puszta* farmhouse. (☎575 112. Entrees 1000-2000Ft. Breakfast included. Doubles 9000Ft.) While Bugac tourism focuses on seeing horses, not riding them, there are a few opportunities to take the reins. **Táltos Reiterpension,** Nagybugac 135, offers **horseback riding** for 2000Ft per hour in the *puszta* or 1800Ft per hr. around their property. On the main road from the park, turn right and walk 150m. (☎372 633. Open daily 9am-5pm.) *Buses (45min., 11 per day, 600Ft) and trains (45min., 3 per day, 450Ft) depart from Kecskemét. The train leads to the village of Bugac, not the puszta 5km away. Get off the bus at the second-to-last stop, just after the bus turns left at the entrance to Bugacpuszta. From the stop, walk down the road (15-20min.) to the entrance. Take the carriage to the museum and stables (2500Ft), or make the short trek from the entrance by foot (entry 1100Ft).*

gathered to listen to live music. The first night I heard a doo-wop-esque rock band in matching blue-striped suits. When I retuned the next evening, I caught the end of a performance by a drum quintent, playing complex rhythms on large plastic vats.

For me, festivals were the best way to get a taste (literally and figuratively) of local life. So head to southern Hungary in the summer—as you never know what you might encounter.

Some of the many festivals that enliven the towns of rural Hungary throughout the year with music, dance, theater, film, and folk culture include: the **Pécs Weeks of Art and Gastronomy** (late June-early July); the **Szeged Open Air Festival** (July to Aug.) and the **Thealter** alternative theater festival (end of July); the **Békéscsaba Sausage Festival** (Oct.), the **Gyula Castle Theatre Festival** (July-Aug.); the **Kecskemét Spring Festival** (Mar.), **Animation Film Festival** (late June), and the **International Kodaly Festival** (mid-July to Aug.); the **Szentendre Summer and Theater** festival (July-Aug.; the **Esztergom Castle Theatre Festival** (June-Aug.); and the **Hódmezővásárhely Saint George Day Shepherd Contest** (Sept.). For more information, consult www.artsfestivals.hu or www.hungarytourism.hu.

—Amelia Atlas

LATVIA

LATVIA (LATVIJA)

The serenity and easy charm of Latvia belie centuries of suffering. The country has been conquered and reconquered so many times that the year 2004 was only the 35th year of Latvian independence—ever. These days, Latvia's vibrant capital, Rīga, is under siege by a new force: tourism. Cheap flights have brought so many Western visitors that the Rīga Old Town can feel like one big British bachelor party on summer weekends. You don't have to wander far from the beaten path, however, to discover the allure of Rīga's Art Nouveau elegance and student nightlife, its stunning seacoast, and the wild beauty of its Gaujas Valley National Park.

DISCOVER LATVIA: SUGGESTED ITINERARIES

THREE DAYS. Settle into **Rīga** (2 days; p. 351) to enjoy stunning **Art Nouveau** architecture, **cafe culture,** and the best **music and performing arts** scene in the Baltics. Finish with a daytrip to **Rundāle Palace** (1 day; p. 362).

ONE WEEK. Begin your Latvian tour in seaside **Liēpaja** (2 days; p. 364). After three days in **Rīga** (p. 351), head to **Cēsis** (2 days; p. 370) to enjoy **Cēsis Castle** and the wilds of **Gaujas Valley National Park.**

FACTS AND FIGURES

Official Name: Republic of Latvia.

Capital: Rīga.

Major Cities: Daugavpils, Rēzekne.

Population: 2,253,000.

Time Zone: GMT +2, in summer GMT +3.

Language: Latvian.

Religions: Lutheran 55%, Roman Catholic 24%, Russian Orthodox 9%.

National Bird: White Wagtail.

Years of Compulsory Education: 9.

ESSENTIALS

WHEN TO GO

Latvia is wet year-round, with cold, snowy winters and short, rainy summers. Tourism peaks in July and August; if you'd prefer not to experience central Rīga in the company of throngs of British stag parties, late spring or early fall is the best time to visit. Still, much of the seacoast stays untouristed even in summer.

DOCUMENTS AND FORMALITIES

EMBASSIES AND CONSULATES. Foreign embassies and consulates to Latvia are in **Rīga** (p. 353). Latvian embassies and consulates abroad include: **Australia,** Honorary Consul, 2 Mackennel St., East Ivanhoe, VIC 3079; send mail to: P.O. Box 23, Kew VIC 3101 (☎61 39 49 96 920; latcon@ozemail.com.au); **Canada,** 350 Sparks St., Ste. 1200, Ottawa, ON K1R 7S8 (☎613-238-6014; embassy.canada@mfa.gov.lv); **Ireland,** 92 St. Stephen's Green, Dublin 2 (☎35 31 42 83 320; http://www.am.gov.lv/en/ireland/); **New Zealand,** Honorary Consul, 161 Kilmore St., Amsterdam House, Level 3, P.O. Box 13600, Christchurch (☎64 03 36 53 505; lrconsulate@ebox.lv); **UK,** 45 Nottingham Place, London W1U 5LY (☎442 073 120 040; www.london.am.gov.lv).

ENTRANCE REQUIREMENTS.

Passport: Required for citizens of Australia, Canada, New Zealand, and the US. EU citizens only need to display identity cards.

Visa: Not required for stays of under 90 days for citizens of Australia, Canada, the EU, New Zealand, and the US.

Letter of Invitation: Not required for citizens of Australia, Canada, Ireland, New Zealand, the UK, and the US.

Inoculations: Recommended up-to-date on DTaP (diphtheria, tetanus, and pertussis), Hepatitis A, Hepatitis B, MMR (measles, mumps, and rubella), polio booster, tick-borne encephalitis, and typhoid.

Work Permit: Required of all foreigners planning to work in Latvia.

International Driving Permit: Required for all those planning to drive in Latvia.

VISA AND ENTRY INFORMATION. Citizens of Australia, Canada, the EU, New Zealand, and the US do not need a visa for stays of up to 90 days. Those wishing to stay for a longer period must submit an Aim of Residence form to the Visas Divison, Office of Citizenship and Migration Affairs, Alunāna iela 1, Rīga, LV-1050 (☎67 21 96 51; www.ocma.gov.lv), to receive a visa for either temporary or permanent residence. Application forms vary based on country of origin; consult the website for further details. All travelers must display a passport valid for three months beyond the duration of their planned stay in Latvia and must also be able to give proof of a valid insurance policy to cover potential health service needs while in Latvia. The best way to enter Latvia is by plane, train, or bus to Rīga.

TOURIST SERVICES

Offices of the state-run **tourist bureau**, can be found in nearly every town and city in Latvia. Employees of such establishments typically speak English, Russian, and German. Tourists offices distribute free maps and brochures, often help with booking private rooms, and can assist with translation questions.

LATVIA

MONEY

LATU (LS)		
	AUS$1 = 0.44LS	1LS = AUS$2.28
	CDN$1 = 0.49LS	1LS = CDN$2.05
	EUR€1 = 0.70LS	1LS = EUR€1.43
	NZ$1 = 0.39LS	1LS = NZ$2.54
	UK£1 = 1.03LS	1LS = UK£0.97
	US$1 = 0.52LS	1LS = US$1.93

The Latvian unit of currency is the **lats** (Ls), plural *latu*, which is divided into 100 **santīmu** (singular *santīms*). Although Latvia has been a member of the EU since 2004, persistent inflation has rendered it unlikely that it will switch to the Euro until 2012 at the earliest. The **inflation** rate in 2007 was 3.7%, representing a significant decrease over the past three years. Most banks **exchange currency** for 1% commission, except for Hansabanka, which does not charge fees. **ATMs** are common in Rīga and may also be found in larger towns. Some businesses, restaurants, and hotels accept **MasterCard** and **Visa. Traveler's checks** are harder to use, but both AmEx and Thomas Cook checks can be converted in Rīga. It's often difficult to exchange non-Baltic currencies other than US dollars or euro.

HEALTH AND SAFETY

EMERGENCY	**Ambulance:** ☎03. **Fire:** ☎01. **Police:** ☎02. **General Emergency:** ☎112.

Although some private clinics provide adequate medical supplies and services, Latvian medical facilities generally fall below Western standards. Emergency medical services are free; other services are chargeable or may be paid for by private medical insurance. Latvia has been hotlisted by the World Health Organization for its periodic outbreaks of incurable varieties of **tuberculosis,** though none have been reported since 2000. As a precaution, drink **bottled water** (available at grocery stores and kiosks and often carbonated) or boil tap water before drinking. **Pharmacies** *(aptieka)* in Latvia are generally privately owned and fairly well stocked with antibiotics and prescription medication produced in Latvia or other Eastern European countries; travelers should be aware that products may have different names than in the West, and instructions are frequently not printed in English. Pharmacies carry tampons *(tampons)*, sanitary napkins *(sieviešu paketes)*, and condoms *(prezervatīvs)*. **Restrooms** are marked with an upward-pointing triangle for women, downward for men.

Although violent **crime** in Latvia is rare, travelers should be on their guard for pickpockets and scam artists. A common scam is to dupe foreigners into ordering outrageously expensive drinks in bars; travelers should always verify the price of drinks in advance. Both men and women should avoid walking alone at night. If you feel threatened, say *"Ej prom"* (EY prawm), which means "go away"; *"Liec man miera"* (LEEtz mahn MEE-rah; "leave me alone") says it more forcefully, and *"Ej bekot"* (EY bek-oht; "go pick mushrooms") is even ruder. **Women** travelers may be verbally hassled at any hour, especially if traveling alone, but usually such harassment is unaccompanied by physical action. After dark in Rīga, it is best to take a cab home. **Minorities** in Latvia are rare; incidents of verbal and physical harassment have been known to occur, although generally there is little discrimination. Travelers with **disabilities** may encounter some difficulties; they should contact the Latvian Society of Disabled People (☎37 12 61 45 16; nnazarova@csb.lv) or the Disabled Peoples' Association of Latvia (☎37 17 54 87 56) if they require further assistance. Although **homosexuality** is legal in Latvia, public displays of affection may result in violence. Women walk down the street holding hands, but this is strictly an indication of friendship and does not render Latvia gay-friendly. Safe options for GLBT travelers include **gay and lesbian clubs,** which advertise themselves freely in Rīga. Expect less tolerance outside the capital.

TRANSPORTATION

BY PLANE. Airlines flying to Latvia use the Rīga international airport. **Air Baltic, Finnair, Lufthansa, Ryanair, SAS,** and others make the hop to Rīga from their hubs. Round-trip fares typically run to US$900-1000 during the summer months.

BY TRAIN. Trains link Latvia to Berlin, GER; Lviv, UKR; Moscow, RUS; Odessa, UKR; St. Petersburg, RUS; Tallinn, EST; and Vilnius, LIT. Trains are cheap and efficient, and stations are clearly marked. Latvia is not covered by **Eurail.** The Rīga **commuter rail** is very good and provides extensive service. For daytrips from Rīga, it's best to take the **electric train.** The Latvian word for departures is *atiet;* arrivals is *pienāk.*

BY BUS. Buses, often adorned with the driver's collection of icons and stuffed animals, are faster than trains for travel within Latvia. The major bus company servicing Latvia is **Eurolines** (www.eurolines.lv). Book tickets in advance by phone or online. Some crowded trips may leave you standing for long hours without a seat. Generally, however, buses are faster, cheaper, and more comfortable than trains.

BY CAR AND BY TAXI. All travelers planning to drive in Latvia are required to carry an **International Driving Permit.** These can be obtained from the national automobile association in your home country. Road conditions in Latvia are improving after years of deterioration, and urban and rural road conditions are generally fair. Consult the Latvian Road Administration (www.lad.lv) for more details. That said, Latvia has one of the highest levels of traffic fatalities in Europe, and travelers should watch out for local drivers disregarding the rules of the road, as well as for oblivious, drunken pedestrians. **Taxis** are considered safe in Latvia. Taxi stands in front of hotels charge higher rates.

BY BIKE AND BY THUMB. Recreational cycling is popular in Latvia. Tourist offices can provide information about local bike rentals and routes. A bicycle service is also run by **Gunārs Šauriņš** (☎371 26 32 23 58). **Hitchhiking** is not common, and is especially unsafe for women. Let's Go does not recommend hitchhiking.

KEEPING IN TOUCH

PHONE CODES	**Country code:** 371. **International dialing prefix:** 011. From outside Latvia, dial international dialing prefix (see inside back cover) + 371 + city code + local number. Inside Latvia, dial city code + local number, even when calling from within the city.

EMAIL AND INTERNET. Internet access is readily available in Rīga but rarer elsewhere and averages 1Ls per hour at Internet cafes; many libraries and cafes offer free service. Internet cafes, however, are more prevalent, and typically offer a range of services including printing, laminating, and CD burning.

TELEPHONE. To make local or international calls, you must purchase a **phone card,** which come in 3, 5, and 10Ls denominations from post offices, telephone offices, kiosks, and state stores and have instructions in English. To operate a phone, dial 0, then press 1 or 2 for English and follow the instructions. For international calls, **Tele 2** has the best rates. Cell phones receive free incoming calls; they are very prevalent and can be purchased from Tele 2 for prices starting at 20Ls. International access codes include **AT&T Direct** (☎800 2288), **MCI** (☎800 2171), and **Nobel** (☎800 3019). For domestic calls, if a number is six digits, dial a 2 before it; if it's seven, you needn't dial anything before it. To call abroad from an analog phone, dial 1, then 00, then the country code. If it's digital, dial 00, then the country code. Phone offices have the latest info on changes to the phone system.

MAIL. Latvia's postal system is reliable; it generally takes mail 10-12 days to reach the US or Canada from Latvia. All post offices have information desks where English is spoken. The standard rate for a letter to the US or Canada is 0.50Ls. Mail can be received through **Poste Restante,** though this is not especially prevalent. Envelopes should be addressed as follows: first name LAST NAME, POSTE RESTANTE, post office address, Postal Code, city, LATVIA.

ACCOMMODATIONS AND CAMPING

LATVIA	❶	❷	❸	❹	❺
ACCOMMODATIONS	under 9Ls	9-14Ls	15-19Ls	20-24Ls	over 24Ls

Hostels are common in Latvia, as are hotel chains, bed and breakfasts, and family-run guesthouses. Hostels are unfortunately prone to being overrun by large and raucous British stag parties, especially on summer weekends. The **Latvian Youth Hostel Association,** Aldaru 8, Rīga LV-1050 (☎921 8560; www.hostellinglatvia.com), is a useful resource for info on hostels in Rīga and elsewhere. **College dormitories** are often the cheapest option, but are open to travelers only in the summer. Rīga's array of **hotels** satisfies any budget. Most small towns outside the capital have at most one hotel in the budget range; expect to pay 3-15Ls per night. **Campgrounds** exist in the countryside. Camping outside marked areas is illegal.

FOOD AND DRINK

LATVIA	❶	❷	❸	❹	❺
FOOD	under 2Ls	3-5Ls	6-7Ls	8-12Ls2	over 12Ls

Latvian food is heavy and starchy—and therefore delicious. Tasty specialties include *maizes zupa* (soup made from cornbread, currants, and cream) and the warming *Rīgas* (or *Melnais*) and *balzams* (a black liquor). Dark rye bread is a staple. Try *speķa rauši*, also known as *pīrāgi*, a warm pastry, or *biezpienmaize*, bread with sweet curds. Dark-colored *kaņepju sviests* (hemp butter) is good but too diluted for "medicinal" purposes. A particularly good Latvian beer is Porteris, from the Aldaris brewery. Cities offer foreign, **kosher,** and **vegetarian** cuisine.

LIFE AND TIMES

HISTORY

STUCK IN THE MIDDLE WITH YOU. Like her Baltic sisters, Latvia has often struggled under the yoke of foreign rule. The saga began when the Germans arrived in the late 12th century to convert the locals to Christianity. Then, in 1237, the Teutonic Knights established the **Confederation of Livonia,** which ruled a territory that included present-day Latvia and Estonia for nearly 300 years. Then Russian Tsar **Ivan IV** (the Terrible) invaded and the confederation collapsed, giving rise to the harsh **Livonian War** (1558-83) and a half-century of partition.

ARTIFICIAL SWEDENER. Things calmed down a bit when the 1629 **Truce of Altmark** gave control of eastern Livonia to the Poles, and that of Rīga and the northern regions to the Swedes. The following period of relative stability and freedom is known as the **Swedish Interlude.** Sweden, however, was forced to grant its Livonian territories to **Peter the Great** under the 1721 **Peace of Nystad,** and, with the third partition of Poland in 1795, the Russians swallowed up the Polish territory as well. The Latvian peasantry, however, strengthened by the 1861 **abolition of serfdom,** continued the struggle for freedom from the Russian Empire in the 19th century. **Nationalism** sprang up with particular strength during the Russian Revolution of 1905.

THE WAR YEARS. Reacting to the Bolshevik coup of the previous year, the **Latvian People's Council** proclaimed independence on November 18, 1918, establishing a government in Rīga led by agricultural scientist **Kārlis Ulmanis.** The **Constitution of 1922** created a republic governed by a president and unicameral parliament, but the large number of political parties in the legislature, or **Saeima,** kept the political situation unstable. Ulmanis faced difficulties when German elements within Latvia grew sympathetic to the Nazis, and in 1934 he declared a state of emergency. Under the **Nazi-Soviet Nonaggression Pact,** Latvia succumbed to Soviet control in 1939. In 1941, however, Germany reneged on the Pact and occupied Latvia, only to be driven back in 1945 by the Red Army, which promptly annexed its neighbor.

SUPREMELY SOVIET. Latvia entered the **Soviet Union** as one of its wealthiest and most industrialized regions. Under Soviet rule, the state was torn by radical economic restructuring, political repression, and the Russification of its culture. Some 35,000 Latvians, including many members of the intelligentsia, were deported to Russia during the first year of the occupation, while immigrants poured in from the rest of the USSR. Foreigners soon dominated local politics, and, within four decades, ethnic Latvians made up only half the population.

FREE AT LAST. Under **glasnost** and **perestroika,** Latvians, along with citizens of the other Baltic nations, protested in large numbers against the communist regime and created the **Popular Front** in 1988. Unsurprisingly, the communists were trounced in the 1990 elections. On May 4, 1990, the new legislature declared independence, but Soviet intervention sparked violent clashes in Rīga in 1991 between soldiers and Latvian demonstrators. Following the failed Moscow coup in August, the Latvian legislature reasserted its independence.

TODAY

Latvia has a unicameral **parliament,** the 100-seat **Saeima** (Supreme Council), and is governed by a **prime minister** representing the ruling party. The **president,** who is elected by parliament for a three-year term, holds limited power as head of state. Latvia has over 20 political parties; most governments are formed by coalition. Latvia solidified its relationship with the West by becoming a member of the **European Union** (EU) and **NATO** in 2004. Meanwhile, Latvian relations with both **Russia** and the large Russian minority at home remain thorny: laws mandate the teaching of Latvian in primary schools, while former President **Vaira Vike-Freiberga** (1999-2007, the first woman to hold such a post in Eastern Europe) demanded that Russia concede that its occupation of the Baltic states was unlawful.

Internal politics remain turbulent, with numerous parties jockeying for position in the Saeima. After Europe's first **Green Party** leader, **Indulis Emsis,** resigned in 2004 upon losing a budget vote, **Aigars Kalvītis** became prime minister of a four-party center-right coalition government. Such rapid political turnovers, spurred in part by conflict over the fast pace of privatization in telecommunications and energy, have caused delays in economic reform. Widespread allegations of corruption that rocked the Latvian government in 2007 will test the leadership of the incoming president, orthopedic surgeon **Valdis Zatlers.**

PEOPLE AND CULTURE

DEMOGRAPHICS. Nearly 30% of the country's population is **Russian,** leaving a bare 57% ethnic Latvian majority. **Belarusians** constitute a sparse 4% portion, and **Poles** and **Ukrainians** combined make up an additional 5%. Latvia has one of the lowest birth rates in the world. A majority of ethnic Latvians are **Evangelical Lutherans.** There are also sizable **Roman Catholic** and **Russian Orthodox** minorities.

LANGUAGE. Heavily influenced by German, Russian, Estonian, and Swedish, **Latvian** is one of two languages (the other is Lithuanian) in the Baltic language group. **Russian** is acceptable and widespread in Rīga; it is still spoken in the countryside, but its popularity is waning. Many young Latvians study **English;** older ones know some **German.** For a phrasebook and glossary, see **Appendix: Latvian,** p. 798.

CUSTOMS AND ETIQUETTE. Expect to be bought a drink if you talk with someone for a while; repay the favor in kind. If you're invited to a meal in someone's home, bring a **gift** for the hostess (an odd number of flowers is customary). **Handshaking** is expected when meeting new people or greeting a friend. **Shops** sometimes close for a break between noon and 3pm. When **toasting,** be sure to look your partner in the eye. A common toast is *"Augsā, lejā, prieksā, ieksā!"* ("Up, down, to the front, inside!" with accompanying hand gestures) or, simply *"Priekā!"* ("To happiness!") **Tipping** in Latvia is not obligatory, although leaving a 10% tip is not uncommon; pay attention to your bill: some restaurants will add the 10% service charge for you.

THE ARTS

LITERATURE. The mid-19th century brought a national awakening as the country asserted its literary independence in works such as *Lāčplēsis (Bearslayer)*, **Andrējs Pumpurs's** 1888 national epic. Realism and social protest became important in the **New Movement** in the late 19th century, and writer **Jānis Rainis** used folk imagery to critique contemporary problems. **Aleksandrs Čaks** detailed everyday life and gave a haunting account of WWI. Many Latvian writers turned to psychological detail in the 20th century. **Anšlāvs Eglītis,** in particular, reveled in intensifying human traits to the point of absurdity. Following WWII, the Soviets imposed **Socialist Realism,** mandating that texts promote revolutionary ideals. **Jānis Medenis**, exiled to a Siberian labor camp, wrote in his poetry of his longing for a free Latvia. **Mārtiņs Zīverts,** author of *Kāds Kura Nav (Someone Who Is Not)* is regarded as the best 20th-century Latvian dramatist.

MUSIC. Latvia has a rich tradition of folk music, centered around the *dainas*, a genre of short folk song based on a strict unrhymed verse-form. The folk music tradition influenced the late 19th-century works of **Jāzeps Vītols** and **Andrejs Jurjāns,** the country's first major composers. Rock music grew in popularity during the 1970s, when it served as a focal point for citizens desiring social change. Particularly influential were the rock songs of **Imants Kalniņš,** who is also considered one of Latvia's most important 20th-century composers. An important venue for classical music is the **International Chamber Choir Festival,** held each September in Rīga. Pop music, however, represented by such artists as 2000 Eurovision contestants **Brainstorm (Prāta Vētra),** is the most popular genre today.

THE VISUAL ARTS. Rīga is the **Art Nouveau** capital of Europe, with blocks upon blocks of buildings designed in this style dating back to the turn of the 20th century. Although the long period of mandated Socialist Realism forced the Latvian art scene into hibernation, the national liberation in the 1990s brought renewed creativity and engagement with the international art scene. Contemporary painter **Miervaldis Polis** has begun to enjoy acclaim for his hyper-realist art and is best known for his painting *A Golden Man.*

HOLIDAYS AND FESTIVALS

Holidays: New Year's Day (Jan. 1); Good Friday (Mar. 21, 2008; Apr. 10, 2009); Easter Monday (Mar. 24, 2008; Apr. 12, 2009); Labor Day (May 1); Ligo Day (June 23); St. John's Day (June 24); Independence Day (Nov. 18); Christmas (Dec. 25); Boxing Day (Dec. 26); New Year's Eve (Dec. 31).

Festivals: Midsummer's Eve is celebrated across the Baltic states every June 23-24. An updated calendar of cultural events is available at http://latviatourism.lv. Dziesmu Svētki, a large song festival, will pack the streets of Rīga in summer 2008. Check out their website for updated dates and other details: www.dziesmusvetki2008.lv.

RĪGA ☎8(2)

Rīga (REE-ga, pop. 756,000) is the unquestioned center of Latvia's cultural and economic life. The city's calendar is filled with music, theater, and opera festivals, while bright costumes and colors dominate the streets during holidays and celebrations. Founded in 1201 by the German Bishop Albert, Rīga is also an architectural treasure: medieval church spires dominate the Old Town, while early 20th-century Art Nouveau masterpieces line the city's newer streets. The large Russian minority contributes to the dynamic interaction of languages and cultures that characterizes this city.

The phone code in Rīga is 2 for all 6-digit numbers; there is no phone code for 7-digit numbers. Dial ☎116 for a Latvian operator and 115 for an international operator. Still confused? Call ☎800 8008 for info or 118, 722 2222, or 777 0777 for directory services.

INTERCITY TRANSPORTATION

Flights: Lidosta Rīga (Rīga Airport; ☎720 7009; www.riga-airport.com), southwest of Vecrīga. The easiest way to get to the Old Town is to take a bus (30min., about every 15min., 30Ls) from 13-Janvara iela, at the far right side of the airport parking lot. Bus #22 goes to the south edge of the Old Town, and #22a (express) stops by the Orthodox Cathedral. A taxi to Vecrīga is 6Ls. **Air Baltic** (☎720 7777; www.airbaltic.com) flies to many European cities. **Finnair** (☎720 7010; www.finnair.com) flies to **Helsinki, FIN. Lufthansa** (☎750 7711; www.lufthansa.com) flies to **Frankfurt** and **Munich, GER.**

Trains: Centrālā Stacija (Central Station), Stacijas laukums (☎723 3113; www.ldz.lv), next to the bus station south of the Old Town; head toward the clock tower. International trains arrive at platform 2. Note that trains are marked by both *perons* (platforms) and *cels* (tracks). Open daily 4:30am-midnight. The **info center** at the train station charges 0.10Ls per question, but a 2nd info center (marked with a yellow "i") is located near cash desk #15 and offers free help. Open daily 8am-1pm and 2-8pm. **Tickets** for domestic trains can be bought from counters #1-13, to the right of the main entrance to the station. If you have trouble deciphering your ticket, ask at information to find your platform. International train tickets are sold at counters #1-6 beside the pricey information desk. To: **Moscow, RUS** (18hr., 1 per day, 11Ls); **St. Petersburg, RUS** (14hr., 2 per day, 9Ls); and **Vilnius, LIT** (8hr., 2 per day on odd-numbered days, 10-14Ls). **Baltic Express** also goes to **Berlin, GER** and **Warsaw, POL.**

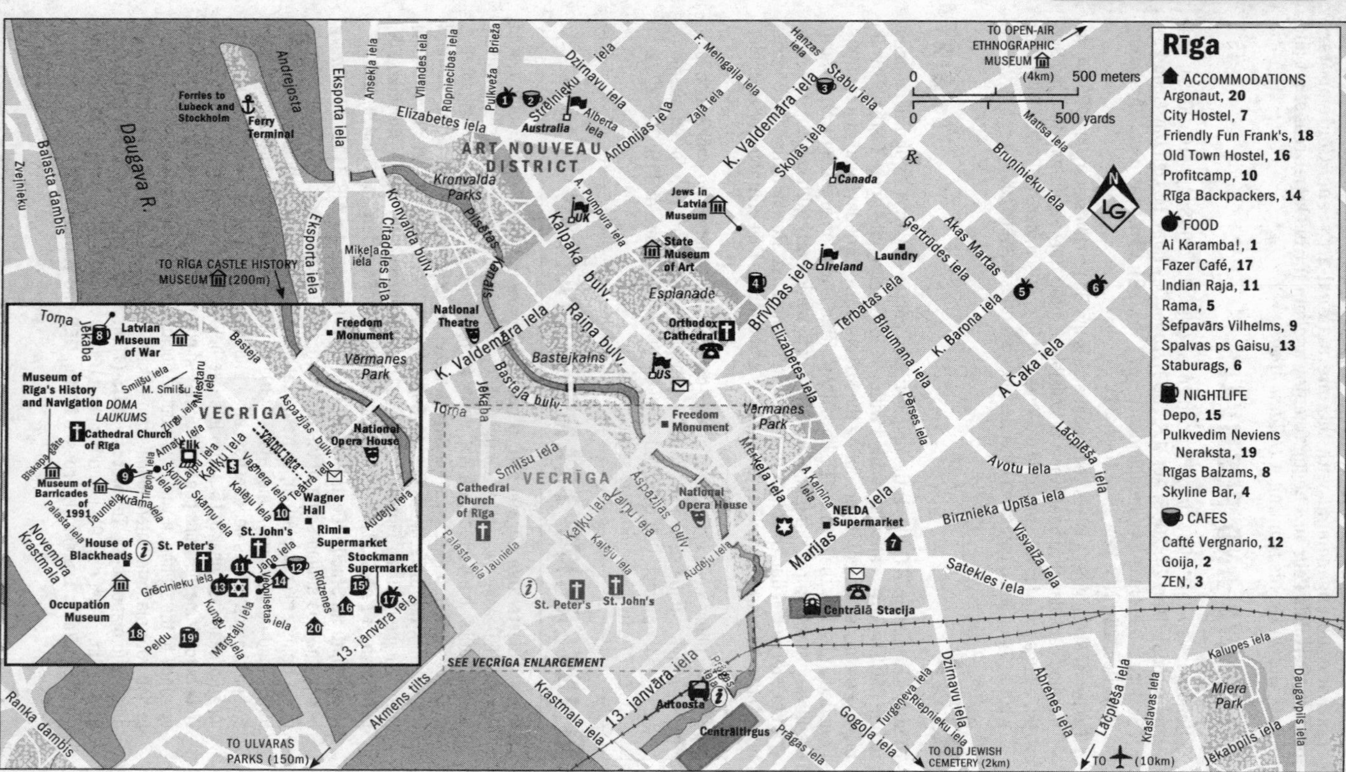
Rīga
ACCOMMODATIONS
Argonaut, 20
City Hostel, 7
Friendly Fun Frank's, 18
Old Town Hostel, 16
Profitcamp, 10
Rīga Backpackers, 14
FOOD
Ai Karamba!, 1
Fazer Café, 17
Indian Raja, 11
Rama, 5
Šefpavārs Vilhelms, 9
Spalvas ps Gaisu, 13
Staburags, 6
NIGHTLIFE
Depo, 15
Pulkvedim Neviens
Neraksta, 19
Rīgas Balzams, 8
Skyline Bar, 4
CAFES
Cafté Vergnario, 12
Goija, 2
ZEN, 3
0
500 meters
0
500 yards
TO OPEN-AIR ETHNOGRAPHIC MUSEUM (4km)
ART NOUVEAU DISTRICT
VECRĪGA
SEE VECRĪGA ENLARGEMENT
Daugava R.
Ferries to Lubeck and Stockholm
Ferry Terminal
Andrejosta
TO RĪGA CASTLE HISTORY MUSEUM (200m)
TO ULVARAS PARKS (150m)
TO OLD JEWISH CEMETERY (2km)
TO (10km)
Centrālā Stacija
Centrāltirgus
Autoosta
Freedom Monument
National Opera House
National Theatre
Orthodox Cathedral
State Museum of Art
Jews in Latvia Museum
Cathedral Church of Rīga
St. Peter's
St. John's
Latvian Museum of War
Museum of Rīga's History and Navigation
DOMA LAUKUMS
Museum of Barricades of 1991
House of Blackheads
Occupation Museum
Wagner Hall
Rimi Supermarket
Stockmann Supermarket
NELDA Supermarket
Laundry
Australia
Canada
Ireland
UK
US
Vērmanes Park
Kronvalda Parks
Miera Park
Esplanade
Bastejkalns
Pilsētas Kanāls
Akmens tilts
Brīvības iela
K. Valdemāra iela
Elizabetes iela
Kalpaka bulv.
Raiņa bulv.
Aspazijas bulv.
Basteja bulv.
13. janvāra iela
Krastmala iela
Dzirnavu iela
Lāčplēša iela
Marijas iela
Merķeļa iela
Gogoļa iela
Eksporta iela
Kronvalda bulv.
Citadeles iela
Balasta dambis
Ranka dambis
Zvejnieku
Novembra Krastmala
Satekles iela
Visvalža iela
Birznieka Upīša iela
Avotu iela
A. Čaka iela
K. Barona iela
Blaumaņa iela
Tērbatas iela
Ģertrūdes iela
Akas Martas
Bruņinieku iela
Matīsa iela
Skolas iela
Stabu iela
Antonijas iela
Strēlnieku iela
Abrenes iela
Kalupes iela
Daugavpils iela
Jēkabpils iela
Krāslavas iela
Prāgas iela

Buses: Autoosta (Bus Station), Prāgas 1 (☎900 0009; www.autoosta.lv). From the train station, face the Old Town and go left 100m, crossing under the train tracks. Across the canal from the central market. Open daily 5am-midnight. To: **Kaliningrad, RUS** (9-10hr., 1 per day, 14Ls); **Kaunas, LIT** (5-6hr., 2 per day, 8Ls); **Klaipėda, LIT** (6hr., 4 per day, 8Ls); **Minsk, BLR** (12hr., 1 per day, 14Ls); **Prague, CZR** (25½hr., 1 per week); **Tallinn, EST** (4-6hr., 11per day, 6-8Ls); **Tartu, EST** (4hr., 2 per day, 6Ls); **Vilnius, LIT** (5hr., 5 per day, 7Ls). **Ecolines** (☎721 4512; www.ecolines.lv) books buses to **Moscow** (17hr., 2 per day). Book other international destinations through **Eurolines** (☎721 4080; www.eurolines.lv).

ORIENTATION

Chaotic in their names and numbers, the streets of Rīga twist and turn and can prove disorienting for even the most seasoned traveler. Be patient: even if you get lost, you'll be sure to stumble upon something worthwhile—though it can help to keep a few key landmarks in mind. The city is divided in half by **Brīvības iela,** which leads from the outskirts to the **Freedom Monument** in the center and continues through **Vecrīga** (Old Rīga) as **Kaļķu iela.** The **Daugava River** borders Old Rīga on the west, while the smaller canal separates Old from New Rīga on the east. To reach Vecrīga from the train station, turn left on Marijas iela, cross the street, and go right on one of the small streets beyond the canal. If all else fails, just head toward the towering spires. **K. Valdemāra iela** cuts through Vecrīga roughly parallel to Brīvības; from the river, it passes the National Theater on the left and the Art Museum on the right. The semi-circular **Elizabetes iela** surrounds Vecrīga and its adjoining parks. *Rīga In Your Pocket* (1.20Ls), available at kiosks and travel agencies, has **maps** and up-to-date listings. Similarly, *Rīga This Week* is free at most major hotels and some hostels.

LOCAL TRANSPORTATION

Trains: (www.ldz.lv). Suburban trains, running as far as the border with Estonia at **Valka/Valga,** leave from the smaller building of the train station. The Lugaži line includes **Cēsis** and **Sigulda.** Buy same-day tickets at counters #1-15 or advance tickets in the **booking office** next to the information center to the right of counter #15 (☎583 3397). Open daily 8am-1pm and 2-8pm. Purchase tickets on board for a 0.30Ls surcharge.

Public Transportation: (www.ttp.lv). **Buses, trams,** and **trolleys** run daily 5:30am-midnight. Buy tickets on board from the ticket collector (0.30Ls).

Taxis: All licensed taxis have a yellow license plate. Private taxis have a green light in the windshield. **Rīga Taxi** (☎800 1010). 0.30Ls per km during the day; 0.40Ls per km midnight-6am. Insist that the meter is turned on, or agree on a price beforehand.

Bike Rental: Gandrs, Kalnciema 28 (☎761 4775; www.gandrs.lv). Take bus #22 or tram #4 or 5 from the Old Town to the intersection of Slokas and Kalnciema. From the tram stop, turn left on Kalnciema and continue 100m. Helmets and equipment available. 1Ls per hr., 6Ls per day. Open M-F 10am-7pm, Sa-Su 10am-5pm. MC/V.

PRACTICAL INFORMATION

TOURIST AND FINANCIAL SERVICES

Tourist Office: City of Rīga Information Centre, Ratslaukums 6 (☎67 03 79 00; www.rigatourism.com), next to the House of Blackheads and the Occupation Museum. English, German, Latvian, and Russian spoken. Open daily in high season 9am-7pm;

in low season 10am-6pm. Most hotels and travel agencies sell the **Rīga Card,** which gives restaurant, museum, and transit discounts. Unless you can cram all of Rīga's museums into 1-2 days, the card likely isn't worth it.

Embassies and Consulates: Australia, Alberta iela 13 (☎733 6383; acr@latnet.lv). Open Tu 10am-noon, Th 3-5pm. **Canada,** Baznīcas 20/22 (☎781 3945; www.dfait-maeci.gc.ca/canada-europa/baltics). Open Tu and Th 10am-1pm. **Ireland,** Valdemāra 21 (☎67 03 52 86; fax 67 03 53 23). Open M-Tu and Th-F 10am-noon. In an emergency, citizens can call or stop by M-Tu and Th-F 10am-6pm. **Russia,** Antonijas iela 2 (☎733 2151; rusembas@delfi.lv, www.latvia.mid.ru). Entrance on Kalpaka bul. Open M-F 8:30am-5:30pm. **UK,** Alunāna iela 5 (☎777 4700; www.britain.lv). Open M-F 9:30am-noon. **US,** Raiņa bulv. 7 (☎703 6200; www.usembassy.lv). Open M-Tu and Th 9-11:30am. US citizen services Tu-Th 2-4pm. In an emergency, citizens can stop by M and F 9-11:30am and 2-4pm or call an officer at ☎920 5708.

Currency Exchange: At any kiosk labeled **"valutos maiņa." SEB Unibanka,** Pils iela 23 (☎67 21 53 99; www.seb.lv). MC/V **cash advances** and cashes AmEx and Thomas Cook traveler's checks for no commission. Open M-F 9am-5pm. **Marika** 24hr. currency exchange desks are at Bastēja bul. 14, Brīvības 30, and at almost all of Rīga's casinos.

LOCAL SERVICES AND COMMUNICATIONS

Luggage Storage: At the **bus station,** near the Eurolines office. 0.50Ls per 10kg bag for 1st hr., 0.20Ls per hr. thereafter. Open daily 6:30am-10:30pm. At the **train station,** under the stairs in front of the main exit. 0.50-1.50Ls per bag per day. Open 4:30am-midnight. At the **airport,** left of the exit. Arrange drop-off or retrieval with the red phone. 0.60Lt per day. Open M-Tu, Th, Sa 4:30am-midnight; W, F, Su 5:30am-midnight.

English-Language Bookstore: Globuss, Vaļņu iela 26 (☎722 6957). English-language classics and bestsellers. Open M-F 9am-8pm, Sa 10am-7pm, Su 10am-5pm. MC/V.

GLBT Resources: Check out **www.gay.lv** for a complete list of gay clubs, hotels, and resources in Rīga.

Laundromat: Nivala, Akas iela 4 (☎728 1346), between Ģertrūdes iela and Lāčplēša iela. Self-service 4Ls per load. Open 24hr.

24hr. Pharmacy: Vecpilsētas Aptieka, Audeju 20 (☎721 3340). English spoken.

Telephones: A cluster of public phones is located on **Brīvības,** next to the brown Laima clock. Phone booths are available throughout the city, and require you to purchase a 2Ls or 5Ls card, available at the post office and numerous shops and kiosks.

Internet: Internet cafes dot the Old Town. **Elik,** Kaļķu iela 11 (☎722 7079; www.elikkafe.lv), is a centrally located option. 47 computers. Beer and snacks. 0.50Ls per hr., 1Ls per 3hr., 3-4Ls per day. Open 24hr. Branch at Čaka iela 26 (☎728 4506). Lattelecom's Wi-Fi networks blanket the Old Town. Look for establishments with the Lattelecom logo in the window to purchase an access card (0.94Ls per hr.).

Post Office: Stacijas laukums 1 (☎701 8804; www.riga.post.lv), near the train station. Open M-F 7am-8pm, Sa 8am-6pm, Su 8am-4pm. Branches at Brīvības 19 (☎67 01 87 71; open M-F 7am-10pm, Sa-Su 8am-8pm) and Aspāzijas bul. 24 (☎67 01 87 71; open M-F 8am-8pm, Sa 8am-6pm). **Poste Restante** at window #9, or ask at any counter if window #9 is closed. **Postal Code:** LV-1050.

ACCOMMODATIONS

Lovers express their affection publicly along Rīga's streets in summer. You could tell them to get a room, but they probably can't find one. Though hostels have proliferated in Rīga, travelers should make reservations months in advance, especially in summer and on weekends. For a homestay (from 22Ls) or an apartment near the center (31-52Ls), try **Patricia,** Elizabetes iela 22. (☎728 4868, 24hr. 721 0180; www.patriciahotel.com. Open M-F 9am-6pm, Sa-Su 11am-4pm.)

Old Town Hostel, Vaļņu iela 43 (☎722 3406; www.rigaoldtownhostel.lv). This hostel is equipped with a lively pub that will keep you awake until the wee hours, whether you like it or not. The bright, freshly painted dorms and sparkling clean beds make sleep easier. Fully equipped kitchen, free Internet and Wi-Fi, and a sauna (2Ls). English spoken. Friendly, chatty staff. Safes in rooms. Check-in noon. 12-person dorms from 8Ls; 6-person dorms 10Ls. Prices vary by season, group size, and length of stay. MC/V. ❷

Argonaut, Kalēju 50 (☎614 7214; www.argonauthostel.com). Adorned with rock posters, this hostel offers key-card door access and gigantic lockers in each room. The dorms are slightly dark, and your room may contain some mosquitoes in summertime, but the staff is friendly and helpful. Try an "Argonaut Adventure," such as bobsledding with the Latvian national team. Free Internet. 12-bed dorms from 8Ls; 8-bed dorms 9Ls; 4-bed dorms 12Ls. Prices vary by season and day of the week. MC/V. ❷

City Hostel, Elizabetes 101 (☎728 0124; www.cityhostel.lv). Go north on Marijas and turn left on Elizabetes; City Hostel is on the left. These tidy dorms offer new wooden bunk beds that make for a soothing stay near the train station and Old Town. Kitchen, common room, and free Internet. 10-bed dorms 8Ls, 6-bed 11Ls. Cash only. ❷

Friendly Fun Frank's, 18. Novembra krastmala 29 (☎599 0612; www.franks.lv). From the bus and train stations, walk toward the river and go right on Novembra krastmala. Continue to the large peach building with a small koala beside the buzzer. Don't be surprised if at 3am you're the first one home. This party hostel offers nightly outings to pubs and clubs in Rīga, as well as 1 free beer when you arrive. Spacious dorms, common room, and Internet. 10-bed dorms from 9Ls. Cash only. ❷

Profitcamp, Teatra iela 12 (☎721 6361; www.profitcamp.lv). This friendly hostel often serves as overflow when dorm beds are in high demand. Rooms are dark, but the convenient location in the Old Town is a significant plus. Breakfast included. Safes in rooms, kitchen. Free luggage storage, Internet, and Wi-Fi. 6- to 20-person dorms 8-12Ls. Prices vary depending on size of group and length of stay. MC/V. ❷

Rīga Backpackers, Mārstaļu 6 (☎67 22 99 22; www.riga-backpackers.com). This historic hotel, fit with ornate glass chandeliers and high ceilings, offers rare elegance for budget travelers. Watch TV in a common room reminiscent of an 18th-century palace, relax in the clean rooms, and chat with the helpful staff. Free Internet and luggage storage. Singles 30Ls; doubles 35Ls; triples 30Ls. Cash only. ❺

FOOD

Rīga's diverse culinary offerings (including Japanese, Turkish, Spanish, Russian, and other international fare) add flavor to the city's cosmopolitan atmosphere, particularly in the Old Town. For 24hr. food and liquor, try **Nelda,** Marijas 5. (☎722 9355. Cash only.) The central supermarket **Rimi,** Audēju 16, stocks the basics (☎701 8020; open daily 8am-10pm; MC/V), while the **Stockmann department store,** 13. Janvara iela 8, next to the bus station, carries an enormous selection of Latvian and Western brands alike. Occupying five zeppelin hangars behind the bus station, **Centrālais Tirgus** (Central Market) is one of the largest markets in Europe. Fresh fruits and vegetables are sold in stalls outside of the main buildings, while bread, meat, and dairy are sold inside. Beware of pickpockets. (Open M and Su 8am-4pm, Tu-Sa 8am-5pm.)

Rama, Barona iela 56 (☎727 2490), between Ģertrūdes and Stabu. Eat well for about 1Lt at this Hare Krishna cafeteria, serving a wide variety of vegetarian Indian food. Main courses like stewed vegetables or soy salad are sold by weight, while spicy samosas are sold individually (0.20Ls). Proceeds go to feed the poor. Open M-Sa 11am-7pm. ❶

Indian Raja, Vecpilsētas iela 3 (☎721 2614). This undiscovered establishment serves incredibly authentic Indian and Thai food in a romantic, lavishly decorated hidden basement in the Old Town. Chat away with travelers and expats over excellent chicken tikka (6Ls) and lamb vindaloo (6.65Ls). Entrees 8-11Ls. Open daily noon-11pm. MC/V. ❹

Šefpavārs Vilhelms (Chef William), Šķūņu iela 6. Look for the chef statue outside this pancake house that offers greasily delicious self-serve meat, potato, apple, banana, cheese, and plain pancakes. Slather on fruit jam or sour cream, grab a glass of milk, and find a seat along walls decorated to look like pancake batter. You'll feed yourself for under 2Lt. Open M-Th 9am-10pm, F-Sa 10am-11pm, Su 10am-10pm. Cash only. ❶

Staburags, A. Čaka iela 55 (☎729 9787). Follow A. Čaka iela away from Vecrīga. Servers in 19th-century serf costumes dish out portions fit for a tsar. Impressive interior features replicas of rural Latvian dwellings, complete with log tables, miniature waterfalls, and a maze of tiny rooms. Excellent house beer 1.50Ls per 0.5L. Entrees 3-6Ls. Open daily noon-midnight. Cash only. ❷

Ai Karamba!, Pulkveža Brieža 2 (☎733 4672). Walk away from the train station and the center on Elizabetes iela, and turn right on Pulkveža Brieža; the diner is on the right. Decorated with license plates from Canada and the US, the diner has a delicious all-day breakfast menu and lunch and dinner specials. Omelettes 1-3Ls. BLTs 1Ls. Entrees 2-4Ls. Open M-Th 8-midnight, F-Sa 8am-1am, Su 10am-midnight. MC/V. ❷

Spalvas Pa Gaisu (Feathers in the Air), Grēcinieku 8 (☎67 22 03 93). This stylish restaurant, fit with colorful floor lights and a well-stocked bar, serves gourmet chicken pockets (3.25Ls), roast pork (3.09Ls), herring rolls (2.35 Ls), and other elegant entrees at reasonable prices. Don't miss their unique and delicious soups (1-2Ls). Live music and a hip crowd surround the bar for early evening mixed drinks. Open Su-Tu 11am-midnight, W-Th 11am-2am, F-Sa 11am-5am. MC/V. ❷

Fazer Cafe, 13. Janvāra 8, on the top floor of the Stockmann shopping center (☎67 07 12 99). Help yourself to large portions of Italian buffet in this modern penthouse cafe. The diverse, fresh selection of entrees, salads, pastas, breakfast foods, desserts, and mixed drinks offers something for everyone. Feast on a soup and an entree with the lunch special (11am-3pm) for only 4Ls. Open daily 9am-10pm. MC/V. ❷

CAFES

Summer in Rīga is all about being outside—breakfast, lunch, dinner, and drinks are enjoyed on the many terraces and beer gardens throughout town.

Goija, Strēlnieku iela 1a (☎703 3370), just off Elizabetes. Dark lighting, rich Asian decor, and pillows galore make this unique teahouse a refuge from the bustling streets. Magnifying glasses allow you to inspect each kind of tea available (from 1.50Ls). Has board games and books. Free Internet. Open M-Th and Su 11am-2am, F-Sa 11am-5am.

ZEN, Stabu iela 6 (☎731 6521). Follow Brīvības east from the Old Town. Turn left on Stabu and walk for 1½ blocks. Slip off your shoes and relax among pillows, candles, and lanterns. Your choice of tea is brewed slowly, right before your eyes. The black tea (1.30Ls) is said to prolong your life. Water pipes 5-8Ls. Open daily 2pm-2am. MC/V.

Caffé Vergnano, Jāņa iela 18 (☎67 22 56 99). Sink into a cozy arm chair and bask in the afternoon sun shining through the many skylights. This sleek, Mediterranean cafe serves up pasta, salads, light snacks, and some of the richest coffees and teas in the Old Town. Open daily 11am-11pm.

SIGHTS

VECRĪGA

The city's most famous landmarks are clustered in tiny Vecrīga (Old Town), a maze of crowded cobblestone streets mostly off-limits to automobiles. Vecrīga hasn't kept capitalism out, however, as the golden arches at the eastern entrance attest. As you move from site to site, don't forget to admire the distinctive buildings that have made Rīga the architectural capital of Eastern Europe.

ST. PETER'S CHURCH (SV. PĒTERA BAZNĪCA). Built in 1209 by the Livs who accepted Christianity, this church is best known for its spire. In 1666, it toppled to the ground and crushed locals to death; it was shelled by Germans on St. Peter's Day, June 29, 1941. The spire was rebuilt in 1973, and according to local lore, is haunted by the ghost of a soldier who guarded the church in the 18th century. Visitors can wander through an excellent exhibition of local art on the ground floor, admire the intricate brickwork in the interior, or take an elevator to the tower for awe-inspiring views of Rīga. *(Open May-Sept. Tu-Su 10am-6pm; Oct.-Apr. Tu-Su 10am-5pm; staff sometimes shuts ticket office for lunch break 12:50-2:30pm. Exhibits 0.50Ls. Spire accessible via elevator; last elevator to the top 20min. before closing. 2Ls, students 1Ls.)*

CATHEDRAL CHURCH OF RĪGA (DOMA BAZNĪCA). This awe-inspiring house of worship is the largest church in the Baltics and houses a legendary organ of over 6700 pipes, whose beauty inspired Franz Lizst to compose a piece in its honor. Wander the pews of the cathedral to see stonework and masonry from the original structure, or go outside and into the Cross-Vaulted Gallery, a museum in the courtyard. On display are a Salaspils stone head and a statue of Bishop Albert, the German missionary who founded Rīga in 1201. The original 1897 statue was moved to St. Petersburg during WWII and then disappeared. This 2001 replica commemorates Rīga's 800th anniversary. *(Gallery open May-Oct. Tu-F 11am-4pm, Sa 10am-2pm. English captions. 1Ls, students 0.50Ls. Separate payment for cathedral and gallery.)*

LATVIAN RIFLEMEN MONUMENT (LATVIEŠU STRĒLNIEKU LAUKUMS). Looming over the Museum of the Occupation, this granite monument is a controversial reminder of Latvia's Soviet past. The Socialist-Realist statue depicts three soldiers guarding the square, honoring those who served as Lenin's bodyguards during and after the Revolution. Many locals would like to see the monument torn down, while others see it as an important tribute to the Latvians who fought in WWI.

HOUSE OF THE BLACKHEADS (MELNGALVJU NAMS). One of Rīga's most prized architectural treasures, this Gothic building with a Dutch-Renaissance facade was originally erected in 1334. In 1687, the building was purchased by the Blackheads, a group of bachelor merchants who adopted the quirky name to honor their patron saint, dark-skinned St. Maurice. Portraits and statues of Maurice can be found inside, and his symbol decorates the interior furniture. The intricate cream-pink second-floor assembly hall, open to the public, is also used for official state functions. The basement houses a museum that displays artifacts from the original house. The building was severely damaged during WWII and demolished by the Soviets in 1948, but was rebuilt and completed in 2001. *(Ratslaukums 7, in the town square by the Occupation Museum. ☎704 4300; melngalv@rcc.lv. Open Tu-Su May-Sept. 10am-5pm; Oct.-Apr. 11am-5pm. House and museum 1.50Ls, students 0.70Ls. Tours in English, French, German, or Russian 5Ls.)*

RĪGA CASTLE. In 1487, locals destroyed the castle on the banks of the Daugava in a rebellion against the ruling Livonian Knights. The Livonians forced city dwellers to rebuild the structure in 1515. It has since been expanded, and served as the presidential residence of Karlis Ulmanis during the country's brief period of independence between the world wars. Inside the castle, the **History Museum of Latvia** is incomprehensible to those who can't read Latvian. *(Pils laukums 3, off Valdemāra iela. ☎722 8147. Open W-Su 11am-6pm. Free. Tours in English, German, and Russian 5Ls.)*

POWDER TOWER (PULVERTORNIS). The German student fraternity Rubonia once held its debaucherous parties inside this 14th-century fortress, and nine cannonballs are still lodged in its walls (curiously enough on the side facing the city).

No frat parties take place here anymore: the tower houses the **Latvian Museum of War** (Latvijas Kara Muzejs), which provides a good shorthand account of Rīga's history, packed into four floors of photographs and exhibitions. The second floor displays of Latvia's post-WWI effort to win independence, and the fourth-floor exhibit detailing the fall of communism are particularly captivating. Only these two sections have English captions. *(Smilšu iela 20. ☎ 722 8147. Open W-Su May-Sept. 10am-6pm; Oct.-Apr. 10am-5pm. Museum 0.50Ls, students 0.25Ls. Tours in English 3Ls.)*

NEW RĪGA

FREEDOM MONUMENT (BRĪVĪBAS PIEMINEKLIS). This beloved monument depicts Liberty raising her arms skyward surrounded by throngs of singing, working Latvians. Dedicated in 1935, during Latvia's brief period of independence, the monument—affectionately known as Milda—survived the subsequent Russian occupation by masquerading as a Soviet symbol. The stars in Mighty Milda's palms represent the three main regions of Latvia (Kurzeme, Latgale, and Vidzeme), but the Soviets claimed it represented Mother Russia supporting the three Baltic states. Today, locals frequently leave flowers at her base—an act that was punished by deportation to Siberia during Soviet rule. Two steadfast guards protect her honor daily 9am-6pm; the changing of the guard occurs on the hour. *(At the corner of Raiņa bul. and Brīvības iela.)*

BASTEJKALNS (BASTION HILL). Rīga's busy central park, surrounded by the Old City moat (Pīlsētas kanāls), houses the ruins of the Old City walls. Five red stone slabs around the canal commemorate the five Latvians killed on January 20, 1991, when Soviet special forces stormed the Interior Ministry on Raiņa bul. At the northern end of Bastejkalns, on K. Valdemāra iela, is the **National Theater.** Latvia first declared independence here on November 18, 1918. Benches along the pathways and riverbanks are popular with couples in summertime. *(Kronvalda bul. 2. ☎ 732 2759. Open daily 10am-7pm.)*

ORTHODOX CATHEDRAL. Surrounded by Esplanade Park, Rīga's Byzantine **Orthodox Cathedral** (Pareizticigo Katedrāle) was built between 1876 and 1884. Soviets closed the church in 1961 and revamped it as a "house of atheism," which contained a cafe, lecture hall, library, and planetarium. Restoration of the interior is currently underway, and the church is frequented by worshippers and tourists alike. *(Brīvības iela 23. ☎ 721 2901; www.svet.lv. Open daily 7am-6pm. Services M-F 8am, 5pm; Sa 7, 9:30am, 5pm; Su 8, 10am, 5pm. Donations requested.)*

JEWISH RĪGA

Jews were barred from Rīga until the 18th century. By 1935, the more than 40,000 Jews who lived in the city comprised about 10% of Rīga's total population; only about 150 remained at the end of WWII. Although many returned during Soviet times, the fall of communism brought about a new migration. Today, between 10,000 and 15,000 Jews reside here.

JEWS IN LATVIA MUSEUM. Funded largely by non-Jewish German philanthropists, this museum contains photographs and biographical information on Rīga's most famous Jewish residents, including intellectuals, teachers, musicians, and athletes. A sobering, black-painted room is filled with graphic photographs of the Terror Against the Jews, beginning in 1941. Exhibits tell the story of local Christians who sheltered Jews from the Nazis. *(Skolas 6, 3rd fl., at the intersection with Dzirnavu. ☎ 728 3484; ebreji.latvija@apollo.lv. Open M-Th and Su noon-5pm. Donations requested.)*

OLD JEWISH CEMETERY. Before the graveyard was established in 1725, local Jews had to cart their dead all the way to Poland for burial. On July 4, 1941, much of the cemetery was destroyed by Nazi soldiers and used as a mass grave for the ghetto. The

Soviets converted it into a public park. A **monument** was erected after the fall of communism. Most of the Hebrew grave inscriptions have worn away, but the large Star of David carved into granite is still surrounded with flowers and candles. *(2/4 Līksnas iela. Tram #15 stops near the intersection of Ludzas and Līksnas.)*

BIĶERNIEKI FOREST. Erected in 2001 by the German War Graves Commission, this beautiful, powerful memorial commemorates the Jews who were murdered here between 1941 and 1944. A central altar is inscribed with Job's words, "O earth, do not cover my blood, and let there be no resting place for my cry." Around the altar, rocks jut out of the ground, representing the cities from which Jews were taken. Quiet forest paths branch out from the monument. *(Take tram #14 from Brīvības to "Keguma"; do not get off at "Bikernicku." Walk straight 1km and you will see a white gate leading to the memorial. The memorial extends into the woods on the left side of the road, 600m closer to the tram stop.)*

SYNAGOGUE. Built in 1905, the only Latvian Synagogue to remain standing after WWII is today the center of Rīga's Jewish community. The Nazis used it as a warehouse and would have burned it but for its close proximity to the residential areas of Old Rīga. Luckily, the Synagogue's sacred artifacts and scrolls were hidden away by members of the community and escaped destruction; they are on display today. *(Peitavas 6/8. Hebrew services M-F and Sa 9:30am, Su 9am. Open 10am-4pm. Donations requested.)*

MUSEUMS

OCCUPATION MUSEUM (OKUPĀCIJAS MUZEJS). This compelling museum guides visitors through Latvia's tortured history under the Soviets, then the Nazis, and then the Soviets again. It takes at least an hour to go through the gripping displays, and may require more than a day to fully explore. The exhibits include a re-creation of gulag barracks and movies and photographs about the atrocities committed by the KGB and the Checka, a Soviet squad of informants and tribunals. The museum offers a sobering account of Latvian Nazi sympathizers' role in the slaughter of the country's Jewish population. Collections of personal items from those shipped off to gulags are particularly poignant. *(Strēlnieku laukums 1, in the black building behind the Latvian Riflemen Monument. ☎ 721 2715; www.occupationmuseum.lv. Open May-Sept. daily 11am-6pm; Oct.-Apr. Tu-Su 11am-5pm. English captions. Admission Free; donations requested. Free audio tours in English, German, and Russian.)*

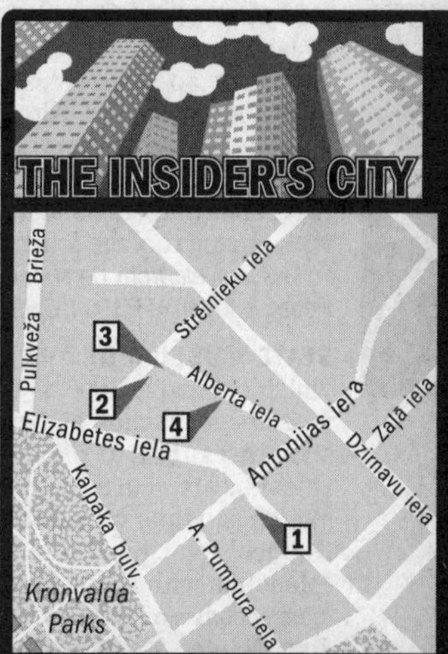

ART NOUVEAU RĪGA

Riga's remarkable architecture makes its Old Town a sight in itself. About 40% of the downtown area is built in the unique Art Nouveau style, characterized by stylized, curvilinear designs and floral motifs. To see the most impressive buildings, many of which were designed by Russian architect Mikhail Eisenstein in the early 20th century, take this walk:

1. From K. Valdemara iela, turn left on Elizabetes iela to reach 10b, on your left. Admire the work from across the street.

2. Turn right on Strelnieku for the blue-and-white 1905 student hostel at 4b, now the Stockholm School of Economics.

3. Next door is the massive, cream-colored corner edifice at Alberta iela 13, with fine details and pointed turrets.

4. Turn on Alberta iela. Numbers 2, 2a, 4, 6, and 8, in various states of repair, showcase a colorful and impressive catalogue of Art Nouveau balconies and intricate brickwork.

MUSEUM OF BARRICADES OF 1991. Vecrīga morphed into a medieval fortress in January 1991, when locals built makeshift walls to defend the city center from Red Army special forces. The barricades didn't stop the Soviets from firing on unarmed protesters. Although the tiny museum doesn't seem like much, it provides an incredibly interesting snapshot of Rīga's short resistance. Displays include information about those killed during the resistance, as well as maps of Latvia and Rīga documenting those 10 days. Don't miss the 35min. English video with jarring footage taken by a Latvian TV crew during the gunfight. *(Krāmu iela 3. Follow Jauniela from Doma laukums; knock on door #1 on the 2nd fl. ☎721 3525; www.barikades.lv. Open M-F 10am-5pm, Sa 11am-5pm. Free; donations requested.)*

STATE MUSEUM OF ART (VALSTS MĀKSLAS MUZEJS). This majestic building, which opened in 1905, is as interesting as the treasures within it, but don't let the magnificent salmon-and-green colored entrance overshadow the art. The museum showcases 18th- to 20th-century works by Latvian artists and a large collection of Russian art. Turn-of-the-century collages share space with ink-and-pencil sketches, while oil paintings dominate the rooms. Highlights include Nicholas Roerich's blue-hued Himalayan landscapes, on the first floor, and Karlis Padego's "Madonna with a Machine Gun" upstairs. *(Valdemāra iela 10a, near the Elizabetes iela intersection. ☎67 32 50 51; www.vmm.lv. Open Apr.-Oct. M and W-Su 11am-5pm, Th 11am-7pm; Oct.-Apr. M and W-Su 11am-5pm. 0.70Ls, students 0.30Ls. English audio tours 1Ls.)*

MUSEUM OF RĪGA'S HISTORY AND NAVIGATION (RĪGAS VĒSTURES UN KUĢNIECĪBAS MUZEJS). A dazzling collection of 500,000 items fills this Neoclassical history museum established in 1773. The museum helped preserve Latvian culture during the Soviet era; it now gives a complete history of Rīga until 1940. Don't miss the giant statue of Latvia's patron saint, St. Christopher, on the top floor, and the lavish exhibit "Rīga and its Citizens, 1918-1940." *(Palasta iela 4, next to Dome Cathedral. ☎721 1358; www.vip.latnet.lv/museums/riga. Open W-Su May-Sept. 10am-5pm; Oct.-Apr. 11am-5pm. 1.20Ls, students 0.40Ls. Tours in English, German, and Russian 3Ls.)*

OPEN-AIR ETHNOGRAPHIC MUSEUM (ETNOGRĀFISKAIS BRĪVDABAS MUZEJS). Nearly 100 historic 18th- and 19th-century buildings from all over Latvia are gathered here at one of the oldest, most realistic ethnographic museums in Europe. Here you can still see local artisans churning out traditional wares, from wooden spoons to pottery. *(Brīvības 440. Bus #1 from Merķela iela to "Brīvdabas Muzejs." ☎799 4106. Open daily 10am-5pm. 1Ls, students 0.25Ls. Tours 8/5Ls; call ahead.)*

RĪGA MOTOR MUSEUM (RĪGAS MOTORMUZEJS). A wax figure of Stalin sits in the seat of his armored ZIS-1155 at this bizarre museum, housed in a building designed to look like a radiator, which showcases an impressive collection of over one hundred 20th-century cars, including classic limos and sports and military vehicles. Particularly noteworthy is the 1966 Rolls Royce Silver Shadow that Brezhnev crashed in 1980; see the wax-figure bureaucrat gasping after denting his wheels. The museum is a treat for car-lovers and Sovietophiles. *(6 S. Eizensteina iela. Take tram #14 from Brīvības iela to Gailezers Hospital. Cross the street and follow Gailezera iela over the river 400m. Go right at the T-intersection. ☎709 7170; rmm@apollo.lv. Open daily 10am-6pm. Some English captions. 1Ls, students 0.50Ls.)*

ENTERTAINMENT AND NIGHTLIFE

Rīga offers the best array of music and performance art in the Baltics. Theaters close from mid-June through August, but the **Opera House** hosts summer events. The **Latvian National Opera** (☎707 3777; www.opera.lv) performs in the Opera House, Aspāzijas bul. 3. Richard Wagner once presided as director, and you can catch concerts for 2-30Ls. The **Latvian Symphony Orchestra** (☎722 4850) has frequent concerts in the Great and Small Guilds off Filharmonija laukums. Smaller ensembles perform throughout the summer in **Wagner Hall** (Vāgnera zāle), Vāgnera iela 4 (☎721 0817). The topnotch **Rīga Ballet** carries on the dance tradition of native star Mikhail Baryshnikov. The **ticket offices,** at Teātra 10/12 (☎722 5747; open daily 10am-7pm) and Amatu iela 6 (☎721 3798), on the first floor of the Great Guild, serve most local concerts. The fantastic and mostly free **Rīgas Ritmi** is a street music festival early in July. Check out www.rigasritmi.lv for dates. Nightlife is centered on **Vecrīga,** where 24hr. casinos and *diskotekas* flourish. For a mellower evening, join Rīgans at their beer gardens on Līvu lakums.

Skyline Bar, Elizabetes iela 55, 26th fl. (☎777 2222), in the Reval Hotel Latvija. Arrive by 8pm for a coveted "Vecrīga window seat" with a stunning view of the Old Town and Baltic Sea. Retro decor, comfortable couches, and a well-stocked bar keep the crowd of foreigners lively until late. Guinness and other foreign beers on tap (3Ls). Mixed drinks include classics like White Russians (4.20Ls). Salmon and caviar canapés 1-3Ls; other snacks 2-6Ls. Open M-Th and Su 3pm-2am, F-Sa 3pm-3am. MC/V.

Pulkvedim Neviens Neraksta (Nobody Writes to the Colonel), Peldu 26/28 (☎721 3886; www.pulkvedim.lv), off Kungu iela. Taking its name from a popular novel, this industrial bar is popular with Rīga's young, cool crowd for its alternative, funk, and fusion music scene. The dance floor upstairs can get crowded—mostly with locals—but downstairs the bravely color-uncoordinated lounge plays salsa and chill-out mixes. Beer 1-3Ls. Cover F-Sa 3Ls. Open M-Th noon-3am, F-Sa noon-5am, Su 4pm-1am. MC/V.

Cetri Balti Krekli (Four White Shirts), Vecpilsētas iela 12 (☎721 3885; www.krekli.lv), off Kaleju and around the corner from Sue's Indian Raj. Hidden from the Old Town's crowds, this cellar club fills quickly with locals and visitors alike. Latvians come well dressed and ready to party. Live music F-Sa. No sneakers. Cover Tu-Th 1-2Ls, F-Sa 5Ls. Open M-F noon-5am, Sa 5pm-5am, Su 5pm-3am. MC/V.

Rīgas Balzams, Torņa iela 4 (☎721 4494), in the Old Town, 100m east of the Powder Tower. This cozy pub is in the cellar of the long yellow building. In winter, take advantage of the warm, intimate atmosphere to enjoy Latvia's potent national liquor. In summer, relax on the terrace and choose from a range of mixed balsams (3-5Ls), beer, and mixed drinks. Open M-Th and Su 11am-midnight, F-Sa 11am-1am. MC/V.

Depo, Valņu 32 (☎67 22 01 14). Known for its underground music scene, this raucous club is—appropriately enough—located underground. Garage bands and well-known alternative groups from around Europe mix with techno for a dynamic dance floor. The upstairs cafe is a great place to cool off. Cover 5Ls. Open Th-Sa 8pm-5am. MC/V.

DAYTRIPS FROM RĪGA

SALASPILS MEMORIAL

Electric trains run to Dārziņi along the Ogre line (20min., 14 per day, 0.22Ls). Do not take the train to "Salaspils." The last train back to Rīga is around 10pm. In the woods behind the Dārziņi station house is a paved pathway. Turn right and continue 1km. Go left after the soccer field.

The Salaspils Memorial marks the meager remains of the Kurtenhof concentration camp, where an estimated 100,000 Jews and ethnic minorities were killed by the Nazis. As is the case at other Soviet-era Holocaust memorials, communist officials omitted any references to religion and referred to the dead obliquely as "victims of the Fascist terror." Today, a huge concrete wall marks where the camp entrance once stood. The inscription over the entrance reads, "Here the innocent walked the way of death. How many unfinished words, how many unlived years were cut short by a bullet." All that remains of the barracks are the foundations, but visitors can walk a cold, somber pathway to a small display of woodcuts and a map of concentration camps in the area. Four sculptures—Motherhood, Solidarity, the Humiliated, and the Unbroken—watch over the Way of the Suffering, the circular path connecting barracks foundations, while an eerie metronome ticks constantly in memory of those murdered.

RUNDĀLE PALACE

The palace is 10km west of Bauska. From Rīga, take the bus (1hr., about every 30min., 1.35Ls) to Bauska. Ask for an express bus, or choose one from scheduled departure times marked with an "E." From there, take a bus (15min., 5 per day, 0.20Ls) or taxi (3Ls) to Rundāles. Buses are infrequent; check the schedule before you leave the station at Bauska. ☎621 97; www.rpm.apollo.lv. Gardens, palace, and exhibit open daily June-Aug. 10am-7pm; Sept. and May 10am-6pm; Nov.-Apr. 10am-5pm. 2.50Ls, students 1.50Ls. Park 0.50Ls. Other exhibits 0.10-0.50Ls.

The expansive Rundāle Palace long served as a countryside retreat for local nobility. A Russian empress, Anna Ioanova, built the palace as a gift to one of her advisers, Ernst Johann von Bühren, a Baltic German noble. The palace was designed by Italian architect Bartolomeo Rastrelli, who also designed St. Petersburg's Winter Palace, and required the work of 15,000 laborers and artisans. Construction began in 1730 but stalled after Anna's death in 1740. Catherine the Great finished the palace in 1767. Accordingly, images of Catherine's life adorn the majestic interior, allowing you to trace her growth—in power and in girth. Spend some time wandering through the palace's opulent 138 gilded rooms. Most impressive is the **Gold Room** (Zelta Zāle), which contains the throne, murals, and soldiers' graffiti from 1812. The upstairs exhibit describes the palace's 1971-2002 restoration. Panels in each room date and name every piece of art, furniture, and porcelain. The magnificent **White Hall** shouldn't be missed. Quiet benches on your way out offer a vantage point for admiring the extensive gardens.

WESTERN LATVIA

JŪRMALA ☎(8)77

The sandy resort of Jūrmala (YOUR-mala; sea shore; pop. 60,000) has been a holiday destination for decades. Composed of 14 small towns, the region is bordered by 32km of busy shore and calm, forested land. A short jaunt from Rīga, Jūrmala is popular for restorative spas and for its young, tanned, and toned beach bums.

THE REAL DEAL. Jūrmala is known as Rīga's playground, but the sandbox is a bit crowded. Getting to and from the "Latvian Riviera" is a sticky, sweaty, and squishy train ride. The beach is littered with cigarette butts and crowded with people knocking soccer balls in your direction. For a real Latvian seaside experience, take a bus to the coast and walk along the beautiful white sands of Liepāja or Ventspils. You'll feel welcome and relaxed, and you won't be fighting dozens of British stag parties for space.

TRANSPORTATION AND PRACTICAL INFORMATION. A **commuter rail** (30min.; every 30min. 5am-11:30pm; 0.50Ls, 0.80Ls on board; platforms #3 and 4) runs from **Rīga.** Ride the Tukums-bound line to **Majori station** (☎583 0315). Minibuses depart form the central minibus station opposite the train station every 5min. from 6am-11pm. **Public buses** (0.20Ls), **microbuses** (0.50Ls), and the same commuter rail connect Jūrmala's towns. Rent a **bike** along the beach (2-3Ls per hr.) or at Juras iela 24. (☎911 9091. 6Ls per day. Open daily 10am-7pm.)

From the **train station** in **Majori,** follow the pedestrian boulevard Jomas iela east 100m to reach the **Tourism Information Center,** Jomas iela 42 (☎776 4276; www.jurmala.lv). The English-speaking staff distributes **free maps** and brochures, sells guides, and books private rooms for a 1Ls fee. The free *Jūrmala Visitor's Guide* offers extensive regional info. MasterCard and Visa **ATMs** abound on Jomas iela in **Dzintari,** the town immediately to the East of Majori. There is one outside **Hansabanka,** Jomas 37 (☎781 1482). For the 24hr. **currency exchange** at the eastern end of Jomas, head toward Jomas iela 62. To the east of Majori lies **Dzintari,** where a 24hr. currency exchange can be found at 92 Jomas iela. Get there by following Jomas iela past the TIC and continuing for 1km. A **pharmacy,** Majori Aptieka, can be found at Jomas 41. (☎776 4413. Open daily 9am-8pm.) There is an **Internet** cafe, **Digitorklubs,** at Jomas 62. (☎781 1411. Open daily 10am-9pm.) **Dubulti,** the town immediately to the west of Majori, has a **post office** at 16 Strelnieku pr. (☎776 2430. Open M-F 8am-5pm, Sa 8am-4pm.)

ACCOMMODATIONS AND FOOD. The **TIC** books rooms in local hotels and hostels from 6Ls per night. The TIC has no service charge and usually provides the best rates. **Elina ❺,** Lienes 43, has bright, clean doubles with private baths above a pleasant cafe. Heading east on Jomas, turn right on J. Pliekšāna iela; it's 200m down on the right. (☎776 1665; www.elinahotel.lv. Doubles 25Ls. Cash only.) Despite its looming concrete facade, travelers find comfortable, spacious rooms with private baths, tea sets, and fridges inside **Dzintari ❷,** Piestatnes 6/14, in Dzintari. (☎775 4539. Singles 12Ls; doubles 14Ls; triples 23Ls. MC/V.) **Rakstnieku nams ❷,** Dubulti, Akas 4, is an old-fashioned guesthouse with tidy rooms. During your stay, watch for the former president of Latvia; she has a house just a few doors down. (☎776 9965. Singles 15-20Ls; doubles 20-30Ls. Cash only.)

Cafes line Jomas iela, particularly in the summer, when nearly every inch of open space in town becomes a beer garden. For spectacular seafood by the shore, head to **Jurus Zakis ❷,** Vienibas 1, in Bulduri. Follow Dzintari eastward from Jomas. After 2km, Dzintari becomes Bulduri. Continue to Vienības and turn left. (☎775 3005. Entrees 3-6Ls. Open daily noon-11pm. MC/V.) **Sue's Asia ❷,** Jomas 74, has authentic spicy Indian, Thai, and Chinese cuisine. (☎775 5900. Entrees 3-10Ls. Open M-Th noon-11pm, F-Su noon-late. MC/V.) Head to **Dukats ❶,** Dubulti, Baznīcas 12/14 (☎776 4267), for hearty homemade soups and entrees for less than 2Lt. Don't forget to grab a delicious pastry on your way out. Try Latvia's famous beer, Uzavas, and traditional cuisine at **Zem Burām ❶,** Bulduri, Vidus prospekts 38/7, for less than 3Ls (☎775 5127).

SIGHTS AND ENTERTAINMENT. Jūrmala's main attraction is its beach. Powder-fine sand, warm waters, and festive boardwalks have drawn crowds since the late 19th century. A **statue of Lāčplēsis the Bear Slayer** protects the street across from the Majori train station. In the summer, don't miss the **The Antique Car Museum,** which has a large collection of shiny, classic automobiles and motocycles dating back to 1907. (Open May-Sept. 11am-6pm. Donations requested.) The **Rainis and Aspazija Memorial Summer House,** J. Pliekšāna iela 5-7, was home to **Janis Pliekshans** (1865-1929), known by the pen name **Rainis.** The poet and playwright was exiled by the tsar for participating in the 1905 Russian Revolution, but returned to Majori after Latvia gained independence. The two-story cottage now contains Rainis and his wife Aspāzija's personal library, sculptures, exquisite furniture, and original editions of their work. From the TIC, follow Jomas east 400m and turn left. (☎776 4295. Open W-Su 10am-6pm; closed last F of each month. 0.70Ls, students 0.30Ls. Tour 0.20Ls.)

Take a left on Turaidas and head toward the beach to reach the **Dzintari Concert Hall,** Turaidas 1. US and Soviet diplomats met here in 1986 for negotiations over the USSR's occupation of Latvia. The open-air stage hosts a stream of summertime performances, including **chamber music concerts,** an international youth **singing contest** in July, and youth piano contest in May. Posters across town advertise the monthly line-up of cultural events, which take place daily in high season.

VENTSPILS (8)36

The colorful cobblestone streets and perfectly manicured gardens of Ventspils (pop. 44,000) give little sense of the city's recent industrial past. Once a base for Russian oil exports, this wealthy port city is now home to the cleanest, most beautiful coastlines in Latvia. Bask in the sunset on the western shore at the **Blue Flag Beach,** internationally recognized for its high water safety and cleanliness. 1km south is a co-ed **nude beach.** Nearby, the **Seaside Open Air Museum,** Rinka iela 2, showcases the history of fishing in Ventspils, including extensive exhibits of boats and cabins, as well as the largest anchor collection in the world. (☎362 4467. Open May-Oct. 10am-6pm; Nov.-Apr. M-F 11am-5pm. 0.60Ls, students 0.30Ls.) Stroll along the Ostas iela, a waterfront promenade lined with sculptures and fountains, to see the gigantic **Touring Cow.** To get a closer look at the impressive industrial facilities of Ventspils, head out on **Hercogs Jēkabs excursion boat** (sails every hr. between 10am-7pm, 0.50Ls). The boat departs just west of the **Livonian Order Castle,** Jāņa iela 17, built in 1290 and the oldest-standing medieval fortress in Latvia. It now houses the **Ventspils Museum,** which features a small exhibit on the history of Ventspils. In the summertime, knights duel in the courtyard. (☎362 2031; www.ventspilsmuzejs.lv. 1Ls, students 0.50Ls.)

Head up Kulīgas iela to the center of Ventspils to reach the **dormitory of the vocational secondary school No. 20 ❶,** which offers basic, clean dorms with a shared shower and WC for just 4Ls a night (☎362 4468; 20_avc_ventspils@inbocx.lv). The **Guesthouse at Meza Street ❶,** Mezu iela 13, is a family-run guesthouse with charming, clean rooms surrounded by lovely private gardens. (☎29 42 24 07. Shared bath and shower. Breakfast 2Ls. Laundry 8Ls. Singles 8Ls; doubles 12Ls.) Dine on embroidered tablecloths near overflowing flowerboxes at **Krodziņs Don Basil ❷,** Annas iela 5. This classy Italian restaurant serves enormous pasta plates (2-4Lt), salads, and excellent coffee for 0.80Ls. (☎26 56 32 09. Open 11am-11pm.) **Cits Ostgals ❷,** Ganibu 19, a pub popular with sailors and tourists alike, is one of the few places to try the local Uzava beer. (☎951 4321. Open noon-2am.)

Buses depart from Ventspils for Rīga (17 per day, 4Ls), Liepāja (6 per day, 2-4Ls), and Kuldīga (7 per day, 1.40Ls). With your back to the bus station, turn left on Kuldīgas iela and make a quick right on Sofijas. Walk straight past St. Nicholas's Orthodox church and down Tirgus iela to reach the center and the **Tourism Information Center,** Tirgus iela 7, which hands out free maps. (☎362 2263; www.tourism.ventspils.lv. Open M-F 8am-7pm, Sa 10am-5pm, Su 10am-3pm.) Cash **traveler's checks** and **exchange currency** at **Hansabankas,** Kuldīgas iela 25a. (Open M-F 9am-5pm.) An **ATM** is outside. The **post office** is at Platā iela 8. (Open M-F 8am-6pm, Sa 8am-4pm.) **Postal Code:** LV-3601.

LIEPĀJA ☎(8)34

The westernmost and third-largest city in Latvia, Liepāja (Lee-EP-ay-a; pop. 86,500) is a relatively undiscovered coastal retreat. Bordered by sea, canals, and an estuary, the city maintains a calm, quiet air and offers a wealth of spectacular beaches. The northern suburb of Karosta, site of a naval port and prison (and off-limits to civilians) during most of its hundred-year history, is now a haven for artists and adventurous visitors.

TRANSPORTATION AND PRACTICAL INFORMATION. Buses from Rīga (3-5hr., 12 per day, 4Ls) arrive at Liepāja Bus Station, Stacijas laukums. (☎342 7552; www.aslap.lv. Ticket window open daily 5am-9:30pm.) Bus connections to Ventspils (2½hr., 3 per day, 2.40-3.40Ls) and Klaipėda, LIT (2hr., 4 per day, 2.10-3Ls) are also available. Don't forget to validate your ticket on board after buying it from the driver. **Buses** (25Ls), **microbuses** (30Ls), and **trams** (24Ls) make travel within the city easy between the hours of 6am and 11pm.

With your back to the bus station, walk to your right down Rīgas iela for about 1km, or take any tram along the way. **Lielā iela** continues from the bridge to the center of the **Old Town.** From the city center, Jūras iela eventually becomes Kūrmājas prospekts and leads to the promenade and the beach. North of the bridge, in the New Town, Raiņa iela becomes O. Kalpaka iela, which runs parallel to the shore and eventually leads to **Karosta tilts,** the moveable bridge that must be crossed to reach Karosta. **Atmodas bulvāris** leads north through Karosta.

The **Lejaskurzemes Tourist Information Center (TIC),** Rozu laukums 5/6, provides free maps. (☎63 48 08 08; www.liepaja.lv/turisms. Open daily May-Sept. 9am-7pm; Oct.-Apr. 9am-5pm.) Just before the tourist office, **Latvia Tours,** offers **American Express** services. (☎342 7173; www.latviatours.lv. Open M-F 8am-noon and 1-7pm.) **Exchange money** or get MasterCard and Visa **cash advances** at **Unibanka,** Brivības iela 4/6. (☎340 1300. Open M-F 9am-5pm.) Centra Aptieka, a **pharmacy,** can be found at K. Zāles laukums 6. (☎342 3595. Open M-F 7:30am-9pm, Sa 8:30am-8pm, Su 9am-6pm. MC/V.) Find **Internet access** at **Sapņu Sala,** Liela 12. (Enter around the corner. ☎348 5333; www.sapnu-sala.lv. 0.50Ls per hr., ISIC discount. Open daily 10am-10pm.) The **post office,** Pasta iela 4, has **Western Union** services. (Open M-F 7:30am-6:30pm, Sa 7:30am-4:30pm.) **Postal Code:** LV-3401.

ACCOMMODATIONS AND FOOD. The **TIC** distributes free handouts with useful information about accommodations and attractions in the Liepāja region. If you're willing to stay outside the Old Town, head to **Brīze ❶,** O. Kalpaka 68/70. Its recently renovated, spacious rooms are an excellent value. Modern kitchens boast filtered drinking water, and the common area has a TV. Bathrooms are communal. The hotel is on the main bus route, and there is a small vegetable market behind the building. (☎344 1566; www.brizehostel.lv. Singles 8Ls; triples and quads 18Ls. MC/V.) Centrally located **Līva ❷,** Lielā iela 11, is on the left after crossing the bridge to the Old Town. Economy rooms are small and can be stuffy in the heat, but have TVs, phones, and sinks. Hallway showers and toilets, though clean, are far from some rooms. (☎342 0102; www.liva.lv. Reserve ahead for July-Aug. Economy singles 10Ls; doubles 15Ls. Singles 25Ls; doubles 45Ls; triples 39Ls; quads 60Ls. MC/V.) In **Karosta,** the **K@2 Hostel ❶,** Katedrāles 2, provides comfortable beds and delicious breakfast in an unusual setting. A gargantuan key opens the old, heavy front door to an eclectically decorated building, with a terrace and cafe out back. The dorm bunks are comfortable and the staff is fantastic. Microbuses #1 and #3 run past the building, which is just off Atmodas bulv. (☎974 7962; www.karosta.lv/hostel. Breakfast included. Rooms 6Ls.)

A large **RIMI hypermarket,** 8 K. Zāles laukams, is to the left of the bridge after crossing into the Old Town. (Open daily 8am-midnight.) **Peter's Market,** Kursu 5/7/9, just off Zivju, sells dairy and meat products inside, and fruits and vegetables in outdoor stalls. (Open M-Sa 8am-6pm, Su 8am-2pm.) **Rock Cafe ❷,** Stendera 18/20, an impressive four-story cafe, offers excellent international food, drinks, pool tables, and Old Town people-watching. Chow down on a range of entrees (1.20-4Lt), including a number of vegetarian dishes. Rock Cafe is also one of the few places that serves the local Līvu beer (0.80Ls per 0.5L). Live music is featured most nights. (☎348 1555. Open daily 9am-4am. MC/V.) **Fontaine Delisnack ❶,** Dzirnavu 4,

HOSTILE HOSTEL

t's generally a good idea to avoid oreign prisons, but if you'd like o take home a very special souvenir—your own prison ID card, complete with mug shot—try to spend a night at Karosta Prison *Karostas cietums)*. Guests pay only 5Ls for the privilege of being reated like a criminal: the package includes a set of black-and-white prison clothes, a bed of vooden planks with a bedroll, and a night of verbal abuse and egular cell checks.

The prison, located in the desolate naval port north of Liepaja, began incarcerating political prisoners in 1905. When the Soviets ook over Karosta, they placed the entire area on lockdown, even denying civilians access to the seashore. Prisoners were killed in he very courtyard where guests vill be marched, yelled at, and nade to do exercises in the dead of night. Men in uniform will interrogate you, criticize your form, and pull you aside for extra punishment if you give them any attitude. Once back in the prison, guests will be sent to pitch-black cells and interrogation chambers, vhere the original prisoners' pained emotions are still engraved on the walls. Breakfast, ittingly, is not included.

Book your night "Behind the Bars" at www.karostascietums.lv. Ask or English translators to participate with you. Karosta Prison, 4 nvalidu iela (☎636 9470).

is an excellent 24hr. joint that serves up everything from stir-fried noodles to hamburgers and Tex-Mex. Entrees, at just 1-2Ls, leave your stomach and your pocket satisfied. (☎63 48 85 23. MC/V.) **Baltā bize** (The White Braid) ❷, Kūrmājas prospekts 8/10, to the right after crossing the bridge, is a popular self-service restaurant with whitewashed wooden furniture and country charm. The extensive menu offers such delicacies as chicken liver ragout in a pastry basket (1.50Ls) and cod filet seared in white wine for 3Ls. (☎342 4588. Open M-F 8am-7pm, Sa-Su 11am-7pm. MC/V.) Grab a seat in **Kiss Me** ❶, Lielā 13, a long corridor encased in glass next to the Kurzeme shopping center, and enjoy coffee (0.60Ls) and dessert (0.60-3Ls) while watching the crowds on the main thoroughfare. (☎342 5464. Open daily 8am-10pm.)

SIGHTS AND ENTERTAINMENT. Turn right after you cross the bridge to the Old Town and continue to the beach. Alternatively, take the promenade along the harbor to the **beachfront.** The beach at Liepāja is internationally recognized with a Blue Flag, indicating high water safety and cleanliness; moreover the soft sandy shore is never too crowded. Parallel to the beach is **Jūrmalas Park,** which throbs late into the summer nights with live music and sprawling beer gardens. The bright, Art Nouveau wooden cottages lining the park are nearly 100 years old. **Karosta,** a naval port built by Tsar Alexander III from 1890-1904, was home to the first Baltic submarine fleet. During Soviet times, Liepāja's strategic importance kept it completely off-limits to civilians, but today unique Karosta beckons tourists. You can reach the suburb on buses #1 and 3. When you're there, rent a bicycle from **K@2,** Ģenerāļa Dankera 1, to explore the streets. The helpful staff at the office provide maps and suggest routes. (☎979 8224. 0.50Ls per hr., tandem bicycle 1Ls per hr. Open daily 9am-5pm.) In Karosta, the massive **St. Nicholas Orthodox Cathedral,** Katedrāles 7 (☎345 7634), shines above endless blocks of Soviet army housing. Though the cathedral has no internal support beams, extra-strong walls keep it standing. **Karosta Prison,** Invalīdu 4, was built as a hospital in 1900 but used to hold prisoners from the Revolution of 1905. The last prisoner left in 1997, and today you can tour the prison (0.50Ls), participate in "Behind the Bars," a chilling experience during which you'll be taken into the prison and treated as an inmate (5Ls), or even spend the night incarcerated (see left). Knowledgeable "prison wardens" brief you on the history of the prison and offer you the chance to ask questions after they've broken you in. (☎636 9470; www.karostascietums.lv. Bookings must be made in advance. 8Ls per person. Group rates 5Ls, 10-person minimum.) Enjoy a walk along the 2km long **Northern Pier** to get some fresh air after you break out. For updates on events and happenings in Karosta, check out www.karosta.lv.

Back in the Old Town, **Holy Trinity Church,** Lielā 9, looks unassuming from the outside, but its bright white-and-gold interior is breathtaking. Built between 1742 and 1748, the church's most impressive feature is its incredible organ, whose 7000 pipes and 131 registers made it for a time the largest in the world. (☎943 8050. Open daily 10am-6pm. Church free; donations suggested. Tower 1Ls.) The **Liepāja Museum** (Liepājas muzejs), Kūrmājas prospekts 16/18, displays a rare collection of Stone and Bronze Age artifacts, Viking weapons, and 20th-century paintings inside an ornate 20th-century space. Don't miss the serene sculpture garden out back. (☎342 2337. Open W-Th and Sa-Su 10am-6pm, F 11am-7pm. Free.) The small museum **Liepāja Under the Regimes of Occupation,** K. Ukstina 7/9, south of the market, provides a sobering account of the city's brutal 20th-century history. Upstairs in the same building is an impressive collection of vintage Kodak cameras and photographic equipment. (☎342 0274. Open W-Th and Sa-Su 10am-6pm, F 11am-7pm. No English captions. Free.)

Outside town, the trail in Lake Pape Nature Park offers 30km of splendid hiking, biking, and other outdoor activities. The World Wildlife Fund organizes guided wild-life-viewing excursions (☎349 4850; www.rucava.lv). The park is virtually inaccessible without a car, but you can ask at Tourist Information for maps and suggested routes.

KULDĪGA ☎8(33)

The sleepy town of Kuldīga (KOOL-di-ga; pop. 13,500) maintains an authentic Old Town of red-tiled roofs and pockmarked streets. Visitors come to this rarely traveled area for relaxation and to see Latvia's widest waterfall, **Ventas rumba.** In the summer the wide falls provide a number of opportunities for boating, swimming, and walking along the river. Just downstream, Kuldīga's red brick bridge, the largest of its kind in Europe and the site of numerous film scenes, provides excellent vistas. The **Kuldīga District Museum,** 5 Pils iela, is housed in a natural wood building from the Paris World Fair. Its collection of over 85,000 artifacts, photographs, and contemporary pieces provide insight into the archaeological and ethnographic history of Kuldīga. (☎33 32 23 64. Open Tu-Su 11am-5pm. 0.50Ls, students 0.30Ls.) The museum includes the **Card Room,** 10 Smilšu iela, which offers a collection of historic playing cards. (Open Tu-Sa 10am-4pm.) The nearby **sculpture park,** on the site of the castle ruins, provides a shady vantage from which to watch the waterfall. The **Sculpture Hall,** 19 Mucenieku iela, at the back of the building, is a miniature studio space for traveling artists. (Open Sa-Su 11am-4pm.) The exciting **NEKAC** (Center for Non-Commercial Culture), Vijolīšu iela 24 (www.nekac.lv), often has rock and experimental concerts on weekend evenings. Check website for schedules.

From the center, walk along Kalna iela to reach the **bridge** and the **waterfall.** Cross the bridge to stay at **Ventas Rumba ❶,** Stendes iela, a hostel named for its proximity to the waterfall. Clean, renovated rooms and dorms are available in a house with a kitchen and dining area. (☎332 4168; www.ventasrumba.lv. **Bike rental** 6Ls per day. Boat rental 2Ls per hr. Dorms 6Ls; rooms 20Ls.) At the **Sport School ❶,** Kalna iela 6 (☎332 2465), 1.50Ls gets you a bed in a shared room, with hallway bathrooms. A **Saulīte** grocery store is at the corner of Liepājas iela and Piltenes iela. (Open daily 8am-10pm.) Near the waterfall, **Pīlādzītis ❶,** Stendes 2a, offers coffee (0.50Ls) and light snacks. (☎928 3859. Open daily 9am-late.)

Buses from Rīga (3hr., 5 per day, 3Ls) arrive at the bus station, a short walk from town. Buses also run to Liepāja (2hr., 5 per day, 3Ls) and Ventspils (2hr., 5 per day, 2Ls). With your back to the station, turn right on Stacijas iela and left on Jēlgavas iela. Bear to the right and turn left when you see an information sign. The **Tourist Information Center,** Baznīcas iela 5, provides **free maps,** accommodation listings, and info about outdoor activities. (☎332 2259; tourinfo@kuldiga.lv. Open M-F 9am-5pm, Sa 10am-4pm, Su 10am-2pm.) Cash **traveler's checks** and **exchange currency** at **Hansabankas,** Liepājas iela 15. (Open M-F 9am-5pm.) An **ATM** is outside. Farther down is a **pharmacy,** Meness Aptieka. (☎332 2473. Open M-Sa 8am-9pm, Su 10am-8pm.) Across the street, the **post office** is at Liepājas iela 34. (Open M-F 8am-6pm, Sa 8am-4pm.) **Postal Code:** LV-3301.

INLAND LATVIA

In inland Latvia, the Gauja, Latvia's longest river, flows past the ruins of the medieval castles of Cēsis and Sigulda. The country's most naturally diverse setting, the lush Gauja Valley is a goldmine at any time of year for those looking to hike, camp, and spend time outdoors.

SIGULDA ☎(8)79

Situated in the Gaujas Valley National Park, Sigulda feels worlds away from hectic Rīga. The Knights of the Sword, the Germanic crusaders who Christianized much of Latvia in the 13th century, made this their base. Today, the town remains popular for its castle ruins, hiking and biking trails, and beautiful surrounding scenery.

TRANSPORTATION AND PRACTICAL INFORMATION. **Trains** from Rīga run on the Rīga-Lugaži commuter rail line (1hr., 9 per day, 0.80Ls). **Buses** from Rīga (1hr., 14 per day, 1-1.50Ls) go to the bus station, Raiņa iela 3. (☎721 06. Open daily 6am-8pm. Ticket office open M-Sa 8am-1:30pm and 2-5:30pm.) Buses to **Cēsis** may stop on the south edge of Sigulda along Highway A2; backtrack toward Rīga and turn right on Gāles to reach the center. The best way to explore Sigulda is by bicycle, but mind the erratic drivers who share the road. Choose from a variety of **bikes** at **Tridens,** Cēsu iela 15. Follow Raina from the bus station and turn left just before the tourist center onto Cēsu; continue past the green space, and the building will be on the left. (☎964 4800. 1Ls per hr., 5Ls per day. Open daily 10am-8pm.)

From the bus and train stations, Raiņa iela runs 1km north to the **Gauja National Park Visitor Centre,** Baznicas 3, which has a knowledgeable, English-speaking staff and free **maps** of Sigulda. They also sell essential maps (1.50Ls) of the park. (☎797 1345; www.gnp.gov.lv. Open M 9am-5:30pm, Tu-Su 9am-7pm.) **Exchange money,** cash **American Express Traveler's Cheques,** and find **Western Union** services next door at **Latvijas Krajbanka,** K. Valdemāra iela 1a. From Raiņa iela, turn right onto Ausekla iela; the bank is on the corner, two blocks down. (Open M-F 9am-5pm.) A block closer to the bus station is a **pharmacy,** Pils iela 3. (☎797 0910. Open M-F 7:30am-9:30pm, Sa 9am-8pm, Su 9am-6pm. MC/V.) For **Internet** access, go around to the back of the pharmacy building, through the unmarked gray metal door, and up one flight of stairs. (1Ls per hr. Open daily 10am-10pm.) Across the street is the **post office,** Pils iela 2. (☎797 2177. **Telephones** outside. Open M-F 8am-7pm, Sa 8am-4pm.) **Postal Code:** LV-2150.

ACCOMMODATIONS AND FOOD. The **GNP Visitors Centre** helps locate campsites and **private rooms;** if you're looking for the latter, they'll most likely send you to **Viesu Nams Livonija ❷**, P. Brieža iela 55. Just 10min. from the bus and train stations, this hostel offers pleasant rooms with baths; the spacious shared-bath singles are in a separate house. Kitchen facilities, a common room, and a sauna are also available. From the bus station, head down Raiņa iela toward the train station, turn right on

Ausekla iela, and cross the tracks at the pedestrian signs; continue down Gāles iela and turn left on P. Brieza. (☎797 3066; hotel.livonija@lis.lv. Breakfast 2Ls. Singles 14Ls, with shared bath 7Ls; doubles 16-20Ls.) **Aparjods ❺**, Ventas iela 1A, decorated like a modern home, offers luxurious rooms with saunas and satellite TVs. With your back to the Visitors Centre, head left down Ausekla iela, right on R. Blaumaņa, left on Strēlnieku, and left on Ventas iela. (☎67 97 22 30; www.aparjods.lv. Singles 35Ls; doubles 40Ls. MC/V.)

Pilsmuižas Restorāns ❸, Pils iela 16, serves generous portions of Latvian food. Try the pork chops with red bilberry jam (6Ls). The restaurant is located in the 19th-century Pilseta Dome of Sigulda Castle. (☎797 1425. Entrees 4-12Ls. 10% service charge. Open daily noon-2am. MC/V.) Rustic **Aparjods ❸**, Ventas iela 1a, is crammed full of old clocks and traditional Latvian antiques. The food is some of the best in town; order the stuffed pheasant (6Ls) or pork for 7Ls. (☎67 70 52 42. Entrees 4-12Ls. Open daily noon-1am. MC/V.) A newer, brighter cafeteria is **Elvi ❶**, Vidus iela 1, which shares a building with a bowling alley and a supermarket of the same name. Hot dishes, soups, and salads are available by weight, and you can easily fill up on 1Ls worth of food. Follow Ausekla iela, keeping the train tracks to your left; the building is beside the large parking lot on your right. (☎797 3539. Open daily 7am-11pm.) **Saulīte,** a large grocery store, is at Paegles iela 3. (☎797 1463. Open daily 8am-10pm. MC/V.)

SIGHTS AND ENTERTAINMENT. Sigulda's main attraction is the **Turaidas Museum Reserve,** 3km after the bridge. This 42-hectare site includes an impressive stone castle, historic churches, and endless forests. The reserve can be reached on bike or by bus #12 (1 per hr., 0.20Ls) from the station. A **cable car** (5min.; 2 per hr. 10am-7pm; M-F 1.50Ls, Sa-Su 2Ls) runs from the Sigulda side of Gaujas to Krimulda Castle. From Sigulda, cross the river and follow **Turaidas** 1.5km until you reach the turn-off for **Gutman's Cave** (Gūtmaņa Ala), the largest cave in the Baltic region. It is inscribed with coats of arms and scribblings dating from the 17th century. Farther down the path is the enormous, red brick **Turaida Castle** (Turaidas Pils). Inside, a **museum** chronicles the saga of Kaupo, chieftain of the Livs, a pagan group who maintained a castle here in the late 12th century. The wily Kaupo converted to Christianity in 1203 before plundering his tribe's fortress. Archaeological finds and artifacts are now on display. (Info in English, German, and Russian. Tower open daily 9am-8pm. Museum open daily

THE SLEEPING WOLF

Order yourself a shot of balzams, Latvia's national liquor, and you're in for a head-clearing experience. The strong black liquid, usually only taken in mixed drinks, is crafted from an 18th-century recipe for cough syrup. With more than 24 ingredients, including roots, berries, and flowers, the drink is aged in oak barrels to foster an acidic, bittersweet taste. Black balzams is rumored to have cured the illnesses of Catherine the Great, but be warned: large quantities are not medically advisable. Try a sip or take it with cola, lemon juice, or soda. Hot drinks prepared with this liquor are especially popular during the winter. Bring home a bottle and try these recipes.

Balzams Black Currant
1 measure Black Balzams
3 measures black currant juice
grenadine to taste

Innocent Balzams
1 measure Black Balzams
2 measures ice cream
2 measures peach juice

Sleeping Wolf
1 measure Black Balzams
1 tablespoon honey
3 measures milk
1 egg yolk

For the Sleeping Wolf, heat balzams, honey, and milk together. Add yolk and mix it with a blender.

May-Oct. 10am-6pm; Nov.-Apr. 10am-5pm. Free with ticket from Turaidas Museum Reserve.) Left of the caves, climb 366 steps to a vigorous, forested hike that eventually leads to the scant ruins of 13th-century **Krimulda Castle** (Krimuldas Pilsdrupas), juxtaposed with the refurbished, Neoclassical Krimulda manor and nearby pristine gardens. (Open M-F 11am-6pm, Sa-Su 10am-6pm.) A cable car leads from the ruins back across the river to Sigulda. On the Sigulda side of the river, on a ridge behind Gauja National Park headquarters, is the 19th-century **Pilsētas Dome** (Castle Dome), the "new" castle-palace where the Russian Prince Kropotkin once lived. The immense ruins of the once glorious **Sigulda Castle Ruins** (Siguldas Pilsdrupas) are behind the palace. Constructed between 1207 and 1226, the castle was destroyed in the Great Northern War (1700-21) between Russia and Sweden. The castle also forms the backdrop for the **Opera Festival** (☎727 7900; www.lmuza.lv/sigulda) in late July.

OUTDOOR ACTIVITIES. An Olympic-sized **bobsled run** plummets from Sveices iela 13. You can take the plunge year-round; in summer, you'll be on wheels. **Skis** are available in the wintertime. (☎739 44; fax 790 1667. Open Sa-Su noon-5pm. 3Ls.) To go **bungee jumping,** head to the cable car and sign a release. (☎725 31; fax 722 53; www.lgk.lv. Open F-Su 6:30pm-last customer. F 17Ls, Sa-Su 20Ls.) Watching jumpers from the bridge is a popular pasttime on weekend evenings.

DAYTRIP FROM SIGULDA: GAUJA NATIONAL PARK. Named after the river at its center, this lush park, established in 1973, is home to some of Estonia's most pristine natural scenery and a plethora of diverse wildlife. Grab a bag lunch and spend the day canoeing, picnicking, and wandering hiking trails of all skill levels. In the winter, the trails are marked for **cross-country skiing.** The **Līgatne Nature Trail** (Līgatne dabas takas; round-trip from Sigulda 41km) takes visitors on a 5.5km loop past captive bears, elk, deer, and hares. The wooden pathway leads to viewing towers, where you can observe the wildlife without disturbing it. Climb **Zvartes Rock** behind the Information Center for beautiful open views of the river and park. The park doesn't provide equipment, but **Makars Tourism Agency,** Peldu 1, located in the park, rents equipment, **tents** (4-7Ls per day), and **boats** (7-70Ls per day) and arranges **rafting trips** starting at 7Ls per hour. From Gaujas iela, go left on Peldu before you cross the river. (☎924 4948; www.makars.lv. Open M-F 10am-5pm, Sa-Su 9am-6pm. MC/V.)

Buses to the park are infrequent; check the schedule at the TIC. The park's entrance is located off Raiņa iela, 1km north of Sigulda. From Sigulda's TIC, follow Ausekla iela east and turn left on Raiņa iela; follow it for 1km. The **Gauja National Park Information Centre** is located at the entrance. Stop here for free maps; they're vital to finding your way around the park. (Park entrance fee 1Ls, students 0.5Ls. Park and Information Center open M 9am-5:30pm, Tu-Su 9am-7pm.)

CĒSIS ☎(8)41

Quiet Cēsis (TSEH-siss; pop. 17,500), Latvia's second oldest city after Rīga, is famous for castle ruins, medieval architecture, and the local brew, Cēsu, which enjoys nationwide popularity. Crusading Germans arrived in the area in 1209 and built **Cēsis Castle,** which has suffered a complicated history ever since. When Russia's **Ivan the Terrible** laid siege in 1577, the castle's defenders filled the cellars with gunpowder and blew themselves up to avoid surrendering. Although the castle was later rebuilt, a 1703 attack by **Peter the Great** returned it to ruins. The nearby **Cēsis New Castle,** built as the personal estate of an 18th-century Baltic-German nobleman, now houses the **Cēsis Museum of History and Art,** which has comprehensive displays on the town's history. Museum admission includes access to the new castle's **Lademahers Tower,** as well as the old castle's **ruins.** For the latter, put on a hard hat and grab a candle-lantern to climb narrow medieval staircases or descend to the dungeon before emerging into the castle gardens. At the garden entrance, a fallen Lenin statue lies in a wooden coffin. (☎412 2615. Open mid-May to Sept. Tu-Su 10am-6pm; Nov. to mid-May W-Su 10am-5pm. Tours in English, German, Latvian or Russian 15Ls.) Ivan also destroyed the nearby **Āraiši Castle,** which remains in ruins. This castle, on the near shore of the picturesque Lake Āraiši, is part of the **Open-Air Archaeological Museum,** an odd collection of reconstructed buildings and huts. Steps away from the Āraiši castle is a reconstruction of medieval **Latgale settlement** as well as a small reconstruction of a **Stone Age reed dwelling.** Āraiši is easily reached by bike: head out of town on Piebalgas iela, take a right on P20 (in the direction of Rīga), then take a left when you see a sign post for the museum. Infrequent buses leave Cēsis for Drabeši, stopping at Āraiši. (☎419 7288. English captions. Open mid-Apr. to Dec. daily 11am-5pm. 0.80Ls, students 0.40Ls.)

Hotel Birzes ❷, Miglas iela, has clean, inexpensive rooms equipped with TVs, private baths, and nice views. (☎26 55 59 58; www.hotelbirzes.viss.lv. Doubles 10Ls. Stop at the TIC for directions. Cash only). **Hotel Cēsis ❷,** Vienības laukums 1, is luxurious, with huge beds and sparkling clean private baths. (☎412 0122; www.danlat-group.lv. English spoken. Singles June-Aug. 12Ls; Sept.-May 9Ls. MC/V.) The hotel's lively **Cafe Popular ❶** serves superb Latvian food by the kilo. (☎412 2392. Entrees 1-2Ls. Open M-Th and Su 11am-11pm, F-Sa 11am-midnight. MC/V.) **Madara '89,** Raunas 15, is a basic **supermarket.** (Open daily 8am-10pm.)

Cēsis is accessible by infrequent **trains** from Rīga via **Sigulda** on the Lugazi line (1½-2hr.; 5per day; 1.38Ls, bikes 0.41Ls). **Buses** from Rīga (2hr., 1-2 per hr. 6am-9pm, 1.30Ls) are more convenient. Call ahead if you want to reserve a **bike** (6Ls per day) at **Cēsu Tourism Inventory,** Lenču iela 6 (☎942 3270). It is a 2-3hr. bike ride to Sigulda each way. **Public transportation** in Sigulda consists of two buses (0.20Ls): bus #9 runs west to the Gauja River, while bus #11 runs east along **Jāņa Poruka iela** and down **Lapsu iela. Raunas iela** heads to the town center from the station and opens onto the main square, **Vienības laukums. Rīgas iela** and **Valnu iela** go downhill at the square's south end and meet at **Līvu laukums,** the original 13th-century heart of the town. **Lenču iela,** which leads from Vienības laukums, travels to Cēsis Castle (Cēsu Pils). The English-speaking staff at the **Tourist Information Center,** Pils laukums 1, across from the castle, arranges **private rooms** in the region or elsewhere in Latvia (1Ls fee) and has **free maps** and one computer with **Internet.** (☎412 1815; www.tourism.cesis.lv. 1Ls per hr. Open mid-May to mid-Sept. M-F 9am-6pm, Sa-Su 10am-5pm.) **Exchange currency** at **Unibanka,** Raunas iela 8, which cashes **traveler's checks** and gives MasterCard and Visa **cash advances** for 1% commission. (☎220 31. Open M-F 9am-5pm.) There are 24hr. **ATMs** on Rīgas iela. (☎412 2762. Cash windows open 6am-8pm.) The **post office** is at Raunas iela 13. (☎227 88. **Western Union.** Open M-F 7:30am-6pm, Sa 7:30am-4pm.) **Postal Code:** LV-4101.

LITHUANIA (LIETUVA)

Lithuania has always been an offbeat place. Once the last pagan outpost in Christian Europe, today the tiny country continues to forge an eccentric path, from the breakaway artists' republic and Frank Zappa statue in its spectacular capital, Vilnius, to the drifting sand dunes, the quirky folk art, and even a decaying Soviet missile base in the countryside. More conventional treats include the wild beauty of the unspoiled coast and the Baroque architecture of Vilnius's Old Town. Lithuania became the first Baltic nation to declare independence from the USSR in 1990. Having gained EU membership in 2004, it continues to push ahead with optimism, growing more Western with every passing year but retaining its unique character.

DISCOVER LITHUANIA: SUGGESTED ITINERARIES

THREE DAYS. Head straight to the **Baltic Coast** to enjoy the stunning—and the stunningly tourist-free—coastal sands of the **Drifting Dunes of Parnidis** (1 day; p. 409) and the bike and hiking trails of **Nida** (1 day; p. 409); then leave the **Curonian Spit** and head up the coast to the haunting **Soviet Missile Base** (p. 405).

ONE WEEK. After three days on the **Baltic Coast,** go inland to the unique **Hill of Crosses** outside lively **Šiauliai** (1 day; p. 399). Continue to cosmopolitan **Vilnius** (3 days; p. 379), where you can explore the cobblestoned **Old Town,** wander offbeat **Užupis,** and take a daytrip to the ancient capital of Lithuania, **Trakai Castle** (p. 390).

FACTS AND FIGURES

Official Name: Republic of Lithuania.
Capital: Vilnius.
Major Cities: Kaunas, Klaipėda.
Population: 3,575,000.
Time Zone: GMT + 2, in summer GMT +3.
Language: Lithuanian.
Religion: Roman Catholic (79%).
Land Area: 65,200 sq. km.
Number of Tractors: 101,300.
Vehicle Density: 18.5 per sq. km.

ESSENTIALS

WHEN TO GO

Summer is brief but glorious in Lithuania, while winter is long and cold. Tourist season peaks between June and September, especially along the coast, where temperatures reach 22°C (72°F). A winter visit also has its charms, especially if you're headed for Vilnius, but be aware that many establishments along the coast close in the low season due to temperatures below 0°C (32°F).

DOCUMENTS AND FORMALITIES

EMBASSIES AND CONSULATES. Foreign embassies to Lithuania are in Vilnius (p. 379). Lithuanian embassies and consulates abroad include: **Australia,** 40B Fiddens Wharf Rd., Killara, NSW 2071 (☎02 94 98 25 71); **Canada,** 130 Albert St., Ste. 204, Ottowa, ON K1P 5G4 (☎613-567-5458; amb.ca@urm.lt); **Ireland,** 90 Merrion Rd., Ballsbridge, Dublin 4 (☎1 668 8292); **New Zealand,** 17 Koraha St., Remuera, Auckland 1005 (☎9 524 9463; jurgispec@hotmail.com); **UK,** 84 Gloucester Pl., London W1U 6AU (☎20 74 86 64 01; amb.uk@urm.lt); **US,** 4590 MacArthur Blvd., Ste. 200 NW, Washington, D.C. 20007 (☎202-234-5860; amb.us@urm.lt). Check www.lithuania.embassyhomepage.com for more embassy info.

ENTRANCE REQUIREMENTS.

Passport: Required for all travelers.

Visa: Not required for stays under 90 days for citizens of Australia, Canada, Ireland, New Zealand, the UK, and the US.

Letter of Invitation: Not required for citizens of Australia, Canada, Ireland, New Zealand, the UK, and the US.

Inoculations: Recommended up-to-date on DTaP (diphtheria, tetanus, and pertussis), Hepatitis A, Hepatitis B, MMR (measles, mumps, and rubella), polio booster, and typhoid.

Work Permit: Required of all foreigners planning to work in Lithuania.

International Driving Permit: Required for all those planning to drive in Lithuania for periods of under 90 days except citizens of the US.

VISA AND ENTRY INFORMATION. Citizens of the EU do not need visas to travel to Lithuania. Citizens of Australia, Canada, New Zealand, the UK, and the US do not need a visa for stays of up to 90 days. Long-term visas for temporary residence (€60) can be purchased from the nearest embassy or consulate. Avoid crossing through Belarus to enter or exit Lithuania: not only do you need to obtain a transit visa (US$50) for Belarus in advance, but guards may hassle you at the border.

TOURIST SERVICES AND MONEY

LITAI (LT)		
	AUS$1 = 2.14LT	1LT = AUS$0.47
	CDN$1 = 2.32LT	1LT = CDN$0.43
	EUR€1 = 3.45LT	1LT = EUR€0.30
	NZ$1 = 1.97LT	1LT = NZ$0.51
	UK£1 = 5.08LT	1LT = UK£0.20
	US$1 = 2.81LT	1LT = US$0.36

Major cities have official **tourist offices. Litinterp** (www.litinterp.lt) reserves accommodations and rents cars, usually without a surcharge. Kaunas, Klaipėda, Nida, Palanga, and Vilnius each have an edition of the *In Your Pocket* series, available at kiosks and some hotels. Employees at tourist stations often speak English.

The unit of currency is the **Lita** (Lt; 1Lt=100 Centų), plural Litai or Litų. The Lita is fixed to the euro at €1 = 3.45Lt until the euro replaces the Lita altogether after 2010. The rapidly expanding economy (growing at over 7% anually) has created **inflation** of over 3% in recent years. Exchange bureaus near the train station usually have poorer rates than **banks.** Most banks cash **traveler's checks** for 2-3% commission. Visa **cash advances** can usually be obtained with minimum hassle. **Vilniaus Bankas,** with outlets in major cities, accepts major credit cards and traveler's checks for a small commission. Most places catering to locals don't take credit cards. Additionally, some establishments that claim to take MasterCard or Visa may not actually be able to do so. **ATMs** are readily available in most cities, though few accept American Express.

HEALTH AND SAFETY

EMERGENCY	**Ambulance:** ☎033. **Fire:** ☎011. **Police:** ☎022. **General Emergency:** ☎112.

Lithuania's medical facilities are quickly catching up to Western standards. However, while most hospitals are stocked in basic medical supplies, there is a shortage of doctors. Many doctors, too, expect immediate payment in cash.

Well-stocked **pharmacies** are common and carry most medical supplies, tampons, condoms, and toiletries. Drink bottled mineral water, and **boil tap water** for 10min. before drinking. A triangle pointing downward indicates men's **restrooms;** one pointing upward indicates women's restrooms. However, many bathrooms are nothing but a hole in the ground; carry toilet paper. Lithuania's **crime rate** is generally low, especially when it comes to violent crime against tourists, though cab drivers will think nothing of ripping you off, and petty crime is rampant. Nevertheless, Vilnius is one of the safer capitals in Europe. Lithuanian **police** are helpful but understaffed, so your best bet for assistance in English is your **consulate.**

Women traveling alone will be noticed but shouldn't encounter too much difficulty. Skirts, blouses, and heels are far more common than jeans, shorts, tank tops, or sneakers, but showing skin is acceptable primarily in the club scene. **Minorities** traveling to Lithuania may encounter unwanted attention or discrimination, though most is directed toward Roma (gypsies). Lithuania has made little effort to provide services or facilities for **disabled** travelers. **Homosexuality** is legal but not always tolerated. Lithuania has numerous nightclubs, hotlines, and services for **GLBT** travelers to the Baltics (see **Vilnius: GLBT Resources,** p. 382).

TRANSPORTATION

BY PLANE. AirBaltic, Delta, Finnair, LOT, Lufthansa, SAS, and other **airlines** fly into Vilnius, and RyanAir flies into Kaunas. Many discount airlines offer cheap connections through London. However, if you're already near the Baltic, buses and trains are unbeatable.

BY TRAIN. **Trains** are more popular for international and long-distance travel. Two major lines cross Lithuania: one runs north-south from Latvia through Šiauliai and Kaunas to Poland; the other runs east-west from Belarus through Vilnius and Kaunas to Kaliningrad, branching out around Vilnius and Klaipėda.

BY BUS AND FERRY. Domestic **buses** are faster, more common, less crowded, and only a bit more expensive than trains. Whenever possible, try to catch an express bus; such buses are normally marked with an asterisk or an "E" on the timetable. They are typically direct and can be up to twice as fast. Vilnius, Kaunas, and Klaipėda are easily reached by train or bus from Estonia, Latvia, Poland, and Russia. **Ferries** connect Klaipėda with Arhus and Aabenraa, DEN; Kiel, Zasnicas, and Mukran, GER; Baltijskas, RUS; and Ahus and Karlshamn, SWE.

BY CAR AND BY TAXI. All travelers planning to **drive** in Lithuania must purchase a Liability Insurance Policy at the Lithuanian border (79Lt for the 15-day minimum). These policies may only be purchased with Litas, so make sure to convert some cash before reaching the border. Headlights are required while driving from November until March. US citizens may drive with an American driver's license for up to three months; all other motorists must have an International Driving Permit. There are inexpensive **taxis** in most cities. Agree on a price before getting in, or make sure that the meter is running.

BY BIKE AND BY THUMB. **Biking** is a great way to get to see the Lithuanian countryside. Many companies offer tours throughout the country; check out **ScanTours** (www.scantours.net) and the European Cyclists' Federation (www.ecf.com) for some ideas. **Hitchhiking** is common; locals line up along major roads leaving large cities. Many drivers charge a fee comparable to local bus or train fares. Let's Go does not recommend hitchhiking.

KEEPING IN TOUCH

PHONE CODES	**Country code:** 370. **International dialing prefix:** 00. From outside Lithuania, dial international dialing prefix (see inside back cover) + 370 + city code + local number. Within Lithuania, dial 8 + city code + local number. Within cities, just dial the 6-digit number.

EMAIL AND INTERNET. **Internet** access and Wi-Fi are widely available in Lithuania, even in small towns. Most well-located Internet cafes charge 3Lt per hour and also offer a range of services including copying, laminating, and CD burning.

TELEPHONE. To use public phones, travelers must purchase a **Tele2** card. These come in 9, 13, 16, and 30Lt denominations and can be purchased at kiosks or at the post office. Cell phones are very prevalent and receive free incoming calls; they can be found at Tele2 stores or Omnitel. SIM cards are also easy to install; once again, Tele2 is the best option, with competitive international rates of 1.85Lt per minute. International access numbers include: **AT&T Direct** (☎880 090 028); **Canada Direct** (☎880 090 004); and **Sprint** (☎880 095 877).

MAIL. Airmail **letters** abroad cost 1.30Lt (postcards 1.20Lt) and take about one week to reach the US or Canada. Post offices are generally open M-F 11am-5pm as well as Saturday until 4pm in Vilnius and Kaunas. It is not generally difficult to find English service. **Poste Restante** is available in Vilnius but hard to find elsewhere. Address the envelope as follows: first name LAST NAME, POSTE RESTANTE, post office address, Postal Code, city, LITHUANIA.

ACCOMMODATIONS AND CAMPING

LITHUANIA	❶	❷	❸	❹	❺
ACCOMMODATIONS	under 40Lt	41-70Lt	71-120Lt	121-180Lt	over 180Lt

Lithuania has many youth **hostels,** particularly in Vilnius and Klaipėda. HI membership is nominally required, but an LJNN guest card (10.50Lt at any of the hostels) will suffice. The head office is in Vilnius (see **Vilnius: Practical Information,** p. 381). Their *Hostel Guide* has maps and info on bike and car rentals and hotel reservations. **Hotels** across the price spectrum abound in Vilnius and most major towns. **Litinterp,** with offices in Vilnius, Kaunas, and Klaipėda, assists in finding homestays or apartments for rent. **Camping** is restricted by law to marked campgrounds; the law is well enforced, particularly along the Curonian Spit.

FOOD AND DRINK

LITHUANIA	❶	❷	❸	❹	❺
FOOD	under 8Lt	8-17Lt	18-30Lt	31-40Lt	over 40Lt

Lithuanian cuisine is heavy and sometimes greasy. Keeping a **vegetarian** or **kosher** diet is difficult but not impossible. Restaurants serve various types of *blynai* (pancakes) with *mėsa* (meat) or *varske* (cheese). *Cepelinai*—translated as "zeppelins"—are heavy, potato-dough missiles of meat, cheese, and mushrooms; *saltibarščiai* is a beet-and-cucumber soup prevalent in the east; *karbonadas* is breaded pork fillet; and *koldunai* are meat dumplings. Lithuanian **beer** flows freely. Kalnapis is popular in Vilnius and most of Lithuania, Baltijos reigns supreme around Klaipėda, and the award-winning Utenos is everywhere. Lithuanian **vodka** *(degtinė)* is also popular.

LIFE AND TIMES

HISTORY

PAGAN AND PROUD OF IT. The Baltic people settled in the region 2000 years before the Christian era. The **Žemaičiai** tribe occupied the western part of Lithuania, and the **Aukštaitiai** inhabited the east. Defiantly pagan Lithuania was the last country in Europe to accept Christianity (in 1387). The Lithuanian tribes united briefly under Aukštaitiai leader **Mindaugas,** who became **Christian** in 1251 and was named the country's first Grand Duke by Pope Innocent IV. Mindaugas was assassinated, likely by pagan princes, in 1263. In the 14th century, Lithuanian territory swelled as **Grand Duke Gediminas** consolidated power.

UNDERAGE IN THE MIDDLE AGES. Jogaila, Gediminas's grandson, married the 12-year-old Polish Princess Jadwiga and became Wladisław II Jagiełło, King of Poland, in 1385. With this union, Jogaila introduced **Roman Catholicism** to Lithuania: the Aukštaitiai were baptized in 1387 and the Žemaičiai in 1413. Jogaila forged a bond between Lithuania and Poland lasting 400 years that rivaled the power of Muscovy. Jogaila left control of Lithuania to his onetime rival **Vytautas Didysis,**

most famous for his defeat of the Teutonic Knights at the 1410 **Battle of Grunwald.** Together, they expanded their empire until Vytautus's death in 1430, at which point Lithuanian territory included present-day Belarus and Ukraine, stretching from the Baltics to the Black Sea and from Vilnius to within 160km of Moscow. Lithuania solidified its ties to Poland with the 1569 **Union of Lublin,** which created the **Polish-Lithuanian Commonwealth,** heralding a period of prosperity and cultural development. Along with the alliance came further class division, as the nobility became steeped in Polish culture while the peasantry held on to the old customs.

DECLINE AND FALL. In the 18th century, the growing power of Russia and Prussia led to the three **Partitions of Poland** (see p. 418), which ceded most of Lithuania to Russia. By 1815, Russia had complete control of the territory. Nationalist uprisings in Poland in 1830-31 and 1863 provoked intensified campaigns of **Russification** in Lithuania, such that by 1864 the Lithuanian alphabet itself was outlawed. German troops returned to Lithuania in 1915, 500 years after the defeat of the Teutonic Knights, before being expelled at the end of 1918. The Lithuanians next beat the Red Army in 1919 and shortly thereafter declared **independence.** But while the army was occupied, Poland took **Vilnius**—the population of the city being predominantly Polish—and refused to release it. A dispute also arose with Germany over the port of **Klaipėda,** a predominantly German city that was Lithuania's only viable harbor on the Baltic. Germany won, claiming the city as their own.

STUCK IN THE MIDDLE AGAIN. Deprived of its capital and primary port, Lithuania did not remain independent for long. The country's parliamentary democracy collapsed in 1926 in a coup, as dictator **Antanas Smetona** banned opposition parties. Whatever autonomy remained disappeared with the 1939 **Nazi-Soviet Non-Aggression Pact,** which invited the Soviets to invade. In June 1941, the Soviets began to exile Lithuanians to remote regions of the USSR. Some 35,000 people were displaced. Nazi occupation caused even greater devastation, as Lithuania lost another 250,000 citizens to war and concentration camps, including most of its Jewish population.

POLITICAL FREE-FOR-ALL. The Soviets returned in 1944, opposed by Lithuanian guerrilla fighters—at their height 40,000 strong—into the early 1950s. It was not until the 1960s that **Antanas Sniečkus** managed to solidify Soviet rule. Even then, resistance persisted through the stagnation of the 1970s and 1980s, as the republic generated more *samizdat* ("self-made" dissident publications) per capita than any other region in the Soviet bloc. **Mikhail Gorbachev's** democratic reforms were eagerly received, and on March 1, 1990, Lithuania seceded from the USSR. Moscow retaliated, futilely attempting to disconnect the region's oil and gas resources. In what has come to be known as the "Lithuanian massacre," the Soviets launched an assault on Vilnius's radio and TV center, killing 14. In the wake of the failed Soviet *putsch* of August 1991, Lithuania finally achieved independence.

TODAY

Although still poor relative to the rest of Central Europe, Lithuania got off to an early start on economic reforms, and has been labeled by investors as one of Eastern Europe's economic "tigers." Having joined both the **EU** and **NATO** in the spring of 2004, Lithuania is attempting to break from its Russia-dominated past. But then again, recent Prime Minister **Algirdas Brazauskas,** who held the post from 2001-06, and his successor, **Gediminas Kirkilas,** are both former Communists. President **Rolandas Paksas,** who was elected in 2003, made history by being the first modern European head of state to be impeached. He was dismissed in April 2004, and in a special election in June, former President **Valdas Adamkus** was returned to office.

PEOPLE AND CULTURE

LANGUAGE. Lithuanian is one of only two Baltic languages (Latvian is the other). All "r"s are trilled. **Polish** is helpful in the south and **German** on the coast. **Russian** is understood in most places, although it is not as prominent as in Latvia. Most Lithuanians understand basic English phrases. If someone seems to sneeze at you, he might be saying *ačiu* (ah-choo; thank you). For a phrasebook and glossary, see **Appendix: Lithuanian,** p. 798.

DEMOGRAPHICS. The population of Lithuania is 83% **Lithuanian,** 6% **Russian,** and 7% **Polish.** The vast majority (79%) of Lithuanians are **Roman Catholic.**

CUSTOMS AND ETIQUETTE. Reserve informal greetings for those you know personally. Say *"laba diena"* ("good day") whenever you enter a shop. In polite company, you can never say *"prašau"* too many times (pra-sho; both "please" and "you're welcome"). Lithuanians usually **tip** 10%. **Bargaining** is acceptable at street booths and for taxis, but is not at shops and restaurants.

THE ARTS

LITERATURE. The earliest Lithuanian writings were the *Chronicles of the Grand Duchy of Lithuania,* written in an East Slavic dialect. The first book in Lithuanian, a Lutheran catechism, was printed in 1547. The year 1706 saw the appearance of secular literature with the publication in Lithuanian of *Aesop's Fables.* A Lithuanian translation of the **New Testament** was published in 1701 and a Lithuanian Bible in 1727. Despite a 1864 Tsarist ban on publishing Lithuanian works in Latin letters (as opposed to Cyrillic), many writers continued to write in their native tongue, seeking to overthrow Russian political and Polish cultural control. Known for both dramatic and lyric poetry, **Jonas Mačiulis** (a.k.a. Maironis) launched modern Lithuanian poetry with his 1895 *Voices of Spring (Pavasario balsai).* During the interwar period, ex-priest **Vincas Mykolaitis-Putinas** pioneered the modern Lithuanian novel with *In the Shadows of the Altars (Altorių šešėly).* After WWII, Soviet rule gagged and shackled Lithuanian writers; however, the poetry of **Alfonsas Nyka-Niliunas** and the novels of **Marius Katiliskis** flouted propagandistic Soviet Socialist Realism. *Pre-Dawn Highways,* by **Bronius Radzevicius,** is considered the strongest work of the late Soviet period.

MUSIC AND VISUAL ARTS. Both Lithuanian **music** and **painting** have been heavily influenced by traditional folk culture. Much of the visual arts' development has centered on the **Vilnius Drawing School,** founded in 1866, in which painter **Mikalojus Čiurlionis** was a central figure. **Folk songs,** called *dainos,* are essential to Lithuanian music, and are often accompanied by a the *kanklė,* a zither-like instrument, and the *lumzdelis,* which sounds like a whistle. The traditional *rateliai* is a circular dance, usually unaccompanied by music. During Soviet rule, **rock music** was seen as symbolic of a decadent, corrupt society, and was discouraged; only in the last two decades has it become popular. Even so, some rock bands, such as Vilnius's **Žalvarinis,** still draw on folk music for their inspiration and their beats.

FILM. Lithuanian-American independent filmmaker **Jonas Mekas** is best known for his 1976 film *Lost Lost Lost*—the story of his arrival in New York and contact with New York counter-culture icons of the 50s, like Allen Ginsberg and Frank O'Hara.

HOLIDAYS AND FESTIVALS

Holidays: New Year's Day and Flag Day (Jan. 1); Epiphany (Jan. 6); Independence Day (Feb. 16); Restoration of Independence (Mar. 11); Easter (Mar. 23-24, 2008; Apr. 12-13, 2009); Labor Day (May 1); Statehood Day (July 6); Assumption (Aug. 15); All Saints' Day (Nov. 1); Christmas (Dec. 25-26).

Festivals: Since the 19th century, regional craftsmen have gathered to display their wares each Mar. in Vilnius at the Kaziukas Fair. In the fall, the capital also hosts the Vilnius Jazz Festival and the avant-garde theater festival, SIRENOS (during the last few weeks in Sept.). Beautiful Trakai Castle hosts classical music concerts in July and Aug. during the Trakai Festival. During spring's Užgavėnės festival, citizens dress as animals or demons and burn an image of winter in effigy.

VILNIUS ☎(8)5

The top of Gediminas's Hill, where an iron wolf is said to have appeared to the Grand Duke in a dream and inspired him to found the city in 1323, is a good vantage point for taking in the extraordinary breadth of Lithuania's capital, which has turned its gaze resolutely toward modernity. Down in the city, the decades of decaying ruins are steadily giving way to stucco facades, Prada storefronts, and recently refurbished Baroque, gothic, and Neoclassical architecture. Increased tourism is expected in 2009, when Vilnius will serve as one of the European Union's European Capitals of Culture.

TRANSPORTATION

Flights: Vilnius Airport (Vilniaus oro uostas), Rodūnės Kelias 10a (info ☎230 6666; www.vilnius-airport.lt), 5km south of town. Buy a bus ticket (1.10Lt) from the Lietuvos Spauda kiosk on your right as you exit the departure hall. Take Bus #1 to the Geležinkelio Stotis train station to reach the Old Town. Airlines include: **Air Baltic** (☎235 6000; www.airbaltic.com); **Austrian Airlines** (☎273 9305); www.austrianairlines.lt); **British Airways** (☎273 1416; www.ba.com); **Czech Airlines** (☎232 9292; www.czech-airlines.com); **Finnair** (☎261 9339; www.finnair.com); **Lithuanian Airlines** (☎273 9305; www.lal.lt); **LOT** (☎273 9020; www.lot.com); **Lufthansa** (☎292 9290; www.lufthansa.com); **SAS** (☎235 6000; www.scandinavian.net).

Trains: Geležinkelio Stotis, Geležinkelio 16 (☎269 3722; www.litrail.lt). Domestic tickets are sold to the left and international to the right. Tickets for trains originating outside of Lithuania can be bought between 3hr. and 5min. before departure. Open daily 6-11am and noon-6pm. Most international trains pass through Belarus, which requires a Belarusian transit visa. To: **Berlin, GER** (22hr., 1 per day, 305Lt); **Kaliningrad, RUS** (7hr., 14 per day, 48Lt); **Minsk, BLR** (6hr., 2 per day, 20-60Lt); **Moscow, RUS** (17hr., 3 per day, 110Lt); **Rīga, LAT** (8hr., 1 per day, 118Lt); **St. Petersburg, RUS** (18hr., 3 per day, 90Lt); **Warsaw, POL** (8hr., 2 per day, 85Lt).

Buses: Autobusų Stotis, Sodų 22 (☎290 1661, reservations 216 2977; www.toks.lt), opposite the train station. Tickets for bus travel within Lithuania can be bought at the row of kiosks to the left of the information center. **Eurolines Baltic International** (**EBI;** ☎215 1377; www.eurolines.lt) offers routes to **Berlin, GER** (17hr., 1 per day, 187Lt); **Minsk, BLR** (5hr., 3 per day, 30Lt); **Rīga, LAT** (5hr., 4 per day, 45Lt); **St. Petersburg, RUS** (18hr., 4 per day, 129Lt); **Tallinn, EST** (9hr., 2 per day, 81Lt); **Warsaw, POL** (9-10hr., 3 per day, 105Lt); and other points west. Buy tickets in EBI kiosks to the right of the main entrance to the bus station. English spoken at most EBI kiosks. Student discount with valid ISIC. Open daily 6am-10pm.

Public Transportation: Buses and **trolleys** link downtown with the train and bus stations and the suburbs. Most lines run daily 6am-midnight. Buy tickets for state-owned buses at any kiosk (1.10Lt) or from the driver (1.40 Lt). Punch your ticket in the boxes on the state-owned buses to avoid a 10Lt fine—tickets are checked reasonably often.

Taxis: Martino (☎240 0004, from a mobile 1422). Although slightly more expensive than other taxi companies (roughly 10Lt for a trip in Old Town), it is said to have the

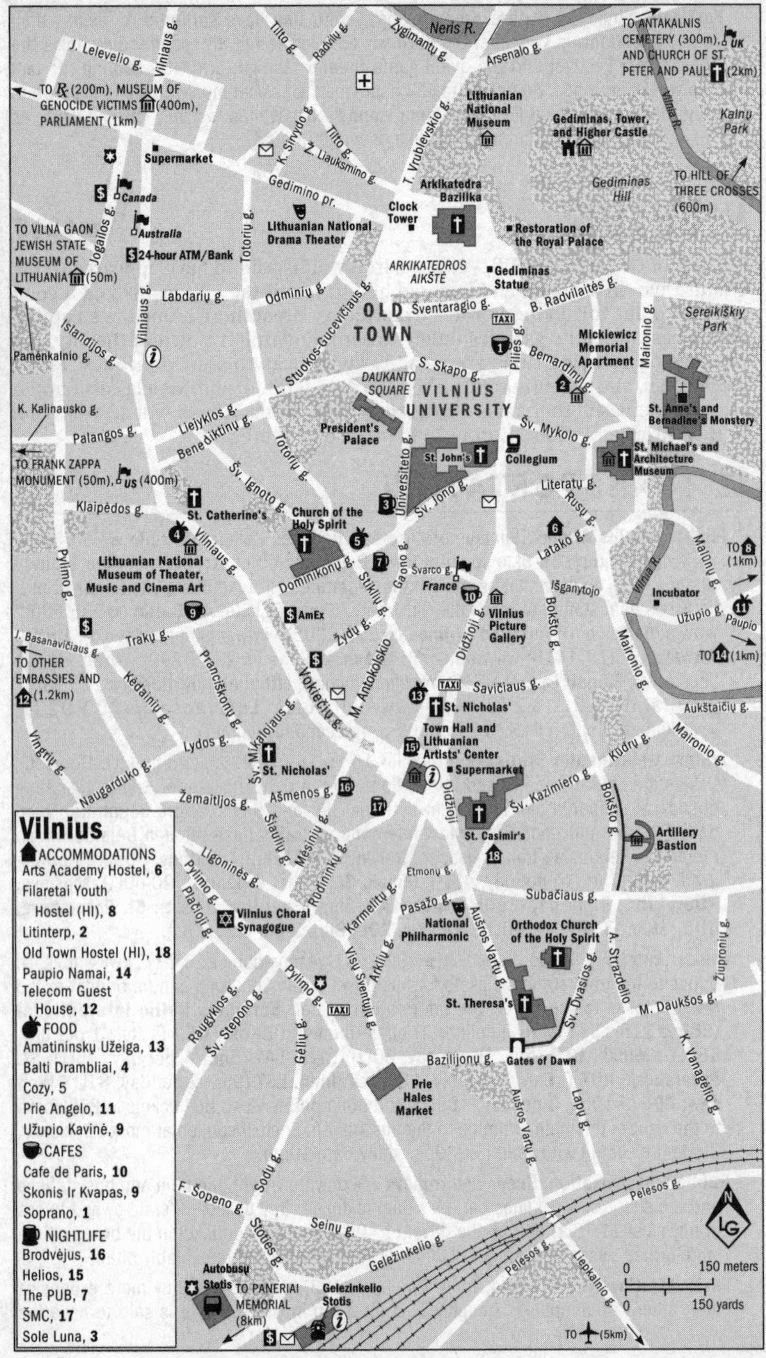
Neris R.
TO ANTAKALNIS CEMETERY (300m), UK AND CHURCH OF ST. PETER AND PAUL (2km)
TO ℞ (200m), MUSEUM OF GENOCIDE VICTIMS (400m), PARLIAMENT (1km)
Supermarket
Canada
Australia
24-hour ATM/Bank
TO VILNA GAON JEWISH STATE MUSEUM OF LITHUANIA (50m)
Lithuanian National Museum
Gediminas, Tower, and Higher Castle
Kalnų Park
Gediminas Hill
TO HILL OF THREE CROSSES (600m)
Arkikatedra Bazilika
Clock Tower
Lithuanian National Drama Theater
Restoration of the Royal Palace
ARKIKATEDROS AIKŠTĖ
Gediminas Statue
OLD TOWN
Sereikiškių Park
Mickiewicz Memorial Apartment
DAUKANTO SQUARE
VILNIUS UNIVERSITY
President's Palace
St. Anne's and Bernadine's Monstery
St. John's
Collegium
St. Michael's and Architecture Museum
TO FRANK ZAPPA MONUMENT (50m), US (400m)
St. Catherine's
Church of the Holy Spirit
Lithuanian National Museum of Theater, Music and Cinema Art
France
Vilnius Picture Gallery
Incubator
Paupio
AmEx
TO OTHER EMBASSIES AND 12 (1.2km)
St. Nicholas'
Town Hall and Lithuanian Artists' Center
Supermarket
St. Nicholas'
St. Casimir's
Artillery Bastion
Vilnius Choral Synagogue
National Philharmonic
Orthodox Church of the Holy Spirit
St. Theresa's
Gates of Dawn
Prie Hales Market
Autobusų Stotis
TO PANERIAI MEMORIAL (8km)
Gelezinkelio Stotis
TO (5km)
0 150 meters
0 150 yards
J. Lelevelio g.
Vilniaus g.
Tilto g.
Radvilų g.
Žygimantų g.
Arsenalo g.
T. Vrublevskio g.
K. Sirvydo g.
Ž. Liauksmino g.
Gedimino pr.
Jogailos g.
Totorių g.
Labdarių g.
Odminių g.
Šventaragio g.
B. Radvilaitės g.
Islandijos g.
Paménkalnio g.
L. Stuokos-Gucevičiaus g.
S. Skapo g.
Pilies g.
Bernardinų g.
Maironio g.
K. Kalinausko g.
Palangos g.
Liejyklos g.
Benediktinų g.
Šv. Mykolo g.
Universiteto g.
Šv. Ignoto g.
Šv. Jono g.
Literatų g.
Rusų g.
Klaipėdos g.
Latako g.
Malūnų g.
TO 8 (1km)
Pylimo g.
Dominikonų g.
Stiklių g.
Gaono g.
Švarco g.
Išganytojo
Vilnia R.
Užupio g.
TO 14 (1km)
Didžioji g.
Bokšto g.
J. Basanavičiaus g.
Trakų g.
Žydų g.
Pranciškonų g.
Vokiečių g.
M. Antokolskio
Savičiaus g.
Aukštaičių g.
Kėdainių g.
Šv. Mikalojaus g.
Lydos g.
Vingrių g.
Naugarduko g.
Kūdrų g.
Maironio g.
Žemaitljos g.
Ašmenos g.
Šv. Kazimiero g.
Didžioji
Šiaulių g.
Mėsinių g.
Rūdininkų g.
Ligoninės g.
Etmonų g.
Subačiaus g.
Pylimo g.
Plačioji g.
Karmelitų g.
Pasažo g.
Aušros Vartų g.
A. Strazdelio
Žiupronių g.
Visų Šventųjų g.
Arklių g.
Šv. Dvasios g.
M. Daukšos g.
Raugyklos g.
Šv. Stepono g.
Gėlių g.
Bazilijonų g.
K. Vanagėlio g.
Lapų g.
Sodų g.
F. Šopeno g.
Seinų g.
Stoties g.
Geležinkelio g.
Pelesos g.
Liepkalnio g.
Vilnius
ACCOMMODATIONS
Arts Academy Hostel, 6
Filaretai Youth Hostel (HI), 8
Litinterp, 2
Old Town Hostel (HI), 18
Paupio Namai, 14
Telecom Guest House, 12
FOOD
Amatininskų Užeiga, 13
Balti Drambliai, 4
Cozy, 5
Prie Angelo, 11
Užupio Kavinė, 9
CAFES
Cafe de Paris, 10
Skonis Ir Kvapas, 9
Soprano, 1
NIGHTLIFE
Brodvėjus, 16
Helios, 15
The PUB, 7
ŠMC, 17
Sole Luna, 3

MINIBUSES. White **minibuses** are small privately owned vans that follow the same routes as city buses. Hail them from the side of the street and tell the driver where you want to go. Minibuses are a bit more expensive (2Lt, paid to the driver), but are quicker, safer, and less crowded than city transport.

most reliable service. Vilnius drivers are notorious for overcharging foreigners who hail cabs from the side of the street. If you're at a cafe or restaurant, ask your server to call for a cab, as the fare will likely be half the rate you would have paid if you tried to hail one yourself.

ORIENTATION

The **train** and **bus stations** are located on opposite sides of **Geležinkelio.** With your back to the train station, turn right on Geležinkelio and walk 300m until you reach the base of a hill with an overpass on your right; turn left onto Aušros Vartų, which runs north through the **Aušros Vartai** (Gates of Dawn) into **Senamiestis** (Old Town). Aušros Vartų becomes Didžioji and then Pilies—both partially blocked for construction until summer 2008—before reaching the base of **Gediminas' Hill**. The Gediminas Tower of Higher Castle presides over **Arkikatedros Aikštė** (Cathedral Sq.) and the banks of the **Neris River.** Beyond Gediminas Hill to the east, the small **Vilnia River** winds north to the bigger Neris River. The commercial artery, **Gedimino,** leads west from the square in front of the Cathedral.

PRACTICAL INFORMATION

TOURIST AND FINANCIAL SERVICES

Tourist Offices: Tourist Information Center (TIC) maintains 3 branches with English-speaking staff. All offer excellent **free maps** as well as train and bus schedules, free Wi-Fi, and souvenirs. Bicycles are for rent at the Vilniaus location (1Lt per day), Vilniaus 22 (☎262 96 60; www.turizmas.vilnius.lt), 50m north of the Radvilai Palace. Branches at Didžioji 31 (☎262 6470), at the northeast corner of the Town Hall, and at Geležinkelio 16 (☎269 2091), in a kiosk inside the train station. Open M-F 9am-6pm, Sa-Su 10am-4pm. **Kelvita Tourism Agency,** Geležinkelio 16 (☎210 6130; fax 210 6131), in a kiosk inside the train station at window #30. German and English spoken. Turnaround is quick for visas to Russia. American visas 470Lt for 24hr. wait or 260Lt for 8-day wait. Citizens of other English-speaking countries pay roughly 20% less. Open M-F 8am-6pm.

Embassies and Consulates: Australia, Vilniaus 23 (☎212 3369). Open Tu 10am-1pm, Th 2-5pm. **Canada,** Jogailos 4 (☎249 0950; www.canada.lt). Visas M, W, F 9am-noon. Open daily 8:30am-5pm. **UK,** Antakalnio 2 (☎246 2900, emergency mobile 869 83 70 97; www.britain.lt). Visas M-F 8:30am-11:30am. Open M-Th 8:30am-5pm, F 8:30am-4pm; **US,** Akmenų 6 (☎266 5500; www.usembassy.lt). Visas M-Th 8:30am-11:30am. Open M-F 8am-5:30pm.

Currency Exchange: Most currency kiosks exchange British pounds, euro, Latvian lats, Swedish crowns, Swiss francs, and US dollars. **Parex Bankas,** Geležinkelio 6 (☎233 0763), to the left with the train station behind you, doesn't offer the best rates, but changes several currencies not accepted at other banks. Open 24hr. **Vilniaus Bankas,** Vokiečių 9 (☎/fax 262 7869). Gives MC/V **cash advances** at no commission and cashes AmEx and Thomas Cook **traveler's checks.** Open M-F 8am-6pm. **Bankas Snoras** has good exchange rates, cashes traveler's checks, and gives Visa cash advances for a small commission. Look for blue-and-white kiosks throughout town. Open M-F 8am-7pm, Sa 9am-2pm. **ATMs** offer the best exchange rates and are everywhere.

LOCAL SERVICES

Luggage Storage: The storage center in the bus station near the main entrance charges 3Lt per bag per day. Open M-F 5:30am-9pm, Sa-Su 7am-9pm. A better option is the self-service, electronic facility beneath the train station (2Lt per 12hr., less thereafter). Take the stairs down from the ground fl. and turn right. Save the receipt: you will need the PIN to retrieve your baggage. Open 24hr., no time limit. Many hostels also provide luggage storage for a fee (3-5Lt).

English-Language Bookstore: Prie Halés, Pylimo 53, below the hill from the bus station (☎262 4528; prie-hales@masiulis.lt). Maintains a small section of English-language fiction, textbooks, and guidebooks. Open M-F 9am-6pm, Sa 9am-3pm.

Laundromat: Nearly all hostels and hotels in Vilnius offer full-service laundry, often even if you are not staying there (10-30Lt).

Bike Rental: Some hostels lend bikes to guests for free. For touring the Old Town, rent a bicycle for 1Lt per day from the **Tourist Information Center** at Vilniaus 22. Bicycle must be returned by 6pm. For more extensive trips, rent online from www.bicycle.lt, a website maintained by **Du Ratai** (Two Wheels), a branch of the Lithuanian Cyclists' Community. The energetic Baltic cyclist can even rent in Lithuania and return the bicycle in Latvia or Estonia (or vice-versa). Rates start at €9 per day, and decrease to €7.50 per day for rentals of 15 days or more. Further discounts available for group or extended rentals.

GLBT Resources: Gay and Lesbian Information Line (☎233 3031; www.gay.lt). Info about organizations and events for gay and lesbian travelers. The **Lithuanian Gay and Lesbian Homepage** (www.gayline.lt) and **The Gay Club** (☎998 50 09; vgc@takas.lt) list gay and lesbian establishments in Lithuania.

EMERGENCY AND COMMUNICATIONS

24hr. Pharmacy: Gedimino Vaistinė, Gedimino pr. 27 (☎261 0135).

Medical Services: Baltic-American Medical and Surgical Clinic, Nemenčinės 54a (☎234 2020 or 69 85 26 55; www.bak.lt). Accepts major American, British, and other international insurance plans. Open daily 7am-11pm. Doctors on call 24hr.

Telephones: Public **phone booths** are omnipresent in Vilnius. Except for emergency and toll-free lines, you must use a phone card, available from street kiosks. See www.nautel.lt for more information.

Internet: Free Internet is offered at many hostels and some cafes, as well as at the **British Council Library,** Jogailos g. 4 (☎264 4890; www.britishcouncil.lt). In Old Town, **Collegium,** Pilies 22 (☎261 8334; www.dora.lt) is centrally located and the fast computers carry a wide selection of software. 3Lt an hour. Also offers Wi-Fi, photocopying, printing, binding, and laminating. Open M-F 8am-10pm, Sa-Su 11am-10pm.

Post Office: Lietuvos Paštas, Gedimino 7 (☎261 6759; www.post.lt), west of Arkikatedros Aikštė (the Cathedral). **Poste Restante** at the window labeled "iki pareikalavimo." Open M-F 7am-7pm, Sa 9am-4pm. **Postal Code:** LT-01001.

ACCOMMODATIONS

LITINTERP, Bernardinų 7/2 (☎212 3850; www.litinterp.lt). This travel agency and hostel places guests in Old Town B&Bs or in its own beautiful, spacious rooms. English spoken. Breakfast included. Reception M-F 8:30am-5:30pm, Sa 9am-3pm. Reserve ahead. Singles 80-140Lt; doubles 140-160Lt; triples 180-210Lt. 5% ISIC discount. MC/V. ❸

Arts Academy Hostel, Latako 2 (☎212 0176). From June-Sept., this Soviet-style concrete edifice offers some of the cheapest beds in town. Utilitarian rooms come equipped with desks, cupboards, and kettles. Linens 5Lt. Common area with kitchen and TV. 5-person dorms 18Lt; singles 43Lt; doubles 76Lt; triples 72-76Lt. Cash only. ❶

Old Town Hostel (HI), Aušros Vartų 20-10 (☎262 5357; www.balticbackpackers.com), in a courtyard 100m south of the Gates of Dawn. A great place to meet hard-partying English-speakers. 4-person rooms lack lockers, but free coffee, Internet, and helpful English-speaking staff make up for it. Clean, colorful communal kitchen, common room, and shared showers. Linens 2-5Lt, laundry and bike rental. Reservations recommended. Dorms 34Lt, HI members 32Lt; doubles 50Lt; quads 40Lt. MC/V. ❶

Filaretai Youth Hostel (HI), Filaretų 17 (☎215 4627; www.filaretaihostel.lt). Take #34 bus from the train station to Filaretai, the 7th stop. Renovated, spacious dorms are clean and shared bathrooms are well kept. The 1km hike from the Old Town is dark at night, but there are free bike loans. Kitchen, laundry facilities, common room, free Internet, luggage storage (3Lt). Dorms 39Lt; doubles 46t; triples 56Lt; quads 80Lt. Oct.-Apr. prices drop by 5Lt. 3Lt discount after 1st night. 4Lt discount for members. MC/V. ❶

Paupio Namai, Paupio 31a (☎264 3113; www.hotel.paupio.lt). Take #34 bus from the train station to "Filaretai," the 7th stop; on foot from downtown, go east on Užupio across the Vilnia River. Turn right on Paupio, walk over the footbridge, and Paupio Namai is on your right. This large, family-style manor offers basic, clean rooms, a communal kitchen, linens, and free Internet and Wi-Fi. Price includes a hearty breakfast spread each morning. Dorms 50Lt; singles 80Lt; doubles 130Lt, triples 150Lt. MC/V. ❸

Telecom Guest House, A. Vivulskio 13a (☎264 4861; www.telecomguesthouse.lt). From the city center, follow Trakų, which turns into J. Basanavičiaus. Just before the green-domed church, turn left on Algirido, then right on A. Vivulskio; the guesthouse is located in a courtyard. Clean, new rooms with private bathrooms, TVs, minibars and A/C make Telecom worth the 20min. walk into Old Town. English spoken. Hot and cold breakfast. Singles 240Lt; doubles 280 LT. MC/V. ❺

FOOD

The streets of Vilnius are bursting with inexpensive restaurants dishing out both regional cuisine and fare from the far corners of the globe. Cafes offer delicious meals at almost any hour, but budget travelers might find supermarkets and picnic lunches the most economical. Several **Iki** supermarkets (www.iki.lt) on the outskirts of Vilnius stock local and Western brands. One convenient location is Sodu 22, opposite the bus station. (Open daily 8am-10pm.) There are seven **Ikiukas** (literally "little Iki") minimarts inside the city, including branches at Uzupio 7, Pylmio 21, and A. Vivulskio 15. (Open daily 8am-11pm.) The centrally located **Rimi** supermarket, at Didžioji 28, is across the street from the Town Hall.

For an authentic Lithuanian shopping experience, visit **Halés Market,** a sprawling indoor market at the corner of Pylmio and Bazilijonv. Inside the expansive building, rows of vendors offer freshly cut meat, homemade cheeses, fruits, vegetables, and baked goods. Walk south out of the Old Town through the Gates of Dawn; go right on Bazlijonu and continue for 250m. Look for locals selling flowers from baskets on the sidewalk. (Open M-W 9am-2am, Th 9am-4am, Sa 10am-4am, Su 10am-2am.)

Balti Drambliai (White Elephant), Vilniaus 41 (☎262 0875; www.baltidramblai.com). Offers a range of options for vegetarians and vegans. Lanterns hanging from a canopy in an outdoor courtyard are perfect for dinner and drinks on long summer nights. Vegetable curry with spinach and paneer (9Lt) is complex and flavorful, while the less adventurous

GALLERIES IN VILNIUS

Vhile Vilnius gears up for its desgnation as a 2009 European Capital of Culture, its growing community of avant-garde artists continues to fuel the city's burgeoning art scene. Not confined o museums, the energy spills out o free street-side galleries run by ocal artists and students eager to alk about their work.

The **Contemporary Art Centre** is a must see. Boasting huge nstallations and video art, this arge space showcases the forerunners in the field. Tucked away n a dark alleyway, the **Vilnius Graphic Art Centre** is filled with computer-generated graphics. **Gallery Vartai** is one of the most prestigious private galleries in Vilnius, while **Art ma galleria** showcases a large underground scene. For both black-and-white and contemporary photography, stop by **Prospekto Galerija** and he **Photograph Gallery.** Finally, he **Amber Gallery** houses amber art and jewelry. Call beforehand o set up an amber-molding workshop with a local artist, starting at just 5Lt an hour.

The Contemporary Art Centre; Vokieciu 2 (☎261 7097). Vilnius Graphic Art Centre, Latako g. 3 (☎261 1995). Gallery Vartai, Vilniaus 39 (☎212 2949, www.galerijavartai.lt). Prospekto Galerija, Gedimino 43 (☎261 3338). Photograph Gallery, Didzioji 19 (☎261 1702). Amber Gallery, Šv. Mykolo g. (☎120 1124).

might enjoy one of many vegetarian pizzas (from 5Lt). English menu. Live music many nights at 8pm. Open M-F 11am-midnight, Sa-Su 7pm-midnight. MC/V. ❶

Užupio Kavinė, Užupio 2 (☎212 2138). Offers a peaceful patio overlooking the Vilnia river and the opportunity to enjoy beer with breakfast. The extensive menu includes pages of salads (7-12Lt) and entrees (14-35Lt), including the "Ruins of Užupis," a pork-and-vegetable dish. English menu. Open daily 10am-11pm. MC/V. ❷

Amatininskų Užeiga, Didžioji 19, #2 (☎261 7968). Sample traditional Lithuanian fare at this centrally located steetside cafe. The cold beetroot soup (5-8Lt) and meat-filled pancakes (11-32t) are quite filling. Also offers a wide selection of Western fare. English menu. Open M-F 10am-5am, Sa-Su 11am-5am. Cash only. ❷

Prie Angelo, Užupio 9 (☎215 3790). Across from the Užupis Angel, this small restaurant serves everything from thin-crust pizza (from 8Lt) to meat plates (58Lt). English menu. Entrees 10-28Lt. Open M-Th and Su 10am-11pm, F-Sa 10am-midnight. MC/V. ❸

Cozy, Dominikonų 10, (☎261 1137; www.cozy.lt). The ultra-70s decor, complete with artsy photography and orange furniture transport patrons back to a funkier era. Try the mussels stewed in cider cream sauce (16Lt) or enjoy free Wi-Fi while you sip from a wide variety of coffees and teas. English menu. Open M-W 9am-2am, Th 9am-4am, Sa 10am-4am, Su 10am-2am. ❷

CAFES

Cafe De Paris, Didžioji 1 (☎261 1021; www.cafedeparis.lt). An eclectic mix of electronica playlists and French-style decor, this funky cafe serves up sweet crepes and savory breakfast sandwiches (5-11Lt). Join the crowds for cocktails in the evenings when de Paris turns on the club lights and hosts music performances. See website for details. Open M-Tu 11am-midnight; W-Th and Su 11am-2am; F, Sa 11am-4am. MC/V. ❶

Skonis Ir Kvapas, Trakų 8 (☎212 2803). Tucked away in a quiet courtyard near the heart of the Old City, this cafe offers a fan-shaped menu of exotic teas (mug 3-5Lt, pot 8Lt). The name means "taste and smell," and, accordingly, servers will let you sniff your tea before ordering. Also offers a diverse breakfast menu; try an egg boiled in green tea (5Lt) or blueberry pancakes (5-7Lt). English menu. Open daily 9:30am-11pm. MC/V. ❶

Soprano, Pilies 3 (☎212 6042). At the end of the pedestrian thoroughfare, this cafe serves desserts to die for. The coffee is great, but it's the hazelnut or grapefruit gelato (2.5Lt cone, 3Lt bowl) that will keep you coming back for more. Flavors to please every ice cream connoisseur. M-Th and Su 10am-11pm, F-Sa 10am-midnight. MC/V. ❶

SIGHTS

SENAMIESTIS AND BEYOND

HIGHER CASTLE MUSEUM AND GEDIMINAS'S TOWER. Behind the cathedral (see below), a winding stairway leads to the top of the hill, from which visitors can enjoy awe-inspiring views of Vilnius. The hilltop fortification, whose origins go back to 200BC, is an excellent example of 13th-century Gothic architecture. The **Higher Castle Museum** (Aukštutinės Pilies Muziejus) showcases Lithuanian medieval history with a diverse display of old maps, scale models of the castle, and photographs of the ruin dating from the turn of the 19th and 20th centuries. The main attraction, however, is an even more magnificent view of Senamiestis and Gedimino available from the top of **Gediminas's Tower.** Now a funicular runs from the base to the tower. *(Castle Hill, Arsenalo 5. ☎61 74 53. Open Mar.-Oct. daily 10am-7pm; Nov.-Feb. Tu-Su 11am-5pm. Museum 4Lt, students 2Lt. Funicular 1/2 Lr one way/return.)*

CATHEDRAL SQUARE (ARKIKATEDROS AIKŠTĖ). Once a gothic shrine to the pagan god Perkūnas, this 13th-century Neoclassical structure is thought to be Lithuania's first Christian church. The remains of Casmir, Lithuania's patron saint, lie on the cathedral's southern side. The freestanding bell tower west of the cathedral dates to the 16th century, although the six bells inside were donated in 2002. Between the bell tower and the Cathedral, look for a small tile inscribed with the word "stebuklas" (miracle). This marks the site of one end of the 1989 human chain that stretched from Vilnius to Tallinn, made up of about 2,000,000 Estonians, Latvians, and Lithuanians protesting Soviet rule. *(At the end of Pilies and Universiteto. ☎261 1127. Open daily 7am-7pm.)* The **statue** of Grand Duke Gediminas, founder of Vilnius (see **History,** p. 376), was erected in 1996. To the east of the cathedral is the **Royal Palace,** which the city is hoping to rebuild in time for the 2009 millennial celebration of Lithuania's first mention in written records. *(Open daily 11am-6pm.)*

TOWN HALL SQUARE (ROTUŠĖS AIKŠTĖ). Located on Didžioji, Town Hall Square is an old marketplace dominated by the columns of the 18th-century **Town Hall**, now home to the **Lithuanian Artists' Center** (Lietuvos Menininkv Rumai). A small exhibit of popular local artists and gallery work is now on display. After a 2002 visit by US President George W. Bush, during which he declared that "anyone who would choose Lithuania as an enemy has also made an enemy of the United States of America," his words were immortalized in an engraving at the northeast corner of the hall. *(Didžioji 31. ☎261 8007. Open M-F 8am-6pm.)* The **Church of St. Nicholas** (Šv. Mikalojaus Bažnyčia), north of the Town Hall, is the oldest standing church and gothic structure in Lithuania. It was built in 1320 by German merchants while Lithuania was still a pagan nation. *(Didžioji 12. ☎261 8559. Open daily 10am-6pm.)*

CHURCH OF ST. ANNE AND CHURCH OF ST. FRANCIS AND BERNARDINES. These beloved churches, both dating from the 15th century, provide a beautiful architectural contrast. The Gothic exterior of St. Anne (Šv. Onos bažnyčia) may be the most frequently featured image on Vilnius postcards. Napoleon, arriving in the city triumphantly in the summer of 1812, supposedly said he wanted to carry the small church back to Paris in the palm of his hand. St. Francis and Bernardines (Bernardinų bažnyčia) housed the Vilnius Art Academy during Soviet times. It is worth a visit to see the intricately laid brickwork, faded paintings on the chipped plaster walls, and the musty interior that maintains faint traces of past glory. *(Maironio 8, at the end of Bernardinų. Services M-Sa 4:30pm; Su 9, 11am, 4:30pm.)*

CHURCH OF ST. PETER AND PAUL (ŠV. APAŠTALŲ PETRO IR POVILO BAŽNYČIA). According to local lore, Italian stucco-workers built the incredibly ornate Baroque interior of this church after its commissioner, the Grand Hetman of the Lithuanian armies, decided that Lithuanian sculptors were inferior. Its beautiful halls are now home to more than 2,000 stuccoed statues representing various mythical and biblical scenes. Note the chandelier, crafted from glass and brass beads and styled like a sailing ship. *(Antakalnio 1. Take tram #2, 3, or 4 from Senamiestis. Alternatively, head to the northeastern edge of the Old Town, where the Neris and Vilnia Rivers intersect, and follow T. Kosciuškos 2km until you reach the church. ☎234 0229.)*

ANTAKALNIS CEMETERY (ANTAKALINO KAPINES). This stunning graveyard 3km outside the Old Town is a resting place for Lithuania's national heroes and artistic luminaries. Graves marked with folk art crosses are mixed with large memorials to soldiers killed in WWI and WWII, as well as a sculpture commemorating the Lithuanians who died in clashes with the Soviet Army in 1991. Once inside, take the path to your left to see a hill filled with rows of crosses marking Polish Legionnaire graves. *(Facing the Church of St. Peter and Paul, walk up Antakalnio, on your left, and continue 150m until the road forks. Bear right onto Sapiegos and continue 400m; at the archway, turn right onto Jūratės. Take the 1st left onto Kuosų, then the 1st right onto Kariu Kapu. Continue to a grassy hill with steps leading to the cemetery. Open daily, dawn until dusk.)*

HILL OF THREE CROSSES (TRJIŲ KRŽIŲ KALNAS). Avid hikers will enjoy the winding path that ends in a view to rival that from Gediminas Hill, but in the company of fewer tourists and more Lithuanians, many of whom will be making out. From the northeast edge of the Old Town, cross the Arsenalo bridge and turn right up a winding road. Where the road diverges in front of an amphitheater, go right to reach the crosses and catch a breathtaking view of the area. Legend says that in the 13th century, pagans crucified Franciscan monks on the hill. Four centuries later, locals erected crosses to commemorate the martyrs; Stalin dismantled the monuments in 1950. They were rebuilt in 1989 to both memorialize the martyred monks and honor the Lithuanians who were deported to Siberia under the Soviets.

VILNIUS UNIVERSITY (VILNIAUS UNIVERSITETAS). Regarded as the oldest university in Eastern Europe, this assembly of perfectly trimmed lawns and beautifully restored buildings samples nearly every architectural style since its founding by Jesuits in 1579. Distinguished alums include 19th-century bard Adam Mickiewicz and Polish poet Czesław Miłosz, a Nobel Laureate in literature. *(3Lt, students 1Lt. Open M-Sa 9am-6pm.)* **St. John's Church** (Šv. Jonų bažnyčia), Šv. Jono 12, off Pilies, was once a science museum under Soviet rule and now houses a small collection of rare books dating back to the 14th century. *(Universiteto 3. ☎261 7155. Open M-Sa 10am-5pm.)* The 17th-century **Astronomical Observatory,** once rivaled in importance only by Greenwich and the Sorbonne, is opposite St. John's.

ST. CASIMIR'S CHURCH (ŠV. KAZIMIERO BAŽNYČIA). Named after Lithuania's patron saint and topped with a golden crown to symbolize Casimir's royal bloodline, this is the oldest Baroque church in Vilnius. Built by the Jesuits in 1604, the church has endured a painful history: Napoleon used it to store grain, tsarist authorities of the Russian Orthodox faith seized it from Catholics in 1841, invading Germans declared it a Lutheran house of worship in WWI, and the Soviets converted the church into an atheist monument. The church returned to Catholic control in 1989, and little evidence of its painful history remains. *(Didžioji 34. ☎222 1715. English info. Open M-Sa 4-6:30pm, Su 9am-1pm.)*

GATES OF DAWN (AUŠROS VARTAI). The Gates of Dawn, the only surviving portal of the city walls, have guarded the Old Town since the 16th century. Perhaps one of Vilnius's most beautiful examples of neo-classical architecture, the gates are a popular pilgrimage site for Eastern European Catholics. It is common practice for locals to cross themselves or pray before walking through. After entering the Old Town, pass through a door to the right and climb the stairs; the gold-laced **portrait of the Virgin Mary** on the 2nd floor is said to have miraculous powers *(Open daily 9am-6pm. Free.)* The highly decorated **St. Theresa's Church** (Šv. Teresės bažnyčia) was built between 1633 and 1652. The **Orthodox Church of the Holy Spirit** (Šv. Dvasios bažnyčia) is the seat of Lithuania's Russian Orthodox archbishop. The preserved bodies of St. Antonius, Ivan, and Eustachius, martyred in 1347 by pagan militants, are clothed in black during lent, white during Christmas and red during the remaining year, with the exception on June 26, when they are displayed naked. *(Aušros Vartų 10. ☎212 3513.)*

PARLIAMENT. In January 1991, the world watched as Lithuanians raised barricades to protect their parliament from the Soviet army. President Ladsbergis later said that all of the deputies expected to give their lives on the night of the Soviet invasion. West of the building, toward the river, a section of the barricade remains. Crosses, flowers, and photographs honor the fourteen unarmed civilians who were killed as the Red Army tried to occupy the 326m tall TV Tower on Jan. 13, 1991. *(Gedimino 53, just before the Neris River.)*

FRANK ZAPPA MONUMENT. Built by Konstantinas Bogdanas, a sculptor who once created busts of Lenin, this monument is reputed to be the only sculpture of Zappa anywhere in the world. Though the rock musician never visited Vilnius, his anti-authority message struck a chord among a population buckling under Soviet oppression. Today, he is immortalized through a bust of his head elevated on a 3m pole in a parking lot. Perhaps the most random monument in Eastern Europe, it was installed in 1995 by members of the Republic of Užupis (p. 391). *(Off Pylimo between Kalinausko 1 and 3.)*

JEWISH VILNIUS

Vilnius, known in Yiddish as "Vilna," was once called "Jerusalem of the North," and served as a center of Jewish learning and culture. It was a stronghold of the "Mitnagdim," the scholarly rabbis who resisted the Chasidic movement in the 18th century. Jews accounted for 100,000 of the city's 230,000 population at the outbreak of WWII. Only 6000 remained when the Red Army retook the city in 1944.

VILNA GAON JEWISH STATE MUSEUM OF LITHUANIA. Named for the 18th-century Talmudic scholar Elijah Ben Shlomo Zalman (known as the *gaon*, or genius), this three-site museum seeks to preserve Vilnius's Jewish heritage and commemorate victims of the Holocaust. The Green House's jarring exhibit, "Catastrophe," details the elite Nazi *Einsatzkommando* units' extermination of the city's Jews. The museum contains a collection of photographs and maps that reveal the terror of life in the Jewish Ghetto, before and after the German invasion. The last room includes a tribute to Chiune Sugihara, "the Japanese Schindler," a diplomat who helped 6000 Jews escape from Poland and Lithuania. *(Pamėnkalnio 12. Walk up a cobblestone drive on the south side of the street and look for a small sign or a green house. ☎261 3128; www.jmuseum.lt. Open M, W, F 2-6pm; Tu and Th 10am-2pm. English captions. Donations requested.)* The Tarbut Gymnasium pays homage to the 550,000 Jews—many of Lithuanian descent—who fought for the US Army in WWII. The Gallery of the Righteous (Teisuoliu Galerija) honors Lithuanians who sheltered Jews during WWII, and documents the life of the great violin player Jascha Heifetz, who grew up and was partly trained in Vilnius. *(Pylimo 4. ☎261 7917. Open in summer M-Th 9am-5pm, F 9am-4pm, Su 10am-4pm; in winter M-Th 9am-5pm, F 9am-4pm. English captions.)* The Tolerance Center contains a permanent exhibition of fragments and artifacts from Vilnius's Great Synagogue, as well as Jewish contemporary art. *(Naugarduko 10. ☎231 2356. Open in summer M-Th 10am-4pm, F 10am-4pm, Su 10am-4pm; in winter M-F 11am-4pm. 4Lt, students 2Lt.)*

PANERIAI MEMORIAL (PANERIŲ MEMORIALAS). Hidden at the end of a desolate dirt road 8km southwest of the Old City, this quiet forest is where Nazis butchered 100,000 Lithuanians, including 70,000 Jews. The Gestapo found that the oil pits the Soviets had drilled made convenient mass graves. Scattered throughout Paneriai Forest, the pits are marked with large stone circles. Inscriptions at the memorial are in Hebrew, Lithuanian, and Russian. You can reach the memorial by rail (10min.); most trains bound for Trakai and Kaunas from Geležinkelio Stotis, Vilnius's main station, will make their first stop in Panerai. Inquire about tickets (0.90Lt) at the windows to the left of the central entrance of the station. *(From Panerai's small yellow station house, turn right on Agrastų, continuing for 2km until you reach the memorial. Return to Vilnius by train or catch a bus close to the station house that will be labeled "Stotis"—ask the bus driver to be sure you're headed to Vilnius.)* There is a museum with English captions, but if you find it closed, a large map on the door can act as a guide to the memorials. *(Agrastų 17. ☎ 260 2001. Open M and W-F 11am-6pm. Free.)*

LITHUANIA

VILNIUS CHORAL SYNAGOGUE (SINAGOGA). Vilnius was once home to more than 100 Jewish houses of worship, including the majestic Great Synagogue, which Napoleon likened to Notre Dame. The Vilnius Choral Synagogue, built in 1903, is the only Jewish holy site that was not destroyed in WWII. The synagogue was closed in 2004, partially due to security concerns, but restoration efforts in recent months have restored much of its ornate interior. *(Pylimo 39. ☎ 261 2523.)*

CHABAD LUBAVITCH CENTER. This Jewish cultural center provides kosher meals (8Lt) for travelers; call or email at least a week in advance. The only resident rabbi in Lithuania, American-born Sholom Ber Krinsky, coordinates community service and aids Jews visiting Vilnius with genealogical research. *(Šaltinių 12. ☎ 21 50 38 72; krinsky@jewish.lt; www.jewish.lt. Open daily 9am-6pm.)*

MUSEUMS

MUSEUM OF GENOCIDE VICTIMS (GENOCIDO AUKŲ MUZIEJUS). The horrific realities of the Soviet regime are highlighted at the former KGB headquarters, which also served as a Gestapo outpost during WWII. This eye-opening museum's insightful explanations and historical frankness will leave an impact on all. The basement prison remains as it was in 1991; its chilling holding cells, isolation rooms, and torture chambers are open to the public. Truly mortifying is the execution cell, which provides a glimpse into Soviet punishment methods. The upstairs exhibit documents Lithuanian resistance fighters and a 20th-century history of the city and country. *(Aukų 2a. Turn left after Gedimino 40, the building inscribed with names of KGB victims. ☎ 249 6264. Open Tu-Sa 10am-5pm, Su 10am-3pm. English captions. Museum 4Lt; W free. 50% discount for students June-Sept. English audio tour 8Lt.)*

LITHUANIAN NATIONAL MUSEUM OF THEATER, MUSIC, AND CINEMA ART (LIETUVOS TEATRO, MUZIKOS, IR KINO MUZIEJUS). Chronicling the unique history of Lithuanian performing arts over the past 200 years, this museum provides a peerless glimpse into the country's cultural vibrancy. Impressive collections include musical instruments crafted in the Baltics, as well as exquisite costumes and shoes worn by famous Lithuanian thespians and dancers. Upstairs, fascinating rooms are filled with movie cameras and gramophones. *(Vilniaus 41. ☎ 262 2406. English captions. Open Tu-F noon-6pm, Sa 11am-4pm. 4Lt, students 2Lt.)*

MUSEUM OF APPLIED ART (TAIKOMOSIOS DALIĖS MUZIEJUS). In spacious, dome-like rooms, this museum holds over 270 pieces of ornate gold, silver, and jeweled religious objects. Hidden in the cathedral walls on the eve of the Russian invasion in 1655, these treasures were only rediscovered in 1985. The top floor features sacred art from the 17th through 20th centuries, including oak crosses, portable altars, and inscribed books. *(Arsenalo 3a, next to the National Museum. ☎212 1813; www.tdm.lt. Open Tu-Sa 11am-6pm, Su 11am-4pm. 4Lt, students 2Lt.)*

LITHUANIAN NATIONAL MUSEUM (LIETUVOS NACIONALINIS MUZIEJUS). This impressive display is the definitive collection of artifacts detailing Lithuanian ethnographic history. Relics depict traditional Lithuanian life, with an emphasis on rural areas around the time of the emancipation of the serfs. Farming, fishing, and crafting tools are accompanied by early 20th-century photographs of rural Lithuanian life. *(Arsenalo 1, behind the Gedimino Tower. Enter Arsenalo 3 through courtyard. ☎262 9426; www.lnm.lt. English captions. Open Tu-Sa 10am-5pm, Su 10am-3pm. 4Lt, students 2Lt.)*

MICKIEWICZ MEMORIAL APARTMENT (MICKEVIČIAUS MEMORIALINIS BUTAS). The Lithuanian-Polish poet Adam Mickiewicz (p. 420) lived in this apartment in 1822; his possessions, including a collection of desks, medals, and early editions of his books, remain. Although Mickiewicz wrote in Polish, Lithuanians cherish him for penning their national epic, Pan Tadeusz. *(Bernardinų 11. ☎279 1879. Open Tu-F 10am-5pm, Sa-Su 10am-4pm. English captions. 5Lt.)*

ARTILLERY BASTION (BASTEJA). Home to the alleged Vilnius Basilisk, these narrow, seldom-trodden corridors are a maze where explorers' feet make deep echoes. The wall was built for defense against the Swedish and Russian armies in the 17th century, and since then has played many roles, enclosing an orphanage in the 19th century, a German ammunitions cache during WWII, and a post-war vegetable cellar. Visitors can enjoy a panoramic view of the city from just outside. *(Bokšto 20/18. ☎261 2149. Open Tu-Sa 10am-5pm, Su 10am-3pm.)*

ENTERTAINMENT

Check the Lithuanian-language morning paper *Lietuvos Rytas* for event listings. The **Tourist Information Center (TIC)** also has info on obtaining tickets. English-language movies are shown at **Lietuva Cinema,** Pylimo 17 (☎262 3422), which has several "seats for lovers" (2 seats not separated by an arm rest) and the biggest screen in Lithuania. Catch a flick at the ultra-swanky **Coca-Cola Plaza,** Savanoriu 7 (☎261 1567; www.forumcinemas.lt). **Skalvija,** Goštauto 2/15 (☎261 0505), is the best independent film theater. *Lietuvos Rytas* and the website *www.skalvija.lt* list locations and showtimes.

Lithuanian National Philharmonic (Lietuvos Nacionalinė Filharmonija), Aušros Vartų 5 (☎266 5210; www.filharmonija.lt). Student pricing available during the regular season. Performances W-Sa 7pm, Su noon. Organizes the **Vilniaus Festivalis,** a month of symphonic and operatic performances beginning in late May. Tickets 25-190Lt. Box office open Tu-Sa 10am-7pm, Su 10am-noon. MC/V.

Opera and Ballet Theater (Operos ir Baleto Teatras), Vienuolio 1 (☎262 0727; www.opera.lt). Concrete Soviet exterior with magnificent classical hall. Box office open Sept.-June M-F 10am-7pm, Sa 10am-6pm, Su 11am-3pm; closed in summer.

Lithuanian National Drama Theater (Lietuvos Nacionalinis Dramos Teatras), Gedimino 4 (☎262 9771; www.teatras.lt). Look for the 3 muses in the entrance hall carved in black stone. Most performances in Lithuanian, with occasional shows in English. Dance performances and an annual summer drama festival. Box office open M-F 11am-7pm, Sa-Su 11am-6pm.

NIGHTLIFE

The Vilnius bar and club circuit is vibrant and diverse, but also small. If you linger long in town, you'll begin to recognize names and faces. Keep an eye out in cafes for postcards advertising upcoming events and club nights throughout the city. Look to the **Lithuanian Gay and Lesbian Homepage** or the **Gay Club** (see **GLBT Resources,** p. 382) for the latest in Vilnius's gay nightlife scene.

Brodvėjus (Broadway), Mėsiniu 4 (☎210 7208), in the Old Town. Pub by day, club by night, Brodvėjus is extraordinarily popular with foreigners and is the place from which many backpackers stumble home in the early morning. Boasting 2 bars, live music, and the most popular local DJs, the dance floor is active all night. Cover 10Lt; includes 2 drinks. No sneakers. Open M noon-3am, Tu noon-4am, W-Sa noon-5am, Su noon-2am. MC/V.

ŠMC, Vokiečių 2 (☎261 7097). Tucked behind the Contemporary Art Center, this bar is filled each evening with the artsy, hip, and interesting. Dance amongst the latest installation art on the outdoor patio or drink beer (6Lt) at funky tables fashioned from rubber tires (beer 5Lt). Open M-Th and Su 11am-midnight, F 11am-3am, Sa noon-4am. MC/V.

The PUB (Prie Universiteto Baras), Dominikonų 9 (☎261 8393; www.pub.lt). Frequented by students from the nearby Vilnius University, this late-night pub is a raucous dancing and drinking frenzy. Enjoy the lively crowd and last year's summer hits. The extensive drink menu includes beer (8-12Lt) and 6 types of vodka; the food is pub fare, including onion rings (4Lt). Open M-Th and Su 11am-2am, F-Sa 11am-4am. MC/V.

Helios, Didžioji 28 (☎261 5040). This all-night sushi bar dazzles from ceiling to floor with a swanky display of electronic lights. Thumping house music and a hip young crowd makes this scene one of the hottest spots in town. Dress code. 21+. Cover 15Lt. English menu. Open Tu-Sa 10pm-5am.

Sole Luna, Universiteto 4 (☎212 0925). Step off the gray streets of Vilnius and into this vibrant Mediterranean-style bar. Come night, music blasts and crowds pour into the spectacular courtyard next to the Presidential Palace, making this one of the liveliest nightspots in town. English menu. Open M-W 11am-midnight, Th-F 10:30am-3:30am, Sa noon-4am. MC/V.

DAYTRIPS FROM VILNIUS

TRAKAI CASTLE

Buses run to Trakai, 28km west of Vilnius (40min., 2 per hr. 6:45am-9:30pm, 3Lt). Last bus back departs at 9:30pm. Check the bus schedule for changes. Bus station (☎90 00 16 61) open daily 4am-midnight. The castle is 3km north of the bus station. Facing Lake Totoriskia, turn right from the bus station and follow Vytauto g. Within 100m, you will reach a map of the area. Continue along the street to reach the castle. The Tourist Information Center, Vytauto 69 (☎52 851 934; www.trakai.lt), 1km from the bus station, offers free maps, bus schedules, and English-language guides. Open M 8:30am-noon and 12:45-4:15pm, Tu-F 8:30am-noon and 12:45-5:30pm, Sa 9am-noon and 12:45-3pm. Castle and museum open daily 10am-7pm. 8Lt, students with ISIC 4Lt. 1hr. tours in English 50Lt. English captions in most places. Travelers can see Lake Galve by paddleboat for around 14Lt per hr. Rental stands are just before the castle footbridge. The best way to explore the region is via bike (10Lt at the Tourist Information Center) on the breathtaking 14km bike trail that runs around the entire peninsula.

Surrounded by tranquil waters and gorgeous hills, Trakai is Lithuania's ancient capital. The red-brick **Insular Castle** served as home to the Teutonic Knights, who ruled Lithuania and Poland in the late medieval era. Following the defeat of the Teutonic Order at the Battle of Grunwald in 1410, Trakai became the capital of the Grand Duchy of Lithuania (see **History,** p. 376). In 1665, the Russians plundered the town and razed the castle, which remained in ruins until the 1980s.

The original stone foundations are visible, but unfortunately the castle is mostly a 20th-century reconstruction. Still, busloads of tourists, young and old, flock to see the castle and grounds. Tickets are valid for both the 30m brick watchtower and the **City and Castle History Museum.** Actors dressed as knights sword fight in the courtyard during **Medieval Days** each June. In July and August, the castle is a dramatic backdrop for concerts at the **Trakai Festival** (☎528 262 0727; www.trakaifestival.lt).

Trakai is also home to one of the last remaining community of Karaites, a breakaway sect of Judaism which sprung up in the Byzantine Empire during the eighth century. In 1398, Grand Duke Vytautas the Great granted the Karaites religious freedom and brought a small group to Trakai to serve as his bodyguards. Visitors can explore rows of their vibrantly colored houses, each with three windows: one for God, one for the Grand Duke, and one for the family that resides inside. Stop by the **Karaite Ethnographic Museum** for an array of artifacts and history, near Trakai Castle, Karaimų 22. (☎528 225 5286. Open W-Sa 10am-6pm. English captions. 4Lt, students 1Lt.) North 50m is the **Kenesa**, Karaimų 30, a Karaite house of worship. (Open Th-Sa 11am-6pm. English pamphlet.) Try traditional Karaite fare at **Kybynlar ❷**, Karaimų 29, across from the museum. Their homemade beer (3.50Lt per 0.5L) is especially good. (☎528 285 5179; kybynlar@takas.lt. MC/V.)

EUROPOS PARKAS

Take the #5 trolley (departs 3-10 times per hr.) from the train station to the 3rd stop after the Neris River. Then, at the adjacent bus stop (by the kiosk), change to the #36 bus (leaves every 10-20min.) and continue to the last stop, which will drop you off about 3km away (30min. walk). Continue down the main road to the park. There are also public transportation minibuses which run 4-7 times daily and leave from the same location as the #36 bus, but go directly to the park. Last minibus leaves the park M-F 6:30pm and Sa-Su 4:45pm, but be sure to check the schedule as times may change. Park includes a restaurant, post office, and gift shop. ☎237 7077; www.europosparkas.lt. Open daily 9am-sunset. Guided tours in English, Lithuanian, or Russian; 50Lt. Park 21Lt, students 8Lt.

In 1989, the French National Geographic Institute made a rather earth-shattering calculation: the geographical center of continental Europe does not lie in Budapest, Kraków, or even Prague. Rather, Europe's center is in a remote forest outside of Vilnius. In light of this discovery, Gintaras Karosas, a Lithuanian sculptor and artist, spearheaded the construction of a sculpture park. By the time the

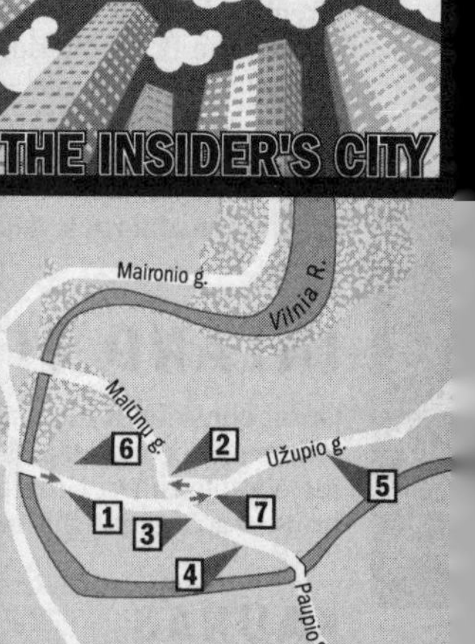

REPUBLIC OF UŽUPIS

Cross over the Vilnia River, and you'll find residents of an off-beat artists' community that declared itself the independent Rebublic of Užupis in 1997; it has its own president, flag, constitution, and army of 12 men. Although many of its eccentric citizens are fleeing rising prices, the remaining studios and landmarks make its winding streets still worth a visit.

Greet the **Užupis Angel (1)** in the town square. This massive statue, unveiled in 2002 on April Fool's Day, the Republic's national holiday, symbolizes the rebirth of artistic freedom. The offbeat **Constitution (2)** is just around the corner, engraved in French, English, and Lithuanian. You might catch a local goldsmith working at the **Užupis Galerija (3),** or chat up some young artists at the **Incubator (4),** a graffitied artists' workshop and hangout by the river. Finally, rest your feet and enjoy thin-crust pizzas at **Prie Angelo (5).** (Entrees 10-28 Lt. Open M-Th and Su 10am-11pm, F-Sa 10am-midnight. MC/V.)

USSR fell and Lithuania achieved its independence, Europos Parkas had become a reality. Karosas's poignant sculpture, reminiscent of the equator line in Ecuador, or the Prime Meridian line in Greenwich, indicates the center of Europe. The park gives the distance to all of Europe's capitals, and there are about 90 contemporary sculptures, created by artists from over 70 countries, spread across 55 acres of secluded, forested hills. Particularly impressive is the fallen statue of Lenin at the center of the park. Other sights include a wire-frame chair, a 6m pyramidal rock, and assorted other sculptural oddities.

INLAND LITHUANIA

Often considered the nation's cultural bedrock, inland Lithuania is home to the country's second largest city, Kaunas, as well as more secluded sights like the memorable Hill of Crosses, near Šiauliai. With plenty of folk dancing, music, and brew to go around, this region has a much more relaxed pace of life than Vilnius.

KAUNAS ☎37

From 1920 to 1939, while Vilnius languished under Polish rule, Kaunas (KOW-nas, pop. 361,000) was the capital of independent Lithuania. During those glorious decades, the city became the center of Lithuania's cultural and intellectual life, a legacy that lives on in its eclectic collection of museums and its mismatched set of castles and modern buildings. Add to the mix ample green spaces, cobblestone streets, and the 35,000 resident college students who fuel some of Lithuania's best nightlife, and you've got some idea of the atmosphere in this exciting, out-of-the way urban center.

TRANSPORTATION

Trains: MK Čiurlionio 16 (☎27 29 55; www.litrail.lt), at the end of Vytauto, where it intersects with MK Čiurlionio. Trolley buses #3, 5, 7, 14 directly across from the station go directly through Old Town. Open 24hr. To: **Vilnius** (1½-2hr., 21 per day, 10Lt); **Warsaw, POL** (7½hr., 4 per day, 86Lt); **Kaliningrad, RUS** (4hr., 6 per day, 32Lt). Other connections include **Tallinn, EST** and **Rīga, LAT.** All international trains run through Vilnius. Check schedule for time changes.

Buses: Buses leave from Vytauto 24/26 (☎40 90 60, international reservations 32 22 22). Open daily 5:45am-8:45pm. To: **Klaipėda** (2½-4hr., 14 per day, 32-40Lt); **Palanga** (2½-6½hr., 7 per day, 34-36Lt); **Šiauliai** (2½-3½hr., 8 per day, 30Lt); **Vilnius** (1½hr., every 30min., 18Lt). For bus schedules or advance tickets, visit **EuroLines,** Laisvės 36 (☎20 98 36; www.kautra.lt). Open M-F 9am-1pm and 2-6pm, Sa 9am-1pm.

Public Transportation: Bus and **tram** tickets are available from kiosks (0.90Lt) or from the driver (1Lt). Bus #7 runs parallel to Laisvės, never more than a block away from the main street. Monthly passes 35Lt. The best way to get around the city is by one of the **maršrutinis taksis** vans (1.5Lt, at night 2Lt) that zip along bus routes. Hail one from the street and tell the driver where you want to get off.

Taxis: Like everywhere else in Lithuania, you will pay a much more reasonable fare if you call a taxi (or have your waiter or hostel receptionist phone) than if you hail one at the side of the street. In Kaunas, expect to pay about 1.8Lt per km. The major taxi companies are **Forsarus** (☎33 88 88), **Merulos Taksi** (☎34 11 55), and **Zaibiškas Taksi** (☎33 30 00).

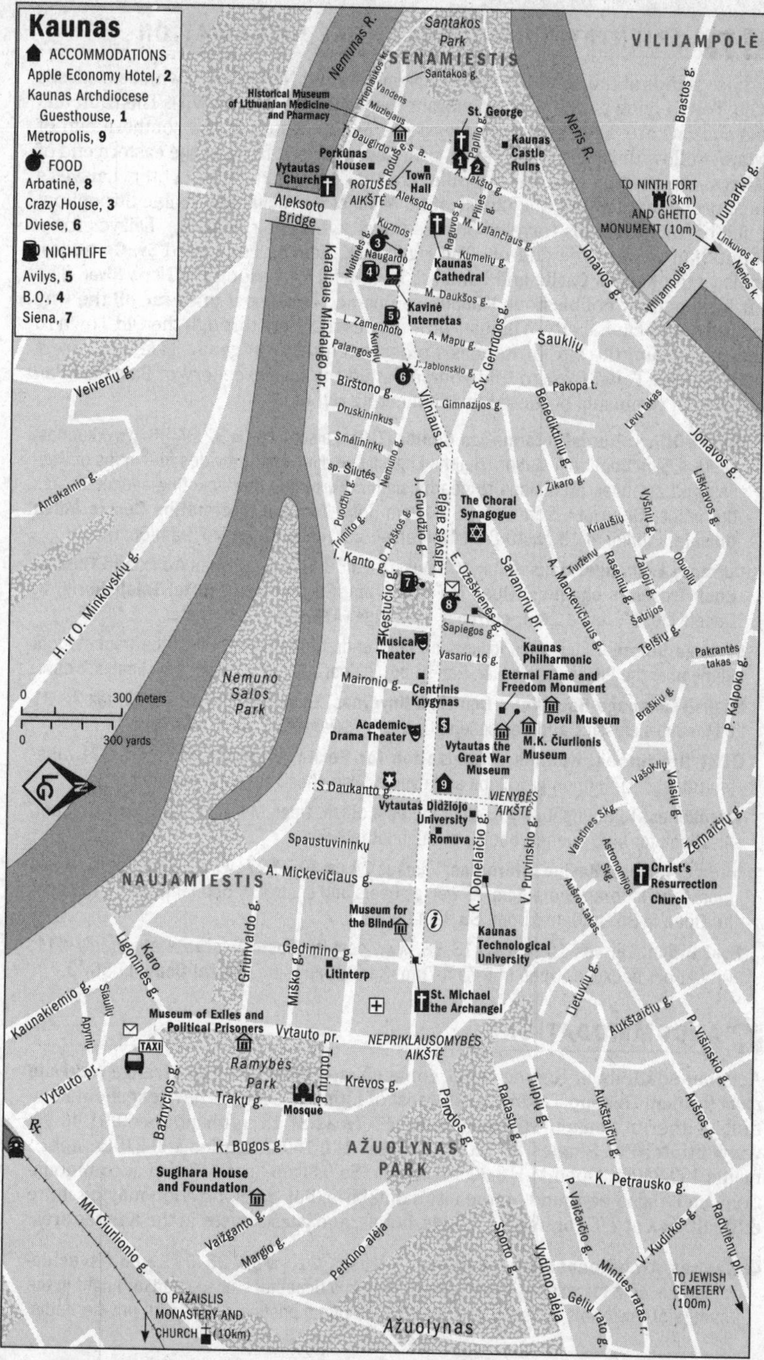
Kaunas
ACCOMMODATIONS
Apple Economy Hotel, 2
Kaunas Archdiocese Guesthouse, 1
Metropolis, 9
FOOD
Arbatinė, 8
Crazy House, 3
Dviese, 6
NIGHTLIFE
Avilys, 5
B.O., 4
Siena, 7
SENAMIESTIS
VILIJAMPOLĖ
NAUJAMIESTIS
Santakos Park
Nemuno Salos Park
Ramybės Park
AŽUOLYNAS PARK
Historical Museum of Lithuanian Medicine and Pharmacy
St. George
Kaunas Castle Ruins
Perkūnas House
Vytautas Church
Town Hall
ROTUŠĖS AIKŠTĖ
Aleksoto Bridge
Kaunas Cathedral
Kavinė Internetas
TO NINTH FORT (3km) AND GHETTO MONUMENT (10m)
The Choral Synagogue
Musical Theater
Kaunas Philharmonic
Eternal Flame and Freedom Monument
Centrinis Knygynas
Devil Museum
Academic Drama Theater
Vytautas the Great War Museum
M.K. Čiurlionis Museum
VIENYBĖS AIKŠTĖ
Vytautas Didžiojo University
Romuva
Christ's Resurrection Church
Museum for the Blind
Kaunas Technological University
Litinterp
St. Michael the Archangel
Museum of Exiles and Political Prisoners
NEPRIKLAUSOMYBĖS AIKŠTĖ
Mosque
Sugihara House and Foundation
TO PAŽAISLIS MONASTERY AND CHURCH (10km)
TO JEWISH CEMETERY (100m)
0 300 meters
0 300 yards
Nemunas R.
Neris R.
Laisvės alėja
Vilniaus g.
Karaliaus Mindaugo pr.
Savanorių pr.
Jonavos g.
Vytauto pr.
K. Donelaičio g.
Gedimino g.
A. Mickevičiaus g.
S Daukanto g.
Maironio g.
Vasario 16 g.
Šauklių
Žemaičių g.
K. Petrausko g.
Ažuolynas
MK Čiurlionio g.
H. ir O. Minkovskių g.
Veiverių g.
Antakalnio g.
Kaunakiemio g.
Vydūno alėja
Perkūno alėja

ORIENTATION AND PRACTICAL INFORMATION

Kaunas stands at the confluence of the Nemunas and Neris rivers, with **Senamiestis** (Old Town) lying to the west of vibrant **Naujamiestis** (New Town). The train and bus stations are 300m apart, southeast of the city center, at the southern end of **Vytayo.** Follow this busy street north, past **Ramybes Park,** to meet the eastern end of **Laisvės,** the lengthy pedestrian boulevard that bisects the city center. Laisvės's most prominent feature, the **Church of St. Michael the Archangel,** visible throughout much of Kaunas, helps travelers across the city find their bearings. Laisvės forks about 2km west of the church. The right fork, heavily congested **Šv. Gertrūdos,** leads to the **Kaunas Castle** and **Santakos Park,** which overlook the **Neris River.** The left fork, narrow cobblestone **Vilniaus**—so named because it once ran all the way to Lithuania's capital city, Vilnius—now carries travelers through the Old Town to **Rotušės Square,** the site of Kaunas's oldest architectural gems. Take any street from the Old Town west to find yourself amid the lush greenery of **Santakos Parkas,** a quiet peninsula bordered by the meeting rivers.

Tourist Office: Tourist Information Center (TIC), Laisvės 36 (☎32 34 36; www.kaunastic.lt), 1.5km from train station. Helpful English-speaking staff provides free maps of Kaunas and arranges excursions to nearby sights. **Eurolines** bus ticketing agency shares the office. Open M-F 9am-6pm, Sa 10am-6pm. **Tourism Information Centre Müsu Odisëja,** Čiurlionio 15 (☎40 84 14) arranges car rental. Open M-F 9am-6pm.

Currency Exchange: Hansabank, Vilniaus 13 (☎68 44 44). Cashes **AmEx and Thomas Cook Travelers cheques.** Open M-F 8am-7pm, Sa 9am-3pm. **Hotel Taioji Neris,** K. Donelaičio 27, has a 24hr. **currency exchange. ATMs** are everywhere.

Luggage Storage: Electronic lockers on both ends of the main hall of the train station. Remember the PIN to your locker. Rates from 3Lt per 12hr. of storage; time limit is 2 days.

English-Language Bookstore: Centrinis Knygynas, Laisvės 81 (☎22 95 72; fax 22 31 01), stocks classics and bestsellers. Open M-F 10am-7pm, Sa 10am-5pm.

GLBT Resources: Kaunas Organization for Sexual Equality (☎70 57 37; robejona@takas.lt). Info on gay clubs and events. Also check out www.gayline.lt.

Telephones: To the right as you enter the post office. Open M-F 7am-7pm, Sa 7am-5pm. Also look for blue-and-red booths throughout the city.

Internet Access: Kavinė Internetas, Vilniaus 24 (☎40 74 27, www.cafenet.ot.lt). Offers more than a dozen computers, as well as beers and snacks. 1.5Lt per 20min., 4.5Lt per hr. Open M-Sa 8:30am-10pm, Su 9am-9pm.

Post Office: Laisvės 102 (☎40 13 68, www.post.lt). **Poste Restante** at window #11; 0.50Lt per package. Open M-F 7am-7pm, Sa 7:30am-5pm. **Postal Code:** LT-3000.

ACCOMMODATIONS

Accommodations in Kaunas don't come cheap. Travelers can arrange a **private room** through **Litinterp,** Gedimino 28. Most of Litinterp's rooms have excellent locations, either in Senamiestis or on Laisvės. (☎22 87 18, after-hours 69 91 46 90; www.litinterp.lt. Singles 80-120Lt; doubles 140-160Lt; triples 180-210Lt; apartments 180-240Lt. Open M-F 8:30am-5:30pm, Sa 9:30am-3pm.) Cheap accommodation can be also be found on the city's outskirts, but transportation may be more difficult. Ask at TIC for info on motels, hotels, and guesthouses in the Kaunas area.

Kaunas Archdiocese Guest House, Rotuses 21 (☎32 25 97; email sveciunamai@kn.lcn.lt for reservations). Tucked away in a beautiful stucco courtyard right in the middle of town, this godsend of a guesthouse offers pristine rooms with private baths.

Free linens, Internet, and guidebooks. The only catch? Alcohol and cigarettes are strictly prohibited. Singles 50Lt; doubles 80Lt; triples 110 Lt; quads 130Lt. Cash only. ❷

Apple Economy Hotel, M. Valanciaus 19 (☎32 14 04; www.applehotel.lt). Following Sv. Getrudos toward Kaunas Castle, turn left on M. Valanciaus. Hotel is in a courtyard on the right. Well-worn rooms with linoleum floors are well-kept. Reserve ahead in summer. Singles and doubles 135-180Lt. MC/V. ❹

Metropolis, S. Daukanto 21 (☎20 80 81; www.takiojineris.com), just off Laisvės in the center of town. If the musty charm of former splendor is what you're looking for, then the mint-green enamel bathtubs, mismatched tile, and cigarette-smoke-scented rooms of this hotel will delight. Soviet-era TV and bath in each room. Singles 90Lt; doubles 100Lt-120Lt; triples 170Lt. MC/V. ❸

FOOD

Arbatinė, Laisvės 100 (☎32 37 32). Look for the green-and-white striped canopy. This vegetarian and vegan cafe attracts locals with freshly baked pastries (1-2Lt). Sit inside the small but bright space at a white picnic table to enjoy a range of healthy entrees (5-6Lt). Open M-F 8:30am-8pm, Sa 10am-6pm. ❶

Dviese, Vilniaus 8 (☎20 36 38). Don't let the run-down exterior fool you: inside Dviese is a sleek little restaurant that serves up delicious Lithuanian eats. Their hearty lunch special (main course, soup, and tea) for only 6.50Lt is a steal. For dinner, try the "piquant pizza" with ham and pineapple (8Lt) or choose from the wide array of hot dishes (5-14Lt). Open M-Sa 10am-midnight, Su 10am-11pm. Cash only. ❶

Crazy House, Viliniaus 16 (22 11 82; www.crazyhouse.lt). Crazy House lives up to its name with decor featuring moaning mannequins and moving ceilings. Fortunately, the menu of Western and Lithuanian fried food is much saner, with no-nonsense entrees in the 14-26Lt range. Don't be the one stuck sitting on the toilet-shaped seat. Open M-Th and Su 11am-midnight, F-Sa 11am-2am. MC/V. ❷

SIGHTS

Sights in Kaunas cluster around the two ends of Laisvės, the city's main pedestrian boulevard. St. Michael's Church and Unity Sq. lie at the eastern end, while Senamiestis and its cathedral, town hall, and smaller attractions are at the opposite end.

ST. MICHAEL THE ARCHANGEL CHURCH (Š. MYKOLO ARCHANGELO BAŽNYČIOJE). Originally built for the tsar's Russian Orthodox troops at the end of the 19th century, this breathtaking neo-Byzantine structure became a Catholic church in the 1990s. Its striking silver domes are visible throughout the city, but access inside is limited. Out front, don't miss the suggestive **Statue of Man** by Petras Mozuras. *(Nepriklausomybės aikštė 14, at the east end of Laisvės. ☎22 66 76. Open M-F 9am-3pm, Sa-Su 8:30am-2pm. Services M-F noon, Sa 10am, Su 10am and noon. Free.)*

UNITY SQUARE (VIENYBĖS AIKŠTĖ). On the south side of the square, Vytauto Didžiojo University and the older Kaunas draw a local student population of more than 16,000. Across the street, an outdoor shrine to Lithuanian statehood displays busts of political and literary figures. These flank a corridor leading from the **Freedom Monument** (Laisvės paminklas) to an eternal flame commemorating those who died in the liberation struggle of 1918-20. Take a funicular (0.50Lt) from Putvinskio and Aušros up the hill northeast of the square, home to the **Christ's Resurrection Church.** In the Soviet era, the towering structure acted as a paper warehouse and a radio factory; finally, after 70 years of restoration, it was consecrated by the Catholic Church in 2004. Take the elevator to the top (5Lt) to enjoy the panoramic views of Kaunas and a rooftop cafe.

KAUNAS CATHEDRAL (KAUNO ARKIKATEDRA BAŽNYČIA). Lithuania's largest Gothic church—but with the floor plan of a basilica—is Kaunas Cathedral. The breathtaking interior boasts nine main altars with Renaissance and Baroque influences. The church is thought to have been built during the 1408-13 Christianization of Lower Lithuania, and several damaging fires in its history have necessitated a series of recent renovations. Next to the altar, the neo-Gothic **Chapel of St. John the Baptist** holds the tomb of Maironis, a famous Kaunas priest and nationalist poet. *(Vilniaus 1, just before Rotušės Aikštė. ☎32 40 93. Open daily 7am-7pm. Free.)*

OLD TOWN SQUARE (ROTUŠĖS AIKŠTĖ). Just past the cathedral, the **town hall,** a stylistic melange constructed from 1542 to 1771, presides over Old Town Square. Access is limited. Today, it is used primarily for weddings. Behind and to the left of the town hall stands a **statue of Maironis.** His hand hides his clerical collar, a ploy that duped the atheist Soviets into allowing the city to erect a statue of the priest. On the south side of the square is the **St. Francis Church and Jesuit Monastery,** which, in the years since its construction in 1666, has been used as an ammunitions storehouse by Napoleon's army, converted into an Orthodox church in the mid-19th century, and employed as a sports hall under the Soviet regime. The Jesuits regained control in 1990, and today it's a chapel once more. Follow Aleksoto toward the river to reach the 15th-century **Perkūnas House** (Perkūnas namas), said to be the most Gothic structure in Lithuania. It was built on the site of a temple to Perkūnas, pagan god of thunder. *(Open M-F 8am-5pm.)* Breeze through the Gothic **Vytautas Church** (Vytauto bažnyčia), at the end of the street, also built in the early 1400s. According to legend, when Vytautas's army was defeated by the Tatars in 1398, the Lithuanian leader pledged to erect a church in the Virgin Mary's honor if his life was spared. *(☎20 38 54. Services Tu-Th 6pm; Su 10am, noon, 6pm.)*

NINTH FORT (IX FORTAS). The tsar's troops built this defensive installation in the late 19th century to protect Russia from an impending German invasion. Ironically, the fort eventually facilitated the mass murder of Jewish and other Lithuanians, Russians, and Europeans. During WWII the Nazis exterminated 50,000 people, including 30,000 Jews, in the surrounding fields. Begin your visit at the architecturally innovative **new museum,** which houses the ticket booth for both parts of the site and features an extensive display of blotchy photographs on the deportation of Lithuanians to Siberia during Stalin's rule. Inside the fort, the **old museum's** Cell no. 5 still contains inscriptions carved by French Jews who were held there before being executed in May 1944. Past the fort, an enormous Soviet-era sculpture commemorates "the victims of fascism," as the Holocaust dead were called in Soviet jargon. To your right as you approach the sculpture, a series of commemorative plaques includes one placed there by the city of Munich, which reads, "in sorrow and shame, and appalled by the silence of the bystanders." *(Žemaičių Plentas 73. Telsai-bound buses from the main station stop in front of the fort; 20 min., 1.70Lt. Return on the same bus, which stops every 10-30min. on the highway in front of the new museum. ☎37 77 15. Open M and W-Su 10am-6pm. Each museum 2Lt, students 1Lt. Hire a guide to explore the tunnel connecting the prison with the barracks for 20Lt.)*

JEWISH KAUNAS. Kovno, as Kaunas is known in Yiddish, was home to 37,000 Jews on the eve of WWII. Most were slaughtered at the Ninth Fort during Hitler's occupation, and just 2500 Jews remained when the Soviets arrived in 1944. The Slobodka district, now known as Vilijampole, north of the Neris, traditionally served as home to the city's Jews. Little remains of the WWII ghetto except for a small **monument** in Lithuanian to its former residents. To get there, cross the Jurbarko bridge and turn right at the end. At the first fork, bear left on Linkuvos and continue 50m to the intersection of Ariogalos and Krisciukaicio. The **Choral Synagogue** is renowned for its gold-trimmed *bimah* (altar). Inside is a memorial to Jewish soldiers who died fighting for Lithuanian independence between 1918 and 1920, as well as a memorial for the children killed at the Ninth Fort. Kaunas's remaining Jewish community cannot support a rabbi for this historic site, but the synagogue is open daily for prayer. *(E. Ozeskienes 17. ☎20 68 80. Open M-F and Su 5:45-6:30pm, Sa 10am-noon.)* The forsaken remains of two other synagogues are located on Zamenhofo 7 and 9. The **cemetery** (senosios Žydu kapinės), located 2km from the city center, was neglected after the near-total extermination of Kaunas's Jewish community during WWII and is now a haunting, forsaken site overgrown with vegetation. *(Go east down Parados, turn left on K. Petrauskro and continue 750m, then turn right onto Radvilėnų. The cemetery is 500m down, at the intersection with J. Basanaviciaus.)*

PAŽAISLIS MONASTERY AND CHURCH. This vibrant, fresco-filled, Baroque complex sits on the right bank of the Nemunas 10km east of central Kaunas. Originally designed by three Florentine masters in the 17th century, the church was a KGB-run "psychiatric hospital" before being returned to the Catholic Church in 1992. The **Pažaislis Music Festival,** featuring classical music concerts, is held from June to early August; there are other **musical performances** year-round. Visit the website for up-to-date concert listings. *(Mausiulio 31. Take tram #5 from the train station to the end of the line; the monastery is 1km down the road past a small beach. ☎75 64 85; www.pazaislis.lt. Open Tu-Su 11am-6:30pm, but hours vary; call ahead. Free tour Tu-Su after 11am mass.)*

FUN WITH FUNICULARS. Instead of spending an entire day trudging up and down the hills of Kaunas, take a ride on one of its two **funiculars.** These rare machines from the 1930s consist of paired box cars; when one is going downhill, the second makes use of the first one's momentum to ascend. The price hasn't changed in about 70 years either: tickets are only 0.50Lt. Breathtaking views of the city await you at the top. (Funicular between Putvinskio and Aušros open 8am-8pm; funicular between Veiveriv and Skriaudziv open M-F 7am-noon, 1pm-4pm.)

MUSEUMS

DEVIL MUSEUM (VELNIŲ MUZIEJUS). This wacky and daring museum devoted to the devil is the only of its kind in the world. According to Lithuanian folklore, the devil was a guardian figure until the advent of Christianity came to rain on the satanic parade. Painter Antanas Žmuidzinavičius (1876-1966) attributed his own longevity to his obsession with the devil, and over the course of his life he amassed the 2000 devil images now on display at the museum. Although a full exploration of the collection should take no more than 30min., it should include the painting *The Division of Lithuania,* which depicts a satanic Stalin chasing a horned Hitler across skull-covered Lithuania. *(V. Putvinskio 64. ☎22 14 17. Open Tu-Su 11am-5pm. 5Lt, students 2.50Lt. English tours 25Lt.)*

MUSEUM OF EXILES AND POLITICAL PRISONERS (REZISTENCIJOS IR TREMTIES MUZIEJUS). This fascinating museum contains a collection of photographs, improvised tools, and artifacts from the resistance to Soviet rule and has an exhibit on the daily life of Siberian exiles. Get a first-hand account from the curator himself, who was exiled for 10 years and gives tours in Lithuanian, German, and Russian. *(Vytauto 46, at the corner of Ramybės Park, a short walk from St. Michael's. ☎32 31 79. Open W-Su 11am-5pm. Donations requested. English brochure free.)*

VYTAUTAS THE GREAT WAR MUSEUM (VYTAUTO DIDŽIOJO KARO MUZIEJUS). Named after the 15th-century Lithuanian ruler, who conquered much of Eastern Europe, this horrific museum houses all sorts of weapons, images of bloodshed, and war equipment ranging from 17th-century armor to 19th-century cannons. Gun enthusiasts will be delighted with the oak-and-glass-encased pistols and rifles on the second floor. The museum also holds the shattered remains of the airplane Lituanica, in which two Lithuanian-Americans, Steponas Darius and Stasys Girė nas (both featured on the 10Lt banknote), attempted to fly nonstop from New York to Kaunas in 1933. Both men were killed in a crash near Soldin, Germany. *(Donelaičio 64, in Unity Sq. behind 2 soccer-playing lions. ☎32 09 39. Open W-Su mid-Mar. to mid-Oct. 10am-6pm; mid-Oct to mid-Mar. 9am-5pm. 2Lt, students 1Lt.)*

M.K. ČIURLIONIS MUSEUM (M.K. ČIURLIONIS MUZIEJUS). The works of painter and composer M.K. Čiurlionis (1875-1911) reflect Symbolist and Surrealist influences. His symphonies—both musical and visual—draw from Lithuanian folk art. Art enthusiasts and historians alike will enjoy this museum's extensive portfolio of Čiurlionis's paintings, in addition to temporary exhibits and permanent displays of Lithuanian folk art. Lithuanian cross-making, a tradition that dates to pre-Christian times, is a particular focus of the museum. *(Putvinskio 55, in Unity Sq. ☎22 97 38. Open Tu-Su 11am-5pm. English captions. 5Lt, students 2.50Lt.)*

SUGIHARA HOUSE AND FOUNDATION. Chiune Sugihara, the so-called "Japanese Schindler," served as Tokyo's consul in Kaunas at the beginning of WWII. In violation of government orders, Sugihara issued more than 6000 visas for Polish and Lithuanian Jews to travel to Kobe, Japan in 1940. The museum at his former home features powerful tributes from Jews who escaped death because of Sugihara's courage. *(Valzganto 30, at the eastern edge of Naujamiestis. From Vytauto, follow Totoriu east to a mosque. Turn right, then left on Putino. Climb the stairs with the green railing, then turn right and walk 100m to the Japanese Studies Center. ☎33 28 81; sugihara@takas.lt. Open May-Sept. M-F 10am-5pm, Sa-Su 11am-6pm; Oct.-Apr. M-F 11am-3pm. English captions. Free.)*

MUSEUM FOR THE BLIND. Despite its name, this museum in fact caters to sighted people, trying to provide them with the opportunity to experience life without vision. Bells, smells, and sounds guide visitors through this haunting experience that leads in total darkness through the catacombs of St. Michael the Archangel church. Entrance through the back of the church. *(Nepriklausomybės aikštė 14, at the east end of Laisvės. Open W 11am-3:30pm, Sa 11am-1:30pm. Admission 3Lt.)*

MUSEUM OF THE HISTORY OF LITHUANIAN MEDICINE AND PHARMACY. This jarring glimpse into the medical practices of the 19th and early 20th centuries will leave visitors thankful they weren't born a century earlier. Feast your eyes on rows of specimens suspended in strange liquids, recipes for potions, and terrifying contraptions used for surgeries and experiments. For a particularly gruesome experience, check out jars of ground up flesh on the top floor, once thought to hold the cure for epilepsy. Captions provide an informative history of medicine in Lithuania. *(Rotuses 28. ☎20 15 69; lmfmuziejus@med.kmu.lt. Open W-Su 10am-6pm. English captions. Admission 3Lt; English tours 20lt.)*

ENTERTAINMENT AND NIGHTLIFE

Although many theaters take a summer break, musical events will be announced on posters plastered along Laisvės. The **Musical Theater** (Muzikinis Teatras), Laisvės 91, performs operettas. (☎22 71 13. Box office open Tu-Sa 11am-6pm.) The **Academic Drama Theater** (Akademinis Dramos Teatras), Laisvės 71, stages dances and plays in Lithuanian and Russian. (☎22 40 64; www.dramosteatras.lt. Box office open daily 10am-7pm.) The **Kaunas Philharmonic** (Kauno filharmonija), Sapiegos 5, has classical concerts. (☎22 25 58. Schedule posted at box office. Box office open daily 2-6pm.) Cinemas with American films, usually in English, can be found at www.cinema.lt. The large screen at **Cinamon,** Islandijos 32 (☎70 07 01 11) is the biggest theater in town and shows mainstream flicks. Tickets average 12Lt, although matinees are cheaper than evening shows. Kaunas nightlife is hidden away in the cellars of clubs and pubs, and in the courtyards and side streets of the Old Town. Walk along **Laisvės** and up **Vilniaus** and listen for thumping bass.

Avilys, Vilniaus 34 (☎20 34 76; www.avilys.lt). This old-fashioned, candlelit beer hall serves Tibetan teas (4Lt), and attracts a jovial crowd for eating, drinking, and making merry. 2 excellent house beers on tap, including "Honey Beer" (4Lt per 0.25L), brewed on site. Dine next to their brass barrels and ask a friendly server to show you how it's brewed. Open M-Th 11am-midnight, F-Sa noon-2am, Su noon-midnight. MC/V.

B.O., Multines 9 (☎20 65 42). This vivacious Old Town bar overcomes its unfortunate name to attract a fun student crowd. The lengthy, bright bar serves crowds long into the night and will ensure a lively evening. Beer 4.50Lt per 0.5L. Live music Th 9pm. Open M-Th 10am-2am, F 10am-3am, Sa 3pm-3am, Su 3pm-2am. MC/V.

Siena (Wall), Laisvės 93 (☎42 44 24; www.siena.lt), beneath Miesto Sodas. The spacious main dance floor fills quickly, and the bar gets busy as DJs spin techno. The 2nd room is an upbeat night cafe. Open Th-Sa 9pm-4am. MC/V.

LITHUANIA

DAYTRIP FROM KAUNAS

ŠIAULIAI AND HILL OF THE CROSSES

Take a bus (3hr., 12 per day, 23Lt) to the bus station in the nearby town of Šiauliai (shoo-LAY), Tilžės 109 (☎52 50 58). Last bus back to Kaunas at 6:30pm. Luggage storage is available at the train station, a short walk across the green-railed overpass, and along Dubijos. (3Lt per bag per day. Open daily 8am-10pm.) To reach the Hill from the bus station, transfer to a Joniškis-bound bus, which stops at Domantai, at the trailhead to Kryžių Kalna (8 per day, last returning shuttle at 5:20pm). You can also reach the Hill by bike. The friendly staff at the Šiauliai Tourist Information Center (Šiauliu Turizmo Informacijos Centras), Vilniaus 213 (☎52 31 10; tic@siauliai.lt), rent bicycles (2-3Lt per hr.), provide free maps, and store luggage for free. To get to the TIC from the bus station, turn left on Tilžės and continue 300m to Vilniaus, then turn left and continue 50m. Once you have your bike, return to the intersection of Vilniaus and Tilžės and turn left; follow the road out of town 10km until you reach a brown sign marked "Kryžių Kalna." Turn right and continue 2km to the Hill of the Crosses. Note that although there is a designated bicycle path for most of the journey, these are busy roads, and TIC does not rent helmets.

The quiet city of Šiauliai, in northern Lithuania, is most prominently known as the gateway to the **Hill of the Crosses.** Tucked away in the countryside, 12km outside of town, the famous site attracts thousands of visitors each year, including throngs of Catholics who make the pilgrimage to the remote location on Easter. Former pope John Paul II visited in 1993, and postcards commemorating his visit are scattered among the numerous crosses, memorials, and relics planted on the hill. Some say the hill's history reaches back to the Middle Ages, when—according to legend—Lithuanians built a fort there to hold back the Teutonic Knights. In the 19th century, crosses dotted the hill as a memorial to those killed in the Lithuanian struggle for independence from tsarist rule. After the Soviet Union seized the country in WWII, Lithuanians planted crosses on the site to mourn loved ones who had been sent off to Siberian prison camps. Soviet authorities responded by burning the crosses, but Lithuanians persisted in replacing the symbols. Today, the hill is a dense forest of wooden crucifixes. Every cross is dated, and some have inscriptions and entire stories to tell. Vendors selling wooden crosses allow travelers to add to the collection by planting a cross of their own.

The quiet city of Šiauliai is home to a pedestrian thoroughfare, lined with cafes and vendors. The most popular attraction within the city is the majestic cathedral, known as the **Church of St. Peter and Paul** from 1625 until it became the seat of the local bishop in 1997 and was designated a cathedral. From the bus station, turn left on Tilžės and continue 400m. Once inside, notice the gunports that line the balcony level, vestiges of the church's use as a defensive structure. The TIC can provide a map of accommodations in the city. The conveniently located **Youth Hostel of Šiauliai College ❷**, Tilžės 159, is across from the cathedral. (☎41 52 37 64; administracija@siauliaukolegija.lt. Doubles 70Lt, 60Lt for 1 person; triples 80lt; suites 100Lt.) Wander along the cheery pedestrian street Vilniaus to find a pub or cafe. The familiar but tasty selection at **Brodvejus ❷**, Vilniaus 146, includes pizza (7-30Lt) and Lithuanian pancakes (5.50-8Lt) to fill you up before a night of revelry. (☎41 50 04 12. Open M-Th 10am-11pm, F-Sa 10am-midnight, Su 11am-11pm.)

COASTAL LITHUANIA

Walk along Lithuania's luscious Baltic beaches and you'll see why Germany, Russia, and Latvia have all coveted these shores. Dance the night away in Palanga's glittering discos, shed your swimsuit and sunbathe on Smiltynė's bawdy beaches, and climb the sand dunes that extend from Nida to the Russian border. The coast is an extraordinarily tourist-friendly region in summer. Outside Klaipėda, winter traveling in these parts can be bleak.

KLAIPĖDA ☎(8)46

Lithuania's most important port city and a popular seaside escape, Klaipėda bustles with activity year-round. Famous as the birthplace of Lithuania's most popular beer, Švyturys, the brewery remains the pride and joy of the city. The shores of the Danė River offer a quiet place to sit and relax, although tourists arrive by the boatload during summer. Stray outside the Old Town, however, and you'll find yourself surrounded by towering cranes and a sea of industrial factories. Teutonic Knights and Prussian dukes kept Klaipėda in German hands from 1252 until 1919, except during brief periods of Swedish and Russian rule. France gained control of the city after WWI, but promptly surrendered it to newly independent Lithuania. The city was lost to invading Nazis in 1939 and subsequently fell under Soviet control until 1990. The German-language captions in Klaipėda museums reflect the city's continued popularity with German visitors.

TRANSPORTATION

Trains: Geležinkelio stotis, Priestocio g. 1 (☎29 63 85). Station open daily 5:30am-11pm. Ticket booth open daily 6am-6pm. **Vilnius** (5-6½hr., 2 per day, 40-47Lt).

Buses: Autobusų stotis, Butkų Juzės 9 (☎41 15 47, reservations 41 15 40). Station open daily 4:30am-10:30pm. From the station, take #8 bus into the center of Old Town. To: **Kaunas** (3hr., 12 per day, 38Lt); **Palanga** (30-40min., every hr., 4.50Lt); **Šiauliai** (2½-3hr., 6 per day, 25Lt); **Vilnius** (4-5hr., 10-14 per day, 49Lt); **Kaliningrad, RUS** (4hr., 3 per day, 28Lt); **Rīga, LAT** (6hr., 2 per day, 40Lt).

Ferries: Old Castle Port Ferry Terminal, Žvejų 8 (☎31 42 57, info 31 11 17; www.keltas.lt). Ferries to **Smiltynė** (7min.; every 30min. 5am-3am; 2Lt, students 1.50Lt; round-trip 2.75Lt). Microbuses in Smiltynė connect to **Juodkrantė** (30min., 5.50Lt) and **Nida** (1hr., 7Lt). The **International Ferry Terminal** (☎39 50 50) is south of the city. Ships dock here from a number of countries, including **DEN, GER,** and **POL.** A taxi to town from the terminal costs about 12Lt; microbus 8a to city center 3Lt.

Public Transportation: City buses (0.80Lt, 1Lt from the driver) are surprisingly rare, but the wonderfully convenient **maršrutinis taksis** (6am-11pm 1.70Lt, 11pm-6am 2Lt) run all over town. *MarŠrutinis taksi* #8 goes from the train station down H. Manto through Taikos.

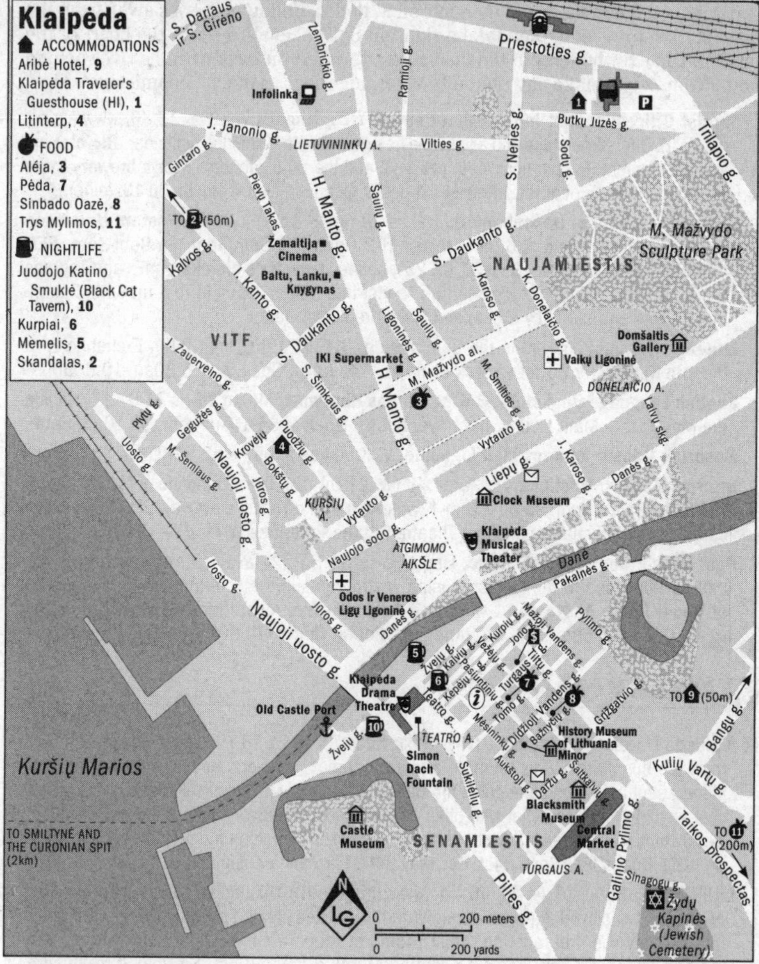

Taxis: (☎006). The small size of the city makes walking convenient, and public transport covers most areas. Standard taxi fare 1.20Lt per km. The cabs of several **private companies** roam the streets and charge 1-1.50Lt per km. Try to have your waiter or hostel receptionist call ahead for a taxi, which will be cheaper than hailing one on the street.

ORIENTATION AND PRACTICAL INFORMATION

The **Danė River** divides the city into south **Senamiestis** (Old Town) and north **Naujamiestis** (New Town). **H. Manto,** the main artery, becomes **Tiltų** as it crosses the river into Senamiestis, and **Taikos** as it enters the more modern part of the city. **Kuršių Marios** (Curonian Lagoon) to the west cuts off **Smiltynė,** Klaipėda's Kuršių Nerija (Curonian Spit) quarter. All of mainland Klaipėda lies close to the bus and train stations, which are separated by **Priestocio.** Facing away from the bus station, turn right on **Butkų Juzės** and then left on **S. Nėries.** Follow S. Nėries away from the train station to its end, then take a right on S. Daukanto to reach the heart of the city. As you exit the ferry at **Old Castle Port,** turn left on **Žvejų** with the river behind you. From Žvejų, make any right after crossing Pilies to reach Senamiestis.

Tourist Offices: Tourist Information Center (TIC), Turgaus 7 (☎41 21 86; www.klaipedainfo.lt). Offers **free maps** and a valuable free **guidebook,** "Exploring Klaipėda." **Bicycles** are available for rent (8Lt per hour, 40Lt per day), and the TIC organizes Švyturys **brewery tours** for groups (min. 5 people). **Internet** 2Lt per hr. Open M-F 9am-7pm, Sa-Su 10am-4pm.

Currency Exchange: Hansabankas, Taikos 22 (☎48 46 37). Offers **Western Union** services. Branch at Turgaus 6, next to the TIC. Open M-F 8am-6pm, Sa 9am-3pm. **SEB Vilniaus Bankas,** Darzu 13 (☎31 09 25), cashes **traveler's checks** (AmEx and Thomas Cook). Branch at Turgaus 15, near the Tourist Info Center. Open M-Th 8am-6pm, F 8am-5pm. **ATMs** and currency exchange kiosks are everywhere.

Luggage Storage: Lockers in the train station. 3Lt per 12hr.; limit 24hr. Exchange Lt at the info window for Soviet kopeck coins to store bags. Open daily 5:30am-10:30pm.

English Language Bookstore: Baltos Lankos Knygynas, Manto 21 (☎31 07 17). Inside the Mega Store Mall. Fiction and travel books. Open M-Sa 10am-8pm, Su 10am-6pm.

Hospital: Odos ir Veneros Ligų Ligoninė, V. Kurdikos g. 99 (☎52 42 57).

Internet Access: Infolinka, H. Manto 46 (☎ 21 04 42). Fast connections for 2Lt per hr. Open M-F 8am-11pm, Sa-Su 11am-11pm. Also at the **TIC** (see above). 2Lt per hr. Many cafes and public places, such as Theatre Square, offer free Wi-Fi.

Post Office: Central Post Office, Liepų 16 (☎31 50 22; fax 31 50 45). Houses a 48-bell **carillon** (one of the largest musical instruments in the country), which rings Sa-Su at noon. **Poste Restante** at window #4. 0.50Lt fee. Also offers **Western Union** services. Open M-F 8am-7pm, Sa 9am-4pm. **Postal Code:** LT-5800.

ACCOMMODATIONS

Klaipėda Traveler's Guesthouse (HI), Butkų Juzės 7-4 (☎21 18 79; oldtown@takas.lt.), 50m from the bus station. This intimate and cozy home's spacious dorms, hot showers, and friendly staff are welcome features for the weary traveler. Make yourself a cup of tea, check your email for free, and chat with other backpackers. Owners organize excursions, including weekly trips to the nearby Soviet Missile Base. Lockers, common room, basic kitchen. Laundry 12Lt. Dorms June-Sept. 44Lt; Oct.-May 34Lt. Discount for members 2Lt. Cash only. ❷

Litinterp, Puodžių 17 (☎41 06 44; www.litinterp.lt). Distinctive rooms with exposed beams and brickwork have been renovated to provide clean, spacious living, with breakfast delivery. Central location. Most rooms overlook a small, quiet courtyard. Cheery red-and-white-tiled bathrooms. Reception M-F 8:30am-5:30pm, Sa 9am-3pm. In summer singles 70-100Lt; doubles 120-160Lt; triples 180-220Lt. MC/V. ❸

Aribė Hotel, Bangų 17a (☎49 09 40; hotel@aribe.lt; www.aribe.lt). Heading away from the Danė River on Tiltų, go left on Kulių Vartų and again on Bangų. Reserve 1 week ahead for this small hotel a short walk from the center. Clean rooms have baths, Internet, phones, and TVs. Breakfast included. Singles 130Lt; doubles 170-190Lt. MC/V. ❹

FOOD

The **central market** is on Turgaus aikštė; follow Tiltų through Senamiestis and take a sharp right at the first rotary. Go inside the main building to find meat, or wander the assortment of surrounding stalls for fresh vegetables, fruit, and flowers. (Open daily 8am-6pm.) **Iki supermarket,** M. Mažvyado 7/11, is within walking distance of Senamiestis. (Open daily 8am-10pm.) The largest Iki in the Baltics is on Taikos.

Sinbado Oazė, Didzioji Vandeus 20 (☎21 17 86). Phenomenal falafel (9Lt) can be enjoyed while smoking a variety of hookahs in this exotic basement den. Perhaps the most comfortable restaurant seating in town, with velvet couches and cushions lining the walls. English menu. Open M-Th and Su 11am-midnight, F-Sa 11am-2am. Cash only. ❷

Trys Mylimos, Taikos 23 (☎41 14 79), 500m southeast of the Old Town. This traditional, antique-cluttered beer hall dishes out gargantuan portions of deep-fried regional cuisine. Locals gather here to wash down dishes such as veal liver and fried apples (11Lt) with a heavy mug of beer (5Lt per 0.5L). English menu. Entrees 8-20Lt. Live music F-Sa 8-11pm. Open daily 11am-midnight. MC/V. ❷

Pėda, Targaus 10 (☎41 07 10). Most art museums wouldn't let you bring food inside, but this charming basement cafe and gallery is different. Patrons can admire the works of Lithuanian metal sculptor Vytautas Karčiauskas while sipping coffee (2Lt), or enjoy a delicious entree (10-18Lt) at an alcove table. Upstairs and around the corner, find the full gallery. Open M-Th and Su 11am-11pm, F-Sa 11am-midnight. MC/V. ❷

Aleja, M. Mažvyado 8 (☎41 57 63). This underground cafe offers the standard menu of traditional Lithuanian food, but at the best prices around. Savory breakfast crepes (2-3Lt), omelettes (4-5Lt), and hot entrees (5-9Lt) will fill you for the rest of the day. Even better, their central location and lightning-fast service makes it one of the most convenient eats in town. Open M-Sa 8:30am-11pm, Su 11am-11pm. MC/V. ❶

SIGHTS AND MUSEUMS

MAINLAND KLAIPĖDA

One would never guess that the lush, cheery **M. Mažvydas Sculpture Park** (M. Mažvydo Skulptūrų Parkas), between Liepų and S. Daukanto, was once the town's central burial ground. When Soviet authorities demolished the cemetery in 1977, townspeople saved some of intricately crafted crosses from the graves, which are now displayed at the **Blacksmith Museum,** (Kalvystės muziejus), Saltkalviu 2. This is a real working forge, where visitors can catch a sweaty glimpse into the blacksmith's trade. Finished products on display include unique metal crosses and weathervanes. (☎41 05 26; www.mlimuziejus.lt. Open Tu-Sa 10am-5:30pm. 2Lt, students 1Lt.) Art aficionados will enjoy the exhibits by Lithuanian and international artists at the impressive **P. Domšaitis Gallery** (P. Domšaicio paveikslų galerija), Liepų 33, across the park heading away from the bus station. The house features a magnificent sculpture courtyard, contemporary artwork in a variety of media, and a permanent exhibit of Lithuanian art from 1920-1940. Don't miss the collection of avant-garde pre-World War II postcards. (☎41 04 12. Open Tu-Sa noon-6pm, Su noon-5pm. English captions. 4Lt, students 2Lt.) Exiting the gallery, continue right down Liepų to the **Clock Museum** (Laikrodžių Muziejus), Liepų 12. This off-beat, unique collection is worth a visit. The museum displays every conceivable timekeeping device, from Chinese candle clocks to a modern atomic clock. Out back, the spacious garden courtyard is decorated with stone sundials and zodiac symbols. (☎41 04 17. Open Tu-Sa noon-5:30pm, Su noon-4:30pm. English pamphlet in each room. Museum 4Lt, students 2Lt.)

The 1857, Neoclassical **Klaipėda Drama Theater** (Klaipėdos Dramos Teatras), Teatro aikštė, on the other side of H. Manto, is famous for being one of Richard Wagner's favorite haunts and infamous for being the site where Hitler proclaimed the town's incorporation into the Reich in 1939. (Tickets ☎31 44 53. Box office open Tu-Su 11am-2pm and 4-7pm.) In front, the **Simon Dach Fountain** spouts water over Klaipėda's symbol, a statue of Ännchen von Tharau. The original statue disappeared during WWII. Some say it was removed by the Nazis, who didn't want the statue's back to face Hitler during his speech. The copy standing today was erected by German expatriates in 1989. The **History**

Museum of Lithuania Minor (Mažosios Lietuvos Istorijos Muziejus) features miscellaneous relics and fading photographs of Klaipėda's more recent German past. (☎41 05 24. Open Tu-Su 10am-5:30pm. Few English captions. 2Lt, students 1Lt; W free.) The **Klaipėda Castle Museum,** Pilies 4, beyond the port-authority building, features the remains of the 13th-century castle and alongside 16th to 18th century furnishings. The ammunition storage areas in the back contain small exhibits on the history of the city and castle. (☎31 33 23. Open Tu-Sa 10am-5pm. 4Lt, students 2Lt.) **Aukštoji,** near the history museum, is one of the best-preserved areas of Senamiestis, lined with the exposed-timber *Fachwerk* buildings for which prewar Klaipėda was famous. Past the central market, Aukstoji leads into **Sinagogu,** once the heart of Klaipėda's Jewish Quarter. On the eve of Hitler's invasion, Jews accounted for 17% of Klaipėda's population; today, just 300 remain. The historic **Jewish cemetery** is 150m from the market. Few gravestones or markers remain, but the park is the quietest part of the city. The gray and blue building next to the cemetery is home to the **Jewish Community Centre,** Ziedu 3, which has a Synagogue, library, and Sunday school. (☎49 37 58. Open M-Sa 10am-3pm. Shabbat services Sa 10am.)

SMILTYNĖ

The shifting sands of Smiltyne, desecrated by a fire in May of 2006, are now home to less crowded beaches and dunes. As you get off the ferry (see p. 400), make a right on Smiltynės and follow it along the lagoon 200m to the **Tourist Information Center (TIC),** Smiltynės 11. (☎40 22 56; www.nerija.lt. Open M-F 8am-noon and 1-5pm, Sa 9am-4pm, Su 9am-2pm.) Buses from the ferry terminal (1.5Lt) carry passengers straight to the **Lithuanian Sea Museum** (see below), and horse-drawn buggies (parked to the right as you exit the ferry) charge 15Lt for the trek. The best way to see Smiltynė is to walk the 1km from the ferry terminal to the northern end of the Spit. Flanking the TIC on both sides is the three-house **Kuršių Nerija National Park Museum of Nature** (Kušrių Nerijos Nacionalinis Parkas Gamtos Muziejus), Smiltynės 9-12. The rather sparse museum details the Spit's prominence as a site for tracking migratory birds. (Open June-Aug. Tu-Su 11am-6pm; Sept. and May Tu-Su 11am-5pm. 2Lt, students 1Lt, with ISIC free.) Just down the road, three ships sit on pillars as representatives of **Old Fishing Vessels** (Senieji Žvejybos Laivai). The nearby **Fishermen's Farmstead** (Ethnografinė Pajūrio Žvejo Sodyba), a reconstructed late 19th-century settlement, includes a rustic boathouse, granary, smokeshed, and cattleshed that houses a small exhibition with photographs and relics showing the progression of fishing over time. (Open 24hr. Free.) Go to the end of Smiltynės for the main attraction, the **Lithuanian Sea Museum** (Lietuvos Jūrų Muziejus), Smiltynės 3. It is housed in an 1860s fortress that once guarded Klaipėda's bustling port. Seals, sea lions, and penguins now frolic in the moat. Don't miss the highly amusing, slightly cheeky **sea lion show,** in which the feisty mammals shoot basketball hoops. (Shows 15min.; 11:15am, 1:15, 2:15, 3:15pm. 5Lt.) Dolphins leap, paint, and dance at the museum's **Dolphinarium.** (Shows 40min.; noon, 2, 4pm. 12Lt, students 6Lt.) Watch where you sit: rows 1-6 get soaked. (☎49 07 54; www.juru.muziejus.lt. Open June-Aug. Tu-Su 10:30am-6:30pm; Sept. and May W-Su 10:30am-6:30pm; Oct.-Apr. Sa-Su 10:30am-5pm. 8Lt, students 4Lt.) If you're still not wet enough, follow the forest paths 500m from the Fishermen's Village to the **beaches** along the Spit's western coast. To the left is a 1.5km long public bathing area. Straight ahead is the **women's beach** (clothing optional), and south is a **co-ed nude beach.** Lines separate the areas, but bathers close to the latter section don't always respect the boundaries.

ENTERTAINMENT AND NIGHTLIFE

Klaipėda Musical Theater (Muzikinis teatras), Danės 19, hosts operas and other musical events. (☎39 74 02; www.muzikinis-teatras.lt. Season Oct.-May; brief series mid-Aug. Box office open Tu-Su 11am-2pm and 3-6pm. Performances F 7pm, Sa-Su 6pm. Tickets range from 25-120Lt.) **Žemaitija Cinema,** H. Manto 31, shows Hollywood films with Lithuanian subtitles. (☎31 40 90. 12Lt. MC/V.) The best barhopping is on **H. Manto.**

Kurpiai, Kurpių 1a (☎41 05 55; www.jazz.lt), in the middle of Senamiestis. This superb jazz club is a mix between a traditional tavern and a jazz museum, attracting groups from Lithuania and a mixed clientele of locals and foreigners. Adding to the fun is the multi-level maze of platforms and rooms. Live music nightly, usually at 9:30pm. Beer 7Lt per 0.5L. Cover F-Sa 10Lt. Open M and Su noon-midnight, Tu-Sa noon-2am. MC/V.

Memelis, Žvejų 4 (☎40 30 40; www.memelis.lt), on the river across the street from the ferry port. It's a tough call between the 2 lines of "Memelio": Sviesusis (light beer) and Juodasis (dark beer) are brewed in 2 large vats behind the bar. Try them both (6Lt per 0.5L). Upstairs, talented DJs spin as young Klaipėdans dance and mix with expats until early in the morning. No cover. Open M and Su noon-midnight, Tu-Th noon-2am, F-Sa noon-3am. MC/V.

Skandalas, I. Kanto 44 (☎41 15 85; www.skandalas.info). Statues of cowboys, Native Americans, and highway cops crowd this hopping New Town restaurant and bar. Well-prepared American food (entrees 14-29Lt) will cure any American traveler suffering a bout of homesickness. The french fries are spectacular (3Lt). Live bands F-Sa 9pm provide a great backdrop for kicking back with beers and meeting fellow travelers. Open M-Th noon-1am, F-Sa noon-2am, Su noon-midnight. MC/V.

Juodojo Katino Smuklė (Black Cat Tavern), Žveju 21/1 (☎41 11 67). This expat staple is the perfect place to go for cold beers and good food, but the main attraction is its regular, fun-loving, and raucous crowd. Open 10am-midnight. MC/V.

DAYTRIP FROM KLAIPĖDA: SOVIET MISSILE BASE AT PLOKSTINE RESERVATION. Tucked away in the forested Plokstine Reservation inside Zematijia National Park, the remains of an underground **Soviet missile base,** are among the most remarkable sites in Lithuania. The large, gated field, and concrete mounds look unremarkable on the surface, but underground, visitors will be transported back to feel the fear and military power of the Soviets. Soviet leader Nikita Krushchev ordered the construction of this site in September 1960. Lithuania was the ideal location for such a facility, as missiles fired here could have reached as far as Turkey and Spain. The base was put on high alert during the Czechoslovakian Revolution of 1968. During its working years, the base was home to thousands of soldiers, but the Soviets abandoned the site in 1978 after signing the SALT (Strategic Arms Limitation Treaties) with the US. Locals looted the facility for scrap metal during the lean years of the 1980s; as a result, much of the site is falling apart, and only one of the four silos is open to tourists. As a visitor, you will walk through the dark, dripping corridors and see the remnants of computer operating rooms, massive machinery and engines, electric generators, and the plumbing systems necessary to cool the missile silos after firing. Crawl through a small door to peer down the 30m hole that once held warheads five times the strength of the atomic bomb dropped on Hiroshima. The structure is deteriorating so quickly that the reservation is constantly struggling to maintain scheduled renovations.

The best route to the base is by organized excursion with the lovely **Jurga,** the owner of the Klaipėda Traveler's Guesthouse. Email or call in advance to arrange a trip. (3hr. including travel time and Jurga's English-language tour. Usually Tu,

Th, or F afternoon 160Lt per car, 4 people per car, 40Lt per person.) If you decide to go on your own, contact the **Zematija National Park Information Center** in advance to ensure that the base will be open and to organize a tour (30Lt) in English, as there are no English guides on hand. (☎844 849 231; znp@plunge.omnitel.net. Open M-Sa 9am-noon and 1-5pm.) Go to Plungė from Klaipėda by **bus** (1hr., about 6 per day, 10Lt) or train (1hr., 2 per day, 6.40-8.30Lt). From there, board a **minibus** to the tiny town of Plateliai and ask the driver to let you off at Militarizmo Expozicija. You will be dropped off at a trailhead 5km from the site. Take the path and head left at the fork. (Tours daily June-Aug. every 2hr. 10am-6pm. Most guides speak only Lithuanian. Tours 5Lt, students 3Lt. Admission free.)

PALANGA ☎(8)460

The day starts late in Palanga, and the night runs long. Spectacular sea and sand are the city's focus, and rightly so: kilometers of pristine beach are bordered by equally serene woods. In the late 17th century, Jan Sobieski, King of Poland and Grand Duke of Lithuania, invited English merchants to build a harbor along Palanga's shallow shores. Rampaging Swedes destroyed the merchants' efforts in 1701, but Palanga still warmly welcomes English speakers to its beaches: almost all street signs and menus are translated. In the summer, Palanga's beaches and pedestrian thoroughfare attract throngs of foreign tourists and Lithuanians alike.

TRANSPORTATION AND PRACTICAL INFORMATION. Palanga is a short ride from Klaipėda. Buses depart from both cities every 30min. until 11:30pm (20min., 4.70Lt). The **bus station** (☎533 33) also sends buses to: Kaunas (3hr., 10 per day, 34Lt); Klaipėda (30min., every 30min., 2.50Lt); Šiauliai (2½-3hr., 7 per day, 20Lt); Vilnius (4hr., 11 per day, 47Lt); Rīga, LAT (5-6hr., 2 per day, 40Lt). Speedier **microbuses** also run to Klaipėda (20min., depart as they fill, 3Lt). During summer, **bike** rental kiosks line **J. Basanavičiaus, Vytauto,** and **Jūratės.** Pedestrian areas and paths through the woods and along the coast make for pleasant rides. (Helmets not available. Rates average 8Lt per hr. or 30-40Lt per day.)

The **bus station** and Tourist Information Center share the corner lot at the intersection of **Kretingos** with **Vytauto,** one of Palanga's main streets, which runs parallel to the beach. With your back to the bus station, turn left on Vytauto and continue to reach **J. Basanavičiaus,** which eventually runs into the long **pier,** a favorite spot for watching the sunset. The looming tower on the **Church of the Assumption,** facing the bus station, is a good point of reference near the center of town. The **tourist office,** Kretingos 1, adjacent to the bus station *kasa*, gives out **free maps,** rents bikes (8Lt per hr.) and books **private rooms** with no service charge. (☎488 11; www.palangatic.lt. Open M-F 9am-6pm, Sa 9am-4pm, Su 9am-3pm.) **Hansabankas,** Juratės 15/2, **exchanges currency,** cashes **traveler's checks,** and gives MasterCard **cash advances.** (☎412 12. **Western Union** inside. **ATM** outside. Open M-Th 8am-4pm, F 8am-3:30pm.) Racks in the bus station, just to the right of the ticket counter, provide **luggage storage.** (1Lt per bag, limit 1 day. Open daily 7am-1pm and 2-10pm.) **Internet** cafes line J. Basanavičiaus, including **Klubo Kaimynas,** along J. Basanavičiaus near intersection with S. Daukanto. (6Lt per hr. noon-midnight, 4Lt per hr. midnight-noon. Open 24hr.) The **post office,** Vytauto 53, has **Poste Restante** at window #1. **Western Union** services are also available. (☎488 71. Open M-F 9am-6:30pm, Sa 9am-4pm.) **Postal Code:** LT-00134.

ACCOMMODATIONS. Hotel prices rise considerably in the peak months of July and August. In the low season, you'll pay a pittance for luxurious digs near the beach. Arrange a private room (from 80Lt per night) through the TIC. **Palanga Welcome Host,** Vytauto 21, arranges rooms, many of which can be viewed online. The staff speaks limited English, but a catalog has English listings and pictures. Study it closely, and you'll find prices much lower than those printed in the agency's thinner pamphlet. (☎487 23; www.palangawelcomehost.lt. Doubles June €15-20; July €20-25; Aug. €25-30.) Budget travelers who haven't planned ahead can head to Neries St across form the bus station, which is lined with households that rent rooms, often for half the price of a hotel. Look for homes with "kambariu numoa" or "nuoma" in the window. **Mėguva ❷,** Valančiaus 1, just west of the Church of the Assumption, has charmless and slightly musty rooms with private baths and TVs. What it lacks in style, however, it makes up for with its suberb location close to the bus station and the center of Palanga's pedestrian area. (☎488 39. June singles 50Lt; doubles 80Lt. July-Aug. 60/120Lt. Sept.-May 40/60Lt. Cash only.) Near the Botanical Gardens, **Palangos Dailė ❷,** S. Daukanto 33, has quiet, basic rooms near the the Botanical Park with TVs, refrigerators, and Wi-Fi. The English-speaking staff is helpful. Reserve in advance (☎538 87, www.palangosdaile.lt. Singles 40-80Lt, doubles 60-150Lt, triples 80-170Lt. MC/V.) **Vyturys ❷,** S. Dariaus ir S. Girėno 20, is a huge complex well equipped with safes, a library, and a sunny cafe where visitors can play chess and meet fellow travelers. Book in advance for the best rates. (☎491 49; www.baltijahotal.lt. Singles 60-105Lt; doubles 90-150Lt; triples 102-189Lt. MC/V.)

LITHUANIA

FOOD. In true seaside-resort style, Palanga's streets are lined with vendors selling cotton candy, ice cream, chocolate dipped waffles, and Lithuanian snacks such as *čeburekai* (meat-filled pastries; around 4Lt). On **Vytauto** and **J. Basanavičiaus,** cafes and restaurants blare music across outdoor patios. There are several supermarkets in the center of town, including **Prekybos Centras,** J. Basanavičiaus 23. (Open daily 9am-2am.) A large **Maxima** supermarket is behind the bus station on Vytauto. (Open daily 8am-midnight.) The most popular **local beer** is HBH Vilkmerges, brewed just 7km from Palanga. The town is divided between adherents of the dark and light varieties. You'll find both on tap (3.50Lt per 0.5L) at **Dvitaktis ❷,** Vytauto 80, a thatch-roofed lean-to that also offers meals. (Entrees 9-26Lt. Open noon-midnight.) For a quick bite, head to **Café Ruta ❶,** Vytauto 94, right next to the bus station. The healthy, traditional breakfast and lunch fare is served promptly, straight from the stove to your plate. (☎516 04. Salads 3-6Lt. Breakfast and lunch entrees 3-8Lt. Coffee and tea 1-2Lt. English menu.) **Monika ❷,** J. Basanavičiaus 12, has earned a name for itself as one of the most popular places on J. Basanavičiaus for its Lithuanian and Italian fare. Try the 6Lt potato *bliny*, or the meat dumplings with pork rinds and sour cream for 8Lt. (☎525 60. Entrees 6-30Lt. Open daily 10am-midnight. MC/V.)

SIGHTS. Palanga's pride and joy is the world's first **Amber Museum** (Gintaro muziejus), housed in a neo-Renaissance style palace, which showcases the fossilized resin known as "Baltic Gold." Those with an interest in biology will be thrilled by nearly 29,000 "inclusions," pieces of amber with primeval flora and fauna, such spiders, mosquitoes, and even a lizard, trapped inside. (☎513 19. Open June-Aug. Tu-Sa 10am-8pm, Su 10am-7pm; Sept.-May daily 11am-4:30pm; ticket office closes 1hr. earlier June-Aug., 30min. Sept.-May. English captions. 5Lt, students 2.50Lt.) The surrounding estate grounds are now home to the **Palanga Botanical Gardens,** a vast and beautifully landscaped forested area, perfect for stealing away from the crowds for a quiet stroll. Through the main entrance to the gardens, on the corner of Vytauto and S. Dariaus ir S. Girėno, is one of the nation's most famous sculptures: **Eglė,** Queen of the Serpents. According to local lore, a serpent thrust himself on Eglė and forced her to marry him. When she did, he morphed into a charming prince. Eglė's brothers then slaughtered her husband, and in despair, she turned herself into a tree. Inside the garden, along a forest path behind the Amber Museum, stands **Birutė Hill.** Archaeologists recently found the remains of a 14th-century pagan temple on the site; a 19th-century **chapel** stands atop the hill today. Less than 1km south of the Botanical Gardens, along tree-lined Vytauto, is a 1m high black marble marker pointing toward the secluded **Holocaust Mass Graves** (Holokausto Auku Kapai). Follow the path into the woods, bear left at the fork, and continue 500m. A large grey stone, with worn words and a still-visible Star of David, marks the site. Palanga's Jewish community was among the first to be exterminated by the Nazi *Einsatzgruppe A* in June 1944.

Toward the center of town, you will find the **Dr. Jonas Šliūpas Memorial Gardens and House,** Vytauto 23a, set back from the street behind a yellow-and-green house. Sliupas, a physician, newspaper editor, and politician, spent much of his life in the US and played a leading role in the Union of Lithuanian Socialists in America in the early 20th century. The house is filled with his miscellaneous, dusty belongings, including his typewriter and letters, as well as exquisite furnishings and a photo album of 20th-century postcards of the region. (Open in high season daily noon-7pm; in low season Tu-Su 11am-3pm. Captions in Lithuanian only. 2Lt.)

A bit farther north on Vytauto, turn left on Kęstučio to reach the **Antanas Mončys House-Museum** (Antano Mončio Namai-Muziejus), a blue-and-white building at S. Daukanto 16. The renowned sculptor left Lithuania for France in 1944 and sent his work home for 45 years. On display is a unique collection of his sculptures, drawings, graphic art, advertising posters, and parts of his diary. As specified in Mončys's will, visitors may touch any of his abstract wooden sculptures. (☎493 66. Open June-Aug. Tu noon-5pm, W-Su 2-9pm; Sept.-May Th-Su noon-5pm. 4Lt, students 2Lt, with ISIC 1.50Lt.) At the end of J. Basanavičiaus 12, visitors can walk amidst the local fishermen on the lengthy seaside **Pier** for a superb view of Palanga's coast and dunes.

ENTERTAINMENT AND NIGHTLIFE. Summer visitors flock to the beach, the hallmark of any Palanga excursion; take a dip in the chilly Baltic on the tourist-packed beaches, or enjoy a private bit of sun between the hilly dunes. Beach volleyball and pickup games of soccer happen close to the pier. Palanga also seems to be part amusement park, with arcades and midway games lining its pedestrian streets. Play **minigolf** across from J. Basanavičiaus 42. Thrill-seekers can take a ride on the **bungee chair** (80Lt for 2 people) at J. Basanavičiaus 22. The **Summer Theater** (Vasaraos Estrada), at Vytauto 43, hosts **concerts** by the Lithuanian National Philharmonic and the Klaipėda Philharmonic, as well as visiting performers. (☎522 10. Box office open daily 3-9pm; check TIC for prices & concert schedules.) Cafes on **J. Basanavičiaus** and **Vytauto** feature live bands, many of which make a living covering Eurovision songs. **Kinoteatras Naglis,** Vytauto 82, shows Hollywood flicks (8Lt) with Lithuanian subtitles.

The **choir festival** opens at the end of May. The opening of the **summer season** takes place the first weekend of June, with theater, fireworks, and a giant feast to declare Palanga the summer capital of Lithuania. **Night Serenades,** evenings of classical music, are held every night during the first week of August at the Amber Museum and Botanical Gardens. On the first weekend of August, the **Palanga Cup,** a beach volleyball competition, draws crowds.

Palanga has no shortage of nightlife, as almost everyone here is on vacation and almost every restaurant morphs into a club at dusk. The night scene centers on J. Basanavičiaus, where dozens of street musicians battle for attention. Travelers hit the dance floor at **Honolulu Night Club,** S. Nerіės 39, north of J. Basanavičiaus. (☎356 41. Cover 20Lt. Open 10pm-2am.) Escape the crowds for an evening at **Kupeta,** S. Dariaus ir Gireno 13, just north of the Botanical Gardens. The bar makes good use of the large courtyard it shares with an art gallery, and hosts a steady stream of local and international bands, including a number of funky jazz groups. (☎400 14; www.feliksas.lt. Occasional cover 5-10Lt. Open daily 9am-midnight.)

CURONIAN SPIT (NERINGA)

A product of glaciers from the last Ice Age, the Lithuanian section of Curonian Spit is a 52km long sandbar lined with majestic dunes and crisscrossed by lush forests. It is bordered by the Baltic Sea to the west and the beautifully calm Curonian Lagoon to the east. Outside of Nida and Juodkrantė, endless kilometers of untouched waterfront are perfect for exploration. Take the ferry to Smiltynė, rent a bike in Nida, and keep pedaling until you're ready for a dip in the chilly Baltic.

WITCHES' HILL

Goblins, devils, and mortals frolic on **Witches' Hill** (Raganų Kalnas) in Juodkrantė. On the way to Nida, set aside an hour to wander the worn trail through the dense wood lined with 71 wooden sculptures in high Lithuanian folk-art style. Carved between 1979 and 1981, the works were crafted by local artists who spent their summers in Juodkrantė. Take a detour through the forest and head toward the sound of crashing water to reach the quiet **beach** on the Baltic side of the Spit. While Juodkrantė is always a site of mirth and ritual, Witches' Hill is especially popular on **Midsummer's Eve** and **St. John's Day** (June 23-24). **Buses** run hourly from 6am to 10pm along the Nida-Klaipėda (via Smiltynė) route and stop in the center of town; from the bus stop, walk south along L. Rėzos until you see a large wooden sign and a creature pointing toward the start of the path. (30min., 5Lt to Nida. 15min., 3Lt to Smiltynė.)

NIDA ☎(8)469

Bike trails, hiking paths, and miles of rolling dunes are Nida's main attraction. Settlers have lived in this section of the Curonian Spit since the late 14th century, but shifting dunes have buried their villages as often as every 50 years. These days, 50,000 tourists pack tiny Nida (pop. 1550) each summer. Hike a couple of kilometers south from town, however, and you'll find yourself all alone in a dune-filled desert. Don't go too far, though: 4km south of Nida's center, a militarized border separates Lithuania from the Russian region of Kaliningrad. Head straight to the stunning **Drifting Dunes of Parnidis** for splendid views and a quiet place to bask in the sun. These vast dunes rise high above Nida, though they sink 30cm each year. Hikers will enjoy the footpaths winding between the dunes and deep into the forest. Walk south along the beach or down forest paths to reach the base of the sand dunes (bike trails end here). A moderate climb will lead you to the peak of the tallest sand dune (69m), marked by the remains of an immense sundial. It was smashed by a hurricane in 1999, but its site offers awesome views of the coastline. On the far side of the dunes is the **Valley of Death,** which was used by Prussia—the Spit's former owner—as a prison camp for French soldiers in the early 1870s. The **wooden houses** clustered along Lotmiško, the lane leading back to town, are classified as historical monuments; dozens more are buried under the sand.

From the town center, go 500m north on Pamario to the Gothic-style **Nida Evangelical Lutheran Church** (Evangelikų liuteronų bažnyčioje), Pamario 43, built in 1888. Soviet authorities left it standing but looted the wooden pews to fuel a sauna. The handful of Nida's remaining Lutherans shares the house of worship with local Catholics, and concerts are held at the church during summer. (Open daily 10am-6pm. Check the TIC for schedules.) Just 100m farther, the **Neringa Museum of History** (Neringos Istorijos Muziejus), Pamario 53, presents a thought-provoking exhibit on Neringa's fishing community. (☎511 62. Open June-Aug. M-Su 10am-6pm; 2Lt, students 0.50Lt.) Bear right on Skruzdynės and climb the 3rd wooden staircase on the left to reach the renovated **Thomas Mann House** (Thomo Manno Namelis) at #17. The German Nobel laureate built this cottage in 1930.

Today it houses a small history exhibit. (☎522 60. Open June-Aug. daily 10am-6pm; Sept.-May Tu-Sa 10am-5pm. No English captions. 2Lt, students 0.50Lt.) The **Thomas Mann Cultural Center** puts on classical concerts for the mid-July **Thomas Mann Festival,** which also includes art exhibits, films, and lecture series.

Hotel and guesthouse prices on the Curonian Spit rise during the summer season, but if you're willing to be away from the action at Nida, staying in Juodkrantė will save you some cash. The **TIC** arranges **private rooms** (40-50Lt, 5Lt fee) and is the best option for inexpensive accommodations. If you are in the market for a hotel, try **Jurates ❷,** Pamario 3, located in the center of town. The rooms don't directly overlook the water, so they are cheap during the low season. (☎526 18; juratenida@takas.lt. Singles 80-125Lt; doubles 120-180Lt.) **Miško Namas ❷,** Pamario 10, is a family-run hotel complete with a communal kitchen, private gardens, and helpful staff. (☎522 95; www.miskonamas.lt. Doubles 80-180Lt.) To get to **Kempingas** (Camping) **❶,** Taikos 45a, walk beyond the path to Urbo Kalnas and continue until you see a road signpost on your left. Kempingas offers a taste of the outdoor experience, but with showers, flushing toilets, an adjacent Chinese restaurant, and the opportunity to rent sporting equipment. (☎370 68 24 11 50; www.kempingas.lt. 15Lt per person, 10Lt per site. Sleeping-bag rental 5Lt. Tents 10Lt.)

The regional specialty is *rūkyta žuvis* (smoked fish), served with bread. Stop by **Fischbrotchen ❶,** in a yellow hut next to the bus station, for a 7Lt herring sandwich. (Open daily 11am-8pm.) Nida's largest grocery store is **Kuršis,** Naglių 29, just north of the bus station. (Open daily 8am-10pm.) Its **cafe** serves a great breakfast (5-10Lt) for early risers. (Open daily 8am-midnight. MC/V.) At family-run **Baras Po Vyšniom ❶,** Nagilų 10, you can find locals devouring snacks and fish dishes.

Buses run from the **bus station,** Naglių 18e (☎528 59), to Klaipėda and Smiltynė (45min., 1 per hr., on the hr., 7Lt); Kaunas (4½hr., 1 per day, 44Lt); and Kaliningrad, RUS (2½-4hr., 2 per day, 18Lt). **Bikes** are available for rent at many different points along the lagoon shore. (5-8Lt per hr., 30-40 Lt per day.) From the water, **Taikos** runs inland. Perpendicular to it, **Naglių** eventually becomes **Pamario.** The **Tourist Information Center (TIC),** Taikos 4, opposite the station, arranges **private rooms** (5Lt fee) and has **free maps,** transport info, and slow but free **Internet access.** (☎523 45; www.neringainfo.lt. English spoken. Open June-Aug. M-F 10am-8pm, Sa 10am-6pm, Su 10am-3pm; Sept.-May M-F 9am-1pm and 2-6pm, Sa 10am-3pm). **Hansabankas,** Taikos 5, **exchanges currency,** gives MasterCard and Visa **cash advances,** cashes **traveler's checks,** and has **Western Union** services. (☎522 41. Open M-Th 8am-4pm, F 8am-3:30pm.) Buy phone cards at kiosks or the **post office,** Taikos 13, farther up the road, past the police station on your left. (☎526 47. Open M-F 9am-noon and 1-5:30pm, Sa 9am-1pm.) **Postal Code:** LT-5872.

POLAND (POLSKA)

Poland is a sprawling country in which history casts a long shadow. Plains that stretch from the Tatras Mountains in the south to the Baltic Sea in the north have seen foreign invaders time and time again and the contrast between Western cities like Wrocław and Eastern outposts like Białystok is a reminder of Poland's subjection to competing empires. After a century of destruction, however, Poland is finally self-governed, and the change is marked. Today's Poland is a haven for budget travelers, where the rich cultural treasures of medieval Kraków and bustling Warsaw are complemented by wide Baltic beaches, rugged Tatras peaks, and tranquil Mazury lakes.

POLAND

DISCOVER POLAND: SUGGESTED ITINERARIES

THREE DAYS. In **Kraków,** enjoy the stunning **Wawel Castle** (p. 443), the medieval grace of **Stare Miasto** (p. 444), and the bohemian nightlife of **Kazimierz** (p. 445). Take a day in the sobering **Auschwitz-Birkenau** death camp (p. 447).

ONE WEEK. After three days in **Kraków,** head up to **Warsaw** (2 days; p. 420), the capital city, where the medieval Old Town and new **Uprising Museum** (p. 433) and edgy **nightlife** (p. 435) can't be missed; head north to wander the cosmopolitan streets and sights of **Gdańsk** (2 days; p. 487) and soak up the sun on the beach of **Sopot** (p. 495).

BEST OF POLAND, THREE WEEKS. Begin with five days in **Kraków,** including daytrips to **Auschwitz-Birkenau** and the **Wieliczka** salt mines (p. 447). Spend two days in lovely **Wrocław** (p. 461), then enjoy the mountain air of **Karpacz** (p. 467; 1 day). After stopping off for a night at the edgy bars and clubs of **Poznań** (p. 475), head east to up-and-coming **Łódź** (2 days) and dynamic **Warsaw** (4 days). In **Gdańsk** (4 days), don't miss **Sopot** or **Malbork Castle** (p. 495). Spend your last two days in either eastern **Białowieża** (p. 502) or western **Międzyzdroje** (p. 485), enjoying Poland's natural wonders.

FACTS AND FIGURES

Official Name: Republic of Poland.

Capital: Warsaw.

Major Cities: Katowice, Kraków, Łódź.

Population: 38,518,000.

Time Zone: GMT +1, in summer GMT +2.

Language: Polish.

Religions: Roman Catholic (90%, 75% practicing).

Annual Pork Consumption Per Capita: 83.2 lb.

ESSENTIALS

WHEN TO GO

Poland has cold, snowy winters, and warm summers, though summer weather can be unpredictable and rain is frequent in July. The tourist season runs from late May to early September, except in mountain areas, which also have a winter high season (Dec.-Mar.). Though rain is a risk in late spring and early autumn, these months are pleasantly mild, so travelers may want to visit in late April, September, or early October. Many attractions are closed from mid-autumn to mid-spring.

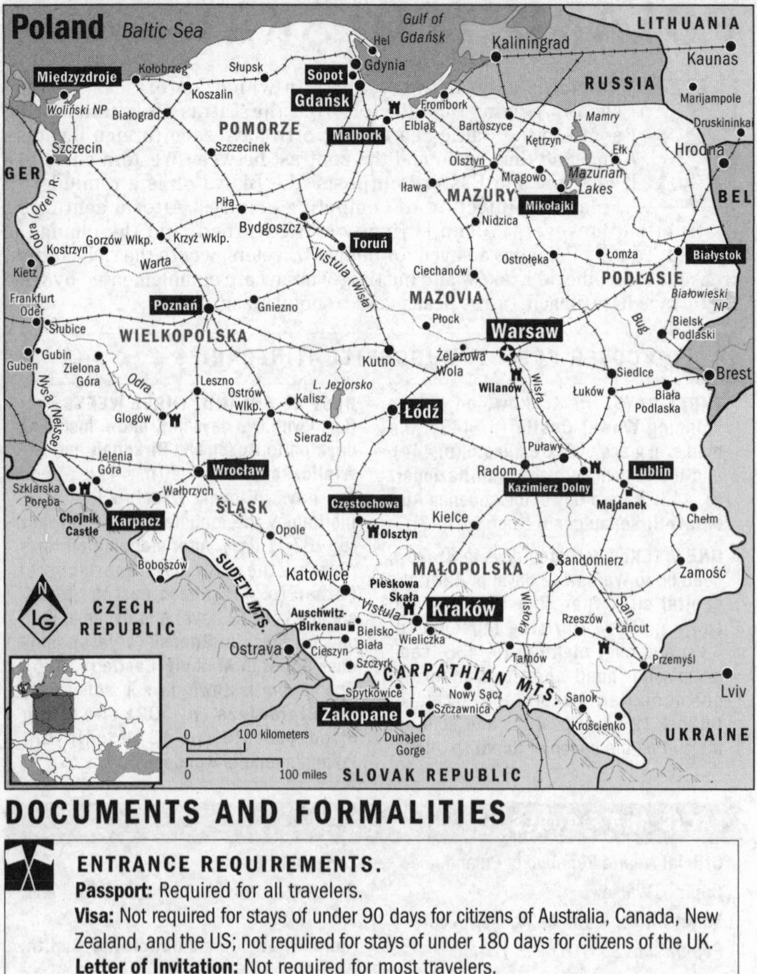

DOCUMENTS AND FORMALITIES

ENTRANCE REQUIREMENTS.

Passport: Required for all travelers.

Visa: Not required for stays of under 90 days for citizens of Australia, Canada, New Zealand, and the US; not required for stays of under 180 days for citizens of the UK.

Letter of Invitation: Not required for most travelers.

Inoculations: Recommended up-to-date on DTaP (diphtheria, tetanus, and pertussis), Hepatitis A, Hepatitis B, MMR (measles, mumps, and rubella), rabies, polio booster, and typhoid.

Work Permit: Required for all foreigners planning to work in Poland, except EU citizens.

International Driving Permit: Required for all those planning to drive in Poland except for EU citizens.

EMBASSIES AND CONSULATES. Foreign embassies to Poland are in Warsaw and Kraków. For Polish embassies and consulates abroad, contact: **Australia,** 7 Turrana St., Yarralumla, Canberra, ACT 2600 (☎02 62 73 12 08; www.poland.org.au); **Canada,** 443 Daly Ave., Ottawa, ON K1N 6H3 (☎613-789-0468; www.polishembassy.ca); **Ireland,** 5 Ailesbury Rd., Ballbridge, Dublin 4 (☎01 283 0855; www.polishheritage.co.nz);

New Zealand, 51 Granger Rd., Howick, Auckland 1705 (☎09 534 4670); **UK,** 47 Portland Pl., London, W1B 1JH (☎020 75 80 43 24; www.polishembassy.org.uk); **US,** 2640 16th St., NW, Washington, D.C. 20009 (☎202-234-3800; www.polandembassy.org).

VISA AND ENTRY INFORMATION. Citizens of Australia, Canada, and the US need a visa for stays of over 90 days. EU citizens do not require a visa but will need to apply for temporary residence after 90 days. Visas for US citizens are free. Processing may take up to two weeks, but express visas can be processed within 24 hours. You must be ready to present ample documentation concerning your stay, including verification of accommodation reservations, sufficient funds for the duration of your stay and confirmation of health insurance coverage.

TOURIST SERVICES

City-specific **tourist offices** are the most helpful. Almost all provide free info in English and help arrange accommodations. Most have good free **maps. Orbis,** the state-sponsored travel bureau, operates hotels in most cities and sells transportation tickets. **Almatur,** a student travel organization with offices in 15 major cities, offers ISICs, arranges dorm stays, and sells discounted transportation tickets. The state-sponsored **PTTK** and **IT** bureaus, in nearly every city, are helpful for basic traveling needs. Try **Polish Pages,** a free guide available at hotels and tourist agencies.

MONEY

ZŁOTYCH (ZŁ)		
	AUS$1 = 2.49ZŁ	1ZŁ = AUS$0.40
	CDN$1 = 2.70ZŁ	1ZŁ = CDN$0.37
	EUR€1 = 4.02ZŁ	1ZŁ = EUR€0.25
	NZ$1 = 2.30ZŁ	1ZŁ = NZ$0.44
	UK£1 = 5.92ZŁ	1ZŁ = UK£0.17
	US$1 = 3.28ZŁ	1ZŁ = US$0.31

The Polish currency is the **złotych** (zwah-tee; zł); the plural is złoty. Inflation is around 2%, so prices should be reasonably stable. Bank PKO SA and Bank Pekao have decent exchange rates; they cash **traveler's checks** and give cash advances. **ATMs** *(bankomaty)* are common, and generally offer the best rates; MasterCard and Visa are widely accepted at ATMs. Budget accommodations rarely accept credit cards, but some restaurants and upscale hotels do. Normal business hours in Poland are 8am-4pm. **Tipping** varies, but is generally a few additional złoty.

HEALTH AND SAFETY

EMERGENCY	**Ambulance:** ☎999. **Fire:** ☎150. **Police:** ☎158. **Cell Phone Emergency Number:** ☎112.

Medical clinics in major cities have private, English-speaking doctors who are generally high-quality but are not uniformly up to Western standards. Expect to pay at least 50zł per visit. Pharmacies are well stocked, and some stay open 24hr. Tap water is theoretically drinkable, but bottled mineral water will spare you from some unpleasant metals and chemicals.

Crime rates are low, but tourists are sometimes targeted. Watch for muggings and pickpockets, especially on trains and in lower-priced hostels. Cab drivers may attempt to cheat those who do not speak Polish. **Women** traveling alone should take usual precautions and avoid dangerous places at night or revealing that they

are traveling without a companion. Those with darker skin may encounter discrimination due to long-standing prejudice against the **Roma** people. There may be lingering prejudice against Jews despite governmental efforts to change this; anti-Semitic remarks are heard frequently. Like many Eastern European nations, Poland is not widely **wheelchair-accessible,** but interest groups, newly armed with EU funds, are working to change that. **Warsaw** in particular, with its multitude of steep, winding steps, is difficult to access. **Homosexuality** is not widely accepted; discretion is advised. GLBT travelers might find www.gay.pl a useful resource.

TRANSPORTATION

BY PLANE. The Polish national airline, **LOT,** flies to major cities, as do many discount airlines. Many major international airlines, including **Allitalia, Finnair,** and **Lufthansa** fly into either Warsaw or Kraków's **John Paul II Airport.** United States airlines generally do not fly directly to Warsaw and are probably more expensive: the tickets start around US$600 but commonly run up to US$1000. Look for special deals through discount carriers like Easyjet, especially during high season.

BY TRAIN. . It's usually better to take a train than a bus, as buses are slow and uncomfortable. For a timetable, see www.pkp.pl. *Odjazdy* (departures) are in yellow, *przyjazdy* (arrivals) in white. InterCity and *ekspresowy* (express) trains are listed in red with an "IC" or "Ex" in front of the train number. *Pośpieszny* (direct; in red) are almost as fast and a bit cheaper. Low-priced *osobowy* (in black) are the slowest and have no restrooms. If you see a boxed "R" on the schedule, ask the clerk for a *miejscówka* (reservation). Students and seniors buy *ulgowy* (half-price) tickets instead of *normalny* tickets. Beware: foreign travelers are not eligible for discounts on domestic buses and trains. Eurail is not valid in Poland. Look for Wasteels tickets and Eurotrain passes, sold at Almatur and Orbis for discounts. Buy tickets in advance or wait in long lines. Stations are not announced and are often poorly marked. Theft frequently occurs on overnight trains; avoid night trains if possible, especially the heavily-touristed Kraków-Warsaw and Prague-Kraków.

BY BUS. The semi-state-run PKS buses are cheap and fast for short trips; there are *pośpieszny* (direct; in red) and *osobowy* (slow; in black). In the countryside, PKS markers (yellow steering wheels that look like upside-down Mercedes-Benz symbols) indicate stops. Buses have no luggage compartments. Polski Express, a private company, offers more luxurious service, but does not run to all cities. Ferries run throughout the Baltic area.

BY CAR AND BY TAXI. For taxis, either arrange the price before getting in (in Polish, if possible) or be sure the driver turns on the meter. The going rate is 1.50-3zł per km. Arrange cabs by phone if possible. Rental cars are readily available in Warsaw and Kraków. All but EU citizens must possess an international driver's license to drive in Poland.

BY BIKE AND BY THUMB. Bike rental is available in most cities and outdoor-oriented towns. Though legal, **hitchhiking** is rare and dangerous for foreigners. Hand-waving is the accepted sign. Let's Go does not recommend hitchhiking.

KEEPING IN TOUCH

PHONE CODES	**Country code:** 48. **International dialing prefix:** 00. From outside Poland, dial international dialing prefix (see inside back cover) + 48 + city code + local number. Within Poland, dial city code + local number, even when dialing inside the city.

EMAIL AND INTERNET. Internet access is readily available in most of Poland, costing from 5-15zł per hour.

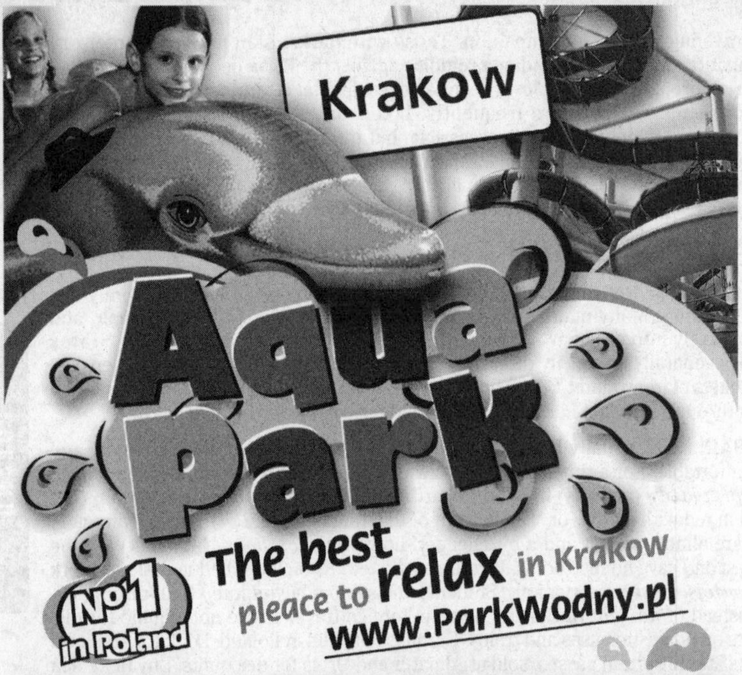
Krakow
Aqua Park
No1 in Poland
The best pleace to relax in Krakow
www.ParkWodny.pl

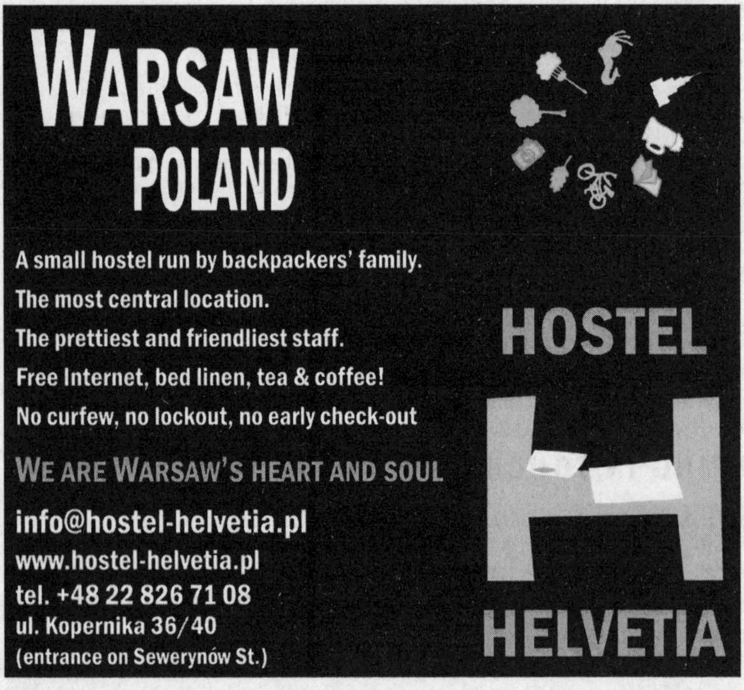
WARSAW
POLAND
A small hostel run by backpackers' family.
The most central location.
The prettiest and friendliest staff.
Free Internet, bed linen, tea & coffee!
No curfew, no lockout, no early check-out
WE ARE WARSAW'S HEART AND SOUL
info@hostel-helvetia.pl
www.hostel-helvetia.pl
tel. +48 22 826 71 08
ul. Kopernika 36/40
(entrance on Sewerynów St.)
HOSTEL
HELVETIA

TELEPHONE. Card telephones are standard. To make an international call, you can purchase a long distance card (Telegrosik is a popular brand) at many places, including grocery stores. To operate the phone, either start dialing the numbers you're given or insert the magnetic card first. International access numbers include: **ATT Direct** (☎00 800 111 111); **Australia Direct** (☎00 80 06 41); **Canada Direct** (☎080 01 11 41 18); **MCI** (☎00 800 111 2122); and **Sprint** (☎00 800 11 3115). Cell phones are very prevalent and receive incoming calls for free. They can be found at any media store (e.g. Empik). You can get a cheap one for 100zł or so. Make sure you get one "*na karte*" (for prepaid cards), and avoid "*abunament.*" SIM cards are also easy to obtain, and can be purchased at Empik for 10zł. Long-distance cards for cell phones are rare.

MAIL. Mail in Poland is admirably efficient. Airmail *(Poczta lotnicza)* takes two to five days to Western Europe and seven to 10 days to Australia, New Zealand, and the US. Surface mail is far less reliable. Mail can be received via **Poste Restante.** English services are not prevalent, though generally one can simply give hand over the letter or package and wait to be told the postage cost. Useful terms are *priorytet* (priority mail), *paczka* (package), *list* (pronounced "least"; letter). Envelopes should be addressed: First name, LAST NAME, POSTE RESTANTE, post office address, Postal Code, city, POLAND. Letters to the US or Canada cost about 3.20zł. To pick up Poste Restante, customers should show their passports.

POLAND

ACCOMMODATIONS AND CAMPING

POLAND	❶	❷	❸	❹	❺
ACCOMMODATIONS	under 50zł	51-65zł	66-80zł	81-120zł	over 120zł

Hostels *(schroniska młodzieżowe)* cost 30-60zł per night. Call at least a week ahead. **PTSM** is the national hostel organization. **University dorms** become budget housing in July and August; these are an especially good option in Kraków. The **Almatur** office in Warsaw arranges stays throughout Poland. **PTTK** runs **hotels** called Dom Turysty, which have multi-bed rooms and budget singles and doubles and generally cost 80-180zł. **Private rooms** *(wolne pokoje)* are available most places, but be careful what you agree to; they should only cost 20-60zł. **Homestays** can be a great way to meet locals; inquire at the tourist office. **Campsites** average 10-15zł per person or 20zł with a car. *Polska Mapa Campingów*, available at tourist offices, lists campsites. Almatur runs a number of sites in summer; ask them for a list. Camp only in official campsites or risk a night in jail.

FOOD AND DRINK

POLAND	❶	❷	❸	❹	❺
FOOD	under 8zł	8-18zł	19-30zł	31-45zł	over 45zł

Polish cuisine derives from French, Italian, and Slavic traditions. Meals begin with **soup,** while **main courses** include *gołąbki* (cabbage rolls with meat and rice), *kotlet schabowy* (pork cutlet), *naleśniki* (crepes filled with cheese or jam), and *pierogi* (dumplings). Following a **vegetarian** diet can be accomplished by sticking to dumplings and crepes, but **kosher** eating is next to impossible, as even most Jewish restaurants are not kosher. Poland offers a wealth of **beer, vodka,** and **spiced liquor.** *Żywiec* is the most popular beer. Even those who dislike beer might enjoy sweet **piwo z sokiem,** beer with raspberry syrup. *Wyborowa*, *Żytnia*, and *Polonez* are popular *wódka* (vodka) brands, while *Belweder* (Belvedere) is a major alcoholic export. *Żubrówka* vodka, also known as "Bison grass vodka," comes packaged with a strand of grass from the Białowieża forest. It's often mixed with apple juice *(z sokem jabłkowym)*. *Miód* (beer made with honey) and *krupnik* (mead) are old-fashioned favorites; as is *nalewka na porzeczce* (black currant vodka).

LIFE AND TIMES

HISTORY

THE NASCENT STATE. In AD 966, **Prince Mieszko I** accepted Christianity and unified the tribes the local tribes; his son, **Bolesław Chrobry** was crowned Poland's first king in 1025. The conglomeration of states was devastated by the Mongols in 1241, but it recovered by the 14th century. It then became more prosperous, particularly under **King Kazimierz III Wielki** (Casimir the Great). Under Casimir's tolerant reign, Poland became a refuge for Jews expelled from Western Europe.

PROSPERITY. After Casimir III's death in 1370, the **Teutonic Knights** took over East Prussia and cut off the Baltic Sea. To combat them, Polish nobles allied with Lithuania by marrying Casimir's only child, Princess Jadwiga, to the powerful Grand Duke of Lithuania, **Jogaila.** The duke was crowned King Władysław II Jagiełło of Poland. The new **Polish Commonwealth** lasted 187 years and defeated the Teutonic Order in 1410. In the 16th century, under King Zygmunt I Stary, the **Renaissance** reached Poland. The spirit of the age found fertile ground at Kraków's **Jagiellonian University** (founded in 1394), where **Copernicus** developed the revolutionary heliocentric model of the solar system.

DELUGE. Poland and Lithuania became stronger allies when the 1569 **Union of Lublin** established the **Polish-Lithuanian Commonwealth** with an elected king, a customs union, and a legislature. **King Zygmunt III Waza** moved the capital from Kraków to Warsaw; he and his successors embroiled the state in wars with Sweden, Turkey, and Muscovy throughout the 17th century. Poland only survived this devastating period, known as the **Deluge,** because of great military commanders like **Jan Zamoyski** and **Stanisław Żółkiewski.** Yet belligerent nobles, separate Polish and Lithuanian administrations, and a weakened monarch hobbled the Polish state.

THE PARTITIONS. Fearing Russian encroachment, nationalist Poles formed the **Confederation of Bar** in opposition to the weak Polish king in 1768. The resulting civil war threw Poland into anarchy. While France and Turkey aided the confederates, Russia backed the monarchy and supported Prussian ruler Frederick the Great's schemes to shrink Polish lands. In the 1772 **First Partition of Poland,** Austria, Prussia, and Russia each claimed a sizable chunk. In 1788, Polish noblemen produced a constitution calling for a parliamentary monarchy. Signed on May 3, 1791, it established Catholicism as the national religion, set up a plan for political elections, and provided for a standing army. Nervous at the prospect of a newly powerful state, Russia and Prussia incited the **Second Partition of Poland** (1793). The following year, **Tadeusz Kościuszko** led an uprising against Russian rule. He ended up in prison, and Poland was divided again in the **Third Partition** (1795). Poland would remain dominated for the next 123 years, while Russia attempted to crush all traces of Polish nationalism and identity. Poland did not regain independence until 1918, when **Marshal Józef Piłudski** repulsed the Red Army. A delegation led by **Roman Dmowski** worked **Polish statehood** into the Treaty of Versailles one year later.

WWII AND THE RISE OF COMMUNISM. The 1939 **Nazi-Soviet Non-Aggression Pact** secretly divided Poland between the two powers, rendering Poland's defense treaties obsolete. Nazi and Soviet forces attacked simultaneously, with Germany occupying the western two-thirds of the country and the USSR seizing the rest. **Concentration camps** were erected throughout Poland, and over six million Poles, including three million Jews, were killed during **WWII.** In April 1943, a group of approximately 750 Jews organized the **Warsaw Ghetto Uprising,** valiantly rebelling against the Nazis for almost a month before the revolt was brutally suppressed. In

1944, the Polish Resistance staged the similarly heroic—and doomed—**Warsaw Uprising,** after which the Nazis leveled the entire city. When Red tanks rolled in, they "liberated" the rubble of Warsaw. The first years of **communism** brought mass migrations and political crackdowns. The country grudgingly submitted, but **strikes** broke out in 1956, 1968, and 1970; all were violently quashed.

SOLIDARITY. In 1978 **Karol Wojtyła** became the first Polish pope, taking the name **John Paul II.** His visit to Poland the next year helped to unite Catholic Poles; it also served as an impetus for the 1980 birth of **Solidarność** (Solidarity), the first independent workers' union in Eastern Europe. Led by **Lech Wałęsa,** an electrician from Gdańsk, Solidarity's anti-Communist activities resulted in the declaration of **martial law** in 1981. Wałęsa was jailed, and was released only after the movement disbanded and outlawed by the government in 1982. In 1989, however, Poland spearheaded the peaceful fall of Soviet authority in Eastern Europe. **Tadeusz Mazowiecki** was sworn in as Eastern Europe's first non-Communist premier in 40 years. In December 1990, Wałęsa became the first elected president of post-Communist Poland. The new government cut subsidies, froze wages, and devalued the currency. This threw the economy into **recession,** creating widespread unemployment. Poland has since rebounded toward stability and prosperity.

TODAY

In 2003, Poland voted to accept its invitation to the **EU,** which it joined in May 2004. In October 2005, Poles elected former child-actor **Lech Kaczyński** as president. Parliamentary elections, also held that fall, took a surprising turn. An expected coalition between two right-leaning parties **Prawo i Sprawiedliwość (PiS),** or **Law and Justice, and Platforma Obywatelska (PO),** or Civic Platform, failed partly due to latent campaign resentments. The PiS ultimately defeated the PO, creating a minority government with Kazimierz Marcinkiewicz as prime minister, instead of the party leader. While the new government initially enjoyed strong public support, one blight was the forced resignation of Marcinkiewicz, following a rift with **Jarosław Kaczyński.** Kaczyński, who is Lech's identical twin and his co-star in the 1962 film *The Two Who Stole the Moon*, replaced Marcinkiewicz as Prime Minister. That's right—Poland is now run by identical twins who are former child actors.

PEOPLE AND CULTURE

DEMOGRAPHICS. The homogenization that set in following WWII continues: 97% of today's population is ethnically Polish. Officially recognized ethnic minorities include Germans, Ukrainians, Lithuanians, Jews, and Belarusians.

RELIGION. Poland is one of the most **Catholic** countries in the world and the Church enjoys immense respect and political power. Polish Catholicism was bolstered in 1978 by the election of the Polish Pope John Paul II—and again in 2005 by his death. **Protestant** groups are generally confined to German-border areas. Only traces of the rich pre-war **Jewish** culture are still apparent, with about 30,000 Jews compared to Poland's prewar population of 3,000,000.

LANGUAGE. Polish is a West Slavic language written in the Latin alphabet, and is closely related to **Czech** and **Slovak.** The language varies little across the country. The two exceptions are in the region of **Kaszuby,** where the distinctive Germanized dialect is sometimes classified as a separate language, and in **Karpaty,** known for highlander accents. In western Poland and Mazury, **German** is the most common foreign language, although many Poles in big cities, especially young people, speak **English.** Most can understand other Slavic languages if they're spoken slowly. The older generation may speak **Russian.** Finally, the English word "no" means "yes" in Polish. For a phrasebook and glossary, see **Appendix: Polish,** p. 799.

CUSTOMS AND ETIQUETTE. In restaurants, tell the server how much change you want and leave the rest as a **tip** (10-15%). In taxis, just leave the change. In any establishment, say *"dzień dobry"* (hello) as you enter, and *"do widzenia"* (goodbye) when you leave. Your waiter will often say *"smacznego"* when he serves you food; reply with *"dziękuję"* (thank you). But be careful: if you say *"dziękuję"* after receiving the bill, the waiter will assume you don't want change. When arriving as a guest, bring a female host an odd number of flowers. Smoking is often prohibited indoors. Always give up your seat to an elderly person, woman, or child.

LITERATURE

Poland's medieval texts, mostly religious works, were written in Latin. Self-taught 16th-century author **Mikołaj Rej** was the first to write consistently in Polish and is considered the father of Polish literature. The 18th-century partitions paved the way for **Romanticism,** which idealized the notion of statehood. The great poet **Adam Mickiewicz's** national epic *Pan Tadeusz* is considered a masterpiece from that era.

The pessimistic early 20th-century **Młoda Polska** (Young Poland) movement yielded **Stanisław Wyspiański's** drama *Wesele* (The Wedding) which addressed many of Poland's problems. In the years following WWII, many Polish writers published abroad. Nobel Laureate poet **Czesław Miłosz** penned *Zniewolony Umysł* (The Captive Mind), a commentary on Communist control of thought in the mid-1950s. In response to attempts to enforce **Socialist Realism,** the "thaw" brought an explosion of new work depicting Poland under communism. Later, the **Generation of '68** ushered in a wave of works addressing life at an historical crossroads. In 1996, the poet **Wisława Szymborska** received the Nobel Prize. Numerous contemporary Polish poets, among them **Zbigniew Herbert, Sławomir Mrożek, Adam Zagajewski,** and **Stanisław Barańczak,** have garnered praise at home and abroad. Journalist **Ryszard Kapuściński** and essayist **Adam Michnik** have also received critical acclaim.

HOLIDAYS AND FESTIVALS

Holidays: New Year's Day (Jan. 1); Easter Holiday (Mar. 24, 2008; Apr. 13, 2009); May Day (May 1); Constitution Day (May 3); Pentecost (May 11, 2008; May 31, 2009); Corpus Christi (May 22, 2008; June 11, 2009); Assumption Day (Aug. 15); All Saints' Day (Nov. 1); Independence Day (Nov. 11); Christmas (Dec. 25-26).

Festivals: Unsurprisingly, in highly Catholic Poland, many of the festivals revolve around religious holidays. A two-month carnival season precedes Lent. Easter is also a particularly large festival, during which revelers splash water on one another—sometimes by the bucketful. Uniquely Polish festivals include all-night bonfire merrymaking before St. John's Day in June, as well as an annual August folk festival in Kraków complete with entertainers and artisans peddling their goods.

WARSAW (WARSZAWA) ☎(0)22

Construction cranes dominate the Warsaw skyline and the smell of wet concrete fills the air of the busy, youthful Polish capital. Massive rebuilding is nothing new for a city that raised itself from rubble at the end of World War II, when two-thirds of the population was killed and 80% of the city was destroyed by the Nazis in revenge for the 1944 Warsaw Uprising. Having weathered the further blow of a half-century of communist rule, Warsaw has now sprung back to life as a dynamic center of business, politics, and culture. With Poland's recent accession into the European Union, Warsaw is transforming its culture and landscape at an even faster pace. Now is the time to visit this compelling and grossly underrated city.

INTERCITY TRANSPORTATION

Flights: Port Lotniczy Warszawa-Okęcie ("Terminal 1"), Żwirki i Wigury (info desk ☎650 4100, reservations 0 801 300 952). Take bus #175 to the city center (after 10:40pm, bus #611); buy tickets at the *Ruch* kiosk at the top of the escalator in the arrivals hall. Open M-F 5:30am-10:30pm. If you arrive past 10:30pm, it is possible to buy tickets from the bus driver for a 3zł surcharge (students 1.50zł). The **IT** (Informacja Turystyczna) office is at the top of the escalator in the arrivals hall (see **Tourist Offices,** p. 424). Open M-F 8am-8pm. Airlines include: **Air France,** Nowy Świat 64 (☎584 9900, open M-F 9am-4pm; at the airport ☎846 0303, open M-Sa 5am-7pm, Su 7:30am-7pm); **American Airlines,** al. Ujazdowskie 20 (☎625 3002; open M-F 9am-6pm); **British Airways,** Krucza 49, off al. Jerozolimskie (☎529 9000; open M-F 9am-5pm; at the airport ☎650 4520, open daily 6am-6pm); **Delta,** Królewska 11 (☎827 8461; open M-F 9am-5pm); **LOT,** al. Jerozolimskie 65/79 (from mobile ☎22 95 72, from landline 08 01 70 37 03; www.lot.com; open M-F 9am-7pm, Sa 9am-3pm) in the Marriott; **Lufthansa,** Sienna 39 (☎338 1300; www.lufthansa.pl; open M-F 9am-5pm).

Trains: There are 3 major train stations; the most convenient is **Warszawa Centralna** (Central Station), al. Jerozolimskie 54 (☎94 36; www.pkp.pl). Most trains also stop at **Warszawa Zachodnia** (Western Station), Towarowa 1, and **Warszawa Wschodnia** (Eastern Station), Lubelska 1, in Praga. Warszawa Centralna has cafes, a 24hr. **pharmacy, ATMs, pay phones, luggage storage,** and a **post office.** On the main level, international counters are to the left and domestic to the right. Write down where and when you want to go, along with *"Który peron?"* (Which platform?). Yellow signs list departures *(odjazdy);* white signs arrivals *(przyjazdy).* To: **Gdańsk** (4hr., 20 per day, 47-90zł); **Kraków** (2½-5hr., 30 per day, 47-89zł); **Łódź** (1½-2hr., 11 per day, 31zł); **Lublin** (2½hr., 17 per day, 35zł); **Poznań** (2½-3hr., 20 per day, 46-89zł); **Szczecin** (5½-6½hr., 8 per day, 53-114zł); **Toruń** (2½-5hr., 5 per day, 40zł); **Wrocław** (4½-6hr., 11 per day, 50-96zł); **Berlin, GER** (6hr., 6 per day, €29-45); **Budapest, HUN** (10-13hr., 1 per day, 280zł); **Prague, CZR** (9-12hr., 2 per day, 270-310zł); **St. Petersburg, RUS** (25-30hr., 1 per day, 300zł). Remember that many international trains originate outside Poland; for these trains you cannot make a reservation.

Buses: Both Polski Express and PKS buses run out of Warsaw.

Polski Express, al. Jana Pawła II (☎854 0285), in a kiosk next to Warszawa Centralna. Faster than PKS. Kiosk open daily 6:30am-10pm. To: **Białystok** (4hr., 1 per day, 41zł); **Częstochowa** (5½hr., 1 per day, 41zł); **Gdańsk** (6hr., 2 per day, 60zł); **Kraków** (8hr., 2 per day, 69zł); **Łódź** (2½hr., 7 per day, 25zł); **Lublin** (3hr., 7 per day, 41zł); **Toruń** (4hr., 9 per day, 50zł).

PKS Warszawa Zachodnia, al. Jerozolimskie 144 (☎822 4811, domestic info 03 00 30 01 30, from cell phones ☎720 8383; www.pks.warszawa.pl), connected by tunnels to the Warszawa Zachodnia train station. Cross to far side al. Jerozolimskie and take bus #127, 130, 508, or E5 to the center. Open daily 6am-9:30pm. To: **Białystok** (4hr., 3 per day, 27zł); **Częstochowa** (4½hr., 12 per day, 30zł); **Gdańsk** (5-7hr., 16 per day, 35-51zł); **Kazimierz Dolny** (3½hr., 3 per day, 22zł); **Kraków** (5½-7hr., 8 per day, 40zł); **Lublin** (3hr., 9 per day, 22-30zł); **Toruń** (4hr., 10 per day, 32zł); **Wrocław** (6½-8½hr., 3 per day, 43zł); **Kyiv, UKR** (14½hr., 1 per day, 155zł); **Vilnius, LIT** (9½hr., 3 per day, 115zł).

Centrum Podróży AURA, al. Jerozolimskie 144 (☎ 659 4785; www.aura.pl), at the Zachodnia station left of the entrance. Books international buses on various private bus lines. Number of connection a day depends on the day, the bus lines, and when you're booking. Open M-F 9am-6pm, Sa 9am-2pm. Also at al. Jerozolimskie 54 (☎628 6253), at Warszawa Centralna. International buses to: **Amsterdam, NED** (23hr., 2 per day, 209-279zł); **Geneva, SWI** (27hr., 2 per day, 269-320zł); **London, BRI** (27hr., 3 per day, 280-450zł); **Paris, FRA** (25hr., 1-3 per day, 220-334zł); **Prague, CZR** (28hr.; 3 per week; 115-145zł); **Rome, ITA** (28hr., 1 per day, 249-418zł). Most buses leave from Warszawa Stadion, the Palace of Culture, and others.

POLAND

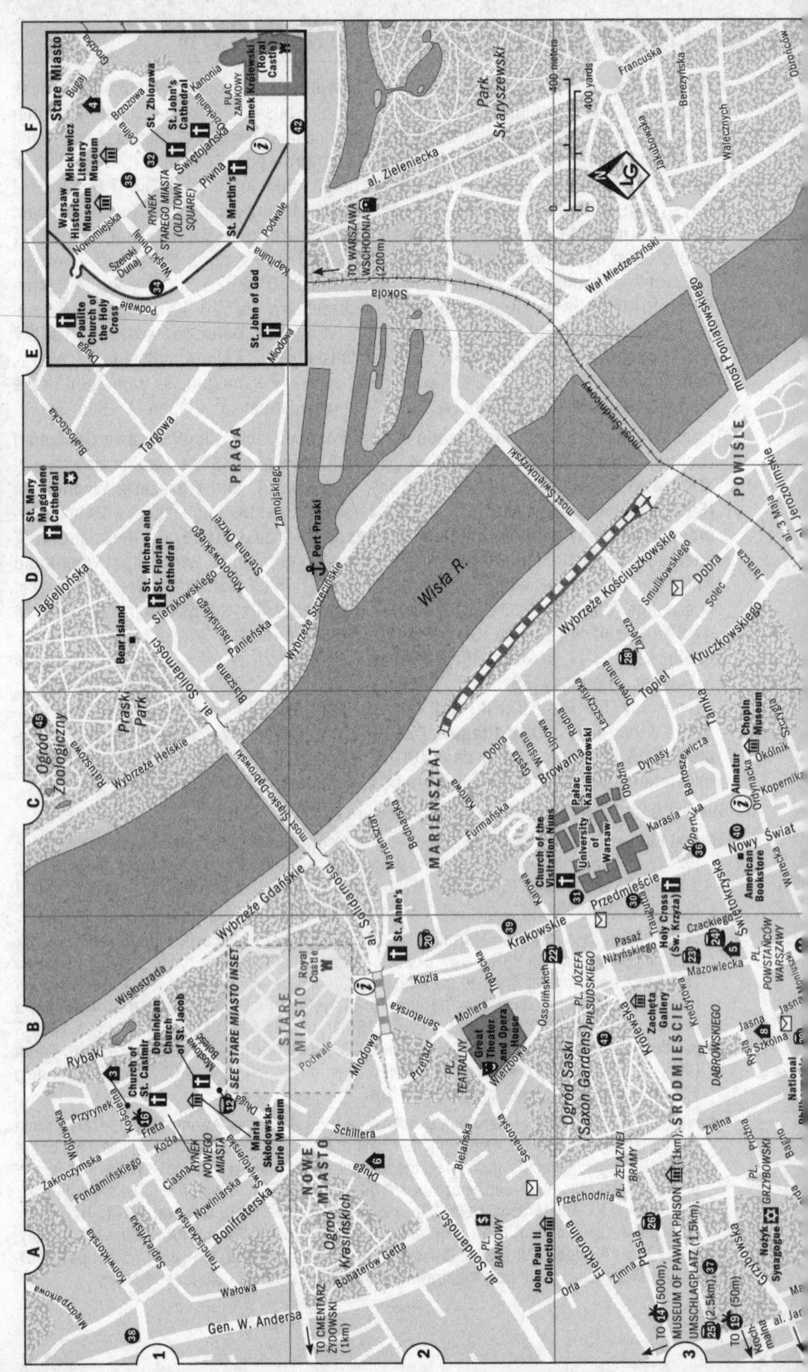

Stare Miasto
Warsaw Historical Museum
Mickiewicz Literary Museum
RYNEK STAREGO MIASTA (OLD TOWN SQUARE)
St. John's Cathedral
St. Martin's
Zamek Królewski (Royal Castle)
PLAC ZAMKOWY
Paulite Church of the Holy Cross
St. John of God
PRAGA
St. Mary Magdalene Cathedral
St. Michael and St. Florian Cathedral
Bear Island
Praski Park
Ogród Zoologiczny
Port Praski
Wisła R.
Park Skaryszewski
TO WARSZAWA WSCHODNIA (200m)
POWIŚLE
MARIENSZTAT
Pałac Kazimierzowski
University of Warsaw
Church of the Visitation Nuns
Chopin Museum
Almatur
American Bookstore
Nowy Świat
St. Anne's
STARE MIASTO
Royal Castle
SEE STARE MIASTO INSET
Dominican Church of St. Jacob
Church of St. Casimir
Maria Skłodowska-Curie Museum
RYNEK NOWEGO MIASTA
NOWE MIASTO
Ogród Krasińskich
PL. TEATRALNY
Great Theater and Opera House
Ogród Saski (Saxon Gardens)
PL. JÓZEFA PIŁSUDSKIEGO
Zachęta Gallery
Holy Cross (Św. Krzyża)
PL. POWSTAŃCÓW WARSZAWY
ŚRÓDMIEŚCIE
PL. DĄBROWSKIEGO
PL. BANKOWY
John Paul II Collection
PL. ŻELAZNEJ BRAMY
MUSEUM OF PAWIAK PRISON (1km)
UMSCHLAGPLATZ (2.5km)
PL. GRZYBOWSKI
Nożyk Synagogue
TO CMENTARZ ŻYDOWSKI (1km)
al. Solidarności
most Śląsko-Dąbrowski
most Świętokrzyski
most Średnicowy
most Poniatowskiego
Wybrzeże Gdańskie
Wybrzeże Kościuszkowskie
Wybrzeże Szczecińskie
Wybrzeże Helskie
Krakowskie Przedmieście
al. Zieleniecka
Wał Miedzeszyński
Targowa
Jagiellońska
Gen. W. Andersa
al. Jerozolimskie
400 meters
400 yards

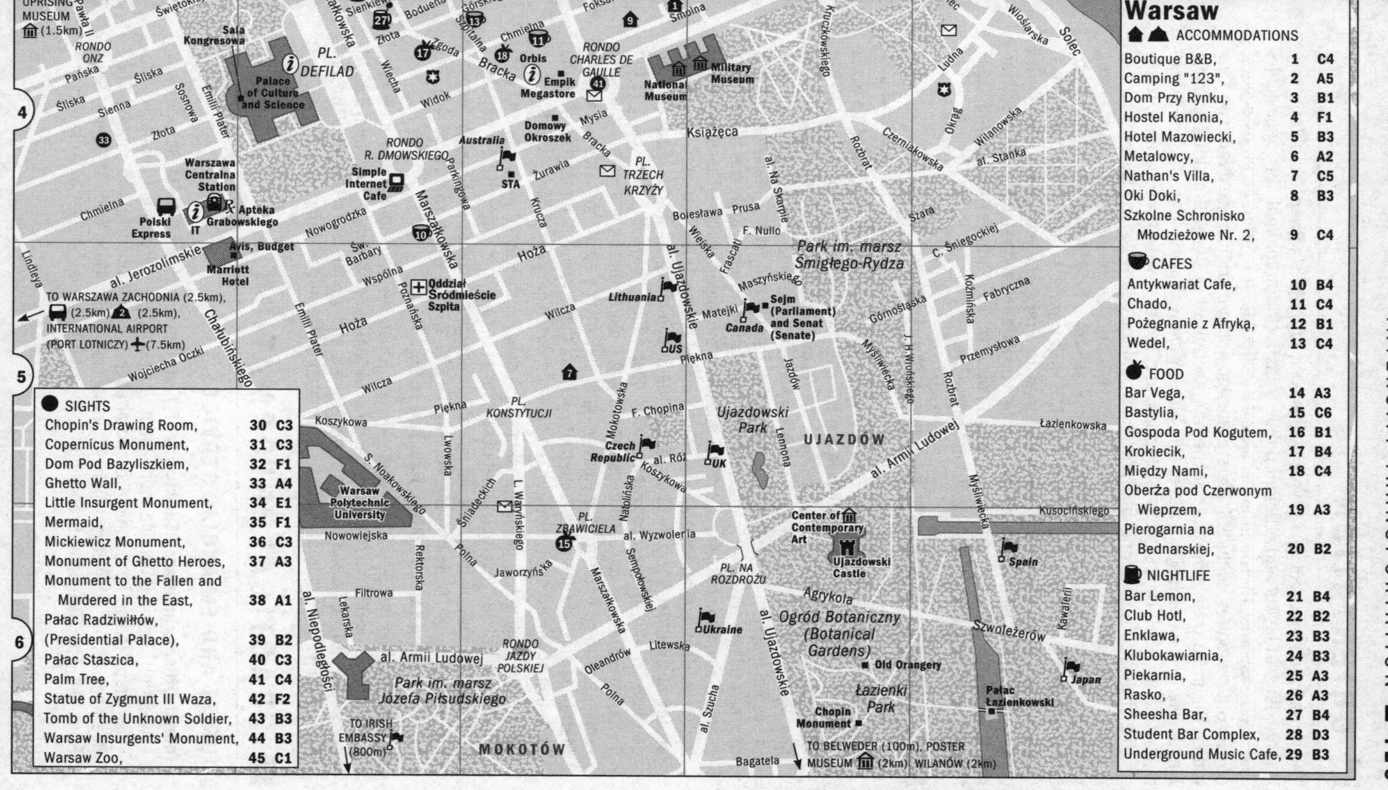
Warsaw
ACCOMMODATIONS
Boutique B&B, 1 C4
Camping "123", 2 A5
Dom Przy Rynku, 3 B1
Hostel Kanonia, 4 F1
Hotel Mazowiecki, 5 B3
Metalowcy, 6 A2
Nathan's Villa, 7 C5
Oki Doki, 8 B3
Szkolne Schronisko Młodzieżowe Nr. 2, 9 C4
CAFES
Antykwariat Cafe, 10 B4
Chado, 11 C4
Pożegnanie z Afryką, 12 B1
Wedel, 13 C4
FOOD
Bar Vega, 14 A3
Bastylia, 15 C6
Gospoda Pod Kogutem, 16 B1
Krokiecik, 17 B4
Między Nami, 18 C4
Oberża pod Czerwonym Wieprzem, 19 A3
Pierogarnia na Bednarskiej, 20 B2
NIGHTLIFE
Bar Lemon, 21 B4
Club Hotl, 22 B2
Enklawa, 23 B3
Klubokawiarnia, 24 B3
Piekarnia, 25 A3
Rasko, 26 A3
Sheesha Bar, 27 B4
Student Bar Complex, 28 D3
Underground Music Cafe, 29 B3
SIGHTS
Chopin's Drawing Room, 30 C3
Copernicus Monument, 31 C3
Dom Pod Bazyliszkiem, 32 F1
Ghetto Wall, 33 A4
Little Insurgent Monument, 34 E1
Mermaid, 35 F1
Mickiewicz Monument, 36 C3
Monument of Ghetto Heroes, 37 A3
Monument to the Fallen and Murdered in the East, 38 A1
Pałac Radziwiłłów, (Presidential Palace), 39 B2
Pałac Staszica, 40 C3
Palm Tree, 41 C4
Statue of Zygmunt III Waza, 42 F2
Tomb of the Unknown Soldier, 43 B3
Warsaw Insurgents' Monument, 44 B3
Warsaw Zoo, 45 C1
UPRISING MUSEUM (1.5km)
TO WARSZAWA ZACHODNIA (2.5km), (2.5km) (2.5km), INTERNATIONAL AIRPORT (PORT LOTNICZY) (7.5km)
TO IRISH EMBASSY (800m)
TO BELWEDER (100m), POSTER MUSEUM (2km) WILANÓW (2km)
Palace of Culture and Science
Warsaw Polytechnic University
Ujazdowski Park
Park im. marsz Śmigłego-Rydza
Park im. marsz Józefa Piłsudskiego
Ogród Botaniczny (Botanical Gardens)
Łazienki Park
UJAZDÓW
MOKOTÓW
POLAND

ORIENTATION

The most prominent section of Warsaw lies west of the **Wisła River.** Though the city is large, its grid layout and efficient public transportation make it very accessible. The main east-west thoroughfare is **aleja Jerozolimskie.** It is intersected by several north-south avenues, including **Marszałkowska,** a major tram route. **Warszawa Centralna,** the main train station, is at the intersection of al. Jerozolimskie and **aleja Jana Pawła II,** the north-south street one block west of Marsza kowska. The northern boundary of pl. Defilad is **Świętokrzyska,** another east-west thoroughfare. Intersecting al. Jerozolimskie one city block east of Marsza kowska and the city center, the **Trakt Królewski** (Royal Way) takes different names as it runs north-south. Going north it first becomes **Nowy Świat** and then **Krakowskie Przedmieście** as it leads into **Stare Miasto** (Old Town; just north of al. Solidarności overlooking the Wisła). Going south, the road becomes **aleja Ujazdowskie. Praga,** the part of the city on the east bank of the Wisła, is accessible by tram via **aleja Jerozolimskie** and **aleja Solidarności.** In Praga, the most trafficked north-south thoroughfares are **Targowa,** near the zoo, and **Francuska,** south of al. Jerozolimskie.

LOCAL TRANSPORTATION

Public Transportation: (info line ☎94 84; www.ztm.waw.pl). Warsaw's public transit is excellent. Daytime **trams** and **buses** 2.40zł, with ISIC 1.25zł; day pass 7.20/3.70zł; weekly pass 26/12zł. Punch the ticket in the yellow machines on board or face a 120zł fine. Bus, tram, and subway lines share the same tickets, passes, and prices. It's wise to keep a supply of tickets because many corner stores and bright green *Ruch* booths that sell tickets are only open during the day; when drivers supply the tickets they charge a small commission. Bus #175 goes from the airport to Stare Miasto by way of Warszawa Centralna and Nowy Świat. Watch out for pickpockets. There are also 2 **sightseeing bus routes:** #180 (M-F) and #100 (Sa-Su). Purchase an all-day ticket and you can hop on and off the bus. **Night buses** cost double, have "N" prefixes, and run 11:30pm-5:30am. If you need to use one, ask at a tourist bureau or accommodation to explain how to order them, as without an order they won't stop at most stops. Warsaw's **Metro** has only one line going north-south; it is not that convenient for tourists. With the exception of limited night buses, urban transport buses run daily 4:30am-11pm.

Taxis: Overcharging is a problem; ask a Polish speaker to arrange pickup and to confirm the price. The government sets cab fare at 2zł per km; with privately run cabs, stated prices may be lower but the risk of overcharging is greater. It helps to keep an eye on the meter. State-run: **ME.RC. Taxi** (☎677 7777), **Wawa Taxi** (☎96 44). Privately run: **Euro Taxi** (☎96 62), **Halo Taxi** (☎96 23).

Car Rental: Avis (☎630 7316), at the Marriott. Open M-F 8am-8pm, Sa-Su 8am-4pm. Airport office (☎650 4870). Open daily 7am-11pm. From 340zł per day, from 1200zł per week. **Budget** (☎868 3336), at the Marriott and the airport (☎650 4052). From €77 per day. Open daily at the hostel 8am-4pm, at the airport 7am-10pm.

PRACTICAL INFORMATION

TOURIST AND FINANCIAL SERVICES

Tourist Offices: Informacji Turystyczna (IT), al. Jerozolimskie 54 (☎94 31; www.warsawtour.pl), inside Centralna train station. English-speaking staff is informative. Provides **maps** (some free, some 4zł) and arranges accommodations (no charge). Their free booklets list popular restaurants and special events. Open daily May-Sept. 8am-8pm; Oct.-Apr. 8am-6pm. **Branches:** Krakowskie Przedmieście 39. Open daily, same hours. In the airport, open daily, same hours. Pl. Zamkowy 1/13, outside the Stare Miasto. Open M-F 9am-6pm, Sa 10am-6pm, Su 11am-6pm.

Budget Travel: Almatur, Kopernika 23 (☎826 3512). Offers discounted plane and bus tickets. ISIC 69zł. Open M-F 9am-7pm, Sa 10am-3pm. AmEx/MC/V. **Orbis,** Bracka 16 (☎827 3857), entrance on al. Jerozolimskie. Sells plane, train, ferry, and international bus tickets. Open M-F 8am-6pm, Sa 9am-3pm. **Branch** at Świętokrzyska 23/25 (☎831 82 99; orbis.bis@pbp.com.pl). Open M-F 9am-6pm, Sa 10am-3pm. MC/V.

Embassies: Most are near al. Ujazdowskie. **Australia,** Nowogrodzka 11 (☎521 3444; fax 627 3500; ambasada@australia.pl). Open M-F 9am-1pm and 2-5pm. **Canada,** al. Matejki 1/5 (☎584 3100, fax 584 3192; wsaw@international.gc.ca). Open M-F 8:30am-4:30pm. Open M-F 8:30am-4:30pm. **Ireland,** Mysia 5 (☎849 6633, fax 849 8431; ambasada@irlandial.pl). Open M-F 9am-1pm. **UK,** al. Róż (☎311 0000). Open M-F 8:30am-4:30pm. **US,** ul. Piękna 12 (☎625 1401 or 504 2784; fax 504 2122). Open M, W, F 9am-noon; Tu and Th 9am-3pm.

Currency Exchange: Except at tourist sights, *kantory* (exchange booths) have the best rates for exchanging currency and traveler's checks. 24hr. **currency exchange** at Warszawa Centralna or at al. Jerozolimskie 61. Many 24hr. *kantory* offer worse rates at night. **Bank PKO SA,** pl. Bankowy 2 (☎521 84 40), in the blue glass skyscraper, or Grójecka 1/3 (☎59 88 28), in Hotel Sobieski, cashes AmEx/V **traveler's checks** for 1-2% commission and gives MC/V **cash advances.** All branches open M-F 8am-6pm, Sa 10am-2pm. 24hr. **ATMs,** called *bankomat,* accept Cirrus and Plus. **Branches** can be found in banks and stores. Try to stick to ATMs associated with major banks and chain stores: unfamiliar-looking ATMs have turned out to be fakes used for identity theft.

POLAND

LOCAL SERVICES

Luggage Storage (Kasa Bagażowa): At Warszawa Centralna train station. 5zł per item per day, plus 2.25zł per 50zł of declared value if you want insurance. To sidestep the language barrier and retain more control over your bag, choose a locker. Open 24hr.

English-Language Bookstores: American Bookstore (Księgarnia Amerykańska), Nowy Świat 61 (☎827 4852). Eclectic and pricey selection of fiction, history, and maps. Open M-Sa 10am-7pm, Su 10am-6pm. AmEx/MC/V. **Empik Megastore,** Nowy Świat 15-17 (☎627 0650). Great selection of maps. Those clerks who speak English have British flags on their nametags. Open M-Sa 9am-10pm, Su 11am-7pm.

GLBT Resources: Lambda, (☎628 5222; www.lambda.org.pl), in English and Polish. Open Tu-W 6-9pm, F 4-10pm. Other info can be found at the English-language site http://warsaw.gayguide.net. The GLBT scene in Warsaw is discreet and lacks wide-spread political support.

EMERGENCY AND COMMUNICATIONS

24hr. Pharmacy: Apteka Grabowskiego "21" (☎825 6986), upstairs at Warszawa Centralna train station. AmEx/MC/V.

Medical Services: Centrum Medyczyne LIM, al. Jerozolimskie 65/79, 9th fl. (24hr. **emergency line** ☎458 7000, 24hr. **ambulance** 430 3030; www.cm-lim.com.pl), at the Marriott. English-speaking doctors. Open M-F 7am-9pm, Sa 8am-4pm, Su 9am-6pm, Holidays 9am-1pm. **Branch** at Domaniewski 41 (☎458 7000). Open M-F 7am-9pm, Sa 8am-8pm. **Central Emergency Station,** Hoża 56 (☎999) has a 24hr. ambulance.

Telephones: Phones are at the post office, train station, and scattered throughout the city. All but very few accept only cards, available at the post office and many kiosks. Ask for a *karta telefoniczna.* Directory assistance ☎11 89 13.

Internet: Simple Internet Cafe, Marszałkowska 99/101 (☎628 3190), at the corner of al. Jerozolimskie, has English-speaking staff and good hourly rates. The largest Internet cafe in Warsaw. Rates vary from 1zł per hr. late at night to 4zł per hr. midday. Open 24hr. Internet cafes line the bowels of Centralna train station.

Post Office: Main branch, Świętokrzyska 31/33 (☎827 00 52). Take a number at the entrance. For stamps and letters push "D"; packages "F." For **Poste Restante,** inquire at window #42. Open 24hr. *Kantor* open daily 7am-10pm. Most other branches open 8am-8pm. **Postal Code:** 00 001.

ACCOMMODATIONS

Warsaw accommodations are improving rapidly, but demand still exceeds supply, so reserve in advance, especially on weekends in high season (July and Aug.). Conveniently located mid-range hotels are particularly hard to come by. The tourist office **(IT)** can get you a **university dorm** ❶ (25-30zł) if you're traveling between July and September. They also maintain a list of lodgings, including **private rooms.**

POLAND

HOSTELS

Oki Doki, pl. Dąbrowskiego 3 (☎826 5112; www.okidoki.pl). From pl. Defilad, head 1 block east on Świętokrzyska and take a left; the sign will point you to this chic and artistic hostel. The friendly staff serve beer (5zł) and breakfast (10zł) in the dining room, which doubles as a bar (open until 1am). Bike rental 30zł per day, 6zł per hr. Laundry 10zł. Free Internet. Reception 24hr. Check-in 3pm. Check-out 11am. Reserve ahead. May-Aug. dorms 45-60zł; singles 110zł; doubles 135zł, with baths 185zł. Sept.-Apr. prices tend to increase by around 5zł. 5MC/V. ❶

Nathan's Villa, Piękna 24/26 (☎05 09 35 84 87; www.nathansvilla.com). From pl. Defilad, take any tram south on Marszałkowska to pl. Konstytucji. Go left on Piękna; the hostel is on the left. Though guests have been known to pass out on the lawn of this relentlessly hard-partying hostel, the rooms gleam with bright colors and brand-new furniture. Staff will be happy to point you to clubs and cheap places to eat (many of which offer discounts for Nathan's customers). Breakfast included. Free laundry. Free Internet. Reception 24hr. Flexible check-out. Dorms 45-60zł; rooms 120-140zł. MC/V. ❶

Hostel Kanonia, ul. Jezuicka 2 (☎635 0676; www.kanonia.pl). Tucked into an alley right in the thick of Stare Miasto, this hostel's cheery yellow paint and gleaming wood trim soften the spartan rooms. Kitchen. Breakfast 10zł. Free Internet. Check-in noon. Check-out 10am. Dorms 45-60zł; doubles 150zł. ISIC discount. Cash only. ❶

Dom Przy Rynku, Rynek Nowego Miasta 4 (☎831 5033; www.cityhostel.net). Take bus #175 from pl. Defilad to Franciszkańska. Turn right on Franciszkańska, then right into the main square; it's downhill on the left. This school for disadvantaged children supports itself by renting rooms in the summer. Reception 24hr. Flexible lockout 10am-4pm. Open July to late Aug. daily; Sept.-May F-Su. 2- to 4-bed dorms 40zł. Cash only. ❷

Szkolne Schronisko Młodzieżowe nr. 2, Smolna 30 (☎827 8952), 2 blocks up Smolna from Nowy Świat. From Centralna Station, take any tram east on al. Jerozolimskie and get off at Rondo Charles de Gaulle. This sunny hostel maintains small but well-kept rooms, and the central location can't be beat. Large kitchen. A/C. Free lockers and linen. Reception 24hr, but doors are locked midnight-6am. Lockout 10am-4pm. Curfew midnight. Dorms 36zł; singles 65zł. Cash only. ❶

HOTELS AND CAMPING

Boutique Bed and Breakfast, Smolna 14/7 (☎829 4801). From the center, take any tram east on al. Jerozolimskie to Rondo Charles de Gaulle. Smolna is a half block north on Nowy Świat. Enter through the unmarked double-doors, then the first door on your left, or dial 72 and someone will let you in; reception is on the 3rd floor. With homey touches like fresh flowers, sophisticated Boutique B&B is like your rich aunt's apartment in the city. Rooms have separate entry from the stairwell. Shared kitchen, dining room, and office. Breakfast included. Rooms from 70zł. MC/V. ❸

Hotel Mazowiecki, Mazowiecka 10 (☎827 2365; www.mazowiecki.com.pl), just north of Świętokrzyska between Marszałkowska and Nowy Świat. The curtains are faded and the rooms smell vaguely of cigarette smoke, but moderate prices and a location in the middle of the hottest nightlife in town recommend Mazowiecki. Book ahead in summer. Breakfast included. Check-in 2pm. Check-out noon. Singles 150zł, with bath 198zł; doubles 200/248zł. Weekend discount 20%. AmEx/MC/V. ❺

Metalowcy, Długa 299 (☎635 5460; www.metalowcy.emeteor.pl). The cheapest hotel rooms in Warsaw, and you get what you pay for. An incongruously grand marble staircase takes you to cramped but clean rooms with peeling paint, creaky furniture, and rotary-dial phones that appear to pre-date Solidarity. Check out 10am, check-in from 2pm. Singles 70zł, with bath 86zł. Doubles with bath 128zł, Quads with bath 256zł. ❸

Camping "123," Bitwy Warszawskiej 15/17 (☎822 9121). From Warszawa Centralna, take bus #127, 130, 508, or 517 to Zachodnia bus station. Cross to the far side of al. Jerozolimskie and take the pedestrian path west to Bitwy Warszawskiej; turn left. The campground is on the right. Tranquil Camping "123" is close to the center and provides reliable service but few amenities. Guarded 24hr. Open May-Sept. 12zł per person, 14zł per tent, 55-65zł for camper spots with electricity (labeled "stream.") Spartan 4-person bungalows: singles 40zł; doubles 70zł; triples 100zł; quads 120zł. Am/Ex/MC/V. ❶

POLAND

FOOD

The local street food of choice is the **kebab,** a pita stuffed with spicy meat, cabbage, and pickles (5-10zł). Excellent versions can be had at **Kebab Bar,** Nowy Świat 31, and **Kebab Tureck,** Marszałkowska 81. Food poisoning is a reality of the Warsaw kebab scene: try to stick to stands that draw crowds of non-intoxicated locals. **Bakery stands** offer delicious treats. In spring and summer, farmers sell **fresh produce** on Warsaw streets: the best is found in Praga. Grocery stores **MarcPol** on pl. Defilad, and **Albert** at al. Jerozolimskie 56, facing Marszałkowska, are open until 10pm.

Gospoda Pod Kogutem, Freta 48 (☎635 8282; www.gospodapodkogutem.pl). A rare find in touristy Stare Miasto: generous portions of delectable local food. Enjoy the barn-themed interior or sit outside on Freta. The place to try something shamelessly traditional, like Polish-style pig's knuckle (*golonka*; 21zł) or *smalec*, surprisingly tasty fried bits of lard. Entrees 15-40zł. Open M noon-midnight, Tu-Su 11am-midnight. MC/V. ❷

Oberża pod Czerwonym Wieprzem (Żelazna 68, ☎850 3144; www.czerwonywieprz.pl). Waitresses in bright red ties welcome you to this beautifully capitalist exploitation of Poland's communist past, with a gigantic mural of Lenin along one wall and Soviet flags all over. Each part of the menu is split into sections with cheaper food "for the proletariat" (13-22zł) and more expensive dishes "for dignitaries and the bourgeoisie" (26-44zł). Other touches include dishes such as Mao's Chicken (24zł) and Fidel's Cigar (rolls of ground meat in "Cuban" sauce; 23zł). M-Su 11am-midnight. MC/V. ❷

Bar Vega, al. Jana Pawła II 36c (☎652 2754), near the former Ghetto. Secluded from the bustle of al. Jana Pawła II street vendors, Bar Vega serves a full vegetarian Indian meal for the price of a coffee on Nowy Świat (small plate 8zł, big plate 12zł). The inexplicably cheap cafeteria-style offerings allow you to sample a variety of *pakoras* and *koftas*. Funds a nonprofit for homeless children. Open daily noon-8pm. Cash only. ❷

Krokiecik, Zgoda 1 (☎827 3037). When a constant diet of *pierogi* and kebab have got you down, come to Krokiecik and try *krokiety*, Polish-style pancake wraps (6-7zł). Popular among area businessmen. More traditional main dishes (8-19zł), a chocolate *naleśnik* dessert 5zł. Open M-Sa 9am-9pm, Su 10am-7pm. Cash only. ❷

MILK IT FOR ALL IT'S WORTH

In the Soviet era, locals flocked to Warsaw's subsidized cafeteria-style milk bars out of pure necessity, and they remain the cheapest meal in town. Named because of their dairy-heavy offerings, these establishments still receive large subsidies, making it cheaper to buy home-style cooking here than to cook it at home. Patrons range from the homeless or elderly to students and young professionals looking for a quick, cheap meal. There are between 10 and 20 milk bars in Warsaw, and the number will continue to fall along with subsidy-levels.

Milk bars can be a challenge to those who don't speak Polish. First, choose your meal from the big board: some form of kotlet, or meat cutlet, is a safe bet, with zemniaki (potatoes) and perhaps a surówka (salad). Then tell the cashier what you want, pay, and get a receipt. Give the receipt to the cooks at the next window and they'll get you what you want.

***Bar Uniwersytet,** Krakowskie Przedmiescie 20/22, has an authentic camp-like interior, long lines, and extremely traditional dishes. Bar Mleczny Familijny, ul. Nowy Swiat 39, allows you to enjoy beautiful Nowy Swiat for cheap. Bar Kubus, Ordynacka 13, serves great soups and has a friendly staff. Zlota Kurka, Marszalkowska 55/73, is a favorite among students at the nearby Polytechnic.*

Między Nami, Bracka 20 (☎828 5417; www.miedzynami-cafe.com). Packed art-house crowd favorite serves a rotating menu of light pastas, traditional soups, and seasonal salads. A hotbed of photography and fashion, this cafe-pub publishes its own in-house magazine. Friendly, attentive, English-speaking staff. Homemade cake (8zł) is excellent. Entrees 15-25zł. Open M-Th 10am-10pm, F-Sa 10am-midnight, Su 4-11pm. MC/V. ❷

Pierogarnia na Bednarskiej, ul. Bednarka 28/30 (☎828 0392), on a side street west of ul. Krakówscie Przedmiescie. Locals get their *pierogi* fix at this tiny, pleasant, and fragrant shop; you don't even have to wait, as they keep new *pierogi* boiling constantly. 3 pierogi 6zł, 6 *pierogi* 12zł. Open daily 11am-9pm. Cash only. ❶

Bastylia, pl. Zbawieciela 3/5, enter from around the corner on Mokotowska (☎825 0157). Excellent French-style crepes (9.50-13.50zł) are served under a picture of the Eiffel tower at this crêperie. Sidewalk seating available. Gay-friendly, with a helpful staff that will point you to gay clubs and other resources. Open daily 8am-10pm. MC/V. ❷

CAFES

Poland's is more of a tea than a coffee culture, but the cafes of the capital city offer excellent takes on both drinks, as well as exquisite hot chocolate. The local equivalent of Starbucks is **Coffee Heaven**, with locations wherever you look in the city's center, including one on Nowy Świat 46.

Pożegnanie z Afryką (Out of Africa), Freta 4/6. This Polish cafe chain brews consistently incredible coffee (8-15zł). Worth the wait for 1 of 4 tables in the candlelit interior. In warm weather, enjoy Stare Miasto sidewalk seating and iced coffee (8zł). Branches throughout the city. Open daily 11am-9pm. Cash only.

Antykwariat Cafe, Żurawia 45 (☎629 9929). Antykwariat ("Antiquarian") recalls an inviting old personal library, with its sloppily shelved books, antique piano, and engravings of pre-war Warsaw. The cafe mesmerizes patrons with delicate cups of coffee (5-17zł) and many varieties of tea (5zł) served with a wrapped chocolate. Also serves beer, wine, and desserts. Plush wicker chairs and outdoor seating invite lingering. Open M-F 11am-11pm, Sa-Su 1-11pm. Cash only.

Wedel, Szpitalna 17 (☎827 2916). The Emil Wedel house, built in 1893 for the Polish chocolate tycoon, was one of the few buildings to survive WWII, and its 1st fl. now houses an elegant dessert cafe. Delicious hot chocolate (8zł).The adjacent **Wedel Chocolate** company store has a whimsical diorama of elves making chocolate. Open M-Sa 10am-10pm, Su noon-5pm. AmEx/MC/V.

Chado, ul. Chmielna 11 (☎828 5374). Chado lives up to its slogan, "nie tylko herbata" ("not only tea") by offering coffee (from 7zł) and other beverages. But its tea (from 12zł) is definitely what sets Chado apart. Its menu features 15 pages of different varieties and presentations of exotic teas, stored in the tins upon tins lining the walls. Open 10pm-late (often past midnight). AmEx/MC/V.

SIGHTS

At first glance, Warsaw offers three strains of architecture: impeccably restored historical facades, Soviet-era concrete blocks, and gleaming modern skyscrapers. But Warsaw holds out its most compelling sights, ranging from cutting-edge art installations in a rebuilt castle to the sobering stillness of the Jewish Cemetery, to those who delve beneath the surface. The tourist bus routes #100 and 180 are convenient; they begin at pl. Zamkowy and run along pl. Teatralny, Marszałkowska, al. Ujazdowskie, Łazienki Park, and back up the Royal Way, then loop through Praga before returning to pl. Zamkowy.

STARE AND NOWE MIASTO

Warsaw's reconstruction shows its finest face in the cobblestone streets and colorful facades of Stare Miasto (Old Town), so expertly restored that it is the only complete reconstruction to be recognized as a UNESCO World Heritage Site. The brick red Royal Castle anchors the neighborhood, and the reconstructed fortifications of the Barbican mark the old city walls. Both the Stare Miasto and its little cousin the Nowe Miasto (see below) were rebuilt using large fragments of the original buildings. For many, the rubble from which they were made serves as a reminder of the Polish blood shed in the Warsaw Uprising, when nearly all of these buildings were destroyed. *(Take bus #175 or E3 from the center to Miodowa.)*

ST. JOHN'S CATHEDRAL. Decimated in the 1944 Uprising, Warsaw's oldest church (Katedra Św. Jana) was rebuilt in the Vistulan Gothic style and features white walls trimmed with brick vaulting. Its **crypts** hold the dukes of Mazovia and such famous Poles as Nobel Laureate Henryk Sienkiewicz and Gabriel Narutowicz, the first president of independent Poland. A side altar contains the tomb of Cardinal Stefan Wyszyński, primate of Poland from 1948 to 1981. *(On Świętojańska and pl. Zamkowy. Open daily 10am-1pm and 3-5:30pm. Entrance to crypts 1zł.)*

OLD TOWN SQUARE. A stone plaque at the entrance commemorates the most impressive reconstruction of Stare Miasto, the reconstituted square (Rynek Starego Miasta), finished in 1954. The square bustles with sidewalk cafes and souvenir peddlers, and the statue of the Warsaw **Mermaid** (Warszawa Syrenka) still marks the center. According to legend, a merchant kidnapped the mermaid from the Wisła River, but local fishermen rescued her. In return, she swore to defend the city and now protects Warsaw with her shield and raised sword. On the square's southeast side at #1/3, Dom Pod Bazyliszkiem immortalizes the Stare Miasto **Basilisk,** a reptile famous for its fatal breath and deadly stare. *(On Świętojańska.)*

NOWE MIASTO. The Barbican opens onto Freta, the edge of Nowe Miasto. The "New Town," established at the beginning of the 15th century, had its own separate town hall until 1791. Mostly destroyed during WWII, its 18th- and 19th-century buildings have enjoyed an expensive facelift. The great physicist and chemist **Maria Skłodowska-Curie,** winner of two Nobel prizes, was born at Freta 16 in 1867 (p. 434). Freta leads to New Town Square (Rynek Nowego Miasta), a smaller brother of the Old Town Square, and to the Baroque dome of the **Church St. Casimir,** founded in 1688 to commemorate King Jan III Sobieski's 1683 victory over the Turks. *(www.sakramentki.opoka.org.pl. Open daily dawn-dusk. Free.)*

TRAKT KRÓLEWSKI

The 4km Trakt Królewski (Royal Way) begins on pl. Zamkowy at the entrance to Stare Miasto. From Krakowskie Przedmieście, Trakt Królewski becomes Nowy Świat (New World Street). The Royal Way, so named because it leads to Poland's former capital of Kraków, is lined with palaces, churches, and convents built when the royal family moved to Warsaw. The name New World Street dates to the mid-17th century, when a new settlement of working-class people was started here. It was not until the 18th century that the aristocracy started moving in and sprucing the place up with ornate manors and residences.

UNIVERSITY OF WARSAW. Continue down Krakowskie Przedmieście, and the main entrance to the **University of Warsaw** (Uniwersytet Warszawski) will be on your left. Founded in 1816 on Enlightenment principles, the university was closed by Russian Nicholas I in 1831 as punishment for its contribution to the November Uprising of Polish military cadets against the Russian occupiers. Professors taught in private apartments during the WWII bombings, their courses' frequent changes of location giving the University the nickname "Flying University." Duck in the gate to find a courtyard surrounded by elegant Enlightenment edifices.

POLAND

HEART AND SOUL: HOLY CROSS CHURCH (KOŚCIÓŁ ŚW. KRZYŻA). Back outside, heading along the Trakt Królewski, you'll find on your right the Holy Cross Church, fronted by a giant sculpture of Jesus carrying the cross. Inside you'll find Chopin's heart—literally. Although the composer died abroad at 39, his heart belongs to Poland: it's in an urn in the left nave. Nobel Prize-winning writer Władysław Reymont left his here, too. *(Krakowskie Przedmieście 3. Open daily dawn-dusk.)*

ŁAZIENKI PARK

The palaces and their park were built in the 18th century for Stanisław August Poniatowski, Poland's last king, but peacocks and schoolchildren now rule the meandering paths. Rose bushes and benches ring the **Chopin Monument.** A nearby amphitheater, its stage across a bridge on an island in the center of the park's lake, hosts free **Chopin concerts** performed by acclaimed Polish and international musicians. (Open mid-May to Sept. Su noon and 4pm). The Neoclassical palace outbuildings host rotating exhibits of contemporary Polish art. The tranquil 1822 **Temple of Diana** (Świątynia Diany) perches above a wooded pond. *(Park borders al. Ujazdowskie and Trakt Królewski. Take bus #100 from Marszalkowska, #116, 180, or 195 from Nowy Świat, or #119 from the pl. Defilad to Bagatela. Open daily dawn-dusk.)*

PAŁAC ŁAZIENKOWSKI. Farther into the park is the striking Neoclassical Pałac Łazienkowski, also called the **Palace on Water** (Pałac na Wodzie) or **Palace on the Isle** (Pałac na Wyspie). Surrounded by water, peacocks, and leafy boughs, this breathtaking building was the joint creation of King Stanisław August and his architect Dominik Merlini. Displays of period furnishings and views of the park are concentrated in this small space. Before entering, put protective slippers over your shoes and check any bags (storage available to the left of the entry). *(Open Tu-Su 8:30am-3:30pm. 12zł, students 9zł. Guided tour in English 80zł.)*

OTHER SIGHTS. Warsaw University's enchanting **Botanical Garden** (Ogród Botaniczny) welcomes visitors with a fragrant path lined by lilac trees. Student gardeners tend to this perpetual work-in-progress, which exhibits native and foreign plants. Highlights include the butterfly garden, alpine garden, and medicinal plants. The nearby Neoclassical **observatory** (Gmach Obserwatorium) was rebuilt in 1944 and shadows more exotic greenhouses. *(☎553 05 11. Open Apr.-Aug. M-F 9am-8pm, Sa-Su 10am-8pm; Sept. daily 10am-7pm; Oct. daily 10am-6pm. 4.50zł, students 2.50zł.)* **Belweder,** an 1818 palace just south of Łazienki, was built for the Russian tsar and was Józef Piłsudski's home. Now a residence for visiting heads of state, Belweder is closed to the public. Just north of Łazienki along al. Ujazdowskie is the

Ujazdowski Castle (see **Museums,** p. 433), built in 1637 for King Zygmunt III Waza. Continue toward the center along al. Ujazdowskie and go right on Matejki to reach the **Sejm** (Parliament) and the **Senate building.** *(Both closed to the public.)*

THE FORMER WARSAW GHETTO

The term "ghetto" refers to the Jewish district sealed off from 1939-45; the modern Muranów (walled) neighborhood, north of the center, displays few vestiges of the nearly 400,000 Jews who comprised one-third of the city's pre-war population. During WWII the Ghetto shrank continually as its residents were deported to death camps, and parts of it, including the **Nożyk Synagogue,** were "re-Aryanized" long before the war's end. The Nazis razed the entire area after the 1943 Ghetto Uprising, and Soviet-era concrete block housing now fills much of it. In the former Ghetto, absence, emptiness, and ruin tell the story for the silenced.

JEWISH CEMETERY. A haunting testament to the near-total annihilation of Jewish Warsaw is this final resting place of 250,000 Polish Jews. The 19th-century walled cemetery (Cmentarz Żydowski) lies in sad disrepair, as most of those buried here have no descendants to care for their graves. Notable figures buried here include Rabbi Szlomo Lipszyc (d. 1839), actress Ester Kamińska (d. 1925), and Ludwik Zamenhof (d. 1917), the creator of Esperanto. *(Okopowa 49/51, in the western corner of Muranów. From the center of town, follow al. Jana Pawła II north to Anielewicza and take a left. Or, take tram #22 from the center to Cm. Żydowski. ☎838 2622; www.jewishcem.waw.pl. Open Apr.-Oct. M-Th 10am-5pm, F 9am-1pm, Su 11am-4pm; Nov.-Mar. closes at dusk. Closed Jewish holidays. 4zł.)* Nearby, the **Monument of Common Martyrdom of Jews and Poles,** Gibalskiego 2, marks the site of mass graves from WWII. *(Follow the street south of the cemetery to Gibalskiego, then turn left before the Nissenbaum building.)*

NOŻYK SYNAGOGUE. This restored synagogue is a living artifact of Warsaw's Jewish life. Used as a stable by the Nazis, it was the only synagogue to survive the war. The delicate white interior closely approximates the original decor. Today it serves as the spiritual home for 500 observant Jews who remain in Warsaw and also hosts meetings for Jewish student groups. There's a small kosher store in the basement. Men must wear traditional head-covering provided at the entrance; tight security includes a mandatory bag search. *(Twarda 6. From the center, take any tram along al. Jana Pawła II to Rondo Onz. Turn right on Twarda and left at the Jewish Theater, Teatr Żydowski. ☎620 1037. Open M-F and Su, Apr.-Oct. 10am-5pm; Nov.-Feb. 10am-3pm. Closed Jewish holidays. 5zł. Morning and evening prayer daily.)*

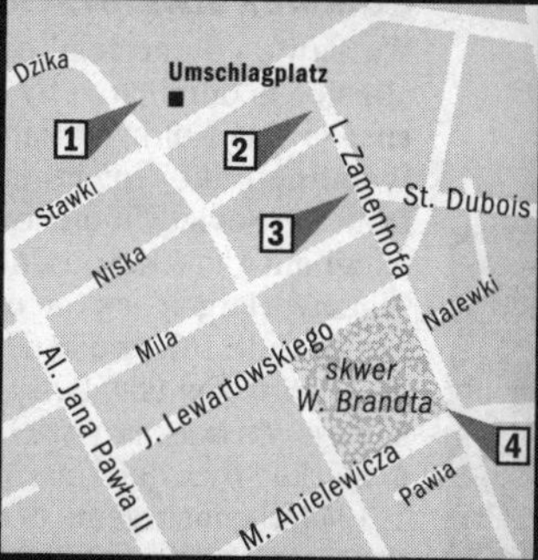

THE GHETTO UPRISING

The monuments that mark some of the most important sites of the heroic Warsaw Ghetto Uprising of 1943 are small and easily missed:

1 In 1942 and 1943, the Nazis gathered Jews from the Warsaw Ghetto at the **Umschlagplatz** (Trans-Shipment Square) for transport to death camps. *(Corner of Dzika and Stawki.)*

2 A series of **black stone blocks** along Zamenhofa commemorates the leaders of the Ghetto Uprising.

3 At Mila 18, where a **command bunker** once housed the headquarters of ŻOB, the Jewish fighting organization, a small **monument** honors Mordechaj Anielewicz and Arie Wilner, the ŻOB leaders who committed suicide when the Nazis discovered the bunker.

4 On Zamenhofa between Lewartskiego and Anielewicza, the **Monument to the Heroes of the Ghetto** is carved from stone originally intended for a Third Reich victory monument.

GHETTO WALL. Early in the occupation of Warsaw, the Nazis built a wall around the entire neighborhood, confining the Jews to the Ghetto until the entire area was liquidated in 1943 following the uprising. A small section of the original Ghetto wall still stands between two buildings on Sienna and Złota, west of al. Jana Pawła II. *(Enter at Sienna 55; the wall is on the left.)*

COMMERCIAL DISTRICT

Warsaw's commercial district (next to the train station, southwest of Stare Miasto) is dominated by the 52-story Stalinist Gothic **Palace of Culture and Science** (Pałac Kultury i Nauki, PKiN), Poland's tallest structure. Nicknamed "The Wedding Cake" for its unattractive multi-tiered architecture, this 1955 "gift" from the Soviet Union now houses offices, exhibition facilities, theaters, and the excellent Cafe Kulturalna. The view from the observation deck is the best in Warsaw (largely, as the old Varsovian joke goes, because you can't see the Palace of Culture). *(☎656 6000. Open daily 9am-8pm. Observation deck on 33rd fl. 20zł, students 15zł; after 9pm 20zł.)* Below lies **pl. Defilad** (Parade Sq.), Europe's largest square. *(On Marszałkowska.)* **Warsaw Insurgents' Square** (pl. Powstańców Warszawy) is marked by a dark marble memorial barely elevated off the ground. On August 1, 1944, the insurgents of the Warsaw Uprising began their ill-fated battle against the Germans here. *(On Świętokrzyska, between Marszałkowska and Krakowskie Przedmieście.)* The new **Warsaw Uprising Monument,** composed of larger-than-life sized statues of rebels rising out of the streets, in on the corner of Długa and Bonifraterska Streets, in front of the intriguingly modern new **Supreme Court Building.** Interesting **neighborhood walks** include the daily **open-air market** on al. Jana Pawła II; the hillside **Mariensztat** neighborhood (between Stare Miasto and the University of Warsaw); and the **stores** along Chmielna and pedestrian Nowy Świat.

PRAGA

Cross the **Wisła River** to Warsaw's east bank and you will be rewarded with graceful parks, a gargantuan open-air market, and two of the most attractive churches in Warsaw. Often maligned as poorer and less safe than the rest of the city, Praga has become more fashionable in recent years, though many locals still recommend traveling there only in groups after dark. Settled in the seventh century and converted into a suburb of Warsaw in the 16th century, Praga survived WWII relatively intact. During the Warsaw Uprising, the Red Army stopped its westward advance in Praga and stood by as the Germans and Poles battled across the river: some buildings were looted and bombed, but Praga escaped utter annihilation.

ST. MARY MAGDALENE CATHEDRAL. This sumptuous Russian Orthodox Church, built in 1869, inspires awe in even the casual viewer. Bright frescoes and gold-framed icons adorn the walls, complementing the horizontal altar. The telltale onion domes hint at the pre-Soviet Russian presence in Warsaw. *(Al. Solidarności 52. From Russian Market, take tram #2, 8, 12, or 25 to intersection of Targowa and al. Solidarności: church is across the street on the left. ☎619 8467. Open M and Su 1-4pm, Tu-Sa 11am-3pm.)*

PRASKI PARK. Built on the ruins of Napoleonic fortifications, the park was completed in 1871 and spans 45 acres. The entrance to Praski Park contains the **Island of Bears,** or Bear Run, a manmade island on which bears have been kept since 1949. This tiny island opens onto al. Solidarności and is a mini-zoo in its own right. The bears may appear harmless, but they have been known to maul intruders. Let's Go does not recommend feeding or wrestling the bears. *(Enter on Floriańska, across the street from St. Michael and St. Florian Cathedral. Free.)*

WARSAW ZOO. Built in 1928, the zoo (Ogród Zoologiczny) originally bred many rare species, but the animals of Warsaw fared no better than its citizens, and the zoo was bombed during WWII. Surviving animals escaped, were eaten by desperate locals, or were sent to Germany. Zoo director Jan Zabinski used the grounds to hide Jews throughout the war. Today, popular sections include the petting zoo, aquarium, cougars, monkeys, and reptiles. You won't find any English captions, but zoo maps with pictures instead of words are convenient for children and foreigners alike. *(Ratuszowa 1/3. ☎619 4041. Open daily 9am-4pm. 12zl, students 6zl.)*

MUSEUMS

While some of Warsaw's museums are dreary leftovers from Communist times, with unexplained displays and little attempt made to interest visitors, a new generation of curators are revamping Warsaw's most prominent museums along the lines of Western museums, with new, more engaging means of presenting materials and multimedia exhibits. Visitors to Warsaw's museums should enjoy this opportunity to see the city in the process of reconsidering its approach to the past.

WARSAW UPRISING MUSEUM. This new museum has won praise as one of Poland's finest. Recorded testimonials, artifacts, letters, and interactive images of the tragic 1944 Uprising are arranged in themed rooms that include full-scale replica bunkers and ruins haunted by the sound of approaching bombs emanating from hidden speakers. No natural light filters through, completing the experience of this jagged and disorienting landscape. Wander through dark tunnels guarded by heavy rubber flaps to find the "red room," dedicated to the spread of Communism during WWII. This powerful museum manages to be educational without being pedantic and somber without being heavy-handed. *(Grzybowska 79, enter on Przyokopowa. From the center, take tram #12, 20, or 22 to Grzybowska: the museum will be on your left. ☎539 7901; www.1944.pl. Open W and F-Su 10am-6pm, Th 10am-8pm. Excellent English captions. 4zł, students 2zł; Su free. Cash only.)*

ROYAL CASTLE. In the Middle Ages, the castle (Zamek Królewski) was home to the Dukes of Mazovia. In the late 16th century, it replaced Kraków's Wawel as the official royal residence; later it became the presidential palace, and in 1939 it was burned down and plundered by the Nazis. Following its destruction, many Varsovians risked their lives hiding the castle's priceless works. Some of the treasures were retrieved after WWII, but it took 40 years—and contributions from Poles, expats, and dignitaries, including Pope John Paul II—to restore this symbol of national pride. *(Pl. Zamkowy 4. ☎657 2170; www.zamek-krolewski.art.pl. Tickets and guides at the kasa inside the courtyard. Open M and Su 11am-6pm, Tu-Sa 10am-6pm. 20zł, students 13zł. Highlights tour Su 11am-6pm free. Tour in English M-Sa, 85zł per group. AmEx/MC/V.)*

CENTER OF CONTEMPORARY ART AT UJAZDOWSKI CASTLE. Illustrating the phrase *Nowe jest stare* ("what is new is old") etched on a museum wall, this reconstructed 17th-century castle speaks volumes about the interplay of modernity and tradition that infuses contemporary Polish art. The castle's winding cellars exhibit cutting-edge art installations; don't miss the panoramic view of Lazienki Park or the exhibits in the Laboratorium outbuilding. Ujazdowski Castle also hosts modern dance and literary presentations, and is home to KinoLab, which screens art films, as well as the Artistic Kitchen, which serves up innovative cuisine. *(Al. Ujazdowskie 6. Take the same buses as to Łazienki, but get off at* pl. Na Rozdrożu; *the museum is past the overpass. ☎62 81 27 13; www.csw.art.pl. Open Tu-Th and Sa-Su 11am-7pm, F 11am-9pm. 12zł, students 6zł. Cash only.)*

WILANÓW. Half an hour south of the city, this extraordinary residence is Warsaw's answer to Versailles. In 1677, King Jan III Sobieski bought the sleepy village of Milanowo and rebuilt the existing mansion as a palace; today, it has recently been revamped into one of Warsaw's most attractive museums. The French-influenced gardens feature elegant topiary. *(Take bus #180 from Krakowskie Przedmieście or #516 or 519 from Marszalkowska south to Wilanów. From the bus stop, cross the highway and follow signs for the Pałac. ☎842 0795. Open mid-May to mid-Sept. M and W-Su 9:30am-4:30pm; mid-Sept. to mid-May M and Th-Sa 9:30am-4pm, W 9:30am-6pm, Su 9:30am-7pm. Last entrance 1½hr. before closing. 20zł, students 10zł. Th free. Highly recommended audio tours 6zł. Gardens open M and W-F 9:30am-dusk. 4.5zł, students 2.5zł. Cash only.)*

POSTER MUSEUM. Polish artists have long been producing stunning poster art, and the medium rose in prominence under Communism. The rotating exhibits are well worth the trip to Wilanów. The museum hosts the International Poster Biennale in summers of even-numbered years. Phone ahead, since the museum closes between exhibitions. *(Stanisława Potockiego 10/16, by Pałac Wilanowski. ☎842 4848. Open M noon-4pm, Tu-Su 10am-4pm. Last entry 30min. before close. 8zł, students 5zł; M free.)*

POLAND

ZACHĘTA GALLERY. Warsaw's most impressive contemporary art gallery features photography, film, sculpture, and painting. Many rotating exhibits display works by foreign artists and include everything from photography to design. The impressive building has played its own role in history: in 1922, Gabriel Narutowicz, first president of the Second Polish Republic, was assassinated in the exhibition hall. *(Pl. Malachowskiego 3. Buses #100 toward pl. Zamkowy and #160 toward Targowek from the center both stop at Zachęta. ☎827 58 54; www.zacheta.art.pl. Open Tu-Su 10am-8pm. 10zł, students 7zł; Tu free. Guided tour in Polish 60zł, in English 80zł; call 2 days in advance. Cash only.)*

NATIONAL MUSEUM. Poland's largest museum (Muzeum Narodowe) was looted by the Nazis in WWII but has since rebuilt an impressive, well-presented collection of Polish art alongside a weaker collection of European art. The prolific Polish art community asserts its strength in the early 20th-century collection; the contrast between Socialist Realist and more innovative art from the same period is especially interesting. *(Al. Jerozolimskie 3. ☎629 3093, tours in English 629 5060; www.mnw.art.pl. Open Tu-Su 10am-5pm. Permanent exhibits 12zł, students 7zł; special exhibits 17zł, students 10zł. English audio tours 17zł, students 12zł; guided tour in English 50zł; call 1 week in advance. AmEx/MC/V.)*

MARIA SKŁODOWSKA-CURIE MUSEUM. Founded in 1967, on the 100th anniversary of the two-time Nobel Laureate's birth, the exhibit (Muzeum Marii Skłodowskiej-Curie) chronicles Maria Skłodowska's life in Poland, immigration to France, and marriage to scientist Pierre Curie, with whom she discovered radium, polonium (named after Poland), and brief marital bliss. Eclectic exhibits include a diorama of her lab and a shrine to Alfred Nobel. *(Freta 16, in Skłodowska's former house. ☎831 8092. Open Tu-Sa 10am-4pm, Su 10am-2pm. 6zł, students 3zł.)*

FRÉDÉRIC CHOPIN MUSEUM. A small but fascinating collection of original letters, scores, paintings, and keepsakes, including the composer's last piano; his first published piece, the *Polonaise in G Minor* (penned at the ripe old age of seven); and his last composition, *Mazurka in F Minor*. A brief tour will interest those unacquainted with his music, and even casual visitors will be transfixed by the haunting bronze mold of his left hand. The museum (Muzeum Fryderyka Chopina) also hosts the International Chopin Festival, with concerts on selected days in July and August. *(Okólnik 1, in Ostrogski Castle. Enter from Tamka. ☎827 5475. Open Tu-Su, 10am-6pm. Last entry at 5:30pm. 8zł, students 4zł. English-language guides 100zł, Polish-language 50zł. Concerts 15zł, students 10zł. Cash only.)*

ADAM MICKIEWICZ MUSEUM OF LITERATURE. Old sketches, letters, books, a shrine room, and Mickiewicz's original inkpot take visitors through his life and work. While there are some captions in English, the excerpts of Mickiewicz's poetry are unfortunately only in Polish. A rotating exhibit of Polish art is found on the first floor. *(Rynek Starego Miasta 20. ☎831 4061. Open M-Tu and F 10am-3pm, W-Th 11am-6pm, Su 11am-5pm. 6zł, students 5zł, Su free.)*

MUSEUM OF PAWIAK PRISON. Built in the 1830s as a prison for common criminals, Pawiak (Muzeum Więzienia Pawiaka) later served as Gestapo headquarters. From 1939 to 1944, over 100,000 Poles, 10% of Warsaw's entire population, were imprisoned and tortured here. One room has been converted into a museum that exhibits photography and poetry as well as prisoners' possessions. The catacomb-like hallways lead to preserved cells. A dead tree outside bears the names of some of the 30,000 prisoners killed at Pawiak during the war. *(Dzielna 24/26. ☎/fax 831 13 17. Open W 9am-5pm, Th and Sa 9am-4pm, F 10am-5pm, Su 10am-4pm. Donations requested.)*

ENTERTAINMENT

Warsaw boasts a wide array of live music including free outdoor concerts in summer. Classical music performances are rarely sold out; standby tickets for major performances run as low as 10zł. Inquire at the **Warsaw Music Society** (Warszawskie Towarzystwo Muzyczne), Morskie Oko 2 (☎849 5651). Take tram #4, 18, 19, 35, or 36 to Morskie Oko from Marszałkowska. The **Warsaw Chamber Opera** (Warszawska Opera Kameralna), al. Solidarności 76B (☎831 2240), hosts a **Mozart Festival** in early summer. Łazienki Park has free Sunday concerts at the **Chopin Monument** (Pomnik Chopina; concerts mid-May to Sept. Su noon and 4pm). The **Opera Narodowa,** pl. Teatralny 1 (☎692 0200), founded in 1778, hosts several operas each week, with standby tickets as low as 15zł. The first week of June brings the **International Festival of Sacred Music,** with performances at historic churches. **Jazz Klub Tygmont,** Mazowiecka 6/8 (☎828 3409), hosts free jazz concerts. From July through September, the Old Market Square of Stare Miasto draws locals with nightly free jazz at 7pm. For tickets to rock concerts, call **Empik Megastore** (☎625 1219).

Teatr Wielki, in the same building as **Opera Narodowa,** the main opera and ballet hall, has regular performances. (☎826 3288; www.teatrwielki.pl. Tickets 10-100zł. AmEx/MC/V.) **Teatr Dramatyczny,** in the Pałac Kultury, has a stage for big productions and a studio theater playing more avant-garde works. (☎620 2102; standby tickets 11-17zł.) **Teatr Żydowski** (pl. Grzybowski 12/16; ☎620 7025), is a Jewish theater with shows mostly in Yiddish. **Kinoteka** (☎826 1961), in the Pałac Kultury, shows Hollywood blockbusters in a Stalinist setting. **Kino Lab,** al. Ujazdowskie 6 (☎628 1271), features independent films.

NIGHTLIFE

Warsaw's night scene is accessible, exuberant, and constantly changing. New bars and clubs are emerging at fever pace, so check *Aktivist* or *Warsaw in Your Pocket* for the latest listings. Many locals arrive at bars as midnight approaches, and don't hit the clubs until the wee hours. While some gay clubs have become raucous places of interest for the "mixed" crowd, most remain discreet. For info, call the gay and lesbian **hotline** (see **GLBT Resources,** p. 425).

Piekarnia, Młocińska 11 (☎636 4979). Take the #22 tram to Rondo Babka and backtrack on Okopowa. Make a right on Powiązkowska, a right on Burakowa, and a right on Młocińska. The unmarked club will be down the road on your left. Boasting a host of resident DJs and a constant stream of guests, Piekarnia is proud to have been a pioneer as one of the first modern clubs in Poland. These days the so-hip-it-hurts scene really picks up around 4am. The selective bouncer, packed dance floor, and progressive house music make this a local institution. Cover F 20zł, Sa 25zł. Open F-Sa 10pm-late.

Klubokawiarnia, Czeckiego 3 (www.klubo.pl). An authentic Communist-era sign advertising "coffee, tea, and cold beverages" hangs over the bar, while portraits of Lenin gaze down from the bright red walls in this ironic take-off of the bad old days. Despite the nostalgic decor however, Klubokawiarnia's DJs spin the hottest new tracks for a stylish young crowd. Special events on occasion, such as a "Caribbean Night" with imported sand. Cover varies. Open daily 10pm-late. Cash only.

Sheesha Bar, ul. Sienkiewicza (☎825 2528). Those who need a break from the barrage of house and techno will find a welcome respite in Warsaw's Sheesha Bar, where the DJs spin Middle Eastern dance music for a largely expatriate crowd. The main attraction, however, is the set of cushioned booths, where you can relax with a hookah (25-50zł per bowl). Cover F-Sa 20zł includes free drink. Open T-Su 4pm-late. AmEx/MC/V.

Student Bar Complex, Dobra 33/35, at the corner of Dobra and Zajęcza. 3 popular student bars are grouped in this complex built from squat concrete storage huts. **Duina** plays pop and 80s music to keep the bargoers singing. Next comes **Aurora,** a full-fledged dance club that flashes colorful lights through circular windows and chiefly plays house music. **Klub Czarny Lew** rounds out the group with an industrial atmosphere that plays on the utilitarian roots of this onetime warehouse. Open M-Tu and F-Su 7pm-late, W-Th 5pm-late. Cash only.

Enklawa, Mazowiecka 12 (☎827 3151). An elite crowd of expats, locals, students, and young professionals cough up hefty cover charges for a spot on the sexually charged dance floor. Hot but unintimidating, this place gets going by 11pm. Chat someone up in English and take in mainstream hip hop and techno. Check out the plasma video screens in the bathrooms. Cover W-Th men 10zł, women 5zł; F-Sa before 11pm 20zł, after 11pm 30zł. Open M-Th and Su 9pm-3am, F-Sa 9pm-4am. AmEx/MC/V.

Underground Music Cafe, Marszałkowska 126/134 (☎826 7048; www.under.pl). Behind the large McDonald's; walk down the steps. This 2-level dance club is a guaranteed weeknight party. Casual, young student crowd keeps the smoky dance floor completely packed until 4am. Beer 5zł 11pm-midnight. M-Tu and Su old-school house; W and Sa hiphop; Th 70s and 80s. Cover W and F 10zł, students 5zł; Th 10zł, Sa 20/10zł. No cover M-Tu and Su. Open M-Sa 1pm-late, Su 4pm-late.

Bar Lemon, Sienkiewicza 6 (☎829 5544). On weekends, Lemon is a popular spot for Warsaw's smart set to dance to house music spun by visiting DJs. The chic interior has clean lines and yellow accents, and the crowd schmoozes until the dancing picks up around midnight. Beer 7zł. Open daily 9pm-late. MC/V. Next door, **Cafe Lemon** serves contemporary meals 24hr.

Rasko, Krochmalna 32A (☎890 0299; www.rasko.pl). 1 block north of Grzybowska, turn left on Krochmalna; the bar is 2 blocks down on your right near a small sign and blue unmarked door. Small, secluded, and artsy Rasko serves Warsaw's largely underground GLBT scene. Laid-back but cautious bouncer ensures that Warsaw's less tolerant elements stay out. The close-knit and friendly staff will be happy to direct you to other GLBT establishments and organizations. Beer 7zł. Open daily 5pm-3am. Cash only.

MAŁOPOLSKA (LESSER POLAND)

Małopolska, marked by gentle hills and medieval castle ruins, stretches from the Kraków-Częstochowa Uplands in the west to Lublin in the east. Kraków, which suffered minimal damage during WWII, remains Poland's cultural and social center. Lublin, with its many universities, is an intellectual hub. The surrounding area contains some of humanity's most beautiful and most horrific creations: the artistry of the Wieliczka salt caves and the serenity of the Pieskowa Skała castle contrast the remnants of Auschwitz-Birkenau and Mąjdanek concentration camps.

KRAKÓW ☎(0)12

Although Kraków (KRAH-koof; pop 758,000) only recently emerged as a trendy international capital, it has long been Poland's darling. The regal architecture, rich cafe culture, and palpable sense of history that now bewitch throngs of foreign visitors have drawn Polish kings, artists, and scholars for centuries. The maze-like Old Town and the old Jewish quarter of Kazimierz hide scores of museums, galleries, cellar pubs, and clubs; 130,000 students add to the spirited nightlife. Still, the city's gloss and glamor can't completely hide the scars of the 20th century: the nearby Auschwitz-Birkenau Nazi death camps provide a sobering reminder of the atrocities committed in the not-so-distant past.

INTERCITY TRANSPORTATION

Flights: Balice Airport (John Paul II International Airport; Port Lotniczy im. Jana Pawła), Kapitana Medweckiego 1 (☎411 19 55; airport@lotnisko-balice.pl), 18km from the center. Connect to the main train station by bus #192 (40min.) or 208 (1hr.). Or take the airport train that leaves from the train platform #1 on W and F-Sa, at least once per hour. A taxi to the center costs 50-60zł. Carriers include **British Airways, Central Wings, German Wings, LOT, Lufthansa,** and **Sky Europe.** Open 24hr.

Trains: Kraków Główny, pl. Kolejowy 1 (☎393 5409 info, 1580; www.pkp.pl). Ticket office open 5am-11pm. Go to Kasa Krajowej for domestic trains and Kasa Międzynardowa for international trains. You can reserve spaces on the train ahead of time. AmEx/MC/V. To: **Gdańsk** ("Gdynia"; 7-10hr., 10 per day, 60-100zł); **Poznań** (6-8hr., 2 per day, 50-81zł); **Warsaw** (3hr., 15 per day, 81-127zł); **Zakopane** (3-5hr., 17 per day, 30-50zł); **Bratislava, SLK** (8hr., 1 per day, 188zł); **Budapest, HUN** (11hr., 1 per day, 159-208zł); **Kyiv, UKR** (22hr., 1 per day, 240zł); **Odessa, UKR** (21hr., 1 per day, 240zł); **Prague, CZR** (9hr., 2 per day, 128-165zł); **Vienna, AUT** (8½hr., 2 per day, 157-194zł). Let's Go does not recommend traveling on night trains.

Buses: Bosacka 18 (☎300 300 150). Open daily 5am-11pm. To: **Bielsko-Biała** (2½-3½hr., 28 per day, 14zł); **Łódź** (5hr., 5 per day, 50zł); **Warsaw** (6hr., 3 per day, 50zł); **Wrocław** (5hr., 2 per day, 43zł); **Zakopane** (2hr., 33 per day, 16zł). AmEx/MC/V.

ORIENTATION

The heart of the city is the huge **Rynek Główny** (Main Marketplace), in the center of **Stare Miasto**. Stare Miasto is encircled by the **Planty** gardens and, a bit farther out, a broad ring road, which is confusingly divided into sections with different names: **Basztowa, Dunajewskiego, Podwale,** and **Westerplatte.** South of Rynek Główny looms the celebrated **Wawel Castle.** The **Wisła River** snakes past the castle and borders the old Jewish district of **Kazimierz.** The train station sits northeast of Stare Miasto. A large, well-marked underpass cuts beneath the ring road and into the Planty gardens; from there a number of paths lead into the Rynek (10min.). Turn left from the train station to reach the underpass.

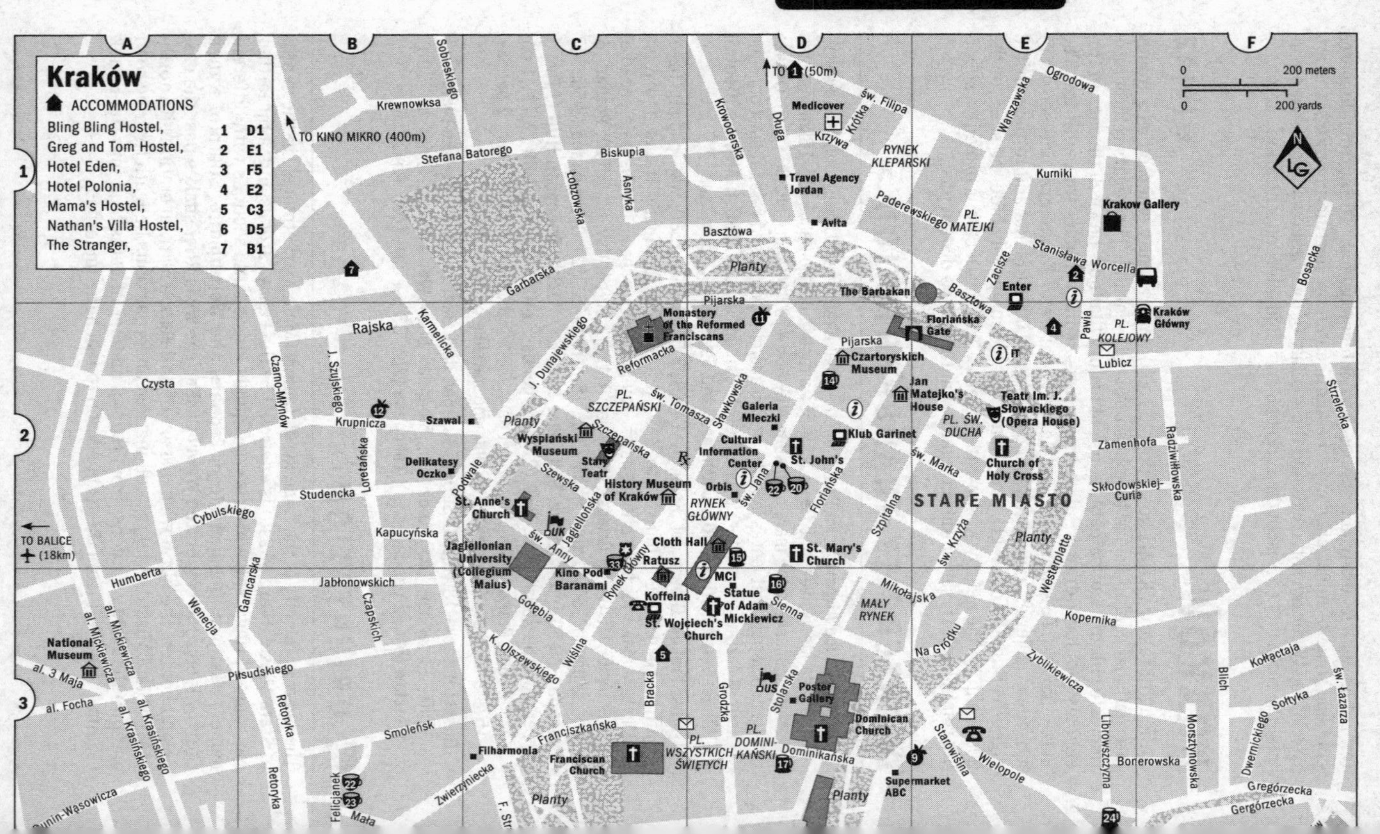

Kraków
ACCOMMODATIONS
Bling Bling Hostel, 1 D1
Greg and Tom Hostel, 2 E1
Hotel Eden, 3 F5
Hotel Polonia, 4 E2
Mama's Hostel, 5 C3
Nathan's Villa Hostel, 6 D5
The Stranger, 7 B1
200 meters
200 yards
TO KINO MIKRO (400m)
TO 1 (50m)
TO BALICE (18km)
Krakow Gallery
Kraków Główny
PL. KOLEJOWY
Medicover
Travel Agency Jordan
Avita
The Barbakan
Floriańska Gate
Enter
Teatr Im. J. Słowackiego (Opera House)
Church of Holy Cross
Jan Matejko's House
Czartoryskich Museum
Klub Garinet
St. John's
Monastery of the Reformed Franciscans
Galeria Mleczki
Cultural Information Center
Orbis
History Museum of Kraków
Cloth Hall
MCI
Ratusz
Statue of Adam Mickiewicz
St. Wojciech's Church
St. Mary's Church
Koffeina
Kino Pod Baranami
Wyspiański Museum
Stary Teatr
St. Anne's Church
Jagiellonian University (Collegium Maius)
Szawal
Delikatesy Oczko
Filharmonia
Franciscan Church
Dominican Church
Poster Gallery
Supermarket ABC
National Museum
STARE MIASTO
RYNEK GŁÓWNY
MAŁY RYNEK
RYNEK KLEPARSKI
PL. MATEJKI
PL. SZCZEPAŃSKI
PL. ŚW. DUCHA
PL. DOMINIKAŃSKI
PL. WSZYSTKICH ŚWIĘTYCH
Planty
Strzelecka
Bosacka
Radziwiłłowska
Ogrodowa
Warszawska
Kurniki
Worcella
Stanisława
Pawia
Lubicz
Zacisze
Basztowa
Zamenhofa
Skłodowskiej-Curie
Westerplatte
Kopernika
św. Łazarza
Sołtyka
Kołłątaja
Dwernickiego
Blich
Morsztynowska
Librowszczyzna
Bonerowska
Gregórzecka
Gergórzecka
Zyblikiewicza
Wielopole
Starowiślna
Na Gródku
św. Krzyża
św. Marka
Szpitalna
Mikołajska
Floriańska
Sienna
Stolarska
Dominikańska
Grodzka
Bracka
Wiślna
Franciszkańska
Gołębia
św. Anny
Jagiellońska
Szewska
Szczepańska
św. Tomasza
Sławkowska
św. Jana
Rynek Główny
Pijarska
Reformacka
J. Dunajewskiego
Garbarska
Krowoderska
Długa
Krzywa
Krótka
św. Filipa
Paderewskiego
Asnyka
Biskupia
Łobzowska
Stefana Batorego
Sobieskiego
Krewnowksa
Karmelicka
Rajska
Podwale
Kapucyńska
Loretańska
Krupnicza
J. Szujskiego
Studencka
Jabłonowskich
Czapskich
K. Olszewskiego
Smoleńsk
Zwierzyniecka
F. Str
Felicjanek
Mała
Retoryka
Piłsudskiego
Czarno-Młynów
Garncarska
Cybulskiego
Czysta
Wenecja
Humberta
al. Mickiewicza
al. Krasińskiego
al. 3 Maja
al. Focha
Wąsowicza

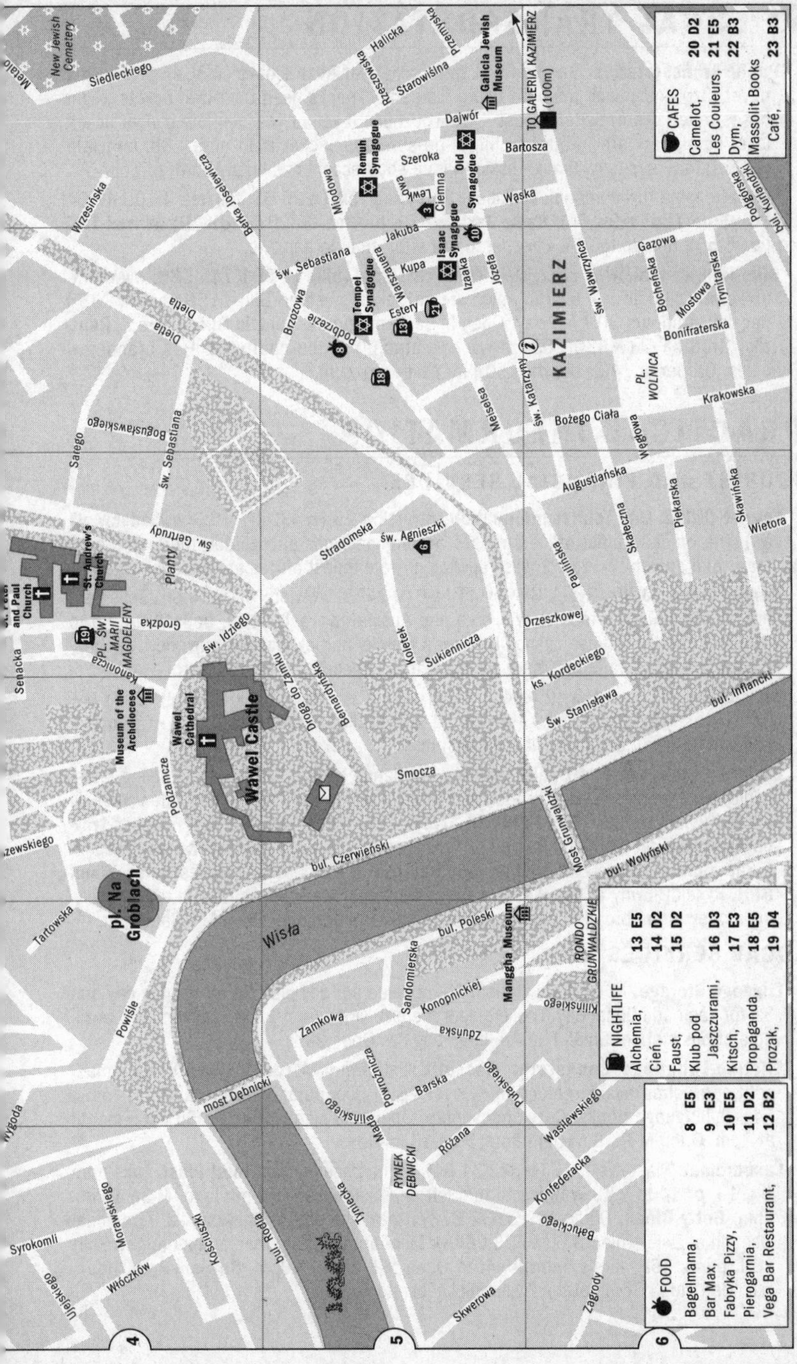
FOOD
Bagelmama, 8 E5
Bar Max, 9 E3
Fabryka Pizzy, 10 E5
Pierogarnia, 11 D2
Vega Bar Restaurant, 12 B2
NIGHTLIFE
Alchemia, 13 E5
Cień, 14 D2
Faust, 15 D2
Klub pod Jaszczurami, 16 D3
Kitsch, 17 E3
Propaganda, 18 E5
Prozak, 19 D4
CAFES
Camelot, 20 D2
Les Couleurs, 21 E5
Dym, 22 B3
Massolit Books Café, 23 B3
KAZIMIERZ
Wawel Castle
Wawel Cathedral
Museum of the Archdiocese
St. Peter and Paul Church
St. Andrew's Church
PL. ŚW. MARII MAGDELENY
pl. Na Groblach
Wisła
Manggha Museum
RONDO GRUNWALDZKIE
RYNEK DĘBNICKI
PL. WOLNICA
Tempel Synagogue
Remuh Synagogue
Isaac Synagogue
Old Synagogue
Galicia Jewish Museum
TO GALERIA KAZIMIERZ (100m)
New Jewish Cemetery
most Dębnicki
Most Grunwaldzki
bul. Czerwieński
bul. Poleski
bul. Wołyński
bul. Inflancki
4
5
6

POLAND

LOCAL TRANSPORTATION

Public Transportation: Buy **bus** and **tram** tickets at Ruch kiosks (2.50zł) or from the driver (3zł) and punch them on board. Large backpacks need their own tickets. Night buses (after 11pm) 5zł; day pass 11zł; 100zł fine if you or your bag are caught ticketless. Foreigners are frequently fined–be sure your ticket is in order. Student fare (1.35zł) for Poles only, though asking with a good accent has been known to work.

Taxis: Reliable taxi companies include: **Barbakan Taxi** (☎96 61, toll-free 08 00 40 04 00); **Euro Taxi** (☎96 64); **Radio Taxi** (☎919, toll-free 08 00 50 09 19); **Wawel Taxi** (☎96 66). It is up to 30% cheaper to call a taxi than to hail one.

Bike Rental: Kraków is a bicycle-friendly city. **Rentabike** (☎501 745 986; www.rentabike.pl) will deliver a bike to anywhere in Kraków's center. Bikes 15zł per 3hr., 35zł per day, students 30zł per day. Open M-Sa 9am-8pm. **Eccentric Bike Tours & Rentals,** Grodzka 2 (☎430 2034; www.eccentric.pl) in the courtyard. Has brand-new bikes. 6zł per hr., 40zł per day, 50zł for next-day return.

PRACTICAL INFORMATION

TOURIST AND FINANCIAL SERVICES

Tourist Office: City Tourist Information, Szpitalna 25 (☎432 01 10; www.krakow.pl/en). The official tourist office arranges accommodations and guided tours, and sells maps and guides (7-12zł). English spoken. Private tourist offices are throughout town.

Budget Travel: Orbis, Rynek Główny 41 (☎619 2449; www.orbis.krakow.pl). Sells train tickets and arranges trips to Wieliczka and Auschwitz (each 120zł, both 238zł; up to 50% ISIC discount). Also cashes **traveler's checks** and **exchanges currency.** Open M-F 9am-7pm, Sa 9am-3pm. There are many travel agencies in Stare Miasto.

Consulates: UK, św. Anny 9 (☎421 5656, 7030; ukconsul@bci.krakow.pl). Open M-F 9am-4pm. **US,** Stolarska 9 (☎424 51 00; krakow.usconsulate.gov). Open M-F 8:30am-4:40pm; citizen services until 3pm.

Currency Exchange and Banks: *Kantory* (exchange kiosks) have widely varying rates. Avoid those around the train station and near Floriańska Gate. Also check rates carefully around Rynek Główny. **Bank PKO SA,** Rynek Główny 31 (☎424 3732). Cashes **traveler's checks** for 2% commission (20zł min.) and gives MC/V **cash advances.** Open M-F 8am-6pm, Sa 9am-2pm. **ATMs,** found all over the city, offer the best rates. **Bank BPH,** Rynek Główny 4, has **Western Union Services.** Many banks require those receiving money from abroad to change it into złotych at a bad rate. Open M-F 8am-6pm.

LOCAL SERVICES

Luggage Storage: At the train station. 1% of value per day plus 5zł for the 1st day and 3zł for each additional day. Lockers near the exit. Open 5am-11pm. Lockers also available at bus station. Small bag 4zł, large bag 8zł. Open 24hr.

English-Language Bookstore: Massolit, Felicjanek 4 (☎432 4150; www.massolit.com). Impressive selection of over 25,000 popular, classic, and academic English-language books. Cozy atmosphere. Open mic night every 3rd Su each month at 7pm. Open M-Th, Su 10am-8pm; F-Sa 10am-9pm.

Laundromat: Piastowska 47 (☎622 31 81), in the basement of **Hotel Piast.** Take tram #4, 13, or 14 to WKS Wawel and turn left on Piastowska. 40zł per load. M-Sa 10am-6pm. **Betty Clean,** Długa 17 (☎632 6787), past the end of Sławkowska. Additional location at Zwierzyniecka 6 (☎423 0848). More a dry-cleaner than a laundromat. Shirt 10zł, pants 15zł, nun's habit 25-40zł. Open M-F 8am-7:30pm, Sa 8am-2pm. Hours extended until3:30pm at the Zwierzynicka location on Sa.

EMERGENCY AND COMMUNICATIONS

Emergency: In the event of an emergency, contact the police by calling ☎158

Pharmacy: Apteka Pod Żółtym Tygrysem, Szczepańska 1 (☎422 9293), just off Rynek Główny. Posts a list of 24hr. pharmacies. Open M-F 8am-8pm, Sa 8am-3pm. MC/V.

Medical Services: Medicover, Krótka 1 (☎616 1000). Ambulance services available. English spoken. Open M-F 7am-9pm, Sa 9am-2pm.

Telephones: At the post office and throughout the city. Buy phone cards at any kiosk or at **Telekomunikacja Polska,** Wielpole 2 (☎421 6457). Open M-F 10am-6pm, Sa 10am-2pm. Some Internet cafes, such as **Internet Cafe,** Bracka 4 and Rynek Główny 23, offer very cheap (0.25zł per min. to US and UK) calls over the Internet, although the quality can be inconsistent.

Internet: You can't throw a rock in Stare Miasto without hitting an Internet cafe. (Let's Go does not recommend rock-throwing.) **Koffeina Internet Cafe,** Rynek Główny 23. 2zł per 30min., 3zł per hr. Open 24hr. **Telekomunikacja Polska** offers free Internet, but has standing room only.

Post Office: Westerplatte 20 (☎422 24 97). **Poste Restante** at counter #1. Open M-F 7:30am-8:30pm, Sa 8am-2pm. **Postal Code:** 31 075.

POLAND

ACCOMMODATIONS

Kraków has a growing range of affordable hotels and conveniently located hostels, but travelers still outnumber beds during high season, and prices have been rising, so call ahead. **Travel Agency Jordan,** Długa 9, arranges accommodations, including guest rooms above their office. (☎421 2125; www.jordan.krakow.pl. Open M-F 8am-6pm, Sa 9am-2pm. Singles 140zł; doubles 210zł; triples 280zł. AmEx/MC/V.) Locals also rent rooms; watch for signs at the train station. It is advisable to see the room before agreeing to pay. **University dorms** open up in July and August. All hostels listed have English-speaking staff, and all supply linens. Except where noted, free breakfast, storage, and laundry facilities are provided.

HOSTELS AND DORMITORIES

Nathan's Villa Hostel, św. Agnieszki 1 (☎422 35 45; www.nathansvilla.com). From Kraków Główny, take tram #10 toward Wawel and get off at the 3rd stop. Kraków's most social hostel—at times akin to living in a frat house—has expanded following the addition of 4 new upstairs rooms and a great new cellar bar with ping-pong and pool. Kitchen available. Breakfast until 1pm. Wi-Fi. Reception 24hr. Dorms 50-60zł. MC/V. ❶

Mama's Hostel, Bracka 4 (☎429 5940; www.mamashostel.com.pl). From the southern side of the Rynek, Mama's is a half-block down Bracka on the left. The most centrally located hostel in Kraków, Mama's boasts 46 sturdy and comfortable wooden beds, 4 bathrooms, a common room with 2 computers and a flat-panel TV, as well as a beautiful kitchen—all in a 15th-century building with a small flower-lined balcony. Breakfast until 1pm. Reception 24hr. Flexible check-in and check-out. Luggage storage available. 10-bed dorms 45zł; 6-bed dorms 60zł. MC/V; 3% surcharge. ❶

The Stranger, Kochanowskiego 1 (☎634 2516; www.thestrangerhostel.com). A social atmosphere and simple, clean dorms characterize this hostel. The laid-back common room's entertainment system includes an 8-speaker sound system, a wide selection of DVDs, 2 computers, and free Wi-Fi. The friendly staff does guests' laundry daily. Kitchen available. Reception 24hr. Dorms 55-60zł. Cash only. ❷

Greg and Tom Hostel, Pawia 12/15 (☎422 4100; www.gregtomhostel.com). 2nd location on Warszawska 16/5. 30 seconds from the train station, Greg and Tom is perfect for late-night arrivals. Look past the climb to the 4th fl. of a weary Soviet-era building:

this small hostel is clean and attractive, and one of the few in Kraków without bunkbeds. Kitchen available. Free Wi-Fi available in the salmon-pink common room. Reception 24hr. Dorms 50zł; doubles 60zł. AmEx/MC/V. ❷

Bling Bling Hostel, Pędzichów 7 (☎634 0532; www.blingbling.pl). From the train station, take the underpass to Basztowa and turn right on Długa. Bear right on Pędzichów. Simple wooden beds, sparkling bathrooms, and a homey kitchen. Breakfast until 10am. Free Internet. Reception 24hr. Flexible check-in and check-out. Dorms 55zł. MC/V. ❷

HOTELS

Hotel Polonia, Basztowa 25 (☎422 1233; www.hotel-polonia.com.pl), across from the train station, 5min. from Rynek Główny. Features a Neoclassical exterior, modern rooms, and a great location. Quirky, see-through bathtubs in the suites. Breakfast 18zł, included for rooms with bath. Reception 24hr. Check-in 2pm. Check-out noon. Singles 100zł, with bath 295zł; doubles 119/303zł; triples 139/409zł; suites 526zł. MC/V. ❹

Hotel Eden, Ciemna 15 (☎430 6565; www.hoteleden.pl). From Rynek Główny, follow Sienna, which becomes Starowiślna near Kazimierz. Bear right on Dajwór, then turn right onto Ciemna. In a restored 15th-century building, Eden offers the only *mikvah* (Jewish ritual bath) in Poland, kosher meals, and tours of Kazimierz. Rooms include baths, telephones, and satellite TVs. Kosher breakfast included. Internet. Wheelchair-accessible. Singles 260zł; doubles 350zł; triples 430zł; suites 550zł. AmEx/MC/V. ❺

POLAND

FOOD

While Warsaw has turned its attention to international cuisine, Kraków remains solidly rooted in local culinary tradition. The restaurants and cafes on and around the **Rynek** satisfy locals and tourists. **Grocery stores** surround the train station and dot the center. Two 24hr. grocery stores, **Delikatesy Oczko,** Podwale 4, and **Avita,** pl. Kleparski 5, off Bracka, are near the Rynek. **Plac Nowy,** in Kazimierz, boasts an **open-air market** with fresh fruits and vegetables. (M-F 6am-8pm, Sa 7am-1pm.) Alternatively, head to Rynek Kleparski, next to pl. Matejki, to find a food and a **flea market,** called Stary Kleparz. (Open M-F 7am-8pm, Sa 7am-6pm, Su 7am-3pm.)

Bagelmama, Podbrzezie 2 (☎431 1942), facing the Tempel Synagogue. Poland is the mother of the bagel; here the blessed foodstuff returns home in triumph. At this tiny bagel shop, an American-Polish couple serves delicious bagels with a variety of fresh spreads (3.50zł, with cream cheese or hummus 6-9zł). They also make some of the best burritos in Kraków (12-15zł). Open Tu-Su 10am-9pm. Cash only. ❷

Pierogarnia, Sławkowska 32 (☎422 7495). By the counter in this miniscule dumpling outpost, a window reveals a cook rolling dough and shaping *pierogi.* Meals range from classic cheese-and-potato *ruskie* to the more daring groats-and-liver. Also serves excellent *gołąbki* (cabbage rolls; 8zł) and 15 fruit juices, including cherry and black currant (4zł). Remarkably fast service. *Pierogi* 7-8zł. Open daily 10am-10pm. Cash only. ❶

Vega Bar Restaurant, Krupnicza 22 (☎430 0846). Fresh flowers set the mood for munching on delightful, largely vegetarian cuisine (3-10zł). Faux-meat dishes like the cheese-and-soy *kotlety* (cutlet; 5zł) will please pining carnivores; the *fasola z grzybami* (beans with mushrooms; 7zł) is another great spin on a traditionally meat-based Polish favorite. 32 varieties of tea (2.50zł). Open daily 9am-9pm. Students 10% off. MC/V. **Branch** at św. Gertrudy 7 (☎422 3494). ❶

Fabryka Pizzy, Józefa 34 (☎433 8080). This wildly popular Kazimierz pizza place lives up to its hype. Excellent pizzas (12-20zł) and fabulous breadsticks and calzone (5-8zł). Can be difficult to find a seat early in the day on weekends. Open M-Th and Su 11am-11pm, F-Sa noon-midnight. MC/V. ❷

Bar Max, św. Gertrudy 5. Don't be fooled by its similarity to tram-ticket booths: Bar Max offers a filling Polish version of a cheeseburger (7zł) that can feed 2 people. Its hamburger (3zł) is popular with the weekend crowd through the wee hours of the morning. Open M-Th 10am-2am, F-Sa 10am-4am, Su 11am-1am. Cash only. ❶

CAFES

Dym (Smoke), św. Tomasza 13 (☎429 6661). A hub for sophisticated locals, Dym earns high praise for unbeatable coffee (5zł), though many prefer to enjoy the relaxed atmosphere over beer (5.50zł). The cheesecake (6zł) is divine. The watery, green-blue walls also display artworks. Open M-F 10am-midnight. Cash only.

Camelot, św. Tomasza 17 (☎421 0123). The literati flock to Camelot, one of Stare Miasto's legends. The space is cluttered with paintings and photos, and the occasional 17th-century document; soothing jazz plays in the background. Coffee 6-11zł. Breakfast 6-16zł. Sandwiches 3-6zł. Salads 19-21zł. Music, readings, or cabaret F 8:15pm, downstairs at Loch Camelot. English menu. Open daily 9am-midnight. Cash only.

Massolit Books Café, Felicjanek 4 (☎432 4150). Great wood-lined bookstore cafe with a 1920s atmosphere. This tiny expat hangout has only 4 tables, but with desserts as decadent as the carrot cake (8zł), that hardly matters. Coffee 4zł. Open mic night every 1st and 3rd Su at 7pm. Open M-Th and Su 10am-8pm, F-Sa 10am-9pm. MC/V.

Les Couleurs, Estery 10 (☎429 4270). Begin your day at this Parisian cafe with buttery croissants (4zł), fresh-squeezed juice (9zł), and French newspapers. By afternoon the back patio fills with laid-back coffee drinkers (5zł), while Kazimierz regulars nurse beers at the bar (*Żywiec;* 6zł). Lively late at night. Open daily 7am-2am. Cash only.

SIGHTS

WAWEL CASTLE AND CATHEDRAL

Entry is limited and only 10 tickets become available every 10min., so you may have to wait. It's advisable to buy tickets early in the morning because they often sell out, especially in summer. English info and tickets to all buildings except the cathedral at the main kasa. Tourist Service Office (BOT) ☎422 1697; www.wawel.krakow.pl.

WAWEL CASTLE (ZAMEK WAWELSKI). The Wawel Castle and Cathedral complex is arguably the most impressive sight in Poland. Begun in the 10th century and remodeled in the 1500s, the castle contains 71 chambers and a magnificent sequence of tapestries. The star of the collection is **Szczerbiec,** the coronation sword used from 1230 to 1734. The **Lost Wawel** exhibit traces Wawel Hill's evolution from the Stone Age, displaying fragments of ancient Wawel. You can also visit the **Oriental Collection** of Turkish military regalia, the spoils of Polish military victories, and Asian porcelain. *(Open Apr.-Oct. M 9:30am-1pm, Tu, W and Sa 9:30am-3pm, Th-F 9:30am-4pm, Su 10am-4pm. Nov.-Mar. Tu-Sa 9:30am-4pm, Su 10am-4pm. Royal Private Apartments and Oriental Collection closed M. Wawel Castle 15zł, students 8zł; M free. Lost Wawel and Oriental Collection 7/4zł each. Royal Apartments and Treasury and Armory 20/15zł each.)*

WAWEL CATHEDRAL (KATEDRA WAWELSKA). For centuries, the magnificent Wawel Cathedral, on Wawel Hill beside the castle, witnessed the coronations of Polish kings and queens. John Paul II, who held mass here when he was Archbishop of Kraków, canonized the cathedral in 1997. Ascend the tower to **Sigismund's Bell** for an unbeatable view of Kraków. The huge bell can supposedly be heard for up to 50km. Descend to the **Royal Tombs** through the Czartoryskich Chapel. The underground maze contains elaborately carved sarcophagi of royals and acclaimed military leaders, including generals Tadeusz Kościuszko and Józef

Piłsudski. *(Cathedral open M-Sa 9am-2:45pm, Su and holy days 12:15-2:45pm. Buy tickets at the kasa across from the entrance. 10zł, students 5zł. Cathedral Museum 5/2zł.)*

DRAGON'S DEN. Home to Kraków's erstwhile menace, the **dragon's den** is in the southwest corner of the complex. According to legend, the dragon held the people of Kraków in terror, eating livestock and virgins, until a shepherd put a fake sheep full of sulfur outside its cave. Upon devouring the trap, the reptile became so thirsty that it drank water from the Wisła until it burst. Enjoy the cave, or skip the den and walk down to the path that borders the castle walls to see a wonderfully ugly metal statue of the fire-breathing dragon. *(Open daily May-Oct. 10am-5pm. 3zł.)*

STARE MIASTO

At the center of Stare Miasto (Old Town) spreads **Rynek Główny,** the largest market square in Europe, and at the heart of the Rynek stands the **Sukiennice** (Cloth Hall). Surrounded by multicolored row houses and cafes, it's a convenient center for exploring the nearby sights. The Royal Road (Droga Królewska), traversed by medieval royals on the way to coronations in Wawel, starts at **St. Florian's Church** (Kościół św. Floriana), crosses pl. Matejki, passes the **Academy of Fine Arts** (Akademia Sztuk Pięknych), and crosses Basztowa to the **Barbakan.** The Gothic-style Barbakan, built in 1499, is the best preserved of the three such defensive fortifications surviving in Europe. *(Open daily 10:30am-6pm. 6zł, students 4zł.)* The royal road continues through **Floriańska Gate,** the old city entrance and the only remnant of the city's medieval walls. Inside Stare Miasto, the road runs down Floriańska, past the Rynek and along Grodzka, which ends with **Wawel** in sight. A **map** marking all the points can be found in front of Floriańska Gate.

ST. MARY'S CHURCH (KOŚCIÓŁ MARIACKI). This church, home to the oldest Gothic altar in the world, barely survived WWII. Dismantled by the Nazis, it was discovered by Allied forces at the war's end and reassembled. Look down from the exquisite, star-flecked ceiling to see a 500-year-old wooden altar. Every hour, the blaring Hejnał trumpet calls from the taller of St. Mary's two towers and cuts off abruptly to recall the near-destruction of Kraków in 1241, when invading Tatars shot down the trumpeter as he attempted to warn the city. Visitors can ascend both towers. *(At the corner of the Rynek closest to the train station. Open daily 11:30am-6pm. Icon unveiled daily M-F 11:50am-6pm, Su and holidays 2-6pm. Cover shoulders and knees. No photography. Altar 4zł, students 2zł. Video or photo camera 5zł. Wieża Mariacka open Tu, Th, Sa 9am-5:30pm. 5zł. Smaller tower open daily 10am-1:15pm and 2-5pm. 5zł, students 2.50zł.)*

JAGIELLONIAN UNIVERSITY (UNIWERSYTET JAGIELLOŃSKI). Established in 1364, Kraków's Jagiellonian University is the third oldest university in Europe. Among its celebrated alumni are astronomer **Mikołaj Kopernik (Copernicus)** and painter Jan Matejko. The picturesque Collegium Maius is the university's oldest building. It became a museum in 1964 and now boasts an extensive collection of historical scientific instruments. Call ahead to join or arrange a tour. *(Jagiellońska 15. ☎422 0549. Open M-W and F 10am-2:30pm, Th 10am-5:20pm, Sa 10am-2pm. Guided visits only; tours begin every 20min. Tour in English daily 1pm. 12zł, students 6zł.)*

CLOTH HALL (SUKIENNICE). In the Rynek, the yellow Cloth Hall remains as profit-oriented today as when medieval cloth merchants used it. The ground floor is lined with wooden stalls selling crafts. Upstairs, the Cloth Hall Gallery houses 18th- and 19th-century art. During the academic year, students fill the area. *(☎422 1166. Open Tu and F-Sa 10am-6pm. 8zł, students 5zł; Th free.)*

CZARTORYSKICH MUSEUM. This museum exhibits countless artifacts, ranging from 16th-century Polish battle armor to Egyptian sarcophagi and includes **Leonardo da Vinci's** *Lady with an Ermine* and **Rembrandt's** *Landscape with a*

Merciful Samaritan. Da Vinci's piece harbors several secrets: historians have debated whether the lady portrayed is Beatrice d'Este, the Duchess of Milan or Cecilia Gallerani, the Duke of Milan's 16-year-old mistress. Also debatable are the painting's authenticity and location prior to its 1800 purchase by Polish prince. *(św. Jana 19. ☎422 55 66. Open Tu, Th 10am-4pm; W, F 11am-7pm; Sa-Su 10am-3pm; closed last Su of each month. 10zł; students 5zł; Th free.)*

OTHER SIGHTS. The main branch of the **National Museum** *(Muzeum Narodowe)* has permanent exhibits of armory and 20th-century art, and hosts acclaimed temporary exhibits. *(Al. 3 Maja 1. Take tram #15 to Cracovia. ☎634 3377; www.muz-nar.krakow.pl. Open Tu, Th 10am-4pm, W, F, Sa 10am-7pm; Su 10am-3pm. Permanent exhibit 8zł, students 9zł. Temporary exhibits 6/3zł. Th Free. Cash Only.)* The **History Museum of Kraków,** a branch of the National Museum, displays ceiling frescoes and centuries-old documents from Kraków. *(Rynek Główny 35. ☎619 2300. Open daily 10am-5:30pm. 9zł, students 6zł.)* Both a store and gallery, **Galeria Autorska Andrzeja Mleczki** features satirical, funky, and fun drawings, offering a glimpse into Polish politics. *(Św. Jana 14. Open M-F 11am-7pm, Sa 10am-5pm. MC/V.)* For an even funkier experience, visit the **Poster Gallery** to view locally printed posters. *(Stolarska 8. ☎421 2640. Open M-F 11am-6pm, Sa 11am-2pm. AmEx/MC/V.)*

POLAND

KAZIMIERZ: THE OLD JEWISH QUARTER

Southeast of the Rynek and Wawel. The 15min. walk from the Rynek leads down Sienna past St. Mary's Church. Eventually, Sienna turns into Starowiślna. After 1km, turn right on Miodowa and take the 1st left onto Szeroka.

In 1495, King Jan Olbrecht moved Kraków's Jews to Kazimierz in order to remove them from the city proper; most continued to live here through the beginning of World War II, when most of Kraków 68,000 Jews were forced out by the Nazis. The 15,000 remaining were resettled in the Podgórze ghetto in 1941, and deported to death camps by 1943. Only about 100 practicing Jews now live here, but Kazimierz, is now a favorite haunt of Kraków's intellectuals and the center of a resurgence of Central European Jewish culture. The **Jarden Bookstore,** the only Jewish bookstore in Poland, organizes guided **tours,** including a 2hr. tour of Kazimierz and the Płaszów death camp, that traces the sites shown in the film *Schindler's List.* Płaszów, south of Kraków, was destroyed by the Nazis on their retreat and is now an overgrown field. *(Szeroka 2. ☎421 1166; www.jarden.pl. Open M-F 9am-6pm, Sa-Su 10am-6pm. Kazimierz tour 110zł, with ghetto 140zł. Schindler's List tour 195zł. Car tour of Auschwitz-Birkenau 360zł, private guide 160zł. 20% student discount. AmEx/MC/V.)*

GALICIA JEWISH MUSEUM. Galicia, a region that includes much of southern Poland, was once the heart of Eastern European Jewish culture. In this unconventional museum, photojournalist Chris Schwarz uses photographs of contemporary Poland to document the past and present of Jewish life in Galicia with images of ruins, abandoned cemeteries, and surviving traces of Jewish culture. A spare converted warehouse houses the museum, a cafe, and a bookstore. The non-profit organization also offers Yiddish language lessons and lectures on Judaism. *(Dajwór 18. ☎421 6842; www.galiciajewishmuseum.org. Open daily 9am-7pm. 7zł, students 5zł.)*

OLD SYNAGOGUE (STARA SYNAGOGA). Poland's earliest example of Jewish religious architecture, the Old Synagogue houses the **Kraków Jewish History and Culture Museum,** depicting the history, tradition, and art of the local community. Historic religious objects and nostalgic prewar photographs are counterposed with WWII-era documents of segregation and deportation. *(Szeroka 24. ☎422 0962; fax 431 0545. Open Apr.-Oct. M 10am-2pm, Tu-Su 9am-5pm; Nov.-Mar. M 10am-2pm, W-Th and Sa-Su 9am-4pm, F 10am-5pm. English captions. 7zł, students 5zł. M free. Cameras 10zł.)*

REMUH SYNAGOGUE AND CEMETERY (SYNAGOGA I CMENTARZ REMUH). Rabbi Moses Isserles, a great scholar better known as the Remuh, founded this tiny synagogue in 1553 in honor of his wife, who had died in the plague of 1551-52. The Remuh, now buried under a tree to the left of the cemetery's entrance, is believed to have caused strong winds to cover the cemetery with sand, protecting it from 19th-century Austrian invaders. Many of the gravestones remained buried through WWII. Though the Nazis used the small cemetery as a garbage dump, the sands protected it from total destruction. Much of the site has been painstakingly reconstructed but remains relatively untouristed. *(Szeroka 40. Open M-F and Su 9am-6pm. Services F at sundown and Sa morning. 5zł, students 2zł.)*

CENTER FOR JEWISH CULTURE. The center organizes cultural events, heritage tours, lectures, and concerts. Free exhibits are across from the info desk. *(Meiselsa 17. ☎430 6449; www.judaica.pl. Open M-F 10am-6pm, Sa-Su 10am-2pm.)*

NOWA HUTA. For a sharp contrast with both the tourist crowds and the beauty of Wawel Hill, head to eerie **Nowa Huta** (New Steelworks), one of only two full-scale Soviet planned communities ever realized. Just 20min. by tram from Stare Miasto, Nowa Huta was fashioned by the Soviet Union beginning in 1949 in a bid to stir communist spirit in Catholic, intellectual Kraków. With broad streets, plentiful greenery, and imposing architecture, the town is a surreal relic of the Soviet era. From the outset, the hyper-planned community backfired on its planners. The **Lenin Steelworks,** operating the biggest blast furnace in Europe in its heyday, showered industrial pollution on Kraków; the community's residents, meanwhile, launched a 20-year campaign to have a parish church built in Nowa Huta. By the 1980s, the 40,000 steelworkers of Nowa Huta were at the forefront of dissent against the Communist regime, frequently striking in protest of government policies. Visitors can take in the modernist **Church of Mary of Fatima,** finally built in 1977, tour the Steelworks by appointment, and stroll along the streets where Andrzej Wajda set his seminal film about Communist Poland, *Man of Marble. (To reach Nowa Huta from Kraków center, take tram #4 or 15 from the train station to the pl. Centralny stop. www.nh.pl. For a guided tour in an authentic East German Trabant, contact Crazy Guides, ☎500 091 200; www.crazyguides.com. Tour 119zl per person.)*

ENTERTAINMENT AND FESTIVALS

The **Cultural Information Center,** św. Jana 2, sells the monthly guide *Karnet* (4zł) and directs visitors to box offices. (☎421 7787. Open daily 10am-6pm.) The city jumps with jazz; check out **U Muniaka,** Floriańska 3 (☎423 1205; open daily 6:30pm-2am) and **Harris Piano Jazz Bar,** Rynek Główny 28 (☎421 57 41; shows 9pm-midnight; open daily Tu-Su 1pm-2am.) Classical music-lovers will relish the **Sala Filharmonia** (Philharmonic Hall), Zwierzyniecka 1. (☎422 9477, ext. 31; www.filharmonia.krakow.pl. Box office open Tu-F 12-7pm, Sa-Su 1hr. before performance; closed June 9-Sept. 20.) The **opera** performs at the **Słowacki Theater,** św. Ducha 1. (☎424 4525. Box office open M-Sa 9am-7pm, Su 4hr. before performance. Tickets 30-50zł, students 25-35zł.) The **Stary Teatr** (Old Theater) has a few stages that host films, plays, and exhibits. (☎422 4040. Open Tu-Sa 10am-1pm and 5-7pm, Su 5-7pm. Tickets 30-60zł, students 20-35zł.) Enjoy a relaxing evening and catch a movie at **Kino Pod Baranami,** Rynek Główny 27. (☎423 0768. Tickets M 9.90zł; Tu-Th 15zł, students 13zł; F-Su 16/14zł. Drop by at noon everyday for a 10zł movie.) **Kino Mikro,** Lea 5, shows European films. (☎634 2897. Open daily 30min. before 1st showing. M 10zł, Tu-Su 13zł, students 11zł.)

Notable festivals include the **International Short Film Festival** (late May), **Wianki** (the Floating of Wreaths on the Wisła; June), the **Festival of Jewish Culture** (early July), the **Street Theater Festival** (early July), and the **Jazz Festival** (late July).

NIGHTLIFE

Kraków in Your Pocket has up-to-date info on the club and pub scenes, and the free monthly English-language *KrakOut* magazine has day-by-day event listings. Most dance clubs are in Stare Miasto, while bohemian pubs and cafes cluster in Kazimierz. Visit www.cracow-life.com/drink/pubs_cafes.php for more info. Kraków's night establishments have a high turnover rate. For tips on Kraków's **gay nightlife,** see http://gayeuro.com/krakow or www.cracow.gayguide.net.

Alchemia, Estery 5 (☎421 2200). Candles twinkle in this pleasantly disheveled bar, which includes bizarre and fascinating decor–one of the many rooms is decorated to look like a 1950s kitchen. Frequented by students, artists, and Brits downing beer (*Żywiec;* 6.5zł) and lingering until dawn. During the day, this Kazimierz bar masquerades as a smoky cafe. Occasional live music and film screenings. Open daily 9am-4am.

Prozak, Dominikańska 6 (☎429 1128; www.prozak.pl). With more dance floors, bars, and intimate nooks than you'll be able to count–including a shisha bar–Prozak is one of the top clubs in town. Hipster students, porn star look-alikes, and large groups of foreigners lounge on low-slung couches. Pass on the undersized mixed drinks (5-20zł) for pints of beer (7-10zł). No sneakers or sandals. Cover F-Sa 10zł. Open daily 7pm-late.

Kitsch, ul. Wielopole 15 (☎698 613 790), located between the Rynek and Kazimierz. This gay-friendly establishment, in the same building as 3 other clubs, offers a convenient location and great dancing atmosphere. Drinks start at 8zł. Boys night on W, student Night Th, with beer at 5zł for men and students, respectively. Open 5pm-late.

Cień, św. Jana 15 (☎422 2177). The underground vaults of the "Shadow" fill with Kraków's beautiful people, who come here to see and be seen. The club plays mostly house techno and can be selective at the door. Mixed drinks 10-20zł. No sneakers or sandals. Open Tu-Th 8pm-5am, F-Sa 8pm-6am. MC/V.

Faust, Rynek Główny 6, entrance off of Sienna St. (☎423 8300). Sell your soul in this underground labyrinth, where a raucous, friendly crowd sits at massive wooden tables or dances unabashedly to pop and techno hits. Beer 4-8zł. Disco W-Sa. Cover F-Sa 5zł. Open M-Th and Su noon-1am, F-Sa noon-4am. Cash only.

Propaganda, Miodowa 20 (☎292 0402). Despite the candles and wobbly tables, Propaganda's take on Kazimierz bohemia has a punk-rock feel. Decor mixes posters of Stalin with guitars of Polish rockers, some of whom have been known to tend bar here. Open daily 2pm-late. Cash only.

Klub pod Jaszczurami (Club under the Lizards), Rynek Główny 8 (☎292 2202). A cafe by day and thumping club party by night. Familiar tunes fill the dark dance floors as smoke wafts above the tables of chatting 20-somethings. Beer 6.50zł. Open M-Sa 10am-late, Su 11am-late.

DAYTRIPS FROM KRAKÓW

AUSCHWITZ-BIRKENAU

Tourist offices in Kraków organize trips that include transportation and guides. Buses (1½-2hr., 5 per day, 10-15zł; get off at Muzeum Oświęcim) run to the town of Oświęcim from Kraków's central bus station. The bus back to Kraków leaves from a different stop across from the parking lot. Trains run from Kraków Płaszów (7-10zł). From outside the Oświęcim train station, buses #2-5, 8-9, and 24-29 drop visitors off at the Muzeum Oświęcim stop. Alternatively, turn right as you exit the station, go 1 block, and turn left on Więźniów Oświęcimia; the Auschwitz camp is 1.6km down the road.

An estimated 1.5 million people—mostly Jews—were murdered, and thousands more suffered unthinkable horrors in the infamous Nazi death camps at **Auschwitz**

(Oświęcim) and **Birkenau** (Brzezinka). As the largest and most brutal of the camps, their names are synonymous with the Nazi death machine. In 1979, the complexes were added to the UNESCO World Heritage List.

AUSCHWITZ I. In 1940, the Nazis built the first and smaller of two death camps on the grounds of a Polish Army garrison. Originally consisting of 20 buildings, the camp grew as prisoners were forced to build additional barracks to house the growing number of arriving prisoners. In 1942, Auschwitz became the center of extermination of Jews, Roma, and other peoples deemed "inferior" by the Nazis. The eerily tidy red brick buildings seems silent and unremarkable until the bitter irony of the inscription on the camp's gate—*Arbeit Macht Frei* (Work Shall Set You Free)—sinks in. Surviving barracks showcase victims' ghostly remnants: suitcases, shoes, eyeglasses, and even hair provide a terrifyingly personal look at Nazi atrocities. The lynching post and gas chamber also remain on the grounds. At 11am and 1pm, the building at the entrance shows a 15min. English-language film (3.50zł) with footage recorded by the Soviet Army when it liberated the camp in January 1945. Children under 14 are strongly advised not to visit. *(☎843 2022. Open daily June-Aug. 8am-7pm; Sept. and May 8am-6pm; Oct. and Apr. 8am-5pm; Nov. and Mar. 8am-4pm; Dec.-Feb. 8am-3pm. Tour in English daily 10, 11am, 1 and 3pm. Free. 3½hr. tours with guide 26zł; film and bus included. English guidebook 3zł.)*

POLAND

AUSCHWITZ II-BIRKENAU. Auschwitz II-Birkenau was built when the mass influx of prisoners to Auschwitz motivated the Nazis to pursue a more "efficient" method of killing. Little is left now of the 300 barracks that spanned the 425-acre camp, which the Nazis destroyed before it was liberated in 1945. The reconstructed railroad tracks beneath the original SS watchtower glide past the rows of selection barracks where individuals were singled out for work or death. The tracks end among piles of rubber, former gas chambers, and crematoria. Beyond the ruins, a memorial paying tribute to those who died in the Auschwitz camps is a place for quiet reflection. Near the monument is a pond, still gray from the ashes deposited there more than half a century ago. *(Birkenau is 3km from Auschwitz I. Shuttle runs every hr. 11:30am-5:30pm from the Auschwitz parking lot. To walk to Birkenau, turn right from the parking lot, follow the path for about 1.5km, then turn left at the sign for the road. Cross the bridge and continue for about 1km. Open daily 8am-dusk. Free.)*

AUSCHWITZ JEWISH CENTER AND SYNAGOGUE (CENTRUM ŻYDOWSKIE WOŚWIĘCIMIU). The center is next to the restored prewar synagogue. Exhibits focus on prewar Jewish life in the town. Oświęcim offers study and research opportunities, discussion groups, and video testimonials of Auschwitz survivors. The center also provides guidance for those interested in exploring their Jewish roots. Auschwitz guides are available for hire. *(Pl. Ks. Jana Skarbka 5. From the train station take bus #1, 3-6, 8, or 28 to the town center, get off at the stop after the bridge and backtrack, taking the 1st right and then a left to pl. Ks. Jana Skarbka. Alternatively, take a taxi for about 17zł. ☎844 7002; www.ajcf.pl. English spoken. Open M-F and Su 8:30am-8pm.)*

WIELICZKA

Danilowicza 10. Many companies, including Orbis, organize trips to the mine. The cheapest way to go is to take one of the minibuses that leave from between the train and bus stations. (30min., "Contrabus" every 15min., 2.5zl.) In Wieliczka, follow the old path of the tracks and then the "do kopalni" signs. ☎278 7302; www.kopalnia.pl. Open daily Apr.-Oct. 7:30am-7:30pm; Nov.-Mar. 8am-5pm; closed holidays. Admission with guided tours only. Polish tours 45zl, students 30zl. Tours in English daily 8:30am-6pm; June and Sept. 8 per day, July and Aug. every 35 people; wait should be no longer than 1hr. 50zl, students under 25 40zl; Nov.-Feb. 20% off. 1hr. museum tours 9zl, students 4.50zl; M free. Wheelchair-accessible. MC/V.

Thirteen kilometers southeast of Kraków and 100m below the tiny town of Wieliczka lies the 700-year-old **Wieliczka Salt Mine.** Follow the footsteps of Goethe, one of the attraction's first tourists, and see how miners and artists transformed the salt deposits into a maze of chambers full of sculptures and carvings. Though salt has not been manually excavated here since July 1996, it still exports 20,000 tons of salt per year through natural processes. In 1978, UNESCO, declared it one of the 12 most priceless monuments in the world. Amazingly, the mine once provided a third of Poland's GDP. The 2hr. tour passes spectacular underground lakes and sculptures of beloved Poles like Copernicus and the late Pope John Paul II. The most impressive sight is **St. Kinga's Chapel,** with an altar, chandeliers, and religious relics, all carved from salt. At the end of the tour, take the lift 120m back to the surface or go to the **underground museum,** Muzeum Żup Krakowskich, which gives a more detailed history of the mines and features 14 additional chambers. Bring a sweater—the mine is chilly.

CZĘSTOCHOWA

Trains run directly to Częstochowa from Krakow Glowny (2-3hr., 4 per day; 18-32zł). The train and bus stations lie across the post office parking lot from each other and are near the town center between al. Wolnosci and Pilsudskiego. Al. NMP links them to Jasna Góra, whose spire is visible throughout town. From either station, go right on Wolnosci to get to al. NMP. Go left to reach Jasna Góra (Bright Mountain).

Since 1382, Częstochowa (chen-sto-HO-va) has been defined by a four-foot tall icon housed in the Jasna Góra monastery overlooking the city. The **Black Madonna** (Czarna Madonna, also known as Matka Boża Częstochowska), the most sacred of Polish icons, draws millions of Catholic pilgrims every year. It is displayed in the ornate 15th-century **Basilica** (Bazylika) inside the small **Chapel of Our Lady** (Kaplica Matki Bożej), which has twice been extended to house more pilgrims. The icon is veiled and revealed several times per day, accompanied by solemn festivities. (Chapel open daily 5am-9:30pm. Icon revealed May-Oct. M-F 6am-noon and 1-9:15pm, Sa-Su and holidays 6am-1pm and 3-9:15pm; Nov.-Apr. M-F 6am-noon and 3-9:15pm; Sa-Su and holidays 6am-1pm and 3-9:15pm. Free; donations requested.) To get a better understanding of the Madonna's history and significance, as well as the history of the monastery itself, it's worth grabbing an audio tour from the stand in the courtyard. (Audio tours 14zł, students 10zł, family of four 36zł.)

Częstochowa's restaurants and ice cream stands keep both pilgrims and locals well fed. The gigantic **Elea SuperMarket,** in the red building across from the bus station, is a good place to stock up on supplies. (Open M-F 8am-9pm, Sa 8am-8pm, Su 9am-4pm.) **Restauracja and Bar Dom Pielgrzyma ❶,** Wyszyńskiego 1, is a devout variation on the milk bar that serves meaty *pierogi* and *kotlety* (3-6zł), various soups (2-5zł), and non-alcoholic beverages (3-6zł) to pilgrims who don't mind the school gym ambience. (☎377 7564. Open M-Th and Su 7am-6pm, Sa 7am-8pm.)

TRAIL OF EAGLES' NESTS (SZLAK ORLICH GNIAZD)

Trains run directly to Częstochowa from Krakow Glowny central train (2-3hr., 4 per day; 18-32zł). From Częstochowa, take bus #58 or 67 to Olsztyn-Rynek (40min.; appx. 1 per hr.; 3.30zł, students 1.60zł) from Piłsudskiego, across from the Częstochowa train station. Castle tower open May-Oct. daily 10am-8pm. 2zł, students 1zł.

Crags of Jurassic limestone erupt from green hills along the narrow 100km strip of land known as the **Kraków-Częstochowa Uplands** (Jura Krakowska-Częstochowska). These breathtaking rocks helped fortify the 12th-century castles built in the area, whose cliff-side perches next to the nests of eagle owls earned them the name "eagles' nests." The fortifications proved no match for the artillery of the invading Swedes, however, and by the end of the 17th century, the fortresses had badly deteriorated. Today, only a few, including Wawel Castle in Kraków, remain whole. The ruins of the rest lie along the uplands, waiting to be discovered.

The two biggest attractions on the trail, the **Olsztyn Castle** and the **Pieskowa Skała Castle,** are half-day trips from Częstochowa and Kraków, respectively. Constructed in the 12th and 13th centuries, the castle that stands in the pastoral town of Olsztyn has lost much of its former glory. In 1655, the Swedish army ransacked the complex. A century later, the locals took bricks from the castle to rebuild the town church. The preserved sections are in the upper castle, where the imposing watchtower and stockier square tower still stand among smaller fragments of the former castle walls. The castles are rumored to be haunted by the ghosts of a young bride who got lost in the dungeon and Maćko Borkowic, who was starved to death in the circular tower for his rebellion against King Kazimierz the Great. The lack of formal paths surrounding the sprawling ruins and rock caves invites exploration. Kebab and ice cream stands along ul. Zamkowa, leading from the square to the castle, provide cheap eats. **Pod Zamkiem ❷,** ul. Zamkowa 3, serves up pizza for 12-16zł. (Open Su-Th noon-10pm, F-Sa noon-11pm. Cash only.)

There are 20 hiking trails that run along the entire 100km route: the full hike takes about seven days. The trail is a rewarding, if challenging, **bicycle route** with five variations. There are also two choice **equestrian trails.** Kraków and Częstochowa branches of PTTK provide maps. The trail, covering a broad range of terrain, is marked by red blazes with maps posted along the way. The route leads through 12 different castle ruins between Kraków and Częstochowa, and passes through several small towns that can provide food and accommodations.

WADOWICE

Take 1 of 8 daily buses from Kraków PKS station (1½hr., 5-10zł). From the Wadowice bus station, follow the path behind the ticket office through the park. Turn left on Sienkiewicza, then right on Lwowska to reach pl. Jana Pawła II. Wojtyła House open May-Oct. Tu-Su 9am-1pm and 2-6pm; Nov.-Apr. Tu-Su 9am-noon and 1-4pm. Free, donations requested.

In the midst of rolling hills teeming with pheasants lies the birthplace of Poland's beloved Karol Wojtyła, Pope John Paul II. Since the pope's death, Wadowice has seen a deluge of tourists and pilgrims both Polish and foreign. Accommodation and food options are limited, but the town offers a glimpse of Poland's adoration of its great modern hero. The two primary sites of interest for visitors are the house where Wojtyła was born and raised and the basilica where he was baptized and ordained. The **Wojtyła House** at Kościelna 7 is half a block from the large pl. Jana Pawła II. If you can brave the crowds and long lines, especially on weekends, you will find a house with six small rooms (only three of which the Wojtyła family lived in), including the one where baby Karol was born on May 18, 1920. The rooms are now filled with black-and-white photos and personal items that trace Wojtyła's early life and career. A few buildings over stands the large **Minor Basilica** (Bazylika Mniejsza), where the pope's baptismal font rests alongside the reputedly miraculous icon Our Lady of Perpetual Help. Both items were blessed by the pope during a 1999 visit and now attract reverent visitors. The Wadowice tourist information office, ul Kościelna 4, will provide info on other sights in town related to the papal childhood. (☎03 38 73 23 65. Open M-F 8am-4pm, Sa 10am-4pm.

LUBLIN ☎0(81)

The main attraction of Lublin (LOO-blin; pop. 400,000) is its centuries of history, made tangible in buildings that emerged largely unscathed from the bombings which razed so much of the country during World War II. But the Old Town isn't the only well-preserved feature of Lublin: more unsettlingly, the Majdanek concentration camp on the city's outskirts preserves the gas chambers where so many died in the Holocaust. During the Communist era, Lublin was the stronghold of Polish Catholic resistance: its Katolicki Uniwersytet Lubelski was the country's only independent university, and the only church-run university in the Eastern Bloc. The church's presence remains palpable, and today nuns and priests share Lublin's streets with an exuberant student population.

TRANSPORTATION

Trains: Pl. Dworcowy 1 (☎94 36). To: **Częstochowa** (6hr., 1per day, 47zł); **Gdańsk** (7hr., 3 per day, 54zł); **Kraków** (4hr., 2 per day, 47zł); **Poznań** (10hr., 2 per day, 56zł); **Toruń** (8hr., 3 per day, 50zł); **Warsaw** (3hr., 9 per day, 34zł); **Wrocław** (9½hr., 2 per day, 54zł); **Berlin, GER** (11hr., 1 per day, 153-226zł).

Buses: Tysiąclecia 4 (☎77 66 49, info 934). To: **Kraków** (6hr., 4 per day, 40zł); **Warsaw** (2¼hr., 20 per day, 25-30zł); **Wrocław** (8hr., 2per day, 60zł). **Polski Express** (☎02 28 54 02 85; www.polskiexpress.org) runs buses to: **Warsaw** (3hr., 7 per day, 41zł).

Public Transportation: Buy tickets for buses and trolleys at kiosks. 2zł, students 1zł.

POLAND

ORIENTATION AND PRACTICAL INFORMATION

The city's main drag, **Krakowskie Przedmieście,** connects **Stare Miasto** (Old Town) in east Lublin to the **Katolicki Uniwersytet Lubelski** (KUL; Catholic University of Lublin) and **Uniwersytet Marii Curie-Skłodowskiej** (Marie Curie-Skłodowska University) in the west. It passes the urban oasis of the **Ogród Saski** (Saxon Garden) and becomes **al. Racławickie.** Take bus #5, 10, or 13 into town from the bus station. From the castle, **Zamkowa** runs out the gates and through Stare Miasto, becoming **Grodzka** and then **Bramowa.** The street runs through the Rynek and emerges from the Stare Miasto through **Brama Krakowska** (Kraków Gate), intersecting Krakowskie Przedmieście. From the train station, take trolley #150 or bus #13 to the city center.

Tourist Office: IT, Jezuicka 1/3 (☎532 4412; itlublin@onet.pl), near the Kraków Gate. Sells **maps** (5zł) and has train and bus info. Open May-Aug. M-Sa 9am-6pm, Su 10am-3pm; Sept.-Apr. M-F 9am-5pm, Sa 10am-4pm, Su 10am-3pm. **Orbis,** Narutowicza 31/33 (☎532 2256), books tours and transportation, provides travel insurance, and helps with visas. Open M-F 9am-6pm, Sa 9am-2pm. AmEx/MC/V.

Currency Exchange: Bank PKO S.A., Królewska 1 (☎532 1016; fax 532 6069), cashes **traveler's checks** for 1.5% commission and offers MC/V **cash advances.** Open M-F 8am-6pm, Sa 10am-2pm. **ATMs** are all over town.

English-Language Bookstore: Empik, Krakowskie Przedmieście 59 (☎/fax 534 3286), offers a small selection of English-language books, magazines, maps, CDs, and DVDs (25-40zł). Open M-F 9:30am-8pm, Su 10:30am-6pm. AmEx/MC/V.

Pharmacy: Apteka, Bramowa 2/8 (☎535 3997). Window open 24hr. Store open daily 8am-8pm. AmEx/MC/V.

Hospital: PSK 1, Staszica 16 (☎532 3935).

Telephones: Inside and outside the post office; inside bus and train stations. Purchase a phone card from the tellers inside the post office, or at kiosks around town.

Internet: Net-Box, Krakowskie Przedmieście 52 (☎532 5220) 1.5zł per 15min. Open M-F 9am-9pm, Sa 10am-9pm, Su noon-9pm. Sesja, Akademicka 4 (enter from the side; ☎504 619 553), a self-proclaimed "cafe drink bar" offers free Wi-Fi. Beer 3.50zł. Open daily 10am-10pm.

Post Office: Krakowskie Przedmieście 50 (☎/fax 532 2071). Fax at window #3. **Poste Restante** at window #1. Open M-F 7am-9pm, Sa 7am-2pm. **Branch** at Grodzka 7. Open M-F 9am-4pm. **Postal Code:** 20-950.

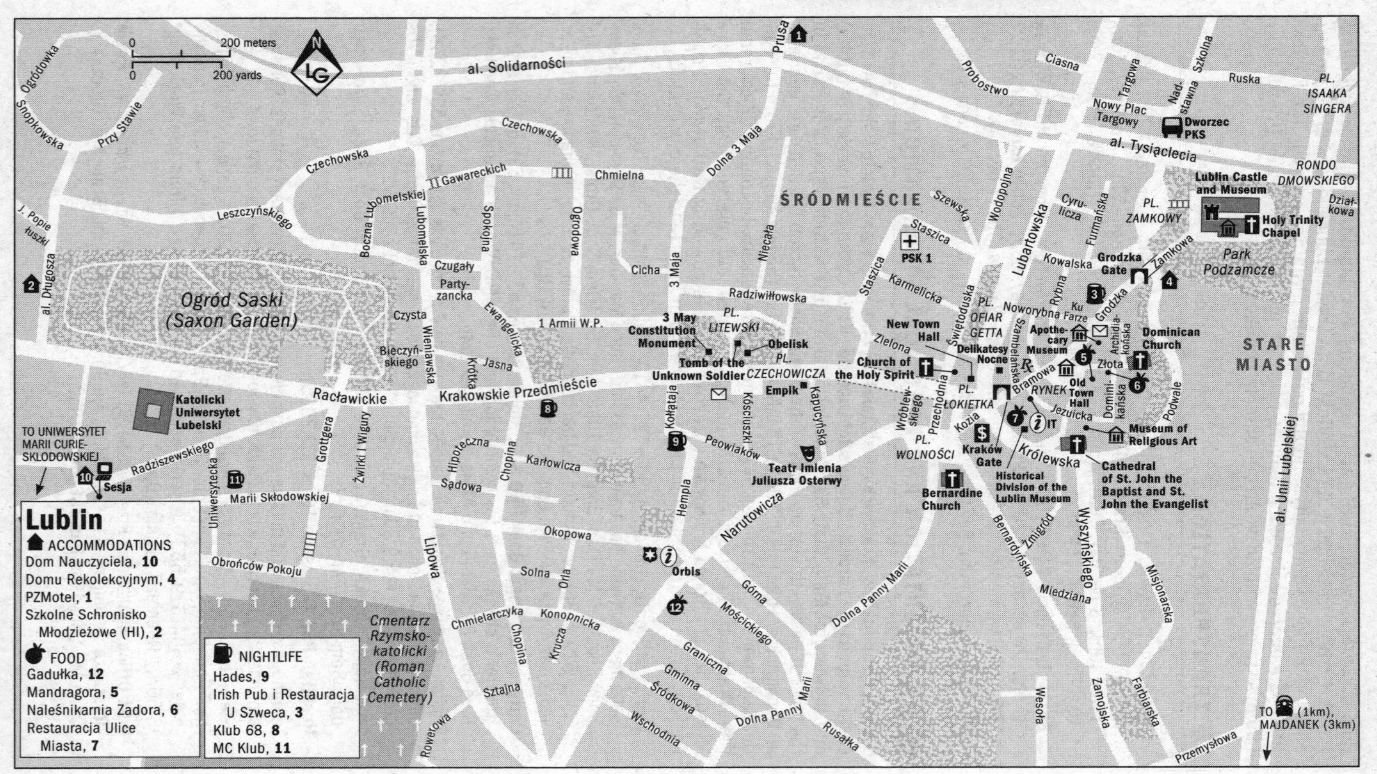
Lublin
ACCOMMODATIONS
Dom Nauczyciela, 10
Domu Rekolekcyjnym, 4
PZMotel, 1
Szkolne Schronisko Młodzieżowe (HI), 2
FOOD
Gadułka, 12
Mandragora, 5
Naleśnikarnia Zadora, 6
Restauracja Ulice Miasta, 7
NIGHTLIFE
Hades, 9
Irish Pub i Restauracja U Szweca, 3
Klub 68, 8
MC Klub, 11
STARE MIASTO
ŚRÓDMIEŚCIE
Lublin Castle and Museum
Holy Trinity Chapel
Park Podzamcze
Dworzec PKS
Grodzka Gate
Dominican Church
Apothecary Museum
Old Town Hall
Museum of Religious Art
Cathedral of St. John the Baptist and St. John the Evangelist
Historical Division of the Lublin Museum
Kraków Gate
Bernardine Church
New Town Hall
Church of the Holy Spirit
Delikatesy Nocne
PSK 1
Teatr Imienia Juliusza Osterwy
Empik
Obelisk
Tomb of the Unknown Soldier
3 May Constitution Monument
Orbis
Ogród Saski (Saxon Garden)
Katolicki Uniwersytet Lubelski
Cmentarz Rzymsko-katolicki (Roman Catholic Cemetery)
TO UNIWERSYTET MARII CURIE-SKŁODOWSKIEJ
TO MAJDANEK (3km)
Sesja
200 meters
200 yards
al. Tysiąclecia
al. Solidarności
Lubartowska
Krakowskie Przedmieście
Racławickie
Lipowa
Narutowicza
al. Unii Lubelskiej

ACCOMMODATIONS

Domu Rekolekcyjnym, Podwale 15 (☎532 4138). From the train station, take bus #1 to Lubartowska. Buzz the doorbell marked "director." Don't be surprised to see friendly nuns in full habit in this bright, inviting convent in the middle of Stare Miasto. The nuns won't cramp your style, though unmarried co-eds can't share rooms. Breakfast 7zł. Flexible check-out. Quiet hours after 10pm. If arriving on Su, try to make arrangements in advance. Rooms usually 20-40zł. Cash only. ❶

Szkolne Schronisko Młodzieżowe, Długosza 6 (☎/fax 533 0628), west of the center near the KUL. Standard dorm rooms offer few luxuries, and the exterior looks like a 1970s elementary school, but SSM remains a favorite of Polish university students, and is often full in summer. Guests gravitate to the front-lawn picnic tables and the comfortable lounge chairs of the TV lounge. Kitchen. Linen 6zł. Lockout 10am-5pm. Flexible curfew 10pm. 10-bed dorm 24zł, students 16zł; triples 84/69zł. Cash only. ❶

Dom Nauczyciela, Akademicka 4 (☎533 8285). Offering discounts for Polish elementary and high school teachers, Dom Nauczyciela has comfortable and relatively cheap rooms with TVs and baths at a great location. Singles 90-126zł, depending on amenities; doubles 88-154zł. 20% weekend discount. MC/V. ❹

PZMotel, Prusa 8 (☎533 4232; fax 747 8493). From train station, take bus #1 to the bus station. The bright and well-kept interior is more than you might expect from a motel next to a gas station. In-house restaurant *Fiesta* on the ground floor. Squeaky-clean rooms with TVs. Breakfast included. Check-out noon. Singles 120zł; doubles 160zł; triples 249zł; 2-person apartment 350zł. MC/V. ❺

POLAND

FOOD

Those who prefer to assemble their own meals can find supplies at **Delikatesy Nocne,** ul Lubartowska 3, a reasonably priced grocery store right outside Kraków Gate. (Open daily 8am-midnight.) As always, the cheapest option is kebab stands; **Lunch Bar Kebab,** Krakowskie Przedmieście 11, is a solid option on the main drag. (Small kebab 6zł, large 9zł; open 9am-midnight. Cash only.)

Naleśnikarnia Zadora, Rynek 8 (☎534 5534). Hidden in a cool, comfortable courtyard accessible from both the Rynek and Grodzka, Zadora offers dozens of varieties of *naleśniki.* Savory *naleśniki* (9-19zł) feature meats such as salami and ham, but also include vegetarian options like the 3-cheese *naleśnik*. Sweet desert *naleśnik* (5-13zł) include the banana and Nutella naleśnik (12zł); you can also order up a personalized *naleśnik* (priced by topping). Open daily 10am-11pm. AmEx/MC/V. ❷

Mandragora, Rynek 9 (☎536 2020). Menorahs, stars of David, and pictures of Israel cover the walls of this self-proclaimed "Jewish Pub," which offers traditional Jewish dishes such as gefilte fish (15zł) and Israeli favorites (falafel 18zł). Owned by an effusive Polish-Israeli woman whose picture and manifesto grace the back of the menu. Entrees 18-20zł. Kosher, with a special Shabbat menu F-Sa. Open daily 1-11pm. ❸

Gadułka, Narutowicza 32. This small white nook furnished with white plastic patio furniture belies a true cafe spirit, with excellent coffee and fruit tarts (3zł) for a third of the going Krakowskie Przedmieście rate, and massive cream puffs run a mere 2zł. This far away from the tourist center, don't expect an English menu. Open M-Sa 9am-7pm, Su 10am-6pm. Cash only. ❶

Restauracja Ulice Miasta, pl. Łokietka 3 (☎534 0592; www.ulicemiasta.com.pl). Tucked into a corner next to Kraków Gate. Regional cuisine in Stare Miasto. Meat-heavy dishes such as "the gamekeepers' money bag" (cutlet with mushrooms; 23zł) and *forszmak* meat soup (9zł) dominate the menu. Dinner special (3-course fixed dinner) 18/23zł M-F 12-6pm. Open Su-Th 9am-11pm, F-Sa 9am-1am. AmEx/MC/V. ❸

SIGHTS AND FESTIVALS

The ochre facades of **Krakowskie Przedmieście** lead into medieval Stare Miasto. Pl. Litewski showcases an **obelisk** commemorating the treaty, signed in Lublin in 1569, unifying Poland and Lithuania into what was then the largest country in Europe. The square also displays a monument to Józef Piłsudski, a statue honoring the **Third of May Constitution** (Pomnik Konstytucji 3 Maja), and a **Tomb of the Unknown Soldier** (Płyta Grobu Nieznanego Żołnierza). The 1827 **New Town Hall** (Nowy Ratusz), the seat of Lublin's government, sits on pl. Łokietka, east of pl. Litewski. To the right begins Królewska, which runs around the corner to the grand **Cathedral of St. John the Baptist and St. John the Evangelist** (Katedra Św. Jana Chrzciciele i Św. Jana Ewangelisty). Inside the church, a crypt holds the open coffins of 18th-century religious figures, and near the building's exit hangs a full-size replica of the Shroud of Turin, a 2003 gift from the late pope John Paul II. (Open daily 10am-4pm. Crypt 2zł per 1.50zł; crypt and treasury 4zł, students 3zł.) The **Archdiocesan Museum of Sacred Art** (Muzeum Archidiecezjalne Sztuki Sakralnej) occupies the 17th-century **Trinitarska Tower** beside the cathedral, which contains statues of saints, cherubs, and roosters. A side gallery halfway up the tower holds a 16th-century Madonna. Your reward comes 320 stairs later: a panoramic view of Lublin from the top. (☎444 7450. Open Mar. 25-Nov. 15 daily 10am-5pm. 5zł, students 3zł.)

Krakowskie Przedmieście runs through pl. Łokietka to the fortified **Kraków Gate,** which houses the **Historical Division of Lublin Museum** (Muzeum Historii Miasta Lublina), pl. Łokietka 3. Exhibits highlight town history from 1585 to present, with a special focus on WWII. (With your back to pl. Łokietka, enter through the side door on the right. ☎532 6001. Open W-Sa 9am-4pm, Su 9am-5pm. 3.50zł, students 2.50zł. One day each week is arbitrarily free.) Across the gate, Bramowa leads to the Rynek (market square) and the nearby Renaissance houses. For an unusual treat, stop in the **Apothecary Museum** (Muzeum Zakładu Historii Farmacji), Grodzka 5a, for a collection of medical artifacts seasoned with drying herbs. (☎747 6416. Open Tu-F 11am-4pm. Free.) In the Rynek's center stands the 18th-century **Old Town Hall** (Stary Ratusz). A walk along Grodzka leads through the 15th-century **Grodzka Gate** to Zamkowa, which runs to **Lublin Castle** (Zamek Lubelski). Most of the structure was built in the 14th century by King Kazimierz the Great. The castle retains a sinister air: during WWII, it functioned as a Gestapo jail and the region's Nazi headquarters; in the decade that followed, the Soviets tortured and killed political prisoners there. After dusk, the flickering votive candles of **Cmentarz Rzymskokatolicki,** Lublin's oldest cemetery, make for a stirring experience. Poles have a well-established Sunday tradition of visiting the graves of their loved ones after mass. Benches accompany most recent gravestones, and fresh flowers and offerings reveals how frequently these sites enjoy visits. The mossy headstones of the older sections are engraved in Cyrillic. (Open daily dawn-dusk. Free.)

Festivals abound in Lublin. June brings a month-long festival called **Uncover Lublin: Lublin Days** (Odkryjmy Lublin: Dni Lublin). The city hosts musical performances and art exhibits. Schedules are available in English in the tourist office. For more info visit the festival's website at www.odkryjmylublin.pl.

NIGHTLIFE

Lublin's nightlife concentrates in several distinct areas. Boisterous students fill spots clustered near **Radziszewskiego** and along less-traveled streets such as **Peow-**

iaków, while an older crowd keeps to the bars of **Grodzka** in Stare Miasto. The two scenes mingle on **Krakowskie Przedmieście.** Travelers can catch independent films and even the odd Hollywood blockbuster at **Kino "Bajka,"** Radziszewskiego 8. (☎533 8872. 15zł, students 13zł.) The **Teatr Imienia Juliusza Osterwy,** Narutowicza 17, puts on classic shows. (☎ 532 4244. Ticket window open Tu-Sa noon-7pm, Su 4-7pm. Most shows start at 7pm. 21-30zł, students 13-20zł.)

Klub 68, Krakowskie Przedmieście (☎534 2991). One of a few hot new clubs that have popped up along this street, Klub 68's 2 dance floors are separated by 2 dungeon-like lounges with bars and wall-to-wall brightly colored leather couches. With different DJs spinning a different type of music on each dance floor, there's something here to satisfy most tastes. Open daily 9pm-late. Cover Th-Sa 10zł. Cash only.

MC Klub, MC Skłodowskiej 5 (☎743 6516; www.mcklub.pl); enter beneath the city philharmonium. Aiming to please the hordes of students who pack the place from wall to glow-in-the-dark wall on weekends, DJs spin mainstream Polish pop music. If dancing isn't your thing, relax on couches amid the stylish Art Deco decor. Drinks 5-10zł. Cover 10zł; Th men 10zł, students 5zł, women free; no cover Tu-W and Su.

Hades, Peowiaków 12 (☎532 5641; www.hades-lublin.pl), in the basement of the Centrum Kultury. Hades draws a mixed crowd with pub and grub in crypt-like rooms and on the stone dance floor. The DJ spins techno, house, and Polish pop. Admission enters you in a nightly raffle for large bottles of vodka. Beer 6zł. Cover Th men 8zł, women 4zł; F men 10zł, women 8zł; Sa men 12zł, women 10zł. Open Th-Sa 7pm-late. AmEx/MC/V.

Irish Pub i Restauracja U Szweca, Grodzka 18 (☎532 8284). Still lively when the other Stare Miasto beer gardens are closing up for the night. The decor of this "Irish Pub" may not be very authentic, but its commitment to heavy drinking is. Conveniently, Lublin's best make-out spot is a brief stumble across the street. Żywiec 5zł. Beamish Stout and Guinness 10zł. Open M-Th and Su noon-midnight, F-Sa noon-1am. MC/V.

DAYTRIPS FROM LUBLIN

MAJDANEK

Take bus #28 from the train station, trolley #153 or 156 from al. Racławickie, or trolley #156 from Królewska. Or simply walk the 4km from Lublin on Królewska, which becomes Wyszyńskiego and then Zamojska, before bearing left at the roundabout onto Fabryczna, which becomes the Droga Męczenników Majdanka *(Road of the Martyrs of Majdanek; 45min.). ☎744 2648; www.majdanek.pl. Open Tu-Su except for national holidays Apr.-Oct. 8am-6pm; Nov.-March 8am-3pm. Free. Children under 14 not permitted. Tours in Polish 60zł per group; in English, German, or Russian 100zł per group. Detailed English guide (7zł) available at the ticket office; helpful English-language map pamphlets free.*

During WWII, the Nazis used Lublin as their eastern base and built Europe's second-largest concentration camp in the suburb of Majdanek. About 78,000 died here. The **Majdanek State Museum** (Państwowe Muzeum Na Majdanku) was founded in 1944 after the Soviet liberation of Lublin; the Soviets, however, kept part of the camp operational in order to intern Polish political prisoners. Since the Nazis didn't have time to destroy the camp in their retreat, the original structures stand untouched, including gas chambers, crematorium, prisoners' barracks, watchtowers, and the electrified barbed-wire perimeter. On November 3, the camp holds a memorial service commemorating the day in 1943 when over 18,400 Jews were executed as part of a two-day plan to kill about 40,000 in operation "Erntefest" (Harvest Festival); it was the largest mass execution of the Holocaust.

KARPATY (THE CARPATHIANS)

Once home to only the reclusive and culturally distinct *Górale* (Highlanders), the Carpathians now lure millions every year to superb hiking and skiing trails. Zakopane, the heart of the region, provides easy access to excellent trails.

ZAKOPANE ☎(0)18

Zakopane (zah-ko-PAH-neh; pop. 28,000) is set in a valley surrounded by jagged peaks and alpine meadows. Although this outdoor adventure haven swells to a population of over 100,000 during the high season (late June-Sept. and Dec.-Feb.), it retains its mountain village charm thanks to its log cabins, sweeping scenery, and native Highlander culture.

TRANSPORTATION

Trains: Chramcówki 35 (☎201 45 04). To: **Częstochowa** (4hr., 3 per day, 24-30zł); **Kraków** (3-4hr., 19 per day, 18-20zł); **Poznań** (11hr., 3 per day, 50-55zł); **Warsaw** (8hr., 8 per day, 46-80zł).

Buses: Kościuszki 25 (☎201 46 03). To **Bielsko-Biała** (3½hr., 2 per day, 20zł), **Kraków** (2-2½hr., 28 per day, 14zł), and **Warsaw** (8½hr., 2 per day, 53zł). An **express bus** runs to **Kraków** (2hr., 10 per day, 14zł); buses leave from the "Express" stop on Kościuszki, 50m toward Krupówki from the bus station.

Taxis: Interradio Taxi (☎96 21). **Radio Taxi** (☎919). **Zielone Taxi** (☎96 62).

Bike Rental: Villa Anna, Nowotarska 21 (☎502 137 512). Bikes 10zł per hr., 50zł per day. Cash only. **Rental Bikes and Scooters,** Piłsudskiego, just over the bridge. Bikes 10zł per hr., 40zł per day; scooters 35zł per hr., 120zł per day. AmEx/MC/V.

ORIENTATION AND PRACTICAL INFORMATION

The main street in town is **Krupówki,** where you'll find most of the city's shopping, eating, and nightlife. The **bus station** is at the intersection of **Kościuszki** and **Jagiellońska** and faces the **train station.** The town center is 15min. down Kościuszki, which intersects Krupówki. The **Tatras** spread around Zakopane.

Tourist Offices: Centrum Informacji Turystyczniej (CIT), Kościuszki 17 (☎201 22 11). Provides regional info on topics from dining to hiking. Sells **maps** (5-9zł) and **guides** (11-28zł) and partners with Centrum Turystyki "Tatry" (☎201 37 44) to book rafting trips on the Dunajec (70-80zł). Open daily July-Sept. 8am-8pm; Oct.-June 9am-6pm.

Currency Exchange: Bank PKO SA, Krupówki 71 (☎201 40 48), cashes **traveler's checks** for 1.5% commission (10zł min.) and gives AmEx/MC/V **cash advances.** Open M-F 9am-5pm. **Bank BPH,** Krupówki 19 (☎132 13 21), offers **Western Union** services. Open 8am-6pm. **Kantory** and **ATMs** line Krupówki.

Luggage Storage: 4zł for a large bag, 8zł for a large bag per day, plus 0.5zł per 50zł declared value. In lockers at the train station, bags are said to be kept all in one big room. Open daily 7am-1pm and 1:30-9pm. Also located at the bus station. 3zł for small bag and 8zł for large bag per day; exact change required. Open daily 8am-7pm.

Pharmacy: Apteka Zdrowie, Kościuszki 10 (☎201 38 30). Open M-F 8am-8pm, Sa 9am-3pm. AmEx/MC/V.

Medical Services: Ambulance ☎992. **Mountain Rescue Service (TOPR),** Piłsudskiego 3a (☎206 34 44). **Samodzielny Publiczny Zakład Opieki Zdrowotnej** (Independent Public Enterprise of Healthcare), Kamieniec 10 (☎201 20 21).

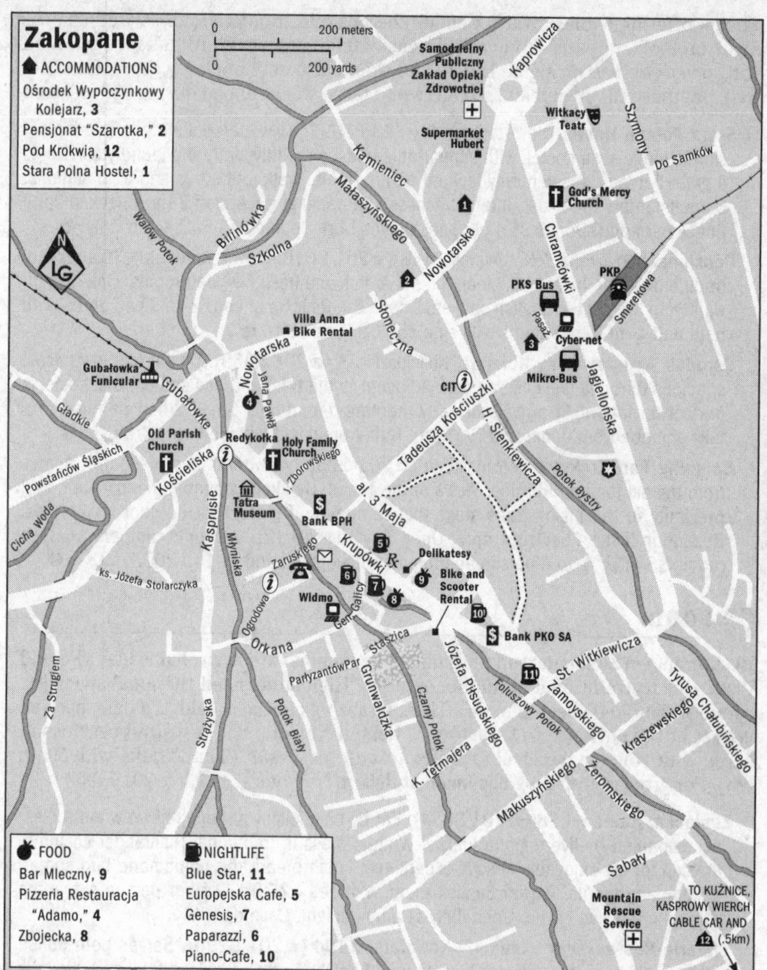

Telephones: Telekomunikacja Polska, Zaruskiego 1. Phones outside. Open 24hr.

Internet: Widmo Internet Cafe, Gen. Galicy 8 (☎206 43 77). 3zł per 30min., 5zł per hr. Open M-F 7:30am-midnight, Sa-Su 9am-midnight. **Cyber-Net**, Kościuszki 24a. 4.5 zł per hour. Open M-Sun 7am-10pm.

Post Office: Krupówki 20 (☎206 3858). **Poste Restante** at *kasa* #5. Open M-F 7am-8pm, Sa 8am-2pm, Su 10am-noon. **Postal Code:** 34500.

ACCOMMODATIONS AND CAMPING

Lodgings in Zakopane are not difficult to find, and reservations are generally unnecessary. While peak season (June-Sept. and Dec.-Feb.) sees an influx of tourists and a steep hike in prices, more **private rooms** (35-70zł) become available.

POLAND

Locals offering rooms swarm outside the bus and train stations as well as post signs on their property. You can also easily find homes with rooms for rent; look for *noclegi* or *pokoje* signs. Hikers and skiers also stay in *chaty* (mountain cabins), but these fill up quickly, so call two to three weeks ahead during high season.

Stara Polana Hostel, Nowotarska 59 (☎206 8902, www.starapolana.pl). This hip yet simple lodge-style hostel, with comfortable beds, a friendly staff, and laundry service, is a great bargain. It is centrally located and a 10min. walk to the bus and train stations. Complimentary breakfast, Internet access and parking. Reception 24hr. Check-in 2pm. Check-out noon. Dorms 35zł per bed; singles 55zł; doubles 45-50zł. Cash Only. ❶

Pensjonat "Szarotka," Notowarska 45G (☎201 3618; www.szarotka.pl). This rugged, traditional lodge has small, clean, no-frill rooms and fresh new bathrooms. Only 10min. walk from the center. English spoken. Linens 5zł. Reserve ahead. 2- to 3-bed dorms with bath and 4- to 8-bed dorms with sink 35-40zł. Cash only. ❶

Ośrodek Wypoczynkowy Kolejarz, Kościuszki 23 (☎201 5468). Despite its low prices, spacious Ośrodek feels like a hotel. Adjacent to the train and bus station, this hostel is perfect for late-night arrivals or early morning departures. Small 2-bed dorms with a fully-equipped bathroom and TV (55zł). Buffet breakfast included. AmEx/MC/V. ❷

Camping Pod Krokwią, Żeromskiego (☎201 2256; www.mati.com.pl/camp), across from the ski jump in Kuźnice. Views of the Tatras, well-kept grounds, friendly staff, and proximity to the hiking trails make this campground perfect for outdoor adventures. Reception 24hr. Check-out 4pm. Open July-Aug. 10-12zł per tent; campers 16-30zł; rooms 35-40zł; 4- to 6-person apartments with kitchen and TV 140-200zł. MC/V. ❶

POLAND

FOOD

Restaurants in Zakopane run the gamut from familiar Western chains like KFC and Pizza Hut to traditional mountain eateries. Highlanders sell the local specialty, *oscypek* (smoked sheep cheese). This tantalizing cheese is sold at a daily **open-air market** at the entrance to Onbatówka, behind Nowotarska. If warm beer doesn't agree with you, try the local favorite, *herbata ceperska* (25mL vodka with 50mL tea). For groceries stop by **Supermarket Hubert,** Nowotarska 79. (☎ 201 7455.)

Zbójecka, Krupówki 28 (☎201 3854). Eat by candlelight on rough-hewn wood tables, accompanied by live regional music. Waiters dress in traditional Highlander costume, making for an enjoyably kitschy experience. Fresh bread and homemade lard spread accompany meals. Partial English menu. Entrees 12-30zł. 2zł per person surcharge when there is live music. Open daily 10am-midnight. Cash only. ❷

Pizzeria Restauracja "Adamo," Nowotarska 10d (☎201 5290). Serves both Polish dishes and pizza in a lodge-style restaurant furnished with dark wood tables. *Danie dnia* (daily special; 11am-3pm; 14-17zł) includes soup, entree, coffee, and dessert. Pizza 8-22zł. Entrees 7-31zł. Open daily 11am-midnight. AmEx/MC/V. ❷

Bar Mleczny, Weteranów Wojny 2 (☎206 6257), off Krupówki. The unaffected atmosphere of this milk bar matches its simple, delicious cooking. For a taste of Polish cuisine, try *pierogi ruskie* (potato-and-cheese dumplings; 5zł) or the *omlet* (pancake with berries and whipped cream; 6zł). Entrees 3-7zł. Open daily 9am-7pm. Cash only. ❶

SIGHTS AND ENTERTAINMENT

Zakopane primarily serves as a gateway to the Tatras, but the picturesque town itself is also worth a visit. Architect and artist **Jan Witkiewicz** designed seven houses along Kościeliska; the most famous of these was occupied by the writer **Stanisław Ignacy Witkiewicz** in the 1930s. Stop by the **Tytus Chałubiński Tatra Museum**

(Muzeum Tatrzańskie), Krupówki 10, for an in-depth look at the geography and ecology of the Tatras. The museum displays traditional Highlander home interiors, antiques, and regional costumes. (☎201 5205. Open Tu-Sa 9am-5pm, Su 9am-3pm. Closed on Tuesdays during the off-season. 6.42zł, students 5.35zł; Su free.)

In the evening, the cafes of **Krupówki** fill with locals and tourists. At **Piano-Cafe,** Krupówki 63, you can burrow into a corner couch or sit on a swing chair. (Tea 3zł. 0.5L *Żywiec* 4.50zł. Open daily 3pm-midnight. Cash only.) Alternatively, join the sharp young crowd at **Paparazzi,** Gen. Galicy 8, a popular pub with a slick glass bar and decorated with black-and-white photos. (☎206 3251. Open M-F 4pm-1am, Sa noon-2am. Cash only.) To experience Polish hits from the 60s, check out the retro-chic **Europejska Cafe,** Krupówki 37, where a slightly older crowd unwinds over frosty beers on weekdays and rocks out on weekends. (☎201 2200. Beer 5zł. Desserts 4-6zł. Open daily 8am-11pm; open later during high season. MC/V.) Those looking to dance the night away should try **Blue Star,** Tetmajera 2, on the corner of Krupówki, which blares Europop hits tailored to its clientele. (21+. Cover 10zł. Open F-Sa 9pm-4am. Cash only.) **Genesis: Music and Dance Club,** Plac Niepodległości 1, on the corner of Krupówki, with its smoke machines, snazzy lighting and modern music, is a techno-lover's dream. (18+. Cover 20 zł. Women free on Fridays. Open all week 9pm-5am. Cash only.)

Park Linowy (☎06 02 49 56 50) is a destination for the more adventurous tourist, featuring a high ropes course 8m off the ground. Thanks to additional lighting, the course can be your playground at all hours. (On J. Piłsudskiego, before you reach the ski jump. 20zł. Open daily 10am-last customer.) From mid- to late August, Zakopane is filled with the sounds of the **International Festival of Highlander Folklore** (Międzynardowy Festival Folkloro ziem Górskich). Highland groups from around the world perform along Krupówki.

POLAND

HIKING

Magnificent **Tatra National Park** (Tatrzański Park Narodowy; 3.6zł, students 1.6zł) is Zakopane's main attraction. Before heading out, consult a good map, such as the **Tatrzański Park Narodowy: Mapa Turystyczna** (7zł), and choose trails that fit your experience and ambitions. The best—and most popular—place to begin many of the challenging and scenic hikes is **Kuźnice.** Go uphill on **Krupówki** to Zamoyskiego; continue as it becomes Chałubińskiego and then Przewodników Tatrzańskich; the trailheads are 1 hr. from Zakopane's center. You can also reach Kuźnice by *mikrobus* (2zł) from in front of the bus station. From Kuźnice, start one of the hikes listed below, or try the 1987m **Kasprowy Wierch cable car,** which leads to the amazing views atop Kasprowy Mountain, where you can wander over the border to the Slovak Republic. *(Open July-Aug. 7am-7pm; June and Sept. 7:30am-6pm; Oct. 7:30am-3pm. Round-trip 29zł, students 19zł; up 19/14zł, down 15/10zł.)* Alternatively, instead of going to Kuźnice, you can take the **funicular** to **Gubałówka** from Zakopane *(1120m, located off Koscieliska. Open daily Dec. 15-31 7:30am-10pm; July-Aug. 8am-10pm; Jan.-Mar. 7:30am-9pm; Apr.-June and Sept. 8:30am-7:20pm; Oct.-Dec. 15 8:30am-6pm; Round-trip 14zł; up 8zł.)*

VALLEY OF THE FIVE POLISH TARNS. Called the Dolina Pięciu Stawów Polskich, this hike is perfect if you have time for only one trail. It covers all the major highlights of the Tatras. An intense full-day hike takes you past five lakes between sharp peaks: Wielki, Czarny, Przedni, Zadni, and Mały. Start this beautiful and rewarding hike at **Kuźnice** and follow the yellow trail through **Dolina Jaworzynka** (Jaworzynka Valley) until you reach the steep blue trail, which leads to **Hala Gasienicowa** (2½hr.) and the nearby mountain hut **Schronisko Murowaniec.** *(☎201 2633. Dorms 28-34zł).* From the mountain shelter, the trail continues to **Czarny Staw,** a tranquil lake whose glassy surface reflects the tallest peaks of the Tatras. Continue on the blue trail to **Zawrat Peak,** where you'll have to use mountain chains and natural holds. Once you cross Zawrat, breathtaking views of the valley and its lakes await, along with **Schronisko Dolina Pięciu Stawów** (4hr.), where you can refuel or spend the night. *(☎207 76 07. Linen 5zl. Beds 21-25zł.)* Those ready to continue can take the blue trail (2hr.) to **Morskie Oko** and the popular **PTTK Mountain Shelter,** which rests on its shores. *(☎207 7609. Linen 7zł. Beds with sheets 44zł; space on floor 34zł. Low season 34/24zł.)* From here you can take a microbus down, hike down, or hike onward. A **shorter version** of the hike (4-6hr.) begins at **Palenica Białczańska.** *(Take bus from Zakopane station.)* Head toward Morskie Oko, as described above. The green trail breaks off to the right, leads past the crashing **Mickiewicza Waterfalls,** and ends on a small bridge near the Schronisko Dolina Pięciu Stawów, merging into the blue trail. Follow the blue trail to the majestic Morskie Oko.

POLAND

SEA EYE (MORSKIE OKO). Glacial Morskie Oko Lake, surrounded by dramatic peaks, dazzles herds of tourists each summer. Take a bus from the PKS station to Palenica Białczańska (45min., 11 per day, 4zł) or a private microbus from across the street (30min., 5zł). A 9km paved road leads to the lake, which is fabled to connect to the Baltic Sea. Alternatively, at Schronisko Dolina Roztoki, 1¾hr. up road from Palenica Białczańska, take the green trail to the blue trail for an astounding view of Morskie Oko (1406m, 4hr.). From Morskie Oko, hike the red trail to reach the highest mountain lake, **Czarny Staw pod Rysami** (30min.).

GIEWONT. This popular trail traverses Giewont, a mountain whose silhouette resembles a man lying down. Local legend holds that the mountain is a sleeping prince who will awaken and defend the town of Zakopane if it is in danger. A local priest placed an enormous iron cross on the peak in 1901. The moderately difficult blue trail (7km, 3hr.) leads to the summit from **Kuźnice.** The path becomes much rockier toward **Hala Kondratowa,** where a variety of fast-food restaurants and local stalls awaits weary travelers. The trail wraps around the ridge of Giewont's peak and leads to the tricky final ascent; here, chains and footholds come to your aid. The summit offers a striking view of Zakopane and the icy peaks of the Tatras. From the peak, take the yellow trail to Kondracka Kopa to reach the **Red Peaks** (45min.), or return to Zakopane on the red trail to **Dolina Strążyska.** For a shorter and steeper ascent, take the red trail up from Dolina Strążyska (2-3hr.).

STRĄŻYSKA VALLEY (DOLINA STRĄŻYSKA). This trail from Zakopane is pleasant and easy to navigate. Walk down Koscieliska and head left on Kasprusie, which becomes Strążyska, to the entrance to the **Tatras National Park** (30-45min.). Follow the lush, forested path along streams until it ends at the dramatic **Siklawica waterfall.** Back up and take the path to your right to **Mt. Sarnia Skała.** The peak offers unspoiled views of Zakopane and Mt. Giewont. The trail takes 4-5hr.

RED PEAKS (CZERWONE WIERCHY). This less rocky range is full of mild dips and ascents, during which the trail criss-crosses the Polish-Slovak border. Three of the **Red Peaks** that follow Kasprowy Wierch have trails that allow tired hikers to return to Zakopane, while the trail along the last peak, **Ciemniak** (3hr.), continues to **Schronisko na Hali Ornak.** *(☎207 0520. Beds 27-35zł. Cash only.)* Take a right on the red trail at the top of Kasprowy Wierch. The trail passes through **Kościeliska Valley.** For a direct descent, follow the red trail to its end at **Kiry** (3hr.). The heights of the ridge are known as the "Red Peaks" because native plants blossom throughout the area each autumn, coloring the rocks.

DAYTRIP FROM ZAKOPANE: DUNAJEC GORGE

Take a microbus to Kąty (across from the bus station, 1-1½hr., 14zł). It is advisable to schedule an outing through a tourist agency. Many packages include trips to Dunajec Castle. Rafting tickets at Dunajec Gorge 35zł plus 4zł entrance fee, 2zł for students. English-speaking tour guides usually available.

Both residents and tourists raft along the Dunajec in **Pieniński National Park** (☎262 9721). The tranquil ride traces the steep peaks and rolling forests dividing Poland from Slovakia. To complement the scenery, guides sport traditional Highlander garb. Travelers shouldn't exactly expect death-defying rafting—the smooth ride is virtually splashless. The waters, however, offer unparalleled views of **Trzy Korony** (Three Crowns Peak) and **Dunajec Castle,** where Polish fighters supposedly ran through the tunnels leading out of the castle to attack enemy soldiers. Unaccompanied rafting is not permitted. Visits to the 13th-century castle are best arranged through tourist agencies in Zakopane.

The end of the 2hr. excursion deposits you in the town of Szczawnica. While Szczawnica is armed with souvenir stands and crowded bars, those seeking to savor the outdoors can rent bikes to tour the city or take leisurely rides near the river. **Rent bikes** at Pienińska 6, a left turn from the raft drop-off point. (☎262 1246. 3zł per hr., 20zł per day. Open daily 7am-9pm.) Riding along the Polish riverside, one crosses into Slovakia. Alternatively, walkers can follow the pathway that runs along the river for splendid views of the hills by the border. Those wishing to wander off the path can take the chair lift (9am-7:30pm, 10zł) and explore mountain paths with views of Szczawnica.

On the way back to Zakopane, the church in Dębnie is a small, worthwhile gem. Built solely out of wood in the 1300s, the church is adorned with old relics. Despite being stuck with an artillery shell during a WWII retreat, the fragile church did not explode. For preservation reasons, the church is closed during humid weather and opens only for groups or during mass. Info in English is available.

POLAND

ŚLĄSK (SILESIA)

Poles treasure Śląsk, which spent centuries under Prussian and, later, German rule, for the rough-hewn beauty of its limestone crags, pine forests, and medieval castles. The region's industrial lowlands bear scars from the multiple brutal Five-Year Plans of the Communist era, but the mountains remain pristine and lightly touristed, with hiking and biking trails fanning west into Karkonosze National Park and east into the Jura Uplands.

WROCŁAW ☎(0)71

Wrocław (VROTS-wahv), the capital of Lower Silesia (Dolny Śląsk), is a graceful city of Gothic spires and stone bridges, islands, and gardens. Breathtaking sights and vibrant nightlife make Wrocław one of the most alluring destinations in Eastern Europe. The tranquil main square, however, belies centuries of turmoil. Passed among competing powers for centuries, Wrocław gained infamy at the end of WWII as "Festung Breslau," one of the last Nazi holdouts on the retreat to Berlin. Today, investment has rejuvenated the city, which enjoys one of the fastest development rates in Poland and is gearing up for an onslaught of tourism as cheap airlines turn it into a prime stag destination.

TRANSPORTATION

Trains: Wrocław Główny, Piłsudskiego 105 (☎367 5882). 24hr. **currency exchange** inside. International tickets at counter #20. MC/V. To: **Częstochowa** (2½hr., 4 per day, 34zł); **Gdynia** (8hr., 4 per day, 54zł); **Jelenia Góra** (3¼hr., 8 per day, 16-31zł); **Kołobrzeg** (6½hr., 2 per day, 50zł); **Kraków** (4½-5hr., 13 per day, 43-82zł); **Łódź** (6¼hr., 3 per day, 42zł); **Poznań** (3¼hr., 25 per day, 21-55zł); **Szczecin** (5hr., 8 per day, 49-

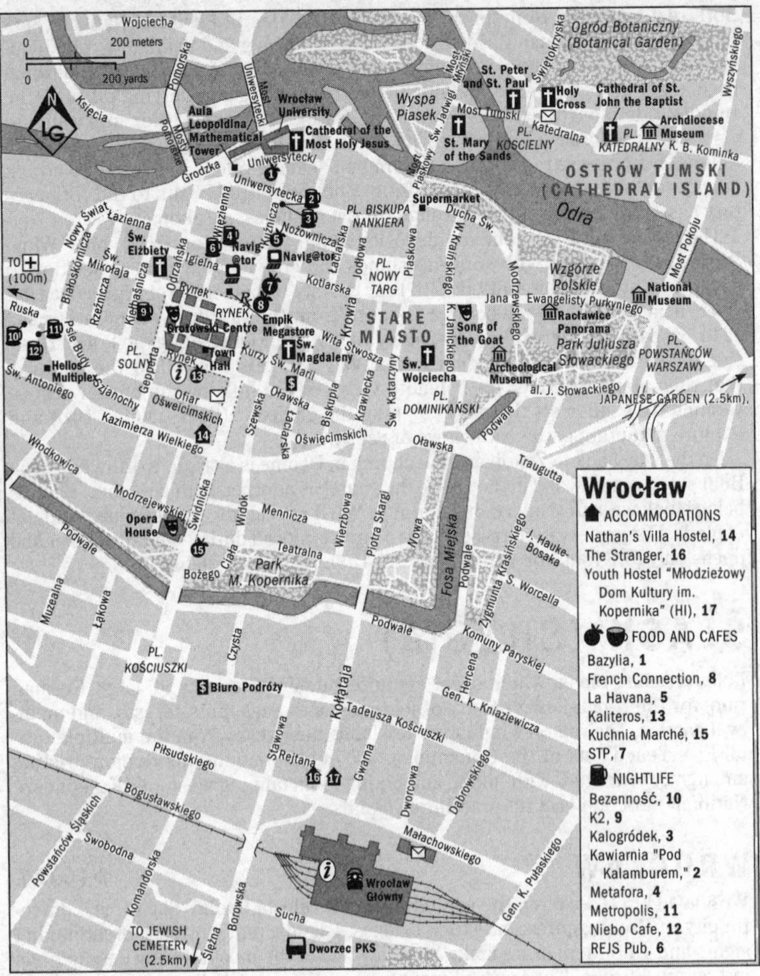

52zł); **Warsaw** (4¼-6hr., 8 per day, 49-88zł); **Berlin, GER** (5½-6¼hr., 2 per day, 185zł); **Dresden, GER** (4½hr., 4 per day, 120zł).

Buses: Station at Sucha 1 (☎361 2299), behind the trains. Waiting room open daily 5am-11pm. Buses run to: **Częstochowa** (4¼hr., 10 per day, 26zł); **Gdańsk** (8hr., 2 per day, 64zł); **Jelenia Góra** (2hr., 28 per day, 24zł); **Karpacz** (3hr., 4 per day, 23zł); **Kraków** (6hr., 7 per day, 37zł); **Łódź** (5hr., 5 per day, 33zł); **Poznań** (4hr., 5 per day, 26zł); **Warsaw** (6hr., 7 per day, 48zł).

Public Transportation: Most lines run 5am-midnight. **Tram** and **bus** tickets cost 2zł per person, 1zł per student, 2zł per backpack. 1-day pass 6.60zł, students 3.30zł; 10-day pass 24/12zł. Express buses (marked by letters) 2.40zł. Night buses 3/1.50zł.

Taxis: ZTP (☎96 22) is reliable. A ride from the train station to the Rynek costs around 15zł. Always make sure the meter is running or agree on a price beforehand.

ORIENTATION AND PRACTICAL INFORMATION

Filled with bustling restaurants and shops, the **Rynek** (Market Square) is the heart of Wrocław. From the train and bus stations, turn left on **Piłsudskiego,** take a right on **Świdnicka,** go past **plac Kościuszki,** over the **Fosa Miejska** (City Moat), through the pedestrian lane beneath Kazimierza Wielkiego, and into the Rynek.

Tourist Offices: IT, Rynek 14 (☎344 3111; www.dolnyslask.info.pl). **Maps** 6-16zł. Free Internet. Bike rental 10zł for 1st hr., 5zł thereafter, 50zł per day (11hr.); 400zł deposit. Open daily 9am-9pm. AmEx/MC/V. **Centrum Informacji Kulturalnej,** Rynek-Ratusz 24 (☎342 2291; www.okis.pl). The cultural branch of the IT, specializing in info for events and festivals. Open M-F 10am-6pm, Sa 9am-2pm.

Currency Exchange: Bank Pekao SA, Oławska 2 (☎371 6124). Cashes **traveler's checks** for 1.5% commission (10zł min.) and gives MC/V **cash advances.** Open M-F 8am-6pm, Sa 9am-2pm.

Western Union: Biuro Podróży, Kościuszki 27 (☎344 8188). Open M-F 10am-6pm, Sa 10am-3pm.

Luggage Storage: Lockers in the train station 4-8zł per day. Also in the kiosk in the back of the bus station. 5.50zł per day plus 1zł per 50zł value. Open daily 6am-10pm.

English-Language Bookstore: Empik Megastore, Rynek 50 (☎343 3972). Open M-Sa 9am-10pm, Su noon-8pm. MC/V.

Pharmacy: Apteka Podwójnym Złotym Orłem, Rynek 42/43 (☎343 4428). Open M-F 8am-9pm, Sa 9am-8pm.

Hospital: Szpital Im. Babińskiego, pl. 1 Maja 8 (☎341 0000).

Internet: Internet Klub Navig@tor Podziemia, Kuźnicza 11/13 (☎343 7069). 2zł per 30min., 3zł per hr. Open daily 9am-10pm.

Post Office: Małachowskiego 1 (☎344 7778), to the right of the train station. **Poste Restante** at window #22. **Telephones** inside and outside. Open M-F 6am-8pm, Sa-Su 9am-3pm. Branch at Rynek 28. Open M-F 6:30am-8:30pm. **Postal Code:** 50-900.

ACCOMMODATIONS

Rooms are plentiful in Wrocław, but reserve ahead for reasonable accommodations near the center of town. Check with the tourist office for info and to make reservations in **student dorms,** which rent rooms July through August (20-50zł), just a tram ride from the Rynek in pl. Grunwaldski.

The Stranger Hostel, Kołłątaja 16/3 (☎634 1206), opposite the train station, on the 3rd fl. behind an unmarked wooden doorway (ring buzzer #3). True to their motto "the stranger, the better," this new hostel is filled with quirky touches, from decorated glass toilet seats to a raised platform in the common room. Dorms are large and feature eclectic, comfortable stylings. Entertainment center, beautiful kitchen, free laundry, free Internet. Reception 24hr. Dorms 50zł. AmEx/MC/V. ❷

Nathan's Villa Hostel, ul. Swidnicka 13 (☎344 1095), conveniently located just outside the old square, is a vast affair filling the top 3 floors of a large building. Beautifully designed dorms and private rooms complement a large kitchen and an attic TV room. Free breakfast, Internet, and laundry. Shampoo, toothbrushes, and other supplies 2zł-5zł apiece. Dorms 45-60zł; private rooms 75-95zł per person. AmEx/MC/V. ❶

Youth Hostel "Młodzieżowy Dom Kultury im. Kopernika" (HI), Kołłątaja 20 (☎343 8856), opposite the train station. The lime green walls of this institutional but cheerful hostel are plastered with student artwork. Kitchen and shared bathrooms. Sheets 7zł. Lockout 10am-5pm. Curfew 10pm. Reserve in advance. Dorms 22zł; doubles 58zł. Discount for stays over 1 night. Cash only. ❶

POLAND

FOOD

Stock up on food at **Hala Targowa,** at the corner of Piaskowa and Ducha Sw., where you'll find a massive selection of fresh produce, meats, and pirated DVDs, housed in a towering 1908 building. (Open M-F 8am-6:30pm, Sa 9am-3pm.)

La Havana, Kuźnicza 12 (☎343 2072). This tongue-in-cheek presentation of Cuban Communism is wildly popular with locals. Enjoy tasty Cuban-influenced Polish dishes (entrees 10-20zł) in the company of a packed student crowd, images of Che and Castro, and plastic palm trees. Large tropical mixed drinks 12-18zł. Open M-Th and Su 11am-11:30pm, F-Sa noon-1am. Reservations recommended on weekends. MC/V. ❷

Bazylia, Kuźnicza 42 (☎375 2065). Under the glass facade and chic metal decor of a businessman's bistro, Bazylia serves students cheap, homestyle meals. Order at the counter from the long list of milk bar classics. Prepare for a language barrier if you don't speak Polish. Entrees 3-7zł. Open M-F 7am-7pm, Sa 8am-5pm. Cash only. ❶

Kaliteros, Rynek 20/21 (☎343 5617). One of a surprising number of "Mediterranean" restaurants, Kaliteros impresses with colorful frescoes and comfortable sidewalk seating on the Rynek. While Greek entrees (18-59zł) are not particularly authentic, they are perfectly cooked. Open M-Th 11am-11pm, F-Su 11am-midnight. ❸

French Connection, ul. Kuźnicza 63/64. Right off the market square, this new cafe-bistro offers a bewildering variety of both sweet and savory *naleśniki* (6-11.50zł; extra toppings 0.50-2zł) stuffed with fillings in a sparsely decorated but elegantly French-themed setting. Entrees 6-12zł. Open daily 10am-10pm. MC/V. ❷

STP, ul. Kuźnicza 10 (☎344 5449). STP has a great concept: food priced by the kilogram. Just walk in, grab a large plate, fill it up with an array of Polish specialties such as pierogi, potato pancakes, and *schabowy,* and weigh the plate at the end of the line to pay. 23.90zł per kg, half-price after 9pm. Open daily 10am-11pm. MC/V. ❶

Kuchnia Marché, Świdnicka 53 (☎343 9565). Value, freshness, and a market-themed interior make this spot popular with a hip, young crowd. At scattered food stations, the Marché offers fresh pastries (1-3zł), pasta cooked before your eyes (8-11.50zł), smoothies (2.50zł), and salads (1.50-4zł). Accumulate stamps on a card and pay after you eat. Open M-F 9am-8pm, Sa-Su noon-8pm. MC/V. ❶

SIGHTS

RACŁAWICE PANORAMA AND NATIONAL MUSEUM. The 120m by 15m Panorama wraps viewers in the action of the 18th-century peasant insurrection against Russian occupation. This painting depicts the legendary victory of the underdog Poles led by Tadeusz Kościuszko (p. 418). Damaged by a bomb in 1944, it was hidden in a monastery for safekeeping, and was displayed only publicly after the rise of Solidarity in the 1980s. The 30min. showings include audio narration; free headsets are available in eight languages. *(Purkyniego 11. Facing away from the town hall, bear left on Kuźnicza for 2 blocks and then right on Kotlarska, which becomes Purkyniego. ☎344 2344. Open Tu-Su 9am-5pm; viewings every 30min. 9:30am-5pm. 20zł, students 15zł. A ticket to the Panorama includes entrance to National Museum.)* The **National Museum** is in the massive ivy-clad building across the street and to the left. Permanent exhibits include installations by 20th-century Polish artists Magdalena Abakanowicz and Józef Szajna, medieval statuary, and 18th- and 19th-century paintings. Check out the all-white atrium. *(Pl. Powstanców Warszawy 5. ☎343 8839. Open W, F, Su 10am-4pm, Th 9am-4pm, Sa 10am-6pm. 15zl, students 10zl; Sa free.)*

POLAND

OSTRÓW TUMSKI. Ostrów Tumski, the oldest part of Wrocław, occupies the islands and far shore of the Odra and was the site of the founding of the Wrocław bishopric in the year AD 1000. A thousand years later, the neighborhood remains largely devoted to archdiocesan buildings, and priests and nuns frequent its lovely and quiet streets. Biking and pedestrian paths connect the islands. The sky-piercing spires of the 13th-century **Cathedral of St. John the Baptist** (Katedra Św. Jana Chrzciciela) dominate Ostrów Tumski's skyline. Inside, light filters through stained-glass windows, shrouding the Gothic interior with shadows. Climb the tower or take the elevator for a view of the surrounding churches. *(Open M-Sa 10am-5:30pm, Su 2-4pm. 4zł, students 3zł.)* Nearby, the Church of **St. Mary of the Sands** (Najświętszej Marii Panny) houses a 14th-century icon of Our Lady of Victory that medieval knights carried into battle. The real attraction, however, is the incredible Chapel of the Blind, Deaf, and Dumb (Kaplica Niesłyszących i Niewidomych), in the right of the nave, where the altar has been adorned with thousands of children's toys. Ask a nun to hit the switch, and the toy village comes to life. *(Open daily 10am-6pm. Daily services for the disabled. Donations requested.)* The **Archdiocese Museum** (Muzeum Archidiecezjalne), pl. Katedralny 16, contains a undistinguished grab bag of religious art and the earliest surviving sentence written in the Polish language. *(☎327 1178. Open Tu-Su 9am-3pm. 4zł, students 3zł.)* From pl. Katedralny, go north on Kapitulna to reach the enchanting **Botanical Garden** (Ogród Botaniczny). Sculptures of oversized acorns and pine cones are scattered throughout the garden, along with students from the nearby university studying on benches and tables facing the stream. *(Open daily 8am-6pm. 5zł, students 3zł.)*

WROCŁAW UNIVERSITY (UNIWERSYTET WROCŁAWSKI). Wrocław's cultural life houses several architectural gems. **Aula Leopoldina,** an 18th-century frescoed lecture hall, is the most impressive. *(Pl. Uniwersytecka 1, 2nd fl. ☎375 2618. Open M-Tu and Th-Su 10am-3pm. See all of the university sights for 8zł, students 6zł.)* Climb the **Mathematical Tower** for a sweeping view of the city. You can also see **Longchamps Hall,** which displays the university's history, and the **Oratorium,** the slightly less decadent cousin of the Aula. The breathtaking 17th-century **Cathedral of the Most Holy Jesus** (Kościół Najświętszego im. Jezusa), built on the site of Piast castle, retains much of its original interior. The colonialist, 18th-century sculptures on the vaults depict the Christianization of African, American, and Asian indigenous people. *(Open to tourists M-Sa 11am-3:30pm. 3zł, students 2zł.)*

AROUND THE RYNEK. The Rynek and its Gothic **town hall** *(ratusz)* are the heart of the city. Inside the town hall, the **Museum of Urban Art** (Muzeum Sztuki Mieszczańskiej), displays both ancient and contemporary art in a medieval building whose decorations are equally engaging. Around the corner, you can enjoy the sights and sounds from a **horse-drawn carriage.** *(☎374 1693. Open W-Sa 11am-5pm, Su 10am-6pm. Museum 12zł, students 8zł; W free. Carriage 5-10zł.)*

JEWISH CEMETERY (CMENTARZ ŻYDOWSKI). That this Jewish Cemetery is one of the best-preserved in Poland is a sad comment on the state of Poland's Jewish sights. Among the faded and damaged headstones, the cemetery holds the remains of socialist Ferdinand Lasalle, the families of physicist Max Born and chemist Fritz Haber, and the wife of writer Thomas Mann. A walk around this shaded enclave reveals fragments of Jewish tombstones dating from the 13th century. *(Ślężna 37/39. From the stops along Kołłątaja and Piotra Skargi, take tram #9 and get off at Ślężna. ☎791 5904. Free guided tours in Polish and English Su noon. Open Apr.-Oct. daily 9am-6pm. 5zł, students 3zł.)* The oldest Jewish tombstone in Poland, dated 1203 and discovered at the site of the now-vanished Wrocław Old Jewish Cemetery, is on display at the **Archaeology Museum.** *(Cieszynskiego 9. ☎347 1696.)*

OTHER SIGHTS. The only of its kind in Poland, the **Japanese Garden** (Ogród Japoski) is a carefully trimmed and symmetrical version of paradise. *(Located 3km east of the Rynek. ☎347 5140. Open daily 9am-9pm. 3zł, students 1.50zł.)* Also worth visiting is the Architecture Museum, with displays on both modern and medieval architecture and models of Wrocław in various stages of its development, all set in a beautiful old monastery and gutted church. The carefully tended cloister garden is a highlight. *(Ul. Cieszynskiego 9. ☎347 1696. Open W-Sa 11am-5pm, Su 10am-6pm. 7zł, students 5zł. Cash only.)*

ENTERTAINMENT AND NIGHTLIFE

For event info, pick up *City Magazine* or *Co jest grane?* (What's Going On?). Visit **Centrum Informacji Kulturalnej** (p. 463) for info on Wrocław's experimental theater, which continues the work of local pioneer Jerzy Grotowski. The **Song of the Goat Theater** (Teatr Pieśń Kozła), Purkyniego 1 (☎342 7110), and the **Grotowski Theater,** Rynek-Ratusz 27 (☎343 4267), are two prominent outlets. An extremely popular festival, **Wrocław Non-Stop** (www.wroclawnonstop.pl) transforms the city in the last week of June and first week of July into a celebration of the visual and performance arts. The more than 100 events at the festival include free concerts, gallery openings, fireworks, and film screenings. Poland's largest international film festival, **Nowe Horyzonty,** comes to town in late July, bringing hundreds of screenings and directors from around the world.

Wrocław's nightlife encompasses a wide range of options. The unquestioned center of student nightlife is **Ruska,** near the intersection with Nowy Świat, where a large complex around a courtyard at Ruska 51 contains several clubs and bars that are filled every night of the week.

Bezenność (Insomnia) serves up a raucous mix of dance, hiphop, and rock in a large, loft-like hall split down the middle by the bar. A mannequin dressed as an old woman gazes eerily down from one corner, while patrons relax in soft upholstered chairs. Cover F-Sa 5zł. Beer 6zł. Open M-Th and Su 6pm-1am, F-Sa 6pm-4am. Cash only.

Kawiarnia "Pod Kalamburem," Kuźnicza 29a (☎372 3571, ext. 32). This bar and cafe was founded by the experimental theater group that used to occupy its Art Nouveau building in the university quarter. Among many claims to fame, the biggest festival of avant-garde theater in Europe was hosted here in the 1970s and 80s, an impressive feat under the Communist yoke. Beer and mixed drinks 3-15zł. Open M-Th 1pm-midnight, F-Sa 1pm-late, Su 4pm-midnight. Cash only.

Niebo Cafe (☎342 9867), across the street from Bezenność. Offers occasional free rock shows in a lovingly worn interior filled with plush velvet chairs. Patrons can play DJ with the alt-rock CD collection at the bar. Beer 4.50zł. Open M-F 1pm-late, Sa-Su 5pm-late. Cash only.

Metropolis (☎343 1373), with its winding blacklight lit hallways, serves as an intense dance spot for house and techno, while 80s and 90s pop blare in the basement. Beer 6zł. Cover F 5zł; Sa men 10zł, women 5zł. Open daily 8pm-late. AmEx/MC/V.

Kalogródek, Kuźnicza 29b (☎372 3571.), offers darts, foosball, and beer. Open M-Th and Su 11am-11pm, F-Sa 11am-late.

REJS Pub, Kotlarska 32a (☎509 796 771). This tiny bar caters to self-described "alternative" students and locals who down cheap beer and enjoy the movie soundtracks playing. Beer 4.50zł. Open M-Sa 9:30am-late, Su 11am-late. Cash only.

K2, Kiełbaśnicza 2 (☎372 3415). In the farm-themed interior of this cafe nestled in an alley, you'll find an encyclopedic array of teas, delicious homemade cakes, and a surfeit of charm. Try a fruit tea with preserves for 6.50zł. Open daily 11am-11pm.

Metafora, Więzienna 5b (☎79 50 98), caters to the more pensive set. The small but high-quality menu fortifies conversationalists who recline for hours on leather couches. Coffee 5zł. Open daily noon-midnight. MC/V.

POLAND

KARPACZ

☎(0)75

Mountains cast long shadows over the thickly forested valleys of Karpacz in Poland's southeast. The landscape is stunning, even when glimpsed from within the village itself. Trails and slopes lure visitors to the Czech border year-round.

TRANSPORTATION AND PRACTICAL INFORMATION. Most **buses** to Karpacz originate in, or at least pass through, Jelenia Góra and run to either the train station or the bus station. There is no bus station in Karpacz. Konstytucji 3 Maja is the main thoroughfare for buses—eight stops dot the way to Karpacz Górny, the top of town (45min., every 30-60min., 5.50-7zł). Catch any bus to ride among stops within Karpacz (1.50-3zł). The poorly marked stops are named for local landmarks. A scenic **bicycle path** also traverses the 28km from Jelenia Góra to Karpacz; maps are available at the Jelenia Góra tourist info office.

Karpacz is a vertical town: most of its restaurants and sights line a single road, **Konstytucji 3 Maja,** which meanders uphill parallel to the ridge of the Karkonosy Mountains. Poorly marked side streets provide steeply sloped shortcuts. Uphill from Biały Jar, a large circular bus stop with a restaurant and hotel (not to be confused with Biały Jar, the valley 1½hr. into the black trail), the road changes names to **Karkonoska.** Get off incoming buses at **Karpacz Bachus** and go downhill to the **tourist office,** 3 Maja 25, which is distinguished from the myriad private tourist offices by a large blue circle with "it" in white. The staff sells **maps,** reserves rooms, and has info about bicycling, skiing, rock climbing, horseback riding, and camping. (☎761 8605; www.karpacz.pl. English spoken. Open M-Sa 9am-5pm.) **Exchange currency** at *kantors* in most of the tourist bureaus that dot Konstytucji 3 Maja. Hotel Orbis Skalny, Obrońców Pokoju 5, rents **bicycles.** (☎752 7000. 10zł per 3hr., 18zł per 6hr., 25zł per 12hr. Open daily 7am-9pm.) **Szkoła Górska,** Na Śnieżkę 16, in **Schronisko Samotnia** (☎761 9376), two hours into the blue trail, offers rock-climbing lessons, equipment, and excursions, as well as ski and ice-climbing lessons in winter. Call ahead to make arrangements. **Bank Zachodni,** 3 Maja 43, cashes **traveler's checks** for a 30zł commission and has a MasterCard and Visa **ATM** and **Western Union** services. (☎/fax 753 8120. Open M-F 9am-4:30pm.) There is a **K-Med pharmacy** at 3 Maja 33. (☎761 8669. Open M-F 9am-7pm, Sa 9am-5pm, Su 9am-1pm.) The **post office** is at 3 Maja 23. (☎761 9220; fax 761 9585. Open M-F 8am-6pm, Sa 9:30am-3pm.) **Postal Code:** 58-540.

ACCOMMODATIONS AND FOOD. Reservations are not necessary in Karpacz. **Private pensions** (25-70zł) can be found on Kościelna just downhill from Karpacz Bachus. Unfortunately, some are open only part of the year—inquire at the tourist office. As a general rule, the better deals are farther uphill. **Hotel Karpacz ❹,** 3 Maja 11/13, has comfortable, large rooms with TV and bath, and a generous breakfast buffet from 9-11am. (☎761 9728. Check-in noon-3pm. Check-out noon. Singles 85zł; doubles 160zł; triples 125zł. Prices fall by as much as 25zł in winter.) **D.W. Szczyt ❶,** Na Śnieżkę 6, is at the uphill end of town just a few steps from Świątynia Wang (p. 468). Take the bus to Karpacz Wang and make the steep climb toward Świątynia Wang—the hike from the center of town (1hr.) is impossible with luggage. Both the view and the great prices will leave you breathless—as will the 200m haul from the bus stop. Rooms are simple and worn, but the offbeat staff, tiny resident dog, and sweeping views make it a solid value. Call the tourist office to reserve. (☎761 9360. Singles 25zł; doubles 50zł; triples 75zł; quads 100zł.) Though the occasionally steep grade makes it challenging to reach with a full pack, popular **Schronisko Samotnia ❶,** overlooking the stunning Mały Staw lake, a 1¼hr. (2hr. with full pack) hike along the blue trail from town, offers secluded accommodations halfway up the mountain. Call the tourist office to reserve. (☎761 9376; www.samotnia.com.pl. Dorms 19-32zł; singles 31-37zł; doubles and triples 29-35zł. Check-out 10am. Cash only.)

Food in Karpacz is unpretentious and filling, an ideal conclusion to a long day of hiking or skiing. It can be difficult to tell the touristy from the extremely touristy, but there are great deals to be had. The grocery store **Delikatesy,** 3 Maja 29, has everything you need for a picnic in the mountains. (☎761 9259. Open M-Sa 8:30am-10pm, Su 10am-8pm. AmEx/MC/V.) Green-roofed **Karczma Śląska ❷,** Rybacka 1, just off 3 Maja, specializes in yard art and mouth-watering pork (11-12zł). Pool tables (2zł per game) can be found at the restaurant's "Bar Oscar." (☎761 9633. Pool 19-20zł; entrees 5.50-39zł. Open daily noon-10pm.) The seriously old-school **Zagroda Góralska ❶,** 3 Maja 46, offers meats, sauerkraut, and potatoes (3-7zł per serving) from massive grills on the counter; you may see a pig on a spit. The sturdy wood lean-to seems gimmicky, but the food is popular with locals. (Open daily 10am-late. Cash only.) The *pierogi* at **U Petiego ❷,** Parkowa 10, are made with so much care that the chef's thumbprints are visible on the creases (12zł); more substantial entrees are heavy on meat and sauerkraut. (☎643 9220. Entrees 6.50-19zł. Open daily noon-10pm. Cash only.)

SIGHTS AND OUTDOOR ACTIVITIES. The uphill hike to **Wang Chapel** (Świątynia Wang), Śnieżki 8, takes hours from the center of town but is worth the effort. Follow 3 Maja and side streets marked by a blue blaze. Alternatively, take the bus to Karpacz Wang (10min.) and follow the signs. This Viking church was built in Norway at the turn of the 12th century. In the 1800s, the church sorely needed a restoration that no one could afford, so Kaiser Friedrich Wilhelm III of Prussia sent it to Karpacz for the Lutheran community there to enjoy. Carved dragons, lions, and plants adorn the building. From the garden, look to the mountains for a glimpse of the peak, Śnieżka. (☎752 8291. Open Apr. 15-Oct. 31 M-Sa 9am-6pm, Su 11:30am-6pm; Nov.-Apr. 14 closes 1hr. earlier. 4.50zł, students 3.50zł.)

Hikers aim for the crown of **Śnieżka** (Mt. Snow; 1602m), the highest peak in Poland. The border with the Czech Republic runs across the summit. Śnieżka and the trails lie within **Karkonosze National Park** (5zł, students 3zł; 3-day pass 10/5zł). All park trails lead to **Pod Śnieżka** (1394m), the last stop under the peak. Even during summer the peak averages 10°C, so bring a sweater. To get there as quickly and painlessly as possible, take the Kopa chairlift, Olimpijska 4, off Turystyczna. Follow the black trail from Hotel Biały Jar until you see the lift on the left. From the top it's a rigorous 40min. hike to the peak. (☎761 9284. Runs daily June-Aug. 8:30am-5pm; Sept.-May 8am-4pm. Before 1pm 19zł, students 15zł; round-trip 23/19zł. After 1pm 16/11zł; round-trip 19/14zł.) There are several hiking routes up Śnieżka, all of which originate in Świątynia Wang or Biały Jar. The easiest route to Śnieżka is the **blue-blazed path** (3hr.) from Świątynia Wang. This trail is also suited to vigorous biking up to Spalona Strażnica. Follow the stone-paved road to **Polana** (1080m, 35min.), then hike one hour up to scenic **Mały Staw** (Small Lake). From there, it's an hour to **Spalona Strażnica** (Burned-down Guardhouse), then 30min. to **Pod Śnieżka.** From Polana, endurance hikers should continue along the **yellow trail** (2½hr.) to another rock protrusion at **Słonecznik** (Sunflower; 1hr. from Polana). This stretch, along a rocky stream bed, is a challenging, vertical haul and not for the weak of ankle. Turning left here takes you to the red trail, which leads to **Pod Śnieżka** (1hr.). The red trail meanders along the length of the ridgeline from the Czech side to **Spalona Strażnica,** where it meets the yellow trail for the difficult hike above the treeline to **Pod Śnieżka;** it then continues along the ridgeline east, wandering back and forth along the border. The most physically challenging and least scenic of the trails, the **black trail** (2¼hr.) heads up from behind Hotel Biały Jar's parking lot, shooting straight up the ski slopes in an exhausting trek to **Pod Śnieżka** (1½hr.) at the top, where it meets the red again for the final 30-minute push.

From Pod Śnieżka, two trails lead to Śnieżka. The black **Zygzag** goes straight up the north side; look for the rubble path. The blue trail, **Jubilee Way,** takes an easier,

30-minute route winding around the peak. If incredible views of the Sudety aren't enough, climb to the **observatory** for the most expansive view. (Open daily June-Aug. 9am-5pm; Sept.-May 9am-3pm. 2zł, students 1zł.) Winter brings snow and skiers. Lift and equipment rental info can be found at the tourist office and from **Kopa,** in the Ski Complex Śnieżka, Turystyczna 4. (☎761 8619; www.kopa.com.pl. Day pass 60zł, students 45zł. Ski rental 50zł; snowboard 45zł.) The longest lift is 2229m and leads to the Kopa peak. Back in town, the alpine slide **CRiS-Kolorawa,** Parkowa 10, is almost equally terrifying. (☎761 9098; www.kolorowa.pl. 6zł per person per ride; 5 rides 20zł, 10 rides 35zł. Open daily 9am-8pm, weather permitting.)

WIELKOPOLSKA

The birthplace of the Polish nation, blessed with rich agricultural land and a strategic position between Berlin and Warsaw, has seen tanks roll across its green plains many times. In these quieter days, the westward-looking cities of Wielkopolska hum with commerce, while the countryside remains serene.

ŁÓDŹ ☎(0)42

Łódź (WOODGE; pop. 813,000), Poland's second-largest city, is anything but a tourist town. Most of the factories that once fueled Łódź have shut down, leaving it with a soaring unemployment rate that is finally starting to come back down to earth; today Łódź is struggling to reinvent itself as a modern cultural and commercial center, with lofts and tech industry outposts replacing the textile factories of old. Yet stop for a drink in one of Łódź's legendary bars, and you'll find that an offbeat music, film, and fashion scene thrives in what locals boast is American filmmaker David Lynch's favorite city. Beneath the soot and graffiti, the ruins of industrial Łódź hide many surprises and a charisma all their own.

TRANSPORTATION

Trains: There are 2 main train stations in town. **Łódź Fabryczna,** pl. B. Sałacińskiego 1 (☎664 5467). To **Białystok** (one transfer, 6hr., 3 per day, 46zł) and **Warsaw** (2hr., 12 per day, 31zł). **Łódź Kaliska,** al. Unii Lubelskiej 1 (☎41 02). To: **Częstochowa** (2hr., 4 per day, 33zł); **Gdańsk** (7½hr., 5 per day, 49zł); **Kraków** (3¼hr., 1 per day, 46zł); **Warsaw** (2hr., 3 per day, 31zł); **Wrocław** (3¾hr., 3 per day, 42zł). The information hotline serving both stations can be reached at ☎94 26.

Buses: Łódź Centralna PKS, pl. B. Sałacińskiego 1 (☎631 9520), attached to the Fabryczna train station. To: **Częstochowa** (2¼hr., 18 per day, 23zł); **Kraków** (5hr., 10 per day, 40zł); **Warsaw** (2½hr., 14 per day to Warsaw West, 5 to Warsaw Central, 24zł). **Polski Express** (☎02 28 54 02 85; www.polskiexpress.org) runs buses to **Warsaw** (2½hr., 7 per day, 36zł) and **Gdańsk** (4hr., 1 per day, 57zł).

Public Transportation: Trams and **buses** run throughout the city 4am-11pm. 10min. ticket 1.70zł, 30min. 2.40zł, 1hr. 3.60zł; students 0.75/1.10/1.65zł. Prices double at night. 1-day pass (8.80zł, students 4.40zł) and 7-day pass (35/17.50zł) available. A few late-night buses, designated by numbers over 100, run 11pm-4am.

ORIENTATION AND PRACTICAL INFORMATION

Piotrkowska is Łódź's 3km main thoroughfare. Its shop-lined pedestrian-only section stretches from **plac Wolności** to **aleja Marsz. Piłsudskiego** and is an attraction in its own right. Bicycle ricksaws will ferry you up and down Piotrkowska for 3zł or

4zł at night. From **Łódź Fabryczna,** cross under Jana Kilińskiego and head toward Łódźki Dom Kultury, a large building across the way. Continue on Traugutta to Piotrkowska. From **Łódź Kaliska,** cross under al. Włókniarzy via the tunnel; the second exit on the left leads to the tram stop. Take tram #12 or 14 toward Stoki and get off at Piotrkowska, or take tram #10 to Zielona.

Tourist Office: IT, Piotrkowska 87 (☎638 5955; www.cityoflodz.pl). **Free maps,** brochures, and accommodations info. Open Sa 9am-1pm, May-Sept. M-F.

Currency Exchange: Bank Pekao SA, al. Kościuszki 47 (☎637 5236). Cashes **traveler's checks** for 1.5% commission and gives MC/V **cash advances.** Open M-F 8am-6pm, Sa 10am-2pm.

Luggage Storage: Locked rooms in Łódź Fabryczna and Łódź Kaliska. 4zł per item per day. Open daily 5am-10pm. Key lockers next to the ticket counter. 8zł per 24hr. for large items, 4zł for small items. After 72hr. bags are removed and placed in storage.

English-Language Bookstore: Empik, Piotrkowska 81 (☎631 1998). Classic fiction, maps, and magazines. Offers **cash back.** Open M-Sa 9am-9pm, Su 11am-7pm. MC/V.

Pharmacy: Apteka Pod Białym Orłem, Piotrkowska 46 (☎/fax 630 0068). One of the oldest pharmacies in Łódź. Open M-F 8am-8pm, Sa 10am-3pm.

Medical Services: Szpital Barlickiego, Kopcińskiego 22 (☎677 6950). English spoken. **Medicover,** al. Piłsudskiego 3 (☎639 6666). 24hr. **emergency line** (☎96 77).

Internet: Łódź is wired; Internet cafes dot the alleys off Piotrkowska. **Meganet Caffe,** al. Piłsudskiego 3 (☎636 3376; biuro@meganetcaffe.pl), on the 2nd floor of the Silver Screen complex. 0.90zł per 20min., 2.40zł per hr. Open daily 8am-midnight. **One-21 Club,** Piotrskowska 121 is a cafe/bar with free Wi-Fi. Open M-F 10am-late, Sa 1pm-late, Su 1pm-10pm. AmEx/MC/V.

Post Office: Tuwima 38 (☎633 9452; fax 632 8208). Take a ticket as you enter: "A/B" for stamps, "C" for international packages, "D" for fax services. **Telephones** are inside. **Poste Restante** at window #19. Post office open 24hr., Poste Restante M-F 7am-9pm, Sa 8:30am-3:30pm. Poste Restante M-F 7am-6pm. **Postal Code:** 90-001.

ACCOMMODATIONS

IT maintains a list of **private rooms** and, in summer, rooms in **university dorms.** Beds in three-bed shared rooms begin at 25zł, while singles with bath run 45-65zł. Call from the train station, and they can make arrangements for you.

PTSM Youth Hostel (HI), Legionów 27 (☎630 6680; www.yhlodz.pl). Take tram #4 toward Helenówek from Fabryczna station to pl. Wolności at one end of Piotrkowskal; walk on Legionów the rest of the way. Large, institutional hostel with clean rooms but few amenities. Free locked storage until 10pm. Reception open 6am-11pm. Check out 10am, curfew 10pm. 1 bathless single 45zł, singles with bath and TV 65zł; doubles with TV 80zł; triples with TV 120zł. MC/V. ❶

PTSM Łódź SSH (HI), Zemahowa 13. A more centrally located branch of the hostel chain. The building is in worse shape, with linoleum floors and old furnaces in the corners of the dorms, made up for by the convenience of its lack of curfew and 24hr. reception. Dorm 30zł, students 20zł; single 45zł. Parking 10zł. AmEx/MC/V. ❶

Hotel Reymont, Legionów 81 (☎633 8023; www.hotelreymont.com), 2 blocks down from the PTSM Youth Hostel. From pl. Wolności, take bus #43 along Legionów. The grand Art Deco lobby gives way to small, colorful rooms. Each room has bath, phone, radio, cable TV, microwave, and refrigerator. Color-coordinated floors and access to a gym and free sauna. Breakfast included. Check-out 11am. Singles 173-181zł; doubles 218-280zł; apartment 298-310zł. 25% off Sa-Su. MC/V. ❺

Hotel Savoy, Traugutta 6 (☎32 93 60, fax 632 9368). A stylish hotel right off Piotrkowska, with small but comfortable rooms. Prices are more reasonable if you eschew amenities such as a private bath. Singles 99-179zł, doubles 204-259zł, parking in garage 25zł/night. ❹

Hotel Polonia, Narutowicza 38 (☎632 8773). From Fabryczna, take tram #1, 4, or 5 to Narutowicza. The Hotel Polonia offers decent rooms a short walk from the station. Newer rooms have crisp linens and a muted color-scheme; cheaper singles aren't as well coordinated. Unless you're craving the sights and sounds of rattling trams, request a room that doesn't face the street. Check-in 2-10pm. Check-out noon. Singles 75zł, with bath 125-175zł; doubles with bath 140-270zł. 10% off Sa-Su. AmEx/MC/V. ❷

FOOD

Large servings and low prices mark the Łódź restaurant scene, and culinary diversity has recently begun to arrive. Vegetarian and healthier options are changing the ways of the sooty, hard-drinking city. The majority of restaurants are along **Piotrowska. Albert,** Legionów 16, is one of several grocery stores along Legionów. (☎633 4836. Open M-Sa 7am-9pm, Su 9am-2pm.) A decent kosher meal for a reasonable price can be found at **Cafe Tuwim,** Pomorska 18, next to the Jewish Community Center. (☎631 1471. Entrees 11-30zł. Open daily 10am-10pm. MC/V.) Budget eaters can grab a large sandwich or shawarma (4.50-6.50zł) at one of many **Kebab House** ❶ locations along Piotrkowska; a full meal with sides and a drink is 9-15zł. Piotrkowska 91 (☎632 2005. Open 11am-late. AmEx/MC/V.)

ŁÓDŹ KALISKA

Chances are, most of the bars you know don't have manifestos. In Lódz, however, the line between a bar and an art movement can be blurry. Not just any drink-tank, Lódz Kaliska is named for the art movement founded in Lódz in 1979 and has a seasoned cult following: if you're here on the weekend, you may run into some of Poland's most acclaimed actors and artists taking a flaming shot off the club's tilted bar. Lódz Kaliska, the group, was originally created as an anti-Communist art group. Under martial law in the 80s the group printed a secret art magazine, Tango, and screened films in a hidden location.

Once a perennial object of criticism for both the political and the artistic establishment, today the group enjoys respect from scholars and bargoers alike. The walls and furniture of Łódź Kaliska—the bar—are adorned with the group's influential work, and the unusual toilets, along with the Bartender's Special Shot, are among this playful local institution's artistic touches. Spend an evening here to understand why people drive all the way from Warsaw to drink at Kaliska—and why many locals consider this the best bar n Poland.

***Łódź Kaliska,** Piotrkowska 102 (Group ☎63 06 95 51; www.lodzkaliska.pl. Club: www.klub.lodzkaliska.pl). F-Sa disco. Open M-Sa noon-3am, Su 4pm-3am.*

Anatewka, 6 Sierpnia 2/4 (☎630 3635). Meals start with complimentary matzah and a taste of wine at quietly elegant Anatewka, where Ashkenazi Jewish cuisine is served on lace tablecloths beneath 19th-century Yiddish etchings. Here's a chance for travelers to give the *pierogi* a break with delicate entrees such as chicken with honey and ginger (19zł). Entrees are don't come with sides; the waitress will remind you to order one for a full meal. Not kosher. Entrees 15-45zł. Open daily 11am-11pm. Call ahead F-Sa. MC/V. Second location in Manufaktura (see **Sights,** p. 472). ❸

Green Way Bar Wegetariański, Piotrkowska 80 (☎632 0852). Green Way pioneered vegetarian eating in Łódź and remains the city's leading outpost of all things green and tasty. Menu changes almost daily to include fresh seasonal produce. Berry and yogurt *koktajly* (fruit smoothies; 1.50-3zł), rich coffee (3.50-4.50zł), and *naleśniki* with fruit (6.50zł) complement hefty portions of international options and veggie versions of traditional Polish favorites. Entrees 7.50zł. Open daily 10am-9pm. Cash only. ❶

Presto Pizza, Piotrkowska 67 (☎630 8883), in the alley across from Hotel Grand. Alongside solid renditions of pizza standbys like the margarita (9zł), Presto offers traditional Italian food including a variety of pasta dishes (13-20zł, depending on the sauce) and gnocchi (16.50zł). A *mała* (small) pizza is large enough for two. Open M-Sa noon-midnight, Su 12am-11pm. MC/V. Second location at Piotrkovska 27. ❷

U Chochoła, Traugutta 3 (☎632 5138), across the street from Hotel Savoy. Locals can't get enough of the heaping portions, waitstaff in folk costumes, and *Staropolski* (Old Polish) menu. Even the restroom adheres to the rustic theme. The pork loin with bone and cabbage (21zł) is a treat. Veggie options 8-13zł. 20-*pierogi* variety platter (20zł) is for serious eaters. Open M-Th and Su noon-11pm, F-Sa noon-midnight. AmEx/MC/V. ❷

SIGHTS

MANUFAKTURA. The same red brick and wrought-iron factories that were the heart of Łódź's textile industry at the turn of the 20th century have now become its newest and most impressive commercial and cultural hub. Since the last holdout finally closed its doors in 1997, some of the industry's oldest classic buildings have been cleaned out and refurbished, opening up 120,000 square meters of state of the art shopping, restaurants, movie theaters, gyms, and even a climbing wall and skating rink, all within the original factory walls. Completed in the summer of 2007, the factories' rebirth offers a glimpse into Łódź's own struggles to move beyond its fading industrial past. Don't miss the complex's small but fascinating **Museum of the Factory,** which offers a detailed multimedia look at the history of Łódź's textile industry, with emphasis on the harsh existence of textile workers at the turn of the 20th century and the role the industry has played in the development of the city and the country. If asked, museum staff will demonstrate the working industrial machines. (*ul. Ogrodowka 17 in the passageway opposite Cinema City. ☎664 9293; www.muzeumfabryki.manufaktura.com. Open Tu-Fr 9am-1pm, 3pm-7pm; Sa 11am-7pm; Su 10am-6pm. 2zl. Cash only.)*

JEWISH CEMETERY (CMENTARZ ŻYDOWSKI). Eerily beautiful, the sprawling Jewish cemetery, established in 1892, is the largest in Europe. There are more than 200,000 graves and 180,000 tombstones, some elaborately engraved although worn and overgrown. Instead of the flowers and memorial candles found in Christian cemeteries, visits here are marked with cobwebbed stones. Especially noteworthy is the colossal Poznański family crypt with its gold-mosaic ceiling. Near the entrance to the cemetery is a memorial to the Jews killed in the Łódź ghetto: signs lead the way to the **Ghetto Fields** (Pole Ghettowe), which are lined with the faintly marked graves of the 43,527 Jews who died there. The cemetery is difficult to find and its gates are often locked during so-called open hours, so contact the helpful and English-speaking tourist information bureau ahead of time for assistance. *(Take tram #1 from Kilińskiego or #6 from Kościuszki or Zachodnia north to the last stop, 20min. away. Continue up the street; make a left onto Zmienna, a small stone road off Inflancka; and head to the small gate on your right. It is better to try this entrance than the main gate on Bracka, which is usually locked. ☎656 7019. Open May-Sept. M-Th and Su 9am-5pm, F 9am-3pm; Oct.-Apr. M-F and Su 8am-3pm. Closed Jewish holidays. 4zł; free for those visiting the graves of relatives.)* In the center of town, the **Jewish Community Center** (Gmina Wyznaniowa Żydowska) has info on those buried in the cemetery. *(Pomorska 18. ☎633 5156. English spoken. Open M-F 10am-2pm. Services daily.)*

POZNAŃSKI PALACE AND SCHEIBLER PALACE. Prewar Łódź, a hub of European industry, thrived at the intersection of Polish, Jewish, and German culture. In the late 19th century, factory magnates Izrael Poznański and Karol Scheibler competed fiercely for dominance of the city's lucrative textile industry. Striving to outdo one another, Jewish Poznański and German Scheibler each built lavish residences adjacent to their factories. The intact interiors of the two palaces are now home to two Łódź's most notable museums: the Historical Museum is in the Poznański Palace, and the Scheibler Palace holds the Museum of Cinematography. *(See listings below for directions to and locations of palaces.)*

ŁÓDŹ HISTORICAL MUSEUM (MUZEUM HISTORII MIASTA ŁODZI). Preserving the Poznański family home's Gilded Age splendor, this museum boasts an ornate neo-Baroque palace ballroom, gorgeously furnished salons and rooms, and exhibits on Łódź's famous sons and daughters, including pianist Artur Rubinstein and writers Jerzy Kosiński and Władysław Reymont. Factory walls and workers' quarters are visible outside the palace. *(Ogrodowa 15. Take tram #4 toward Helenówek or #6 toward Strykowskar to intersection of Nowomiejska and Północna. Turn left on Północna, which becomes Ogrodowa. ☎654 0082. Open Tu and Th 10am-4pm, W 2-6pm, F-Su 10am-2pm. 7zł, students 4zł; Su free.)*

MUSEUM OF CINEMATOGRAPHY (MUZEUM KINOMATOGRAFII). International film giants Krzysztof Kieślowski, Roman Polański, and Andrzej Wajda all got their start at Łódź's famous film school—the city, sometimes called "HollyŁódź," has its own "Avenue of the Stars" on Piotrkowska. Contributing to this tradition, the museum has acquired props and sets from recent Polish films and rebuilt them in and around the building. With neo-Baroque cherubs lolling on the ceilings and Venetian mosaics underfoot, the style of Scheibler Palace is best described as Industrial Magnate Eclectic. Museum highlights include a massive 1900 animation machine called the *fotoplastikon* and the animation sets on the second floor, and a tribute to Krzysztof Kieślowski, complete with his international awards and letters from the Academy. The basement and a room above the foyer host rotating photography exhibits. *(pl. Zwycięstwa 1, behind a park off Piłudskiego. ☎674 0957; www.kinomuzeum.pl. Open Sept.-June Tu 10am-5pm, Th 10am-6pm, W and F-Su 9am-4pm; July-Aug. Tu-W and F-Su 10am-4pm. 5zł, students 3zł.)*

ENTERTAINMENT AND NIGHTLIFE

As a hub of Polish film, Łódź hosts several annual film festivals. The most famous of these are the **International Festival of the Art of Cinematography,** "Camerimage" (late Nov. to early Dec.) and the **International Film and Television School Festival** "Media School" (mid-Oct.). The **Dialogue of Four Cultures** (Festiwal Dialogu Czterech Kultur) in early September includes film, theater, and music presentations. Łódź prides itself on extraordinary nightlife. **Piotrkowska** turns into publand a little after 9pm, though plenty of drinking is already underway by mid-afternoon.

Łódź Kaliska, Piotrkowska 102 (☎630 6955). This local legend–bar, club, offbeat art space, and occasional theater venue–has such a cult following that people drive from Warsaw to drink here for the night. Beer 8zł. Open M-Sa noon-3am, Su 4pm-3am (see **Łódź Kaliska,** p. 472).

Port-West, Piotrkowska 102 (☎632 5606). The wrought-iron and concrete industrial theme of Łódź's hottest new nightclub is offset by the waterfalls and neon lights that line its walls. Check your coat (1zł) at the door and cross a small bridge to the large dance-floor, complete with strobe lights and a fog machine. Others look on from the balconies and bars above. 18+. Until 11pm free, afterwards Th men 5zł, students and women free; F men 10zł, women free, students 5zł and free beer; Sa men 15zł, women 10zł, students 5zł and free beer. Open F-Sa 9pm-late. Cash only. Next to **Łódź Kaliska.**

Quo Vadis, Piotrkowska 65 (☎632 1919). Named for the 1896 novel by Nobel Prize-winner Henryk Sienkiewicz, Quo Vadis offers a Polish epic of a different sort: the house specialty drink is a towering 5L glass of beer (48zł; also available in 7.5L for those with a death wish). In summer, this sidewalk patio is a stronghold of the Łódź party scene. Open daily 10am-late. MC/V.

Klub Muzyczny Riff Raff, Roosevelta 10 (☎637 5889; www.riffraff.com.pl). Pub/club Riff Raff blends foosball, rock, and beer with the flickering fluorescent lighting of the cigarette and beer signs lining its walls to create an atmosphere as appealingly gritty as Łódź itself. DJ and dancing every F and Sa after 8pm. 21+. No cover. Pub downstairs open daily from 4pm, club upstairs Th-Sa 8pm-late. Cash only.

HOLLYŁÓDŹ

Although Poland's film industry has come to international prominence through the films of directors Andrzej Wajda, Roman Polański, and Krzyśztof Kieslowski, few might realize that all three filmmakers graduated from a film school in the grimy industrial town of Łódź.

Łódź's national film school (the awkwardly named Panstwowa Wyzsza Szkola Filmowa, Telewizyjna i Teatralna im. Leona Schillera w Lodzi) permitted a degree of freedom of expression unheard of in the Eastern Bloc of the 1950s and 1960s. Although the school tried to clamp down in 1968, it was too late: in the 70s and 80s Wajda and Kieślowski created devastating cinematic critiques of the communist regimes that reached international audiences.

As Łódź has given the West some of its best filmmakers, it has in turn attracted the enigmatic director David Lynch, who visited the city in 2000 for a film festival and liked it so much that in 2005 he filmed his epic *Inland Empire,* ostensibly set in Los Angeles, mostly in Lódz with many Polish actors and actresses.

Visit the Museum of Cinematography for exhibits on Lódz's famous film-makers. 1 Zwyciestwa Sq. ☎04 26 74 09 57; www.kinomuzeum.pl. Open W and F-Su 9am-4pm, Tu 10am-5pm, Th 11am-6pm. 5zł per person.

POZNAŃ ☎(0)61

Poznań (POZ-nayn; pop. 590,000) is a city of many faces. Influenced by the Prussians and the Germans, Poznań is a buzzing economic hub, especially during its many international trade fairs. The romantic Stare Miasto (Old Town) swells with meandering tourists in summer, and a lively arts scene thrives just below the all-business surface. On the edges of Stare Miasto, a constant stream of construction speaks to the rapid changes that the cosmopolitan city is undergoing.

TRANSPORTATION

Trains: Dworcowa 1 (☎866 1212). International tickets *Kasa* 7. Open 24hr. To: **Częstochowa** (5-7hr., 2 per day, 46zł); **Gdynia** (4½hr., 9 per day, 47zł); **Gniezno** (1hr., 26 per day, 10-20zł); **Kołobzreg** (4hr., 6 per day, 26-43zł); **Kraków** (5hr., 9 per day, 50-79zł); **Łódź** (5hr., 6 per day, 25-42zł); **Szczecin** (2hr., 17 per day, 36-62zł); **Toruń** (2½hr., 6 per day, 20-33zł); **Warsaw** (3-4½hr., 12 per day, 46-89zł); **Wrocław** (2-3hr., 26 per day, 21-60zł); **Berlin, GER** (3½hr., 6 per day, 92-125zł).

Buses: Towarowa 17 (☎833 1511). Open 5:30am-10:30pm. To: **Jelenia Góra** (5½hr., 3 per day, 40zł); **Kraków** (9¾hr., 4 per day, 47zł); **Łódź** (3-4hr., 8 per day, 34-38zł); **Malbork** (5½hr., 1 per day, 45zł); **Szczecin** (4¼hr., 5 per day, 33zł); **Warsaw** (4-5hr., 3 per day, 38zł); **Wrocław** (2½-3½hr., 5 per day, 28zł).

Public Transportation: Tickets 1.20zł per 10min., 2.40zł per 30min. Students 0.65zł per 10min. Large luggage needs its own ticket. Prices double 11pm-4am. **Night buses** and **trams** distinguished by 3-digit route numbers.

Taxi: Radio Taxi (☎9191).

POLAND

ORIENTATION AND PRACTICAL INFORMATION

Poznań is sprawling, but almost everything you want can be found in **Stare Miasto.** The **train station,** Poznań Główny, is on **Dworcowa** at the edge of Stare Miasto. The **bus station** is on **Towarowa.** To get to the **Stary Rynek** (Old Market Square), exit the train station, climb the stairs, turn left on the bridge, and turn right on **Roosevelta.** After several blocks, turn right on **Śweti Marcin.** Continue to **aleja Marcinkowskiego,** go left, and turn right on **Pąderewskiego.** Alternatively, catch any **tram** going to the right along Św. Marcin from the end of Dworcowa. From Roosevelta, trams #5 and 8 run to Stare Miasto. Get off at Marcinkowskiego.

Tourist Offices: Centrum Informacji Turystycznej (CIT), Stary Rynek 59/60 (☎852 6156; fax 855 3379). Provides free **maps** and accommodation info and arranges tours (220zł). Open June-Aug. M-F 9am-8pm, Sa 10am-8pm, Su 10am-6pm; Sept.-May M-F 9am-5pm, Sa 10am-2pm. **Glob-Tour,** Dworcowa 1 (☎/fax 866 0667), in the train station. Offers tourist info, maps (6-8zł), and **currency exchange.** Open 24hr.

Currency Exchange: Bank Pekao S.A., Św. Marcin 52/56 (☎855 8558), cashes **traveler's checks** for 1% commission. Open M-F 8am-6pm, Sa 10am-2pm. **Bank Zachodni,** Fredry 12 (☎853 0416). Has **Western Union.** Open M-F 8am-6pm.

Luggage Storage: At the train station. 2zł plus 0.15% of declared value. Open 24hr. Lockers also available at the train and bus stations. Large 8zł, small 4zł.

English-Language Bookstore: Omnibus Bookstore, Św. Marcin 39 (☎853 6182). Open M-F 10am-7pm, Sa 10am-4pm. AmEx/MC/V. **Empik,** ul. Ratajczaka 44, has English-language newspapers and magazines. Open M-Sa 9am-10pm, Su 10am-6pm. AmEx/MC/V.

24hr. Pharmacy: Apteka Centralna, 23 Lutego 18 (☎852 2625). MC/V.

Hospital: Szpital Miejski, Szkolna 8/12 (☎858 5600).

Internet: Pięterko, Nowowiejskiego 7 (☎662 3845). 2.50zł per hr. Open M-Sa 10am-midnight, Su noon-midnight.

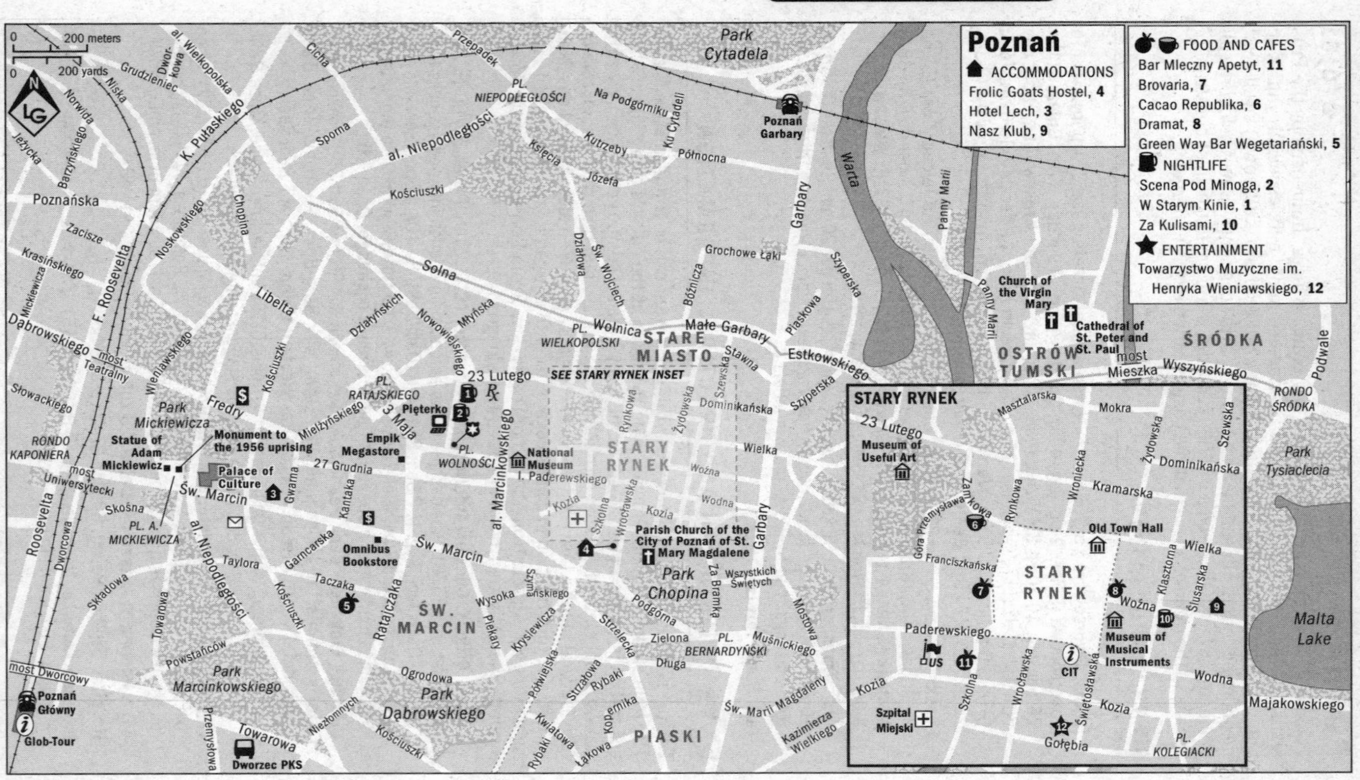

Poznań
ACCOMMODATIONS
Frolic Goats Hostel, 4
Hotel Lech, 3
Nasz Klub, 9
FOOD AND CAFES
Bar Mleczny Apetyt, 11
Brovaria, 7
Cacao Republika, 6
Dramat, 8
Green Way Bar Wegetariański, 5
NIGHTLIFE
Scena Pod Minogą, 2
W Starym Kinie, 1
Za Kulisami, 10
ENTERTAINMENT
Towarzystwo Muzyczne im. Henryka Wieniawskiego, 12
STARY RYNEK
Museum of Useful Art
Old Town Hall
Museum of Musical Instruments
CIT
Szpital Miejski
Cathedral of St. Peter and St. Paul
Church of the Virgin Mary
OSTRÓW TUMSKI
ŚRÓDKA
RONDO ŚRÓDKA
Park Tysiaclecia
Malta Lake
Warta
Park Cytadela
Poznań Garbary
STARE MIASTO
SEE STARY RYNEK INSET
National Museum
Parish Church of the City of Poznań of St. Mary Magdalene
Park Chopina
PIASKI
ŚW. MARCIN
Park Dąbrowskiego
Empik Megastore
Omnibus Bookstore
Pięterko
Monument to the 1956 uprising
Palace of Culture
Statue of Adam Mickiewicz
Park Mickiewicza
Park Marcinkowskiego
Dworzec PKS
Poznań Główny
Glob-Tour
RONDO KAPONIERA
PL. WOLNOŚCI
PL. WIELKOPOLSKI
PL. NIEPODLEGŁOŚCI
PL. RATAJSKIEGO
PL. A. MICKIEWICZA
PL. BERNARDYŃSKI
PL. KOLEGIACKI
al. Niepodległości
al. Marcinkowskiego
Św. Marcin
F. Roosevelta
Garbary
Wielka
Wroniecka
Kramarska
Szewska
Dominikańska
Żydowska
Wodna
Woźna
Rynkowa
Wrocławska
Szkolna
Kozia
Paderewskiego
23 Lutego
27 Grudnia
Ratajczaka
Kościuszki
Fredry
Solna
Towarowa
Dworcowa
200 meters
200 yards

Post Office: Kościuszki 77 (☎853 6743; fax 869 7408). For **Poste Restante,** go to windows #6 or 7 upstairs. Open M-F 7am-9pm, Sa 8am-6pm, Su 9am-5pm. Branch next to the train station open 24hr. **Postal Code:** 61890.

ACCOMMODATIONS

During trade fairs, which occur all year except July-August and December, businesspeople fill the city and some prices double. A cheap room is almost impossible to find without calling ahead. You can find the dates of all fairs online at www.mtp.com.pl. The helpful staff at **Przemysław** ❶, Głogowska 16, rents comfortable **private rooms** near the center. (☎866 3560; www.przemyslaw.com.pl. Singles 42zł, during fairs 68zł; doubles 64/96zł. Open M-F 8am-6pm, Sa 10am-2pm; open 2hr. later during fairs; July-Aug. closed some Sa.)

Frolic Goats Hostel, Wrocławska 16/6. (☎501 144 704) Poznań's new backpacker hostel, with its great location and clean baaaths, is by far the best value in the city. The kitchen and common area with sofas, TV, and sound system will remind you of your living room back home. Dorms 50-60zł, private rooms 70-100zł per person. Breakfast included. Free Internet. Reception 24hr. MC/V. ❸

Nasz Klub, Woźna 10 (☎851 7630; www.naszklub.pl). From the train station, take tram #5 or 8 to Marcinkowskiego and cross the Rynek to Woźna; hotel is in a covered driveway on the left. Nasz Klub offers newly furnished rooms above a spacious restaurant. Rooms have baths, telephones, and TVs. Breakfast included. Reception 24hr. Check-in and check-out noon. Singles 135zł; doubles 195zł; triples 255zł. AmEx/MC/V. ❺

Hotel Lech, Św. Marcin 74 (☎853 0151; www.hotel-lech.poznan.pl). With a history in hospitality that predates WWI, this lime-green hotel on busy św. Marcin has airy, modern rooms. Communications amenities cater to business travelers: all rooms have satellite TV, telephone, Internet, and baths. Breakfast buffet included. Singles 162zł, students with ISIC 72zł; doubles 244zł; suites 254zł. During fairs singles 240-310zł; doubles 370-430zł. Sa-Su 20% discount. MC/V. ❺

FOOD

Along Wielka there are several **24hr. grocery stores.** In summer, enjoy the homemade treats and locally grown fruits of the **open-air market** in pl. Wielkopolski, off 23 Lutego. (Open M-Sa 7:30am-afternoon.)

Brovaria, Stary Rynek 73-74 (☎858 6869). Poznań's only micro-brewery and one of Poland's few brew-pubs, Brovaria's high-quality beers include a honey beer (8zł), a pils (7.50zł), and a rotating special. Exquisite dishes are served in a loft-like hall with gleaming copper brewing tanks. Cheaper dishes include pork knuckle simmered in beer (26zł), beerwurst (18zł), and ribs in a hops sauce (24zł). Entrees 18-49zł. Open daily 11am-1pm. MC/V. ❸

Dramat, Stary Rynek 41 (☎856 0936). A rarity among the many overpriced Stary Rynek restaurants, Dramat serves good *naleśniki* at reasonable prices. If you find the multitude of sauces dizzying, ask your server for a recommendation. Beer 5.50-6.50zł. Breakfast 9.50zł. Main course *naleśniki* 6.50-9.50zł. Open daily 10am-midnight. Bar open 2pm-midnight. MC/V. ❶

Green Way Bar Wegetariański, Taczaka 2 (☎853 6912). Branch at Zeylanda 3 (☎843 4027). A rainbow of juice and smoothie pitchers lines the counter at this vegetarian favorite, where the servings are generous and the friendly staff make perfect *samosas* (7.50zł). Rotating menu of soy dishes, lasagnas, and hearty pastas and salads. Entrees 5-9zł. Open M-F 11am-7pm, Sa noon-7pm, Su noon-5pm. Cash only. ❶

POLAND

Bar Mleczny Apetyt, ul. Skolna 4. This perfectly located milk bar just off the Rynek adds new specialties like varied *naleśniki* and *kotleciki serowe* (fried cheese curds; 4.12zł) to the usual milk bar offerings, in a clean setting with friendly staff. Entrees 4-8zł. Open M-Sa 8am-10pm, Su 10am-10pm. Cash only. ❶

Cacao Republika, Zamkowa 7 (☎855 4378). The steady whir of hot-chocolate mixers reveals the house specialty (5-8zł), sipped on wicker seats amid antique decor. The Romantic upstairs is strewn with plush red couches and low tables, where mixed drinks (7-13zł) flow freely. Open M-Sa 10am-midnight, Su 10am-10pm. Cash only. ❶

SIGHTS

Ostentatious 15th-century merchant houses, notable for their rainbow paint jobs, line the fountain-filled **Stary Rynek.** The houses surround the multicolored **Old Town Hall,** a triumph of Renaissance architecture. Every day at noon a crowd gathers outside the clock tower to watch two **mechanical billy goats** emerge from a door above the clock and butt heads a dozen times. According to legend, the cook hired to prepare a feast celebrating the clock's 1511 completion burnt the venison that was to be served to the governor. Frantic, the cook stole two goats to cook instead, but they exposed his ruse when they escaped to the clock tower and began fighting in front of the guests. The **Historical Museum** (Muzeum Historii) in the town hall chronicles the region's history since the 13th century, but the most captivating sight is the building itself, with painted ceilings and 15th-century stone doorways leading to grandiose meeting halls. You can also find the 1913 version of the mechanical goats. (☎852 5613. Open M-Tu 10am-4pm, W 11am-6pm, F 9am-4pm, Sa-Su 10am-3pm. 5.50zł, students 3.50zł; Sa free.) The vast **National Museum** (Muzeum Narodowe), Marcinkowskiego 9, contains a marvelous collection of 13th- to 19th-century Western European paintings; the top floor is devoted to an intriguing collection of modern Polish art. (☎856 8000; fax 851 5898. Open Tu 10am-6pm, W 9am-5pm, Th and Su 10am-4pm, F-Sa 10am-5pm. 10zł, students 6zł; Sa free.) One of the National's daughter museums is the **Museum of Musical Instruments** (Muzeum Instrumentów Muzycznych), Stary Rynek 45, which features antique and exotic instruments, as well as a piano that once belonged to Chopin. (☎852 0857. Open Tu-Sa 11am-5pm, Su 11am-3pm. 5.50zł, students 3.50zł; Sa free.) Its sister museum, the **Museum of Useful Art,** Góra Przemysława 1, on the hill by Stary Rynek, highlights the creativity of design, including exhibits of 13th- to 18th-century swords and modern household objects (☎852 2035. Open Tu-W and F-Sa 10am-4pm, Su 10am-3pm. 5.50zł, students 3.50zł; Sa free.)

One stop from the Old Town on trams #1, 4, 8, or 16 in **Ostrów Tumski** stands the **Cathedral of St. Peter and St. Paul** (Katedra Piotra i Pawła), the first cathedral in Poland. The original 10th-century church is said to have been the site of Poland's symbolic baptism, when Mieszko I, the first prince of the Piast dynasty, abandoned paganism in 966. In its ornate **Gold Chapel** (Kaplica Złota) lie the tombs of two Piast rulers: Prince Mieszko I and his oldest son, Bolesław the Brave, Poland's first king. (Cathedral open M-Sa 9am-6pm, Su 1:15-6:30pm.)

Within the striking rose-colored **Parish Church of the City of Poznań of St. Mary Magdalene,** at the end of Świętosławska off Stary Rynek, sculpted ceilings and columns spiral toward heaven. (Free concerts Sa 12:15pm.) **Plac Mickiewicza** commemorates the 1956 clash between workers and government troops over food prices, which resulted in 76 deaths. Two stark crosses knotted together with steel cable are emblazoned with the dates of five additional Communist-era worker uprisings. A recording tells the story from a console in front of the monument. (In several languages, including English and Esperanto. Free.)

ENTERTAINMENT AND FESTIVALS

The monthly *Poznański Informator Kulturalny, Sportowy i Turystyczny* (IKST; 3.90zł) contains an English supplement on cultural events (sold at bookstores and some kiosks.) The **Towarzystwo Muzyczne im. Henryka Wieniawskiego** (Music Society), Świętosławska 7, provides classical concert info. (☎852 2642; fax 852 8991. English spoken. Open M-F 9am-5pm. Ring the bell.) The huge **International Theater Festival** comes to Malta Lake in late June and early July. Other festivals include the **Jazz Festival** in early March, the **International Blues Festival** in late May and early June, and a **folk art festival** in July. For tickets and info on these and other cultural events, contact **Centrum Informacji Miejskiej,** Ratajczka 44, next to the Empik Megastore. (☎94 31. Open M-F 10am-7pm, Sa-Su 10am-5pm.) Poznań's experimental performances and film screenings are concentrated along Nowowiejskiego. For current listings, check the free Mapa guide (www.czyli.info).

POLAND

NIGHTLIFE

Bars and cafes—many of them inexplicably Wild West-themed—surround the Rynek, and dance clubs dot Stare Miasto. A more avant-garde scene thrives on **Nowowiejskiego,** where bars serve up attitude and drinks until the early morning.

W Starym Kinie, Nowowiejskiego 8 (☎852 2241; www.wstarymkinie.iq.pl). An antique film projector on the bar and a gregarious crowd welcome patrons to the magical "Old Cinema." Relax in old movie theater seats at the bar downstairs; head upstairs to take in one of the frequent film screenings, rock and jazz concerts, or innovative DJ sets. Beer 6.50zł. Tu movie night, W "Classic Vinyl," F Disko Inferno. 18+. Open M-Sa 10am-1am, Su 6pm-midnight. Cash only.

Za Kulisami (Behind the Curtains), Klasztorna 8 (☎853 2397). With a slew of letters taped to the bar and a broken-in collection of wooden furniture, relaxed Za Kulisami is a favorite haunt of Poznań's young artists. Comedian regulars spice up the bar conversation, and blues and jazz patter lightly in the background. Beer 5zł, but a staggering 1.5L goes for a mere 15zł. Open daily 4pm-late. Cash only.

Scena Pod Minogą, Nowowiejskiego 8 (☎852 7922). Exuberant Pod Minogą is a student dance favorite. Rooms wind through 2 floors of a rambling house. Frequent live music upstairs ranges from piano and bagpipes to jam sessions—you won't hear house or techno on this dance floor. The bartenders work all sorts of magic with grenadine. Beer 6zł. M Karaoke night. 18+. Open M-Sa 10am-late, Su 4pm-midnight. Cash only.

DAYTRIP FROM POZNAŃ

LICHEŃ

From Poznań, take one of 9 daily buses to Konin (2hr., 19zł). From the intracity bus stop in the Konin bus station parking lot, hop on one of many daily microbuses or PKS buses to Lichen (25min.; microbus 3-5zł, bus 3.20zł). Microbus stops at the main entrance, Klasztorna 4, while the PKS bus stops just before—make sure to let the PKS driver know you want to get off at Licheń. To return to Konin, catch one of the same buses from the bus stop 100m from the main entrance. A few daily buses run from Konin back to Poznań, but you're better off hopping off the bus from Licheń at the Konin train station and taking one of 15 daily trains back to Poznań (1-2hr., 16zł). ☎270 8100; www.lichen.pl.

With a theme park's sprawling acreage, the **Sanctuary of Licheń** is one of the world's most grandiose pilgrimage sites. A petite masterpiece rests in the **Chapel of Saint Dorothy,** the brick church to the right at the end of the entrance drive. The image of the **Madonna Licheńska** is said to have revealed itself in an

1813 apparition to Tomasz Kłossowski, a Polish soldier wounded near Leipzig, Germany, while fighting for Napoleon. Kłossowski survived and sought her likeness, which he found in the tiny town of Lgota. In 1852, the icon was moved to Licheń, and when Nazis took over the church during WWII, the painting was hidden and escaped damage. Today, the stunningly beautiful icon has been moved to a special hall in the much larger basilica (see below), but the chapel remains an important destination for pilgrims. In contrast with the subtle beauty of the Madonna Licheńska, the colossal gold dome of the **Licheń Basilica** looms as Poland's largest temple. Begun in 1994 and completed in 1999, this massive structure impresses viewers with its sheer scale. Visitors can access the basilica only by way of the **Path of the Cross,** a flower-lined procession through the Stations of the Cross (10min., to the left at the end of the entrance drive). The altar is an overwhelming sight, with marble detailing and the iridescent words *jestem który jestem* ("I am who I am") over the altarpiece. The grounds boast enormous fountains, sculptures, and grottoes, including a stylized reconstruction of Golgotha that visitors are invited to climb up. Food options are limited—fast food can be found at street stands outside the entrance, but bringing a bag lunch is a better option.

TORUŃ ☎(0)56

Toruń (pop. 210,000), extols itself as the birthplace of Mikołaj Kopernik, a.k.a. Copernicus. Even before the local genius came to fame, the mercantile medieval city was known far and wide: it was called "beautiful red Toruń" for its impressive brick-and-stone structures. Today, parishioners pray in 500-year-old churches, and children scramble through the ruins of a Teutonic castle, while visitors stroll through the city's cobblestone streets and linger along the riverwalk.

TRANSPORTATION

Trains: Toruń Główny, Kujawska 1 (☎94 36). Open M-F 7am-5pm, Sa-Su 7am-2pm. To: **Gdańsk** (3¼hr., 7 per day, 38zł); **Łódź** (3hr., 9 per day, 21-34zł); **Poznań** (2¼hr., 7 per day, 20-33zł); **Szczecin** (4½hr., daily, 46zł); **Warsaw** (2¾hr., 6 per day, 40zł).

Buses: Dworzec PKS, Dąbrowskiego 26 (☎655 5333). Open 4am-midnight to: **Gdańsk** (3½hr., 2 per day, 34zł); **Kołobrzeg** (7hr., 5 per day, 40zł); **Łódź** (3¼hr., 13 per day, 27zł); **Szczecin** (6½hr., 1 per day, 47zł); **Warsaw** (4hr., 6 per day, 32zł). **Polski Express** (☎228 445 555) runs buses from the Ruch kiosk north of pl. Teatralny to: **Kołobrzeg** (6¾hr.; 1 per day; 60zł, students 30zł); **Łódź** (3hr., 1 per day, 37/22zł); **Szczecin** (5¼hr., 2 per day, 60/30zł); **Warsaw** (3½hr., 9 per day, 55/27.50zł).

Public Transportation: (☎655 5200). **Bus** tickets 2.10zł, students 1.05zł. Surcharge if you buy from the driver instead of at a kiosk. Prices rise annually. Luggage needs its own ticket.

Taxis: ☎91 91, wheelchair-accessible transport 91 96. To avoid being overcharged, make sure the driver uses a meter.

Bike Rental: Emporium, Piekary 28 (☎657 6108). Bikes 5zł per hr.; document deposit required. Also provides free walking-tour maps; biking-tour maps come with rental. Open M-F 10am-6pm, Sa-Su 10am-4pm. MC/V.

ORIENTATION AND PRACTICAL INFORMATION

The tourist office and most sights are in and around **Rynek Staromiejski** (Old Town Square). To get to the Rynek from the train station, take bus #22 or 27 across the **Wisła River** to **plac Rapackiego.** Head through the park, with the river on your right, to find the square. On foot, take Kujawska left from the train station, turn right

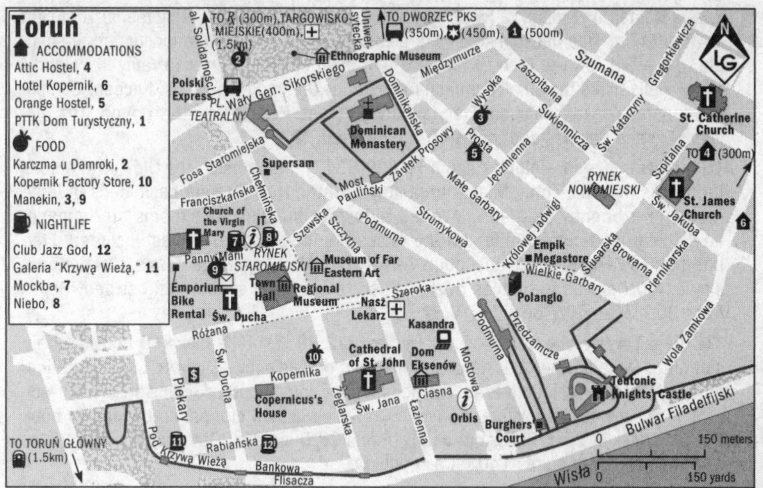

onto al. Jana Pawła II, and hike over the Wisła. Pl. Rapackiego is on the right, after Kopernika. From the bus station, walk through the park and take a left on Uniwersytecka. Continue along the street and turn right on Wały Gen. Sikorskiego. At **plac Teatralny,** turn left onto Chełmińska, which leads to Rynek Staromiejski. **Szeroka** and **Królowej Jadwigi** run to **Rynek Nowomiejski** (New Town Square).

Tourist Office: IT, Rynek Staromiejski 25 (☎621 0931; www.it.torun.pl). Has free **maps,** including a map of bus and tram system, and sells others (5.50-7zł). Open May-Aug. M and Sa 9am-4pm, Tu-F 9am-6pm, Su 9am-1pm; Sept.-Apr. M and Sa 9am-4pm.

Currency Exchange: Bank PKO, Szeroka 14. Gives Visa **cash advances,** and cashes **American Express Travelers Cheques** for a small commission. Open M-F 8am-6pm, Sa 9am-1pm. ATMs line Szeroka, and *kantors* are scattered throughout the Old Town.

English-Language Bookstore: Polanglo, Wielkie Garbary 19 (☎/fax 621 1222; www.polanglo.pl). A lot of English fiction in addition to an array of school books. Open M-F 10am-6pm, Sa 10am-2pm. MC/V. **Empik,** ul. Wielkie Garbary 18, has a good selection of English-language papers and magazines. Open M-Sa 10am-7pm, Su 11am-5pm. AmEx/MC/V.

Pharmacy: Apteka Panaceum, Odrodzenia 1 (☎622 4159), off al. Solidarności, is open fairly late on weekdays. Open M-F 8am-10pm, Sa 8am-3pm, Su 10am-2pm. AmEx/MC/V.

Medical Services: Szpital Bielany, św. Józefa 53/59 (☎610 1100). Take bus #11. **Nasz Lekarz** has registration at Szeroka 25 (☎622 6189). Physicians' offices are around the corner at Szczytna 1. Open M-F 8am-8pm, Sa 8am-2pm.

Internet: Kasandra Internet Cafe, ul. Mostowa 15 (☎652 1266). 4zł per hr. Open M-Sa 10-midnight, Su noon-midnight. Cash only.

Post Office: Rynek Staromiejski 15 (☎621 9100). **Telephones** inside. **Poste Restante** at window #9 open M-F 8am-8pm. Open 24hr.; 9pm-6am enter from Piekary 26. Branch at train station open M-Sa 6:30am-8:30pm. **Postal Code:** 87100.

ACCOMMODATIONS

There are a number of reasonably priced accommodations in the center, but they fill up fast, so call ahead. Inexpensive hotels are often the best-situated budget option, but deal-seekers can check the **IT** (see above) for far-flung rooms in university dorms in July and August. (Singles 45zł; doubles 60zł.)

Orange Hostel, ul. Prosta 19 (☎652 0033; www.hostelorange.pl). Ring the buzzer to get in. Toruń's first true backpacker hostel gets everything right, from a location in the middle of the Old Town to laundry facilities that even include a dryer (a rarity in Poland). Mirror walls make the small common-room/lobby feel more spacious. Kitchen. Complimentary breakfast 7am-noon. Free laundry. Internet. Reception 24hr. Dorms 30zł; singles 50zł and doubles and triples 40zł per person. ❶

Attic Hostel, ul. gen. Chłopickiego 4 (☎659 8517), just outside the Old Town, across the tracks from the Toruń Miasto train station. Attic Hostel offers basic beds in large rooms in a brightly painted converted industrial building. The rooms are immaculately clean and comfortable and the prices are incredible. Breakfast included. Free Internet. Towels provided. Reception 7am-10pm. May-Aug. large dorms 30zł per bed, singles 70zł per bed, doubles 50zł per bed, triples and quads 40zł per bed. Sept.-Apr.: 25zł/35zł/40zł/50zł. MC/V. ❷

PTTK Dom Turystyczny, Legionów 24 (☎/fax 622 3855). Take bus #10 from the train station to Dekerta, then backtrack toward town on Legionów. Close to the bus station. Although this is a trek from town, the helpful staff and smoothed linens of Dom Turystyczny make the dorms inviting. A favorite of Polish school groups, so be sure to book ahead. Check-in 2pm. Check-out noon. Dorms 28zł; singles 60zł; doubles 76zł; triples 94zł; quads 112zł; quints 140zł. Cash only ❶

Hotel Kopernik, Wola Zamkowa 16 (☎659 7333; fax 652 2573). From the Rynek, follow Szeroka, go right on św. Jakuba, and left on Wola Zamkowa. At the edge of Stare Miasto beside the Teutonic Knights' Castle, Kopernik has a friendly staff, fluffy towels, and satellite TV. Rooms are spacious and spotless. Sausage-happy breakfast buffet 14zł. Check-in and check-out 2pm. Singles 96-136zł depending on bath facilities, weekends 71-101zł; doubles 121-176zł/86-131zł; apartments 246zł. AmEx/MC/V. ❹

FOOD

Toruń still offers its centuries-old treat of **gingerbread** *(pierniki)*. The original cakes, tough and unsweetened, were considered a medicine rather than a snack. Toruń kept its gingerbread recipe a secret for centuries, and even today many gingerbread-makers guard their recipes closely. When selecting gingerbread, bear in mind that the intricately designed breads in the shapes of historical figures and buildings are more decorative than edible. The smaller breads in simpler shapes are the soft, sweetened, modern form of gingerbread. **Supersam,** Chełmińska 22, is a 24hr. grocery store. An international bazaar and a farmer's market offering an unusual collection of fruits, baked goods, and cheap clothing make up **Targowisko Miejskie.** Two square blocks of bartering sprawl on Chełmińska, offering mild chaos and unparalleled bargains. (Open daily 8am-3pm.)

Kopernik Factory Store, Żeglarska 25 (☎621 0561), and Rynek Staromiejski 6 (☎622 8832). Collect gingerbread likenesses of your favorite Polish historical figures. Highlights include heart-shaped *katarzynki* and gingerbread-filled boxes in the shapes of Toruń's most beautiful buildings. From 0.70zł for a small taste to 26zł for top-of-the-line historical figures. Sold by weight (about 12zł per kg) or pre-packaged. Open M-F 9am-7pm, Sa-Su 10am-2pm. MC/V. ❷

Manekin, Wysoka 5 (☎652 2885). Although somewhat confused in its country-western-mannequin-garden decor, Manekin sustains throngs of students on massive and delicious square *naleśniki* made to order. Sweet and savory are cooked up in endless varieties, but with gargantuan servings you'll be lucky to finish dinner, let alone dive into dessert (*naleśniki;* 3-11.50zł). The curry chicken-and-cheese (8.50zł) is a favorite. A variety of veggie options (6.50-9.50zł). 2nd location at Rynek Staromiejski. Open M-Th and Su 10am-10pm, F-Sa 10am-11pm. Cash only. ❶

Karczma u Damroki, al. Solidarności 1 (☎622 3660), in a Kashubian farmhouse in the Ethnographic Park. In medieval times, a *karczma* was an eatery for knights and peasants alike. Skirted by garden patios, Karczma u Damroki accurately recreates traditional dishes. The mushroom soup (6.50zł) and liver with apple and onion (14.50zł) are both popular, but the cult favorites are esoteric mixed drinks like "Elvis Lives!!!" (10.50zł). Curiously translated English menu. Entrees 8-28zł. Open daily 11am-11pm. MC/V. ❸

SIGHTS

An astounding number of attractions are packed into Toruń's ramparts, particularly in the 13th-century **Stare Miasto** (Old Town), built by the Teutonic Knights.

COPERNICUS'S HOUSE (DOM KOPERNIKA). The likely birthplace of astronomer Mikołaj Kopernik showcases astronomical instruments, Kopernik family documents, and artifacts from some of the astronomer's lesser-known activities, such as improving the defenses of Olsztyn Castle and translating Greek poetry to Latin. A sound-and-light show centered on a miniature model of the city (c. 1550) plays every 30min. and features an excellent video about the town's early history. Choose from eight languages, including English. *(Kopernika 15/17. ☎622 7038, ext. 13. Open W, F, Su 10am-4pm; Tu, Th, Sa noon-6pm. English captions. 10zł, students 6zł. Sound-and-light show 10/6zł. Both 18/11zł.)*

TOWN HALL (RATUSZ). One of Europe's finest examples of burgher architecture, this 14th-century building dominates the Rynek Staromiejski. The building once contained the lively trading stalls of the 15th-century merchants who crowded Toruń selling spices, spirits, and fish. The hall also hosted clandestine meetings in which citizens chaneled their grievances against the Teutonic Order into a regional uprising. The Ratusz now contains the **Regional Museum** (Muzeum Okręgowe). Exhibits include a famous 16th-century portrait of Copernicus, artifacts from Toruń's many craft guilds, and a rich collection of 20th-century Polish art, as well as early sacred art and stained glass. The neighboring tower provides a panorama of Toruń's most charming architecture. *(Rynek Staromiejski 1. ☎622 7038. Museum open May-Aug. Tu-W and Sa noon-6pm, Th and Su 10am-4pm; Sept.-Apr. Tu-Su 10am-4pm. 10zł, students 6zł; Su free. Tower open May-Sept. Tu-Su 10am-8pm. 10/6zł.)* Outside, a statue of Copernicus watches over the city. Another local "hero," the Raftsman ringed by gold frogs, also flanks the Ratusz. Legend has it that his flute charmed animals, delivering the city from a pesky frog plague; he was rewarded with marriage to the mayor's daughter.

TEUTONIC STRUCTURES. The 13th-century **Teutonic Knights' Castle** survived for two centuries before the burghers burned it to the ground in a 1454 revolt. The knights were originally called into the area to help defeat invading pagans, but soon established their own oppressive rule. The insurgent revolt against the castle set off a number of uprisings around the region, and hostilities continued for 20 years before Toruń was taken under the rule of the Polish king. The castle ruins house a booth where you can try your hand at archery for 4zł. *(Przedzamcze. ☎622 7039. Open daily 9am-8pm. Free.)* The nearby **Burghers' Court,** at the end of Podmurna, was built in 1489 from bricks of the destroyed Teutonic castle and served as a medieval social and sporting center. Today, it hosts cultural events listed on the door and at the IT. Across town, to the right as you face the river, stands the **Krzywą Wieżą** (Leaning Tower), built in 1271 by a knight as punishment for breaking the Order's rule of celibacy. The assumption was that the tower's "deviation" would remind the knight of his own. The less imaginative credit the shifting, sandy ground beneath. Either way, the 15m tower doesn't lean enough to scare away entrepreneurs, who have opened a bar and a cafe inside. *(Krzywą Wieżą 17; see Nightlife section below for info on cafe-bar.)*

CHURCHES. The **Cathedral of St. John the Baptist and St. John the Evangelist** (Bazylika Katedralna pw. Św. Janów) is the most impressive of the many Gothic churches in the region. Built between the 13th and 15th centuries, it mixes Gothic, Baroque, and Rococo elements. In 1473, the baby Kopernik was baptized in the **baptismal font.** The tower holds Tuba Dei, the oldest bell in Poland. *(At the corner of Żeglarska and Św. Jana. Open Apr.-Oct. M-Sa 8:30am-5:30pm, Su 2-5:30pm. 2zł, students 1zł. Tower 6/4zł.)* The **Church of the Annunciation of our Lady** (Kościół Św. Marii), with its slender stained-glass windows and patterned ceilings, is less ornate than many Polish churches and somewhat dusty. The chancel holds the mausoleum of Swedish queen Anna Wazówna, while a small shrine next to the entrance memorializes Stefan Wincent Frechilowski, a young priest who was imprisoned in a concentration camp and died ministering to his fellow inmates. *(On Panny Marii. Open M-Sa around 8am-5pm. Recorded info 2zł.)* The untouristed, beautiful **St. James Church** (Św. Jakuba) contains dramatically lit icons and the "Tree of Life" crucifix. *(Sw. Jakuba just off Rynek Nowomiejski. Open daily noon-3:30pm.)*

POLAND

OTHER SIGHTS. Just north of the Old Town in the Ethnographic Park, the **Ethnographic Museum,** Wały Sikorskiego 19, eschews the usual dry displays for a much more exciting reconstructed peasant village, complete with two mills, a blacksmith's workshop, and barns and farmhouses. Furnishings are authentic, and one farmhouse hosts rotating exhibits on subjects such as the history of beekeeping. *(☎622 7038. Open M, W, F 9am-4pm; Tu, Th, Sa-Su 10am-6pm. 8.50zł, students 5.50zł. Polish language guide 30zł. Photography permit 5zł. Cash only.)* A well-preserved old townhouse on the Rynek now hosts the Museum of Far Eastern Art, an eclectic collection of Chinese crystal dragons, samurai swords, delicate screens and other curiosities. The first floor holds a rotating Far Eastern photography exhibit. *(☎622 3078. 5.50zl, students 3.50zl. Open Tu-Su 10am-5pm. Cash only.)*

FESTIVALS AND NIGHTLIFE

In May, Toruń hosts **Probaltica,** a celebration of chamber music and arts, and the "Kontakt" **International Theater Festival.** Eastern European folk musicians converge in early June for the **Folk Music Festival.** In June and July, during the **Music and Architecture Festival,** classical concerts are held in different historic buildings each weekend. July and August usher in the annual **Summer Street Theater** series, which stages weekly performances in July and August. Check **IT** for more info. Nightlife, especially at student bars and clubs, is lively.

Niebo, Rynek Staromiejski 1 (☎621 0327). Niebo (heaven) may be an odd name for a subterranean cafe, but this Gothic cellar beneath the Ratusz proves itself worthy with celestial *szarlotka* (3zł) and classy decor. Run by a local singer-songwriter, Niebo hosts live jazz and cabaret. Open M-Th and Su noon-midnight, F-Sa noon-2am. Check out the folk art at the adjacent pub **Piwnica pod Aniołami** (Cellar Beneath the Angels; ☎658 5482). Beer 4-5zł. Open M-F 10am-1am, Sa-Su 10am-4am. Cash only.

Mockba, Rynek Staromiejski 22. With stylish all-red decor and stylized mock-Russian posters of tanks and starlets, this cellar off the Rynek has quickly become Toruń's chicest club. Laid-back door-policy results in a completely packed house by midnight. Cover F-Sa 10zł. Open daily 10am-late. Cash only.

Club Jazz God, Rabiańska 17 (☎65 22 13 08; www.jazzgod.torun.com.pl). With free live jazz Su 10pm, this stone cellar does justice to its name. The rest of the week, students fill scattered seats for lively conversation and thunderous rock, reggae, and Polish pop. The party starts around 8:30pm. Open M-Th and Su 5pm-2am, F-Sa 5pm-4am.

Galeria "Krzywą Wieżą," Pod Krzywą Wieżą 1/3. On the 2nd and 3rd floors of the Leaning Tower, whose cramped and ancient interior is full of odd angles and crooked doors. The toilets occupy a 14th-century women's prison. A must in summer for students and professors alike. A terrace precariously attached to the ramparts offers views across the Wisła. Beer 4.50-6zł. Open M-F 1pm-1am, Sa-Su 10am-2am.

WOLIN ISLAND: MIĘDZYZDROJE ☎(0)91

On the Baltic Coast near the German border, Wolin Island cradles glacial lakes, sweeping sea bluffs, and a bison preserve. The largest of the island's resort towns, Międzyzdroje (myen-dzi-ZDROY-eh), lures visitors with a gorgeous stretch of coast and access to the hiking and cycling trails of pristine Woliński National Park. With a base in Międzyzdroje, intrepid visitors can explore the island's many hidden corners, from the scattered ruins of forts and churches to windswept marshes.

TRANSPORTATION. Trains run to: Kraków (12hr., 4 per day, 60zł); Poznań (4hr., 7 per day, 46-82zł); Świnoujście (20min., 19 per day, 4-7.50zł); Szczecin (1½hr., 16 per day, 14-42zł); Warsaw (7-9hr., 3 per day, 57-97zł); Wrocław (9½hr., 4 per day, 52-56zł). **Buses** run to: Kołobrzeg (3hr., 9 per day, 21zł); Świnoujście (20min., 44-65 per day, 4zł); Szczecin (2hr., 2 per day, 18zł); Warsaw (8hr., 1 per day, 36zł). Buses travel to points along the hiking trails, including the towns of Kołczewo, Wolin, and Wisełka (10-30min., 6:30am-8pm, 6zł).

ORIENTATION AND PRACTICAL INFORMATION. To reach the center from the **train station,** walk downhill and go left on Norwida. The **PKS bus stop** is on Niepodległości in front of the Muzeum WPN, near the corner of Kolejowa. Pedestrian **plac Neptuna,** at the intersection of Niepodległości and Kolejowa, harbors many restaurants and shops. Several blocks north, the beach promenade along Bohaterów Warzsawy and Promenada Gwiazd is alive with fried fish stands, cotton candy, and a new pier. **PTTK,** Kolejowa 2, sells **maps** (9-12zł) and provides info about the region and local accommodations. (☎328 0462. No English spoken. Open M-F 7am-4pm.) A conveniently located *kantor* with great hours can be found at Niepodległości 2A. (Open M-F 9am-7pm, Sa 9am-6pm, Su 10am-4pm.) An **ATM** is outside the Polino Hotel at Zwycięstwa 1. **Luggage storage** is at the train sta-

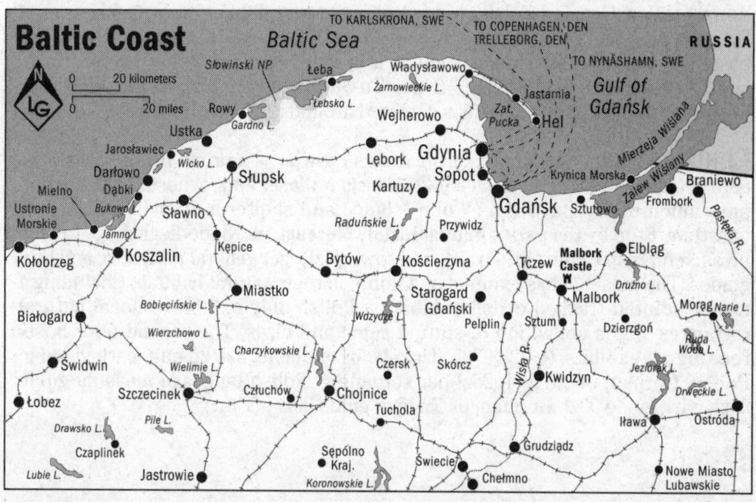

tion. (5zł per item per day. Open daily 7am-9:30pm.) A **pharmacy** is at Zwycięstwa 9. (☎328 0090. Open M-F 8am-7pm.) Use the web at **Internet Cafe,** Norwida 17. (☎328 0421. 5zł per hr. Open daily 9am-10pm.) The **post office** is at Gryfa Pomorskiego 7. (☎328 0140. Open M-F 8am-8pm.) **Postal Code:** 72-500.

ACCOMMODATIONS AND FOOD. Watch for *wolne pokoje* (rooms available) signs, particularly along Gryfa Pomorskiego. Call ahead in July and August. Alternatively, consult **PTTK,** Kolejowa 2, which arranges **private rooms** and runs the **PTTK Hotel Dom Turysty ❶,** in the same building as the office. Quirky rooms are variously outfitted with old radios and tropical-themed lanterns. (☎328 0382. June-Aug. singles 35zł, with bath 60zł; doubles 60/110zł; triples 90/165zł. Sept.-May singles 25/40zł; doubles 50/80zł; triples 75/120zł. Cash only.) To get to **Camping Gromada ❶,** Bohaterów Warszawy 1, follow Kolejowa as it becomes Gryfa Pomorskiego. Take the right fork to Mickiewicza and turn left. A block from the beach, Gromada has aluminum cabins with small shaded rooms. (☎328 1083. Complimentary beach towels. Reception 8am-10pm. Curfew 10pm. Campground open May-Sept. 1- to 4-person cabins with bath 30-59zł per person. Tents 9zł per person, students 7.50zł. Electricity 7.50zł. MC/V.) The curious decor at **Dolce Vita ❷,** pl. Neptuna 2, involves bouquets of uncooked spaghetti. The eatery serves generous portions of tasty if unadventurous pizza and pasta with a range of toppings and sauces. A pleasant terrace opens in summer. (☎328 1770. Entrees 12-59zł; smaller but cheaper Polish menu has meals for 18-19zł. Open daily 10am-midnight. MC/V.) Cheery **Restauracja Cafeteria Centrum ❷,** pl. Neptuna 7/9, dishes up meaty *naleśniki* (9-12zł), pizza (12-39zł), and Polish breakfasts including omelettes and grilled meats. (☎328 1162. Open daily 10am-late. Cash only.) To grab some quick food, head to the 24hr. convenience store **Sklep Smakasz,** Norwida 4.

BEACHES AND NIGHTLIFE. Most are drawn to Międzyzdroje for its beautiful beaches. The promenades of Bohaterów Warszawy and Promenada Gwiazd run the town's length and a 390m curving, tourist-accessible pier (*molo* in Polish) divides it cleanly in half. Promenada Gwiazd (Promenade of the Stars), the part of the promenade running east of the *molo*, is a miniature Polish hall of fame, with handprints and stars dedicated to Polish film and TV stars. The nearby **Wax Museum** (Gabinet Figur Woskowych), just off the beach at Bohaterów Warszawy 20, contains a fascinating collection of figures both international (Hitler, Osama bin Laden, Einstein, and an oddly effeminate likeness of Bruce Willis) and domestic (Lech Wałęsa and other Polish heavyweights). The basement contains specimens such as a bearded woman, a three-legged man, and "the world's ugliest woman." (Open Tu-Su 10am-5pm. 10zł, 16 and under. 5zł. Cash only.) The dismal nightlife is centered around the beachfront area.

HIKING. Although Międzyzdroje draws crowds as a prime beach resort, the true accolades belong to adjacent **Woliński National Park,** whose wilds encompass much of Wyspa Wolin (Wolin Island) and shelter a dramatic stretch of coastline. Stop by the park's **Natural History Museum,** ul. Niepodległości 3, to pick up a useful map of the park, trails, and town (5zł); get general park info; and hire guides. The museum has exhibits of wildlife in their natural habitats (including a rather pointed trashed beach exhibit), a Polish-only exhibit on local natural resources, and a collection of stuffed game and birds. The second floor hosts rotating art exhibits. (☎328 0737. Tickets 5zł, students 3zł. 20 min. park video in Polish, German or English 25zł per screening. Polish language museum guide 25zł, park guide 35zł. German, or English guide 50zł per hr.)

POLAND

The park is immaculately kept, with **hiking and bicycling trails** marked on trees and stones. The black and red trails begin at the end of **Promenada Gwiazd,** and the green at the end of **Leśna.** The blue trail begins on **Cmentarna** near the train station. These hikes are not very strenuous—don't expect Tatras trailblazing. Rent a **bike** at friendly **Willa 5,** Bohaterów Warszawy 16. (☎328 26 10. 5zł per hr. ID required. Open M-F 9:30am-8pm.) The demanding **black trail** climbs the seaside cliffs to **Góra Kawcza** (61m), a lookout point with a breathtaking view of the Baltic, where you just might glimpse one of the park's famed eagles *(bieliki)*. Just after Góra Kawcza, the trail hits a closed military area; backtrack a few steps and follow the trail into the woods. It eventually intersects the green trail and returns to Międzyzdroje. Lapping waves and secluded beach spots follow the **red trail,** a relaxed but beautiful route starting at the beach in Międzyzdroje and following a 15km stretch of coastline beneath the cliffs. Just 2km from the pier, the crowds are replaced by fishermen. The trail passes under the highest of the Baltic's cliffs at **Góra Gosan** (93m), then turns back into the woods and passes the lakeside town of Wisełka, the Kikut lighthouse, and another scenic cliff at **Strażnica** (74m) before intersecting the green trail, where you can loop back around or continue off the island by way of Międzywodzie. The 15km **green trail,** which begins as a road and has an extensive set of **bike paths,** though including stretches of less rewarding territory between the highlights, leads past glacial lakes into the heavily forested park center. Just 1.2km from the trailhead is the popular **bison preserve.** (☎328 0737. Open May-Sept. Tu-Su 10am-6pm; Nov.-Apr. Tu-Su 8am-4pm. 5zł, students 3zł.) The trail passes the villages of Warnowo (5km), Kołczewo (7km), and **Lake Czajcze.** The green trail ends where it hits the red trail, 3km past Kołczewo. The **blue trail** winds all the way from Swinoujscie on the German border through Międzyzdroje to Szczecin. At 74.5km, this trail is more conducive to bicycling than hiking. The tame stretch near Międzyzdroje heads south along the edge of the Park, passing ruins, nature preserves, and lookout points. It leaves the island at the small town of Wolin.

TRI-CITY AREA (TRÓJMIASTO)

World-class beaches, a flurry of cultural life, and stunning Hanseatic architecture have made portside Trójmiasto (pop. 755,000) Poland's summer playground of choice. The three cities on the Baltic are a study in contrasts: the restored splendor of old Gdańsk hides a turbulent millennium of history. Sopot basks in beachfront glitz, and the trade-rich port town of Gdynia fuels the area's economy. Great public transportation makes it easy to sleep in one city and explore the others.

GDAŃSK ☎(0)58

At the mouth of the Wisła and Motława Rivers, Gdańsk (gh-DA-insk; pop. 458,000) has flourished for more than a millennium as a crossroads of art and commerce. This former Hanseatic trade city was treasured as the "gateway to the sea" during Poland's foreign occupation in the 18th and 19th centuries. Gdańsk has faced its challenges admirably—WWII left 90% of the ancient city center in ruins, yet today its street opera, graceful brick buildings, and meandering waterways have all been restored. The rise of Lech Wałęsa's Solidarity movement, before its brutal suppression by the imposition of martial law in 1981, brought 16 months of hope to the now-famous shipyards and to all of the Eastern Bloc. Now reconstructed and revitalized, with its amber-filled beaches, cobblestone alleys, and sprawling construction sites, the heart of the Trójmiasto displays both beauty and brawn.

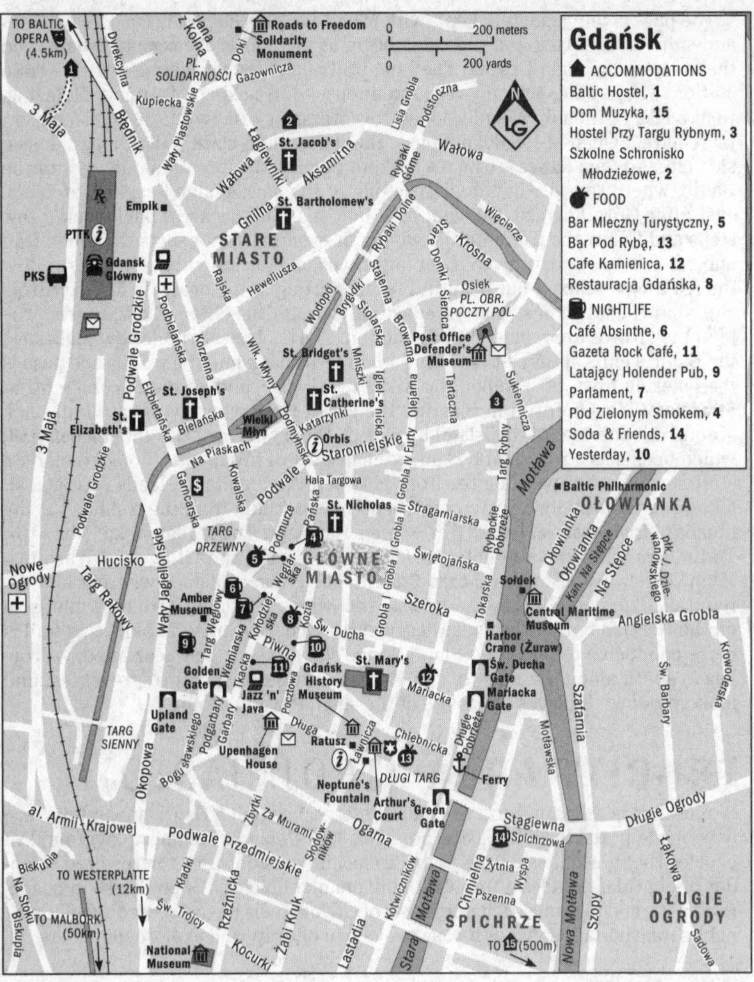

TRANSPORTATION

Trains: Gdańsk Główny, Podwale Grodzkie 1 (☎94 36). To: **Białystok** (7½hr., 3 per day, 52zł); **Częstochowa** (8hr., 7 per day, 55zł); **Kołobrzeg** (3½-5hr., 5 per day, 42-71zł); **Kraków** (7-11hr., 15 per day, 59-105zł); **Łódź** (8hr., 6 per day, 49zł); **Lublin** (7hr., 3 per day, 54-98zł); **Malbork** (50min., 40 per day, 10-32zł); **Mikołajki** (5hr., 1 per day, 43zł); **Poznań** (4-5hr., 7 per day, 46zł); **Szczecin** (5¾hr., 5 per day, 22-47zł); **Toruń** (3¼hr., 6 per day, 38zł); **Warsaw** (4hr., 22 per day, 50-82zł); **Wrocław** (6-7hr., 4 per day, 52zł). **SKM** (Fast City Trains; ☎628 5778) run to **Gdynia** (35min.; 4zł, students 2zł) and **Sopot** (20min., 2.80/1.40zł) every 10min. during the day and less frequently at night. Buy tickets downstairs. Punch ticket in a *kasownik* machine before boarding.

Buses: 3 Maja 12 (☎302 1532), behind the train station, connected by an underground passageway. To: **Białystok** (9hr., 1 per day, 51zł); **Częstochowa** (7½hr., 1 per day, 60zł); **Kołobrzeg** (6hr., 1 per day, 42zł); **Łódź** (8hr., 1 per day, 45zł); **Malbork** (1hr., 8 per day, 10-13zł); **Toruń** (2½hr., 2 per day, 32zł); **Warsaw** (5¾hr., 9 per day, 45zł); **Kaliningrad, RUS** (6-7hr., 2 per day, 28zł). Comfortable **Polski Express** buses run to **Warsaw** (4½hr., 2 per day, 45zł).

Ferries: Żegluga Gdańska (☎301 4926; www.zegluga.gda.pl) runs ferries (May-Sept.) to domestic destinations, from **Zielona Brama** (The Green Gate). To: **Gdynia** (2hr.; 2 per day; 52zł, students 36zł); **Hel** (1½-3hr., 2 per day, 60/42zł); **Sopot** (1hr., 5 per day, 44/30zł); **Westerplatte** (50min., 9 per day, round-trip 43/22zł). **Polferries,** Przemysłowa 1 (☎343 0212), in Gdańsk-Brzeźno. To **Nynäshamn, SWE** (19hr., 3 per week, 250zł).

BLOWN AWAY. If you're planning to take a ferry around the Trójmiasto or to Hel, be sure to call ahead and check if the ferry is running that day—even on clear days, ferries can be canceled abruptly due to wind on the bay or at the ports. Even if one ferry is canceled, though, call around—the ferry from the next town over is technically run by a different company, and so may still be running.

POLAND

Public Transportation: Gdańsk has an extensive **bus** and **tram** system. Buses run 6am-10pm. Tickets are priced by the minute. 10min. 1.40zł; 30min. 2.80zł; 1hr. 4.20zł; day pass 9zł. **Night buses,** designated by "N," run 10pm-6am. 3.30zł, students 16.5zł; night 5.50/2.75zł.

Taxis: To avoid paying inflated tourist rates for taxis, book a cab by phone or over the Internet at the state-run **MPT** (☎96 33; www.artusmpt.gda.pl).

ORIENTATION AND PRACTICAL INFORMATION

Although Gdańsk sits on the Baltic Coast, its commercial center is 5km inland. From the Gdańsk Główny train and bus stations, the center is just a few blocks southeast, bordered on the west by Wały Jagiellońskie and on the east by the Motława River. Take the underpass in front of the station, go right, and turn left on Heweliusza. Turn right on Rajska and follow the signs to **Główne Miasto** (Main Town), turning left on Długa, also called **Trakt Królewski** (Royal Way). Długa becomes Długi Targ as it widens near the Motława. Gdańsk has several suburbs, all north of Główne Miasto. Piwna and Sw. Ducha are Główne Miasto's other main thoroughfares and are parallel to Długa just to the north.

Tourist Offices: PTTK Gdańsk, Długa 45 (☎301 9151; www.pttk-gdansk.com.pl), in Główne Miasto, has **free maps.** Tours May-Sept. for groups of 3-10, 80zł per person. Open May-Sept. M-F 9am-5pm, Sa-Su 9am-3pm; Oct.-Apr. M-F 9am-6pm.

Budget Travel: Almatur, Długi Targ 11, 2nd fl. (☎301 2403; www.almatur.gda.pl), in Główne Miasto. Sells **ISIC** (59zł), offers hostel info, and books international air and ferry tickets. Open M-F 10am-6pm, Sa 10am-2pm.

Currency Exchange: Bank Pekao SA, Garncarska 31 (☎801 365 365). **Cashes traveler's checks** for 1% commission and provides MC/V **cash advances** for no commission. Open M-F 8am-6pm, first and last Sa of each month 10am-2pm.

Luggage Storage: In the train station. Locked room downstairs (4zł plus 0.45zł per 50zł declared value, min. 6.25zł) or lockers upstairs (small 4zł, large 8zł). Lockers in bus station (small 4zł, large 8zł). Both open 24hr.

English-Language Bookstore: Empik, Podwale Grodzkie 8 (☎301 6288, ext. 115). Sells maps. Open M-Sa 9am-9pm, Su 11am-8pm.

24hr. Pharmacy: Apteka Plus (☎763 1074), at the train station. Ring bell at night.

Medical Services: Private doctors, Podbielańska 16 (☎301 5168). Sign says "Lekarze Specjaliści." 50zł per visit. Open daily 7am-7pm. For **emergency care,** go to **Szpital Specjalistyczny im. M. Kopernika,** Nowe Ogrody 5 (☎302 3031).

Internet: Jazz'n'Java, Tkacka 17/18 (☎305 3616; www.cafe.jnj.pl), in the Old Town. 3zł per 30min., 5zł per hr. Open daily 10am-10pm. **Internet Cafe,** Podwale Grodzkie 10 (☎320 9230), inside the movie theater across the street from the train station. 5zł per hr. Open M-Sa 9am-1am, Su 9:30am-1am.

Post Office: Długa 23/28 (☎301 88 53). **Exchanges currency** and has **fax** service. For **Poste Restante,** use the entrance on Pocztowa. **Telephones** inside. Open M-F 8am-8pm, Sa 9am-3pm. **Postal Code:** 80-801.

POLAND

ACCOMMODATIONS

Gdańsk has limited accommodations, especially for those on a budget; it's best to reserve ahead. In July or August you can stay in a **university dorm.** Consult **PTTK. Private rooms** (20-80zł) can be arranged via **PTTK** or **Grand-Tourist** (Biuro Podróży i Zakwaterowania), Podwale Grodzkie 8, linked to the train station by the tunnel, near Empik. (☎301 2634; www.grand-tourist.pl. July-Aug. daily 8am-8pm; Sept.-June M-Sa 10am-6pm. Singles 50-60zł; doubles 80-100zł; apartments 180-280zł. Cash only.)

Hostel Przy Targu Rybnym, Grodzka 21 (☎301 56 27; www.gdanskhostel.com), off Targ Rybny, on the waterfront south of Podwale Staromiejskie and across from the *baszta* (tower). In this bright hostel, guests enjoy a chummy common room with free crackers and (occasionally) beer. Hilariously bitchy staff. Free coffee, and Internet. Breakfast included. Bicycles 20zł per day. Reception 24hr. Dorms 50zł; doubles 200-250zł; triples, quads, and quints 240-350zł. Cash only. ❷

Baltic Hostel, 3 Maja 25 (☎721 96 57; www.baltichostel.com), 3min. from the station. From train station, take the KFC underpass to the bus station, then go right on 3 Maja and take the pedestrian path on the right. Inside an aging brick apartment building, the renovated Baltic has excellent rooms, and its bright colors, hardwood floors, and eclectic furnishings bustle with backpackers. Crowded bathroom gives little privacy, and the main hostel doors are often left unlocked. Free breakfast, towels, laundry, Internet, and bike and kayak use. Reception 24hr. Dorms 35-40zł; doubles 50zł. Cash only. ❶

Szkolne Schronisko Młodzieżowe, Wałowa 21 (☎301 2313). From the train station, follow Karmelicka from City Forum; go left on Rajska and right on Wałowa. Dorms feature new furnishings, and baths have enough showers and sinks to clean a small army. Full kitchen and common room set the facilities a cut above most HI hostels, but the living is as clean as the rooms: there's no smoking or drinking, and there is a midnight curfew. Reception 8am-10pm. Dorms 13-20zł; singles 23-30zł. Cash only. ❶

Dom Muzyka, Łąkowa 1/2 (☎300 9260). From the train or bus station, take tram #8 or 13 to the Akademia Muzyczna stop. Dom Muzyka is on the corner of Łąkowa and Podwale Przedmiejskie, behind the gate of the yellow building. Just across the Motława from the Old Town, Muzyka offers large, newly furnished, lyre-bedecked rooms that do their namesake proud. Rooms include TVs, phones, and Internet, as well as a generous breakfast buffet. Singles 165zł; doubles 230zł; triples 280zł. MC/V. ❺

FOOD

For fresh produce, try **Hala Targowa,** on Pańska, in the shadow of Kościół św. Katarzyny, just off Podwale Staromiejskie. Row upon row of stands sell everything from dried fruits to raw meat. (Open May-Aug. M-F 9am-7pm, Sa 9am-5pm; Sept.-Apr. M-F 9am-6pm, Sa 9am-3pm.) The supermarket, **Esta,** is nearby at Podwale Staromiejskie 109/112, in Targ Drzewny. (Open M-Sa 10am-10pm, Su noon-10pm.)

Cafe Kamienica, Mariacka 37/39 (☎301 1230). Antique couches and an elegant stone patio complement relaxed meals, with fresh, delicate entrees, like salad with grilled chicken (14zł). Tea 5zł. Superb coffee drinks 6-11zł. Entrees 7-30zł. Open daily June-Sept. 9am-midnight; Oct.-May 10am-10pm. AmEx/MC/V. ❷

Jadalnia Pod Zielonym Smokiem, ul. Szeroka 125 (☎320 7865). This basement eatery serves elegant, sophisticated dishes for prices that won't break the bank. A rowdy student crowd keeps the place going until late. Try the excellent salmon in blue cheese sauce (16zł). Entrees 6-16zł. Open daily 10am-3am. Cash only. ❷

Restaurancja Gdańska, ul. Sw. Ducha 16/24. Crowded walls covered in clocks, oil paintings, and figurines add a sense of Baroque topsy-turvy to crystal cut elegance. A favorite of local celebrities, including former president Lech Wałesa (try his "favorite ribs," a restaurant specialty; 25zł). Entrees 18-60zł. Open daily 11am-midnight. ❸

Bar Pod Rybą (Bar Under the Fish), Długi Targ 35/38/1 (☎305 1307). With an unusual take on a Polish staple, Pod Rybą serves huge baked potatoes with addictive fillings (6-20zł) that run the gamut from chicken shawarma to chili (4-7.50zł). The Hungarian sausage topping is top-notch. Keep an eye out for the collection of antique coat-hangers. Open daily July-Aug. 11am-10pm; Sept.-June 11am-7pm. AmEx/MC/V. ❶

Bar Mleczny Turystyczny, Szeroka 8/10 (☎301 6013). The brightly painted walls and gleaming new wood tables of this renovated milk bar complement truly delicious Polish staples. *Gołąbki* (tasty stuffed cabbage; 4.20zł), are among the meaty specialties (3-6zł). Eat alongside deal-seeking workers and vacationing families. Open M-F 7:30am-6pm, Sa-Su 9am-4pm. Cash only. ❶

POLAND

SIGHTS

ROADS TO FREEDOM (DROGI DO WOLNOŚCI). In the Gdańsk Shipyard where the Solidarity (Solidarność) movement was born, a powerful permanent exhibit documents the rise of the Eastern Bloc's first trade union. This moving multimedia journey begins with the early struggle against Soviet rule in the 1950s and chronicles the censorship, police surveillance, and propaganda that marked the era. Slides, films, and photographs trace the changing fortunes of Solidarity from the strikes of 1980 and the brutal period of martial law to the sweeping victory of 1989. Outside the shipyard can be found the **Solidarity Monument,** 3 towering crosses made out of ship's steel topped with anchors. *(Doki 1, in the Shipyard. ☎308 4280. Open Tu-Su 10am-5pm. 6zl, students 4zł; W free.)*

NATIONAL MUSEUM (MUZEUM NARODOWE). Housed in the vaulted chambers of a former Franciscan monastery, this museum displays Flemish and Polish sacred art, alongside small collections of 18th- to 20th-century china and 18th-century Polish paintings. The jewel of the museum, Hans Memling's *Last Judgment* altar triptych, has a checkered history. In 1473, it was intercepted by Gdańsk pirates en route to England. The 20th century saw it ricochet between the Nazis and the Soviets before coming to rest in Gdańsk in 1956. If the massive triptych is your style, don't miss Jacob van Swanenburgh's *Sybil and Aeneas in the Underworld*, similarly punctuated by fantastical creatures and damned nudes. *(Toruńska 1, off Podwale Przedmiejskie. ☎301 70 61; www.muzeum.narodowe.gda.pl. Open June to mid-Sept. Tu-F 9am-4pm, Sa-Su 10am-5pm; mid-Sept. to May Tu-Su 9am-4pm. 10zł, students 6zł; Sa free.)*

AMBER AND TORTURE MUSEUM. A renovated former medieval prison now hosts a museum devoted to Gdańsk's signature fossil resin. Multimedia displays trace amber's history back from ancient times (when, as the English captions explain, the stone was thought to originate from "the feces of mythical beasts, wax produced by giant ants, the fossilized spawn of some unknown fish, or elephant semen") to the present day. Exhibits include a vast collection of magnified natural amber with fossilized "inclusions" and two rooms devoted to the use of amber in modern fashion. Across the courtyard can be found a set of eerie cells where, in keeping with the building's former occupation, life-size statues demonstrate various methods of torture. *(Targ W glowy 26. ☎326 21 53. Open Tu-Sa 10am-6pm, Su 11am-6pm. 10zł, students 5zł. Cash only.)*

DŁUGI TARG (LONG MARKET). The handsome main square, Długi Targ, is the heart of the painstakingly restored Główne Miasto. Gdańsk's characteristic row houses, adorned with dragon's head gutter spouts, line the surrounding cobblestones. The stone Upland Gate and elegant blue-gray Golden Gate, emblazoned with gold-leaf moldings and the shields of Poland, Prussia, and Germany, mark the entrance to Długa. Ornate mechanical clocks and graceful sundials are a common sight. The 14th-century **Ratusz** (Town Hall), Długa 47, houses a branch of the **Gdańsk History Museum.** Baroque paintings adorn the ceiling of the museum's fantastic Red Chamber. Exhibits span Gdańsk's long history, from the first mention of the city to its reduction to rubble in WWII, and include a large collection of amber art. Nearby, the 16th-century facade of **Arthur's Court** (Dwór Artusa), Długi Targ 43/44, now houses a second branch of the History Museum, which contains a massive, elegant-but-quirky meeting hall with 3D paintings, suspended model ships, and a 16th-century stove. The palace faces **Neptune's Fountain,** where the sea god stands astride a giant shell. Closer to the city gates, the History Museum's third branch, Rococo **Upenhagen House** (Dom Uphagena), Długa 12, is an 18th-century merchant's home. Inside you'll find immaculately restored Rococo furnishings and a museum tracing the oft-forgotten history of mechanical clockmaking, which saw its golden age in Gdańsk from 1631-1775. *(Town Hall ☎301 4871, Arthur's Court 301 4359, Upenhagen House 301 2371. Ratusz open June-Sept. M 11am-3pm, Tu-Sa 10am-6pm, Su 11am-6pm; Oct.-May Tu-Sa 10am-4pm, Su 11am-4pm. Arthur's Court open Tu-Su 10am-3pm. Upenhagen House open Tu-Sa 10am-6pm, Su 11am-6pm. Each 8zł, students 5zł; combined ticket 15/7zł; W free.)*

NAUTICAL SIGHTS. The **Central Maritime Museum** (Centralne Muzeum Morskie) spans both banks of the Motława, including a museum, the medieval **Żuraw** (Harbor Crane), and the ship **Sołdek.** The crane, an oft-photographed symbol of the city, towers over the riverside promenade **Długie Pobrzeże.** An exhibit beside the crane displays traditional boats of Asia, Africa, and South America, while the main museum offers an exhaustive tour through maritime Poland and Joseph Conrad's life at sea. *(To reach the Sołdek and the museum, take the shuttle boat, which runs every 15min. 10am-6pm, or walk from the end of Długi Targ, cross 2 bridges, and bear left. ☎301 8611. Open June-Aug. daily 10am-6pm; Sept.-May Tu-Su 9:30am-4pm. Crane 6zł, students 4zł. Museum 6/4zł. Sołdek 6/4zł. Shuttle boat round-trip 3/1.50zł. All museums and shuttle boat 14/8zł. English guide 20zł per group; call ahead.)*

CHURCHES. Massive Gothic **St. Mary's Church** (Kościół Mariacki) is made of 25,000 red bricks. Don't miss the gigantic 1464 astronomical clock atop the church. Climb the 405 steps for a panoramic view of the city. *(Open June-Aug. M-Sa 9am-5:30pm, Su 1-5:30pm; low-season hours vary. 3zł, students 1.50zł.)* In the foreground on Wielkie Młyny, the 13th-century **St. Nicholas's Church** (Kościół św. Mikołaja) was the only church in Gdańsk not gutted during WWII. Behind it is the 12th-century **St. Catherine's Church** (Kościół św. Katarzyny), which preserves a cemetery dating from AD 997 that is the resting place of astronomer **Jan Heweliusz.** Sixty-six steps above, the Baroque **Tower Clocks Museum** displays antique clocks and a 49-bell carillon that has rung the hour since the 50th anniversary of the outbreak of WWII. Keep an ear out for carillon concerts every Friday at 11am. *(☎305 6492. Museum open June-Sept. Tu-Su 10am-5pm. Cemetery 1zł. Museum 8zł, students 4zł; W free.)*

MUSEUM OF THE DEFENSE OF THE POST OFFICE. This museum inside Gdańsk's reconstructed former Polish post office recognizes the workers who bravely defended the building (a Polish outpost in the inter-war "Free City of Gdańsk") against the Germans in one of the first battles of WWII. On September 1st, 1939, postal employees resisted the German army until the building was engulfed in flames. Those who survived the blaze were executed or sent to concentration camps. Interesting displays include a collection of modern art depicting Polish POWs and a world map with Poland at its center. A moving **Memorial to the Defenders of the Post Office** (Obrońców Poczty) stands outside. *(From Podwale Staromiejskie, go north on Tartaczna and turn right onto Obrońców Polskiej Poczty 1-2. ☎301 7611. Open Tu-F 10am-4pm, Sa-Su 10:30am-4pm. 3zł, students 2zł; Tu free. The exhibit on the post office defense has a narrative in English; otherwise, captions are in Polish.)*

WESTERPLATTE. When Germany attacked Poland, the little island fort guarding the entrance to Gdańsk's harbor gained unfortunate distinction as the first target of WWII. Outnumbered 20 to one, the Polish troops held out for a week until a lack of food and munitions forced them to surrender. **Guardhouse #1** has been turned into a museum with a small exhibit recounting the fateful battle. *(☎343 69 72. Open daily May-Sept. 9am-7pm. 3zł, students 2zł. English booklet 6zł.)* The main attraction lies beyond the guardhouse, down the path leading past the bunker ruins to the massive **Memorial to the Defenders of the Coast.** The words *Nigdy Więcej Wojny* ("Never More War") are inscribed at the base of the monument, perched on a tall hill overlooking the entire city. *(From the train station, take bus #106 or 606 south to the last stop. The bus stop is to the right of the station entrance in front of the KFC. Żegluga Gdańska also runs a 50min. ferry; every hr. 10am-6pm; round-trip 34zł, students 18zł. ☎301 4926. Board by the Green Gate, Zielona Brama, at the end of Długi Targ.)*

ENTERTAINMENT

Of the three cities that line this stretch of the Baltic, Gdańsk offers the most traditional entertainment. The **Baltic Philharmonic,** Ołowianka 1 (☎305 20 40), performs free riverside concerts in summer. Opera-lovers can check out the **Baltic Opera** (Opera Bałtycka), al. Zwycięstwa 15 (☎341 4642). Tickets to the Philharmonic and the Opera run 8-40zł. The **Church of the Blessed Virgin Mary** has organ concerts (20zł, students 10zł) every Friday at 8:15pm in July and August. Special summer events include the **Feta Street Theater Festival** (mid-July), **Shakespeare Festival** (Aug.), and

SOCCER STEP UP

Europe is well known for its soccer fanaticism, and Poland is no exception. Still, the joint Polish and Ukrainian bid for the 2012 World Cup was considered a long shot. The former soviet Bloc countries were not only said to lack the necessary infrafrasture, they were also competing for hosting a traditionally Western-European dominated sport.

But after referee scandals and bad crowd behavior marred front-runner Italy's 2006 World Cup win, the field opened up, and several dignitaries, including former Polish President Lech Wałęsa, lobbied for hosting rights. The 2007 announcement that Poland and the Ukraine had won the bid was greeted with an outpouring of national pride. But once the cheers subsided, it was clear that the hard part was about to begin-Poland will spend over US$2.7 billion building new stadiums in Gdańsk, Warsaw, and Wrocław. (The other Polish host cities are Chorzów, Kraków, and Poznań.) Another major obstacle is improving transportation between the host countries. Government officials, however, are putting their best foot forward. The Polish Interior Development Minister said that the games will provide the impetus Poland needs to improve its infrastructure, adding, "then, all we need to do is to win the championships."

International Organ Music Festival (late June to late Aug.), at nearby Gdańsk Oliwa. For three weeks beginning in the last week of July, the Old Town welcomes the immense **Dominican Fair,** begun in the 15th century when monks came to trade their handcrafts. Today you can buy homemade souvenirs, art, and jewelry.

NIGHTLIFE

When the sun sets, crowds turn to the party spots of Długi Targ. Gdańsk tends more toward pubs than clubs, and plays second fiddle to Sopot's nightlife, but a few worthy establishments keep the local students loaded with music, art, and beer. *City* lists events in the Tri-City Area, and *Gdańsk in Your Pocket* offers updated club listings.

Cafe Absinthe, ul. w. Ducha 2 (☎320 3784), down an alley behind Parlament (see below), next to Teatr Wybrze e. Gdańsk's modernistic new hot spot attracts ruminating intellectuals by day and a rambunctious, absinthe-imbibing set by night. Absinthe (10-13zł) is served flaming blue with a sugar cube on top. Open daily 10am-4am. MC/V.

Parlament, św. Ducha 2 (☎302 1365). This popular club entices a wild young crowd with an extensive bar, a fog machine, and a maze of voyeuristic balconies overlooking the dance floor. The sleek crowd arrives comes in droves for hip hop (F) and clubbing hits (Sa). Beer 5zł. 18+. Cover Th after 10pm 5zł; F-Sa before 10pm 5zł, after 10 pm 10zł. Purchases at the bar must be made with non-refundable "prepaid cards" purchased at the entrance. Open Tu-Sa 8pm-late. Dance floor open Th-Sa 10pm.

Latający Holender Pub, Wały Jagiellońskie 2/4 (☎802 0363), near the end of Długa. An affable den of oddities, where an easygoing student crowd packs onto velvet couches beneath an array of flying machines. Drinks 4-22zł. Open daily noon-midnight.

Yesterday, Piwna 50/51 (☎301 3924). Almost every surface of this popular student bar is painted with notables ranging from the Beatles to Mao, with a few bronze animal masks thrown in for good measure. Alternative rock gives way to pop and techno as dancing picks up around midnight in the cellar. Beer 6zł. Open daily 7pm-3am.

Soda and Friends, Chmielna 103/104 (☎346 3861), across the 1st bridge at the end of Długi Targ, to the right. Hidden under a tame-looking restaurant, the basement of Soda and Friends is a pleasure palace outfitted with graffiti and porcelain theater masks. Known to host illustrious drag parties, the dance floor and neon bar fill with partygoers eager for hip hop and hard liquor. Beer 6-9zł. Open daily 10am-late. MC/V.

DAYTRIP FROM GDAŃSK

MALBORK

Trains (40-60min.; 40 per day; 9.30zł, express 32zł) and buses (1hr., 8 per day, 9.40-13zł) run from Gdańsk to Malbork. From the station, turn right on Dworcowa, then left at the fork. Go around the corner to the roundabout and cross to the street across the way, Kościuszki. Follow it, then veer right on Piastowska, where signs for the castle appear. ☎556 470 800; www.zamek.malbork.com.pl. Castle open May-Sept. Tu-Su 9am-7pm; Oct.-Apr. Tu-Su 9am-3pm. Courtyards, terraces, and moats open May-Sept. Tu-Su 9am-8pm; Oct.-Apr. Tu-Su 9am-4pm; kasa open 8:30-7:30pm. English tours leave at 11am, 1:30, 3:30pm. Castle 30zł, students 18zł; 3hr. Polish tour included. English booklet 7zł. Tour in English 5zł. Tour required to enter the castle, but you can wander off on your own once inside. M free; with Polish tour 5zł, English-speaking guide 150zł. Sound-and-light show mid-May to mid-Oct. 10pm; 5zł. AmEx/MC/V.

The largest brick castle in the world, **Malbork** is a stunning feat of restoration and a rich lens onto the turbulent history of the surrounding region. The **Teutonic Knights** built Malbork as their headquarters in the 1300s. The Teutons first came to the region in 1230 when Polish Duke Konrad Mazowiecki requested their assistance in Poland's struggle against the Prussians. The Knights double-crossed the Poles, however, establishing their own state in 1309. In their heyday, the celibate order of warrior-monks marauded across the region, forcibly converting Lithuanians to Christianity and hunting bison in the forest surrounding Malbork. The knights' vows of poverty fell by the wayside, and while the Poles won several 15th-century battles against the order, it was the lavish lifestyle of the Teutonic Knights that lost them Malbork. In 1457, the Teutons had to turn over the castle to mercenary knights for outstanding debts, and the mercenaries promptly sold the castle back to the Poles. During WWII, the castle was under German control, and housed a POW camp (Stalag XXB). Soviet bombing razed the castle at the war's end, but one of the world's largest works of reconstruction has since pieced the bricks of Malbork back together. The most beautiful rooms in the castle are the unfurnished **Grand Master's Chambers,** notable for columns in the shape of palm trees. The tour winds through the **High, Middle,** and **Low Castles** and visits the treasures of the **amber collection** and **weapons collection** as well as the remains of the unreconstructed castle church. Keep an eye out for the **castle ghost,** Hans von Endorf, who has wandered Malbork's halls since he killed himself in 1330 out of guilt for the murder of his brother, the Grand Master.

In a cellar off the castle courtyard, **Restauracja Piwniczka ❷** offers surprisingly reasonably-priced traditional Polish specialties. (☎552 733 668. Veggie dishes from 10zł. Mouth-watering meat dishes from 25zł. MC/V.) If you need to stay the night, consult the **IT tourist office** outside the castle at Piastowska 15, or look for the ubiquitous signs advertising **private rooms** (from 30zł). (☎552 734 990. Open May-Sept. Tu-F 10am-6pm, Sa-Su 10am-2pm.)

POLAND

SOPOT ☎(0)58

Poland's premier resort town, magnetic Sopot (pop. 50,000) draws throngs of visitors to its sandy beaches. Restaurants, shops, and street musicians dot the graceful pedestrian promenade, Bohaterów Monte Cassino, and the longest wooden pier in Europe rewards seaside amblers with spectacular Baltic views. Sopot's superb nightlife is renowned throughout Poland.

TRANSPORTATION. The **commuter rail (SKM)** connects Sopot to Gdańsk (20min.; 2.80zł, students 1.40zł) and Gdynia (15min.; 2.80/1.40zł) and runs 24hr. Trains leave from platform #1 every 10min. during peak hours and every hr. at night. Stamp your ticket in the box or risk 50-100zł fines. **PKP trains** run to: Białystok (7¾hr., 3 per day, 52zł); Kołobrzeg (3½hr., 5 per day, 42-71zł); Kraków (7-10hr., 8 per day, 59-97zł); Lublin (7hr., 3 per day, 54-98zł); Łódź (8hr., 6 per day, 49zł); Malbork (1hr., 34 per day, 10-32zł); Poznań (4-5hr., 7 per day, 46zł); Szczecin (5¾hr., 5 per day, 22-47zł); Toruń (3¾hr., 6 per day, 38zł); Warsaw (4hr., 20 per day, 47-82zł); Wrocław (6-7hr., 4 per day, 52zł); Berlin, GER (9¾hr., 1 per day, price varies). **Ferries** (tamwaj wodny; ☎551 12 93) from the end of the pier go to **Gdańsk** (1hr.; 4 per day; 8zł, students 4zł). For a **taxi,** call the state-run **MPT** or order a taxi over the Internet through their website. (☎96 33; www.artusmpt.gda.pl. Base 5zł, 2zł per km.)

ORIENTATION AND PRACTICAL INFORMATION. Dworcowa begins at the train station and heads left to the pedestrian **Bohaterów Monte Cassino,** which runs toward the *molo* (pier). Almost everything lies on or near Bohaterów Monte Cassino. The **tourist office IT,** Dworcowa 4, across from the train station, provides **maps** (free-5zł) of the area, and arranges accommodations. (☎550 3783; www.sopot.pl. Open daily June-Aug. 9am-8pm; Sept.-May 10am-6pm.) An **accommodations office** is in the same building. (☎551 2617. Open June-Sept. 15 daily 10am-5pm; Sept. 16-May M-F 10am-3pm.) PKO Bank Polski, Monte Cassino 32/34,

exchanges currency, gives MC/V **cash advances,** cashes **traveler's checks** for 1.5% commission (10zł min.), and has a MC/V **ATM.** (☎666 8567. Open M-F 8am-7pm, Sa 9am-1pm.) A **pharmacy,** Apteka pod Orlem, is at Monte Cassino 37. (☎551 1018. Open M-F 8am-9pm, Sa 8am-8pm.) Head to NetCave, Pułaskiego 7a, for **Internet** access. (3zł per 30min., 5zł per hr.; students 1/4zł. Open daily 10am-9pm.). During July and August, **WP.pl** also runs a free 24hr. outdoor Internet cafe at the base of the pier (free Wi-Fi also provided). The **post office,** Kościuszki 2, has **telephones** outside. (☎551 1784. Open M-F 8am-8pm, Sa 9am-3pm.) **Postal Code:** 81-701.

ACCOMMODATIONS AND FOOD. Sopot is one of Poland's most popular and expensive resort towns, so reservations are important in summer. Staying in Gdańsk will probably be cheaper and is a must for hostel accommodations. Consider renting a **private room,** which frequently requires a minimum three-day stay; visit **IT** for help. Beware of aggressive taxi drivers outside the IT offering **private rooms**—they operate illegally, and the quality of their rooms is dubious. **Hotel Wojskowy Dom Wypoczynkowy (WDW) ❶,** Kilińskiego 12, off Grunwaldzka (reception in the building marked "Meduza") offers the cheapest sea views in Sopot from its pastel rooms, clustered in five buildings spread out over a gated campus. The rooms have TVs and well-kept baths, and the premises include tennis courts. (☎551 0685; www.wdw.sopot.pl. Breakfast included. Check-in 2pm. Check-out noon. Reserve at least 1 month ahead July-Aug. "Tourist Class" rooms without baths or breakfast 35zł; singles 74-120zł; doubles 134-220zł; triples 168-310zł; apartments 300-380zł.) For travelers without the foresight to reserve a room months in advance, centrally located university dorms are a good option. **Uniwersytet Gdański "Łajba" ❸,** Armii Krajowej 111, provides clean, spacious, newly renovated rooms with generous shared baths, and neighbors some of the most popular student bars. (☎550 9164. Check-out 10am. Singles 80zł; doubles 110zł.) **Willa "Muszelk" ❸,** ul. Hofera 90, offers very cheap but well-appointed rooms about a 15min. walk from Monte Cassino. (☎551 3349. Singles with bath 60zł; doubles 100zł; triples 120zł. Sept.-May 10zł per person discount.) Find camping at **Camping nr. 19 ❶,** Zamkowa Góra 25. Take the commuter rail (3min., every 10-20min., 1.25zł) to Sopot-Kamienny Potok, then go down the stairs, turn right, and cross the street. The site is behind the gas station on your left. Nr. 19 is a small, well-groomed, and friendly campground with clean bathrooms and a playground. (☎550 0445. Parking 7zł. Gates locked 10pm-7am. Open May-Sept. 10zł per person, 4-9zł per tent; 4-person bungalows 95-150zł.)

Monte Cassino is riddled with fashionable cafes and inexpensive food stands. A small 24hr. grocery, **Non-stop,** Monte Cassino 62 (☎551 5762), is steps away from the pier. **Błękitny Pudel ❷** (Blue Poodle) is at Monte Cassino 44. The garden of this quirky cafe is lovely in summer, and the interior, chock-full of tapestried chairs and antique curiosities, is as charismatic as the food. (☎551 1672. *Pierogi* 18zł. Entrees 12-26zł. Open daily July-Aug. 9am-last customer; Sept.-June noon-last customer. AmEx/MC/V.) Local institution **Przystań ❶,** al. Wojska Polskiego 11, along the beach, serves grilled and fried seafood under fishing nets and hung blowfish. (☎550 0241; www.barprzystan.pl. Fresh fish 4.20-8zł per 100g. Fish salads from 3.20zł per 100g. Open daily 11am-11pm. Cash only.) For good, dirt-cheap Polish food served in simple elegance, try **Bar Elita ❷,** ul. Podjazd 3, just across the tracks from ul. Dworcowa. (☎551 0620. *Pierogi* 7.90zł-11.90zł. Open 11am-last customer. Cash only.) **U Przyjaciół ❷,** Polna 55, 150m from the beach, offers rich traditional Polish food. Pigs' knuckles (30zł) are house specialties, served among nostalgic bookcases beside a giant fireplace. (☎551 7725; www.uprzyjaciol.pl. Entrees 18-48zł. Open daily noon-10pm. AmEx/MC/V.)

ENTERTAINMENT. Sopot's popularity stems from its vast white-sand **beach,** which offers endless recreation, from waterslides to outdoor theater. Stands along the beach rent equipment for watersports. **Copacabana,** the makeshift compound of huts that shows up on the beach next to the pier from June through August, rents windsurfing equipment (35zł per hr., with lessons 65zł per hr.) and kayaks. The most popular sands lie at the end of Monte Cassino, where the 1827 wooden **pier** (*molo* in Polish), extends 512m into the sea, a European legend. (☎551 0002. M-F 2.50zł, Sa-Su 3.30zł.) Sopot also contains great **biking trails.** Get a free map from IT; all paths begin west of al. Niepodległości. Rent **bikes** and 4-wheel dune buggies outside of **Hotel Zhong Hua Hotel,** al. Wojska Polskiego 1, just off the beach. (☎508 109 018. 8zł per hr., 20zł per 3hr., 30zł per 5hr., 40zł per day. Open daily 9am-8pm. Cash only.) **Opera Leśna** (Forest Opera), Moniuszki 12, is an open-air theater with some of the best acoustics in Europe. Its rock and pop music festival, the **International Song Festival** (☎555 8400) dominates the area in late August or early September, bringing in international stars. For tickets or info, call the theater or contact **IT Teatr Atelier,** Franciszka Mamuszki 2, which stages independent theater on its beachside stage. (☎559 1001. Show schedule at IT. Tickets 24-34zł.)

NIGHTLIFE. Sopot is the Ibiza of the Eastern Bloc—in all of Poland, only Warsaw and Kraków can hold a candle to its nightlife. The beach town's legendary hedonism runs the gamut from exclusive discos to historic cafe-pubs. The flurry of cafes, pubs, and discos along Monte Cassino bears testament to Sopot's status as one of the hardest-partying towns in Poland. During the summer months, the hottest party is naturally enough right on the beach itself, at **Copacabana,** a thatched-roof temporary construction that turns at night into a fully outfitted club of choice for Poland's young and famous. (www.copacabanasopot.pl. Cover some nights after 10pm. Open 24hr. Restaurant and yacht club open during daylight hours. MC/V.) **Soho clubogaleria,** Monte Cassino 61, brandishes art and attitude at every turn, playing jazz and alt-rock during the week and full-on house and techno on Fridays and Saturdays. Edgy, mildly disaffected students crowd the retro bar in the basement and the velvet couches upstairs. Exhibitions by local artists rotate bimonthly. (☎551 6927. Beer 6.50zł. Open daily July-Aug. 10am-late; Sept.-June noon-5am.) **Józef K,** Kościuszki 4/1b, on the corner of Dworcowa and Kościuszki, is on the first floor of a 19th-century apartment building. The copper-plated bar dispenses beer, wine, and mixed drinks at surreally good prices (4-11zł) in the midst of whitewashed wooden beams, stacks of books, and antique toys. During the day, Józef K. doubles as a charismatic cafe. (☎509 598 737. Open M-Sa 10am-late, Su 11am-midnight.) **Mandarynka,** Bema 6, off Monte Cassino, offers three floors of partying, each of which brings faster music and even faster drinking. The comfy cushions and large retro lamps of the ground floor are ideal for casual drinking and conversation, while the third floor's disco swells with dancing students on weekends. (☎550 4563. Beer 6zł. Open M 1pm-late, Tu-Su noon-late.) **Papryka,** Grunwaldzka 11, lives up to its name with a spicy red interior outfitted in streamlined couches and offset by a few black antiques. Students and young entrepreneurs chat to varied musical accompaniment. (☎551 7476. Open 3pm-late. 21+. MC/V.) **Sfinks,** Powstańców Warszawy 18, not to be confused with the popular Polish restaurant chain of the same name, saw its heyday in 2003 as one of the country's hottest clubs. Today, vaguely Asian decor, strong liquors, and a lively crowd make a potent mix. In summer, monthly avant-garde theater and traveling DJs clinch Sfinks's position as a local favorite. (☎802 5626. Cover F-Sa 15zł. Open daily 10pm-late. Disco open F-Sa 6pm-late.) For the latest on Sopot's emerging GLBT scene check *Gdańsk in Your Pocket.*

MAZURY

A train ride through the rolling hills of Mazury reveals an achingly beautiful landscape of pine groves, poppy fields, and glassy lakes. East of Pomorze, the "land of a thousand lakes" region actually cradles more than 4000 lakes. Small, quiet towns like Mikołajki offer visitors waters to canoe, kayak, and sail.

MIKOŁAJKI (0)87

Serene little Mikołajki is a gateway to Poland's largest lake, Lake Śniardwy. In the center of town, a statue of a crowned fish leaps from a fountain, honoring Mikołajki's unlikely aquatic hero. Legend has it that the people of Mikołajki were bullied by a giant fish named Król Sielaw, who broke their nets and capsized boats until a fisherman caught him in a steel net. Król Sielaw said that if he were spared, Lake Mikołajskie would always be full of fish. He kept his word. Today the lakeside town boasts all the amenities, all in close proximity to the beautiful Mazury lakes.

TRANSPORTATION AND PRACTICAL INFORMATION. Mikołajki is isolated from the rest of the country; make connections in Olsztyn. **Trains,** Kolejowa 1 (☎421 6238), go to Ełk (1½hr., 3 per day, 18zł), Olsztyn (2hr., 4 per day, 14-22zł), and Poznań (8hr., 1 per day, 49zł). **Buses,** pl. Kościelny, go to Olsztyn (2hr., 6 per day, 16zł) and Warsaw (4-5hr., 9 per day, 58zł).

To reach the center from the train station, turn left on **Kolejowa,** away from the train tracks, and then before you hit the bridge, turn left on 3 Maja, which leads to **plac Wolności,** the center of town. The bus stop is at the intersection of Kolejowa and 3 Maja, at the Protestant church. To get to the **lake,** take any right from pl. Wolności. **Aleja Kasztanowa** and **aleja Spacerowa,** pedestrian streets bordering the lake, Król Sielaw with restaurants and cafes. In the center, the **IT office,** pl. Wolności 3, provides visitors with **maps** (8zł) and info about accommodations and cultural events. (☎421 6850; www.mikolajki.pl. Open June-Sept. daily 8am-8pm.) **Bank Spółdzielczy,** ul. Kajki 1, cashes **traveler's checks** for a small commission and provides MasterCard and Visa **cash advances.** (☎421 6316. Open M-F 8am-7pm, Sa 9am-4pm. Cash only.) A **pharmacy** is at 3 Maja 3. (☎421 6316. Open M-F 8am-9pm, Sa 9am-6pm, Su 10am-4pm. MC/V.) Since the demise of Mikołajki's one Internet cafe, Internet is available only at the **public library,** located at the intersection of Szkolna and Kolejowa streets. (Open Tu-F 10am-5pm, Sa 10am-2pm. Free.) The **post office,** 3 Maja 8, has **telephones** outside; **Poste Restante** is available at window 4. (Open M-F 8am-8pm, Sa 8am-2pm). **Postal Code:** 11730.

ACCOMMODATIONS AND FOOD. Yellow signs point the way to **private rooms** and pensions. The best budget rooms are along Kajki. Decent lakeside accommodations run 30-50zł per person, depending on the season and the location. Inquire at the **IT office** (see above) for a list of places with open rooms. Once meeting with a room owner, do not be afraid to haggle: owners often start out by proposing higher prices to foreigners. **Pensjonat Mikołajki ❹,** Kajki 18, is a family-run business with stellar service and an amazing location on the banks of Lake Mikołajskie. From pl. Wolności, continue down 3 Maja until it turns into Kajki. Their generous breakfast will make *naleśniki*-lovers swoon. (☎421 6437; www.pensjonatmikolajki.prv.pl. Bike rentals 8zł per hr., 30zł per day. Singles June-Aug. 130zł; doubles 200zł. Steep low season discount of up to 50zł, depending on room. Discounts also available for stays over 3 days. Cash only.) Nearby **Noclegi ❷,** Kajki 8, offers inexpensive spic-and-span lakeside rooms. (☎421 6362. Doubles and triples with bath 50zł per person. Cash only.)

As in many Polish towns, decent home-style Polish food can be had for cheap at the local milk bar, in this case the colorfully decorated **Kaskada** ❶, ul. 3 Maja 6. (Entrees 3.50zł-9.50zł. Open daily 9am-9pm. Cash only.) In a comfy green interior decorated with coconuts and modern art, **Pizza "Teja"** ❶, 3 Maja 18, dishes out pizzas, fries, and *zapiekanki* to patrons who have escaped the grip of the overpriced lakeside. (☎421 6541. Pizza 8-12zł. Entrees 4.50-12zł. Open daily 10am-9pm. Cash only.) For cheap *naleśniki* and excellent fried fish in a comfortable setting, try local favorite **Bar Okoń** ❶, 11 pl. Wolności. (*Naleśniki* from 6.90zł. Fish from 7zł per 100g. Entrees from 13zł. Open 10am-10pm. MC/V). You can find fresh produce, not to mention the cheapest souvenirs in town, in the stalls behind Hotel Caligula, pl. Handlowy. (Open daily 9am-3pm.) **Tawerna Żagel,** Kowalska 3, boasts the best lake view in town from its terrace and hosts all-night house and techno dance parties in July and August. (☎421 5037. Beer 4zł. Dance parties F-Sa 9pm-dawn. Open daily noon-late.) The town's only nightclub is **Kon-tiki,** pl. Wolności 9 (enter from the lake side). The large dance floor is brightly decorated with sweeping windows that frame a beautiful view of the lake just outside. (☎421 5353. Club open in high season daily 9pm-late, F-Sa 9pm-late in low season. MC/V.)

SIGHTS AND OUTDOOR ACTIVITIES. The **Kościół sw. Trójcy** (Church of the Holy Trinity), one the few Protestant churches in Poland, has a small museum with Protestant documents from Poland and beyond, and provides an example of elegantly understated architecture. (☎421 6810. Museum open daily 9am-3pm. Services Su 10:30am. Museum 4zł, students 2zł.)

Żegluga Mazurska, pl. Wolnosci 15, on the shore on al. Żeglarska, offers excursions on Lake Sniardwy and round-trip ferry service to various Mazurian cities for 25-75zł. (☎421 6102. Students 18-55zł. Ticket office open May-Sept. 8:30am-6pm). For more lakeside adventure, **Wioska Żeglarska Mikolajki,** farther down the shore at Kowalska 3, above Tawerna Pod Zlamanym Pagajem, rents yachts. Although the law prevents anyone without a Polish sailing license from renting a sailing craft, travelers can still charter a skippered boat. (☎421 6040. Sailboats 20zl per hr., 150zl per day. Mandatory skipper 30zł per hr.) Skippered motorboats can be rented next door at Szekla (☎421 5703; www.szekla.mazury.pl) for 350zl per hr., but those who prefer to skip the skipper can head across the lake to Port Rypitwa, ul. Okrężna, which rents them more cheaply. The staff also provides itinerary suggestions. (☎421 6163; www.portrybitwa.pl; 85-150zł per hr., from 425zł per

WÓNDERFUL WODKA

Poland's vodkas are distinguished not only by their exceptional quality, but also often by their unusual ingredients. One of Poland's most popular vodkas, for instance, is Zubrówka, made from rye and flavored with bison grass. Each bottle contains a long blade of the characteristic grass, which aficionados say is the source of its silky smooth finish.

The Trójmiasto is known for a more glitzy specimen, Goldwasser. In addition to over 20 various herbs, Gdańsk's emblematic vodka contains flakes of real gold, small enough to float enticingly in the liquor. The glamorous drink been a favorite of European royalty since the 17th century, and now makes an excellent gift for the erudite alcoholic in the family.

Chopin, meanwhile, considered by many to be among the best vodkas in the world hasn't forgotten its roots: unlike the rest of the upper echelon, however, Chopin isn't made from wheat, but from Poland's favorite ingredient-the humble potato.

Zubrówka can be found at any bar or liquor store in Poland. Sadly, in the US, stringent FDA regulations mean that the only Zubrówka available in stores is artificial. Many Polish liquor stores carry Goldwasser, and it can be found throughout the Tri-City. Chopin can be found in any upscale liquor store worth its salt anywhere in the world.

day.) Those willing to splurge can water-ski with **Marek Żesko,** ul. Kajki 26, by the lake. (☎06 03 69 58 61. Water-skiing 100zł per 20min.; knee-boarding and other activities also available. Open May-Aug. 10am-8pm.) Or, you may simply want to join hundreds of Poles in renting a kayak or paddle-boat (typically 10zł per hr., 40zł per day) along the lakeside. The city also runs a free makeshift beach, at the end of ul. Okrężna, with sand and a volleyball net on the lakeshore. Fishing supplies are available at Sklep Wędkarski, 3 Maja 17. (Open M-Sa 9am-7pm. Cash only.) Travelers who want to explore the surrounding countryside can rent bicycles inside the Walkuski Hotel, 3 Maja 13a. (☎421 6628. 8zł per hr., 35zł per day.)

DAYTRIP FROM MIKOŁAJKI: LAKE ŁUKNAJNO

Just 5km outside of Mikołajki, Lake Łuknajno is easily accessible by car, bike, or foot. Follow ul. Szkolna out of Mikołajki as it becomes Jana Pawła II and then ul. Łabędza. The small village that will be your jumping-off point for exploring the lake is just across the small bridge over the waterway connecting the Lake Łuknajno to Lake Śniardwy. By bike or by foot you can also take the red trail out of Mikołajki, with beautiful views of Lake Śniardwy along the way. The trail meets up with the road 1km before the bridge

POLAND

If the throngs of tourists that swarm Mikołajki during high season start to wear you out, you may want to escape to serene Lake Łuknajno, just 5km away and easily accessible by bike or foot. The ornithological sanctuary that contains the lake is home to 175 different species of birds, including up to 2000 of the mute swans unique to the area, as well as a variety of frogs, newts, and other small creatures. UNESCO recognized the lake as a Biosphere Sanctuary in 1977. The lake is connected to the much larger Lake Śniardwy by a small marshy waterway. The main road here crosses the waterway by the small bridge used by locals for fishing. The village of Łuknajno is over the bridge, just south of the lake. The trailhead is in the village just off the main road. The left hand trail leads over a wooden-plank path to an observatory tower, where travelers are treated to an view overlooking the lake and the chance to do some birdwatching. A bit farther down, the road branches off the right-hand trail, which runs 8km through picturesque meadows and forests along the lake, with the ruins of an 18th-century settlement. If the hike leaves you hungry, you can grab a bite of traditional Polish food in the renovated country manor of **Folwark Łuknajno,** ul Łuknajno 2), which, along with its attendant stables and barn, dominates the village. (Entrees 14-30zł. Bicycles, canoes, kayaks 8zł per hr., 30zł per day. Open 11:30am-11pm. July-August, singles 130zł; doubles 200zł; triples 240zł. Sept.-June: 90/150/190zł. Tent spot 15zł per day; camper spot 25zł per day.)

BIAŁYSTOK ☎(0)85

For many tourists, Białystok is known mainly as the gateway to the outstanding national parks of Podlasie. While its town center is steadily transforming into a pedestrian center typical of modern Polish cities, much of the city remains an unsightly jumble of Soviet-era concrete high-rises, with only faint traces of a once-prosperous town at the crossroads of Polish, Russian, and Tartar cultures. Poland's accession to the EU may have put a stop to Białystok's once booming trade in used AK-47s from Belarus and Ukraine, but the town's atmosphere remains palpably eastern.

TRANSPORTATION. The train station, **Białystok Główny** (☎94 36), is on Kolejowa 9. **Trains** run to: Gdynia (7¾hr., 3 per day, 52zł); Kraków (5hr., 2 per day, 54zł); Olsztyn (4hr., 2 per day, 43zł); Szczecin (9 or 13hr., 3 per day, 60zł); Warsaw (2hr., 10 per day, 34zł). The bus station (☎94 16) is across the tracks from the train station on Bohaterów Monte Cassino 10. **Buses** run to: Gdańsk (9hr., 1 per day, 51zł); Lublin (6hr., 2 per day, 34zł); Olsztyn (4½hr., 2 per day, 35zł); Warsaw (3½hr., 3 per day, 30zł); Wrocław (13hr., 1 per day, 62zł); Minsk, BLR (8hr., 1 per day, 60zł). Comfortable Polski Express buses run to Warsaw (4hr., 1 per day, 41zł). **Local buses** cost 1-2zł. For a **taxi,** call ☎91 91.

ORIENTATION AND PRACTICAL INFORMATION. The city center and most sights lie along a spine defined by **Lipowa.** To reach the center from the stations, catch city bus #2, 4, 10, or 21S from the far side of Bohaterów Monte Cassino. The **tourist office, IT,** ul. Malmeda 6, sells **maps,** and has info about Białystok and the national parks. (☎732 6831; www.podlaskieit.pl. Open M-F 9am-5pm.) **PKO Bank Polski,** Rynek Kościuszki 16, **exchanges currency,** has a 24hr. **ATM,** cashes **traveler's checks** for 1.5% commission, and gives MasterCard and Visa **cash advances.** (☎678 61 00. Open M-W and F 8am-7pm, Th 10am-5pm, Sa 8am-2pm.) **Luggage storage** is in the tunnel below the bus station. (3zł per day, 4zł per 2 days. Open daily 6am-5pm.) **Lockers** (4zł per small bag, 8zł per large bag) are in the train station. **Apteka Przy Rynku,** Rynek Kościuszki 18, is a conveniently-located **pharmacy** just off the main square. (☎732 1522. Open M-F 8am-8pm, Sa 9am-4pm, Su 10am-2pm. AmEx/MC/V). For **Internet access,** head to **Cafe Piramida,** Grochowa 2, near Lipowa. (☎742 1818; piramida.net@interia.pl. 3zł per 30min. Open M-F 8am-midnight, Sa-Su 9am-midnight.) The **post office,** Kolejowa 15, has **telephone** and **fax** services. For **Poste Restante,** go to window #4. (☎652 6191. Open daily 6am-7pm; basic postal services 24hr.) **Postal Code:** 15900.

POLAND

ACCOMMODATIONS AND FOOD. Białystok's few budget options rarely fill up. **SSM "Podlasie"** ❶ is at al. Piłsudskiego 7b. From the bus station, turn left on Bohaterów Monte Cassino and take a right on św. Rocha. Take the roundabout to al. Piłsudskiego, then follow the signs. Primary-color decor and curiously undersized tables and chairs give this friendly, impeccably clean hostel a nursery-school feel. The eager staff are a treasure trove of information about Podlasie, and the kitchen has a homey feel. (☎652 4250; www.ssm.bialystok.ids.pl. Curfew midnight. Dorms 25zł, discounts based on ISIC or HI card, age, and duration of stay. Cash only.) **Zajazd Starodworski** ❸ is at Warszawska 7. From the train station take city bus #2, 21, or 21S to Warszawska. This tired old cement building hides a family-run collection of comfortable rooms, each complete with TV and a bathroom. (☎653 7418. No breakfast, but tea and coffee available. Reserve ahead in high season. Singles 80zł, doubles 120zł. Cash only.) As far as Białystok's dining scene goes, **Hokus Pokus** ❶, Kilińskiego 12, takes pride in gale-force air conditioning that keeps the hanging lanterns swaying. A better reason to visit is the tasty range of "American" pizzas, salads, and sandwiches, not to mention the surprisingly pleasant decor of mirrors, faux fur, and metal. (☎741 6348. Entrees 7-18zł. Open M-Sa 10am-11pm, Su noon-11pm. MC/V.) **Bar Podlasie** ❶, Rynek Kościuszki 15, buffered from the beer gardens by a small park, is the most popular lunch spot downtown. Serving traditional Eastern Polish dishes with rich sauces and thick soups, this bare-bones milk bar dishes out high-quality food at such low prices that diners happily partake of the Polish pastime of yore: waiting in line. (☎742 2504. Entrees 3-7zł. Open daily 8am-8pm. MC/V.)

SIGHTS AND NIGHTLIFE. From Lipowa, take a right on Sienkiewicza to get to the gardens of **Branicki Palace** (Pałac Branickich). A pretender to the Polish throne, Hetman Branicki, set out in the 18th century to build a palace that would compare to Versailles. Although Branicki fell short of his goal, the formal gardens and Baroque palace are an impressive feat of hubris. The best view of the garden is from the second-floor **Dzierżyński Balcony,** where Felix Dzierżyński proclaimed the Polish Soviet Republic in 1920. (Open daily 8am-8pm. Free.) The **Military Museum** (Muzeum Wojska), Kilińskiego 7, off Lipowa, displays artifacts from the

THE FOREST PRIMEVAL

Ever wonder exactly where that degree in forestry was going to take you? The answer could be Poland. The **Białowieża National Park** takes on international volunteers to help with a range of conservation and research efforts, from investigating amphibians to helping preserve the local bison, vole, and red deer population. Backgrounds in biology or related fields are not required: volunteers specializing in anything from cultural anthropology to public administration can contact the park and local research institutions, who are in constant need of volunteers.

At 10,502 hectares, the Białowieża Primeval Forest is a natural wonder, and has long been treasured as such. The earliest recorded legislation to protect the land dates to 1538. Russian tsars were the last private owners, giving up the land in 1917. WWI brought German troops who hunted the wild bison. Just one month before Polish forces expelled the Germans from the forest in 1919, the Germans killed the last of the park's wild bison. Today the bison have been brought back to Europe's last old growth forest, and the park is an incredible ecological site.

Volunteers can expect to pay for accommodations, board, and personal travel. Stints of at least 2 months are requested. Contact park authorities for info at Park Palacowy 11, 17-230 Bialowieza. ☎856 812 306. You can also

city's embattled history, including the original declaration of the 1944 Białystok ghetto uprising and a series of silver eagles showing the evolution of Poland's national symbol. Military aficionados will love the 13th-century weaponry and jumble of WWII gear. (☎741 5448. Open Tu-Su 9:30am-5pm. 5zł, students 3zł.) The large student population in Białystok makes for some decent nightlife, though more sophisticated venues are hard to come by. You'll find most bars on **Lipowa** or tucked among its branching side streets. *Gazela Magazyn* has detailed info and is available free in most bars. Unmarked **Metro,** Białówny 9, has the telltale fluorescent lights and imposing bouncers of the hottest disco in a small town. (☎746 0129. Cover after 10pm 10zł. Open Th-Sa 6pm-late.) **Antidotum,** Akamemicka 26a, with its red walls, urban black-and-white photography, and a diverse playlist featuring both R&B and jazz legends, is a sign that things might be turning around for Białystok nightlife. Although relatively new, it's already a hit with local students, who fill the secluded garden nightly. (☎744 7006. Beer 5zł. Open daily noon-late.)

DAYTRIP FROM BIALYSTOK: BIAŁOWIESKI NATIONAL PARK

Białowieża Primeval Forest (Puszcza Białowieska), Europe's last remaining primeval forest, is a sprawling natural treasury of centuries-old oak trees, European bison, and 12,000 species of fauna. Once the hunting ground of Polish kings, the park has been named a UNESCO World Heritage Site and attracts visitors from around the world. Bordering Białowieża is the park's main attraction, the **Strict Preserve** (Obszar Ochrony Ścisłej), where 300 bison roam freely. The last wild bison were killed in 1919, but captive-bred Lithuanian bison were introduced to the park in 1929 and have thrived ever since. Only **guided tours** can enter this section of the park. Although you will be lucky to see any large mammals, the informative tour winds deep into the preserve and will leave you with a sound understanding of the forest's complex ecology and biodiversity. Consider buying repellent before the tour: the park has dozens of species of mosquitoes and ticks. Between Białowieża and the Strict Preserve is the small **Palace Park** (Park Pałacowy), a carefully crafted park with two small artificial ponds which once contained a palace of the Russian tsars (since burned down by the Nazis). Just inside the park, the **Park Museum** (Muzeum Przyodniczo-Leśne) has exhibits on the park and an observatory tower, as well as a multimedia show on park history and local biology. The permanent multimedia show is 55zł, and English-speakers with whom to split the price are few and far between; most opt for the Strict Preserve instead. (☎681 2275. Open M-F 9am-4:30pm, Sa-Su 9am-5pm. 12zł, students 6zł.) To guarantee a view of the bison, head to the small **bison preserve** (Rezerwat Pokazowy Żubrów), 4km from the trailhead, where bison and other animals are kept in tighter quarters resembling a small zoo. It is accessible via the yellow trail (2hr.), which splits off from the main road 2km from the PTTK office. (Open daily 8am-4pm. 6zł, students 3zł.) The yellow, red, green, and blue trails offer great biking and walking paths through the fields and forests.

Most park visitors stay overnight in the town of Białowieża. Either IT in Białystok or PTTK in Białowieża can arrange accommodations. **Szkolne Schronisko Młodzieżowe ❶,** Waszkiewicza 6, across from the Orthodox church, is the most popular budget option in town, with comfortable dorm rooms, both large and small, and an knowledgeable staff who put PTTK to shame. (☎681 2560. Reserve ahead in summer. 10- to 12-bed dorms 19zł; 4- to 6-bed dorms 22zł; triples 26zł; doubles 40zł per person. ISIC discounts available.) For tourist information, check out the national park's **IT office,** just inside the park at Park Pałacowy 1. (☎681 2901. Open M-F 8am-4pm, Sa-Su 8am-3pm. Decent free Polish maps available; English maps 7-8zł.). The office helps travelers find **ecotourist rooms,** essentially **private rooms** arranged by local retired farmers, most of whom also rent bikes. Most ecotourist rooms are along Waszkiewicza, the main road, and Tropinka, one block north. (Rooms 30-45zł.) After a day of hikes, enjoy decent *pierogi* at **Unikat ❸,** Waszkiewicza 39. (☎681 2774. Entrees 8-25zł. Open daily 8am-10pm.)

Direct **buses** run from Białystok to Bialowieża (3hr., 2 per day, 19zł). The last return bus from Bialowieża is at 7:05pm. For quick access to the Palace Park, IT, and hostel, get off at the main bus stop in front of the Orthodox church; for **private rooms,** wait and exit at the next stop. In the gateway of the park entrance, **PTTK,** Kolejowa 17, arranges guides for the Strict Preserve. From the Orthodox church, walk through the Palace Park and turn left at the circle, taking the bridge between the two ponds. The price for the guide is 165zł, so during the tourist season it's a good idea to get there early and wait until a few English-speakers show up. (☎681 22 95; www.pttk.bialowieza.pl. Maps 10-12zł. Open daily 8am-4pm. AmEx/MC/V.) The only **ATM** in town is at the Best Western Hotel next to PTTK, Kolejowa 15.

ROMANIA (ROMÂNIA)

Devastated by the lengthy and oppressive reign of Nicolae Ceauşescu (in office 1965-1989), modern Romania remains in the midst of economic and political transition. This condition of flux, combined with a reputation for poverty and crime, sometimes discourages foreign visitors. But travelers who dismiss Romania do themselves a disservice—it is a budget traveler's paradise, rich in history, rustic beauty, and hospitality. Romania's fascinating legacy draws visitors to Dracula's dark castle and to the famous frescoes of the Bucovina monasteries. Meanwhile, modern Romania is embodied by Bucharest, where visitors can explore the imposing remnants of Ceauşescu's reign, as well as by the heavily touristed Black Sea Coast, where resorts entice throngs of vacationers each summer.

DISCOVER ROMANIA: SUGGESTED ITINERARIES

THREE DAYS. Head for **Transylvania** (p. 524) to relax in the Gothic hillside towns of **Sighişoara** (1 day; p. 528) and **Sinaia** (1 day; p. 522), hike in the spectacular, jagged **Făgăraş Mountains** (p. 532), and explore the wild ruins of **Râşnov** castle (1 day; p. 528).

ONE WEEK. After 3 days in darkly intriguing **Transylvania,** head to medieval **Sibiu** (1 day; p. 530) and stylish **Braşov** (1 day; p. 524), before ending in **Bucharest** (2 days; p. 512), the complex and enigmatic capital, home to imposing communist architecture and wild nightlife.

FACTS AND FIGURES

Official Name: Romania.
Capital: Bucharest.
Major Cities: Iaşi, Timişoara, Constanţa.
Population: 22,276,000.
Land Area: 237,500 sq. km.
Time Zone: GMT + 2, in summer GMT + 3.
Language: Romanian.
Religions: Eastern Orthodox (87%).
First European city with electric streetlamps: Timişoara.

ESSENTIALS

WHEN TO GO

Romania's varied climate makes it a year-round destination. The south has hot summers and mild winters, while in the northern mountains, winters are harsher and summers are cooler. Tourist season peaks sharply in July and August only along the Black Sea Coast; elsewhere, travelers will find a refreshing lack of crowds even in mid-summer. They would do well to remember, however, that summer can be brutally hot in much of Romania.

DOCUMENTS AND FORMALITIES

EMBASSIES AND CONSULATES. Foreign embassies to Romania are in Bucharest (p. 512). Romanian embassies abroad include: **Australia,** 4 Dalman Crescent, O'Malley, Canberra, ACT 2606 (☎262 862 343; www.canberra.mae.ro); **Canada,** 655 Rideau St., Ottawa, ON K1N 6A3 (☎613-789-3709; www.ottawa.mae.ro); **Ireland,** 26 Waterloo Rd., Ballsbridge, Dublin 4 (☎016 681 085; www.dublin.mae.ro);

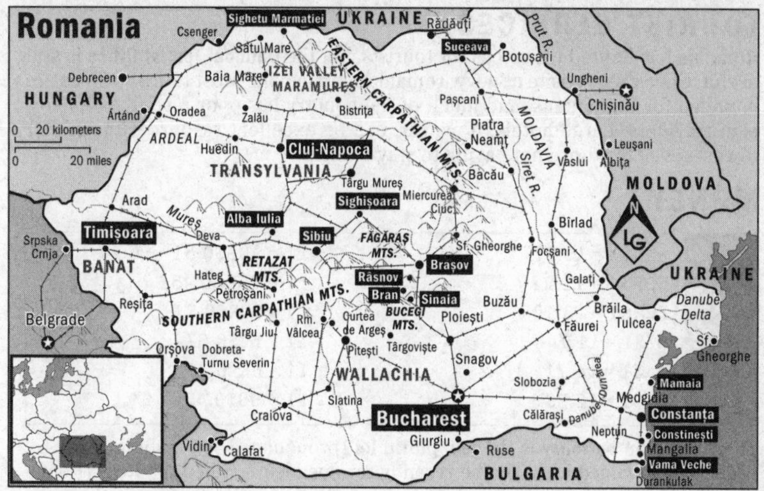

ENTRANCE REQUIREMENTS.

Passport: Required for all travelers.

Visa: Not required for stays under 90 days for citizens of Australia, Canada, the EU, Ireland, New Zealand, the UK, and the US.

Letter of Invitation: Not required for citizens of Australia, Canada, Ireland, New Zealand, the UK, and the US.

Inoculations: Recommended up-to-date on DTaP (diphtheria, tetanus, and pertussis), Hepatitis A, Hepatitis B, MMR (measles, mumps, and rubella), polio booster, rabies, and typhoid.

Work Permit: Required of all foreigners planning to work in Romania.

International Driving Permit: For stays longer than 90 days, all foreigners must obtain an International Driving Permit or a Romanian driver's license.

UK, 4 Palace Green, London W8 4QD (☎020 79 37 96 66; www.london.mae.ro); **US,** 1607 23rd St., NW, Washington, D.C. 20008 (☎202-332-4848; www.roembus.org). Romania maintains an honorary consulate in **New Zealand,** 53 Homewood Ave., Karori, Wellington (☎044 676 883; giffpip@xtra.co.nz).

VISA AND ENTRY INFORMATION. Romanian **visa** regulations change frequently; check with your embassy or consulate for the most current information. Citizens of Australia, Canada, Ireland, New Zealand, the UK, and the US can visit Romania for up to 90 days without visas. In all cases, passports are required and must be valid for six months after the date of departure. Travelers should consult the Romanian embassy in their country of origin to apply for a long-term visa. For citizens of the US, a single-entry visa costs US$40; multiple-entry US$75. Visas are not available at the border. **Visa extensions** and related services are available at police headquarters in large cities or at Bucharest's **Visas for Foreigners Office** (☎01 650 3050), Str. Luigi Cazzavillan 11. Long lines are common at the border for customs. In order to avoid being scammed, travelers should be aware that there is no entry tax for Romania. For additional information on visas and a list of Romanian embassies and consulates abroad, check out www.mae.ro.

TOURIST SERVICES

Romania has limited resources for tourists, but the **National Tourist Office** is still useful. Check its website at www.romaniatourism.com. Most tourist offices are intended for Romanians, and much of the country has poor resources for foreign travelers. Large hotels, however, can be excellent resources in smaller towns—even for those not paying to stay in them.

MONEY

LEI (L)		
	AUS$1 = L1.97	L1 = AUS$0.51
	CDN$1 = L2.21	L1 = CDN$0.45
	EUR€1 = L3.19	L1 = EUR€0.31
	NZ$1 = L1.74	L1 = NZ$0.57
	UK£1 = L4.71	L1 = UK£0.21
	US$1 = L2.33	L1 = US$0.43

The Romanian **currency** is the **leu,** plural lei (pronounced "lay"; abbreviated L), which was revalued in 2005. The recently revalued leu is called the RON (Romanian New Leu), whereas the old leu is called the ROL (Romanian Leu); 1RON=10,000ROL. Banknotes are issued in denominations of L1, L5, L10, L50, L100, and L500; coins come in amounts of 1, 5, 10, and 50 bani (singular ban; L1=100bani). Romania joined the EU in 2007, and Romanian officials are currently aiming to adopt the **euro** by 2014. As the leu strengthens, **inflation** rates continue to drop dramatically and now hover around 5%, though this statistic is liable to fluctuate. Romania has a 19% **value added tax (VAT) rate** on goods and services. **ATMs** are the best way to exchange or withdraw money. As identity theft rings sometimes target ATMs, travelers should use machines located inside banks and check for evidence of tampering. **Private exchange bureaus,** which often offer better exchange rates than **banks,** are everywhere and deal in common foreign currencies. However, few take **credit cards** or **traveler's checks.** Changing money on the street is both illegal and a surefire way to get cheated. It is a good idea to carry plenty of cash when traveling in small cities and less-touristed regions, as few establishments in these locations accept **traveler's checks** or **credit cards.**

HEALTH AND SAFETY

EMERGENCY	**Ambulance:** ☎961. **Fire:** ☎981. **Police:** ☎955. **Toll-Free General Emergency:** ☎112

If possible, avoid Romanian **hospitals,** as most are not up to Western standards. Your embassy can recommend a good private doctor. Some **European medical clinics** in Bucharest have English-speaking doctors and will require **cash payments.** *Farmacii* (pharmacies) stock basic medical supplies. *Antinevralgic* is for headaches, *aspirină* or *piramidon* for colds and the flu, and *saprosan* for diarrhea. *Prezervative* (condoms), *tampoane* (tampons), and *şerveţele igienice* (sanitary napkins) are available at all drugstores and many kiosks. **Public restrooms** are relatively uncommon in Romania and often lack soap, towels, and toilet paper. Though water in Romania is less contaminated than it once was, avoid untreated **tap water** and do not use **ice cubes;** boil water before drinking it or drink imported **bottled water.** Beware of contaminated vendor food.

Violent **crime** is not a major concern, but petty crime against tourists is common. Be especially careful on public transport and night trains. Pickpocketing, money exchange, and taxi scams are prevalent in Romania. Beware of distracting children and con artists dressed as policemen who ask for your passport or wallet. If someone shows a badge and claims to be a plainclothes policeman, he may be lying and trying to scam you. No police officer would ask to see credit cards or cash. When in doubt, ask the officer to escort you to the nearest police station. Taxis should be avoided if possible, as scams are very, very common. If it is necessary to take a taxi, particularly an inter-city taxi, it is advisable to call for a taxi, verify that the meter is operational, and agree on a price beforehand. Solo **female travelers** shouldn't go out alone after dark, should say they are traveling with a male, and should dress conservatively; tank tops, shorts, and sneakers may attract attention. Sexual harassment is a problem in Bucharest. **Minorities**, and especially those with dark skin, may encounter unwanted attention, as they may be mistaken for Roma (gypsies), who face much discrimination in Romania. **Homosexuality** is now legal in Romania, but discrimination remains; public displays of affection may incite violence. Most Romanians hold conservative attitudes toward sexuality, which may translate into harassment of **GLBT** travelers and often manifests itself in the form of anti-gay propaganda in major cities. For more information about gay and lesbian clubs and resources, check out **www.accept-romania.ro.**

TRANSPORTATION

BY PLANE. Many international **airlines** fly into **Bucharest Henri Coanda International Airport** (☎021 204 1200). It is often cheaper, however, to fly into another major European city, such as Budapest or Prague, and then to catch a train to Bucharest. **TAROM** (Romanian Airlines; ☎21 201 4000; www.tarom.ro) and **CarpatAir** (☎256 300 900; www.carpatair.com) fly to a number of European and Middle Eastern destinations and smaller airports within Romania, including Cluj-Napoca, Constanța, Iași, Sibiu, Suceava, and Timișoara.

BY TRAIN. **Trains** are faster and more efficient than buses for international travel and tend to be less expensive than flights. **Eurail** is accepted in Romania, but **Eastpass** is not. To buy tickets for the national railway, go to the **CFR** (Che-Fe-Re) office in larger towns. You must buy international tickets in advance. Train stations sell domestic tickets 1hr. in advance. The English-language timetable *Mersul Trenurilor* (hardcopy L12; www.cfr.ro) is very useful. There are four types of trains: *InterCity* (indicated by an "IC" on timetables and at train stations); *rapid* (in green);

ROMANIA TOP TEN

1. Best place to meet a vampire: Sighișoara's **medieval citadel,** with its huge graveyard and the only crypt in Transylvania (p. 530).
2. Best moonshine brandy, worst hangover: *palincă,* which tastes smooth but hits you like a 120-proof brick.
3. Best waste of space: the **Parliamentary Palace** in Bucharest, the world's second largest building, most of which stands empty (p. 518).
4. Best flashback: the super-traditional **Iza Valley,** where life continues as it has for several hundred years (p. 542).
5. Best student nightlife: Cluj-Napoca, packed to the gills with students (p. 533).
6. Best fairytale setting: the stunning spires and towers of **Peleș Castle,** set against a backdrop of mountains and forests (p. 523).
7. Best place to be a carnivore: Transylvania, where game meats, including boar, venison, and bear, are affordable (p. 524).
8. Best place to rage against the system: the Black Sea coast town of **Vama Veche,** which attracts alternative youths of all types to its annual free concert on the beach (p. 551).
9. Best mountaintop experience: hiking in the cloud-topped **Făgăraș Mountains** (p. 532).
10. Best place to debate religion: **Bucovina,** with its miraculously preserved frescoes and monasteries. Chemistry or divine intervention? (p. 545).

accelerat (red); and *personal* (black). International trains (blue) are indicated with an "i." *InterCity* trains stop only at major cities. *Rapid* trains are the next fastest; *accelerat* trains are slower and dirtier. The sluggish and decrepit *personal* trains stop at every station. The difference between **first class** (*clasa întâi;* 6 people per compartment) and **2nd class** (*clasa doua;* 8 people) is small.

BY BUS. Traveling to Romania by **bus** is often cheaper than entering by plane or train. Tourist agencies may sell timetables and tickets, but buying tickets from the carrier saves commission and is often cheaper. **Local buses** can be cheaper than trains but are packed and poorly ventilated. Minibuses are a good option for short distances, as they are often cheaper, faster, and cleaner than trains.

BY FERRY AND BY TAXI. In the Danube Delta, boats are the best mode of transport. A **ferry** runs down the new European riverway from Rotterdam, Netherlands to Constanţa, and in the Black Sea between İstanbul, Turkey and Constanţa. If taking a **taxi** is necessary, only use cars that post a company name, phone number, and rate per kilometer. Agree on a fee beforehand and be sure the driver uses the meter. Your ride should cost no more than L6 per km plus a L7 flat fee.

BY THUMB. Although Let's Go does not recommend **hitchhiking,** travelers report that it is very common in rural Romania and, in some places, is the only way to get around without a car. Hitchhikers stand on the side of the road and put out their palm, as if waving. Drivers generally expect a **payment** similar to the price of a train or bus ticket for the distance traveled; L1 for every 10km is a fair price.

KEEPING IN TOUCH

PHONE CODES	**Country code:** 40. **International dialing prefix:** 00. From outside Romania, dial international dialing prefix (see inside back cover) + 40 + city code + local number. Within Romania, dial 0 + city code + local number. For calls within a city, just use the local number, unless on a cell phone, in which case the city code is always required.

EMAIL AND INTERNET. Internet cafes are relatively common—though not always easy to find—in cities and larger towns and cost L3 per hr.

TELEPHONE. Most public phones are orange and only accept **phone cards,** sold at telephone offices, Metro stops, and some post offices and kiosks. These cards are only accepted at telephones of the same brand; the most prevalent is **Romtelecom.** Rates run around L1.20 per min. to neighboring countries, L1.60 per min. to most of Europe, and L2 per min. to the US. Phones operate in English if you press "i." At an analog phone, dial ☎971 for international calls. You may need to make a phone call *prin comandă* (with the help of the operator) at the telephone office; this takes longer and costs more. International access codes include: **AT&T** (☎02 18 00 42 88); **British Telecom** (☎02 18 00 44 44); **Canada Direct** (☎02 18 00 50 00); **MCI WorldPhone** (☎02 18 00 18 00); and **Sprint** (☎02 18 00 08 77).

MAIL. At the post office, request *par avion* for **airmail,** which takes two weeks for delivery. For postcards or letters, it costs L3 to mail within Europe and L5 to mail to the rest of the world. For **Poste restante,** address envelopes as follows: LAST NAME, first name, Oficiul Postal nr. 1 (post office address), city-, Romania, Postal Code. Major cities have **UPS** and **Federal Express.**

ACCOMMODATIONS AND CAMPING

ROMANIA	❶	❷	❸	❹	❺
ACCOMMODATIONS	under L41	L41-70	L71-100	L101-200	over L200

Many **hostels** are fairly pleasant, and some have perks like free beer and breakfast. While some **hotels** charge foreigners 50-100% more, lodging is still inexpensive (US$7-20). Reservations are helpful in July and August, but you can usually get by without them. **Guesthouses** and **pensions** are simple and comfortable but rare. In summer, many towns rent low-priced rooms in **university dorms. Private rooms** and **homestays** are a great option, but hosts rarely speak English. Look at the room and fix a price before accepting. **Bungalows** are often full in summer; reserve far in advance. Hotels and hostels often provide the best info for tourists.

FOOD AND DRINK

ROMANIA	❶	❷	❸	❹	❺
FOOD	under L8	L8-12	L13-16	L17-25	over L25

A complete **Romanian meal** includes an appetizer, soup, fish, an entree, and dessert. Lunch includes **soup,** called *supă* or *ciorbă* (the former has noodles or dumplings, the latter is saltier and with vegetables), an entree (typically grilled meat), and dessert. Some restaurants **charge by weight** rather than by portion; although prices may be listed per 50 or 100 grams, the actual serving can be up to 300 grams. Some servers will attempt to charge tourists extra; if the menu is not specific, always ask. *Garnituri*, the extras that come with a meal, are usually charged separately. This means you're paying for everything, even a bit of butter or a dollop of mustard. Pork rules in Romania, so keeping **kosher** is difficult. **Vegetarian** eating is feasible if you are willing to stick to foods that are not traditionally Romanian. Local **drinks** include *ţuică*, a brandy distilled from plums and apples, and double-distilled *palincă*, which approaches 70% alcohol. A delicious liqueur called *vişinată* is made from wild cherries. Romania produces high-quality wine, which is often only served by the bottle in restaurants. Always verify, however, that the server brings the exact vintage that was ordered; some will attempt to substitute a more expensive wine and, when questioned, claim that the restaurant ran out of the other.

LIFE AND TIMES

HISTORY

GROWING PAINS. Getian tribes inhabited ancient Romania until the second century AD, when Rome conquered the territory and reorganized its lands into the province of Dacia. Almost no architectural or written evidence remains from the period following the fall of Rome until the founding of the first Romanian state, **Wallachia,** in the south during the early 14th century AD. The second Romanian state, **Moldavia,** sprang up east of the Carpathians. The fledgling states constantly fought against the **Ottoman Turks,** who ruled Transylvania and other nearby lands. Moldavia's **Ştefan cel Mare** (Stephen the Great; 1457-1504) was most successful in warding off the attacks. During his 47-year rule, he built 42 monasteries and churches, one for each of his victories in battle. Successful resistance, however, died with Ştefan, and Moldavia and Wallachia became Turkish provinces.

TURMOIL. For the next 400 years, Austria-Hungary, Poland-Lithuania, Russia, and Turkey fought over the region. Wallachia's **Mihai Viteazul** (Michael the Brave) succeeded in briefly unifying Romanians to create an autonomous state in 1600, but Hungarian, Ottoman, and Polish attacks decimated the country. Moldavia and Wallachia united again under **Alexandru Ioan Cuza** in 1859. **King Carol I** then reduced corruption, built railroads, and strengthened the army that won Romania its independence in 1877. After Austria-Hungary's defeat in **WWI,** independent Romania gained Bessarabia (now Moldova), Bucovina, and Transylvania. Under the 1941 **Nazi-Soviet Non-Aggression Pact,** Romania lost its new territory to the Axis powers. Hoping the Nazis would preserve an independent Romania, dictator **General Ion Antonescu** supported Germany in WWII. In 1944, **King Mihai** orchestrated a coup and surrendered to the Allies, but the bid for Western alliance was unsuccessful. The Soviets moved in and proclaimed the **Romanian People's Republic** in late 1947.

THE EXECUTION WILL BE TELEVISED. The government violently suppressed opposition in the postwar era. Over 200,000 died in the **purges** of the 1950s, and farms were forced to collectivize. In 1965, **Nicolae Ceauşescu** took control of the Communist Party. He won praise for attempting to distance Romania from Moscow, but his ruthless domestic policies deprived his citizens of basic needs. By the late 1980s, Ceauşescu had turned Romania into a police state. When the dreaded **Securitate** (Secret Police) arrested dissident priest **Laszlo Tokes,** a violent protest erupted in **Timişoara,** and Romania was soon in a state of full-scale revolt. The 1989 **revolution** was as merciless as Ceauşescu himself. In December, clashes in Bucharest brought thousands of protesters to the streets. Ceauşescu was arrested, tried, and executed—on TV—all on Christmas Day. The enthusiasm following these days didn't last, as **Ion Iliescu's National Salvation Front,** composed largely of former communists, won the 1990 elections. Iliescu made some reforms but received international criticism for using violence and terror to repress student protests.

TODAY

In November 1996, **Emil Constantinescu** succeeded Iliescu in the country's first democratic transfer of power. Romania joined **NATO** in May 2004 and has subsequently amended its constitution and taken other steps toward a more open democracy. In December 2004, **Traian Basescu** was elected president and **Calin Popescu Tariceanu** was elected prime minister. Although Romania joined the EU in January 2007, the government still needs to address rampant corruption in order to avoid losing much-needed international aid.

PEOPLE AND CULTURE

DEMOGRAPHICS. Ethnic tensions trouble Romania, which is almost 90% ethnically **Romanian.** The 7% **Hungarian** minority, concentrated in Transylvania, and the 2.5% **Roma** minority both complain of discrimination. Most Romanians (87%) are **Eastern Orthodox;** most of the remainder are **Protestant** (7%) or **Catholic** (6%).

LANGUAGE. Romanian is a Romance language. Those familiar with French, Italian, Portuguese, or Spanish should be able to decipher many words. Romanian differs from other Romance tongues in its Slavic-influenced vocabulary. **German** and **Hungarian** are widely spoken in Transylvania. Throughout the country, **French** is a common second language for the older generation, while **English** is common among the younger. Avoid **Russian,** which is often understood but disliked. For a phrasebook and glossary, see **Appendix: Romanian,** p. 800.

CUSTOMS AND ETIQUETTE. It is customary not to give small change for purchases; restaurants usually round up to the nearest L1 or give candy instead of change. Locals generally don't **tip,** but foreigners are expected to tip 5-10% in restaurants. Hotel porters and helpful concierges are generally tipped modestly. It is unnecessary to tip **taxis.** In all cases, tipping too much is inappropriate. **Bargain** over taxi fares and accommodations if there is no posted rate. Try for one third off in open-air markets. Romanians take pride in their **hospitality.** Most will be eager to help and offer to show you around or invite you into their homes. Bring your hostess an odd number of flowers; even-numbered bouquets are only brought to graves. In rural areas, men should wear pants and closed-toed shoes, and women should wear dresses; for those over 30, these guidelines also apply in cities.

THE ARTS

LITERATURE. While the Roman poet **Ovid** wrote his last works in exile near Constanţa, Romanian literature did not flourish until the **Văcărescu family** invigorated it in the late 1700s: grandfather **Ienăchiţă** wrote the first Romanian grammar, father **Alecu** wrote love poetry, and son **Iancu** is considered the master of Romanian poetry. **Grigore Alexandrescu's** 19th-century fables and satires are also well-known. The next generation of writers ushered in a golden age of Romanian literature. **Mihai Eminescu,** a member of the **Romantic** movement, is widely considered Romania's national poet; his face appears on the 500-lei banknote. The end of WWII brought **Socialist Realism. Geo Bogza** and **Mihail Beniuc** were prominent adherents whose writings glorified the archetypal worker. Some sought freedom in other lands and languages—absurdist dramatist **Eugen Ionescu,** scholar of religion **Mircea Eliade,** writer **Elie Wiesel,** and father of Dada **Tristan Tzara** are the best known.

ROMANIA

MUSIC. Romanian clubs typically blast European house and techno, although the country's own DJs, including Projekt, Akcent, and Morandi, are common. Folk music remains very popular today.

THE VISUAL ARTS. Contemporary artists include painter **Nicolae Grigorescu,** who studied art in France before setting out to immortalize the Romanian countryside. **Constantin Brâncuşi** is considered one of the world's greatest Modernist sculptors. Although historically lacking an international audience, edgy, realist **Romanian cinema** is gaining recognition, especially through the popular Film Festival Cottbus and its dominance at the 2007 Cannes Film Festival, at which a Romanian film, **4 Months, 3 Weeks, and 2 days,** won the top prize.

HOLIDAYS AND FESTIVALS

Holidays: New Year's Holiday (Jan. 1-2); Epiphany (Jan. 6); *Mărţişor* (Mar. 1); Orthodox Easter Holiday (Apr. 27-28, 2008; Apr. 19-20, 2009); Labor Day (May 1); National Unity Day/Romania Day (Dec. 1); Christmas (Dec. 25-26).

Festivals: *Dragobete* (Feb. 24), known as "the day when the birds are getting engaged," is a traditional Romanian fertility festival. For *Mărţişor* (Mar. 1), locals wear *porte-boneurs* (good-luck charms) and give snow-drop flowers to friends and lovers. During the second weekend in July, Sighişoara hosts a popular medieval festival. Concerts, recitals, exhibitions, and movies are shown in Bucharest's Piaţa Revolutiei for the biannual George Enescu International Festival and Competition (Sept. 1-23). At the beginning of September, Cluj-Napoca hosts a competitive international film festival. Romania Day (Dec. 1), commemorates the day in 1918 that Transylvania became a part of Romania.

BUCHAREST (BUCUREȘTI) ☎(0)21

Once a fabled beauty on the Orient Express, Bucharest (booh-kooh-RESHT; pop. 2,100,000) is now infamous for its heavy-handed transformation under dictator Nicolae Ceaușescu. During his 25-year reign, Ceaușescu nearly ruined the city's splendor by replacing historic neighborhoods, grand boulevards, and Ottoman ruins with concrete blocks, wide highways, and communist monuments. Adults remember and may have participated in the 1989 revolution, but all citizens have since endured a mix of communist nostalgia and break-neck capitalism. Though Bucharest retains only glimmers of the sophisticated city it once was, life here is now as fascinating as it is frustrating.

TRANSPORTATION

Flights: Henri Coanda (Otopeni) Airport (☎204 1200; www.otp-airport.ro). Avoid taxis outside the terminal; the FlyTaxi company has exclusive rights to the space and charges several times the normal rate. Call a cab or buy a bus ticket (L5 per 2 trips) from the corner kiosk at the exit from the airport. Bus #783 runs from the airport to Pța. Unirii (45min., every 30min. 5:23am-11:53pm). It departs from the level beneath the international arrivals hall. Flying into Bucharest can be expensive; often, a better idea is to fly into Budapest or Zagreb and enter Romania via train or bus.

Trains: Gara de Nord (☎223 0880, info 95 21). M1: Gara de Nord. To: **Brașov** (2½-4hr., 26 per day, L26); **Cluj-Napoca** (8hr., 6 per day, L56); **Constanța** (5hr., 9 per day, L41); **Sighișoara** (4-5hr., 10 per day, L49); **Timișoara** (8-10hr., 9 per day, L74); **Budapest, HUN** (14hr., 3 per day, L172); **Kraków, POL** (27hr., 1 per day, L299); **Prague, CZR** (36hr., 1 per day, L336); **Sofia, BUL** (11hr., 2 per day, L95). **CFR,** Str. Domnița Anastasia 10-14 (☎313 2643; www.cfr.ro), books domestic and international tickets. Open M-F 7am-8pm, Sa 9am-1:30pm. Cash only. **Wasteels** (☎317 0369; www.wasteels.ro), inside Gara de Nord, books international tickets. English spoken. Open M-F 8am-7pm, Sa 8am-2pm. AmEx/MC/V.

Buses: The profusion of bus services, both private and public, in Bucharest makes taking a bus notoriously difficult; trains are preferable for domestic travel. There are 6 official bus stations in Bucharest; each serves a different sector of the city and sends buses to destinations in that sector's direction. Near the center, **Filaret** station, Cuțitul de Argint 2 (M2: Tineretului; ☎336 0692), serves the greatest number of domestic destinations but few tourist destinations. There are also countless smaller bus stations, some no more than parking lots serving just 1 location. Internationally, however, buses are the best way to reach **Athens, GCE** and **İstanbul, TUR.** Multiple bus companies located near the train station sell tickets to most of Europe. **Toros,** Calea Griviței 134 (☎223 1918), outside the station, sends 2 buses per day to İstanbul for L125. English spoken. Open daily 7am-5pm. Cash only. Next door at Calea Griviței 136-138, **Transcontinental** (☎202 9030; www.tci.ro) sends 2 buses per week to Athens for €73. They also sell Eurolines bus tickets, which cover most of Western Europe. English spoken. Open daily 9am-5pm. Cash only.

Public Transportation: Buses, trolleys, and **trams** cost L1.10 and run daily 5:30am-11:30pm. Validate tickets by sliding them into the small boxes to avoid a L30 fine. The transportation system is invaluable, but figuring out how it works is a chore. **Express buses** take only magnetic cards (L5 per 2 trips, L20 per 10 trips). Tickets and magnetic cards are sold at R.A.T.B. kiosks, often near bus stops. Pickpocketing is a problem during peak hours. The **Metro** offers reliable, less-crowded service (L2 per 2 trips, L7 per 10). Runs 5am-11:30pm. Maps of the public transportation system, which include a detailed city map, can be purchased from kiosks. They also appear in the free English-language publication *București What, Where, When,* available at many hotels, hostels, and restaurants.

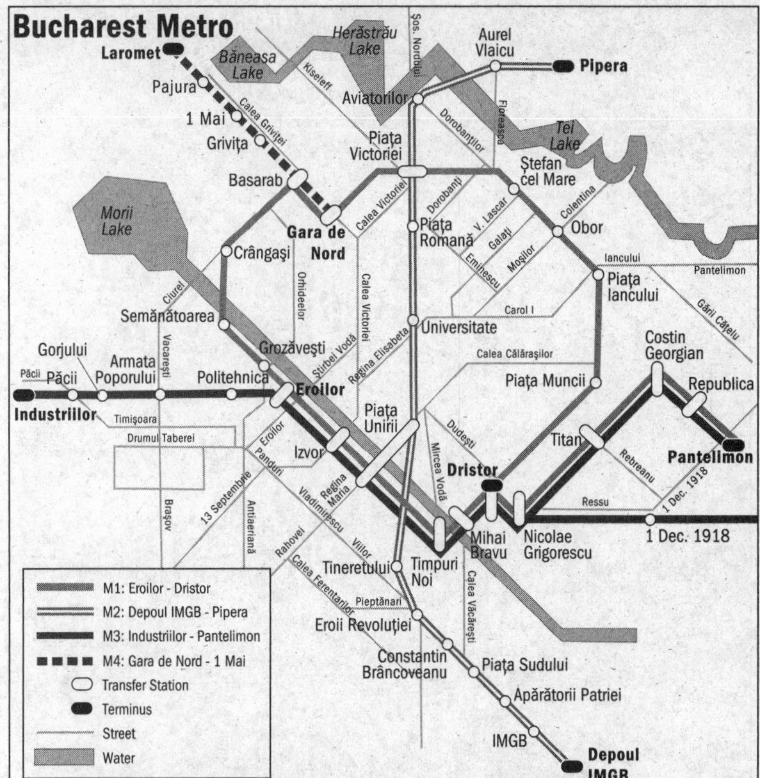

Taxis: Taxi drivers in Bucharest will cheerfully charge you 10 times the regular fare, especially from airports, train stations, shopping centers, and hotels. Especially beware private *(privat)* taxis. Normal rates should be around L1 base fee and L1.4 per km. The base fee is often posted; look for the *"tarif."* Only use taxis that have a company name, phone number, and rate posted. Some fake taxis have started posting counterfit company stickers and phone numbers, making it difficult to identify authentic and established companies; as a definite precaution, avoid taxis that post the number "9403," as this is a commonly used fake number. In general, have a local call a cab for you whenever possible. Few drivers speak English, so carry a good map and directions to your hotel or hostel, written in Romanian. Reliable companies include **Meridien** (☎94 44), **ChrisTaxi** (☎94 61), and **Taxi2000** (☎94 94).

ORIENTATION

Bucharest's main street changes its name from **Şosea Kiseleff** to **Bulevard Lascăr Catargiu** to **Bulevard General Magheru** to **Bulevard Nicolae Bălcescu** to **Bulevard I.C. Brătianu** as it runs north-south through the city's four main squares: **Piaţa Victoriei, Piaţa Română, Piaţa Universităţii,** and **Piaţa Unirii.** Another thoroughfare, running parallel, is **Calea Victoriei,** which crosses **Piaţa Revoluţiei.** The **Metro** M1 line forms a diamond that encloses the city center. The M3 passes horizontally along the bottom of this diamond, while M2 pierces it vertically, stopping at the main squares.

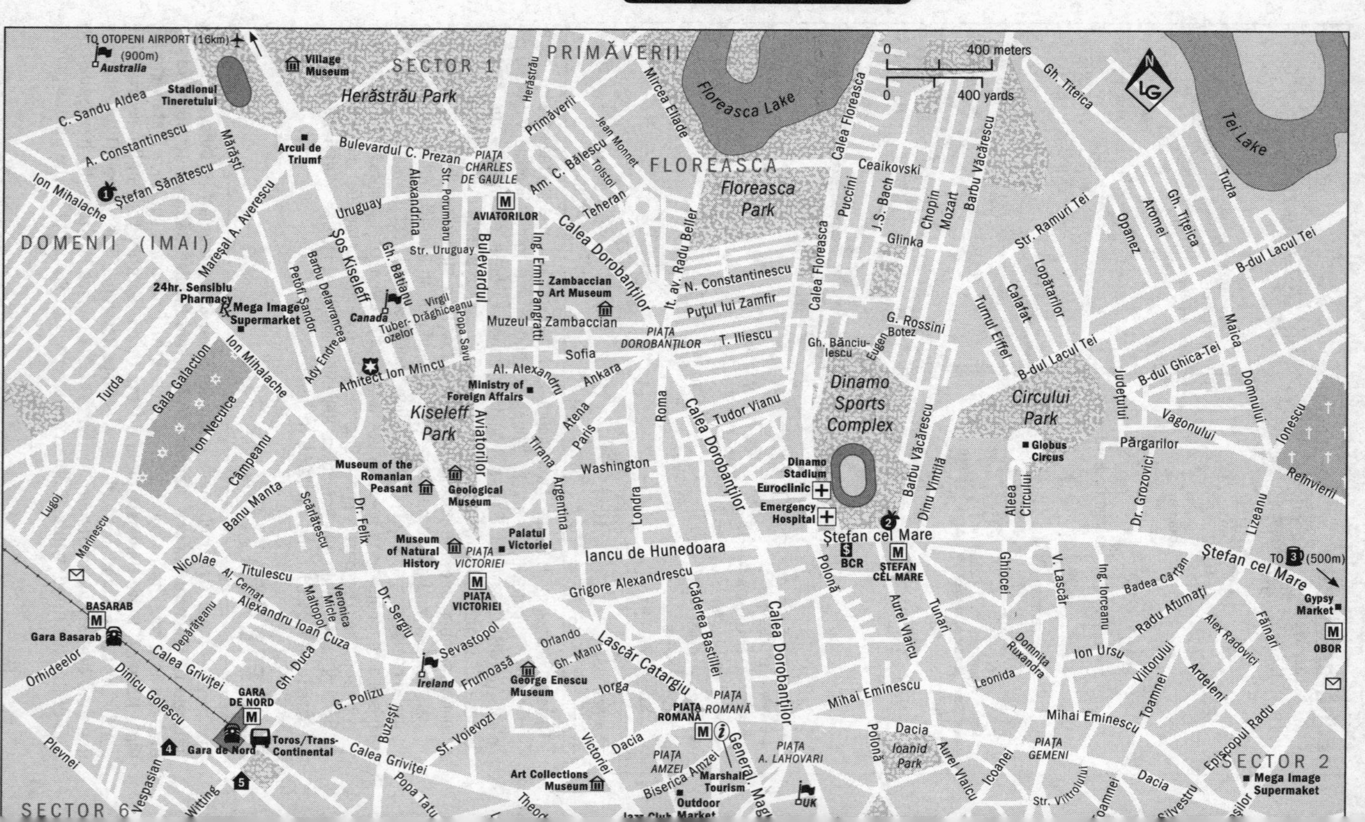

TO OTOPENI AIRPORT (16km)
(900m)
Australia
Village Museum
SECTOR 1
PRIMĂVERII
Herăstrău Park
Stadionul Tineretului
C. Sandu Aldea
A. Constantinescu
Mărăşti
Arcul de Triumf
Bulevardul C. Prezan
PIATA CHARLES DE GAULLE
AVIATORILOR
Ion Mihalache
Ştefan Sănătescu
DOMENII (IMAI)
Mareşal A. Averescu
Uruguay
Alexandrina
Str. Porumbaru
Str. Uruguay
Bulevardul
Ing. Ermil Pangratti
Zambaccian Art Museum
Muzeul Zambaccian
Calea Dorobanţilor
24hr. Sensiblu Pharmacy
Mega Image Supermarket
Petöfi Şandor
Barbu Delavrancea
Şos Kiseleff
Gh. Bătianu
Canada
Virgil
Tuber-ozelor
Drăghiceanu
Popa Savu
Ady Endre
Arhitect Ion Mincu
Al. Alexandru
Ministry of Foreign Affairs
Kiseleff Park
Aviatorilor
Sofia
Ankara
Atena
Paris
Tirana
Argentina
Washington
Londra
Roma
Tudor Vianu
PIATA DOROBANŢILOR
T. Iliescu
Puţul lui Zamfir
N. Constantinescu
lt. av. Radu Beller
Teheran
Tolstoi
Am. C. Bălescu
Primăverii
Herăstrău
Jean Monnet
Mircea Eliade
Floreasca Lake
FLOREASCA
Floreasca Park
Calea Floreasca
Puccini
Ceaikovski
J.S. Bach
Chopin
Mozart
Glinka
Barbu Văcărescu
0 400 meters
0 400 yards
Gh. Titeica
Tei Lake
Tuzla
Gh. Tiţeica
Aromei
Opanez
Str. Ramuri Tei
B-dul Lacul Tei
Lopătarilor
Calafat
Turnul Eiffel
Maica
Domnului
B-dul Ghica-Tei
Judeţului
G. Rossini
Eugen Botez
Gh. Bănciu-lescu
Dinamo Sports Complex
Circului Park
Globus Circus
Vagonului
Pargarilor
Ionescu
Reînvierii
Dr. Grozovici
Lizeanu
Aleea Circului
Dinu Vintilă
Dinamo Stadium
Euroclinic
Emergency Hospital
Ştefan cel Mare
BCR
ŞTEFAN CEL MARE
TO (500m)
Gypsy Market
OBOR
Gala Galaction
Ion Neculce
Turda
Câmpeanu
Banu Manta
Lugoj
Marinescu
Scărlătescu
Dr. Felix
Museum of the Romanian Peasant
Geological Museum
Museum of Natural History
PIATA VICTORIEI
Palatul Victoriei
Iancu de Hunedoara
Nicolae Titulescu
Al. Cernat
Alexandru Ioan Cuza
Veronica Micle
Maltopol
Dr. Sergiu
Grigore Alexandrescu
Căderea Bastillei
Polonă
Aurel Vlaicu
Tunari
Ghiocei
V. Lascăr
Ing. Iorceanu
Badea Cârţan
Radu Afumaţi
Alex Radovici
Făinari
BASARAB
Gara Basarab
Orhideelor
Depărăţeanu
Calea Griviţei
Gh. Duca
Dinicu Golescu
GARA DE NORD
Gara de Nord
Toros/Trans-Continental
Plevnei
Vespasian
Witting
SECTOR 6
G. Polizu
Buzeşti
Sf. Voievozi
Ireland
Frumoasă
Sevastopol
George Enescu Museum
Orlando
Gh. Manu
Iorga
Lascăr Catargiu
PIATA ROMANĂ
General Magheru
Victoriei
Dacia
Popa Tatu
Art Collections Museum
PIATA AMZEI
Biserica Amzei
Marshal Tourism
Outdoor Market
PIATA A. LAHOVARI
UK
Mihai Eminescu
Ioanid Park
Leonida
Domnita Ruxandra
Ion Ursu
Viitorului
Toamnei
Ardeleni
Icoanei
PIATA GEMENI
Str. Viitorului
Episcopul Radu
SECTOR 2
Mega Image Supermaket
Silvestru

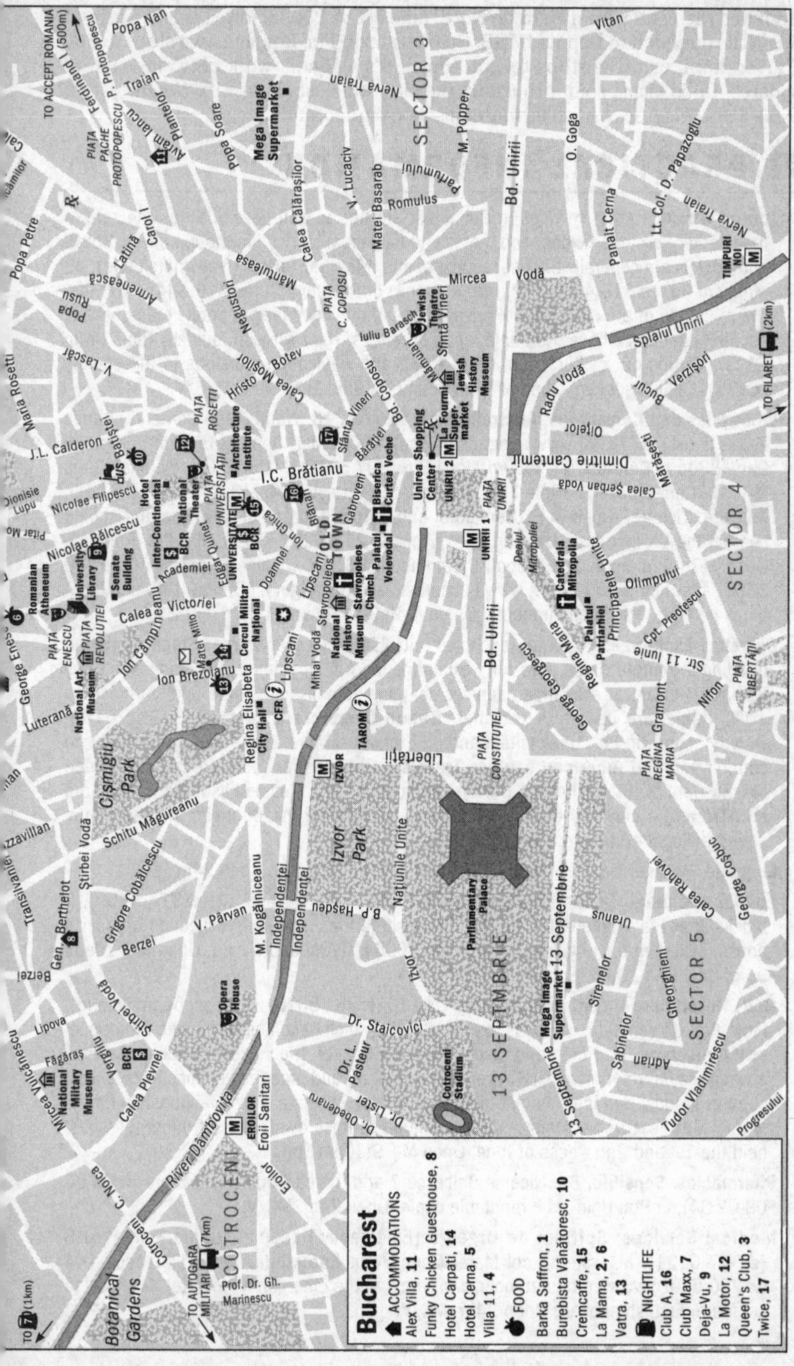

Bucharest

ACCOMMODATIONS

- Alex Villa, 11
- Funky Chicken Guesthouse, 8
- Hotel Carpati, 14
- Hotel Cerna, 5
- Villa 11, 4

FOOD

- Barka Saffron, 1
- Burebista Vânătoresc, 10
- Cremcaffe, 15
- La Mama, 2, 6
- Vatra, 13

NIGHTLIFE

- Club A, 16
- Club Maxx, 7
- Deja-Vu, 9
- La Motor, 12
- Queen's Club, 3
- Twice, 17

To reach the center from Gara de Nord, take M1 to Pța. Victoriei, then change to M2 in the direction of Depoul IMGB. Go one stop to Pța. Română, two stops to Pța. Universității, or three stops to Pța. Unirii. It's a 15min. walk between each of squares. Good **maps,** sold throughout the city, will cost about L15. *Bucharest in Your Pocket* is free at hostels, museums, bookstores, and hotels.

PRACTICAL INFORMATION

Tourist Office: Tourist services in Bucharest are not as well developed as they are in many other Romanian cities, and there is no municipal tourist information office. Hotels and hostels are generally the best source of info. **Marshal Turism** (www.marshal.ro), 43 Magheru Bd. (☎319 4455; M2: Pța. Romană) or Bd. Unirii 20 (☎319 4445; M2: Pța. Unirii), is one of the most helpful private firms in the city. Marshal books plane tickets, accommodations all over Romania, and car rentals. The staff also runs city tours (from €11), daytrips out of Bucharest (from €16), and weeklong excursions to the country (€375). English spoken. Open M-F 9am-6pm, Sa 9am-1pm. AmEx/MC/V.

Embassies and Consulates: Australia, Pța. Montreal 10, World Trade Center, entrance F, 1st fl. (☎316 7553; www.austrade.gov.au). M4: 1 Mai. Open M-Th 9am-5:30pm, F 9am-2:30pm. **Canada,** Str. Tuberozelor 1-3 (☎307 5000). M1 or 2: Pța. Victoriei. Open M-Th 8:30am-5pm, F 8:30am-2pm. **Ireland,** Str. Buzești 50-52, 3rd fl. (☎310 2131). M2: Pța. Victoriei. Open M-F 10am-noon and 2-4pm. Citizens of **New Zealand** should contact the UK embassy. **UK,** Str. Jules Michelet 24 (☎201 7279). M2: Pța. Romană. Open M-Th 9am-noon and 2-6pm, F 9am-noon. **US,** Str. Nicolae Filipescu 26 (☎200 3300, after hours 200 3433; www.bucharest.usembassy.gov). M2: Pța. Universității. A block behind Hotel Intercontinental. Open M-Th 9-11am and 1-3pm, F 9-11am.

ROMANIA

Currency Exchange: Exchange agencies and **ATMs** are everywhere. Stock up before heading to remote areas, but don't exchange more than you'll need–many won't buy *lei* back. Beware of exchange agencies charging commission; some take as much as 10%. Banks are usually a safe bet. **Banca Comercială Română** (☎312 6185; www.bcr.com), in Pța. Universității and on Ștefan cel Mare, exchanges currency for no commission and **American Express Travelers Cheques** for 1.5% commission. Open M-F 8:30am-5:30pm. The Pța. Universității location, Bd. Regina Elisabeta 5, has both an **ATM** and a currency exchange machine, available 24hr. Changing money on the street is illegal and almost always a scam.

Luggage Storage: Gara de Nord. L3 per bag, L6 per large bag. Open 24hr.

English-Language Bookstore: Cărturesti, Pictor Arthur Verona 13 (☎317 3459), 2 blocks after Pța. Romană toward Pța. Universității. Has a sizeable collection of English books, including travel guides, in addition to CDs, DVDs, and a cafe. Open M-F 10am-9pm, Sa 11am-10pm, Su 1-7pm. MC/V.

GLBT Resources: Accept Romania, Str. Lirei 10 (☎252 5620; www.accept-romania.ro). From Pța. Universității, walk east on Bd. Carol I, which becomes Bd. Pache Protopopescu; turn left on Str. Horei, and then right onto Str. Lirei. The English-speaking staff has a wealth of information on GLBT events in the center and organizes counseling services, support groups, and informal get-togethers. Accept Romania is also responsible for the annual **Gay-Fest,** a weeklong festival intended to raise awareness of minority issues, held the 1st and 2nd weeks of June. Open M-F 9:30am-5pm.

Pharmacies: Sensiblu, Bd. Nicolae Balcescu 7 and Unirea Department Store (☎08 00 08 02 34), in Pța. Unirii, is a reputable chain. Open 24hr. MC/V.

Medical Services: Spitalul de Urgență (Emergency Hospital), Calea Floreasca 8 (☎317 0121). M1: Ștefan cel Mare. Open 24hr. **Euroclinic,** Calea Floreasca 14A (☎200 6800; www.spitaluleuroclinic.ro), next to the Emergency Hospital. M1: Ștefan cel Mare. English spoken. Open 24hr. MC/V.

Telephones: Public pay phones are orange and take prepaid phone cards, which come in L10, L15, and higher denominations, and can be bought at kiosks and convenience stores. These work for domestic calls and are a simple but expensive way to place international calls. **Internet cafes** often have low overseas rates.

Internet: Internet cafes are everywhere. **Jazz Club,** Calea Victoriei 120 (☎312 4841). M2: Pţa. Romană. 7am-11pm L3 per hr., 11pm-7am L2 per hr. Printing L0.50 per page. Scanning L1 per page. CD burning L2 per disc. Open 24hr. Free **Wi-Fi** available at all KFC and Pizza Hut locations in the city.

Post Office: Central Post Office, Str. Matei Millo 10 (☎315 8793). M2: Pţa. Universităţii. From Bd. Regina Elisabeta, go north on Calea Victoriei and turn left on Str. Matei Millo. Like most branches, this one has **Poste Restante.** Open M-F 7:30am-1pm and 1:30-8pm. **Postal Code:** 014700.

ACCOMMODATIONS

Bucharest doesn't have many private rooms, and its hotels are more expensive than those in other Romanian cities. The established hostels are fairly cheap, very international, and comfortable. Beware of people at Gara de Nord who claim to work for hostels—often they are con-artists trying to scam you.

Alex Villa, Str. Avram Iancu 5 (☎312 1653). M2: Pţa. Universităţii. From Gara de Nord, take trolley #85 to Calea Moşilor. Follow Bd. Carol I to Pţa. Pache Protopopescu, then go right on Str. Sf. Ştefan. At the playground, take a left on Avram Iancu. This new hostel, formerly Elvis' Villa, is in a quiet, historic neighborhood. Rooms have big windows, brightly painted walls with bold designs, and A/C. Diverse international clientele. Breakfast, laundry, and Internet included. 4-bed dorms €10. Cash only. ❶

Funky Chicken Guesthouse, Str. General Berthelot 63 (☎312 1425). From Gara de Nord, go right on Calea Griviţei, right on Str. Berzei, and left on Str. General Berthelot. Bucharest's most centrally located hostel, near Cişmigiu Park and Pţa.Revoluţiei. The cheapest prices in town draw a colorful mix of people. Well-placed couches make bedrooms decorated with contemporary paintings comfortable and intimate. Small kitchen. Laundry included. Call ahead in summer. 4- to 8-bed dorms €8. Cash only. ❶

Hotel Carpati, Str. Matei Millo 6 (☎315 0140; fax 312 1857). M2: Universităţii. From Pţa. Universităţii, it's a short walk down Bd. Regina Elizabeta to Str. I. Brezoianu. Turn right; the hotel is at the 2nd corner. This budget hotel boasts a central location, neat rooms, new furnishings, balconies, and an English-speaking staff. Modest breakfast included. Check-in after 2pm. Check-out noon. Reserve ahead. Singles with shared bath L118; doubles with shared bath L160, with private bath L220. MC/V. ❸

Villa 11, Str. Institut Medico Militar 11 (☎07 22 49 59 00). M1 or M4: Gara de Nord. From the train station, take a right on Bd. Dinicu Golescu, then left on Str. Vespasian. This villa is a bit older, but you'll get a home-cooked breakfast every morning and a quiet respite from the sometimes-rowdy hostel scene. A winding staircase, piano, and paintings add a warm personal touch. English spoken. 3- to 8-bed dorms L45; singles with shared bath L80; doubles with shared bath L100. Cash only. ❷

Hotel Cerna, Str. Dinicu Golescu 29 (☎317 8564), across from Gara de Nord. Clean, decently sized rooms (some with balcony) and a very convenient location make this Soviet-era hotel a deal. English spoken. Breakfast included. Check-out noon. Singles with shared bath L75, with private bath L105; doubles L120/180. Cash only. ❷

FOOD

Restaurants serve a wide range of international cuisine, including American, Chinese, French, Greek, Hungarian, Indian, Italian, and, of course, Romanian. A meal here will cost you roughly twice what it would anywhere else in the country. To save some lei, look for the fruit and vegetable stands all over the city or head to the conveniently located **open-air market** at Pţa. Amzei, near Pţa. Română. (Open M-F 6am-9pm, Sa 6am-7pm, Su 6am-3pm. Cash only.) **La Fourmi Supermarket,** in the basement of Unirea Shopping Center on Pţa. Unirii, is well-stocked with fresh meats, fruits and vegetables, frozen foods, and a sizeable alcohol section. (Open M-F 8am-9:30pm, Sa 8:30am-9pm, Su 10am-6pm. MC/V.)

Burebista Vânătoresc, Str. Batiştei 14 (☎211 8929; www.restaurantburebista.ro). M2: Pţa. Universităţii. Across from the US embassy. The dining room recreates a medieval tavern, complete with tapestries, stuffed bears and wild boar, and candelabra. Guests are treated to music by a live folk band after 8pm. Menu features tasty wild game, including, as it happens, bear and wild boar (L35 each). English menu. Full bar. Entrees L13-70. Open daily noon-midnight. MC/V. ❹

Cremcaffe, Str. T. Caragiu 3 (☎313 9740; www.cremcaffe.ro). M2: Pţa. Universităţii, just off Bd. Regina Elisabeta. The gritty realities of Bucharest melt away in this elegant Italian coffeehouse, which features delicious focaccia sandwiches (from L14) and coffee. On occasion, the relaxing background music gives way to mini-concerts on the house piano. English menu available. Coffee/liqueur blends L11-19. Ice cream L10-15. Open M-F 7:30am-midnight, Sa-Su 9am-midnight. Cash only. ❷

ROMANIA

Vatra, Str. Brezoianu 23-25 (☎315 8375; www.vatra.ro). M2: Pţa. Universităţii. From Pţa. Universităţii, head down B-dul. Regina Elisabeta towards Cişmigiu Park. A block before reaching the park, turn right down Brezoianu. Traditionally attired waitstaff serves authentic Romanian cuisine in a lively dining room with rough-hewn wooden tables. English menu. Beer L4-6. Entrees L9-24. Open daily noon-midnight. Cash only. ❸

La Mama, Str. Barbu Văcărescu 3 (☎212 4086; www.lamama.ro). M1: Ştefan cel Mare. Branches at Str. Delea Veche 51 (☎320 5213; M1: Pţa. Muncii) and Str. Episcopiei 9 (☎312 9797; M2: Pţa. Universităţii). Living up to its motto "like at mom's house," La Mama serves Romanian favorites for low prices in a down-to-earth atmosphere immensely popular with both locals and tourists. Vegetarian options. No English menu. Entrees L9-28. Beer and wine from L2.90. Call ahead for reservations. Open M-Th and Su 10am-2am, F-Sa 10am-4am. AmEx/MC/V. ❸

Barka Saffron (Saffron Boat), Str. Ştefan Sănătescu 1 (☎224 1004), at the intersection with Bd. Ion Mihalache. M2: Aviatorilor. A hike from the center: consider calling a taxi, or take the 15-20min. walk from the Aviatorilor Metro stop. Walk down Bul. Prezan to Arcul de Triumf; take Averesu and turn right onto Mărăşti, then left onto Sănătescu. Delicious Indian and Thai cuisine in a relaxed, stylish atmosphere with a great bar and temporary art exhibits. English menu. Appetizers L10. Vegetarian options from L11. Entrees L15-26. Open M-F noon-11:30pm, Sa-Su 10am-11:30pm. MC/V. ❹

SIGHTS

PARLIAMENTARY PALACE (PALATUL PARLAMENTULUI). With 16 levels and nearly 100,000 rooms totaling 365,000 sq. m, the Parliamentary Palace is the **world's second-largest building,** after the Pentagon in Washington, D.C. Starting in 1984, 20,000 laborers and 700 architects worked around the clock to construct the so-called **House of the People** (Casa Poporuli); as much as 80% of Romania's GDP was consumed by the project during its construction. Built to the scale of Ceauşescu's ego, it is far too large to be fully used; today, many rooms sit empty. Intended to serve as home for Romania's Communist functionaries, the building now houses the **Parliament.** Extending eastward from the Parliamentary Palace is **Bulevard Unirii,** a mammoth gray scar that was intentionally built 1m wider than Paris's Champs Elysées. Many of the apartment blocks on the west end sit nearly empty. *(M1 or 3: Izvor. M2: Unirii. Visitors entrance is on the north side of the building by the river. Open daily 10am-4pm. 40min. tours in English L15. Photo L30. Cash only.)*

CIŞMIGIU PARK (PARCUL CIŞMIGIU). One of Bucharest's oldest parks, Cişmigiu Park is the peaceful, tree-filled eye of central Bucharest's storm of gray modernity. Stroll among carefully tended flower gardens, statues, cobblestone pathways, and fountains that surround the small lake. *(M2: Pţa. Universităţii. Bus #61 or 336. Open 24hr. Rowboats and paddleboats L10 per hr. Open M-Th 11am-9pm, F 11am-midnight, Sa 10am-midnight, Su 10am-9pm. Cash only.)*

HISTORIC NEIGHBORHOODS. In northern Bucharest, the peaceful, tree-lined side streets between Pţa. Victoriei and Pţa. Dorobanţilor (M2: Victoriei) are full of beautiful villas from pre-Ceauşescu Bucharest. What remains of Bucharest's **Old Town** lies near Str. Lipscani and Str. Gabroveni (M2: Piaţa Universităţii). The narrow, curving avenues, now pedestrian-only zones, contain the city's oldest church, **Biserica Curtea Veche** (Old Court Church), where Wallachian princes were crowned for centuries. The soot-stained frescoes, dating from the 16th century, are original, but most are now obscured by scaffolding due to ongoing restoration. *(No captions. Open 10am-6pm. Free.)* Next to the church are the ruins of **Palatul Voievoda,** a palace built in the 14th century and once inhabited by the notorious Impaler, Vlad Ţepeş (see **Son of a...,** p. 526). Much remains of the palace walls, including an almost entirely intact ground floor, and some arches of the second floor. *(☎314 0375. English captions. Open daily 10am-5pm. L2.04, students L1.02. Cash only.)* During his aesthetic assault, Ceauşescu inexplicably spared **Dealul Mitropoliei,** the hill southwest of Pţa. Unirii. Atop the hill is the small but old **Catedrala Mitropolia,** with a very imaginative depiction of Judgment Day on its portico. *(M1, 2, or 3: Pţa. Unirii. Up Aleea Dealul Mitropoliei. No captions. Church open daily 7am-7pm. Free.)*

SIGHTS OF THE REVOLUTION. Crosses and plaques throughout the city commemorate the *eroii revoluţiei Române*, "heroes of the Romanian revolution," and the year 1989. The first shots of the revolution were fired at **Piaţa Revoluţiei** on December 21, 1989. In the square are the **University Library,** the **National Art Museum,** and the **Senate Building** (former Communist Party Headquarters) where Ceauşescu delivered his final speech. Afterward, he fled the roof by helicopter but didn't get very far; shortly thereafter, he was captured by his pursuers and executed on national television. A white marble triangle with the inscription *Glorie martirilor noştri* ("Glory to our martyrs") commemorates the rioters who overthrew the dictator. *(M2: Pţa. Universitatii. Turn right on Bd. Regina Elisabeta and then right on Calea Victoriei.)* **Piaţa Universităţii** overlooks memorials to victims of the revolution and the 1990 protests of the corrupt government that replaced Ceauşescu. Crosses line Bd. Nicolae Bălcescu—the **black cross** lies where the first victim died.

HERĂSTRĂU PARK. This immense park, north of downtown, surrounds a lake of the same name; its diversions include rowboat rentals in the booths along the lakeshore (open M noon-8pm, Tu-Su 10am-8pm; L40 per hr.), ferry rides (L4, students L2), and a traveling-circus-style amusement park for children, open weekends. At the southern end of the park on Şos. Kiseleff, the massive **Arcul de Triumf** (Triumphal Arch) commemorates Romania's reunification in 1918 and honors those who died in WWI. *(M2: Aviatorilor. Bus #131 or 331 from Pta. Romana.)*

MUSEUMS

VILLAGE MUSEUM (MUZEUL SATULUI). This open-air museum, a replica 18th- to 19th-century village, contains nearly 100 houses, churches, mills, and even a sunflower-oil factory, all carted in from villages across Romania. Festivals with musicians in traditional garb take place most weekends in spring and summer. The English map from the museum giftshop (L2) is extremely helpful. *(Şos. Kiseleff 28-30. M2: Aviatorilor. ☎222 9068; www.muzeulsatului.ro. English captions. Open M 10am-5pm, Tu-Su 9am-7pm. L5, students L2.50. Cash only.)*

NATIONAL ART MUSEUM (MUZEUL NATIONAL DE ARTA AL ROMÂNIEI). This two-wing museum was built in the 1930s as a royal residence. The **European exhibit** presents an impressive overview of European art history, including works by **El Greco, Monet, Rembrandt,** and **Renoir.** The highlight, however, is the **Romanian section,** which houses an extensive collection of medieval, modern, and contemporary art. *(Calea Victoriei 49-53, in Pța. Revolutiei. M2: Pța. Universitatii. ☎313 3030. English captions. Open W-Su May-Sept. 11am-7pm; Oct.-Apr. 10am-6pm. Both wings L15, students L7.50; one wing L10/L5; free 1st W of every month. Cash only.)*

NATIONAL HISTORY MUSEUM (MUZEUL NAȚIONAL DE ISTORIE). Chronicling Romania's long and turbulent history through a huge collection of artifacts, many of this museum's exhibits may be appealing only to those most interested in Romanian history. Two exhibits, however, make this museum worth the trip: *Traian's Column*, a Roman triumphal marble monument of awesome proportions, and the dazzling Treasure Room, which contains the country's greatest precious metal and gem wealth, including the diamond-encrusted court jewelry of the last monarchs of Romania. *(Calea Victoriei 12. M1 or 2: Pța. Unirii. ☎315 8207; www.mnir.ro. Some English captions. Open W-Su 10am-6pm. L7, students L2. Photo L20. Cash only.)*

ENTERTAINMENT

Bucharest hosts numerous festivals and rock concerts every summer—Michael Jackson once greeted screaming fans here with "Hello, Budapest!" Check local guides, like the *Șapte Seri* or *B 24 FUN* booklets, available in hotels, hostels, and restaurants, for upcoming events. Fans of the classical arts will appreciate the **opera, symphony orchestra,** and **theater,** which are world class and dirt cheap; seasons run September to June. Tickets can be purchased at the on-site box offices; a good rule of thumb is to stop by or phone five to six days before a performance.

Romanian National Opera House (Opera Națională Română), B-dul. Kogalnicanu 70-72 (☎314 6980, box office 313 1857; www.operanb.ro). M1 or M3: Eroilor. Hosts performances of the National Opera Company and the Romanian National Ballet. Performances run most weekends and some weekday nights starting at 6:30pm. Box office open daily 10am-1pm and 2-7pm. Tickets L4.20-26. Cash only.

Atheneum (Ateneu Român), Str. Franklin 1-3 (☎315 2567, box office 315 6875; www.fge.org.ro), near Pța.Revoluției. M2: Pța. Universității. The home of the Romanian Philharmonic George Enescu, this beautifully designed rotunda, with its world-renowned acoustics, usually holds symphony performances Tu-Su at 7pm. Box office open M-F 10am-6pm. Tickets for symphony L16-40, for chamber music L3.50-15. Cash only.

National Theater (Teatru Național), B-dul. Nicolae Bălcescu 2 (☎313 9175, box office 314 7171; www.tnb.kappa.ro). M2: Pța. Universității. Imposing Soviet-era theater featuring some of the best drama in the city. Box office open M-F 10am-6pm. Tickets L5-27. Cash only.

NIGHTLIFE

Bucharest has countless bars, pubs, and watering holes. The club scene, in particular, is one of the best in Romania. Many venues are in the old town center and in the student district by M1: Grozăvești. Bring cab fare and directions to your hotel, written in Romanian, as public transit shuts down by midnight. For info on **GLBT nightlife,** ask at **Accept Romania** (see **Orientation and Practical Information,** p. 516).

Twice, Str. Sfânta Vineri 4 (☎313 5592). M2: Pța. Universității. This large, multi-leveled club, long a popular Bucharest nightspot, boasts a top and bottom floor that pound away to beats ranging from techno to hip hop, while a chill outdoor terrace sells pizza and provides a place to relax. Beer L3-10. Mixed drinks L10-18. Pizza L3-12. Cover men W L5; F-Sa L10. Open Th-Su 9pm-5am. Cash only.

ROMANIA

Club A, Str. Blănari 14 (☎315 6853; www.cluba.ro). M2: Pţa. Universităţii. Walk down Bd. Brătianu and take 3rd right by Kenvelo clothing store. A Bucharest institution since 1969. A student crowd moshes nightly to rock bands while school's in session. Beer from L2.40. Cover M-W and Su men L3; Th men L4; F-Sa men L5, women L2. Open M-Th 10am-5am, F 10am-6am, Sa 9pm-6am, Su 9pm-5am. Cash only.

Deja-Vu, Bd. Nicolae Bălcescu 25 (☎311 2322). M2: Pţa. Universităţii. Bring all the comrades to this faux-communist bar, decked out in propaganda and plenty of red paint. Plays mostly Club hits with some Russian pop favorites. Beer from L10. Mixed drinks L15-25. Open Su-Th 8pm-2am, F-Sa 8pm-5am. Cash only.

La Motor/Lăptăria, Bd. Nicolae Bălcescu 1-3 (☎315 8508; www.laptaria.totalnet.ro), on top of the National Theater. M2: Pţa. Universităţii. La Motor, on the outdoor terrace between the 3rd and 4th fl., becomes indoor Lăptăria in winter. In summer, students flock here for the the night air and cheap beer (L3-5) from the cabana-style bar. Bands occasionally play a variety of music at free open-air concerts at 9:30pm in the summer. Open M-Th and Su noon-2am, F-Sa noon-4am. Cash only.

Club Maxx, Str. Independenţei 290 (☎316 2435; www.clubmaxx.ro). M1: Grozăveşti. This giant room fills every night with crowds of raucous university students ready to enjoy the club's 2 bars and mix of blasting hip hop and house. The thriving night scene here in the student quarter, with several bars and clubs to choose from, is an alternative to the often more expensive and pretentious city center scene. Theme nights include F "Wet and Wild" Foam Party, Sa "Dancers Night," and Su "Ladies Night," when girls get free cocktails. Beer from L5. Attached pizza parlor; pizza from L6.50. Cover F-Sa men L15, women L5; F students free. Open daily 10pm-5am.

Queen's Club, Str. Mihai Bravu 32 (☎07 22 75 42 93; www.queen-s-club.ro). M1: Obor. From the Metro station head down Bravu. After the 3rd apartment block on the right, turn right into the yard and head to La Piazzetta restaurant. Queen's Club is in the restaurant's basement; ask the staff to point you to the stairs. This is the only GLBT nightspot in central Bucharest that seems to have any staying power longer than a few months. Flashing lights, a sizeable dance floor, loud house music, lots of guest DJs, drag performances, and theme nights make the club a favorite with the GLBT and straight crowd alike. Beer from L5. Mixed drinks from L12. Cover F midnight-close and all Sa L20; includes one drink. Open Th 9pm-5am, F-Sa 11pm-5am, Su 10pm-5am.

ROMANIAN MOONSHINE

If you're tired of basic local plum brandy, commonly served in restaurants and touted as the major local drink, you may want to branch out and try the stronger version, *palincă.* This locally produced moonshine, widely available—but never in stores—is a triple-distilled version of tamer *ţuică.* The alcohol content of *palincă* often exceeds 60%.

In towns, *palinca* is usually sold in produce markets along with all the other wholesome farm goods; in the countryside it is sold everywhere. It is commonly dispensed in old plastic drinking water bottles with labels removed. It has a light-yellow color, and its smell is deceptively weaker than one would imagine. Prices vary, but L10 per liter is usually fair.

As with any home-brew, a lot of caution is in order. Watch to see if a vendor's product is popular. If other locals are drinking it, chances are you can too. Still, *palincă*'s power lies in the fact that it goes down easily and disorients its drinker quite quickly, so know your limits. If you stay in a private home in Romania, especially in the countryside, you're more than likely to be offered a shot of the powerful pale brandy. If you accept, you'll be getting a real taste of the local culture—but those who taste too much might regret it in the morning.

WALLACHIA (ȚARA ROMÂNEASCĂ)

Known simply as "the Romanian Land," Wallachia is the heart of the country, the homeland of its royalty, and the seat of its capital. Along with Transylvania and Moldavia, it is one of Romania's three historical regions. Here, a giant plain of sunflowers rolls gently from the Carpathians down to the Black Sea.

SINAIA ☎(0)244

A few centuries ago, only monks had access to the striking natural beauty of Sinaia (see-NAH-yah; pop. 15,000), a small mountain town in the heart of the Carpathians. In the second half of the 19th century, however, the first king of Romania, Carol I, decided to move to the tiny monastic settlement for six months each year. Now Romania's preeminent mountain resort, the town is full of luxury hotels and restaurants catering to the summer vacationers who flock here for excellent hiking, beautiful views, and a royal palace unmatched in southeastern Europe.

TRANSPORTATION AND PRACTICAL INFORMATION. Sinaia's train station, on Str. Gării, down the hill from Bd. Carol I, sends **trains** to Brașov (1hr., 33 per day, L15), Bucharest (1½-2½hr., 27 per day, L30), and Cluj-Napoca (6hr., 6 per day, L54). The **CFR** office at the train station sells tickets. (☎54 20 80. Open M-F 9am-4pm. Cash only.) Cheap, quick **buses** run from the train station to Brașov and Bucharest (every 30min. 7am-9pm, L10).

To reach Sinaia's main street, **Bulevard Carol I,** from the station, simply walk up the stairs across the street from the station's main entrance. The street's commercial stretch is to the left. The helpful, English-speaking staff at the **tourist bureau,** Bd. Carol I 47, provides info about hiking, skiing, accommodations, and restaurants, as well as free hiking and city maps; more detailed maps are available for L15. (☎31 56 56; www.infosinaia.ro. Open M-F 8:30am-4:30pm, occasionally Sa or Su 10am-12:30pm. Cash only.) **Banca Comercială Română,** Bd. Carol I 49, cashes **traveler's checks** for a 1.5% commission (€5 min.) and has a 24hr. **ATM** and a 24hr. **currency exchange** machine. (☎31 01 25. Open M-F 8:30am-5:30pm, Sa 8:30am-12:30pm.) **Store luggage** at the train station. (Fewer than 4hr. L2; over 4hr. L4. Open daily 7:30am-7:30pm. Cash only.) A **pharmacy, Sensiblu,** Bd. Carol 8, is in the Hotel Sinaia complex. (☎31 25 25. Open M-F 8am-10pm, Sa 9am-9pm, Su 9am-2pm. MC/V.) 24hr. emergency medical services are available at the **Adult Emergency Centre,** Str. Cuza Voda 2, a block off of Bd. Carol I (☎31 38 88). An **Internet cafe** is in the shopping center at Bd. Carol I 41; follow the signs and go down the stairs outside the building. (☎31 30 30. L3 per hr. Open M-Sa 10am-10pm, Su noon-10pm. Cash only.) The **post office,** Bd. Carol I 33, has **Western Union** services. (Open M-F 7am-8pm, Sa 8am-1pm.) **Postal Code:** 106100.

Be wary of establishments in Sinaia billing themselves as "hostels." While some may have common areas like lounges and kitchens, they offer only private rooms, not dorm-style lodgings, and can be as expensive as *pensiunes.*

ACCOMMODATIONS AND FOOD. Though hotels in Sinaia typically run around €100 a night and even pensions generally cost €25, Sinaia does offer some budget options. Cheap mountain **cabanas** have reasonably priced dorms, singles, and doubles, but visitors should be aware that lifts up the mountain typically stop running at 5pm and mountain paths can be steep and are often dangerous in the dark. **Cabana Miorița ❶,** at Cota 2000, is equipped with a bar, restaurant, comfortable mattresses, and stunning views of mountain sunsets. (☎31 22 99. Reception 24hr. 12-bed dorms L20; 7-bed dorms L30; private rooms L40-50. Cash only.) If you'd like to avoid dealing with the lift schedule, **Hotel Intim ❶**, Str. Furnica 1, across from the main entrance of the monastery, is one of the cheapest options in town. Rooms in this old villa are bright, if slightly worn. (☎31 55 57. English spoken. Check-out noon. Singles L56; doubles L80; triples L75. Cash only.)

The **open-air market** (Piaţa Centrala Sinaia) is on Pţa. Unirii, just off Bd. Carol I next to the tourist bureau. (Open M-Sa 7am-9pm, Su 7am-5pm. Cash only.) **Restaurant Bucegi ❷**, Bd. Carol I 22, recreates the Carpathian wilderness with walls decorated in animal skins and rough-hewn wooden chandeliers. The staff serves traditional Romanian cuisine and—fittingly—specializes in game meat, including grilled bear and wild boar for L12. (☎31 39 02. English menu. Entrees L5.50-27. Beer from L3.50. Open daily 9am-10pm. MC/V.) The leather sofas of candlelit **Old Nick's Pub ❸**, Bd. Carol I 8, are a great place to kick back after a day of hiking and palace-gazing, whether it be for a drink or some great thin-crust pizza and pub fare. The most popular watering hole in town, Old Nick's recently opened a summer garden bar just inside the entrance to Park Dimitrie Ghica, where Bd. Carol meets Str. Octavian Goga. (☎31 24 91; www.oldnickpub.ro. Open daily 9am-2am. Pizza L11-18. Entrees L10-18. Beer from L5-12. Cash only.)

SIGHTS. Carol I, Romania's first king, designed the breathtaking **Peleş Castle** (Castelul Peleş) himself. A fantastic exterior of spires, colonnades, and Greco-Roman statuary is surpassed only by the interior. Visitors enter through a red-carpeted marble staircase, paneled in carved walnut and topped by a retractable stained-glass skylight. Every room has its own spectacular theme; no expense was spared in creating opulent Florentine halls, Turkish lounges, and Moorish parlors. Just down the road, **Pelişor Castle** (Castelul Pelişor) is modest only by comparison. It was built by King Carol I for his nephew and successor, Prince Ferdinand, and decorated by Ferdinand's wife Maria, in Art Nouveau style, with paintings by noted Romanian artists. An accomplished artist, Maria's works can be seen in the palace. Tours of Peleş are available in English and are included in the price of admission, while English-speaking visitors to Pelişor receive a sheet of info explaining the highlights of each room. Signs throughout town point toward the castles; both are a short walk up Str. Pelişului from the main road, Bd. Carol I. (☎31 09 18; www.peles.ro. Open June-Aug. Tu 11am-5pm, W-Su 9am-5pm; Sept.-May W-Su 9am-5pm; ticket office closes 4pm. Peleş L12, students L5. Pelişor L9/3. Photography L30. Cash only.)

The **Sinaia Monastery** (Mânăstirea Sinaia), at the intersection of Aleea Nifon and Aleea Carmen Silva, just off Str. Mânăstirii, was the area's first settlement when it was founded in 1695. It has housed monks ever since. There are two interior courtyards: the older one centers on a simple white chapel dating to the monastery's founding; visitors, however, are not allowed inside. The other courtyard features a church in the Byzantine-Moldovan style, which hides several political messages in its decor. A small **museum** houses religious artifacts and the first Bible printed in Romanian. (☎31 49 17. Monastery open daily 9:30am-6pm. English captions. Free. English pamphlet L3. Museum open July-Sept. Tu-Sa 9am-5pm. L4, students L2.)

HIKING. There are numerous **hiking** and **skiing** opportunities in this mountain village; the trails are dotted with **cabanas** that offer beds (L5-50) and meals (from L5). **Cable cars** are the best way to get to the trails; **Telecabină**, the base station, is a short walk uphill from Bd. Carol, behind the Hotel New Montana. The first leg of the cable car runs to the Cota 1400 station, which contains a luxury hotel, a *cabana*, and a few restaurants, including a snack stop with cheap meat grills (L1.50-8.50). The second leg goes to the Cota 2000 station, which contains the Salvamont station, Cabana Mioriţa, and a small restaurant. (☎31 19 39. Cars run June-Aug. and Dec.-Feb. M 10:30am-5pm, Tu-Su 8:30am-5pm; Sept.-Nov. and Mar.-May Tu-Su 8:30am-5pm; last car usually 4:45pm. Sinaia-Cota 1400 or Cota 1400-Cota

ROMANIA

2000 L12, round-trip L20; Sinaia-Cota 2000 L21/40. Cash only.) Several trails start from the Cota 2000 station, marked by posts with colored stripes. The **yellow stripe trail** is a 4-5hr. hike past **Mt. Babele** (2200m; 2-2½hr.) to **Mt. Omu** (2505m), the Bucegi range's highest peak. **Cabana Omu,** the highest-altitude chalet in Romania, offers meals and inexpensive lodging year-round (☎02 44 32 06 77. Meals from L8. Beds from L20.) The **yellow cross trail** is a 2-2½hr. hike downhill to **Cabana Zanoaga** (☎07 45 77 21 76; 1400m) along a river that runs off from the mist-shrouded, mirror-like mountain lake **Lacul Bolboci.** The **red stripe trail** toward **Cabana Padina** (☎07 23 31 59 11; 1525m) is a 2-2½hr. journey into a valley past the Pestera caves. Serious hikers can trek 6-8 hr. to **Bran Castle** (p. 527) by taking the yellow stripe trail to the summit of Mt. Omu, and then transferring to the red stripe trail down to Bran. **Salvamont,** the mountain-rescue organization, can be reached at ☎31 31 31.

TRANSYLVANIA (TRANSILVANIA)

ROMANIA

Though the name evokes images of a dark, evil land of black magic and vampires, Transylvania (also known as Ardeal), with a history of Saxon settlement dating back to the 12th century, is a relatively Westernized region that sees the biggest share of tourists in Romania. Its green hills and mountains descend from the rugged Carpathians in the south to the Hungarian Plain in the northwest. The vampire legends do, however, resonate with the region's architecture: Transylvanian buildings are tilted, jagged, and more sternly Gothic than anywhere else in Europe. Medieval cities make this area a favorite of travelers, while hikers revel in the untamed wilderness of the misty Făgăraş Mountains.

BRAŞOV ☎(0)268

The historic center of Braşov (BRAH-shohv; pop. 281,400) is a kaleidoscopic maze of 800-year-old buildings. Surrounded by the Carpathian mountains, Braşov's Old Town is dominated by the gothic Black Church and filled with picturesque squares, tiny, winding streets, and broad tree-lined boulevards, making it the perfect place for a nighttime stroll. The town is also the natural base camp for excursions to Poiana Braşov's ski slopes, Bran Castle, and the ruins at Râşnov.

TRANSPORTATION. The train station (☎41 02 33) is along Bd. Gării, southwest of the Old Town. **Train** destinations from Braşov include Bucharest (2½-3hr., 26 per day, L40), Cluj-Napoca (5hr., 8 per day, L53), and Sibiu (2½-3½hr., 10 per day, L31). Buy tickets at **CFR,** Bd. 15 Noiembrie 43. (☎47 06 96. Open M-F 7am-8pm. Cash only.) Braşov has two main bus stations: Autogară 1, next to the train station, is the main depot; Autogară 2 (☎42 72 67), Str. Avram Iancu 114, called "Gara Bartolomeu," runs **buses** to Râşnov and Bran. To get there, take bus #12 from the main bus stop at center of town, Livada Postei, at the west end of Bd. Eroilor. Buy tickets (L1.50 per ride) for **city buses** at "R.A.T." kiosks scattered throughout town.

ORIENTATION AND PRACTICAL INFORMATION. The city is divided into the picturesque Old Town, wedged in a valley between two tall mountains, and the surrounding communist-era sprawl. The Old Town includes two districts. The old Saxon center, called **Kronstadt,** lies at the mouth of the valley and centers on **Piața Sfântului** and **Biserica Neagră** (Black Church). **Schei,** the old Romanian district, is farther up the valley and centered on the smaller **Piața Unirii.** To get to the Old Town from the train station or from Autogară 1, take bus #4 to the last stop, Livada Postei. From there walk along Str. Mureşenilor for just a few short minutes to reach Piața Sfântului. Alternatively, take bus #51 from the station to the last stop, Piața Unirii. On foot, cross the street in front of the train station and head down

Bulevard Victoriei. Turn right on **Strada Mihai Kogălniceanu,** then bear right on **Bulevard 15 Noiembrie,** which becomes **Bulevard Eroilor. Strada Republicii** and **Strada Mureşenilor** branch off 1km apart, both converging on Pţa. Sfantului. Taxi fare from the train station to the Old Town should be L5-6.

The multilingual staff at the **tourist information bureau,** housed in the yellow clock-tower building in Pţa. Sfatului, offers free **maps,** English pamphlets, and information about accommodations and hiking. (☎41 90 78; www.brasovcity.ro. Open daily 9am-5pm.) More detailed maps and **hiking maps** are sold at *librarie* (bookstores) along Str. Republicii; try **Libraria Ralu,** Str. Republicii 54, which sells maps for L8-15. (☎47 39 32. Open M-F 10am-7pm, Sa 10am-5pm. MC/V.) **Banca Comercială Română,** Pţa. Sfatului 14, cashes **American Express Travelers Cheques** for a 1.5% commission, **exchanges currency,** and has a 24hr. **ATM.** (☎47 71 09. Open M-F 8:30am-5pm, Sa 8:30am-12:30pm.) A **pharmacy,** Aurofarm, is at Str. Republicii 27. (☎47 56 27. Open daily 8am-midnight. V.) **Non-stop Internet** is at Str. G Bariţiu 8, just off Pţa. Sfatului. (Open 24hr. L2 per hr. Cash only). The **post office,** Nicolae Iorga 1, on Pţa. Revolutiei, provides **Western Union** services. (☎41 22 22. Open M-F 7am-8pm, Sa 8am-1pm. Cash only.) **:** 500001.

ACCOMMODATIONS AND FOOD. The market for **private rooms** is booming. In high season, vendors go tourist hunting in the train station. Look at the room and agree on a price (€15 is reasonable) before you accept. For a sure thing, head to **Kismet Dao Villa Hostel ❶,** Str. Democraţiei 2b, formerly known as Elvis's Villa Hostel. From Pţa. Unirii, walk up Str. Bâlea and turn right. Comfortable rooms with balconies complement plentiful common space and a social, international atmosphere. Free perks include Internet access, Wi-Fi, breakfast, laundry, and one beer, soda, or bottled water per day. (☎51 42 96; www.kismetdoa.com. English spoken. Check-out noon. Daytrip to Bran, Râşnov, and Peleş Castle L60. 8- to 10-bed dorms L40; 6-bed dorms L42-45; doubles L110. MC/V.) For Romanian hospitality and spacious rooms, try **Eugene Junior ❷,** Str. Neagoe Basarab 1. The house benefits from the personal warmth of the family's decor, including woven cloth, carpets, and paintings. From Bd. 15 Novembrie, turn on Str. Matei Basarab; it's at the intersection with Str. N. Basarab. (☎07 22 54 25 81; ejrr68@yahoo.com. Call or email ahead, and Eugene, who speaks English, will pick you up. Kitchen facilities. Useful hand-drawn map free. Breakfast L5. Laundry L5. Doubles L100; triples L129; quads L160. Min. 2 night stay in the summer. Cash only.)

ROMANIAN HOLIDAY

While most castles close to tourists at night, one member of the Translyvanian aristocracy has decided to change the rules. Count Tibor Kalnoky, descended from an ancient line of Magyar nobles, has converted one of his family's ancestral homes, located in the quiet village of Micloşoara, north of Braşov, into a guesthouse.

When the communists came to power, Count Kalnoky's aristocratic family relocated to America and were stripped of their possessions. After the fall of communism and a lengthy battle to reclaim their property, however, the family has returned to its ancestral lands—and they've invited guests along for the ride. For €125 per day, guests get royal treatment in the stunning rooms of a centuries-old manor home, including three restaurant meals, free-flowing wine, activities like horseback riding and hiking, and tours to numerous destinations in Transylvania. But, more importantly, guests also earn bragging rights; they stayed in the same rooms that once hosted members of the British royal family, not to mention the Kalnoky line since the Middle Ages.

☎07 42 20 25 86; www.transylvaniancastle.com. Bed and breakfast €49; all-inclusive €125.

SON OF A...

'es, Dracula did exist—sort of. He vas not the ruler of Transylvania, but of Wallachia; he was not a count, but a *voivode* (a local governor or "prince"); and he was not a vampire. Still, the truth about Vlad Țepeș (1431-1476) is enough to make anyone lock the id to his or her coffin at night.

Dracula's story begins with his ather, the ruthless Vlad Basarab, vho became known as Vlad Dracul (dragon) for his membership in the Order of the Dragon. Drac" in Romanian can be transated as either dragon or, fittingly, devil. In a diplomatic move, Dracul sent his 10-year-old son, Dracula (Son of the Dragon), to he Ottoman Empire as a hostage n 1442. There, Vlad learned his preferred method of torture: mpalement. Victims of impalement—which involved the insertion of a large wooden stake into he victim's body, avoiding piercing the vital organs—begged for a swift death throughout the slow, agonizing process of blood loss and exposure to the elements.

Known as Vlad the Impaler, Dracula impaled not only murderers, thieves, and political rivals but also the destitute and the crippled n a bid to rid his territory of poverty. His crowning achievement, however, was in turning the Turks' gruesome practice against them. n 1462, the invading Turks turned ail at Wallachia's border, which had been decorated with 20,000 of their impaled countrymen.

The open-air market, **Agro Central,** and a 24hr. supermarket are conveniently located next to each other at Str. Nicolae Balcescu 62. (Open daily dawn-dusk. Cash only.) The **supermarket** is sizeable and well stocked. (☎41 98 28. 24hr. AmEx/MC/V.) More upscale options surround Pța. Sfatului. **Bella Muzica ❸,** Str. G Barițiu 2, is across Pța. Sfatului from Str. Mureșenilor. Make your way through the music store and downstairs to a candlelit wine cellar. Bella offers an eclectic Romanian-Hungarian-Mexican menu, including the Romanian peasant dish "Maramureșan Bulz" (maize pudding with bacon and a fried egg; L13). Free chips and a free shot of *palincă* (Romanian plum moonshine) complete the meal. (☎47 69 46. English menu. Entrees L9-45. Open daily noon-11pm. MC/V.) **Taverna ❹,** Str. Politechnicii 6, is also near the city center. From Pța. Sfatului, walk up Str. Republicii and go right. This classy restaurant, with warm red walls, has a menu that features a long list of Romanian, Hungarian, and French dishes. (☎47 46 18. English menu. Entrees L11-44. Open daily noon-midnight. AmEx/MC/V.)

SIGHTS. The area surrounding Pța. Sfatului is perfect for a stroll, as is Str. Republicii, the main pedestrian drag. Jagged and aging, Romania's largest Gothic cathedral looms above the square along Str. Gh. Barițiu. The **Black Church** (Biserica Neagră, or Schwartzen Kirche) earned its name in 1689 when it was charred by the Great Fire that destroyed most of Brașov. Inside, the classically austere gothic interior is decorated with a renowned collection of 119 Anatolian carpets, compliments of 17th- and 18th-century German merchants, and an enormous 4000-pipe silver organ, the largest in southeastern Europe. (Open June 15th-Sept. 15th M-Sa 10am-5pm; Sept. 16th-June 14th M-Sa 10am-3:30pm. L4, students L2. Organ concerts June and Sept. Tu 6pm; July-Aug. Tu, Th, Sa 6pm. L4. Cash only.) The expansive view from the summit of **Mt. Tâmpa** shows the stark contrast between the spires and cobblestone of old Kronstadt and the concrete of new Brașov. Follow the red triangle markings to hike to the top (1½hr.), or take the *telecabina* (cable car). From Pța. Sfatului, walk down Apollonia Hirscher, go left on Str. Castelui, then right on Suișul Castelui, and head upstairs. (Cable car runs M noon-5:45pm, Tu-F 9:30am-5:45pm, Sa-Su 9:30am-6:45pm. L5, round-trip L7. Cash only.) Follow the blue stripe trail (15min.) to the peak. Pța. Unirii is home to **St. Nicholas's Church** (Biserică Sfântu Nicolae), built in 1495. The church's jagged black spires shelter a low-roofed interior filled to the brim with icons and colorful murals. **Romania's First School** (Prima Școală Românească), now a museum on the church grounds, traces the history of Romanians in old Saxon Kronstadt and displays the first Romanian books printed in the Latin alphabet. (☎51 14 11. No English captions. Church open daily 8am-6pm. Liturgy 9am, vespers 6pm. Free. School open daily 9am-5pm. L5, students L3. Cash only.)

ENTERTAINMENT AND NIGHTLIFE. Braşov's artistic offerings are rich and cheap; the season runs Sept.-July. For the **opera** and **orchestra,** tickets are sold at the box office on Str. Gh. Bariţiu 20, the **Agencia Teatrală de Bilete.** Shows are usually once or twice a week. (☎47 18 89. Open Tu-F 10am-5pm, Sa 10am-2pm. Opera tickets L8-10, students L3; orchestra tickets L10/5. Cash only.) The **Opera House** (Opera Braşov) is at Str. Biserica Române 51 (☎41 59 90; www.operabrasov.ro); the **Cercul Militar Braşov** hosts the Filarmonica Braşov orchestra at Str. Mureşenilor 29 (☎47 30 58). For **theater** tickets, go to the **Teatrul Dramatic** at Pţa. Teatrului 1, along Bd. Eriolor going away from the city center. (☎41 88 50. Performances usually F, Sa, Su at 7pm. Box office open Tu-F 11am-7pm, Sa-Su 3-7pm. L4-9. Cash only.) The summer months bring both the **International Chamber Music Festival,** held the first week of September, and the **Golden Stag Festival** (Cerbul de Aur; www.cerbuldeaur.ro), held in Pţa. Sfatului at the end of August, which showcases a wide variety of Romanian and international pop musicians.

Saloon, Str. Mureşenilor 11, is a tourist favorite by day (decent pizza L8.50-15) and a hotspot by night, offering a selection of imported beers (L4-10) and mixed drinks (L8-13). On Friday and Saturday nights, Saloon opens its popular basement lounge, **Harley,** a techno and hip-hop club full of black leather couches and with a steel bar only vaguely reminiscent of the motorcycle brand. (☎41 77 05. Saloon open daily 9am-2am. Harley open 11pm-6am. Cash only.)

ROMANIA

DAYTRIPS FROM BRAŞOV

BRAN CASTLE

From Braşov, take a taxi or city bus #12 to Autogara 2. From there, catch an intercity bus to Bran (45min., every 30-60min. 7am-11:30pm, L3.50.) Get off when you see the souvenir market or the "Cabana Bran Castle—500m" sign. Backtrack along the road; the castle is on the right amid souvenir shops. ☎23 83 33; www.brancastlemuseum.ro. English captions. Castle and village open M noon-6pm, Tu-Su 9am-6pm. L12, students L6. Cash only.

Ever since Bram Stoker's novel identified **Bran Castle** with **Count Dracula,** castle and legend have been linked in popular imagination. But the history of this small turreted castle is more complicated than fables suggest. Residents of Bran built the castle in the 14th century to guard against Turkish invaders and to serve as a tollbooth along the trade route through Transylvania. In the early 15th century, the Hungarian king gave the castle to local ruler Mircea the Old, the grandfather of Vlad Ţepeş, or **Vlad the Impaler**—the historical model of the count-vampire. During his own reign, Vlad never ruled from Bran Castle; his only tie to it was his one-time imprisonment here by the Hungarian king in 1462. The restored castle commands a good view of both Bran and the surrounding countryside, and contains furnished rooms from the Middle Ages through the 20th century. Despite the absence of Dracula in the castle's exhibits, dozens of stands outside sell vampire paraphernalia, from toy stakes to "blood wine," at what is very much a tourist attraction.

RÂŞNOV FORTRESS

Most buses to Bran stop in Râşnov (25min.), and direct buses to Râşnov depart from Autogara 2 every 30min. (L2.50). From the bus stop, follow Str. Republicii past an open-air market. Following the signs for Muzeu Cetate, go right and then left through an arch. ☎23 02 55. English captions. Open daily 9am-7pm. L10.

On a windswept hill near **Râşnov** sits a **ruined fortress** topped by an immense wooden crucifix. Much of the fortress has been renovated recently, with whole towers, gates, inner cottages, rooms, and dungeons restored, but work continues on the topmost portion, which shows every one of its nearly 800 years. Drop a coin down the spectacularly deep well (146m), dug in 17 years by two Turkish prisoners in exchange for their freedom, which enabled the fortress to withstand sieges throughout its centuries of use. The small museum houses a collection of the weapons used to protect the fortress over the ages. The experience is less touristy than Bran, and the panoramic view from the top is breathtaking.

POIANA BRAŞOV

Take Braşov city bus #20 (25min., 2-3 per hr. 7am-10pm, L3.50) from Livada Postei, at the western end of Bd. Eroilor. Make sure to buy a special ticket for Poiana Braşov from the R.A.T. kiosk, as it both looks and is priced differently than a normal city bus ticket. A taxi from town costs L30.

If Sinaia is Romania's longstanding summer alpine resort, Poiana Braşov (POY-ah-nah BRAH-shohv) is its younger winter sibling. Nine ski slopes served by three big cable-car lifts, picture-perfect mountain vistas, and four- and five-star lodging attract an international crowd in winter, with a similar (although smaller) crowd during the summer. **Ski rental** starts at €10 per day, with daytime lift tickets from L80 and lessons from €15 per hr. **Equipment rental** is available at the base; nearly all staff are multilingual. The **Centru de Echitaţie** (Equestrian Center), down the road toward Braşov from the main resort area, has **horseback riding** for L40 per hr. To avoid the throngs of luxury hotels, a budget traveler can book a room in cheaper Braşov or rent a two-floor **cabin** from the equestrian center. (☎26 21 61. Horse rental daily 8am-noon and 2-5pm. Kitchenettes, baths, and cable TV. 3-person cabins L200; 4-5 person cabins L300. Cash only.)

In the summer months when snow is in short supply, the scene revolves around hiking and bicycling, playing tennis, and lounging about on the meadows. Those feeling motivated to conquer the mountain can take the **red cross trail** from the base up to the summit of Vf. Cristianul Mare (1690m; 1½hr.). Alternatively, one of the ski lifts, **Kanzel,** operates in the summer and takes visitors to the summit in just 5min. Go right on the main road from the bus stop past the stadium. (Open 9am-4:20pm. L13, round-trip L20. Cash only). From the top of the Kanzel lift, the **blue stripe trail** goes over the ridge of the mountain, with stunning drop-offs on either side, to the summit of Vf. Postvaru (1799m; 15-30min.). The trail then continues on downhill to the town of Timisu de Jos (2½hr.). From the base of the mountains, the **red stripe trail** takes hikers back to Bran (1hr.).

SIGHIŞOARA ☎(0)265

Known as the "Pearl of Transylvania" and the birthplace of Vlad Ţepeş, the "real" Dracula, Sighişoara (see-ghee-SHWAH-rah; pop. 32,200), looks just like you'd imagine Dracula's hometown: cobblestone streets wind around Gothic spires, and a centuries-old Saxon clock tower houses a torture chamber. One of the best-preserved medieval citadels in Europe crowns the hillside town. And no visit to Transylvania is complete without a nighttime stroll among the tombs of Sighişoara's enormous hilltop graveyard, which is enough to make even the most stout-hearted believe, if only just for a moment, in vampires.

TRANSPORTATION AND PRACTICAL INFORMATION. Trains run from Str. Libertăţii 51 to: Alba Iulia (1½hr., 4 per day, L25); Bucharest (4½hr., 10 per day, L49) via Braşov (1½-2½hr., 19 per day, L30); and Cluj-Napoca (3hr., 7 per day, L41). **Buses** leave from Str. Libertăţii 57 for Sibiu (5 per day, L13) and other locations.

(Ticket offices open 6am-8pm.) To rent **bikes,** either head to **Gia Hostel** on Str. Libertății 41, near the train station (☎77 24 86; www.hotelgia.com; L30 per day; open daily 8am-late; cash only) or to the **Cultural Heritage Info Center** (see below) in the citadel. (Bike rental ☎07 47 35 68 10. €1 per hr. Cash only.)

The walk from the train or bus station to the center is about 10min.; turn right on Str. Libertății, then left on Str. Gării. Veer left at the cemetery, go right through the church courtyard, cross the pedestrian bridge over the river **Târana Mare,** and turn left on **Strada Morii.** A right at the fork leads to **Strada O. Goga,** the **citadel** *(cetatea)*, the center of the modern town, and Str. Oberth. If all else fails, aim for the highly visible clock tower. A left leads to the main street, **Strada 1 Decembrie 1918.** For free detailed **maps** of Sighișoara and numerous other Romanian cities, visit the UNESCO-sponsored **Cultural Heritage Info Center,** Str. Muzeului 6, in the citadel and across from the Monastery Church. The helpful English-speaking staff provides info on everything from restaurants and sights to hay-rides in the countryside and all types of accommodations. (☎07 88 11 55 11; sighisoara@dordeduca.ro. Open daily 9am-6pm.) **Banca Transilvania,** Str. Oberth 15, **exchanges currency,** cashes **traveler's checks** for 1.5% commision (min. US$5), and has **Western Union** and a 24hr. **ATM.** (☎77 27 19; www.bancatransilvania.ro. Open M-F 9am-5pm, Sa 9:30am-12:30pm.) The train station has **luggage storage.** (L4. Open 24hr.) The **Aescalop pharmacy** is at Str. Oberth 22. (☎77 99 13. Open M-F 9am-7pm, Sa 9am-2pm. Cash only.) **Culture Cafe,** in the citadel, attached to Burg Hostel, has **Internet** access. (☎77 84 89. L3.50 per hr. Open daily 7am-late. MC/V.) The **telephone office** (☎77 77 01; open M-F 9am-6pm, Sa 9am-1pm; MC/V) and the **post office** are at Str. Oberth 16-17. The post office has **Western Union** services and **Poste Restante** at window #5. (☎77 41 10. Open M-F 7am-8pm.) **Postal Code:** 545400.

ACCOMMODATIONS AND FOOD. **Private rooms** (US$10-15) are available in the Old Town. Check out the room and negotiate the price before agreeing to anything. The storied **Nathan's Villa Hostel ❶,** Str. Libertății 8, a right turn out of the train station, is one of Transylvania's leading party hostels, attracting rambunctious travelers from all over the world. Ask the charismatic American owner to make his famous punch. (☎77 25 46; www.nathansvilla.com. Breakfast and laundry included. 12-bed dorms L35; doubles L80. Cash only.) In the the citadel is HI-affiliated **Burg Hostel ❶,** Str. Bastionului 4-6, in the square near the clock tower. An international crowd fills rooms with comfortable bunk beds upstairs and a joint bar and Internet cafe in the exposed brick cellar. (☎77 84 89; www.ibz.ro. English spoken. Breakfast L12; lunch L18; dinner L15. Beer L3-5. Laundry L5. 24hr. reception. Check-out noon. 5- to 7-bed dorms L35; single with shared bath L53, with private bath L83; doubles L83/100; triples L105/120. 10% HI discount. MC/V.) **Pensiune Chic ❶,** directly across from the train station at Str. Libertății 44, offers clean, spacious, and brightly decorated rooms at reasonable prices. (☎77 59 01; www.sighisoara-tourism.com. Check-out noon. Singles with shared bath L45; doubles with shared bath L59-69, with private bath L95. Cash only.)

Grocery stores line Str. 1 Decembrie 1918. An **open-air market** in Pța. Agroalimentară has a good selection of produce and cheeses; from the train station, follow Str. Libertății and cross the bridge. (Open daily dawn-dusk.) **Cafe Rustic ❷,** Str. 1 Decembrie 1918 5, serves Transylvanian dishes in a dark wood-and-brick-paneled dining room that is, indeed, rustic. The cafe turns into an quiet, atmospheric bar at night. (Entrees L5.50-28. Beer L3-4. Open M-Th 9am-midnight, F-Su 9am-1am. Cash only.) In the Citadel, try **Casa Vlad Dracul ❹,** Str. Cositorarilor 5, under the big metal dragon sign. Vlad was indeed born here in 1431 and lived here for the next five years. The medieval decor is fittingly spooky, and the traditional dishes are top-notch. (☎77 15 96. Entrees L11-41. Open 24hr. Cash only.)

SIGHTS AND FESTIVALS. The **Citadel,** built by the Saxons in 1191, is a truly fantastic medieval city-within-a-city. Enter through the **Clock Tower** (Turnul cu Ceas), Pţa. Muzeului 1, off Str. O. Goga, which houses the eclectic **Museum of History.** Climb to the top to see the clock's mechanism and painted figurines representing the days of the week. The deck above provides an expansive view of the area. On the way up to the top of the clock tower, each floor features exhibits on the city's history. To the left as you leave the tower, the **Museum of Medieval Armory** (Colecţia de Arme Medievale) displays weapons from all over the world and maintains a small exhibit on Vlad Ţepeş. Underneath the clock tower, the **Torture Room** (Camera de Tortura) houses a tiny but gruesome collection of pain-inflicting instruments and shackles. (☎77 11 08. Open M 10am-4:30pm, Tu-F 9am-6:30pm, Sa-Su 9am-4:30pm. Some English captions. Clock tower and Museum of History L5, students L2.5. Museum of Medieval Armory L4/2. Torture room L3. All 3 museums L10. Photography L30 per museum. Cash only.) Across the street at Str. Cositorarilor 13, the 13th-century Lutheran **Monastery Church** (Biserica Mănăstrii) was originally built by Dominican monks, who cleared out when the Reformation came to Transylvania. Turkish rugs donated by passing German merchants hang on the walls. Organ concerts are held Friday afternoons at 6pm. (☎77 11 95. English pamphlets. Open Tu-Sa 10am-5pm, Su 11:15am-3pm. L2, students L1. Organ concerts L4.) A left up Str. Şcolii reveals the long, tunnel-enclosed 179-step **stairway,** built in 1642 to help children get to school. At the top is the Gothic **Church on the Hill** (Biserica din Deal), Str. Scării 10, which dates to the 15th century. Its walls were once covered in medieval frescoes: many were destroyed by overzealous Reformers, but some have since been restored. The **crypt** under the altar, the only crypt in existence in Transylvania, is now just an empty shell. Don't miss the huge, spooky hilltop graveyard—and remember your wooden stake. (Church and crypt open daily 10am-6pm. L2, students L1. No cameras.) The second weekend in July brings the **Medieval Festival** to Sighişoara. The **Folk Art Festival** arrives in late August.

SIBIU ☎(0)269

The one-time capital of Transylvania, Sibiu (SEE-bee-oo; pop. 154,800) remains a town of medieval monuments and ornate architecture. The city's colorful Old Town and proximity to some of the best hiking in the country, as well as its reign as the European Cultural Capital in 2007, have recently led to the town's reinvention as a major tourist destination. But if the center ever feels too crowded, an escape to the stunning Făgăraş mountains is just a short trip away.

TRANSPORTATION. Trains run to: Braşov (2½-3½hr., 10 per day, L31); Bucharest (5hr., 4 per day, L53); Cluj-Napoca (4hr., 1 per day, L41); Timişoara (5-6hr., 3 per day, L53). **CFR,** Str. N. Bălcescu 6, past Hotel Împăratul Romanilor from Pţa. Mare, sells tickets. (☎21 20 85. Open M-F 7am-8pm. Cash only.) **Buses** run to: Braşov (3hr., 4 per day, L20); Bucharest (5hr., 7 per day, L34); Cluj-Napoca (3½hr., 4 per day, L20) via Alba Iulia (1½hr., 4 per day, L12); Timişoara (5½hr., 2 per day, L32). The bus station, Autogara Transmixt, is beside the train station; incoming microbuses can drop off in Pţa. Unirii or elsewhere. **Microbuses** run by C&I Transport (☎02 63 21 36 21), which stop in front of Hotel Parc, 10min. from Pţa. Unirii, are a cheap, fast option. They run to numerous destinations, including Sighişoara (2½hr., 3 per day, L13).

ORIENTATION AND PRACTICAL INFORMATION. The train and bus stations are at Pţa. 1 Decembrie 1918, about 2km east of the city center. Bus #5 runs to the center (L1; buy tickets from R.A.T. kiosks or the tourist office), and a taxi to the center will cost about L5. From the station, turn left on **Strada General Magheru** to reach the center. At the small square with a statue of Nicolaus

Olahus, either take the left fork or bear right on **Strada Avram Iancu.** Both routes lead to the main square of the Old Town, **Piața Mare.** To the right, through the tunnels, is **Piața Mică.** To reach **Piața Unirii,** the modern main square, proceed through Pța. Mare and down **Strada Nicolae Bălcescu.**

The English-speaking staff at Sibiu's **tourist information center,** Pța. Mare 7, provides detailed free **maps** of the city. (☎20 89 13; www.sibiu.ro. Open M-F 9am-5pm; Sa 10am-1pm.) **Librăria Friedrich Schiller,** Pța. Mare 7, sells city and hiking guides and maps for L7-14. (☎20 89 13. Open M-F 10am-7pm, Sa 10am-6pm, Su 11:30am-6pm. Cash only.) **Banca Comercială Română,** Str. Bălcescu 11, cashes **traveler's checks** for 1.5% commission (€5 min.), and has a 24hr. **ATM** and **currency exchange machine.** (☎21 83 45. Open M-F 8:30am-5:30pm, Sa 8:30am-12:30pm.) MasterCard and Visa **ATMs** are on Str. Bălcescu, on Calea Dumărăvii, and in Pța. Unirii. **Farmacia Farmasib** is at Str. Bălcescu 53. (☎21 78 97. Open M-F 7am-9pm, Sa-Su 8am-9pm. Open 24hr. for emergencies. MC/V.) The **telephone office** is at Str. Bălcescu 13. (☎20 41 10. Open M-F 9am-6pm, Sa 9am-1pm. MC/V.) For **Internet** access, try to find the **Hidden Internet Cafe** on Str. N. Bălcescu 51. (☎03 69 11 01 039. 7am-11pm L1.70 per hr., 11pm-7am L1.25 per hr. Open 24hr. Cash only.) The **post office,** Str. Metropoliei 14, has **Western Union** and **Poste Restante** at window #2. (☎23 22 22. Open M-F 7am-8pm, Sa 8am-1pm.) **Postal Code:** 550450.

ACCOMMODATIONS AND FOOD. At just about the most convenient and central location in town, **Old Town Hostel (HI) ❷,** Pța. Mică 26, has very spacious rooms with high ceilings, plenty of comfy armchairs, and big windows overlooking the square. (☎21 64 45; www.hostelsibiu.ro. Laundry L7. Free Internet. Bike rental L35 per day. 7- to 12-bed dorms L45. Cash only.) **Pensiuna Ela ❷,** Str. Nouă 43, is a bit of a walk from the city center, but worth it for thick mattresses and well-decorated, spacious rooms with TVs, private baths, kitchen, and peaceful backyard terrace. From Pța. Mare, proceed through the clock tower, across Pța. Mica, and down a hill. Continue on Str. Ocnei and make a right on Str. Nouă. (☎21 51 97; www.ela-hotels.ro. English spoken. Breakfast L15. Book ahead. Singles L110; doubles L125; triples L160. MC/V.) To reach hotel **Pensiune Leu** (Lion) **❷,** Str. Moș Ion Roată 6, walk along Str. S. Brukenthall from Pța. Mare until it ends, and continue down the staircase on the right. Follow the road, looping back to Str. Moș Ion Roată. This centrally located hotel offers low prices, bright rooms, free laundry service, a bar, and hot showers. (☎21 83 92. Reception 24hr. Singles L50; doubles L100; triples L150. Cash only.)

To find the large **open-air market,** in Pța. Cibin, walk north from the city center down Str. Turnului. (Open dawn-dusk. Meat and dairy section open M-F 7am-8pm, Sa 7am-4pm, Su 7am-1pm.) Past the open-air market, across the bridge on Str. Reconstructiei 2a, is **Supermarket Cora.** (☎07 28 15 98 30. Open 24hr. Cash only.) For authentic, cheap eats, head to **Crama Ileana ❷,** Pța. Teatrului 2, downhill and to the left from Pța. Unirii, off a side street called Str. Berariei. The food's as traditional as it gets, with a wide variety of rural dishes in a setting that looks like an old peasant's cabin. (☎43 43 43. English menu. Entrees L7.50-24. Open daily noon-midnight. Cash only.) For even cheaper Transylvanian food, walk north on Str. Turnului, pass the open-air market, cross the bridge, and veer left onto Str. Reconstructiei, which will turn into Str. Tudor Vladimescu, to get to **Kon-Tiki ❷,** Str. Tudor Vladimirescu 12. Don't be fooled by the no-frills decor: the absolutely delicious *ciorbă de burtă* (pork soup; L5) is a local favorite. (☎22 03 50. Entrees L5-15. Open M-Sa 10am-10pm, Su noon-10pm. Cash only.)

SIGHTS AND FESTIVALS. The biggest attraction lies just outside of town. The **ASTRA Museum of Traditional Folk Civilization** (Muzeul Civilizatiei Populare Tradiționale ASTRA), in a forest preserve surrounding a lake south of the center, is one of the country's finest open-air exhibits. It's a 4km hike from Pța. Unirii along Calea Dumbravii; your best bet is a taxi (about L10) or bus T1 from the bus station to its final stop (1 per hr. from 9:40am). At 96,000 sq. km, the museum occupies a fair bit of local forest and displays a large collection of buildings from across the country, such as mills, peasant farmsteads, taverns, a dancing pavilion, and an old plum brandy distillery. The museum's 17th-century **Orthodox church,** billed as the "Sistine Chapel of Wooden Churches," is covered inside with original paintings. (☎24 25 99. Open Tu-Su 10am-6pm. Few English captions. L15, students L4. English guidebooks L2. Tours in English L30 per hr. Call ahead to reserve. Cash only.) Back in the city center, the city's beautiful 14th-century Gothic cathedral, Pţa. Huet 1, now a **Lutheran Church,** is topped by unusually colorful, tiled towers with golden orbs. (☎21 12 03. Some English captions. Open M-Sa 9am-8pm, Su 11am-8pm. L3, students L1. Cash only.) **Muzeul Naţional Brukenthall,** Str. Metropoliei 2 and Pţa. Mare 7-9, has two branches. The building on Str. Metropoliei houses a history museum that features an impressive armory, Roman statuary, and various treasures from the House of Brukenthall, a branch of the Habsburgs whose head served as Governor of Transylvania. (☎21 81 43; www.brukenthalmuseum.ro. Open Tu-Su 10am-6pm. Some English captions. L12, students L3.) The royal palace on Pţa. Mare displays a genuinely impressive art collection, including several notable Renaissance paintings, and furnished rooms which have been restored to their former royal glory. (☎21 76 91. Some English captions. Open Tu-Su 9am-6pm. L12, students L3.) The **International Theater Festival,** in the first week of June, attracts groups from around the world. **Summer Fest** rages June 15 to September 15 near Pţa. Unirii, with free open-air concerts Thursday and Friday nights. The **Medieval Festival** arrives in the last two weeks of August.

HIKING. The **Făgăraş Mountains** extend about 70km from the Olt Valley to the Piatra Craiului Mountains, with a sharp ridge running east-west above the treeline. Wildflower meadows, cloud-shrouded summits, and superb views of Wallachian plains and Transylvanian hills have earned the Făgăraş renown among Romanian hikers. For food, shelter, and basic supplies, **cabanas** dot the area. Most are 500m up in the lowlands, where facilities are more posh, or the middle uplands (1500m); few are above the treeline (2000m). Some offer sleeping sacks (L10-15); others have doubles with baths (L30-80).

Before hiking, stop by the tourist office (see **Orientation and Practical Information,** p. 530), or Salvamont (see below), for info about various trails and to inquire about hiring guides. Trail maps and hiking guidebooks can be purchased at **Librăria Friedrich Schiller** (see **Orientation and Practical Information,** p. 530). There are two ways to get to the mountains: by car or by *personal* (slow) train. **Advantage Rent-A-Car** is at Str. N. Bălcescu 37, Apt. #5; you'll need a valid driver's license and two years driving experience. (☎21 69 49; www.advantage-rentacar.ro. English spoken. Open M-F 9am-8pm, Sa 10am-5pm. €37-90 per day. MC/V.) Driving all the way across the ridge is only possible July to September: the upper parts of the road and the tunnel on the Trans-Făgăran highway traversing the mountains are closed the rest of the year. The **train** route from Sibiu to Braşov (1-3hr.) stops in the villages of Avrig, Ucea, Arpaşu de Jos, Porumbaca de Jos, and Cărta, any of which makes a good base for hiking. For Mt. Negoiu, stop off at Avrig or Porumbaca de Jos; for Mt. Moldoveanu, try Ucea. The town of Victoria is a popular base camp, accessible by bus from Ucea (25min., 9 per day, L3).

Short hikes are in short supply for those without a car, as the towns on the Sibiu-Braşov railway line are still 10-15km from the start of the mountains. Some travelers catch a ride from Cărta, a stop on the railway, although Let's Go does not recommend hitchhiking. The tourist office can also organize a car (about €25 per person) to drive visitors up and back down the mountain, usually to **Bâlea Lac** (2027m), a stunning glacial lake above the treeline, or **Bâlea Cascada.** The shorter **blue triangle trail** (2-2½hr.) leads from Cascada to Lac, while the longer, meandering **red cross trail** (3hr.) is more picturesque. From **Bâlea Lac,** the **blue stripe trail** (1½hr.) gently slopes uphill, circling around the lake on the surrounding slopes, leading up to the summit of Curmătura Balei (2202m), and providing gorgeous vistas of the lake below and the jagged peaks above. From the summit, hike 15min. downhill along the red cross trail to reach **Cabana Bâlea Lac ❸,** whose restaurant and terrace overlook the water, for a picturesque view and traditional Romanian food. (☎07 45 07 26 02; www.balealac.ro. Entrees L8-52. Beer L4-8. Open daily 7:30am-11:30pm. Cash only.)

One possible longer trip is a three-day, two-night excursion from Sibiu. Take a train to **Avrig,** 16km (4hr. hike) from **Cabana Poiana Neamţului** (☎02 69 52 32 61; iliestoica@yahoo.com) and a road-accessible town at the foot of the mountains. Taxis are rare in Avrig, so many visitors traverse this stretch by hitchhiking, though Let's Go does not recommend it. You can also walk—follow the red cross markings from the train station. Continue up the mountains on the same trail (3hr.) as it separates from the road, and spend the night at **Cabana Bărcaciu ❶.** (☎07 40 03 98 05; www.barcaciu.ro. English spoken. On-site restaurant and bar. 6- or 20-bed dorms €5. Cash only.) Then, take the blue dot trail to glacial **Lake Avrig** (3hr.), and connect with the red stripe to the **Puha Saddle** (Şaua Puha). **Custura Sărăţii** (1hr. east of the Puha Saddle), the trail's most spectacular and difficult portion—a 2hr. path sometimes less than 30cm wide, with drops on either side—is only for experienced hikers. Stay the night at **Cabana Negoiu ❶,** a 2hr. descent down the blue cross trail. (☎02 69 21 06 07; www.negoiu.ro. English-speaking reception. On-site restaurant and bar. 10-bed dorms L22; 6-bed dorms L25, 4-bed dorm L27; doubles L32. Cash only.) Descend the blue triangle trail (1½hr.) and walk for 4hr., or catch a bus to **Porumbaco de Jos,** where trains return to Sibiu.

The most prized hike for serious hikers is across the entire Făgăraş ridge, which takes roughly seven days—10 for the less experienced—with a guide, going from west to east. The weather can be cold year-round. You can buy food at the *cabanas* along the way, but it's less expensive in the mountain villages. Call **Salişte-Bâlea Turism** (☎21 17 03) in Sibiu at Str. Zaharia Boiu 2, to make reservations. In an emergency or for help planning a trip, contact the mountain-rescue organization **Salvamont,** Nicolae Balcescu 9 (☎21 64 77); if given enough notice, they will even serve as guides for excursions into the mountains.

ROMANIA

CLUJ-NAPOCA ☎(0)264

Cluj-Napoca (KLOOZH nah-POH-kah; pop. 300,000) is Transylvania's unofficial capital and undisputed student center. While the beautiful but faded Old Town recalls the region's past, the university students who fill the cafes, bars, and parks—as well as every square inch of space on and around the city's monuments—make Cluj-Napoca a city on the move. With its high-spirited nightlife, imposing cathedrals, and graceful town squares, the city offers a cultural experience that is at once contradictory and thrilling.

TRANSPORTATION. International Airport Cluj-Napoca (☎41 67 02; www.airportcluj.ro) offers domestic flights to **Bucharest** and **Timişoara,** as well as regional flights to Austria, Germany, Hungary, and Italy. The easiest way to the airport from the center is by **taxi** (about L12). A city bus (marked "Aeroportul") also makes this trip, leaving from Pţa. Mihai Viteazul, behind the statue. For train tickets, go to **CFR,** Pţa. Mihai Viteazul 19. (Domestic ☎42 30 01, international 53 40 09. Open M-F 7am-8pm. Cash only.) **Trains** run to: Bucharest (8-12hr., 6 per day, L59) via Braşov (5-7hr., L36); Sibiu (4hr., 1 per day, L38); Sighetu Marmatiei (5-6hr., 2 per day, L30); Timişoara (5-7hr., 6 per day, L37); Budapest, HUN (7hr.; 2 per day; L114, under 27 L104). **Intercity Buses** are privately operated and leave from either the train station or the bus station *(autogara)*, Str. Giordano Bruno 3. Check with

tourist agencies for times and prices. Buy tickets (L1.30 per trip) for **local buses, trams,** and **trolleybuses** at **RATUC** kiosks, often located by the busier stops. (Public transportation runs M-F 5am-11pm, Sa-Su 6am-11pm.)

ORIENTATION AND PRACTICAL INFORMATION. From the **train station** *(gara)*, walk right and make another right, crossing the overpass to reach the intercity **bus station** *(autogara)*, Str. Giordano Bruno 3. To get to the main square, **Piața Unirii,** from the train station, take city bus #9 (buses depart just across the street from the train station), or walk down **Str. Horea,** which becomes **Regele Ferdinand** after it crosses the river. Pța. Unirii is on the right at its end. **Hotel Melody-Central,** Pța. Unirii 29 (☎59 74 65), has a full-service **tourist bureau** with English-speaking staff that book flights and accommodations and arrange tours. (☎45 91 69. Open daily 8am-6pm.) **Banca Transilvania,** Bd. Eroilor 36, near Pța. Avram Iancu, has **Western Union** services, **exchanges currency,** and cashes **American Express Travelers Cheques** for no commission and other traveler's checks for a small commission. (☎30 13 00. Open M-F 9am-8pm, Sa 9:30am-12:30pm.) MasterCard and Visa **ATMs** line Bd. Ferdinand. **Farmacia Clematis** is at Pța. Unirii 10. (☎40 71 00. Open M-Sa 8am-8pm. MC/V.) An **Internet** cafe, **Total Net Soft,** is at Str. Emil Isac 2. (7am-11pm L1.50 per hr., 11pm-7am L1 per hr. Open 24hr. Cash only.) **Flowers Tea House,** Pța. Unirii 25, offers its patrons **free Wi-Fi.** (Drinks from L2. Open M and Sa-Su 10am-10pm, Tu-F 8am-10pm. Cash only.) The main **post office** is at Bd. Ferdinand 33. (Open M-F 7am-8pm, Sa 8am-

1pm.) Another post office is at Str. Aurel Vlaicu 3. (☎43 11 21. Open M-F 8am-2pm.) Both offer **Poste Restante. Postal Code:** 400110. **Postal Code:** 400110.

ACCOMMODATIONS AND FOOD. **Retro Youth Hostel (HI) ❷,** Str. Potaissa 13, is both clean and bright, with modern bathrooms and showers and a kitchen. Located next to the Old Town walls, the hostel is only a few minutes' walk from the center. The English-speaking staff arrange daytrips and longer excursions around Transylvania. (☎45 04 52; www.retro.ro. Breakfast L14. Laundry L10. Free Internet. 6-bed and 8-bed dorms L44; triples L58-63. HI, ISIC, IYTC, ITIC discount 5%. MC/V.) Though it looks like a grand hotel from the street, **Hotel Melody-Central ❹,** Pţa. Unirii 29, in the heart of the city, sports a modern interior, with white walls and basic amenities, plus a tourist bureau in the lobby. (☎59 74 65; www.hcm.ro. Breakfast included. Free Internet. Singles L160; doubles L320. MC/V.)

Roata ❸, Str. Alexandru Ciurea 6a, hidden off Str. Emil Isac through the arch in a tan building, serves traditional Romanian dishes in a garden and in several wood-trimmed rooms. (☎19 20 22. Entrees L11-30. Open Su-M 1-11pm, Tu-Sa noon-11pm. Cash only.) If you're looking for cheap eats, look no further than the streets. **Pastry shops** are everywhere and sell baked goods for about L1. **Lugano ❸,** Str. Clemenceau 2, boasts an extensive menu of Italian food that caters both to travelers on a budget and to those willing to splurge. (☎59 45 93. Entrees L13-55. Restaurant open daily 11am-1am; bar 8pm-1am. MC/V.)

SIGHTS. Begin at **Piaţa Unirii,** dominated by the Gothic **St. Michael's Church** (Biserica Sf. Mihail). The 80m steeple of this Catholic church sits atop some of the country's largest and most exquisite stained-glass windows. (Open to the public until late afternoon; during times of worship, the church is closed to visitors.) The church shares the square with a large and imposing **statue** of Hungarian King Matthias Corvinus, pointedly surrounded by six large Romanian flags. Standing between the church and the statue, **Bánffy Palace,** Pţa. Unirii 30, houses the **National Museum of Art** (Muzeul National de Arta Cluj), which specializes in Romanian painting ranging from old religious icons to modern works. The museum houses a sizable collection of the works of arguably the most famous Romanian painter, **Nicolae Grigorescu,** who is renowned for his depictions of peasant life. (☎59 69 53; www.maccluj.ro. Open W-Su May-Sept. 10am-5pm; Oct.-Apr. 11am-6pm. L4. Cash only.) Stroll down Bd. 21 Decembrie 1989 to Pţa. Avram Iancu, home to the **Orthodox Cathedral,** which is adorned with elaborate mosaics, an unusual sight in Romanian churches. (Open 6am-8pm.) Next to the church looms a giant statue of **Avram Iancu,** revered for defending Romania from the Turks in the 19th century. From Pţa. Avram Iancu, head back to Pţa. Unirii, down Bd. Regele Ferdinand, and then turn left onto Str. E. Zola to reach Pţa. Muzeului. There, the **History Museum** (Muzeul de Istorie), Str. Constantin Daicoviciu 2, traces Transylvanian history from the Bronze Age to the present, albeit without English captions. Displays of medieval Transylvanian suits of armor and an ornately carved pulpit are highlights. (☎004 0264. Open Tu-Su 10am-4pm. L6, English guide L13. Cash only.) For a dazzling view of the city, head to **Cetăţuie Hill.** Walk up Bd. Regele Ferdinand, cross the bridge, turn left onto Str. Drăgalina, and persevere through the long climb up the stairs on your right.

ENTERTAINMENT AND NIGHTLIFE. The **National Theater and Opera** (Teatrul Naţional şi Opera Română), in Pţa. Ştefan cel Mare, imitates the architecture of the Garnier Opera House of Paris and hosts performances ranging from Broadway to ballet. The box office is across the street, at n. 14. (☎59 53 63. Box office open Tu-Su 11am-5pm. Theater and opera closed July-Sept. 15. Opera L10, students L3; theater L15/2.50. Cash only.)

For the latest on Cluj's nightlife, pick up the free Romanian *Şapte Seri* from hotels, hostels, or tourist agencies. **Art Club Cafe,** Pţa. Ştefan cel Mare n. 12, with its makeshift wallpaper of movie, concert, and performance posters, is frequented by an alternative student crowd. (☎59 50 32. Open M-Sa 9am-midnight, Su noon-midnight. Cash only.) Clubbers might prefer **Diesel,** Pţa. Unirii 17, which occasionally hosts popular Romanian bands and international DJs. Although there is technically no dance floor, patrons dance between tables in the downstairs rooms or relax in the all-white lounge. (☎43 90 43; www.dieselclub.ro. Mixed drinks L7-20. Open daily 9pm-3am. Cash only.) **Kharma Club,** Pţa. Lucian Blaga 1-3, caters to a diverse crowd, with a mellow outdoor seating area, a classy indoor lounge, and a dance floor that plays thumping house on the weekends but more low-key music on the weekdays. It also doubles as a restaurant during the day. (☎07 46 36. Food from L5. Beer from L4. Mixed drinks from L7. Open daily 8pm-4am. Cash only.)

ALBA IULIA ☎(0)258

Alba Iulia (AHL-bah YOO-lee-ah; pop. 66,360), set in the rolling hills of Transylvania, is capped by an ancient citadel that many consider the spiritual center of Romania. Outside the citadel gates, on the magnificent Pţa. Tricolorului, the Great Assembly of Transylvania voted for union with Romania on December 1, 1918, while inside the walls, in a grand cathedral built for the occasion, King Ferdinand I was crowned the first king of Romania. To this day, Alba Iulia retains a special place in the hearts of Romanians—and tourists from across Europe.

ROMANIA

TRANSPORTATION AND PRACTICAL INFORMATION. Most daily **trains** running in this area stop in Alba. Destinations include: Bucharest (6hr., 5 per day, L31); Cluj-Napoca (2hr., 3 per day, L12); Sighişoara (2hr., 4 per day, L25); Timişoara (5 hr., 4 per day, L34). **Buses** depart from the "Autotrans" Autogara (☎81 29 67), across from the train station, for numerous destinations, including Bucharest (6 per day, L36); Cluj-Napoca (14 per day, L12); Sibiu (11 per day L12); Timişoara (3 per day, L25). To get from the train and bus stations to the citadel and the center, take city bus #3 or 4. Buy tickets on board (L1). **Taxis** line up outside the train station; ask to go to Str. Mihai Viteazul, which runs directly through the citadel (around L5). On foot, turn right from the stations and walk north along Bd. Ferdinand I to the center. Turn left on Str. Mihai Viteazul to get to the citadel.

In front of the Orthodox Cathedral, **Piaţa Tricolorului** leads to the intersection of Bd. Transilvania and Bd. 1 Decembrie, which are lined with most services. **BCR,** Bd. Transilvania 25, has a 24hr. outdoor **currency exchange** machine and **ATM,** and cashes **traveler's checks** for 1.5% commission. (☎83 45 22. Open M-F 8:30am-5pm, Sa 8:30am-12:30pm.) **Librăria Mircea Eliade,** at the intersection of Bd. 1 Decembrie and Str. Closca, sells **maps** for L8-15. (Open M-F 9:30am-5:30pm, Sa 9:30am-1:30pm. Cash only.) **Farmacia Sic-Volo,** Bd. Decembrie 1, is a 24hr. **pharmacy.** (☎83 03 95. MC/V.) **Internet** access can be found at the aptly named **Internet Cafe,** Bd. Transilvania 9. Turn left into the yard behind the apartment building at Bd. Transilvania 9 just after the Fornetti Pastries on Bd. Transilvania; the cafe is at the back of this building, to your right. (☎07 48 85 06 85. L2.50 per hr. Open 24hr. Cash only.) The **post office,** Bd. Transilvania 12, has **Western Union.** (Open M-F 7am-8pm, Sa 8am-1pm.) **Postal Code:** 510097.

ACCOMMODATIONS AND FOOD. **Pensiune Flamingo ❶,** Str. Mihai Viteazul 6, is in the green villa just to the right of citadel Gate #1. It has simple rooms, free-flowing hot water, and a small attached restaurant and bar. Enter through the bar if the front door is locked. (☎81 63 54; www.flamingo.3x.ro. Shared baths. Check-out noon. Singles L60; doubles with private bath L100; triples L90; quads L120. Cash only.) Although 2km from the city center, **Pensiune MA ❸,** Str. Arieşului 51, makes up for its less than convenient location with big, bright rooms; brand-new, modern bathrooms; a helpful English-speaking staff, and a delicious and affordable on-site restaurant and bar. Following the signs for the *pensiune*, head down B-dul. Tudor Vladimirescu, turn left at B-dul. Republicii, and make a final left onto Str. Arieşului; MA is on the left. (☎83 15 02; www.mahotels.ro. Breakfast included. Check-out noon. Singles L140; doubles L160. MC/V.) Fresh **fruit and vegetable stands** cluster near the intersection of Bd. 1 Decembrie and Bd. Transilvania; look for signs that say "Legume Fructe." **Pizzeria Roberta ❷,** Str. Tudor Vladimirescu 4, next to the bank, serves the best pizza in town in an upscale dining room. (☎82 35 92. Pizzas L4-19. Entrees L8-26. Open daily 9am-midnight. Cash only.) A more Romanian choice, **Restaurant Transilvania ❷,** Pţa. Iuliu Manilu 22, attached to Hotel Transilvania, serves traditional entrees on wooden tables. (☎81 20 52. English menu. Entrees L6-18. Open daily 7am-11pm. Cash only.)

SIGHTS AND ENTERTAINMENT. To get to the star-shaped **citadel** *(cetatea)*, home to nearly all the town's sights, walk left from the train and bus stations along Str. Mihai Viteazul to Gate #1. (Open 24hr. Free.) Continue to Gate #2 to enter the inner citadel. Helpful orange-and-gray English signs, courtesy of the EU, mark the path. In the large square at the heart of the citadel, you'll see an imposing statue of **Mihai Viteazul** (Michael the Brave), who unified Romania in 1599-1601. Past the statue and to your right on Str. Mihai Viteazul 12-13, two grand old military buildings house museums: **Union Hall** (Sala Unirii) and the **National Union Museum** (Muzeul Naţional al Unirii). The National Union Museum, on the left side of the street, traces the history of Romania from Dacian rule through Roman, Byzantine, medieval, and modern times, and showcases an excellent collection of Roman statuary. Vlad Ţepeş is included among the great men of Romanian history who crowd the murals on the walls of the Union Hall, on the right side of the street. It was here that Aurel Lazar ushered in Romanian unity in October 1918, by drafting the Transylvanian declaration of self-determination. (☎81 33 00. Hall open daily 9am-5pm. Museum open daily 10am-6pm. No English captions. Hall and museum each L5, students L2.50. English tour of hall and museum L20. Photography L10 each. Cash only.) Beside the twin museums sit twin cathedrals, the **Catholic Cathedral** (Catedrala Sfântul Mihail) and the Orthodox **Reunification Cathedral.** Construction on the Catholic Cathedral began in the 13th century; its Gothic style reflects Western influences, while the interior, filled with Hungarian flags, bears witness to the Magyar influence in the area. (Open M-Sa 6:30am-9:30pm, Su 7am-9:30pm. English captions. Free.) Colonnades, a bell tower, and a sculpture-dotted courtyard skirt the bronze cupolas and yellow walls of the Reunification Cathedral. Murals and plaques depicting the greatest hits of Romanian history adorn the interior. (Open daily 7am-11:30pm. English captions. Free.)

Kick back after a hard day of sightseeing at **Pub 13,** built into the citadel wall on Str. Mihai Viteazul between Gates #1 and 2. Look for the little bridge across the moat. In the dark and atmospheric interior of the exposed stone of the citadel wall, an international crowd packs the dance floor, which plays anything from retro to techno. The outdoor terrace offers an unparalleled view of the city. (☎83 95 55; www.pub13.ro. English menu. Beer L2.50-18. Mixed drinks L5-12. Entrees L4.50-28. Open daily noon-2am. Cash only.)

BANAT

Romania's westernmost province, Banat lies squarely on the plains beyond the Carpathian mountains, weathering hot, dry summers that contrast with the cooler temperatures of the surrounding mountains. Heavily influenced by its former Austrian and Hungarian rulers, today, its population is more ethnically diverse than that of the rest of Romania, with large Magyar and German minorities. Accordingly, the area feels decidedly more Western European than much of the country.

TIMIŞOARA ☎(0)256

In 1989, 105 years after becoming the first European city with electric street lamps, Timişoara (tee-mee-SHWAH-rah; pop. 307,300) ignited the revolution that left Romanian communism in cinders. Romania's westernmost city, both geographically and politically, it earned the name of Little Vienna for the elegance of its grand old boulevards, magnificent town squares, peaceful riverside cafes, and well-groomed parks and gardens.

TRANSPORTATION AND PRACTICAL INFORMATION. If going by train to Timişoara, get off at **Timişoara Nord.** Buy tickets at **CFR**, Str. Măcieşilor 3, just off Pţa. Victoreii. (☎49 38 06. Open M-F 7am-8pm. Cash only.) **Trains** run to: Alba Iulia (4½-5hr., 4 per day, L35); Braşov (9hr., 1 per day, L48); Bucharest (8-11hr., 8 per day, L74); Cluj-Napoca (5-7hr., 6 per day, L39); Sibiu (5-6hr., 3 per day, L53); Budapest, HUN (5hr.; 2 per day; L104, under 26 L90). The intercity **bus station** (☎49 34 71) is across the river from the center, at Str. Vladimirescu and Str. Iancu Văcărescu. **Buses** depart regularly to numerous destinations, including Alba Iulia (6hr., 1 per day, L35); Braşov (9hr., 2 per day, L55); Bucharest (11hr., 4 per day, L51); Sibiu (6½hr., 5 per day, L35); Sighetu Marmatiei (8hr., 2 per day, L38); Suceava (14hr., 1 per day, L58).

The train station is less than 2km west of the city center. From the station, turn left down Bd. Republicii. Alternatively, take city bus #11 or 14, heading to the center of town (L2.50 for 2 trips; buy tickets at RATT kiosks). Get off when

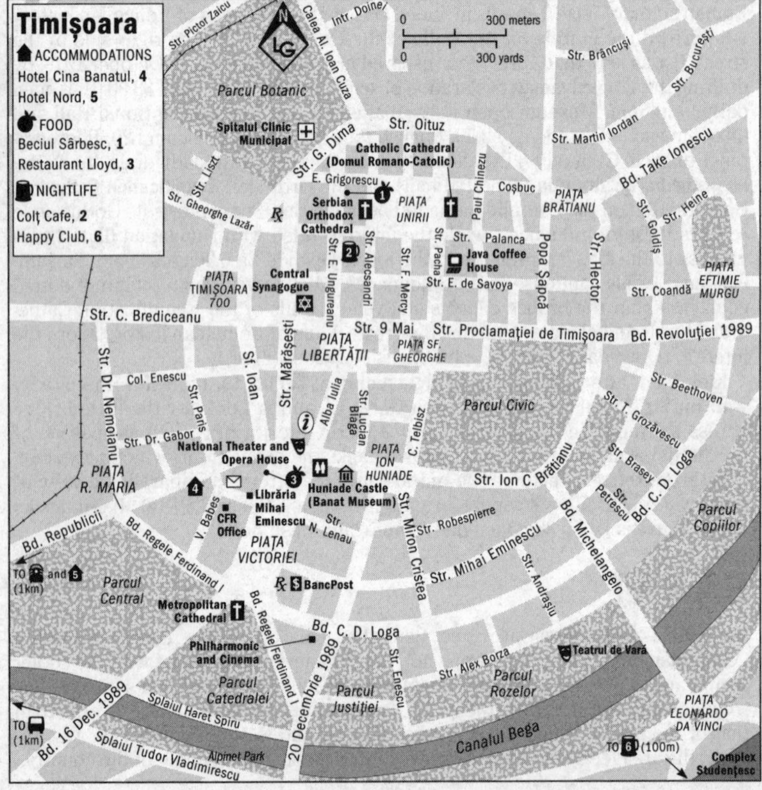

you see Pţa. Victoriei, the main square, with its multicolored cathedral. The old center is compact and circular, originally built within fortifications, which are now mostly gone. You'll find nearly everything you need in the main square, **Piaţa Victoriei.** The **tourist information center** (Info Centrul Turistic Timişoara), Str. Alba Iulia 2, in the Opera building to the left of the main entrance, provides free **maps** and books accommodations. (☎43 79 73. English spoken. Open June-Aug. M-F 9am-8pm, Sa 9am-5pm; Sept.-May M-F 9am-6pm, Sa 10am-3pm.) **Banc Post,** Bd. Mihai Eminescu, just off Pţa. Victoriei, has **Western Union** services, **exchanges currency,** and cashes **traveler's checks.** (☎40 79 01. Open M-F 9am-5pm.) **Vlad Pharmacy** (☎20 18 89; MC/V), Str. Lazăr 8, near the hospital, is open 24hr. Seek **medical assistance** at **Spitalul Clinic Municipal,** Str. G. Dima 5 (☎43 36 12). For **Internet** access, try **Java Coffee House,** Str. Augustin Pacha 6, just below Pţa. Unirii, which doubles as a stylish cafe. (☎43 24 95. L3.50 per hr. Open 24hr.) The **post office,** Str. Craiului 1, Bd. Republicii and Pţa. Victoriei, offers **Western Union** and **Poste Restante** services. (Open M-F 8am-7pm. Cash only.) **Postal Code**: 300000.

ACCOMMODATIONS AND FOOD. Convenient **Hotel Nord ❸,** Str. Gen. Ion Drăgălina 47, is one of the best values in town, with low-priced modern rooms that boast TVs and fridges. It's the bright yellow-and-pink building across the street from the train station. (☎49 75 04; www.hotelnord.ro. Breakfast included. Singles with shared bath €29, with private bath €32; doubles €58/74; apartments €50 per person. MC/V.) Centrally located **Hotel Cina Banatul ❸,** Bd. Republicii 7, pampers guests with thick mattresses and plush carpets. All rooms have fridges, private baths, and TVs. (☎49 19 03. Check-out noon. Singles L120; doubles L140; apartments L200. Cash only.)

The enormous **open-air market,** Pţa Timişoara 700, along Str. C. Brediceanu, hawks everything that your heart does or does not desire. (Open daily dawn-dusk.) Restaurants with outdoor seating line Pţa. Victoriei. **Restaurant Lloyd ❸,** on Pţa. Victoriei 2, overlooks the square. The daring can select frogs' legs (L27) or grilled shark (L30) from an English menu in the sumptuous paneled-and-mirrored interior. (☎29 49 49; www.lloyd.ro. Entrees L6-60. Open 24hr. AmEx/MC/V.) **Beciul Sârbesc ❸,** Str. G. Ungureanu 14, near the Serbian Orthodox Church, serves Serbian food, a popular culinary tradition in Timişoara. Stained glass windows give this establishment a decidely refined air, while the food is a welcome variation on Romanian cuisine. (☎07 24 27 73 70. English menu. Entrees L10-40. Live music 7pm. Open daily 10am-late. Cash only.)

SIGHTS AND ENTERTAINMENT. Beautiful **Piaţa Victoriei** is flanked by the **National Theater and Opera** (Teatrul Naţional şi Opera Română) and the **Metropolitan Cathedral** (Catedrala Mitropolitană). A fountain, flower garden, and statue of Romulus and Remus grace its regal center. Near the church, a modern sculpture commemorates the victims of the 1989 Revolution. The cathedral itself is a spectacular blend of Byzantine and Moldavian styles, capped by 13 green-and-gold spires. This Orthodox church, the largest in Romania, contains sculpted chandeliers, an awe-inspiring pure gold iconostasis, and the bones of St. Joseph of Partos, the patron saint of Banat. As of August 2007, the museum downstairs is closed indefinitely for repairs. (Open daily 6:30am-8pm. Liturgy M-F 7:30am, Su 7 and 10am; vespers M-F and Su 6pm. Museum open W-Su 10am-3pm. Cathedral free. Museum L1, students L0.50.) The **Park of Roses** (Parcul Rozelor), along the riverbank, holds frequent free concerts; inquire at the tourist office. The unbelievably cheap shows at the **National Theater and Opera** are enhanced by the theater's stunning Neobyzantine interior. (☎20 11 17. Box office open daily Sept. to mid-June 10am-1pm and 5-7pm. Theater L10-20. Opera L5-15. Cash only.)

HIDDEN TREASURE. Some of the real treasures of Timişoara's cathedral are cleverly hidden away in the basement. Open a small door on the right side of the front of the church—really, you're allowed in—then turn right and open an even smaller door. Go down the staircase to find a large collection of priceless artifacts, including the first Bible printed in Romanian and a golden Madonna and Child icon given to a Romanian princess by the Russian tsar. Ask one of the priests to show you around, but don't ask what the names of the icons are. It's sacrilege to write them down, or even to speak them!

In the square to the right of Pţa. Victoriei, as you face the opera, the old **Huniade Castle** houses the **Banat Museum** (Muzeul Banatului), which traces Timişoara's history from ancient times through WWII. Check out the **sculpture garden.** The original antique electric **lamp posts** outside are the first in Europe. (☎49 13 39. Open Tu-Su 10am-4pm. Two floors; L2 per floor, students L1.) North of Victoriei, the increasingly gentrified Old Town stretches to **Piaţa Unirii,** where a fountain spouts water said to remedy stomach ailments. West of the square sits the delicate pale yellow **Serbian Orthodox Church** (open only for services); the deep yellow **Catholic Cathedral** (Domul Romano-Catolic), built in a *fin-de-siècle* revival style, stands over the eastern flank. (Open daily 7am-8pm. Free.) The **Botanical Park,** northwest of Pţa. Unirii, is a good place to picnic. The elusive entrance is on Str. G. Dima. (Open daily June-Aug. 7am-10pm; Sept.-May 10am-8pm. Free.)

ROMANIA

At night, the place to be is the student district, **Complex Studenţesc.** From the main square, head down Bd. I.C. Brătianu, make a right on Bd. Michelangelo, and cross the bridge. At Pţa. Leonardo da Vinci, turn onto Aleea F.C. Ripensia. Veer left onto the busy Aleea Studenţilor, lined with fast-food joints, bars, and clubs. Smoky **Happy Club,** A. Studenţilor 4, earns its name with a packed terrace, intense drinking, and dancing to house and techno. (☎29 52 99. Open 24hr. Cash only.) For those who don't want to trek to the student district, a hot spot in the center is slick **Colţ Cafe,** Str. Ungureanu 10, near Pţa. Unirii. The split level cafe and bar with stylish green chairs and chill background music is a perfect place to sit back and relax. (☎22 93 85. Beer and shots L5-14. Mixed drinks L10-13. Sandwiches L4.20-6. Open 24hr. Cash only.)

MARAMUREȘ

Entering Maramureş (mah-rah-MOO-resh) is like stepping into a time capsule: life here proceeds as it did 50 or 100 years ago. The population is famous for its loyalty to traditional dress, especially during feasts and holidays, and takes pride in its ancient Dacian roots. Few visitors venture to the region on account of its location far north of the Romanian capital, but those who do are richly rewarded.

SIGHETU MARMAȚIEI ☎(0)262

Just across the Tisa River from Ukraine, Sighetu Marmaţiei (SEE-get-oo Mahr-MA-tzee-ay; pop. 45,000), is both the birthplace of Holocaust-survivor and novelist Elie Wiesel and host to several stellar museums. Maramureş's cultural center, the town is, nevertheless, not as traditional as the rural areas around it. Signs on the town's beautiful main street still warn drivers to beware of horse-pulled carts, making life here a dynamic mix between modernization and conservatism.

TRANSPORTATION AND PRACTICAL INFORMATION. CFR is at Pţa. Libertăţii 25. (☎31 26 66. Open M-F 7am-7:30pm. Cash only.) **Trains** run to: Bucharest (14hr., 1 per day, L59), Cluj-Napoca (6hr., 2 per day, L30), and Timişoara (13hr.,

1 per day, L59). The **bus station** is located next to the train station. (☎31 15 12. Ticket office open M-F 7am-7pm, Sa-Su 8am-2pm.) Destinations include Cluj-Napoca (6hr., 5 per day, L26), Oradea (5hr., 1 per day, L33), and Săpânţa (40min., 2 per day, L4). **Minibuses** leave for Budapest, HUN from in front of the Hotel Coroana; inquire at the hotel desk and reserve in advance. (8hr., daily 5am and 7:30pm, L82.) **Taxis** are fairly common and frequent Pţa. Libertăţii.

Head straight out of the train station and bear right (but not the sharp right) down **Strada Iuliu Maniu.** At the T-intersection right before the church (about 1km), go left on **Strada 22 Decembrie 1989** to reach **Piaţa Libertăţii,** the main square. For info about Sighet and its surroundings, head to **Pangaea Proiect Turism** office, Pţa. Libertăţii 17. The English-speaking staff book accommodations and car tours and provide maps and pamphlets for a fee. (☎31 22 28. www.pangaeaturism.ro. Open M-F 9am-5pm. Cash only.) **BCR,** Str. Iuliu Maniu 32, cashes **traveler's checks** at 0.5% commission (min. US$5) and **exchanges currency;** an **ATM** is outside. (☎31 14 04. Open M-F 8:30am-5:30pm, Sa 8:30am-12:30pm.) **Farmacia Minerva** is at Pţa. Libertăţii 23. (☎31 19 77. Open M-F 8am-8pm. Cash only.) Find **Internet** access at **Zifer Serv,** Str. Iuliu Maniu, across the street from BCR. (☎50 29 80. L1.50 per hr. Open M-F 8am-6pm, Sa 9am-5pm. Cash only.) The **post office** is at Str. Bogdan Vodă 2, just off the main square, and has **Western Union** services and **Poste Restante.** (☎93 93 11. Open M-F 7am-8pm, Sa 8am-noon.) **Postal Code:** 435500.

ROMANIA

ACCOMMODATIONS AND FOOD. Staying in **private villas** (from L30), which can be rented from proprietors waiting at the train station, is an inexpensive option in Sighet. The charm of Maramureş, however, is in its countryside. To properly take it in, ask the staff at Pangaea Proiect Turism (see above) to book a room in a village guesthouse, often called a *pensiune*. (L30-60. Cash only.) **CobWobs Hostel ❶,** close to the city center at Str. 22 Decembrie 1989 42, in the yard behind a small orange building (look carefully for a sign on the street), seems more like a home than a hostel. The English-speaking proprietors, who live downstairs with their family, built and decorated most of the house themselves and organize various tours, including trips to a Ukrainian market, mushroom picking in the countryside, and tours of the nearby Iza Valley (see p. 542). (☎745 615 173, 740 635 673. Laundry L6. Free Internet. 4- or 6-bed dorms L30. Cash only.) The popular **Perla Sigheteana ❸,** Str. Avram Iancu 65a, located in a new building on the edge of town, offers comfortable doubles with TVs, private baths, and balconies that provide great views of the surrounding hills. (☎31 06 13. Breakfast included. Call ahead, as it is often full. Doubles L150. MC/V.)

The **open-air market,** one block up from the main square (turn off at the Farmacia Minerva) sells fresh fruits and vegetables, as well as cheap clothing and other random wares. (Open daily dawn-dusk. Cash only.) Affordable cafes and pizzerias can be found on or near the main square. The nicest place in town is **Casa Iurca de Călineşti ❷,** Str. Dragoş Vodă 14, next to the Elie Wiesel house. Waiters in traditional dress serve food from an excellent Romanian menu, and, occasionally, a troop of folk singers and musicians serenades the clientele. (☎31 88 82. www.casaiurca.com. English menu. Extensive vegetarian options. Entrees L7-25. Open daily 7:30am-10pm. MC/V.) For tasty Romanian and international food and a beautiful view of the hills surrounding Sighet—in either an indoor or outdoor setting—try **Restaurant Perla Sigheteană ❷,** inside the eponymous hotel. (☎31 06 13. Entrees L5-15. Open daily 7am-midnight.)

SIGHTS. Sighet's **Memorial Museum** (Muzeul Memorialui), Str. Copusu 4, south of the main square, is a unique and sobering testament to the abuses of the Communist regime in Romania. In the period after WWII, the building was a top-secret political prison that held former political leaders, famous intellectuals, high-ranking Catholic clergy, and even high school students. The museum now contains a variety of exhibits, from a re-creation of the prison's torture chamber and isolation "punishment" cells to pictures, sculptures, and paintings that exemplify the cult of Nicolae Ceauşescu. (☎31 68 48, 94 24; www.memorial-sighet.ro. Limited English captions. Open Apr. 15-Oct. 15 daily 9:30am-6:30pm; Oct. 16-Apr. 14 Tu-Su 9:30am-4:30pm. L5, students L2.50; tour in English included.) The **Maramureş Museum** has two branches. The first is an **ethnographic wing** (Muzeul Maramureşan), Str. Bogdan Vodă 1, opposite the post office, which is notable for its collection of the fantastic, horned devil costumes used in the town Christmas drama (Dec. 25-26). The second is an **open-air village museum** (Muzeul Satului), 6km from the town center at the end of Str. Bogdan Vodă, filled with traditional Maramureşan buildings from the 17th-19th centuries. Follow the signs from Str. Bogdan Vodă just before the little bridge, or take a taxi for L6. (Some English captions. Open Tu-Su 9am-7pm. L4, students L2. English book L5.) **Casa Elie Wiesel,** the light blue house on Str. Drogoş Vodă, one block up from Str. Traian on the corner of Str. Tudor Vladimirescu, is the childhood residence of the 1986 Nobel Peace Prize winner, best known for his Holocaust memoir *Night.* Wiesel, a Transylvanian Jew, lived in this house until he was 15. His family was then deported, and Wiesel subsequently spent WWII in concentration camps. The museum contains samples of Wiesel's writings, displays about the fate of the region's Jews, and a few rooms restored to their pre-WWII appearance. (Limited English captions. Open Tu-Su 10am-6pm. L4, students L2.)

ROMANIA

DAYTRIP FROM SIGHETU MARMATIEI: SĂPÂNŢA. For an exuberant outlook on death, head to Săpânţa, home of the world-famous **Merry Cemetery** (Cimitirul Vesel; CHEE-mee-teer-ool Veh-SEL). Take a left off the road from Sighet onto the only other paved road and go up 200 yd. to get to the cemetery. The cemetery, near the local church, is a sea of colorfully painted wooden grave markers that depict scenes from the lives of the deceased and are engraved with witty poems—often in first person—using archaisms and slang. In 1935, local artisan Stan Ion Patras, drawing on rich traditions of folk art and woodworking, began carving these unique headstones; the tradition continues today, and new crosses are still being added. The crosses and markers have attracted worldwide attention and have been displayed in many foreign galleries. Despite its fame, this tiny village maintains a traditional lifestyle; its inhabitants sport straw hats and head scarves, and still prefer the horse-and-cart as their primary means of transportation. (No English captions. Cemetery open daily dawn-dusk. L4.)

Buses run from **Sighet** train station (40min., 2 per day, L3-4). Many buses going elsewhere, including the bus to Satu Mare, will stop in Săpânţa; ask the driver. **Hitchhiking** from Str. Avram Iancu at the western edge of Sighet, by the hospital, is very common (about the price of a bus ticket, L3-5), as a taxi costs significantly more (round-trip L45) and buses are scarce. Let's Go does not recommend hitchhiking.

IZA VALLEY AND ENVIRONS

Those seeking to experience real Romanian country life—rather than simply imagine it at the Open-Air Village Museum in Sighet (see above)—should head to the **Iza Valley.** In villages where traditional dress is the norm and homes are still crafted from interlocking logs, ornately carved wooden gateposts and churches abound. Visitors soak up the mountain-village atmosphere while enjoying the people's renowned hospitality and authentic meals. At the valley's mouth, 7km from Sighet, is **Vadu Iza** (VAHD-wee-zah), the commercial hub. Although the town offers numerous accommodations, it lacks the traditional feel of the other villages. Particularly stunning is **Ieud,** home to the tall wooden steeple of the 1716 **Church of the Wood** (Biserica de Lemn), on the main street, and the 1364 **Church on the Hill,** the oldest wooden church in Maramureş. The latter is located east along the dirt road that juts off north of the village council building; this building, for its part, is the oldest of its kind and also contains a small museum (L1). The village churches are often locked; ask around, and locals will find a key. **Bârsana** is home to a traditional monastery that now houses up to 12 nuns, has a museum of religious artifacts, and boasts stunning wooden architecture and hourly bell-ringing. At the eastern end of Maramureş, the old mining center of **Borsa** is a gateway to the Rodna mountains; a small ski area lies to the east. Food and lodgings are available at the many B&Bs in the villages for L30-60 per person. Book rooms through the Pangaea Proiect Turism in Sighet (see p. 540) or look for signs.

Transportation within the Iza Valley is highly variable. **Buses,** which stop in front of the train station, run from **Sighet** to various villages within the valley. (30min.-2hr., in summer 6-8 per day, L4.) Once in the villages, however, tourists are sometimes stranded; very few villagers speak English, and the buses between the villages and back to Sighet can be very difficult to navigate. Pangaea Proiect Turism sells **maps** of the area for L5. Hitchhikers commonly stand in two places, depending on their destination: for Vadu Iza and Baia Mare, in front of the Unicarm supermarket in Sighet, a few blocks from the central square on Str. Bogdan Vodă, and for Borsa, on Str. Dragos Vodă, at the crossroads with Str. Traian near the church. Buses also stop at each of these locations, although the stops are unmarked. Let's Go does not recommend hitchhiking. A good alternative to public transportation or hitchhiking is renting a private car tour, which is more expensive but also often more rewarding. Many owners of guesthouses in the valley will serve as a guide for guests for about L2 per km, including the time spent at stops. Pangaea Proiect Turism can make arrangements.

ROMANIA

MOLDAVIA (MOLDOVA)

Eastern Romania once included the entire Moldovan territory, but the Bessarabian section is now the independent Republic of Moldova. Due to its flat landscape, Romanian Moldavia, which extends from the Carpathians to the Prut River, doesn't offer the stunning vistas of the rest of the country. Still, travelers from around the world come to see the masterfully painted monasteries in the hills of Bucovina. Forty-seven of them were built 500 years ago by national hero Ştefan cel Mare—rumor has it that he built one after every victory over the Turks—while others were built by later rulers. These exquisite structures are perfect examples of Moldavian architecture, a unique mix of Byzantine, Roman, and Gothic styles. They served as isolated outposts against Turkish and Tatar marauders, acquiring massive walls and towers over the years. After being repressed under Communism, the monasteries once again house large communities of nuns or monks.

Moldavia and Moldova are not the same place. While Moldavia is the northeastern part of Romania, Moldova is a separate country between Russia and Romania. The distinction is further confused because the region of Moldavia is known as "Moldova" in Romanian. Although as of 2007, US citizens no longer need a visa to enter Moldova, Australians and New Zealanders still do. Make sure you don't accidentally book a bus that passes through Moldova unless you have proper documentation.

SUCEAVA ☎(0)230

The capital of Moldavia under Ştefan cel Mare, Suceava (soo-CHYAH-vah; pop. 107,500) is the biggest town in monastery country and a good base for exploration. The town, however, has more than just proximity to offer the monastery-seeker: among the concrete Soviet buildings that dominate Suceava, there are still intriguing museums, historic churches, and the ruins of Ştefan's citadel to explore.

TRANSPORTATION. Gara Suceava Nord, the main station, sends **trains** to: Brașov (8hr., 1 per day, L44); Bucharest (6-7hr., 6 per day, L35); Cluj-Napoca (6-7hr., 6 per day, L36); Gura Humorului (1hr., 6 per day, L8). **Gara Suceava,** another train station, serves Gura Humorului (1hr., 9 per day, L8) and Sighetu Marmației (11-14hr., 5 per day, L28) via Salva, Dej Calatori, or Beclean pe Someș. Buy tickets at **CFR,** Str. N. Bălcescu 4. (☎21 43 35. Open M-F 7:30am-8:30pm. Cash only.) The **bus station** (☎52 43 40), at the intersection of Str. N. Bălcescu and Str. V. Alecsandri, sends buses to: Bucharest (8hr., 5 per day, L25); Cluj-Napoca (7hr., 2 per day, L37); Constanța (8 hr., 1 per day, L40); Gura Humorului (1hr., 12 per day, L5).

ORIENTATION AND PRACTICAL INFORMATION. From the Suceava Nord train station, take city bus #5 (L1) or any of the **Maxi taxis** (L1) waiting outside to reach the center, **Piața 22 Decembrie.** As you walk up the square **Strada Nicolae Bălcescu** is on your right. **Strada Ștefan cel Mare** crosses in front of the concrete theater (Casa de Cultura a Sindicatelor) on the square. **Bilco Agenția de Turism,** Str. N. Bălcescu 2, organizes car tours to the monasteries and books accommodations. (☎52 24 60. Tours €60-100 per car. Private guides available. L8 maps of Bucovina, but not of Suceava. Open in summer M-Sa 8:30am-7pm; in winter M-F 9:30am-5pm, Sa 9:30am-3pm. MC/V.) **Banca Românească,** Str. N. Bălescu 2b, cashes **American Express Travelers Cheques** for no commission, offers **Western Union** services, **exchanges currency,** and has a 24hr. **ATM.** (☎20 61 44; www.banca-romaneasca.ro. Open M-F 9am-4:30pm. Western Union open 9am-4:30pm, Sa 9am-1pm.) **Luggage storage** is at the train stations. (L4 per day. Open 24hr.) **Librăria Lidana,** on Str. C. Porumbescu behind the theater in the main square, sells **maps** of Suceava. (☎37 73 24. Maps L14. Open M-F 9am-6pm, Sa 9am-3pm.) **Farmacia Centrală** is at Str. N. Bălcescu 2b. (☎21 72 85. Open daily 7am-9pm. Cash only.) **Internet** access is available at **Assist Computers,** Str. Tipografiei 1. The entrance is in the back of the the tower on Pța. 22 Decembrie, at the corner with Bd. Ana Ipătescu. (☎52 30 44. CD burning, printing, and scanning available. L2 per hr. Open daily 9am-10pm. Cash only.) To get to the **post office,** Str. Dimitrie Onciul 1, turn right off Str. N. Bălescu after passing the Banc Post building. **Poste Restante** is available at window 5. (☎53 06 53. Open M-F 8am-7pm, Sa 8am-1pm.) **Postal Code:** 720290.

ROMANIA

ACCOMMODATIONS AND FOOD. Despite its remote location on the edge of town, the new **High Class Hostel ❷,** Str. Aurel Vlaicu 195, draws budget travelers on account of its spacious rooms, extremely helpful English-speaking staff, and excellent cooking. The owner is also a licensed tour guide who runs car tours of the monasteries (L90 per person for 1-day tour). As of summer 2007, the High Class Hostel will move to a new location near the city center at Str. Mihai Eminescu 19. (☎78 23 28; www.classhostel.ro. Free maps. Breakfast L10. Dinner L25. Vegetarian dishes available. Laundry L10. Free Internet. Dorms L50. MC/V.) To reach **Villa Alice ❸,** Str. Simion Florea Marian 1b, take a left off Str. Nicolae Bălcescu in front of Cinema Modern and follow the signs. This hotel is located in a quiet neighborhood and offers tastefully decorated rooms with cable TV, fridges, and balconies. A sauna (L40-60) and heath club (L15) are also available. (☎28 78 98; www.villaalice.ro. Free Internet. Singles L120; doubles L150. MC/V.)

The freshest fruits, vegetables, and baked goods in town are at the **open-air market,** Pța. Agroalimentara on Str. Petru Rareș, off the pedestrian end of Str. Ștefan cel Mare. (Open daily dawn-dusk. Cash only.) **Pub Chagall ❷,** on the corner of Str. N. Bălescu and Str. Ștefan cel Mare, in the courtyard of the apartment block, serves excellent Romanian and international food in a dark-wood-and-brick cellar. (☎53 06 21. No English menu. Beer L3. Mixed drinks from L9. Entrees L6-18. Open M-Sa 10am-midnight, Su 11am-midnight. Cash only.) **Latino ❸,** Curtea Domnească 9, left of the pedestrian side of Str. Ștefan cel Mare, serves Italian food, including the best pizza in town, in a stylish interior or on an outdoor terrace. (☎52 36 27. Pasta and pizza L10-15. Entrees L13-29. Open daily 9am-11pm. MC/V.)

SIGHTS AND ENTERTAINMENT. The mammoth **statue** of Ştefan cel Mare, the most celebrated King of Moldavia, is visible from Pţa. 22 Decembrie, across Bd. Ana Ipătescu, and can be reached by taking the pedestrian path right next to the McDonald's by the main square. A few minutes' walk from this hill stands the ancient **Citadel of the Throne** (Cetatea de Scaun). The citadel was built in 1388 by Petru Muşat I, who moved Moldavia's capital to Suceava; it was refortified by his great-great-grandson, Ştefan cel Mare, and withstood the 1476 siege by Mehmet II, conqueror of Constantinople. The citadel is a 10min. walk through the valley, which can be reached by the pedestrian path from the square (see above). Although the citadel was partially destroyed by the Turks, a significant portion of the walls and a tower remain, making it a great place for exploring. (Open daily in summer 8am-8pm; in winter 10am-5pm. L2, students L1. Cash only.) The adjacent **Bucovina Village Museum** (Muzeul Şatului Bucovinean) displays 18th- through 20th-century houses, churches, workshops, and inns with their interiors re-created true to the style of the region. (Some English captions. Open M-F 10am-6pm, Sa-Su 10am-8pm. L2, students L1. Photography L5. Cash only.) The **Monastery of St. Ioan the New** (Mânăstirea Sf. Ioan cel Nou), completed in 1522 by Bogdan III, one of Ştefan's many sons, holds beneath its colorful roof and frescoes the body of St. Ioan, martyred in 1330 for refusing to join the Zoroastrian faith. In late June, his silver casket is opened and the faithful can kiss his bones. To get there, walk past the McDonald's on Str. Ana Ipătescu and take the first left on Str. Ion Vodă Viteazu, right before the church Sfânta In Viere. (Open daily 5am-10pm. Free. English pamphlet L4.) On the same street, walk in the opposite direction past the McDonald's and bus shelter; turn left on the pathway to reach Str. Curtea Domnească, where you'll find **St. Demeter Church** (Biserica Sf. Dumitru). The interior is covered with brilliantly colorful frescoes dating from 1535 and featuring a particularly vicious Hellmouth on the portico. (Open daily 8am-7pm. Free. English pamphlet L2.)

The **Shock Club,** Str. Aleea Saturn 7, a two-level carnival of smoke machines and flashing lights centered on an enormous, crowded dance floor surrounded by balconies and bars, is the most popular club in town. It's also, however, quite a hike from the center; taking a taxi (L5) is worthwhile. (☎52 86 60. Beer from L5. Open Th-Su 10pm-late. Cash only.) **Club Night,** at Str. Curtea Domneasca 10, plays grinding techno music but is filled with comfortable seashell-style couches. (☎94 44 88. Open W-Su 10pm-late. Drinks from L3. Cash only.)

MONASTERIES AND CONVENTS

Many visit Bucovina just for the painted monasteries, hidden in hard-to-reach but beautifully untouched villages. Voroneţ and Humor are relatively accessible by public transportation; getting to Moldoviţa and Putna is harder; reaching the others is very, very difficult but extremely rewarding. Hitchhiking is common, but Let's Go does not recommend it. A car tour, with a licensed guide, is by far the easiest way to see the monasteries. Tours cost €40-100 per car; arrange them in Suceava. Most monasteries only give tours to official tour groups, but some sell booklets (L5-20). It is considered respectful to wear long pants or skirts and to avoid tight-fitting clothing. Those breaking dress code will be required to don one of the monastery's skirts (regardless of gender), or will be denied entrance.

MOLDOVIŢA. Moldoviţa is a beautiful community of 40 nuns, who have surrounded the church inside their stone walls with a vibrant garden. Though the complex was destroyed shortly after Alexandru cel Bun (Alexander the Good) constructed it in 1402-10, the monastery was rebuilt in 1532-37, and the frescoes that adorn the church's outside walls have braved the elements since that time. The frescoes are among the best preserved in Romania, leading many to call their survival a miracle. After viewing these monumental works, visitors enter the church in a strange sort of limbo, as the doorway to the church is incorporated into the portrayal of the Last Judgment; it functions as the space between salvation and damnation. Inside, the walls are covered with a fully illustrated calendar. In chronological order, each day is frescoed with the story of its Saint. *(From Suceava, catch a train to Vama; 1hr., 8 per day, L4. Then to Vatra Moldoviţei; 40min., 3 per day, L2.30. If you want to return the same day, take the earliest train out of Suceava at around 7:30am. Open daily 7am-8pm. L4, students L2. Photo L6.)*

SUCEVIŢA. Suceviţa, the youngest of the monasteries at 407 years old, is as much a fortress as a convent. After passing 4m-thick walls and a watchtower, visitors enter through a tiny door meant to hinder mounted attackers. The frescos on the church's outside walls are so well preserved—even on the northern wall, which is stripped bare in almost every other monastery—that scientists debate the presence of a microclimate surrounding the high tower. On the southern wall there is another feature unique among the monasteries: a frescoed procession of ancient Greek philosophers instead of Saints. This wall also depicts a 30-step ladder to heaven, with each step representing the virtues one must attain to acquire a heavenly crown. While most of the monastery is painted in bright colors, particularly emerald green, the western wall remains incomplete—it is said that the artist fell to his death from a scaffold, and his ghost prevents the fresco's completion. *(Suceviţa lies 32km north of Moldoviţa. Public transportation is unavailable, but many car tours run out of Suceava. Hitchhiking from Moldoviţa is common, but Let's Go does not recommend it. Open daily 7am-8pm. L4, students L2. Photo L6.)*

ROMANIA

VORONEŢ. In 1488, it took Ştefan cel Mare precisely three months, three weeks, and three days to erect Voroneţ. But it was Petru Rareş, his illegitimate son, who, in 1524, added the frescoes that have earned it the title "Sistine Chapel of the East" and made it the most famous and visited of the monasteries. The rich **Voroneţ Blue** pigment, which changes shades depending on the humidity, still baffles art historians. Some believe the paint's secret ingredient to be crushed powder from the gemstone lapis lazuli, but many locals insist that divine intervention is the key ingredient. *(The monastery is accessible by foot from Suceava. Take Str. Ştefan cel Mare away from the center of town; following the signs, head left on Cartierul Voroneţ; the monastery is 5km down the road. A one-way cab should be L8. Open daily 7am-8pm. L4, students 2. Photo L6.)*

AGAPIA. All of Agapia's paintings inside the church are by Nicolae Grigorescu, the 19th-century Neoclassical master on the shortlist of Romania's greatest artists. After winning a nationwide contest, he spent 1858-61 producing icons, canvases, and a famous altar screen for the 14th-century church. Grigorescu is best known for his scenes of peasant life, and Agapia is his only foray into religious art. It is said that after painting in Agapia, he went to France to perfect his painting, and could never paint religious subjects with the same beauty again. Today, Agapia is a village of 160 nuns with their own houses and vegetable plots. It also houses an Orthodox high school for girls. *(Buses run from the Suceava autogara to Târgu Neamt, 9km from the monastery; 1½ hr., 3 per day, L7. From the bus station at Târgu Neamt, take a bus out to the monastery; 20min., 4 per day, L2. Monastery L3, students L1.50.)*

PUTNA. Ştefan cel Mare's first creation and final resting place, the white plaster-and-stone 1469 Putna Monastery was not completely rebuilt until 1982. Only one of the original towers has survived the ravages of fires, earthquakes, and attacks. No original frescoes remain, but repainting of the inside began in 2001 to celebrate the 500th anniversary of Ştefan's death, and is now close to completion. The church contains the marble-canopied **tomb** of Ştefan cel Mare and is thus one of the most revered churches in Romania. According to legend, the king left Putna's location up to God; climbing a nearby hill, he shot an arrow into the air. A slice of the oak that it struck is on display at the museum. Take your first right in the direction of town from the monastery to climb **Dealul Crucii** (Hill of the Cross), Ștefan's shooting point, for a fantastic view. Two hills are marked with crosses—Ștefan's is the smaller one. *(Trains run from Suceava directly to Putna, 75km to the northwest; 2½hr., 4 per day, L6. The monastery is 1km from the train station. Turn right as you exit the platform and then left at the 1st intersection. Open daily 6am-8pm. Free. Photo L6. Museum open daily 9am-8pm. L4, students L2.)*

BLACK SEA COAST (DOBROGEA)

Controlled at different times by Greeks, Romans, and Ottoman Turks, the land between the Danube and the Black Sea has endured a turbulent history that has made it Romania's most ethnically diverse region. A stunning coastline stretches south, while the interior valleys hold the country's best vineyards. The sun-kissed beaches draw crowds of Romanians and foreigners in the summer, especially in peak season, July 1-August 15.

CONSTANȚA ☎(0)241

Constanța (COHN-stahn-tsah; pop. 307,500), the largest city on the Romanian Black Sea coast, has a dual identity: home to Romania's busiest port and its naval fleet, it is also the gateway city from which hordes of tourists explore the numerous resorts just kilometers away. Its museums, broad boulevards, and Roman ruins, however, also offer travelers a respite from beaches and crowds.

TRANSPORTATION. The **airport** (☎25 83 78), Aeroportul Internațional Constanța Mihail Kogălniceanu, Str. Tudor Vladimirescu 4, has daily flights to Bucharest, but catching the train to the city is much cheaper. Gara Costanța, the **train station,** at the end of B-dul. Ferdinand, has trains to: Brașov (7hr., 2 per day, L51); Bucharest (4-6hr., 7 per day, L38); Cluj-Napoca (13hr., 1 per day, L86); Suceava (9hr., 1 per day, L52); Timișoara (13hr., 1 per day, L86). Buy tickets at **CFR,** Vasile Canarache 4. (☎61 49 50. Open M-F 7:30am-7:30pm, Sa 8am-2pm. International booth open M-F 9am-4pm. Cash only.) **Minibuses** to Mangalia (every 20min., L5) leave from next to the train station on the opposite side of the building from the bus station; pay on board. Most stop in various beach resorts on the way, so ask the driver. Private companies run buses to a variety of domestic and international destinations from Autogara Sud, the **bus station,** Str. Theodor Burada, next to the train station. (Open daily

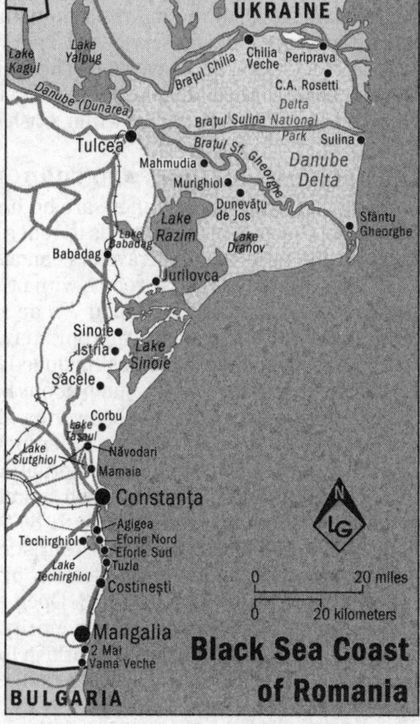

Black Sea Coast of Romania

5am-11pm.) **Ozlem, Condor,** and **Niş-Tur** (☎63 83 43) go to İstanbul, TUR (11hr., L100) via Varna, BUL (3½hr., L40). Local **buses, trolleybuses,** and **trams** run 5am-11:30pm along the city's main streets and connect the city center, the train and bus stations, and Mamaia (see p. 549). Buy tickets (L1 per trip) in advance from the few **RATUC** kiosks on the main streets. **Taxis** (☎55 55 55) should cost L1 per km and are common in the center and by the train station.

ORIENTATION AND PRACTICAL INFORMATION. To reach the city center from the train station, either walk straight ahead along B-dul. Ferdinand or take city bus #2, 4, or 5. The beach is only a short distance from **Piața Ovidiu,** the main square; walk north down Str. Mircea cel Bătrân and make any right turn. The quarterly English-language What, Where, When Constanța, in museums and hotels, has **maps** of the city and surrounding resorts. Most tourist agencies in town do not provide information about the Romanian Black Sea coast. For official information about the region, check out www.infolitoral.ro or call ☎55 50 00, but don't be fooled by the signs pointing you to a non-existent "official" office on Str. Traian. Instead try the Litoral **tourist office,** B-dul. Tomis 133. The English-speaking staff is exceptionally helpful and provides great maps, despite the fact the office is technically geared toward complete tours for tourists from abroad. (☎83 11 63; www.litoral.info.ro. Open M-F 9am-5pm.) **Banca Transilvania,** B-dul. Mamaia 134, **changes currency,** cashes **traveler's checks** for a 1.5% commission (€4 min.), and has a 24hr. **ATM.** (☎66 42 43. Open M-F 9am-6pm, Sa 9am-4pm.) **Luggage Storage** is in the basement of the train station. (L4 per day, L8 for a large bag. Open daily 6am-10pm.) **Heliofarm,** a **pharmacy,** is at B-dul. Tomis 80. (☎41 45 31. Open daily 7:30am-9pm. Cash only.) The **telephone office, Romtelecom,** B-dul Tomis 79-81, is right next door to the post office. (Open M-F 9am-6pm, Sa 9am-1pm. MC/V.) **Net Cafe Capitol,** B-dul. Mamaia 69, at the intersection with B-dul. Ferdinand, has **Internet** access and offers **copying** and **fax** services. (L3 per hr. Open 24hr. Cash only.) Several cafes around Pța. Ovidiu. also have **Wi-Fi.** The main **post office,** B-dul. Tomis 79-81, offers **Western Union** services and has **Poste Restante** at window #7. (☎66 46 34. Open M-F 7am-1pm and 1:30-8pm, Sa 8am-1pm. Cash only.) **Postal Code:** 8700.

ROMANIA

ACCOMMODATIONS AND FOOD. Budget accommodations are hard to come by in Constanța, and there are no hostels as of yet on the Romanian Black Sea coast. One option, however, is to rent a **private room** (from L20) from one of the locals at the train station. Travelers can also try **Hotel Tinerețului ❷,** B-dul. Tomis 20-26, for affordable, sparse rooms with private baths. While not much can be said for the hotel's dark hallways and 70s decor, its location—just a block from the main square—is unbeatable. Appropriately, there is also a disco downstairs. (☎61 35 90. English spoken. Breakfast included. Wi-Fi L2 per 2hr. Singles L84; doubles L94. Cash only.) Other hotels jump about L100 in price.

Cheap fast food, pizza, and shawarma abound in Constanța, particularly on B-dul. Tomis by Pța Ovidiu. For a classier meal, head to **Terassa Colonadelor ❸,** Str. Traian 57, where Romanian and international food is served in outdoors seating overlooking the sea. Try the fresh bakery for breakfast, or come during the evening for soothing live music. (☎61 80 58. Entrees L9-25. Open daily 9am-midnight. MC/V.) **On Plonge ❷,** Tomis Touristic Harbor, offers surprisingly affordable seafood considering its prime location overlooking Modern Beach and the Old Quarter. (☎60 19 05. Entrees L4-13. Open daily 10am-midnight. Cash only.) For a taste of one of Constanța's chief minority cuisines, try **Restaurant Nur ❹,** B-dul. Tomis 48, which offers authentic Turkish food, decor, and music. (☎91 21 21. Hookahs available. Entrees L15-26. Open daily 8am-midnight. Cash only.)

SIGHTS. Begin by strolling along the beautiful pedestrian walkway that lines the Black Sea from the commercial to the touristic port. On the way, you'll pass several statues honoring the city's history, ranging from fishermen to poets. Near the end of the walkway is the **Genoese lighthouse,** which was erected in the 19th century in honor of Genoese merchants who dominated the port's commerce during the 10th through 13th centuries. After the walkway is the Touristic Harbor and, a bit farther, **Modern Beach.** While not as clean or large as neighboring resorts, Modern Beach is convenient and provides a good view of the city. For a bit of intellectual exercise, head back to Piaţa Ovidiu for the **Museum of National History and Archaeology** (Muzeul Naţional de Istorie şi Arheologie Constanţa), Pţa. Ovidiu 12, which illustrates the city's history from Roman times to the present. Don't miss the fascinating 2nd-century Glykon Serpent, a snake which has the hair of a woman. (☎61 87 63. Open during high season daily 8am-8pm; low season W-Su 9am-5pm. L10, students L5. Photography L10. Cash only.) Next door, the museum's **Roman Mozaic Building** (Edificiul Roman cu Mozaic) showcases the remains of the intricate mosaic floor of the old Roman baths. (Hours same as museum. L5. Photography L10. Cash only.) Nearby, the **Museum of Art** (Muzeul de Artă), B-dul. Tomis 82-84, exhibits the work of 19th- and 20th-century Romanian artists, with a particularly sizable collection of Grigorescu's paintings displayed in a light inner atrium. (☎61 80 19. Open in high season daily 9am-8pm; low season W-Su 9am-5pm. L9, students L4.50. Photography L10.) The Muslim presence in the city is manifested chiefly in the **Great Mosque,** Str. Arhiepiscopiei 5. Built in 1823, the mosque's architecture is an interesting fusion of Egyptian-Byzantine and Romanian architecture. While the interior isn't very impressive, the view of the city from atop the 47m minaret is fantastic. (Open daily 9:30am-9:30pm. L4, students L2. Cash only.)

ENTERTAINMENT AND NIGHTLIFE. Operas, ballets, dramatic theatre, traveling shows, and festivals are performed on the stage of the **Teatrul National de Opera şi Balet "Oleg Danovski,"** Str. Mircea cel Bătrân 97. The box office is across the street through the park, on B-dul. Tomis 97. (☎48 14 60. Open M-F 9:30am-6pm, Sa-Su 10am-1pm and 3-6pm. Tickets from L40. Cash only.) For extensive and up-to-date nightlife listings, the weekly Romanian-language *Zile şi Nopţi* is available in many hotels and restaurants. Cafes line the streets in Constanţa, but if you're looking for a more upscale evening of drinking, head to **Cafe D'Art,** B-dul. Tomis 97, right next to the National Opera and Ballet Theater. A cultured crowd sips drinks outdoors in wrought-iron chairs, but radio hits playing in the background keep the atmosphere lively. (☎44 51 80. Beer L4-7. Cocktails L12-15. Open daily 10am-late. MC/V.) For those in the mood for dancing, **Club "No Problem,"** in Complex Dacia on B-dul. Tomis, draws a young crowd for the latest hits. (☎51 33 77. Cover L10 when live music. Open Th-Sa 10pm-5am. Cash only.)

MAMAIA ☎(0)241

The all-purpose behemoth of Romanian resorts, crowded Mamaia (Mah-MAH-yah) is located on a narrow spit of land running north and south between the Sea and Lake Suitghiol and is easily accessible for a quick beach holiday. Of all the Romanian Black Sea resorts, it features the widest array of watersports, bars, and clubs. Soak up rays on the long stretch of **beach,** which is less crowded at the northern and southern ends (although a fishery at the southern edge makes the northern end the less smelly choice). At **Aqua Magic,** a full-scale waterpark located on the far southern end of the beach, next to Hotel Perla, visitors enjoy inner tubes, waterslides like the "Space Bowl" and the "Black Hole," and, of course, island bars. (☎83 31 83; www.aquamagic.ro. Open June 15th-Sept. daily 10am-7pm.

L40, those under 1.5m tall L20. Cash only.) For a great view of the sea, or to avoid walking back to the hotel after an exhausting day of sunbathing, the **Telegondola** offers a leisurely ride above the resort between the Perla Hotel, on the south end of Mamaia, and Hotel Albatros, in the middle of the strip. (Open daily 10am-10am. L8, round-trip L15. Cash only.) Nightlife centers around the countless **"summer clubs,"** open-air bars right on the beach. These are built each June and taken down when the crowds depart at the end of the summer.

Unless you come with a tour group, be prepared to seek your own accommodations by asking directly at hotels. If at all possible, call ahead, particularly on the weekends, as rooms fill up quickly. The small rooms at **Hotel Delta ❷**, on the southern half of the beach and past the waterpark, are covered in the Black Sea coast's ubiquitous 70s decor but also offer private, new bathrooms and balconies. (☎83 19 65. Doubles L120-130. Cash only.) **Hotel Ovidiu ❷**, a few hotels past Delta and one of the cheaper options in Mamaia, offers basic accommodations in tiny rooms with balconies and private bathrooms. Ask for a room on a higher floor; these are significantly nicer than ground-floor accommodations. (☎83 15 90. Doubles L80; triples L100. Cash only.) Toward the northern end of the strip, there are several **campgrounds** and **bungalow colonies. Tourist Camping ❷**, at the northern end of Mamaia proper, rents bungalows that include TVs and refrigerators. (☎83 11 45. Reception 24hr. Doubles L100; triples L120. Tent sites L8 per person. Cash only.) Vacationers in Mamaia survive mostly on carnival food. If you're looking for a more serious meal, try **Balans Steakhouse ❸**, near the middle of the strip, which serves good international food outdoors in comfortable swings. (☎72 91 08 51 29. Entrees L9-40. Open daily 11am-midnight. Cash only.) To reach Mamaia from **Constanța**, take the #23E or #41 city bus. (20min. from train station; L1.)

ROMANIA

COSTINEȘTI ☎(0)241

Costinești (coh-stee-NEHSHT), crowded during high season with boisterous young Romanians, offers a great, wide beach by day and loud fun by night. Historically a youth resort, Costinești still provides a vacation at a low price—relative to to the rest of the coast, that is. The main road, **Strada Tineretului**, runs parallel to much of the beach, but veers away towards the railroad tracks, where it turns into **Str. Principala.** Walk downhill from the main road to get to the beach, which features views of the wreckage of *Evangelia*, a 1960s Greek shipping boat. A paved walkway runs along the shore and past Costinești's artificial **lake**, where you can rent **boats** and **hydrobikes.** (Booth is on the lakeshore. L10 per hr. Cash only.) One of the most popular **nightclubs** along the walkway is the outdoor **Disco Ring**, where Romanian youth dance to the latest hits among smoke machines and strobe lights. (Beer L4. Cover L5. Open daily 9pm-late.)

Along the walkway and past the lake, you'll find several hotels, most of which are aging, overpriced, or both. Any one of the new villas springing up on the north end of the beach are a better option, as they are clean, nicely decorated, and conveniently located. **Villa Vicky ❷**, Str. Profesor Georgi Alexianu 1, a white house towards the north end of the beach near the shipwreck, offers large new rooms with private baths and balconies with beautiful sea views. (☎29 95 99. Doubles L80. Cash only.) For those seeking less expensive accommodations, a number of bungalow colonies line the pedestrian walkway on the southern section of the beach. All offer small rooms and shared baths. Most bungalow rooms cost about L20 per person, but singles are hard to come by, and a double will automatically run you L40. Another possibility is a private room; look for signs reading *Cazare* or *Camere Libere* outside houses. Hot running water isn't a sure thing in Costinești, so check before booking accommodations. Cheap meals abound near the train station, on the main street, and on the terraces overlooking the coast. A swankier option is the traditional **Rustic Poienița ❸**, along the beach on Str. Marii, with plenty of outdoor seating at carved wooden tables. Try the *tigaie picanta* (L13), a frying pan full of delicious pork, beef, chicken, and veggies. (☎43 75 01. No English menu. Pizza L8-13. Entrees L9-23. Cash only.)

If you are arriving by **train**, get off at "Costinești Tabără," head down Str. Tineretului, and take any right turn to get to the beach. Trains go to Constanța (50min., 9-20 per day, L3). **Microbuses** stop at the shelter near the red post office on the main street. Check in Constanța to be sure your bus is stopping in Costinești. Return buses depart for Constanța (30min., every 15min., L5).

VAMA VECHE ☎(0)241

A tiny fishing village just a few kilometers from the border with Bulgaria, **Vama Veche** (Vah-mah VEH-key; pop. 200) was spared the massive touristic buildup of the rest of the Romanian Black Sea coast due to communist concern over border control. As a result, intelligentsia flocked here for their summer vacations, attempting to live a Bohemian lifestyle far from the intrusive eyes of the repressive Ceaușescu regime. To this day, Vama Veche remains a destination for Romania's counterculture, with hippies, punks, and goths flocking to camp on the **nude beach** and rock out under the stars. Although some hotels have sprung up in recent years, a campaign to stop the touristic buildup—termed Save Vama Veche—has begun; its advocates hold an annual rock concert on the beach in July. For evening entertainment, try **El Comandante Club**, which plays *musica para la resistencia*—which basically amounts to rock and 80s music. Young Romanians swig beer and bask in their own edginess at this chill bar on the north end of the beach. (Beer L4.50. Open high season 24hr.; low season 10am-late. Cash only.)

Despite the relative lack of tourists, prices of hotels and bungalows are as expensive here as on the rest of the coast, so make like the locals and bring a tent for **camping** on the beach (L3 per person). Another budget option is to rent a **private room** (from L15 per night); look for *Cazare* signs outside houses. If you do need a hotel room, however, head to the **Dispecerat de Cazare** midway along the main street; they book rooms during the high season. (☎88 90 87. L80-200. Open 9am-6pm. Cash only.) Vama Veche doesn't offer many dining options beyond fast food stands, so head into nearby Mangalia for more choice.

To get to Constanța from Vama Veche, first catch the **minibus** to Mangalia (15min., 1 per hr. 6am-7pm, L2), and then take a **bus** or minibus to Constanța (40min., 3 per hr. 5am-8pm, L5). Buses and minibuses leave across the street from the bus and train stations in Mangalia; they cost the same as the train but are faster and run more often.

RUSSIA (РОССИЯ)

Over a decade since the fall of the USSR, mammoth Russia still struggles to redefine itself. Between fierce, worldly Moscow and graceful, majestic St. Petersburg lies a gulf as wide as any in Europe—and a swath of provincial towns that seem frozen in time. Rich in history, mysterious, and inexpensive, with good public transportation and scores of breathtaking sights, Russia is in many ways an ideal destination for the adventurous budget traveler. While the legacy of Communism endures through present-day bureaucratic headaches, the fragile situation in neighboring Chechnya raises tensions, Russia remains the epitome of Eastern European grandeur. Opulent tsarist palaces, fossilized Soviet edifices, and a bounty of storied theaters and museums bear witness to one of the richest cultural heritages on Earth.

DISCOVER RUSSIA: SUGGESTED ITINERARIES

ONE WEEK. Explore the many remains of the Soviet Empire in newly cosmopolitan **Moscow** (3 days; p. 562). Then hop the train to **St. Petersburg** (3 days; p. 587) to explore the city's literary, architectural, and artistic grandeur. If you can tear yourself away from the glorious canals, take a day to visit **Peterhof** (p. 610), the stunning residence of the former tsars.

TWO WEEKS. After five days in **Moscow,** head to historic **Suzdal** (2 days; p. 583) to gawk at medieval riches, before taking the train to **St. Petersburg** (4 days). After a day at **Peterhof,** visit the imperial palaces of **Pavlovsk** (1 day; p. 611) and **Tsarkoye Selo** (1 day; p. 611) or head straight for peaceful **Novgorod** (2 days; p. 612), a capital of Kievan Rus.

RUSSIA

FACTS AND FIGURES

Official Name: Russian Federation.

Capital: Moscow.

Major Cities: St. Petersburg, Nizhniy Novgorod, Novosibirsk, Yekatarinburg.

Population: 141,378,000.

Time Zone (Western Russia): GMT +3.

Language: Russian.

Religions: Russian Orthodox (72%), Muslim (15%).

Chess Grandmasters: 156.

Oil Refining Ability: 6,600,000 barrels per day.

ESSENTIALS

WHEN TO GO

It may be wise to plan around the high season (June-Aug.). Autumn and spring (Sept.-Oct. and Apr.-May) are more appealing times to visit; the weather is mild and flights are cheaper. If you intend to visit the large cities and linger indoors at museums and theaters, the bitter winter (Nov.-Mar.) is most economical. Keep in mind, however, that some sights and accommodations close or run reduced hours. Another factor to consider is hours of daylight—in St. Petersburg, summer light lasts almost to midnight, but in winter the sun sets at around 3:45pm.

DOCUMENTS AND FORMALITIES

ENTRANCE REQUIREMENTS.

Passport: Required for all travelers.

Visa: Required for all travelers.

Letter of Invitation: Required for all travelers.

Inoculations: Recommended up-to-date on DTaP (diphtheria, tetanus, and pertussis), Hepatitis A, Hepatitis B, MMR (measles, mumps, and rubella), polio booster, rabies, and typhoid.

Work Permit: Required of all foreigners planning to work in Russia.

International Driving Permit: Required of all those planning to drive in Russia.

RUSSIA: PROJECT SURVIVAL

It's common knowledge that tourists should never go anywhere in Russia without certain essential items: passports, visas, bulletproof vests, and some 500R in case of unexpected "fines" from the police.

Another item, however, should now be added to the list. Upon entering the country, you'll fill out two immigration cards: one you'll immediately give away, and the other you'll keep.

But I didn't keep it. Upon registering my visa with a travel company in St. Petersburg, I gave away my card in exchange for a small slip of gray paper I assumed was more important. Some three weeks later, however, I arrived in Novgorod after dark and attempted to check in to my hotel. I was told that they could not legally board me—with or without my 500 rubles—and was turned away into the dark. After a long night best forgotten, I arrived at the Novgorod tourist office in the morning and found my guardian angel. Three hours of phone calls and a chauffeured trip to a government office later, I recieved another card and realized just how vital it was—and how lucky I had been.

The moral of the story? In Russia, documents are a basic need without which there can be no survival. Hold on to them for dear life. Oh, and I'm kidding about the bulletproof vest. Mostly.

—Alina Mogilyanskaya

EMBASSIES AND CONSULATES. Foreign embassies to Russia are in Moscow (p. 562); consulates are in St. Petersburg (p. 587). Russian embassies and consulates abroad include: **Australia,** 78 Canberra Ave., Griffith, ACT 2603 (☎662 959 033; www.australia.mid.ru); **Canada,** 285 Charlotte St., Ottawa, ON K1N 8L5 (☎613-235-4341; www.rusembcanada.mid.ru); **Ireland,** 184-186 Orwell Rd., Rathgar, Dublin 14 (☎14 92 20 48; www.ireland.mid.ru); **New Zealand,** 57 Messines Rd., Karori, Wellington (☎44 76 61 13, visa info 476 9548; www.rus.co.nz); **UK,** 13 Kensington Palace Gardens, London W8 4QX (☎20 72 29 36 28, visa info 229 8027; www.great-britain.mid.ru); **US,** 2650 Wisconsin Ave., NW, Washington, D.C. 20007 (☎202-298-5700; www.russianembassy.org).

VISA AND ENTRY INFORMATION. Almost every visitor to Russia needs a visa. The standard tourist visa is valid for 30 days, while a business visa is valid for up to three months. Both come in single-entry and double-entry varieties. All applications for Russian visas require an **invitation.** Hostels and hotels often provide invitations for tourist visas. If you have an invitation from an authorized travel agency or Russian organization and want to get a visa on your own, apply for the visa in person or by mail at a Russian embassy or consulate; for same-day processing, however, you must apply in person. (Download an application form at www.ruscon.org.) Prices vary by processing speed. Single-entry visas US$100-300; double-entry US$150-350, except on 10-day processing; multiple-entry US$100-450. **Visa services** and **travel agencies** can also provide business and tourist visa invitations (US$30-80), as well as secure visas in a matter of days (from US$160). **Host Families Association (HOFA),** 3 Linia 6, V.O., St. Petersburg 199053, Russia (☎91 19 14 27 62, 81 22 75 19 92; www.hofa.us), arranges homestays, meals, and transport. Visa invitations for Russia, Ukraine, and Belarus cost US$30-40. **VISAtoRUSSIA.com,** 309A Peters St., Atlanta, GA 30313, USA (☎800-339-2118, in Europe 749 59 56 44 22; www.visatorussia.com), provides Russian visa invitations from US$30.

The best way to cross the **border** is to fly directly into Moscow or St. Petersburg. Another option is to take a train or bus into one of the major cities. Upon arrival, travelers must fill out an **immigration card,** part of which must be kept until departure from Russia, and **register** their visa within three working days. Registration can be done at your hostel or hotel, or for a fee at a travel agency. As a last resort, head to the central **OVIR** (ОВИР) office to register. Though many travelers skip this nuisance, fines for visa non-registration run about US$150. When in Russia, carry your passport at all times; never, ever give it to anyone, except to hotel or OVIR staff during registration.

TOURIST SERVICES

There are two types of Russian tourist offices—those that only arrange tours and those that offer general travel assistance. Offices of the former type are often unhelpful with general questions, but those of the latter are usually eager to assist, particularly with visa registration. While Western-style tourist offices are rare, big hotels often house tourist agencies with English-speaking staff. The most accurate maps are sold by street kiosks. A great online resource is www.waytorussia.net.

MONEY

RUBLES (R)		
	AUS$1 = 21.72R	10R = AUS$0.46
	CDN$1 = 24.07R	10R = CDN$0.42
	EUR€1 = 34.85R	10R = EUR€0.29
	NZ$1 = 19.27R	10R = NZ$0.52
	UK£1 = 51.57R	10R = UK£0.19
	US$1 = 25.45R	10R = US$0.39

The Russian unit of currency is the **рубль** (ruble; R), plural рубли (ru-BLEE), which come in banknote denominations of 5, 10, 50, 100, 500, and 1000 and in coin denominations of 1, 2, and 5. Each ruble is divided into 100 **копейки** (kopecks; k), singular копейка, which comes in denominations of 1, 5, 10 and 50. Government regulations require that you show your passport when you exchange money. Find an **Обмен Валюта** (Obmen Valyuta), hand over your currency—most will only exchange US dollars and euro—and receive your rubles. **Inflation** runs around 9%. Do not exchange money on the street. **Banks** offer the best combination of good rates and security. **ATMs** (банкоматы; bankomaty) linked to all major networks can be found in most cities. As identity theft rings sometimes target ATMs, however, travelers should use machines located inside banks and check for evidence of tampering. Banks, large restaurants, and currency exchanges often accept major **credit cards,** especially Visa. Main branches of banks will usually accept **traveler's checks** and give **cash advances** on credit cards. It's wise to keep a small amount of money (US$20 or less) on hand. Most establishments don't accept torn, written-on, or crumpled bills, and Russians are wary of old US money; bring new bills. Keep in mind, however, that establishments that display prices in dollars or euro also tend to be much more expensive.

HEALTH AND SAFETY

EMERGENCY	**Ambulance:** ☎03. **Fire:** ☎01 **Police:** ☎02.

In a **medical emergency,** either leave the country or go to the American or European Medical Centers in Moscow or St. Petersburg; these clinics have English-speaking, Western doctors. Water is drinkable in much of Russia, but not in Moscow or St. Petersburg; buy **bottled water.** Men's **toilets** are marked with an "M," women's with a "Ж." The 0.5-5R charge for public toilets generally gets you a hole in the ground and maybe a piece of toilet paper. **Pharmacies** abound and offer a range of Western products; look for the "Аптека" (apteka) signs.

Crimes against foreigners are on the rise, particularly in Moscow and St. Petersburg. Although it is often difficult to blend in, try not to flaunt your nationality. Seeming Russian may increase your chances of police attention, but keeps you safer among the citizenry. Avoid interaction with the police unless an emergency necessitates it. It is legal for police to stop anyone on the street, including foreigners, to ask for documentation; **carry your passport and visa with you at all times.** If you do not (and sometimes even if you do), expect to be taken to a police station and/or to be asked to pay a fine. Although Let's Go does not endorse bribery, some travelers report that such "fines" are negotiable and, for minor infractions, should not amount to more than 500-1000R. Do not let officials go through your possessions; some travelers have reported incidences of police theft. If police try to detain you, threaten to call your embassy ("*ya pozvonyu svoyu posolstvu*"). Sometimes, it may be simpler and safer to go ahead and pay.

The concept of **sexual harassment** hasn't yet reached Russia. Local men will try to pick up lone **women** and will get away with offensive language and actions. The routine starts with an innocent-sounding "*Devushka...*" (young lady); say "*Nyet*" (No) or simply walk away. Women in Russia tend to dress quite formally, often wearing skirts or dresses rather than pants and tight-fitting blouses rather than T-shirts. This is especially true in St. Petersburg and Moscow. Those who do not speak Russian will also find themselves the target of unwanted attention. The authorities on the Metro and police on the street will frequently stop and question dark-skinned individuals, who may also receive rude treatment in shops and restaurants. Although **violent crime** against foreigners is generally rare, anti-Semitic and racist hate crimes—including murder—are on the rise. **Homosexuality** is still taboo even in the larger cities; it is best to be discreet.

TRANSPORTATION

BY PLANE. Most major international carriers fly into **Sheremetyevo-2** in Moscow or **Pulkovo-2** in St. Petersburg. **Aeroflot,** Leningradskiy Prospect 37, Building 9, Moscow 125167 (☎49 52 23 55 55; www.aeroflot.org) is the most popular domestic carrier. The majority of domestic routes are served by Soviet-model planes, many of which have poor safety records. From London, England, Aeroflot offers cheap flights into Russia. A number of European budget airlines land in Tallinn, Estonia (easyJet; www.easyjet.com), Rīga, Latvia (Ryan Air; www.ryanair.com), or Helsinki, Finland, from which you can reach Russia by bus or train.

BY TRAIN AND BY BUS. In a perfect world, all travelers would fly into St. Petersburg or Moscow, skipping customs officials who tear packs apart and demand bribes, and avoiding Belarus entirely. Nevertheless, many travelers find themselves headed to Russia on an eastbound train. If that train is passing through Belarus, you will need a US$100 transit visa to pass through the country. If you wait until you reach the Belarusian border to get one, you'll likely pay more and risk a forced no-expense-paid weekend getaway in Minsk. Trains, however, are a cheap and relatively comfortable way to travel to Russia from Tallinn, Estonia, Riga, Latvia, and Vilnius, Lithuania. Domestically, trains are generally the best option. Weekend or holiday trains between St. Petersburg and Moscow sometimes sell out a week in advance. The best class is *lyuks*, with two beds, while the 2nd-class *kupeyny* has four bunks. The next class down is *platskartny,* an open car with 52 shorter, harder bunks. Aim for places 1-33; they're farthest from the bathroom. Day trains sometimes have a very cheap fourth class, "*opshiya,*" which typically only provides hard wooden benches. Hotels and tourist offices are invaluable resources for those who don't speak Russian; almost no train station officials speak English, and train schedules are impossibly complicated. **Women** traveling alone can try to buy out a *lyuks* compartment or can travel *platskartny* with the regular folk and depend on the crowds to shame would-be harassers into silence. *Platskartny* is a better idea on the theft-ridden St. Petersburg-Moscow line, as you are less likely to be targeted in that class.

Buses, less expensive than trains, are better for very short distances. Russian roads are in poor condition; by bus, long-distance trips can be bumpy. Buses are often crowded and overbooked; oust people who try to sit in your seat.

BY BOAT. Cruise ships stop in the main Russian ports: St. Petersburg, Murmansk, and Vladivostok. However, they usually allow travelers less than 48hr. in the city. In December 2002, a regular ferry route opened between Kaliningrad and St. Petersburg (1-2 per week; for schedules and fares see www.balticline.ru/eng/translubeca.htm). Kaliningrad ferries also operate to **Poland** and **Germany.** A river cruise runs between Moscow and St. Petersburg.

BY CAR AND BY TAXI. Although it is sometimes necessary to reach Russia's more remote regions, renting a car is both expensive and difficult, and poor road conditions, the necessity of bribing traffic inspectors, dangerous driving practices, and the frequency of automobile crime make the experience particularly stressful. If you must drive, however, remember to bring your **International Driving Permit. Avis, Budget,** and **Hertz** rent cars in Russia. Hailing a **taxi** is indistinguishable from **hitchhiking,** and should be treated with equal caution. Though it is technically illegal, most drivers who stop will be private citizens trying to make a little extra cash; even cars labeled taxis may not be official. Those seeking a ride should stand off the curb and hold out a hand into the street, palm down; when a car stops, riders tell the driver the destination before getting in; he will either refuse altogether or ask "*Сколько?*" (Skolko?; How much?), leading to negotiations. Non-Russian speakers will get ripped off unless they manage a firm agreement and are well-aware of the fair price—if the driver agrees without asking for a price, you must ask "*skolko?*" yourself (sign language works too). Never get into a car that has more than one person in it. Let's Go does not recommend hitchhiking.

KEEPING IN TOUCH

PHONE CODES	**Country code:** 7. **International dialing prefix:** 810. From outside Russia, dial the international dialing prefix (see inside back cover) + 7 + city code + local number. Within Russia, dial 8 + city code for intercity calls and simply dial the local number for local calls.

EMAIL AND INTERNET. Internet cafes are prevalent throughout St. Petersburg and Moscow, but aren't as popular outside these cities, where connections are less reliable. Internet typically costs 35-70R per hour.

TELEPHONE. Most public telephones take phonecards, which are sold at central telephone offices, Metro stations, and newspaper kiosks. When you are purchasing phonecards from a telephone office or Metro station, the attendant will often ask, "На улицу?" (*Na ulitsu?;* On the street?) to find out whether you want a card for the phones in the station or for outdoor public phones. Be careful: phone cards in Russia are very specific, and it is easy to purchase the wrong kind. For five-digit numbers, insert a "2" between the dialing code and the phone number. Make direct **international** calls from telephone offices in St. Petersburg and Moscow. Most new **mobile phones** are compatible with Russian networks and cell phone shops are common, but service can be costly. On average, a minute costs US$.20 and users are charged for incoming calls. Major providers Megafon, BeeLine GSM, and MTS have stores throughout the cities, as do rental chains like Euroset and

Svyaznoy. International access codes include: **AT&T,** which varies by region (see www.consumer.att.com/global/english/access_codes.html for specific info); **British Telecom** (☎08 00 89 07 00); **Canada Direct** (☎810 800 110 1012); **MCI,** which varies by region (see www.consumer.mci.com/international/english/resourcesaccessnos2.jsp for specific info); and **Sprint** (in Moscow ☎747 3324, outside Moscow 8095 747 3324).

MAIL. Mail service is more reliable leaving the country than coming in. Letters to the US arrive one to two weeks after mailing; letters to other destinations take two to three weeks. **Airmail** is "авиа" *(avia)*. Send mail "заказное" (*zakaznoye;* certified; 40R) to reduce the chance of it being lost. Most post office employees do not speak English; it can be helpful to say *"banderoley,"* which signifies international mail, and to know the Russian name of the country of destination. **Poste Restante** is *Pismo Do Vostrebovaniya.* Address envelopes: LAST NAME, first name, Postal Code, city, Письмо До Востребования, Россия.

ACCOMMODATIONS AND CAMPING

RUSSIA	❶	❷	❸	❹	❺
ACCOMMODATIONS	under 500R	501-750R	751-1200R	1201-2000R	over 2000R

The **hostel** scene in Russia averages US$18-25 per night. Some hostels will only accept Russian guests. **Hotels** offer several classes of rooms. "Люкс" *(Lyux)*, usually two-room doubles with TV, phone, fridge, and bath, are the most expensive. "Поли-люкс" *(Polu-lyux)* rooms are singles or doubles with TV, phone, and bath. The lowest-priced rooms are "без удобств" *(bez udobstv)*, which means one room with a sink. As a rule, only cash is accepted as payment. In many hotels, **hot water**—and sometimes all water—is only turned on for a few hours each day. In the larger cities, **private rooms** and **apartments** can often be found for very reasonable prices (about 200R per night). Outside major train stations, there are usually women offering private rooms to rent—bargain with them and ask to see the room before agreeing. **Camping** is very rare in Russia.

FOOD AND DRINK

RUSSIA	❶	❷	❸	❹	❺
FOOD	under 100R	101-200R	201-300R	301-500R	over 500R

Russian cuisine is a medley of dishes both delectable and unpleasant; tasty *borshch* (борщ; beet soup) can come in the same meal as *salo* (сало; pig fat). The largest meal of the day, *obed* (обед; lunch), includes: *salat* (салат; salad), usually cucumbers and tomatoes or beets and potatoes with mayonnaise or sour cream; *sup* (суп; soup); and *kuritsa* (курица; chicken) or *myaso* (мясо; meat), often called *kotlety* (котлеты; cutlets) or *bifshteks* (бифштекс; beefsteaks). Other common foods include *shchi* (щи; cabbage soup) and *bliny* (блины; potato pancakes). **Vegetarians** and **kosher** diners traveling in Russia will probably find it easiest to stick to the cuisine in large cities and to eat in foreign restaurants.

On the streets, you'll see a lot of *shashliki* (шашлики; barbecued meat on a stick) and *kvas* (квас), a slightly alcoholic dark-brown drink. Beware of any meat products hawked by sidewalk vendors; they may be several days old. *Russkiy Standart* (Русский Стандарт) and *Flagman* (Флагман) are the best **vodkas;** the much-touted *Stolichnaya* is made mostly for export. Among local **beers,** *Baltika* (Ђалтика; numbered 1-7 according to brew and alcohol content) is the most popular and arguably the best. *Baltika 1* is the weakest (5%), *Baltika 7* the strongest (7%). *Baltikas 4* and *6* are dark; the rest are lagers.

LIFE AND TIMES

HISTORY

THE NOT-SO-GOLDEN AGE. The earliest recorded settlers of European Russia were the Scandinavian **Varangians,** or **Rus,** in the ninth century AD. In 862, several of these Slavic tribes chose as their leader **Ryurik,** who established **Novgorod** and **Kyiv** as centers of power, thus founding the Russian state. In 1223, Batu Khan, the grandson of Genghis Khan, and the Mongol **Golden Horde** invaded, creating the world's largest empire. In 1480, however, the Mongol Khanate fell to civil war.

A TERRIBLE EPOCH. Duke of Muscovy **Ivan III** (1462-1505) filled the void left by the departure of the Mongols and began a drive to unify all East Slavic lands—parts of present-day Belarus, Russia, and Ukraine—under his rule. His grandson **Ivan IV** (the Terrible) was the first to take the title "tsar." Ruthless in both his public and personal life, Ivan killed his own son in a fit of rage, and his decrees led to the deaths of tens of thousands of his people. After Ivan's son Fyodor died childless in 1598, **Boris Godunov** became tsar until the **boyars** (nobles) deposed him. Instability followed until **Mikhail Romanov** ascended the throne in 1613, ushering in the dynasty that ruled until the 1917 Bolshevik Revolution. Mikhail's grandson **Peter the Great,** whose reign began in 1682, created a Westernized elite, expanded Russia's borders to the Baltic Sea, and built European-style St. Petersburg.

FRENCH INVASION. After resisting the French during Napoleon's invasion in 1812, Russian officers and young liberals launched the unsuccessful **Decembrist coup** on December 14, 1825. Russia's loss to the West in the **Crimean War** (1853-1856) spurred some of the reforms that the Decembrists had demanded 25 years earlier including the **liberation of the serfs** in 1861. **Alexander II,** "The Great Emancipator," was assassinated by populists two decades later.

WAR AND PEACE. The famine, peasant unrest, terrorism, and strikes of the late 1800s culminated in the failed **1905 Revolution,** but the forces of change were more successful twelve years later, when the February Revolution of 1917 deposed Tsar Nicholas II. Shortly after, **Vladimir Ilyich Lenin,** leader of the Bolsheviks, led the October Revolution, which turned the nation Communist. A **Civil War** followed the October Revolution, but the Communists won and the **Union of Soviet Socialist Republics (USSR)** was formed in 1922. After Lenin's death in 1924, **Josef Stalin** emerged triumphant from a period of infighting and proceeded to eliminate his rivals in a bloodthirsty reign that would kill as many as 20 million Russians and ethnic minorities. Stalin forced **collectivization** of Soviet farms and filled **Siberian gulags** (labor camps) with political prisoners.

BACK IN THE USSR. Stalin was able to find an ally only in **Adolf Hitler,** with whom he signed the **Nazi-Soviet Non-Aggression Pact** in August 1939. Hitler, however, broke the treaty and invaded Russia in 1941, catching the Soviet forces completely unprepared. Hitler's invasion was stymied by the long winter and his own tactical errors, however. In 1945, the Soviets took **Berlin** and gained status as a postwar superpower. Feeling abandoned by the Allies, Stalin reneged on agreements made at the **Yalta Conference** and refused to allow free elections in the nations of Eastern Europe. The USSR left its army in Eastern Europe as far west as East Germany, and the **Iron Curtain** descended on the continent.

BEHIND THE CURTAIN. In 1949, in response to the US-led Marshall Plan for European economic rehabilitation, the Soviet Union formed the **Council for Mutual Economic Assistance (COMECON),** which reduced the Eastern European nations to satellites of the Party's headquarters in Moscow. In his 1956 **"Secret Speech," Nikita**

Khrushchev denounced the terrors of the Stalinist period. He also inaugurated the space race with the US by launching **Sputnik,** the first space satellite, into orbit in 1957. A brief political and cultural "thaw" followed, lasting until 1964, when Khrushchev was ousted by **Leonid Brezhnev.** Over the coming decades, the Party elites aged and weakened, and the geriatric regime finally gave way to 56-year-old firebrand **Mikhail Gorbachev** in 1985. Gorbachev began an age of political and economic reform symbolized by the new ideals of **glasnost** (openness) and **perestroika** (rebuilding). Despite hopes of regaining superpower status, the country gradually turned into a bewildering hodgepodge of near-anarchy, economic crisis, and cynicism. Discontent with reforms, coupled with a failed right-wing coup in August 1991, led to the **dissolution of the Soviet Union** on December 25, 1991.

THE PARTY'S OVER. Presiding over a freer but still-poor country, Russia's first president, **Boris Yeltsin,** instituted chaotic free-market reforms that resulted in widespread corruption and economic disparity. Any successful policies came crashing down in the financial crisis of August 1998, and **inflation** skyrocketed. In 1991, Russia banded together with many of the other former Soviet republics to create the **Commonwealth of Independent States (CIS),** but the largely symbolic organization has only begun to act as a common economic area.

TODAY

Yeltsin's resignation on January 1, 2000 marked the first-ever voluntary transfer of power by a Russian leader—Soviet leaders had maintained the tsarist tradition of either being forced from office or leaving in a casket. He passed on the presidency to his prime minister, ex-KGB official **Vladimir Putin,** who made economic growth a priority and helped stabilize the ruble. The "road to democracy," however, remains bumpy: Putin's domestic reform policies sometimes smack of the old regime. The government continues to shut down independent news sources and, in 2007, began to demand that 50% of the news covered by the press be "positive." Likewise, corruption and bribery persist; in 2005, bribes were estimated to have reached US$316 billion per year, double the government's yearly revenue. Meanwhile, a series of attacks by rebels from neighboring **Chechnya,** including the horrific siege and massacre at a Beslan school in 2004, has prompted Russia to escalate its war on terrorism. A rebel cease-fire declared in 2005 seems to have done little to calm high tensions.

Although Putin is due to leave office in 2008, he remains hugely popular, and some citizens have called on the government to alter the constitution so that he can serve a—currently illegal—third term in office.

PEOPLE AND CULTURE

DEMOGRAPHICS. Since the fall of the USSR, **Russian Orthodoxy,** headed by **Patriarch Aleksey II,** has emerged from hiding. Despite the Patriarch's claim that the Orthodox Church does not seek state-status, the Russian state has favored the Orthodox Church by making it difficult for other religious groups to own property or worship in public. Despite the homogeneity of its western regions (including Moscow and St. Petersburg), Russia is a very diverse country, home to over 85 ethnic groups. Most Tatar and Turkish groups in Russia, such as the **Turkmen** of the Caspian Sea region and the **Tatars** around Kazan, are **Muslim; Asiatic Inuits** practice **animism,** and Mongolian-speaking groups, such as the **Buryat,** are **Buddhist.**

LANGUAGE. Russian is an East Slavic language written in the Cyrillic alphabet. Once you get the hang of the Cyrillic alphabet, you can pronounce just about any Russian word, even if you think you sound like an idiot. Although **English** is increasingly common among young people, don't expect English to be spoken by anyone over the age of 30 or to find English resources anywhere outside of the largest cities; come equipped with at least a few helpful Russian phrases. For a phrasebook and glossary, see **Appendix: Russian,** p. 802.

CUSTOMS AND ETIQUETTE. Bribery and corruption are as ubiquitous as vodka in Russia. While officials and police are largely respectful and honest, do not give them a reason to hassle you: always carry your passport and visa, obey the law, and follow their instructions. If you are asked for a bribe, remain calm; travelers report that such bribes should be negotiable and not steep: for minor "infractions," this means 500-1000R. Be aware of transaction fees associated with being foreign, which are often legal. On **public transportation,** it's polite to give one's seat to the elderly, pregnant women, and women with children. **Loud talking** and **whistling** in public is disrespectful, while the "ok" sign (made by touching the thumb and forefinger) may be seen as a **vulgar gesture.** Russians rarely sit on the ground or floor.

Women should wear skirts and cover their heads when visiting Orthodox churches. Locals note that criminals spot foreigners by their sloppy appearances; Russian women in particular dress quite formally. Women should avoid leaning with their backs to the wall with one leg bent so that the foot is flat against the wall, as this is the posture typically assumed by a prostitute. Russians wear blue jeans but never wear **shorts.** When at a dinner table, put your wrists on the edge of the table. If you are served **vodka** and do not wish to drink it, in order to avoid offending your hosts, invent a medical excuse, claim to be an athlete, or say you will have to drive later. In restaurants, a 5-10% **tip** is becoming customary.

THE ARTS

LITERATURE. Ever since Catherine the Great exiled **Alexander Radishchev,** whose *Journey from St. Petersburg to Moscow* (1790) documented the dehumanizing nature of serfdom, Russian literature and politics have been closely intertwined. The country's most beloved literary figure, **Alexander Pushkin,** was not allowed to publish for five years after some of his poems were discovered among the papers of the Decembrists. Under the influence of literary critic **Vissarion Belinsky,** the 1840s turned toward Realism. The absurdist works of **Nikolai Gogol** were read as masterful social commentary in his own time: *Dead Souls* in particular exposed the corruption and decay of Russian feudal society. **Fyodor Dostoevsky's** psychologically penetrating novels, such as *Crime and Punishment* and *The Brothers Karamazov*, remain classics worldwide. The same can be said for the sweeping epics of **Leo Tolstoy,** who wrote *Anna Karenina* and *War and Peace.* Realism's last great voice belonged to **Anton Chekhov,** whose bleak domestic dramas and short stories distilled the power of his more long-winded predecessors.

At the beginning of the 20th century, with the influence of French symbolism drifting east, Russian poetry entered its **Silver Age,** led by **Alexander Blok.** The metaphysical vagueness of the Symbolists was soon challenged, however, by other movements and poets: **Anna Akhmatova** became known for her haunting, melancholic love verses, while the **Futurists** embraced the furious onset of technology in their verse. In the 1920s the state mandated **Socialist Realism,** a coerced glorification of socialism, and began a devasting crackdown on artistic freedom. Known for his classicism and lyrical density, **Osip Mandelstam** was imprisoned for writing a satirical poem about Stalin; he composed some of his works in exile before dying in a Siberian *gulag,* a fate he shared with numerous authors who wrote during the violent and oppressive 1930s. **Boris Pasternak** was awarded the Nobel Prize for his Civil-War-epic *Doctor Zhivago,* but the Soviet government forced him to decline its acceptance. The political "thaw" of the early 1960s allowed **Joseph Brodsky** to publish his verse and **Alexander Solzhenitsyn** to publish his *One Day in the Life of Ivan Denisovich*, a novel detailing life in a labor camp. The repressive measures of Premier Leonid Brezhnev, however, plunged the arts into an ice age from which Russia has yet to fully recover.

MUSIC. The early 20th century brought revolutionary ferment and artistic experimentation, as evidenced by the collaboration of composers **Igor Stravinsky** and **Sergei Diaghilev,** impresario of the Paris-based **Ballets Russes,** with choreographer **Vatslav Nizhinsky.** Despite repeated falls from favor, **Dmitri Shostakovich** maintained his stylistic integrity, often satirizing the unwitting Soviet authorities in his famous symphonies. His contemporary **Sergei Prokofiev** enjoyed more approval from the government. Virtuoso pianist and composer **Sergei Rachmaninov** fused the traditional romanticism of the Western school with a unique Slavic lyricism.

THE VISUAL ARTS. In the years immediately following the Revolution, painting and photography in the USSR blossomed, producing internationally-acclaimed artists such as **Wassily Kandinsky,** Belarussian-born **Marc Chagall,** Supremitist **Lev Malevich,** and neo-Primitivist **Natalya Goncharova.** Kandinsky, of Russian and Mongolian ancestry, and Malevich are acknowledged as pioneers of **Abstraction.** Soviet-period artists, confined by the strictures of **Socialist Realism,** were limited to painting canvases with such bland titles as "The Tractor Drivers' Supper." The young Soviet Union produced filmmakers of international stature, such as **Sergei Eisenstein** and his successor **Andrei Tarkovsky.**

HOLIDAYS AND FESTIVALS

Holidays: New Year's Holiday (Jan. 1-2); Orthodox Christmas (Jan. 7); Orthodox New Year (Jan. 14); Defenders of the Motherland Day (Feb. 23); Orthodox Easter Holiday (Apr. 27, 2008; Apr. 19th, 2009); Labor Day (May 1); Victory Day (May 9); Independence Day (June Accord and Reconciliation Day; Nov. 7); Constitution Day (Dec. 12).

Festivals: The country that perfected the "workers' rally" may have lost Communism but still knows how to Party. Come April, St. Petersburg celebrates Music Spring, an international classical music festival, which has a twin in Moscow (Apr. through May). In June, the city stays up late to celebrate the sunlight of White Nights (*Beliye Nochi;* mid-June to early July), with concerts, and fireworks. The Russian Winter Festival is celebrated in major cities from late Dec. to early Jan. with folklore exhibitions and vodka. People eat pancakes covered in honey, caviar, fresh cream, and butter during *Maslyanitsa* (Butter Festival; end of Feb.), a farewell to winter.

MOSCOW (МОСКВА) ☎(8)495

Change happens quickly in Moscow (pop. 12,600,000). Western visitors may feel like they're suspended between the high life and the underworld. When communism began to crumble, it left behind dust, drab Soviet housing complexes, and countless statues of Lenin. Yet, on 16th-century side streets, it's possible to glimpse the same golden domes that Napoleon saw after reaching the city in 1812. Invading Europe's largest city today is a thrilling, intense experience, flashier and costlier than Petersburg, and undeniably rougher too. Despite the threat of street crime and terrorism, and the bribes demanded of foreigners, President Putin's emphasis on security has made Moscow safer for visitors than ever before. Slowly, Moscow is re-creating itself as one of the world's most urbane capitals and embracing innovation with the same sense of enterprise that helped it command and then survive history's most ambitious social experiment.

Although the area code for most Moscow numbers is still 495, others now have a 499 area code. When dialing such numbers, always dial 8 + 499 + the local number, even from within Moscow.

INTERCITY TRANSPORTATION

Flights: International flights arrive at **Sheremetyevo-2** (Шереметьево-2; ☎956 4666). Take the van under the "автолайн" sign in front of the station to M2: Rechnoy Vokzal (Речной Вокзал), or take bus #851 to M2: Rechnoy Vokzal or bus #517 to M8: Planyornaya (Планёрная; 15R). Both buses and the Metro stop running at 1am. Purchase bus tickets at the *kassa* (касса) at **Tsentralnyy Aerovokzal** (Центральный Аэровокзал; Central Airport Station), Leningradskiy pr. 37 (Ленинградский), corpus 6 (☎941 9999), 2 stops on almost any tram or trolley from M2: Aeroport. **Taxis** to the center tend to be overpriced; bargain down to 750R. **Yellow Taxi** (☎940 8888) has fixed prices (base fare usually 400R). Cars outside the departures level charge 350-500R; agree on a price before getting in.

Air France, Korovyy Val 7 (Коровый Вал; ☎937 3839; fax 937 3838). M5: Dobryninskaya (Добрынинская). Open M-F 9am-6pm. Branch at Sheremetyevo-2, 2nd fl. (☎231 4748). Open 5-8am, 9am-4pm, and 5-8pm.

British Airways, 3-y Lesnoy per. 4, 5th fl. (3-й Лесной; ☎363 2525; fax 363 2507; www.britishairways.com). M2: Belorusskaya (Белорусская). In the large building with the "Capital Group" sign. Open M-F 9am-6pm.

Delta, 11 Gogolevskiy bul., 2nd fl. (Гоголевский; ☎937 9090; www.delta.com). M1: Kropotkinskaya (Кропоткинская). Open M-F 9-5:30pm.

Finnair, Kropotkinskiy per. 7 (Кропоткинский; ☎933 0056; www.finnair.com). M1 or 5: Park Kultury (Парк Культуры). Open M-F 9am-5pm.

Lufthansa, Posledniy per. 17 (Последний; ☎980 9999; www.lufthansa.ru). M6: Sukharevskaya (Сухаревская). Open M-F 9am-6pm, Sa 10am-3pm.

SAS, 1-ya Tverskaya-Yamskaya 5, 3rd fl. (1-я Тверская-Ямская; ☎775 4747; www.flysas.ru). M2: Mayakovskaya. Branch at Sheremtyevo ☎231 4747. Open M-F 9am-5:30pm.

Trains: Moscow has 8 train stations arranged around the M5 (circle) line. Tickets for international and longer domestic trips can be bought at the **Moskovskoye Zheleznodorozhnoye Agenstvo** (Московское Железнодорожное Агенство; Moscow Train Agency; Russian destinations ☎266 9333, international destinations 262 0604; www.mza.ru; MC/V), on the far side of Yaroslavskiy Vokzal from the Metro station. Tickets specify your name, wagon, seat, and station (вокзал; vokzal) of departure. Cyrillic schedules of trains, destinations, departure times, and station names are posted on the left side of the hall. *Kassa* open M-F 8am-1pm and 2-7pm, Sa 8am-1pm and 2-6pm. 24hr. service is available at the stations.

Belorusskiy Vokzal (Белорусский), pl. Tverskoy Zastavy 7 (Тверской Заставы; ☎266 0300). M2: Belorusskaya (Белорусская). To: **Berlin, GER** (27hr., 1 per day, 3820R); **Minsk, BLR** (7½-11hr., 3 per day, 550-1230R); **Prague, CZR** (32hr., 1 per day, 3800R); **Vilnius, LIT** (14½hr., 1 per day, 1360-1700R); **Warsaw, POL** (21hr., 2 per day, 2200R).

Kazanskiy Vokzal (Казанский), Komsomolskaya pl. 2 (Комсомольская; ☎266 2300). M5: Komsomolskaya. Opposite Leningradskiy Vokzal. To **Kazan** (10-12hr., 2 per day, 660-1550R).

Kiyevskiy Vokzal (Киевский), pl. Kiyevskogo Vokzala 2 (Киевского Вокзала; ☎84 99 24 07 071). M3 or 5: Kiyevskaya (Киевская). To destinations in Ukraine, including **Kyiv** (10-14hr., 4 per day, 760-2100R), **Lviv** (24hr., 1 per day, 1200-2600R), and **Odessa** (23hr., 1 per day, 1060-2500R).

Kurskiy Vokzal (Курский), Zemlyanoy Val 29/1 (Земляной Вал; ☎266 5310). M3: Kurskaya (Курская). To **Sochi** (38hr., 1 per day, 1300-3320R), **Sevastopol, UKR** (25hr., 3 per day, 1280-2600R), and destinations in the **Caucasus.**

Leningradskiy Vokzal (Ленинградский), Komsomolskaya pl. 3 (☎262 9143). M1 or 5: Komsomolskaya. To: **Pskov** (12hr., 1 per day, 800-1200R); **Novgorod** (8hr., 1 per day, 450-2000R); **St. Petersburg** (8hr., 10-15 per day, 500-2100R); **Helsinki, FIN** (14hr., 1 per day, 3500R); **Tallinn, EST** (16hr., 1 per day, 1300-2300R).

Paveletskiy Vokzal (Павелецкий), Paveletskaya pl. 1 (☎950 3700). M2: Paveletskaya. Serves the **Crimea** and eastern **Ukraine.**

Rizhskiy Vokzal (Рижский), pr. Mira 79/3 (пр. Мира; ☎631 1588). M6: Rizhskaya. To **Rīga, LAT** (16hr., 2 per day, 800-4000R) and destinations in **Estonia.**

Yaroslavskiy Vokzal (Ярославский), Komsomolskaya pl. 5a (☎921 5914). M1 or 5: Komsomolskaya. The starting point for the legendary **Trans-Siberian Railroad.** To **Novosibirsk** (48hr., every other day, 1900R-4900R), **Yaroslavl** (4hrs., 1-2 per day, 220-500R), **Siberia,** and the **Far East.**

Buses: Uralskaya ul. 2 (Уральская; ☎468 0400 or 468 3401). M3: Shchelkovskaya (Щелковская). Open 6:30am-11pm. Sends buses to: **Novgorod** (8½hr., 2 per day, 385R); **Pskov** (15hr., 3 per week, 600R); **St. Petersburg** (13hr., 2 per day, 740-751R); **Vladimir** (4hr., 2-4 per day, 156R); **Yaroslavl** (5hr., 5-6 per day, 260-311R).

ORIENTATION

A series of concentric rings radiates from the **Kremlin** (Кремль; Kreml) and **Red Square** (Красная площадь; Krasnaya ploshchad). The outermost street, the **Moscow Ring** (Московское Кольцо; Moskovskoye Koltso), marks the city limits, but Muscovites divide the world into two regions: the area that lies within the **Garden Ring** (Садовное Кольцо; Sadovnoe Koltso), and the area that doesn't. Most sights are within. The tree-lined **Boulevard Ring,** made up of 10 short, wide boulevards, makes an incomplete circle within the center. **Tverskaya** (Тверская), considered Moscow's main street, begins just north of Red Square and continues northwest along the green line of the Metro. The **Arbat** (Арбат) and **Novyy Arbat** (Новый Арбат), Moscow's hippest and most commercialized streets respectively, lie west of the Kremlin. **Zamoskvareche** (Замоскварече) and **Krymskiy Val** (Крымский Вал), the neighborhoods directly across the **Moscow River** to the south of Red Square, are home to numerous pubs, museums, mansions, and monasteries. To the east of Red Square is the ninth-century **Kitai-Gorod** (Китай-Город) neighborhood, packed with towering churches and bustling thoroughfares. English and Cyrillic **maps** (35-60R) are sold at kiosks and bookstores all over; look for "печать" and "книги" signs. See this book's color insert for maps of the Metro and the city center. Note that the Metro station Izmailovskiy Park, located on line 3, has changed names to Partizanskaya (Партизанская). Be careful when crossing streets, as drivers are notoriously oblivious to pedestrians; for safety's sake, most intersections have an underpass (переход; perekhod).

LOCAL TRANSPORTATION

Public Transportation: The **Metro** (Метро) is fast, clean, and efficient—a masterpiece of urban planning. A station serving more than 1 line may have more than 1 name. The M5 is known as the Circle Line (кольцевая линия; koltsevaya liniya). Trains run daily 6am-1:30am; changes between stations close at 1am. Rush hours are 8-10am and 5-7pm. Buy fare cards (17R; 5 trips 75R, 10 trips 140R) from *kassy* in stations. Buy **bus** and **trolleybus** tickets (15R) at kiosks labeled "проездные билеты" (proyezdnyye bilety), and from the driver (25R). Punch your ticket when you board or risk a 100R fine. Buses run 6am-1am. Monthly passes (единые билеты; yedinyye bilety), valid for buses, trolleybuses, trams, and the Metro, are sold at Metro *kassy* after the 18th of the month (1080R), as are unlimited 30-day Metro passes (770R).

METRO MADNESS. Moscow's subway system can seem bewildering. *Let's Go* has tried to simplify navigation by artificially numbering each line; for correspondences, consult this guide's color map of the Moscow Metro. When speaking with Russians, however, use the color or name, and not the number.

Taxis: Most taxis do not use meters and overcharge. **Yellow Taxis** (☎940 8888) have fixed rates (base fare 400R). Instead of taking a taxi, many locals "catch a car," called **gypsy cabs** (частники; chastniki), which are typically cheaper than cabs: they flag down a car on the street, determine where it's going, agree on a price, and hop a ride. Moscovites hold an arm out horizontally; when the driver stops, they tell him their destination and haggle over the price. Within the Garden Ring, a ride to almost anywhere is 100R; shorter trips cost around 50R. Be aware that even if you hail a car marked "taxi," you may still have to haggle, as many drivers use taxi markings simply to attract riders. If you're not fluent, be prepared to gesture. To be safe, never get into a taxi or car with more than 1 person already in it. Let's Go does not recommend hitchhiking.

PRACTICAL INFORMATION

TOURIST AND FINANCIAL SERVICES

Tours: The folks with loudspeakers on the northern end of Red Square hawk Russian-language walking tours of the area (1½hr., every 30min. 9am-2pm, 200R) and bus tours of the city's main sights (1hr., every 45min., 300R). Translators are sometimes available for an extra charge.

Patriarshy Dom Tours, Vspolnyy per. 6 (Вспольный; from the US ☎65 06 78 70 76, in Russia 49 57 95 09 27; www.russiatravel-pdtours.netfirms.com). M5 or 7: Barrikadnaya (Баррикадная). Offers a selection of English-language tours, including "Stalin's Moscow," which traces evidence of his personality throughout the city, and "Bulgakov in Moscow," which visits the principal settings of the novel *Master and Margarita* (510-2380R). A schedule of tours is available at various hotels and expat hangouts, including the Starlite Diner (see **Food,** p. 570). They also help with airline booking and offer visa support. Open M-F 9am-6pm. Cash only.

Capital Tours, Ilyinka 4 (Ильинка; ☎232 2442; www.capitaltours.ru), in Gostinyy Dvor, entrance 6. M3: Ploshchad Revolyutsii (Площадь Революции). Offers 3hr. English-language bus tours of the city center, covering everything from Cathedral of Christ the Savior to the Bolshoy Theater. Tours daily 11am and 2:30pm (750R). 3hr. tours of the Kremlin and Armory M-W and F-Su 10:30am and 3pm (1400R). 15% ISIC discount. MC/V.

Budget Travel: Student Travel Agency Russia (STAR), Baltiyskaya 9, 3rd fl. (Балтийская; ☎797 9557; www.startravel.ru). M2: Sokol (Сокол). Discount plane tickets, ISICs, and worldwide hostel booking. Branch at Mokhovaya 9 (Моховая), near the Kremlin. Open June-Aug. M-F 10am-7pm, Sa 11am-4pm, Su 11am-4pm; Sept.-May M-F 10am-7pm, Sa 11am-4pm.

Embassies: Australia, Podkolokolnyy per. 10/2 (Подколокольный; ☎956 6070; www.australianembassy.ru). M6: Kitai Gorod (Китай Город). Open M-F 9am-12:30pm and 1:10-5pm. **Canada,** Starokonyushennyy per. 23 (Староконюшенный; ☎105 6000; www.canadianembassy.ru). M1: Kropotkinskaya (Кропоткинская) or M4: Arbatskaya (Арбатская). Open 9am-3pm. **Ireland,** Grokholskiy per. 5 (Грохольский; ☎937 5911). M5 or 6: Prospekt Mira (Проспект Мира). Open M-F 9:30am-5:30pm. **New Zealand,** Povarskaya 44 (Поварская; ☎956 3579). M7: Barikadnaya (Барикадная). Open M-F 9am-12:30pm and 1:30-5:30pm. **UK,** Smolenskaya nab. 10 (Смоленская; ☎956 7200; www.britemb.msk.ru). M3: Smolenskaya. Open M-F 9am-1pm and 2-5pm. **US,** Novinskiy 21 (Новинский; ☎728 5000; www.usembassy.ru). M5: Krasnopresnenskaya (Краснопресненская). Open M-F 9am-6pm. **American Citizen**

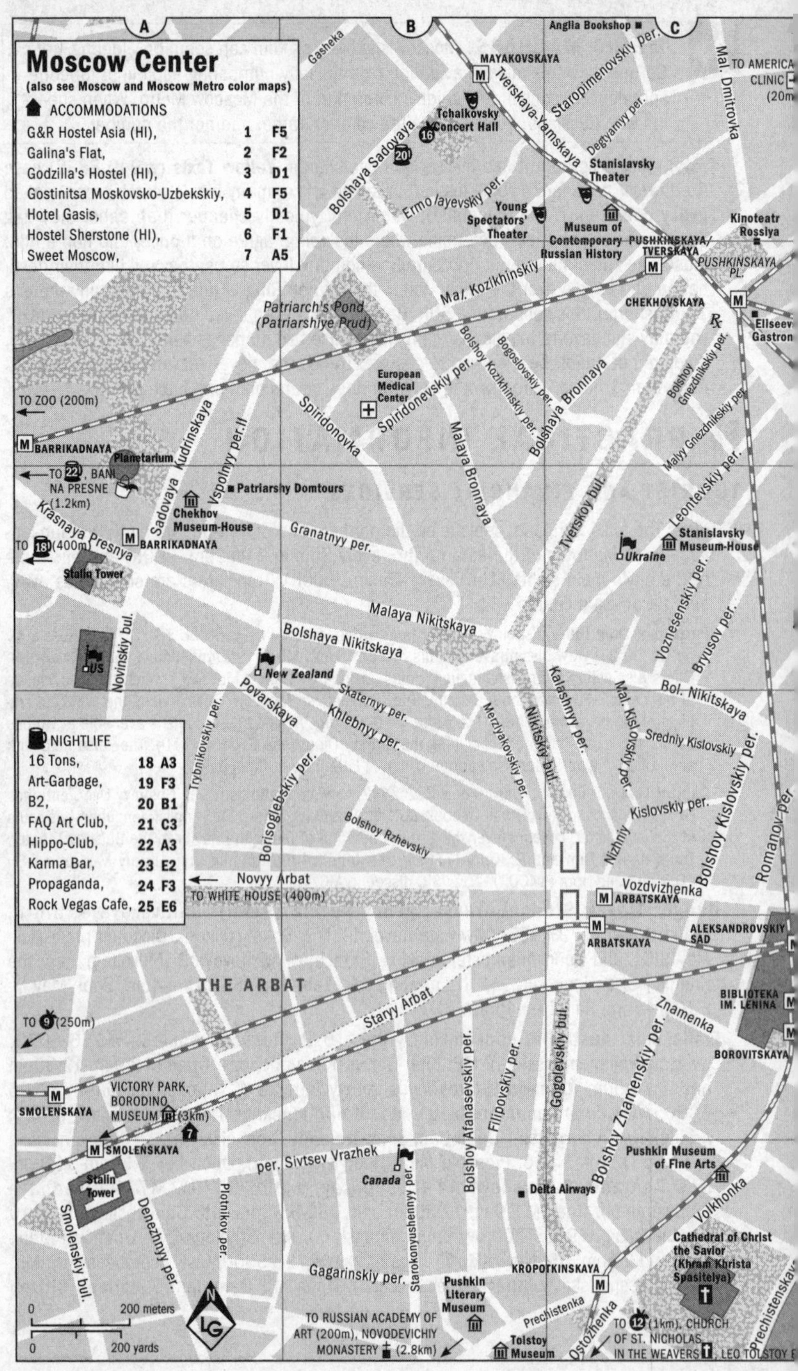
Moscow Center
(also see Moscow and Moscow Metro color maps)
ACCOMMODATIONS
G&R Hostel Asia (HI), 1 F5
Galina's Flat, 2 F2
Godzilla's Hostel (HI), 3 D1
Gostinitsa Moskovsko-Uzbekskiy, 4 F5
Hotel Gasis, 5 D1
Hostel Sherstone (HI), 6 F1
Sweet Moscow, 7 A5
NIGHTLIFE
16 Tons, 18 A3
Art-Garbage, 19 F3
B2, 20 B1
FAQ Art Club, 21 C3
Hippo-Club, 22 A3
Karma Bar, 23 E2
Propaganda, 24 F3
Rock Vegas Cafe, 25 E6
A
B
C
Gasheka
Anglia Bookshop
MAYAKOVSKAYA
Tverskaya-Yamskaya
Staropimenovskiy per.
Mal. Dmitrovka
TO AMERICA
CLINIC
(20m
Tchaikovsky
Concert Hall
Bolshaya Sadovaya
Degtyarnyy per.
Stanislavsky
Theater
Ermolayevskiy per.
Young
Spectators'
Theater
Museum of
Contemporary
Russian History
PUSHKINSKAYA/
TVERSKAYA
Kinoteatr
Rossiya
PUSHKINSKAYA
PL.
Mal. Kozikhinskiy
CHEKHOVSKAYA
Eliseev
Gastron
Patriarch's Pond
(Patriarshiye Prud)
Bolshoy Kozikhinskiy per.
Bogoslovskiy per.
Bolshaya Bronnaya
Bolshoy Gnezdnikskiy per.
Malyy Gnezdnikskiy per.
European
Medical
Center
Spiridonovka
Spiridonevskiy per.
Malaya Bronnaya
TO ZOO (200m)
BARRIKADNAYA
Planetarium
TO 22, BANI
NA PRESNE
(1.2km)
Sadovaya Kudrinskaya
Vspolnyy per.
Patriarshy Domtours
Chekhov
Museum-House
Tverskoy bul.
Leontevskiy per.
Stanislavsky
Museum-House
Ukraine
Granatnyy per.
Krasnaya Presnya
TO 18 (400m)
BARRIKADNAYA
Stalin Tower
Malaya Nikitskaya
Novinskiy bul.
US
Bolshaya Nikitskaya
New Zealand
Voznesenskiy per.
Bryusov per.
Bol. Nikitskaya
Skaternyy per.
Povarskaya
Khlebnyy per.
Trybnikovskiy per.
Borisoglebskiy per.
Merzlyakovskiy per.
Nikitskiy bul.
Kalashnyy per.
Mal. Kislovskiy per.
Sredniy Kislovskiy
Bolshoy Kislovskiy per.
Kislovskiy per.
Nizhniy
Bolshoy Rzhevskiy
Romanov per.
Novyy Arbat
TO WHITE HOUSE (400m)
Vozdvizhenka
ARBATSKAYA
ARBATSKAYA
ALEKSANDROVSKIY
SAD
THE ARBAT
Staryy Arbat
BIBLIOTEKA
IM. LENINA
Znamenka
TO 9 (250m)
Bolshoy Afanasevskiy per.
Filipovskiy per.
Gogolevskiy bul.
Bolshoy Znamenskiy per.
BOROVITSKAYA
SMOLENSKAYA
VICTORY PARK,
BORODINO
MUSEUM (3km)
SMOLENSKAYA
per. Sivtsev Vrazhek
Canada
Pushkin Museum
of Fine Arts
Stalin
Tower
Starokonyushennyy per.
Delta Airways
Volkhonka
Smolenskiy bul.
Denezhnyy per.
Plotnikov per.
Cathedral of Christ
the Savior
(Khram Khrista
Spasitelya)
Gagarinskiy per.
KROPOTKINSKAYA
Pushkin
Literary
Museum
Prechistenka
Prechistenskaya
0
200 meters
0
200 yards
TO RUSSIAN ACADEMY OF
ART (200m), NOVODEVICHIY
MONASTERY (2.8km)
Tolstoy
Museum
Ostozhenka
TO 12 (1km), CHURCH
OF ST. NICHOLAS
IN THE WEAVERS, LEO TOLSTOY

RUSSIA

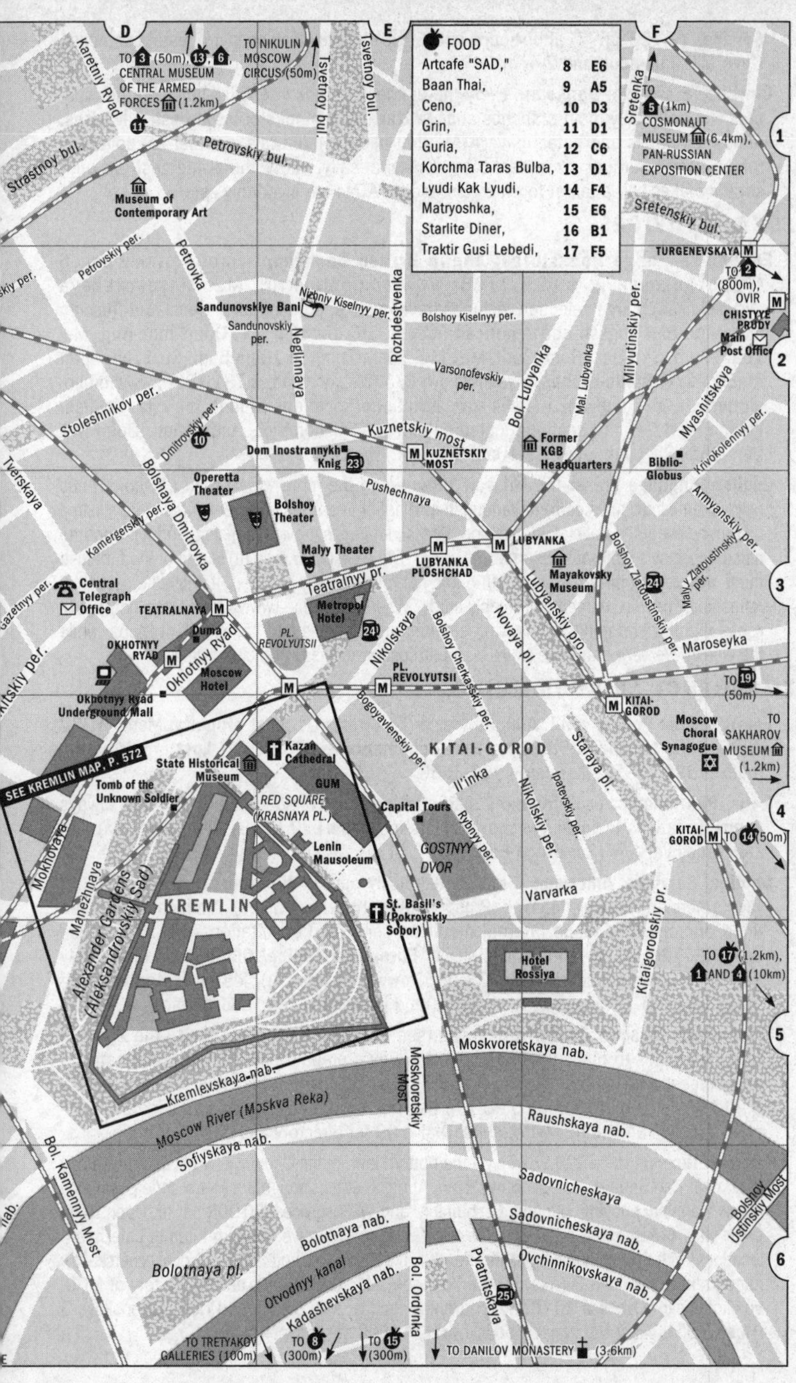
FOOD
Artcafe "SAD," 8 E6
Baan Thai, 9 A5
Ceno, 10 D3
Grin, 11 D1
Guria, 12 C6
Korchma Taras Bulba, 13 D1
Lyudi Kak Lyudi, 14 F4
Matryoshka, 15 E6
Starlite Diner, 16 B1
Traktir Gusi Lebedi, 17 F5
TO 3 (50m), 13, 6, CENTRAL MUSEUM OF THE ARMED FORCES (1.2km)
TO NIKULIN MOSCOW CIRCUS (50m)
TO 5 (1km) COSMONAUT MUSEUM (6.4km), PAN-RUSSIAN EXPOSITION CENTER
Museum of Contemporary Art
Sandunovskiye Bani
Dom Inostrannykh Knig
Former KGB Headquarters
Biblio-Globus
Operetta Theater
Bolshoy Theater
Malyy Theater
Central Telegraph Office
Mayakovsky Museum
Metropol Hotel
Duma
Moscow Hotel
Okhotnyy Ryad Underground Mall
Kazan Cathedral
State Historical Museum
Tomb of the Unknown Soldier
SEE KREMLIN MAP, P. 572
RED SQUARE (KRASNAYA PL.)
GUM
Capital Tours
Lenin Mausoleum
KREMLIN
St. Basil's (Pokrovskiy Sobor)
Hotel Rossiya
KITAI-GOROD
GOSTNYY DVOR
Moscow Choral Synagogue
TO SAKHAROV MUSEUM (1.2km)
TO 14 (50m)
TO 17 (1.2km), 1 AND 4 (10km)
TO 19 (50m)
TO 2 (800m), OVIR
Main Post Office
TURGENEVSKAYA
CHISTYYE PRUDY
KUZNETSKIY MOST
LUBYANKA
LUBYANKA PLOSHCHAD
TEATRALNAYA
OKHOTNYY RYAD
PL. REVOLYUTSII
KITAI-GOROD
Moscow River (Moskva Reka)
Bolotnaya pl.
TO TRETYAKOV GALLERIES (100m)
TO 8 (300m)
TO 15 (300m)
TO DANILOV MONASTERY (3.6km)

RUSSIA

Services (☎728 5577, after hours 728 5000) lists English-speaking establishments. Open M-F 9am-noon and 2-4pm.

Currency Exchange: Banks are everywhere; check for ads in English-language newspapers. Typically only main branches change **traveler's checks** or issue **cash advances.** Almost all banks and hotels have **ATMs** that allow withdrawals in either US dollars or rubles. Avoid outdoor machines; they work erratically, and withdrawing cash on busy streets makes you a target for muggers. Indoor ATMs are invariably safer.

LOCAL SERVICES

English-Language Bookstores: Anglia British Bookshop, Vorotnikovskiy per. 6 (Воротниковский; ☎699 7766; www.anglophile.ru). M2: Mayakovskaya (Маяковская). Large selection includes travel guides, phrasebooks, translated Russian literature, and English and American fiction. ISIC discount 5%. Open June-Aug. M-F 10am-7pm, Sa 10am-6pm; Sept.-May M-F 10am-7pm, Sa 10am-6pm, Su 11am-5pm. AmEx/MC/V. **Biblio-Globus,** Myasnitskaya 6/3 (Мясницкая; ☎781 1900; www.biblio-globus.ru). M7: Lubyanka (Лубянка). Additional locations around the city. English, French, and German sections including classics, dictionaries, and fiction. Open M-F 9am-9pm, Sa 10am-9pm, Su 10am-8pm. MC/V.

English-Language Press: The *Moscow Tribune* and the more widely read *Moscow Times* (www.themoscowtimes.com) have foreign and national articles and weekend sections listing upcoming events, a travel guide section, English-language movies, housing, and job opportunities. Moscow's infamous "alternative" paper, *The eXile* (www.exile.ru) is one of the funniest, most irreverent publications on earth but is not for the easily shocked. Its nightlife section is refreshingly candid, though undeniably crude. *Where* magazine (www.whererussia.com) publishes monthly shopping, dining, and entertainment listings and has excellent maps, while the weekly *Element* magazine (www.elementmoscow.ru) has good club listings.

RUSSIA

EMERGENCY AND COMMUNICATIONS

Emergencies: Police: ☎02. **Ambulance:** ☎03. **Fire:** ☎01. **Lost property:** Metro ☎222 2085, other transport 298 3241. **Lost documents:** ☎200 99 57. **Lost credit cards:** AmEx ☎933 6635, other cards 956 3556.

24hr. Pharmacies: Look for signs marked "круглосуточно" (kruglosutochno; always open). Locations include: Tverskaya 17 (Тверская; ☎629 6333), M2: Tverskaya; and Zemlyanoy Val 1/4 (Земляной Вал; ☎917 0434), M5: Kurskaya (Курская).

Medical Services: American Clinic, Grokholskiy per. 31 (Грохольский; ☎937 5757; www.americanclinic.ru). M5 or 6: Prospekt Mira (Проспект Мира). American board-certified doctors; family and internal medicine services. Consultations US$120. House calls US$220. Open 24hr. AmEx/MC/V. **European Medical Clinic,** Spiridoniyevskiy Per. 5/1 (Спиридониевский; ☎933 6555; www.emcmos.ru). M5 or 7: Barrikadnaya (Баррикадная). Gynecological, pediatric, and psychiatric care. Consultations 4320R.

Telephones: Moscow Central Telegraph (see **Post Offices,** below). Go to the 2nd hall with telephones to place international calls. Buy a prepaid phonecard for international and domestic calls. Collect calls and calling card calls not available. Calls to the US 0.90-18R per min., to Europe 0.90-14R per min. **Local calls** require phone cards, available at kiosks and some Metro stops. Dial ☎09 for directory assistance.

Internet: Timeonline (☎223 9687), on the bottom level of the Okhotnyy Ryad (Охотный Ряд) mall, near Red Square. M1: Okhotnyy Ryad. At night, enter through the Metro underpass. Also offers scanning, copying, printing, CD-burning, and Wi-Fi services. 50-90R per hr. Open 24hr. Cash only. **Cafemax** (☎787 6858; www.cafemax.ru). Massive, modern Internet cafe has 4 locations, with English-speaking staff: Pyatnitskaya 25/1 (Пятницкая; M2: Novokuznetskaya); Akademika Khokhlova 3 (Академика Хохлова; M1: Universitet), on the territory of MGU; Volokolamskoye shosse 10 (Волоколамское шоссе; M2: Sokol); and Novoslobodskaya 3 (Новослободская; M9: Novoslobodskaya). 24-100R per hr. Open 24hr. MC/V.

Post Offices: Moscow Central Telegraph, Tverskaya ul. 7 (Тверская), uphill from the Kremlin. M1: Okhotnyy Ryad (Охотный Ряд). **International mail** at window #23. **Faxes** at #11. Bring packages unwrapped; they will be wrapped and mailed for you. Open M-F 8am-2pm and 3-8pm, Sa-Su 7am-2pm and 3-7pm. **Postal Code:** 125009.

ACCOMMODATIONS

Hostels in Moscow are expensive. Although the best deals are often found in Soviet standard-issue hotels, these tend to have receptionists with very limited English. Older women standing outside major rail stations often rent **private rooms** (сдаю комнату) or apartments (сдаю квартиру); be prepared to haggle.

Godzilla's Hostel (HI), Bolshoy Karetniy 6/5 (Большой Каретний; ☎699 4223; www.godzillashostel.com). M9: Tsvetnoy Bulvar (Цветной Бульвар). Social, hip hostel with great location, 7min. from Pushkin Sq. and 20min. from the Kremlin. English spoken. Kitchen available. Co-ed dorms unless you specify otherwise in advance. Free Internet. Reception 24hr. Check-out noon. Dorms 725R; doubles 1740R. ❷

Galina's Flat, Chaplygina 8, 5th fl., #35 (Чаплыгина; ☎921 6038; galinas.flat@mtu-net.ru). M1: Chistyye Prudy (Чистые Пруды). Head down Chistoprudnyy bul., turn left on Bol. Kharitonevskiy per., then right on Chaplygina. Go into the courtyard at #8 and enter the building with the "KB35-36" sign. Superb location. English-speaking Galina provides home-like hospitality to an international group. Airport transport 1000R. Breakfast 50R. Reserve ahead. Dorms 400R; singles 800R; doubles 1000R. Cash only. ❶

G&R Hostel Asia (HI), Zelenodolskaya 3/2 (Зеленодольская; ☎378 0001; hostel-asia@mtu-net.ru). M7: Ryazanskiy Prospekt (Рязанский). On the 5th fl. of the Gostinitsa Moskovsko-Uzbekskiy (see below). Clean rooms with TVs and refrigerators. Friendly staff will help with rail, theater, and tour reservations. Visa invitations €30. Airport transport €25-45. Free luggage storage and safe. Internet 40R per hr. Reception 9am-10pm. Singles €35-60; doubles €50-60; triples €80. 10th day and 10th person free. MC/V. ❸

Hostel Sherstone (HI), Gostinichny pr. 8 (Гостиничны; ☎783 3438; www.sherstone.ru). M9: Vladykino (Владыкино). Walk along the railway, turning left from the Metro, go under the overpass, walk a block, then take a right at the post office. Be careful at night. On the 3rd fl. of the Hotel Sherstone. Young backpackers crowd this professional hostel, which resembles a hotel more than a traditional hostel; all rooms are equipped with refrigerator, phone, and TV. English spoken. Visa invitations €30-35. Airport transport €30-55. Internet 3R per min. Reception (room 324) 8am-midnight. Dorms €27; singles €69; doubles €74. €1 HI discount. MC/V. ❸

Sweet Moscow, Stariy Arbat ul. 51, 8th fl. #31 (☎241 1446; www.sweetmoscow.com). M4: Smolenskaya. Turn right on Smolenskaya pl. out of the Metro, then left at the McDonald's onto Stariy Arbat. The hostel is located across from Hard Rock Cafe; no signs are displayed, so ring the buzzer. In the middle of the city's most famous pedestrian street. Laundry 150R per load. Free Internet. Extremely helpful English-speaking reception 24hr. 6-, 8-, and 10-bed dorms US$25. Cash only. ❷

Gostinitsa Moskovsko-Uzbekskiy, Zelenodolskaya 3/2 (Зеленодольская; ☎378 3392 or 77 03 01). M7: Ryazanskiy Prospekt (Рязанский). Exit the Metro near the back car of the outbound train. A "Гостиница" sign will be visible on top of the hotel to your left. A wide range of rooms; non-renovated ones are clean and ultra-cheap. English spoken. Singles 1050-2350R; doubles 1450-2400R. V. ❷

Gasis (Гасис), Bolshaya Pereslavskaya 50 (Большая Переславская; ☎510 3250 or 680 7647). M5 or 6: Prospekt Mira (Проспект Мира). Take a right off pr. Mira onto Bannyy per. (Банный) and go left on Pereyaslavskaya. Simple rooms in a large, Soviet-style building for relatively low prices. Breakfast included. Check-out noon. Rooms in 5-room block 600-940R; singles 1400-2200R; doubles 2600-3200R. MC. ❷

RUSSIA

A NEW SORT OF CHEMISTRY CLASS

If you have an extra several thousand rubles handy, you also have the chance to try the newest and perhaps strangest gastronomic experience to hit Moscow since the creation of *okroshka*, soup flavored with *kvas*. These days, chef Anatoly Komm has introduced Russians—the people of hearty meals— to the newest fad: molecular cuisine.

Owning four high-class restaurants in Moscow, Komm holds tasting events with such suggestive titles as "The Alchemy of Taste" and "Frost and Sea Molecular Spectacle." Diners are asked to turn off their cell phones, not to smoke, and to keep their minds open before being presented with between 10 and 20 courses of visionary taste treasures.

Komm's kitchen is better likened to a scientific laboratory. The basic principle behind these meals is purely scientific: by breaking food down into its smallest components, one can later put these particles back together in combinations that will excite the tastebuds in new ways. For some 6000R, you can try a *Russkaya Zakuska* (Russian Appetizer), a tequila glass of liquid that combines the tastes of every traditional Russian appetizer—a thought that is at once disturbing and intriguing.

For more info, see www.anatolykomm.ru, or visit Grin (p. 571)

FOOD

Restaurants range from the expensive to the outrageous. Many higher-priced places offer business lunch specials (бизнес ланч; typically noon-4pm; US$5-10). For fresh produce, head to a **market;** try the ones by the **Turgenevskaya** and **Kuznetskiy Most** Metro stations. (Open daily 10am-8pm.) To find grocery stores, look for "продукты" *(produkty)* signs.

REGIONAL CUISINE AND CAFES

Lyudi Kak Lyudi (Люди как Люди; "People like People"), Solyanskiy Tupik 1/4 (☎921 1201). Enter from Solyanka. A hip atmosphere in dimly lit rooms makes this cafe a favorite of young Russians. Business lunch is very cheap (soup, salad, and sandwich or *pierogi;* 130R). English menu. Smoothies 100R. Sandwiches 90-100R. Open M-Th 8am-11pm, F 8am-6am, Sa 11am-6am, Su 11am-10pm. Cash only. ❶

Korchma Taras Bulba (Корчма Тарас Бульба), Sadovaya-Samotechnaya 13 (Садовая-Самотечная; ☎694 0056, 24hr. 778 3430; www.tarasbulba.ru). M9: Tsvetnoy Bulvar (Цветной Бульвар). From the Metro, turn left and walk up Tsvetnoy bul. Any place with a 24hr. feedback hotline obviously takes service seriously. Delicious Ukrainian specialities served by waitresses in folk dress. English menu. Entrees 75-550R. Open 24hr. 12 locations. MC/V. ❸

Matryoshka (Матрёшка), Klimentovskiy per. 10 (Климентовский; ☎953 9400). M6: Tretyakovskaya (Третьяковская). As you exit the Metro, the restaurant is on nearby Klimentovskiy, off bul. Ordynka. Inexpensive traditional Russian entrees (from 135R) in a winter setting. Business lunch noon-4pm 220R. Open noon-midnight. Branch at Triumfalnaya 1 (Триумфальная; ☎49 99 78 16 60). V. ❷

Guria (Гуриа), Komsomolskiy pr. 7/3 (Комсомольский; ☎246 0378), opposite St. Nicholas of the Weavers. M1 or 5: Park Kultury (Парк Культуры). Authentic Georgian fare for some of the city's lowest prices in an atmosphere that is at once classy and traditional. Private, green-roofed gazebo tables in the garden. English menu. Entrees 200-500R. Open daily noon-midnight. MC/V. ❸

Artcafe "SAD" (Арткафе "САД"), Bul. Tolmachevskiy per. 3 (Толмачевский; ☎239 9115), near the Tretyakov Gallery. M2, 6, or 8: Tretyakovskaya. Hip Muscovites dine in a setting to match. English menu. Weekday business lunch noon-4pm 160-330R. Sushi rolls 70-290R. Entrees 160-600R. Open 10am-midnight. AmEx/MC/V. ❸

Traktir Gusi Lebedi (Трактир Гуси Лебеди), Nikoloyamskaya 28/60 (Николоямская; ☎502 9908). M5 or 7: Taganskaya (Таганская). Walk down Zemlyanoy Val and go left on Nikoloyamskaya. Modeled after a hunting lodge. Waitresses wear cartridge belts, but, as far as we know, they're not actually packing heat. English menu. Business lunch noon-5pm 200R. Entrees 220-1000R. Open daily 11am-8pm. MC/V. ❸

Ceno (Сено; "Hay"), Kamergerskiy per. 6 (Камергерский; ☎692 0452). 5min. from the Kremlin and Teatralnaya Ploshchad, this cafe offers some of the cheapest and most delicious Russian and European food to be found in Moscow, served cafeteria-style. English menu. Salads 20-50R. Hot dishes 60-250R. Open M-Th and Su 10am-11pm, F-Sa 10am-midnight. MC/V. ❷

INTERNATIONAL CUISINE AND CAFES

Grin (Грин), Petrovka 30/7 (Петровка; ☎290 7373; www.anatolykomm.ru). Creations by master chef Anatoly Komm are served in the simple elegance of this high-class restaurant. Dishes are as delicious and innovative as they are expensive. English menu. Oysters 230-300R. Entrees 450-3850R. Open noon-midnight. AmEx/MC/V. ❺

Baan Thai, Bolshaya Dorogomilovskaya 11 (Большая Дорогомиловская; ☎499 0597; www.baanthai.ru). M3, 4, or 5: Kiyevskaya (Киевская). Turn left out of the Metro, take the first right, then turn left after 2 blocks. Pricey but authentic Thai cuisine in a romantic setting. Pad Thai 430R. Open daily noon-midnight. MC/V. ❹

Starlite Diner, Bolshaya Sadovaya 16 (Большая Садовая; ☎260 9638), in the small park of the Mossoveta Theater, near the Tchaikovsky Concert Hall. M2: Mayakovskaya (Маяковская). American diner serves cheeseburgers with fries (210-310R) and delicious shakes (180-230R). Packed with expats on weekends. Wi-Fi 300R per hr. All-day breakfast. Entrees 410-795R. Open 24hr. Branch at Korovyy Val 9a (Коровый Вал; ☎959 8919), M6: Oktyabrskaya (Октябрьская). AmEx/MC/V. ❺

SIGHTS

Moscow's sights reflect the city's interrupted history: because St. Petersburg was the tsar's seat for 200 years, there are 16th-century churches and Soviet-era museums, but little in between. Though Moscow has no grand palaces, and 80% of its pre-revolutionary splendor was demolished by the Soviet regime, the city's museums contain the very best of Russian art and contemporary history.

THE KREMLIN

Enter through Borovitskaya gate tower in the southwest corner if you're going to the Armory; otherwise, enter between the kassy off Mokhovaya ul. (Моховая). Buy tickets at the kassa in Alexander Gardens. ☎202 3776; www.kremlin.museum.ru. M1, 3, 4, or 9: Aleksandrovskiy Sad (Александровский Сад). Open M-W and F-Su 10am-5pm; kassy open 9:30am-4:30pm. Entrance to the Kremlin territory and all cathedrals 300R, students 50R. Audio tours 220R. English-speaking guides offer expensive tours; haggle away. Buy separate tickets for the Armory (350R, students 70R). No large bags. Bag check (60R, camera 30R) is in the Alexander Gardens, under the arch (see map). MC/V.

The Kremlin (Кремль; Kreml) is Moscow's center and the birthplace of much of Russia's political and religious history. It was here that Napoleon simmered while Moscow burned and here that the Congress of People's Deputies dissolved itself in 1991, breaking up the USSR. Much of the triangular complex is closed to tourists; the watchful police will blow whistles if you stray into a forbidden zone.

ARMORY MUSEUM AND DIAMOND FUND. The most beautiful treasures of the Russian state can be found in the Armory and Diamond Fund (Оружейная Палата и Выставка Алмазного Фонда; Oruzheynaya Palata i Vystavka Almaznogo Fonda). Room 2, on the second floor, holds the legendary Fabergé eggs and the royal silver. Room 6 holds pieces of the royal wardrobe. The thrones of Ivan the Terrible and Elizabeth stand imposingly next to the hats of

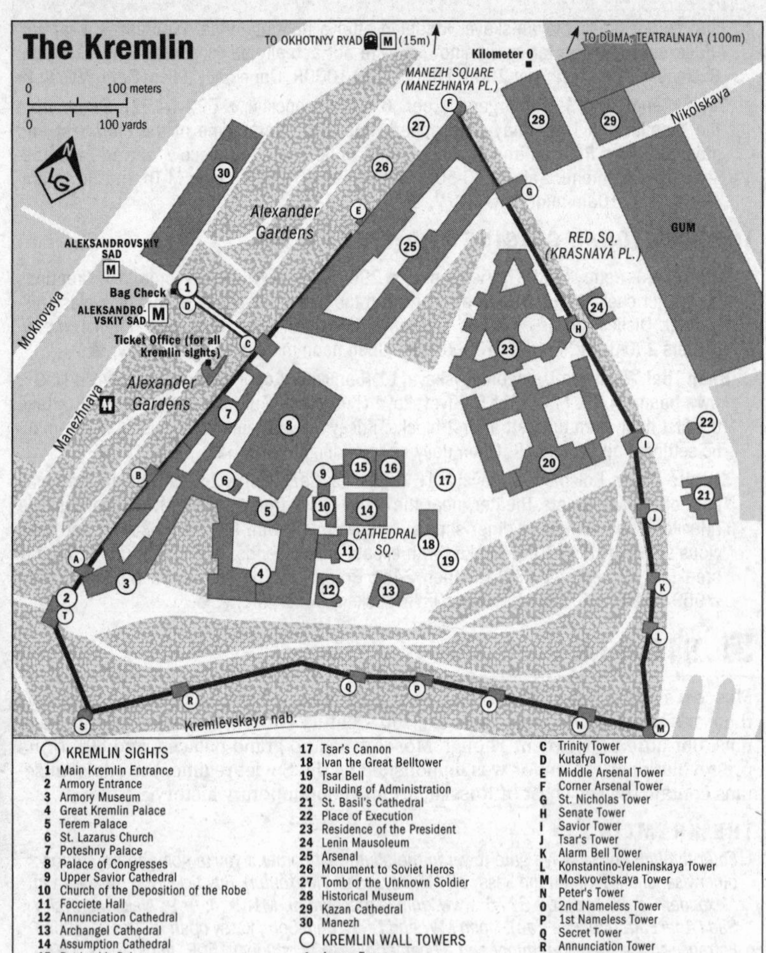

Peter the Great and Vladimir Monomakh in Room 7. The **Diamond Fund** has still more glitter, including a 190-carat diamond given to Catherine the Great by Gregory Orlov, a "special friend." Among the emerald necklaces and ruby rings of the tsars are Soviet-era finds, including the world's largest chunks of **platinum.** *(To the left as you enter the Kremlin by the Armory entrance. ☎202 4631. Open M-W and F-Su. Armory lets in groups for 1½hr. visits at 10am, noon, 2:30, 4:30pm. 350R, students 70R. Diamond Fund lets in groups every 20min. 10am-1pm and 2-6pm. 350R, students 250R. Group size is limited; buy tickets early. Bags and cameras must be checked before entering Diamond Fund.)*

CATHEDRAL SQUARE. From the Armory, head to Cathedral Square, home of the most famous golden domes in Russia. The first church to the left, **Annunciation Cathedral** (Благовещенский Собор; Blagoveshchenskiy Sobor), guards what might be the loveliest iconostasis in the country, with luminous icons by Andrei Rublyov and

Theophanes the Greek. Originally only three-domed, the cathedral was enlarged and gilded by Ivan the Terrible. Ivan's seven marriages made him ineligible to enter the church; as penance, he was forced to stand on the porch during services. Across the way, the **Archangel Cathedral** (Архангельский Собор; Arkhangelskiy Sobor), with its vivid icons, colorful frescoes, and metallic coffins, is the final resting place of many tsars who ruled before Peter the Great. Ivans III (the Great) and IV (the Terrible) rest beside the iconostasis; Mikhail Romanov is by the front right column. The center of Cathedral Square is **Assumption Cathedral** (Успенский Собор; Uspenskiy Sobor), one of the oldest religious buildings in Russia, dating from the 15th century and modeled after the Assumption Cathedral in Vladimir. Napoleon used it as a stable in 1812. Today, its spacious interior is covered in warm-toned frescoes and elaborately detailed icons; it also holds the wooden Tsar's Pew and the white-stone Patriarch's Pew. To the right of Uspenskiy Sobor stands the **Ivan the Great Belltower** (Колокольная Ивана Великого; Kolokolnaya Ivana Velikogo), which holds rotating exhibitions. The tower is visible from over 30km away.

OTHER KREMLIN SIGHTS. Directly behind the bell tower is the world's largest bell, the **Tsar Bell** (Царь-колокол; Tsar-kolokol). It has never rung; an 11½-ton piece broke off after a 1737 fire. Behind Assumption Cathedral stands the **Patriarch's Palace** (Патриарший Дворец; Patriarshiy Dvorets), site of the **Museum of 17th-Century Russian Applied Art and Life** and the **Cathedral of the Twelve Apostles** (Собор Двенадцати Апостолов; Sobor Dvenadtsati Apostolov). It contains a variety of metalwork and textiles, as well as a small religious space. To the left of Assumption Cathedral and next to the Patriarch's Palace is the small **Church of the Deposition of the Robe,** which contains a small but interesting exhibit of wooden religious sculptures. The only other building inside the Kremlin that you can enter is the **Kremlin Palace of Congresses,** a square white monster built by Khrushchev in 1961 for Communist Party congresses. Now used as a **theater** for the Kremlin Ballet Company and other performances, the giant bas-relief of Lenin that once dominated it has been removed.

RED SQUARE

Red Square (Красная Площадь; Krasnaya Ploshchad) has been the site of everything from a giant farmer's market to public hangings. On one side of the 700m long square is the **Kremlin;** on the other is **GUM,** once the world's largest purveyor of Soviet "consumer goods," and now an upscale mall. **St. Basil's Cathedral,** the **State Historical Museum,** the **Lenin Mausoleum,** and **Kazan Cathedral** flank the square. You can buy a combined ticket (230R, students 115R) for St. Basil's Cathedral and the State Historical museum at either location.

ST. BASIL'S CATHEDRAL. There is nothing more symbolic of Moscow—or Russia—than the colorful onion domes of St. Basil's Cathedral (Собор Василия Блаженного; Sobor Vasiliya Blazhennogo). Commissioned by Ivan the Terrible to celebrate his 1552 victory over the Tatars in Kazan, it was completed in 1561. The cathedral bears the name of a holy fool, Vasily (Basil in English), who correctly predicted that Ivan would murder his own son. The labyrinthine interior, unusual for Orthodox churches, is filled with both decorative and religious frescoes. *(M3: Ploshchad Revolyutsii (Площадь Революции). Buy tickets from the* kassa *to the left of the entrance, then proceed upstairs. ☎698 3304, tours 698 3304. Open daily 11am-6pm;* kassa *closes 5:30pm. 100R, students 50R. Services Su 10am. Tours 1000R; call 2 weeks ahead. English-language audio tour 120R. Photo 100R, video 130R.)*

LENIN'S TOMB. Lenin's likeness can be seen in bronze all over the city, but here he appears eerily in the flesh. In the glory days, this squat red structure

(Мавзолей В.И. Ленина; Mavzoley V.I. Lenina) was guarded fiercely, and the wait to enter took hours. Today's line is still long and the guards are still stone-faced, but visitors now exude curiosity, not reverence. Entrance includes access to the **Kremlin wall,** where Stalin, Brezhnev, Andropov, Gagarin, and John Reed (founder of the American Communist Labor Party) are buried. During the hours that the mausoleum is open, access to Red Square is limited. The line to see Lenin forms between the Historical Museum and the Kremlin wall; arrive at least by noon to have a chance of making it through. *(Open Tu-Th and Sa-Su 10am-1pm. Free. No cameras or cell phones; check them at the bag check in the Alexander Gardens.)*

STATE DEPARTMENT STORE GUM. Built in the 19th century, GUM (Государственный Универсальный Магазин (ГУМ); Gosudarstvennyy Universalnyy Magazin) was designed to hold 1000 shops. Its arched, wrought-iron and glass roofs resemble a Victorian train station. During Soviet rule, GUM's 1000 empty shops were a depressing sight. Today, it's depressing only to those who can't afford the designer goods—that is, almost everyone. The renovated complex is an upscale arcade of boutiques and restaurants. *(M3: Ploshchad Revolyutsii (Площадь Революции). From the Metro, turn left, then left again at the gate to Red Square. ☎788 4343. Open daily 10am-10pm.)*

STATE HISTORICAL MUSEUM. This comprehensive collection traces Russian history from the Neanderthals through Kyivan Rus to modern Russia. One of the largest museums in the country, the State Historical Museum (Государственный Исторический Музей; Gosudarstvennyy Istoricheskiy Muzey) provides info and audio tours (100R) in English to help visitors make sense of its vastness. Though it may be bewildering at first, the museum promises something of interest to virtually everyone. *(Krasnaya pl. 1/2. M1: Okhotnyy Ryad (Охотный Ряд). Entrance by Red Square. ☎692 3731; www.shm.ru. Open M and W-Sa 10am-6pm, Su 11am-8pm; kassa closes 1hr. earlier; closed 1st M of the month. 150R, students 60R. Photo 80R, video 100R.)*

RUSSIA

NORTH OF RED SQUARE

AREAS FOR WALKING. Just outside the main gate to Red Square is an elaborate gold circle marking **Kilometer 0,** the spot from which all distances from Moscow are measured. But don't be fooled by this tourist attraction—the real Kilometer 0 lies below the Lenin Mausoleum. Around the corner, the **Alexander Gardens** (Александровский Сад; Aleksandrovskiy Sad) are a respite from the urban bustle of central Moscow. At the north end of the gardens is the **Tomb of the Unknown Soldier** (Могила Неизвестного Солдата; Mogila Neizvestnogo Soldata), where an **eternal flame** burns in memory of the catastrophic losses suffered in WWII.

AREAS FOR SHOPPING. Bordering Red Square are two other major squares. On the west side is **Manezh Square** (Манежная Площадь; Manezhnaya Ploshchad), recently converted into a pedestrian area. The Manezh, which formerly served as the Kremlin stables and an exhibition hall, burned down in March 2004 and was rebuilt to look exactly the same. The famous **Moscow Hotel,** demolished in late 2004 and restored to its original state, separates Manezh Square from the older, smaller **Revolution Square** (Площадь Революции; Ploshchad Revolyutsii). The squares are connected in the north by **Okhotnyy Ryad** (Охотный Ряд; Hunters' Row), once a market for wild game. Now a ritzy underground mall, Okhotnyy Ryad is full of new trends. Across Okhotnyy Ryad from the Moscow Hotel stands the **Duma,** the lower house of Parliament; across from Revolution Square, **Theater Square** (Театральная Площадь; Teatralnaya Ploshchad), home of the **Bolshoy** and **Malyy Theaters** (see

Entertainment, p. 580). Lined with chic stores, government buildings, and the homes of Moscow's richest, **Tverskaya** is the closest the city has to a main street.

RELIGIOUS SIGHTS

If the grime and bedlam get to you, escape to one of Moscow's houses of worship. Before the revolution, the city had more than 1000 churches. Today, there are fewer than 100, though many are being restored. *(No shorts. Women should cover their heads and shoulders with scarves and wear knee-covering skirts.)*

CATHEDRAL OF CHRIST THE SAVIOR. Moscow's most controversial landmark is the enormous, gold-domed Cathedral of Christ the Savior (Храм Христа Спасителя; Khram Khrista Spasitelya). Stalin demolished Nicholas I's original cathedral on this site to make way for a huge Palace of the Soviets, but Khrushchev abandoned the project and built a heated pool instead. In 1995, after the pool's water vapors damaged works in the nearby Pushkin Museum, the city built the US$250 million cathedral in five years. The staggeringly spacious cathedral contains enormous frescoes, ornate gold patterning, and marble walls recounting the deeds of the Russian heroes of the Napoleonic Wars. Downstairs is a museum detailing the history of the cathedral and showcasing some recent religious art. *(Volkhonka 15 (Волхонка), near the Moscow River. M1: Kropotkinskaya (Кропоткинская). Open daily M 1-6pm, Tu-Sa 10am-6pm, Su 8:30am-6pm. Services M-F 8am and 6pm; Sa 8, 9am, and 5pm; Su 9, 10am, and 5pm. Cathedral and museum free. No cameras, shorts, or hats.)*

NOVODEVICHY MONASTERY AND CEMETERY. Moscow's most famous monastery (Новодевичий Монастырь; Novodevichiy Monastyr), also a UNESCO World Heritage Site, is hard to miss thanks to its high brick walls, golden domes, and tourist buses. In the center, the **Smolensk Cathedral** (Смоленский Собор; Smolenskiy Sobor) shows off icons and frescoes. As you exit the gates, turn right and follow the exterior wall back around to the cemetery (кладбище; kladbishche), a pilgrimage site that holds the graves of such famous figures as Krushchev, Bulgakov, Chekhov, Shostakovich, and Stanislavsky. *(M1: Sportivnaya (Спортивная). Take the Metro exit that does not lead to the stadium, then turn right. ☎246 5607. Open M and W-Su 10am-5:30pm; kassa closes 4:45pm; closed 1st M of month. Cathedral closed on rainy and humid days. Cemetery (☎246 0832) open daily 9am-5pm. Cathedral and special exhibits each 150R, students 55R. Photo 80R, video 170R.)*

DANILOV MONASTERY. Founded in 1282, the monastery (Данилов Монастырь; Danilov Monastyr) has historically been as much a fortress as a house of worship. During the Stalinist Terror, the monks were all shot and the monastery fell into ruin. It has since been restored to its former glory and is now home to the Patriarch, head of the Russian Orthodox Church. The only thing missing from this perfect picture of ecclesiastical renewal are the bells. During the Revolution, they were sold to an American industrialist, who donated them to Harvard University. Harvard has agreed to return them if the Orthodox Church paid to move them and have a replica set built. The money has been raised and the replica built; the new bells were transported to Harvard in the summer of 2007, while the old bells will return in 2008. *(M9: Tulskaya (Тульская). Exit the Metro near the last car on the outbound train. From the square, cut through the small park with the chapel, then follow the trolley tracks down Danilovsky val. ☎955 6749. Open daily 6am-8pm. Services M-F 6, 7am, 5pm; Sa-Su 6:30, 9am, 5pm. Museum ☎958 0502. Open W, F, and Su 11am-1pm and 1:30-4pm.)*

MOSCOW CHORAL SYNAGOGUE. Constructed in the 1870s, the yellow synagogue with white columns provides a break from the city's ubiquitous onion domes. Its interior is even more refreshing, with two stories supported by multiple columns, white chandeliers, and intricately patterned artwork. Though it remained open during Soviet rule, all but the bravest Jews were deterred by KGB agents who photographed anyone who entered. Today, more than 200,000 Jews live in Moscow. Services are increasingly well attended, but the occasional graffiti is a sad reminder that Russian anti-Semitism did not die with the USSR. *(M6 or 7: Kitai-Gorod (Китай-Город). Go north on Solyanskiy Proyezd (Солянский Проезд) and take the first left. Open M-F 7am-11pm, Sa-Su 7am-1am. Services M-F 8:30am, Sa-Su 9am; evening services at sunset daily. A cafe on the 2nd floor serves kosher food. English menu. Entrees 150-300R.)*

AREAS TO EXPLORE

MOSCOW METRO. Most cities put their marble above ground and their cement below, but Moscow is not most cities. The Metro (Московское Метро) is worth a tour of its own. Each station is unique: those inside the circle line have sculptures, stained glass, elaborate mosaics, and unusual chandeliers. See the Baroque elegance of **Komsomolskaya** (Комсомольская), the stained glass of **Novoslobodskaya** (Новослободская), and the bronze statues of farmer and factory worker in **Ploshchad Revolyutsii** (Площадь Революции), all for the price of a Metro ticket.

PAN-RUSSIAN EXPOSITION CENTER. The enormous center (Всероссийский Выставочный Центр; Vserossiyskiy Vystavochniy Tsentr) has changed a great deal since its conception. Formerly the Exhibition of Soviet Economic Achievements (VDNKh), this World's Fair-like park, filled with pavilions and amusement park rides, has become a giant shopping and recreation area. Each of the buildings is filled with small shops selling wares ranging from hand-crafted swords and Celtic music to aquariums, electric guitars, and computer equipment. If you can dream it, they've probably got it. *(M6: VDNKh (ВДНХ). Exiting the Metro to "ВВЦ," go left down the kiosk-flanked pathway, and cross the street. Most shops open 10am-7pm.)*

THE ARBAT. Now a commercial pedestrian shopping arcade, the Arbat (Арбат) was once a showpiece of *glasnost* and a haven for political radicals, Hare Krishnas, and *metallisty* (heavy metal rockers). Old flavor lingers in the streets in the form of performers and guitar-playing teenagers, though today the Arbat is mostly populated by pricey souvenir stalls and shops. Intersecting but nearly parallel runs the bigger, newer, and uglier **Novyy Arbat,** lined with gray high-rises, foreign businesses, and massive stores. *(M3: Arbatskaya; Арбатская.)*

PUSHKIN SQUARE. Pushkin Square (Пушкинская Площадь; Pushkinskaya Ploshchad) has inherited the Arbat's penchant for political fervor. During the Cold War's thaw, dissidents came here to protest and voice their visions of a democratic Russia. Today, missionaries evangelize while unknown politicians hand out petitions. Follow Bolshaya Bronnaya downhill, turn right, and follow Malaya Bronnaya to Patriarch's Pond (Патриарший Пруд; Patriarshiy Prud). This area is popular among artsy students and domino-playing men. *(M7: Pushkinskaya; Пушкинская.)*

PARKS

VICTORY PARK. Past the **Triumphal Arch,** which celebrates the 1812 defeat of Napoleon, is Victory Park (Парк Победы; Park Pobedy), built as a monument to WWII. It includes the **Museum of the Great Patriotic War** (Музей Отечественной Войны; Muzey Otechestvennoy Voyny) and the **Church of St. George the Victorious** (Храм Георгия Победаносного; Khram Georgiya Pobedanosnova) which honors the 27,000,000 Russians who died in WWII. *(M3: Park Pobedy.)*

KOLOMENSKOYE SUMMER RESIDENCE. The tsars' summer residence (Коломенское) sits on a wooded slope above the Moskva River. The centerpieces of the grounds are the cone-shaped, 16th-century **Assumption Cathedral** (Успенский Собор; Uspenskiy Sobor) and the seven blue-and-gold cupolas of the nearby **Church of Our Lady of Kazan** (Церковь Казанской Богоматери; Tserkov Kazanskoy Bogomateri). The park's nine small museums include Peter the Great's

1702 **log cabin,** which has exhibits about the history and treasures of the estate. *(M2: Kolomenskaya (Коломенская). Follow the exit signs to "к музею Коломенское," turn left to go out of the Metro, then right, and walk down the tree-shaded path, through the small black gate, and 10min. uphill on the leftmost path. ☎615 2768. Museums open Tu-Su 10am-5pm; kassa closes 30min. earlier. Grounds open daily Apr.-Oct. 8am-10pm; Nov.-Mar. 8am-9pm. Museums 40-300R, students 20-100R. Grounds free. Photo and video 60R.)*

IZMAILOVSKIY PARK. Your one-stop shop for souvenirs from Soviet kitsch to lacquer boxes, Izmailovskiy Park (Измайловский Парк) and its colossal art market, **Vernisazh** (Вернисаж), are best visited on Sunday afternoons, when vendors want to go home and are willing to make a deal. Compare prices and bargain hard, but beware of pickpockets. *(M3: Partizanskaya (Партизанская), formerly Izmailovskiy Park. Go left and follow the crowd to what looks like a theme park. Open daily 8am-6pm.)*

GORKY PARK. Established in 1928, the park (Парк Горкого; Park Gorkogo) gained fame in the West through Martin Cruz Smith's novel of the same name and the film it inspired. In summer, out-of-towners and young Muscovites relax and ride the roller coaster at Moscow's main amusement park. In winter, paths are flooded to create a park-wide ice rink. Those seeking an American-style theme park will be disappointed, as ice-cream kiosks outnumber attractions. Still, the park's main draw is its rides, which include a giant ferris wheel, a mediocre roller coaster, and an original Buran spacecraft. It is mostly frequented by children and teenage couples. *(M1 or 5: Park Kultury (Парк Культуры) or M5 or 6: Oktyabrskaya (Октябрьская). From the Park Kultury stop, cross Krymskiy Most (Крымский Мост). The park is across from the New Tretyakov Gallery (see below). Open daily Apr.-Sept. 10am-2am; Oct.-Mar. 10am-10pm. Ice rink open Nov.-Apr. Admission 50R, students 20R. Most rides 80-160R.)*

RUSSIA

MUSEUMS

Moscow's museums are by far the most patriotic part of the city. Government museums and small galleries alike proudly display Russian art, and dozens of historical and literary museums are devoted to the nation's past.

ART GALLERIES

STATE TRETYAKOV GALLERY. A treasure chest of 18th- to early 20th-century Russian art, the Tretyakov Gallery (Государственная Третьяковская Галерея; Gosudarstvennaya Tretyakovskaya Galereya) also has a superb collection of icons, including works by Andrei Rublev and Theophanes the Greek. *(Lavrushinskiy per. 10 (Лаврушинский). ☎951 1362; www.tretyakov.ru. M8: Tretyakovskaya (Третьяковская). Turn left out of the Metro, left again, then take an immediate right on Bolshoy Tolmachevskiy per.; turn right after 2 blocks onto Lavrushinskiy per. Open Tu-Su 10am-7:30pm; kassa closes 6:30pm. 250R, students 150R. English audio tour 300R.)*

NEW TRETYAKOV GALLERY. Where the first Tretyakov chronologically leaves off, the new gallery (Новая Третьяковская Галерея; Novaya Tretyakovskaya Galereya) begins. The collection starts on the third floor with early 20th-century art and moves through the neo-Primitivist, Futurist, Suprematist, Cubist, and Social Realist schools. The second floor holds temporary exhibits that draw huge crowds; it's best to go on weekday mornings. Behind the gallery lies a graveyard for Soviet statues. *(Krymskiy Val 10 (Крымский Вал). ☎283 1378; www.tretyakov.ru. M5: Oktyabraskaya (Октябрьская). Walk toward the big intersection at Kaluzhskaya pl. (Калужская) and turn right onto Krymskiy. Open Tu-Su 10am-7:30pm; kassa closes 6:30pm. 250R, students 150R. Sculpture garden open daily 9am-10pm. 100R.)*

PUSHKIN MUSEUM OF FINE ARTS. Moscow's most important collection of non-Russian art, the Pushkin Museum (Музей Изобразительных Искусств им.

А.С. Пушкина; Muzey Izobrazitelnykh Iskusstv im. A.S. Pushkina) houses major Renaissance, Greco-Roman, and Egyptian works. As of August 2007, the second floor is closed indefinitely for renovations. *(Volkhonka 12 (Волхонка). ☎203 9578; www.gmii.com. M1: Kropotkinskaya (Кропоткинская). Open Tu-Su 10am-7pm; kassa closes 6pm. 60R, students 30R.)* The smaller building to the right of the main entrance houses the **Pushkin Museum of Private Collections** (Музей Личныч Коллеций; Muzey Lichnych Kolletsiy), with art by Kandinsky and Rodchenko. *(Open W-Su noon-7pm; kassa closes 6pm. 100R, students 50R.)* The other, smaller building to the left of the main entrance contains the **Gallery of European and American Art** of the last two centuries, which displays works by Chagall, Picasso, Van Gogh, and Degas. *(Open Tu-Su 10am-7pm; kassa closes 6pm. 300R, 150R. English audio tour 250R.)*

CENTRAL HOUSE OF ARTISTS. Part art museum, part gallery, and part gift shop, this house (Центральный Дом Художника; Tsentralnyy Dom Khudozhnika) attracts browsers and serious collectors alike with cutting-edge exhibits from new names and opportunities to acquire older artists' work. *(Krymskiy Val 10. In the same building as the New Tretyakov Gallery. M1 or 5: Park Kultury (Парк Культуры), or M5: Okyabraskaya. ☎238 9634. Open Tu-Su 11am-8pm; kassa closes 7pm. 200R, students 100R.)*

HISTORICAL MUSEUMS

KGB MUSEUM. Documenting the history and strategies of Russian secret intelligence from Ivan the Terrible to Putin, the KGB Museum (Музей КГБ; Muzey KGB) gives visitors a chance to quiz a current agent from the FSB, one of the KGB's four successors. As of August 2007, the museum is closed for restoration. *(Bul. Lubyanka 12 (Лубянка). M1: Lubyanka. Behind the concrete behemoth on the northeastern side of the square. By tour only. Patriarshy Dom Tours, p. 565, leads 2hr. group tours; US$18 per person.)*

CENTRAL MUSEUM OF THE ARMED FORCES. The fascinating Armed Forces Museum (Центральный Музей Вооруженных Сил; Tsentralnyy Muzey Vooruzhennykh Sil) exhibits weapons, uniforms, and artwork dating from the reign of Peter the Great to the Chechnyan conflict. The yard behind the museum holds more than 150 examples of war machinery. *(Sovetskoy Armii 2 (Советской Армии). M5: Novoslobodskaya (Новослободская). Walk to the end of Seleznyovskaya (Селезнёвская), turn left after the theater, and bear right at the fork. ☎681 6303. Open W-Su 10am-5pm. Last entrance 4:30pm. Call ahead for English tours, 2000R for groups under 25. English information booklet 10R. 50R, students with ISIC 30R. Photo and video 100R.)*

RUSSIA

MUSEUM OF THE GREAT PATRIOTIC WAR. This impressive collection (Музей Отечественной Войны; Muzey Otechestvennoy Voyny) was built to immortalize those who died fighting Germany in WWII. After the Hall of Memory and Sorrow, though, the emphasis shifts from death to glory. *(Pl. Pobedy (Победы). M3: Park Pobedy. Behind the tall black WWII obelisk in Victory Park. ☎142 4185. Open Tu-Su 10am-7pm; kassa closes 6pm; closed last Th of month. English tours 390R, students 240R. 120R, students 70R. Photo 100R, video 200R.)* In the **Exposition of War Technology** (Експозиция Военной Техники; Ekspozitsiya Voyennoy Tekhniki), a large display of aircraft and weaponry sits behind the museum. *(Open Tu-Su 10am-7pm. 80R, students 50R.)*

MUSEUM OF CONTEMPORARY HISTORY. Housed in the former Moscow English Club mansion, the gallery (Центральный Музей Современной Истории России; Tsentralnyy Muzey Sovremennoy Istorii Rossii) thoroughly covers Russian history from the late 19th century to the present. *(Tverskaya 21 (Тверская). M7: Pushkinskaya (Пушкинская). A large red building across the street and 1 block down from Pushkin Sq. ☎699 3078; www.sovr.ru. Open Tu and F 10am-6pm; Th and Sa 11am-7pm; Su 10am-5pm; last admission 30min. before closing; closed last F of the month. 150R, students 100R. English tours 4 people or fewer 2000R, 15 people or fewer 4500R.)*

COSMONAUT MUSEUM. The tall, aesthetically challenged, and suggestive obelisk that stands atop the museum is the **Monument to Soviet Space Achievements.** Inside the museum (Музей Космонавтики; Muzey Kosmonavtiki) is a fascinating collection on Sputnik and life in space. The 15min. movie answers a burning question: yes, Russian cosmonauts do feast on freeze-dried *borshch.* As of August 2007, the museum is closed for renovation. *(Pr. Mira 111 (Проспект Мира). M6: VDNKh (ВДНХ). ☎683 7914. Open Tu-Su 10am-6pm; closed last F of month. 30R, students 14R.)*

HOUSES OF THE LITERARY AND FAMOUS

Russians take immense pride in their literary history, and preserve authors' houses in their original state, even down to half-full teacups on the mantelpiece. Each is guarded by a team of fiercely loyal *babushki* who often outnumber visitors to the museum in their trust. Be aware, however, that many of these sights are demonstrations of hero-worship rather than archives of interesting artifacts.

MAYAKOVSKY MUSEUM. This four-story work of Futurist Art illustrates the biography of the Revolution's greatest poet. From 1919 to 1930, Mayakovsky lived—and, by his own hand, died—in a communal apartment on the 4th floor. His room is preserved at the top of the building, and the rest of the museum (Музей им. В.В. Маяковского; Muzey im. V.V. Mayakovskogo), which includes a vast and bewildering array of abstract art, was built around it as a poetic reminder. *(Lubyanskiy pr. 3/6 (Лубянский). M1: Lubyanka. Behind a bust of Mayakovsky on Myasnitskaya (Мясницкая). Open M-Tu and F-Su 10am-6pm, Th 1-9pm; closed last F of the month; kassa closes 1hr. earlier. 90R, students 50R.)*

PUSHKIN LITERARY MUSEUM. Fifteen rooms in this beautiful, modern building (Литературный Музей Пушкина; Literaturnyy Muzey Pushkina) lead you through the key points in Pushkin's life and work. Portraits of the author, along with his personal possessions, will delight any Pushkin worshipper and scare away the unconverted. *(Prechistenka 12/2 (Пречистенка). Entrance on Khrushchevskiy per (Хрущевский). M1: Kropotkinskaya (Кропоткинская). Open Tu-Su 10am-6pm; closed last F of the month; kassa closes 5:30pm. 60R.)*

DOSTOEVSKY HOUSE-MUSEUM. This museum (Дом-Музей Достоевского; Dom-Muzey Dostoyevskogo) in Dostoevsky's childhood home displays some of his family's original furniture, books, and photographs. *(Dostoyevskogo 2 (Достоевского). M5: Novoslobodskaya (Новослободская). From Seleznevskaya (Селезневская), take a left at the trolley tracks onto Dostoyevskiy per. and follow the tracks onto Dostoyevskogo; the museum is on the left. ☎681 1085. Open W and F 2-7pm, Th and Sa-Su 11am-6pm; closed last day of the month; kassa closes 30min. earlier. English info available upon request. 40R, students 30R.)*

TOLSTOY MUSEUM. This museum (Музей Толстого; Muzey Tolstogo), in the neighborhood of Tolstoy's first Moscow residence, displays original texts, paintings, and letters. *(Prechistenka 11 (Пречистенка). M1: Kropotkinskaya (Кропоткинская). ☎637 7410; www.tolstoymuseum.ru. Open Tu-Su 10am-6pm; closed last F of month; kassa closes 30min. earlier. 150R, students 50R.)*

LEO TOLSTOY ESTATE. The celebrated author lived here during the winters of 1882-1901. Each room has been laid out as it would have been during his time, with the original possessions of Tolstoy and his family. *(Lva Tolstogo 21 (Льва Толстого). M1 or 5: Park Kultury (Парк Культуры). Exiting the Metro, walk down Komsomolskiy pr. toward the colorful Church of St. Nicholas of the Weavers; turn right at the corner on Lva Tolstogo. ☎246 9444. Open Tu-Sa 10am-5pm; closed last F of month. Exhibits in English. 200R, students 60R.)*

CHEKHOV HOUSE-MUSEUM. This museum (Музей-дом Чехова; Muzey-dom Chekhova) re-creates the literary atmosphere of the late 19th and early 20th cen-

RUSSIA

tury with pictures of Chekhov and family, in addition to showcasing artifacts from Chekhov's career. *(Sadovaya-Kudrinskaya 6 (Садовая-Кудринская). M7: Barrikadnaya. From the Metro, turn left on Barrikadnaya, and left on Sadovaya-Kudrinskaya. ☎291 6154. Open M-Tu, Th, and Sa-Su 11am-5pm, W and F 2-8pm; closed last day of the month; kassa closes 1hr. earlier. English info available. 40R, students 30R. English tours 1000/700R.)*

ENTERTAINMENT

PERFORMING ARTS

From September through June, Moscow boasts some of the world's best **theater, ballet,** and **opera,** as well as excellent **orchestras.** Most of the performance venues are in the northern part of the city center. If you buy **tickets** days in advance and don't demand front row center, you can attend quite cheaply (US$5). Beware, however, of steep mark-ups for foreigners. Tickets can often be purchased online or from the *kassa* located inside each theater, which is usually open from noon until curtain. Kiosks around the city sell tickets and programs for the following two months. During July and August, Russian companies are on tour, and the only groups playing in Moscow are touring productions from other cities, which, with the exception of those from St. Petersburg, tend to be of lower quality. Check www.moscowtimes.ru for schedules.

Bolshoi Theater (Большой Театр), Teatralnaya pl. 1 (Театральная; ☎250 7317; www.bolshoi.ru). M2: Teatralnaya. Home to the opera and the world-renowned ballet company. Main stage closed in summer 2005 and is set to undergo renovations until at least 2008. Performances daily Sept.-June 7pm, with occasional noon performances. *Kassa* open daily 11am-3pm and 4-8pm. Tickets 50-5000R. AmEx/MC/V.

Malyy Theater (Малый Театр), Teatralnaya pl. 1/6 (☎623 2621; www.maly.ru), just to the right of the Bolshoy. M2: Teatralnaya. Moscow's 1st dramatic theater, with an affiliate at Bolshaya Ordynka 69 (Большая Ордынка; ☎237 3181). Performances daily Oct.-June 7pm. *Kassa* open daily Sept.-May 10am-8pm; June-Aug. noon-7pm; closes 1hr. earlier on non-performance days. Tickets 70-1500R.

Tchaikovsky Concert Hall, 4/31 Triumfalnaya pl. (Триумфальная; ☎232 5353). M2: Mayakovskaya (Маяковская). Classical music performances Sept.-June by premier international musicians. *Kassa* open daily 11am-2pm and 3-7pm. Tickets (150-2000R) go on sale 30-45 days in advance.

Old Moscow State Circus (Tsirk Nikulina), Tsvetnoy bul. 13 (Цветной Бульвар; ☎625 8970). M9: Tsvetnoy Bulvar. Turn right and walk half a block; the circus is on the right. Animal acts in the 1st half and glittery acrobatics in the 2nd. Performances M and W-Su 7pm, Sa 2:30pm. Buy tickets 2-3 days in advance. *Kassa* open M-F 11am-2pm and 3-7pm, Sa-Su 11am-12:30pm and 1:30-7pm. Tickets 200-1000R.

BANYAS (RUSSIAN BATHS)

Sandunovskiye Bani (Сандуновские Бани), Neglinnaya 14 (Неглинная; ☎625 4631; www.sanduny.ru). M7: Kuznetskiy Most (Кузнетский Мост). Enter on Zvonarskiy per. (Звонарский). Moscow's oldest *banya* features high ceilings, cavernous rooms, and classical statues. 2hr. sessions 800-1000R, but worth every ruble. Private rooms start at 1000R. Open daily 8am-10pm; *kassa* closes at 8pm.

Bani Na Presne (Бани На Пресне), Stolyarnyy per. 7 (Столярный; mens' ☎255 5306, womens' 253 8090). M7: 1905 Goda. Stolyarnyy per. is the 1st right on Presnenskiy Val (Пресненский Вал) from the Square. Large, modern, and reasonably priced *banya* fills up on weekends. Also offers spa, salon, and restaurant/bar. 2hr. sessions M-F 500R, Sa-Su 600R. Open M and W-Su 8am-10pm, Tu 2-8pm.

NIGHTLIFE

Moscow's nightlife, the most Bacchanalian experience this side of the Volga, is varied and often expensive. Some clubs enjoy flaunting their high cover charges and face-control policies. Several more sedate venues draw bohemians and absinthe-seeking students with cheap prices. Check the *Moscow Times*'s Friday pull-out section, *Element*, or the *eXile*'s nightlife section (www.exile.ru) for excellent synopses of the week's events and up-to-date reviews of clubs. Those looking for something tamer can head to the English-language theater **American Cinema,** 2 pl. Yevropy (Европы; ☎941 8747; M3: Kievskaya), inside the Radisson SAS Slavyanskaya Hotel. **35MM,** Pokrovka 47/24 (Покровка; M5: Kurskaya), is Moscow's only independent movie theater and shows films in their original languages with Russian subtitles.

SAVE FACE. When navigating the hostile, exclusive world of Moscow nightlife, our researchers have found that there is only one proven technique to ensure that "face control" (bouncer) doesn't ruin the night before it even starts: become a wealthy, tall, blonde model in high Russian style. More realistically, try to find friends in Moscow. Otherwise, dress up, go early, and get ready to have your face controlled.

Propaganda (Пропаганда), Bolshoy Zlatoustinskiy per. 7 (Большой Златоустинский; ☎624 5732; www.propogandamoscow.com). M6 or 7: Kitai Gorod (Китай-Город). Exiting the Metro, walk down Maroseyka and take a left on Bolshoy Zlatoustinsky per. Get down to house music at this Moscow hotspot without feeling like you're in a meat market. Go early to eat (and avoid strict face control). Dancing after midnight. Th DJ night. Su gay night. Beer from 100R, after 11pm from 60R. Open daily noon-6am.

FAQ Art Club, Gozetniy per. 9/2 (☎629 0827; www.faqclub.ru). M2: Teatralnaya. Chill with Moscow's young and alternative crowd on the tented patio or in house-themed rooms—drawings for the "children's room" are accepted and appreciated. Entrees 115-420R. Beer from 115R. Mixed drinks from 130R. Hookahs from 500R. Jazz concerts Su 8pm, 300R. Call ahead to reserve a table. Open daily 7pm-6am.

Karma Bar, Pushechnaya 3 (Пушечная; ☎624 5633; www.karmabar.ru). M1 or 7: Kuznetzkiy Most (Кузнетский Мост). With your back to the Metro, walk through the arch on your left and turn right on Pushechnaya. Crowd-pleasing dance music keeps the crowd, both foreign and local, lively. Beer 110-170R. Vodka 150-160R. Mixed drinks 260-320R. Latin dance lessons 9pm-midnight. Su hip hop. Cover F-Sa men 300R, women 200R; free before 11pm. Open Th-Sa 9pm-6am, Su 11pm-6am.

Art-Garbage, Starosadskiy per. 5 (Старосадский; ☎628 8745; www.art-garbage.ru). M6 or 7: Kitai Gorod (Китай-Город). Art gallery, restaurant, and club, Art-Garbage is refreshingly more laid-back than many of the chic and trendy Moscow establishments. Better for drinking on the inviting patio than for dancing. Shots from 60R. Beer from 70R. Cover F-Sa 150-500R. Open noon-6am.

B2, Bolshaya Sadovaya 8 (Большая Садовая; ☎650 9918; www.b2club.ru). M5: Mayakovskaya. This multistory complex truly has it all, and without the face control: a quiet beer garden, restaurant, sushi bar, karaoke, jazz club, billiard room, several dance floors, and weekend disco. Beer 80-180R. Hard alcohol from 100R. Concerts F-Sa from 300R; some free with ISIC; check website. Open noon-6am. MC/V.

Hippo-Club (Гиппопотам; Gippopotam), Mantulinskaya 5/1 (Мантулинсая; ☎256 2346, www.rosingfer.ru). M7: Ulitsa 1905 Goda (Улица 1905 года). Exit the Metro onto ul. 1905 Goda, then walk downhill beside the park. Take a right on Mantulinskaya; entrance is around back. The hip hop, R&B, and soul keeps a diverse group of clubbers moving. Beer 100-170R. Mixed drinks from 130R. Th Latin night, F-Sa R&B party, Su Tarzan body show. Cover men 330R, women 100R. Open W-Su 10pm-6am.

16 Tons, Presnenskiy Val 6 (Пресненский Вал; ☎253 5300; www.16tons.ru). M7: Ulitsa 1905 Goda (Улица 1905 года). Drink the bar's own patented beer with New Russians on weeknights and rock out to Russian electronic and alternative concerts on weekends. Th independent bands; F-Sa more established bands. Cover Th-Sa 300-600R. Open daily 11am-6am. AmEx/MC/V.

Rock Vegas Cafe, Pyatnitskaya 29/8 (Пятницкая; ☎959 5333), next to Pizza Hut. M2, 6, or 8: Tretyakovskaya (Третьяковская). Local students and visitors frequent this expat hangout. Billiards 50R per game. Beer 100-220R. Th 80s disco; F-Sa jazz, blues, and rock concerts. Cover F-Sa men 200R. Open daily noon-6am. MC/V.

DAYTRIP FROM MOSCOW

SERGIYEV POSAD (СЕРГИЕВ ПОСАД)

Take the Elektrichki *(commuter rail) from Yaroslavskiy Vokzal (1½-2hr., every 20-50min., round-trip 168R). Alternatively, purchase a train ticket (84R) and return via the bus leaving from outside the Sergiyev Posad station (1½-2½hr., every 10min., 80R). Buses back to Moscow go to VDNKh. To reach the churches, turn right from the train tracks toward the gold domes and follow the road to the city (10-15min.). Monastery open daily 5am-9pm. Free. Tours in English 260R per person, for groups of 5 or less an extra 300R is included; ☎49 65 40 57 21. Otherwise, book excursions at the kassa to the right, just inside the monastery gates (tours 12:15-3:45pm). Map 50R. Museums open W-Su 10am-5:30pm. 160R, students 80R. On grounds, photo 100R, video 150R. No photography inside cathedrals.*

Russia's famous pilgrimage point, Sergiyev Posad (pop. 200,000), attracts believers to the several churches clustered around its main sight, **St. Sergius's Trinity Monastery** (Свято-Троицкая Сергиева Лавра; Svyato-Troitskaya Sergiyeva Lavra). During Soviet times, Sergiyev Posad was called Zagorsk, and many locals still use this name. After decades of state-propagated atheism, this stunning monastery—founded in the 1340s and one of the Russian Orthodox Church's four *lavras*—has again become a thriving religious center. The Patriarch of the Russian Orthodox Church resided here until 1988, when he moved to Moscow's Danilov Monastery (see **Religious Sights,** p. 575).

Each church is exquisite, but none matches the serene calm **Trinity Cathedral** (Троицкий Собор; Troitskiy Sobor), surrounded in dim light by walls of gilded Andrei Rublyov icons. Nearby, the magnificently frescoed **refectory** (Трапезная; Trapeznaya) houses large, graceful paintings. Be warned, however, that you won't be allowed past the small lobby without a tour guide. The **Chapel-at-the-Well** (Надкладезная Часовня; Nadkladeznaya Chasovnya) was allegedly established on the site of a spring with magical healing powers. Next door, the **Assumption Cathedral** (Успенский Собор; Uspenskiy Sobor) is modeled after the cathedral in Moscow's Kremlin (see **Sights,** p. 572). To the left of the main entrance of the Assumption Cathedral, the **grave of Boris Godunov** and the graves of his family (see **History,** p. 559) lie under the modest white tomb.

THE GOLDEN RING (ЗОЛОТОЕ КОЛЬЦО)

North and east of Moscow lies the Golden Ring (Zolotoye Koltso), a string of towns with some of the most beautiful and beloved churches and kremlins in Russia. Many of the towns reached their zenith in the 12th century, when the Russian empire's center of power shifted from Kyiv to Moscow. The slower, calmer pace of these towns provides a much-needed break from the chaos of Moscow, as well as an alternative perspective on Russian life.

SUZDAL (СУЗДАЛЬ)

☎(8)49231

The beauty of Suzdal (SOOZ-duhl; pop. 12,000), set amid lazy streams, dirt roads, and cucumber fields, lies in its isolation and stillness. In the 12th century, the Rostov-Suzdal principality ruled Moscow and even collected tribute from Byzantium. Nine centuries later, the town's medieval riches are visible everywhere.

TRANSPORTATION AND PRACTICAL INFORMATION. The bus station, avtovokzal (автовокзал; ☎213 43 or 201 47), Vasilevskaya ul. 44 (Васильевская), sends **buses** to Vladimir (50min., every 40min.-1¼hr., 33R). Departure times are listed at the *kassy*. (Open 5am-8pm.) Buses leave Vladimir for Moscow (3½hr.; 25-30 per day, last departure 6:45pm; 156R). **Trains** also leave Vladimir for Moscow's Kurskiy Vokzal (3hr., 15-20 per day, 200-400R). **Taxis** frequent Suzdal's bus station and town center. (☎206 34 or 250 40.)

To reach the **tourist bureau** "Shishilov" (Шишилов), ul. Lenina 57 (Ленина), near the kremlin, turn left onto ul. Vasilevskaya (Васильевская) as you exit the bus station, then right on ul. Lenina. The staff offers maps for 40-50R. (☎206 02; www.shishilov.norod.ru. Open M-Sa 10am-5pm.) **Exchange currency** at Sberbank, ul. Lounskaya 1a (Лоунская), off ul. Lenina. The bank has an **ATM** (2% commission) and cashes **traveler's checks** for 2.4% commission. (☎219 18 or 202 02. Open M-F 8am-12:30pm and 1:30-6pm, Sa 8am-12:30pm and 1:30-5pm.)

ACCOMMODATIONS AND FOOD. For a small town, Suzdal has plenty of accommodations, but most of them are expensive. The most affordable option is **Tourbase Young People** (Турбаза Молодещная; Turbaza Molodeshchnaya) ❷, at ul. Lenina 104 (Ленина), across the street from the Convent of the Deposition of the Robe. The 8- to 15-bed dorm rooms may offer little privacy, but the location and price makes this hostel a worthwhile choice. (☎205 53; suzdal@avo.ru. Dorms 550R. Cash only.) A more beautiful and perhaps more interesting option is **Gostinitsa Rizopolozhenskaya** (Ризоположенская) ❷, ul. Kommunalnyy Gorodok 9 (Коммунальный Городок), located on the grounds of the Convent of the Deposition of the Robe. Enjoy views of the nearby church and cattle from the hotel's cafe. (☎207 06. Singles 920R; doubles 1370-1820R. Cash only.) For a multitude of distinctly Russian foods in a traditional setting, head to **Kharchevnya** (Харчевня) ❷, ul. Lenina 73. (☎207 22. English menu available. Entrees 80-220R. Open daily 9am-11pm. Cash only.) For fancier, Western European fare, try **Trapeznaya** (Трапезная) ❸, behind the museum in the Kremlin. (☎234 80. English menu available. Entrees 170-509R. Open daily 11am-11pm. MC.)

SIGHTS. To reach the **kremlin,** the town's main sight, make a right on ul. Kremlevskaya (Кремлевская) from pl. Lenina (Ленина). Time has softened the profile of the mighty fortress, but the faded, star-studded blue domes of the **Nativity Cathedral** (Рождественский Собор; Rozhdestvenskiy Sobor) still dazzle. The first and main exhibit of the kremlin, the Cathedral's most precious possession, is the 13th-century Golden Gate, which depicts the lives of Jesus and the Virgin Mary in gold. (Open daily 10am-6pm. 80R.) Nearby, the **Archbishop's Palace** houses the other four kremlin exhibits, including the famous 17th-century Canopy of Jordan, used by the Russian Orthodox Church in a ritual blessing of the waters. (Open M and W-Su 10am-6pm; closed last F of each month. Each exhibit 30-80R; combined 200R.) Cross the river, turn left, and head to the **Museum of Wooden Architecture** (Музей Деревянного Зодчества; Muzey Derevyannogo Zodchestva), an outdoor display with windmills, churches, and several houses dating from the 17th through 19th centuries. (Open daily 9am-7pm; closed last W of each month. Entrance 50R; each exhibit 50R.) North of the kremlin lie several **monasteries** and convents. The **Convent of the Deposition of the Robe** (Ризоположенский Монастырь; Rizopolozhenskiy Monastyr) has a picturesque bell tower. The cathedral and its red, flowered Holy Gate date from the 16th and 17th centuries. If you're lucky, you'll catch sight of the monastery's cows. (Grounds open 24hr. Free.)

Farther down ul. Lenina, the **Spaso-Yevfimiyev Monastery** (Спасо-Евфимиев Монастырь) is surrounded by a red stone wall, which encompasses several museums and the green-domed **Cathedral of the Transfiguration.** In addition to incredible murals, the cathedral houses a **museum** that displays 13th- to 20th-century decorative arts and 11th- to 12th-century books, including **Russia's oldest book** (AD 1056) and a huge 17th-century Gospel, **Russia's largest book.** (Open Tu-Su 10am-6pm; closed last Th of each month.) Behind the monastery and across the river stands the beautifully kept and wonderfully tranquil **Convent of the Intercession.** This complex served as a prison for women of the highest class: Peter the Great, Ivan the Terrible, his son, and Basil III each exiled at least one wife here. Today, it contains two white cathedrals, both dating from the 16th century, and numerous wooden houses. (Open 24hr. Free.)

YAROSLAVL (ЯРОСЛАВЛЬ) ☎(8)0852

Yaroslavl (yah-rah-SLAH-vl; pop. 630,000) is one of the most touristed cities in Russia, earning it the nickname "The Florence of Russia." Yaroslavl's numerous churches, pleasant riverside promenades, and proximity to Moscow have made it a regular stop on the tour bus circuit.

TRANSPORTATION. Trains run from **Glavnyy Vokzal** (Главный Вокзал; ☎79 21 11; open 24hr.) to Moscow (4½hr., 15-20 per day, 200-800R) and St. Petersburg (12hr., 2 per day, 550-1500R). **Buses** leave from the **Avtovokzal,** Moskovskiy pr. 80 (Московский; ☎44 18 37), for Moscow (5 hr., 8 daily, 320R), St. Petersburg (13hr., 1 every F, 850R), and Vladimir (5½hr., 2 per day, 278R). Buy **tickets** (8R) for **local buses** from the conductor on board.

ORIENTATION AND PRACTICAL INFORMATION. Yaroslavl lies at the confluence of the **Volga** (Волга) and **Kotorosl** (Которосль) rivers, 280km northeast of Moscow. The center is defined to the south and northeast by the two rivers and on the west by **Pervomaiskaya ulitsa** (Первомайская). Pervomaiskaya runs from **Krasnaya ploshchad** (Красная) to **Bogoyavlenskaya ploshchad** (Богоявленская), the beginning of **Moskovskiy prospekt** (Московский), which runs south across the Kotorosl to the the main bus station. To get to the center from the bus station, cross Moskovskiy pr. and take trolley #5 or 9 three stops to **ploshchad Volkova** (Волкова). To get to pl. Volkova from the main train station, take trolley #1 six stops. Some streets are marked with both their current and former names. For travelers navigating the city, only the topmost name is useful. Cyrillic **maps** (35R) are sold at many print kiosks and book stores for 20-50Rю **Sberbank,** ul. Kirova 16 (Кирова), **exchanges currency** and cashes **traveler's checks** for a 3% commission. (Open M-Sa 8:30am-7pm, Su 10am-3pm; closed last day of each month.) **Store luggage** at the train station. (50R per day. Open 24hr.) There is a **24hr. pharmacy** at ul. Svobody 8. (Свободы. ☎32 95 61. Ring buzzer 8pm-8am. MC/V.) Find **Internet access** and scanning, printing, and copy services at **Punkt Internet Dostupa** (Пункт Интернет Доступа), Komsomolskaya ul. 14 (Комсомольская), second floor. Go through the arch with KOMSOMOL written over it and follow the signs upstairs. (☎30 80 55; idostup@yandex.ru. 32R per hr., students 28R. Open daily 9am-9pm.) The **post office,** Komsomolskaya ul. 22 (Комсомольская), is across the square from the monastery. (☎32 92 79. Open 24hr.) **Postal Code:** 150000.

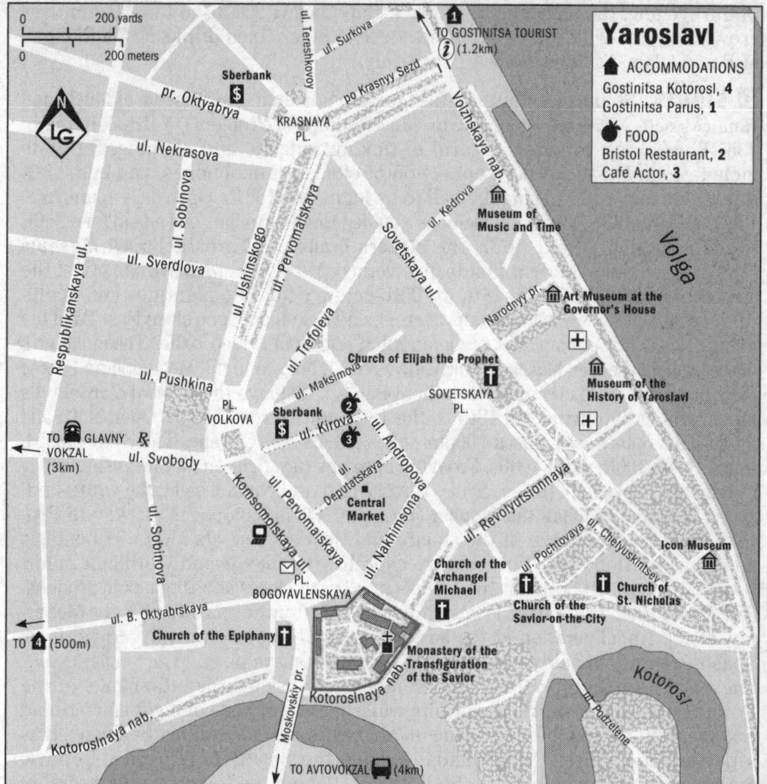

ACCOMMODATIONS AND FOOD. Yaroslavl's hotel prices are high due to the city's popularity, and rooms are scarce in summer. Although a bit dated, **Gostinitsa Parus** (Парус) ❷, Volzhskaya nab. 4 (Волжская), is centrally located and offers relatively large rooms and an intimate atmosphere. Take trolley #1 to Krasnaya pl. (Красная пл.), then walk down to the promenade and turn left. (☎30 41 92. Check-out noon. Singles with sink 600R, with bath 900R; doubles with bath 1300R. Cash only.) Although **Gostinitsa Kotorosl** (Которосль) ❸, ul. Bolshaya Oktyabrskaya 87 (Ђольшая Октябрьская), is located a bit far from the sights, the sauna, tennis courts, ping-pong tables, and decent prices make a stay worthwhile. Walk up ul. Bolshaya Oktyabrskaya for 10-15min. from pl. Bogoayavlenskaya (Ђогоявленская), or take tram #3 from the train station. The hotel is on the left. (☎21 15 81; www.kotorosl@yaroslavl.ru. Some English spoken. Singles 1300-3500; doubles 2200-4200. MC/V.)

Sidewalk cafes sell beer, ice cream, and sweet rolls. Stock up on produce at the **tsentralnyy rynok** (центральный рынок; central market), ul. Deputatskaya 5. (Депутатская. Open daily 8am-6pm.) **Cafe Actor** (Актер; Aktyor) ❸, ul. Kirova 5 (Кирова), serves Russian favorites in an elegant setting. Photographs of Russian actors line the walls in the adjacent bar area. (☎72 75 43. English menu available. Entrees 120-400R. Open 24hr. Cash only.) For excellent Russian and Georgian cuisine in a silver-age ballroom, head to **Bristol Restaurant** ❷, ul. Kirova 10. Later

RUSSIA

in the evening, the ballroom becomes a club playing 80s disco to a 30-and-over crowd. (☎72 94 08. Entrees 110-240R. Beer 45-90R. Mixed drinks 80-300R. Open M-F noon-2am, Sa-Su noon-5am. Cash only.)

SIGHTS. Step inside Russia's first private museum, the **Museum of Music and Time** (Музей Музыки и Времени; Muzey Muzyki i Vremeni), Volzhskaya nab. 33a (Волжская), to enter a world of ticking, ringing, and chiming. Exhibits include John Mastoslavsky's collection of clocks, gramophones, and bells. Fittingly, you may have to ring the bell to be let in. (☎32 86 37. Open daily 10am-7pm. 120R, students 60R. Admission includes a guided tour in Russian; call ahead for a 250R tour in English.) Next door, the **modern branch** of Yaroslavl's **Art Museum** (Художественный Музей; Khudozhestvennyy Muzey), Volzhskaya nab. 23, at the governor's house exhibits 18th- to 20th-century Russian paintings and sculpture. (☎30 34 95; www.artmuseum.yar.ru. Open Tu-Su 10am-6pm; closed last Tu of the month; *kassa* closes 5pm. 50R, students 20R. Photo 100R, video 100R.) The museum's other branch, the **Icon Museum,** Volzhskaya nab. 1, housed in the Metropolitan Palace (Метрополичьи Палаты; Metropolichi Palaty), displays the best of Yaroslavl's icons, which date from the 13th to the 18th century. (☎72 92 87. Open M-Th and Sa-Su 10am-5pm; *kassa* closes 4:30pm. 40R, students 20R. Call ahead for 350R English tours. Photo 100R, video 100R). From the museum, turn right on ul. Chelyushkinstsev to reach Sovetskaya pl (Советская). Yaroslavl's most beautiful sight, the white-and-green **Church of Elijah the Prophet** (Церковь Ильи Пророка; Tserkov Ili Proroka) is the centerpiece of the square and the city. The elaborate iconostasis and frescoes flood this 17th-century church with unexpectedly brilliant color. (Open M-Tu and Th-Su 10am-1pm and 2-6pm; *kassa* closes at 5:30pm. 65R, students 35R. Photo 100R, video 100R.) Down Nakhimosona from Sovetskaya pl. is the **Monastery of the Transfiguration of the Savior** (Спасо-Преображенский Монастырь; Spaso-Preobrazhenskiy Monastyr), Bogoyavlenskaya pl. 25 (Ђогоявленская). Since the 12th century, this fortified monastery has guarded the banks of the Kotorosl. The monastery's high white walls enclose a range of eight educational and recreational exhibits, focusing on art, crafts, and natural history, as well as a petting zoo. Enter the grounds through the **Holy Gate** (Святые Ворота; Svyatyye Vorota), which faces the Kotorosl. Behind the tower, the **Cathedral of the Transfiguration of the Savior** (Спасо-Преображенский Собор; Spaso-Preobrazhenskiy Sobor), built during the reign of Ivan the Terrible, houses a number of unrestored frescoes. (Monastery open daily 8am-10pm. Exhibits open Tu-Su 10am-6pm; closed first M of the month; *kassa* closes at 5pm. Petting zoo open daily 10am-7pm. Cathedral open M and Th-Su 10am-5pm. Admission to monastery grounds 15R, students 5R; free with exhibition tickets. Each exhibit 15-50R, students 5-25R; 80R combined. Petting zoo 90R, students 60R. Photo 100R, video 100R.) Opposite the monastery, the red-brick **Church of the Epiphany** (Церковь Богоявления; Tserkov Bogoyavleniya) includes a museum featuring an ornately carved Baroque iconostasis. (Open May-Sept. 7am-7pm; Oct.-Apr. W-Su 10am-4pm; closed during rain. Services M-F 7:30am and 7pm, Sa-Su 8:30am and 7pm. 30R, students 15R. Photo 100R, video 100R.)

NORTHWEST RUSSIA

The Northwest once held the lion's share of Russia's political power. The kremlins and monasteries of Novgorod and Pskov, along with St. Petersburg's opulent palaces, reflect the region's historical prominence, both religious and secular. Closer to Europe than to the heart of Russia, the Northwest is the geographical and symbolic point of convergence between the European East and the Asian West.

ST. PETERSBURG (САНКТ-ПЕТЕРБУРГ)

☎(8)812

St. Petersburg's wide boulevards, spacious squares, and bright facades are exactly what Peter the Great envisioned when he turned a mosquito-infested swamp into his "window on the West." The Bolsheviks drew the curtains when St. Petersburg (pop. 4,600,000) became the birthplace of the 1917 February Revolution, turning Russia into a Communist state; the city's name was subsequently changed to Leningrad. Since the fall of Communism and its subsequent reversion to its original name, however, the city has rediscovered the genius of former residents like Dostoevsky, Gogol, Tchaikovsky, and Stravinsky, whose legacies (and statues) mingle with the centuries-old buildings, streets, and canals of this remarkable city.

INTERCITY TRANSPORTATION

Flights: The main airport, **Pulkovo** (Пулково), 18/4 Pilotov str. (www.pulkovo.ru) has 2 terminals: Pulkovo-1 (☎704 3822) for domestic flights and Pulkovo-2 (☎704 3444) for international flights. The airport is 17km south of the city. M2: Moskovskaya. From the Metro, take bus #13 for Pulkovo 1 (25min.) or bus #39 for Pulkovo 2 (20min.). Only small bills are accepted to supply bus fare (14R). Hostels can arrange a taxi (usually US$30-35), but taking a little initiative might save a good deal of money. Call a taxi service and request to be picked up (a 20-30min. wait), or learn the Russian name of your destination and you should be able to negotiate a fare of around US$20 at the airport. **Taxi Millionnaya** (Такси Миллионная; ☎100 0000) offers reliable, reasonably priced service. Fare from the center to the airport (including booking and collection) is 550R (non-negotiated fare around US$22) and from the airport to the center 600R (US$23). Millionnaya also runs within the city center (see **Local Transportation,** p. 591). Route taxis *(marshrutki)* also provide transport between the Metro and the airport.

Aeroflot Russian International Airlines, Rubinshteyna ul. 1/43 (Рубинштейна; ☎438 5583). M2: Nevskiy Prospekt. Open M-F 9:30am-7pm, Sa 10am-3pm.

Air France, Malaya Morskaya 23, 4th fl. (Малая Морская; ☎336 2900). M4: Sadovaya. Open M-F 9:30am-5:30pm.

Austrian Airlines, Nevskiy pr. 32, 4th fl. (Невский; ☎331 2005). M2: Nevskiy Propekt. Open M-F 9am-5:30pm.

British Airways, Malaya Konyushennaya 1/3A, office 23B (Малая Конюшенная; ☎380 0626). M2: Nevskiy Prospekt. Walk to the end of Malaya Konyushenna and turn left, then left again into the first black iron gate. Open M-F 9am-5pm.

Delta, Bolshaya Morskaya 36 (☎571 5820). M4: Sadovaya. Open M-F 9am-5:30pm.

Finnair, Malaya Konyushennaya 1/3A, Office B33 (☎331 8884). M2: Nevskiy Prospekt. Same directions as for British Airways. Open M-F 9am-6pm.

SAS, Nevskiy pr. 25, 4th fl. (☎326 2600), in the Corinthia Nevskiy Palace Hotel. M2: Nevskiy Prospekt. Open M-F 9am-5:30pm.

Trains: Tsentralnye Zheleznodorozhny Kassy (Центральные Железнодорожные Кассы; Central Railroad Ticket Offices), Canal Griboyedova 24 (Грибоедова; ☎067). Open M-Sa 8am-8pm, Su 8am-6pm. If you don't speak Russian, the aid of a travel agent or hotel staffer may be necessary to make a reservation; it's often easiest to ask your hostel receptionist to write down your preferred time, train, and destination in Russian and hand it to the person helping you. Many trains sell out in advance. Check your ticket for the station from which your train departs, have your passport ready for inspection, and ask if there are any additional requirements (e.g. transit visas) for your trip. Ticket prices are about 200R more expensive during the high season (June-Sept.).

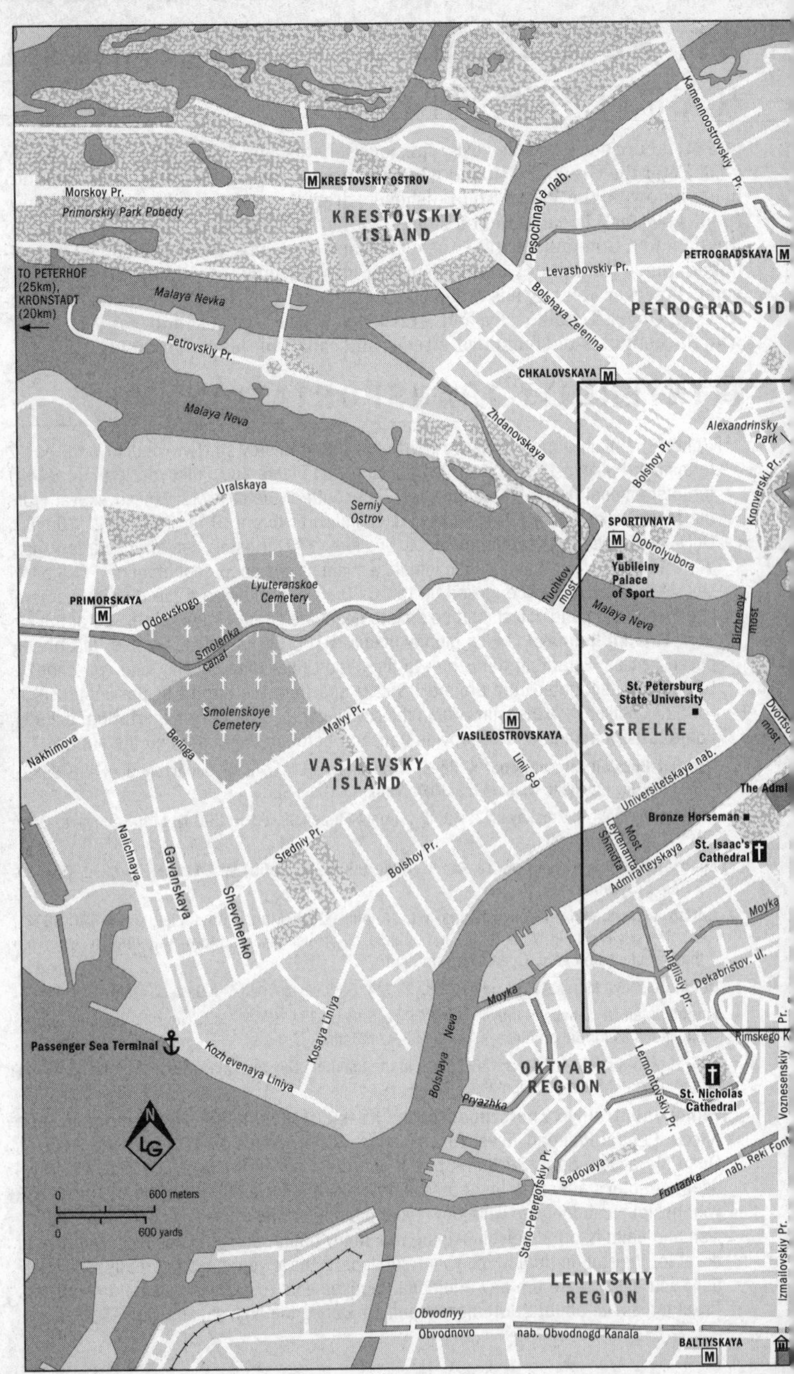

KRESTOVSKIY OSTROV
Morskoy Pr.
Primorskiy Park Pobedy
KRESTOVSKIY ISLAND
Pesochnaya nab.
Kamennoostrovskiy Pr.
PETROGRADSKAYA
Levashovskiy Pr.
Bolshaya Zelenina
PETROGRAD SID
TO PETERHOF (25km), KRONSTADT (20km)
Malaya Nevka
Petrovskiy Pr.
CHKALOVSKAYA
Malaya Neva
Zhdanovskaya
Alexandrinsky Park
Bolshoy Pr.
Kronverski Pr.
Uralskaya
Serniy Ostrov
SPORTIVNAYA
Dobrolyubora
Yubileiny Palace of Sport
Lyuteranskoe Cemetery
PRIMORSKAYA
Odoevskogo
Tuchkov most
Malaya Neva
Birzhevoy most
Smolenka canal
St. Petersburg State University
Smolenskoye Cemetery
Malyy Pr.
VASILEOSTROVSKAYA
STRELKE
Dvortsov most
Nakhimova
Beringa
VASILEVSKY ISLAND
Linii 8-9
Universitetskaya nab.
The Admi
Bronze Horseman
Nalichnaya
Gavanskaya
Sredniy Pr.
Most Leytenanta Shmidta
St. Isaac's Cathedral
Shevchenko
Bolshoy Pr.
Admiralteyskaya
Moyka
Angliiskiy pr.
Dekabristov. ul.
Moyka
Kosaya Liniya
Rimskego K
Passenger Sea Terminal
Kozhevenaya Liniya
Bolshaya Neva
OKTYABR REGION
Lermontovskiy Pr.
St. Nicholas Cathedral
Voznesenskiy
Pryazhka
Sadovaya
Staro-Petergofskiy Pr.
Fontanka
nab. Reki Font
0
600 meters
0
600 yards
LENINSKIY REGION
Izmailovskiy Pr.
Obvodnyy
Obvodnovo
nab. Obvodnogo Kanala
BALTIYSKAYA

RUSSIA

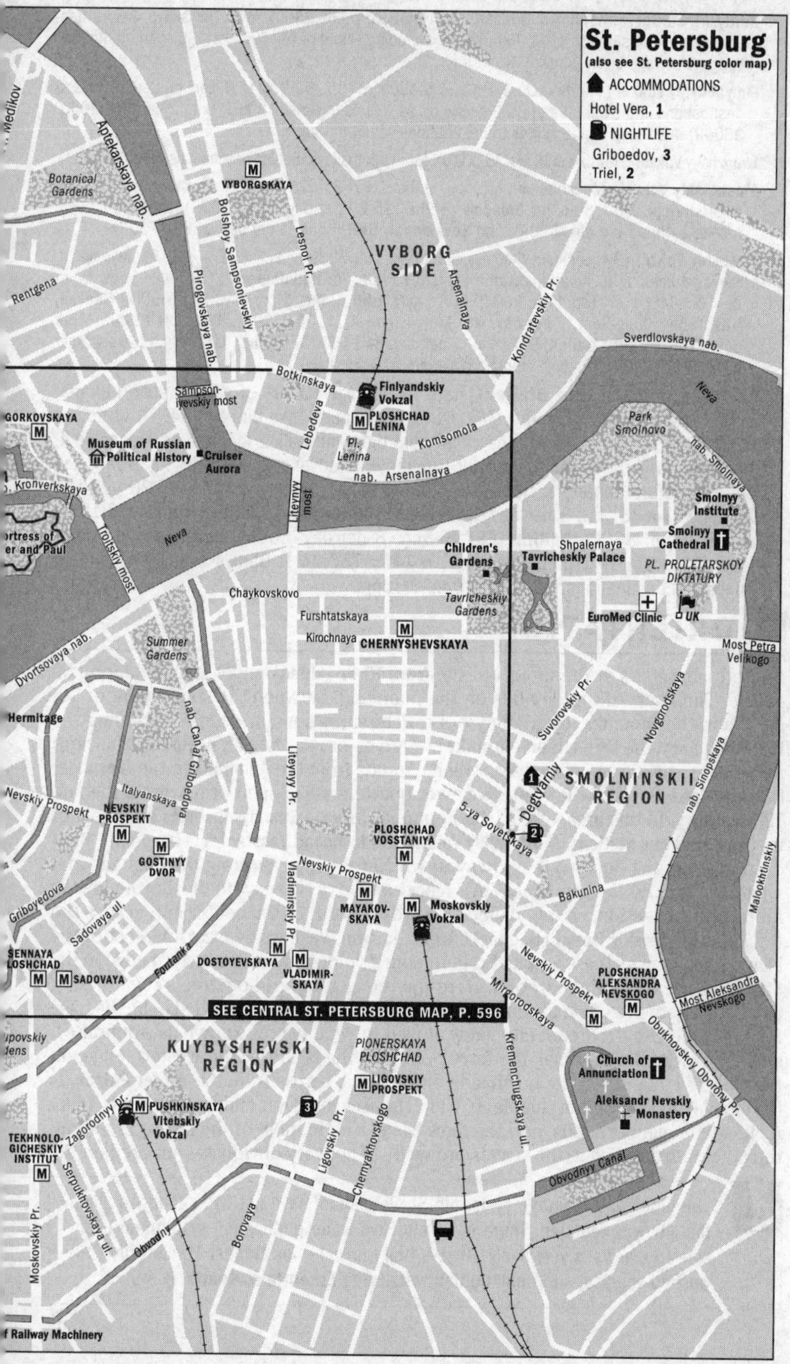

St. Petersburg

(also see St. Petersburg color map)

ACCOMMODATIONS

Hotel Vera, **1**

NIGHTLIFE

Griboedov, **3**

Triel, **2**

Medikov
Aptekarskaya nab.
Botanical Gardens
VYBORGSKAYA
Bolshoy Sampsonievskiy
Lesnoi Pr.
VYBORG SIDE
Arsenalnaya
Kondratevskiy Pr.
Rentgena
Pirogovskaya nab.
Sverdlovskaya nab.
Neva
Botkinskaya
Sampsoniyevskiy most
Finlyandskiy Vokzal
PLOSHCHAD LENINA
Lebedeva
Pl. Lenina
Komsomola
Park Smolnovo
nab. Smolnaya
GORKOVSKAYA
Museum of Russian Political History
Cruiser Aurora
nab. Arsenalnaya
Kronverkskaya
Liteyny most
Smolnyy Institute
Fortress of Peter and Paul
Neva
Troitskiy most
Children's Gardens
Shpalernaya
Tavricheskiy Palace
Smolnyy Cathedral
PL. PROLETARSKOY DIKTATURY
Chaykovskovo
Furshtatskaya
Tavricheskiy Gardens
EuroMed Clinic
UK
Kirochnaya
CHERNYSHEVSKAYA
Most Petra Velikogo
Summer Gardens
Dvortsovaya nab.
Hermitage
nab. Canal Griboedova
Suvorovskiy Pr.
Novgorodskaya
Liteyny Pr.
SMOLNINSKII REGION
Degtyarniy
nab. Sinopskaya
Italyanskaya
Nevskiy Prospekt
NEVSKIY PROSPEKT
5-ya Sovetskaya
PLOSHCHAD VOSSTANIYA
GOSTINYY DVOR
Nevskiy Prospekt
Vladimirskiy Pr.
Malookhtinskiy
Griboyedova
MAYAKOVSKAYA
Moskovskiy Vokzal
Bakunina
Sadovaya ul.
SENNAYA PLOSHCHAD
SADOVAYA
Fontanka
DOSTOYEVSKAYA
VLADIMIRSKAYA
Nevskiy Prospekt
Mirgorodskaya
PLOSHCHAD ALEKSANDRA NEVSKOGO
Most Aleksandra Nevskogo

SEE CENTRAL ST. PETERSBURG MAP, P. 596

Yusupovskiy Gardens
KUYBYSHEVSKI REGION
PIONERSKAYA PLOSHCHAD
Kremenchugskaya ul.
Obukhovskoy Oborony Pr.
Church of Annunciation
LIGOVSKIY PROSPEKT
Aleksandr Nevskiy Monastery
PUSHKINSKAYA
Vitebskiy Vokzal
Zagorodnyy Pr.
Ligovskiy Pr.
Chernyakhovskogo
TEKHNOLOGICHESKIY INSTITUT
Serpukhovskaya ul.
Obvodnyy Canal
Borovaya
Moskovskiy Pr.
Obvodny
Museum of Railway Machinery

Baltiyskiy Vokzal (Балтийский Вокзал; Baltic station; ☎768 2859). M1: Baltiyskaya. Serves destinations in the suburbs of St. Petersburg, including Peterhof (electrichka 48R, 5am-midnight). Luggage storage open 24hr., 51R per day.

Finlyandskiy Vokzal (Финляндский; Finland Station; ☎768 7539). M1: Pl. Lenina. Sells tickets to destinations in the suburbs of St. Petersburg, as well as to **Helsinki, FIN** (6hr., 2 per day, 2000-3600R). Also sells airline tickets to destinations within Russia.

Ladozhsky Vokzal (Ладожский; ☎436 5310). M4: Ladozhskaya. Serves destinations within Russia.

Moskovskiy Vokzal (Московский; Moscow Station; ☎768 4428). M1: Pl. Vosstaniya. 24hr. luggage storage. From 50R. To: **Moscow** (5-9hr., 15-20 per day, 515-2500R); **Novgorod** (*electrichka* 3-4hr., 1 per day, 320R); and **Sevastopol, UKR** (35hr., 1 per day, 1520-2700R).

Vitebskiy Vokzal (Витебский; Vitebskiy Station; ☎168 5939 or 168 3918). M1: Pushkinskaya. Serves numerous destinations within Eastern Europe. To: **Kaliningrad** (26hr.; June-Sept. 1 per day, Oct.-May every two days; 900-2500P); **Kyiv, UKR** (24hr., 1 per day, 990-1450R); **Odessa, UKR** (36hr.; June-Sept. 1 per day, Oct.-May 4 per wk.; 1100-2330R); **Rīga, LAT** (13hr., 1 per day, 1700-2600R); **Tallinn, EST** (8hr., 1 per day, 640-1600R); **Vilnius, LIT** (14hr., 1 every other day, 1070-1790R). Luggage storage available, 51R per day.

Buses: Автовокзал (Bus Station), nab. Obvodnogo Kanala 36 (Обводного Канала; ☎766 3644; www.avokzal.ru). M4: Ligovskiy Prospekt. Take bus #3, 34, 74 or trolleybus #42 to the canal. Facing the canal, turn right and walk 2 long blocks alongside it. The station will be on your right. 10R surcharge for advance tickets; tickets usually sell out 1hr. before departure. Open daily 8am-8pm. To: **Novgorod** (4hr., 15-20 per day, 250R); **Pskov** (5½hr., 3 per day, 380-460R); **Rīga, LAT** (12hr., 2 per day at 7:15pm and 8:30pm, 860R); **Tallinn, EST** (5-8hr., 8 per day, 800R). **Eurolines,** ul. Mitrofanevckoye 2/1 (Митрофаньевское; ☎441 3757). M1: Baltiyskaya. Offers similar prices and destinations. Open daily 9am-8:30pm.

RUSSIA

ORIENTATION

St. Petersburg sits at the mouth of the **Neva River** (Нева) on 44 islands among 50 canals. The heart of the city lies on the mainland, between the south bank of the Neva and the **Fontanka River.** Many of St. Petersburg's major sights—including the Hermitage and the three main cathedrals—are on or near **Nevskiy prospekt** (Невский проспект), the city's main street, which extends from the **Admiralty** to the **Alexander Nevskiy Monastery** and the center's newer quarters, developed primarily in the late 19th century. In this area, east of the Fontanka, are the **Smolnyy Institute** and most of the **train** and **bus stations. Moskovskiy Vokzal** on **Ploshchad Vosstaniya** (Площадь Восстания; Uprising Square) is midway down Nevskiy pr., marking the change from what is called Old Nevskiy (Старый Невский; Staryy Nevskiy) to the thoroughfare's more central section, simply called "Nevskiy." North of the center and across the Neva lies **Vasilevskiy Island** (Василевский Остров; Vasilevskiy Ostrov). Most of the island's sights, which are among St. Petersburg's oldest, sit on its eastern edge in the **Strelka** (Стрелка) neighborhood. Here the rectangular grid of streets recalls early plans for a network of canals on the island that was originally intended to be the base for Peter the Great's dream city, later moved to what is now known as Admiralteyskiy. The city's **Sea Terminal,** the ferry port, is at the island's southwestern edge, on the Gulf of Finland. On the north side of the Neva, across from the **Winter Palace,** is the small **Petrograd Side** archipelago, which houses the Peter and Paul Fortress, quiet residential neighborhoods, and the **Kirov Island** trio. In most of the city's center and the areas surrounding it, the streets are well—if not very obviously—marked on the

The pipes and drainage system in St. Petersburg have not been changed since the city was founded. There is no effective water purification system, so exposure to *giardia* is very likely. Always boil tap water for at least 10min., dry your washed veggies, and drink bottled water. See **Essentials: Health,** p. 28.

sides of buildings. Moving outward from the center, however, street names are less consistent and well-marked; a highly detailed map is recommended if you plan to venture to outlying areas.

LOCAL TRANSPORTATION

Public Transportation: A **transportation card** is good for a specified number of rides on public transportation (excluding *marshrutki*) for a given two-week period or calendar month; purchase one at any Metro station. The monthly card works from the 16th of one month to the 15th of the next, is valid for 70 rides, and costs 880R. A 2-week card works from the 1st to the 15th or the 16th to the end of the month, is valid for 35 rides, and costs 440R.

The **Metro** (Метро), is famous for both its depth (most stations were built 50-75m underground) and efficient design. Stations are open daily from 5:30 or 6am to midnight or 12:30am. The St. Petersburg Metro is generally busy; you may want to avoid peak hours (8-9am and 5-6pm). A Metro **token** (жетон; zheton) costs 14R. Stock up, as lines are long and cutting is common. Multiple-journey tickets are valid for 7, 15, 30, or 90 days. A pocket-size map of the system can usually be bought for 5-10R from a news kiosk after passing through the turnstiles.

Buses, trams, and **trolleys** (14R) run fairly frequently. Stops are posted on the outside of the vehicle, but if you don't read Cyrillic, it is advisable to get directions from your hostel/hotel receptionist. Trolleys #1, 5, 10, and 22 run from Uprising Square to the beginning of Nevskiy pr., near the Hermitage. Bus #7 runs from Vasilevskiy Island, past Palace Square, and along Nevskiy pr. Buses, trams, and trolleys generally run 6am-midnight. Tickets can be purchased from the conductor, who will be walking around the vehicle.

Marshrutki (маршрутки; private minibuses) are an option for Russian speakers. They cost more than buses (15-17R) and are used more by commuters than by tourists, but move much more quickly through traffic and will stop on request (routes and numbers are displayed on the outside windows, price on the inside windows). #147 runs from Vasilevskiy Island, past Palace Square, and along Nevskiy pr. and Suvorovskiy pr.; #46 can be used to get across the Trotsky Bridge to the Peter and Paul Fortress; #15 runs from Lenin Square to the south along Liteynyy pr., Vladimirskiy pr. and Zagorodnyy pr. *Marshrutki* generally operate 7am-10pm, but may work later.

Taxis: Both marked and private cabs operate in St. Petersburg. **St. Petersburg Taxi** is the city's umbrella service. (☎068 from a land line, ☎324 7777 from a mobile phone; 20R per km.) Instead of taking a taxi, many locals "catch a car," called **"gypsy cabs"** (частники): they flag down a car on the street, determine where it's going, agree on a price, and hop a ride. This practice is usually cheaper than taking marked cabs. If you choose to flag down a car, keep in mind that it's a good idea to have some fluency in Russian and a degree of familiarity with the streets along your route. Never get in a car containing more than 1 person. Let's Go does not recommend hitchhiking.

BRIDGE OUT. The bridges over the Neva go up on summer nights to allow boats to pass. It's beautiful to watch, but don't get caught on the wrong side.

PRACTICAL INFORMATION

TOURIST AND FINANCIAL SERVICES

Tourist Office: City Tourist Information Center, Sadovaya 14 (Садовая; ☎310 2822; www.visit-petersburg.com). M3: Gostinyy Dvor. In addition to offering English-language advice and free brochures and maps, the info center sells postcards and souvenirs. Open M-F 10am-7pm, Sa noon-8pm. A smaller office, pl. Dvortsovaya 12 (Дворцовая; ☎982 8253), also has English speakers and souvenirs, but fewer free pamphlets. Located between the Hermitage and the Admiralty. Open daily 10am-7pm. Tourist offices provide the helpful, free English-language publications *Where* and the *St. Petersburg Times* (www.sptimes.ru), which are also available in many hostels and hotels.

RUSSIA

St. Petersburg Metro

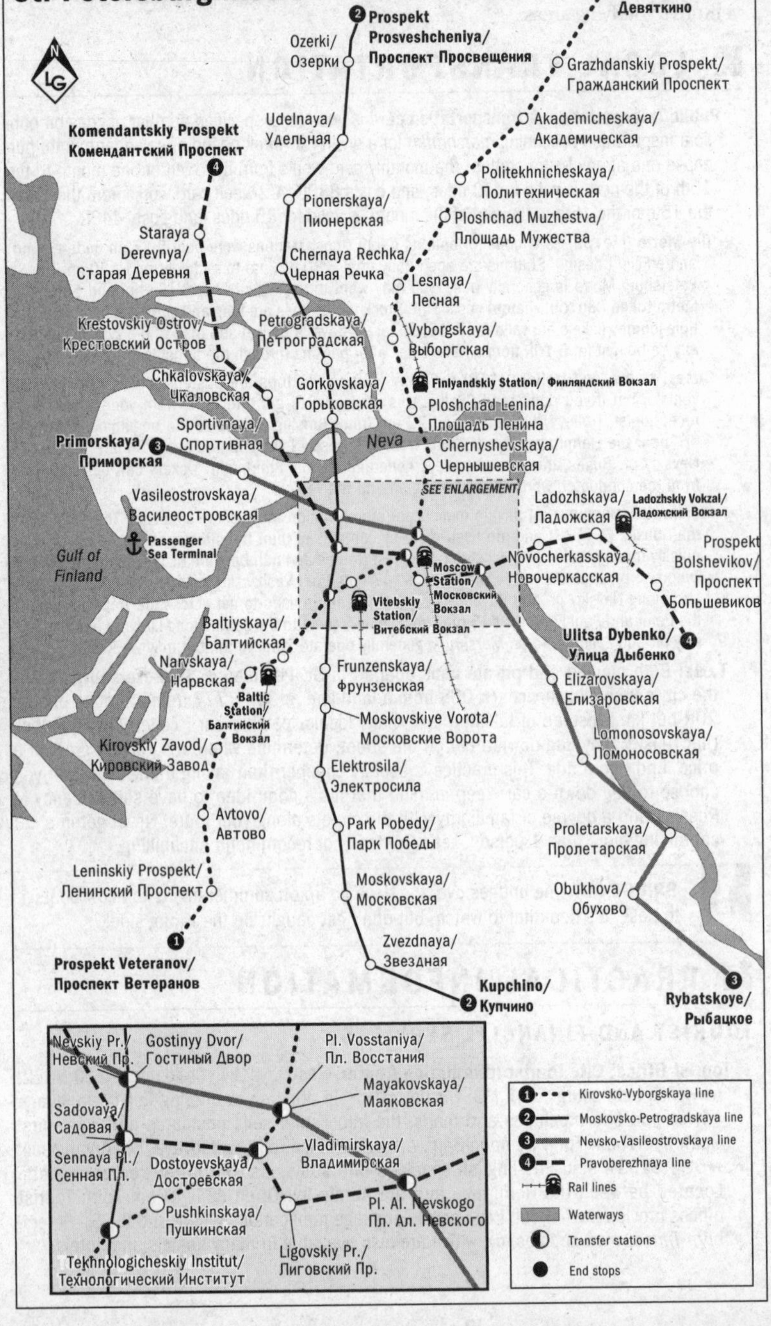

LG

1 Devyatkino/
Девяткино

2 Prospekt
Prosveshcheniya/
Проспект Просвещения

Ozerki/
Озерки

Grazhdanskiy Prospekt/
Гражданский Проспект

Akademicheskaya/
Академическая

Udelnaya/
Удельная

Komendantskiy Prospekt
Комендантский Проспект 4

Politekhnicheskaya/
Политехническая

Pionerskaya/
Пионерская

Ploshchad Muzhestva/
Площадь Мужества

Staraya
Derevnya/
Старая Деревня

Chernaya Rechka/
Черная Речка

Lesnaya/
Лесная

Krestovskiy Ostrov/
Крестовский Остров

Petrogradskaya/
Петроградская

Vyborgskaya/
Выборгская

Chkalovskaya/
Чкаловская

Gorkovskaya/
Горьковская

Finlyandskiy Station/ Финляндский Вокзал

Ploshchad Lenina/
Площадь Ленина

Sportivnaya/
Спортивная

Primorskaya/
Приморская 3

Neva

Chernyshevskaya/
Чернышевская

Vasileostrovskaya/
Василеостровская

SEE ENLARGEMENT

Ladozhskaya/
Ладожская

Ladozhskiy Vokzal/
Ладожский Вокзал

Passenger
Sea Terminal

Gulf of
Finland

Moscow
Station/
Московский
Вокзал

Novocherkasskaya/
Новочеркасская

Prospekt
Bolshevikov/
Проспект
Большевиков

Vitebskiy
Station/
Витебский Вокзал

Baltiyskaya/
Балтийская

Ulitsa Dybenko/
Улица Дыбенко 4

Narvskaya/
Нарвская

Frunzenskaya/
Фрунзенская

Elizarovskaya/
Елизаровская

Baltic
Station/
Балтийский
Вокзал

Moskovskiye Vorota/
Московские Ворота

Kirovskiy Zavod/
Кировский Завод

Lomonosovskaya/
Ломоносовская

Elektrosila/
Электросила

Avtovo/
Автово

Park Pobedy/
Парк Победы

Proletarskaya/
Пролетарская

Leninskiy Prospekt/
Ленинский Проспект

Moskovskaya/
Московская

Obukhova/
Обухово

1
Prospekt Veteranov/
Проспект Ветеранов

Zvezdnaya/
Звездная

2 Kupchino/
Купчино

3
Rybatskoye/
Рыбацкое

Nevskiy Pr./
Невский Пр.

Gostinyy Dvor/
Гостиный Двор

Pl. Vosstaniya/
Пл. Восстания

Mayakovskaya/
Маяковская

Sadovaya/
Садовая

Sennaya Pl./
Сенная Пл.

Dostoyevskaya/
Достоевская

Vladimirskaya/
Владимирская

Pl. Al. Nevskogo
Пл. Ал. Невского

Pushkinskaya/
Пушкинская

Ligovskiy Pr./
Лиговский Пр.

Tekhnologicheskiy Institut/
Технологический Институт

1 Kirovsko-Vyborgskaya line
2 Moskovsko-Petrogradskaya line
3 Nevsko-Vasileostrovskaya line
4 Pravoberezhnaya line
Rail lines
Waterways
Transfer stations
End stops

RUSSIA

Tours: Peter's Walking Tours, 3-ya Sovyetskaya 28 (3-я Советская; www.peterswalk.com), in the International Youth Hostel. M1: Pl. Vosstaniya. Offers a range of 3-6hr. English-language thematic excursions, changeable from season to season. Especially popular during the White Nights is Peter's "Friday Night Pub Crawl," during which your guide takes you to the best party spots in town, then drops you off for more drinking or for bed by 10pm (430R, drinks not included). Tours (430-800R) can be booked online, but those who simply turn up at the pre-arranged departure points (the International Hostel lobby, the Internet cafe Quo Vadis, and Skat Prokat Bike Shop) are welcome. For more information—and to create your own custom tour—visit the website or pick up the widely available pamphlet.

Budget Travel: Sindbad Travel (FIYTO), 2-ya Sovetskaya 12 (2-я Советская; ☎332 2020; www.sindbad.ru). M1: pl. Vostanniya. Housed in a hip and modern building, English-speaking agents sell train and bus tickets to destinations throughout Europe, flights worldwide, and ISICs. Student discounts on plane tickets. Open M-F 10am-10pm, Sa-Su 10am-6pm. The agency also maintains staff at the **ISIC Info Center** in Cafemax, Nevskiy 90-92 (☎273 9401) and at the **ISIC-Petersburg/Sindbad Lufthansa City Center,** ul. Zhukovskov 63 (Жуковского; ☎332 2020 or 332 2439).

Consulates: In an emergency, citizens of **Ireland** and **New Zealand** can call the UK consulate. **Australia,** Italyanskaya 1 (Итальянская; ☎/fax 325 7333; www.australianembassy.ru). M2: Nevskiy Prospekt. Open M-F 9am-6pm. **UK,** Pl. Proletarskoy Diktatury 5 (Пролетарской Диктатуры; ☎320 3200; www.britain.spb.ru). M1: Chernyshevskaya. Open M-F 9am-1pm, 2-5pm. **US,** Furshtatskaya 15 (Фурштатская; ☎331 2600, emergency ☎331 2888; www.stpetersburg-usconsulate.ru). M1: Chernyshevskaya. Open M-Tu, Th-F 2-5pm, W 10am-1pm. Phone inquiries M-Tu, Th-F 10am-1pm, W 3-5pm.

Currency Exchange: ATMs are omnipresent in the most cosmopolitan areas of the city. It's cheaper to take out rubles than other currencies, and many establishments accept only rubles. There are also currency exchange establishments every few blocks on Nevskiy pr., and many of them house Western Union. Look for "обмен валюты" (obmen valyuti) signs everywhere, and don't forget your passport.

English-Language Bookstore: Angliya British Bookshop (Англия), nab. Reki Fontanka 38 (Реки Фонтанки; ☎579 8284). M2: Nevskiy Prospekt. Enter where the sign says Turgenev House; it's on the right. Stocks a large variety of educational, art, and children's books, including books about Russia and the Russian masters in translation. Also offers travel guides and a number of foreign-language books. Open daily 10am-8pm. MC/V.

Dom Knigi (Дом Книги; House of Books), Nevskiy pr. 28 (☎570 6438; www.spbdk.ru). M2: Nevskiy Prospekt. Conveniently located on Nevskiy and housed in the famous Singer house, Dom Knigi is one of the most well-known bookstores in St. Petersburg. Offering a reasonable selection of English books and tourist literature, Dom Knigi also sells a wealth of Russian books, as well as smaller selections of German and French literature. 20min. free **Internet** on the three computers on the first floor; use the one on the very left to launch foreign servers. Open daily 9am-midnight. MC/V.

RUSSIA

EMERGENCY AND COMMUNICATIONS

Be aware of rules about sitting, walking on, or otherwise harming the city's lawns and gardens, even if locals are doing it. You might have to do some quick-stepping to avoid fines. Police may merely take down the names of Russian offenders, but exact hefty fines from foreigners doing the same thing.

Police Services for Foreigners: ☎702 2177.

Pharmacy: Throughout the city center; look for "Аптека" signs accompanied by a green or red cross. **PetroFarm,** Nevskiy pr. 22 (☎314 5401). Stocks an impressive selection of Western medicines, toiletries, and specialized beauty care products. Open 24hr. Pharmacist daily 9am-10pm. MC/V.

Medical Services: American Medical Clinic, nab. Reki Moyki 78 (Реки Мойки; ☎740 2090; www.amclinic.com). M2: Sennaya Pl. Follow per. Grivtsova across Griboyedov Canal and along to the Moyka river. English-speaking doctors provide comprehensive services; house calls can be made by general practitioners, but not specialists. Consultation US$75. Open 24hr., specialist appointments M-Sa 9am-8pm. AmEx/MC/V. **International Clinic MEDEM,** ul. Marata 6 (Марата; ☎336 3333; www.medem.ru). M3: Mayakovskaya. English-speaking doctors provide full medical and dental services. Accepts numerous Russian and foreign insurance providers. Consulation €70, 10% discount on full-body checkup (men 1032R, women 1208R). Open daily 24hr.; specialist appointments M-F 9am-9pm. Pharmacy on the 1st fl., open daily 24hr. AmEx/MC/V.

Internet: Straying from Nevskiy pr. yields far lower rates. **Cafemax,** Nevskiy pr. 90, 2nd fl. (☎273 6655; spb@e-max.ru). M3: Mayakovskaya. Massive, modern Internet cafe. Students 65R per hr., with ISIC 38R per hr., all night (11pm-7am) Su-Th 149R. Fax and copy services available. ISIC sold. Wi-Fi. Open 24hr. **Quo Vadis,** Nevskiy pr. 76 (☎333 0708; www.quovadis.ru). Enter from Liteynyy pr. and go to the 2nd floor; it's the door on the left. Internet 70R per 30min., with ISIC 50R; 130R per hr., with ISIC 90R. English spoken. Fax and printing services and Wi-Fi. Open 9am-11pm. MC/V.

Post Office: Почта России (Pochta Rossii). Main branch at Pochtamtskaya 9 (Почтамтская; ☎312 3954). From Nevskiy pr., turn onto Malaya Morskaya (Малая Морская), which becomes Pochtamtskaya. **Currency exchange** at window 1, information at window 2. **Telephone** service. Internet 50R per 30 min. International mail at windows 8 & 9. Open 24hr. **Postal Code:** 190 000.

RUSSIA

ACCOMMODATIONS

Travelers can choose from a variety of **hostels, hotels,** and **private apartments,** though hotels tend to be very, very expensive. St. Petersburg hostels provide guests with linens and often a towel. The *St. Petersburg Times*, an English-language newspaper, lists apartments for rent; find free copies at the City Tourist Information Center and at numerous hotels and restaurants throughout the city. Hotels and hostels will register your visa upon arrival and in most cases can provide you with the necessary invitation for a fee, usually about 1000-2000R.

Nord Hostel, Bolshaya Morskaya 10 (Большая Морская; ☎571 0342; www.nordhostel.com). M2: Nevskiy Prospekt. Centrally located in a beautiful building, Nord Hostel offers comfortable rooms, many services, and even a piano. International clientele. Kitchen, TV lounge, and laundry (175R per 8kg) available. Breakfast (8am-2pm) included. Free luggage storage. Free Internet. Check-out 11am. 6- to 10-bed dorms Apr.-Jan. €24; Feb.-Mar. €18. Cash only. ❸

Hotel LokoSphinx (Локосфинкс), Canal Griboyedova 101 (Грибоедова; ☎/fax 314 8890; www.lokosphinxhotel.ru). Regally furnished and overlooking the canal, this hotel provides fantastic prices for its location and services. Rooms equipped with TV, phone, and free Wi-Fi. English spoken. Sauna additional charge. Breakfast (8-11am) included. Laundry US$1-2 per item. Check-in 2pm. Check-out noon. Doubles 2000-3900R, for two people 2500R-4450R; apartment 4700/5200R. MC/V. ❹

Sleep Cheap, Mokhovaya 18, apt. 32 (Моховая; ☎115 1304; www.sleepcheap.spb.ru). M1: Chernyshevskaya. When you reach Mokhovaya 18, head into the courtyard; the hostel will be the first black door on your right. The hostel's welcoming, family-like setting complements the many full-size dorm beds and private baths. Airport and train transfer available. Breakfast included. Laundry 150R. 8-bed dorms 700R. Cash only. ❷

Hostel "Zimmer Freie," Liteynyy pr. 46 (Литейный; ☎973 3757; www.zimmer.ru). Walk through the archway at Liteynyy pr. 46 and bear left; enter at the "Fast Link" sign. Clean, apartment-style rooms include showers, TV, refrigerator, and kitchen, and are a great value for the central location. English spoken. Laundry 100R per 4kg. Fast Internet connection 50R per hr. Check-out noon. May 18-Aug. 31 dorms US$28, singles US$56; Sept. 1-May 17 US$20/40. 5% discount with YIHA or ISIC. Cash only. ❷

Hotel Vera (Вера), Suvorovsky pr. 25, 5th fl. (Суворовский; ☎/fax 702 7206; www.hotelvera.ru). Set in a renovated Art Nouveau building, Hotel Vera is both centrally located and warmly decorated. English-speaking staff will help arrange tours, reserve theater seats, and provide transfer services. All rooms equipped with TV, phone, and Internet; small library and DVD collection available. Security cameras and guard. Breakfast included. Laundry 150R. May 1-Sept. 30 single junior 2700R; classic for 1 person 3900R, 2 people 4900R; Oct. 1-Apr. 30 1900/2700/3500R. AmEx/MC/V. ❺

International Youth Hostel (HI), 3-ya Sovetskaya 28 (3-я Советская; ☎329 8018; www.ryh.ru). M1: Pl. Vosstaniya. Walk along Suvorovskiy pr. (Суворовский) for 3 blocks, then turn right on 3-ya Sovetskaya. Rooms are bare, but have large windows, and the hostel is in a quiet neighborhood. English spoken. TV and English movies in common room. Kitchen. Breakfast included. Communal showers 8am-1am. Free lockers and safe. Laundry 120R per 5kg. Internet 1R per min. Reception daily 8am-1am. Check-out 11am. Quiet hours 11pm-8am. 3- to 5-bed dorms 690R; doubles 1680R. 60R discount with HI, 30R with ISIC. Cash only. ❷

FOOD

Market vendors offer fresh produce, meat, bread, pastries, and honey. The biggest **markets** are the **covered market,** Kuznechnyy per. 3 (Кузнечный; open M-Sa 8am-8pm, Su 8am-7pm), just around the corner from M1: Vladimirskaya, and the **Maltsevskiy Rynok** (Мальцевский Рынок), Nekrasova 52 (Некрасова), at the top of Ligovskiy pr. (Лиговский; M1: Pl. Vosstaniya. Open daily 9am-8pm.) The cheapest supermarkets in the city are **Dixie,** indicated by orange and yellow square signs with white lettering. **Nakhodka** (Находка) supermarkets, nab. Reki Fontanki 5 (Реки Фонтанки), at the end of the block, are considered the best. There are **24hr. supermarkets** on side streets off Nevskiy pr. Look for the "24 Часа" (24 hours) signs.

RUSSIAN RESTAURANTS

Cafe Zoom, Gorokhovaya 22 (Гороховая; ☎448 5001; www.cafezoom.ru). With menus detailing world history and geography and small golden theater masks on the walls, this popular eatery caters to the creative and intelligent consumer. English menu. Vegetarian options. Entrees 100-240R. Open M-Sa 11am-midnight, Su 1pm-midnight. Kitchen closes at 10:30pm. 20% lunch discount until 4pm. Cash only. ❷

Literaturnoye Kafe (Литературное Кафе), 18 Nevskiy pr. (☎312 6057). M2: Gostinyy Dvor. Formerly a confectioner's shop, this cafe once boasted a clientele of luminaries from Dostoevsky to Pushkin, who came here the night before his fatal duel. It now caters to tourists, offering an excellent menu and reasonable prices in an elegant setting. English menu. *Bliny* with mushrooms 120R. Entrees 100-600R. Favorite dishes of Pushkin 70-220R. Open daily 11am-11pm. MC/V. ❸

Traktir Shury Mury (Трактир Шуры Муры), ul. Belinskogo 8 (Белинского; ☎279 8550). M2: Gostinyy Dvor. From the Metro, go toward nab. Reki Fontanki and turn left; at the next bridge turn right onto ul. Belinskogo. Russian and European cuisine served to locals in the setting of a traditional Russian countryhouse, or *dacha,* by friendly waitresses in traditional garb. English menu. Try the *Tsarskoye Selo* (Царское Село; chicken with mushroom; 210R). Entrees 110-280R. Open daily 11am-6am. MC/V. ❷

RUSSIA

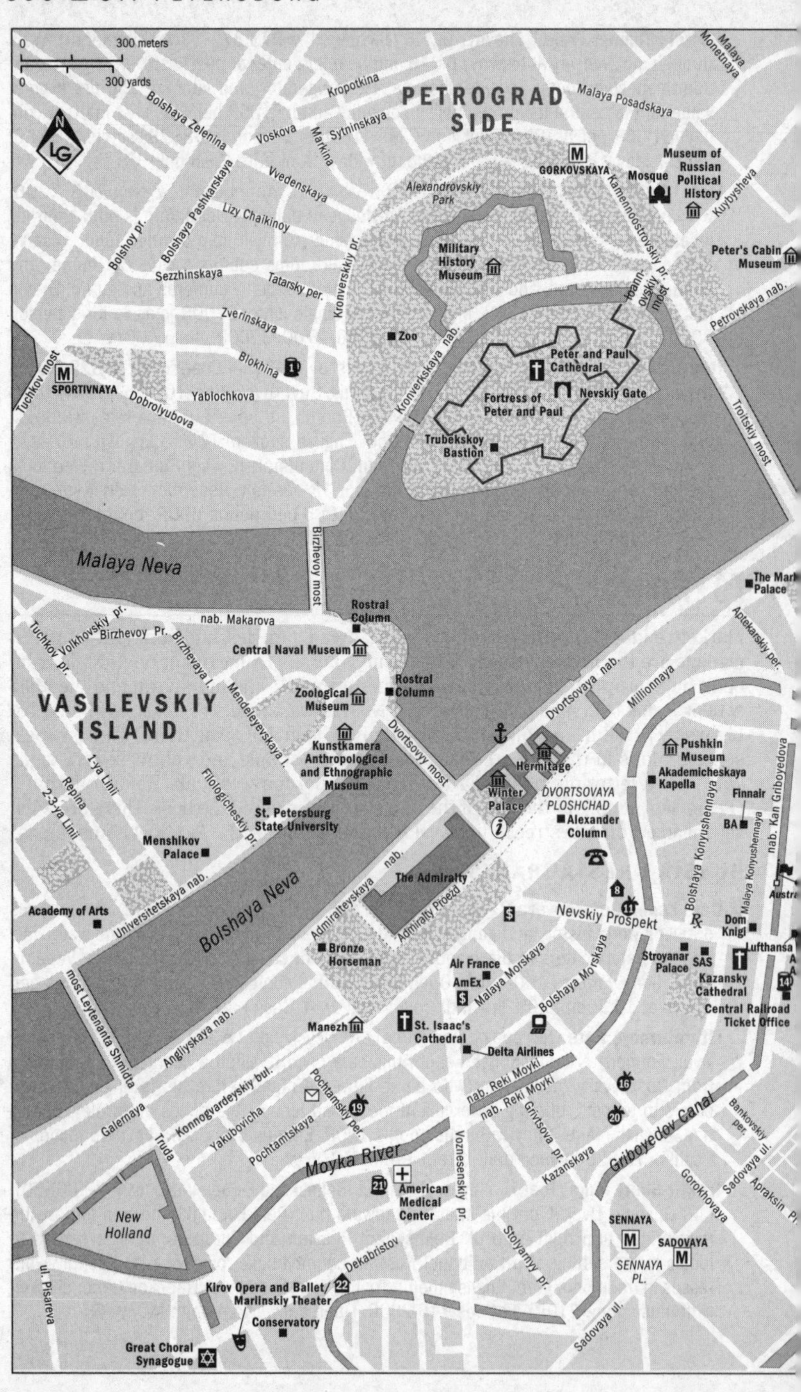

0 300 meters
0 300 yards
PETROGRAD SIDE
VASILEVSKIY ISLAND
Malaya Neva
Bolshaya Neva
Moyka River
Griboyedov Canal
Alexandrovskiy Park
GORKOVSKAYA
SPORTIVNAYA
SENNAYA
SADOVAYA
SENNAYA PL.
DVORTSOVAYA PLOSHCHAD
Museum of Russian Political History
Mosque
Peter's Cabin Museum
Military History Museum
Zoo
Peter and Paul Cathedral
Fortress of Peter and Paul
Nevskiy Gate
Trubekskoy Bastion
The Marble Palace
Rostral Column
Central Naval Museum
Zoological Museum
Kunstkamera Anthropological and Ethnographic Museum
St. Petersburg State University
Menshikov Palace
Academy of Arts
Hermitage
Winter Palace
Alexander Column
The Admiralty
Pushkin Museum
Akademicheskaya Kapella
Finnair
BA
Dom Knigi
Lufthansa
Stroyanar Palace
SAS
Kazansky Cathedral
Central Railroad Ticket Office
Bronze Horseman
Air France
AmEx
Manezh
St. Isaac's Cathedral
Delta Airlines
American Medical Center
New Holland
Kirov Opera and Ballet/ Marlinskiy Theater
Conservatory
Great Choral Synagogue
Kropotkina
Malaya Posadskaya
Malaya Monetnaya
Bolshaya Zelenina
Voskova
Sytninskaya
Markina
Vvedenskaya
Lizy Chaikinoy
Bolshaya Pashkarskaya
Bolshoy pr.
Sezzhinskaya
Tatarsky per.
Kronverskkiy pr.
Kamennoostrovskiy pr.
Kuybysheva
Ioannovskiy most
Petrovskaya nab.
Zverinskaya
Blokhina
Kronverkskaya nab.
Tuchkov most
Yablochkova
Dobrolyubova
Troitskiy most
Birzhevoy most
nab. Makarova
Volkhovskiy pr.
Birzhevoy Pr.
Tuchkov pr.
Birzhevaya l.
Mendeleyevskaya l.
Aptekarskiy per.
Dvortsovaya nab.
Millionnaya
Dvortsovyy most
1-ya Linii
Repina
2-3-ya Linii
Filologicheskiy pr.
Universitetskaya nab.
Admiralteyskaya nab.
Admiralty Proezd
Nevskiy Prospekt
Bolshaya Konyushennaya
Malaya Konyushennaya
nab. Kan Griboyedova
Malaya Morskaya
Bolshaya Morskaya
most Leytenanta Shmidta
Angliyskaya nab.
Galernaya
Konnogvardeyskiy bul.
Yakubovicha
Pochtamtskaya
Pochtamskiy per.
nab. Reki Moyki
Grivtsova pr.
Kazanskaya
Voznesenskiy pr.
Bankovskiy per.
Sadovaya ul.
Apraksin Pr.
Gorokhovaya
Truda
ul. Pisareva
Dekabristov
Stolyarnyy pr.
1
8
11
14
16
19
20
21
22

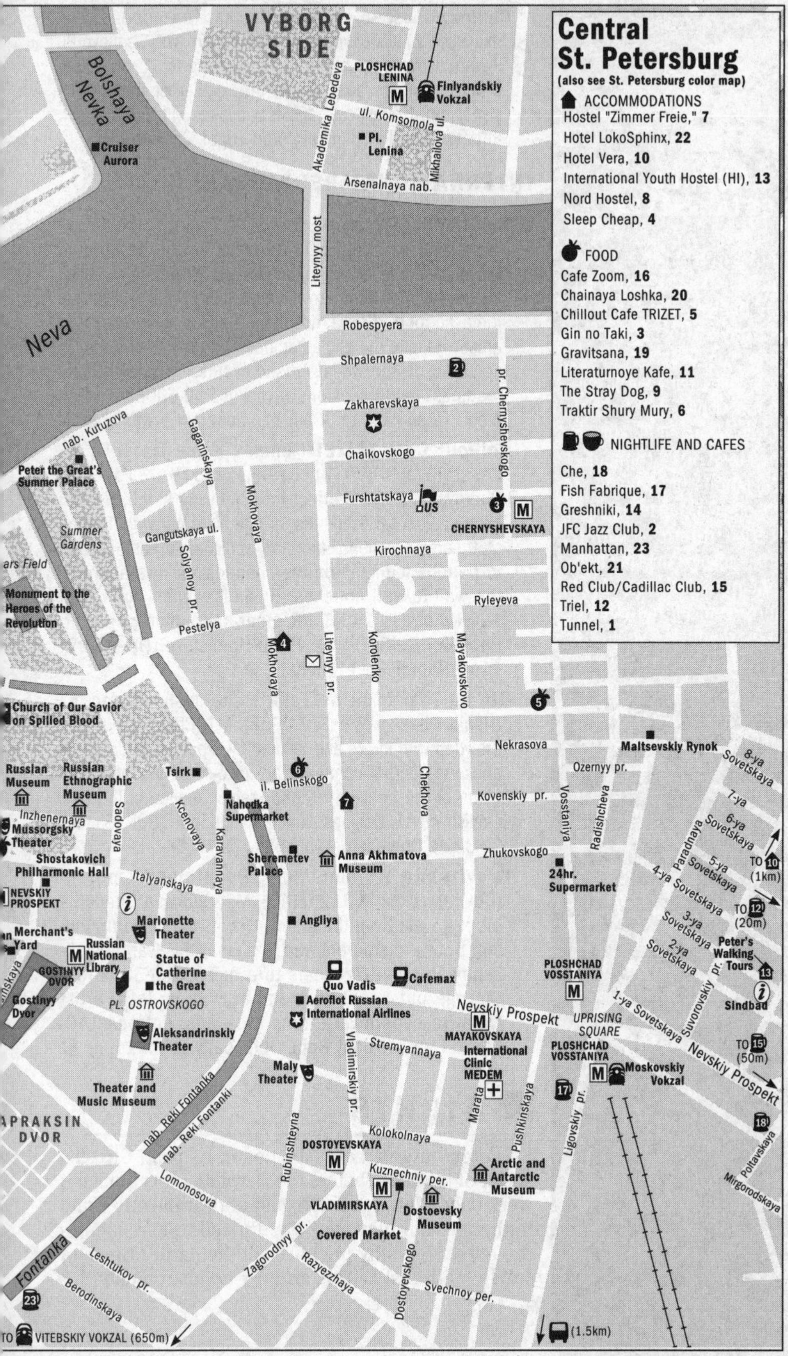
Central
St. Petersburg
(also see St. Petersburg color map)
ACCOMMODATIONS
Hostel "Zimmer Freie," 7
Hotel LokoSphinx, 22
Hotel Vera, 10
International Youth Hostel (HI), 13
Nord Hostel, 8
Sleep Cheap, 4
FOOD
Cafe Zoom, 16
Chainaya Loshka, 20
Chillout Cafe TRIZET, 5
Gin no Taki, 3
Gravitsana, 19
Literaturnoye Kafe, 11
The Stray Dog, 9
Traktir Shury Mury, 6
NIGHTLIFE AND CAFES
Che, 18
Fish Fabrique, 17
Greshniki, 14
JFC Jazz Club, 2
Manhattan, 23
Ob'ekt, 21
Red Club/Cadillac Club, 15
Triel, 12
Tunnel, 1
VYBORG SIDE
Bolshaya Nevka
Cruiser Aurora
PLOSHCHAD LENINA
Finlyandskiy Vokzal
ul. Komsomola
Akademika Lebedeva
Mikhailova ul.
Pl. Lenina
Arsenalnaya nab.
Liteynyy most
Neva
Robespyera
Shpalernaya
Zakharevskaya
pr. Chernyshevskogo
nab. Kutuzova
Gagarinskaya
Chaikovskogo
Peter the Great's Summer Palace
Mokhovaya
Furshtatskaya
US
CHERNYSHEVSKAYA
Summer Gardens
Gangutskaya ul.
Solyanoy pr.
Kirochnaya
ars Field
Monument to the Heroes of the Revolution
Ryleyeva
Pestelya
Liteynyy pr.
Korolenko
Mayakovskovo
Church of Our Savior on Spilled Blood
Nekrasova
Maltsevskiy Rynok
8-ya Sovetskaya
Russian Museum
Russian Ethnographic Museum
Tsirk
il. Belinskogo
Ozernyy pr.
Chekhova
Kovenskiy pr.
Vosstaniya
Radishcheva
7-ya
6-ya Sovetskaya
Inzhenernaya
Mussorgsky Theater
Sadovaya
Ksenovaya
Nahodka Supermarket
Karavannaya
Sheremetev Palace
Anna Akhmatova Museum
Zhukovskogo
24hr. Supermarket
Paradnaya
5-ya Sovetskaya
4-ya Sovetskaya
Shostakovich Philharmonic Hall
Italyanskaya
NEVSKIY PROSPEKT
TO 10 (1km)
TO 12 (20m)
Marionette Theater
Angliya
3-ya Sovetskaya
2-ya Sovetskaya
Peter's Walking Tours
Merchant's Yard
Russian National Library
Statue of Catherine the Great
GOSTINYY DVOR
Gostinyy Dvor
Quo Vadis
Cafemax
PLOSHCHAD VOSSTANIYA
Suvorovskiy pr.
Sindbad
PL. OSTROVSKOGO
Aeroflot Russian International Airlines
Nevskiy Prospekt
UPRISING SQUARE
1-ya Sovetskaya
Aleksandrinskiy Theater
Vladimirskiy pr.
MAYAKOVSKAYA
Stremyannaya
International Clinic MEDEM
PLOSHCHAD VOSSTANIYA
Moskovskiy Vokzal
TO 15 (50m)
Nevskiy Prospekt
Maly Theater
Theater and Music Museum
nab. Reki Fontanka
nab. Reki Fontanki
Marata
Pushkinskaya
Ligovskiy pr.
APRAKSIN DVOR
Rubinshteyna
Kolokolnaya
DOSTOYEVSKAYA
Arctic and Antarctic Museum
Poltavskaya
Mirgorodskaya
Lomonosova
Kuznechniy per.
VLADIMIRSKAYA
Dostoevsky Museum
Covered Market
Zagorodnyy pr.
Fontanka
Leshtukov pr.
Razyezzhaya
Dostoyevskogo
Svechnoy per.
Berodinskaya
TO VITEBSKIY VOKZAL (650m)
(1.5km)

Chainaya Loshka (Чайная Лошка; Tea Spoon), Gorokhovaya 27 (Гороховая; ☎314 3945). M2: Sennaya Pl. Perhaps the best place in Petersburg to go for *bliny*. Branches can be found all over the city. English menu. *Bliny s maslom* (Блины с маслом; pancakes with butter) 26R. Entrees 26-40R. Open daily 9am-10pm. Cash only. ❶

INTERNATIONAL RESTAURANTS

The Stray Dog (Подваль Бродячей Собаки), pl. Iskusstv 5/4 (Искусств; ☎312 8047), to the left of the Russian Museum. The favorite hangout of early 20th-century artists, including Anna Akhmatova's circle, The Stray Dog serves fantastic food in an atmosphere that remains classy and artistic despite the ragged stuffed dogs and the messages scrawled on the walls. Artistic events, including poetry readings, held occasionally (cover 200-600R). English menu. Open daily 11:30am-11:30pm. AmEx/MC/V. ❹

Chillout Cafe TRIZET (Чилайт Кафе ТРИЗЕТ), ul. Vosstaniya 30/7 (Восстания; ☎579 9315). M1: Chernyshevskaya. Perfect for a relaxing lunch, a good evening spent with friends, or late-night partying. Helpful staff serve excellent European and Middle Eastern food to patrons lounging on the countless pillows adorning the wall-to-wall couches. Business lunch noon-6pm 120R. Entrees 140-350R. Beer and liquor from 60R. Hookah 300-500R. DJ Th-Su 9pm-close. Open M-Th 11am-2am, F-Su 11am-5am. ❸

Gin no Taki (Гин но Таки), Chernyshevskogo 17 (Чернышевского; ☎272 0958). M1: Chernyshevskaya. Crowded with locals and favored by expats, this large Japanese restaurant combines an upscale atmosphere with some of the best prices and fastest service in the city. English menu. Business lunch 11am-5pm 180R. Entrees 90-320R. Open daily 11am-6pm. MC/V. ❷

Gravitsana (Гравицана), Pochtamskiy per. 8 (Почтамтский; ☎312 0343). M2: Sennaya. Though a bit of a walk from the Metro, Gravitsana is worth finding. Both a restaurant and jazz club, this warm establishment generally caters to a quiet, over-30 crowd. Strange but beautiful metal artwork by local artist Nataliya Lebedeva adorns the walls. Entrees 140-200R. Live jazz daily 8pm. Open daily 10am-11pm. ❷

SIGHTS

St. Petersburg is a city steeped in its past. Citizens speak of the time "before the Revolution" as though it were only a few years ago, and of dear old Peter and Catherine as if they were good friends. Signs such as the one at Nevskiy pr. 14 recall the harder times of WWII: "Citizens! During artillery bombardments this

PANCAKES, RUSSIAN-STYLE

The French have crepes; the Americans have pancakes; Jewish culture has blintzes. But the Russians also have a lesser-known version: *bliny* (блины).

In pre-Christian, early Slavic cultures, the round *bliny* symbolized the sun and were eaten during the festival of Maslenitsa (pancake week) to celebrate the coming of spring. Despite its pagan origins, the Eastern Orthodox Church absorbed this festival, moving it to the week before Lent, after which celebrations—and all foods containing dairy products—would be forbidden. Maslenitsa, akin to Mardi Gras, thus became a week-long party of sleigh rides, snowball fights, and food, culminating in the burning of Lady Maslenitsa, a straw effigy of a woman.

Despite the festival's new trappings, however, *bliny* still remain its definitive characteristic and an important element of Russian cuisine. Topped with everything from butter and jam to caviar and meat, Russians eat them as a snack, as a dessert, or even as a full meal. In a country that worships beets and cabbage, *bliny* can be a much-appreciated culinary treat for tourists.

Priyatnogo Apetita!

side of the street is more dangerous." The worst effects of those bombings were mitigated by Soviet-era reconstruction, and a more recent wave of projects restored the best sights for the city's 300th anniversary in 2003.

THE HERMITAGE

Dvortsovaya nab. 36 (Дворцовая; ☎571 3420; www.hermitagemuseum.org). M2: Nevskiy Prospekt. Exiting the Metro, turn right and walk down Nevskiy pr. to its end at the Admiralty. Bear right through Dvortsovaya pl., then enter the courtyard through the gates on Palace Square. Allow at least 3hr. to see the museum. Open Tu-Sa 10:30am-6pm, Su 10:30am-5pm; kassa and upper floors close 1hr. earlier. All buildings 350R, students free. 1½hr. tours in English 200R. English audiotour 300R. English museum plan available for free at information desk. Photo 100R, video 350R.

Originally a collection of 225 paintings bought by **Catherine the Great** in 1764, the **State Hermitage Museum** (Эрмитаж; Ermitazh), the world's largest art collection, rivals Paris's Louvre in architectural, historical, and artistic significance. The tsars lived with their collection in the Winter Palace and Hermitage until 1917, when both the palace and the collection were nationalized. Catherine II once wrote of the treasures, "the only ones to admire all this are the mice and me." Fortunately, since 1852 the five buildings have been open to the public. Ask for an indispensable English audio tour at the info desk. The museum is organized chronologically by floor, starting with **prehistoric artifacts** in the Winter Palace and **Egyptian, Greek,** and **Roman art** on the ground floor of the Small and Great Hermitages. On the second floor of the Hermitage are collections of 15th- to 19th-century **European art.** It is nearly impossible to absorb the museum's entire display in a day or even a week—a full tour would cover a distance of 24 mi. and would only reveal 5% of the museum's three-million-piece collection, most of which is in storage due to lack of space. Some of the collection's Russian artifacts are on display at the Russian museum. If you're running late, visit the upper floors first—they close earliest.

WINTER PALACE. Commissioned in 1762, the majestic architecture of the Winter Palace (Зимний Дворец; Zimniy Dvorets) reflects the extravagant Rococo tastes of Empress Elizabeth and the architect Rastrelli. Rooms 190-198 on the second floor are the palace **state rooms.** The rest of the floor houses 15th- to 18th-century **French art** (Rooms 273-297) and 10th- to 20th-century **Russian art** (Rooms 147-151, 153, 157-187). The third floor offers exhibits on Byzantium, 19th- to 20th-century French art, and 19th- to 20th-century European art. The famous **Malachite Hall** (Room 189) contains six tons of malachite columns, boxes, and urns, each painstakingly constructed from thousands of matched stones to give the illusion of having been carved from one massive rock.

OTHER BUILDINGS. By the end of the 1760s, the collection amassed by the Empress had become too large for the Winter Palace, and Catherine appointed Vallin de la Mothe to build the **Small Hermitage** (Малый Эрмитаж; Malyy Ermitazh), a retreat for herself and her lovers. The **Large Hermitage** (Большой Эрмитаж; Bolshoy Ermitazh) was completed in the 1780s. In Rooms 226-227, an exact copy of Raphael's *Loggia*, commissioned by Catherine the Great, covers the walls just as in the Vatican. In 1851, Stasov, a famous imperial Russian architect, built the **New Hermitage** (Новый Эрмитаж; Novyy Ermitazh).

NEAR THE HERMITAGE

ST. ISAAC'S CATHEDRAL. Intricately carved masterpieces of iconostasis find the home they deserve in the awesome **St. Isaac's Cathedral** (Исаакиевский Собор; Isaakiyevskiy Sobor), a 19th-century megalith built during the reign of Alexander I. On a sunny day, the 100kg of pure gold coating the dome can be

RUSSIA

seen for miles. The cost of this opulent cathedral was well over five times that of the Winter Palace, and 60 laborers died from mercury inhalation during the gilding process. Due in part to architect Auguste de Montferrand's lack of experience, construction took 40 years; the superstition that the Romanov dynasty would fall with the cathedral's completion didn't speed things up. The cathedral was completed in 1858 and is one of the world's largest cathedrals. Some of Russia's greatest artists worked on the 150 murals and mosaics inside. Although officially designated a museum in 1931, the cathedral still holds religious services on major holidays. The breathtaking 360° view of St. Petersburg is worth the 260-stair climb to the top of the **colonnade.** *(Isaakievskaya pl. between Admiralteyskiy pr. and Malaya Morskaya (Адмиралтейский пр. and Малая Морская); museum administration ☎315 9732. M2: Nevskiy Prospekt. Exit the Metro, turn left, and go almost to the end of Nevskiy pr. Turn left on Malaya Morskaya. Cathedral open in summer M-Tu and Th-Su 10am-8pm; in winter M-Tu and Th-Su 11am-7pm; kassa closes 1hr. earlier. 300R, students 170R, children under 7 free. Photo 50R, video 100R. Colonnade summer M-Tu and Th-Su 10am-7pm; winter M-Tu and Th-Su 11am-3pm. 150R, students 100R, children under 7 free. Photo 25R, video 50R. Enter on the south side (from Malaya Morskaya). A kassa is to the right, on the northeast side. Cathedral often open at night during the summer M-Tu and Th-Su 8-11pm; kassa closes 30min. earlier. Colonnade open 7pm-5am, kassa closes 30min. earlier. 300R.)*

AN EYE FOR ICONOSTASIS. In a Russian Orthodox church or cathedral, iconostasis is the boundary screening off the sanctuary from the gaze of those in the main part of the church, often likened to a divide between heaven and earth. Its construction is meticulously arranged with up to six tiers, each having a unique significance within the religion.

DVORTSOVAYA PLOSHCHAD. The windswept Palace Square (Дворцовая Площадь) has witnessed many milestones in Russian history. Catherine was crowned here in 1762, and, years later, Nicholas II's guards fired into a crowd of peaceful demonstrators on Russia's "Bloody Sunday," precipitating the 1905 revolution. In October 1917, Lenin's Bolsheviks seized power from Kerensky's provisional government here during the storming of the Winter Palace. Today, the square is used for various events, from concerts to political meetings. Overlooking it all is the angel at the top of the **Alexander Column** (Александрийская Колонна; Aleksandriyskaya Kolonna), which commemorates Russia's 1812 victory over Napoleon. At the base of the column are inscribed the words, "To Alexander I, from a grateful Russia." The 700-ton column took two years to cut from a cliff in Karelia, but when it arrived in St. Petersburg, it was raised in just 40min. by thousands of war veterans using a complex pulley system. At 47m, it is the largest freestanding monument in the world.

THE ADMIRALTY. The only way into the Admiralty (Адмиралтейство; Admiralteystvo) is to become an officer in the Russian Navy, but tourists can admire its impressive exterior and gleaming golden spire, visible throughout St. Petersburg. The Admiralty began life as a fortified shipyard and was reincarnated by architect Andrey Zakharov in 1806 in homage to the successes of the Russian naval force. During WWII, the spire was painted black to hide it from German artillery bombers. Peter supposedly supervised the construction of St. Petersburg from the tower, one of the oldest buildings in the city. The gardens, initially designed as a firing range, now hold statues of important Russian literary figures. Inside, young Russian men live for five-year stints, studying engineering in preparation for military careers. *(Admiralteyskaya nab. 2. M2: Nevskiy Prospekt.)*

BRONZE HORSEMAN. This hulking statue of Peter the Great astride a rearing horse terrorized the protagonists in works by Alexander Pushkin and Andrey Bely by coming to life and chasing them through the streets. In reality, the statue hasn't moved from the site on which Catherine the Great had it set in 1782. *(M2: Nevskiy Prospekt. On the river, from St. Isaac's Cathedral across the Admiralty gardens in Decembrists' Square.)*

VASILYEVSKIY ISLAND. Just across the bridge from the Hermitage, the Strelka (Стрелка; arrow or promontory) section of the city's biggest island (Васильевский Остров; Vasilevskiy Ostrov) juts into the river, dividing it in two and providing a spectacular view of both sides. Peter the Great had intended to make the island home to his new capital's administration, but he abandoned these plans due to the lack of a permanent bridge to the mainland. The former Stock Exchange (now the Naval Museum) dominates the square on the island's east end, and the ships' prows and anchors sticking out of the two red **Rostral Columns** proclaim the glory of Peter's modern navy. St. Petersburg State University and the Academy of Arts, as well as some of St. Petersburg's most interesting museums (see **Museums**, p. 604), are housed on the embankment facing the Admiralty. *(Take bus #7 or trolleybus #10 from Nevskiy pr.)*

FORTRESS OF PETER AND PAUL

M2: Gorkovskaya. Exiting the Metro, bear forward and right onto Kamennostrovskiy pr. (Каменноостровский), the unmarked street in front of you on the left side of the park. Follow it to the river, bear slightly to the right and cross the wooden bridge (Иоанновский Мост; Ioannovskiy Bridge) to the island fortress (☎230 6431; www.spbmuseum.ru). Peter's Cabin is a small brick house along the river on the east side of the fortress. To get there, walk down Petroskaya nab. until you reach a bronze gate with gold trim. Fortress open M and W-Su 11am-6pm (in the summer until 7pm), Tu 11am-4pm. Cathedral open daily 10am-8pm. Peter's Cabin open M 10am-4pm, W-Su 10am-5pm; closed last M of month. Purchase a ticket for most sights (250R, students 130R) at the kassa *in the "boathouse" in the middle of the fortress (10am-7:45pm) or in the smaller* kassa *to the left inside the main entrance (10am-6pm). Fortress free. Russian audiotour 150R, English 250R. English information pamphlet free. Peter's Cabin 200R, students 70R.*

Across the river from the Hermitage are the walls and golden spire of the Fortress of Peter and Paul (Петропавловская Крепость; Petropavlovskaya Krepost). Construction of the fortress, supervised by Peter the Great himself, began on May 27, 1703; the date is now considered to mark the birthday of St. Petersburg. The fortress was originally intended as a defense against the Swedes, but was converted by Peter I into a prison for political dissidents. Inmates' graffiti is still legible on the citadel's stone walls. Arrive early to set your watch by the boom of the cannon that's fired from the spire of the cathedral every day at noon.

PETER AND PAUL CATHEDRAL. The main attraction within the fortress, the cathedral (Петропавловский Собор; Petropavlovskiy Sobor) glows with walls of rose and aquamarine marble. At 122.5m, it's the tallest building in the city. From the ceiling, cherubs keep watch over the breathtaking Baroque iconostasis and the ornate coffins of Peter the Great and his successors. Before the main vault sits the recently restored **Chapel of St. Catherine the Martyr.** The bodies of Nicholas II and his family were entombed here on July 17, 1998, the 80th anniversary of their murder at the hands of the Bolsheviks. Mikhail Shemyakin's controversial bronze **statue** of Peter the Great sits outside.

NEVSKIY GATE AND TRUBETSKOY BASTION. To the right of the statue, the **Nevskiy Gate** (Невские Ворота; Nevskiye Vorota) was the site of numerous executions. The condemned awaited their fate in the fortress's southwest corner at the

RUSSIA

Trubetskoy Bastion (Трубецкой Бастион) prison, where Peter the Great tortured his first son, Aleksey. Dostoevsky, Gorky, and Trotsky spent time here as well.

PETER'S CABIN. Peter the Great supervised the construction of his city while living in this modest cabin (Домик Петра Первого; Domik Petra Pervogo), the oldest building in St. Petersburg (nicknamed the "Small House of Peter I"). The museum contains many of his personal effects, including a boat he built himself, and describes his victories in the Northern War of 1700-1721.

ALONG NEVSKIY PROSPEKT

The easternmost boulevard of central St. Petersburg, Nevskiy pr. is the city's main thoroughfare. In accordance with Peter's vision, the regal avenue runs 4.5km from the Neva in the west to the Alexander Nevskiy Monastery in the east.

CHURCH OF OUR SAVIOR ON SPILLED BLOOD. This church's colorful forest of elaborate "Russian style" domes was built between 1883 and 1907 over the site of Tsar Alexander II's 1881 assassination. Also known as the Church of Christ's Resurrection and the Church of the Bleeding Savior, the cathedral (Спас На Крови; Spas Na Krovi) has been beautifully renovated according to the original artists' designs after 40 years of Soviet neglect. The interior walls are covered with 7000 sq. m of mosaics based mainly on the New Testament. The arrangement of mosaics follows the canons of Orthodox iconography; the southern wall shows events from the Nativity to the Baptism of Christ, while the northern wall displays miracles worked by Jesus. In the adjacent chapel is an exhibit on the life and death of reformist Alexander II. Behind the church and to the left is an outdoor souvenir market popular with tourists. *(2 nab. Kanala Griboyedova, 3 blocks off Nevskiy pr. up Canal Griboyedova from Dom Knigi. M2: Nevskiy Prospekt. ☎315 1636. Open M-Tu and Th-Su in summer 10am-8pm; in winter 11am-7pm; kassa closes 1hr. earlier. Foreigners buy tickets inside. Church 300R, students 170R, under 7 free. Photo 50R, video 100R.)*

KAZANSKY CATHEDRAL. This colossal edifice (Казанский Собор; Kazanskiy Sobor) on the corner of Nevskiy pr. and the Griboyedov Canal was inspired by St. Peter's Basilica in Rome. Completed in 1811, the cathedral was originally created to house the icon Our Lady of Kazan, to whom the Russian general Mikhail Golenshokov Kutuzov prayed before his military campaign. After the Franco-Prussian conflict, Russian soldiers placed the keys of captured French cities and military emblems above Kutuzov's tomb in the cathedral, where they (and he) remain. Ironically, during the Communist era, the cathedral housed the Museum of Atheism. *(Kazanskaya pl. 2. M2: Nevskiy Prospekt. ☎314 4663; www.kazansky.spb.ru. Open daily 8:30am-7:30pm. Services daily 7, 10am, 6pm. Free. Tours daily noon-6pm; for tours in English call ahead ☎570 4528.)*

GOSTINYY DVOR. Built under Catherine the Great, this large yellow 18th-century complex (Гостиныи Двор; Gostinyy Dvor; Merchant's Complex) near the Metro claims to be the oldest indoor shopping mall in the world. The two-floored ring of stores is like an open-air market—but with Western European fashions, souvenirs, and more. Be warned, however, that no one bargains here. *(M3: Gostinyy Dvor. Open M-Sa 10am-10pm, Su 10am-9pm.)*

UPRISING SQUARE. Some of the bloodiest confrontations of the February Revolution, including the Cossack attack on police, took place here (Площадь Восстания; Ploshchad Vosstaniya). The obelisk, erected in 1985, replaced a statue of Tsar Alexander III that was removed in 1937. Across from the train station, the green Oktyabrskaya Hotel bears the words "Город-герой Ленинград" (Leningrad, the Hero-City), recalling the tremendous suffering during the German WWII siege. *(M1: Ploshchad Vosstaniya. Near Moskovskiy Vokzal.)*

ALEXANDER NEVSKIY MONASTERY

Pl. Aleksandra Nevskogo 1 (Александра Невского). M3 or 4: Pl. Aleksandra Nevskogo. The 18th-century Necropolis lies behind and to the left of the entrance archway; the Artists' Necropolis is behind and to the right. ☎274 1112. Grounds open daily 6am-11pm. Cathedral open daily in summer 6am-9pm; in winter 6am-8pm. Annunciation Church open Tu-W and F-Su 11am-5pm. Both necropolises open daily 10am-9pm. Kassa closes 5pm. Services daily 7, 10am, 5pm. Donations requested for upkeep of church and grounds. Both necropolises 100R, students 50R. Photo and video 120R. Museum of Sculpture 70R, students 35R. English map 10R.

A major pilgrimage destination, Alexander Nevskiy Monastery (Александро-невская Лавра; Aleksandro-Nevskaya Lavra) derives its name and importance from St. Alexander of Novgorod, a 13th-century Russian prince who defeated the Swedes and appeased the Mongol overlords without betraying his faith. His body was moved here by Peter the Great in 1724. In 1797, the monastery was promoted to *lavra*, a distinguished status bestowed on only four Russian Orthodox monasteries. A cobblestone path connects the cathedral and the two cemeteries.

TIKHVIN CEMETERY. Also known as the Artists' Necropolis (Некрапол Мастеров Искусств; Nekrapol Masterov Iskusstv), this cemetery (Тихвинское Кладбище; Tikhvinskoye Kladbishche) is the resting place of many famous Russians. Fyodor Dostoevsky could only afford to be buried here thanks to support from the Russian Orthodox Church. His grave, along the wall to the right, is always strewn with flowers. Mikhail Glinka, composer of the first Russian opera, and Mikhail Balakirev, who taught Nikolai Rimskiy-Korsakov, also rest here. Alexander Borodin's grave is graced with a gold mosaic of a composition sheet from his famous *String Quartet no. 1.* The magnificent tombs of Modest Mussorgsky, Anton Rubinstein, and Peter Tchaikovsky are next to Borodin's.

OTHER SIGHTS. Next to the Artists' Necropolis is the **18th-century necropolis,** St. Petersburg's oldest cemetery. Farther along the central path on the left is the **Church of the Annunciation** (Благовещенская Церков; Blagoveshchenskaya Tserkov), the original burial place of the Romanovs, who were moved to Peter and Paul Cathedral in 1998 (see p. 601). The church now houses the graves of military heroes, including **Suvorov** and other members of the royal family. The **Holy Trinity Cathedral** (Свято-Тройтский Собор; Svyato-Troitskiy Sobor), at the end of the path, is a functioning church, teeming with priests and devout *babushki*.

SUMMER GARDENS AND PALACE

The Summer Gardens and Palace (Летний Сад и Дворец; Letniy Sad i Dvorets) are relaxing and intimate spots in an otherwise imposing city. Both the northern and southern entrances lead to long, shady paths lined with replicas of classical Roman sculptures, crafted in the 1720s. In the northeastern corner of the Garden sits Peter's **Summer Palace,** which seems like more of a *dacha* (summer home) than a palace. The decor reflects Peter's diverse tastes: Spanish chairs, German clocks, and Japanese paintings fill the rooms. **Mars Field** (Марсого Поле; Marsogo Pole), named after military parades held here in the 19th century, is now a memorial to the victims of the Revolution and the Civil War (1917-19). A round monument in the center holds an eternal flame. *(M2: Nevskiy Prospekt. Turn right on nab. Kanala Griboyedova (Канала Грибоедова), cross the Moyka, and turn right on Pestelya (Пестеля). ☎314 0374. Garden open daily May-Oct. 10am-10pm; Nov.-Apr. 10am-8pm. Free. Palace open M 10am-4pm, Tu-Su 10am-6pm; closed last M of the month; kassa closes 5pm. Palace signs in English. 300R, students 150R. Photo and video 100R.)*

RUSSIA

SMOLNYY INSTITUTE AND CATHEDRAL

Once a school for aristocratic girls, the **Smolnyy Institute** (Смолный Институт) earned its place in history in 1917 when Trotsky and Lenin set up the headquarters of the **Bolshevik Central Committee** here. In front of the institute stand busts of Engels, Marx, and Lenin, the last of whom lived here 1917-18. Next door, the blue-and-white **Smolnyy Cathedral** (Смолный Собор; Smolnyy Sobor), designed by Rastrelli, combines Baroque and Orthodox Russian styles. Climb to the top of the 68m bell tower to survey the splendor of the city. *(Pl. Rastrelli 3/1 (Растрелли). From M2: Nevskiy Prospekt, take trolley 5 or 7 or bus K147. Or, from the stop across Kirochnaya (Кирочная) from M1: Chernyshevskaya, take bus #46 or 136. Get off after 10-15min. at the blue towers with gray domes. ☎577 1421. Cathedral open M-Tu and Th-Su 10am-6pm. 100R, students 70R. Photo 25R, video 50R. To see the Institute, call to make an appointment.)*

OCTOBER REGION

In the October Region (Октябрьский Район; Oktyabrskiy Raion) the Griboyedov Canal meanders through quiet neighborhoods.

ST. NICHOLAS CATHEDRAL. A striking blue-and-gold structure, St. Nicholas Cathedral (Никольский Собор; Nikolskiy Sobor) was constructed in 18th-century Baroque style. On the inside, the lower church has numerous columns connected by smooth archways, giving the small structure the illusion of spaciousness. *(M4: Sadovaya. Cross the square, head down Sadovaya (Садовая), and turn right onto Rimskogo-Korsakogo (Римского-Корсакого) at the fork. The cathedral is across the canal. Enter through the gate on the right side. Lower church open daily 6:30am-7:30pm; upper church M-F 9:30am-noon, Sa 9:30am-noon and 6pm-vespers' end. Services daily 7, 10am, 6pm.)*

YUSUPOVSKIY GARDENS. On the borders of the October Region, the Yusupovskiy Gardens (Юсуповский Сад; Yusupovskiy Sad)—named after the prince who succeeded in killing Rasputin only after poisoning, shooting, and ultimately drowning him—provide a patch of green in the middle of the urban expanse. Locals come here to relax beside the pond. *(At the intersection of Sadovaya and Rimskogo-Korsakogo. M4: Sadovaya.)*

GREAT CHORAL SYNAGOGUE. Europe's second-largest, the synagogue (Больщая Хоралная Синагога; Bolshchaya Khoralnaya Sinagoga) was built in 1893 with the permission of Tsar Alexander II. Upon its completion, the city outlawed all other Jewish meeting houses, forcing St. Petersburg's 15,000 Jews to meet in a space intended for 2000. Though the Moorish exterior pays tribute to the architectural trends of the time, the interior is more traditional, its main dome covering a two-tiered worship space. The large synagogue holds services only on Shabbat (Saturday) and holidays. The small, adjacent synagogue holds regular services. A small cafe downstairs serves kosher food. *(Lermontovskiy pr. 2 (Лермонтовский). M4: Sadovaya. Turn right off Sadovaya (Садовая), cross the canal onto Rimskogo-Korsakogo (Римского-Корсакого), continue to Lermontovskiy pr., and turn right. ☎713 8186. Open daily 10am-7pm.)*

MUSEUMS

St. Petersburg's museums are famous worldwide, and with good reason. You'll be awed by the opulent extravagance of the palatial residences and the Soviet buildings that house these spectacular collections.

ART AND LITERATURE

RUSSIAN MUSEUM. Containing the world's second-largest collection of Russian art after Moscow's Tretyakov Gallery, this museum (Русский Музей; Russkiy

Muzey) displays 12th- to 17th-century icons, 18th- to 19th-century paintings and sculpture, and Russian folk art, arranged chronologically. The museum's main building, the Mikhailovsky Palace, contains Russian art dating from the 14th to the early 20th century, while the stunning Marble Palace (Millionnaya ul. 5/1; Миллионнаya) is home to exhibitions of Modern and Pop Art, in addition to being an architectural novelty in its own right—32 types of marble decorate its facade. The Stroganov Palace (Nevksiy pr. 17) features a private collection of Russian icons. *(Inzhenernaya ul. 4 (Инженерная). M3: Gostinyy Dvor. In the yellow 1825 Mikhailov Palace (Михайловский Дворец; Mikhailovskiy Dvorets), behind the Pushkin monument. From the Metro, go down Mikhailovskaya ul. past the Grand Hotel Europe. Enter through the basement in the courtyard's right corner; go downstairs and turn left. ☎595 4248; www.rusmuseum.ru. Wheelchair-accessible. Open M 10am-5pm, W-Su 10am-6pm; kassa closes 1hr. earlier. English signs; English map free. 300R, students 150R; inclusive entrance for Mikhailovsky, Marble, and Stroganov palaces 600R, students 300R. English audio tour 300R. Photo and video 100R.)*

ANNA AKHMATOVA MUSEUM. Housed in the apartment where Anna Akhmatova lived from 1927 to 1952 with Nikolai Punin, this museum paints a detailed and beautiful picture of the life and work of Russia's most revered female poet, who lived during the Silver Age of Russian culture. Displays recreate Akhmatova's room and Punin's study and include penetrating exhibits on her works. *(Fontanka emb. 34, enter from courtyard at Liteynyy pr. 53 (Литейный). M1: Chernyshevskaya. ☎272 2211. Open Tu-Su 10:30am-6:30pm; closed last W of the month; kassa closes 1hr. earlier. 100R. English audio tour 100R. Photo 75R, video 100R.)*

ALEXANDER PUSHKIN APARTMENT MUSEUM. Visiting the former residence of Russia's most revered literary figure is a sort of pilgrimage for poetry lovers. The museum (Музей Квартира Пушкина; Muzey Kvartira Pushkina) displays his personal effects and dramatically narrates the tragic story of his last days. In the library where he died, all the furniture is original and the clock is stopped at the time of his death. *(nab. Reki Moyki 12 (наб. Реки Мойки). M2: Nevskiy Prospekt. Walk toward the Admiralty; turn right on nab. Reki Moyki and follow the canal to the yellow building on the right. Enter through the courtyard; the kassa is on the left. If only the small wooden door is open, be careful not to bump your head. Apartment ☎571 3531, literary exhibition 314 0007; www.museumpushkin.ru. Open M and W-Su 10:30am-6pm; closed last F of the month; kassa closes 5pm. Apartment 100R, students 60R; literary exhibition 100/20R. Photo 100R, video 200R. English information free, audio tour 100R. Cash only.)*

RUSSIA

DOSTOEVSKY HOUSE. While Fyodor Dostoevsky wrote some of *The Brothers Karamazov* and his diary in this house (Дом Достоевского; Dom Dostoyevskogo), he was surrounded—unlike most of his troubled characters—by a supportive wife and beloved children, two things he declared constituted 75% of a man's happiness in life. This museum exhibits the author's work while providing moving insight into the writer's domestic and literary existence. *(Kuznechnyy per. 5/2 (Кузнечный), on the corner of Dostoyevskogo (Достоевского), just past the market. M1: Vladimirskaya. ☎311 4031. Open daily 11am-6pm; kassa closes 5pm. 120R, students 60R. English captions and information sheets in each room; audio tour 80R. Photo 40R, video 80R.)*

SCIENCE

KUNSTKAMERA ANTHROPOLOGICAL AND ETHNOGRAPHIC MUSEUM. This museum (Музей Антропологии и Этнографии—Кунсткамера; Muzey Antropologii i Etnografii—Kunstkamera) exhibits the history, lives, homes, dress, and tools of many of the world's ethnic groups. Most excitingly, it also displays Peter the Great's 17th- and 18th-century collection of anatomist Frederik Ruysch's work, including jar after jar of fetuses in various stages, as well as a large variety of malformed ones. Don't miss the embalmed two-headed fetus. *(Universitetskaya nab. 3 (Университетская), across the river from the Admiralty via bus #7 or trolley #10; enter on the left on Tamozheniy per. (Таможенный пер.). ☎328 1412. Captions in English. Open Tu-Su 11am-6pm; closed last Tu of the month; kassa, along the left side of building, closes 5pm. 200R, students 100R. Photo and video 50R.)*

ETHNOGRAPHIC MUSEUM. This museum (Музей Этнографии; Muzey Etnografii) exhibits the art, traditions, and cultures of Russia's 159 ethnic groups, spanning Ukraine and Belarus in the west and stretching across the Caucasus, Central Asia, and Siberia to the Pacific Ocean. Highlights include the "Treasure Room," a collection of pearls and precious metal and stone gifts given to the Imperial family from throughout the Russian Empire. *(Inzhenernaya 4, bldg. 1 (Инженерная). M3: Gostinyy Dvor. ☎570 5421. Open Tu-Su 11am-6pm; closed last F of the month; kassa closes 5pm, 4pm on holidays. 300R, students 150R. Photo 150R, video 300R.)*

HISTORY

CENTRAL NAVAL MUSEUM. The old Stock Exchange building houses the boat that inspired Peter I to create the Russian navy. The museum inside (Центральный Военно-Морской Музей; Tsentralnyy Voyenno-Morskoy Muzey) displays submarines, artwork, and model ships chronicling the development of Russia's modern fleet. Be sure to walk up the stairs winding around Russia's first ballistic missile, which stands two stories high. *(Birzhevaya pl. 4 (Биржевая). Take bus #7 or trolley #10 across the bridge to Vasilevskiy Island and get off at the 1st stop. Walk toward the Peter and Paul fortress; the museum is on the left. ☎328 2501. Open W-Su 11am-6pm; last entry 5:15pm; closed last Th of the month. English info 50R. 320R, students 110R; last W of the month free. Book English tours 5 days ahead; 300R. Photo 60R, video 100R.)*

RUSSIA

MUSEUM OF RUSSIAN POLITICAL HISTORY. Before the Bolsheviks set up shop here, this building was the residence of Matilda Kshesinskaya, prima ballerina of the Mariinskiy Theater and lover of Nicholas II. Today, the museum (Музей Политической Истории России; Muzey Politicheskoy Istorii Rossii) includes a shrine-like memorial to Lenin, in addition to exhibits on Russian political history. *(Kuybysheva 2 (Куйбышева). M2: Gorkovskaya. Go down Kamennoostrovskiy (Каменоостровский) past the mosque; turn left on Kuybysheva. ☎233 7052. Open M-W and F-Su 10am-6pm; kassa closes 1hr. earlier. 150R, students 70R. Tours in English 700R; call two weeks in advance. Photo 100R, video prohibited.)*

MILITARY HISTORY MUSEUM. Military hardware from 15th-century armor to 20th-century tanks is displayed at this enormous museum (Централный Военно-Исторический Музей; Tsentralniy Voenno-Istoricheskiy Muzey). Here's your chance to see genuine AK-47s and medium-range missiles up close. *(Aleksandrovskiy Park 7 (Александровский Парк). M2: Gorkovskaya. Exit the Metro and walk toward the river, then bear right on Kronverskaya nab. (Кронверская наб.); the museum is on the right. ☎232 0296. Open W-Su 11am-6pm; closed last Th of month; kassa closes 1hr. earlier. Museum and esplanade 300R, students 150R; esplanade only 50/20R. Tours in English 300R per person. Photo free, video 100R.)*

ARCTIC AND ANTARCTIC MUSEUM. Science and history blend admirably in this museum (Музей Арктики и Антарктики; Muzey Arktiki i Antarktiki) devoted to expeditions into the extreme conditions of the North and South poles. The museum displays ship models and nautical accoutrements such as a life-size seaplane, an explorer's hut, and archaeological remains from failed expeditions. To fully appreciate the fantastic and fascinating museum, take the tour. *(Marata 24 (Марата). M1: Vladimirskaya. From the Metro, walk down Kuznechnyy per. (Кузнечный) 2 blocks. On the corner of Kuznechnyy per. and Marata. ☎571 2549. Open W-Su 10am-6pm; kassa closes 5pm. Signs in Russian. 100R, students 50R. Tours in English 300R per person; call ahead. Video 150R.)*

SHOPPING

The **souvenir market** behind the Church of Our Savior on Spilled Blood offers variety, but also astronomical prices, which should always be negotiated. The enormous **Gostinyy Dvor** (see **Sights,** p. 598) also sells numerous souvenirs, but many of these are in glass cases and cannot be negotiated. Other, slightly less expensive clothing stores can be found along Nevskiy pr. **Apraksin Dvor** (Апраксин Двор), slightly south of Gostinyy Dvor, sells cheap to decent quality wares for half the price of nicer stores, both in shops and in an outdoor market. Make sure to watch your pockets and bags around Gostinyy and Apraksin yards.

FESTIVALS AND ENTERTAINMENT

Throughout June, when the evening sun barely touches the horizon, the city holds the famed **White Nights Festival.** In late June and early July, ballets and operas play at the theaters in celebration of White Nights. All year long, the former home of Tchaikovsky, Prokofiev, and Stravinsky lives up to its reputation as a mecca for the performing arts. It is fairly easy to get tickets to world-class performances for very reasonable prices. *Yarus* (ярус) are the cheapest seats. The **theater season** ends in May and begins in September, but many theaters have a so-called "tourist season" in summer. The **ticket office** is at Nevskiy pr. 42, near Gostinyy Dvor. (☎571 3183. Schedule 50R.) The Friday issue of the *St. Petersburg Times* has comprehensive listings of entertainment and nightlife and indicates which performances are in English. If this is all too highbrow, head to the movies. Most films are dubbed in Russian, but it is increasingly common for movies to be shown in their original language. **Dom Kino,** Karavannaya 12 (Караванная), plays some movies in English. (M3: Gostinyy Dvor. ☎314 8036; www.domkino.spb.ru. 50-100R.)

BALLET AND OPERA

Mariinskiy Teatr (Мариинский), also called **Kirov Teatr,** Teatralnaya pl. 1 (Театральная; ☎326 4141). M4: Sadovaya. Walk along Griboyedov Canal, then go right into the square. Bus #3, 22, or 27. This building premiered Tchaikovsky's *Nutcracker* and launched the careers of Pavlova and Baryshnikov. Open Sept.-June. Performances 7pm, matinees 11:30am. *Kassa* open Tu-Su 11am-7pm. Tickets (160-4300R) on sale 20-30 days in advance. It is illegal but common to purchase tickets at the entrance 15-30min. before shows. MC/V.

Mussorgskiy Opera and Ballet Theater (Театр имени Муссоргского; Teatr imeni Mussorgskogo), also called the **Maly Theater,** pl. Iskusstv 1 (Искусств; ☎595 4284, 214 3758; www.mikhailovsky.ru). Hosts excellent performances of Russian ballet and opera. Bring your passport; documents are checked at the door. Open July-Aug. when the Mariinskiy is closed. Performances 7pm. *Kassa* open daily 11am-3pm and 4-7pm. Tickets 300-1500R.

CLASSICAL MUSIC AND THEATER

Shostakovich Philharmonic Hall, Mikhailovskaya 2 (Михайловская; ☎710 4290), across the square from the Russian Museum. M3: Gostinyy Dvor. Classical and modern performances by resident and visiting orchestras. Open Sept. 22-July 10. Performances 7pm. *Kassa* open daily noon-3pm and 4-7pm. Tickets 750-2000R.

Akademicheskaya Kapella (Академическая Капелла), nab. Reki Moyki 20 (наб. Реки Мойки; ☎314 1058), off Palace Square. M2: Nevskiy Prospekt. A venue for the Emperor Court Choir Capella, a professional choir that dates back to 1437 and was

BLAST IN THE BANYA

The banya is the real Russian bathing experience—it has been a part of Slavic culture since long before there was a Russia to claim it as Russian. A modern banya is usually single-sex and involves several stages. During the first stage, you enter the *parilka* (парилка), a steam room that reaches temperatures upwards of 70°C. The idea is to stay in the *parilka* as long as you can stand it, then cool down under a shower before going out into the open air. This is repeated several times before a plunge into the icy cold pool (холодный бассейн) is added to the cycle. At this point, it is also customary to offer and receive a beating with a wet birch-tree switch—this actually feels like a pleasant massage.

Bring sandals and a sheet if you have them, or rent them upon arrival. Also bring shampoo and soap for a Western-style shower to wrap things up. Birch switches can be bought on site (100R).

There is a public banya at 11 Bolshoy Kazachiy per. (☎315 0734). M1: Pushkinskaya. Enter the banya through the courtyard of Dom 11. Open Tu-Su 9am-10pm; Tu, Th, Sa women's days 10am-10pm. 50R. A private banya is at Gagarinskaya ul. (☎272 9682), in Dom 32. M1: Chernashevskaya. Call ahead to book. 630R per hr. Open 8am-10pm.

transferred from Moscow to St. Petersburg in 1703. Performances 7pm. *Kassa* open daily noon-3pm and 4-7pm. Tickets 300-2000R.

Aleksandrinskiy Teatr (Александринский Театр), pl. Ostrovskogo 6 (Островского; ☎312 1546). M3: Gostinyy Dvor. Turn right on Nevskiy pr., then right at the park with Catherine's statue. Ballet and theater shows of mostly Western classics like Hamlet and Cyrano de Bergerac. In summer, the theater features evening performances by the St. Petersburg Ballet Company. *Kassa* open daily 11am-7pm. Tickets 100-2500R.

NIGHTLIFE

Pre-*glasnost*, there was only one club—and the Party ran the party. These days, Petersburg is more than making up for lost time. Whether seeking a quiet drink, a rave, or a chance to show off designer duds, travelers as well as locals will be tempted by the siren song of the city's nightlife. Check the Friday issues of the *St. Petersburg Times* and *Pulse* for current events. Note that the trendier clubs often exercise a door policy known as "face and dress control," so be sure to look sharp.

JFC Jazz Club, Shpalernaya 33 (Шпалерная; ☎272 9850; www.jfc.sp.ru). M1: Chernyshevskaya. Go right on pr. Chernyshevskogo (Чернышевского), and continue 4 blocks. Take a left on Shpalernaya and go into courtyard 33. The friendly club offers a wide variety of quality jazz in a relaxed and appreciative atmosphere and holds occasional classical, folk, and funk concerts. Beer from 100R. Hard liquor from 50R. Live music 8-10pm. Cover 150-300R. Arrive early or call ahead for a table. Open daily 7-11pm.

Fish Fabrique, Ligovskiy 53 (Лиговский; ☎264 4857; www.fishfabrique.spb.ru). M1: pl. Vosstaniya. Walk through the courtyard, into the black door directly in front of you, and follow the corridor and stairs to the bar. An almost hidden location and a tight-knit clientele of alternative youngsters make this the perfect hangout. Rock concerts Th-Sa at 11pm. Cover 100-150R. Beer 50-90R. Open 6pm-6am. Cash only.

Che, Poltavskaya 3 (Полтавская; ☎277 7600). M1: Vosstaniya. Walk down Nevskiy pr. toward pl. Aleksandra Nevskogo 2-3 blocks, then make a right on Poltavskaya. Named for the fiery revolutionary, Che is a comfortable place to chill among the young, trendy, and well-to-do while listening to Latin or jazz. Drinks 130-550R. Hookah 500R. English menu. Live music 10pm-2am. Open 24hr. MC/V.

Ob'ekt, nab. Reki Moyki 82 (наб. Реки Мойки; ☎312 1134). This basement bar and club is perfect for drinks after dinner, smoking hookah (250R) with friends, or doing some alternative dancing on weekends. Crowd is young and vivacious any day of the week, but especially during Drum&Bass (from 6pm Th) and Retro (from 11pm F-Sa; don't forget your roller blades) nights. Beer from 70R. Open 24hr.

Manhattan, nab. Reki Fontanki 90 (Реки Фонтанки; ☎713 1945; www.manhattan-club.ru). M4: Sadovaya. Walk into the courtyard; the club is the first door on the right. Formerly catering to artists and literati, this art club is now a down-to-earth place to relax. Music lovers of all ages enjoy daily concerts of rock, folk, acoustic, and jazz, as well as monthly poetry readings (100-250R) and the bi-monthly rotation of photo exhibitions. Beer from 100R. Hard liquor from 40R. Open daily 1pm-midnight. Cash only.

Griboyedov (Грибоедов), Voronezhskaya 2A (Воронежская; ☎764 4355; www.griboedovclub.ru). M4: Ligovskiy Prospekt. Go left exiting the underpass from the Metro. Go left at the intersection onto Konstantina Zaslonova (Константина Заслонова) and walk 2 blocks; take a left on Voronezhskaya. Look for a big mound. This loud house and techno club also invites alternative acts to play in front of a crowd of 20-somethings. The club only really gets going at midnight. Beer 60-100R. Vodka 40-70R. Live DJ daily midnight-6am. 18+. Cover 300-350R. 50% discount with ISIC. Open daily 6pm-6am.

Red Club/Cadillac Club, Poltavskaya 7 (Полтавская; ☎717 0000; www.clubred.ru). M1: Pl. Vosstaniya. Located in a former feed storage house behind Moscow Station. 2 stages attract top club bands, both local and international. The music, as always, determines the audience, but the crowd is always energetic. Th-Su rock concerts at 7pm with DJs following at midnight. Cover 150-500R. Open Th-Su 7pm-6am.

Tunnel, Blokhina 16 (Блохина; ☎572 1551; www.tunnelclub.ru). M4: Sportivnaya. Exit the Metro and turn right to reach Blokhina. At Blokhina 16, turn left at the unmarked street and head for the farthest bunker. Russia's pioneering techno club, located inside a bomb shelter, offers cutting-edge jungle and house over an excellent sound system. Drinks from 50R. Cover Su-Th 50R, F 250R, Sa 300R. Open daily midnight-6am.

Though it's common to spot Russians of all ages sipping from beer bottles at any hour of the day, be aware that it's illegal to consume anything with more than 12% alcohol in public places, including vodka. Doing so can result in a 200-500R (US$7-15) fine.

GLBT NIGHTLIFE

Those interested in finding out more about the gay life of St. Petersburg should pick up a copy of *GAYP*, which can be found in many GLBT establishments throughout the city and lists gay services from clubs to saunas. The website www.xsgay.com is another good resource.

Triel, 5-ya Sovetskaya ul, 45 (5-я Советская; ☎710 2016). M1: Pl. Vosstaniya. Turn left on Suvorovskiy pr. (Суворовский), then right on 5-ya Sovetskaya. St. Pete's only lesbian club plays a mix of Russian pop, industrial techno, and house. Drinks 50-280R. Cover men 200R; F-Sa women 200R. Open W, F, Sa-Su 8pm-5:30am; cafe Tu and Th 6pm-midnight.

Greshniki (Грешники; Sinners), nab. Kanala Griboyedova 28 (Грибоедова; ☎318 4291; www.greshniki.ru), 2 blocks off Nevskiy pr., past Kazanskiy Cathedral. M2: Nevskiy Prospekt. Rocker-dungeon themed 4-fl. gay club, primarily for men. Plays disco, techno, and Europop. Drinks 70-400R. Drag shows daily 2:30am. Male strip shows daily midnight-4am. 18+. Cover for men before 10pm free, afterward Su-Th 100R, F-Sa 150R; women 300R/500R. Open daily 10pm-6am.

DAYTRIPS FROM ST. PETERSBURG

Many residents of the city retreat to a family *dacha* (дача; summer cottage) outside the city to harvest private produce or relax for the weekend. The tsars, of course, took a different approach: many built country houses of their own just outside the city, though "house" hardly evokes the awesome grandeur of these palatial megaliths. The imperial residences at Peterhof, Pushkin, and Pavlovsk were all torched during the Nazi retreat, but Soviet authorities provided staggering sums of money to return these proud monuments to their original state.

PETERHOF (ПЕТЕРГОФ)

In summer, hydrofoils (Damarov ☎311 8694, Meteor 325 6120) leave from the quay on Dvortsovaya nab. (Дворцовая) in front of the Hermitage (30-35min.; every 20min. 9:30am-6pm; 200R, round-trip 360R, children 100R/180R). The less glamorous train runs year-round from Baltiyskiy Vokzal (Балтийский; M1: Baltiyskaya; 35min., every 10-50min., 48R). Buy tickets from the suburban ticket office (пригородная касса; prigorodnaya kassa). Any train to Oraniyenbaum (Ораниенбаум), Kalishche (Калище), or Krasnoflotsk (Краснофлотск) will get you there. Get off at Novyy Petergof (Новый Петергоф), the 11th stop, or Staryy Petergof (Старый Петергоф). From the station, take bus #352, 356, or 359 (10min., 7R) or a van (5min., 10R) bound for Petrodvorets (Петродворец; Peter's Palace); get off when you see the palace. Maps of the territory (20R) and various literature (English available, up to 400R) are available at kiosks all over the territory.

UPPER AND LOWER GARDENS. Through the gates of the grounds lie the **Upper Gardens** (Верхний Сад; Verkhniy Sad). Go right or left of the palace to find a *kassa* where you can pay for entrance to the stunning **Lower Gardens** (Нижний Парк; Nizhniy Park), which contain most of Peterhof's territory, including the parks, fountains, and museums, as well as a beach on the Gulf of Finland. Most of the fountains are reconstructions, as post-war Germany misplaced the stolen originals. *(Gardens open daily 9am-7pm. 300R, students 150R. Fountains operate May-Oct. M-F 11am-5pm, Sa-Su 11am-6pm.)*

GRAND PALACE (ВОЛЬШОЙ ДВОРЕЦ; BOLSHOY DVORETS). In an attempt to create his own Versailles, Peter started building a residence here in 1714. Empresses Elizabeth and Catherine the Great greatly expanded and remodeled it. The rooms reflect the diverse tastes of the various tsars and the changing architectural fashions of their respective ages. Ascend the exquisite main staircase to the second-floor rooms, including the great **Chesme Gallery,** in which artwork depicts the 1770 Russian victory over the Turks. A ship in Catherine's fleet was actually blown up so that her artist, Philip Gaekert, could paint the last scene accurately. Farther along are the **Chinese rooms,** which contain panels restored by Russian artists after WWII, but the vases and one lacquer panel in each room are originals from the tsars' trade with the East. *(☎420 0073. Open Tu-Su 10:30am-6pm; closed last Tu of each month; kassa closes 5pm. Buy tickets inside. Russian tours 500R; if you're lucky, you may find an English-speaking tour guide. Palace 500R, students 250R. Photo 100R, video 200R.)*

GRAND CASCADE (ВОЛЬШОЙ КАСКАД; BOLSHOY KASKAD). The 64 elegant fountains of the Grand Cascade direct their waters to the Grand Canal. The largest of 37 shining gold statues (originally from the early 18th century but mostly recast after WWII), *Samson Tearing Open the Jaws of a Lion*, is a vivid symbol of Peter's victory over Sweden. To enter the impressive stone grotto underneath the fountains, buy tickets just outside the palace. *(Grotto open daily 11am-6pm, kassa open 11am-5:30pm. 110R, students 60R.)*

HERMITAGE PAVILION (ЕРМИТАЖ; ERMITAZH). Russia's first hermitage served to amuse the palace residents. Fans of 17th- and 18th-century European art might enjoy the second-floor room filled floor-to-ceiling with the paintings of various

RUSSIA

lesser-known Belgian, Dutch, French, and German artists. *(Open Tu-Su 10:30am-6pm; kassa closes at 5:30pm. 110R, students 60R. Photo 60R, video 150R.)*

TSARSKOYE SELO (ЦАРСКОЕ СЕЛО)

From Pobedy pl. (пл. Победы; M2: Moskovskaya) take bus #287 or one of the numerous marshrutki, *such as #20, that go to Tsarskoye Selo or Pushkin. Alternatively, the* elektrichka *runs from Vitebskiy Vokzal (M1: Pushkinskaya, 30min., 12R). Buy tickets from the suburban ticket office (пригородная касса; prigorodnaya kassa); walk out of the Metro and around the station to the left. Don't worry that none of the signs say Pushkin; all trains leaving from platforms 1-3 stop there. Get off at Detskoye Selo (Детское Село), the 1st stop outside Petersburg that actually looks like a station, with a large number of people. From the station, take bus #370 or 378 (10min., 5R). Knowing where to get off is tricky; ask the conductor or get off after spotting a thick group of trees right in front of you.*

About 25km south of St. Petersburg, Tsarskoye Selo (Tsar's Village) surrounds Catherine the Great's summer residence, a gorgeous azure, white, and gold Baroque palace overlooking extensive, English-style parks. The area was renamed "Pushkin" during the Soviet era, although the train station, Detskoye Selo (Детское Село; Children's Village) kept its old name. Built in 1756 by the architect Rastrelli in a Baroque style, **Catherine's Palace** (Екатерининский Дворец; Yekaterininskiy Dvorets) was remodeled by Charles Cameron on Catherine's orders. She had the gilding removed from the facade, desiring a modest "cottage" where she could relax. This residence of unbridled opulence was devastated by the Nazis but has been restored. The "golden" suites—named for their lavish Baroque ornamentation—hold original furnishings that survived WWII. (☎456 2196. Open M and W-Su 10am-6pm; closed last M of each month; *kassa* closes 1hr. earlier. June-Aug. 10am-noon and 2-4pm the museum is only open to private tour groups who have reserved well in advance. English tours for groups under 6 people 3000R, over 6 people 540R per person. Palace 520R, students 250R. Cash only.) Rastrelli's **parks** combine the liberating feel of unfenced natural space with well-tended precision of design. Here Catherine would ramble with her dogs—showing affection some believed in excess of that accorded to her children. The dogs now rest in peace beneath the **Pyramid** facing the **Island Pavilion,** which can be reached by ferry during summer. The **Cold Bath Pavilion** stands in front of the palace to the left. Designed by Charles Cameron, it contains the famous Agate Rooms. Across the street from Catherine's Palace, outside the park, is the **lycée** that Pushkin attended from age 12 to 18. (Park open May-Sept. 6am-10pm, paid admission 9am-5pm. 160R, students 80R. All buildings open May-Sept. Bath Pavilion open W-Su 10am-5pm; closed last W of each month. 160R, students 80R. Lycée ☎476 6411. Open M-W and F-Su 10am-6pm; *kassa* closes 5pm. 200R, students 100R. Photo 50R, video 150R.)

PAVLOVSK (ПАВЛОВСК)

Get off the train at Pavlovsk, the stop after Pushkin. To get to the palace from the train station, take bus #370, 383, or 383A. If you have time, cross the street in front of the station and walk the 2km through the park. To go to Pushkin from Pavlovsk, take bus #370, 383, or 493 from the Great Palace. You can also take one of the various marshrutki, *especially #513, which goes between Pushkin and Pavolovsk and makes stops at the rail stations. Or, you can take* marshrutka *#286 or 299 straight from Petersburg, at Pobedy pl. (пл. Победы; M2: Moskovskaya). Gardens open M-Sa 7am-8pm, Su 7am-6pm. 100R. Palace ☎470 2156. Open daily 10am-6pm; Sept. 16-May 14 closed every F and 1st M of the month;* kassa *closes 5pm. 370R, students 185R. English tours 500R. English literature starts at 100R. Photo 150, video 250. Cash only.*

Catherine the Great gave the 600-hectare park and gardens at Pavlovsk to her son Paul in 1777. The **Three Graces Pavilion,** in the small garden behind the palace, is renowned for the beauty of its central sculpture, carved by Paolo Triscorni in 1802 from a single piece of white marble. A few hundred meters before the palace stands the **Monument to Maria Fyodorovna,** the widow of Paul I. Paul's **Great Palace** is not as lavish (or garish, depending on your architectural taste) as his mother's at

Tsarskoye Selo, but is worth a visit. The faux-marble columns and sculpted ceilings of the **Greek Hall** are particularly noteworthy. **Maria Fyodorovna's apartments** are rare examples of modest royal taste. (30R, students 15R.) During the winter, many bring skis or ice skates to enjoy the very, very extensive grounds.

NOVGOROD (НОВГОРОД) ☎(8)8162(2)

Founded in the ninth century by Prince Ryurik, Novgorod (pop. 220,000) blossomed during the Middle Ages. In its medieval heyday, it housed twice its current population, triumphed over the Mongols, and challenged Moscow and Kyiv for Slavic supremacy. Larger and better-restored than Pskov, stunning Novgorod is the ideal location to gain an understanding of early Russian culture.

TRANSPORTATION. Trains depart from the station, Oktyabrskaya ul. 5 (Октябрская; ☎73 90 38) for Moscow (8½hr., 1 per day, 600-1300R) and St. Petersburg (3-4hr., 3 per day, 258-330R). Ticket counters are open 24hr. The bus station (автостанция; avtostantsiya), Oktyabrskaya ul. 5 (Октябрская; ☎73 99 79), is to the right of the train station. *Kassa* open 5am-10pm. **Buses** go to Pskov (4½hr., 2 per day, 278R) and St. Petersburg (3hr., 9-14 per day, 250R).

Novgorod uses both 5- and 6-digit phone numbers. When dialing 6-digit numbers from out of town, drop the last digit (2) from the city code.

ORIENTATION AND PRACTICAL INFORMATION. Novgorod's heart is its **kremlin,** from which a web of streets spins outward on the **west side** of the river. **Prospekt Karla Marksa** (Карла Маркса) runs from the train station to what remains of the walls surrounding old Novgorod. Follow **Lyudogoshchaya ulitsa** (Людогощая) from the walls, through **ploshchad Sofiyskaya** (Софийская) to the kremlin. The east side of the river is home to many churches as well as Yaroslav's court, around which the streets form a rectangular grid.

The **tourist office, Krasnaya Izba** (Красная Изба; Red Wooden Hut), is at pl. Sennaya 5 (Сенная), 1 block down ul. Meretskogo (Мерецкого) from pl. Sofiyskaya. The helpful staff offers **free maps** and will help book accommodations, tours, and train and bus tickets. Call in advance to arrange a 1hr. English-language tour of the kremlin for 360R. (☎77 30 74 or 99 86 86; www.visitnovgord.ru. English-speaking staff. Wheelchair-accessible. Open daily 10am-5pm; available by telephone 24hr.) **Exchange currency** at any placed marked with an "обмен валюты" (obmen valyuty) sign and in all the major banks including Sberbank, on Bolshaya Moskovskaya ul. (Ђольшая Московская), across from Yaroslav's Court. **ATMs** are located in the train station, in the telephone office, and at major banks. A **pharmacy,** Panacea N, is located at bul. Sankt Peterburgskaya 7/2. (Санкт Петербургская; ☎73 82 66. Open daily 8am-10pm. MC/V.) Pre-pay for intercity or international calls at **Novgorod Telecom,** Lyodogoshchaya ul. 2 (Людогощая), at the corner of Lyudogoshchaya ul. and ul. Gazon (Газон), on Sofiyskaya pl. (Open 24hr.) **Internet access** and printing and fax services are available at the tourist office. (100R per hr.) The main **post office** is at Octyabrskaya ul. 13. (Октябрьская; ☎77 35 05. Open M-Th 8:30am-5:30pm, F 8:30am-6:30pm.) **Postal Code:** 173000.

ACCOMMODATIONS AND FOOD. Well-touristed Novgorod offers few budget accommodations. The English-speaking staff, great location, and plethora of services make **Gostinitsa Volkhov** (Волхов) ❹, Predtechenskaya ul. 24 (Предтеченская), a deal. Rooms in this remodeled hotel include TVs and telephones. A sauna, bar, and massage parlor are also available. (☎33 55 05 or 33 55 07; www.novtour.ru. Sauna 800R-1200R. Breakfast included. Check-out noon. Singles

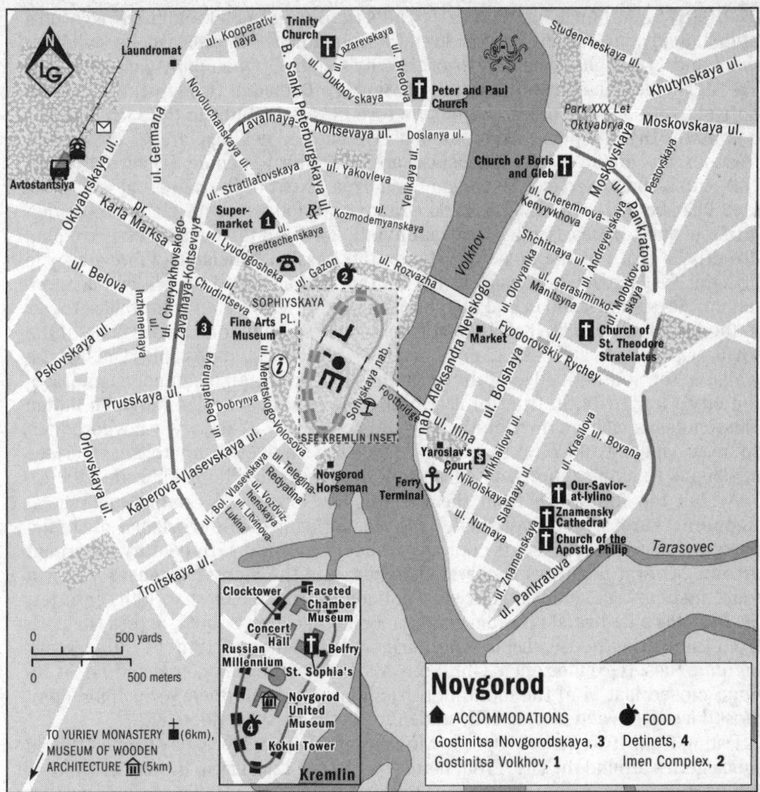

1500-1700R; doubles 2100-2500R. AmEx/MC/V.) **Gostinitsa Novgorodskaya** (Новгородская) ❷, Desyatinnaya ul. 6a (Десятинная), is one of Novgorod's less expensive options and boasts a great location near the kremlin. Simple rooms include TVs, phones, and private baths. To get to the hotel from the train station, take bus # 7, 9, or 27. (☎77 22 60. Singles 1050R; doubles 1100-1300R. MC/V.)

The well-stocked **grocery store Vavilon** (Вавилон), ul. Lyudogoshchaya 10 (Людогощая), is an alternative to fancy dining. (Open M 11am-11pm, Tu-Su 8am-11pm.) There's a produce **market** on ul. Fyodorovskiy Ruchey 2. (Фёдоровский Ручей. Open daily M-F 9am-7pm, Sa-Su 10am-6pm.) In the west wall of the kremlin, **Detinets** (Детинец) ❸, Novgorod's most popular restaurant, serves authentic Russian food in a medieval atmosphere. Climb up the spiral staircase and proceed all the way left to the veranda for a great view of Novgorod. (☎77 46 24. English menu available. Entrees 175-320R. Open M noon-11pm, Tu-Su 11am-11pm. Cash only.) Whatever kind of food you're looking for, **Ilmen Gastronomic Complex** (Ильмень), ul. Gazon 2 (Газон), has it. Inside the complex is a **deli** ❶ (entrees 50R; open daily 10am-9am; cash only) offering baked goods and other snacks, a **bistro** ❶ (☎77 24 96; entrees 50R; open daily 10am-11pm; cash only) for more substantial meals, and an upscale restaurant, **Holmgard** ❸, which offers Viking paraphernalia alongside Russian and Scandinavian food cooked over an open flame. (☎77 71 92. English menu. Entrees 190-570R. Open daily noon-midnight. AmEx/MC/V.)

SIGHTS. Although known as a *detinets* (детинец; small kremlin), Novgorod's pride and joy, its **kremlin** (кремль; kreml), is nonetheless impressive. Its walls, 3m thick and 11m high, protect most of the city's sights. (Open daily 6am-midnight. Free.) The golden-spired Byzantine **St. Sophia's Cathedral** (Софийский Собор; Sofiyskiy Sobor), the oldest stone structure in Russia, built in the 11th century, dominates the complex. Inside, the massive vaulted ceilings, arches covered in frescoes, and an impressive iconostasis are incredible to behold. (Open daily 8am-1pm and 2-10pm. Services 10am and 6pm. Free.) Next to the cathedral is the **Faceted Chamber** (Грановитая Палата; Granovitaya Palata), with elaborate golden artifacts and textiles. (Under renovation until 2009.) In the center of the kremlin, directly in front of the museum, stands the **Russian Millennium** (Тысячелетие России; Tysyacheletiye Rossii). It was built in 1852 as one of three identical monuments; its sisters stand in St. Petersburg and Kyiv. Nearby stands the tallest tower in the kremlin walls, the **Kokui tower,** from whose summit you can see most of the town. (Open Tu-W and F-Su 11am-2pm and 3-7pm. 60R, students 35R.) Outside the walls, at the southern edge of the park, the Novgorod Horseman commemorates the city's longevity. In front of it stretches a clean beach. The **Novgorod United Museum** leads visitors through the city's history. (☎77 37 63; www.novgorodmuseum.ru. Open M and W-Su 10am-6pm; closed last Th of each month; *kassa* closes at 5:30pm. Exhibit captions in English. 90R, students 50R. Photo 30R, video 100R.)

Across the footbridge from the kremlin lies Yaroslav's Court (Ярославово Дворище; Yaroslavogo Dvorishche), the old market center and original site of the Novgorod princes' palace. It contains what's left of the 17th-century **waterfront arcade,** several beautiful **medieval churches,** and the **Market Gatehouse,** now a museum housing exhibits on Christian antiquities from the ninth to 19th centuries. **St. Nicholas's Cathedral** (Никольский Собор; Nikolskiy Sobor), across the path from the market house, displays an intriguing collection of 12th- to 18th-century ceramic tiles. (Grounds open 24hr. Free. Market Gatehouse open M and Th-Su 10-6pm; closed last M of the month. St. Nicholas' museum open W-Su 10am-6pm; closed last F of each month. 60R, students 35R. Photo 30R, video 50R.)

Dating from 1030, **Yuriev** (Юрьев Монастырь; Yuryev Monastyr) is one of three monasteries around the city. From here, you can see **Lake Ilmen,** the site of Ryurik's 9th-century court, where the state of Russia first took shape. The twin-domed **St. George's Cathedral** (Георгиевский Собор; Georgiyevskiy Sobor), founded in 1119, houses icons and a large collection of frescoes from the 12th century, as well as a *kafedra* (кафедра), a unique round pulpit. In the summer, the grounds are especially enjoyable. To get to the monastery, take bus #7 or 7a (20min., every 20-30min., 10R) from the stop on Meritskogo (Меритского) between Chudintseva (Чудинцева) and Prusskaya (Прусская). Go well past the airport and get off when you see the monastery on your right. (Open daily 10am-8pm. Free. Cathedral 60R, students 35R. Services at 6:30, 9am, and 6pm. Photo 10R, video 30R.)

PSKOV (ПСКОВ) ☎(8)8112(2)

Pskov (pop. 200,000) was established in AD 903, 800 years earlier than neighboring St. Petersburg. Pskov was so successful that by the Middle Ages, Father Piotrowski, the chronicler of the Polish king Stephen Bathori, likened the city to Paris. Though it would be difficult to make such a comparison today, Pskov maintains its own quiet appeal. Full of lush parks and housing age-old religious sights, Pskov provides a welcome break from cold and imposing St. Petersburg.

TRANSPORTATION. It was at Pskov's train station, ul. Vokzalnaya 23 (Вокзальная; ☎66 00 00), that Tsar Nicholas II officially abdicated on March 2, 1917. *Kassa* open 24hr. **Trains** run to: Moscow (12hr., 1-2 per day, 600-2500R); St. Petersburg (6hr., 2-3 per day, 350-800R); Minsk, BLR (16hr., 2 per week on W and

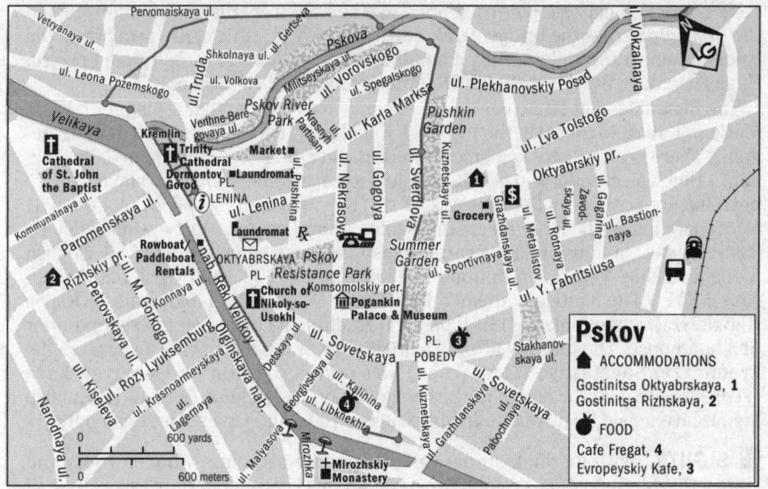

Su, 700-1500R); Rīga, LAT (8hr., 1 per day, 500-2000R); Vilnius, LIT (9hr., every 2 days, 630-1250R). The bus station, ul. Vokzalnaya 21 (Вокзальная; ☎73 55 02), is open daily 5:45am-8pm and located next to the train station. **Buses** go to Novgorod (4hr., 2 per day, 278R) and St. Petersburg (6hr., 4 per day, 380R).

ORIENTATION AND PRACTICAL INFORMATION. **Ulitsa Vokzalnaya** (Вокзальная) intersects **Oktyabrskiy prospekt** (Октябрьский), Pskov's main axis, two blocks to the right as you exit either the bus or the train station. Oktayabrskiy pr. intersects **Sovetskaya ulitsa** (Советская), which runs north to the kremlin, at **Oktyabrskaya ploshchad**. The Velikaya (Великая) and Pskova (Пскова) rivers meet at the kremlin's northernmost. To get to the town center from the train station, catch bus #17, which stops at Gostinitsa Oktyabrskaya (see **Accommodations,** p. 615), near Gostinitsa Rizhskaya, and at the kremlin. Buy tickets (9R) on board.

The **tourist bureau,** pl. Lenina 1 (Ленина), offers free booklets and maps, and helps arrange English tours of the city and kremlin. (☎/fax 72 45 68. Open M-F 10am-5pm.) The **exchange office,** Oktyabrskiy pr. 23/25 (Октябрьский пр.), next to Sberbank (Сбербанк), cashes **American Express Travelers Cheques** for 3% commission. (☎69 87 83. Open M-F 8am-8pm, Sa-Su 9am-3pm.) You can find better exchange rates at most kiosks with "обмен валюты" (obmen valyuty) signs. **ATMs** are located at the train station, in the telephone office, in Gostinitsa Oktyabrskaya, and in Gostinitsa Rizhskaya. The **telephone office,** ul. Nekrasova 17 (Некрасова), is in a large gray building with an additional entrance on Oktyabrskiy pr. (☎66 24 25. Calls 18R per min. to the US; fax 46R per page to the US.) **Internet** access is available inside the **post office,** Sovetskaya ul. 20 (Советская), obscured by trees on north side of Oktyabrskaya pl. Send international mail from the office in the courtyard on the right side of the building. (☎66 05 56. Internet access 30R per hr. Open M-F 8am- 9pm, Sa 8am-8pm, Su 9am-6pm.) **Postal Code:** 180000.

ACCOMMODATIONS AND FOOD. Pskov has an abundance of Soviet-style budget hotels. **Gostinitsa Oktyabrskaya** (Октябрьская) ❶, Oktyabrskiy pr. 36, accessible by the #1, 11, 14, or 17 bus from the train station, has comfortable rooms, many with TVs, phones, and sinks. (☎16 42 46; fax 16 42 54. 2- to 7-bed dorms 300-390R; singles 500-550R, with bath 850R; doubles with bath 1200-1500R. Cash only.) Though simply decorated, the rooms in **Gostinitsa Rizhskaya** (Рижская) ❷, Rizhskiy pr. 25, have private baths, TVs, phones, and fridges; the hotel also has a beauty center and a grocery shop downstairs. Take bus #17 from the train station (9R) to the first stop across the bridge. Walk down Rizhskiy pr. (Рижский) away from the bridge, then to the right across a small square. (☎46 22 23; hotelr@com.psc.ru. English spoken. Singles 820R-2100R; doubles 1400-3400R. Cash only.)

The **Central Market** (Центральный Рынок; Tsentralnyy Rynok) is on ul. Karla Marksa (Карла Маркса) at the top of ul. Pushkina (Пушкина). (Open daily 10am-4pm.) There is a well-stocked **grocery store** at Oktyabrskiy pr. 19. (Open daily 8am-9pm.) Blue velvet seats and gentle classical music set the scene for relaxed, European-inspired cuisine at **Yevropeyskiy Kafe** (Европейский Кафе) ❸, pl. Pobedy 1 (Победы), inside the large green-and-white cultural center. Most evenings (Tu-Sa 8:30-11:30pm), a house band covers English-language music. (☎16 55 80. English menu available. Vegetarian options 74-180R. Entrees 180-300R. Open daily noon-1am. MC/V.) The nautically themed **Cafe Fregat** ❸, ul. Karla Libknekhta 9 (Карла Либкнехта), serves salads (110-190R) and traditional cuisine on the second floor of a boathouse. The balcony affords a great view of the river. Walk away from the kremlin on Sovetskaya (Советская) and take a right on ul. Geogiyevskaya (Георгиевская). At the end of the street, go left on Libknekhta. (☎62 13 17. English menu. Live music F-Sa 8pm-midnight. Entrees 160-390R. Open 24hr. Cash only.)

SIGHTS. With its thick stone walls topped by authentic wooden roofs and spires, this ninth-century kremlin (кремль; kreml) keeps modernity (as well as all of its associated noise) well outside its arched portals. Follow the cobblestone pathway up to the main grounds. In the courtyard stand the ruins of **Dovmont's City** (Довмонтов Город; Dovmontov Gorod), named for Prince Dovmont, who ruled here from 1266 to 1299. The gold- and black-domed **Trinity Cathedral** (Троицкий Собор; Troitskiy Sobor), built in the 17th century, boasts an elaborate iconostasis and frescoes, which exemplify the Pskovian school of icon painting. An archway at the far right end of the grounds leads through the **kremlin wall** and opens up to an especially beautiful view of the natural terrain below, including the Pskov River. From the train station, take bus #17 or any bus to pl. Lenina (Ленина); get off when you see the kremlin walls. (Kremlin open daily 6am-10pm. Museum open Tu-Su 11am-6pm. Museum 80R, students 60R. Photo 150R, video 250R. Church open daily 8am-8pm. Services daily 9-11am and 6-8pm. Donations appreciated.)

RUSSIA

The neat grounds of **Mirozhskiy Monastery** (Мирожский Монастырь; Mirozhshkiy Monastyr) overlook the Velikaya River. The walls enclose the **Cathedral of the Transfiguration** (Спасо-Преображенский Собор; Spaso-Preobrazhenskiy Sobor), which dates from 1156 and still contains an amazing 80% of its original frescoes. Take bus #2 or 8 from the corner of ul. M. Gorkogo (Горького) and Rizhskiy pr. (Рижский) for 5min. (3 stops); get off at Krasnoarmeyskaya ul. (Красноармейская) and walk forward until you reach a fork; make a hard left and follow the curving, badly paved road until you see the blue sign indicating the monastery 200m to the left. (☎46 73 02. Open Tu-Su 11am-6pm; closed last Tu of the month and during rain and fog. 200R, students 150R. Photo 100R, video 75R. English tours 900R, students 700R. Call ahead.) Nearby, paddleboats and rowboats are available for rent (70R per 30min.) at the stand by the river on the opposite side of the Rizhskiy pr. bridge (Рижский) from the kremlin.

The wealth and heritage of Pskov rest in **Pogankin Palace and Museum** (Поганкины Палаты и Музей; Pogankiny Palaty i Muzey), Nekrasova 7 (Некрасова), originally the home of a 17th-century merchant. The second floor of the old building is often populated by students meticulously copying the numerous 16th-century icons on display. Traditional costumes and jewelry await visitors on the first floor. Enter through the new wing door on Komsomolskiy per. (Комсомольский). The newer wing houses a picture gallery and an exhibit on Pskov's role in WWII. (☎66 33 11. Open Tu-Su 11am-6pm; closed last Tu of the month; *kassa* closes 5:40pm. Palace and museum 150R, students 120R. Photo 50R, video 100R. For tours in English call ahead; 1400-1800R for groups.)

SLOVAKIA (SLOVENSKO)

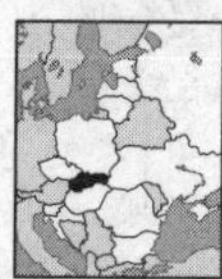

Slovakia is a nation of split personalities. Known for its beautiful mountain ranges, vibrant folk culture, and generous hospitality, Slovakia appeals especially to hikers and lovers of rural life. But the country also enjoys rapid industrialization and one of the fastest-growing economies in the former Eastern Bloc. Only hours away from the sophisticated, up-and-coming capital await a multitude of scenic, serene villages.

DISCOVER SLOVAKIA: SUGGESTED ITINERARIES

THREE DAYS. Devote your stay to a leisurely exploration of **Bratislava** (p. 623). Make sure to check out **Primate's Palace** (no monkeys, unfortunately; p. 629). Also stop by the **UFO,** atop New Bridge, to see if there's a party going on (p. 629).

ONE WEEK. From **Bratislava** (3 days), head to **Starý Smokovec** (4 days, p. 640) via **Poprad.** There you can mountain bike, hike, or ski the grand **High Tatras.** Leave time for a daytrip to **Štrbské Pleso** (p. 642), with its waterfalls and rigorous hikes.

FACTS AND FIGURES

Official Name: Slovak Republic.

Capital: Bratislava

Major Cities: Košice

Population: 5,448,000.

Time Zone: GMT + 1, in summer GMT + 2

Languages: Slovak (84%), Hungarian (11%).

Religions: Roman Catholic (69%), Protestant (11%), Greek Catholic (4%).

Known Mammal Species: 85.

ESSENTIALS

WHEN TO GO

Slovakia is blissfully free of massive crowds during any season. The Tatras draw the most tourists during peak season from July to August, and for good reason: the summer is a much more pleasant (and safe) time for hiking the beautiful mountain range than the cold winter weather. To avoid any crowds, explore the Tatras in the two months before or after high season.

DOCUMENTS AND FORMALITIES

ENTRANCE REQUIREMENTS.

Passport: Required of all travelers.

Visa: Not required for stays of under 90 days of citizens of Australia, Canada, New Zealand, and the US.

Letter of Invitation: Not required of citizens of Australia, Canada, Ireland, New Zealand, the UK, and the US.

Inoculations: Recommended up-to-date on DTap (Diphtheria, tetanus, and pertussis) Hepatitis A, Hepatitis B, MMR (measles, mumps and rubella), polio booster, rabies, and typhoid.

Work Permit: Required of foreigners planning to work in Slovakia.

International Driving Permit: Required of all those planning to drive in Slovakia except for UK citizens, who only need an International Driving Permit to rent cars.

SLOVAKIA

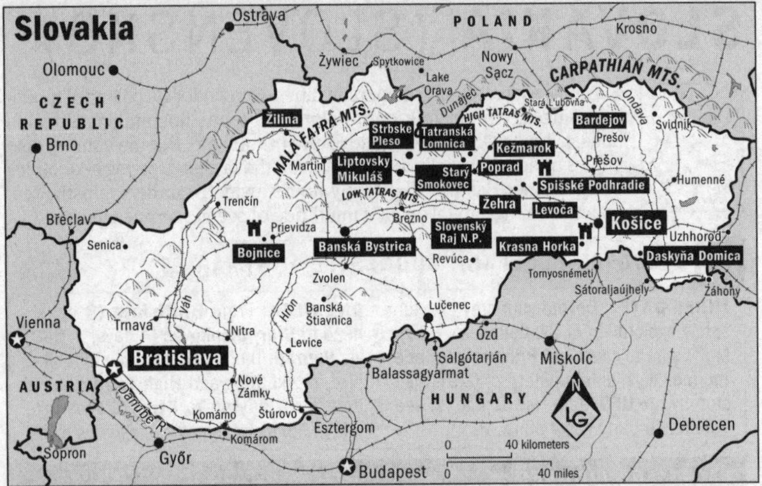

EMBASSIES AND CONSULATES. Foreign embassies to Slovakia are in Bratislava (p. 623). Slovak embassies abroad include: **Australia,** 47 Culgoa Circuit, O'Malley, Canberra, ACT 2606 (☎262 901 516; www.slovakemb-aust.org); **Canada,** 50 Rideau Ter., Ottawa, ON K1M 2A1 (☎613-749-4442; www.ottawa.mfa.sk); **Ireland,** 20 Clyde Rd., Ballsbridge, Dublin 4 (☎33 56 66 00 12; fax 660 0014); **UK,** 25 Kensington Palace Gardens, London W8 4QY (☎020 73 1364 70; www.slovakembassy.co.uk); **US,** 3523 International Ct., NW, Washington, D.C. 20008 (☎202-237-1054; www.slovakembassy-us.org).

VISA AND ENTRY INFORMATION. Citizens of Australia, Canada, Ireland, New Zealand, the UK, and the US can travel to Slovakia without a visa for up to 90 days. Those traveling for business, employment, or study must obtain a temporary residence permit. There are many kinds of visas, including single- and multiple-entry, as well as long term, and range in price from US$37-154.

TOURIST SERVICES

The **Slovak Tourist Board** (☎484 136 146; www.sacr.sk) provides useful information on Slovakian accommodations, natural resources, and culture. Public tourist offices are marked by a white "i" inside a green square. English is often spoken at tourist offices, which usually provide maps and information about transportation. If booking accommodations at an office, be wary of handing over cash on the spot.

MONEY

KORUNY (SK)		
	AUS$1 = 23.85SK	10SK = AUS$0.42
	CDN$1 = 26.01SK	10SK = CDN$0.38
	EUR€1 = 38.60SK	10SK = EUR€0.25
	NZ$1 = 22.04SK	10SK = NZ$0.45
	UK£1 = 56.86SK	10SK = UK£0.18
	US$1 = 31.70SK	10SK = US$0.32

Although Slovakia is now a member state of the EU, the **Slovak koruna** (Sk), plural koruny, remains the main unit of currency and comes in denominations of 20, 50, 100, 200, 500, 1000 and 5000 koruny. Slovakia's changeover to the euro is slated for early 2009. The koruna is divided into 100 *halier*, issued in standard denominations of 50 *halier*. Bear in mind that smaller establishments may not be able to break 5000Sk bills. **Credit cards** are not accepted in many Slovak establishments, but MasterCard and Visa are the most useful, followed by American Express. Inflation is down to about 4.5%, which means prices are relatively stable. ATMs are plentiful and give the best exchange rates, but also tend to charge a flat service fee; it is most economical to withdraw large amounts at once. Banks **Slovenská-Sporitełňa** and **Unibank** handle MC/V cash advances. Banks require that you present your passport for most transactions.

HEALTH AND SAFETY

EMERGENCY	**Ambulance and General Emergency:** ☎112. **Fire:** ☎150. **Police:** ☎158.

Medical care varies a great deal in Slovakia. Few doctors speak English and many facilities require cash payment upon service. European Health Insurance Card (EHIC) and Slovakian National Insurance are the only kinds accepted; to obtain Slovakian insurance one may visit www.apollo.sk, or www.szp.sk, among others. In an emergency, dial ☎112 for English and German operators. **Tap water** varies in quality and appearance but is probably safe, though bottled water is always safest. If water comes out of the faucet cloudy, let it sit for 5min; air bubbles may be probably to blame. *Drogerii* (drugstores) stock Western brands. Bandages are *obväz*, aspirin *aspirena*, tampons *tampony*, and condoms *kondómy*. **Petty crime** is common; be wary in crowded areas and secure passports and other valuables at all times. **Violent crimes** are not unheard of, but tourists are rarely the targets. Accommodations for **disabled** travelers are rare. **Women** traveling alone are rarely harassed, but may encounter stares. Dress modestly and avoid walking or riding public transportation at night. **Minority** travelers with darker skin may encounter discrimination and should exercise caution. **Homosexuality** is not accepted by all Slovaks; GLBT couples may experience stares or insults.

TRANSPORTATION

BY PLANE. Flying to Bratislava may be inconvenient and expensive, as many international carriers have no direct flights. Flying to Vienna, AUS and taking a bus or train is often much cheaper and the only option. Another good option is to take an indirect flight and then fly from within Europe to Bratislava with a budget airline, such as SkyEurope (www.skyeurope.com) or Ryanair (www.ryanair.com).

BY TRAIN. EastPass is valid in Slovakia, but **Eurail** is not. *InterCity* or *EuroCity* trains are faster but cost more. A boxed "R" on the timetable means that a *miestenka* (reservation; 7Sk) is required; there is a fine for boarding an international train without a reservation. Reservations are recommended and often required for *expresný* (express) trains and first-class seats, but are not necessary for *rychlík* (fast), *spešný* (semi-fast), or *osobný* (local) trains. Both first and second class are relatively comfortable and considered safe. Buy tickets before boarding the train, except in small towns. For up-to-date train info, check www.zsr.sk. Master schedules *(cestovný poriadok)* for **ŽSR,** the national rail company, are available for sale at information desks and are posted on boards in most stations.

BY BUS. In hilly regions, **ČSAD** or **Slovak Lines buses** are the best and sometimes the only option. Except for very long trips, buy tickets on board. You can probably ignore most footnotes on schedules, but the following are important: **x** (crossed hammers) means weekdays only; **a** is Saturday and Sunday; **b** means Monday through Saturday; **n** is Sunday; and **r** and **k** mean excluding holidays. *"Premava"* means "including"; *"nepremava"* is "except"; following those words are often lists of dates. Check www.slovaklines.sk for updated schedules.

BY CAR AND BY TAXI. The International Driving Permit is required for foreigners driving in Slovakia, except for UK citizens, who need one only to rent cars. Larger cities have car rentals that are comparably much cheaper than those in the rest of Europe. **Taxis** are common in Bratislava, but travelers should look for taxis that carry the name of a specific company on the roof, not just a yellow light. Taxis are more expensive if they are hailed, rather than called; if you do hail a cab, it is advisable to negotiate the fare beforehand or to make sure the meter is running.

BY BIKE AND BY THUMB. Rambling wilds and ruined castles inspire many bike tours, and renting a bike in Bratislava is becoming easier. Biking is popular among the Slovaks, especially in the Tatras, the foothills of western Slovakia, and Šariš. **VKÚ** publishes color bike maps (70-80Sk). Although Let's Go does not recommend hitchhiking, it is common and generally considered safe in Slovakia. Hitchhikers going to major cities are advised to write their destination on a sheet of paper or cardboard; for a list of city codes, visit www.slovensko.com/about/hitchhiking.

KEEPING IN TOUCH

PHONE CODES	**Country code:** 421. **International dialing prefix:** 00. From outside Slovakia, dial international dialing prefix (see inside back cover) + 421 + city code + local number. Within Slovakia, dial city code + local number for intercity calls and simply the local number for calls within a city.

EMAIL AND INTERNET. Internet access is common in Slovakia, even in smaller towns. **Internet** cafes usually offer cheap (1Sk per min.), fast access.

TELEPHONE. Recent modernization of the Slovak **phone** system has required many businesses and individuals to switch phone numbers. The phone system is still somewhat unreliable; try multiple times if you don't get through. Some public phones allow international calls, while others do not. The international and national phones exist in each city, but there is no good way to distinguish between them. **Card phones** are common and are usually much better than the coin-operated variety. Purchase cards (100-500Sk) at the post office. Be sure to buy the "Global Phone" card if you plan to make international calls.

MAIL. Mail service is generally efficient. Letters abroad take two to three weeks. Letters to Europe cost 11-14Sk; letters to the US cost 21S Almost every post office ***(pošta)*** provides express mail services. To send a package abroad, go to a customs office ***(colnice)***. Address envelopes for **Poste Restante** as follows: First name LAST NAME, POSTE RESTANTE, post office address, Postal Code, city, Slovakia.

ACCOMMODATIONS AND CAMPING

SLOVAKIA	❶	❷	❸	❹	❺
ACCOMMODATIONS	under 300Sk	300-550Sk	550-850Sk	850-1100Sk	over 1100Sk

Beware of scams and overpricing, as foreigners are often charged much more than Slovaks for accommodation. Finding cheap rooms in Bratislava before student dorms open in July is very difficult. Without reservations, you may also have a great deal of trouble in Slovenský Raj and the Tatras. In other regions, finding a bed is relatively easy if you call ahead. The tourist office, **SlovakoTourist,** and other tourist agencies can usually help. Slovakia has few hostels, most of which are found in and around Bratislava. These usually provide towels and a bar of soap. **Juniorhotels (HI)** tend to be a bit nicer than hostels. **Hotel** prices are dramatically lower outside Bratislava and the Tatras, with budget hotels running 300-600Sk. **Pensions** *(penzióny)* are smaller and less expensive than hotels.

Campgrounds are common. They are located on the outskirts of most towns and usually rent bungalows to travelers. Camping in national parks is illegal. In the mountains, *chaty* (mountain huts) range from plush quarters around 600Sk to friendly bunks with outhouses (about 200Sk).

FOOD AND DRINK

SLOVAKIA	❶	❷	❸	❹	❺
FOOD	under 120Sk	120-190Sk	190-270Sk	270-330Sk	over 330Sk

The national dish, *bryndzové halušky* (small dumplings in sauce), is a godsend for **vegetarians** and those sticking to a **kosher** diet. Pork products, however, are central to many traditional meals. *Knedliky* (dumplings) or *zemiaky* (potatoes) frequently accompany entrees. Enjoy *kolačky* (pastry), baked with cheese, jam or poppy seeds, and honey, for dessert. White **wines** are produced northeast of Bratislava, while *Tokaj* wines (distinct from Hungarian *Tokaji Aszú*) are produced around Košice. The favorite Slovak beer is the slightly bitter *Spis*. Another popular alcohol is *slivovica*, a plum brandy with an alcoholic content of well over 50%; it is reputed to not leave hangovers because it is so concentrated.

LIFE AND TIMES

HISTORY

EARLY CIVILIZATION AND HUNGRY HUNGARY. In 174 **Marcus Aurelius** conquered more of the territory, creating the empire's most northern border; it was on the banks of a Slovak river that he wrote his philosophical treatise, *Meditations*. After the fall of the Roman Empire, possession of Slovak lands was violently contested. The Slavs eventually won power, and a new state formed in 833 under **Prince Mojmír of Moravia,** who brought Christianity to Slovakia. Despite unification, the Slavs could not fend off the Magyars. After their defeat in the 907 **Battle of the Bavarians,** the state was made part of the Hungarian Kingdom.

ESCAPING HUNGARY'S GRASP. The Tatar invasions of 1241-43 devastated the already weakened Hungarian Kingdom, which finally fell to the Ottomans in 1526. With the Empire divided, the Austrian Habsburgs gained control of Slovak lands. For the next 200 years, Slovakia was the front line in a continuous struggle between the Habsburgs and the Turks. A Slovak nationalist movement emerged in the 18th century; however, Hungarian power continued to grow, thanks in part to the 1867 establishment of the **Austro-Hungarian Dual Monarchy.** The Hungarian government intensified its Magyarization policies, which only further provoked the Slovak nationalist movement. On October 28, 1918, Slovakia, Bohemia, Moravia, and Ruthenia combined to form independent **Czechoslovakia.**

ENTER GERMANY. After Czechoslovakia was abandoned by Britain and France in the **Munich Agreement** of 1938, the Slovaks clamored for autonomy. While Hitler occupied Prague, Slovakia declared independence in 1939 as a nationalist Christian state under the leadership of **Monsignor Jozef Tiso.** The Tiso government's allied with Nazi Germany, and over 70,000 Slovak Jews were sent to concentration camps. A resistance emerged, culminating in August 1944 with the ill-fated two-month **Slovak National Uprising,** a bloody, armed struggle against Nazi invasion.

THE AFTERMATH. After WWII, the Slovaks again became a part of democratic Czechoslovakia. In February 1948, as the National Front government fell apart, the communists seized control in a coup. Discontent simmered beneath the surface of communist Czechoslovakia until the late 1960s, when Slovak **Alexander**

Dubček steered the regime away from Moscow's grip. During the 1968 **Prague Spring,** Dubček sought to liberalize the regime. Soviet tanks immediately rolled into Prague and reinstated totalitarian rule.

BREAKING UP IS HARD TO DO. The Communists remained in power until the 1989 **Velvet Revolution** (see p. 161), when Czech dissident **Václav Havel** was elected president; he introduced a pluralistic political system and market economy. Slovak nationalism emerged victorious with a **Declaration of Independence** on January 1, 1993. Coming out of the 1993 **Velvet Divorce** with only 25% of the industrial capacity of former Czechoslovakia, Slovakia has had trouble adjusting to the post-Eastern Bloc world. Matters were worsened by **Vladimír Mečiar,** who has been thrice elected—and removed—as prime minister. During his tenure he violated the constitution and failed to reform the economy.

TODAY

Rudolf Schuster became president in May 1999. His election, along with the appointment of Prime Minister **Mikuláš Dzurinda,** brought much-needed economic reforms, which have attracted foreign investment. Now, the economy is in fairly good shape aside from high unemployment rates. In 2004, the World Bank declared that Slovakia had the world's fastest-transforming economy. The same year, the country gained accession into both **NATO** and the **European Union (EU),** and **Ivan Gašparovič,** a hardline nationalist, was elected president. Gašparovič's election was controversial at the time due to his membership in the unpopular, early '90s **Movement for a Democratic Slovakia;** his popularity, however, has since increased. **Robert Fico,** a left-wing leader, was elected Prime Minister in 2006. Racially motivated violence remains a problem in Slovakia, and **minorities** face substantial discrimination.

PEOPLE AND CULTURE

LANGUAGE. Slovak is a West Slavic language written in the Latin alphabet. It is closely related to the other languages in this group—Czech and Polish—and speakers of one will understand the others. Attempts to speak Slovak itself, however, will be appreciated. Older people will speak a little Polish. English is common among Bratislava's youth, but German is more prevalent outside the capital. Russian is occasionally understood but is sometimes unwelcome. The golden rules of speaking Slovak are to pronounce every letter and stress the first syllable. Accents over vowels lengthen them. For a phrasebook and glossary, see Appendix: **Slovakian,** p. 804.

DEMOGRAPHICS. Ethnic Slovaks comprise 86% of the population of Slovakia, with a significant Hungarian minority accounting for another 11%. Roma, Germans, and various Slavs make up the remainder.

CUSTOMS AND ETIQUETTE. Tipping is common in restaurants, though the rules are ambiguous. Most people round up to a convenient number by refusing change when they pay. Bargaining is unacceptable—special offense is taken when foreigners attempt the practice. Most bus and train stations and some restaurants are non-smoking, though many Slovaks smoke. Social mores tend to be conservative; dress neatly and be polite.

THE ARTS

LITERATURE. Slovak remained formally undistinguished from Czech until the end of the 18th century, when nationalist writers like **Josef Ignác Bajza** began to draw upon Slovak dialects. **Anton Bernolák** subsequently wrote a grammar and six-volume dictionary of the language. A full-blown literary tradition only began after 19th-century linguist **Ľudovít Štúr's** "new" language, based on Central Slovak dialects, inspired a string of national poets. Foremost among these was **Andrej Sládk-**

ovič, author of the Slovak national epic, *Marína* (1846). In the wake of WWI, Slovak nationalism and literature matured concurrently. Cosmopolitan influences appeared alongside Romanticism: **Emil Boleslav Lukáč** experimented with Symbolism while **Rudolf Fábry** championed Surrealism. Novelist **Janko Jesenský** satirized the interwar government in *The Democrats* (*Demokrati;* 1934-37). After WWII, the Slovak literati reacted to communist rule. **Ladislav Mňačko,** author of the 1968 novel *The Taste of Power (Ako chutí moc)*, openly opposed Stalin early on.

MUSIC. Slovak folk music uses instruments such as the flute-like *fujara* and Slovak bagpipes, called *gajdy.* Many folk songs relate the adventures of Juraj Jánošík, a Slovak bandit reminiscent of Robin Hood. Classical music is also popular, and famous composers like **Mikuláš Moyzes** and **Andrej Ocenáš** worked folk themes into their music in the early 20th century. Both the **Bratislava Philharmonic Orchestra** and the **Slovak Chamber Orchestra** enjoy international reputations. Contemporary American music is popular in Slovakia, as is rock and pop music. Meanwhile, a Slovakian version of American Idol has taken the country by storm; young people leave bars early on weekends to catch it.

THE VISUAL ARTS. Folk art is a vital part of Slovakian tradition, as is baroque art and gothic art. **Art Slovakia,** held in the nation's capital, is a festival that showcases a variety of up-and-coming talent in far ranging from decorative art to hand-woven carpets and rugs.

FILM. The 1921 film *Jánosík* was one of the world's first full-length features. The **Czechoslovak New Wave** of the late 1960s was arguably the most important film movement to emerge from Eastern or Central Europe in the latter half of the 20th century. Ján Kadár, a Slovak involved in the movement, directed *The Shop on Main Street (Obchod na korze)*, which won an Academy Award in 1965. Despite the current lack of both funding and facilities for filmmaking, Slovakian directors **Martin Šulík** and **Štefan Semjan** are well known internationally.

HOLIDAYS AND FESTIVALS

Holidays: Independence Day of Slovakia (Jan. 1); Epiphany (Jan. 6); Good Friday (Mar. 21 in 2008; Apr. 10 in 2009); Easter Holiday (Mar. 24, 2008; Apr. 13, 2009); May Day (May 1); Sts. Cyril and Methodius Day (July 5); Anniversary of Slovak National Uprising (Aug. 29); Constitution Day (Sept. 1); Our Lady of the 7 Sorrows (Sept. 15); All Saints' Day (Nov. 1); Day of Freedom and Democracy (Nov. 17); Christmas (Dec. 24-26).

Festivals: Bojnice's Festival of Ghosts and Spirits, in late spring, is a celebration of the dead and the ghosts that are said to haunt the castle. Bratislava hosts Junifest, a 10-day beer festival that includes hundreds of performances by artists, in early June. Near Poprad, the Vychod Folk Festival occurs in mid-summer.

BRATISLAVA ☎(0)2

The booming Slovak capital, with a GDP is 20% greater than the EU average, surprises visitors with high-caliber entertainment and cuisine. Bratislava (pop. 500,000) has many of the amenities of modern towns, with a burgeoning downtown district. Yet it's still possible to escape the cosmopolitan bustle: villages, vineyards, and castles lace the outskirts.

TRANSPORTATION

Flights: M.R. Štefánik International Airport (☎48 57 11 11), 9km northeast of town. To reach the center, take bus #61 (1hr.) to the train station and then take tram #1 to Poštová on nám. SNP. Most airlines frequent the airport in Vienna, but the following carriers cross the Slovak border: **Austrian Airlines** (☎54 41 16 10; www.ava.com); **ČSA** (☎52 96 10 42; www.czech-airlines.com); **Delta** (☎52 92 09 40; www.delta.com); **LOT** (☎52 96 40 07; www.lot.com); **Lufthansa** (☎52 96 78 15; www.lufthansa.com). A few **budget airlines** service the city as well: **SkyEurope** (☎48 50 11 11; www.skyeurope.com) and **easyJet** (www.easyjet.com) which flies from Bratislava to **Luton, ENG.**

Trains: Bratislava Hlavná Stanica, at the end of Predstaničné nám., off Šancová. **Železnice Slovenskej republiky** (☎20 29 11 11; www.zsr.sk) posts schedules on its website. To: **Banská Bystrica** (3-4½hr., 1 per day, 292Sk); **Košice** (5-6hr., 10 per day, 518Sk); **Poprad** (4¾hr., 2 per day, 420Sk); **Žilina** (2¾hr., 6 per day, 260Sk); **Prague, CZR** (4½-5½hr., 3 per day, 400Sk); **Vienna, AUT** (1hr., every hr., 283Sk round-trip).

Buses: Mlynské nivy 31 (☎55 42 16 67, info 09 84 22 22 22). Bus #210 runs between the train and bus stations. Check your ticket for the bus number (č. aut.); several depart from the same stand. **Eurolines**-offers a 10% discount to those under 26. To: **Banská Bystrica** (3-4½hr., 2-3 per hr., 290-450Sk); **Poprad** (6-7¾hr., 7-8 per day, 380-462Sk); **Žilina** (3-4hr., 11-15 per day, 250Sk); **Belgrade, SMN** (12hr., 1 per day, 1200Sk); **Berlin, GER** (12hr., 1 per day, 2200Sk); **Budapest, HUN** (4hr., 2 per day, 610Sk); **Prague, CZR** (4¾hr., 5 per day, 520Sk); **Vienna, AUT** (1½hr., every hr., 400Sk).

GETTING AROUND SLOVAKIA. If you're traveling by bus to destinations outside of the city, purchase tickets by telling the driver your intended destination. If you are taking the train, buy tickets at the cash register *(kasa)* inside the train station before you board.

Hydrofoils: Lodná osobná doprava, Fajnorovo nábr. 2 (☎52 93 22 26; www.lod.sk), across from the **Slovak National Museum.** Hit the Danube in style. Open daily 8:30am-5:30pm. To: **Devín Castle** (1½hr., Tu-Su 2 per day, 150Sk); **Budapest, HUN** (4hr.; 1 per day; €79, students €69); and **Vienna, AUT** (1¾hr., 2 per day, 550Sk).

Local Transportation: Tram and **bus** tickets (10min. 14Sk, 30min. 18Sk, 1hr. 22Sk) are sold at kiosks and at the orange *automaty* in bus stations. Use an *automat* only if its light is on. Stamp your ticket when you board; the fine for riding ticketless is 1200Sk. Trams and buses run 4am-11pm. **Night buses,** marked with blue and yellow numbers and an "N" run midnight-4am. Some kiosks and ticket machines sell **passes** (1-day 90Sk, 2-day 170Sk, 3-day 210Sk).

Taxis: BP (☎169 99); **FunTaxi** (☎167 77); **Profi Taxi** (☎162 22).

SLOVAKIA

ORIENTATION AND PRACTICAL INFORMATION

The **Dunaj** (Danube) flows eastward across Bratislava. Four bridges span the river; the main **Nový Most** (New Bridge) connects Bratislava's center, **Staromestská** (Old Town), in the north, to the commercial and entertainment district on the river's southern bank. **Bratislavský Hrad** (Bratislava Castle) towers on a hill to the west, while the city center sits between the river and **námestie Slovenského Národného Povstania** (nám. SNP; Slovak National Uprising Square). When arriving by train, make sure to get off at **Hlavná Stanica,** the main train station. To reach the center from the **train station,** take tram #2 to the 6th stop or walk downhill, take a right, then an immediate left, and walk down Stefanikova (15-20min.) From the **bus station,** take trolley #202, or turn right on Mlynské nivy and walk to Dunajská, which leads to **Kamenné námestie** (Stone Square) and the center of town (15-20min.)

TOURIST, FINANCIAL, AND LOCAL SERVICES

Tourist Office: Bratislava Culture and Information Center (BKIS), Klobúčnicka 2 (☎161 86; www.bkis.sk). Books **private rooms** and hotels (800-3000Sk, 50Sk fee); sells **maps** (free-80Sk) and books **tours** (1200Sk per hr.; max. 19 people). Open June-mid-Oct. M-F 8:30am-7pm, Sa 9am-6pm, Su 9:30am-6pm; mid-Oct.-May M-F 8am-

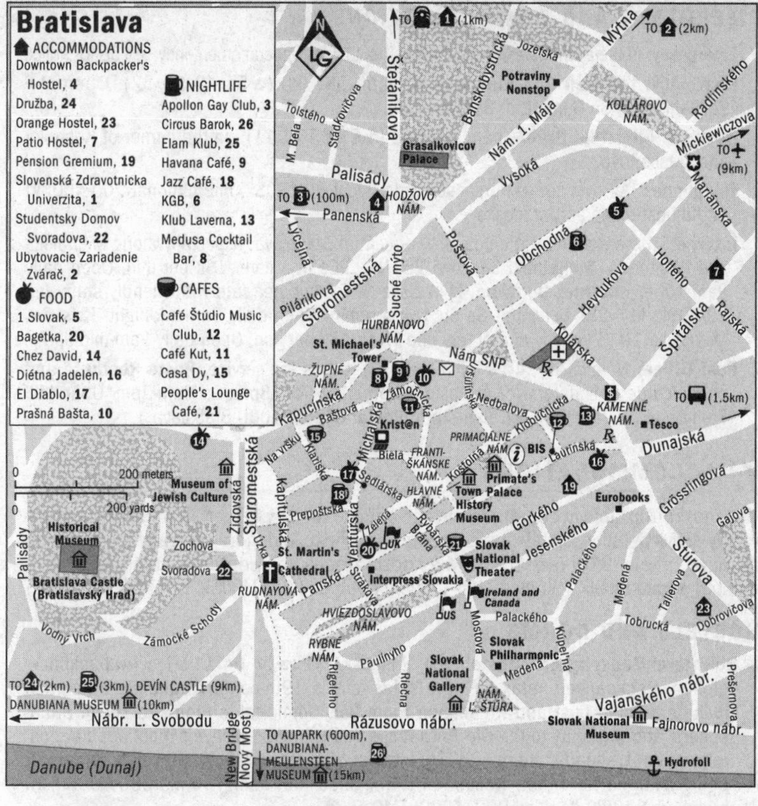

6pm, Sa 9am-4pm, Su 10am-3pm. **Branch** in train station annex open M-F 8am-2pm and 2:30-7pm, Sa-Su 8am-2pm and 2:30-5pm.

Embassies: Citizens of **Australia** and **New Zealand** should contact the UK embassy in an emergency. **Canada,** Mostová 2 (☎59 20 40 31; ambassador resides in Prague). Open M-F 8:30am-noon and 1:30pm-4:30pm. **Ireland,** Mostová 2 (☎59 30 96 11; bratislava@dfa.ie). Open M-F 9am-12:30pm. **UK,** Panská 16 (☎59 98 20 00; www.britishembassy.sk). Visa office open M-F 8:30-11am. **US,** Hviezdoslavovo nám. 5 (☎54 43 08 61, emergency 09 03 70 36 66; www.usembassy.sk). Open M-F 8am-noon and 2pm-3:30pm.

Currency Exchange: Ľudová Banka, nám. SNP 15 (☎59 21 17 63, ext. 760; www.luba.sk) cashes American Express **traveler's checks** for 1% commission and offers MC/V **cash advances.** Open M-F 8am-8pm. 24hr. MasterCard and Visa **ATMs** are at the train station and throughout the center.

Luggage Storage: At the bus station 25-35Sk. Open M-F 7am-noon, 12:30-7pm, 7:30-9pm; Sa-Su 7am-noon and 12:30-6pm. At train station 30-40Sk. Open daily 5:30am-midnight.

English-Language Bookstores: Eurobooks, Jesenského 5-9 (☎90 55 66 973; www.eurobooks.sk). Large selection of English-language literature and guidebooks. Open M-F 10am-6pm, Sa 9am-1pm. AmEx/MC/V. **Interpress Slovakia,** Sedlárska 2 (☎44 87 15 01; interpress@interpress.sk), on the corner with Ventúrska, has foreign magazines (110-447Sk) and newspapers (60-120Sk). Open M-Th 7am-10pm, F 7am-11pm, Sa 9am-11pm, Su 10am-10pm. MC/V; min 100Sk.

EMERGENCY AND COMMUNICATIONS

Emergency: In the event of an emergency, call ☎112 for General emergency; ☎158 for Police

Pharmacy: Lekáreň Pod Manderlom, nám. SNP 20 (☎54 43 29 52). Open M-F 7:30am-8pm, Sa 8am-7pm, Su 9am-7pm.

Hospital: Milosrdni Braha, nám. SNP 10 (☎57 88 71 11), on the corner of Kolárska and Treskoňova.

Telephones: All over town. Purchase cards (local 80-120Sk, international 200-400Sk) at the post office and at kiosks.

Internet: There are Internet cafes all over central Bratislava, especially along Michalská and Obchodná. **Megainet,** Šancová 25. New PCs in a cafe. 1Sk per min. Open daily 9am-10pm. **Internet Centrum,** Michalská 2. 6-computer cafe with friendly staff. Tea 20-30Sk. M-F 2Sk per min., Sa-Su 1Sk per min. Open daily 9am-midnight. **Krist@n,** Michalská 10. 2 speedy computers and Wi-Fi. 1Sk per min. Open daily 9am-midnight.

Post Office: Nám. SNP 34 (☎59 39 31 11). Offers **fax** service. **Poste Restante** and phone cards at counters #2-4. Poste restante M-F 7am-8pm, Sa 7am-2pm. Open M-F 7am-8pm, Sa 7am-6pm, Su 9am-2pm. **Postal Code:** 81000 Bratislava 1.

ACCOMMODATIONS

The most affordable accommodations lie outside the city center. In mid-summer, **university dorms** open as hostels, where rooms are cheap and more centrally located than at many hotels. **BKIS** (see p. 624) has dorm prices and contacts, and books well-located **private rooms.** (Singles 1100-1700Sk; doubles 1390-2400Sk. Booking fee 50Sk.)

HOSTELS AND DORMS

Downtown Backpacker's Hostel (HI), Panenská 31 (☎54 64 11 91; www.backpackers.sk). Backpackers relax on worn sofas in this 19th-century building. Amenities include a Lenin bust and a common room bar. Comfortable rooms, a social atmosphere, and proximity to the Old Town make this one of Bratislava's most popular hostels, so book ahead. Laundry 200Sk. Internet 2Sk per min. Some travelers report not being charged for either. Reception 24hr. Check-out noon. Dorms 500-600Sk, HI members 540Sk; doubles 800/720Sk. MC/V. ❸

Patio Hostel, Špitálska 35 (☎52 92 57 97; www.patiohostel.com). Clean and comfortable, with a lime-green common room lined with Warhol prints. Windows let in plenty of natural light. Free Internet. Check-in 1pm. Check-out 10pm. 2- to 12-bed dorms 600-800Sk. MC/V. ❸

Slovenská Zdravotnicka Univerzita, Limbová 12 (☎59 37 01 00; www.szu.sk). From the train station, take bus #32 or electric cable bus #204 5 stops to Nemocnica Kramárel, then climb the steps to the right. This green tower is far from the center, but rooms are clean and comfy, and the doubles are a deal. New baths. Shared kitchen. Breakfast 70Sk. Reception 24hr. Check-out 10am. Singles 380Sk; doubles 760Sk; apartments 1600Sk. Tourist tax 30Sk. Cash only. ❷

Ubytovacie Zariadenie Zvárač, Pionierska 17 (☎49 24 66 00; www.vuz.sk). Take tram #3 from the train station or #5 or 11 toward Raca-Komisárky to Pionierska. Backtrack to the intersection, then turn right. Inside this concrete-chic university dorm, rooms are pleasant and beds are comfortable. Shared baths, kitchen, and common room TV. Breakfast included from 7am-8:30am. Reception 24hr., ring bell after midnight. Check-in noon. Check-out 10am. Singles 730Sk, with bath 930Sk; doubles 1160/1460Sk. Tourist tax 30Sk. MC/V. ❸

Studentský Domov Svoradov, Svoradova 13 (☎0918 664 041), shares the hilltop with the Bratyslavký Hrad. During the summer, these university dorms are converted into cheap lodgings. Shared bathroom and showers are the only things that promote a sense of community, but it's difficult to complain at this price. Reception 24hr. Single or double dorms 400Sk; with ISIC 289Sk. Cash only. ❷

SLOVAKIA

Orange Hostel, Dobrovičova 14 (☎908 567 092; www.hostelinbratislava.com). A quick walk from the main square. Cozy beds in dorms. Laundry 50Sk. Free Internet. Reception 24hr. Check-out 9am. Open early July to late Aug. Dorms 550Sk. MC/V. ❸

HOTELS AND PENSIONS

Pension Gremium, Gorkého 11 (☎54 13 10 26; www.gremium.sk), off Hviezdoslavovo nám. Sparkling showers, English-speaking receptionists, a cafe, and an exceptional location make this a great find. Baths, fridges, phones, and TVs. Kitchen available. Breakfast in the cafe downstairs €1.70-4. Check-in until 5pm. Check-out 11am. Call ahead. Singles 950Sk; doubles 1650Sk. 30Sk tax. AmEx/MC/V. ❹

Družba, Botanická 25 (☎65 42 00 65; www.hotel-druzba.sk). Take tram #1 or 5, from the train station toward Pri Kríži to Botanická Záhrada, cross the pedestrian overpass, and go to the farther of the 2 red-blue-and-green concrete blocks. Stick to the remarkably cheap dorms at this combination hotel and university dorm. Dorm reception 24hr. Open July-Aug. Call ahead. 2- to 3-bed dorms 170Sk, 30Sk tourist tax. Hotel open year-round. Singles 790Sk; doubles 1966Sk. MC/V. ❷

FOOD

Prices are substantially higher in Bratislava than elsewhere in Slovakia, but now is your chance to indulge in international cuisine. Head to **Tesco,** Kamenné nám. 1, for groceries. (Open M-F 8am-10pm, Sa 8am-8pm, Su 9am-8pm. MC/V.) Or, try the nearby indoor **fruit market** at Stará Trzníćá, Kamenné nám. (Open M-F 7am-6pm, Sa 7am-1pm.) For late-night grocery needs, check out **Potraviny Nonstop,** nám. 1. Mája 15. (Open 24hr. MC/V.)

TRADITIONAL FOOD

1 Slovak Pub, Obchodná 62 (☎09 05 35 32 30). Join the student crowd at one of Bratislava's largest and cheapest Slovak restaurants. Each of the many wooden rooms has a different theme; the reconstructed country cottage is particularly well-done. Lunch until 5pm. Lunch entrees 35-89Sk. Dinner entrees 79-250Sk. Open M-Th 10am-midnight, F-Sa 10am-2am, Su noon-midnight. Cash only. ❷

Prašná Bašta, Zámočnícka 11 (☎54 43 49 57). Sit outside on the leafy terrace or head downstairs to sculptures and slick wooden decor. A 20-something crowd enjoys large portions of Slovak cuisine. Entrees 85-325Sk. Open daily 11am-11pm. MC/V. ❸

Diétna Jadelen, Laurinská 8. A popular lunchtime destination. Consider the long lines an opportunity to deliberate over your choices–the terrific food is worth the wait. English menu. Entrees 49-85Sk. Open M-F 11am-3pm. Cash only. ❶

INTERNATIONAL

El Diablo, Sedlárska 6 (☎904 556 886; www.mexicana.cz). The hankering for Mexican food draws tourists in droves to this restaurant decorated with Wild West memorabilia. El Diablo is the best place in Bratislava to down tequila (109-299Sk) and delicious fajitas (289-439Sk). Huge portions. Entrees 180-600Sk. Open M-Sa 9am-3am, Su 11am-1am. Kitchen open until midnight. MC/V. ❹

Bagetka, Zelená 8. A small, simple, and relaxed sandwich bar, Bagetka is an ideal escape from the busy main streets and a great place to pick up something to go. Limited seating. Entrees 50-90Sk. Open M-Sa 9:30am-9pm, Su 2-9pm. Cash only. ❶

Chez David, Zámocká 13 (☎54 41 38 24). A restaurant in a quarter steeped in Jewish culture. Elegant decor and delectable dishes. Matzah ball soup 57Sk. Entrees 67-397Sk. Open daily 7am-11pm. AmEx/MC/V. ❷

THE BLOODY COUNTESS

400 years ago in Slovakia, status and wealth meant you could get away with murder. Or at least it did for Elizabeth Bathory, one of the most infamous criminals in Slovakian history. As a Hungarian countess (her former castle is in modern-day Slovakia at Čachtice-near the town of Trenčín and a short bus ride from Bratislava), Bathory is said to have terrorized as many as 650 young women between 1580 and 1610. Her husband was often away and Bathory grew bored; teaming up with her two maids, one of whom became her lover, she found entertainment by torturing peasant girls, whom she lured into the castle by hiring them for work.

It wasn't until she made the mistake of kidnapping girls from the lower gentry that a local count launched an investigation. As the investigators moved through the castle, they found evidence of Bathory's brutality everywhere: various girls, some dead and some half-dead, were drained of their blood, their bodies marked up by Bathory's beatings and piercings.

Bathory was put on trial in 1610, but her noble status as a countess prevented her from execution, unlike her accomplices. Instead, she was kept under house arrest in her castle, where she died a natural death at the age of 54.

CAFES

Bratislava's burgeoning cafe culture is rapidly improving in quality and diversity, though cafes generally lack a bohemian ambience.

Café Kút, Zámočnícka 11 (☎54 43 49 57), connected to Prašná Bašta. Tucked behind an archway, this hidden cafe invites visitors to join locals on the comfortable wooden chairs and let the hours fly by. Live music 7pm-10pm. Occasional live reggae one F per month. Espresso 30-40Sk. Open M-F 8am-11pm, Sa-Su 4-11pm. Cash only.

Café Štúdio Music Club, Laurinská 11 (☎09 04 95 14 52). Vinyl LPs line the walls and parted curtains adorn a small stage. Even the rows of wooden seats look like they were taken from an early 20th-century theater. M-Tu and Th-Sa music. Šaris 27-45Sk. Pastries 20-30Sk. Open M-W 11am-1am, Th-F 11am-3am, Sa 4pm-3am. Cash only.

People's Lounge Café, Gorkého 1 (☎54 64 07 77), near the State Theater, where ambient music and slick modern decor proves popular with the people. Espresso 50-60Sk. Mixed drinks 120-250Sk. Open daily 10am-11pm. AmEx/MC/V.

Casa Dy, Klariská 7 (☎54 43 22 69). A simple, stylish haunt of Italian expats, bathed in Mediterranean yellows and reds. Espresso 44-55Sk. Panini 69-79Sk. Open M-F 8am-10pm, Sa 10am-10pm. Kitchen open M-F 10am-noon and 1-7pm, Sa 9am-2pm.

SIGHTS

DEVÍN CASTLE (HRAD DEVÍN). Perched on an imposing cliff 9km west of the center, the stunning castle ruins overlook the confluence of the mighty Danube and Morava rivers. Since 5000 BC, the hilltop settlement has changed hands many times and was repeatedly razed and rebuilt until Napoleonic armies blew it up for good in 1809. With the advent of communism, Devín became a functioning symbol of totalitarianism: sharpshooters hid in the ruins with orders to open fire on anyone who tried to traverse this area. Today, visitors can walk along the paths, through the rocks and ruins. A museum details the castle's history. *(Bus #29 from Nový Most to the last stop. ☎65 73 01 05. English info 35Sk. Open July-Aug. Tu-F 10am-5pm, Sa-Su 10am-7pm; May-June and Sept.-Oct. Tu-Su 10am-5pm. Last entry 30min. before closing. Museum 90Sk, students 40Sk.)*

BRATISLAVA CASTLE (BRATISLAVSKÝ HRAD). Visible from the Danube banks, the four-towered castle is Bratislava's defining landmark. Ruined by a fire in 1811 and finished off by WWII bombings, the castle's current stark and boxy form is largely a communist-era restoration that doesn't quite capture its 18th-century glory. Its **Historical Museum** (Historické Muzeum) examines art history from clockmaking to interior design. The spectacular view from the **Crown Tower** (Korunná Veža) is a highlight of the visit. *(From underneath Nový Most, climb the stairs to Židovská, then turn left onto the Castle Stairs and climb up the steps to the* hrad. *Castle open daily Apr.-Sept. 9am-8pm; Oct.-Mar. 9am-6pm. Free. ☎54 41 14 44; www.snm-hm.sk. Open Tu-Su 9am-5pm. Last entry 4:15pm. 100Sk, students 70Sk. Call ahead for 1-1½hr. tour in English; 400Sk.)*

HVIEZDOSLAVOVO NÁMESTIE. With the feel of a central square, this restored promenade is graced by a sliver of a park and surrounded by stunning 19th-century edifices, including the Philharmonic building. Grab a bench, head to the popular cafes, or frolic in the beautiful and refreshing fountain. In the evenings, the square fills with tourists coming to watch ballets and operas at the 1886 Slovak National Theater (Slovenské Národné Divadlo; see p. 630), by the square. *(From Hlavné nám., follow Rybárska Brana until the road ends at Hviezdoslavovo nám.)*

GRASALKOVICOV PALACE (GRASALKOVIČOV PALÁC). Guarded by two unyielding soldiers, the former Hungarian aristocratic residence now houses the offices of the Slovak president. Behind the palace, a peaceful park is a popular destination for lovers' strolls, family picnics, and friendly bocce games; it also hosts the occasional modern art display. Enter through the second gate in the back to avoid irking the presidential security staff. *(Hodžovo nám. Gardens open daily May-Sept. 8am-10pm. Apr.-May 10am-10pm; Jan.-Mar. 10am-7pm; Oct.-Dec. 10am-7pm.)*

ST. MICHAEL'S TOWER (MICHALSKÁ VEŽA). The emerald-green St. Michael's Tower is the only gateway that survived the 1775 demolitions of the town's medieval fortifications, aimed at unifying suburbs with the inner city. Most visitors rush through the **Museum of Arms and Fortifications,** which exhibits a small display of weapons and army uniforms, to reach the real treat—the amazing view of the castle and surrounding Old Town. *(On Michalská, near Hurbranovo nám. ☎54 43 03 44. English info. Open May-Sept. Tu-F 10am-5pm, Sa-Su 11am-6pm; Oct.-Apr. Tu-Su 9:30am-4:30pm. Last entry 10min. before closing. 60Sk, students 20Sk.)*

ST. MARTIN'S CATHEDRAL (DÓM. SV. MARTINA). When war with the Ottoman Empire forced the Hungarian kings to flee Budapest, this Gothic church became their coronation cathedral. Perched precariously atop the Cathedral's steeple, a golden replica of St. Stephen's crown reminds churchgoers of its glorious past. A highway now runs only a few feet from the Cathedral, which must undergo frequent repairs to combat automotive pollution. *(Open M-F 10-11:30am and 2-4:30pm, Sa 10-11:30am, Su 2-4:30pm. 40Sk. Mass in Latin Su 9am.)*

NEW BRIDGE (NOVÝ MOST). Built by the Communist government in 1972, Nový Most is one of the most unusual, prominent sights in Bratislava. Its space-age design was intended to balance the antiquated presence of Bratislava Castle. The bridge is suspended from two angular, concrete towers that are capped by what looks like a giant flying saucer. The UFO, as it is known, contains a viewing deck and a restaurant. *(☎62 53 03 00; www.u-f-o.sk. Deck open daily 10am-10pm. 50Sk, free with restaurant reservations. Restaurant open M-F and Su 10am-1am, Sa 10am-10pm.)*

MUSEUMS

PRIMATE'S PALACE (PRIMACIÁLNY PALÁC). The pink Baroque palace on Primaciálne nám. houses the city magistrate and a small art gallery full of intricate 17th-century tapestries. There are a few eccentricities, too: stare nervously at the dog in Jana Fyta's *Polovnícke zátisie* as its eyes follow you around the room, or watch yourself reflect away to infinity in the **Hall of Mirrors** (Zrkadlová Sieň). Ponder any resulting impressions in the impressive Chapel of St. Ladislaus, which is adorned with beautiful frescoes. *(Primaciálné nám. 1. Buy tickets on 2nd fl. Open Tu-Su 10am-5pm. 40Sk, students free. English pamphlets 40Sk.)*

DANUBIANA-MEULENSTEEN ART MUSEUM. Established in September 2000, this red, blue, and silver contemporary art museum is a piece of modern art in itself. Situated on a small peninsula near the Hungarian border, the museum is surrounded by a small park decorated with sculptures. The remote location prevents crowding, so you can admire cutting-edge exhibits at your leisure. *(Take bus #91 from beneath Nový Most to the last stop, Cunovo; 35min., 20Sk. Follow the signs 3.5km to the museum. ☎09 03 60 55 05; www.danubiana.sk. Open Tu-Su May-Sept. 10am-8pm; Oct.-Apr. 10am-6pm. 80Sk adults, 40Sk students. MC/V.)*

OLD TOWN HALL (STARÁ RADNICA). The hall's **Town History Museum** has an impressive exhibit on Bratislava's political, commercial, and social development, displaying a range of artifacts from ancient pottery to medieval jewelry to 18th-century paintings. The rooms themselves are of considerable interest. The town council once took their oaths of office in the stark Gothic chapel. In the next room, frescoes adorn the walls of the pink, blue, and gold Court Hall. The "Feudal Justice" exhibit, in a subterranean dungeon, showcases relics of medieval torture, trials, and executions, including thumb screws and an executioner's hat. Climb the stairs to the tower for a view of the orange tile roofs of the Old Town. *(Hlavné nám. 1. From Primaciálne nám., head down Kostolná away from the tourist office. ☎59 20 51 30. Borrow an English guidebook. Open Tu-F 10am-5pm, Sa-Su 11am-6pm. 50Sk, students 20Sk.)*

SLOVAK NATIONAL GALLERY (SLOVENSKÁ NARODNÁ GALÉRIA). Focused on Slovak art from the 15th to 18th century, the museum displays a fine collection of Gothic and Baroque sculptures, frescoes, and paintings. There is also a small collection of Renaissance and Baroque British, Italian, and Spanish art. Temporary exhibits tend toward modernism. *(Rázusovo nábr. 2. ☎54 43 45 87; www.sng.sk. Open Tu-Su 10am-5:30pm. 80Sk, students 40Sk. English tour guide 500Sk per hr.)*

MUSEUM OF JEWISH CULTURE (MÚZEUM ŽIDOVSKEJ KULTÚRY). Inside a former synagogue, this new museum chronicles the culture of Bratislava's dwindling Jewish population; Schlossberg, the Jewish quarter, was bulldozed in the 1970s in the name of "progress." *(Židovská 17. ☎54 41 85 07; www.slovak-jewish-heritage.org. Open M-F and Su 11am-5pm. Last entry 4:30pm. 200Sk, students 60Sk.)*

ENTERTAINMENT

BIS carries the monthly *Kam v Bratislave*, which lists film, concert, and theater schedules, and in the summer the *Kultúrné Leto*, an all-inclusive arts calendar. The weekly English newspaper, *Slovak Spectator*, also has current events info. **Slovenské Národné Divadlo** (Slovak National Theater), Hviezdoslavovo nám. 1, puts on ballets and operas that draw crowds from afar. (☎54 43 30 83; www.snd.sk. Box office open M-F 8am-5:30pm, Sa 9am-1pm. Closed July-Aug. 100-200Sk.) The **Slovenská Filharmónia** (Slovak Philharmonic), Medená 3, has two to three performances per week in fall and winter. The **box office,** Palackého 2, is around the corner. (☎54 43 33 51; www.filharm.sk. Open M-Tu and Th-F 1-7pm, W 8am-2pm. 100-200Sk.) Posters everywhere announce concerts and festivals. The annual **Music Festival** (late Sept. to early Oct.), brings international performers to Bratislava to play everything from pop to house. It is followed by the **Bratislava Jazz Days** festival. For **shopping,** try **AuPark** (cross Nový Most and go left).

NIGHTLIFE

By day, the Old Town bustles with tourists shopping and devouring *bryndza*. By night, it's filled with young people priming for a night out. Nightlife in Bratislava is relatively subdued, but there is no shortage of places to party. The GLBT scene is Slovakia's biggest, but is small by Western European standards. For info on **GLBT nightlife,** pick up a copy of *Atribut* at any kiosk.

Klub Laverna, Laurinská 19 (☎54 43 31 65; www.laverna.sk), entrance from SNP street. Expect a floor packed with a young crowd at this dance hotspot. A slide transports drunken clubbers from the upper level to the floor. Mixed drinks 75-230Sk. Weekend cover 100Sk. Open daily 9pm-6am.

Medusa Cocktail Bar, Michalská 33, just after St. Michael's Tower. This happening bar embodies chic with its posh decor and huge selection of delicious but expensive drinks (109-240Sk). Open M-Th 11am-1am, Sa 11am-3am, Su 11am-midnight. AmEx/MC/V.

Krčma Gurmánov Bratislavy (KGB), Obchodná 52 (☎52 73 12 79). Stashed in a red-brick basement, KGB is where hip local students go to partake of rock music and beer (22-52Sk) beneath pictures of Lenin. Open M-Th 11am-1:30am, F 11am-3:30am, Sa 3:30pm-1:30am, Su 3:30-11pm. Kitchen closes 11:30pm.

Jazz Café, Ventúrska 5 (☎54 43 46 61; www.jazz-cafe.sk). Praiseworthy mixed drinks and live jazz draw tourists and local sophisticates. Beer 45Sk. Jazz Th-Sa 9pm-1am. Cafe open daily 10am-2am. MC/V.

Apollon Gay Club, Panenská 24 (www.disco.sk). Go through the archway and turn left. A crowd mostly of gay men lounge and chat at this pub, providing a laid-back atmosphere—until the disco starts. Beer from 39Sk. Disco cover F-Sa 50Sk. Pub open M-Tu and Th 8pm-3am, W and F-Sa 8pm-5am, Su 9pm-1am. Disco open W-Sa from 10pm.

Circus Barok, Razusovo Nábrezie (☎54 64 20 91). Popular club floating on the Danube. This boat is usually packed—if possible, make your way to the beach-bar top deck. Pop, hip-hop, or disco. Drinks 58-145Sk. Cover 50Sk. Open M-Th and Su 11am-4am, F-Sa 11am-6am.

Elam Klub, Staré Grunty 53 (☎65 42 63 04; www.elam.sk). Take bus #31 or 39 from nám. 1. Mája to the last stop. Start walking uphill and veer left, keeping Club Palmyra on your left. Take the path up on your left, pass Grill 53, and go into Akademická Póda on your left. Good music and a lively atmosphere keep the university crowd dancing until dawn on the huge floor. Liveliest during the school year. Drinks 30-160Sk. Cover 39Sk. Open daily 9pm-6am.

Havana Cafe, Michalská 26 (☎910 797 222), just after St. Michael's Tower. Dance until the wee hours to salsa and reggaeton—and don't forget to sign the wall to prove you were here. Drinks 65-160Sk. DJ Tu-Sa. Open M-F 11am-2am, Sa 11am-3am, Su 11am-midnight. MC/V.

CENTRAL SLOVAKIA

It may be tempting to speed through the Central Slovakia on the way to the Tatras, but think twice. The area, rarely visited by tourists, is steeped in folk tradition and affords endless hiking and biking opportunities.

BANSKÁ BYSTRICA ☎(0)88

Banská Bystrica (BAHN-skah bis-TREE-tsah; pop. 84,280) is a well-functioning, mid-sized town boasting gorgeous scenery. The lively Old Town is packed with terraced cafes, shops, and folk-art boutiques, while the hills of the outskirts are an ideal playground for outdoor enthusiasts.

TRANSPORTATION. The **train** and **bus stations** lie next to each other on c. K. Smrečine. **Trains** (☎436 1473) run to: Bratislava (3-4hr., 5 per day, 292Sk); Košice (4hr., 5 per day, 300Sk); and Budapest, HUN (5-7hr., 5 per day, 500Sk). **Buses** (☎422 2222) go to: Bratislava (3½hr., 11-20 per day, 220-280Sk); Košice (4-5hr., 3-5 per day, 280Sk); Liptovsky-Mikuláš (2hr., 4 per day, 120Sk); Prešov (9hr., 5 per day, 350Sk); Žilina (2hr., 6-7 per day, 120Sk). For cabs, try **Fun Taxi** (☎167 77) or **BB Taxi** (☎411 5757). Buy tickets for **local buses** from the driver (15Sk).

ORIENTATION AND PRACTICAL INFORMATION. The **Hron River** cradles the city's southeastern edge. The train and bus stations lie east of the square, and suburban neighborhoods sprawl in all directions. To reach the center, go behind the bus station and cross **Cesta K. Smrečine** into the gardens. Take the pedestrian underpass below the highway and continue straight to **námestie Slobody.** Or, from the train station, head straight on 29 Augusta, turn left on Trieda SNP, then right onto **námestie Slobody.** From nám. Slobody, a left on Horná takes you through **námestie Š. Moyzesa** to **námestie SNP,** the town center (15min.). Alternatively, take a local bus to Narodna (5min., 15Sk) and walk uphill to **námestie SNP.**

Kultúrne a Informačné Stredisko (KIS), nám. SNP 14, between Horná and nám. SNP, has **maps** (10-190Sk) and accommodations info. The staff organizes city tours (1hr., 600Sk) and books **private rooms** for 300-400Sk. (☎415 2272. Open mid-Sept. to mid-May M-F 9am-6pm, Sa 9am-1pm; mid-Sept. to mid-May M-F 9am-5pm.) **Exchange currency** and cash **traveler's checks** for a 1% commission at **OTP Bank,** nám. SNP 15. (☎430 1244. Open M-F 8am-6pm.) MasterCard and Visa **ATMs** pervade the town; there is one outside the tourist office. **Luggage storage** is available at the train station. (20Sk, bicycles 30Sk, heavy bags 40Sk. Open daily 7am-7pm.) **Interpress Slovakia,** Dolná 19, sells newspapers (90-130Sk) and magazines (110-400Sk) in English. (☎412 3075. Open M-F 7am-6pm, Sa 8am-1pm.) The **pharmacy, Lekáreň Nádej,** Dolná 5, posts a list of local pharmacies that remain open after it closes. (☎412 6203. Open M-F 7:30am-5:30pm, Sa 8am-noon.) Cheap **Internet** access can be found at **Internet Centrum,** nám. SNP 3, through the arch. (☎475 6597. 20Sk per hr. Save your password; it is valid for one week. Open M-F 9am-9pm, Sa-Su 1-9pm. Cash only.) There are phonecard-operated **phones** outside the **post office,** Horná 1. **Poste Restante** is upstairs at window #24. Packages are at window #1. (☎432 6211. Open M-F 8am-7pm, Sa 8am-noon.) **Postal Code:** 97401.

ACCOMMODATIONS AND FOOD. KIS books **private rooms** (singles 300-350Sk; doubles 500-600Sk) for 25Sk and has info on hotels, hostels, and dorms. **Ubytovna Stavoprojekt ❸,** Robotnícka 6, offers pleasant, mid-range rooms in a great location 2min. from nám. SNP. Follow directions to Horná, but turn left onto Robotícka just before the Prior. (☎414 2929. Reception 24hr. Check-out noon. Singles 660Sk; doubles 920Sk. Cash only.) The popular **Študencké Domovy 4 ❶,** Trieda SNP 53, is near the center and stations. From the stations, head straight on 29 Augusta and turn right on Trieda SNP. The dorm is ahead on the left. Rooms are basic student dorms. (☎471 1516. Check-out noon. Open July-Aug. 2- to 3-bed rooms 238Sk, with ISIC 218Sk. Cash only.)

In this landlocked country, locals and visitors alike can still find excellent seafood at **Restaurant Fishmen ❸,** Dolna 5. The generic decor downstairs is spruced up by a fountain and an aquarium full of tropical fishes. Dishes range from basic *Pstruh Masle* (buttered trout; 95Sk) to *Zrolcie Platky* (shark slices in olive sauce; 195Sk) but also include Mexican, Italian, and Slovak foods. (☎412 5105. Entrees 99-390Sk. Open M-Sa 10am-11pm, Su 11am-10pm. MC/V.) **Rictárova Pivnica ❶,** Lazovná 18, off nám. SNP, serves up traditional Slovak food; its *bryndza* is delicious. (☎415 4300. Entrees 50-140Sk. Open M-Sa 10am-10pm. Cash only.) At **Červený Rak ❷,** nám. SNP 13, the menu features something for everyone: pizza, salads, fish, pasta, and traditional Slovak dishes. (☎415 3882; www.cervenyrak.sk. Entrees 79-219Sk. Open M-Th 10am-10:30pm, F 10am-midnight, Sa noon-11pm. Cash only.) Look for groceries at **Prior,** on the corner of Horná and c. K. Smrečine. (Open M-F 8am-7pm, Sa 8am-2pm. MC/V.) You can also head to **Billa Supermarket,** just across from the bus station. (Open M-Sa 7am-7pm, Su 8am-5pm. MC/V.) Get fresh fruits and vegetables at the **open-air market** in front of the Prior building.

SIGHTS. Turn right out of the tourist office and take the immediate left onto Kapitulská to reach the **Museum of the Slovak National Uprising,** which chronicles the country's struggles during WWII. Banská Bystrica was home to the underground resistance after the Nazis breached the Slovak border on August 29, 1944. Uniforms and weapons make up the bulk of the exhibition, alongside informational movies about the war. (☎412 3258; www.muzeumsnp.sk. Open daily May-Sept. 9am-6pm; Oct.-Apr. 9am-4pm. 50Sk, students 20Sk. 1hr. tours in English by request; 300Sk.) A cluster of the town's oldest buildings stands on nám. Š. Moyzesa. The restored **Pretórium,** now the **Stredoslovenská Galéria,** nám. Š. Moyzesa 25, hosts a temporary Slovak avant-garde exhibits. (☎412 4167. Open Tu-F 10am-5pm, Sa-Su 10am-4pm. 40Sk, students 10Sk. Free English pamphlet.) Behind the Galéria is the Romanesque **Church of the Virgin Mary.** Breathtaking frescoes adorn the Baroque ceiling, but the real attraction is the Gothic altarpiece, by Master Pavol of Levoča, which is housed in the church's **Chapel of St. Barbora.** The church is open only for services (Su 7, 8:30, 11am, 4:30pm). Walk toward the square from the Galéria to find the **Museum of Central Slovakia,** nám. SNP 4. The small collection features a noteworthy furniture and folk-costume exhibit. (☎412 5897. Open mid-June to mid-Sept. M-F and Su 9am-noon and 1-5pm, Sa 9am-1pm; mid-Sept. to mid-June M-F and Su 8am-4pm. 30Sk, students 15Sk.) The restored 18th-century villa of local artist Dominik Skutecký (1848-1921), **Dom Skutecký,** Horná 55, now displays his work. Committed to capturing the lives of ordinary people in his paintings, Skutecký focused on folk scenes. Head left from the tourist office on Horná to reach the museum. (☎412 5450. Open Tu-Su 10am-4pm. 40Sk, students 15Sk.)

NIGHTLIFE. Banska's nightlife draws tourists and young locals to the Old Town each night. With walls cluttered by black and white photographs and an eclectic mix of knick-knacks, the **Irish Pub,** Horná 45, draws rebels of all ages to worn wooden chairs and tattered but comfortable couches. (☎09 10 90 30 97. Pilsner 30Sk per 0.5L, Guinness 59Sk per 0.33L. Live rock Sa 8pm. Open M-Sa 11am-2am, Su 2pm-2am.) Escape to **Jazz Club U Smadnedio Mnicha** (Jazz Club at the Thirsty Monk), Dolná 20, a popular local stop with a laid-back crowd. (Beer 17-59Sk. Live jazz Tu nights. Open M-Th noon-1am, F noon-4am, Sa 4pm-2am, Su 4pm-midnight.) Another relaxing refuge is **Kapitol Pub,** Kapitulska 10, which has a lively courtyard and an underground cellar. (☎415 2667. Beer 25-40Sk. Open M-Th 10am-2am, F 10am-4am, Sa noon-4am, Su 6pm-midnight.) Banská Bystrica's dance central, **Arcade,** nám. ŠMP 5, draws a twenty-something crowd looking to let loose and get down. (☎430 2600. Occasional cover F 50Sk. Open W and F 1pm-4am, Sa 6pm-4am.) If you're starved for hiphop, join the teens at **Kaktus Bar,** Horná 4. (Beer 20-30Sk. Open daily 6pm-5am.) To escape the bar scene and watch a Hollywood film (sometimes dubbed into Slovak, but usually subtitled), visit **Kino Korzo,** in Dome Kultúry on c. K. Smrečine. (☎415 2466. Shows daily 6:30, 9pm. Open 30min. before showtime. M 70Sk, Tu-Su 25-85Sk.)

OUTDOOR ACTIVITIES. Banská Bystrica offers ample outdoor adventures. Visit the tourist office for current info or purchase the guide to Banská Bystrica and its environs. For **whitewater rafting** check out **Lodenica na Mlynčoku** in Slovenska Lupča that range from 180Sk for an evening trip to 1000Sk for two days. (☎0905 953 097; www.splavhrona.sk) To get to Slovenská L'upča take a city bus from the station (20-30min., 15 per day 25Sk). **Chivas Ranč** is 5km from town and offers horseback riding for all levels. Follow Stefánikovo nábr. and take a right onto Ul. 9 Mája and go straight. (☎418 00 52; www.chivasranc.sk. 350Sk per hr., 1050Sk per 5hr. Open daily 10am-10pm.)

DAYTRIP FROM BANSKÀ BYSTRICA: BOJNICE. Many Slovak castles survive only as ruins or reconstructions, but **Bojnice Castle** remains a real-life fairy tale that dazzles with its splendor and opulence. Originally a 12th-century wooden fortress for a Benedictine monastery, the castle later became a royal residence. Guided tours through the post-Romantic, late-Gothic building lead through galleries, gardens, hunting rooms, and bedrooms; from there, visitors climb a citadel, descending into a crypt, and from there, climb the depths of a 26m underground natural **cave.** The most memorable stops are the intricate **Oriental Saloon,** with magnificent 17th-century Turkish architecture; the **Music Room,** where 183 cherubs stare down from the golden ceiling; and the **chapel.** (☎543 0624; www.bojnicecastle.sk. Open July-Aug. M-Sa 9am-5pm; May-Sept. Tu-Sa 9am-5pm. Oct.-Apr. Tu-Su 10am-3pm. Mandatory guided tour 1¼hr.; call ahead for tours in English, 10-person min.; 400Sk. Grand Tour 140Sk, with ISIC 70Sk. Night tours July-Aug. F-Sa 9pm; otherwise call 3 days ahead to arrange; 200Sk, students 150Sk. Photography 50Sk, video 150Sk.) Ghost enthusiasts can attend the nightly tour, or visit the castle in early May for the **International Festival of Ghosts and Spirits** (180Sk, students 90Sk), when evening festivities include a candlelight ceremony for the Rising of the Dead. During the second weekend in September, **Knight's Days** festival features sword fighting and jousting (110Sk, students 60Sk). Various classical music concerts come to town in summer; tickets start at 30Sk. *(Take the bus to Prievidza from Banská Bystrica 1-2hr., 7-8 per day, 115-120Sk. With the station to your right, walk to the stop on the right. Take bus #3 to the "Bojnice" stop and get off at the park next to a stretch of small shops. 7min., 12Sk. Buses #15, 51, and 90 also go to Bojnice but don't stop next to the castle.)*

MALÁ FATRA MOUNTAINS

SLOVAKIA

The Malá Fatra range is an exhilarating medley of alpine meadows, steep ravines, and limestone peaks, offering hikes for adventurers of all abilities. Many hikes are challenging, however, and it is important to be prepared. Visit for the day or stay overnight in one of the *chaty* (mountain huts).

ŽILINA ☎(0)41

Žilina (ZHI-li-na; pop. 87,000), is a convenient base for exploring the nearby Malá Fatras. The picturesque setting and fountain-rich town square make it an inviting place for an extended stay.

Hotel Slovan ❹ A. Kmet'a 2, has small, well-furnished rooms with clean bathrooms and soft beds. The location is also great, just off nám. Andreja Hlinku. From the train station, go to the square, then turn right just past Tesco. Walk down Hurbanova; the hotel is on the right. (☎562 0134. Reception 24hr. Check-out noon. Singles 1200Sk; doubles 2200Sk. MC/V.) Ten minutes south of the city center at Hlinská 1, **Domov Mládeže ❶,** offers spartan university dorms year-round. Rooms are divided between Block III and V, set amid a field of indistinguishable concrete apartment blocks. Take bus #1, 2, 7, or 13 to the Hlinská stop, then cross the street and enter through the gate. Block III is the first on the left, and Block V is the second on the right. Both dorms have kitchens, shared showers, and small 2- to 3-person rooms, but the Block III beds are bunked. (Block III ☎723 3912, Block V 723 3914. Reception 24hr. Check-out 10am. Dorms plus tourist tax 270Sk. Cash only.)

While tourists eat in the square, locals prefer the calmer **Restaurácia a Vináreň na Bráne ❶,** Botová 10, which serves some of the town's finest Slovak food. With your back to the church in Mariánske nám., go to the far right corner and take the street to your right. (English menu. Lunch 48-79Sk. Dinner 79-120Sk. Open M-F 8:30am-10pm, Sa 9am-10pm. Cash only.) For simple, wholesome sandwiches (45-89Sk), visit the popular **Bageteria ❶**, Hlinkovo nám. 5. (Open M-Sa 7am-9pm, Su 9am-9pm. MC/V.) Those looking to relax should stop by **Fontána-Drink Pub ❷**, Mariánske nám. 25, and grab a beer (25Sk before 10pm; 35Sk after.) Also serves pizza (85-100Sk) and salads from 44Sk. (☎09 05 31 80 81. Open M-Th 7:30am-1, F-Sa 7:30am-3am, Su 8am-midnight. Cash only.) There is an enormous **Tesco** supermarket in nám. Andreja Hlinku. (Open M-F 7am-8pm, Sa 7am-6pm, Su 8am-6pm. MC/V.) There's also an **open-air market** at Starý Trh-Geronetova. (Open M-Sa 8am-6pm.)

The **train station,** Hviezdoslava 7, is northeast of the center. (☎229 5161. MC/V.) Trains run to: Bratislava (3hr., 12 per day, 268Sk); Košice (3¼hr., 11 per day, 316Sk); Poprad (2hr., 15 per day, 200Sk); Budapest, HUN (4¼-7hr., 2 per day, 710Sk); Prague, CZR (7hr., 6 per day, 710Sk). The **bus station,** Jana Milca 23 (☎562 0950), is on the corner of Hviezdoslava and 1 Mája. Buses run to: Banská Bystrica (2hr., 20 per day, 116-128Sk); Bratislava (3-4hr., 9 per day, 250-270Sk); Liptovský Mikuláš (1¾-2hr., 9 per day, 130Sk); Prague, CZR (5-7hr., 12 per day, 410-550Sk). For **local transportation,** buy train or bus tickets at kiosks or orange vending machines (12Sk).

The bus and train stations lie northeast of the center; budget accommodations are to the southwest. From the bus station, go left on **Hviezdoslava** to reach the train station. Take the underpass to **Narodná,** which runs into **námestie Andreja Hlinku,** the attractive New Town square where a church towers over a spacious, gardened plaza. Cross the square and take the stairs to the right of the church to **Farská,** which opens onto **Mariánske námestie,** the lively and touristy Old Town square. The tourist office **Selinan,** Burianova Medzierka 4, is on a street parallel to Farská, on the left. Buy hiking (VKU #110, 115Sk) or town **maps** (free-94Sk), or ask about accommodations in Žilina or nearby Terhová, where there are many beautiful trailheads. (☎562 0789; www.selinan.sk. Open M-F 8:30am-5pm.) **Exchange currency** and cash **traveler's checks** for a 1% commission at **OTP Banka,** Sládkovičova 9. (☎562 09 40. Open M and W 8am-6pm; Tu and Th-F 8am-5pm.) **Luggage storage** is in the underpass in front of the train station. (30Sk per day. Open M-Su 6am-10pm.) The pharmacy **Lekáreň na Bráne,** Bottova 7, posts the hours of nearby pharmacies that remain open late. (Open M-F 8:30am-noon and 12:30-5pm.) Public **telephones** are at the post office. Calling-card phones are at kiosks and at the post office. Try the slick **Internet Cafe,** Kálov 3, which also serves drinks. (8Sk per 15min. Excellent mixed drinks 45-120Sk. Open daily 11am-10pm.) The **post office,** Sládkovičova 14, has phone cards and **Poste Restante.** Facing the church in nám. A. Hlinku, go right and veer right with the street. (☎512 6259. Poste Restante M-F 8am-noon and 12:30-6pm. Open M-F 7am-7pm, Sa 8-noon.)

HIKING

Before departing for hikes, it's important to remember a few crucial details. Pack food and be ready for cold weather and fickle storms that can turn dirt roads into mud. Check conditions at the tourist office. **Emergency rescue** (☎569 5232) is available, although pay phones are not found on most trails. Trail markings are generally accurate but can be erratic. VKÚ **map** #110, sold at tourist agencies, is vital.

MOUNT VEĽKÝ ROZSUTEC. Though not the highest mountain in the range, **Veľký Rozsutec** (1609m) boasts some of the most exciting and challenging slopes. The **Štefanová** trail is possibly the best hike in the region, but the thrilling route is tricky and should not be attempted by amateurs. Take the Terchova-Vrátna bus from platform #10 in Žilina to Štefanová (1hr., every 1-2hr., 43-47Sk) and follow the yellow trail through lush woodland paths to **Sedlo Vrochpodžiar** (30min.). Take a right to start down the blue trail, where steep metal ladders, narrow bridges, and chains take you around, over, and occasionally through a slippery mass of tumbling waterfalls and rapids known as **Horne Diery** (Upper Hole). Continue on the blue trail to **Sedlo Medzirozsutce** (1½hr.). Take a right on the red trail to reach the **summit** (1¼hr.). To descend, follow the red trail to its intersection with the green trail near **Sedlo Medziholie** (1hr.). Turn right: the rocky green trail alternates between grass fields and towering pines, eventually returning to **Štefanová** (1¼hr.; total trip 7hr.). For a less vigorous hike, follow the blue trail from Sedlo Medzirozsutce around the summit until it meets the green trail near Sedlo Medziholie (1hr.). A right here leads across a field to the green trail and back to Štefanová (1¼hr.).

MOUNT VEĽKÝ KRIVÁN. At 1709m, **Veľký Kriván** is the highest peak in the range. Take the bus from platform #10 in Žilina to **Terchová-Vrátna** (43Sk), and get off at Chata Vrátna. The taxing hike begins with the green trail, which heads straight up to **Snilovské Sedlo** (1¾hr.); from there, turn right on the red trail to reach the **summit** (1hr.). To save your strength, take the **Lanová Dráha Vrátna Chleb** chairlift to the red trail and enjoy a splended view of the tree-lined peaks on the way up. (☎569 5642. 10% ISIC discount. 270Sk, round-trip 310Sk. Open daily 8am-4pm.) Turn left off the green trail to follow the red trail along 4km of beautiful vistas to **Poludňový Grúň** (1460m; 1½hr.). From Poludňový Grúň, turn left on the easier yellow trail to return to Chata Vrátna (1¼hr.).

LOW TATRAS (NÍZKE TATRY)

Though not quite as impressive as the High Tatras, the Low Tatras (Nízke Tatry) are still majestic, and benefit from being far less touristed. They and their peaceful valleys contain an extensive trail system as well as beautiful caves and streams. Hikers in these parts enjoy colorful promenades and unparalleled views.

LIPTOVSKÝ MIKULÁŠ ☎(0)44

Liptovský Mikuláš (LIP-tohv-skee mee-koo-LASH; pop. 33,000) is a great base from which to explore the magnificent surrounding mountains. On a rainy day, explore the lovely square and cafes that crowd the center. Go down Štúrova and cross nám. Osloboditeľov, and after 100m you'll see the **Galéria Petra Michala Bohúna,** Transovského 2 on your right. This gallery displays about 4500 works, ranging from 15- to 19th-century paintings to contemporary photography, video, and sculpture. (☎552 2758. Open Tu-Su 10am-5pm. Combined ticket 60Sk, students 30Sk; each exposition hall 20/10Sk.) Housed in a former synagogue, **Múzeum Janka Kráľa,** nám. Osloboditeľov 31, offers a look at the city's past through historical artifacts, antique books, early photographs, and even a doll collection. (☎552 2554; www.lmikulas.sk. Open mid-June to mid-Sept 10am-5pm; mid-Sept. to mid-June M-F 9am-4pm, Sa 10am-5pm. Entrance every 30min. 40Sk, students 20Sk.)

SLOVAKIA

Private rooms fill quickly during the high season, but hotels usually have a few vacancies. **Hotel Kriváň ❷,** Štúrova 5, opposite the tourist office, offers small, centrally located rooms. (☎552 2414. Reception 24hr.; knock after midnight. Check-in 2pm. Check-out 10am. Singles 350Sk, with bath 450Sk; doubles 550/770Sk; quads with bath 1140Sk. Cash only.) **Hotel Garni ❶,** Nešporova 120, 25min. from the center, offers big rooms, comfy beds, and shared showers. From the train station, take bus #2, 7, 8, 9, 10 or 11 to #1. Mája, at the Maytex bus stop (10Sk). Backtrack and take the first left, then the first right. (☎562 5659; www.garni.sk. Reception 24hr. Check-out noon. Singles 300Sk, doubles 400Sk. 10Sk tourist tax. Cash only.) Restaurants are limited, though some are clustered along **námestie Osloboditel'ov.** The **Liptovská Izba Reštaurácia ❶,** nám. Osloboditel'ov 22, serves delicious local dishes in a pleasant setting. (☎551 4853. Entrees 35-135Sk. Open M-Sa 10am-10pm, Su noon-10pm. Cash only.) Stock up on supplies at **Coop Supermarket,** 1 Mája 54, in the Prior building on nám. Mieru. (Open M-F 7am-8pm, Sa 7am-7pm, Su 8am-5pm. MC/V.) For fresh fruits, vegetables and clothes check out the **open-air market** to the right of the tourist office. (Open M-F 8am-4pm, Sa 8am-noon.)

The **train station** (☎551 2484) is at Štefánikova 2, and the **bus station** (☎551 8121) just outside. Bus information can be found in the base of the small white tower (8am-3pm). **Trains** run to: Bratislava (4hr., 12 per day, 364Sk); Košice (2hr., 15 per day, 220Sk); Poprad (30min., 5 per day, 82Sk); Žilina (1hr., 7 per day, 200Sk); Prague, CZR (8½hr., 4 per day, 1128Sk). **Buses** run to: Bratislava (5hr., 10 per day, 400Sk); Košice (3½hr., 1 per day, 300Sk); Poprad (1hr., 20 per day, 100Sk); Žilina (2hr., 13-14 per day, 120Sk). To reach the center, turn left out of the train station on **Štefánikova.** Turn right onto **M.M. Hodžu,** which crosses **Štúrova** at the square **námestie Mieru.** Turn left to reach **námestie Osloboditeľov,** the main square. The friendly staff at **Informačné Centrum,** nám. Mieru 1, in the Dom Služieb complex, books **private rooms** (250-400Sk), **exchanges currency,** and sells hiking **maps,** including VKÚ maps (110-125Sk). Ask for the *Orava Liptov Horehronie,* a hiking and cycling map (146Sk). They also organize full-day guided excursions (1-3 people 1500Sk, 4-8 2000Sk, 8+ 2500Sk) in the Low Tatras. (☎552 2418; www.mikulas.sk. Open mid-June to mid-Sept. M-F 9am-6pm, Sa 8am-noon, Su 11am-4pm; mid-Sept. to mid-Dec., Apr. to mid-June M-F 9am-6pm, Sa 8am-noon; mid-Dec. to Mar. M-F 9am-6pm, Sa 8am-noon.) **Exchange currency** for no commission at **Slovenska-Sporiteľňa,** Štúrova 1, adjacent to nám. Osloboditeľov. (☎551 3203. Open M-F 8am-5pm.) A **pharmacy** is at **Lekáreň Sabadilla,** nám. Mieru 1, in Dom Služieb. (☎552 1318. Open M-F 8am-5pm. MC/V.) **Z@vinác Internet Bar,** nám. Osloboditeľov 21, has **Internet** acess. (1Sk per min. Open M-Sa 10am-10pm, Su 2pm-10pm. **Telephones** are outside the cafe. Open M-Sa 10am-11pm, Su 2-10pm). The **post office** is on M.M. Hodžu 3, near nám. Mieru. Phone cards and **Poste Restante** are at windows #3 and 4. (☎552 2642. Open M-F 8am-6pm, Sa 8am-11am.) **Postal Code:** 03101.

HIKING IN THE LOW TATRAS

DEMÄNOVSKÁ JASKYŇA SLOBODY (DEMÄNOV CAVE OF LIBERTY). Named for its role in WWII, this cave stored supplies for the Slovak Uprising. The 45min. tour of the two-million-year-old cave covers 1.5km and passes through underground chambers, lakes, and a waterfall, all carved out of rock long ago by water falling at a rate of one drop per day. The 2hr. tour includes another 2km of corridors. Bring a sweater. *(For a short hike, take the bus from platform #3 in Liptovský Mikuláš to Demänovská Dolina and get off at "Demänovská jaskyňa slobody"; 20-35min., 1 per hr. 6:25am-5pm, 20Sk and walk to the cave on the blue trail toward Pusté Sedlo Machnate for 1½hr. ☎559 1673; www.ssj.sk. Open Tu-Su June-Aug. 9am-4pm, entrance every hr.; Sept.-Nov. 15 and Dec. 15-May 9:30am-2pm, entrance every 1½hr. 45min. tour 180Sk, with ISIC 160Sk. 2hr. tour 390/340Sk.)*

MOUNT ĎUMBIER AND CHOPOK. The gentle blue trail winds along the calm Štiavnica River until it reaches the Svidovské Sedlo by Chata generála M. R. Štefanika (5hr.). For a strenuous hike, go right on the red trail (2hr. from Liptotvský Ján) and climb Sedlo Javorie (1½hr.). You'll pass two beautiful, oft-cloud-covered peaks, Tanenica (1680m) and Prašivá (1667m). From here, head left on the yellow trail to summit Mt. Ďumbier (2½hr.). Continue on the red trail on your right along the ridge past the intersection with the green trail to reach the range's second-highest peak, Chopok (2024m), where you will be able to gaze at spectacular views of the surrounding mountains and green valleys. From Chopok, walk down the blue trail to the bus stop at Otupné, behind Hotel Grand (1¾hr.), or ride down on the chairlift. Chairlift box office in Jasná open 8:30am-3:40pm; follow the signs from Hotel Grand. (Chairlift daily every 30min. June-Sept. 8:30am-5pm, 240Sk, students 200Sk.) *To conquer Mt. Ďumbier (2043m), catch an early bus from platform #11 in Liptovský Mikuláš to Liptovský Ján (25-30min., every 1-2hr., 16-20Sk).*

DEMÄNOVSKÁ L'ADOVÁ JASKYŇA (DEMÄNOV ICE CAVE). This ice cave rests midway between Liptovský Mikuláš and Jasná. The cave was probably inhabited in the Stone Age, but the site first drew tourists after a set of large bear bones was mistaken for the remnants of a **dragon.** The 25km cave contains a wall signed by some 18th-century visitors and a frozen waterfall that drapes over bleached stone. *(Take the bus from Liptovský Mikuláš to Jasná, get off at "Kamenná chata"; 20-30min., 1 per hr., 20Sk. Follow the signs to the cave entrance for 15min. ☎554 8170; www.ssj.sk. Open Tu-Su June-Aug. 9am-4pm, entrance every hr.; May and Sept. 9:30am-2pm, entrance every 1½hr. 180Sk, students 160Sk.)*

HIGH TATRAS (VYSOKÉ TATRY)

Spanning the border between the Slovakia and Poland, the High Tatras are the highest peaks in the Carpathian range and create mesmerizing valleys. Despite its popularity with hikers and tourists, the High Tatras region retains a small-town Slovak charm, with affordable accommodations and welcoming locals. Starý Smokovec is a popular base for excursions and short hikes, but the most hard-core hikers seek shelter in mountain huts *(chaty)*. Many of the lower slopes on the Slovakian side of the High Tatras were devastated by a freak storm in the fall of 2004, and vast swaths of forest are nothing but thickets of broken pine trees. The upper regions, however, escaped largely unscathed.

POPRAD ☎(0)52

Poprad (pop. 56,000) is one of the Slovakia's major tourist centers and transportation hubs. While Poprad provides amusement for a few hours, travelers may find it more pleasant simply to pass through en route to their final destination.

TRANSPORTATION. Trains run to Bratislava (5hr., 12 per day, 420Sk), Košice (1½hr., 21 per day, 154Sk), and Žilina (2½hr., 21 per day, 200Sk). The clean, efficient **Tatranská elektrická železnica** (TEŽ) runs between Poprad and the various Tatran resorts (10min.-1hr., every 20min., up to 40Sk). From the bus station at the corner of Wolkerova and Alžbetina (☎776 25 55), **buses** go to: Banská Bystrica (2½hr., 9 per day, 150Sk); Bratislava (7hr., 15 per day, 400Sk); Kežmarok (25min., 20-25 per day, 23Sk); Košice (2½hr., 7 per day, 150Sk); Žilina (3hr., 13-14 per day, 200Sk); Frankfurt, GER (18hr., 2 per day, 2100Sk); Prague, CZR (11hr., 12 per day, 680Sk); Vienna, AUT (8hr., 2 per day, 1000Sk). Call **Rádio Taxi** at ☎776 8768.

ORIENTATION AND PRACTICAL INFORMATION. To reach the center, exit right from the train station, turn left on **Alžbetina,** and follow it away from the **bus station.** Turn left again on **Hviezdoslavova,** then right on **Mnoheľova,** which leads to **námestie sv. Egídia.** To reach the old square from the train station, walk up Alžbetina, then turn left on **Štefánikova.** Continue about 2km and turn left on **Kežmarská.** Keep right as the road forks and head up into **Sobotské námestie.** At **Mestska Informačná Agentúra (MIC),** nám. sv. Egídia 15, the English-speaking staff sells **maps** and offers info. (☎772 1394; www.poprad-online.sk. Open July-Aug. M-F 8am-6pm, Sa 9am-1pm, Su 2-5pm; Sept.-June M-F 9am-5pm, Sa 9am-1pm. **Private rooms** 300Sk.) **VÚB,** Mnoheľova 9, cashes **traveler's checks** and **American Express Travelers Cheques** for 1% commission. (☎713 1111. English spoken. Minimum 200Sk. Open M-F 8am-5pm.) Find 24hr. MC/V **ATMs** all over town. There's a 24hr. **currency exchange** desk in the lobby of **Hotel Satel,** Mnohel'ova 5 (☎527 1611; www.satel-slovakia.sk.). **Store luggage** at the train station, opposite the ticket windows. (15Sk per bag, 30Sk per bag over 15kg.) **Internet access** can be found at **Slovak Telecom,** nám. sv. Egídia 16 (free; open M-F 8am-5pm) and **T-Mobil,** nám. sv. Egídia 82 (upstairs; 20Sk per 30min.; open M-F 9am-6pm). **Postal Code:** 05801.

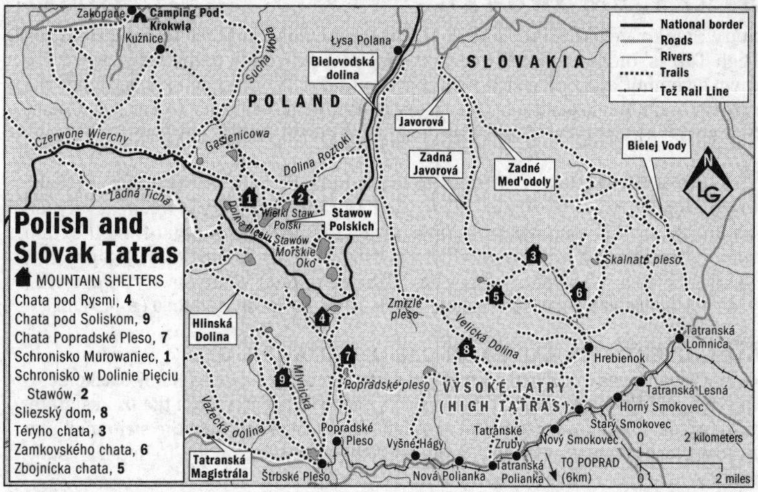

! In winter, a guide is necessary for hiking in the Tatras. To hire one, check with the local tourist information office in your town. The snowfall is very deep and avalanches are common. Dozens of hikers die each winter, often on "easy" trails. Even in summer, many hikes are extremely demanding and require experience. Before you begin, obtain a map and info about the trail. Updated information on trail and weather conditions is available at www.tanap.sk, but at the highest elevations, weather changes frequently and abruptly. Check with a mountain rescue team, a local outdoors store, or a tourist office before going anywhere without an escort. Always let the receptionist at your hostel or hotel know your hiking route and the estimated time of your return.

ACCOMMODATIONS AND FOOD. A student dorm during the school year, **Domov Mładeze ❶**, Karpatská 9, offers the cheapest rooms in town. Walk down Alžbetina from the train station and take the second right on Karpatská. (☎776 3414. Reception 24hr. Call ahead. Open July 1-Aug. 20th. 2- and 3-bed dorms 250Sk; singles with bath 300Sk. Cash only.) Affordable and right by the bus and train stations, **Hotel Europa ❷**, Wolkierowa 1, offers well-worn, spartan rooms. All rooms have sinks; baths are shared. (☎772 1897. Reception 24hr. Check-out 10am. Singles 490Sk; doubles 800Sk; triples 1200Sk. Tourist tax 15Sk. Cash only.) A more luxurious accommodation option, the grand **Hotel Satel ❹**, Mnoheľova 5, has comfortable rooms in a relaxing business atmosphere. (☎716 1111. English spoken. Singles 1600Sk; doubles 2000Sk. AmEx/MC/V.)

Pizza places and traditional restaurants line the central square. An appetizing option is **Slovenska Restauracia ❷**, 1 Mája 7, which serves *bryndzové havlušky* (sheep cheese dumplings; 70Sk), and other traditional Slovak dishes. (☎772 2870. English menu. Entrees 40-260Sk. Open daily 10am-11pm. AmEx/MC/V.) **Egídius ❸**, Mnoheľova 18, near the bus and train stations, specializes in *knedle* (dumplings with plums, 103Sk) served with meat. (☎772 2898. Entrees 40-480Sk. Open daily 9:30am-11:30pm. AmEx/MC/V.) Buy groceries at the **Billa Supermarket,** on the far side of the bus station parking lot. (Open M-Sa 7am-9pm, Su 8am-8pm. MC/V.)

STARÝ SMOKOVEC ☎(0)52

Starý Smokovec (STAH-ree SMOH-koh-vets), founded in the 17th century, is the High Tatras' oldest and most central base resort. Hiking paths originate at the town's summit and connect it with the mountains. While signposts with a dozen arrows and nameless streets may seem daunting, it's difficult to get lost—Starý Smokovec was developed along the main road and is easy to navigate.

TRANSPORTATION. TEŽ **trains** go to Poprad (30min., 1 per hr., 20Sk), Štrbské Pleso (45min., every 30-50min., 30Sk), and Tatranská Lomnica (15min., every 25-40min., 20Sk). The bus station is 2min. away; follow the path right from the train station. **Buses** go to Bratislava (6hr., 2 per day, 409Sk); Košice (3hr., 2-3 per day, 143Sk); Levoča (20-50min., 2-4 per day, 67Sk); Poprad (30min., every 30min.-1hr., 41Sk). A **funicular** runs to Hrebienok (see p. 641). For **taxis,** call **Rigo** (☎442 2525).

ORIENTATION AND PRACTICAL INFORMATION. Starý Smokovec's essential services are mostly along the main road that leads to **Horný Smokovec** to the east and **Nový Smokovec** to the west. To get to the center from the train station, walk uphill to the main road and turn left. Cross the road past the strip mall and head toward the white building, Dom Služieb, where signs point to hotels, restaurants, and services. The **hiking trails** are farther uphill.

The helpful staff of **Tatranská Informačná Kancelária (TIK),** on the closer side of the strip mall toward the train station, provides weather and hiking info and free town **maps;** sells hiking guides and the crucial **VKÚ map #113** (110Sk); and points visitors to hotels, pensions, and **private rooms.** (☎442 3440; www.zcrvt.szm.sk. Open July-Aug. daily 8am-8pm; Sept.-Dec. 26 and Jan. 12-June 1 M-F 9am-noon and 12:30-4pm, Sa 9am-1pm; Dec. 27-Jan. 11 daily 8am-5pm. English spoken. Private rooms 250-400Sk.) **Slovenská Sporiteľňa,** located in the commercial strip on the way to Dom Služieb, **exchanges currency** and has a 24hr. MasterCard and Visa **ATM** outside. (☎442 2470; www.slsp.sk. Open M-F 8am-noon and 12:30-3:30pm.) A **pharmacy, Lekáreň U Zlatej Sovy,** is on the first floor of Dom Služieb. (☎442 2165. Open M-F 8am-noon and 12:30-4:30pm, Sa 9am-noon. MC/V.) **Internet** is available in the **Rogalo** restaurant to the left of the main entrance of Dom Služieb. (☎442 5043. 1Sk per min. Open daily 9am-10pm.) The **post office** is the squat white building uphill to the left of the train station before the main road. **Poste Restante** is at the first window to the left. **Telephones** are located outside. (☎442 2471. Open M-F 8am-1pm and 2-4pm, Sa 8-10am.) **Postal Code:** 06201.

SLOVAKIA

ACCOMMODATIONS AND FOOD. Uphill from the train station on the way to Dom Služieb, an electronic **InfoPanel** lists current vacancies in the greater Smokovec area. The **TIK** (see above) lists available **private rooms** (250-400Sk). Although **Hotel Palace ❷** won't win any awards for its ambience or off-yellow exterior, its rooms are spacious and comfortable—especially those with baths. To get there, turn left out of the TEŽ station onto the main road, walk past the church, and head uphill past Penzión Gerlach; Palace will be on your right. (☎442 2454. Reception 24hr. Singles 450Sk, with bath 980Sk; doubles 900-1200Sk. MC/V.) To reach the family-run **Penzión Gerlach ❸,** follow the directions to Hotel Palace; Gerlach is on the right, after the church. Central location and fabulously furnished rooms ensure comfort in style. (☎442 2577; www.penziongerlach.sk. English spoken. Breakfast included. Reception daily 10am-6pm. Reserve ahead in high season. Singles 800Sk; doubles 1000-1200Sk; triples 1500-1600Sk. Prices drop 200Sk in low season. Cash only.) Just behind Penzión Gerlach lies the beautifully decorated **Villa Dr Szontagh ❺,** whose angular roof and turret suggest a cottage married to a small fort. Each room has a fridge and a balcony. (☎421 44 33; szontagh@isternet.sk. Singles

1100Sk; doubles 1500Sk. Extra person 300Sk. MC/V.) More budget options lie in the nearby hamlet of **Horný Smokovec,** two TEŽ stops away.

Most restaurants in the area are hard to distinguish, serving up typical Slovak dishes like *bryndza* or cabbage-and-sausage soup. For an excellent blend of Slovak and international cuisine, as well as fast and friendly service, try **Restaurant Tatra ❷,** just above the bus station. The *pastiersky syr* (fried cheese; 110Sk) is scrumptious. (Beer 45Sk. Entrees 90-260Sk. Open daily 11:30am-8:30pm. Cash only.) Popular with tourists and locals alike, **Restaurant Pizzeria La Montanara ❷** offers huge portions of traditional Italian food at appealing prices. From the train station, cross the street and go up a hill to your right for about 40m; the restaurant is behind a row of shops. (☎442 5171. Entrees 90-350Sk. Open daily 11am-10pm. MC/V.) Exceptional quality makes up for the relative priciness at **Restaurant Koliba ❸,** a spacious mountain cabin decorated with rough-hewn wooden tables, timber beams, and wagons. Facing downhill, cross the parking lot to the right of the train station and then cross the tracks. (☎442 2204. Entrees 125-285Sk. Open daily 3pm-midnight. AmEx/MC/V.) Hikers can stock up on supplies at the **Supermarket** in the strip mall just above the train station. (Open M-F 7:45am-5:45pm, Sa-Su noon-6pm. MC/V.) Another supermarket, located in the shopping complex opposite the bus station, carries slightly cheaper items. (Open M-F 8am-6pm, Sa-Su 8am-12:30pm.)

OUTDOOR ACTIVITIES. T-ski, in the funicular station behind **Grand Hotel,** offers everything from ski classes to Dunajec river-rafting (470Sk, min. 5 people), and rents sleds and snowboards. (☎442 3265. Sleds 100Sk per day; skis 290Sk; snowboards 590Sk. Individual classes 990Sk, 2 people 400Sk each, groups of 5 or more 250Sk; guides from 500Sk per day. Open daily 9am-6pm. Cash only.) **Tatrasport,** uphill from the bus lot, rents **mountain bikes.** (☎442 5241; www.tatry.net/tatrasport. 200Sk per 5hr., 299Sk per day. Open daily 8am-6pm. MC/V.)

The **funicular** to **Hrebienok** (1285m) runs to the crossroads of numerous hiking trails. (July 2-Sept. 4 ride up 130Sk, ride down 40Sk, round-trip 150Sk; Sept. 5-July 1 80/30/90Sk. Open daily 7:30am-7pm). The six skiing trails vary in difficulty, and lengths range 100-530m. (Morning 440Sk, afternoon 540Sk, full day 690Sk.) Hike the somewhat uninspiring first leg of the **green trail** behind **Hotel Grand** to reach Hrebienok (45min.). Another 20min. down the green trail lie the **Volopády studeného potoka** (Cold Stream Waterfalls); from here you can take the **yellow trail,** a subdued and tranquil route that meanders along the river to Tatranská Lesná (1¾hr.). The popular **red trail,** the **Tatranska Magistrála,** runs east-to-west along the Slovakian Tatras, through or above most of the resort towns. From Hrebienok, follow the red trail just past **Rainerova Chata** (20min.), then head right on the eastward **blue trail** to descend gradually through towering pines to Tatranská Lomnica (1¾hr.). Or, turn left and take the blue trail westward on an intense hike past **Zbojnícká Chata** (3hr.; ☎09 03 63 80 00; 400Sk, includes breakfast) and up **Sedlo Prielom** (2290m, 1¼hr.), then turn onto the green trail (30min.) and ascend **Sliezsky dom** (1670m, 1½hr.). Alternatively, continue on the red trail to **Zamkovského Chata ❷** (☎442 2636; 1475m, 20min., 260Sk), and then take the fairly relaxed green trail through the **Malá studená dolina** (Little Cold Valley) to **Téryho Chata ❷** (☎442 52 45; 2015m; 2hr.; 280Sk, with breakfast 390Sk). If you stick to the red trail, you will eventually reach **Skalnaté Pleso** and an awaiting *chata;* a cable car leads to great views atop **Lomnický Štít** (2½hr.; p. 643).

Heading away from Rainerova Chata, the red trail eventually reaches **Sliezký dom ❸.** (1670m, 6hr. ☎442 5261. Breakfast and dinner included. 675Sk.) Or, zig-zag farther down through the valley to reach the sharp ascent (5hr.) to **Chata Popradské Pleso ❸,** which is on a stunning lakefront. (☎449 27 65; www.horskyhotel.sk. 370-670Sk; in low season 320-550Sk.) Continue farther on the red trail for a pine-tree-lined descent to **Štrbské Pleso** (1355m, 1hr.). Weary hikers can hop off the wandering *magistrála* on one of the many trails that descend to the resort towns below. From **Sliezský dom,** the green trail leads to **Tatranská Polianka** (2hr.). Another hour down the red trail, the yellow trail branches off and descends to **Vyšné Hágy** (2hr.); both towns are on the TEŽ. A difficult blue path branches from the *magistrála* 20min. west of Hrebienok to one of the highest peaks, **Slavkovský Štít.** (2452m, 8hr. round-trip from Hrebienok. Don't attempt without a full day and good weather.)

ŠTRBSKÉ PLESO

Hotels, ski jumps, and souvenir stands clutter calm **Štrbské Pleso** (SHTERB-skay PLEH-soh; Štrbské Lake), which offers some of the most cherished hikes and views in the Tatras. Peaceful trails reveal Štrbské Pleso's natural beauty among awe-inspiring mountains. In summer and winter, a lift carries visitors to **Chata pod Soliskom** (1840m), which overlooks the lake and the valleys that spread behind Štrbské Pleso. (☎449 2221. 150Sk, 90Sk for students; round-trip 230Sk/120Sk. Open daily 8:30am-4pm; last lift up 3:30pm.) To reach the lift, take the road from the train station and follow the signs, or take the yellow trail instead.

Two magnificent day hikes loop out from Štrbské Pleso. Both can get cold, so bring layers as well as food and water. From the **Informačné Stredisko Tanapu** (Information Center; across from TEŽ station) and the bus station, walk past the souvenir lot and head left at the junction. Continue uphill on the challenging **yellow trail** and along **Mlynická dolina** past several enchanting mountain lakes and the dramatic **Vodopády Skok** waterfalls. The path (6-7hr.) involves some strenuous ascents, including mounting **Bystré Sedlo** (2314m) and **Veľké Solisko** (2412m). At the end of the yellow trail, turn left onto the red trail to complete the loop and return to Štrbské Pleso (30min.). The scenery justifies the effort.

The second, even more difficult hike takes you to the top of **Rysy** (2499m), on the Polish-Slovak border; this is Poland's highest peak and the highest Tatra scalable without a guide. From Štrbské Pleso, follow the *magistrála* (red trail) and experience the awe-inspiring views and imposing grandeur of the Tatran peaks. The **green trail** branches off the *magistrála* and rolls by the **Hincov potok** (stream) to an intersection (45min.) where you can continue up on the **blue trail** or take a 2min. detour to the hotel **Chata Popradské Pleso** (see above). After 40min. on the blue trail, take the red branch to tackle Rysy (3-4hr. round-trip). Along the way, you can stop at **Chata pod Rysmi ❶** (2250m), where hot soups (40Sk) are available. (☎442 2314. Rooms 250Sk.) From the start of the red branch, backtracking along the blue then green trails to Štrbské Pleso should take 1½-2hr. Allow 8-9hr. for the round trip. This hike is for advanced hikers and should be attempted in good weather only. (☎524 467 676; www.tatry.sk.)

From the Chata Popradské Pleso, head south 30min. on the yellow trail to the **Symbolic Cemetery** (Symbolický cintorín; 1525m). Built between 1936 and 1940 by painter Otakar Štafl, the field of wooden crosses, metal plaques, and broken propeller blades serves as a memorial to the hikers who have died attempting the great Tatras. (Cemetery open July-Oct. daily dawn-dusk.) The trail ends at a paved blue path where the weary descend to reach the Popradské Pleso TEŽ stop (45min.). Those hardy souls looking to hike back to Štrbské Pleso will be rewarded with striking views from the steep descent. The *magistrála* continues from the *chata* for over 5hr. along scenic ridges to **Hrebienok.**

This stunning region is also popular among skiers of all abilities; the slopes of Štrbské Pleso boast excellent ridges and snow. The six downhill trails range 80-2300m. (Morning 400Sk, afternoon 500Sk, full day 650Sk. Open Dec. 15-March 15.) Many other slopes are accessible from this region, including a fairly gentle ski from Chata Solisko on Predné Solisko, where a lift awaits. For a more challenging ride, take a cable car from the base and ski down a red trail.

Most people choose to stay in **Starý Smokovec** or **Tatranská Lomnica,** as there aren't many places available in Štrbské Pleso. Those intent on staying out late on the trails can find a bed at **Hotel Toliar ❺**, on the first floor of the shopping center across from the train station. (☎449 2690. English spoken. Breakfast, swimming pool, and sauna included. Reception 24hr. Check-out 10am. 1 single 1180Sk; doubles 1600Sk; triples 2000Sk. MC/V.) Cheap beds without much class can be found at **Ubytovňa ŠKP ❸**, on the far end of the main parking lot off the train station. (☎923 76. 11 beds; 210Sk. Call ahead.) A few **private rooms** are available; watch for *Zimmer frei* signs (300-450Sk). Before starting a hike, stock up at the **grocery store** across from the train station. (Open daily 7am-7pm. MC/V.)

Take the TEŽ **train** (30min. from Starý Smokovec, 1-2 per hr., 20Sk). The **tourist office** across the from the stations is open M-Sa 8-11:30am and noon-4pm; hours are shorter in low season. **Internet access** is available in the lobby of Hotel Taliar. Open daily 8am-9pm. 30Sk per 30min.

TATRANSKÁ LOMNICA

Though often dwarfed by the more lively and central Starý Smokovec, Tatranská Lomnica (TA-tran-ska LOM-nee-tsa) has a charming serenity. The town is little more than a scattering of buildings that dot the perimeter of a lush park. From Penzión Bělín (see below), take the road uphill and follow the signs to the Kabinkowá Lanová Dráha lift (10min.), which rides up to the glacial lake of **Skalnaté Pleso.** (1751m. July 3-Sept. ride up 240Sk, ride down 190Sk, round-trip 390Sk. Open daily 8:30am-6pm. Last ascent 4pm.) From the lake, a large gondola ascends to the summit of **Lomnický Štít** (2632m), the second highest peak in the Tatras. The gondola runs only once every 50min., and tickets for the unparalleled view sell out fast, so buy them a few hours in advance at the base (390-550Sk). From **Skalnaté Pleso** there is also a four-person chairlift to **Lomnické Sedlo.** (Open daily 8:30am-6pm, last ascent at 5:45pm. 150Sk). Alternatively, hike up to **Skalnaté Pleso** via the green trail (1½hr. up, 1¼hr. down). Much of the green trail runs through areas that were devastated by the 2004 storms.

In the winter, you can purchase a day ticket (690Sk) in **Skalnaté Pleso** to **ski** the excellent trails down to Tatranská Lomnica. On a clear day, the peak offers a staggering view of the mountains and valleys and makes for a fabulous picnic spot. At **Skalnaté Pleso,** the low-slung wooden *chata* (☎446 7075, 250Sk) is a great spot to begin or end an adventure on the **Tatranská magistrála,** although the hiking is generally better and the views more memorable from Starý Smokovec or Štrbské Pleso. The *magistrála* (red trail), heading from Skalnaté Pleso toward **Lomnická vyhliadka,** a great place to admire the view

DECIPHERING THE TRAILS

A splatter of red. A dash of green. A yellow line criss-crossing the page. Standing in the middle of nowhere, I scrutinized my map and despaired. This looked less like something that would lead me off the trail before nightfall than a work of abstract art. I kept walking. About 500m ahead, I gave a sigh of relief: there was a tiny green mark painted faintly on a tree. I studied the map again—at least I was going the right way.

Trail signals in the Tatras are not as easy as they seem. A yellow line signals a short path connecting major trails. Blue means long—and generally easier—trails that connect sights, like caves or lakes. Green marks connect larger trails but, unlike yellow, tend to lead to famous natural sights or historical attractions. A red mark means that the trail will be challenging and steep, with ledges and slippery slopes.

Keep your eyes peeled, as the marks are often sporadic. The standard trail mark shows the color (red, green, yellow, or blue), bordered by two white stripes. A colored arrow indicates that the trail forks or looks uncertain, and a colored square with the top corner missing means that you have reached a tourist attraction. A white square or circle with a colored square inside means that the trail has been completed.

There you go. Study up, and good luck! *—Calum Docherty*

(1524m, 50min.), and then to **Zamkovského Chata** (1¼hr.), is challenging, but remarkable mountaintop views reward your efforts (see **Hiking: Starý Smokovec,** p. 641). The **blue trail** leads to a gentler hike; follow it from **InfoPanel,** at the center of Tatranská Lomnica, to **Vodopády studeného potoka** (cold stream waterfalls; 1¾hr.), then take the yellow trail to Tatranská Lesná (1hr.) or double back along the blue trail (1¼hr.). The terrain here is flat enough to bike.

Many of the hotels and pensions in Tatranská Lomnica are cheaper than what you would find in Starý Smokovec, and you can also book **private rooms** or look for *Zimmer frei* signs. **Penzión Bělín ❶,** in the center of town, is cheap and comfortable. From the InfoPanel above, take the path across the street into the park. Take the first left and then a right onto the street ahead. Penzión Bělín is the large mustard-colored building to the right. (☎446 7778; belin@tatry.sk. Reception daily 7am-9pm. Check-out 10am. July-Aug. 2- and 4-person rooms 280Sk. MC/V.) Dining options in town are limited. **Stará Mama ❷,** behind the train station, is a bargain that's worth visiting for the decor alone—the bar is designed to look like the exterior of a folk house. (☎446 7713. English menu. Entrees 56-334Sk. Open daily 9am-12am. AmEx/MC/V.) **Grill-Pub ❷,** above the train station, has Slovak meat dishes and vegetarian options. (English menu. Entrees 50-220Sk. Open M-Su 11am-10pm. Cash only.) Stock up on snacks at **Supermarket Sintra,** just down the hill behind the train station. (Open M-F 7:45am-6pm, Sa 7:45am-3pm, Su 8am-1pm. MC/V.)

To get to Tatranská Lomnica, take the TEŽ **train** (15min. from Poprad, 16 per day, 30Sk). The bus station is 50m to the right, when facing the street from the train station. Uphill from the station, behind Uni Banka, get help from the English-speaking staff at **Tatranská Informačná Kancelária.** (☎446 8119; www.tatry.sk. Open July-Aug. M-F 8am-6pm, Sa-Su 9am-2pm; Sept.-June M-F 9am-4pm.) The **InfoPoint,** just outside the exit to the right of the train station, has a map of the town and a list of accommodations. The **Sports Shop,** in the town center, sells last-minute hiking supplies. They also rent bikes. (100Sk per hr., 500Sk per day. Open daily 7am-6pm. MC/V.) **Internet** is available at **Townson Travel,** in **Hotel Slalom** near the center of town. (1Sk per min. Open M-F 9am-6pm.)

SLOVENSKÝ RAJ NATIONAL PARK ☎(0)58

The peaks of Slovenský Raj National Park, southeast of the Low Tatras, don't match their neighbors in height, but they make up for it in beauty. Here, dazzling forests, dramatic waterfalls, and deep limestone ravines earns these mountains their title: Slovenský Raj means "Slovak Paradise." Still, the area is not very touristed, and life moves slowly in the tiny mountain hamlets even as hikers and skiers speed through nearby trails.

TRANSPORTATION. Reaching the park is difficult. Nestled by the shores of Lake Palčmanská Maša, **Dedinky** (pop. 400) is the largest town on Slovenský Raj's southern border. Its sublime location makes it a favorite among hikers. Catch a train from Poprad to Spisska Nová Ves (30min., 7-10 per day, 22Sk) where buses head to Dedinky (1¼-1½hr., 8-9 per day, 71Sk). Alternatively, go straight from Poprad by catching the **bus** toward Rožňava (1hr., 4 per day, 47Sk). The bus stops first at the Dobšinská ľadová jaskyňa, where you can catch a train to Dedinky (25min., 7-8 per day, 15Sk), then at the village, and finally at a junction 2km south of Dedinky. From here, follow the yellow trail that branches off to the right about 150m from the bus stop. When you reach the road at the bottom, turn left, cross the dam, and walk left toward the visible lakeside town (25min.).

ORIENTATION AND PRACTICAL INFORMATION. The bus station is in the middle of Dedinky, while the train station is 15min. away, on the far side of the lake by the dam. The best trail guide is the **VKÚ map #4.** Pick up a copy at the

Mlynky tourist office or Dedinky grocery store (125Sk). To find the **Sedačková Lanová Dráha tourist office,** head to **Mlynky,** a town neighboring Dedinky. From the train station, cross the dam, follow the road, and veer left as it descends to Mlynky. Signs point to **Penzión Salamander** at the bottom of the hill to the right (5-10min.). In Salamander's reception room, the tourist office staff sells VKÚ #4 (120Sk), has info on 200-400Sk **private rooms,** and rents **bikes** for 40Sk per hour. (☎449 3545. Open 24hr. AmEx/MC/V.) Bus and train schedules available at the reception of Hotel Priehrada. Behind Hotel Priehrada, a **chairlift** runs to Chata Geravy. (☎058 798 1212. 1 per hr. May-Aug M 9am-3pm, Tu-Su 9am-4pm; Sept.-Oct. daily 9am-2pm and 2:45pm. 90Sk, round-trip 150Sk.) **Tókóly Tours,** 200m from Hotel Priehrada, rents **boats** and **bikes.** (☎90 55 92 30 11. Rowboats, paddleboats, canoes, or bikes 100Sk per hr. Open daily July-Aug. 9am-6pm; June 15-30 and Sept. 1-15 1-6pm.) There are **telephones** in the entryway of Hotel Priehrada (international calls require payment by coin). Dedinky's **post office** is behind the wooden tower near the bus stop. (☎05 87 98 11 34. **Poste Restante.** Open M-F 8-10am, 12:30-1:30pm, and 2-3pm.) **Postal Code:** 04973.

ACCOMMODATIONS AND FOOD. Book at least two weeks ahead in January, July, and August, or plan on getting a **private room** (200-400Sk). They rarely fill up, and they're often the cheapest and best options. Look for *privat*, *ubytowanie*, or *Zimmer frei* signs. **Penzión Pastierňa ❷,** Dedinky 42, offers spacious rooms furnished with unvarnished pine floors, beds, and tables, all with private baths. From the bus station, go uphill past the grocery store, and straight to the end of the street. (☎798 1175. Reception daily 8:30am-9:30pm. Check-out 11am. 2- to 4-bed rooms 400Sk. Tourist tax 15Sk. Cash only.) **Hotel Priehrada ❷,** Dedinky 107, rents older rooms with new, well-kept baths. It also runs a **campground** by the lake. (☎798 1212; fax 788 1682. Reception 24hr. Strict check-in 2pm. Check-out 10am. Singles 400Sk; doubles 930Sk. Camping 60Sk per person, 40Sk per tent, 50Sk per car. Tax 15Sk. MC/V.) Or, look for lodging in nearby **Mlynky.** From the Dedinky train stop, cross the dam and turn right. When the road splits, veer left toward Mlynky. **Turisticka Ubytovna NITA ❶,** Pakmanslá Maša 295, 50m behind Penzión Salamander, has simple but comfortable rooms and a pleasant staff. (☎/fax 449 3279. Shared baths. Check-in 2pm. Check-out 10am. Call ahead. 2- to 4-bed rooms 200Sk, with breakfast and dinner 350Sk. Cash only.) Restaurants are few here and most hikers prefer to stock up on trail food before heading off. In Dedinky, the restaurant in **Penzión Pastierňa ❷** serves Slovak standards, including fresh lake *pstruh* (trout; 160Sk) and vegetarian options. (Entrees 60-180Sk. Open daily 8am-11:30pm. Cash only.) Or, stock up on *potraviny* (groceries) across from the bus station. (☎798 1121. Open M-F 8am-noon and 2-6pm, Sa 7-11am. Cash only.)

SIGHTS. Discovered in 1870, the **Dobšinská Ice Caves** (Dobšinská ľadová jaskyňa) contain over 110,000 cubic meters of beautifully held frozen water from as long ago as the last Ice Age. The caves hide awe-inspiring sights: hall after hall of frozen columns, gigantic ice walls, and hardened waterfalls. Dress in layers—the cave temperature hovers between -6°C and +0.5°C year-round. To get here from Dedinky, take the 10am **bus** from the Dedinky bus stop (20min., 20Sk) to the ice-cave parking lot; from there the blue trail leads up the steep forest incline to the cave, 15-20min. away. Or take one of seven daily trains (first 5:40am, last 6:40pm) toward Červana Skala for two stops. (15min., 15Sk.) Follow the road leading from the station to the main road. Turn left, and then right after you pass the restaurant; the parking lot of Restaurant Ľadová Jaskyňa is up ahead. (☎788 1470; www.ssj.sk. Open July-Aug. 9am-4pm, entrance every hr.; May 15-June and Sept. 1-15 9:30am-2pm, entrance every 1½hr. by guided tour only; 40-person min. for tour in English. Closed M. 180Sk, students with ISIC 160Sk.)

HIKING. Camping and fires are prohibited in all Slovak national parks except at registered campsites and some *chaty*. Tourists must stick to the clearly marked trails. Having a map is advisable, as cascade trails are one-way—you can go up, but not down them. All cascade trails are closed from November to June except to those accompanied by certified guides. Guides can be hired from nearby resorts, *chaty*, and travel agencies (3000-4000Sk). **Biele vody** (White Waters; 45min.-1¾hr.) is a moderately difficult cascade hike up a series of rapids. Watch your footing on slippery and loose rocks, ladders, and bridges. From the parking lot to the right of Hotel Priehrada, take the red trail to **Mlynky** (25min.) and then join the relaxed blue cross-country ski trail around **Biele vody** (788m; 1-2hr.). Alternatively, from Mlynky take the moderately difficult blue trail up Chata Geravy (1027m; 2hr.). Although the route up can leave you tired, you will be able to take in the beautiful sights. At the top, the **Chata Geravy** or a chairlift await the weary, while the green trail leads the energetic back down (50min.). **Veľký sokol** (Big Falcon; 6½hr.) is a demanding hike into the heart of Slovenský Raj and up its deepest gorge. Follow the road west from Stratená (1hr.) or east from the ice caves (with your back to the caves, take a right; 30min.). At the U-bend, follow the green trail until it meets the road (30min.) and then take the red path. After another 15min., cross the parking lot and take the yellow trail through the rocky Veľký sokol cascade, with magnificent views of the surrounding gorge, up to **Glacka Cesta** (971m; 2½hr.). From the top, a right on the red path returns to **Chata Geravy** (1hr.) and the chairlift or the green trail (50min.) down to **Dedinky.** An even more intense trek through Slovenský Raj, **Sokolia dolina** (Falcon Valley; 7hr.) mounts the highest of the park's waterfalls (70m). From Chata Geravy, take the red trail to the green trail and turn right (1¼hr.). After 20-30min., hang a right onto the yellow trail at **Pod Bykárkou.** Continue until you meet the green trail (1hr.) and head left toward Sokolia and Kamenná dolina. At Sokolia dolina (45min-1hr.) begin the arduous ascent up to the cascade (2hr.), from which you will have a dazzling view of the waterfall. When you reach the bottom, go left on the green trail to **Pod Bykárkou** (20min.) and retrace your steps back to Chata Geravy (1¾hr.). Alternatively, begin another tough ascent by turning right onto the green trail, taking it to the yellow trail, and then continuing on the yellow trail all the way to **Glac** (20-30min.). From there, make a left onto the blue path and head to **Malá Polana** (10min.). Make sure to then go right and follow the red trail to **Sokol** and **Diablova Polka** (1½hr.), not Geravy. When you reach the parking lot, head onto the yellow trail to Velky sokol (2-2½hr.; see above).

SPIŠ

For centuries, Spiš was an autonomous province of Hungary. It was later absorbed into Czechoslovakia and, after the Velvet Divorce in 1993, into Slovakia. Its eastern flatlands are filled with quiet towns where time moves at about the same pace as farmers walking their cows. The medieval charm of Kežmarok, Levoča, and the sprawling ruins of Spišský Castle recall the region's rich past.

KEŽMAROK ☎(0)52

The town of Kežmarok (KEZH-ma-rok; pop. 18,000) boasts colorful buildings, friendly locals, a storied history, and a vibrant atmosphere. From Hlavné nám., go down Hviezdoslavova to reach the **Wooden Articulated Church** (Drevený Artikulárny Kostol). Built in 1717, the church is shaped like a Greek cross in accordance with laws mandating that Protestants build their churches from wood, outside town walls, without solid foundations, and without towers or bells. Northern European Protestants sent money and craftsmen to help construct the church, and it was completed in a mere three months. The porthole-shaped windows and the numbers on the pews still bear the marks of the Swedish sailors who helped build them. Adjacent to the Wooden Articulated Church is a light-green-and-red colossus, the **New Evangelical Church** (Nový Evanjelický Kostol), which eclectically blends Byzantine, Middle Eastern, Renaissance, and Romanesque styles. (Both open June-Sept. daily 9am-noon and 2-5pm; Oct.-May Tu and F 10am-noon and 2-4pm. Buy tickets for both at the Wooden Church, 40Sk.) Down Hlavné nám. is the impressive **Kežmarok Castle,** Hradné nám. 42. Renaissance decor adorns a stocky Gothic frame. The courtyard contains the foundations of a 13th-century Saxon church. (☎452 2618; www.muzeum.sk. Open Tu-F 9am-4pm, Sa-Su 9am-noon and 1pm-4pm. 1hr. tours every 30min-1hr. 70Sk, students 30Sk. English pamphlet 8Sk, guidebook 20-35Sk. Cash only.) During the second weekend in July, the **European Folk Arts Festival** brings craftsmen from all over Europe to present their work in glass, gold, iron, wood, and wool.

The tourist office (see below) books **private rooms** (250Sk). Locals and tourists pack the popular **Cellar Classica Restaurant ❶,** Hviezdoslavova 2, to enjoy cheap drinks (20-45Sk) and tasty Italian food. (☎52 36 93. Entrees 79-159Sk. Open daily 11am-11pm. Cash only.) There's a **grocery store** at Alexandra 35. (Open M-Sa 7am-10pm, Su 8am-10pm. Cash only.)

Trains (☎452 3298) run to Poprad (25min., 12 per day, 20Sk) from the hilltop at the junction of Toporcerova and Michalská. **Buses** leave from under canopies behind the Lidl supermarket, to the right when exiting train station; destinations include Banská Bystrica (7-10 per day, 200Sk), Levoča (1hr., 6-8 per day, 40Sk), and Poprad (20-30min., every 10-40min., 22Sk). Buy bus tickets on board and train tickets at the station. To reach the center, take the pedestrian bridge to the left of the train station and follow **Alexandra** to **Hlavné námestie.** The tourist office, **Kežmarská Informačná,** Hlavné nám. 46, in an alcove, offers tips, arranges **private rooms,** and sells **maps** for 100-130Sk. (☎524 524 047; www.kezmarok.net. Open M-F 8:30am-5pm, Sa 9am-1pm; also July-Aug. Su 9am-1pm.) **Slovenská Sporteľňa,** Baštová 28, **exchanges currency.** (☎45 27 87 92 30; www.slsp.sk. Open July-Aug. M-F 8:30am-5pm, Sa-Su 9am-1pm; Sept. June M-F 8:30am-5pm, Sa 9am-1pm.) A MasterCard and Visa **ATM** is outside on the side of the building. The **post office,** Mučeníkov 2, where Hviezdoslavova becomes Mučeníkov, is past the hospital. (☎452 2021. Open M-F 8am-6pm, Sa 8-10am.) **Postal Code:** 06001.

SLOVAKIA

LEVOČA ☎(0)53

Levoča (LEH-vo-cha; pop. 14,000), the current administrative hub and former capital of Spiš, gained fame through the 16th-century "Law of Storage," which forced merchants to remain in town until they sold all their goods. The new wealth fostered a movement to form craft guilds led by Master Pavol, a renowned sculptor responsible for many of the detailed works that adorn Spiš's churches. With its rich artistic legacy, cobblestone-paved Old Town, and nearly intact medieval walls, Levoča is perfect for those seeking some quiet R&R. During the first weekend in July, the Festival of Marian Devotion attracts countless pilgrims.

TRANSPORTATION AND PRACTICAL INFORMATION. The best way to reach Levoča is by bus. **Buses** run to: Košice (2hr., 8 per day, 128Sk); **Poprad** (50min., 18 per day, 40Sk); Prešov (1hr., 5-9 per day, 90Sk); Starý Smokovec (1-1½hr.; M-F 4 per day, Sa-Su 1-3 per day; 55Sk). To reach the center, take a right out of the station, go straight through the intersection, and continue uphill as the road curves around a small park. Follow Nová up to the main square, nám. Majstra Pavla (15min.). To catch the infrequent local bus, turn left out of the train station and follow the road to the red-and-white **Zastavka** sign.

The **tourist office,** nám. Majstra Pavla 58, has **maps** of the city center (free-32Sk) and recommends **private rooms,** which start at 250Sk. (☎161 88; www.levoca.sk.

Open May-Sept. M-F 9am-5pm, Sa 10am-4pm, Su 11am-3pm; Oct.-Apr. M-F 9am-4:30pm.) **Slovenská Sporiteľňa,** nám. Majstra Pavla 56, gives MasterCard and Visa **cash advances** (50Sk min., 1000Sk max.) for 1% commission. A MasterCard and Visa **ATM** is outside. (☎451 0533. Open M and F 8am-3:30pm, Tu and Th 8am-3pm, W 8am-4:30pm.) The **pharmacy, Lekáren K Hadovi,** nám. Majstra Pavla 13, posts the addresses and hours of other pharmacies. (☎451 2456. Open M-F 7:30am-5pm, Sa 8am-noon.) At **Cafe,** nám. Majstra Pavla 38, Internet passes are valid for up to 15-30 days. (36Sk per hr., Sa-Su 30Sk per hr. Open daily 10am-10pm.) The **post office** is at nám. Majstra Pavla 42. (☎451 2489. **Poste Restante** at any window. Open M-F 8am-noon and 1-5pm, Sa 8-10:30am.) **Postal Code:** 05401.

ACCOMMODATIONS AND FOOD. Though choices are limited, finding accommodations is usually not difficult. Book well in advance for the Festival of Marian Devotion; your best bet is to stay in Poprad and travel to Levoča. Those looking to spend the night can inquire at the tourist office (see above), where the English-speaking staff can help book lodging at **pensions** (350-800Sk) and nearby **campsites.** Check out **Klub turistov a horolezcov ❶,** Vysoká 4 (☎09 03 68 55 52), a minute away from the main square. This pension, run by an extremely pleasant, helpful couple, has a mountain-lodge feel. The rooms are very clean and comfortable, and the guest-book—full of signatures of guests who intended to stay for a day and ended up staying much longer—speaks for itself. (Call ahead. Access to kitchen and laundry. Dorms 220Sk per person.) The family-run **Penzión Šuňavský ❷,** Nová 59, is in the Old Town and has an idyllic garden. Rooms are clean and comfortable. Follow the directions to the town center; the pension is on the left side of Nová. (☎451 4526. Breakfast 150Sk. Laundry 200Sk. Call 2 days ahead in August. 3- to 4-person dorms with shared baths 400Sk per person; spacious 2-person apartments 1400Sk.)The more luxurious **Penzión U Leva ❹,** nám. Majstra Pavla 24, is in the heart of the main square and offers elegant rooms with TVs, kitchenettes, and access to a fitness center and sauna. The apartments are well-appointed, offering kitchens, satellite TVs, and large baths. (☎450 2311; www.uleva.szm.sk. Reception 24hr. Singles 1,250Sk; doubles 1800Sk. Apartments for 1 person 2300Sk, for 2 people 2800Sk. Tourist tax 15Sk.)

Billa Supermarket, next to the bus station, has a huge selection of food and drinks. (Open M-F 7am-9pm, Sa-Su 8am-8pm. MC/V.) For restaurant dining, **U3 Apoštolov ❷,** nám. Majstra Pavla 11, serves large portions of traditional and vegetarian Slovak dishes. Patrons can relax on a beautiful terrace or find refuge from the sun indoors. (☎450 2311. Entrees 59-220Sk. English menu. Open daily 9am-10pm. AmEx/MC/V.) Popular with locals for special occasions, **Restaurant Janusa ❶,** Kláštorská 22, specializes in *pierogi* (73-79Sk) and serves other traditional Slovak dishes. (☎09 66 45 92; www.slovakiaguide.sk. Entrees 70-138Sk. Open daily 10am-10pm. Sa-Su reservations only.)

SIGHTS. Levoča's star attraction is the 14th-century **St. Jacob's Church** (Chrám sv. Jakuba), home to the world's tallest Gothic altar (a staggering 18.62m), beautifully carved by Master Pavol between 1507 and 1517. Almost as dramatic as the altar are the frescoes on the left wall, depicting the seven heavenly virtues and the seven deadly sins. (☎09 07 52 16 73. Buy tickets across the street. Entrance every 30min.; Sept.-June every hr. after 1pm. Open July-Aug. M 11am-5pm, Tu-Sa 9am-1pm and 2-5pm, Su 1-5pm; Sept.-June Tu-Sa 9am-4pm. 60Sk, students 30Sk. Dress appropriately. Brief English-language informational tape 5Sk.) Three branches of the **Spišské Museum** dot nám. Majstra Pavla. In addition to exhibits, the museums feature a worthwhile video about Levoča's history (20min., available in English). **Dom Majstra Pavla,** nám. Majstra Pavla 20 (☎451 2824), details Pavol's life and work; displays include high-quality facsimiles of his greatest pieces. The most interesting branch is housed in the beautiful **Town Hall** *(radnica)* and provides a candid look at Levoča's past, displaying everything from regal chandeliers to basic torture instruments. Enter the museum through the stairs to the right of the town hall's main entrance. Next to the museum entrance stands the **Cage of Shame** (Klietka Hanby), in which accused "ladies of the night" were humiliated in the 16th century. The Spišské Museum's third branch (☎451 2786), at #40, has a small collection of portraits, ceramics, and statues. (www.snm.sk. All open daily May-Oct. 9am-5pm; Nov.-Apr. 8am-4pm. 60Sk, students 30Sk. English brochure 120-129Sk.)

SPIŠSKÉ PODHRADIE AND ŽEHRA

If you visit only one Slovak castle, make it **Spišské Castle** (Spišský hrad) in Spišské Podhradie (SPISH-skay POD-hra-dyeh). The site has been home to fortified settlements for two millennia; the ruins crowning the hilltop today are remnants of a Hungarian castle that was claimed as national property in 1945, long after a 1780 fire left it deserted. The view of the surrounding villages from the castle is well worth the climb, and its free **museum** exhibits interesting war relics like musket balls, cannons, suits of armor, and grisly torture devices. (☎454 1336. Entrance with an English-speaking guide every 30min., min. 15 people. Open daily May-Oct. 9am-6pm. 120Sk, students 60Sk.)

West of town stands the region's religious capital, **Spišské Kapitula.** Facing the bus station departure board, turn right, walk through the gardens, and cross the river. The winding road eventually leads to the Cathedral (15min.). Completely encircled by medieval walls, the 13th-century monastery contains a seminary, bishop's quarters, and **St. Martin's Cathedral** (Katedrála sv. Martina). More impressive for its historical and cultural significance—like hosting the Pope in 1995—than for its aesthetics, the Cathedral weathered a sacking by invading Tatars in 1241 and a stint as a police academy under Soviet rule. Get tickets at the souvenir shop in the small bell tower, 50m from the church. (☎09 08 38 84 11; www.spiskap.sk. Tours every hr. on the hr. Open May-Sept. M-Sa 9am-4pm, Su 9-11am and 1pm-4pm; Oct.-Apr. M-Sa 9am-4:30pm, Su 11am and 1-3pm. 30Sk, students 20Sk. Knees and shoulders must be covered.) To escape the beer gardens and touristy restaurants, head along the road past the monastery for 10-15min. to **Spišský Salaš ❷,** Levočská cesta 11. This wooden cottage, serving traditional Slovak foods, is a local favorite. Enjoy great views of the surrounding countryside and the dubious English translations on the menu: do you dare to try the "Domestic Slaughter" (a lot of pork; 150Sk)? (☎454 1202. Beer 30Sk. Entrees 69-250Sk. Open daily 10am-9pm. MC/V.)

A long, tranquil walk from the castle brings you to the ancient village of **Žehra,** home of the **Church of the Holy Spirit.** Built in a late Romanesque/early Gothic style, it's not to be missed if you can manage the two hour trek to its doors. Though faded and in need of restoration, its UNESCO-protected murals have made it famous; they were painted in five stages during the 12th to 15th centuries and uncovered in the 1950s. From the castle entrance, descend to the closer parking lot and take the yellow trail—it is only recognizable by its closely cut grass. Continue past the limestone crags and bear left into the valley below. The church's brown, onion-domed tower is easy to spot. (Open M-F 9:30-11:30am with entrance every 30min. and 1-4pm with entrance every hr.; Su 2-4pm. 50Sk, students 30Sk. Call Pani Orlovska (☎448 5027) to let you in if the church is closed.)

Buses come from Levoča (30min., 1 per hr., 22Sk), Poprad (1hr., 9 per day, 53Sk), and Prešov (1½hr., 1 per hr. until 6pm, 57Sk). Many uphill paths lead to the castle (check the info map at the castle end of the main square). Or, turn left from the bus departure board and head through the tall grass to the main square. Turn left onto the bridge leading out of town, go immediately left, then right up the narrow road that passes the cemetery. For an easier dirt path up to the castle, follow previous directions, but continue straight after the bridge and take the first left.

ŠARIŠ

More than just the home of Slovakia's most popular beer, Šariš is a region of natural wonder and cosmopolitan flair. Hidden away in the green hills of the eastern Slovak Republic, Šariš was long a buffer against Turkish invasions before spending the last century keeping mostly to itself. Šariš's cities tend to have lovely Old Towns surrounded by unattractive industrial sprawl.

KOŠICE ☎(0)55

Lying only 20km north of Hungary, Košice (KO-shih-tseh; pop. 236,000) is the Slovak Republic's second-largest city. Košice is the place to visit if you want to see a typical Slovak Old Town without giving up the amenities and nightlife of a major city. Outside the Old Town, however, communist-era concrete blocks mar the area's otherwise beautiful landscape.

TRANSPORTATION

Trains: Predstaničné nám. (☎181 88). To: **Banská Bystrica** (4hr., 292Sk); **Bratislava** (6hr., 13 per day, 518Sk); **Poprad** (1¼hr., 10 per day, 154Sk); **Prešov** (45min., 10 per day, 42Sk); **Rožňava** (1hr., 12 per day, 112Sk); **Budapest, HUN** (4hr., 3 per day, 662Sk); **Kraków, POL** (6-7hr., 3 per day, 756Sk); **Prague, CZR** (10hr., 4 per day, 1100Sk).

Buses: (☎625 1445), to the left of the train station. Destinations include: **Banská Bystrica** (4½hr., 7 per day, 280Sk); **Bardejov** (2hr., 12-20 per day, 100Sk); **Bratislava** (7-12hr., 20 per day, 500Sk); **Levoča** (2hr., 10 per day, 120Sk); **Poprad** (2½hr., 5 per day, 150Sk); **Prešov** (30min., 30 per day, 47Sk); **Rožňava** (1¼hr., 37 per day, 100Sk); **Prague, CZR** (10-12hr., 18 per day, 300-800Sk).

Public Transportation: Trams and **buses** cross the city and suburbs 5:30am-11pm. Night buses run every hr. midnight-3:50am. Tickets from kiosks and yellow boxes at bus stops (12Sk) or from driver (14Sk). Extra charge for large backpacks (6Sk). Punch ticket upon boarding. Fines for riding ticketless up to 1000Sk.

Taxis: Taxis wait on almost every corner. **Classic Taxi** (☎622 2244), **CTC** (☎633 33 33), and **Radio Taxi** (☎163 33).

SLOVAKIA

ORIENTATION AND PRACTICAL INFORMATION

To get to the heart of Košice's **Staré Mesto** (Old Town), exit the train station and follow the "Centrum" signs across the park. Walk down **Mlynská** to reach the main square, **Hlavná námestie** (10min.).

Tourist Office: Informačna Centrum Mesta Košice, Hlavná 59 (☎625 8888; www.kosice.sk/icmk). Provides helpful information on accommodations and cultural attractions and sells **maps** (free-104Sk.) Open M-F 9am-6pm, Sa 9am-1pm, Su 1-5pm.

Currency Exchange: VÚB branches are everywhere; the one at Hlavná 8 (☎622 6250) gives MC/V **cash advances** and cashes **traveler's checks** for 1% commission and a hefty 200Sk min. Also **exchanges currency,** but *kantory* along Hlavná generally give better rates. Open M-F 8am-6pm, Sa 9am-noon. There are many 24hr. MC/V **ATMs** along Hlavná.

Luggage Storage: At the train station. 25-35Sk per day. Open 3:30am-12:30am. Small 24hr. lockers 5Sk.

English-Language Bookstore: Glossa, Hlavná 97 (☎623 3676), through the arch and up the stairs. Small selection of popular and classic English-language literature (100-600Sk). Open M-F 9am-6pm, Sa 10am-1pm.

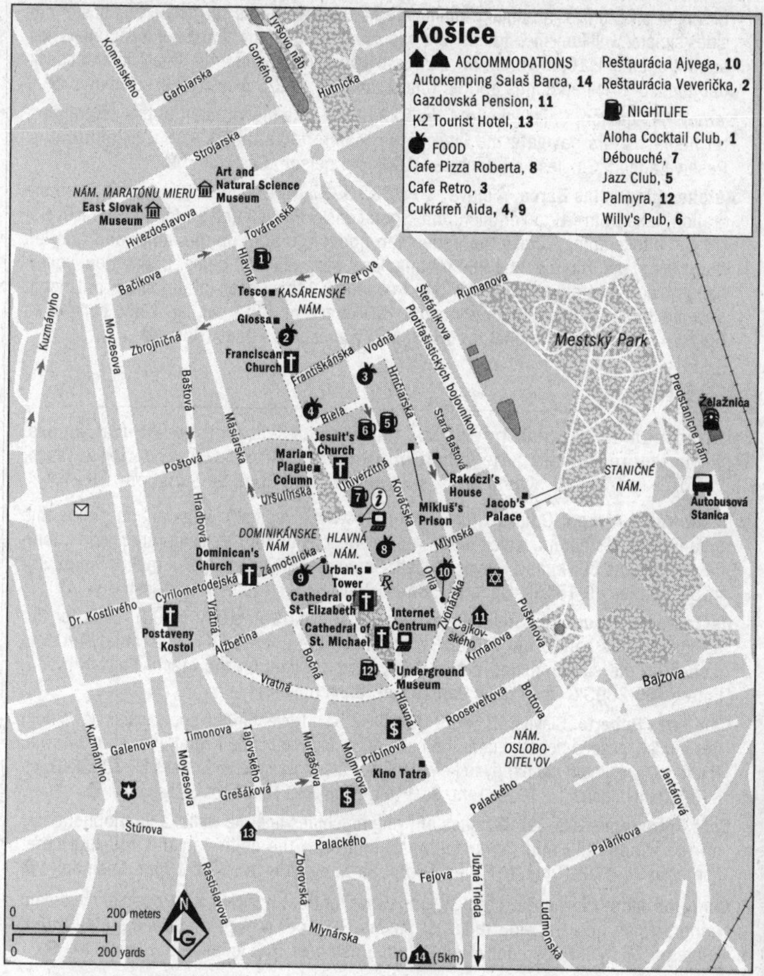

Pharmacy: Lekáreň Pri Dóme, Mlynská 1. Open M-F 8am-6pm, Sa 9am-noon. MC/V.

Telephones: Along Hlavná and outside the post office (see below).

Internet: At the central **tourist office** (see above), 10Sk per 20min. Or, try **Internet Centrum,** Hlavná 9 (www.kosez.sk). 50Sk per hr. Open daily 9am-10pm. Or try the cheaper **Maxim Internet,** Hlavná 48 (through the archway). 25Sk per hr. Open daily 9am-8pm.

Post Office: Poštová 20 (☎617 1401). **Poste Restante** at window #16. Open M-F 7am-7pm, Sa 8am-noon. **Postal Code:** 04001.

ACCOMMODATIONS

K2 Tourist Hotel, Štúrova 32 (☎625 5948). Take tram #6 or bus #16, 21, or 30 from the train/bus station to the "Dom Umenia" stop, or follow Hlavná from the main square and turn right on Štúrova. A bargain within walking distance of the Old Town, this hostel provides simple, well-furnished rooms—although somewhat poorly lit and hot in summer. Restaurant open M-F 10am-10pm, Su 11:30am-10pm. Reception 24hr. Check-in and check-out noon. 3- to 4-bed dorms 350Sk. Tourist tax 25Sk. MC/V plus a 50Sk surcharge. ❷

Gazdovská Pension, Ćajkovského 4, (☎622 8894). The friendly staff at this central hostel helps visitors navigate the city. Clean, comfortable rooms with well-kept baths. Reserve ahead. Singles and doubles 810Sk per person. Cash only. ❸

Autokemping Salaš Barca, Alejová st. (☎623 3397; www.eurocampings.net). From the station, take tram #6 to Ferrocentrum/Spoločenský Pavilón and switch to tram #9. Get off at "Autokemping," cross the pedestrian bridge, go 20m up the ramp, and turn left down the stairs. Simple 2-bedroom bungalows with well-kept baths. Badminton, volleyball, soccer, and ping-pong available. Reception 24hr. Check-in and check-out noon. Reserve 3 days ahead. 80Sk per person, 60Sk per tent, 80Sk per car. 2-bed bungalows 600Sk; 3-bed 900SK. Tourist tax 25Sk. MC/V accepted 10am-10pm. ❶

FOOD

With restaurants on rooftop terraces, under arches, and on the central square, Košice has more culinary variety than any other Slovak city. Get groceries at **Tesco,** Hlavná 109. (☎670 4810. Open M-F 7am-8pm, Sa 7am-6pm, Su 8am-6pm. MC/V.)

Reštaurácia Ajvega, Orlia 10 (☎622 0452; www.ajvega.sk). Vegetarians praise this organic-food restaurant, which offers veggie versions of both Mexican (enchiladas, tortillas, and tacos 89Sk) and Slovak dishes. Some meat dishes. English menu. Soups 30-40Sk. Entrees 89-155Sk. Open M-F 8am-10pm, Sa-Su 11am-10pm. Cash only. ❶

Reštaurácia Veverička (Squirrel Restaurant), Hlavná 95 (☎622 3360). Look for the pair of rodents carved out of dark wood above the doorway. Enjoy a variety of local dishes on the sun-drenched patio. Sadly, squirrel isn't on the menu. English menu. Entrees 65-289Sk. Open daily 9am-10pm. Cash only. ❷

Cafe Pizza Roberta, Hlavná 45 (☎09 05 67 82 31). Delight in the spectacular views from this touristy pizzeria, located near the base of St. Elizabeth's Cathedral and Urban's Tower. The friendly waitstaff are happy to help decipher the Slovak menu. Entrees 59-135Sk. Open M-Th 10am-midnight, F 10am-1am, Sa 11am-1am, Su 11am-11pm. Cash only. ❶

Cafe Retro, Kovácska 49. Sketches of flying-machines line the walls, a gramophone sits on the windowsill, and model blimps hang from the ceiling in this relaxing cafe. Espresso 28-43Sk. Open M-F 8am-10pm, Sa 2pm-midnight, Su 2-10pm. Cash only. ❷

Cukráreň Aida, Hlavná 81. Indulge your sweet tooth at Košice's most popular ice-cream parlor, which offers a wide range of flavors (8Sk per scoop) and sweets (10-80Sk). Espresso 18-29Sk. Open daily 9am-10pm. Cash only. 2nd location at Hlavná 44. ❶

SLOVAKIA

SIGHTS

The **Cathedral of Saint Elizabeth** (Dom Sv. Alžbety) dominates much of the Old Town. Begun in 1378 as a high-Gothic monument, the Cathedral has undergone repeated renovations. It is now a unique mixture of Western styles with an impressive altar. The church's North Tower offers a stunning view of the Old Town and a spectacular look at the intricate roof. (☎09 18 69 05 46. Crypt open M-F 9am-5pm, Sa 9am-1pm. Tower open Apr.-Nov. M-F 9am-5pm, Sa 9am-1pm. Admission to exhibit 20Sk, students 15Sk. Admission to Tower 35/20Sk. Cathedral tours 30/15Sk.) Nearby, a fountain dazzles crowds with musical water-dances. At the start of Hlavná is the **Underground Museum,** which was founded after construction workers accidentally discovered the remains of medieval fortifications in 1995. Two years of excavation revealed a series of archaeological wonders dating from the 13th century. (Open

Tu-Su 10am-6pm. 25Sk, students 15Sk. English pamphlet 10Sk.) Take a right at the **State Theater** onto Univerzitná to arrive at a branch of the **East Slovak Museum, Mikluš's Prison**. Housed in the former city jail, the museum details life behind bars from the 17th to 19th century. Haunting images of violence can be found in the photography collection in the reconstructed chambers—one woman, who killed her illegitimate baby, was thrown into her grave before a stake was driven into her heart. (Hrnčiarska 7. Some English info. Open Tu-Sa 9am-5pm, Su 9am-1pm. Ticket office behind the gate at Hrnčiarska. Mandatory tours in Slovak; 30Sk, students 15Sk.) At nám. Mieru Maratónu, in the ornate building closest to the runner's statue, stands the **archaeological branch** of the East Slovak Museum, which displays tools, bones, and photographs that detail the history of the Šariš region. The museum's best exhibit, in the vault downstairs, is a bowl filled with 2920 medieval gold *thaler* coins, discovered in 1935 while workers were laying foundations for new finance headquarters. (Hviezdoslavova 2. ☎622 0309. Open Tu-Sa 9am-5pm, Su 9am-1pm. 50Sk, students 25Sk. English guidebook 30Sk.) Across the street, is the **Art and Natural Science Museum.** The large taxidermy exhibit could churn some stomachs but provides a fascinating introduction to Carpathian fauna. Upstairs, exhibits chronicle art from the ancient Roman empire to the Middle Ages. (Hviezdoslavova 3. ☎622 3061. Open Tu-Sa 9am-5pm, Su 9am-1pm. 30Sk, students 15Sk.)

NIGHTLIFE

Jazz Club, Kováčska 39 (☎622 4237). This stylish club might not play much jazz, but it still deserves its popularity. Disco dominates Tu and Th-Sa, drawing young cats looking to cut a rug. Beer 27-55Sk. Disco cover 50Sk. Open M, W, and Su 4pm-2am, Tu and Th-Sa 8pm-4am. Cash only.

Willy's Pub, Kováčska 49 (☎09 03 24 31 30). Chill out at this underground bar before heading to the hopping Jazz Club across the street. An excellent choice for cheap pints. The jukebox (5Sk) is equipped with modern songs of all genres. Beer 15-35Sk. Open M-Th 10am-10pm, F 2pm-2am, Sa 4pm-midnight. Cash only.

Aloha Cocktail Club, Hlavná 69 (☎623 1405). This Caribbean-themed club attracts a younger crowd with a loud mix of R&B, hip-hop, and pop. Party until dawn on the cavernous, sky-blue dance floor with the help of Aloha's exhaustive selection of mixed drinks (60-140Sk). Open M-Th noon-midnight, F-Sa noon-2am, Su 3-11pm. Cash only.

Palmyra, Hlavná 24. Relaxed 20-somethings swing to the beats of dance music under a disco ball. If dancing isn't your thing, enjoy the pounding music from comfy booths. Beer 38Sk. Open M-Tu 9pm-2am, W-Th 9am-3pm, F-Sa 9am-4pm. Cash only.

Débouché, Hlavná 69 (☎09 05 99 76 10). Located on the main square, this is the place where young people go for mixed drinks (40-125Sk). Lounge in a booth, or play a game of pool (15Sk per game) or foosball (10Sk per game). English spoken. Open daily 4pm-2am. Cash only.

DAYTRIPS FROM KOŠICE

JASKYŇA DOMICA. Jaskyňa Domica is a challenge to reach, but the breathtaking caverns are worth the effort. Stalactites and stalagmites jut from three-million-year-old cave walls, creating complex patterns in the spacious chambers, the largest of which measures 48,000 cubic meters. When underground water levels permit, the longer tour includes a boat ride covering 1.5km of the cave. The shorter tour covers only 780m of the grand expanse. Only 5km of the 23km cave lie on the Slovak side—the rest is accessible from Hungary. If you want to see more, travel 1km (10min. on foot, above ground) across the border to the **Hungarian** entrance.

(Take a bus to Plešivec (1½hr., 7-10 per day, 128Sk) then catch the connecting bus (3Sk) to Jaskyňa Domica. Check the timetable across from the cave entrance for return buses. Be prepared to wait; it may be 1-2hr. between buses. The friendly, English-speaking TIC staff also have info about buses that make the trip to Plešivec and the caves. ☎ 788 2010; www.domica.sk. Mandatory tours June-Aug. Tu-Su 9am-4pm every hour; Sept.-Dec. and Feb.-May 9:30, 11am, 12:30, 2pm. 45min. tour (min. 4 people) 140Sk, students 120Sk. 1½hr. tour 180/160Sk. Cash only.)

KRASNA HORKA CASTLE. The beautifully restored Krasna Horka Castle looms over the picturesque village of Rožňava. One of Slovakia's best preserved castles, the imposing Krasna Horka was built in the Gothic style in the 14th century. Inside, the 1hr. tour takes you through 31 finely decorated rooms. Highlights include a former money counterfeiting shop and an eerie chapel where a mummified body, clad in black lace, lies in a glass sarcophagus with one arm raised. *(Take the bus to Dobšiná and get off at "Krásnohorské Podhradie" (2hr., 108Sk). Check the timetable for return buses. Walk up the path to the castle. ☎ 732 4769. Open May-Oct. M-F 8:30am-4:30pm. Mandatory 1hr. tours every hr. 100Sk, students 50Sk.)*

BARDEJOV ☎ (0)54

Although scenic Bardejov (bahr-day-YOW; pop. 38,000) is a favorite destination for Slovak newlyweds, life here hasn't always been a honeymoon. Having endured earthquakes, fires, and the occasional Turkish invasion, this former trade center underwent a complete reconstruction in 1986—a feat that earned it the UNESCO Heritage Gold Medal. Relaxing Bardejov attracts visitors who delight in the town's main attraction, its soothing baths.

TRANSPORTATION AND PRACTICAL INFORMATION. Trains, Slovenská 18 (☎ 472 3605) go to: Košice (1¾-2¼hr., 3 per day, 120Sk) and Prešov (1hr., 5 per day, 58Sk). The best way to reach Bardejov is by **bus** (☎ 723 353). Buses head to: Banská Bystrica (4hr., M-F 5 per day, 300Sk); Bratislava (11hr., 4 per day, 560Sk); Košice (1¾hr., 5 per day, 100Sk); Poprad (2-2½hr., M-F 9 per day, 130Sk); Prešov (1hr.; M-F 10 per day, Sa-Su 4 per day; 58Sk); Rožňava (3½hr., 3 per day, 180Sk). From the train and bus station, cross the parking lot, go to the left and turn right onto the cobblestone path just after the T-shaped intersection. Continue up the path past the ruined lower gate of **Staré Mesto** (Old Town), then turn right on **Paštová** to reach **Radničné námestie,** the main square. The **tourist office,** Radničné nám. 21, sells **maps** (60-159Sk) and provides useful info on accommodations and attractions. (☎/fax 474 4003. Open May-Sept. M-F 9am-6:30pm, Sa 9am-5pm; Oct.-Apr. M-F 10am-4pm.) Get MC/V **cash advances** and **Western Union** services or cash American Express and Visa **traveler's checks** (min. 200Sk) for 1% commission at **VÚB,** Kellerova 1. A 24hr. **ATM** stands outside. (☎ 472 2671. Open M-F 8am-5pm.) A **pharmacy, Lekáreň Sv. Egídia,** Radničné nám. 43, posts the addresses and hours of other pharmacies. (☎ 472 7562. Open M-F 7:30am-5pm.) **Internet** access is available at **Golem,** Radničné nám. 35. (29Sk per hr. Open M-F 9am-11pm, Sa 1pm-midnight, Su 1pm-9pm.) The **post office,** Dlný rad 14, sells phone cards; **telephones** are outside. (☎ 472 4062. Open M-F 7am-6pm, Sa 7:30-10:30am.) **Postal Code:** 08501.

ACCOMMODATIONS AND FOOD. Accommodations are limited in Bardejov. Book rooms in advance June through September. More **private rooms** and **pensions** (200-300Sk) lie outside of town but are poorly connected. The tourist office can help book lodging.The Kaminsky family runs **Penzión Semafór ❸,** Kellerova 13, and welcomes visitors with unmatched hospitality. Spacious rooms have TVs, private baths, and a shared kitchen. From the train station, cross the parking lot

SLOVAKIA

and exit on Nový sad. Walk 300m and turn right on Kellerova; the pension is ahead on the left. (☎09 05 83 99 84. Free tea or coffee. Breakfast 90Sk. Laundry 100Sk. Singles 725Sk; doubles 950Sk; apartment with kitchens 1050Sk; extra bed 250Sk. Cash only.) **SOU Pod Vinbargom ❶**, with balconies, nice beds, and well-kept baths, is a comfortable base near the train station. Turn left from the bus stop and follow the road as it curves. The hotel is on the left, past the supermarket. (☎488 0150. Reception 24hr. Call ahead. 250Sk per person in singles, doubles, and triples.)

Though restaurants have besieged Radičné nám., few are more than snack bars and pubs. The classy and romantic **Roland ❷**, Radičné nám. 12, fuses Italian and Slovak flavors by day and takes on a pub-like atmosphere at night. Go through the arch and to the back to reach the patio, or sit amid the medieval decor in the cellar restaurant and pub. (☎472 9220. Entrees 85-149Sk. Open M-Th 7:45am-11pm, F 7:45-1am, Sa 11am-midnight, Su 11am-11pm. Cash only.) **Cafe Restaurant Hubert ❷**, Radničné nám. 6, serves beef, game meats, and fish. (☎474 2603. English menu. Entrees 63-199Sk. Open M-Th 8am-11pm, F 8am-2am, Sa noon-1am, Su noon-11pm. Cash only.) Locals satisfy their sweet tooth with ice cream (7Sk per scoop) and desserts (15-18Sk) at **Oaza ❶**, Radničné nám. 23. (☎474 6470. Open daily 8:30am-9pm.) **Billa Supermarket,** next to the train station, offers a huge selection of groceries. (Open M-Sa 7am-9pm, Su 8am-8pm.)

SIGHTS. The waters of the **Bardejov Baths** (Bardejovské Kúpele) are rumored to have curative powers—powers so great the strong acidic taste doesn't deter the crowds who fill bottles here. The wives of Tsar Alexander I of Russia, Joseph II of Austria-Hungary, Napoleon Bonaparte, and Austrian Emperor Franz Josef frequented the baths. For a dip in 28°C spring waters, head to the *kupalisko* (swimming pool) at the end of the park. (To reach the baths, which lie just outside the Bardejov city center, take bus #1, 6, 7 or 12 from the station to the end of the line; 20min., 9Sk. ☎472 2070. Open May 10-Sept. 22 M-F 1-7pm, Sa-Su 9am-7pm. Tu-F 8am-noon patients with prescription only. M-F 50Sk, students 25Sk; Sa-Su 100/50Sk.) Or, drop into any of the hotels for various **spa treatments.** Near the baths, there is also the open-air **Museum of Folk Architecture,** which consists of 24 full-scale buildings taken from villages across Slovakia and reassembled here. Highlights include a rustic wooden church and a smith's workshop. (Open M-F 10am-5pm. 40Sk, students 20Sk.)

Back in town, the **Church of St. Egidius** (Kostol sv. Egídia), Radničné nám. 47, contains 11 Gothic wing altars crafted between 1450 and 1510 by Master Pavol. The largest of these, the detailed 15th-century **Nativity Altar,** was consecrated by St. Gilles, patron saint of the town and church. (Open M-F 10am-5pm, Sa 10am-4pm, Su for services and visits 11:30am-4pm. 30Sk, students 20Sk. Tower 40/20Sk.)

Head out from the end of the main square on Františkănov and turn right onto Mlynská to reach Bardejov's **Jewish quarter,** where there is a closed **synagogue** and a moving memorial plaque to the more than 7000 Jews from Bardejov who perished during the Holocaust. Twelve **bastions** mark the perimeter of the Old Town. Veterna ends at one of the remaining bastions, which served as a crossroads beacon and, later, as the local beheading stock. The **icon exhibit,** Radničné nám. 27, boasts a small collection of miniature religious figures and models of nearby wooden churches, striking in their detail. The collection's treasure is the gorgeous original **iconostasis** from the altar of a wooden church that stood in Zboy. (☎472 2009. Open M-F 9am-noon and 12:30-4:30pm. 40Sk.) The **town hall** Radničné nám. 48 (☎474 6038), now serves as a **museum,** displaying historic trinkets. Among them is the key to the city, which the treacherous mayor's wife lent to her Turkish lover in 1697. The aptly named "Nature of Northeastern Slovakia" display, in the **Prirodopisne Museum,** Rhodýho 4, across from the entrance to the icon exhibit, will tickle the taxidermist in you, with finely detailed flora and fauna exhibits. Take note of the **Quail trees** at the uphill end, a gift from the US, brought by former Vice President Dan Quayle in 1991. (☎472 2630. Both museums open May-mid-Sept. daily 8:30am-noon and 12:30-5pm; Oct.-Apr. Tu-Su 8am-noon and 12:30-4pm. 25Sk, students 10Sk.) The **Museum of Svidník,** Bardejovska 14, gives an overview of the WWII Battle for the Dukla Pass. The adjacent **battlefield** is hauntingly littered with abandoned tanks, artillery, and other vestiges of the brutal encounter. Don't stray from the dirt paths: some landmines remain in the field. A bus runs from Bardejov to Svidník (30min., 60Sk); a connecting bus runs to Dukla (20Sk). From behind the station, turn left and walk 10min. (☎05 47 42 13 98. Open Tu-F 8am-3:30pm, Sa-Su 10am-2pm. 35Sk; students, children, and soldiers 15Sk.)

NIGHTLIFE. Evenings in Bardejov are subdued, and nightlife is based around the beer gardens in the main square. Those determined to party late should head to **Morca Cafe,** Radničné nám. 37, where a mid-20s crowd chats under neon lights. (☎090 897 68 81. Open daily 7pm-4am.) The shamrock-lined **Irish Pub,** Radničné nám. 32, is like many such Irish bars in Slovakia: largely inauthentic, but strangely popular and the only place in town to find Guinness. (☎09 05 97 18 34. Guinness 70Sk. Open M-Th 11am-11pm, F 11am-1pm, Sa 10am-1am, Su 1-11pm.)

SLOVENIA (SLOVENIJA)

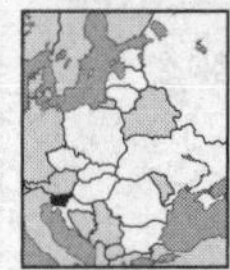

The first and most prosperous of Yugoslavia's breakaway republics, tiny Slovenia revels in republicanism, peace, and independence. With a historically westward gaze, Slovenia's liberal politics and high GDP helped it gain early entry into the European Union, further eroding its weak relationship with Eastern Europe. Fortunately, modernization has not adversely affected the tiny country's natural beauty and diversity: it is still possible to go skiing, explore Slovenia's stunning caves, bathe under the Mediterranean sun, and catch an opera—all in a single day.

DISCOVER SLOVENIA: SUGGESTED ITINERARIES

THREE DAYS. The cafe culture and nightlife of eclectic **Ljubljana** are worth at least a two-day stay, to be followed by a tranquil digression in the fairytale alpine lake town of **Bled** (1 day; p. 670).

ONE WEEK. After spending two days in **Ljubljana** and a day in **Bled,** head to tranquil lake-town **Bohinj** (1 day; p. 673). Take a train to **Piran** (2 days; p. 677), a mini-Venice, and explore the nearby **Škocjanske Caves** (1 day, p. 669).

FACTS AND FIGURES

Official Name: Republic of Slovenia.
Capital: Ljubljana.
Major Cities: Maribor, Celje, Kranj.
Population: 2,009,000.
Time Zone: GMT +1.
Language: Slovenian.
Religion: Roman Catholic (58%).
Tractors per 100 people: 6.

ESSENTIALS

WHEN TO GO

July and August are the peak months in Slovenia; tourists flood the coast, and prices for accommodations rise. Go in spring or early autumn, and you will be blessed with a dearth of crowds and great weather for hiking and exploring the countryside. Skiing is popular from December to March.

DOCUMENTS AND FORMALITIES

ENTRANCE REQUIREMENTS.

Passport: Required for all travelers.
Visa: Not required for stays of under 90 days for citizens of Australia, Canada, Ireland, New Zealand, the UK, and the US.
Letter of Invitation: Not required.
Inoculations: Recommended up-to-date on DTaP (diphtheria, tetanus, and pertussis), Hepatitis A, Hepatitis B, MMR (measles, mumps, and rubella), polio booster, and typhoid.
Work Permit: Required of all foreigners planning to work in Slovenia.
International Driving Permit: Required of those planning to drive in Slovenia.

EMBASSIES AND CONSULATES. Foreign embassies to Slovenia are in Ljubljana. Embassies and consulates abroad include: **Australia,** Level 6, 60 Marcus Clarke St., Canberra, ACT 2601 (☎262 434 830; vca@gov.si); **Canada,** 150 Metcalfe St., Ste. 2101, Ottawa, ON K2P 1P1 (☎613-565-5781; www.gov.si/mzz-dkp/veleposlanistva/

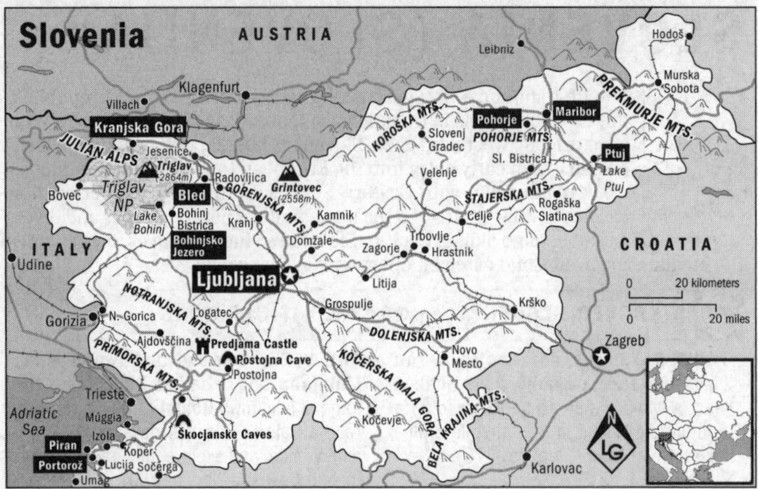

eng/ottawa/embassy.shtml); **Ireland,** Morrison Chambers, 2nd fl., 32 Nassau St., Dublin 2 (☎1 670 5240; vdb@mzz-dkp.gov.si); **UK,** 10 Little College St., London SW1P 3SJ (☎020 72 22 57 00; www.gov.si/mzz-dkp/veleposlanistva/eng/london/events.shtml); **US,** 1525 New Hampshire Ave., NW, Washington, D.C. 20036 (☎202-667-5363; www.gov.si/mzz-dkp/veleposlanistva/eng/washington). Citizens of **New Zealand** should seek assistance from the Slovenian Embassy to Australia.

VISA AND ENTRY INFORMATION. Citizens of Australia, Canada, Ireland, New Zealand, the UK, and the US do not need **visas** for stays of up to 90 days. Visas take four to seven business days to process (US$45 for all types). Visas are not available at the border.

TOURIST SERVICES AND MONEY

There are **tourist offices** in most major cities and tourist destinations. Staff members generally speak English or German and, on the coast, perfect Italian. They can usually find accommodations for a small fee and generally give advice and maps for free. **Kompas** is the main tourist organization.

The **euro (€)** has replaced the *tolar* in Slovenia. SKB Banka, Ljubljanska Banka and Gorenjska Banka are common **banks.** American Express Travelers Cheques and Eurocheques are accepted almost everywhere, but major credit cards are not consistently accepted. MasterCard and Visa **ATMs** are everywhere.

HEALTH AND SAFETY

EMERGENCY	**Ambulance** and **Fire:** ☎112. **Police:** ☎113.

Medical facilities are of high quality, and most have English-speaking doctors. EU citizens receive free medical care with a valid passport; other foreigners must pay cash. **Pharmacies** are stocked according to Western standards; ask for *obliž* (band-aids), *tamponi* (tampons), and *vložki* (sanitary pads). **Tap water** is safe to drink. **Crime** is rare in Slovenia. **Women** should, as always, exercise caution and avoid being out alone after dark. There are few **minorities** in Slovenia, but minorities generally just receive curious glances. Navigating Slovenia with a **disability** can be difficult and requires patience and caution on slippery cobblestones. **Homosexuality** is legal, but may elicit unfriendly reactions outside urban areas.

TRANSPORTATION

BY PLANE. Flights arrive at **Ljubljana Airport** (LJU). Most major airlines offer connections to the national carrier, **Adria Airways** (www.adria-airways.com). To enter inexpensively, consider flying into Vienna, Austria and taking a train to Ljubljana.

BY TRAIN AND BY BUS. First and second class differ little on **trains.** Those under 26 get a 20% discount on most international fares. ISIC holders should ask for the 30% *popust* (discount) off domestic tickets. Schedules often list trains by direction. *Prihodi vlakov* means arrivals; *odhodi vlakov* is departures; *dnevno* is daily. **Eurail** is not accepted in Slovenia. Though often more expensive than trains, **buses** may be the only option in mountainous regions, and they're the best way to reach Bled, as the train station is far from town.

BY CAR AND BY FERRY. Car rental agencies in Ljubljana offer reasonable rates, and Slovenia's roads are in good condition. A regular **ferry** service connects Portorož to Venice, Italy in the summer.

BY BIKE AND BY THUMB. Nearly every town in Slovenia has a bike rental office. While those who partake in it insist that it is safe and widespread in the countryside, hitchhiking is not recommended by Let's Go.

KEEPING IN TOUCH

PHONE CODES	**Country code:** 386. **International dialing prefix:** 00. From outside Slovenia, dial the international dialing prefix (see inside back cover) + 386 + city code + local number. Within Slovenia, dial city code + local number for intercity calls and simply the local number for calls within a city.

EMAIL AND INTERNET. Internet access is fast and common. Though free Internet is hard to find anywhere but in the biggest cities, there are Internet cafes in most major tourist destinations. Expect to pay approximately €2-4 per hour.

TELEPHONE. All phones take **phonecards,** sold at post offices, kiosks, and gas stations. Dial ☎115 for collect calls and ☎1180 for the international operator. Calling abroad is expensive without a phonecard (over US$6 per min. to the US). Use the phones at the post office and pay when you're finished. **British Telecom** (☎080 080 832) offers one of the only international access codes in Slovenia.

MAIL. Airmail *(letalsko)* takes one to two weeks to reach Australia, New Zealand, and the US. To receive mail through Poste Restante, address envelopes as follows: first name, LAST NAME, Poste Restante, post office address, Postal Code, city, SLOVENIA.

ACCOMMODATIONS AND CAMPING

SLOVENIA	❶	❷	❸	❹	❺
ACCOMMODATIONS	under €15	€15-20	€21-25	€26-30	over €30

All establishments charge a nightly **tourist tax. Youth hostels** and **student dormitories** are cheap (€15-20), but generally open only in summer (June 25-Aug. 30). **Hotels** fall into five categories (L, deluxe; A; B; C; and D) and are expensive. **Pensions** are the most common form of accommodation; usually they have private singles as well as inexpensive dorms. **Private rooms** are the only cheap option on the coast and at Lake Bohinj. Prices vary, but rarely exceed US$30. Inquire at the tourist office or look for *Zimmer frei* or *Sobe* signs. **Campgrounds** can be crowded, but most are in excellent condition. Camp in designated areas to avoid fines.

FOOD AND DRINK

SLOVENIA	❶	❷	❸	❹	❺
FOOD	under €5	€6-7	€8-9	€10-11	over €11

For home-style cooking, try a *gostilna* or *gostišče* (country-style inn or restaurant). Traditional meals begin with *jota*, a soup with potatoes, beans, and sauerkraut. Pork is the basis for many dishes, such as *Svinjska pečenka* (roast pork). **Kosher** and **vegetarian** eating is therefore very difficult within the confines of Slovenian cuisine. Those with such dietary restrictions might find pizza and bakery items their best options. Slovenia's **winemaking** tradition dates from antiquity. Renski, Rizling, and Šipon are popular whites, while Cviček and Teran are favorite reds. Brewing is also centuries old; Laško and Union are good beers. For something stronger, try *žganje*, a fruit brandy, or Viljamovka, distilled by monks who closely guard the secret of getting a whole pear inside the bottle.

LIFE AND TIMES

HISTORY

SLAVIC BEGINNINGS. The **Alpine Slavs,** predecessors of the Slovenes, migrated to the eastern Alps in the sixth century and absorbed the existing cultures. After initially resisting German missionaries, the Slovenes converted to **Christianity** in the ninth century. The territory then fell under the rule of Bavarian dukes and Venice until the 14th century, when the **Austrian Habsburgs**—whose influence stifled Slovenian cultural consciousness for centuries to come—assumed control. In the early 1800s, **Napoleon** temporarily displaced Austrian rule in the region, triggering the development of Slovenian **nationalism** and instituting some republican reforms.

PARTISANS AND PARTITIONS. After the collapse of Austria-Hungary following **World War I,** Slovenia agreed to join the newly formed **Kingdom of Serbs, Croats, and Slovenes** (renamed **Yugoslavia** in 1929). The new state was unable, however, to withstand **Hitler's** forces during WWII. When Yugoslavia fell in 1941, Slovenia was partitioned among Germany, Italy, and Hungary. Slovenian resistance groups formed and united under the **Slovenian National Liberation Front,** which soon joined the Yugoslav Partisan Army of **Josip Brož Tito.**

SLOVENIA

WILD WESTERNIZATION. Following WWII, a unified state once again emerged, this time as the communist **Federal People's Republic of Yugoslavia.** Tito liquidated Slovene politicians and leaders who failed to cooperate; tens of thousands of Slovene patriots were murdered at **Kočevje.** After a rift between Tito and Stalin in 1948, Yugoslavia followed its own brand of communism for half a century, slowly opening its doors to Western-style market reforms while retaining a political autocracy. The years following Tito's 1980 death saw a rise in Slovenian nationalism, and in 1990 Slovenia held the first democratic elections in Yugoslavia since before WWII. The new government adopted a Western-style constitution, and on June 25, 1991, Slovenia seceded from Yugoslavia. After a 10-day war with Yugoslavia that claimed the lives of 66 people, a peace treaty was brokered and Slovenia's independence was recognized by the European community in 1992.

TODAY

Slovenia is a parliamentary democracy, consisting of an elected **president,** aided by a council of ministers, and a **prime minister.** The bicameral **legislature** *Skupscina Slovenije* (Slovenian Assembly), consisting of the 90-member *Drzavni Zbor*

(State Chamber) and the 40-member advisory *Drzavni Svet* (State Council), presides over 147 municipalities. In December 2002, long-time prime minister **Janez Drnovšek,** of the **Liberal Democratic Party,** took the presidency from **Milan Kučan,** who had been president since independence. Today's prime minister, **Janez Janša,** heads a center-right coalition government. Slovenia joined **NATO** and the **European Union** (EU) in 2004 and will hold the EU presidency in the first half of 2008.

PEOPLE AND CULTURE

DEMOGRAPHICS. Over 88% of Slovenia's population is Slovenian, and most citizens are Roman Catholic, though a small number are Protestants, Orthodox Christians, Muslims, and Jews. Hungarians and Italians have the status of indigenous minorities under the Slovenian Constitution, which guarantees them seats in the National Assembly, but minorities from former Yugoslavia have had a rougher integration. In 1991, about 18,000 Yugoslav citizens living in newly independent Slovenia were stricken from the population registry because they had not applied for citizenship. A 2004 referendum saw 95% of voters reject the decision of the Constitutional Court to restore resident status to the remaining 4000 countryless citizens, who are known as "the erased." Political leaders and non-governmental organizations have criticized the referendum, and the Ministry of the Interior has already issued thousands of decrees upholding the Court's decision.

LANGUAGE. Slovenian is a South Slavic language written in the Latin alphabet. Most young Slovenes speak at least some English, but the older generations are more likely to understand German or Italian. The tourist industry is generally geared toward Germans, but most tourist office employees speak English. Attempts at speaking Slovenian will be appreciated by locals. For a phrasebook and glossary, see **Appendix: Slovenian,** p. 804.

CUSTOMS AND ETIQUETTE. While not customary, a **tip** is sometimes included in the bill. Generally, 10% is sufficient for good service. Cab drivers won't expect a tip but will be pleased if you round up the fare. Slovenes don't **bargain,** and attempts to do so may cause offense. Shorts are rare in cities but are commonly worn by men on the coast. Jeans are worn everywhere. When hiking, note that trails are marked with a white circle inside a red one. Hikers greet one another on the path. The ascending hiker should speak first: it is considered proper to show respect to those who have already summited.

THE ARTS

LITERATURE. Slovenian literature emerged as an important secular art form in the 19th century with the writings of the country's most beloved poet **France Prešeren** and the codification of the language by **Jernej Kopitar.** The surge in cultural activity during the first half of the century paralleled the period's nationalist interest and set the stage for the country's first political agenda. Throughout the later **Realist** Period (1848-1899), writers such as **Fran Levstik** focused on folkloric themes with a patriotic flavor; the first Slovenian novel, *The Tenth Brother (Deseti brat)*, by **Josip Jurčič,** was published in 1866. Modernist prose flowered with **Ivan Cankar's** 1904 *The Ward of Our Lady of Mercy (Hisa Marije pomocnice)*, while **Expressionist** poetry showed the social and spiritual tensions brought on by WWI through the works of **Tone Seliškar, Miran Jarc,** and **Anton Vodnik.** Soviet **Socialist Realism** crushed many of Slovak literature's avant-garde impulses. Postmodern literary trends emerged in the **Young Slovenian Prose** movement, which has its strongest representation in short prose pieces. Current internationally acclaimed writers include poet **Tomaž Šalamun** and critic and philosopher **Slavoj Žižek.**

THE VISUAL AND MUSICAL ARTS. Contemporaneous with the Modernist and Expressionist movements in Slovenian literature, architect **Jože Plečnik** was a major figure in the development of **Art Deco.** He transformed his otherwise baroque-leaning hometown, Ljubljana, into a cosmopolitan capital (p. 662). Musically, Slovenia experienced a politically minded **folk** revival after WWII. **Laibach,** an adventurous multimedia band, single-handedly ignited an explosion of punk rock. The alternative music movement of the 1980s gave rise to a vigorous **contemporary art** scene, nurtured by the collagist art collectives **Irwin** and **NSK** (*Neue Slowenische Kunst*).

HOLIDAYS AND FESTIVALS

Holidays: New Year's Day (Jan. 1); Culture Day (Prešeren Day; Feb. 8); Easter Holiday (Mar. 23-34, 2008; April 12-13, 2009); National Resistance Day (WWII; Apr. 27); Labor Day (May 1-2); Independence Day (National Statehood; June 25); Reformation Day (Oct. 31); Christmas Day (Dec. 25); Indepedence Day (Dec. 26).

Festivals: Slovenia embraces its alternative artistic culture as much as its folk heritage, which is evident in its lengthy festival calendar. Hitting Ljubljana in July and August, the International Summer Festival is the nation's most famous, featuring ballet, music, and theater. The Peasant's Wedding Day *(Kmecka ohcet),* a presentation of ancient wedding customs held in Bohinj at the end of July, and the Cow's Ball *(Kravji Bal)* in mid-September, which celebrates the return of the cows to the valleys from higher pastures, are a couple of the country's many summertime folk exhibitions.

LJUBLJANA ☎(0)1

Founded by Emperor Augustus in 34 BC, long under Habsburg rule, and revamped in the interwar years by architect Jože Plečnik, Slovenia's capital boasts a rich folkloric history and a mix of old-world Baroque and colorful Art Nouveau architectural styles. Because of its beauty and spirited youth culture, Ljubljana (loob-LYAH-nah; pop. 266,000) deserves to be treated as more than a stopover en route to Budapest or Zagreb. This compact riverside city offers the romantic delight and hip underground vitality of Prague, without the cost or the crowds.

INTERCITY TRANSPORTATION

Flights: Aerodrom Ljubljana-Brnik (☎206 1000; www.lju-airport.si). **Info and Lost and found:** Adria Airways (☎42 36 34 62), other airlines (☎42 06 19 81). **Adria Airways,** Gosposvetska 6 (☎231 3312; www.adriaairways.com), has an airport shuttle, *Avtobusni prevozi Markun* (☎41 67 05 28), to and from the main bus terminal (30min., 8 per day, €8). The slower but cheaper local bus #28 runs from the main bus station (1hr.; M-F every hr. 6am-8pm, Sa-Su every hr. 6-9am and at odd-numbered hours. until 7pm; €3.50); **Austrian Airlines,** Gosposvetska 8 (☎239 1900; www.aua-si.com); **Air France,** Igriška 5 (☎244 3447; www.regional.fr); **British Air,** Trg Republike 3 (☎241 4000; www.ba.com); **ČSA Czech Airlines** (☎206 1226; www.czechairlines.com); **easyJet** (☎42 06 16 77; www.easyJet.com); **JAT,** Slomškova 1 (☎231 4340; www.jat.com); **Lufthansa,** Gosposvetska 6 (☎434 7246; www.lufthansa.com); **Swissair,** Dunajska 156 (☎569 1010).

Trains: Trg OF 6 (☎291 3332). To: **Bled** (1hr., 14 per day, €4) and **Budapest, HUN** (9hr., 3 per day, €50) via **Zagreb, CRO** (2hr., 9 per day, €12).

Buses: Trg OF 4 (☎090 4230; www.ap-ljubljana.si). To: **Bled** (1½hr., every hr. until 9pm, €6.40); **Maribor** (3hr., 10 per day, €12); **Zagreb, CRO** (3hr., 1 per day, €15).

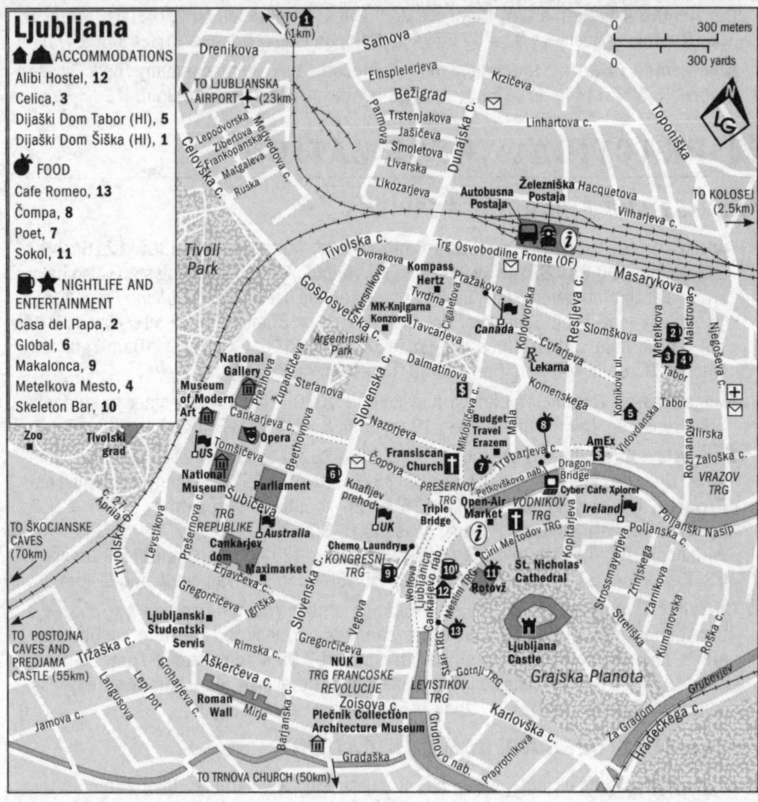

ORIENTATION

The bike-accessible city center is easy to navigate by foot. The curvy **Ljubljanica River** divides the city center, with the picturesque **Stare Miasto** (Old Town) on one bank and 19th- and 20th-century buildings on the other. About a half-mile from either bank, the historic area gives way to a concrete business district. The train and bus stations are next to each other on **Trg Osvobodilne Fronte** (Trg OF). To reach the center from the stations, turn right on Masarykova and left on Miklošičeva c.; continue to **Prešernov trg,** the main square. After crossing the **Tromostovje** (Triple Bridge), you'll see Stare Miasto at the base of Castle Hill. The tourist office is on the left at the corner of Stritarjeva and Adamič-Lundrovo nab.

LOCAL TRANSPORTATION

Buses: Most run until 10:30pm. Drop €1.25 in the box beside the driver or buy cheaper €0.79 (*žetoni*) at post offices, kiosks, or the main bus terminal. Day passes (€4) sold at **Ljubljanski Potniški Promet,** Celovška c. 160 (☎582 2426 or 205 6045). Open M-F 6:45am-7pm, Sa 6:45am-1pm. Pick up a bus map at the **TIC.**

Taxis: ☎97 00 through 97 09. Taxi fares average €0.80 per km.

Car Rental: Avis Rent-a-Car, Cufarjeva 2, in Grand Hotel Union (☎430 8010). **Budget Car Rental,** Miklošičeva 3 (☎421 7340). **Kompas Hertz,** Trdinova 9 (☎434 0147).

Bike Rental: Tir Bar, in the train station. Contact the bike rental company "Bajk Oglasevanje" (☎527 3147). €0.85 per 2hr., €3 per day. Open daily 8am-8pm.

PRACTICAL INFORMATION

TOURIST AND FINANCIAL SERVICES

Tourist Office: Tourist Information Center (TIC), Stritarjeva 1 (☎306 1215; 24hr. English info 090 939 881; www.ljubljana.si). Helpful, English-speaking staff. Also helps arrange accommodations. Pick up **free maps** and the useful, free *Ljubljana From A to Z.* Open daily June-Sept. 8am-9pm; Oct.-May 8am-7pm. Branch, Trg OF 6 (☎/fax 433 94 75), at the train station. Open daily June-Sept. 8am-10pm; Oct.-May 10am-7pm. Box office in TIC open M-F 9am-6pm, Sa-Su 9am-1pm. AmEx/MC/V.

Budget Travel: Erazem, Trubarjeva c. 7 (☎433 1076). Helpful staff cater to students. Open June-Aug. M-F 10am-5pm, Sa 10am-1pm; Sept.-May M-F noon-5pm.

Embassies: Australia, Trg Republike 3 (☎425 4252; fax 426 4721). Open M-F 9am-1pm. **Canada,** Miklošičeva 19 (☎430 3570; fax 430 3577). Open M-F 9am-1pm. **Croatia,** Gruberjevo nab. 6 (☎425 6220, consular department 425 7287; hrvaske@siol.net). **Ireland,** Poljanski nasip 6 (☎300 8970; fax 282 1096). Open M-F 9am-noon. **UK,** Trg Republike 3 (☎200 3910; fax 425 0174). Open M-F 9am-noon. **US,** Prešernova 31 (☎200 5500; fax 200 5555). Open M-F 9am-noon and 2-4pm.

Currency Exchange: Many private exchange offices *(menjalnice)* do not charge a transaction fee. **Ljubljanska banka** exchanges currency for free and cashes **traveler's checks** for a 1.5% commission. Open M-F 9am-noon and 2-7pm, Sa 9am-noon. **ATMs** ("BA" or occasionally "Bankomat") are everywhere. **American Express:** Trubarjeva 50 (☎438 0850). Open M-F 8am-7pm.

LOCAL SERVICES AND COMMUNICATIONS

Luggage Storage: Lockers *(garderoba)* at train station. €2 per day. Open 24hr.

English-Language Bookstore: MK-Knjigarna Konzorcij, Slovenska 29 (☎252 4057). One of the few English-language bookstores in town, Konzorcij offers a wide selection from novels to travel guides. Open M-F 9am-7:30pm, Sa 9am-1pm.

Laundromat: Tič (Student Campus), c. 27 Aprila 31, bldg. 9 (☎257 4397). Self-service. Open M-F 8am-8pm, Sa 8am-2pm. **Chemo Express,** Wolfova 12 (☎251 4404). Convenient location offering services for €5 per kg. Open daily 7am-6pm.

Medical Services: Bohoričeva Medical Center, Bohoričeva 4 (☎232 3060). Open daily 5am-8pm. **Klinični Center,** Zaloška 2-7 (☎522 5050). Take bus #2, 9, 10, 11, or 20 to the Bolnica stop. Open 24hr.

24hr. Pharmacy: Lekarna Miklošič, Miklošičeva 24 (☎231 4558).

Telephones: Outside the post office and all over town. Buy phone cards at the post office and at newsstands (€8).

Internet: Most hostels offer free Internet. **Cyber Cafe Xplorer,** Petkovško nab. 23 (☎430 1991; www.sisky.com), has fast connections and offers Wi-Fi. €2.30 per 30min., students €2. 20% discount 10am-noon. Open M-F 10am-10pm, Sa-Su 2-10pm.

Post Office: Trg OF 5 (☎433 0605). Open M-F 7am-midnight, Sa 7am-6pm, Su 9am-noon. **Poste Restante,** Slovenska 32 (☎426 4668), at *izročitev pošiljk* (outgoing mail) counter. Open M-F 7am-8pm, Sa 7am-1pm. **Postal Code:** 1000.

ACCOMMODATIONS

Finding a bed in Ljubljana is easiest in July and August, when university dorms open to travelers. **Hostelling International Slovenia** (**PZS;** ☎231 2156) has info about hostels. The **TIC** (see **Practical Information,** p. 664) arranges **private rooms** (singles €27-45; doubles €40-75). All establishments have a nightly **tourist tax** of €0.62-1.25.

Celica, Metelkova 8 (☎430 1890; www.hostelcelica.com). In the bohemian neighborhood of Metelkova Mesto, this former prison is now an eclectic work of modern art. Dorms are fully furnished with private bathrooms. Parties and live music performances occur frequently. Internet and a phenomenal breakfast with options from cold cuts to fruit salad are included. Laundry €5. Reception 24hr. Reserve ahead. Dorms €17-20; cells €25. Cash-only deposit €10 per person. MC/V. ❷

Dijaški Dom Šiška (HI), Aljazeva 32 (☎500 7804; www.ddsiska.com). Past Kettejeva on the right side of the street, through the parking lot entrance. It's the last building on the left. Rooms are immaculately kept, if austere, with wooden beds. Breakfast €1. Reception 24hr. Open June-Aug. 25. €14, students €11. Cash only. ❶

Dijaški Dom Tabor (HI), Vidovdanska 7 (☎234 8840; www2.arnes.si/řssljddta4/), 1km from the bus and train stations. Great location in the city center makes this an excellent summer hostel. Shared bathrooms. Breakfast included. Laundry €5. Free Internet. Reception 24hr. Check-out 11am. Open June 25-Aug. 25. Dorms €10, doubles €18, students €16. HI discount €1. Cash only. ❶

Alibi Hostel, Cankarjevo nab. 27 (☎ 251 1244; www.alibi.si). The Alibi Hostel's greatest asset is its unbeatable location beside the candlelit bars that line the river. Rooms are plain, although the stairwell features strange and psychedelic graffiti art. Shared bathrooms. Free lockers and Internet. Reception 24hr. Check-out 10am. Dorms in high season €20, in low season €17. Deposit €20. AmEx/MC/V. ❷

FOOD

There is a grocery store in the basement of the **Maximarket,** Trg Republike 1 (open M-Th 9am-8pm, F 9am-10pm, Sa 8am-3pm.), and an **open-air market** by St. Nicholas's Cathedral. (Open June-Aug. M-Sa 6am-6pm; Sept.-May 6am-4pm). Fast-food stands serve *burek*—dough filled with meat or cheese, usually €2.

Cafe Romeo, Stari trg 6. Popular with local hipsters, this is one of the few places in town that serves food on Su. Outdoor seating supplements a black- and red-leather interior. Snack-oriented menu features burritos (€4.50), and dessert crepes (€3.50). Open daily 10am-1am. Kitchen open M-Sa 11am-midnight, Su 11am-11pm. Cash only. ❶

Sokol, Ciril Metodov trg 18 (☎439 6855), just off Prešernov trg. Take bus #2, 11, or 20 to Metodov. Sokol's pseudo-rustic atmosphere features dried herbs hung on red brick walls and high wood tables. Traditional house specialties include game goulash, served in a miniature kettle hung over a tea candle. Wine €1-38 per bottle. Entrees €5.50-15. Open M-Sa 7am-11pm, Su 10am-11pm. AmEx/MC/V. ❸

Čompa, Trubarjeva 40 (☎40 28 10 52). This family-owned, romantic restaurant is known for its authentic regional cuisine and homey decor. Try the potato-and-goulash *čompa* cheese (€6.50). Complimentary after-dinner drink is highly potent. Open June-Aug. M-Sa 11am-1am, Su noon-10pm; Sept.-May M-Sa 11am-11pm, Su noon-10pm. Cash only. ❷

Pri Pavni, Stari trg 21. Commended by the "Society for the Recognition of Sauteed Potato and Onions as an Independent Dish," Pri Pavni provides heavy and flavorful Slovenian dishes. Try the "smoked meat with turnips and hard-boiled corn mush" (€6.50) with a side of roasted potatoes (€1.50). Cash only. ❷

Poet, Petkovško nab., next to the Triple Bridge. With courteous service and a view of the river, Poet has perfected the art of ice cream concoctions (€3-6) and sandwich creation (€2.30-3.50). Open Apr. 15-Oct. 10. Open daily 9am-midnight. ❶

SIGHTS

One way to see the sights is a 2hr. **walking tour,** in English or Slovenian, that departs from in front of the city hall *(rotovž)*, Mestni trg 1. (July-Aug. M-F 10am, Su 11am; May-Sept. daily 10am; Oct.-Apr. F-Su 11am. €6, students €3.50. Buy tickets at the tour or at TIC.) Consider a three-day Ljubljana card (€13), which offers free or discount tickets to museums, galleries and events as well as free travel on city buses. Ljubljana's open-air **market,** near the Dragon Bridge, opens at dawn (M-Sa). Flea markets pop up along the river on Sundays.

ST. NICHOLAS'S CATHEDRAL (STOLNICA SV. NIKOLAJA). The dazzlingly ornate cathedral occupies the site of a 13th-century Romanesque church, but the current building dates from the 18th century. Aside from the 15th-century Gothic Pietà, little original artwork remains, yet every inch is still a marvelous exploration of the Baroque, with beautiful golden altars and stunning religious artwork. The intricate bronze door, installed to honor the 1996 visit of former pope John Paul II, is especially impressive, as are the writhing figures that seem to rise from the exterior walls. *(On the Stare Miasto side of the river. Walk left to see gorgeous arcades designed by Jože Plečnik. Cathedral is to the right. Open daily 6am-noon and 3-7pm. Free.)*

LJUBLJANA CASTLE (LJUBLJANSKI GRAD). Although the castle's existence was first documented in 1144, most of the present buildings are 16th- and 17th-century renovations. In the past, the castle has served as a prison for high-profile captives such as Slovenia's most famous author, nationalist Ivan Cankar (see p. 661). Head to the top for a view of the city. The **Virtual Museum** presents a 3D version of Ljubljana's history (20min., every 30min., headphones available in multiple languages). The castle hosts exhibitions and performances throughout the year. *(Take 1 of several paths up the hill: from Gornji trg along na Grad, or from Vodnikov trg following Študenska. Tower and Virtual Museum ☎232 9994; www.festival-lj.si/virtualnimuzej. Open daily June-Sept. 10am-dusk; Oct.-May 10am-5pm. €3.50, students €2. Castle open daily May-Oct. 10am-9pm; Nov.-Apr. 10am-7pm. English tours €4.50, students €3.50; 3 people min.)*

PREŠEREN SQUARE (PREŠERNOV TRG). Nestled between Miklošičeva c. and the gorgeous Triple Bridge, Prešernov trg is at the cultural heart of Ljubljana and is one of the city's liveliest spots. A statue pays homage to its namesake, Slovenian poet France Prešeren (see p. 661), author of the country's national anthem; its inclusion of a nude likeness of the poet's muse, however, once aroused local controversy. The enormous pink 17th-century **Franciscan church** (Frančiškanska cerkev) dominates the square and contains an altar designed by local master Francisco Robba. A touch of Art Nouveau is also visible in the facade of the Centromerkur, one of the finer Secessionist buildings that surrounds the square. Don't miss the scale model of Ljubljana on the east side of the square. On warm nights, there are often live music performances. *(A short walk from City Hall, down Stritarjeva and across the Triple Bridge. Church open daily 6:45am-12:30pm and 3-8pm. Free.)*

DRAGON BRIDGE (ZMAJSKI MOST). The striking bronze **dragons** that flank each side of this 1901 Art Nouveau bridge have become the city's symbols, and a popular attraction for visitors. The bridge was designed not by ubiquitous local architect Jože Plečnik but by the Dalmatian Jurij Zaninovič. The nearby open-air market is worth a visit, especially on bustling Saturday mornings.

TRIPLE BRIDGE (TROMOSTOVJE). With its motorway flanked by two footbridges, the Triple Bridge provides a majestic entrance to the Old Town. The current structure was created in the 1930s, when Plečnik modernized the old stone construction, adding Venetian touches like classical balustrades and orbs.

FRENCH REVOLUTION SQUARE (TRG FRANCOSKE REVOLUCIJE). The obelisk that crowns the square commemorates the 1809-1814 Napoleonic occupation of Slovenia. It contains the ashes of a French warrior and is believed to be the only monument in the world dedicated to an unknown soldier from a foreign land. The square's highlight is the beautiful stone **Križanke Summer Theater,** which hosts open-air performances in summer. *(☎241 6026. Box office open M-F 10am-1:30pm and 4-8pm; Sa 10am-1pm; also 1hr. before each performance. Tickets €8.50-21.)*

OTHER SIGHTS. Walk down Zoisova past French Revolution Sq. and take a left on Barjanska c. to see the few ruins of a **Roman wall** preserved from the previous settlement of Emona. Head back up Barjanska to reach Slovenska c., Ljubljana's main shopping area. Behind the **Ursuline Church** on the left is Trg Republike, home to the **Parliament,** its door framed by a distinctive array of naked figures. **Kongresni trg,** on the other side of Slovenska c., is a shaded park just above **Ljubljana University** containing Ljubljana's best nightlife. One block below the University, the **Slovenian Academy of Arts and Sciences** (Slovenska Akademija Znanosti in Umetnosti; SAZU) is a former Baroque palace; the **National Library** (Narodna in Univerzitetna Knjiznica; NUK), another of Plečnik's creations, is across the street. In front of **City Hall** (Rotovž) sits a **fountain** embellished with representations of the Ljubljanica, Sava, and Krka rivers. Tours of the Town Hall, available on Saturdays at noon for €2, let visitors to glimpse the striking Baroque interior of this imposing building.

MUSEUMS

Ljubljana is teeming with little galleries, many of which are located close together. With an underpass to Tivoli Park right in front of the Museum of Modern Art, many locals and travelers like to complete this civilized outing with a picnic.

NATIONAL MUSEUM (NARODNI MUZEJ). Slovenia's oldest museum features exhibits on archaeology, culture, and local history from the prehistoric era to the present. It's full of surprises: as you enter, you'll see statues of eight women sliding down the banister. Impressive stone slabs date from the Roman era. Upstairs, the **Natural History Museum** features a woolly mammoth skeleton and various taxidermied animals. *(Muzejska 1. ☎241 4404; www.narmuz-lj.si. English information, including touchscreens in the Natural History Museum. Open M-W, F, Su 10am-6pm; Th 10am-8pm. Both museums €4, students €3. 1 museum €3/2. First Su of each month free.)*

MUSEUM OF MODERN ART (MODERNA GALERIJA LJUBLJANA). A simple, boxy exterior gives way to a fantastic, high-ceilinged space featuring provocative multimedia work, from paintings and sculpture to videos and projections. The permanent collection is of late 20th-century Slovenian art; rotating exhibits display work by international artists. *(Cankarjeva 15. ☎241 6800; www.mg-lj.si. Open Tu-Su 10am-6pm. €4, students €2; free admission with Ljubljana Tourist card. AmEx/MC/V.)*

PLEČNIK COLLECTION ARCHITECTURE MUSEUM (PLEČNIKOVA ZBRIKA). This small museum chronicles the life and work of Jože Plečnik, Slovenia's premier architect, in a house built by the master himself. Highlights include the artist's well-preserved studio, the wildly intricate furniture that he crafted, and models of ambitious architectural projects that never came to fruition. *(Karunova 4. Walk toward the center on Slovenska; turn left on Zoisova, then right on Emonska. Cross the bridge and* *head behind the church.* ☎*280 1600; fax 280 1605. Open Tu-Th 10am-6pm, Sa 10am-3pm. €4.50, students €2. Mandatory 30min. tour available in English.)*

NATIONAL GALLERY (NARODNA GALERIJA). This handsome Austro-Hungarian building houses works by Slovenian and European painters and sculptors from the Romantic through Impressionist periods, as well as religious icons dating from 1270. The Realist and Modern Art pieces are a special treat. Don't miss the constantly changing exhibitions either. *(Prešernova 24.* ☎*241 5434. Open Tu-Su 10am-6pm. €3.50, students €2.50; Sa afternoon free.)*

ENTERTAINMENT AND FESTIVALS

Pick up a free *Where To?* events listing from the **TIC** (p. 664). **Cankarjev dom,** Prešernov trg 10 (☎241 1764), hosts the **Slovenian Philharmonic.** (Performances Oct.-June. Box office in the basement of Maximarket. Open M-F 11am-1pm and 3-8pm, Sa 11am-1pm and 1hr. before performance. Tickets €8.50-30.) The **Opera House,** Župančičeva 1, also houses the **ballet.** (☎241 1764. Box office open M-F 1-5pm, Sa 11am-1pm, and 1hr. before each performance. Tickets €8.50-40.) In December, the Old Town comes alive with church concerts, street fairs, and New Year's celebrations. **Tivoli Hall,** in Tivoli Park, hosts sporting events and rock concerts. **Kolosej,** Šmartinska c. 152 (☎520 5500; www.kolosej.si), shows English-language movies (€5). Buses #2, 7, and 17 run from the center to the cinema.

The festival season kicks off with the **International Viticulture and Wine Fair** held at the **Fairgrounds** in April. At the end of June and throughout July, the **Festival of Street Theater** (Ana Desetnica) transforms the city streets and squares into impromptu stages. In late June, the alternative arts scene hosts the international, avant-garde **Break 22 Festival;** meanwhile, the **International Jazz Festival** grooves in Cankarjev dom and Križanke in late June; inquire at TIC for a free schedule. The vaguely titled **International Summer Festival,** from mid-June to mid-September, is a conglomeration of music, opera, and theater performances held at Cankarjev dom and other local venues. The **Ljubljana International Film Festival** plays in early November. Don't miss **Križanke Summer Theater,** which hosts open-air music, dance, and theater from June to September. (☎241 6026. Box office open M-F 10am-1:30pm and 4-8pm, Sa 10am-1pm, and 1hr. before performances. Tickets €8.50-20.)

NIGHTLIFE

Cafes and bars line the waterfront, **Trubarjeva, Stari trg,** and **Mestni trg.** For a more energetic scene, try **Metelkova Mesto,** especially on weekends after midnight; for dancing above the city lights, head over to **Global.**

Makalonca, Hribarjevo nab., just past the Triple Bridge. Hidden on a terrace below the waterfront's main drag, an arched stone door leads to this local favorite. The intimate cavern-bar has gorgeous views of the river and an easygoing staff. Sangria €1.60. Mixed drinks €2.50-4.50. Open M-Sa 10pm-1am, Su 10am-3pm.

Metelkova Mesto (www.metelkova.org), the Metelkova block, from Trg OF to the Ethnographic Museum. Formerly part of a military barracks, Metelkova was taken over by squatters in the early 90s when the city threatened to tear it down. Soon it became an artists' colony, with vivid grafitti covering its bars and clubs. The crowd draws local artists and backpackers; while there are gay and lesbian nights at only 2 of these clubs—Tiffany and Monokel, respectively—the whole scene is GLBT-friendly. Little is permanent at this self-proclaimed "autonomous cultural center," as ongoing attempts by the city to demolish the complex attest. Hours vary.

Global, Tomsiceva 2 (☎426 9020; www.global.si). The elevator is on the corner of Slovenska; look for the orange circle that says "Global." Take the glass elevator to the 6th fl. Considered the best dance club in Ljubljana, this trendy rooftop hot spot boasts a 70s disco ambience, an extensive cocktail menu, and views of the castle. On weekends, the action gets going around midnight. Tables can be booked in advance. Mixed drinks €4-6. Cover for men €4.50 after 11pm. Free Wi-Fi. Bar open M-Sa 8am-10pm. Disco open Th-Sa 10pm-5am.

Casa del Papa, Celovška 54a (☎434 3158). This Hemingway- and island-themed bar on the outskirts of the center draws 20- and 30-somethings seeking a change from the packed waterfront nightlife with its Latin beats and Cuban cigars. Beer €1.20-2.30 per 0.25L. Mixed drinks €4.50-5.50. Open M-Sa noon-midnight, Su noon-11pm.

Skeleton Bar, Kljucavnicarska 5, an alley between Cankarjevo and Mestni Trg (☎252 7799). Down the Old Town stone stairs, this dungeon-like bar serves up a host of ghoulish 2-for-1 cocktails (€3.50-6.50) with names like Nuclear Waste and Skeleton Punch amidst skeletons in a range of compromising poses. Open M-Su 8pm-4am.

DAYTRIPS FROM LJUBLJANA

ŠKOCJANSKE CAVES

Trains run from Ljubljana to Divača (1½hr., 10 per day, €6.03). With your back to the train station, turn right and follow the road out of town. Cross the highway on the bridge and walk through a village, following signs that lead to a narrow wooded path and the ticket booth (40min.). Park office ☎057 632 840; www.gov.si/parkskj. Mandatory tours daily June-Sept. every hr. 10am-5pm; Oct.-May 10am, 1, 3:30pm. €11, students €7.50.)

Škocjanske is an amazing system of UNESCO-protected **caverns** with limestone formations and a 120m gorge created by the Reca River. Far less ravaged by tourists than nearby Postojna, the caves offer a stunning gothic 2km walk that dips downward towards the gorge, offering incredible and haunting views. Sights include a giant 250,000-year-old column and a stalactite and stalagmite in the process of joining—currently separated only by 50-100 years, or a waterdrop's breadth. This mysterious underworld is not to be missed.

POSTOJNA CAVES (POSTOJNSKA JAMA)

Trains go to Postojna (1¼hr., 10 per day, €4.55), but the station is far from the caves. Buses are a better option; ask for a ticket to Postojna (1hr., about every 30min., €6). The caves are only a 20min. walk from the bus station. Walk uphill past the ivory-and-green-capped tower to the Tourist Information Center. Make a left at the square and continue; you'll see signs. ☎700 0100; www.postojna-cave.com. Mandatory 1½hr. tours leave May-Sept. daily every hr. 10am-6pm; Oct. and April daily 10am, noon; Nov.-Mar. M-F 10am and noon, Sa-Su every hr. 10am-4pm. €15, students €11.

You'll need to brave the crowds to reach one of Slovenia's greatest natural treasures, but the trip is well worth it. A gentle 2km walk will get you to the stalactites. Although its fame among tourists has turned the caverns into a kind of amusement-park ride, the crowds all but disappear against the array of multicolored rock formations inside the caves. From the train station, an English tour is around the corner on the right. The tour, part on foot, part by train, covers only 20% of the two-million-year-old cave's 20km. Bring something warm, as the temperature inside is a constant 8°C, and a hat, unless you don't mind the occasional drip—the humidity is a constant 90%.

PREDJAMA CASTLE

During the school year, buses go to Bukovje, 2km from the castle (15min.; M-F 7am, 12:35, 1:25, 3:30pm; €1.60). Alternatively, you can take a cab. From Postojna, taxis run to Predjama. (☎031 406 446; about €7.) Call ahead to arrange a visit to the cave below Predjama Castle. (☎756 8260.) Open May-Sept. daily 9am-7pm; Oct. and April daily 10am-5pm; Nov.-Mar. M-F 10am-3pm, Sa-Su 10am-5pm. €4.60, students €3.50. If you plan to visit both the caves and the castle as a single daytrip from Ljubljana, it may be cheaper and more convenient to rent a car (see p. 664).

Though challenging and costly to reach, Predjama Castle (Predjamski Grad), 9km from Postojna, is fascinating. Literally built into a 123m high cave on the side of a mountain, this feat of natural architecture is actually of medieval inspiration, first constructed in the 12th century, and renovated in the 16th century with Renaissance flair. Predjama's most famous inhabitant was Erasmus, a German knight who brazenly supported the Hungarian crown in its wars against the Austrian emperor Friedrich III. Friedrich III sent his entire army after the errant knight and besieged the castle with cannonballs for a year and a day, with nothing to show for it but gifts of cherries and roast bullock from Erasmus. Just as the besiegers were running low on supplies, Erasmus's servant turned the tides by betraying his master. After the servant alerted the Austrians that his master was in the outhouse, a single catapult round earned Friedrich his revenge on the rebel knight, who died in the least honorable of positions.

THE JULIAN ALPS (JULIJSKE ALPE)

Stretching across northwest Slovenia and high into the clouds, the Julian Alps are just as stunning as their Austrian or Swiss counterparts. The serene wilderness around Lake Bohinj, the alpine peaks of Kranjska Gora, and the beauty of Lake Bled and its enchanting island all lie within a short bus ride of one another.

BLED ☎(0)4

Bled (pop. 11,000), perched on the shores of a gorgeous turqouise lake, and ringed by green alpine hills and snow-covered peaks. More and more visitors show up each summer to swim, hike, shop, paraglide. But its beauty is only slightly diminshed by popularity; little on Earth can compare with the crisp perfection of Slovenia's only island and the small but stately castle at its center.

TRANSPORTATION AND PRACTICAL INFORMATION. Bled has no central train station; **trains** to Ljubljana (1hr., 7 per day, €4) depart from the Lesce-Bled station (☎294 4154), 4km from town. To reach Bled from the station, take the frequent **commuter bus** (10min., €1.30), which stops on Ljubljanska and at the bus station, c. Svobode 4 (☎578 0420). **Buses** are more convenient and go to Bohinjsko Jezero (35min., 1 per hr. 7:20am-8:20pm, €3.60), Kranjska Gora (40min., 1 per hr., €4.80), and Ljubljana (1½hr., 1 per hr. 5am-9:30pm, €6.30). A bus runs to Vintgar Gorge's trailhead June 14-Sept. 30 (10am, €2.50).

The town spreads around **Lake Bled,** and most buildings are clustered on the eastern shore. **Ljubljanska,** the main street, leads to the water, where it meets **cesta Svobode,** which circles the lake. To get to the center, with your back to the bus station, turn right on c. Svobode, follow the road uphill and turns into Prešernova c., and turn right on Ljubljanska. From Ljubljanska, the **tourist office,** c. Svobode 10, is on the right, toward the lake and past the Park Hotel. The staff give out **free maps** of Bled and sell hiking maps (€4-10) of the entire region. (☎574 1122 or 574 1555; www.bled.si. Open June-Sept. M-Sa 8am-7pm; Mar.-May 9am-7pm; Nov.-Feb. 9am-5pm.) **Gorenjska Banka,** c. Svobode 15, below the Park Hotel, has a MasterCard **ATM.** (☎574 1300. Open M-F 9am-11:30am and 2-5pm; Sa 8-11am.) **SKB Banka,** Ljubljanska c. 4, accepts all cards. (☎574 2261. Open M-F 8:30am-noon and 2-5pm.) **Zlatarog Pharmacy** is at Prešernova c. 36. (☎578 0770. Open M-F 7am-7:30pm, Sa 7am-

1pm.) **Internet** is available free to guests of most hotels and hostels and at the **library,** Ljubljanska c. 10. (☎575 1600. Max. 1hr. per day. Open M-F 8am-7pm, Sa 8am-noon.) There is an Internet cafe in the shopping center. The **post office** is at Ljubljanska 10. (☎575 0200. Open M-F 7am-7pm, Sa 7am-noon.) **Postal Code:** 4260.

ACCOMMODATIONS AND FOOD. **Agency Kompas,** Ljubljanska 4, on the top floor of the shopping center, books **private rooms.** (☎572 7500; www.kompas-bled.si. Private rooms from €12-33. Open June-Oct. M-Sa 8am-8pm, Su 8am-noon and 4-7pm; Nov.-May M-Sa 8am-7pm, Su 8am-noon and 4-7pm. Tourist tax €1. AmEx/MC/V.) **Globtour,** Ljubljanska 7, also arranges private rooms. (☎574 1821; www.globtour-bled.com. Open June-Sept. 15 and Dec. 21-Jan 4 M-Sa 8am-8pm, Su 9am-noon and 4-7pm. Singles €20-24; doubles €30-70. Stays under 3 nights 30% more. Tourist tax €1. AmEx/MC/V.) To find a room on your own, look for *sobe* signs, which are common outside the center of town. To reach the **Bledec Youth Hostel (HI) ❷,** Grajska c. 17, a 10min. hike from Bled Castle, walk up the street from the bus station. Facing away from the bus station, turn left and walk to the top of the hill, bearing left at the fork. Bledec has a cozy log-cabin feel, with dark wood decor, comfortable beds, and clean bathrooms. (☎574 52 50; bledec@mlino.si. Restaurant and common room available. Breakfast included. Laundry €8.50. Internet €2 per 30min. Reception 24hr. Check-out 10am. Reserve ahead. Open only in high season. Dorms €20, members €19; doubles €25. Tourist tax €1. AmEx/MC/V.) For those who prefer camping, **Camping Bled ❶,** Kidrieva 10c, in a beautiful valley on the west side of the lake, lies about 2.5km from the bus station. From the station, follow c. Svobode downhill, turn left at the lake, and walk 25min. The campground has a store, a restaurant, and a beach. (☎575 20 00; www.camping.bled.si. Laundry €4. Internet €7.50 per hr. Reception 24hr. Check-out 3pm. €6.80-10 per person. Electricity €3. Tourist tax €0.50.)

Most of the restaurants in Bled are touristy and overpriced; your best bet is to pick up supplies at **Mercator,** Ljubljanska c. 13, in the shopping center and find a good picnic spot. (Open M-Sa 7am-8pm, Su 8am-noon.) If days of hostel-made sandwiches have left you feeling extravagant, try **Okarina ❹,** Riklijiva 9, just uphill from the bus station, which specializes in Indian-inspired and vegetarian dishes. Colorful carpets on the wall, Bollywood paraphernalia, and a round open-air courtyard complement the tasty food. The chicken masala (*masala mesna;* €10) with the *parata* (€3.30) should not be missed. (☎574 1458. Entrees €9.50-19. Open M-F 6pm-midnight, Sa-Su noon-midnight.) Excellent service and huge portions of high-quality food distinguish Gostilna pri **Planincu ❷,** Grajska c. 8, diagonally across the street from the bus station. Colorful number plates coat the ceiling and walls of this smoky bar, giving this Bled favorite a distinctly local flavor. (☎574 1613. Crepes €2.50-3.50. Pizza €4.60-11. Open daily 9am-11pm.) Popular with locals, **Slaščičarna Šmon ❶,** Grajska c. 3, between Okarina and the bus station, offers coffee (€1) and desserts (€0.60-2.30). Their *torte* arsenal (€1.50-1.70) includes *grmada,* a chocolate biscuit with vanilla cream, nuts, raisins, and rum. (☎574 2280. Sandwiches €2.10. Pizza €1.25. Open daily 7:30am-10pm.)

SIGHTS. **Bled Castle** (Blejski grad) is of moderate interest, but the view from it is truly beautiful. Built in 1004, Slovenia's oldest citadel rises 100m above the lake, framing a perfect view of Bled's island. The official path to the castle is on Grajska c., but there are several pleasant hikes through the forest. One runs uphill from **St. Martin's Church** (Cerkev sv. Martin), on Kidričeva c. near the lake. Another route begins behind the swimming area; follow blazes marked with a "1" uphill. The shortest path is a 10min. hike from behind the parking lot of Bledec Hostel.

Inside the castle wall, the entrance is through the souvenir shop. Castle tickets include admission to the slight but compelling **History Museum** on the ground floor, stocked with furniture, weapons, and coins from successive historical periods of the Castle's existence. Poke your head into the small printing studio opposite the museum to watch an artist in traditional dress produce medieval, Gutenberg-style prints. Videos in English and interactive touchscreens depict the history of the glacier-formed lake, the castle, and Bled. (☎578 0525. Open daily May-Oct. 8am-8pm, Nov.-Apr. 8am-5pm. €5, students €4.50. MC.)

The town's magnificent centerpiece, wooded Bled Island (Blejski Otok), is home to the **Church of the Assumption** (Cerkev Marijinega Vnebovzetja). Ring the bell in the church to make a wish. There are several ways to reach the island. The supervised swimming area below the castle rents row boats (€10), as does Janez Palak, Koritenska 27. (☎578 0528. 3-seaters €10 for 1st hr., €5 per additional hr.; 5-seaters €12/6. €4 deposit.) You can also cross the lake on gondola-style *plentas*, stationed at the Rowing Center and in Mlino under Hotel Park. (Round-trip 1½hr., 20min. each way, with 30min. on the island; €10 per person.) In summer, swimming to the island is permitted; the closest starting point is the west side of the lake, next to the camping grounds. Or, you can dive in from the **Castle Swimming Grounds** (Grajsko Kopališoe) under Bled Castle. (Day ticket €5, students €3.30; afternoon €3.75/2.90.) In summer, the water averages 21-24°C; in winter, the lake becomes an ice-skating rink. (Open Dec.-Feb. daily 7am-7pm. Lockers €3.)

ENTERTAINMENT AND NIGHTLIFE. The tourist office distributes a free brochure listing local events. The second weekend in July draws together orchestral musicians for **Bled Days** (www.festivalbled.com), which features concerts, arts and crafts, and fireworks on the lake. Bled's nightlife is low-key. Pass up the disco at the shopping center and the casinos and check out **Devil,** c. Svobode 15, under the Park Hotel. With brick walls, red-and-yellow vaulted arches, and wrought iron chairs, it feels delectably dark and medieval. The wooden deck overlooks the lake. (Mixed drinks €1.90-4.50. Wine €1.90. Ice cream €0.70. Open daily 9am-4am. Cash only.) Backpackers mingle with locals on the rustic patio of **The Pub,** c. Svobode 8a, that produces over 100 kinds of mixed drinks for patrons sipping their drinks as they watch the sun set over the lake. The relaxed vibe attracts an older crowd. (☎574 2217. Union €1.70 per 0.3L. Open M-Th 9pm-2am, F-Sa 9-3am.) Once everything has closed, head over to **Stop,** c. svobode 15, beneath the shopping mall, an open terrace that hosts the only disco dancing available in this small town. (Open Tu-Su 9pm-5am in summer.)

OUTDOOR ACTIVITIES. The **Kompas** agency, in the shopping center, rents **bikes** (€3.50 per hr., €8 per ½-day, €11 per day) and offers whitewater rafting trips. (☎572 7500; www.kompas-bled.si. Rafting €25-30 per day. Open 8am-7pm, Su 8am-noon and 4-7pm. AmEx/MC/V.) **Globtour** also rents out bikes (€7 per 1/2 day and €10 per day). Many hiking paths snake from the lake into the hills, each marked with a name and trail number. The tourist office sells detailed trail maps (€8). **3glav Adventures,** Ljubljanska 1, offers some of the most sought-after excursions. Their signature Emerald River Valley tour gives participants an overview of the entire region (€55, with rafting €88). Discounts are available for groups and individuals taking part in three or more activities. (☎168 3184. Open M-Su 8am-7pm.) **LifeTrek Adventures,** Ljubljanska 1, located across the street from Kompas and the shopping center, rents **bikes** and offers guided outdoor excursions around Bled and Triglav National Park, ranging from the tame to the extreme. (☎578 0660; www.sigov.si/trip. Hiking €28-155; climbing €155; rafting €25; paragliding €75. Bikes €4 2hr., €8 per ½ day, €12 per day. Open M-Sa 8am-4pm.)

Traced by the waterfalls and rapids of the Radovna River, nearby **Vintgar Gorge** (Soteska Vintgar) offers one of the best hikes in the area. Walk the 4km instead of taking the bus to the trailhead, and you'll pass small towns and open fields. Bring food: a picnic bench tucked neatly into a nook lies halfway along the hike. The 1.6km gorge carves through the rocks of the nearby **Triglav National Park** (Triglavski Narodni Park). The park info office is at Kidričeva c. 2. (☎574 1188; fax 574 3568.) To get there, go over the hill on Grajska c., away from the center, and make a right at the bottom. Turn left after 100m and follow signs for Vintgar. Alternatively, hop on one of the frequent buses to Podhom (10min., M-Sa 10 per day, €1.30) and follow the 1.5km route. From mid-June through September, **Alpetour** (☎532 0440) runs a bus to the trailhead (15min.; daily 10am; one-way €2.50, round-trip €4.50).

LAKE BOHINJ (BOHINJSKO JEZERO) ☎(0)4

Bohinjsko Jezero (BOH-heen-skoh YEH-zeh-roh; pop. 5,300), 26km southwest of Lake Bled, surpasses its famous neighbor in untouched natural beauty. Protected by the borders of Triglav National Park, the large glacial lake draws aquatic adventurers to its pristine waters. But it is the towering mountains rising right out of the lake that are the most enticing, attracting travelers who yearn to scale or ski these local summits.

TRANSPORTATION AND PRACTICAL INFORMATION. Although **trains** do not run to or from the three villages around Lake Bohinj, the area is still very accessible. You can easily catch a bus to **Bohinjska Bistrica,** the largest town in the area, 6km from the lake, and take a train from there to Ljubljana (2½hr., 8 per day, €5.30) via Jesenice. **Buses,** the more convenient option, run from Hotel Zlatorog in Ukanc to Ribčev Laz (10min., 1 per hr., €1.30) and from Ribčev Laz to Bled (35min., 11-16 per day, €3.60), Bohinjska Bistrica (15min., 1 per hr., €1.60), and Ljubljana (2hr., 1 per hr., €8.30). Buses going to Bohinjsko Jezero (Lake Bohinj) stop at Hotel Jezero in Ribčev Laz or at Hotel Zlatorog in Ukanc. The town nearest the lake is Bohinjska Bistrica, 6km east, but Ribčev Laz, where the bus drops you off, should have everything you need. The lake is surrounded by two other villages, Stara Fužina and Ukanc.

The **tourist bureau,** Ribčev Laz 48, provides maps and transportation info; issues fishing permits, books private rooms (which are cheaper than in Bled), and arranges guided excursions. (☎574 6010; www.bohinj.si. Open July-Aug. M-Sa 8am-8pm, Su 8am-7pm; Sept.-June M-Sa 8am-6pm, Su 9am-3pm.) The nearest bank, **Gorenjska Banka,** Trg Svobode 2B, in Bohinjska Bistrica, **exchanges currency** for no commission and cashes **traveler's checks.** (☎572 1610. Open July-Aug. M-F 8am-6pm, Sa 8-11am; Sept.-June M-F 9-11:30am and 2-5pm, Sa 8-11am.) The closest **pharmacy** is in Bohinjska Bistrica, at Triglavska 15. (☎572 1630. Open M-F 8am-7:30pm, Sa 8am-1pm.) **Internet** is at **Pansion Rožic,** Ribčev Laz 42, just up the street from the TIC. (☎572 3395. €0.10 per min.) It is also available further afield at Bohinjska Bistrica's **Aqua Park** (☎577 0210; www.vodni-park-bohinj.si). The **post office** in Ribčev Laz, Ribčev Laz 47, has a MasterCard and Visa **ATM** outside. (Open July-Aug. M-F 8am-7pm, Sa 8am-noon; Sept.-June M-F 8-9:30am, 10-10:30am, and 4-6pm, Sa 8am-noon.) **Postal Code:** 4265.

HAPPY END. The town of Ukanc ("the end") was so named by locals who once considered it the limit of the natural world. Ironically, it marks the beginning of gorgeous Bohinjska Bistrica.

ACCOMMODATIONS AND FOOD. The tourist bureau arranges **private rooms** and other accommodations in all three villages year-round. (Breakfast €4.60. Rooms €10-15. Tourist tax €1.) **AutoCamp Zlatorog ❶,** Ukanc 2, is on the lake's west side, near the Savica Waterfall and many trailheads, 200m from the

SLOVENIA

cableway. Take a bus to Hotel Zlatorog in Ukranc and then backtrack 300m. The complex, run by Alpinum Tourist Agency, has sports facilities, showers, baths, and a restaurant. Bike and boat rentals are also available. (☎572 3482; fax 572 3446. Reception July-Aug. 24hr.; Sept.-May daily 8am-noon and 4-8pm. Check-out noon. Campsite July-Aug. €7-8 per day; Sept. and May-June €9-12. Tourist tax €0.50. Cash only.) On the way, check out the Mt. Vogel **gondola** (10min.; 2 per hr. 7am-7pm; one-way €7, round-trip €10) that takes you 1535m up to a view of the mountains and lake. **Camping Danica ❶**, Bohinjska Bistrica 4264, is just outside town in a quiet area below the mountains. Get off the bus in Bohinjska Bistrica and backtrack about 75m; the site is on the right. The camp has tennis courts, a restaurant, and showers. The river Sava that runs beside the site is a refreshing antidote to the summer swelter. Danica also organizes folk cultural events in the summer, complete with traditional clothing, music and food. (High season ☎572 1055, low season 574 6010; www.bohinj.si/camping-danica. Campsite July 1-Aug. 18 €10; June 10-30 and Aug. 19-Sept. 1 €8.35; May 1-June 9 and Sept. 2-30 €7. Electricity €2.50. 10% discount on stays longer than 1 week. Tourist tax €0.50. AmEx/MC/V.)

Mercator Supermarket is at Ribčev Laz 49, by the tourist office. (☎572 9534. Open M-F 7am-8pm, Sa 7am-8pm, Su 7am-5pm.) **Gostišče Kramar ❶**, Stara Fužina 3, has a view of the lake, though the menu is limited to pizza (€0.85-5), hot dogs, and other fast food (€1.50-3.75). From Ribčev Laz, walk over the stone bridge and follow the first path on the left through the woods for 7min. (☎572 3697. 0.5L beer €1.70. Open M-Th and Su 11am-midnight, F-Sa 11am-1am.) **Restavracija Center ❷**, Ribčev Laz 50, complements its pizzas (€4.50-6) and the standard "tourist menu" of pastas and meat dishes (€5.80-6.70), which always feature a seafood or vegetarian option, with a log cabin atmosphere. (☎572 3170. Open daily 8am-11pm.)

OUTDOOR ACTIVITIES. The shores of Bohinj are a gateway to a range of outdoor adventures. Good **hiking maps** are available at the tourist office (€7.50) and are highly advisable for those tackling some of the longer treks. The most popular destination is the somewhat overrated **Savica Waterfall** (Slap Savica), which cascades into the Sava Bohinjka River. Take the local bus from Ribčev Laz toward "Bohinj-Zlatorog" and get off at Hotel Zlatorog (15min., 1 per hr. 8am-7pm, €1.30). Follow the signs uphill to Savica Waterfall for 1hr. to the trailhead, Dom Savica, where visitors must pay €2 before heading up to the waterfall (20min. up stairs from the trailhead). In July and August, a bus runs to the trailhead from Ribčev Laz (20min., 4 per day 9am-6pm, €2). If you forgo the bus, turn left at the lake in Ribčev Laz and follow the road along the lake past Ukanc (1½hr.).

If the hiking spirit compels you to continue, cross the bridge by the parking lot and follow the signs up the mountain toward the stunning **Black Lake** (Črno Jezero) at the base of the Julian Alps' highest peaks (1½hr.). Although this is a fun climb, be aware that the hiking is extremely steep; avoid going alone or carrying a pack. Facing the small lake's shore, a trail to the right (Dol Pod Stadorjem) leads to **Mt. Viševnik,** a grassy hillside that overlooks the small peaks. Facing the valley below, veer left and follow the signs and trailblazes to reach **Pršivec** (1½hr., 1761m). Return the way you came or follow the trail east for a quicker and easier return (1hr.) along the ridge through Vogar. When you hit the highway at the base, turn right and proceed via Stara Fužina and Ribčev Laz (2½hr.).

Alpinsport, Ribčev Laz 53, rents **mountain bikes, kayaks,** and **canoes,** and organizes **mountaineering** and **canyoning** trips in nearby gorges. (☎572 3486; www.alpinsport.si. Bikes €4 per hr., €13 per day; kayaks €4/14; canoes €5/27. Open daily July-Aug. 10am-7pm; Sept.-June 10am-5pm.) In winter, Bohinj becomes an enormous **ski** resort with five main slopes: **Soriška Planina, Kobla, Senožeta, Pokljuka,** and **Vogel.** The season runs from late December to mid-April, depending on weather conditions. Vogel, the most popular area, is a hot destination for intermediate and expert skiers. (Morning or afternoon lift pass €15. Day pass €21. Ski rental with boots €16, snowboard and boots €18, poles €3, helmet €4.) Nearby Kobla offers gentler slopes. In winter, **Alpinsport** rents skis and snowboards and holds group and private ski lessons. (Skis and ski boot set rental €17 per day. Private ski lessons €22 per hr. Snowboard set €18 per day.) For more info, contact **Vogel,** Ukanc 6 (☎574 6060; vogel@bohinj.si), or **Kobla,** c. na Ravne 7 (☎574 7100; kobla@siol.net). For more info on outdoor activities, check out **www.bohinj.si.**

KRANJSKA GORA ☎(0)4

The village of **Kranjska Gora** (KRAN-ska GOR-ah; pop. 1500) combines an old-fashioned town center with a serious outdoors scene. Skiers come for Slovenia's best trails, while others will appreciate scenic cycling and hiking in the Karavanke ridge to the north. Beyond this, the town is dominated by picturesque *sobes.* Time your visit to coincide with some of Kranjska's unique festivities, such as their annual Christmas tree drowning and illumination of the Peričnik waterfall, to get a sense of the distinctive character that lurks beneath its resort atmosphere.

For a fairly short hike, take trail #3 (40min., 2.2km) or more difficult #4 (1½hr., 3.5km) to the small village **Podkoren,** 3km from Kranjska Gora, known for its folk architecture. From there, you can pick up trail #12 toward **Rateče,** a tiny town 7km from Kranjska Gora. Rateče sits below **Pec** (1510m), a peak on the border with Austria and Italy, which sports a few restaurants and a modest church. One of the best hikes runs through the **Planica Valley** to **Tamar Valley.** From town, take trail #9 to Planica (2hr., 5km), where you'll see impressive ski runs and enjoy an amazing view of the **Mojstrovka, Travnik, Šita,** and **Jalovec Mountains.** Jalovec peak is considered the most beautiful mountain in Slovenia and is the Alpine Association's official symbol. Continue on the trail past the ski ramps for 45min. to reach the mountain hut **Tamar,** from which Jalovec can be seen.

The nearest **train station** is in Jesenice (24km). **Buses** run to and from: Lesce-Bled Airport (40min., M-F 9:15am and 1:10pm, 2 direct to Bled) and to Ljubljana (2¼hr.; M-F 6 per day, Sa 5; €9). **Sport Point,** Borovška c. 93A, rents **bikes** (€3.50 per hr., €10 per day), **rollerblades** (€2.50/6.50), **trikkes** (like scooters with 3 wheels; €2.50/6.50), and two apartments upstairs (€55-80; prices vary by season). (☎588 4883. Open daily 8am-8pm. AmEx/MC/V.) **Agencija Julijana,** Borovška 93, next to the Prišavik Hotel, arranges **hiking** and **skiing** excursions, and also leads **raft, bike, sled,** and **toboggan** trips. (☎588 1325; www.sednjek.si. Bike rentals €3 per hr., €6.30 per ½-day, €8.50 per day. Rafting trips €30. Open daily 8am-noon and 3-8pm.)

For accommodations, your best budget option is a **private room**—there are plenty available in town, marked by *sobe* signs. The helpful and English-speaking staff at the **tourist office,** on Tičarjeva, arranges rooms for no additional fee and has a comprehensive price list of all hotels and pensions in the city, as well as the bus timetables. (*Sobes* July 28-Aug. 24 €15-19; June 16-July 27 and Aug. 25-Sept. 14 €13-17; Mar. 31-June 15 and Sept. 15-Nov. 30 €11-15. Tax €1.01 per day.) Though pricier than most HI establishments, **HI Pension and Youth Hostel Borka ❸,** Borovška 71, is one of the best options in town. It is located in the city center and is equipped with a TV room, restaurant, and snack bar. (☎587 9100. Breakfast included. 2- to 4-bed suites with bath €25 per person, half-pension €35, full pension €45. Tourist tax €1 per day.) **Hostel Pr' Tatko ❶,** Podkoren 72, is farther afield, about 3km from Kranjska itself, but offers excellent accommodations. At the base of the Julian Alps, it is perfectly situated for day hikes, and is only 2km from Planica's giant ski-jump. With hand-painted walls, Wi-Fi and lessons available in beekeeping and mushroom cultivation, this well-furnished and immaculate alpine villa is a great base for exploring Slovenia's natural surroundings. (☎147 9087. From €13 a day.) The traditionally clad servers at **Gostilna pri Martinu ❸,** Borovška 61, deliver huge portions of Slovenian fare like goulash and polenta for €3.30-9.50. (☎582 0300. Vegetarian plates €4.20-5. Open daily 10am-11pm.) For the standard Italian-influenced menu at the standard prices, but with a touch of class, head to **Kotnik ❶**, Borovška 75. While meals may follow the successful tourist formula, this yellow plaster building with stone interior adds a jazzy texture to the weary adventurer's day. (☎588 1564. Entrees €4.50-12.)

ISTRIA

Slovenia claims only 40km of the Adriatic coast, but its remarkable stretch of green bays and vineyards has a palpably Italian flavor. Reminiscent of the French Riviera or Dalmatian Coast, Slovenian Istria is the site of bustling coastal villages.

PORTOROŽ ☎(0)5

The "Port of Roses" (pohrt-oh-ROHZH; pop. 9,000) is Slovenian Istria's giant resort strip. Streams of visitors have washed away the distinctly Slovenian flavor retained by neighboring coastal towns, but the grassy beach, seaside restaurants, and deep blue tide of Portorož remain unblemished.

TRANSPORTATION. **Buses** go to Ljubljana (2¾hr., 7-8 per day, €12). A **minibus** runs from Lucija through Portorož and on to Piran (every 30min. 5:30am-midnight, €1). **Atlas Express,** Obala 55, has **American Express travel services** and rents **bikes** and **scooters.** (☎674 8821. Open July-Sept. M-F 8:30am-7:30pm, Sa 9am-7pm, Su 10am-1pm.) **Maestral,** Obala 123, rents **boats.** (☎677 9280; www.maestral.si. July-Aug. €100 per 4hr., €180 per day; Sept. and June €90.)

ORIENTATION AND PRACTICAL INFORMATION. Most streets start at **Obala,** the waterfront boulevard. If you arrive by bus, you'll see the **tourist office,** Obala 16, right across the street. (☎674 0231; www.portoroz.si. Open July-Aug. daily 9am-1:30pm and 3-9pm; Sept.-June M-Tu and Th-Su 10am-5pm, W 10am-3pm.) There is also a **tourist information center** where the bus drops passengers off. (Open M-F 9am-3pm, Sa 9am-4pm.) Commission-free **exchange offices** line Obala, and a 24hr. MasterCard and Visa **ATM** is at Obala 32, by Banka Koper. A **pharmacy,** Lekarna Potorož, is at Obala 41. Walk down Obala in the direction of Piran, turn right into the Hotel Palace Courtyard, and follow the sign. (☎674 86 70. Open M-F 8am-8pm, Sa 8am-1pm, Su 9am-1pm. AmEx/V.) **Telephones** line Obala and can be found inside and outside the post office. **Internet** is available at **Planet Pub,** Obala 14, next door to restaurant Paco, a very basic Irish-looking pub with barstools and beer aplenty. The internet is free, although you might be expected to buy some of their beverages (Coffee €0.90. Mixed drinks from €3. Open daily 11am-3am.) Internet is also available at Kapelca, towards the supermaket, a cyber cafe that costs €1.70 for 20min. but has a relaxing leather lounge suite ambience. (☎474 4236.) The **post office,** Stari cesti 1, off Obala past the old Palace Hotel, beside the pharmacy, cashes **traveler's checks** for a 2% commission and has **Poste Restante.** (☎674 60 40. Open M-F 8am-7pm, Sa 8am-noon.) **Postal Code:** 6322.

ACCOMMODATIONS AND FOOD. **Maona Portorož,** Obala 14b, arranges **private rooms.** (☎674 0363; www.maona.si. Singles €18-21; doubles €40-50; apartments €22-27.) **Tourist Service Portorož,** Postajališka 2, right next to the bus station, is another reliable option. (☎674 0360. Open M-Sa 9am-9pm, Su 10am-5pm. Singles €12-20; doubles €19-30; triples €26-40.) **Kamp Lucija ❶,** Seča 204, just beyond the Marina Portorož, is a mid-sized seaside campground with showers and toilets; a restaurant and supermarket are nearby. Hop on a minibus from any point along Obala and ride it away from Piran to the "Lucija" stop. Continue walking away from Piran and turn right at the sign on c. Solinarjev. Follow the street as it curves left into Seča. (☎690 6000; camp@metropolgroup.si. Reception daily 6am-10pm. Guarded 24hr. From €9-12 per person, car €3.) A cheaper option is **Kamp Strujnan** ❶ at €7 per person per night, although it is a kilometer further from town.

Supermarket Mercator, on Obala 8 between Piran and Portorož (open M-F 7am-8pm, Sa 7am-6pm, Su 8am-noon), or Obala 53 next to the bus station in Portorož, is a more wallet-friendly option for beachside picnics. (Open M-Sa 7am-8pm, Su 8-11am.) Beachside **Paco 2** ❷, Obala 18a, delights patrons with excellent food at reasonable prices. The stone exterior gives the checkered tablecloths and log flowerboxes an Istrian air. Choose from pizza (€4.30-7), Slovenian entrees, and seafood (€5-10) under the shade of the thatched roof. (☎674 1020. Open daily 9am-12:30am.) **Plaka** ❶ is a Greek restaurant on the Obala strip with incredibly affordable prices. With €3 salads and €5 *moussaka*, you can afford to be fed while enjoying terrace seating to watch the world go by. (On the Obala strip after the supermarket. Open daily 10am-midnight.)

ENTERTAINMENT AND NIGHTLIFE. For some fun in the sun, head to the manmade sand **beach.** (Open 8am-8pm. Free entrance. Chair rental €3.30 a day, bathing hut €3.30 a day.) When night falls, Obala's main stretch melds into one mammoth beach party. Local favorite **The Club,** at Hotel Belvedere in nearby Izola, is one of the hottest nightclubs in Istria if you're into discotheque—but be prepared to pay for your passion. Take the intercity bus from the station in the direction of Koper (15min.; every hr.; €3.20). Stay until closing to catch an early bus back to Portorož; otherwise a taxi is the only way home. (☎153 9311. Beer €1.50. Open daily 11pm-6am.) Also in Izola, the nightclub **Ambaceda Gavioli** is famous for its wild parties. Particularly well known for the internationally famous house and trance DJs it imports, Amabaceda is the place to be for the dance crowd. The club is not open regularly, so keep your eyes out for flyers advertising an event, or inquire at the tourist office for info. In February, Portorož hosts the **Pust,** a carnival that attracts visitors from all along the coast with its crazy costumes and performances. Portorož also participates in events based in its neighbor Piran, such as the theater-oriented Primorska Summer Festival in July.

PIRAN ☎(0)5

In contrast to its resort-filled neighbor Portorož, the small fishing village of Piran retains an undeniable old-world charm and a distinctly Venetian feel. Dubbed "the pearl of Istria," Piran cradles beautiful churches, crumbling medieval architecture, and a lighthouse that is a beacon for ships on their way along the Istrian coast.

TRANSPORTATION AND PRACTICAL INFORMATION. The streets of Piran radiate from two main squares. **Tartinijev Trg,** named for the native violinist and composer Giuseppe Tartini, is the city's commercial heart and home to its shops and services. From the bus stop, face the sea, turn right, and continue 5min. The square is on the right. Following Verdijeva from Tartinijev Trg leads to the quieter **Trg 1 Maya.** The center of medieval Piran, the square serves as an open-air stage for theater and dance performances during the Primorska Summer Festival. The friendly, English-speaking staff at the **tourist office,** Tartinijev Trg 2, in the far left corner of the square (with your back to the water, facing the square), offer useful **free maps** and bus schedule info. (☎673 0220. Open daily 10am-5pm, later in the summer.) **Banka Koper,** Tartinijev Trg 12, on the opposite corner of the square, **exchanges currency** for no commission, gives MasterCard **cash advances,** and has a

24hr. **ATM** outside. (☎673 3200. Open M-F 8:30am-noon and 3-5pm, Sa 8:30am-noon.) The local **pharmacy, Obalne Lekarne Koper,** is at Tartinijev Trg 4. (☎611 0000. Open M-F 7:30am-8pm, Sa 7:30am-1pm, Su 8am-noon. AmEx/MC/V.) There is one **telephone** right in front of the tourist office. **Internet** is available at **Youth Hostel Val** (see below; €1 per hr., free for guests) or for free at the **library,** Mestna Knjiznica Piran, Tartinijev Trg 1. (30min. limit. Open M-F 10am-6pm, Sa 8am-1pm.) The **post office,** Leninova 1, between the bus station and the main square, **exchanges currency,** cashes **traveler's checks,** and gives MasterCard **cash advances.** (☎673 2688. Open M-F 8am-7pm, Sa 8am-noon.) **Postal Code:** 6330.

ACCOMMODATIONS AND FOOD. Accommodations tend to be pricey. The staff at **Maona Travel Agency,** Cankarjevo nabrezje 7, on the waterfront before Tartinijev Trg, can help you find **private rooms.** (☎673 45 20; www.maona.si. Open daily 8am-7pm. Singles €50-65.) More like a pension than a hostel, **Youth Hostel Val ❷,** Gregorčičeva 38a, has spotless furnished rooms with comfortable beds. From the bus station, follow the waterfront past Tartinijev trg as it curves around and away from the harbor. Look for the sign three blocks up on the right. (☎673 2555; www.hostel-val.com. Shared bathrooms. Reserve ahead. Breakfast and Internet included. Reception daily 8am-10pm. Mid-May to mid-Sept. Dorms €25; mid-Sept. to mid-May €20. HI discount available. €2 additional for stays of fewer than 2 nights in high season.) **Alibi Hostel ❷,** Bonifacijeva 60, a Ljubljana-based company, will probably be your cheapest option. While living arrangements are comfortable, with private bathrooms, kitchenettes and tables in each dorm, broken bathroom doors and and peeling wallpaper are also in evidence. (☎31 363 666; www.alibi.si. Rooms in high season €20.)

There is an open-air **produce market** behind the tourist office at Zelenjavni trg. (Open daily 7am-6pm.) A small but well-stocked **Mercator** supermarket, Levstikova 5, stands one block behind. (Open M-F 7am-8pm, Sa 7am-1pm, Su 8am-noon. AmEx/MC/V.) Many similar waterfront cafes are on the shoreline. **Tri Vdove ❸,** Prešer ovo nab. 4, has delicious seafood, meat, and pasta entrees. The squid stuffed with ham and cheese is especially good. (☎673 0290. Entrees €7-12. Open daily 11am-midnight. AmEx/MC/V.) **Riva Pizzeria ❸,** Gregorčičeva 43, is at the end of the strand. Don't let the name fool you—they sell seafood, too, in a gorgeous setting with a stone interior. (☎673 2180. Pizza €6-10. Open daily 9am-midnight. AmEx/MC/V.) A cheaper and less elegant option is local favorite **Gostiše Pirat ❷,** Župančičeva 26, between Tartinijev trg and the bus station. (☎673 1481. Entrees €5-10. Open M-Sa 10am-10pm, Su noon-10pm.)

SIGHTS AND ENTERTAINMENT. The sea is Piran's primary attraction. Discover the secrets of Piran's seaside past at the **Maritime Museum** (Pomorski Muzej), just off Tartinijev trg on Cankarjevo nab. The three-story building has exhibits on marine archaeology and seamanship, and a collection of ship replicas. (☎671 0040; muzej@pommuz-pi.si. Open Tu-Su in summer 9am-noon and 6-9pm in the summer, in winter 3-6pm. English captions. €3.50, students €2.50.) A short walk uphill from Tartinijev trg leads to the Gothic **Church of St. George** (Crkva sv. Jurja) and the nearby **St. George's Tower,** constructed in 1608, which commands a spectacular view of Piran and the Adriatic. The ornate alabaster and gold used to construct the church is truly exquisite. (Open daily 10am-10pm. Free.) From the tower, head uphill and continue along the shoreline to **Old City walls.** The best views of Piran are along these ancient fortifications—especially at sunrise. The coastal waters offer **scuba diving** opportunities. **Sub-net,** Prešernovo nab. 24, gives certification classes and guided dives. (☎673 2218; www.sub-net.si. Dive with a guide €30, wreck €40. €60 per rental piece. Beginners open-water dive €220. Open Tu-Su

9am-7pm. Cash only.) Meet the ocean critters at the **aquarium,** Kidričeva 4, on the opposite side of the marina. (☎673 25 72. Open daily 10am-noon and 2-7pm. €3, children €2.50.) Piran lacks sand beaches, but paved swimming and sunning areas line the peninsula and, unlike in neighboring Portorož, they're free.

Nightlife in Piran tends to be relaxed. Perched above the old city stage, the beautiful terrace cafe **Teater,** Kidričevo na., a large yellow building on the corner, is a perfect place to relax under the sunset. With flowers and low seated alcoves on the inside, it also makes a romantic getaway. (Mixed drinks €3-5. Open daily 8am-1am. Cash only.) **Da Noi,** Prešernovo nab. 1, draws a laid-back crowd with nightly drink specials. (Sangria €2. Open M-Th and Su 9am-midnight, F 9am-2am.) If you're tired of tourists and looking for something mellow, go down the strand and around the peninsula. **Punta Bar,** Prešernevo na. 24, located next to Sub-net Diving Center, is a simple "beach bar" on the water. (Wine €1.20 per glass. Beer €2. Open daily 9am-midnight. Cash only.) In June, a classic car rally rolls through town, while July brings a regatta of classic boats, as well as the **Primoska Summer Festival,** which features outdoor plays, ballets, and concerts. Inquire at the tourist office for event schedules. In June, the cultural life of the city peaks with the **International Painting Reunion Ex Tempore.** Some of Europe's most promising young painters set up shop in the city's streets and squares.

ŠTAJERSKA

Štajerska's green hills and rolling farmland lie in sharp contrast to the alpine peaks to the west. To Slovenes, the name evokes vineyards, natural springs, and delicious cuisine. The region preserves a strong local character but doesn't hesitate to welcome visitors with open arms and maybe even a bottle of wine.

MARIBOR ☎(0)2

Surrounded by the wine-growing Piramida Hill, the slow Drava River, and the adventuresome ski haven of Pohorje, Maribor (MAHR-ee-bohr; pop. 106,000) brims with youthful energy that belies its deep history. Although second in size to Ljubljana, this 700-year-old university town exudes a pleasingly provincial feel.

TRANSPORTATION. From the train station, Partizanska c. 50 (info ☎292 2100, tickets 292 2164), **trains** run to Ljubljana (1½hr., 12 per day, €7.47-8.91) and Ptuj (1hr., 9 per day, €2.71). The bus station, Mlinska 1 (☎090 7230), sends **buses** to Ljubljana (2½-3hr., 10 per day, €12) and Ptuj (40min., 2 per hr. until 9pm, €3.60).

ORIENTATION AND PRACTICAL INFORMATION. The majority of Maribor's sights lie in the city center, on the north shore of the **Drava River;** this makes it easy to explore the town by foot. From the train station, turn left and follow Partizanska past the large Franciscan **Church of St. Mary** to **Grajski trg,** where you'll see the **Florian Column.** Turn left down Vetrinska, follow it past the shopping complex on the right, and turn right on Koroška cesta to reach Glavni trg. From the main bus station, turn right on Mlinska, follow it to Partizanska, and take a left. Try not to arrive on a Sunday as few businesses open their doors.

Maribor Tourist Information Center "Matic," Partizanska c. 6a, in the center of town, just in front of the Franciscan Church, is stocked with **maps** of both the town and surrounding regions, as well as with brochures for accommodations, tours, and rentals. They can also book your cheapest sleeping option: **private rooms.** (☎234 6611; www.maribor-tourism.si. Rooms €25-35. 90min. city tours W and F 10am, Su 11am; €5. Open M-F 9am-7pm, Sa 9am-5pm, Su 9am-noon.)

Nova KBM, ul. Vita Kraigherja 4, **exchanges currency** for no commission, and **traveler's checks** for 1.5% commission, and has **Western Union** and **American Express** services. (☎062 229 229. Open M-F 8-11:30am and 2-5pm.) A 24hr. **ATM** is at **A-Banka,** Glavni trg 18, perpendicular to Gosposka ul. A 24hr. **pharmacy, Lekarna Glavni trg,** is at Glavni trg 20. Use the side window for night service. You can find a **hospital** at Ljubljanska ul. 5 (☎321 1000). For free **Internet access,** head to **Kibla Multimedia Center,** ul. Kneza Koclja 9. It also has a lively bar and modern art gallery, and stocks the free English-language newspaper *Slovenian Times*. Enter Narodni Dom and go through the large art space on the left. (☎229 4012; www.kibla.org. Open Aug. 15-July 15 M-F 9am-10pm, Sa 4-10pm.) In the summer months, similarly named **Kibla Multimedia,** Glavni trg, next to Benetton, has fast connections. (€0.70 per 30min., €0.90 per hr.) To quench your thirst on the waterfront, head to **Klik Bar and Internet Caffe,** Dravska 7, which, like many Maribor bars, offers free Internet access and Wi-Fi. (Open 9am-11pm.) **Telephones** are located near both **post offices,** Partizanska c. 1 (open M-F 8am-7pm, Sa 8am-noon) and Partizanska c. 54 (open M-F 8am-7pm, Sa 8am-1pm). Both have **currency exchange. Postal Code:** 2000.

ACCOMMODATIONS AND FOOD. "Matic" (see above) can arrange private rooms (singles €17-45; doubles €30-75). **HI Dijaški Dom 26 Junij ❷,** Železnikova 12, is a 15min. walk from the center. From the local bus station in front of the train station, take bus #3 (Brezje) to the "Pokopališče" stop. Cross the street and walk a few paces to the right, then take the first left and follow the road as it curves. Past the Mercator supermarket, you'll see a building with "12" painted on the side. Tidy rooms and quiet environs make this the best deal in town. (☎480 1710. Free Internet access. Check-in 7-10am and 7-11pm. Open June 25-Aug. 25. Singles €15; doubles €25. 20% HI discount.) If you're willing to pay a bit more to be in the center, **Uni Hostel ❸,** Grajski trg 3a, inside the Orel Hotel, has simple singles with private bathrooms. Although the beds are creaky and the fixtures in need of repair, it is a small price to pay for the privacy and a breakfast feast that includes several types of bread, grilled vegetables, cold cuts, marinated mushrooms, olives, and pickles. (☎250 6700; www.teremb.si. €25, HI members €24. AmEx/MC/V.)

Toti Rotov ❷, Glavni trg 14, has savory set meals (€7) and a variety of international dishes, from local specialties to Thai satay, all served in a lovely and atmospheric 16th century townhouse. On Friday and Saturday nights, descend to the stone cellar to dine before dancing the rest of the evening away. (☎228 7650. Entrees €3-15. Open M-Th 8am-midnight, F-Sa 8am-2am. AmEx/MC/V.) A favorite among locals—and one of the only restaurants in town open on Sundays, **Ancora ❷,** Juriciceva 7, offers large portions of delicious seafood, pasta, and brick-oven pizzas. (☎250 2033. Pizza €2.50-5.70. Seafood €4.30-6.90. Open M-Th 9am-midnight, F-Sa 8am-1am, Su 9am-10:30pm.) **Tako's ❷,** Mesarski prehod 3, in a small alley off Glavni trg, serves the freshest salads in town, along with excellent Mexican food at an affordable price. Tequila, burritos, and loud Latin beats draw not only cobblestone-weary travelers but also a host of fashionable locals following the recent craze for all things Mexican. (☎320 3863. Entrees €3-10. Open M-W 11am-midnight, Th-Sa 11am-2am, Su noon-5pm.) For groceries in the center, head to **Mercator,** Partizanska 7 (open M-F 7am-7pm, Sa 7am-1pm) or Mlinska 1, near the bus station (open daily 6am-midnight; both AmEx/MC/V). An **Interspar,** Pobreska 18, can be found in the **Europark** shopping mall on the river. (Open M-F 9am-9pm, Sa 8am-9pm, Su 9am-3pm. MC/V.)

SIGHTS. Maribor's historical neighborhood, **Lent,** runs along the Drava River and is flanked by three old, small towers: **Sodni stolp** (Law Court Tower), built in 1310; **Vodni stolp** (Water Tower); and **Židovski stolp** (Jewish Tower), home to a small art gallery with surrealistic modern pieces (open M-F 10am-7pm, Sa 10am-1pm).

Cross Koroška c. from Glavni trg and take the stairs next to Stari Most down to the river. Face the water and go left to reach Vodni stolp, which used to be the city's major wine cellar. Just up from Vodni stolp is **Židovski trg.** The empty **synagogue** dates from the 14th century. (Open M-F 8am-2:30pm. Free.) Facing the river down Dravška ul. **Stara Trta,** a 400-year-old hanging vine still produces a red wine called Žametna Črnina (Black Velvet), which is only distributed in small bottles as gifts for special visitors to Maribor. Glavni trg centers on the elaborate, beautiful **Plague Memorial,** a gold- and angel-laden monument built in 1743 to commemorate the 1679 epidemic. Up from Grajski trg on ul. Heroja Tomšiča 5, the **Maribor National Liberation Museum** (Muzej Narodne Osvoboditve Maribor) commemorates the city's struggle against Nazi occupation during WWII and contains an exhibit on the Allied bombing of the city. (☎221 1671. Open M-F 8am-6pm, Sa 9am-noon. €1.50, students €1.) To sample some of the Štajerska region's best wines, head to **Vinag,** Trg Svobode 3, a wine cellar with a very knowledgeable staff. The prices are surprisingly reasonable given the excellent quality. (☎220 8113; www.vinag.si. Call ahead for cellar tours. Open M-F 7:30am-7pm, Sa 8am-1pm. AmEx/MC/V.)

NIGHTLIFE AND FESTIVALS. Most nightlife is concentrated in the old **Lent** neighborhood, where lively cafes line the waterfront. **Bongo's Latin Club,** next door to Tako's (see **Accommodations and Food,** p. 680), puts a little fire into the evening with music, salsa, and a lot of tequila. (Sangria €1.70. Mixed drinks €1.70-4.20. Open F-Sa 11am-2am.) Cuban-themed **Cantente,** Pariške Komune 37, serves the best mixed drinks in town in a red-lit underground cafe. (☎331 2989; www.cantante.net. Mixed drinks €2.30-5.20. Open M-Th 7am-midnight, F 7am-2am, Sa 9am-2am, Su noon-midnight.) Hang out with the university crowd at **Študk,** Gosposvetska c. 83, Maribor's most popular disco. Pick your night according to the music, with rock Tuesdays and all things house, dance, and funk Fridays. (☎228 5630; www.gaudeamus.si/stuk. Union beer €1.25. Open M-Tu 8am-2am, W-F 8am-4am, Sa 4:30pm-4am, Su 4:30pm-midnight. Closed mid-July to mid-Aug.) **Kolosej Cinema,** on the river at Blagana, shows English-language Hollywood films and has a bar and pool tables. (☎230 1440; www.kolosej.si. €2.50.) From late June to early July, Maribor's historical waterfront neighborhood explodes in the **Lent Festival.** Theater, dance, and outdoor jazz and folk concerts take place virtually nonstop for 17 days in this Maribor highlight. (Info and tickets ☎229 4000.) The mid-September **International Chamber Music Festival** features classical concerts in Narodni Dom Maribor, ul. Kneza Koclja 9. (☎229 4007; www.nd-mb.si.)

MARIBORSKO POHORJE ☎(0)2

Just a 20min. bus and stunning cable-car ride away from the center of Maribor, the Pohorje hills are an outdoor adventurer's haven. The steep mountains host intense skiing during the winter, and their numerous trails and footpaths make for excellent biking and trekking during the warmer months. Whether you're just passing through on a short hike or enjoying a full ski weekend, Mariborsko Pohorje offers a peaceful respite from the urban bustle of Maribor. The small village of **Bolfenk,** Pohorje's gateway to the wilderness, centers on picturesque stucco **Bolfenk Church.** To take full advantage of the footpaths that crisscross the mountains, pick up a **free trail map** at the church. (☎26 03 42 11. Open W-Su 9:30am-4:30pm.) For a short but scenic **hike** (2.5km), turn right out of the Bolfenk Church and follow the gravel road as it forks up the hill. The trail winds around to the **lookout tower** Razelinski stolp, which provides a panoramic view of the Štajerska valley, before leading to the mysterious black waters of the **waterfall** Slap Skalca.

During the summer, you can also explore the hills by **horseback** (€9 per hr.), **bicycle** (€3-6 per hr., €13-18 per day), or **summer toboggan** (€6.25 per hr.), a contraption that resembles a skateboard with a seat on it. All are available at kiosks directly below the gondola terminal at Hotel Bellevue. From December to March, Pohorje boasts some of Štajerska's most popular **skiing.** The best slopes are just above Bolfenk, accessible by **chairlift** from the village center. For information, contact Sportni Center Pohorje, Mladinska ul. 29. (☎220 8825. 2-day pass €50, students €43; skis €13-21 per day; snowboards €19 per day.) The Bolfenk Church houses the area's only **museum,** with exhibits on the history of Pohorje and a small archaeological collection. (☎603 4211; www.pohorje.org. Open May-June W-F 10:30am-3:30pm, Sa-Su 9:30am-4:30pm; July-Aug. W-Su 9:30am-5:30pm. Free.)

To reach Pohorje, take local bus #6 (€1) from the main station outside the train station in Maribor to the last stop, Vzpenjača. A **free bus map** is available at the Maribor tourist office. From the terminus, a **gondola** runs up the mountain to Pohorje. (Gondola open daily 8am-10pm. One-way trip €5.84, round-trip €7.09.) Because food and accommodations in Pohorje are extremely limited and other tourist services are virtually nonexistent, the most comfortable and economical way to experience the hills is to commute from Maribor, where there are many restaurants, rooms, and bars. If proximity to the slopes is your priority, choose from among a small number of **private apartments** (from €30 per person) on the hill.

PTUJ ☎(0)2

From its beginnings as the Roman town of Poetovio, Ptuj (puh-TOO-ee; pop. 19,000) has been a bastion of culture. Situated on the Amber route that linked the Baltic to the Mediterranean, Ptuj housed a flourishing center of the ancient Roman religion Mithraism and developed a rich winemaking tradition that has kept it thriving through the centuries. Most modern roads tend to bypass this rustic community, but Ptuj benefits from its obscurity, which has enabled the town to preserve its heritage undisturbed.

To reach the beautiful **Ptuj Castle,** head up the hill from Slovenski trg along Grajska. The fortress dates from the 11th century, and was leased to the Lords of Ptuj in 1132, but settlers have occupied its hillsides since 3000 BC. The Counts of Leslie added their own embellishments to the castle, but it was the last owners, the Counts of Herberstein, that created the ornate and intricate rooms that visitors see today. The exquisite structure, and its adjacent courtyard, is one of the best preserved in Slovenia and contains an impressive collection of haunting Gothic and Baroque art. Their collection of musical instruments is the largest in Slovenia and features not only instruments from the famed local famed marching band, but also an array of national and international masters' work. The outlandish **Kurent** (carnival spirit) costumes, also on display, are bizarrely compelling. (☎748 0360. www.pok-muzej-ptuj.si. July-Aug. Daily 9am-6pm and Sa-Su 9am-8pm; May to mid-Oct. daily 9am-6pm; mid-Oct. to Apr. daily 9am-5pm. €4. Guide €10.)

Down the hill, on the opposite side of the castle, is the 13th-century **Dominican Monastery,** Muzejski trg 1, which holds prehistoric and Roman finds from the Ptuj area. (☎748 0360. Open mid-Apr. to Nov. M-F 10am-5pm. €4. Museum and castle €6.) Visit Slovenia's oldest wine cellar to taste the country's best vintages, some dating back to 1917. Established in 1239, the **Ptuj wine cellar,** Vinarski trg 1, is a medieval walk through the region's viticultural history and is well worth the time. Knowledgeable staff can share their expertise on the various wines sold and housed in the cellar, but for English speakers, a brochure might be the best option. (☎787 9810; www.haloze.com.) Ptuj's most famous celebration is **Kurent Carnival,** which takes place in late winter, from Candlemas to Ash Wednesday. Dancing along the streets, the Kurents don sheepskins and headpieces to chase away the evil spirits of winter and beckon spring. Book early to see this sight; crowds typically number over 50,000. After Easter, the **Slovene Farm Produce Exhibition** is the nation's largest country-style cooking exposition. A spectacular fireworks show accompanies the **Ptuj Summer Nights Festival,** the culmination of the **Festival of Slovene Popular Music,** where groups compete for the highly coveted Golden Orpheus.

Kurent Youth Hostel ❷, Osojnikova 9, is situated in the heart of the town, above a disco, a stone's throw away from both the bus and train stations. As a service to the businessmen who are its frequent guests, Kurent has ample work spaces available, but it also organizes daytrips for backpackers. (☎771 0814; www.csod.si. Breakfast included. Free Internet access. Reception 8am-noon and 4pm-8pm. Dorms €16 per night. Tourist tax €1.) **Gostilna Amadeus ❷,** Prešernova 36, across from the library, offers traditional Slovenian entrees. Saffron walls and blue tiles suit the classical elegance of this simple restaurant. The *štruklji* (dumplings with cheese filling; €3.50-4) are phenomenal. (☎771 7051. Entrees €3-9.50. Open M-Th noon-10pm, F-Sa noon-11pm, Su noon-4pm. AmEx/MC/V.) Located in the city center, **Gostilna PP Restaurant ❷,** Novi trg 2, exudes a warm decadence from its dark wood interior in the city center. Vegetarians can look forward to an assortment of salads, but the Ptuj-style roast chicken should not be missed by carnivores. (Entrees €5-12. Open M-F 9am-7pm, Sa 9am-4pm, Su noon-4pm. Cafe open M-Th 7am-10pm, F-Sa 7am-11pm, Su noon-4pm.)

Reach Ptuj from Maribor by **bus** (50min., every 30min. 5am-9pm, €3.60). The heart of Ptuj is **Slovenski trg.** To get there from the bus station, turn right into the Mercator shopping complex, go straight through the parking lot, and turn left on Trstenjakova. Pass the **Ptuj Wine Cellar** and turn right on Ulica h. Lacka, which opens into the main square, Mesti Trg, and the beautiful City Hall. Continue straight to Slovenski trg, passing the stone **Saint Florian Monument,** the **city tower,** and the famous **Orpheus monument** to reach the **tourist office,** Slovenski trg 3, which has helpful English-speaking staff, who can provide free **maps** of town. They can also organize **private accommodations** (private rooms €21-22) and direct you to the hotels and hostels in town. Free **Internet** access is also available, but there is a 15min. time limit. (☎779 6011. Open May-Aug. M-F 8am-8pm, Sa-Su 9am-1pm; Sept.-Apr. M-F 8am-6pm, Sa 8am-noon and 3-6pm, Su 9am-1pm.)

TURKEY (TÜRKİYE)

Turkey is a land rich with history and beauty. Home to some of the world's greatest civilizations—the Hellenes, Hittites, Macedonians, Romans, Byzantines, and Ottomans—Turkey is at the intersection of two very different continents. İstanbul, on the land bridge that connects Europe and Asia, is the infinitely intricate and surprisingly seductive progeny of three thousand years of migrant history. Though resolutely secular by government decree, every facet of Turkish life is graced by the religious traditions of its 99% Muslim population. Tourists cram İstanbul and the glittering western coast, while Anatolia (the Asian portion of Turkey) remains a purist backpacker's paradise of alpine meadows, cliffside monasteries, and a truly hospitable people.

FACTS AND FIGURES

Official Name: Republic of Turkey.

Form of Government: Republican parliamentary democracy.

Capital: Ankara.

Major Cities: Adana, Bursa, Gaziantep, İstanbul, İzmir.

Population: 70,414,000.

Time Zone: GMT +2, in summer GMT +3.

Languages: Turkish.

Religions: Muslim (99.8%).

Number of Roller Coasters: 4.

Largest Skewer of Kebap Meat: Created by the Melike Döner Co. in Osmangazi-Bursa, Turkey on Nov. 6, 2005. Weighed in at 2698kg (5948 lb.).

Number of Army Battle Tanks: 2317.

ESSENTIALS

WHEN TO GO

With mild winters and hot summers, there's no wrong time to travel to Turkey. While most tourists go in July and August, visiting between April and June or September and October brings temperate days, smaller crowds, and lower prices. November to February is the rainy season, so bring appropriate gear.

DOCUMENTS AND FORMALITIES

ENTRANCE REQUIREMENTS.

Passport: Required for all travelers.

Visa: Required for citizens of Australia, Canada, some EU countries, the UK, and the US. Citizens of New Zealand do not need a visa to enter. Multiple-entry visas (around US$20) are available at the border and are valid for up to 90 days.

Letter of Invitation: Not required.

Inoculations: Not required. Recommended up-to-date on DTaP (diphtheria, tetanus, and pertussis), Hepatitis A, Hepatitis B, MMR (measles, mumps, and rubella), polio booster, and typhoid.

Work Permit: Required for all foreigners planning to work in Turkey.

International Driving Permit: Required for all those planning to drive.

EMBASSIES AND CONSULATES. Foreign embassies to Turkey are in Ankara, though many nations also have consulates in İstanbul. Turkish embassies and consulates abroad include: **Australia,** 6 Moonah Pl., Yarralumla, Canberra, ACT 2600 (☎02 62 34 00 00; www.turkishembassy.org.au); **Canada,** 197 Wurtemburg St., Ottawa, ON, K1N 8L9 (☎613-789-4044; www.turkishembassy.com); **Ireland,** 11 Clyde

Rd., Ballsbridge, Dublin 4 (☎668 52 40); **New Zealand,** 15-17 Murphy St., Level 8, Wellington 6011 (☎044 721 290; turkem@xtra.co.nz); **UK,** 43 Belgrave Sq., London SW1X 8PA (☎020 73 93 02 02; www.turkishembassylondon.org); **US,** 2525 Massachusetts Ave., NW, Washington, D.C. 20008 (☎202-612-6700; www.turkishembassy.org).

VISA AND ENTRY INFORMATION. Citizens of Canada and the US may obtain visas at entry points into Turkey for stays of less than three months (paid in cash). For longer stays, study, or work visas, and for citizens of Australia, New Zealand, and countries of the EU, it is necessary to obtain visas in advance (about US$20; Canadians, about US$60), available at Turkish consulates abroad. Travelers must apply at least one month in advance. For more info, check out www.mfa.gov.tr/mfa. If arriving by ferry, expect to pay a port tax of at least €10.

TOURIST SERVICES

In big cities like İstanbul, many establishments that claim to be tourist offices are actually travel agencies. That said, **travel agencies** can often be more helpful for finding accommodations or booking transportation than the official Turkish **tourist offices.** Although it's best to shop around from agency to agency for a deal on tickets, be wary of exceptionally low prices—offices may tack on exorbitant hidden charges. The official tourism website (www.tourismturkey.org) has a list of visa information, helpful links, and office locations.

MONEY

NEW TURKISH LIRA (YTL)		
	AUS$1 = 1.11YTL	1YTL = AUS$0.90
	CDN$1 = 1.22YTL	1YTL = CDN$0.82
	EUR€1 = 1.77YTL	1YTL = EUR€0.57
	NZ$1 = 0.97YTL	1YTL = NZ$1.03
	UK£1 = 2.62YTL	1YTL = UK£0.38
	US$1 = 1.29YTL	1YTL = US$0.77

In response to rampant inflation and ever-confusing prices, Turkey revalued its currency in 2005, dropping 6 zeroes. One million Turkish Lira became 1 **Yeni Türk Lirası** (New Turkish Lira; YTL). One New Turkish Lira equals 100 **New Kuruş,** with standard denominations of 5, 10, 25, and 50. 1YTL are available as both coins and bills, while denominations of 5, 10, 20, 50 and 100YTL come only as banknotes. While Old Turkish Lira are no longer accepted as currency, Turkish Lira banknotes (bills) can be redeemed until 2016 by the Central Bank of the Republic of Turkey (CBRT) and T.C. Ziraat Bank branches. Old Lira coins are no longer redeemable. **Banks** are generally open 8:30am-noon and 1:30-5:30pm. **Inflation** has decreased dramatically in recent years, dropping from 45% in 2003 to an all-time low of 7.7% in 2005 before rising again slightly. The best currency exchange rates can be found at state-run post and telephone offices (PTT). Many places in İstanbul and other major cities accept euro. Turkey has a **value added tax (VAT)** of 18% on general purchases and 8% on food. The prices in *Let's Go* include VAT. Spending more than 118YTL in one store entitles travelers to a tax refund upon leaving Turkey; look for "Tax-Free Shopping" stickers in shop windows.

HEALTH AND SAFETY

EMERGENCY **Ambulance:** ☎112. **Fire:** ☎110. **Police:** ☎155.

Medical facilities in Turkey vary greatly. In İstanbul and Ankara, high-quality hospitals for foreigners and expats provide care for all but the most serious of conditions, and most have adequate medical supplies. Outside the cities, though, it is a different story; try to avoid rural hospitals. **Pharmacies** are easy to find in major cities and are generally well stocked and have at least one professional pharmacist, as they're mandated by the government. Don't drink **water** that hasn't been boiled or filtered, and watch out for ice in drinks. Most local dairy products are safe to eat, but make sure that perishable products are still good before eating them.

Petty crime is common in urban centers, especially in crowded squares, the Grand Bazaar, and on public transportation. Common schemes include distracting travelers with a staged fight while they are being robbed; drugging travelers with tea, juice, or other drinks and then robbing them; or simply presenting travelers with outrageously expensive bills. Pay attention to your valuables, never accept drinks from a stranger, and always ask in advance for prices at bars and restaurants. Though **pirated goods** are sold on the street, it is illegal to buy them, and doing so can result in fines. **Drug trafficking** leads to severe jail time. It is also illegal to show disrespect to Atatürk or to insult the state.

Foreign **women,** especially those traveling alone, attract significant attention in Turkey. Unwanted catcalls and other forms of verbal harassment are common, although physical harassment is rare. Regardless of the signals a foreign woman intends to send, her foreignness alone may suggest a liberal openness to amorous advances. Smiling, regarded in the West as a sign of confidence and friendliness, is sometimes associated in Turkey with sexual attraction. As long as women expect plenty of attention and take common-sense precautions, however, even single travelers need not feel anxious. Although **homosexuality** is legal in Turkey, religious and social norms keep most homosexual activity discreet. Homophobia can be a problem, especially in remote areas; expect authorities to be unsympathetic. Despite the close contact that Turks maintain with same-sex friends, public displays of affection between gay and lesbian travelers should be avoided. Turkey's urban centers have bars and informal cruising areas for men only, though they may not be very overt. **Lambda İstanbul,** a GLBT support group, lists guides to gay-friendly establishments on its website (www.qrd.org/www/world/europe/turkey).

KEEPING IN TOUCH

EMAIL AND THE INTERNET. Like everything in Turkey, the availability of Internet services depends on where in the country you are. In İstanbul, Internet

PHONE CODES	**Country code:** 90. **International dialing prefix:** 00. From outside Turkey, dial international dialing prefix (see inside back cover) + 90 + city code + local number. Within Turkey, dail city code + local number, even when dialing inside the city.

cafes are everywhere; out east, they can be tough to find. Free Wi-Fi is available at hostels and cafes across the city.

TELEPHONES. Whenever possible, use a calling card for international phone calls, as long-distance rates for national phone services are often very high. Mobile phones are an increasingly popular and economical option. Major mobile carriers include **Turkcell, Telsim,** and **Avea.** Direct-dial access numbers for calling out of Turkey include: **AT&T Direct** (☎80 01 22 77); **British Telecom** (☎80 044 1177); **Canada Direct** (☎80 01 66 77); and **Telstra Australia** (☎80 061 1177). For more info on calling home from Europe, see p.39.

MAIL. The postal system is quick and expensive in Turkey. Airmail should be marked *par avion*, and Poste Restante is available in most major cities.

ACCOMMODATIONS AND CAMPING

TURKEY	❶	❷	❸	❹	❺
ACCOMMODATIONS	under 20YTL	20-39YTL	40-59YTL	60-80YTL	over 80YTL

When it comes to lodging, Turkey is a budget traveler's paradise. **Hostels** are available in nearly every major city. **Pensions**—a step above hostels in both quality and price—are also generally available, as are **hotels** in every price range. **Camping** is very common throughout Turkey, and especially on the Aegean coast; campgrounds are generally inexpensive (US$3-10) or free.

FOOD AND DRINK

TURKEY	❶	❷	❸	❹	❺
FOOD	under 8YTL	8-15YTL	16-20YTL	21-30YTL	over 30YTL

Turkish cuisine is as varied as Turkish culture. Strategically located on the land bridge between Europe and Asia, İstanbul is the culinary epicenter of the region, drawing from the dietary practices of many different cultures. **Fish** is a staple in Turkey, especially along the coast, where it is prepared with local spices according to traditional recipes. When it comes to meat, lamb and chicken are Turkish favorites, and are typically prepared as **kebap**—a term which means far more in Turkey than the dry meat cubes on a stick found in most Western restaurants. Despite its strong Muslim majority, Turkey produces good **wines.** More interesting, however, is the unofficial national drink: **rakı.** Translated as "lion's milk," rakı is Turkey's answer to French pastis, Italian sambuca, and Greek ouzo. An anise-flavored liquor, it turns milky white when mixed with water. The strong drink has inspired a Turkish saying: "you must drink the rakı, and not let the rakı drink you."

PEOPLE AND CULTURE

LANGUAGE. Turkish *(Türkçe)*, the official language of Turkey, is spoken by approximately 65 million people domestically and a few million more abroad. Turkish was originally written in Arabic script and exhibited strong Arabic and Persian influences. In 1928, however, Atatürk reformed the language, purging foreign influences (despite using a Romanized alphabet), while leaving some Arabic and Persian words such as *merhaba* (hello). Visitors who speak little or no Turk-

ish should not be intimidated. English is widely spoken wherever tourism is big business—mainly in the major coastal towns. Especially in İstanbul, a small phrasebook will help greatly. For more in-depth study, consult *Teach Yourself Turkish* by Pollard and Pollard (New York, 2004; $17).

DEMOGRAPHICS. Over 99% of the Turkish population is **Muslim.** Jews and Orthodox Christians of Armenian, Greek, and Syrian backgrounds comprise the remainder. While Turkey has no official state religion, every Turkish citizen's national identification card states his or her faith. Although Atatürk's reforms aimed to secularize the nation, Islam continues to play a key role in politics and culture.

CUSTOMS AND ETIQUETTE. Turks value **hospitality** and will frequently go out of their way to welcome travelers. If you are invited to a Turkish house as a guest, it is customary to bring a small gift, often pastries or chocolates, and to remove your shoes before entering. When chatting with Turks, do not speak with any disrespect or skepticism about **Atatürk,** as this is illegal, and avoid other sensitive subjects. In particular, it may be best not to discuss the Kurdish issue, the PKK (the Kurdistan Workers' Party), Northern Cyprus, or Turkey's human rights record.

Many of Turkey's greatest architectural monuments, including **tombs** and **mosques,** have religious significance. Visitors are welcome but should show respect by dressing and acting appropriately. Women must cover their arms, heads, and legs, and both sexes should take off their shoes and carry them inside. There are usually shoe racks in the back of the mosques; otherwise, caretakers will provide plastic bags for carrying shoes. Do not take flash photography, never photograph people in prayer, and avoid visits on Fridays (Islam's holy day). Also forgo visiting during prayer times, which are announced by the *müezzin*'s call to prayer from the mosque's minarets. Donations are sometimes expected.

If **bargaining** is a fine art, then İstanbul has lots and lots of that art. In most places, bargaining is expected. Never pay full price at the Grand Bazaar; start out by offering less than 50% of the asking price. For that matter, bargain just about everywhere—even when stores list prices, they'll usually take around 60-70%. If you're not asked to pay a service charge when paying by credit card, you're probably paying too much for your purchase. Tipping isn't required in Turkey: at bathhouses, hairdressers, hotels, and restaurants, a tip of 5-15% is common, but taxis and *dolmuş* drivers do not expect tips—just try to round up to the nearest YTL.

BODY VIBES. In Turkey, **body language** often matters as much as the spoken word. When a Turk raises his chin and clicks his tongue, he means *hayır* (no). A sideways shake of the head means *anlamadım* (I don't understand), and *evet* (yes) may be signaled by a sharp downward nod. If a Turk waves a hand up and down at you, palm toward the ground, he is signaling you to come, not bidding you farewell. In Turkey, the idle habit of snapping the fingers of one hand and then slapping the top of the other fist is considered obscene; so too is the hand gesture made by bringing thumb and forefinger together (the Western sign for "OK"). However, bringing all fingers toward the thumb is a compliment, generally meaning that something is "good." It is also considered rude to point your finger or the sole of your shoe toward someone. Though public displays of affection are considered inappropriate, Turks of both sexes greet each other with a kiss on both cheeks, and often touch or hug one another during conversation. Turks also tend to stand close to one another while talking.

DRESS. Wearing shorts will single you out as a tourist, as most Turks—particularly women—prefer pants or skirts. Women will probably find a **head scarf** or a bandana handy, perhaps essential, in more conservative regions. Knee-length skirts and lightweight pants, more acceptable, are also comfortable and practical, especially in summer. T-shirts are generally acceptable, though you should always cover your arms when entering mosques or traveling in the more religious parts of the country. Topless bathing is common in some areas along the Aegean and Mediterranean coasts but unacceptable in other regions.

HOLIDAYS AND FESTIVALS

Holidays: New Year's Day (Jan. 1); National Sovereignty Day (Apr. 23); Atatürk Commemoration Day (May 19); Victory Day (Aug. 30); Republic Day (Oct. 29); *Şeker Bayramı* (Ramadan Feast; the 3 days after the end of Ramadan; Sept. 30-Oct. 2, 2008; Sept. 19-22, 2009); *Kurban Bayramı* (Sacrifice Feast; 70 days after Ramadan; Dec. 8-11, 2008; Nov. 17-20, 2009).

Festivals: *Şeker Bayramı* celebrates the end of the month-long fast of Ramadan with socializing and the exchange of sweets. *Kurban Bayramı,* one of the most important religious holidays in Turkey, commemorates the willingness of Abraham to sacrifice Isaac. Animals are sacrificed, and their meat is cooked and given to the needy. Summer fruit festivals celebrate the harvest of strawberries in Bartin (June); wine in Urgup (June); apricots in Malatya (July); and watermelons in Diyarbakir (Sept.).

İSTANBUL

İstanbul is Turkey's heart. In this giant city that straddles Europe and Asia on two intercontinental bridges, the "East meets West" refrain of fusion restaurants, trendy boutiques, and yoga studios returns to its semantic roots. The huge, Western-style suburbs on the Asian side are evidence of rampant modernization, while across the Bosphorus, the sprawling ancient city of mosques and bazaars brims with cafes, bars, and people, day or night. As taxis rush by at mind-boggling speeds, shop owners sip tea with potential customers in shaded corners, and tourists mingle with devout Muslims at magnificent mosques in Sultanahmet. İstanbul is a turbulent place, full of history yet charged with a dynamism and energy that makes it one of the most exciting cities in Europe—and Asia.

INTERCITY TRANSPORTATION

Flights: İstanbul's airport, **Atatürk Havaalanı (IST;** ☎663 6400), is 30km from the city. Buses (3 per hr. 6am-11pm) connect domestic and international terminals. To get to Sultanahmet from the airport, catch the HAVAS bus or the Metro to the Aksaray stop at the end of the line. From there catch a tram to Sultanahmet. A direct taxi to Sultanahmet costs 25YTL. Most hostels and hotels in Sultanahmet arrange convenient airport shuttles several times per day.

Trains: Haydarpaşa Garı (☎21 63 36 04 75 or 336 2063), on the Asian side, sends trains to Anatolia. To get to the station, take the ferry from Karaköy pier #7 (every 20min. 6am-midnight), halfway between Galata Bridge and the Karaköy tourist office. Rail tickets for Anatolia can be bought in advance at the TCDD office upstairs or at any of the travel agencies in Sultanahmet; many of these offices also offer free transportation to the station. Trains go to **Ankara** (6½-9½hr., 6 per day, from 22YTL) and **Kars** (11-13½hr., 1 per day, from 35YTL). Sirkeci Garı (☎527 0050 or 527 0051), in Eminönü, sends trains to Europe via **Athens, GCE** (24hr., 1 per day, 110YTL); **Bucharest, ROM** (17½hr., 1 per day, 65YTL); and **Budapest, HUN** (40hr., 1 per day, 185YTL).

Buses: Modern, comfortable buses run to all major destinations in Turkey and are the cheapest and most convenient way to get around. If you arrange your tickets with any travel agency in Sultanahmet, a free ride is included from there to the bus station. To reach **Esenler Otobüs Terminal** (☎658 0036), take the tram to Yusufpaşa (1.30YTL); then, walk to the Aksaray Metro, and take it to the *otogar* (bus station; 15min., 1.30YTL). Most companies have courtesy buses, called *servis,* that run to the *otogar* from Eminönü, Taksim, and other city points (free with bus ticket purchase). From İstanbul, buses travel to nearly every city in Turkey. Buses run to: **Ankara** (8hr., 6-8 per day, 30YTL); **Antalya** (11hr., 2 per day, 40YTL); **Bodrum** (15hr., 2 per day, 45YTL); **İzmir** (10hr., 4 per day, 35YTL); **Kappadokia** (8hr., 2 per day, 30YTL). International buses run to: **Amman, Jordan** (28hr., daily noon, 100YTL); **Athens, GCE** (19hr.; daily 10am; 130YTL, students 135YTL); **Damascus, Syria** (25hr., daily 1:30pm and 7:30pm, 50YTL); **Sofia, BUL** (15hr., daily 10am and 9pm, 65YTL); **Tehran, Iran** (40hr., M-Sa 1:30pm, 70YTL). To get to Sultanahmet from the *otogar,* take the Metro to the Aksaray stop at the end of the line. From there, catch a tram to Sultanahmet.

Be wary of bus companies offering seemingly ridiculously low prices. Unlicensed companies have been known to offer discounts to Western European destinations and then ditch passengers somewhere en route. To make sure you're going on a legitimate bus, reserve your tickets with a travel agency in advance.

Ferries: Turkish Maritime Lines (reservations ☎252 1700, info 21 22 49 92 22), near pier #7 at Karaköy, to the left of the Haydarpaşa ferry terminal (blue awning marked Denizcilik İşletmeleri). To **İzmir** (16hr., every 2 days, 65YTL) and other destinations on the coast. Many travel agencies don't know too much about ferry connections, so you're better off going to the pier by the Galata Bridge, where you can pick up a free schedule. For more info, call ☎444 4436 or visit www.ido.com.tr. **To and from Greece:** There are 5 main crossing points from Greece to Turkey: Rhodes to Marmaris, Kos to Bodrum, Samos to Kusadasi, Chios to Çeşme, and Lesvos to Ayvalik. Ferries run 1-2 times per day in summer, the ride takes under 2hr., and the tickets are usually €25-34, plus €10 port tax when entering Turkey and a €10-20 visa (see p. 684). If you are visiting a Greek island as a daytrip from Turkey, port taxes are usually waived.

ORIENTATION

Waterways divide İstanbul into three sections. The **Bosphorus Strait** (Boğaz) separates **Asya** (Asia) from **Avrupa** (Europe). The **Golden Horn,** a sizeable river originating just outside the city, splits Avrupa into northern and southern parts. Directions in İstanbul are usually further specified by neighborhood. On the European side, **Sultanahmet,** home to the major sights, is packed with tourists and has plenty of parks and benches and many monuments, shops, and cafes. In Sultanahmet, backpackers congregate in **Akbıyık Caddesi,** while **Divan Yolu** is the main street. Walk away from **Aya Sofya** and the **Blue Mosque** to reach the **Grand Bazaar.** As you walk out of the covered Bazaar on the northern side, you'll reach more streets of outdoor markets that lead uphill to the massive **Suleymaniye Mosque** and the gardens of İstanbul's **University.** To the right, descend through the **Spice Bazaar** to reach the well-lit **Galata Bridge,** where street vendors and seafood restaurants keep the night lively. Across the two-level bridge, narrow, warehouse-filled streets lead to the panoramic **Galata Tower.** Past the tower is the broad main shopping drag **İstiklâl Caddesi,** which takes you directly to **Taksim Square,** modern İstanbul's pulsing center. Sultanahmet and Taksim (on the European side), and **Kadıköy** (on the Asian side) are the most relevant for sightseers. Asya is primarily residential.

TRANSPORTATION

Buses: Run 6am-midnight, less frequently after 10:30pm, arriving every 10min. to most stops. 1-2YTL. Hubs are Eminönü, Aksaray (Yusuf Paşa tram stop), Beyazıt, Taksim, Beşiktaş, and Üsküdar. Signs on the front of buses indicate destination, and signs on the right side list major stops. **Dolmuş** (shared taxi vans) are more comfortable but less frequent than buses. Most *dolmuş* gather on the side streets north of Taksim Sq.

Tram and Cable Car
Metro and Tünel

HALİÇ
(GOLDEN HORN)

BALAT
FENER
KARAGÜMRÜK
ÇARŞAMBA
ZEYREK
KÜÇÜKPAZAR
SÜLEYMANİYE
FATİH
ÇAPA
SARAÇHANE
AKSARAY
YENİKAPI

St. Stephen of the Bulgars
Orthodox Patriarchate
Fethiye Museum
Kariye Camii (Chora Church)
Selimiye Camii
Fatih Camii
Belediye (City Hall)
Yenikapı Seabus Pier
K. Mustafa Paşa Tren. İst.
Old City Walls

EMNİYET
ÇAPA
FINDIKZADE
HASEKİ
YUSUFPAŞA
AKSARAY
LALELİ
ÜNİVERSİTE

Mürselpaşa Cad.
Demirhisar Cad.
Hasköy Yolu
Ibadullah Cad.
Arda Cad.
Savaklar Cad.
Edirnekapı Cad.
Topkapı-
Fevzipaşa Cad.
Yavuz Selim Cad.
Darüşşafaka Cad.
Manyasa Zade Cad.
Fethiye Cad.
Draman Cad.
Kaya Cad.
Salma Tomruk Cad.
Akşemsetin Cad.
Adnan Menderes Bul.
Guraba Hastanesi Cad.
Akdeniz Cad.
Macar Kardeşler Cad.
Horhor Cad.
Atatürk Bul.
Haliç Cad.
Abdülezel Paşa Cad.
Hacıkadın Cad.
Millet Cad.
Oğuzhan Cad.
Ahmet Vefik Paşa Cad.
Gökalp Ziya Sok.
Kızılelma Cad.
Haseki Cad.
Cerrahpaşa Cad.
Hekimoğlu Alipaşa Cad.
Koca Mustafa Paşa Cad.
Küçük Langa Cad.
A. Nafiz Gürman Cad.
Namık Kemal Cad.
Mustafa Kemal Cad.
Bostani Sok.
Kennedy Cad.
Ordu Cad.
Mesih Paşa Cad.
Türkeli Cad.
Şehzadebaşı-Vezneciler Cad.
Cemal Yener Tosyal Cad.
Kirazcımescit Sok.

SEE SULTANAHMET & SÜLEYMANIYE MAP, P. 696

İSTANBUL BOĞAZI (BOSPHORUS)

İstanbul

FOOD

Hacî Abdullah, **1**
Koska Helvacısı, **6**

NIGHTLIFE

Araf Nightclub, **3**
Jazz Stop, **5**
Nayah Music Club, **2**
Sinerji Bar, **4**

0 — 300 yards
0 — 300 meters

PUBLIC TRANSPORTATION. AKBİL is an electronic ticket system that saves you 15-50% on fares for municipal ferries, buses, trams, water taxis, and subway (but not *dolmuş*). Cards (6YTL) are sold at tram stations or ticket offices, and can be recharged in 1YTL increments at the white IETT public bus booths, marked **AKBİL satılır.**

Tram: The *Tramvay* runs from Eminönü to Zeytinburnu every 5min. Make sure to be on the right side of the street, as the carriage follows the traffic. Get tokens at any station and toss them in at the turnstile to board (1.30YTL). The old-fashioned carriages of the **historical tram** run 1km uphill from Tunel (by the Galata Bridge) through İstiklâl Cad. and up to Taksim Sq. They're the same ones that made the trip in the early 20th century.

Metro: İstanbul operates 2 Metro lines (☎568 9970): one from Aksaray to the Esenler Bus Terminal and the other from Taksim Sq. to 4th Levent. A funicular connects the tram stop Cabatas to Taksim Sq. The Metro runs daily every 5min. 5:40am-11:15pm.

Commuter Rail: A slow commuter rail (known locally as *tren*) runs 6am-11pm between Sirkeci Gar and the far western suburbs, as well as the Asian side. The stop in Bostanci is near the ferry to the Princes Islands. Keep your ticket until the end of the journey.

Taxis: Taxi drivers are even more reckless and speed-crazed than other İstanbul drivers, but the city's more than 20,000 taxis offer an undoubtedly quick way to get around. Don't ask the driver to fix a price before getting in; instead, make sure he restarts the meter. Night fares, usually starting at midnight, are double. Rides from Sultanahmet to Taksim Sq. should be around 15YTL, and from the center to the airport around 25YTL.

GETTING A FARE PRICE. While most İstanbul taxis are metered, some cab drivers have an annoying tendency to drive circles around the city before bringing you to your destination. Watch the roads and look out for signs pointing to where you're going. To avoid the risk altogether, take taxis only as far as the Galata Bridge, and walk from there to Sultanahmet or Taksim.

PRACTICAL INFORMATION

Tourist Office: 3 Divan Yolu (☎/fax 518 8754), at the north end of the Hippodrome in Sultanahmet. Open daily 9am-5pm. Branches in Taksim's Hilton Hotel Arcade on Cumhuriyet Cad., Sirkeci train station, Atatürk Airport, and Karaköy Maritime Station.

Budget Travel: İstanbul has many travel agencies, almost all speak English, and most hostels and hotels have started running their own travel services as well. Though most are trustworthy, there are some scams. Always check that the agency is licensed. If anything happens, make sure you have your agent's info and report it to the tourist police.

Fez Travel, 15 Akbıyık Cad. (☎516 9024; www.feztravel.com). İstanbul's most efficient and well informed, Fez's English-speaking staff organizes anything from accommodations to ferries, flights, and buses, as well as their own backpacker-tailored tours of Turkey and Greece. STA-affiliated. Open daily 9am-7pm. MC/V.

Hassle Free, 10 Akbıyık Cad. (☎458 9500; www.anzacgouse.com), right next to New Backpackers. The name is self-explanatory and the young, friendly staff provides the best deals and tips. Books local buses or boat cruises of southern Turkey. Open daily 9am-11pm.

Barefoot Travel, 1 Cetinkaya Sok. (☎517 0269; www.barefoot-travel.com), just off Akbıyık Cad. The English-speaking staff is helpful and offers good deals on airfare, as well as free maps of İstanbul and Turkey. Open daily in summer 8am-8pm; in winter 8am-6pm. AmEx/MC/V.

Consulates: Australia, 15 Asker Ocaği Cad., Elmadag Sisli (☎257 7050; fax 243 1332). **Canada,** 373/5 İstiklâl Cad. (☎251 9838; fax 251 9888). **Ireland,** 26 Cumhuriyet Cad., Mobil Altı, Elmadağ (☎246 6025). **UK,** 34 Meşrutiyet Cad., Beyoğlu/Tepebaşı (☎252 6436). **US,** 2 Kaplicalar Mevkii Sok., Istinye (☎335 9000).

Currency Exchange: Bureaux de change around the city are open M-F 8:30am-noon and 1:30-5pm. Most don't charge commission. **ATMs** generally accept all international cards. Most banks exchange **traveler's checks.** Exchanges in Sultanahmet have poor rates, but are open late and on weekends. There is a yellow **PTT** kiosk between the Aya Sofya and the Blue Mosque that changes currency for no commission. **Western Union** offices are in banks throughout Sultanahmet and Taksim; they operate M-F 8:30am-noon and 1:30-5pm.

English-Language Bookstores: English-language books are all over the city. In Sultanahmet, *köşk* (kiosks) at the Blue Mosque, on Aya Sofya Meydanı, and on Divan Yolu sell international papers. **Galeri Kayseri,** 58 Divan Yolu (☎512 0456), caters to tourists with informational books on Turkish and Islamic history and literature, as well as a host of guidebooks. Open daily 9am-9pm. D/MC/V.

Laundromat: Star Laundry, 18 Akbıyık Cad., between New Backpackers and Hassle Free. Wash, dry, and iron 4YTL per kg. Min. 2kg. Ready in 3hr. Open daily 9am-8pm.

Tourist Police: In Sultanahmet, at the beginning of Yerebatan Cad. (24hr. hotline ☎527 4503 or 528 5369). Tourist police speak excellent English, and their mere presence causes hawkers to scatter. In an **emergency,** call from any phone.

Hospitals: American Hospital, Admiral Bristol Hastanesi, 20 Güzelbahçe Sok., Nişantaşı (☎231 4050), is applauded by locals and tourists. Has many English-speaking doctors. **German Hospital,** 119 Sıraselviler Cad., Taksim (☎293 2150), also has a multilingual staff and is conveniently located for Sultanahmet hostelers. **International Hospital,** 82 İstanbul Cad., Yesilköy (☎663 3000).

Internet Access: Internet in İstanbul is everywhere from hotels to barber shops, and connections are usually cheap and decently fast—notwithstanding the frequent power cuts. Most hostels have free Internet, though many impose a 15min. limit. Some hostels now offer Wi-Fi, as do more upscale hotels and eateries; signs are usually posted on the door. Rates at travel agencies are usually 1YTL per 15min., 3YTL per hr.

Post and Telephone Offices: Known as **PTTs.** All accept packages. **Main branch** in Sirkeci, 25 Büyük Postane Sok. Stamp and currency exchange services open daily 8:30am-midnight. 24hr. phones. Phone cards available for 5-10YTL. There is a yellow PTT kiosk in Sultanahmet between the Aya Sofya and the Blue Mosque, which exchanges currency and sells stamps. Open daily 9am-5pm.

PHONE CODES. The code is **212** on the European side and **216** on the Asian side. All numbers listed here begin with 212 unless otherwise specified.

ACCOMMODATIONS

Budget accommodations are concentrated in **Sultanahmet** (a.k.a. Türist Şeğntral). As Turkey has become a backpacker's must, there has been an explosion of cheap places to stay, turning Akbıyık Cad. into a virtually uninterrupted line of hostels. All offer similar quality and prices. The side streets around **Sirkeci** railway station and **Aksaray** have dozens of dirt-cheap, rundown hotels, while fancier options abound in the more touristy districts. All accommodations listed below are in Sultanahmet. Although you will always find a bed somewhere, reserve ahead for your hostel of choice. Hotels in **Lâleli** are in İstanbul's center of prostitution and should be avoided. Rates can rise by up to 20% in July and August.

TURKEY

Big Apple Hostel, 12 Bayram Fırını Sok. (☎517 7931; www.hostelbigapple.com), down the road from Akbıyık Cad., next to Barefoot Travel. On a quieter side street off of Akbiyik Cad., this hostel offers a fun and relaxing atmosphere for both individuals and groups. Has a large downstairs common room and an upstairs terrace with bean bag

Sultanahmet and Süleymaniye

ACCOMMODATIONS
- Bahaus Guesthouse, 12
- Big Apple Hostel, 11
- İstanbul Hostel, 6
- Metropolis Hostel, 8
- Sultan Hostel, 7
- Sydney Hostel, 10
- Terrace Guesthouse, 9

FOOD
- Doy-Doy, 13
- Muhammad Said Baklavaci, 2
- Pudding Shop, 3
- Trabzon Lokantasi, 1

NIGHTLIFE
- Cheers, 4
- Just Bar, 5

TOPKAPI SIGHTS
1. Imperial Gate
2. Gate of Greeting
3. Kitchens & Porcelain Collection
4. Divan
5. Inner Treasury
6. Gate of Felicity
7. School of the Expeditionary Pages
8. Palace Treasury
9. Pavilion of Holy Relics
10. Circumcision Room
11. Court of the Black Eunuchs'
12. Valide Salon
13. Harem Mosque

Tram
TO GALATA BRIDGE (500m)
TO SIRKECI TRAIN STATION (200m)
TO UNIVERSITE (NOSI) (100m)
PTT
SİRKECİ
CAĞALOĞLU
BEYAZIT
SULTANAHMET
ÇATLADIKAPI
FOURTH COURT
THIRD COURT
SECOND COURT
FIRST COURT
HAREM
Gülhane Park
0 100 yards
0 100 meters
Beyazıt Tower
İstanbul Üniversitesi
Main Gate
Beyazıt Camii
Calligraphy Museum
Grand Bazaar (Kapalı Çarşı) SEE DETAIL MAP
Nuruosmaniye Camii
Çemberlitaş Eczanesi
Çemberlitaş Hamam
ÇEMBERLİTAŞ
Çağaloğlu Hamamı
Vilayet (Government House)
GÜLHANE
Park Entrance
Museum of the Ancient Orient
Çinili Köşkü (Tiled Pavilion)
Archaeological Museum
Aya Irene
Tourist Police
Yerebatan Saray (Underground Cistern)
AYASOFYA MEYDANI
SULTANAHMET
Aya Sofya
Ahmet III Fountain
Four Seasons Hotel
SULTANAHMET SQ.
Law Courts
Adliye Palace
Egyptian Obelisk
İbrahim Paşa Sarayı (Museum of Art)
Serpentine Column
Sultanahmet (Blue) Mosque
Carpet Museum
Hippodrome
Rough Stone Column
Mosaic Museum
Sifa Hamami
Fuat Paşa Cad.
Örücüler Cad.
Mercan Cad.
Mahmutpaşa Yokşu Cad.
Carkcılar Sok.
Tarakcılar Cad.
Tarakçı Cafer Sok.
Hoca Hanı Sok.
Cemal Nadır Sok.
Ebussuut Cad.
Hüdavindigar Cad.
Yeni Saraçhane Cad.
Sultan Mektebi Sok.
Yağlıkcılar Cad.
Tiğcılar Aciçeşme Sok.
Türkocağı Cad.
Ankara Cad.
Hükümet Konağı Sok.
Alemdağ Cad.
Alemdar Cad.
Besim Ömer Paşa Cad.
Bakırcılar Cad.
Çadırcılar Cad.
Ordu Cad.
Yahni Kapan Sok.
Yeni Ceriler Cad.
Mahmut Paşa Mahk Sok.
Şeref Efendi Sok.
Nuruosmaniye Cad.
Prof. K. Ismail Gürkman Cad.
Yerebatan Cad.
Caferiye Sok.
Soğuk Çeşme Sok.
Biloyciler Sok.
Vezirhanı Cad.
Türbedar Sok.
Babiali Cad.
Molla Fenarisk Sok.
Çatal Çeşme Sok.
Ticarethane Sok.
Divan Yolu
Babıhumayun Cad.
İshak Paşa Cad.
Turkanlı S.
Mithatpaşa Cad.
Direkli Camii S.
Beyazit Karakol S.
Sinekli Medr. S.
Pehlivan Yahya Paşa
Tatlı Kuyu Hamamı S.
Gedikpaşa Cad.
Gedikpaşa Camii S.
Dönem S.
Evkaf S.
Ahmet S.
Piyerolti Cad.
Klodfarer Cad.
Imran Öktem Cad.
Atmeydanı Sok.
Peykhane S.
Terzihane Sok.
Kabasakal Cad.
Kutlugün Sok.
Adliye Sk.
Tevfikhane Sok.
Utangaç Sok.
Dalbastı Sok.
Mimar Mehmet Ağa Cad.
Akbıyık Cad.
Katip Sinan S.
Medresesi S.
Çeşmesi S.
Üçler Sok.
Tavukhane Sok.
Arasta Cad.
Torun Sok.
Kadırga Limanı Cad.
Nakilbent Sok.
Küçük Gelinlik Sok.
Ayasofya Cad.
Tomurcuk Sok.
Kaleci Sok.
Fenerli Kapı Sok.
Cankurtaran Cad.
Ahır Kapı

Grand Bazaar (Kapalı Çarşı)

SAHAFLAR ÇARŞISI
Yorgancılar Kapısı
Yorgancılar Cad.
Çadırcılar Cad.
Fesciler Cad.
Fesciler Kapısı
Beyazit Kapısı
Yağlıkcılar Cad.
Kavaflar Sok.
Halıcılar Çarşısı Cad.
Aynacılar Sok.
Güllaç Sokak
Ağa Sok.
Takkeciler Cad.
OLD BAZAAR
Zenneciler Sok.
Keseciler Cad.
Kalpakcılar Başı Cad.
Çarşıkapı Kapısı
Çarşıkapı Sok.
Iskender Boğazı Sok.
Kürçuler Kapısı
Kolancılar Cad.
Candal Bedesteni Sok.
Aynacılar Sok.
SANDAL BEDESTENİ
Nuruosmaniye Kapısı
Nuruosmaniye Kapısı Sok.
Fountain

chairs, beach loungers, a swing, not to mention some of the friendliest staff around. Breakfast (8:30-10:30am), linens, and Internet included. Dorms US$12. MC/V. ❷

Metropolis, 24 Terbıyık Sok. (☎518 1822; www.metropolishostel.com), removed from the hustle of Akbıyık, in a quieter though still central back street. This beautifully kept hostel has comfortable, stylish rooms, friendly staff, and a peaceful location. Guests get a 10% discount at the Metropolis Restaurant and Downunder bar around the corner. Breakfast included. Free Internet. Single-sex dorms 23YTL; doubles 60YTL. ❷

Bahaus Guesthouse, 11-13 Akbıyık Cad. (☎638 6534; www.travelinistanbul.com), across the street from Big Apple. Though its dorm rooms are simple, Bahaus's cozy Anatolian-themed closed terrace and couch-filled open terrace are comfortable and lively. Travelers rave about this place, and the rooms are usually full. Airport pickup available. Breakfast included. Free Internet. Reserve ahead. Dorms €9; doubles €44. ❶

İstanbul Hostel, 35 Kutlugün Sok. (☎516 9380; www.istanbulhostel.net). In business well before Sultanahmet was invaded by backpackers, this hostel has all the usual amenities, as well as a welcoming family feel and an extremely helpful staff. Bar, travel agency, rooftop lounge, and board games also available. The fireplace near the bar makes this a great place for a cozy winter visit. Breakfast included. Free Internet. Beds on the roof 12YTL; dorms 20YTL; doubles 55YTL. ❷

Sultan Hostel, 21 Akbiyik Cad. (☎516 9260; www.sultanhostel.com). Right in the middle of backpacker land, this happening hostel is İstanbul's most famous. With a streetside, rooftop restaurant and comfortable, clean dorms, Sultan's is a great place to meet fellow travelers. Breakfast included. Free safes. Free Internet. Reserve ahead. Dorms €12; singles €30; doubles €30, with bathroom €34; quads €52/56. ❷

Sydney Hostel, 42 Akbıyık Cad. (☎518 6671; fax 518 6672), in the middle of Akbıyık. Despite its central location, Sydney Hostel remains calm, with cheerful sky-blue walls, modern rooms and bathrooms, and much-coveted in-room A/C. Rooftop terrace. Breakfast included. Free safes. Free Internet. Dorms €10; singles and doubles €35. ❶

Terrace Guesthouse, 39 Kutlugün Sok. (☎638 9733; www.terracehotelistanbul.com), behind Akbıyık Cad. Housed in a narrow carpet shop, this elegant hotel has beautifully decorated rooms at affordable prices. The 2 upstairs terraces have spectacular views. Breakfast included. Free Wi-Fi. Singles €50; doubles €60; triples €70. ❺

FOOD

İstanbul's restaurants, like its clubs and bars, often satisfy the golden rule: if it's well advertised or easy to find, it's not worth a visit. Sultanahmet's "Turkish" restaurants are convenient, but much better meals can be found across the **Galata Bridge** and around **Taksim Square.** Small Bosphorus suburbs such as **Arnavutköy** and **Sariyer** (on the European side) and **Çengelköy** (on the Asian side) are the best places for fresh fish. For a cheaper meal, **İstiklâl Caddesi** has all the major Western chains, as well as quick and tasty Turkish fast food. Vendors in Ottoman dress carrying big steel teapots on their backs sell *Vişne suyu* (sour cherry juice), and on any street you'll find plenty of dried fruit and nuts for sale, as well as the omnipresent stalls of sesame bagels (1YTL). The best open-air **market** is open daily in **Beşiktaş,** near Barbaros Cad., while at the Egyptian Spice Bazaar *(Mısır Çarşısı)* you can find almonds, fruit, and—of course—**kebap,** which range from Shawarma-type meat to Western-style meat-on-a-stick.

Doy-Doy, 13 Şifa Hammamı Sok. (☎517 1588). From the southern end of the Hippodrome, walk down the hill around the edge of the Blue Mosque and look for the blue sign. The best in Sultanahmet, 3fl. Doy-Doy has rooftop tables right under the Blue Mosque. On the lower levels, you'll find cushioned floors and plenty of *nargilas* (hookahs). Tasty *kebap* (5-10YTL) and refreshing shepherd salads with *cacik* (yogurt and cucumber; 4YTL). No alcohol served. Open daily 8am-11pm. MC/V. ❷

Trabzon Lokantasi, 10 Dervisler Sok, near Sirkeci. Tucked in an alley off the tram tracks, this small cafe-restaurant features real Turkish home cooking in cheap, plentiful servings, with several vegetarian options. The lentil soup (1.50YTL) is exceptional. Be sure to check out the colorful guestbook, filled with notes from visitors from around the world. Entrees 3-6YTL. Open daily 11am-11pm. ❶

Muhammed Said Baklavaci, 88 Divan Yolu Cad. (☎526 9666). Specializing in homemade Baklava and Turkish Delight of almost every flavor, this small, locally owned bakery is a wonderland of sweets. Prices are reasonable and the quality is exceptional. 1 kilo 20-29YTL. Open daily 9am-10pm. ❸

Hacı Abdullah, 17 Sakizağacı Cad. (☎293 8561; www.haciabdullah.com.tr), down the street from Ağa Camii, in Taksim Sq. This family-style restaurant has been going strong since 1888 and features huge vases of preserved fruit, as well as high-tech bathrooms. Their homemade grapefruit juice is fantastic. Soups and salads 3-7YTL. Entrees 10-20YTL. No alcohol served. Open daily noon-11pm. Kitchen closes 10:30pm. MC/V. ❷

Koska Helvacısı, İstiklâl Cad. 238 (☎244 0877; www.koskahelvacisi.com.tr). This confectionary superstore, which celebrated its 100th anniversary in 2007, is any sugar-lover's dream. Fantastic take-out baklava trays (3YTL) and boxed assortments of sweets (6-20YTL) in all colors and flavors. Open daily 9am-11:30pm. ❷

Pudding Shop, 6 Divan Yolu Cad. (☎522 2970). A major pit stop on the Hippie Trail to the Far and Middle East during the 70s. Young travelers en route to Goa and Kathmandu left messages on a board that's still here. Today, the former setting for the drug deal scene in *Midnight Express* (1978) is a clean and tasty fast-food joint, more nostalgic than exciting. A/C upstairs. Kebap 5-12YTL. Open daily 7am-11pm. ❷

SIGHTS

İstanbul's incomparable array of churches, mosques, palaces, and museums can keep an ardent tourist busy for weeks. Most first-time travelers to İstanbul spend a lot of time in Sultanahmet, the area around the Aya Sofya, south of and uphill from Sirkeci. Merchants crowd the district between the enormous Grand Bazaar, east of the university, and the less touristy Egyptian Spice Bazaar, just southeast of Eminönü. To soak in the city's sights the easy way, hop on one of the small boats on either side of the Galata Bridge and go for a relaxing and panoramic **Bosphorus tour.** Most tours last about 2hr. and return to their starting point.

BARGAINING FOR BEGINNERS. Though the Grand Bazaar is haggling at its finest, bargaining doesn't end at carpets. It's acceptable to bargain for almost anything in İstanbul, including tours. For the best deals on boat trips, bargain with boat owners at the port. Trips shouldn't be more than 20YTL per person for a few hours of floating down the Bosphorus.

AYA SOFYA (HAGIA SOPHIA). When Aya Sofya (Divine Wisdom) was built in AD 537, it was the biggest building in the world. Built as a church, it fell to the Ottomans in 1453 and was converted into a mosque; it remained such until 1932, when Atatürk declared it a museum. The nave is overshadowed by the gold-leaf mosaic dome lined with hundreds of circular windows that make it seem as though the dome is floating on a bed of luminescent pearls. Throughout the building, Qur'anic inscriptions and mosaics of Mary and the angels intertwine in a fascinating symmetry. The gallery contains Byzantine mosaics uncovered from beneath a thick layer of Ottoman plaster, as well as the famed sweating pillar, sheathed in bronze. The pillar has a hole big enough to stick a finger in and collect the odd drop of water, believed to possess healing powers, but the column is often disappointingly dry. *(Open daily 9am-7:30pm. Upper gallery open 9:30am-6:45pm. 10YTL.)*

BLUE MOSQUE (SULTANAHMET CAMİİ). Named for the beautiful blue İznik tiles covering the interior, the extragavant Blue Mosque and its six **minarets** were Sultan Ahmet's 1617 claim to fame. At the time of construction, only the mosque at Mecca had as many minarets, and the thought of rivaling that sacred edifice was considered heretical. The crafty Sultan circumvented this difficulty by financing the construction of a seventh minaret at Mecca. The chandelier structure was intended to create the illusion of tiny starlights floating in the air. The small, single-domed structure in front of the Blue Mosque is **Sultanahmet'in Türbesi,** or Sultan Ahmet's Tomb, which contains the sultan's remains. The reliquary in the back contains strands of the Prophet Muhammad's beard. Behind the mosque, check out the Byzantine-era **Hippdrome.** *(Open M-Th and Sa-Su 9am-12:30pm, 1:45-4:40pm, and 5:40-6:30pm, F noon-2:20pm. Closed to the public for prayer 5 times a day. Scarves are provided at the entrance; women should cover their knees, hair, and shoulders. Inside, don't cross on to the sections limited to prayer. Donations welcome.* *See 689 for more on mosque etiquette.)*

TOPKAPI PALACE (TOPKAPI SARAYI). Towering from the high ground at the tip of the Old City and hidden behind walls up to 12m high, Topkapı was the nerve center of the Ottoman Empire. Built by Mehmet the Conqueror in 1458-1465, the palace became an imperial residence during the reign of Süleyman the Magnificent. The palace is divided into a series of courtyards. The **first courtyard** was the popular center of the palace, where the general public could enter to watch executions and other displays of imperial might. The **second courtyard** leads to displays of wealth, including collections of porcelain, silver, gold, and torture instruments—not to mention crystal staircases. The Gate of Felicity leads to the **third courtyard,** which houses a collection of imperial clothing, as well as the awesome **Palace Treasury.** The **fourth courtyard** is the pleasure center of the palace—it was among these pavilions, gardens, and fountains that the Ottomans really got their mojo working. The most interesting part of Topkapı is the 400-plus-room **harem.** Tours of the harem begin at the Black Eunuchs' Dormitory and continue into the chambers of the Valide Sultan, the sultan's mother and the most powerful woman in the harem. Surrounding the room of the queen mum are the chambers of the concubines. If a particular woman attracted the sultan's affections or if the sultan spent a night with her, she would be promoted to "odalisque" status, which meant that she had to stay in İstanbul forever, but got nicer quarters in exchange for her undying ministrations. *(Palace open M and W-Su 9am-7pm. Harem open 10am-5pm. Audio tour of*

BUMPER CARS, TURKISH STYLE

It happens every year for one glorious week. In early January, the city of Selcuk, Turkey, hosts the country's **Camel Wrestling Championship.**

Maybe "wrestling" isn't quite the appropriate word here. Camels aren't exactly the most vicious of creatures, and their fighting tactics resemble a childhood game of bumper cars more than an all-out war. And while Spain's bulls ultimately reach the sword at the hands of bullfighters, PETA protestors can sleep easy over the fate of Turkey's camels. Perhaps a testament to the camels' true character, the game ends not with death, but when one of the camels runs away, barrelling into the audience and scattering the lounging spectators.

Despite the seeming absurdity of camel-wrestling, the sport has many wealthy supporters and continues to draw crowds despite the reduction in Turkey's camel population. Tickets to the festival's competitions can be bought at the gate, and it's common to gamble on the contestants.

Selcuk is on the Aegean Sea and is accessible by bus from Istanbul or Izmir. Check with travel agencies in İstanbul for tickets and information about the festival.

palace 5YTL. Harem can only be visited on guided tours, which leave every 30min. Lines for tours can be long; arrive early. Palace and harem each 10YTL.)

UNDERGROUND CISTERN (YEREBATAN SARAYI). This underground "palace" is actually a vast cavern whose shallow water eerily reflects the images of its 336 supporting columns. The columns are all illuminated by colored ambient lighting, making the cistern slightly resemble a horror-movie set. Underground walkways originally linked the cistern to Topkapı Palace, but were blocked to curb rampant trafficking in stolen goods and abducted women. At the far end of the cistern, two huge Medusa heads lie upside down in the water. Legend has it that looking at them directly turns people to stone. The cistern's **cafe,** in a dark corner, is a cross between creepy and romantic, and is unsurprisingly overpriced. *(Entrance 175m from the Aya Sofya in a small stone kiosk. Open daily 9am-6:30pm. 10YTL.)*

ARCHAEOLOGICAL MUSEUM COMPLEX. The Archaeological Museum Complex is made of four distinct museums. The **Tiled Pavilion** explains more than you ever wanted to know about the omnipresent İznik tiles. The smaller, adjacent building is the **Ancient Orient Museum.** It houses an excellent collection of 3000-year-old stone artifacts from the ancient Middle East and the Treaty of Kadesh, the world's oldest known written treaty, drafted after a battle between Ramses II of Egypt and the Hittite King Muvatellish. The immense **Archaeology Museum** has one of the world's greatest collections of Classical and Hellenistic art, but is surprisingly bereft of visitors. The highlight is the famous Alexander Sarcophagus, covered with intricate carvings depicting the king in battle. The superb **Museum of Turkish and Islamic Art** features a large and impressive collection of Islamic art. *(150m downhill from the Topkapı Palace's 1st courtyard. All museums open Tu-Su 8:30am-5pm. 5YTL.)*

GRAND BAZAAR. The **Kapalı Çarşısı** (Grand Bazaar) works on a scale unmatched by even the most frenetic of markets elsewhere in Europe. The largest and oldest covered bazaar in the world, the Grand Bazaar began in 1461 as a modest affair during the reign of Mehmet the Conqueror. Today, the enormous Kapalı Çarşısı combines the best and worst of shopping in Turkey to form the massive mercantile sprawl that starts at Çemberlitaş and covers the hill down to Eminönü, ending at the more authentic, less claustrophobic, and cheaper **Mısır Çarşısı** (Egyptian Spice Bazaar) and the Golden Horn waterfront. Rule number one in bargaining: never settle for more than half the first price you are asked. And don't worry if you get lost—there are directional arrows from virtually any spot, so relax and enjoy the ride. *(www.grandbazaar.com. Open M-Sa 9am-7pm.)*

SÜLEYMANİYE COMPLEX. To the north of İstanbul University is the elegant **Süleymaniye Camii,** one of Ottoman architect Sinan's great masterpieces. The mosque is part of a larger **külliye** (complex), which includes **tombs,** an **imaret** (soup kitchen), and several **madrasas** (Islamic schools). After seeing the **royal tombs** of Süleyman I in the **cemetery,** go inside the vast and perfectly proportioned mosque—the height of the dome (53m) is exactly twice the measurement of each side of the square base. The **stained-glass windows** are the sobering work of the master Sarhoş İbrahim (İbrahim the Drunkard). The İznik tile İnzanity all started here: the area around the **mihrab** showcases Sinan's first experiment in blue tiles. *(Open daily except during prayer. Leave your shoes at the entrance. Women must cover their shoulders; men and women should cover their heads. Scarves are available at the entrance.)*

TURKEY

HAMMAMS (TURKISH BATHS)

In the past a man found in a women's bath was sentenced to death, but today's rules have relaxed and it's not rare to find co-ed baths where both genders strip beyond their skivvies. Most baths have separate women's sections or hours, but only some have designated female attendants. If you'd rather have a masseuse of your same sex, make sure to ask at the entrance.

Cağaloğlu Hamami, on Yerebatan Cad. at Babiali Cad. (☎522 2424; www.cagaloglu-hamami.com.tr), near Cağaloğlu Sq. in Sultanahmet. Donated to İstanbul in 1741 by Sultan Mehmet I, this luxurious white-marble bath is one of the city's most illustrious. Self-service bath 20YTL, bath with scrub 30YTL, complete bath and massage 40YTL, luxury treatment with hand-knit Oriental washcloth 60YTL. Slippers, soap, and towels included. Open daily for women 8am-8pm, for men 8am-10pm.

Çemberlitaş Hamamı, 8 Vezirhan Cad. (☎522 7974; www.cemberlitashamami.com.tr). Just a soap-slide away from the Çemberlitaş tram stop. Built by Sinan in 1584, the marble interiors make this place downright regal. Vigorous "towel service" after the bath; guests are welcome to hang around the hot marble rooms afterward. Open daily 6am-midnight.

NIGHTLIFE

İstanbul's intense nightlife falls into three categories. The first includes male-only *çay* (tea) houses, backgammon parlors, and dancing shows. Women are not prohibited but are unwelcome and should avoid these places, which are often unsafe for male travelers as well. Let's Go does not endorse patronage of these establishments. The second category includes the local youth **cafe-bars, rock bars,** and many **backpacker bars.** In **Sultanahmet,** these are crammed within 10m of one another, usually on the rooftop or front tables of the hostels. They have standardized beer prices (5YTL) and are usually Australian-dominated. **Clubs** and **discos** comprise the third nightlife category. Even taxi drivers can't keep up with the ever-fluctuating club scene. The Beşiktaş end of **Ortaköy** is a maze of upscale hangouts. The cheerful **Nevizade** is a virtually uninterrupted row of wine shops and tapas bars, parallel to İstiklâl Cad. İstanbul's local specialty is *balyoz* (sledgehammer or wrecking ball). Getting wrecked won't be difficult: *balyoz* consists of *rakı*, whiskey, vodka, and gin with orange juice. Bottoms up.

Just Bar, 18 Akbıyık Cad. (☎01 23 45 67 89). This bar has become almost as much of a must-see as the Aya Sofya. Outdoor wooden pub tables, rock/funk/R&B music, and free-flowing beer make for a typical backpacker's night, every night. Beer 5YTL. Mixed drinks 7-10YTL. Open daily 11am-4am.

Cheers, next door, flows seamlessly together with Just Bar. Equally popular, friendly, and laid-back. Beer 4-5YTL. Mixed drinks and shots 7-10YTL. Open daily noon-late.

Jazz Stop, at the end of Büyük Parmakkapı Sok., in Taksim. A mixed group of music lovers sits in this large underground tavern while live bands lay the funk, blues, and jazz on thick. The owner, the drummer from one of Turkey's oldest and most respected rock groups, occasionally takes part in the jams. A late-night hangout where the crowds don't build until 2 or 3am. Beer 5YTL. Mixed drinks 7-20YTL. Live music daily 2am. Cover F-Sa 10YTL; includes 1 drink. Open daily 7pm-6am.

Araf, İstiklâl Cad. and 32 Balo Sok. (☎244 8301), across from the entrance to Nevizade. Take the elevator to the 4th fl., then walk upstairs to reach this funky rooftop veranda with international music and freestyle dancing in a birthday-party atmosphere. Beer 4YTL. Mixed drinks 7-20YTL. Open daily 5pm-2am.

Nayah Music Club, Kurabiye Sok. 23 (☎244 1183; www.nayah.org), in Beyoglu. From İstiklâl Cad., take a right onto Mis Sok.; Nayah is 1 block down, on the corner with Kurabiye Sok. This reggae bar is small and relaxed, with rasta bartenders. Customers don't really dance, but instead sit and accompany the music with subtle head bobs. Beer 4YTL. Mixed drinks 7-14YTL. Open M-Th 6pm-2am, F-Sa 6pm-4am.

UKRAINE (УКРАЇНА)

In late 2004, Ukraine's Orange Revolution won international fame for the country. President Viktor Yushchenko and his administration have since enacted important reforms, like firing the notoriously corrupt traffic police en masse. As reforms have slowed down, however, Ukrainian politics have become more muddled. Today, Ukrainians are divided over their own identity: while Western Ukraine speaks Ukrainian, Eastern Ukraine and the Crimea have a decidedly Russian feel, and Kyiv often feels trapped in the middle. This internal struggle to reinvent and yet retain traditions can make Ukrainian culture confusing to navigate. Don't be surprised if a desk clerk and a website provide different prices for a room, and don't expect anyone outside Kyiv to speak much English. Despite these inconveniences, however, Ukraine is captivating. Whole cities are under renovation, and the energy of development spills over into the streets. Ukraine's lack of any viable tourist infrastructure creates an obstacle for the bulk of tourists; get past it, and you'll find a beautiful, delicious, and adventurous place to travel.

DISCOVER UKRAINE: SUGGESTED ITINERARIES

THREE DAYS. Stick to **Kyiv** (p. 724), the epicenter of the Orange Revolution. Check out **Independence Square,** stop by **Shevchenko Park** to enjoy authentic Ukrainian cuisine at **O'Panas** (p. 704), and contemplate your mortality among the mummified monks of the **Kyiv-Cave Monastery** (p. 707).

ONE WEEK. After three days in **Kyiv,** take a 9hr. train to **Lviv** (3 days; p. 725), the cultural capital of Ukraine. Spend time doing nothing at the city's cafes, but don't miss the centuries-old vials and prescriptions of the **Pharmacy Museum** (p. 731); make sure to experience high culture for cheap at the **Theater of Opera and Ballet** (p. 731).

BEST OF UKRAINE, THREE WEEKS. Begin with five days in **Kyiv,** spend another four in **Lviv,** then head to **Carpathian National Natural Park** (3 days; p. 737) to pick mushrooms and hike **Mt. Hoverla,** the tallest point in Ukraine. Next, hit **Odessa** (4 days; p. 740) to visit the **Catacombs** that hid Ukrainian partisans during WWII (p. 744). Spend the rest of your time by the **Black Sea** in **Crimea,** heading first to the relaxed city of **Sevastopol** (2 days; p. 754). Visit the ruins at **Chersonesus** (p. 756) after the beach. Finish in **Yalta** (3 days; p. 748), making sure to sample the stores at the nearby **Massandra Winery** (p. 752). Expect a full day of travel between each leg.

FACTS AND FIGURES

Official Name: Ukraine.

Capital: Kyiv.

Major Cities: Lviv, Odessa, Sevastopol, Simferopol, Yalta.

Population: 46,300,000.

Land Area: 603,700 sq. km.

Time Zone: GMT + 2, in summer GMT + 3.

Language: Ukrainian.

Religions: Ukrainian Orthodox (29%), Orthodox (16%), other (55%).

ESSENTIALS

WHEN TO GO

Ukraine is a huge country with a diverse climate. Things heat up from June to August in Odessa and Crimea, which are just barely subtropical. It is best to reserve in advance at these times. Kyiv enjoys a moderate climate, while the more mountainous west remains cool even in summer. Winter tourism is popular in the Carpathians, but unless you're skiing, spring and summer are probably the best times to visit the country. Book accommodations early around the May 1 holiday.

DOCUMENTS AND FORMALITIES

ENTRANCE REQUIREMENTS.

Passport: Required for all travelers.
Visa: Not required for citizens of Canada, the US, or EU countries, but mandatory for citizens of Australia and New Zealand.
Letter of Invitation: Required for citizens of Australia and New Zealand.
Inoculations: Recommended up-to-date on DTaP (diphtheria, tetanus, and pertussis), Hepatitis A, Hepatitis B, MMR (measles, mumps, and rubella), polio booster, rabies (if you'll be in rural areas for long periods of time), and typhoid.
Work Permit: Required of all foreigners planning to work in Ukraine.
International Driving Permit: Required for all those planning to drive.

EMBASSIES AND CONSULATES. Foreign embassies to Ukraine are in Kyiv (p. 724). Ukrainian embassies and consulates abroad include: **Australia,** Level 12, St.

George Centre, 60 Marcus Clarke St., Canberra, ACT 2601 (☎02 62 30 57 89; www.ukremb.info); **Canada,** 310 Somerset St., West Ottawa, ON K2P 0J9 (☎613-230-2400; www.mfa.gov.ua/canada); **UK,** 60 Holland Park, London, W11 3SJ (☎020 77 27 63 12, visas ☎020 72 43 89 23; www.ukremb.org.uk); **US,** 3350 M St., NW, Washington, D.C. 20007 (☎202-333-0606; www.mfa.gov.ua/usa).

VISA AND ENTRY INFORMATION. Ukraine's visa requirements have changed rapidly since 2005 as the new government works to encourage tourism. **Visas** are no longer required for American or Canadian citizens or citizens of the EU for stays of up to 90 days. All visas are valid for 90 days. Travelers should check with their local embassy or consulate for specific info on visa fees. Citizens of Australia and New Zealand require a letter of invitation, but citizens of Canada, the EU, and the US do not. Make sure to allow plenty of time for processing and to fill out the application thoroughly. You can extend your visa in Ukraine, at the Ministry of Foreign Affairs, 2 Zhytomyska Str., Kyiv, or at the local **Office of Visas and Registration** (ОВИР; OVYR), often located at the police station. When proceeding through **customs** you will be required to declare all cash, traveler's checks, and jewelry regardless of value. Check with your country's Ukrainian embassy for more restrictions. **Do not lose the paper given to you when entering the country to supplement your visa.** Make sure to carry your passport and visa at all times.

TOURIST SERVICES

Lviv's tourist office is extremely helpful, but is unfortunately the only official tourist office in Ukraine. There is no state-run tourist office. The remains of the Soviet giant **Intourist** have offices in hotels, but staff often don't speak English and are accustomed to dealing with groups, to whom they sell "excursion" packages to nearby sights. The official tourist website, **www.traveltoukraine.org,** has a list of "reliable travel agents." While local travel agencies can be helpful, staff rarely speak English and are often delighted to help you lighten your wallet.

MONEY

The Ukrainian unit of currency is the **hryvnya** (hv), and *Obmin Valyut* (Обмшн Валют) kiosks in most cities offer the best rates for **currency exchange. Traveler's checks** can be changed for a small commission in many cities. **ATMs** are everywhere. Most banks will give MasterCard and Visa **cash advances** for a high commission. The lobbies of upscale hotels usually exchange US dollars at lousy rates. **Private money changers** lurk near kiosks, ready with brilliant schemes for scamming you, but **exchanging money with them is illegal.**

HRYVNY (HV)		
	AUS$1 = 3.79HV	1HV = AUS$0.26
	CDN$1 = 4.10HV	1HV = CDN$0.24
	EUR€1 = 6.10HV	1HV = EUR€0.16
	NZ$1 = 3.47HV	1HV = NZ$0.29
	UK£1 = 8.99HV	1HV = UK£0.11
	US$1 = 4.96HV	1HV = US$0.20

HEALTH AND SAFETY

EMERGENCY	**Ambulance:** ☎03. **Fire:** ☎01. **Police:** ☎02.

Hospital facilities in Ukraine are limited and do not meet American or Western European standards. Patients may be required to bring their own medical supplies (e.g., bandages). Travelers must have medical insurance to receive health care; often, however, they have to front the bill themselves. When in doubt, it is advisable to seek aid from your local embassy, and they will find you adequate care or fly you out of the country; medical evacuations to Western Europe cost US$25,000 and upwards of US$50,000 to the US. **Pharmacies** (Аптеки; Apteky) are quite common and carry basic Western products. Aspirin is the only painkiller on hand, but plenty of cold remedies and bandages are available. Anything more complicated should be brought from home. Sanitary napkins (гігієнчні пакети; hihienchni pakety), condoms (презервативи; prezervativy), and tampons (прокладки, prokladky; or in Russian, тампон, pronounced "tampon" with a long "o") are sometimes sold at kiosks. **Boil all water** or learn to love brushing your teeth with soda water. Peel or wash **fruits and vegetables** from open markets. Meat purchased at public markets should be checked carefully and cooked thoroughly; refrigeration is infrequent and insects run rampant. Avoid the tasty-looking hunks of meat for sale out of buckets on the Kyiv Metro. Public restrooms range from disgusting to frightening. **Pay toilets** (платні; platni) are cleaner and might provide toilet paper, but bring your own anyway.

While Ukraine is politically stable, it is poor. Pickpocketing and wallet scams are the most common **crimes** against tourists; instances of armed robbery and assault, however, have been reported. Do not accept drinks from strangers, as this could result in your being drugged and robbed. Credit-card and ATM fraud are rampant; only use ATMs inside of banks and hotels, and avoid using credit cards whenever possible. Also use caution when crossing the street—drivers do not stop for pedestrians. It's wise to **register** with your embassy once you get to Ukraine.

Women traveling alone may receive catcalls on the street, in restaurants, and pretty much anywhere they go, but usually will be safe otherwise. Ukrainian women rarely go to restaurants alone, so expect to feel conspicuous if you do. Women may request to ride in female-only compartments during long train rides, though few do. Although non-Caucasians may experience **discrimination,** the biggest problems stem from the militia, who may stop people who appear non-Slavic. **Disabled** travelers may encounter some difficulty, as few locations are wheelchair accessible. **Homosexuality** is not yet accepted in Ukraine; discretion is advised.

TRANSPORTATION

BY PLANE. It is expensive to travel to Ukraine by plane, and few budget airlines fly in or out of the country. Ground transportation tends to be safer and more pleasant, but it can take a long time to traverse the great distances between cities. If you need to get somewhere quickly, there are several options. **Air Ukraine** flies to Kyiv, Lviv, and Odessa from many European capitals. **Aerosvit, Air France, ČSA, Delta, Lufthansa, LOT,** and **Malév** fly to Kyiv.

BY TRAIN. Trains run frequently and are the best way to travel. They usually run overnight and are timed to arrive in the morning. While *Let's Go* discourages the use of night trains, Ukraine's system is generally safe. When coming from a non-ex-Soviet country, expect a two-hour stop at the border. To purchase train tickets, you must present a passport, driver's license, or student ID. Once on board, you must present both your ticket and ID to the *konduktor*. On most Ukrainian trains, there are three classes: плацкарт, or *platskart*, where you'll be crammed in with *babushki* and baskets of strawberries; купе, or *kupe*, a clean, more private, four-person compartment; and first class, referred to as *CB*, or *SV* (for *Spalny Wagon*), which is twice as roomy and expensive as *kupe*. Unless you're determined to live like a local, pay the extra two dollars for *kupe*. Then again, women traveling alone may want to avoid the smaller, enclosed compartments of *kupe;* in that case, *platskart* may be the safer option. The *kasa* will sell you a *kupe* seat unless you say otherwise. Except in larger cities, where platform numbers are posted on the electronic board, the only way to figure out which platform your train leaves from is by listening to the distorted announcement. In large cities, trains arrive well before they are scheduled to depart, so you'll have a few minutes to show your ticket to cashiers or fellow passengers and ask "plaht-FORM-ah?"

DON'T MESS WITH TRANSNISTRIA. If you're planning a trip from Western Ukraine to the Crimea, make sure that your train or bus route doesn't pass through Moldova on the way. Most of northern Moldova is part of the unrecognized breakaway territory of Transinistra; border guards in Transinistra have been known to demand bribes, confiscate expensive items like laptops and cameras, or simply throw unlucky travelers off of the train. To make sure this doesn't happen to you, check at the ticket counter before buying to make sure your ticket won't take you for an unpleasant ride.

BY BUS. Buses cost about the same as trains, but are often much shabbier. For long distances, the train is usually more comfortable. One exception is AutoLux (АвтоЛюкс), which runs buses with A/C, snacks, and movies. Bus schedules are generally reliable, but low demand sometimes causes cancellations. Buy tickets at the *kasa* (ticket office); if they're sold out, try going directly to the driver, who might just magically find you a seat and pocket the money. Navigating the bus system can be tough for those who do not speak Ukrainian or Russian.

BY TAXI AND BY THUMB. Taxi drivers love to rip off foreigners, so negotiate the price beforehand. In major urban areas, road conditions are fair; in rural areas roads are in disrepair and poorly lit. Few Ukrainians **hitchhike,** but those who do hold a sign with their desired destination or just wave an outstretched hand. Let's Go does not recommend hitchhiking.

KEEPING IN TOUCH

PHONE CODES	**Country code:** 380. **International dialing prefix:** 810. From outside Ukraine, dial the international dialing prefix (see inside back cover) + 380 + city code + local number. Within Ukraine, dial 8 + city code + number. Within a single city, simply dial the local number.

EMAIL AND INTERNET. **Internet cafes** can be found in every major city and typically charge 4-12hv per hour of use. Major cities typically have 24hr. Internet cafes.

TELEPHONE. **Telephone** services are stumbling toward modernity. The easiest way to make international calls is with **Utel.** Buy an Utel phonecard (sold at most Utel phone locations) and dial the number of your international operator (counted as a local call; see the inside back cover). International access codes include: **AT&T Direct** (☎8 100 11); **Canada Direct** (☎8 100 17); and **MCI WorldPhone** (☎8 100 13). Alternatively, call at the central telephone office; estimate the length of your call and pay at the counter, and they'll direct you to a booth. Calling can be expensive, but you can purchase a 30min. international calling card for 15hv. Local calls from gray payphones generally cost 10-30hv. For an English-speaking operator, dial ☎8192. Cell phones are everywhere; to get one, stop at any kiosk or corner store.

MAIL. **Mail** is cheap, reliable, and extremely user-friendly, taking about 8-10 days to reach North America. Sending a postcard or a letter of less than 20g internationally costs 0.66hv. Mail can be received through **Poste Restante** (до запитання; do zapytannya). Address envelopes as follows: First name LAST NAME, post office address, Postal Code, city, UKRAINE.

ACCOMMODATIONS AND CAMPING

UKRAINE	❶	❷	❸	❹	❺
ACCOMMODATIONS	under 75hv	75-150hv	151-250hv	251-350hv	over 350hv

The hostel scene in Ukraine is quickly establishing itself. Though youth **hostels** aren't prevalent in Ukraine, some can be found in Lviv, Kyiv, and Odessa; budget accommodations are often in unrenovated Soviet-era buildings, though they're being renovated at an incredible pace. More expensive lodgings aren't necessarily nicer. Not all **hotels** accept foreigners, and those that do often overcharge them. Though room prices in Kyiv are astronomical, singles run anywhere from 65-110hv in the rest of the country. Standard hotel rooms include TVs, phones, and refrigerators. You will be given a *vizitka* (hotel card) to show to the hall monitor *(dezhurnaya)* to get a key; return it upon leaving. **Hot water** doesn't necessarily come with a bath—ask before checking in. **Private rooms** are the best bargain and run 20-50hv. These can be arranged through overseas agencies or bargained for at the train station. Big cities have **camping** facilities—usually a remote spot with trailers. Camping outside designated areas is illegal, and enforcement is strict.

FOOD AND DRINK

UKRAINE	❶	❷	❸	❹	❺
FOOD	under 15hv	15-35hv	36-55hv	56-75hv	over 75hv

New, fancy restaurants accommodate tourists and the few Ukrainians who can afford them, while *stolovayas* (cafeterias)—remnants of Soviet times—serve cheap, hot food. Pierogi-like dumplings called *vavenyky* are ubiquitous and delicious. **Vegetarians** beware: meat has a tendency to show up in so-called "vegetarian" dishes. Sour cream comes on everything. Finding **kosher** foods can be daunting, but it helps to eat non-meat items. Fruits and veggies are sold at **markets;** bring your own bag. **State food stores** are classified by content: *hastronom* (packaged goods); *moloko* (milk products); *ovochi-frukty* (fruits and vegetables); *myaso* (meat); *khlib* (bread); *kolbasy* (sausage); and *ryba* (fish). Throughout the country, *Kvas* is a popular, barely-alcoholic, fermented-bread drink. Grocery stores are often simply labeled *mahazyn* (store). Beer can be drunk on the streets, but hard liquor can't. The distinction is telling—"I drink beer," goes one Ukrainian saying, "and I also drink alcohol."

LIFE AND TIMES

HISTORY

PREHISTORY AND KYIVAN RUS. The **Cimmerians, Scythians, Sarmatians, Greeks, Huns,** and **Goths** each laid claim the Ukrainian territory over the centuries. The **Slavic** ancestors of modern Ukrainians established the first Kyiv settlement by the 7th century AD. Recorded Ukrainian history begins with the Kyivan Rus dynasty, founded by **Oleh of Novgorod** in 882. Oleh and the Rus elite were Scandanavian Varangians who quickly assimilated into the local Slavic culture. The empire eventually stretched as far north as modern St. Petersburg, reaching its greatest size under **Prince Volodymyr the Great.** In 988, Volodymyr converted to Christianity; the new religion ushered in a written language and various forms of Byzantine culture. Volodymyr's son **Yaroslav** produced the Slavic world's first codified laws and promoted the development of the arts.

SHIFTING BORDERS. Genghis Khan invaded Ukraine in the 1230s; his grandson Batu sacked Kyiv in 1240. By the mid-14th century, Ukraine proper was divided among the **Mongols,** the **Grand Duchy of Lithuania,** and the **Kingdom of Poland.** Mongolian rule persisted as late as 1783 in Crimea. Most of Ukraine soon came directly under Polish rule, and the Polish and Ukrainian nobles forced the Ukrainian peasantry into serfdom. The **1596 Union of Brest-Litovsk** folded Orthodox Ukrainians into the Catholic flock while allowing them to retain traditional liturgy. A fruitless attempt to diffuse growing tension between members of Orthodox and Catholic churches, the agreement ultimately broke down into violence.

THE COSSACKS. In the 15th century, escaped serfs and outcasts gathered on Ukraine's southern frontier. Known as Cossacks (after a Turkish word for "freemen"), they formed a democratic, fiercely militaristic society. Poland valued the Cossacks for the protection they offered from Tatars, Turks, and Muscovites, but considered them a threat during peace time. Such suspicions were well founded: a rebellion led by Cossack commander **Bohdan Khmelnytsky** in 1648 escalated into a full-blown war with Poland. Khmelnytsky's forces—known as the **Zaporozhian Host**—were initially successful, but after subsequent defeat, Khmelnytsky entered into a dissatisfying alliance with Muscovy. Following an era of Cossack organizational disintegration known as "The Ruin," in 1667 Ukraine again found itself divided among foreign powers. Russia won everything east of the Dnipr, including Kyiv and Odessa, while the West went to Poland. The East maintained Cossack autonomy for about a century. By 1775, however, Catherine II had abolished what little power the Cossacks had left.

RUSSIA RUSHES IN. With the decline of Polish power, western Ukraine fell under the authority of Habsburg Austria in 1772; Russia absorbed the rest of Ukraine by 1795. Jews were restricted to the territory formerly controlled by Poland, and numerous pogroms, beginning in 1781, worsened their oppression. Reacting against harsh conditions instituted by the government of Tsar Alexander II—which included bans that censored teaching and publishing—a national movement sprung up in the 1840s. Its major figure was the poet-painter **Taras Shevchenko,** who sought to revitalize the Ukrainian language and establish a democratic state. For his efforts, Shevchenko was arrested and exiled to Central Asia. Conditions improved with the 1905 revolution in Russia: the ban on publishing was dropped, and Ukrainians briefly enjoyed some representation in the Duma, the Russian parliament.

CLAIMING UKRAINE. Caught between two warring nations, Ukraine suffered heavy casualities in WWI. Ukraine declared its independence in 1918, but the **Bolsheviks** set up a rival government in Kharkiv and seized complete power during the Civil War (1918-20). Chaos ensued as one group after another assumed control of Kyiv. Following the war, Ukraine again lay divided: Poland, Czechoslovakia, and Romania each laid claims to the western territory, while the eastern area was reorganized as the **Ukrainian Soviet Socialist Republic.** With the rise of Josef Stalin came the beginning of a long series of tragedies. The new dictator deported nearly 100,000 Ukrainian families to Siberia and Kazakhstan, initiated a program of forced-collectivization that resulted in the 1932-33 famine that claimed millions of lives, and attempted to eradicate Ukrainian culture. Ukrainians outside of the Soviet Union fared better but still chafed at their lack of autonomy; thus, many welcomed the Nazis as liberators. When the brutality of the Nazi regime became apparent, however, partisan cells sprung up in western and northern Ukraine. The country suffered enormous destruction during the war; millions of lives and as much as 40% of the national wealth were lost.

BACK TO THE USSR. The last years of Stalin's regime brought another devastating famine and further Russification. Matters improved under **Nikita Khrushchev,** but attacks on Ukrainian culture intensified during the 1970s. In 1986, the worst nuclear accident in history struck **Chernobyl,** close to Kyiv. Nationalist movements grew during the reign of **Mikhail Gorbachev,** and in a 1991 referendum, more than 90% of voters chose to declare independence from the Soviet Union.

TODAY

The new government struggled to escape economic problems and corruption. Public outcry arose during President **Leonid Kuchma's** second term, amidst widespread allegations that he had engineered the 2001 murder of journalist Grigory Gongadze. In November 2004, **Viktor Yanukovich,** the presidential candidate endorsed by Kuchma and Russian President Vladmir Putin, was declared the winner in a rigged election. Protests erupted across the country, and the Supreme Court mandated an unprecedented additional runoff between Yanukovich and his opponent, reform candidate **Viktor Yushchenko.** Yushchenko soundly won the second round in what is known as the "Orange Revolution," named for the color that Yushchenko had chosen to represent his campaign. Due to internal squabbles in Yushchenko's camp, however, his rival Yanukovich gained enough parliamentary support to be elected prime minister in August 2006.

PEOPLE AND CULTURE

DEMOGRAPHICS. A 78% majority of the population of Ukraine is ethnically **Ukrainian;** 17% is **Russian.** Russians are heavily concentrated in the east and south. No one religious group dominates, though various **Orthodox** churches serve 38% of the population. In western Ukraine, the **Roman Catholic** church predominates.

LANGUAGE. Traveling in Ukraine is much easier if you know some **Ukrainian** or **Russian.** Ukrainian is an East Slavic language written in the Cyrillic alphabet. In Kyiv, Odessa, and Crimea, Russian is more commonly spoken than Ukrainian (although all official signs are in Ukrainian). If you're trying to get by with Russian in western Ukraine, you may run into some difficulty: everyone understands Russian, but some people will answer in Ukrainian out of habit or nationalist sentiment. Try to preface what you say with "I'm sorry, I don't speak Ukrainian." This simple gesture can make a big difference. *Let's Go* provides city names in Ukrainian for Kyiv and western Ukraine, while Russian names are used for Crimea and Odessa. Street names follow a similar convention. For a phrasebook and glossary, see **Appendix: Ukrainian,** p. 805.

CUSTOMS AND ETIQUETTE. A rudimentary knowledge of a few customs can make or break a trip to Ukraine. Several **gestures** that are considered positive in other cultures have a different meaning in Ukraine. The "OK" sign, with the thumb and forefinger touching each other and forming a circle, can be very offensive. The same goes for a shaken fist and a pointed index finger. At the Ukrainian dinner table, hands are usually kept on the table. **Tipping** in restaurants is minimal; never more than 10%. When taking a taxi, bargain the price down and do not give a tip. When on trains, give up seats to the elderly and women with children. In churches, men should wear long pants, and women should cover their heads and shoulders.

THE ARTS

LITERATURE. National literature first flowered in the 19th century. **Taras Shevchenko,** Ukraine's most revered literary figure, emerged from the Romantic movement of this era to ignite nationalist fervor with his poetry (see the Taras

Schevchenko Museum, Kyiv, p. 722). A period of realism gave rise to the work of **Ivano Franko,** who wrote drama, poetry, and short stories. The early 20th century saw an outburst of artistic activity. Major literary movements overtook one another rapidly: the Modernism of **Lesya Ukrainka** gave way to Realism in prose and Symbolism in verse. Another new movement, Futurism, inspired one of Ukraine's greatest poets, **Mykola Bazhan. Mikhail Bulgakov,** author of the famous satire, *The Master and Margarita,* hailed from Kyiv but wrote in Russian.

MUSIC. In addition to a history of church **choral music,** Ukraine boasts a rich **folkloric tradition.** Historical songs called *dumy* are sung a capella or feature folk instruments like the *bandura,* similar to a lute, and the *tsymbaly,* a hammered dulcimer. In classical music, Ukraine's most notable pianist is **Sviatoslav Richter** (1915-1997). In 2004, **Ruslana Lyzhichko** won the Eurovision song contest by infusing pop music with folk techniques from the Hutsul people of the Carpathian mountains. As a result, the pan-European contest was held in Kyiv in 2005, partially contributing to the suspension of visa requirements for EU citizens.

FINE ARTS. Byzantine art had a great influence on early Ukrainian art; mosaics, frescoes, domed buildings, illuminated manuscripts, and above all, iconic paintings mark the centuries between the advent of Christianity and the introduction of more western forms in the 17th century. Taras Shevchenko's paintings typify the realist trend of the 19th century. Following experimentation with avant-garde forms during Ukraine's brief independence in the early 20th century, Socialist Realism dominated the Soviet years. Some artists, like photographer **Boris Mikhailov,** managed to subtly critique Soviet oppression.

A delightful folk art form is the Ukrainian easter egg, called **pysanky.** The eggs are painstakingly decorated with beeswax and multiple treatments of dyes; they feature intricate geometric patterns and styles that differ according to region.

HOLIDAYS AND FESTIVALS

Holidays: New Year's Day (Jan. 1); Orthodox Christmas (Jan. 7); Orthodox New Year (Jan. 14); International Women's Day (Mar. 8); Easter (Apr. 27, 2008; Apr. 19, 2009); Labor Day (May 1-2); Victory Day (May 9); Holy Trinity Day (June 16, 2008; June 8, 2009); Constitution Day (June 28); Independence Day (Aug. 24).

Festivals: One of the most widely celebrated festivals is the **Donetsk Jazz Festival,** usually held in March. The conclusion of the 20th century brought the **Chervona Ruta Festival,** which occurs in different Ukrainian cities each year, celebrating both modern Ukrainian pop and traditional music. The **Molodist Kyiv International Film Festival,** held in the last week of October, sets the stage for student films and film debuts.

KYIV (КИЇВ) ☎(80)44

Since its time as the capital of the Kyivan Rus empire over a millennium ago, Kyiv (KEEV; pop. 4,451,000) has stood as a social and economic center for the region. No stranger to foreign control, the city was razed by the Nazi army only to be rebuilt with extravagant Stalinist pomp by the Soviets. After Ukraine gained its independence from the USSR in 1991, Kyiv has reemerged as a proud capital and cultural center. The streets now buzz with energy, even as the cost of living rises and the new government, elected during the 2004 Orange Revolution, struggles to institute promised reforms.

INTERCITY TRANSPORTATION

Flights: Boryspil International Airport (Бориспіль; ☎490 4777), 30km southeast of the capital. **Polit** (Політ; ☎296 73 67), just to the right of the main entrance, runs buses to Ploshcha Peremohi (the train station) and Boryspilska (the Metro stop). Buy tickets on board (every 30-60min., 17-22hv). A taxi to the center costs 70-100hv. Negotiate with drivers near the Polit bus stop; those stationed outside customs will take you for a ride.

Trains: Kyiv-Pasazhyrskyy (Київ-Пасажирський), Vokzalna pl. (☎005 or 465 4895). MR: Vokzalna (Вокзальна). Purchase tickets for domestic trains in the main hall. For international tickets, go to window #40 or 41 in the newest section of the train station, across the tracks. For the *elektrychka* commuter rail (електричка), go to the **Prymiskyy Vokzal** (Приміский Вокзал; Suburban Station), next to the Metro station. A passport is required for the purchase of any train ticket. Information (довідка; dovidka) windows are located in each section of the train station; some stay open 24hr. Assistance, however, is entirely in Ukrainian or Russian; expect no help in English. There is an **Advance Ticket Office** next to Hotel Express at Shevchenka 38. Trains go to: **Lviv** (10hr., 5-6 per day, 65-100hv); **Odessa** (10hr., 4-5 per day, 60-85hv); **Sevastopol** (20hr., 3 per day, 70-115hv); **Bratislava, SLK** (21hr., 1 per day, 480hv); **Budapest, HUN** (24hr., 1 per day, 595hv); **Moscow, RUS** (14-17hr., 12-15 per day, 280hv); **Prague, CZR** (35hr., 1 per day, 600hv); **Warsaw, POL** (19hr., 2 per day, 370hv).

Buses: Tsentralnyy Avtovokzal (Центральний Автовокзал), Moskovska pl. 3 (Московська; ☎525 5774 or 527 9986), 1 stop away on trolley #1 or 11 from MB: Libidska. Window #1 sells international tickets. Buses run to: **Lviv** (7-10hr., 4 per day, 70hv); **Odessa** (8-10hr., 8 per day, 75hv); **Moscow, RUS** (20hr.; 1 per day, Th-Su; 150hv); **Prague, CZR** (28hr.; 1 per day Tu and Th-F; 380hv). **Avtolyuks** (Автолюкс; ☎536 0055 or 536 0053; www.autolux.ua), left of the main entrance, provides more comfortable domestic buses at a slightly higher price. To **Lviv** (10hr., 4 per day, 75hv) and **Odessa** (8hr., 5 per day, 80hv). Smaller stations are located throughout the city:

Dachna (Дачна), pr. Peremohy 142 (Перемоги; ☎424 15 03).

Darnitsya (Дарниця), pr. Haharyna 1 (Гагарина; ☎559 46 18).

Pivdenna (Південна), pr. Akademika Hlushkova 3 (Академіка Глушкова; ☎257 40 04).

Podil (Поділ), Nizhniy Val 15a (Нижній Вал; ☎417 32 15).

Polissya (Полісся), pl. Shevchenka (Шевченка; ☎430 35 54).

Vydubychi (Видубичі), Haberezhno-Pecherska 10 (Набережно Печерска; ☎524 21 82).

ORIENTATION

Most of Kyiv's attractions and services lie on the west bank of the **Dniper River** (Дніпро; Dnipro). The **train station,** at MR: Vokzalna (Вокзальна) on the western edge of the city center, is three Metro stops from **Khreshchatyk** (Хрещатик), Kyiv's main avenue. Khreshchatyk runs from **Bessarabska Ploshcha** (Бессарабська Площа) to **European Square** (Европейська Площа; Evropeyska Ploshcha) through **Independence Square** (Майдан Незалежності; Maidan Nezalezhnosti), the city's patriotic center and the favorite relaxation spot of locals. Three blocks uphill from Khreshchatyk is **Volodymyrska** (Володимирська), which runs past the **Ukrainian National Opera** (Національна Опера України; Natsionalna Opera Ukrayiny), **Zoloti Vorota** (Золоті Ворота; the city's ancient gate), and the **St. Sophia Monastery.** The area surrounding the square, known as the **Upper City,** was the site of ancient settlement in Kyiv. At the end of Volodymyrska, **St. Andrew's Church** (Андріївська Церква; Andriyivska Tserkva) sits atop winding **Andrew's Rise** (Андріївський Узвіз; Andriyivskyy Uzviz), Kyiv's famous historical street. This in

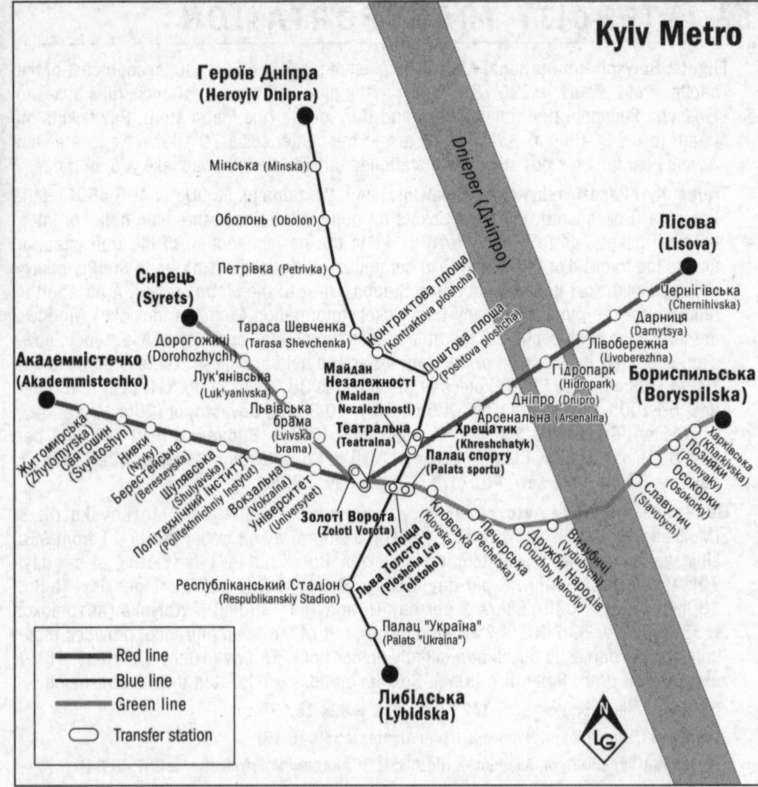

turn leads down to the monument-filled **Podil** (Поділ) district. Along the west bank of the Dniper, **Khreshchatyk Park** covers the slope that runs from the city center to the water's edge. The **Kyiv-Cave Monastery** (Киево-Печерська Лавра; Kyivo-Pecherska Lavra), full of churches and museums, is a 10min. walk from MR: Arsenalna (Арсенальна). The area across the river, near MR: Livoberezhna (Лівобережна; left bank), became a part of Kyiv in 1927 and is now a residential area.

LOCAL TRANSPORTATION

Public Transportation: Most public transport runs 6am-midnight, but some buses and marshrutki run later.

Metro: 3 intersecting lines—blue (MB), green (MG), and red (MR)—cover the city center. Stops can be far apart, but they cover most major tourist attractions, and the Metro is significantly easier to use than other types of public transportation. Purchase tokens (житон; zhyton, 0.50hv) at the window (каса; kasa), or from the machines, which accept only 1hv or 2hv notes. "Перехід" (perekhid) indicates a walkway to another station; "вихід у місто" (vykhid u misto) an exit onto the street; and "вхід" (vkhid) an entrance to the Metro.

Buses (автобуси; avtobusy): Stop at each station. Buy tickets (0.50hv) at kiosks or from conductors on board. Punch your ticket on board to avoid the 10hv fine for riding ticketless.

Marshrutki (маршрутки; marshrutky) are private minibuses that are really only an option for those who speak some Ukrainian or Russian. Numbered vans follow bus routes, usually pulling over just behind corresponding bus stops. They are used more by commuters than by tourists, but move much more quickly through traffic and will stop on request. *Marshrutki* tickets cost 1-3hv and are purchased on board; request stops from the drivers.

Trolleys (Тролейбуси; troleybusy): Like on buses, tickets can be bought on board or from conductors. Routes may differ from identically numbered buses; check signs on the front of the trolley or ask the conductor if you are unsure about a stop.

Taxis: ☎058. Taxis (Taксі; taksi) are everywhere. Always negotiate the price before getting in. Write down your destination if you don't know the name in Ukrainian or Russian. A ride within the city center should be 10hv or less. Owners of **private cars** often act as taxi drivers. Locals hold an arm down at a 45° angle to hail a ride. It is unwise to get in a car with more than 1 person already in it. Let's Go does not recommend hitchhiking.

GETTING A LIFT IN KYIV. To hail a taxi, open the passenger door and tell the driver your destination and a price; the driver will either invite you in or scowl and drive off. Locals often stop several cabs before agreeing on a price. Avoid taking taxis from directly outside nightclubs, as prices tend to be inflated.

PRACTICAL INFORMATION

TOURIST AND FINANCIAL SERVICES

Tourist Offices: Kyiv lacks official tourist services. Representatives of various agencies at the airport offer vouchers, excursion packages, hotel arrangements, and other services. Travel agencies also organize tours. **Carlson Wagonlit Travel,** Khnoelnistkiy 33/34, 2nd fl. (Хноелністкий; ☎238 6156). Open daily 9am-9pm. Also has branch at the US Embassy. **Yana Travel Group,** Saksahanskoho 42 (Саксаганського; ☎490 7373; www.yana.kiev.ua). Open M-F 10am-7pm, Sa 10am-5pm. Students should check out **STI Ukraine,** Proreznaya 18/1 #6, on the 2nd fl. (Прорезная; ☎490 5960). Open M-F 9am-9pm, Sa-Su 10am-4pm.

General Information: The website **www.uazone.net** is an excellent resource for information on Kyiv and all of Ukraine. The **Kyiv Business Directory** (20hv), available in many *Soyuzpechaty* (Союзпечать) and press kiosks (пресса; pressa), lists useful information about dining, shopping, and travel in English and Ukrainian. Several of the major hotels sell **foreign-language newspapers.**

Embassies: Australia, Kominternu 18/137 (Комінтерну; ☎225 7586; fax 244 3597). Open M-Th 10am-1pm. **Canada,** Yaroslaviv Val. 31 (Ярославів; ☎270 7144; kyiv@dfait-maeci.gc.ca). Open M-F 8:30am-1pm and 2-5pm; visa section closed F. **Russia,** Povitroflotskyy pr. 27 (Повітрофлотський; ☎244 0963). Open M-Tu and Th 9am-1:30pm and 3-5pm, W 10am-1:30pm, F 10am-1:30pm and 3-4pm. Visa section at Kutuzova 8 (Кутузова; ☎294 6701; embrus@public.icyb.kiev.ua). Open M-F 10am-1pm, 3-5pm. **UK,** Desyatynna 9 (Десятинна; ☎490 3660; fax 490 3662). Consular section at Glybochytska 4 (Глибочицька; ☎494 3400; fax 494 3418). Open M-Th 9am-1pm and 2-5:30pm, F 9am-1pm and 2-4pm. **US,** Yu. Kotsyubynskoho 10 (Коцюбинського; ☎490 4000; www.usembassy.kiev.ua). Consular section at Pymonenka 6 (Пимоненка; ☎490 4422 or 490 4445; fax 490 4040). From the corner of Maidan Nezalezhnosti (Майдан Незалежності) and Sofievska (Софіевска), take trolley #16 or 18 for 4 stops. Continue on Artema (Артема) until it curves to the right, then take the 1st right, Pymonenka. Open M-F 9am-noon.

Currency Exchange: *Obmin valyut* (обмін валют) windows are everywhere and post their exchange rates outside, but many take only US$, Russian rubles, and EUR€. **Bank Ukoopspilka** (Банк Укоопспілка) on the corner of Instytutska (Инститска) and Khreshchatyk (Хрещатик). Charges 3.5% (4% if in currencies other than US$ or €) commission for all services. Also offers **Western Union** services. Open daily 9am-1pm and 2-8pm. MC/V **ATMs** line Khreshchatyk, and they're also at the post office and at various banks and upscale hotels. Look for bankomat (банкомат) signs.

LOCAL SERVICES

Luggage Storage: At the train station. Look for *kamery skhovu* (камери схову; luggage storage), downstairs outside the main entrance. 8hv per large bag, 5hv per small bag. Open daily 7:30am-noon, 1-7:15pm, 7:30pm-midnight, 1-7:15am. Storage lockers are down a hall to the left of the luggage room. 6hv per locker. At the bus station, look for *Kamera Zberihannya Rechey* (Камера Зберігання Речей), at the back of the main hall. 5hv per large bag, 4hv per medium bag, 2hv per small bag. Open daily 6-11am, 11:30am-5pm, 5:30-10pm.

English-Language Bookstores: Bukva (Буква), Maidan Nezalezhnosti (Майдан Незалежності; ☎585 1141), in the Globus mall by the food court. Carries a small selection of English-language books along with a few maps and guidebooks. Open daily 10am-10pm. MC/V. For English-language maps of Kyiv (10-35hv), visit the nearby **Karty Atlas** (Карти Атлас; ☎537 2276) kiosk, also in the mall at 1-Я. Many expats exchange English-language books at **Baboon Book and Coffee Shop,** B. Khmelnitskoho 39 (Хмелнітского; ☎234 1503; www.baboon.kiev.ua). MR: Universytet.

Laundromats: Komiterna 8 (Комітерна). MR: Vokzalna. Exit the Metro, walk straight, then turn left after McDonald's and walk downhill. In Budynok Pobutu Stolychnyy (Будинок Побуту Столичний), off Victory Square. Dry cleaning (хімчистка; khimchystka) also available. Open Tu-Sa 9am-6pm.

EMERGENCY AND COMMUNICATIONS

Emergencies: Police: ☎02. **Ambulance:** ☎03.

24hr. Pharmacy: Aptechnyy Kiosk (Аптечний Кіоск), at the train station in the corridor that crosses over the tracks.

Medical Services: American Medical Center, Berdychivska 1 (Бердичівска; ☎490 7600; www.amcenters.com). English-speaking doctors will take patients without documents or insurance. Open 24hr. MC/V. Similarly, no documents are required at the **Center of European Medicine,** Shovkovychna 18-a, #2 (Шовковична; ☎253 8219; sokrnta@ln.ua). Appointment recommended. Open Sept.-June M-F 8am-8pm, sometimes Sa 9am-2pm; July M-F 9am-6pm.

Telephones: English operator ☎81 92. **Telephone-Telegraph** (Телефон-Телеграф; telefon-telehraf) around the corner of the post office (enter on Khreshchatyk). Open daily 8am-10pm. Buy cards for **public telephones** (таксофон; taksofon) at any post office. Less widespread than *taksofon,* **Utel phones** are in the post office, train station, hotels, and nice restaurants. Buy Utel cards at the post office and upscale hotels.

Internet: Diadora, Khreshchatyk 48, 2nd fl. (Хрещатик; ☎230 0499). Also has an international calling center. Internet 12hv per hr. Open 24hr. The main **post office** (see below) houses 2 Internet cafes. The cafe to the right of the main hall charges 12hv per hr. and is open M-Sa 8am-8pm and Su 9am-7pm. The other, through the door to the right of the Maidan Nezalezhnosti entrance, is open 24hr. and charges 12hv per hr. 8am-10pm and 9hv per hr. 10pm-8am. **C-Club,** Bessarabskaye pl. 1 (Бессарабскае; ☎247 5647), in the underground mall between Bessarabsky market and the Lenin statue. Over 100 computers. 8hv per hr. Open daily 9am-8am.

Post Office: Khreshchatyk 22 (Хрещатик; ☎278 1167; www.poshta.kiev.ua). Spotless and well-organized office; though signs are in Cyrillic, the helpful staff will point you in the right direction. Some English is spoken at information desk #18. **Poste Restante** at counters #28 and 30. For packages, enter on Maidan Nezalezhnosti. Copy, fax, and photo services available. Open M-Sa 8am-9pm, Su 9am-7pm. **Postal Code:** 01001.

ACCOMMODATIONS

Hotels in Kyiv are expensive. It's worth looking into short-term apartment rentals, which are listed in the *Kyiv Post* (www.kyivpost.com) and other English language guides to the city. These apartments generally start at US$40 per night for a one-room rental. People at the train station offer **private rooms** (from US$5), but quality is inconsistent and bargaining is difficult without Ukrainian or Russian language skills. Check out rooms before agreeing to pay. The telephone service **Okean-9** (Океан; ☎443 6167) helps find budget lodgings. Tell them your price and preferred location, and they'll reserve you a room for free. (Open M-F 9am-5pm, Sa 9am-1pm.) The best budget options are Kyiv's few **hostels,** or apartments on the left bank near the Metro.

International Youth Hostel Yaroslav (Ярослав), Yaroslavska 10 (Ярославська; ☎417 3189). MB: Kontraktova Ploshcha. Take the exit near the front of the train. Follow the underground walkway on the left and exit straight ahead. Turn right on Konstyantynivska (Констянтинівська), then left on Yaroslavska; the hotel courtyard is on the left. In Kyiv's historic Podil district, this small hostel offers clean facilities and a convenient location. Attracts backpackers from around the globe. Communal refrigerator and bath. Ring bell for 24hr. service. Doubles 250hv; 4- to 5-bed dorms 125hv. Cash only. ❸

Youth Hostel Kyiv, Artema 52-A (Артема), building #2 (Корпус; korpus), 5th fl. (☎331 0260). MG: Lukyanivska. From the Metro, walk 15min. to the right on Artema, or take trolley #18 to the Poltavska (Полтавска) stop. From the stop, take a left onto Pymonenka (Пимоненка), and follow it 1 block to the US consulate. The hostel is behind the consulate in a 9-story building with a hostel sign on its entrance (#2). With immaculate 2- to 3-bed dorms, a communal fridge, and baths for every 2 rooms, the hostel's only disadvantage is its distance from the city center. Dorms 120hv. MC/V. ❸

Hotel St. Petersburg (Санкт-Петербург), bul. T. Shevchenka 4 (Шевченка; ☎279 7364; s-peter@i.kiev.ua). MR: Teatralnaya. The hotel has an ideal location, just up the street from Bessarabska Square. Reserve in advance for your choice of rooms and prices. All rooms have TV, fridge, and sink. Many rooms share bathrooms; no hot water June-Aug. Singles 180-500hv; doubles 240-520hv; triples 330hv. Cash only. ❸

Hotel Express (Експрес), bul. Shevchenka 38/40 (☎503 3045; www.expresskiev.com), up Kominternu (Комінтерну) from the train station or MR: Universytet. Clean, expensive rooms with fridges, telephones, toilets, and TVs. Higher floors have panoramic views of the city. Great location, with train tickets sold next door. Internet 4hv per 30min. Singles 235-265hv, with shower 350-430hv; doubles 480-600/540-660hv. MC/V. ❹

Hotel Druzhba, bul. Druzhby Narodiv 5 (Дружби Народів; ☎528 3406; fax 528 3387). From MB: Lybidska, take a left on bul. Druzhby Narodiv and walk 200m; the hotel is on the left. Plain, clean rooms with modern baths, fridges, and TVs. in a quiet area on the edge of town. Singles 300-315hv; doubles 220hv, with bath 315-330hv. Cash only. ❸

FOOD

Kyiv has a large selection of restaurants and **markets,** as well as an army of **street vendors** who sell cheap snacks. Popsicles are a local favorite (1-5hv), and the shawarma (8hv) is particularly delicious. Kyiv is replete with streetside cafes, many of which sell Ukrainian staples such as borscht and vareniki on the cheap (5-30hv). Cafes in the city center tend to cost more than similar establishments in outlying areas. For complete Kyiv restaurant listings, check out *What's On* magazine (www.whatson-kiev.com). High-quality produce can be found at the open-air **Bessarabskyy Rynok** (Бессарабський Ринок), at the intersection of Khreshchatyk and bul. Shevchenka. (Open 24hr.) **King David's** restau-

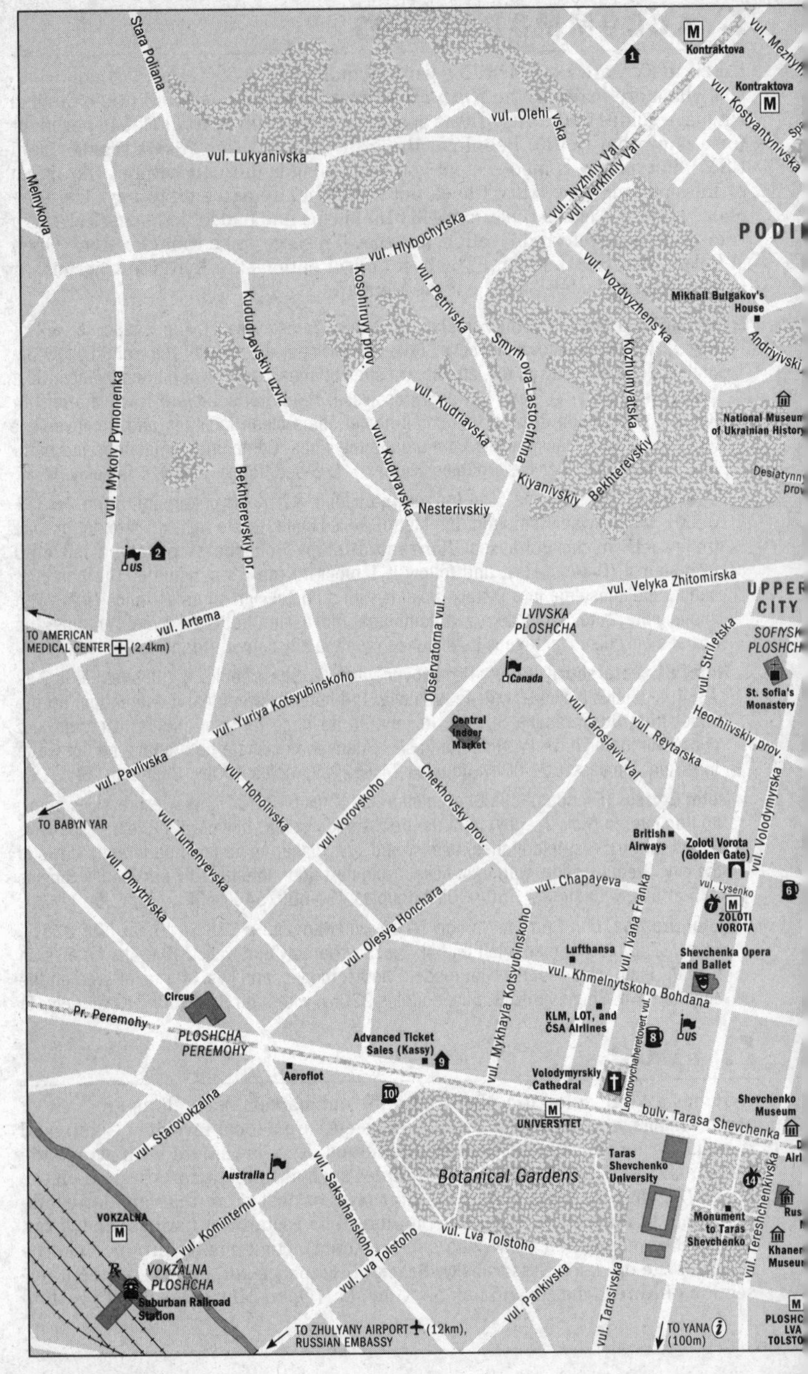
Stara Poliana
Kontraktova
Kontraktova
vul. Mezhyh
vul. Kostyantynivska
vul. Olehi vska
vul. Lukyanivska
vul. Nyzhniy Val
vul. Verkhniy Val
Melnykova
vul. Hlybochytska
PODI
Kosohiruy prov.
vul. Petrivska
vul. Vozdvyzhens'ka
Mikhail Bulgakov's House
Kudryavskiy uzviz
Smyrh ova-Lastochkina
Kozhumyatska
Andriyivski
vul. Kudriavska
National Museum of Ukrainian History
vul. Mykoly Pymonenka
Bekhterevskiy pr.
vul. Kudryavska
Kiyanivskiy
Bekhterevskiy
Desiatynny prov
Nesterivskiy
US
vul. Velyka Zhitomirska
UPPER CITY
TO AMERICAN MEDICAL CENTER (2.4km)
vul. Artema
Observatorna vul.
LVIVSKA PLOSHCHA
vul. Striletska
SOFIYSK PLOSHCH
vul. Yuriya Kotsyubinskoho
Canada
St. Sofia's Monastery
Central Indoor Market
vul. Yaroslaviv Val
vul. Reytarska
Heorhiivskiy prov.
vul. Pavlivska
vul. Hoholivska
Chekhovsky prov.
TO BABYN YAR
vul. Vorovskoho
vul. Volodymyrska
British Airways
Zoloti Vorota (Golden Gate)
vul. Turhenyevska
vul. Dmytrivska
vul. Chapayeva
vul. Lysenko
ZOLOTI VOROTA
vul. Olesya Honchara
vul. Ivana Franka
Lufthansa
Shevchenka Opera and Ballet
vul. Mykhayla Kotsyubinskoho
vul. Khmelnytskoho Bohdana
Circus
Pr. Peremohy
KLM, LOT, and ČSA Airlines
PLOSHCHA PEREMOHY
Advanced Ticket Sales (Kassy)
US
Aeroflot
Volodymyrskiy Cathedral
Leontovychaheretovert vul.
Shevchenko Museum
UNIVERSYTET
bulv. Tarasa Shevchenka
vul. Starovokzalna
Taras Shevchenko University
Australia
vul. Saksahanskoho
Botanical Gardens
vul. Tereshchenkivska
VOKZALNA
vul. Komінternu
Monument to Taras Shevchenko
vul. Lva Tolstoho
Khaner Museu
vul. Lva Tolstoho
VOKZALNA PLOSHCHA
Suburban Railroad Station
vul. Pankivska
vul. Tarasivska
TO ZHULYANY AIRPORT (12km), RUSSIAN EMBASSY
TO YANA (100m)
PLOSHC LVA TOLSTO

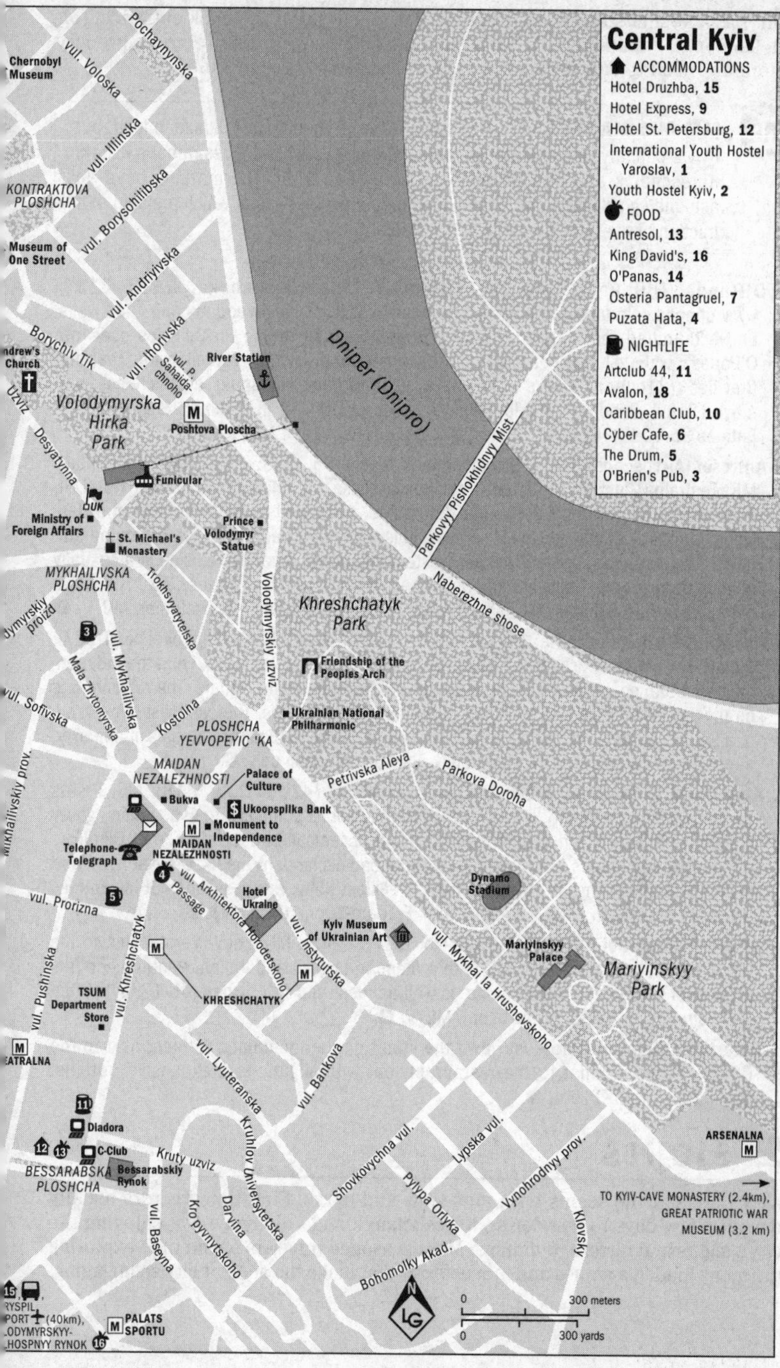
Central Kyiv
ACCOMMODATIONS
Hotel Druzhba, 15
Hotel Express, 9
Hotel St. Petersburg, 12
International Youth Hostel Yaroslav, 1
Youth Hostel Kyiv, 2
FOOD
Antresol, 13
King David's, 16
O'Panas, 14
Osteria Pantagruel, 7
Puzata Hata, 4
NIGHTLIFE
Artclub 44, 11
Avalon, 18
Caribbean Club, 10
Cyber Cafe, 6
The Drum, 5
O'Brien's Pub, 3
Chernobyl Museum
vul. Voloska
Pochaynynska
vul. Illinska
KONTRAKTOVA PLOSHCHA
vul. Borysohlibska
Museum of One Street
vul. Andriyivska
Borychiv Tik
vul. Ihorivska
vul. P. Sahaida-chnoho
River Station
Dniper (Dnipro)
Volodymyrska Hirka Park
Poshtova Ploscha
Desyatynna
Funicular
UK
Ministry of Foreign Affairs
St. Michael's Monastery
Prince Volodymyr Statue
Parkovy Pishokhidnyy Mist
MYKHAILIVSKA PLOSHCHA
Trokhsvyatytelska
Volodymyrskiy uzviz
Khreshchatyk Park
Naberezhne shose
Friendship of the Peoples Arch
vul. Mykhailivska
Mala Zhytomyrska
vul. Sofivska
Kostolna
Ukrainian National Philharmonic
PLOSHCHA YEVVOPEYIC 'KA
MAIDAN NEZALEZHNOSTI
Palace of Culture
Petrivska Aleya
Parkova Doroha
Bukva
Ukoopspilka Bank
Monument to Independence
MAIDAN NEZALEZHNOSTI
Telephone-Telegraph
vul. Arkhitektora Horodetskoho
Passage
vul. Prorizna
Hotel Ukraine
vul. Instytutska
Kyiv Museum of Ukrainian Art
vul. Mykhai la Hrushevskoho
Dynamo Stadium
Mariyinskyy Palace
Mariyinskyy Park
vul. Khreshchatyk
vul. Pushinska
TSUM Department Store
KHRESHCHATYK
vul. Lyuteranska
vul. Bankova
Diadora
C-Club
Kruty uzviz
BESSARABSKA PLOSHCHA
Bessarabskiy Rynok
Kruhlov Universytetska
Shovkovychna vul.
Lypska vul.
Pylypa Orlyka
Vynohrodnyy prov.
ARSENALNA
TO KYIV-CAVE MONASTERY (2.4km), GREAT PATRIOTIC WAR MUSEUM (3.2 km)
vul. Baseyna
Kro pyvnytskoho
Darvina
Klovsky
Bohomolky Akad.
PALATS SPORTU
(40km),
300 meters
300 yards
LG

rant has a kosher supermarket behind it, to the right of the back entrance. (M-Th 9am-7pm, F 9am-5pm, Sa 9am-2pm and 2:30-6pm). For more urban grocery shopping, head to **Furshet** (Фуршет), Yaroslavska 57. (Open 24hr.)

MM MM MARKET. Many restaurants serve "traditional" Ukrainian food, but Kyiv's culinary meccas are its markets, some of which (Bessarabsky Rynok, Khreschatyk and bul. Shevchenka) are open 24hr. The markets have an astounding selection of produce, meats, and pastries—all of which are sold at a fraction of the price of eating in a restaurant.

O'Panas (О'Панас), Tereschenkivska 10 (Терещенківська; ☎235 2132; www.opanas.com.ua), in the Taras Shevchenko Park. Carved wooden chairs, log walls, and a thatched roof help to create a rural Ukrainian theme that carries over into O'Panas's wide selection of traditional Ukrainian food. Try the "Vareniki with Meat and Crackles" (31hv) or "Odarka's Dream," a salad of ham, pineapple, eggs, cheese, and mayo (21hv). A booth outside sells pancakes (1.50-4hv) in summer. English menu. Entrees 35-100hv. Open M-F 8am-1am, Sa-Su 10am-1am. MC/V. ❸

Antresol (Антресоль), bul. T. Shevchenka 2 (Шевченка; ☎235 8347; www.babuin.ua). MR: Teatralna. Just up the street from Bessarabska Sq. on the right, before Hotel St. Petersburg. The cafe and bookstore downstairs, decorated by potted plants and dark wood furniture, offers free Wi-Fi, making this a popular haunt for laptop-bearing students. The restaurant upstairs serves Western-influenced Ukrainian cuisine in a casually elegant atmosphere. English menu on request. Salads 19-45hv. Entrees 30-110hv. Live piano Tu and Su 8-10pm, DJ Th-Sa 8-10pm. Open daily 10am-last customer. MC/V. ❸

Puzata Hata (Пузата Хата; House Full of Food), Khreshchatyk/Zankovetskoyi 15/4 (Хрещатик/Занковемской; ☎279 7683), MR: Maidan Nezalezhnosti. From the Independence Statue, go left down Kreshchatyk toward Bessabarabsky Square. The restaurant is on the left, down a pedestrian street in front of Double Coffee. The capitalist reinvention of a Soviet cafeteria, Puzata Hata features tasty and cheap Ukrainian staples in a relaxed atmosphere. Entrees 3-12hv. Open daily, 8am-11pm. Cash only. ❶

King David's, Esplanadna 24 (Еспланадна; ☎235 7436 or 235 7418). MG: Palats Sportu. Outside the Metro, a 1min. walk from the sports complex. Brocade chairs, gauzy curtains, and a panoramic photographic mural of Jerusalem decorate one of Ukraine's only kosher restaurants. Excellent salads and bread accompany meals. Great service, and menus in Hebrew, English, and Ukrainian. Breakfast 35hv. Business lunch 55hv. Entrees 35-95hv. Open M-Th and Su 10am-11pm, F 10am-10pm. Cash only. ❹

Osteria Pantagruel, Lysenko 1 (Лисенко; ☎278 8142). MG: Zoloti Vorota. Just to the left of the Metro exit on Lysenko. With a menu in English and Italian, Pantagruel offers traditional homemade Italian pasta as well as meat and fish dishes (45-165hv). Open M-F 8am-11pm, Sa-Su 11am-11pm. MC/V. ❹

Osteria Pantagruel Cafe, just down the street on the fountained terrace, next to the Golden Gates. Similar to the restaurant, but with slightly less expensive options. Open daily 10am-11pm. ❸

SIGHTS

Kyiv bursts at the seams with museums and parks. First-time visitors usually devote a few days to wandering Khreshchatyk and Volodymyrska, enjoying the city's sights and historic buildings. More seasoned travelers spend time exploring the many hidden avenues and monasteries that make the ancient city so engaging.

CENTRAL KYIV

INDEPENDENCE SQUARE (МАЙДАН НЕЗАЛЕЖНОСТІ; MAIDAN NEZALEZHNOSTI). Independence Square, often called simply "Maidan," is the unofficial center of Kyiv and has been renamed and redesigned many times over the past century. It hosted a massive tent city through the bitter cold during the Orange Revolution protests of 2004, but its most recent incarnation is as an outdoor park and meeting place, complete with kiosks selling ice cream and beer. The Monument to Independence, a majestic 12m bronze statue of a woman atop a 50m column, was built in 2001 to commemorate the tenth anniversary of Ukraine's independence. Speeches and concerts are held here on national holidays. *(MB: Maidan Nezalezhnosti.)*

KHRESHCHATYK STREET (ХРЕЩАТИК). The people-watching capital of the nation, Kyiv centers on this broad commercial avenue. The houses along Khreshchatyk were destroyed during the Nazi occupation in 1941 and rebuilt during the Soviet era, for better or worse, in distinctive Soviet style. Khreshchatyk is now a place to see and be seen, where amateur fashionistas promenade past students playing guitar on the sidewalks. Beer-drinking Kievans crowd these sidewalks in the evenings, or take to the streets when they're closed to traffic on weekends and holidays. An archway leads to the **Passage** (Пасаж; pasazh), one of Kyiv's most fashionable areas, home to high-priced cafes and bars. *(MR: Khreshchatyk.)*

TARAS SHEVCHENKO BOULEVARD (ТАРАСА ШЕВЧЕНКА; TARASA SHEVCHENKA). Named for the poet who revitalized the Ukrainian language in the mid-19th century (see p. 709), this boulevard is home to bright-red **Taras Shevchenko University,** which still promotes progressive ideas 165 years after its founding. Down the street, the interior of the **Volodymyrskyy Cathedral** is decked with Art Nouveau saints and seraphim. *(Cathedral across from the botanical garden at the intersection with Leontovycha (Леонтовича). MR: Universytet. Open daily 9am-8pm.)*

ST. SOFIA AND ENVIRONS

Take trolley #16 from Maidan Nezalezhnosti or get off at MG: Zoloti Vorota.

ST. SOFIA MONASTERY COMPLEX. The monastery, established in the 11th century, served as the religious and cultural center of Kyivan Rus. The site became a national reserve in 1934, and includes history and architecture museums. Though it seems as if every step you take costs an extra hryvnya, the complex is worth the hassle. Older and less pretentious than other cathedrals, the **St. Sofia Cathedral** still retains impressive golden domes and has a magnificent 260 sq. m of mosaics; some additional mosaics, along with drawings and design plans, are on display in the **architecture museum.** The St. Sofia **bell tower,** 76m above the entrance gate, has an impressive view over central Kyiv; it's a nice reminder that the city does end somewhere, after all. A **statue of Bohdan Khmelnytsky** (see **History,** p. 707) stands near the entrance. *(Volodymyrska 24. ☎ 278 6152 or 278 6262. Monastery grounds open daily 9am-7pm. 2hv. Museums open M-Tu and Th-Su 10am-6pm, W 10am-5pm. Ticket kiosk on the left past the main gate. Ticket for both museums 20hv, students 8hv. Special exhibits 5hv, students 2hv. 45min. 10-person tours in English 30hv.)*

ST. MICHAEL'S MONASTERY (МИХАЙЛІВСЬКИЙ ЗОЛОТОВЕРХИЙ МОНАСТИР; MYHAYLIVSKYY ZOLOTOVERKHYY MONASTYR). This 11th-century monastery was destroyed in 1934 to make way for a government square, the plans for which never materialized. After 60 years as a sports center, the current blue-and-gold-domed monastery was reconstructed in the 1990s. Monks wander the grounds, and visitors are free to stop and talk to them, if their language skills are up to it. *(At the top of Mykhaylivska pl. Open daily 7am-8pm. Free.)* A **museum** in the bell tower leads to the

PLAY THERAPY

Current HIV testing capabilities in Ukraine prevent a diagnosis until a child is 18 months old. In a positive diagnosis, only half of the normal doses of therapy are provided, decreasing life spans and creating resistant strains of the virus. These medical limitations, combined with Ukaine's notoriously underfunded and understaffed orphaned childcare system, leave many AIDS orphans with very little human contact. Orphans spend much of their time alone in Soviet-style concrete buildings, isolated due to their potential medical condition.

Marianna Peipon, an American expat, works with **Ukraine Medical Outreach** to recruit volunteers and engage some of these orphans in "play therapy." "We feed 'em, hold 'em, and just do the things the overworked staff is often not able to do," explains Marianna.

Ukraine Medical Outreach, which started its work in Kyiv in 2001, primarily provides medical services and education. In 2003, Marianna came across seven AIDS orphans in a hospital and has been visiting them ever since. Today, there are 24 AIDS orphans at the hospital, and UMO is searching for volunteers to devote a few hours to "play therapy" with these children.

Contact Marianna Peipon of Ukraine Medical Outreach at www.ukrainemedicaloutreach.org or ☎8 066 746 3550.

chamber of the bells. The bells ring every 15min., and the carillon plays every hour during the day. *(☎278 7068. English captions. Open Tu-Su 10am-6pm; ticket office closes 5pm. 5hv, students 2hv.)* Tryokhsvyatytelska (Трйохсвятительська) runs alongside the monastery and past smaller churches on its way to the **Volodymyrska Hirka Park** (Володимирська Гірка Парк), featuring folk sculptures in a many tiny pavilions.

GOLDEN GATE (ЗОЛОТІ ВОРОТА; ZOLOTI VOROTA). This wood-and-stone gate has marked the entrance to the city for more than a millennium. According to legend, the gate's strength saved Kyiv from the Tatars during the reign of Yaroslav the Wise (see **History,** p. 707), whose statue stands nearby. Inside, a museum devoted to the gate is closed for restoration. *(300m down Volodymyrska from St. Sofia.)*

ANDREW'S RISE AND BABYN YAR

ANDREW'S RISE (ANDRIYIVSKYY UZVIZ). Andrew's Rise is Kyiv's most touristed area. Though vendors hawking jewelry, clothing, and other trinkets crowd the sidewalks, the area retains its old, authentic feel thanks to the steep, winding cobblestone streets, historical buildings, and outdoor cafes. From Mykhaylivska Sq., walk down Desyatynna to get to the top of Andriyivskyy Uzviz. There you'll see **St. Andrew's Church** (Андріївська Церква), conceived by Empress Elizabeth Petrovna in the 18th century and designed by her favorite architect, Italian Bartolomeo Rastrelli. Renovated in the 1970s according to Rastrelli's original plans, the church overlooks the center of Kyiv and the Dniper River. *(☎599 0005 or 278 0928. Open daily 10am-5pm; kasa closes 5pm. 2-5pm 5hv, students 2hv; before 2pm free. Tours in English 30hv; call ahead.)* Down Andriyivskyy Uzviz 100m, steep wooden stairs lead to a great view of **Podil,** Kyiv's oldest district. Farther down are writer **Mikhail Bulgakov's house** (Andriyivskyy uzviz 13) and the **Museum of One Street** (p. 722). Andriyivskyy Rise ends at **Kontraktova Sq.** (Контрактова пл.), the center of Podil.

BABYN YAR (БАБИН ЯР). The monument at Babyn Yar marks the mass grave of the first Ukrainian victims of the Holocaust. More than 33,000 people were murdered at this ravine on September 29 and 30, 1941. Although plaques state that 100,000 Kyivans eventually died here, current estimates double that figure. Many of the victims—most of them Jews—were buried alive. Above the grass-covered pit, a statue shows the victims falling to their deaths. *(MG: Dorohozhychi. Babyn Yar is actually outside Podil, at the intersection of Oleny Telihy (Олени Теліги) and Melnykova (Мелникова) in the park near the TV tower.)*

KYIV-CAVE MONASTERY

Kyiv's oldest and most revered holy site—and one of the most important pilgrimage sites in the world for Orthodox Christians—the Kyiv-Cave Monastery (Киево-Печерська Лавра; Kyivo-Pechersk Lavra) spans a huge labyrinth of churches, museums, souvenir shops, gardens, and functioning monastery buildings. First mentioned in chronicles in 1051, the **monastery** can be viewed in two parts: the churches, bell tower, and museums are all on top of a hill, while the caves are below. Admission to the monastery includes access to the grounds and churches, but the museums and caves cost extra. *(MR: Arsenalna. Turn left as you exit the Metro and walk 10min. down Sichnevoho Povstannya (Січневого Повстання), or take trolley #38. Alternatively, take bus #24 from Bessarabskyy market or along Khreshchatyk. ☎280 3071. Buy tickets for upper grounds and museums at the white kiosks beside main entrance. Tickets for the caves are sold on the grounds. Open daily May-Aug. 9am-7pm, kasa until 6pm; Sept.-Apr. 9:30am-6pm, kasa until 5pm. Monastery 10hv, students 5hv. For tours in English, call ahead.*

UPPER GROUNDS. Most of the monastery's sights are located on the top of the hill and accessed from the main entrance. The 12th-century **Holy Trinity Gate** (Троїцка надбрамна церква; Troyitska Nadbramna Tserkva) contains some beautiful frescoes, a 600kg censer, and the ruins of an ancient church. Step into the operating **Refectory Church,** home to one of the largest and most decorated domes in the complex. The 18th-century **Great Lavra Bell Tower** (Велика Лаврська Дзвінниця; Velyka Lavrska Dzvinnytsya), currently undergoing renovations, offers fantastic views of the river and the golden domes. The **Museum of Historical Treasures of Ukraine** (Музей Історичних Коштовностей України; Muzey Istorychnykh Koshtovnostey Ukrayiny) displays precious stones and metals. *(Open Tu-Su 10am-5:45pm. Kasa closes at 4:45pm.)* The incongruous **Micro-Miniature Exhibit** contains amazingly small books, chess sets, and other oddities. *(Open daily 10am-1:30pm and 2:30-6pm; closes in heavy rain or snow and last Tu of the month. 5hv, students 3hv.)*

CAVES. Monks once lived here in isolation, receiving nothing but food from the outside world. When they died, they were wrapped in cloth, and left in the caves, where the cool air caused their bodies to mummify. Without a guided tour you may view only a 15m section of the caves. All visitors must buy a candle (1hv) and carry it with them. Monks lead the tours, which have a religious tone. Women must wear headscarves and long skirts (both available at the monastery); men must wear long pants and remove their hats. *(☎254 1109; fax 254 3390. Open daily 9am-5:30pm. 50min. tours in Russian every 15min. 10hv, students 8hv. Tours in English 150hv.)*

MUSEUMS

STATE MUSEUM OF FOLK ARCHITECTURE AND LIFE OF UKRAINE (ДЕРЖАВИЙ МУЗЕЙ НАРОДНОЇ АРХІТЕКТУРИ ТА ПОБУТУ УКРАЇНИ; DERZHAVIY MUZEY NARODNOYI ARKHITEKTURY TA POBUTU UKRAYINY). Though it's only 30 minutes from downtown Kyiv, this open-air museum feels much farther. In a hilly countryside sprinkled with thatched-roof houses, green-tipped churches, and wooden windmills, the museum documents the architectural history of seven cultural regions of Ukraine. There are no signs or tours in English. Folk music performances are held on holidays. *(Outside Kyiv in the Pirohiv village. MB: Libidska. Take trolley #11 outside the Metro station to the last stop, 30min.; cross under the road and walk against traffic 30m to the park entrance. A sign reads "Музей." 10min. walk to museum. Or, take marshrutka #156 from outside MB: Respublykanskyy Stadion (Республіканський Стадіон) to its last stop—the museum entrance. Both trolley #11 and marshrutka #156 return to Kyiv. ☎526 5765. Open daily 10am-5pm. 10hv, students under 17 5hv.)*

MUSEUM OF ONE STREET (МУЗЕЙ ОДНІЄЇ ВУЛИЦІ; MUZEY ODNIYEYI VULYTSI). This three-room museum at the bottom of Andriyivskyy Uzviz recounts the famous street's colorful history with photographs and old documents. Great for readers of Russian or Ukrainian; otherwise, save your money. *(Andriyivskyy uzviz 2b. ☎425 0398; mus1str@ua.fm. Open Tu-Su noon-6pm. 10hv. 45min. tours in English 100hv.)*

MUSEUM OF THE GREAT PATRIOTIC WAR (WORLD WAR II). A lesson in Soviet grandeur as well as in the history of World War II, the museum is actually made up of multiple museums, a collection of Soviet military vehicles, an eternal flame, and a 62m metal statue overlooking the Dniper. Located down the hill from the Kyiv Cave Monastery, it spans a large, open park that provides ample space to absorb the military-style music playing in the background and the sculpted images of heroic soldiers that line the pathways. The museum itself is composed of 18 huge marble rooms, designed with all the warmth of a bunker. *(Sicnevoho Ponstannia 44. MR: Arsenalna. From the Metro, turn left and walk 20min. The entrance is on the left, down a hill past the Kyiv-Cave Monastery. Admission to grounds is free. Afghanistan War Museum ☎285 8862. 3hv, students 1hv. World War II Museum ☎285 9452. 5hv, students 1hv.)*

CHERNOBYL MUSEUM (ЧОЕРНОБИЛЬ УКРАЇНСЬКИЙ НАЦІОНАЛЬНИЙ МУЗЕЙ; CHOERNOBYL UKRAYINSKYY NATSIONALNYY MUZEY). In April of 1986, a nuclear reactor exploded in the town of Chernobyl, north of Kyiv near the border with Belarus. Clear and easy to follow, this museum documents the history of that tragedy through poster exhibits, short films, and artifacts from the site. Some English translations are available. *(Provulok Khoryva 1 (Провулок Хорива). MB: Kontraktova. From the Metro, turn left on vul. Verkhniy Val. Walk 1 block and take a right on Mezhyhirska and follow it for 2 blocks. Turn left; the museum is on the left side on the next corner. ☎417 5422. Open M-Sa 10am-6pm; closed last M of each month. 5hv, students with ISIC 1hv. Tours in English 50hv.)*

NATIONAL MUSEUM OF UKRAINIAN HISTORY (НАЦІОНАЛЬНИЙ МУЗЕЙ ІСТОРІЇ УКРАЇНИ; NATSIONALNYY MUZEY ISTORIYI UKRAYINY). This museum, housed in an impressively big stone building, glorifies Ukraine's ancient past and its most recent achievements. *(Volodymyrska 2. At the juncture of Andriyivskyy and Volodymyrska, with St. Andrews Church on the left, bear right on Volodymyrska until reaching a pathway between green construction walls and a large blue building. The museum is down the path, to the right, at the end of a grassy open area. ☎278 2924. Open M-Tu and Th-Su 10am-5:30pm. Kasa closes at 4:45pm. 12hv, students 6hv.)*

TARAS SHEVCHENKO MUSEUM. This museum, dedicated to the exiled poet and artist, contains a huge collection of sketches, paintings, and prints. Housed in a 19th-century mansion, it documents Shevchenko's fascinating life—spent fighting for Ukrainian independence, both political and linguistic—with examples of his own work and relics from his life. Unfortunately, the exhibit is entirely in Ukrainian, making it difficult to grasp the significance of each artifact. *(Bul. Tarasa Shevchenka 12. MR: Universytet. ☎224 2556. Open Tu-Su 10am-5pm; closed last F of each month. 3.50hv, Ukrainian students 1hv.*

ENTERTAINMENT AND FESTIVALS

The last Sunday of May brings **Kyiv Days,** when drama, folklore, jazz, and rock performances are staged all over the city. If you're in town between late spring and fall, don't miss **Dynamo Kyiv,** one of Europe's top soccer teams. (Ticket office in front of the stadium. Tickets 2-50hv.) Hot summer days are perfect for a boat ride down the Dniper or a trip to **Hydropark** (Гідропарк), an **amusement park** and **beach** on an island along the left bank of the Dniper (MR: Hidropark). The beach has showers, toilets, and changing booths. The **National Philharmonic,** Volodymyrsky uzviz 2, holds regular concerts. (☎278 1697. Ticket office open Tu-Su noon-2pm and 3-7pm.) **Shevchenko Opera and Ballet Theater,** Volodymyrska 50, puts on several shows each week. (MR: Teatralna. ☎279 1169. Shows at noon and 7pm. Ticket office open M 3-7:30pm, Tu-Su 11am-2pm and 3-7:30pm.)

NIGHTLIFE

Kyiv's nightlife scene has developed considerably in the past decade, with a lot of new bars and discos, many of which are owned and run by expats. Check out *What's On* (www.whatson-kiev.com), *Kyiv Weekly*, or the *Kyiv Post* (www.kyivpost.com), for the latest hotspots in town. Although homosexuality is not widely accepted in Ukraine, Kyiv's GLBT scene continues to grow. Though many gay men simply dance with each other at the city's mainstream clubs, GLBT clubs remain popular. These clubs tend to favor gay men: they make up the numbers, the drag shows are geared toward them, and "VIP" back rooms cater to them. In summer, the gay scene centers on the **Hydropark;** follow the mob to **Youth Beach** (Молодіжний Пляж; Molodizhnyy Plyazh). Buy a 1hv boat ride to the opposite beach, where the crowd welcomes people of all orientations.

BARS AND CLUBS

Artclub 44, Khreshchatyk pr. 44 (Хрещатик; ☎279 4137), in the basement. Walk into the courtyard; it's through an unmarked brown door on the left. Decorated with dark wood and quirky paintings, Kyiv's most popular jazz club provides live experimental and jazz music nightly 10pm-midnight. Beer 8-18hv. Wine 10-14hv. Cover 10-20hv. Open daily 10am-2am. Cash only.

Caribbean Club, Kominternu 4 (Комінтерну; ☎288 1290). A DJ ensconced in a red-and-white retro convertible spins an addictive mix of salsa music as dancers strut their stuff. The less coordinated look on while enjoying drinks or smoking hookah. Affordable and entertaining. Beer 7-25hv. Mixed drinks 18-40hv. Dance lessons M, W, Su 6:30pm; 20hv. Cover W-Su men 50hv, women 30hv. Open daily 6pm-6am. Cash only.

The Drum, Prorizna 4a (Прорізна; ☎279 2355). MR: Khreshchatyk. On the right on Prorizna, through a gate into the backyard, down the stairs on the left. Owned by a local musician, and decorated with handmade drums and guitars from around the world, this pub features carved-wood chairs and tables, low bluegrass music, and cheap, filling pub-grub. Try the flaming sau-

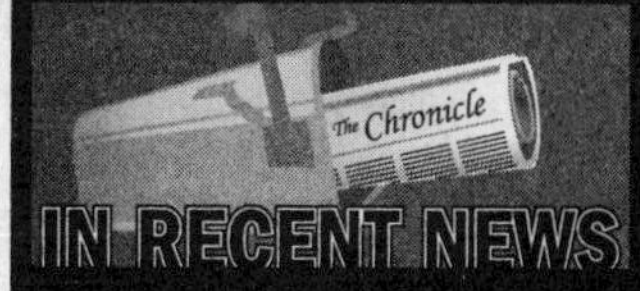

CHERNOBYL REMEMBERED?

April 2006 marked the 20th anniversary of the world's worst nuclear accident. Controversy still exists about the overall effect of the explosion at Chernobyl: a recent Greenpeace study contests the UN's estimate of 4000-9000 cancer deaths, suggesting a staggering figure of over 93,000 casualties.

Today, however, a new trade is beginning in the ghost towns of Chernobyl: tourism. Although radiation levels remain extremely high in the "Dead Zone," several travel agencies have begun leading tours, which cost US$100-400, to look at fateful reactor 4, visit towns in the Dead Zone, and check out radiation-filled tanks.

Despite the influx of tourism, though, Chernobyl is by no means considered safe. Geiger counters find over 50 times the normal radiation. And to make matters worse, the ruins of reactor 4—still filled with nuclear material—are showing signs of breaking down, prompting Ukraine to propose the building of a new steel facility in 2008. Tour agencies press ahead, leading over 500 tourists every year, insising that the danger lies in long-term radiation, not a one-day encounter. Others feel that the name of the Dead Zone speaks for itself.

For info on tours, visit www.tourkiev.com/chernobyl.php, or call ☎405 35 00. Solo East Tours is located at Travneva St. 12.

sages, which are soaked in cognac and set on fire (28hv). English menu. Business lunch M-F 11am-3pm; 26-30hv. Beer 7-16hv. Wine 5-20hv. Entrees 28-46hv. Open daily 11am-11pm. Cash only.

O'Brien's Pub, Mykhaylivska 17a (Михайлівська; ☎229 1584). Kyiv's original Irish pub is a great place to catch sporting events in English or enjoy a casual beer with friends. Satellite TV, darts, billiards, and Irish pub food. Live music daily 9:30pm-midnight. Beer 6-30hv. Fish and chips 70hv. Happy hour 5-7pm. Open daily 8am-2am. AmEx/MC/V.

Avalon, Leontovycha 3 (Леонтовича; ☎234 7494). MR: Universytet. Cross under the street outside the Metro and go left, up the hill on bul. T. Shevchenko. Turn left on Leontovycha after St. Volodymyr's Cathedral. One of Kyiv's many casino-nightclub complexes, this disco's 2 levels fill up on the weekends with dancers in metallic hotpants. High weekend cover (Th-Sa 100hv, Su-W free) and expensive drinks (beer 20hv, mixed drinks from 30hv) dampen the surreal atmosphere. Open 24hr. MC/V.

Cyber Cafe (Сиьер Кафе), Prorizna 21 (Проріэна). MG: Zoloty Vorota toward Khreshchatyk. Housed in the dark, smoky basement of a former Internet cafe, this small club offers nightly Europop and drag shows on the weekends or when the crowds are especially big. Disco daily 10pm-6am, drag shows F-Sa 2am. Cover for men up to 30hv, for women 10-40hv. Open daily 11am-last customer.

DAYTRIP FROM KYIV

CHERNIHIV (ЧЕРНІГІВ)

The best way to get to Chernihiv is from MR: Lisova (Лісова). Exit to the side of the road closest to the Metro and take a marshrutka (1½hr., 15hv). Get off the marshrutka at its first stop in the town center; the churches and historical sights are down Prosp. Miru to the right. Alternatively, take a bus from the same place, but expect the trip to take an extra 30-60min. The main bus station in Kyiv also runs buses to Chernihiv (3hr., 6 per day, 15-18hv. Only 5 per day return to Kyiv). Pick up marshrutki *back to Kyiv from Chernihiv at 90 pr. Peremohy (Перемоги), near Hotel Ukrayina (Україна) and one block off pr. Miru.*

PHONE CODES. To make calls from outside Chernihiv, dial 4622 before five-digit local numbers and 462 before six-digit local numbers.

Situated near the borders with Russia and Belarus, Chernihiv contains churches and monuments dating from the Kyivan Rus empire. Today the city is still noticeably struggling from the collapse of the Soviet Union, but those who look past the box-like concrete Soviet structures will find a beautiful place town with a fascinating history. At the start of Prospekt Myru (Миру), the 18th-century **St. Catherine's Church** has been converted into a small **museum** (Музей Народного Декоративного Мистецтва Чернігівщини; Muzey Narodoho Dekoratyvnoho Mystetsva Chernihivshchyny) displaying a collection of gorgeous regional embroidery. (☎432 36. Open M-Tu and F-Su 9am-4:30pm. 1.50hv.) Across the street, the **Cathedral of the Savior and Transfiguration** (Спасо-Преображенський Собор; Spaso-Preobrazhenskyy Sobor) dates from 1036. To the left of the cathedral, the 12th-century **Cathedral of Boris and Gleb** (Борисо-Глібський Собор; Boriso-Hlibskyy Sobor) houses archaeological artifacts found on the grounds. Continuing left, the 16th-century **Collegium** (Колегіум; Colehium) building displays religious artifacts with English captions. (☎744 63. Open daily 9am-5pm. 3hv. English booklet about Chernihiv 13hv.) The **Chernihiv History Museum,** which contains a copy of the 1581 Osfroh Bible, is located to the right and behind the Cathedral of the Savior of Transfiguration. (☎731 67. Open M-W and F 10am-6pm, Sa-Su 9am-5pm. 2.50hv. Brochure with some English 5hv.)

To get to the **Yeletsky Convent** (Собор Єлецького Монастиря; Sobor Yeletskoho Monastyrya) and its imposing 12th-century Dormition Cathedral, cross back over Pr. Miru past the area in front of St. Catherine's and catch trolley #8 just after the corner on the road's right side. Take the trolley two stops to the foot of the hill leading to the convent. Stop number four brings you to the 17th-century **Monastery of the Holy Trinity,** Tolstogo 92E (Толтого). For a nice view of town, ascend the steps of the monastery's bell tower (2hv, students 1hv).

Backtrack toward town and cross the park to the right to reach the 12th-century **Church of St. Elijah,** beside which loom the enigmatic **Antoniiyevy Caves** (Антонієви Печри; Antoniyevy Pechry). Inside, 318m of labyrinthine paths lead into the **Church of St. Theodosis,** past burial chambers full of red-lit bones. According to legend, these are the remains of monks killed during the Mongol invasion in 1239. (☎462 21. Open M-Th and Sa-Su 9am-4:30pm, F 9am-3:30pm. 3hv, students 1.50hv.)

Options for accommodations and food in Chernihiv are very limited, but you can find everything you need at the **Hradetsky Hotel** ❷ (Градецький), Miru 68. Rates are reasonable, upper floors have great views, and there are almost always rooms available, though it's a little bit of a hike from the town's sights. (☎450 25 or 66 19 22. Marshrutka #33 goes from the hotel to most sights. Singles 95-100hv; doubles 160hv.) Small, cheap dishes are available at Hradetsky's **restaurant** ❶, next to the hotel. (Entrees 3-15hv. Open daily 11am-midnight.) A small cafe and a grocery store are at Pyatnitska 15 (Пятницька) on the corner of pr. Peremohi (Перемоги), a block off pr. Miru. (☎17 67 81. English menu. Entrees 7-22hv. Open daily 9am-11pm. MC/V.)

WESTERN UKRAINE

Proud residents of Western Ukraine will tell you that their region is "the most Ukrainian" part of the country. It has stubbornly maintained its unique identity despite a millenium of shifting nationalities. During WWII, some Western Ukrainians fought against both the Nazis and the Soviets, aiming at independence. Since the fall of the USSR, the western region has earned a reputation as the core of Ukrainian nationalism and Lviv, its largest city, is considered the cultural capital of Ukraine; its world-class music and laid-back vibe draw artists from around the country. Nearby, the beautiful Carpathian Mountains are home to hundreds of intricately carved wooden churches as well as fabulous hiking and skiing.

LVIV (ЛЬВІВ) ☎(80)32[2]

Lviv's star is rising. While Kyiv is the political and economic capital of Ukraine, many consider Lviv (LVEEV; pop. 1,000,000) to be the cultural and patriotic center of the country. Lviv's historic sights were spared from the destruction of World War II, as is evident from its quiet cobblestone streets and untouched picturesque churches. Packed with architecture of nearly every style imaginable, Lviv is becoming a modern city that stretches far beyond its historic center. It is bustling, packed with cafes and surprisingly good nightlife, and located near the beautiful Carpathian Mountains.

PHONE CODES. The area code for Lviv is 322. This number is put directly in front of most phone numbers to call from outside of Lviv. If the number begins with a 2, however, you need only add 32 when dialing from outside of Lviv.

TRANSPORTATION

Flights: Lviv Airport, Lyubinska (Любінська; ☎69 21 12). **Traident** (Траидент), Kopernyka 18 (Коперника; ☎/fax 297 1493 or 297 1332), books tickets for major airlines. **Tourist Agency Mandry** (Мандри), Rynok 44 (Ринок; ☎297 5646, fax 297 1661; www.mandry-travel.lviv.ua), books flights, provides help with other travel arrangements, and plans excursions (3hr., US$35). Open M-F 10am-6pm, Sa 10am-2pm.

Trains: Pl. Vokzalna (Вокзальна; ☎26 11 76, info 005). Tickets at Hnatyuka 20 (Гнатюка; ☎226 1176 or 222 1177), under the "каси" (kasy) sign. Open M-Sa 8am-2pm and 3-8pm, Su 8am-2pm and 3-6pm. Bring your passport. You may have to go to the train station for same-day tickets. Info about trains 2hv. To: **Kyiv** (9hr., 3 per day, 50-100hv); **Odessa** (12hr., 1 per day, 60-110hv); **Simferopol** (25hr.; 1 per day; 60-140hv); **Bratislava, SLK** (22hr., 1 per day, 360hv); **Budapest, HUN** (13hr., 1 per day, 40hv); **Kraków, POL** (8hr., 1 per day, 250hv); **Moscow, RUS** (25hr., 3 per day, 250hv); **Prague, CZR** (32hr., 1 per day, 400hv); **Warsaw, POL** (14hr., 1 per day, 400hv).

Buses: Main station, Stryyska 189 (Стрийська; ☎294 9817). From pl. Halytzka (Галицька) take bus #5 or *marshrutka* #71. To **Kraków, POL** (10hr., 1 per day, 103hv); **Przemyśl, POL** (6hr., 7 per day, 30hv); and **Warsaw, POL** (10hr., 3 per day, 150hv). Lviv also has three **regional stations.** The one at Khmelnytskoho 225 (Хмельницького; ☎52 04 89) can be reached by tram #4 from Shevchenka (Шевченка).

Public Transportation: Maps, available at the English-language bookstore (see **Orientation and Practical Information**), show lines for **trams, trolleys,** and **buses.** Buy tickets (0.50hv for trams and trolleys, 0.60hv for buses, 1hv for *marshrutki*) on board from the conductor. If none is present, simply pass your money to the driver once seated. 10hv fine for riding ticketless. In the Old Town, pl. Halytska is a hub for buses.

Taxis: ☎39 34 34. Agree on the price before you get in. 7-20hv.

ORIENTATION AND PRACTICAL INFORMATION

The center of town is **ploscha Rynok** (Ринок), the old market square. Around it, a grid of streets forms the **Old Town,** where most of the sights are located. Toward the train station, broad **prospect Svobody** (Свободи) runs from the **Opera House** to **ploscha Mitskevycha** (Міцкевича), the Old Town's center of commerce. **Prospect Shevchenko** (Шевченко) extends to the right of pl. Mitskevycha. Trams #1 and 9 and *marshrutka* #68 run from the train station to the Old Town's center; tram #6 runs to the north end of pr. Svobody, behind the Opera. Tram #9 goes from the Old Town to the station. Unlike in Kyiv, streets in Lviv actually have street signs.

Tourist Office: Lviv Tourist Information Center, Pyidvalna 3 (Підвальна; ☎297 5751, 5767; www.tourism.lviv.ua). Enter the building and turn right; it's the door at the end of the hall. Some members of the staff speak English, and all are eager to welcome tourists and provide information. A few brochures are free, but most cost 2-11hv. **Maps** also 2-11hv. City tour 50hv per hr. Open M-F 10am-6pm except for a 1hr. lunch break between 1 and 3pm. For personal, English tours of Lviv and its environs, contact Roman Harbuzyuk (romikon1@hotmail.com; www.ukraine-tour.narod.ru).

Currency Exchange: Western Union services available downstairs at the Post Office in **Availabank,** which also cashes **traveler's checks** (3% commission) and gives MC/V **cash advances.** (☎93 46 77. Open M-F 9:30am-1pm and 2-6pm, Sa 10am-2pm.) Storefronts along pr. Svobody and throughout town exchange currency. Look for the Обмін Валут (Obmin Valut) signs. **ATMs** are marked by Банкомат (bankomat) signs.

Luggage Storage: At the train station. 6hv. Open 24hr.

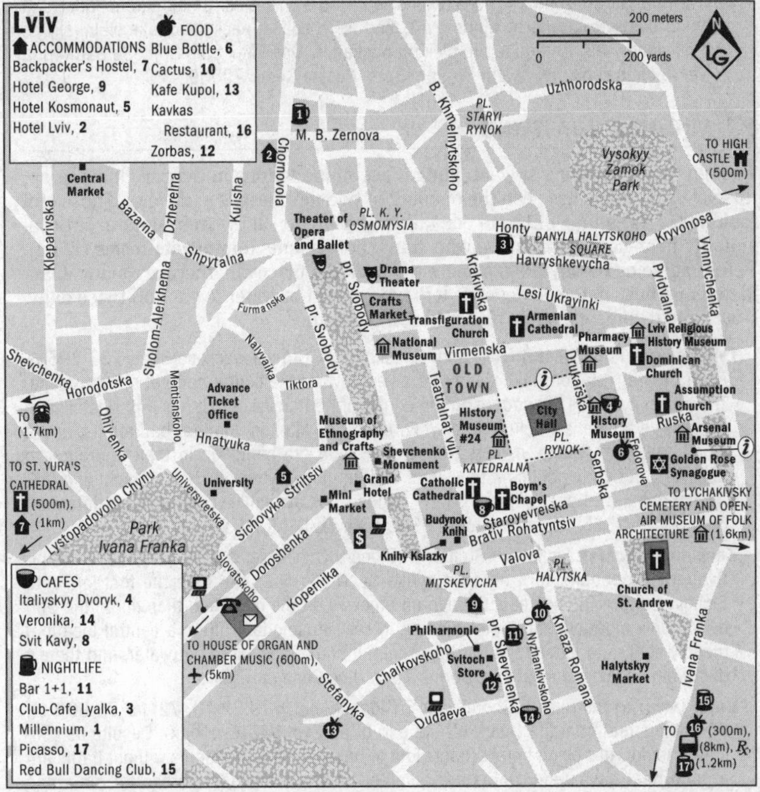

English-Language Bookstores: Budynok Knihi (Будинок Кнігі), Pl. Mitskevycha 8 (☎74 41 64). Go here for city **guidebooks** (30hv) and **maps** (3.50-6hv). Open June-July M-F 10am-7pm, Sa 10am-4pm; Aug.-May M-F 10am-6pm, Sa 10am-3pm. **Knihy Ksiazky** (Кнігі Ксазкц), Pl. Mitskevycha 8 (☎72 27 29), next door to Budinok Knihi. Wide selection of English-language literature 25-160hv, **guidebooks** 40hv, **maps** 3-10hv; same hours as Budynok Knihi.

Emergency: Ambulance ☎03.

City-wide information: ☎09.

24hr. Pharmacy: Добра Аптека (Dobra Apteka), Tyktora 3 (Тиктора; ☎72 50 48). **Apteka #28** (Аптека), Zelena 33 (Зелена; ☎75 37 63).

Telephones: Telecommunication Service Center, Doroshenka 39 (Дорошенка; ☎72 90 12), around the corner from the post office. Farther down are phone booths for long-distance calls, which must be paid for in advance. To place a long distance call, visit the cashier window. State the city being called and number of min. you expect to be on the line. Prices vary by destination. Local telephone cards for pay phones available at the same window. 6hv for 90min. Open daily 7am-11pm.

Internet: Internet Club, Dudaeva 12 (Дудаева; ☎72 27 38). Walk into the alley; the door is on the right. Fast Internet on 25 computers. 4hv per hr., 15min. minimum. Printing services. Open 24hr.

Post Office: Slovatskoho 1 (Словатского; ☎74 40 62), 1 block on right from Park Ivana Franka. **Poste Restante** at window #3, 2nd fl. To collect packages, take claim slip to 1st fl. window #3. ID required to pick up packages. Open M-F 8am-8pm, Sa 8am-4pm; lower fl. open same hours and Su 9am-3pm. **Postal Code:** 79000.

ACCOMMODATIONS

Though they're nothing special, budget accommodations in Lviv are looking up; this past year alone has seen the opening of two new **hostels** in the city. Those still looking for something different can talk to the women at the train station, or occasionally near hotel entrances, who hawk apartments and **private rooms** (25hv). Before agreeing on anything, be sure to check the place out: there are many dilapidated buildings in the city center. It is typical for hot water to shut off twice daily, 6-9am and 6-9pm, and some places lack it altogether.

Lviv Backpackers' Hostel (HI), Kotlyarevskoho 37 (Котляревского 37; ☎237 2053). From the train station, take trolley #1 or #9 toward the center and get off at Kyivska. The hostel is across the square on the corner of Kotliarevskoho; it has a HI-Hostel sign. Impressive amenities include free Wi-Fi, equipped kitchen, modern bathrooms, and a small courtyard. Hostel owners Robert and Yulia are hands-on in their approach to business, debating politics with visitors and running daytrips such as parachuting, AK-47 shooting, and paintballing. Safety deposit box available. Free laundry, detergent 5hv. Dorms US$6-23; private room US$50. AmEx/D/MC/V. ❶

Kosmonaut Hostel, Sichovykh Striltsiv 8 (Січових Стрільців; ☎ 936 554 219) From pr. Svobody (Свободи), turn onto Hnatyuka St. (Гнатюка) and take the first left onto Sichovy Stiltsiv. The hostel is through an archway on the right, and then up on the 2nd fl. The only independent hostel running in Lviv, Kosmonaut offers a central location, friendly staff, and lots of space. Then again, it sometimes lacks hot water, and there's dust from ongoing renovations. Dorms 75-120hv. Cash only. ❷

Hotel Lviv (Готель Львів), Chornovola 7 (Чорновола; ☎79 22 70, 72; fax 72 86 51), down the street from the Opera off the end of pr. Svobody (Свободи). Despite its concrete exterior, this clean hotel attracts lots of backpackers. The rooms without baths are a good deal, and upper floors are quietest. Daytime luggage storage for departing guests 5hv (for use after check-out). Utel phone in the lobby for international calls; reception staff sells cards (27-90hv). Singles75hv, with bath 120-180hv; doubles 130-150/180-300hv; triples without bath 165-195hv; quads 220/320hv. Cash only. ❷

FOOD

The main market is **Tsentralnyy Rynok** (Центральний Ринок; Central Market), also called **Krakivskyy Rynok** (Краківський Ринок; Kraków Market) by locals. (Open M-Sa 9am-6pm.) A 24hr. **Mini Market,** Doroshenka 6 (☎72 35 44), is a block from the Grand Hotel. Lviv is famous for its **Svitoch** (Світоч) confectionery, sold throughout town. For a cheap lunch, stop by one of the hot dog stands on pr. Svobody. (Hot dog with cabbage, corn, ketchup, mayonnaise, mustard 3hv).

Kavarna Pid Synoyu Flyazhkoyu (Каварня Під Синьою Фляжкою; Caverna Blue Bottle), Ruska 4 (Руска; ☎294 9152). On Ruska, turn into a small alleyway marked by a sign with a blue bottle; the restaurant is in the courtyard at the back of the alley. Take a trip back to the Austro-Hungarian Empire in this tiny, five-table restaurant-cafe. Set in a dark room lit only by candles and decorated with trinkets from Austrian Lviv, Pid Synoju offers cheap liquors and sandwiches from every corner of the once-great empire. Tables fill up in the evenings. English menu. Sandwiches 6-8hv. Fondue 35-132hv. Regional liquors 4-10hv. Ice cream and honey 6hv. Open daily 10am-10pm. Cash only. ❶

Bistro Zorbas (Бістро Зорбас), Pr. Shevchenko 14 (Шевченко; ☎261 1973). On Shevchenko, walk away from McDonald's. Zorbas is on the right; look for a Greek flag sign, and go through the walkway into the courtyard. Though its decor leaves a bit to the imagination, Zorbas's food is delicious. The menu is in Ukrainian, but the staff offers recommendations and English translations. The meat, particularly the Souvlaki Pecheni Na Hrili (30hv), is simply succulent. Entrees 20-75hv. Separate salads 7-9hv. Juices 3.50hv. Open daily 10am-11pm. MC/V. ❸

Cactus (Кактус), O. Nyzhankivskoho 18 (О. Нижанківського; ☎74 50 61). Abstract paintings and a blue-tiled mosaic bar complement cast-iron chandeliers and funky broken-glass-covered lights in this offbeat establishment. Dishes named after foreign places such as Beijing, Zurich, and Idaho complete the confused, but strangely appealing postmodern desert motif. Omelettes 17hv. The 3-course business lunch (soup, salad, and an entree; M-F noon-3pm; 29hv) is a good deal. Breakfast daily 7am-noon. English menu. Entrees 25-110hv. Open M-Th and Su 7am-11pm, F-Sa 7am-2am. MC/V. ❹

CAFES

Veronika (Вероніка), pr. Shevchenko 21 (Шевченко; ☎297 8128). Famous for its delicious cakes (8.50-11hv per slice), pastries (5hv), and truffles (5hv). An English menu is available, but most choose from the display case. Outdoor tables in summer. The iced coffee (7.50-18hv) is particularly good. Those tired of the sun can head downstairs to the dark, smoky cellar. Hot appetizers range from pastries (18hv) to *foie gras* with Bordeaux sauce (86hv). Try the sweet Odessa sparkling wine (28hv) with dessert. Soups 27-74hv. Entrees 30-166hv. Vegetarian menu 29-37. Open daily 10am-11pm. MC/V.

Svit Kavy (Світ Кави), pr. Katedralna 6 (Катедральна; ☎297 5675). Tucked away behind the Catholic Cathedral and Boym's Chapel, this small cafe caters mostly to locals, serving hot coffee (7-12hv), small cakes and pastries (4-8hv), and the fruit juice version of a root beer float (8hv). The menu is in Ukrainian, but the staff is helpful, and many of the pastries are on display for selection. Patrons can choose from indoor tables or wicker seats on the porch. Open M-F 8am-10pm, Sa-Su 9am-11pm. Cash only.

SIGHTS

The Old Town is full of churches, squares, and old buildings that show the influence of Armenians, Austrians, Greeks, Hungarians, Italians, Jews, and Poles, among others. Most of the sights and museums are located in or near pl. Rynok. The best time to visit churches is 5-7pm, when the doors are open for services.

PLOSHCHA RYNOK (ПЛОЩА РИНОК). This historic market square lies in the heart of the city, surrounded by richly decorated merchants' homes dating from the 16th to 18th centuries. The *ratusha* (ратуша; town hall) is a 19th-century addition. For a wonderful view of the Old Town, climb the wooden staircase of the **tower** in the middle of the square. *(Ticket office is downstairs, to the left of the main entrance. ☎297 5773. Open Tu-F 10am-5pm, Sa-Su 11am-7pm. 2hv.)*

ARMENIAN CATHEDRAL (ВІРМЕНСЬКИЙ КАФЕДРАЛЬНИЙ). Solemn music adds to the spiritual atmosphere inside this cathedral, built in the 14th century by Lviv's Armenian community. To the left, in the painting *Burial of St. Odelone*, Death holds melting candles to indicate how much longer individuals will live; one man seems slightly worried about the size of his. Near the altar, Judas appears as a shadow in a representation of the Last Supper. A mosaic above the altar is illuminated by the magnificent light that pours into the dome. In the courtyard are a collection of medieval Armenian inscriptions and a cemetery, where each family is permitted only one gravestone. *(Virmenska 7-9 (Вірменска). Open M-F 9am-5pm.)*

GOLDEN ROSE SYNAGOGUE. For centuries, Lviv was an important center of Jewish culture. Unfortunately, little remains of this synagogue, which was built in the late 16th century and destroyed by the Nazis in 1942. A sign in English is posted to the left of the remains of the synagogue's back wall. *(Walk up Staroyevreyska (Староеврейска), or Old Jewish Road; the synagogue is on the left before the Arsenal Museum. Call the tourist office to arrange a guided tour, 50hv per hr., of the city's Jewish heritage sites.)*

OTHER OLD TOWN SIGHTS. Dotting the artsy neighborhoods of Lviv and complementing its quirky vibe are numerous churches. The massive **Assumption Church** (Успенська Церква; Uspenska Tserkva) lies just up Pidvalna (Підвальна); enter through the archway. Next to the church, **Kornyakt's Tower** (Башта Корнякта; Bashta Kornyakta) hangs its bell 60m above ground. The Baroque **Dominican Church** (Домініканський Костел; Dominikanskyy Kostel) is on pl. Muzeyna (Музейна); look for the elliptical dome. The **Church of the Transfiguration** (Преображенська Церква; Preobrazhenska Tserkva), Krakivska 21 (Краківська), is packed with beautiful side altars and icons. The Church's underground passageways run throughout the city, but getting into them requires a researcher's permit. **St. Andrew's Church** at pl. Soborna (Соборна) demonstrates how Greek Catholics blend Orthodoxy and Catholicism.

HIGH CASTLE HILL (ВИСОКИЙ ЗАМОК; VYSOKIY ZAMOK). For a great workout and an impressive view of the city, climb up High Castle Hill, the former site of the Galician king's palace. A Ukrainian flag and a cross, the two most potent symbols of religious, nationalist Lviv, sit at the top of the hill. *(Follow Kryvonosa (Кривоноса) from its intersection with Hotny (готну) and Halytskoho (галитского). Go until you pass #39, then take a left down the road and wind your way up around the hill counter-clockwise.)*

LICHAKIVSKY CEMETERY (ЛИЧАКІВСЬКИЙ ЦВИНТАР; LYCHAKIVSKYY TSVYNTAR). Enter through the main gate of the cemetery and follow the path to the right to visit the graves of famous Ukrainian artists. On the left, a hammer-armed *Stakhanovite* decorates the eternal bed of Ivan Franko (Іван Франко), poet, socialist activist, and celebrated national hero. *(Take tram #4 or 7 from the beginning of Lichakivska (Личаківська) and get off at the 1st stop after the sharp right turn. ☎ 75 54 15. Open daily 9am-6pm. 3hv.)*

IVAN FRANKO PARK (ПАРК ІМ. ІВАНА ФРАНКА; PARK IM. IVANA FRANKA). Walk uphill through Ivan Franko Park to Lystopadovoho (Лустопадового; on the right side of the park), then continue up Lystopadovoho. **St. Yura's Cathedral** (Собор св. Юра; Sobor sv. Yura) is on the right. While the grounds are under construction, the cathedral and its elaborate altar can still be viewed. *(Open daily 7am-1pm and 3-8pm.)* Farther down is **St. Elizabeth's Cathedral.** Constructed by Poles who settled in Lviv, it appears run-down at first glance, but the interior has been fully refurbished and is full of activity. (*From pr. Svobody (Свободи), head down Hnatyuka (Гнатюка), then take a left on Sichovykh Striltsiv (Січових Стрільців) to the park, which faces the columned facade of Lviv University.)*

MUSEUMS

OPEN-AIR MUSEUM OF FOLK ARCHITECTURE AND RURAL LIFE. This outdoor museum (Музей Народноі Архітектури та Побуту у Львові; Muzey Narodnoi Arkhitektury ta Pobutu u Lvovi) at Shevchenkivskiy Hai (Шевченківський Гай) features a collection of Ukrainian buildings made entirely out of wood (скансен; skansen). Though not quite as extensive as the one in Kyiv, it's still impressive and interesting in its own right. Don't miss the 18th-century wooden church. *(From Doroshenka (Дорошенка), take tram #2 or 7 to Mechnykova (Меиникова). Cross the street and follow Krupyarska (Крулярска) all the way up the hill, bearing right at the top. Tours in Ukrainian and Russian ☎ 71 23 60. Open Tu-Su 10am-6pm. 3hv, children 1hv. English map with museum description 5hv.)*

UKRAINE

PHARMACY MUSEUM (АПТЕКА-МУЗЕЙ; APTEKA-MUZEY). This fascinating museum, located in one of Lviv's old pharmacies, details the history of the pharmaceutical business. There are vials of chemicals—including arsenic, opium, and pure cocaine—along with Lviv's earliest written prescriptions and an old wine bar in the basement. Make sure to check out the spooky alchemist's room and the iron wine (iron, according to the conventional wisdom of the day, was supposed to do the body good). A modern pharmacy, which sells "iron wine" (5hv), is located in the front of the building. Very little English spoken. *(Drukarska 2. Друкарска. ☎ 72 00 41. Open M-F 9am-7pm, Sa-Su 10am-5pm. 3hv, students 2hv. MC/V.)*

HISTORY MUSEUM (ІСТОРИЧНИЙ МУЗЕЙ; ISTORYCHNYY MUZEY). Located in a complex of three museums on pl. Rynok, the main building (#6), was the 17th-century home of Polish King Jan III Sobieski. It was here that the "eternal peace" of 1686 was signed, splitting Ukraine in two—the western half went to the Polish empire and the eastern to the Russian empire. The museum at #4 recounts the horrors of WWII and Soviet occupation. The museum at #24 traces the history of the region from Kyivan Rus to annexation by the Polish empire in 1686. *(Pl. Rynok #4, 6, and 24. ☎ 72 06 71. Open M-Tu and Th-Su 10am-5pm. Tours in English 10-15hv, when guides are available. Museum at #4 5hv, students 2hv; museum at #6 3/1.50hv; museum at #24 2hv.)*

NATIONAL MUSEUM (НАЦІОНАЛЬНИЙ МУЗЕЙ; NATSIONALNIY MUSEY). Though it houses a full collection of Ukrainian art from the 12th to 21st centuries, this museum is most famous for maintaining the world's best collection of Ukrainian icons, most of which were created by village amateur artists. They are unusual in that they are painted in the Orthodox style but depict Catholic subjects. *(Pr. Svobody 20 (Свободи). ☎ 74 22 82 or 74 22 18; fax 75 92 93. Open Tu-Su 10am-6pm. 4hv, children 1.50hv. Tours in English 25hv.)*

ARSENAL MUSEUM (МУЗЕЙ АРСЕНАЛ; MUZEY ARSENAL). Housed in a stone fortress dating from the 1600s, this museum has a neatly presented collection of cannons, swords, daggers, guns, and armor gathered from over 30 countries. Artifacts date from the 11th to the 20th centuries. *(Pidvalna 5 (Підвальна). ☎ 72 19 01. Open M-Tu and Th-Su 10am-5:45pm; kasa (каса) closes at 5:15pm. 1.50hv; students, children, and seniors 1hv.)* At Salon Arsenal (Салон Арсенал), in front of the museum, you can get your picture taken with a variety of weapons and armor. *(Open M-F 11am-6pm, Sa-Su 11am-5pm. 15hv, students 10hv.)*

ENTERTAINMENT

After lunch, **prospect Svobody** fills with performers singing to accordion accompaniment. On summer evenings, the sounds of light jazz from sidewalk cafes permeate the avenue, elderly men play chess near the **Shevchenko Monument,** and couples stroll down the walkway leading to the Opera House. Purchase tickets for the opera and other performances at the box offices (театральни касси; teatralny kassy), pr. Svobody 37. (Open M-Sa 10am-1pm and 2-5pm.) During **Lviv City Days** (☎ 97 59 13), held in early May, concerts, theater performances, and competitions are held at venues throughout the city. Easter is celebrated at the **Open-Air Museum of Folk Architecture** with folk and religious traditions and games for children. In late June, the **Lviv Beer Festival** brings locals to the streets and parks for two days of raucous boozing. In September of even-numbered years, the **Golden Lion Theater Festival** takes to the streets with free performances by local and international troupes.

Theater of Opera and Ballet (Театр Опери Та Балету; Teatr Opery Ta Baletu), pr. Svobody 1 (Свободи; ☎ 74 20 80). Many of the world's foremost artists have graced the stage of this theater, which hosts several performances per week. It's a safe bet that the schedule posted in front of the entrance will feature a Tchaikovsky production. Ticket office open daily 11am-7pm, but often closed on days without shows. Tickets 10-75hv.

Philharmonic (Філармонія; Filarmoniya), Chaikovskoho 7 (Чайковского; ☎72 10 42), the next block down on Shevchenka (Щевченка) from Hotel George. The Philharmonic puts on classical music performances by renowned guest performers. *Kasa* open daily Sept.-May 11am-2pm and 3-6pm. Shows start at 6pm. 5-30hv, children's show 2hv.

Organ and Cameral Music (Будинок органноі та камерноі музики; Budynok orhannoi ta kamernoi muzyky), s. Bandery 8 (Бандери). Take tram #2 or 9 down S. Bandery to the Lviv Polytechnic stop. Concerts Sa-Su 6pm. Tickets at the door 1hv.

NIGHTLIFE

Lviv's nightlife centers around its music scene; famous jazz musicians mix with hard-drinking college students in Lviv's bars.

Millennium (Міленіум), Chornovola 2 (Чорновола; ☎40 35 91). From Hotel Lviv, cross Chornovola and take a left; Millennium is a few blocks farther. The largest and arguably most popular dance club in town, Millennium features Europop in a 3-room complex with elaborate light effects. Surrounding the dance floor is plenty of comfortable seating where groups take vodka shots (bottle 30hv) chased with Coca-Cola (6hv). Beer 5hv. Cover up to 50hv on weekends; Tu-W women free. Open Tu-Su 9pm-4am. Cash only.

BUYER BEWARE. Wine prices per glass often look very cheap in Ukraine, especially compared to prices per bottle. But don't be fooled: wine is listed not by the glass, but by grams—usually either as 50 or 100g. An actual glass of wine, which is about 200 grams, will cost 2-4 times the price listed in the menu.

Kult (Култ), Chaikovskoho 7 (Чайковского; ☎242 2242; www.kult.lviv.ua). Right before the Philharmonic. Decked out with photographs of famous Lvivians, and boasting a dark seating area lit by multicolored stagelights, this bar-restaurant-club functions as one of Lviv's only late-night live music venues. With an eclectic variety of acts and a clientele that would fit in at the philharmonic or an all-night pub, Kult succeeds in combining artistic snobbery with laid-back fun for a relaxed, creative atmosphere. Menu in Ukrainian. Beer 9-26hv. Entrees 10-40hv. Shows at 8:30pm. Open daily 11am-2am.

Bar 1+1, pr. Shevchenka 11 (Щевченка; ☎74 37 47), downstairs. With stone walls, a brick ceiling, and carved dark-wood chairs, this bar creates a cozy but smoky atmosphere, marred only by the persistent fashion shows playing on the TV. No English menu. Beer 6-16hv. Mixed drinks 8-30hv. Entrees 10-25hv. Open 24hr. Cash only.

UZHHOROD (УЖГОРОД) ☎(80)312[2]

Uzhhorod (UZH-oh-rohd; pop. 125,000) is tucked at the foot of the Carpathian Mountains along the banks of the Uzh River, only one kilometer from the Slovak Republic and 21km from Hungary. Uzhhorod's proximity to these borders yields a diverse, multilingual populace, though it also facilitates a different kind of exchange—in the form of smuggling. During peaceful evenings, residents stroll along the river and the central pedestrian thoroughfare or lounge at cafes, sipping beer or Italian espresso. The calm town is best used as a base for trips into the nearby mountains; agencies in town arrange excursions.

PHONE CODES. When calling Uzhhorod from outside the city, the area code you should dial depends on the number. For 6-digit phone numbers, use the area code 80 312. For 5-digit numbers, use the area code 80 3122.

TRANSPORTATION. The **train station,** Stantsiyna 9 (Станційна; ☎69 29 62) sends trains to Kyiv (18hr., 2 per day, 50-110hv) and Lviv (7hr., 2 per day, 18-50hv). **Trains** to Hungary and the Slovak Republic, including Bratislava (5½hr., 1 per day, 180hv), leave from the border hub of Chop; to get there, take a **marshrutka** (30min., every 15-30min., 4-10hv) from behind the bus station. Tickets for local trains, including those to Mukachevo, are sold in the small building on the right side of the station. Other tickets are sold at the *kasa*, through the main hall, which is open 24hr. The **bus station,** Stantsiyna 2 (☎321 27), sends buses and *marshrutki* to Ivano-Frankivsk (8hr., 3 per day, 20-41hv) via Mukachevo (2hr., 2-4 per hr., 3-16hv); Lviv (7hr., one per day, 18-40hv); Budapest, HUN (126-246hv); Bratislava, SLK (74-147hv); and Prague, CZR (216-246hv). **City buses** and *marshrutki* within the city cost 0.65-1hv. **Taxis** cost 5-10hv for rides within the city.

ORIENTATION AND PRACTICAL INFORMATION. The **Uzh River** runs east-west through Uzhhorod, dividing the town roughly in half. The Old Town, which includes the castle and the museum, lies on the north side, while the bus and train stations are close together on the south side. To get to the center from the train or bus stations, follow pr. Svobody (Свободи) to Shvabska (Швабска). Take a right on Shvabska and follow it until it ends at a small square. Cross the square and turn left. The first right (pl. Petefi) leads to the walking bridge that ends in the center. Taxis (10hv) and *marshrutki* (to pl. Koryatovycha; Корятовуча) also go to the center. For tourist information and brochures, visit the **Regional Office for Tourism and Resorts,** pl. Narodna 4 (Народна), on the sixth floor in room 612 or 610. The friendly staff has info about Uzhhorod and excursions in the Transcarpathian Region. (☎61 28 39 or 61 28 17; turizm@uzhgorod.ukrsat.ua. Open M-F 8am-1pm and 2-5pm.) **Store luggage** at the train station or at Hotel Zakarpattya (2hv per day). You can find **24hr. pharmacies** at pr. Svobody 40 (Свободи), near Hotel Zakarpattya (☎256 02), and at pl. Koryatovycha 14/16 (Корятовуча), in the center (☎307 82). The **telephone** office, **Ukrtelekom** (Укртелеком), is located near the post office at Nab. Nezalezhnosti 6. (Незалежності; ☎61 11 50. Open daily 8am-8pm.) **Utel** phones can be found inside Hotels Zakarpattya and Uzhhorod. **Internet** is available at **X-net Internet Club** (Х-нет Інтернетклуб), Voloshyna 26 (Волошина), in the center of town. (3hv per hr. Open 24hr.) **A-Club,** at Nab. Nezalezhnosti 1, offers slower access. (3hv per hr. Open 24hr. Enter off Korzo (Корзо) through a stairwell.) The **post office** is at pl. Poshtova 3. (Поштова; ☎340 90. Open M-F 7am-7pm, Sa 7am-6pm, Su 8am-1pm.) **Postal Code:** 88000.

ACCOMMODATIONS AND FOOD. The most pleasant place to stay is **Hotel Atlant** ❷ (Атлант), pl. Koryatovycha 27 (Корятовуча), in the Old Town. In the heart of Old Town, just two blocks from the water, the hotel has modern baths, clean rooms, and a friendly staff. (☎61 40 95 or 61 49 88; www.hotel-atlant.com. Reservations recommended. Rooms 140-365hv. MC/V.) Despite limited hot water (usually 6-10am and 9pm-midnight), **Hotel Zakarpattya** ❷ (Закарпаття), at the intersection of pl. Kyryla (Кирила) and Mefodiya 5 (Мефодія), has great views of the mountains and comfortable rooms. Despite the hotel's harsh concrete exterior, its rooms are clean, relatively spacious, and have private balconies. (☎67 31 43 or 69 72 11; www.intur-zak.com. Singles 90-160hv; doubles 160-210. Cash only.)

There is a large **market** on pl. Koryatovycha (Корятовуча), near Hotel Atlant. (Open M 7am-3pm, Tu-Sa 7am-8pm, Su 7am-2pm; shorter hours in the fall and winter.) A string of cafe-bars with outdoor seating lines the river, near the pedestrian bridge. Cheap beer (3-10hv), a chuck wagon, and blue-jean curtains support the claim that **Cactus** ❷ (Кактус), Korzo 7 (Корзо), provides a "real Old West atmo-

The Carpathians are known for their natural wonders, but one of these is less than wonderful; mosquitoes. Since most hotels use open windows instead of A/C during the summer, be sure to stock up on bug repellent before heading into the countryside. For extra protection, pick up the kind that can be plugged into an outlet, and keep your hotel room happily mosquito-free.

sphere." The food is a mix of classic Texan food and the local flavor, resulting in a menu with dishes like the "Transcarpathian meal" (26hv) and "Redneck" (12hv), a dish of ham, cheese, tongue, and butter. (☎122 95. Wine 10-24hv. Entrees 9-35hv. Live music Th-Su 8-10pm. Open daily 10am-10pm. MC/V.) The somewhat upscale **Atlant restaurant ❷,** on the first floor of Hotel Atlant, has big, filling dishes like "Transcarpathian twisted meat with stuffing," a local specialty of pork stuffed with cheese and mushrooms. Tall, velvet-backed chairs and white tablecloths add class to the otherwise undecorated dining room. (☎61 40 95. English menu. Beer 4-10hv. Entrees 7-25hv. Desserts 5-13hv. Open daily 8am-11pm. Cash only.)

SIGHTS AND ENTERTAINMENT. Uzhhorod's three main attractions are all conveniently clustered just east of the city center. Take Kapitulna (Капітульна) to its end, away from the intersection with Voloshyna (Волошина). Near the top of the hill is the 1644 twin-spired **Catholic Cathedral.** Continue on Kapitulna to number 33, the site of the town's **castle** (замок; zamok); the stone walls date to the Middle Ages, but its facade was built in the 16th century. Inside is a museum showcasing local musical instruments, including two-meter-long mountain longhorns. (☎344 42. Open Tu-Su 10am-6pm. 5hv. Tours in Ukrainian 20hv.) Next door, at Kapitulna 33a, the requisite open-air **Transcarpathian Museum of Folk Architecture and Daily Life** (Закарпатський Музей Народної Архітектури та Побуту; Zakarpatskiy Muzey Narodnoyi Arkhitektury ta Pobutu) displays houses from the region, with textiles and pottery inside. Cute but not spectacular, the museum features the 1777 **St. Michael's Church,** an impressively nail-less, wooden basilica. (☎373 92. Open M and W-Su 9am-5pm. 5hv, children 2hv. Tours in Ukrainian 20/10hv.) **English info booklets** (10hv) are available at the entrances of the three sites.

Of the town's clubs, **Kashtan** (Каштан), Koshytska 22 (Кошицька), is the most popular. International DJs spin hip-hop, trance, and R&B as guests hit the dance floor or lounge on the outdoor terrace. (Beer 4-7hv. Wine 5hv. Cover 50hv. Open F 10pm-3am, Sa 10pm-4am, Su 10pm-2am.) The Transcarpathian region is full of religious, musical, and cultural **festivals** held throughout the year, including January's **Dark Wine Festival,** May's **Blacksmith Festival,** June's **Sheep-Pasturing Festival,** and September's **Local Sheep Cheese Festival.** The festivals take place in Uzhhorod and in smaller towns in the mountains. Exact dates are released about a month in advance; check at the tourist office.

OUTDOOR ACTIVITIES. **Blues** (Блуз; bluz), pr. Svobody 55/63 (Свободи), organizes tours of the region. (☎61 61 16. English spoken.) **Turkul** (Туркул) organizes tours that focus on sustainable development and ecological tourism, including **hiking** and **mountain biking.** (☎341 75; www.turkul.com. Contact at least 2 weeks in advance.) **Boussole Voyage** (Бусоль Вояж; busol voyazh), Vysoka 8 (Висока), runs tours to the **Valley of the Narcissus,** the **Salt Lake,** and various local **castles.** (☎61 66 47 or 61 99 47. Some English spoken.) **Zakarpatturyst** (Закарпаттурист), Koshytska 30 (Кошицька), in Turbaza Svitanok, runs 12 resorts throughout the region. They also organize hiking and sightseeing tours. (☎343 17. Open M-F 8am-noon and 1-5pm.)

For a short **daytrip** from Uzhhorod, visit the **Seredne Castle** (Середне), 12km from town near Kamyanitsya (Камяніця) village. Take *marshrutka* #115 from the bus station and ask the driver to let you off near the castle. Catch the same *marshrutka* on the other side of the street to get back to town (daily 6am-9pm). Cross the bridge and walk up the trail, which quickly turns into a road (20min.). The castle, built during medieval times, was the site of numerous battles in the 16th and 17th centuries, and underwent several transformations before a Transylvanian prince destroyed it in 1644. It was restored in the 1970s and is now a popular tourist attraction. Litter somewhat mars the experience of the ruins, but the view of the Uzh Valley makes up for it. The castle is also the site of an **archaeological excavation** that started in the 1990s and offers volunteer opportunities from May to September. (Contact Olexander Dzembas, head of the ecological-archaeological expedition "Castle of Transcarpathia," Vysoka 8. ☎341 45 or 325 69; centour@mail.uzhgorod.ua. Russian or Ukrainian language skills recommended.)

IVANO-FRANKIVSK ☎(80)342(2)

A transportation hub offering easy access to Chernivtsi and the towns of the Carpathian National Nature Reserve, Ivano-Frankivsk (Івано-Франківск; ee-VAHN-oh frahn-KEEVSK; pop. 240,000) is a necessary stopover for travelers visiting Western Ukraine. Its pedestrian-only centers—traditional **ploscha Rynok** and younger, rowdier **vulytsya Nezalezhnosti**—contain plenty of entertainment, in the form of cafes and illuminated fountains. The main **train, bus,** and **marshrutka stations** are all located in one giant, unwieldy blob on the edge of the town center, in pl. Pryvokzalna (Привокзальа; open 24hr.). The train station, Pryvokzalna 15 (☎253 13), sends **trains** to: Kyiv (14hr., 2-4 per day, 55-91hv); Lviv (4-7hr., 3 per day, 25-48hv); Odessa (18hr., 1 per day, 55-79hv); Simferopol (31hr., 1 per day, 146hv); Uzhhorod (11hr., 1 every other day, 36-48hv). Many towns unreachable by train are easily accessed by **bus** or **marshrutka;** the bus station sells tickets for both, and it is often impossible to tell which the ticket is for until the vehicle arrives. Both go to Chernivtsi (2hr., 10 per day, 8-11hv); Kyiv (18hr., 2 per day, 70hv); Lviv (4-8hr., 10 per day, 20hv); Vorokhta (1-2hr., over 20 per day, 8-10hv); Yaremche (1-2hr., over 20 per day, 8-10hv). Arrive at least 30min. prior to departure to find your bus and seat. Buses arriving in Ivano-Frankivsk do not stop at the central station, but in an empty lot on the outskirts of town. To get to the center, take a **taxi** to vul. Nezalezhnosti (Незалежності; 10-15hv). **Taxi rides** within Ivano-Frankivsk cost 5-15hv.

Those who are stranded for the night can head to **Hotel Nadiya** (Готель Надія) ❹, vul. Nezalezhnosti 40 (Незалежності), which offers a convenient location on the main strip and simple but newly renovated rooms. (☎53 70 77; www.nadia.if.ua. Singles 250-350hv; doubles 300-450hv. MC/V.) **Cafes** and **bars** line vul. Nezalezhnosti, offering beer, hot dogs, pastries, and the best people-watching in town. (Most open daily until 11pm.) During summer, **ice cream vendors** line the streets, serving cheap, tasty treats in many flavors; try the especially delicious yogurt flavor (1hv per scoop). **Postal Code:** 76018.

CHERNIVTSI (ЧЕРНІВЦІ) ☎(80)372(2)

Hilly, green, and filled with students, Chernivtsi is Ukraine's quintessential university town. While tourists rave about the University's complex and somewhat bizarre architecture, it's the students who give the city life. Chernivtsi is filled with small cafes, clubs, parks, and underground bars, all frequented by a casual and trendy student crowd. But it isn't just the students who crowd the town; Chernivtsi's market attracts daily visitors from all over Western Ukraine as well as from Moldova and Romania.

TRANSPORTATION. Chernivtsi's **train station** is located on the northern side of town, close to the banks of the River Prut. A major transportation center, it sends trains to: Ivano-Frankivsk (3½hr., 1 per hr.); Kolomyya (2-2½hr., 2 per day); Kyiv (15hr., 1 per day); Lviv (12hr., 1 per day); Odessa (17hr., 1 per day); Simferopol (32hr., 2 per day); and Uzhhorod (14hr., 1 every other day). Tickets should be bought at the **Advance Ticket Office,** v. Holovna 128. (Головна; ☎429 24. Open M-F 8am-7pm, Sa-Su 8am-5pm.) It is important to note that **most trains going East or South pass through the Moldovan territory of Transnistria,** which requires a difficult-to-obtain visa. To avoid problems at the border, it is better to take a bus to these destinations from Chernivtsi. The **bus station** is on the southern end of town, vul. Holovna (☎416 35). Buses go to: Ivano-Frankivsk (4hr., 1 per day, 21hv); Kamyanets Podilsky (2hr., 7-10 per day, 12-14hv); Kolomyya (2hr., 3 per day, 12hv); Kyiv (10-15hr., 3 per day, 74-77hv); Lviv (8hr., 4 per day, 38-42hv); Odessa (15hr., 1 per day, 101hv); Sevastopol (24hr., 1 per day, 172hv); Simferopol (23hr., 1 per day, 152hv); Uzhhorod (12hr., 1 per day, 60hv); Yalta (30hr., 1 per day, 162hv); and Yaremche (3½hr., 1 per day, 18hv). Chernivtsi's **public transportation** consists of buses and trolleybuses. **Trolleybuses** #3 and 5 go to both the train station and the bus station, as well as at the center.

ORIENTATION AND PRACTICAL INFORMATION. Chernivtsi has two main streets, **vulytsi Holovna** (Головна) and **vulytsi Universitetska.** Vul. Holovna runs from the train station on the northern end of the city through the center to the bus station; vul. Universitetska runs from the University on the western side of town to Ploscha Tsentralna in the center, where it intersects vul. Holovna. Cafes, bars, and pedestrians line both of these streets at any time of day. The bookstore at Pl. Tsentralna 9 sells **maps.** (Maps 6-15hv. Open daily 10am-7pm.) There is a 24hr. **pharmacy,** Holovna 44 (☎223 72), next to Hotel Kyiv. Though there are signs at the Post Office for **Ukrtelecom,** the actual building is at Universytetska 7 (Університетьска), across from the trolley stop. (Open daily 8am-9:30pm. **Utel** office on right. Open daily 8:30am-12:30pm and 1:15-5:30pm.) Only half a block away is the **Internet** cafe Infocom, Universytetska 1. (☎55 27 39; www.chv.ukrpack.net. Internet 5hv per hour. Open daily 8am-7pm.) The **Post Office,** vul. Khudyakova 6 (Худяково), is on a side street just off of Pl. Tsentralna. (☎55 95 81 or 52 63 02. Open M-F 9am-2pm and 3-7pm, Sa 10am-2pm and 3-5pm.)

ACCOMMODATIONS AND FOOD. Chernivtsi has two solid budget options. Cheap rates and a central location make **Hotel Kyiv ❶**, vul. Holovna 46 (Головна), the best option for backpackers. The rooms are clean and the bathrooms are modern; rooms with private baths are a steal. (☎22 24 83. Rooms 60-140hv. MC/V.) Those looking for a bit more class at a reasonable price can head down Holovna to the **Hotel Bukovyna ❷**, vul. Holovna 141. The private rooms, pleasant yellow exterior, and outdoor cafe make this the most comfortable hotel in town. Though close to Chernivtsi's clubs, it's a bit of a walk from the town center. (☎58 56 25; www.hotel.cv.ua. Internet 8hv. Rooms 110-425hv. MC/V.) Pizza is the food of choice at most of Chernivtsi's cafes, and local chain **Pizza Park ❶**, vul. Holovna 85, offers fresh, light pizzas for cheap. (Pizza 3-8hv. Open 10am-3pm, 4pm-11pm.) Outdoor beer garden **Knaus ❷**, vul. Holovna 26a, draws a large local crowd for hearty Ukrainian fare. (☎51 02 55. Beer 3-7hv. Entrees 10-30hv).

SIGHTS. Chernivtsi's famous **university** is renowned for its impressive but incongruous architectural style. Built as a home for the town's Orthodox Church leaders in 1882, it was transformed by the Soviets into a university. Mosaic roofs, bold colors, and brightly landscaped gardens make the university seem like an alternate reality. Only two of the university's buildings are open to the public. On the far left just after entering the gate is **Seminarska Church** (Семінарська); to enter, follow the first path on the left through a small covered walkway and into a courtyard. The entrance is on the right. (Open sporadically; check the schedule of services and try the door.) At the end of the landscaped path beginning at the entrance is the **Palace Residence.** Today it is home to a bank and classrooms. The back right-hand corner, where the bank is located, provides access to a stairwell leading to the **Marble Hallway.** Though only students are allowed up the stairwell, intrepid visitors can try to pass for students, but staff monitoring the stairs are relatively vigilant in weeding out the tourists from the students.

CARPATHIAN NATIONAL NATURAL PARK ☎3434

Fifty-five kilometers long and 20km wide, the Carpathian National Natural Park (CNNP), Ukraine's largest, is one of the most distinctive parts of the country. Thirty thousand people live within the park's borders, including the Hutsul people, who are known throughout Ukraine for their folk art, woodwork, and handmade textiles. In order to protect the park's natural environment against the influx of tourists, its caves, mineral springs, mountain slopes, and green valleys are divided into four zones, each allowing different amounts of human activity. Visitors to the park, however, are unlikely to find their activities hindered; even the most restricted zones allow hikers access, leaving plenty for visitors to explore.

TRANSPORTATION. Visitors to the park are technically expected to pay an **entrance fee** (6hv, children 2hv). Most visitors, however, enter the park on bus or train, neither of which stops to pay the fees. Within the park, there are two towns with lodging for tourists: Vorokhta and Yaremche. Both are accessible by bus or train, and taxis from within these towns travel to other parts of the park. The park itself is serviced by a **railway** line running from Lviv to Rakhiv that stops in Vorokhta, Yaremche, and other towns in the park. **Buses** also run along this line. The inner sections of the park, though, are accessible only by taxi or private car.

CAMPING. Unlike in the rest of Ukraine, **camping is permitted throughout the CNNP.** No special permits are required other than the normal entrance fees, and campers are free to set up on any public land. The banks of the River Prut are popular camping spots. **Campfires are illegal** in the park, though still relatively common. Many parts of the park are protected land, so campers should practice the Leave No Trace ethic (see p. 45) during their stay.

HIKING. Relatively gentle slopes and stunning panoramic views make for fantastic hiking in the Carpathians. Main trails in the area are well marked and easy to follow. Unfortunately, though, they are also inaccessible by public transportation; most require either a private taxi or a tour group. **Mt. Hoverla** (Говерла; 2061m) is the most common destination. The mountain lies to the west of Vorokhta; to get there, head 6km south before taking the right fork, which leads to Zaroslak resort, at the base of the trail. Public transportation ends at Vorokhta; from there, you can take a private taxi, or hire a guide to drive you to the mountain. From Zaroslak, the trail is clearly marked, and usually relatively busy. About 3km each way, it's an easy and enjoyable day hike, so long as it's not swamped by tourists.

SKIING. While hiking draws many summer visitors to the Carpathians, skiing prevails during the winter. There are a number of ski resorts in the area; **www.ski-ukraine.info** offers detailed information (in English) about Ukrainian skiing and provides assistance in booking accommodations. Thirty kilometers west of Yaremche, **Bukovel** offers a European resort experience. With skiing at all levels, it's arguably the most popular resort in Ukraine, and certainly one of the most expensive. (☎372 89; www.bukovel.com. Lift tickets Jan. 12-Dec.28 75-140hv per day; Dec. 29-Jan. 11 89-150hv. Ski Rental 55-330hv.) Buses transport skiers from Yaremche to the slopes and back (Dec.-Apr., 1hr., 5-10hv). Slopeside accommodations start at 1000hv per night (min. 3 nights). For more adventurous skiers, **Drahobrat** offers a true wilderness experience. With a base elevation of 1300m, the resort promises the longest season of any in Ukraine, and plenty of off-piste slopes and steep terrain for advanced skiers. The resort's remote location keeps away the crowds, but makes it unfeasible for daytrips. Visitors to the resort must take a bus (2½hr., 2-4 per day, 10hv) or train (4hr., 1 per day, 12hv) to Yasinya from Ivano-Frankivsk. From Yasinya, special taxis leave from the train and bus stations to Drahobrat (80-120hv per car). Fortunately, Drahobrat offers considerably cheaper lodging and skiing than Bukovel, making it an appealing locale for longer trips. (www.ski.lviv.ua/drahobrat. Lift tickets 25-40hv per day. Ski rental 35-100hv.)

SKIING THE CARPATHIANS FOR POCKET CHANGE. Don't have the cash for the resort high-life? Buy a 3-day lift pass for **Bukovel** (290hv), and rent a standard pair of **skis** (55hv per day). Avoid the expensive resort lodging by taking the Bukovel bus (8hv) back to **Yaremche** in the evening and stay at a local **B&B** (30-100hv per night; check www.karpaty.info/en). Avoid resort-priced lunch by stocking up on food for the day at the local **supermarket;** try Universam, Svobody 256. (Open daily 8am-11pm.)

MUSHROOM PICKING. A local tradition in the Carpathian region, mushroom picking is possible from spring to fall, provided that it rains enough. Locals simply head off into the woods for mushroom hunting, but without excellent knowledge of mushrooms it is unsafe to go picking alone, as many varieties can be poisonous. Those interested should ask at their hotel or inquire at a tourist agency. **Zori Karpat,** Svobody 246, a tour agency based in Yaremche, offers mushroom picking expeditions, conditional on the weather. (☎211 82. Open daily 8am-8pm.)

YAREMCHE (ЯРЕМЧЕ) ☎(80)3434

While it may be famous for its prime skiing and hiking location, Yaremche (yah-REHM-chay; pop. 8000) is anything but a typical resort town. Yaremche is practical, not a tourist haven, and it's filled with a highly friendly locals. Its unpaved roads wind around small, alpine-style houses with colored, slanted roofs; the towering concrete scars of Soviet construction are nowhere to be found. Yaremche is defined by its mountainous natural setting. Starry skies and tree-lined hills exude an atmosphere of both relaxation and adventure; easy access to skiing, biking, hiking, and Ukraine's highest peak, Mt. Hoverla, make it an even sweeter deal.

TRANSPORTATION. The train station, Svobody 268 (Свободи; ☎223 56), in the center of town, sends **trains** to: Ivano-Frankivsk (2hr., 2 per day); Lviv (4hr., 1 per day, 30hv); Vorokhta (45min., 3 per day). (Open daily 8am-noon, 4:30-6:30pm, 9-11pm, and 2-6am.) The bus station, Svobody 234, is down the street, next to the gas station; "Avtovokzal" (Автовокзал) is written on the facade. (☎223 17. Open daily 6:30am-noon and 1pm-7:30pm.) **Buses** go to: Chernivtsi (3hr., 1 per day, 18hv); Ivano-Frankivsk (1½hr., over 20 per day, 8hv); Kyiv (14hr., 1 per day, 74hv); Lviv (6hr., 1 per day, 30hv); Vorokhta (1hr., frequent departures, 3-8hv).

ORIENTATION AND PRACTICAL INFORMATION. Locals describe Yaremche as a large village. Hotels and cottages dot the main corridor, **Svobody** (Свободи), which also houses the town's center. Tourist agency **Zori Karpat** (Зорi Карпат), Svobody 246, organizes hiking tours (150hv) and trips to Mt. Hoverla (320hv), as well as mushroom-picking expeditions. (☎211 82. No English spoken. Open daily 8am-8pm, occasionally closed when staff is leading tours. Cash only.) There is a 24hr. **pharmacy** (Apteka; Аптека) at Dovbusha 5 (Довбуша). The train station has a local pay **telephone. Ukrtelecom** has an office in the same building as the post office, with both local and Utel payphones. (Open daily 8:30am-12:30pm and 1:15-5:30pm.) Yaremche has one **Internet cafe,** Svobody 264, with five computers and a slow dial-up connection. Go straight through the first two doors of the main entrance; the cafe is to the left, marked "Computer Zal." (Open M-F 10am-8pm. Internet 5hv per hour.) The Yaremche **post office** is at Svobody 307, in the center (☎224 31. Open M-F 9am-2pm and 3-5pm, Sa 9am-3pm.) **Postal Codes:** 78500.

ACCOMMODATIONS. Wooden buildings and slanted roofs prevail in Yaremche, and most hotels and B&Bs are on the hillside, so expect to walk. Prices everywhere double or even triple during the popular winter season (Dec.-Mar.). Lone travelers and smaller groups should check out **www.karpaty.info/en** to find a local **Bed & Breakfast ❶.** The website lists English info for over 30 B&Bs in Yaremche (from 30hv in summer). Make sure to book ahead and to arrange transport from the train or bus station, as many of the residential streets are unmarked, and houses can be difficult to find. Those looking for a more secluded option can rent a **private cottage ❷,** just south of town on Svobody 332a. From the bus station, take a *marshrutka* toward Mykulychyn, Tatariv, or Vorokhta, and ask to be let off at the address; or, call ahead to be picked up (5-10hv). (☎312 37. 2- to 4-person rooms 120hv; 2- to 6-person rooms 280hv; 4- to 8-person cottage with full kitchen and sauna 450hv. Cash only.) **Yaroslava ❸** (Ярослава), Svobody 233, 2min. from the train station, has 12 rooms available in Hutsul-style cottages. There's access to a full kitchen, and every room includes a refrigerator, television, and a bathroom with jacuzzi. (☎227 44. No English spoken. Sauna 10-20hv. 2- to 4-person rooms Feb.-Dec. 190-300hv; Jan. from 400hv. Cash only.)

FOOD. Many hotels have restaurants attached, and B&Bs often include breakfast or dinner; independent restaurants are scarce. The town's few restaurants, which cater almost exclusively to tourists, are located in and around the two **souvenir markets,** south of the train station; the one north of Svobody's intersection with the Prum River has several restaurants specializing in supremely touristy "traditional" cuisine. More locals can be found at **Hrazhda** (Гражда) **❷,** down a path to the right of the entrance to the southern souvenir market. The interior of the horseshoe-shaped dining room is simple, with wooden tables. (Entrees 8-30hv. Beer 4-8hv. Wine 20-24hv. Open daily 11am-10pm. MC/V.)

VOROKHTA (ВОРОХТА) ☎(80)3434

The closest town to Mt. Hoverla, Vorokhta (voh-rokh-TAH; pop. 3900) offers convenient lodging for near the slopes and the trails. With a ski jump on the edge of town, a sky lift offering panoramic views of the nearby mountains, and a location smack dab in the middle of the CNNP, Vorokhta is a perfect gateway to the outdoors. Unfortunately, the dreamy landscape is somewhat marred by litter and construction in the town's center, but those who venture out a couple of blocks will find an untouched landscape that both soothes and energizes.

Many resorts and rental cabins are along the road to Vorokhta; most, however, are at least several miles out of town. Luckily, there are a few closer options. At the northern end of Vorokhta, **Ruslana** (Руслана) **❸,** on Halytskoho below the ski jump, offers seven cottages with international themes. The director speaks English and

French. (☎415 42 or 416 99; www.carpathiantours.com. Breakfast included; other meals available. Mountain bike rentals 25hv. Hiking guides 50hv. Minibus to Bukovela (Буковела; p. 737) or to Mt. Hoverla 15hv. July-Aug. cabins 400-800hv; mid-Dec. to Mar. 900-1600hv; Apr. to mid-June and Sept. to mid-Dec. 300hv. Extra person 50hv. Cash only.) Those traveling alone may prefer **Ukraina** (Україна) ❷, Halytskoho 68. Set back from the main road but close to the town center, this large hotel offers very basic but clean rooms. (☎413 74; fax 410 30. Reserve ahead. Rooms 100-300hv. Cash only.) Vorokhta's dining options are sparse. Most cafes serve only the standard hot dog and pizza combination. **Hoverla Cafe** (Говерла) ❶, Halytskoho 14, in the center of Vorokhta, serves sausages (kovbasy; 4-6hv), borscht (3.50hv), and other basic Ukrainian dishes. Seating is on the patio or at indoor tables with wooden benches. (Open daily 10am-midnight. Cash only.)

Vorokhta is a tiny town, concentrated mostly within the three blocks of the town center. **Vulytsya Haltyskoho** runs north-south through the town; the center starts at Halytskoho 10 and ends at about Halytskoho 70. Pedestrian-only **C.M.T. Vorokhta,** which contains the local market, starts across from Hoverla Cafe and ends a block later at the train station. **Avalbank,** Halytskoho 67, **exhanges currency.** (Open M-F 9am-1pm and 2-4:30pm.) In the same building is Vorokhta's only **pharmacy.** (☎414 53. Open M-F 9am-7pm, Sa 10am-6pm, Su 10am-5pm.) There are several **produkti** in the center on Haltyskoho. The **post office** is at Haltyskoho 45. (Open M-F 10am-2pm and 3-6pm, Sa 9am-2pm and 3-4pm.) There is a local **pay phone** across the street from the post office in front of Cafe Karpaty. **Postal Code:** 78595.

The **train station,** located at the end of C.M.T. Vorokhta, one block from the center, sends trains to: Ivano-Frankivsk (3hr., 1-2 per day, 7-23hv); Kolomyya (3hr., 1 per day, 5hv); Lviv (7hr., 1-2 per day, 10-33hv); and Yaremche (1hr., 1-2 per day, 8-19hv). The station is open daily 9am-1pm, 4pm-midnight, and 2-6am. **Marshrutki** run to Ivano-Frankivsk (3-4hr., 10-15hv), Kolomiyya (3hr., 5-6 per day, 8hv), and Yaremche (1hr., 3 per hr., 3hv). Since the town has no bus station, marshrutki leave from the post office; look for signs on *marshrutki* indicating their destination. To reach other destinations, head to Yaremche.

BLACK SEA COAST

Sandwiched between Moldova and the Crimea, the western Black Sea coast is home to beaches and ports that, amazingly, aren't swamped by tourists. Odessa is the region's busy center, home to tasty food and a rocking nightlife.

ODESSA (ОДЕССА) ☎(80)482

Since its founding in 1794 by Catherine the Great, Odessa (pop. 1,100,000) has been a cultural center cursed by pollution and corruption. Stubborn and energetic, Odessans unabashedly love their city, and for good reason. With bustling industry, surging nightlife, nearby beaches, and the best outdoor restaurant scene in Ukraine, Odessa is one of Ukraine's hottest towns. It has served as a backdrop for writers from Alexander Pushkin to local boy Isaac Babel, who in his *Odessa Tales* wrote about Odessa's Jewish mafia. *Let's Go* uses the Russian spelling of the city's name, as most Odessans speak Russian.

TRANSPORTATION

Flights: Ovidiopolskaya Doroga (Овидиопольская Дорога; ☎006 or 21 35 49), southwest of the center. *Marshrutka* #129 runs from the airport to the train station; #101 goes to the city center (Grecheskaya; Греческая).

ODESSA FOR POCKET CHANGE. It's easy to get snared by the tacky, overpriced cafes along Deribasovskaya, or by hotels that provide TVs but lack hot water and decent service. To be one with thrift, rent an apartment (preferably one with its own water heater) from a woman at the train station (p. 743). The beaches we list all have free areas, and museums near the center all cost under 10hv (US$2). You can grab dinner from the **Provoz market** (p. 743), and then catch a ballet or opera for 10hv. If you're strolling down the boardwalk at **Arkadiya** (p. 746), buy your drink for 2.50hv from a stand rather than paying 15hv or more inside the clubs.

Trains: Zheleznodorozhnyy Vokzal (Келезнодорожный Вокзал), pl. Privokzalnaya 2 (Привокзальная; ☎005). International and advance tickets must be purchased at the **service center;** after going through the main entrance, enter the hall on the right, then go left and through the doors to the back room. Expect a long wait. To: **Kyiv** (8hr., 5 per day, 60-80hv); **Lviv** (12hr., 2 per day, 60-80hv); **Simferopol** (12hr., 2 per day, 70-90hv); **Moscow, RUS** (25hr., 2 per day, 215hv); **Warsaw, POL** (24hr., even days, 400hv).

NO TRAVELER LEFT BEHIND. Trains running to and from Odessa and the Crimea are often booked full during summer. To ensure getting a ticket, book your seats at least 3 days in advance; to pick which class to travel in, book at least a couple of weeks in advance.

Buses: Avtovokzal (Автовокзал), Kolontayevskaya 58 (Колонтаевская; ☎004). From the train station, cross the road behind McDonald's and take tram #5 to the last stop. From there, walk down 1 block. To: **Kyiv** (8-10hr., 8 per day, 60hv); **Lviv** (9hr., 2 per day, 58hv); **Sevastopol** (13½hr., 1 per day, 80hv); **Simferopol** (12hr., 2 per day, 65hv); **Yalta** (15hr., 2 per day, 80hv); **Rostov-na-Donu, RUS** (18hr., 2 per day, 140hv). Buy international tickets on the 2nd fl. (☎732 6667). *Kasa* open daily 8am-12:30pm and 1:30-4pm.

Ferries: Morskoy Vokzal (Морской Вокзал), Primorskaya 6 (Приморская; ☎729 3803). To: **İstanbul, TUR** (30-36hr., 2 per wk., 600-1000hv). Open daily 9am-6pm.

Public Transportation: Trams and **trolleys** run almost everywhere 7am-midnight. Buy your ticket (0.50hv) from the badge-wearing conductor. On **buses,** pay as you exit (0.60hv). When entering **marshrutki** (1-1.50hv), look for a sticker that says "обплата при входе" (obplata pri vkhode; payment at entry) or "обплата при выходе" (obplata pri vykhode; payment at exit). If payment is at entry, it's common to sit down first, then pass money to the driver; your change will make its way back to you.

Taxis: ☎070, 345, or 077. Yellow taxis are expensive. Check prices before you ride, and have the driver write it down. Don't pay more than 15hv from pl. Grecheskaya (Греческая) to the train station. When returning from Arkadiya (Аркадия) at night, try to bargain down to 25-30hv.

ORIENTATION AND PRACTICAL INFORMATION

Odessa's center is bounded by the **train station** to the south and the **port** to the north. Almost all streets have been recently renamed and labeled in both Ukrainian and Russian; *Let's Go* lists the Russian names, since they are more commonly used. Numbering of streets begins at the sea and increases as you head inland. **Deribasovskaya** (Дерибасовская) is the main pedestrian thoroughfare. From the McDonald's opposite the train station, take trolley #1 or any of several *marshrutki* to get there. The tree-lined promenade of **Primorskiy bulvar** (Приморский) is separated from the sea terminal by the famous **Potemkin Stairs.** Odessa's **beaches** stretch for miles starting east of the center. **Arkadiya,** the beach-

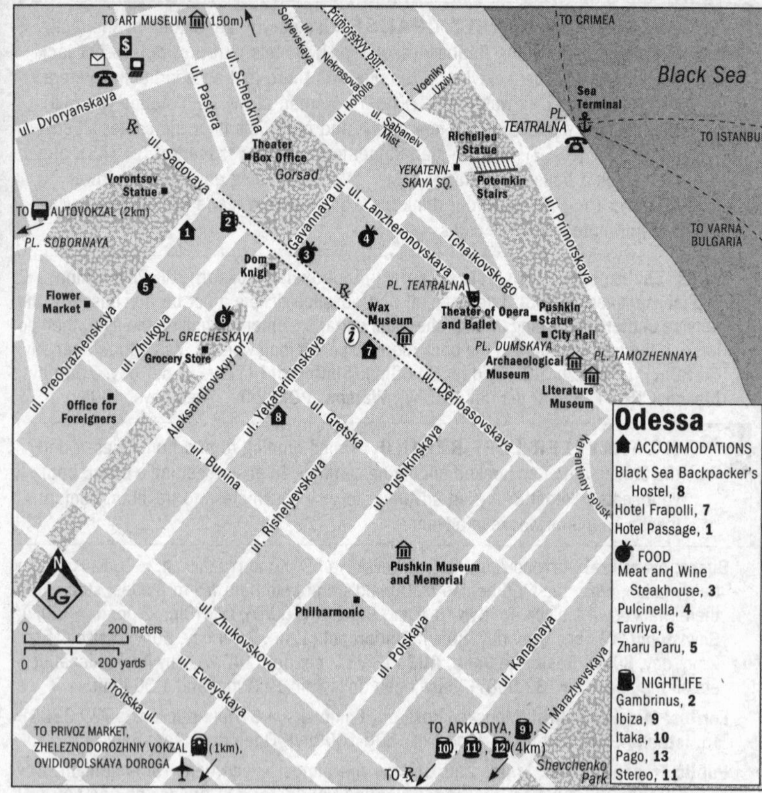

side strip home to all the summer nightlife, is southeast of the city center; take *marshrutka* #195 from Preobrazhenskaya (Преображенская).

Tourist Offices: FGT Travel, Deribasovskaya 13 (Дерибасовская; ☎37 52 01 or 35 68 01; www.odessapassage.com), on the 2nd fl. of Hotel Frapolli. Provides info about accommodations and runs a variety of excursions, including city tours and catacomb tours (each 2½hr., 63hv per person) and wine-tasting tours (100-140hv). Open daily 8:30am-8pm. **Office for Foreigners** (Канцелярия для иностранцев; Kantselyariya dlya inostrantsev), Bunina 37 (Бунина), 2nd fl. (☎28 28 22 or 28 28 46). Visa assistance. Open Tu-Th 10am-12:30pm and 2-4:30pm.

Currency Exchange: There's an *obmen valyut* (обмен валют) on every corner. Rates vary, so check several. **Bank Aval** (Аваль), Sadovaya 9 (Садовая; www.avalbank.com), cashes **traveler's checks** for 2% commission, gives cash advances for 2% commission, and provides **Western Union** services. Open M-F 9am-5pm.

Luggage Storage: Kamera Zberihannya (Камера Зберiгання), outside the train station, 50m down the far right track on the right-hand side. 4hv per bag, 5hv per large bag. Open 24hr. Downstairs in the bus station 3hv per bag. Open daily 5am-midnight. Downstairs in the sea terminal 1.50hv per bag per day, 3hv per night. Open daily 8am-6pm.

English-Language Bookstore: Dom Knigi (Дом Книги), Deribasovskaya 27 (Дерибасовская; ☎22 34 73). Good city maps (6-8hv). Open daily 10am-7pm.

Pharmacy: Apteka Khelp (Аптека Хелп), Admiralskiy Prospekt 37 (Адмиральский Проспект; ☎22 71 27). **Apteka Gayevskogo** (Аптека Гаевского), Sadova 21 (☎22 24 08). MC/V. 24hr. pharmacies also in the train station (☎27 41 65).

Telephones: Ukrtelecom available in kiosks 7-10 at the Post Office. Phone cards 9hv-100hv; phones are in the hallway entrance. At the sea terminal, to the left of the entrance, are 4 phones for long-distance calls. Rates are better 8-11pm and Sa-Su. Open daily 8am-11pm.

Internet: Internet Club Bek 21, Sadovaya 5 (Садовая; ☎728 6479), opposite the post office. 4hv per hr. CD Burning 5hv. Open 24hr.

Post Office: Sadovaya 10 (☎726 7493). Mail letters abroad at window #19. Open M-Sa 8am-2pm and 3-8pm, Su 8am-2pm and 3-6pm. **Fax** service at #22 (☎726 6417). Open daily 8am-1pm and 1:45-5pm. **Photocopies** at window #21. Open M-Sa 8am-8pm, Su 8am-6pm. **Postal Code:** 65001.

ACCOMMODATIONS

New **hostels** in town, offering hot water, Internet access, and included breakfasts, provide a cheap and comfortable way to avoid paying for Odessa's expensive hotels. The city's run-down **budget hotels** are found in the center; many don't have hot water during summer, and room quality varies. **Private rooms** are cheap but not always safe, and most are far from the center. Train station hawkers hold signs reading "Sdayu komnatu" (Сдаю комнату; I'm renting a room). Ask "Skolko?" (Сколько; how much). The asking price is usually 75-100hv; bargain down, and don't pay until you see the room. Apartments are also available from women at the train station, but cost 100hv or more.

Black Sea Backpackers' Hostel, Yekaterinskaya 25, 2nd fl. (Екатеринская; ☎25 22 00 or 24 55 67; www.blackseahostels.com). Go through the archway labeled #25. The stairwell to the hostel is the first door on the right inside the courtyard. With a prime location one block south from Deribasovskaya (Дерибасовская) and numerous amenities, Black Sea is the place to meet other backpackers. Free Wi-Fi, computer access, kitchen use, and laundry. 24hr. hot water. Breakfast included. Excursion to catacombs and Shevchenko Park US$16. US$25 per night. Cash only. ❷

Hotel Passage (Пассаж), Preobrazhenskaya 34 (Преображенская; ☎26 95 37 or 28 55 01; www.passage.odessa.ua), near the corner of Deribasovskaya (Дерибасовская). The grandeur of this old building is somewhat lessened by cracked marble, mismatched furniture, and a cranky plumbing system that occasionally shuts off hot water. However, for cheap, private rooms, Passage is one of the only options, and its great location definitely gives it an edge. Luggage storage 3hv. Singles 100-560hv; doubles 132-558hv. ❷

Hotel Frapolli, Deribasovskaya 13 (Дерибасовская; ☎356 8001; www.odessapassage.com), next to Mick O'Neill's Pub. The price is high, but the prime location and luxurious rooms make it a good option for a splurge. Rooms have A/C, modern bathrooms with hot water, personal computers with Internet access, and satellite TVs. Breakfast included. Reservations recommended. Rooms US$60-195 per person. MC/V. ❺

FOOD

The streets of central Odessa are lined with cafes and restaurants, typically charging about 100hv for a meal. For the budget traveler, Odessa is shawarma (шаурма) town: cheap eats can be found at kiosks along Deribasovskaya (Дерибасовская) and in Arkadiya (Аркадия). There is also a gigantic grocery store in the basement of Galeria Afena in Gretchevskaya Square (open daily 8am-11pm).

Tavriya (Таврія), Ploshcha Grechevskaya, in the basement of Galeria Afena. The motherlode of cafeterias, Tavriya offers Ukrainian food and pizza as well as desserts, drinks, and a large salad bar. There are five seating areas, both smoking and nonsmoking, and one has a stage with live music in the afternoons, with bands playing anything from African folk music to traditional Big Band classics. Drinks 3-8hv. Entrees 6-20hv. Soups 3-5hv. Open daily 8am-11pm. Cash only. ❶

Zharyu Paryu (Жарю Парю), Grechevskaya 45 (Гречевская; ☎33 01 81 or 33 01 91), just down from Hotel Passage. The decor is simple and the prices cheap in this cafeteria. The menu holds no surprises and little variation, but Zharyu is good at what it does. Soups 2.50hv. Salads 2-3hv. Entrees 5-8hv. Open daily 8am-10pm. Cash only. ❶

Pulcinella, Lanzheronovskaya 17 (Ланжероновская; ☎777 3010), between Gavanaya (Гаваная) and Yekaterinskaya (Екатеринская). The cozy Mediterranean decor of this Italian establishment is accentuated by quick, friendly service. It's worth coming just to see meals delivered from the kitchen in a specially heated dumbwaiter. English menu. Entrees 20-100hv. Pizza 20-40hv, group-size 100hv. Open daily 11am-11pm. MC/V. ❹

Meat and Wine Steakhouse, Deribasovskaya 20 (Дерибасовская; ☎34 87 82; www.steak.od.ua). Popular among expats, this classy steakhouse has refined decorations, a relaxed atmosphere, and a menu to make any carnivore's mouth water. International wine list. English menu. Free Wi-Fi. English spoken. Salad bar with a variety of prepared salads 20hv. Steaks 25-80hv. Open daily 9am-midnight. MC/V. ❸

SIGHTS

CATACOMBS. When Catherine the Great decided to build Odessa, the limestone used for its construction was mined from below, leaving the longest catacombs in the world. During WWII, Odessa's partisans hid in these dark, intertwining tunnels, surfacing only for raids against the Nazis. Though the catacombs span a 70km radius around Odessa and its surrounding villages, the only accessible portion of the labyrinths lies under the village of Neribaiskoye (Нерибайское), where the city has set up an outstanding subterranean **museum.** You can enter the catacombs through one entrance only and you must have a guide. At the recreated resistance camp, rocks covered with original partisan's graffiti have been transported to the recreated resistance camp. One declares "Blood for blood; death for death." *(30min. by car from Odessa. Many hotels and tour agencies provide rides and tours. FGT offers 2hr. tours in English; 150hv per guide plus 315hv transportation. Dress warmly.)*

DERIBASOVSKAYA STREET (ДЕРИБАСОВСКАЯ). Odessa's most popular street is filled with cafes, clothing stores, vendors, and performers. During the day, impromptu musical performances pop up unexpectedly; at night, it becomes a preclubbing hotspot. Don't be surprised by the snakes, monkeys, and exotic lizards—some residents make a living by photographing tourists with their odd pets—but steer clear if you don't want to pay. On the east end of the street is the **Gorsad** (Горсад), where artists sell jewelry, landscape paintings, and *matryoshka* dolls.

411TH BATTALION MONUMENT. Far from the busy commercial center lies one of Odessa's more entertaining monuments. Typical armaments of the Soviet forces are spread throughout a large park, where swarms of kids clamber over tanks and torpedoes. There is a small museum by the battleship. The cliffs along the rocky coast are a short walk from behind the bus stop to the left. *(From the train station, take marshrutka #127 30-40min. to the last stop; daily 6am-10pm. Walk straight and take a right at the concrete "411." Museum ☎44 45 27. Open M-Th and Sa-Su 10am-6pm. 1hv.)*

SHEVCHENKO PARK. This large park separates the city center from the sea. At the entrance is a **monument** to the poet Taras Shevchenko (p. 709). Within are the ruins of **Khadzhibey Fortress** and monuments to the dead of the Great Patriotic War (WWII) and the Afghanistan War. An eternal flame burns for an unknown soldier.

PRIMORSKIY BOULEVARD (ПРИМОРСКИЙ). Primorskiy's shaded promenade is home to some of Odessa's finest buildings and most elaborate mansions. The **statue of Alexander Pushkin** turns its back to the City Hall, which refused to help fund its construction. On either side of the hall are Odessa's two symbols: **Fortuna,** goddess of fate; and **Mercury,** god of trade. From Primorskiy, descend the **Potemkin Stairs** (Потомкинская Лестница; Potomkinskaya Lestnitsa) to reach Primorskaya and the Sea Terminal.

MUSEUMS

WAX MUSEUM. This small museum (Музей Восковых Скульптур; Muzey Voskovykh Skulptur) displays wax figures of the city's most famous inhabitants, including Catherine the Great and the Russian poet Pushkin. There is also an exhibition of miniature houses and buildings in Odessa. *(Rishelevskaya 4 (Ришелевская). ☎22 34 36. Open daily 8:30am-10pm. English placards. 12hv. Ticket includes a photo.)*

ART MUSEUM (ХУДОЖНИЙ МУЗЕЙ; KHUDOZHNIY MUZEY). A diverse collection of 19th-century art, including works by Kandinskiy, Ayvazovskiy, and Levitskiy, is displayed in a former palace. One of the rooms, containing golden religious icons, requires an additional ticket. The most exciting part of the museum is the grotto underneath. It is rumored that the underground passageways leading from the palace have been used to conduct secret trysts. Entrance is permitted only with a guide. *(Sofiyevskaya 5a (Софиевская). ☎23 82 72, tours 23 84 62. Open M and W-Su 10:30am-5:30pm; ticket office closes 5pm; closed last F of each month. Museum, icon room, and grotto each 2hv; Ukrainian students 1hv.)*

PUSHKIN MUSEUM AND MEMORIAL. This building was Pushkin's residence during his exile from St. Petersburg from 1823 to 1824. This unique museum (Литературно-мемориальный Музей Пушкина; Literaturno-memorialnyy Muzey Pushkina) displays his manuscripts and possessions, as well as portraits of his family. *(Pushkinskaya 13 (Пушкинская). Enter through the courtyard. ☎25 10 34, tours 22 74 53. Open M-Sa 10am-5pm. Last entry 4:30pm. 3.50hv, students 1.50hv. Tours in Russian 15hv, Ukrainian students 10hv. Tours in English; call ahead.)*

LITERATURE MUSEUM (ЛИТЕРАТУРНЫЙ МУЗЕЙ; LITERATURNYY MUZEY). Odessa prides itself on a strong literary heritage, and this museum provides an intriguing look at the city's intellectual and cultural heritage, with emphasis on writers Pushkin and Gogol. The collection includes the famous letter from the Odessan mayor to the tsar, requesting that Pushkin be expelled "for his own development," because he "is getting the notion into his head that he's a great writer." *(Lanzheronovskaya 2 (Ланжероновская). ☎22 00 02. Open Tu-Su 10am-5pm. 3.50hv per period, students 1.50hv. 10.50hv for all 3, students 4.50hv. Sculpture courtyard 3hv. Tour in English of all periods 75hv.)*

ARCHAEOLOGICAL MUSEUM. The museum (Археологический Музей; Arkheologicheskiy muzey) displays the world's largest collection of artifacts from the Northern Black Sea region as well as Ukraine's only Egyptian collection. *(Lanzheronovskaya 4 (Ланжероновская). ☎22 01 71 or 22 63 02. Open Tu-Su 10am-5pm. 5hv; students, children, and seniors 2hv. Call ahead to arrange a tour in English, 10hv per person.)*

BEACHES

Arkadiya (Аркадия), the city's largest and most popular beach, is the last stop on tram #5, which stops next to the McDonald's at the train station; *marshrutka* #195 also runs to the beach. The shoreline from Shevchenko Park up to Arkadiya is great for an early-morning jog. **Zolotoy Bereg** (Золотой Берег; Golden Shore) is farther from town, but boasts the most impressive beach. Take tram #18 or *marshrutka* #215 or 223 (runs May-Aug.) to the end. Tram #18 also goes to **Riviera** (Ривиера) and **Kurortnyy** (Курортный). Trams #17 and #18 head to **Chaika** (Чайка). Tram #5 stops at **Otrada** (Отрада), where you can avoid the numerous steep steps to the beach by riding the funicular (6hv). To get to **Lanzheron** (Ланжерон), the beach closest to central Odessa, cross Shevchenko Park or take *marshrutka* #253, 233, or 2MT. Some beaches are free, but others charge up to 15hv admission and offer beach chairs, umbrellas, and waiter service.

ENTERTAINMENT

Buy tickets for all shows in town at the **theater box office,** Preobrazhenskaya 28 (Преображенская). Same-day tickets are available until 2pm. (☎22 02 45. Open daily 10am-5pm.)

Theater of Opera and Ballet (Театр Оперы и Балета; Teatr Opery i Baleta), pr. Chaikovskogo 1 (Чайковского; ☎25 24 08), at the end of Rishelevskaya (Ришелевская). Famous, recently renovated 19th-century theater that hosts performances Tu-Su that begin at 6pm or 7pm. Tickets 10-50hv; check with the box office for the schedule. Open Tu-Su 10am-6pm.

Odessa Russian Drama Theater, Grecheskaya 48 (Греческая; ☎24 07 06). Several performances each week. Schedule is posted outside entrance. No shows in English. Shows start at 7pm. Tickets 5-20hv; 10hv tickets are the best value. Box office open daily noon-3pm and 4-7pm.

Philharmonic (Филармония; Filarmoniya), Bunina 15 (Бунина; ☎25 69 03 or 21 78 95; www.odessaphilharmonic.org), on the corner of Pushkinskaya (Пушкинская). The orchestra has won international acclaim for its concerts conducted by American Hobart Earle. Tickets 3-20hv. Box office open 10am-6pm on performance days.

NIGHTLIFE

From May to September, almost all the nightlife is at the beach clubs of **Arkadiya.** To get there, take tram #5 or *marshrutka* #195. After midnight, taxis are the only transportation back to town; a taxi back to the city center is about 25hv. Be prepared to bargain. The glitziest Arkadiya club is **Ibiza,** complete with fashion shows and professional dancers. Call three days ahead to reserve a table near the dance floor. (☎777 0205. Th-Sa live music or other performances 40-50hv. Cover M-W and Su 20hv. Women free before 11pm. Open daily noon-6am.) Not far from Ibiza, and less pretentious, is local favorite **Itaka,** which features live performances and a large dance floor in a faux Greek coloseum. (☎34 91 88. Cover 40-50hv. Open daily 10pm-6am.) Farther down the strip, student-oriented **Pago** offers a less glitzy atmosphere while still blasting standard Russian pop music. (☎715 3830. Cover 35hv. Women only W 9pm-midnight. Cover M-Th and Su 15hv; students M-Th 10hv; F-Sa 25hv. Open daily 9pm-6am.) For house, trance, and big-name DJs from Moscow and London, check out **Stereo.** (☎32 24 23. Cover M-Th and Su 20-30hv; F-Sa 30-40hv. Open daily 10pm-6am.) If you want to stay in town, start your night with folk music at **Gambrinus** (Гамбринус), Deribasovskaya 31 (Дерибасовская), at the corner of Zhukova. (Жукова; ☎26 36 57. Beer 6-38hv. Live folk music M and Th-Su 6-10pm. Tu-W live modern music. Open daily 10am-midnight.)

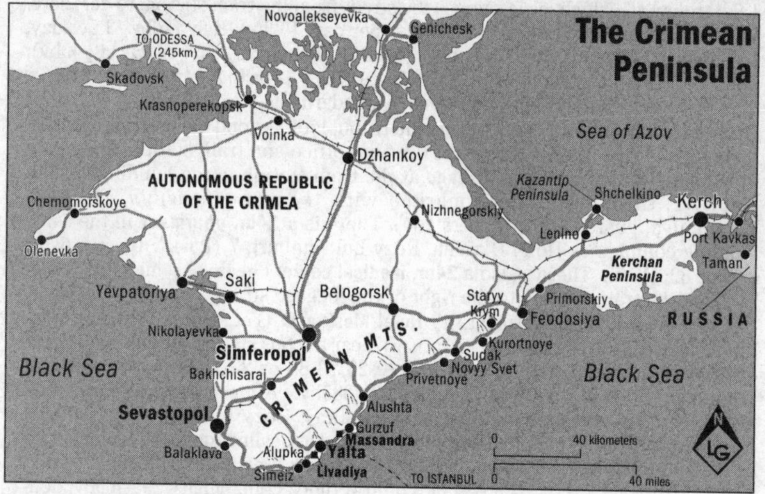

CRIMEA (КРЫМ)

An important trading thoroughfare on the Black Sea Coast, the Crimean peninsula has a 2500-year history of Greek, Turkish, Mongol, and Russian rule. Though bequeathed to Ukraine in 1991, it is autonomously governed and Russian at heart—Crimeans are Russian-speaking, call Ukrainian currency "rubles," and feel closer to Moscow than Kyiv. Striking natural beauty and beaches attract hordes of vacationers, who make hotel rooms scarce and drive up prices in summer. It is best to visit in September, when the crowds have left but the sea is still warm.

PHONE CALLS. Crimea is an autonomous republic within Ukraine, and its phone system mirrors the political situation. Dialing from one Crimean town to another requires special Crimean area codes; the area codes listed in *Let's Go* for each Crimean town work only when calling from outside the peninsula. The intra-Crimean area codes (all preceded by 8) are: Simferopol 22, Bakhchisarai 254, Feodosiya 262, Kerch 261, Yalta 24, Sevastopol 0692.

SIMFEROPOL (СІМФЕРОПОЛЬ) ☎(80)652

Simferopol is the capital of the Autonomous Republic of Crimea and the transport hub of the peninsula. Most trains pass through en route to coastal destinations. The **train station** (вокзал; vokzal) at Vokzalnaya pl. (Вокзальная; ☎005), sends trains to: Kyiv (15hr., 9 per day, 78-120hv); Lviv (27 hr., 2 per day, 88-130hv); Odessa (13hr., 1 per day, 51-73hv); Moscow, Russia (24hr., 7 per day, 245-456hv); and St. Petersburg (31hr., 3 per day, 261-493hv). The **information desk** charges 1hv per question. Tickets for the **elektrichka** (Елекричка; commuter rail) are sold behind the main station at the window marked "пригородный кассы" (*prigorodnyy kassy*). These head to Sevastopol (2-2½hr., 7 per day, 3.10hv) via Bakhchisarai (1hr., 2.30hv). **Buses** and **marshrutki** to various Crimean destinations leave from the square next to the McDonald's. Buses (☎27 34 30) run to: Sevastopol (2hr., 3-4 per hr., 18hv); and Yalta (2hr., 4-5 per hr., 21hv). The 2-3hr. **trolley** #52 ride to Yalta, the longest trolley bus route in the world, costs 10hv. Buses to more distant destinations leave from the central station, across town at Kiyevskaya 4 (Киевская).

Take trolley #6, which leaves across the street from the train station, to get there. Destinations include: Chernivtsi (22hr., 1 per day, 150hv); Kyiv (16hr., 3 per day, 130-136hv); Odessa (12hr., 8 per day, 75-80hv); Yalta (2hr., 15 per day, 12-40hv); Rostov-na-Donu, Russia (13½hr., 2 per day, 107hv). *Marshrutki* are usually faster than buses but charge 5-20hv more than a standard bus.

Currency exchange offices are everywhere, but look beyond the train and bus stations for the best rates. **ATMs** are at the post office and train station, and along Pushkina (Пушкина). **Store luggage** at the train station in the building next to track #1, through the door marked with "камера хранения" (kamera khraneniya; guarded 5hv, lockers 4hv). There is a **24hr. pharmacy** in the same building complex as Hotel Ukraina, Rozy Luksemburg 7 (Розы Луксемкбург; ☎54 56 82; MC/V). There's also a **24hr. medical center** (медпункт; medpunkt; ☎24 21 03) at the train station, to the right of the luggage storage room.

If you need to stay overnight, try **Hotel Moskva** ❸ (Гостиница Москва; Gostinitsa Moskva), Kiyevskaya 2 (Киевская), near the bus station. Rooms have modern bathrooms and simple furniture. (☎23 73 89 or 23 75 20; www.moskva-hotel.com. Singles 200-260hv; doubles 295-385hv.) A nicer place to stay is the newly renovated **Hotel Ukraina** ❹ (Украина), Rozy Luksemburg 7 (Розы Луксемкбург). It has a more central location and appealing rooms, complemented by a grand lobby decked out in dark oranges, forest green, and gold gilding. (☎55 12 44 or 51 01 65; fax 27 84 95; jscukrcomp@crimea.com. Singles 295-460hv; doubles 390-520hv. The **Istanbul Restaurant and Cafe** ❷, Gorikoho 5 (Горикого), is visited primarily by Simferopol's Turkish community, and serves up delicious kebabs, lamb dishes, and baklava (5hv), as well as a popular milk cocktail. (☎52 78 62. Entrees 15-30hv. Open 8am-10pm.) The cafe **Piroga** ❶ (Пирога), Pushkina 4 (Пушкина), specializes in *piroga*, flaky calzones stuffed with meats, vegetables, and cheeses. (Salads 4-6hv. Entrees 7.50-20hv. Open daily 8am-11pm.)

YALTA (ЯЛТА) ☎(8)0654

Yalta is beautiful, crowded, and expensive. Nestled between the arid mountains of the Crimean heartland and the sparkling waters of the Black Sea, the city serves as a playground for the Russian and Ukrainian elite. Tsar Nicholas II summered here, and writers Anton Chekhov and Lesya Ukrainka called Yalta home. In 1945, Yalta's Livadiya Palace hosted the conference at which Churchill, Roosevelt, and Stalin decided the fate of postwar Europe. The only damper to Yalta's enormous appeal is the hordes of wealthy vacationers that flock to the city during July and August, and the high prices they bring with them. Come in the fall or spring, though, and you'll see why Yalta is one of Ukraine's most beloved vacation spots.

TRANSPORTATION

Trains: Yalta is **not accessible by train** but has an Advance Booking office, Ignatenko 14 (Игнатенко; ☎32 43 47), where you can get tickets to depart from **Sevastopol** or **Simferopol.** Purchase tickets in advance (3 week min. in summer). From pl. Lenina (Ленина), walk up Ignatenko and look for the "Железнодорожные Кассы" ("Zheleznodorozhnyye Kassy") sign. Open daily 8am-8pm.

Buses: On Moskovskaya (Московская; ☎34 20 72). To: **Bakhchisarai** (2½hr., 5 per day, 23hv); **Kyiv** (18hr., 1 per day, 110-150hv); **Odessa** (13hr., 2 per day, 88hv); **Sevastopol** (2hr., 2-3 per hr. 7am-9pm, 22hv); **Simferopol** (2hr., 2-6 per hr., 15-22hv). The Yalta **trolleybus** travels to **Simferopol** (2½-3hr., every 20min., 10hv) at dependably slow speeds. The trolleybus station is across from the bus station. **Intourist, LTD.** arranges bus trips to Kyiv during summer.

Ferries: Buy tickets at the waterfront, in front of the docks labeled #7 and 8 (☎32 42 74). To: **Alupka** (1¼hr., July-Aug. 15 per day, 35-40hv) via **Livadiya** (15min., 5-10hv) and **Lastochkino Gnezdo** (45min., 15-20hv). Ferry tickets to **İstanbul, TUR** from **Sevastopol** (33hr.; 1 per week; 1000-1500hv) and **Yalta** (37hr., 1 per week, US$200-250) are available in the main hall of the sea terminal on the left hand side at the window marked "Предприятие Морское" (predpriyatiye morskoye), Ruzvelta 5 (Рузвельта; ☎23 03 02). Open daily noon-3pm.

Public Transportation: Buses and **trolleys** run throughout the city (0.50-0.75hv). Trolley #1 covers most of the central area; it travels from the bus station to pl. Sovetskaya (Советская). From the stop "Kinoteatr Spartak," bus #8 goes to Polyana Skazok and Chekhov's house; bus #24 goes from Chekhov's house to Polyana Skazok. Private **marshrutki** depart from the square at the corner of Moskovskaya (Московская) and Karla Marksa (Карла Маркса). They run the same routes as buses, are faster, and make fewer stops, but cost 0.50-5hv more.

ORIENTATION AND PRACTICAL INFORMATION

Yalta's main drag is the pedestrian **naberezhnaya Lenina** (Ленина), which runs along the Black Sea waterfront (naberezhnaya; Набережная) from **ploshchad Lenina.** From the bus and trolley stations, take trolley #1 toward the center. It runs down Moskovskaya (Московская) past the circus and market to **ploshchad Sovetskaya** (Советская), where Moskovskaya converges with **Klyevskaya** (Киевская). You can get off there and walk two blocks to **ploshchad Lenina.** There, nab. Lenina begins to the right, while a left turn leads to the **Old Quarter.** At the other end of nab. Lenina, both pedestrian **Pushkinskaya** (Пушкинская) and parallel **Gogolya** (Гоголя) run inland to **Kinoteatr Spartak.** Trolley #1 and many *marshrutki* stop there.

Tourist Offices: There are tourist companies with kiosks along the boardwalk that offer excursions around Crimea. Prices and destinations are listed on signs, though many vendors do not speak English. **Intourist, LTD.,** Ruzvelta 5 (Рузвельта; ☎32 76 04; intour@yalta.crimea.ua), beside the sea terminal. Books hotel rooms, arranges tours, offers visa support, provides interpreters, and runs luxury buses to Kyiv in the summer. Open M-F 10am-5pm. **Intourist,** Drazhinskogo 50 (Дражинского; ☎27 01 32; fax 35 30 93), in Hotel Yalta, uphill from Hotel Massandra. Books flights and organizes excursions with English-speaking guides. Open daily 8am-7pm. MC/V.

Currency Exchange: Exchange booths and banks are everywhere, but bad rates make it better to exchange money before arriving in Yalta. **Ukreksimbank** (Укрексимбанк), Moskovskaya 31a (Московская; ☎32 79 35), left of the Tsirk (Цирк; Circus) stop. Cashes **traveler's checks** for 2% commission. Open M-Th 9am-1pm and 2-3pm, F 9am-1pm. **Avalbank** (☎32 03 35), in the central post office (see below), offers **Western Union** services, gives MC/V **cash advances** for 2.5% commission, and cashes **traveler's checks** for 2% commission. Open M-Sa 9am-1pm and 2-6pm; Su 9am-1pm and 2-4pm.

ATMs: At the bus station, the post office (see below), and along nab. Lenina.

Luggage Storage: At the bus station. Look for "Камера-Хранения" (Kamera-Khraneniya) at the bottom of the stairs, in back of the building. 3hv per day. Open daily 8am-7pm.

Pharmacy: Apteka #26, Botkinskaya 1 (Боткинская; ☎32 30 42). From nab. Lenina (Ленина), walk up Pushkinskaya (Пушкинская) and turn right. Open 8am-8pm.

Telephones: Ukrtelecom, Moskovskaya 9 (Московская; ☎32 43 02). One block down the unmarked street, across from the market. Internet 3hv per hr. Open 24hr. **Fax** available 9am-5pm.

Internet: Ukrtelecom has relatively fast connections and cheap prices in a central location. 3hv per hr. Open daily 24hr. For smaller crowds, try **Internet Center,** Yekaterinskaya 3 (Екатеринская; ☎32 30 72). From nab. Lenina, go up Yekaterininskaya, descend steps marked with a sign to the right, and cross courtyard. Slower connections than Ukrtelecom, but less crowded. 4.50hv per hr. Open 24hr.

Post Office: Pl. Lenina (Ленина). **Poste Restante** (Востребования; Vostrebovaniya) at window #4. Open M-F 8am-7pm, Sa 8am-6pm, Su 9am-4pm. **Postal Code:** 98600.

ACCOMMODATIONS

If you plan to stay in a hotel in Yalta during July or August, reserve in advance and be prepared to pay a hefty price. Without a reservation, you may have to negotiate with bus station middlemen for **private rooms ❶** (25-50hv per person). Those who speak Russian or like playing charades can go straight to the *babushki* hawking rooms behind the bus station or along Drazhinskogo (Дражинсково; 25-50hv). During other seasons, hotels are much cheaper, and availability is not a problem.

Pension T.M.M., Lesi Ukrainki 16 (Леси Украинки; ☎/fax 23 09 50; www.firmatmm.ua). From the bus station, take trolley #1 to Sadovaya (Садовая). Backtrack a few steps to a sign pointing toward the pension, uphill to the left. Take the 1st left going uphill, then turn right at the end of the road. The entrance is in an unmarked black fence on the left.

Peaceful, stately pension with views of the sea and its own courtyard with a private swimming pool, outdoor bar, and Russian bath. The airy rooms have balconies, TVs, and private showers. Includes 3 meals per day. Doubles 350-572hv. ❺

Hotel Massandra (Массандра), Drazhinskogo 46 (Дражинсково; ☎27 24 27; fax 27 24 01). Near the beach and a 20min. walk from the town center. Go up Drazhinskogo and left at Avalon Cafe (Авалон) or take *marshrutka* #34 up the hill. Expensive but comfortable, this hotel has comfy rooms with private baths, TVs, and fridges. Doubles June-Oct. 300-600hv; Nov.-May 150-350hv. ❹

FOOD

Most of the cafes and restaurants on and near nab. Lenina (Ленина) are expensive, especially in the summer. Brightly decorated **cafeterias** (столовая; stolovaya) in the city center offer a cheap, quick alternative (10-20hv), though they are often crowded at lunch and have few selections at dinner. **Gastronom** (Гастроном), the grocery store at nab. Lenina 15, sells cheap, fresh bread. The **open-air market,** opposite the circus, has a large selection of fruits and vegetables. To get there, take trolley #1, or walk up Moskovskaya. (Open daily 8am-7pm.)

MENU MIXUPS. Read menus carefully: some places sneak in large surcharges for service and live music or list very expensive wines with names similar to cheaper counterparts.

Cafe Voskhod (Восход), Ignatenko 2 (Игнатенко; ☎23 39 43), near pl. Sovetskaya. (Советская) Turkish dishes, plus some Russian and European cuisine. Try the fresh perch (*sudak;* 25-40hv), or meat dishes (23-27hv), grilled in the dining room. The cafe also has A/C, which is nice in the summer. Entrees 15-45hv. Open June-Sept. 24hr.; Oct.-May daily 9am-midnight. Cash only. ❷

Stolovaya Krym (Столовая), Moskovskaya 1/6 (Московская), next to Gostinitsa Krym. One of Yalta's best self-service cafeterias, serving classic Russian lunch food. The solyanka (meat soup; 5hv) is phenomenal. Entrees 4.50-12hv. Open daily 7am-9pm. Cash only. ❶

SIGHTS

Most of Yalta's impressive sights are outside town. The best way to see the main attractions is to spread them out over three days: one day for the museums and beaches in town; one day for Massandra and the Nikitskiy Botanical Garden, and one day for Livadiya, Swallow's Nest, and Alupka. Absolute must-see sights are the Chekhov House-Museum, the Livadiya palace, and the Massandra winery.

ANTON CHEKHOV HOUSE-MUSEUM. The Russian writer Anton Chekhov lived in Yalta for the final five years of his life. In 1899, he built a house (known as the "white dacha") on a hill overlooking the water. Nearly two decades after his 1904 death from tuberculosis, his sister made the house a museum (Дом Музей А. П. Чехова; Dom Muzey A. P. Chekhova). A modern building displays photo, letters, and manuscripts, as well as the desk at which Chekhov wrote *Three Sisters*, *The Cherry Orchard*, and *Lady with a Lapdog*. Chekhov's **garden** represents "eternal spring"—at any time of year, some plants remain in bloom. The house retains its original furnishings. *(Kirova 112 (Кирова). From the center, take* marshrutka *#8 from Kinoteatr Spartak at the end of Pushkinskaya (Пушкинская). Alternatively, take trolley #1 to Pionerskaya (Пионерская), cross the street, turn left and go down past the two bridges, then turn right* *onto per. Krainiy (Крайний). Go up the steps and turn left on Kirova (Кирова); #112 is on the left. ☎39 49 47. Open June-Sept. Tu-Su 10am-5:15pm; Oct.-May W-Su 10am-4pm; closed last day of each month. 2015hv, students 107hv. English booklet 12hv, English brochure 4hv.)*

OTHER SIGHTS. For a great view of the city, take the **chairlift** (канатная дорога; kanatnaya doroga) up to **Olymp**, a hilltop mock-Greek temple. The lift starts just up from nab. Lenina, to the right of the Gastronom. *(☎32 81 62. Open daily June-Sept. 10am-8pm; Oct.-May 10am-4pm. 14hv, students 7hv.)* The **Museum of Lesya Ukrainka** (Дом-Музей Леси Украинки; Dom-Myzey Lesi Ukrainki), Yekaterinskaya 8 (Екатеринская), honors the famous Ukrainian writer, who lived here briefly in 1897. *(☎32 55 25. Open June-Aug. Tu-Su 11am-7pm; Sept.-May W-Su 10am-5pm. 5hv, students 3hv. Some English spoken.)* The **Yalta Cultural Museum,** in the same building, highlights aspects of local life from the 19th and 20th centuries. The entrance is to the left as you enter. *(Open Sept.-May Tu-Su 11am-6pm. 3hv.)* From June to August, special exhibits take over the Cultural Museum's space. *(☎32 16 34. No English captions. Open daily June-Aug. 11am-6:30pm. 5hv, students 3hv.)*

ENTERTAINMENT AND NIGHTLIFE

Yalta's many **beaches** stretch from both sides of the harbor. (Entrance to most city beaches 2hv, commercial beaches 2-5hv.) Many are crowded and lack sand. There are amusement park rides on nab. Lenina (10-12hv). **Organ concerts** are held in the Roman Catholic church, Pushkinskaya 25 (Пушкинская). (☎23 00 65. July-Sept. M-Su 8pm; Oct. and May-June M-Sa 7:30pm, Su 5pm. Buy tickets on-site.) Enjoy free music and dancing on pl. Lenina in front of the Lenin monument, or walk down nab. Lenina to **Primorskiy beach,** where there are a number of affordable outdoor bars (beer 2-5hv). Capitalizing on Yalta's popularity with wealthy Russians and Ukrainians, glitzy nightclub **Tornado,** nab. Lenina 11, up the stairs through the arch and to the left, features expensive drinks along with house music, nightly laser shows, and a lively clientele. (☎32 20 36. Beer 15hv. Cover 50-100hv. Open June-Sept. daily 10pm-5am; Oct.-Nov. Th-Sa 10pm-5am; Dec.-May F-Sa 10pm-5am.)

DAYTRIPS FROM YALTA

LIVADIYA (ЛІВАДИЯ). The **Great Livadiya Palace,** built in 1911 as a summer residence for Tsar Nicholas II, is famous for hosting the **Yalta Conference** at the end of WWII. At this historic meeting, Winston Churchill, Franklin Roosevelt, and Josef Stalin negotiated post-war claims. The historical exhibits are fascinating and have English captions, salvaging the otherwise unexciting palace. On the first floor is the **White Hall,** where the talks took place. The round table at which the three leaders sat is just outside the hall. The **billiard room,** where the final agreement was signed, looks out onto the **Italian courtyard,** where the famous photo of the "Big Three" was taken. The 2nd floor of the palace houses the **Nicholas II Museum,** which displays the imperial family's living quarters, photographs, and possessions. *(Take bus or marshrutki #11 or 45 from the bus station or from "Kinoteatr Spartak." Bus #13 (1hv) also leaves from "Spartak." Ferries (15min., 1-2 per hr., 10hv) stop at the dock; from there, hike 150m up the hill. Alternatively, a 1hr. hike along the beach from Yalta will get you to Livadiya. Palace ☎31 55 81. Open Apr.-Oct. 13 M-Tu and Th-Su 10am-5pm; Nov.-Mar. 13 Tu and Th-Su 10am-5pm. 20hv, students 10hv. Photography 5hv. English booklet 10hv.)*

MASSANDRA (МАССАНДРА). Founded in 1894, the **Massandra Winery** holds in its cellars one of the largest wine collections in the world—about one million bottles, including a rare 1775 "Jerez de la Frontera" vintage. Much of the collection was hidden under floorboards during WWI, and thousands of bottles were shipped abroad during WWII; thanks to this foresight, much of the collection escaped the German pillagers. Guided tours and tastings are available, and there's a store inside. *(Vinodela Egorova 9 (Винодела Егорова). From Yalta, take* marshrutka *#40 from the downtown station, by the clothing market, to Vinzavod (Винзавод). ☎23 26 62 or 35 27 95. 1hr. tours daily every 2hr. starting at 11am; last tour May-Oct. 7pm, Nov.-Apr. 5pm. Tour 25hv, with wine tasting 55hv, with wine tasting and cellar admission 90hv. Wine tasting only 30hv.)* Overlooking Yalta from atop the hill, the elegant **Massandra Palace** has a past that traces many major historical developments in Crimea. The building served as the tsars' palace until 1920, and later became a base for the Crimean cadet corps, a tuberculosis sanatorium, a German officers' hospital, a Soviet hospital, Stalin's summer residence, and a favorite vacation spot for Soviet officials. The palace was opened to the public as a museum in 1992. *(Take trolley #2 or 3, or* marshrutka *#24 from Yalta, cross the street, and take the road uphill until you see the "Дворец" sign and arrow on the street pointing to a forest path on the left. The path is poorly marked—when in doubt head up and left. ☎32 17 28. Open July-Aug. Tu-Su 9am-6pm; Sept.-Oct. and May-June Tu-Su 9am-5pm, Nov.-Apr. W-Su 9am-4pm. 20hv, students 10hv. English booklet 15hv.)*

NIKITSKIY BOTANICAL GARDEN (НИКИТСКИЙ САД; NIKITSKIY SAD). Founded in 1812, the Nikitskiy Botanical Garden has over 15,000 species of native and foreign flora, including 1000 varieties of roses and many kinds of trees from around the world. A walking path runs between the upper and lower entrances to the garden; follow the blue signs if you're going up, or the green signs if you're going down. Below the lower entrance is a **cactus orangerie,** with a greenhouse and a garden. A stand in the garden sells cacti—pretty, but hard to pack. *(From Yalta, take bus #24 (every 20min.) to the gardens' entrance. It also stops at Massandra. ☎33 55 28. Open daily June-Aug. 8am-8pm; Sept.-May 9am-4pm. 10hv, students 5hv. Cactus orangerie 1hv.)*

ALUPKA (АЛУПКА). The village of Alupka is the site of the **Vorontsov Palace** (Воронцовский Дворец; Vorontsovskiy Dvorets), whose grand stone walls make it an anomaly among Yalta's palaces. The palace has the grandeur and elegance of its English architects' native castles; Winston Churchill remarked that he felt at home when staying here during the Yalta Conference. The interior includes a majestic entrance hall and an indoor winter garden with a fountain and rare plants. The palace **gardens** extend down toward the sea. *(In summer, take a ferry, 1¼hr., 15 per day, 20hv, or* marshrutka *#27, every 20-60min., 3hv, from Yalta. Or the ferry from Livadiya. 9hv. Palace ☎72 22 81 or 72 29 51. Open July-Aug. daily 8am-7:30pm; Sept. to mid-Nov. and Apr.-June daily 9am-5pm; mid-Nov. to Mar. Tu-Su 9am-4pm. 20hv, students and children 10hv. During summer, lines are long but thankfully shaded.)*

AI-PETRI (АЙ-ПЕТРИ). For a great view of the area, go to the nearby village of Miskhor and take the **cable car** (канатная дорога; kanatnaya doroga) 1234m up to the top of **Ay-Petri Mountain** (Ай-Петри). On the way up, get off at the Uchan-Su stop; you will find a viewing platform where you can look at Europe's tallest waterfall. The easiest way to get back from Miskhor is by the ferry from Alupka. To get to Alupka, walk 1km down the coast, and turn right at the castle. Alternatively, you can take a *marshrutka* to Yalta from the top of Ai-Petri. *(Miskhor (Мисхор) cable car ☎72 28 94. Runs every 10min. daily May-Sept. 9am-6pm; Oct.-Apr. 10am-5pm. 16hv. Ferries to Alupka depart Yalta harbor at dock #7. 1hr., 1-2per hr., 40hv. Bus #30 departs from Yalta's main bus station and goes up Ay-Petri, stopping at Uchan-Su waterfall along the way. 3hv.)*

SWALLOW'S NEST. On the coast between Yalta and Alupka is Swallow's Nest (Ласточкино Гнездо; Lastochkino Gnezdo), a popular symbol of the Crimea.

Built for a German businessman in 1912, the cliffside castle is now one of the peninsula's most-photographed sites. Though impressive in pictures and from the water, the castle is far less so at ground level. Today, it functions as an expensive Italian restaurant; those not eating at the restaurant would be best off staying on the ferry and heading back to Yalta or on to Alupka. *(Ferry leaves every 30min. from dock #7 in Yalta harbor; last ferry 7pm. 20hv.)*

SEVASTOPOL (СЕВАСТОПОЛЬ) ☎(80)692

While other Crimean cities have been tourist havens for centuries, Sevastopol (pop. 400,000) has remained hidden, tucked away because of its importance to Russia's Black Sea Fleet. Until the collapse of the Soviet Union, tourists were not permitted to enter Sevastopol. While this prohibition prevented the city from developing a tourist infrastructure, it also preserved Sevastopol's natural beauty and relaxed vibe. Unlike other Crimean port cities, Sevastopol remains refreshingly untouristed, and its large harbor and fresh air make it a pleasant locale for a quieter, historically captivating glimpse of the region.

TRANSPORTATION

Trains: Privokzalnaya pl. 3 (Привокзальная; ☎54 30 77 or 48 79 26). Purchase tickets for non-Crimean destinations several weeks in advance for travel during July and Aug. Advance ticket office across the street from the bus station. Open M-F 7am-6pm; Sa-Su, holidays, and the last day of the month 7:30am-5pm. To: **Kyiv** (18hr., 3 per day, 81-120hv); **Moscow, RUS** (27hr., 3 per day, 248-426hv); and **St. Petersburg, RUS** (35hr., 2 per day, 327-524hv). All Crimean *elektrichki* (commuter rail) connect through **Simferopol** (2-2½hr., 7 per day, 3.10hv). Tickets are sold to the right of the train station. All trolleys at the train station go to the center; #17 and 20 run to the very start of Bolshaya Morskaya (Большая Морская); all others head to pl. Lazaryova (Лазарева; 0.75hv). The trolleybus stop is on the hill above the train station; to get to it, take the bridge that crosses over the train tracks. For a **taxi,** call ☎050.

Buses: Pl. Revyakina 2 (Ревякина; ☎48 81 99). Open daily 6am-9pm. Luggage fee 0.50-8hv. To: **Bakhchisarai** (1hr., 2 per hr. 7am-8pm, 6-7hv); **Feodosiya** (4½hr., 3 per day, 23-35hv); **Kerch** (7½hr., 2 per day, 35-52hv); **Odessa** (13½hr., 1 per day, 68-95hv); **Simferopol** (2hr., over 30 per day, 15-23hv); **Yalta** (1½hr., 1-3 per hr., 12-16hv) via **Alupka; Krasnodar, RUS** (15hr., 1 per day, 100hv); **Rostov-na-Donu, RUS** (18½hr., 2 per day, 84hv).

Ferries: Leave from Artilleriyskaya Bay behind Gostinitsa Sevastopol and from Grafskaya Pristan (Графская Пристань) for the **north shore** (Северная Сторона; Severnaya Storona), landing near pl. Zakharova (Захарова; 20min., 1 per hr., 2hv).

Public Transportation: Less crowded **marshrutki** (1hv) run the same routes as **buses** (0.60hv). *Marshrutki* leave from pl. Zakharova (Захарова) to popular Uchkuyuvka Beach (Үчкуювка). Trolleys (0.75hv; pay on board) are efficient and convenient. #12 runs up Bolshaya Morskaya (Болшая Морская). #17 and 9 circle the center, stopping at the train station. #5 goes up Admirala Oktyabrskogo (Адмирала Октябрского) to the west of the peninsula.

ORIENTATION AND PRACTICAL INFORMATION

The town center is on a peninsula below the Sevastopol harbor. **Pl. Lazaryova** (Лазарёва), up the street from Gostinitsa Sevastopol (p. 755), is a good starting point for exploring the city center. **Generala Petrova** (Генерала Петрова) delves inland, while **prospekt Nakhimova** (Нахимова) curves from here along the peninsula, where it meets **Lenina** (Ленина) at pl. Nakhimova. Lenina runs parallel to the sea until **ploschad Ushakova** (Ушакова). **Bolshaya Morskaya** (Ђольшая Морская) runs back to pl. Lazaryova. Vendors sell **maps** (8-15hv) along nab. Kornilova (Корнилова) and Primorskiy bul. (Приморский).

Tourist Offices: Kiosks along Primorskiy bul. offer city tours (50-80hv). Those near pl. Nakhimova advertise boat tours of the harbor (30min., 20hv).

Currency Exchange: Exchange booths are everywhere. **Oshchadbank** (Ощадбанк; ☎54 12 16), at Bolshaya Morskaya 41 (Большая Морская), cashes AmEx/Thomas Cooke **traveler's checks** and gives MC/V **cash advances,** all for 1.5% commission. **Western Union** services are available here and at the **post office** (see below). Open M-F 8am-1pm and 2-6pm, Sa 8am-4pm.

Luggage Storage: At the bus station, to the right of the main building, next to the cafe. 5-6hv. Open daily 6am-9pm.

Pharmacy: There are pharmacies all over Sevastopol. Try the Apteka (Аптека) at Bolshaya Morskaya 48 (Болшая Морская; ☎54 30 26 or 55 41 75). English "pharmacy" sign. Large selection. Open 24hr.; closed 2nd W of each month. MC/V.

Telephones: There's a telephone office (☎54 55 17; stelecom@stel.sebastopol.ua) to the left of the post office. Open 24hr.

Internet: Absolutnaya Realnost (Абсолутная Реалность; ☎54 40 79), on Bolshaya Morskaya on the 2nd fl. of Kinoteatr Pobeda (Кинотеатр Победа). Go inside the theater's main entrance and up the stairs on the left. 5hv per hr. Open 24hr. **Alpha Club** (☎55 93 09), on the first floor of Hotel Krym. 6hv per hr. Open 24hr.

Post Office: Bolshaya Morskaya 21 (Большая Морская). **Western Union.** Open June-Aug. M-F 8am-7pm, Sa-Su 8am-6pm; Sept.-May M-F 8am-6pm, Sa-Su 8am-5pm. There's also an Internet Cafe in the back room (☎54 59 76; 4.60hv per hr., same hours as post office). **Postal Code:** 99011.

ACCOMMODATIONS AND FOOD

Private rooms and short-term **apartments** are inexpensive and easy to arrange in summer. A desk at the entrance of the bus station sets up accommodations for a 25hv fee. Rooms fill quickly in July and August; the safest option is to reserve well in advance. Elegant Greek columns flank the entrance to **Gostinitsa Sevastopol ❷,** pr. Nakhimova 8 (Нахимова), near the center. Cheaper rooms have shared bathrooms (and hot water), but the central location—steps from the water and right off of trolley routes #1, 3, 7, and 9—is ideal. Many rooms have sea views, and the lobby is downright grand. (☎46 64 00; fax 46 64 09. Hot showers 2.50hv. Singles 80-350hv; doubles 140-350hv; triples 210hv. MC/V.) **Gostinitsa Krym ❸** (Крым), Shestaya Bastionnaya 46 (Шестая Бастионная), is up Admirala Oktyabrskogo (Адмирала Октябрского) from Bolshaya Morskaya (Ђольшая Морская), near pl. Vosstavshikh (Восставших). To get there, take trolley #5, 6, or 10, or hop on any 100-numbered *marshrutka* from the train or bus station. From Bolshaya Morksaya, turn right on Admirala Oktyabrskoga and continue straight until the traffic circle. The hotel is off to the right. All rooms have balconies and private baths; many have sea views. (☎46 90 00 or 55 51 51. Breakfast included. Hot water 7-9am and 7-9pm. Singles 195-340hv; doubles 165-235hv per person.)

The **central market** is downhill from pl. Lazaryova (Лазарёва) at the intersection of Partizanskaya (Партизанская) and Odesskaya (Одесская; open Tu-Su

8pm). A local favorite is **Traktir** ❶ (Трактир), Bolshaya Morskaya 8 (Большая Морская). Waitresses in sailor uniforms serve excellent Ukrainian food and drinks in large portions, including wonderful *solyanka* (meat soup; small 13hv, large 20hv) and *kulebyaka* (pie with meat and cabbage; 14hv). The outdoor terrace is pleasant in summer. (☎54 47 60. English menu. Entrees 15-45hv. Open daily 10am-10pm.) **Pobeda** ❶ (Победа), Divozovskogo 1 (Дивоэовского). Fifties diner chic meets the Soviet Union in this small, brightly colored cafe. Old photographs, cameras, and traffic signs from Ukraine's fifties decorate the walls, while customers sit on fluffy red booths, enjoying hearty diner fare of omelets and *vareniki*. (Salads 2-8hv. Entrees 5-20hv. Open daily 9am-11pm.)

SIGHTS AND ENTERTAINMENT

PANORAMA DEFENSE OF SEVASTOPOL 1854-1855. One of the most impressive sights in Ukraine, the panorama (Панорама Оборона Севастопола; Panorama Oborona Sevastopola) was built in 1905 to commemorate the heroic defense of the city during the Crimean War against Britain and France. Though destroyed during WWII, it was recreated by a team of Moscow artists and reopened in 1954. The display artfully blends a painted backdrop with a realistic 3D foreground. The 360° canvas is 14m high and 115m in circumference. English captions. *(Enter the park at pl. Ushakova (Ушакова) and continue to the end of Istoricheskiy bul. (Исторический). It's the round building, opposite the fountain. ☎49 97 38. Open July-Sept. daily 9:30am-7pm; Oct.-Apr. Tu-Su 9:30am-6pm; May-June daily 9:30am-6pm; ticket office closes 30min. earlier. 20hv, students 10hv. Tours in English 30hv.)*

RUINS AT CHERSONESUS. The austere, beautiful ruins at Chersonesus (Херсонес; Khersones) are 2500 years old. They include an ancient amphitheater, acres of overgrown foundation, and the remains of several basilicas. In the middle stands the modern **St. Vladimir's Cathedral** (Владимирский Собор; Vladimirskiy Sobor), built in the late 19th century and rebuilt in 2001. *(Take minibus #22, labeled "Херсонес"; 1.50hv. ☎24 13 01. Open daily June-Aug. 8am-8pm; Sept.-May 9am-5pm. 10hv, students 5hv. Tour in English 20hv. Tour in Russian 15/10hv.)*

MUSEUM OF THE BLACK SEA FLEET. Russia's Black Sea Fleet has had an enormous impact on Sevastopol, from the Crimean war—during which the city lost an enormous percentage of its population—to the USSR's prohibition of visitors to the city. This museum (Музей Чёрноморского Флота; Muzey Chyornomorskogo Flota) tells the military history of the Black Sea with documents, models, and original weapons. The lower floor displays maps and items recovered from ships. The upper floor has Soviet flags and decorated uniforms. *(ul. Lenina 11 (Ленина). ☎54 22 89 or 54 03 92. Open W-Su 10am-6pm; kassa open 10am-5:30pm; closed last F of each month. Russian captions only. 7hv, students 4hv. Tours in English 12hv, min. 10 people.)*

OTHER SIGHTS. Impressive monuments to Sevastopol's naval heroes decorate the streets and the harbor. In the bay near pl. Nakhimova (Нахимова) is a **monument** to sunken ships: during the Crimean War, the Black Sea Fleet sunk many of its own ships to prevent the enemy from entering the bay. The **obelisk** that marks Sevastopol as a Soviet Hero City is visible from nab. Kornilova (Корнилова); the nearby **Monument to the Black Sea Submariners** can also be seen from there. **Park Pobediy** (Парк Победий) at **Omega Beach** (Пляж Омега; Plyazh Omega) is constantly packed during summer; its bars and discos don't stop until dawn. *(Take trolley #10 to the Plyazh Omega stop.)*

DAYTRIPS FROM SEVASTOPOL

CHUFUT-KALE (ЧУЯУТ-КАЛЕ). Tucked away in the back of dusty Bakhchisarai, Chufut-Kale is a budget traveler's dream. A 1.5km path leads through a valley and past the **Uspenksiy Monastery** (Успенский Монастырь), whose small church is built into the side of the cliff. (Women must cover their shoulders and wear a headscarf to enter.) However, the real treasure is the immense **cave city** built into the top of the plateau. Though a stone path connects both of Chufut-Kale's gates, trails and staircases into multi-level caves branch off of the main path, and Chufut-Kale's sparse landscape and flat plateaus makes getting lost difficult and exploring easy. All sides of the plateau offer stunning, wide views of the valley below and the hills beyond. *(Trains go to Bakhchisarai from Sevastopol. 2hv.* Marshrutki *and buses make the trip for 5-10hv. Buses and* marshrutki *stop at the train station; from there, take a 7-10hv taxi ride or a 1-2hv* marshrutka *to the entrance. From the entrance, continue along the obvious, asphalt path until you reach the Uspenskiy Monastery. 500km, 10min. At the monastery, continue straight along the path as it goes downhill. Stay on the main wide path as it becomes rocky and unpaved, passing a small cemetery on the left, and eventually turning left after a walled, fenced-in path to another cemetery. At this point, the path splits. Both paths go to Chufut-Kale; the path on the left takes a steeper route up the hill; the path on the right, which is the main entry path, is less steep and more shaded but longer. Entrance to the exhibit 12hv, students 6hv. Open 24hr., but no camping permitted. To get back to Sevastopol, retrace your steps down the mountain, and take a taxi or marshrutka to the train station from the street outside the entrance to Chufut Kale. Buses,* marshrutki, *and trains head back to Sevastopol.)*

KHAN'S PALACE. Just up the street from Chufut-Kale, on the way to the train station, is the Khan's Palace, one of the last remaining icons of Tatar rule in the Crimea. Though the palace's glory days are over, it now houses an exhibit on Crimean Tatar culture and many of its buildings are open for tours. The palace is a good complement to Chufut-Kale for daytrippers. *(Open daily 9am-6pm. English captions. 20hv, students 10hv.* Marshrutkas *to Chufut-Kale stop at the palace; tell the driver to let you off at Khanskogo Dvorets.)*

ACCESS POINTS

BELARUS (БЕЛАРУСЬ)

The unwanted stepchild of Mother Russia, Belarus serves as a testament to the glory days of the Soviet Union. Ubiquitous concrete highrises dominate Belarus's sprawling urban landscapes, while the untouched villages of the countryside call back to an earlier period of agricultural beauty and tranquility. Although most visitors are just traveling through, Belarus offers a unique look at a people in transition to those willing to endure the yards of bureaucratic red tape.

FACTS AND FIGURES

Official Name: Republic of Belarus.
Capital: Minsk.
Major Cities: Gomel, Mogilev, Vitebsk.
Population: 9,725,000.
Time Zone: GMT+2.
Language: Belarusian, Russian.
Religions: Eastern Orthodox (80%).
Cinemas per Capita: 0.37.
Number of Injuries from Terrorist Acts, 1968-2005: 0.

ESSENTIALS

WHEN TO GO

Belarus has a temperate climate, with warm and mild summers. Temperatures dip just slightly below freezing during the winter months (Dec.-Jan.). The difficulties of traveling in Belarus ensure that crowds rarely form anywhere, at any time.

DOCUMENTS AND FORMALITIES

ENTRANCE REQUIREMENTS.

Passport: Required of all travelers. Must be valid 90 days after end of intended stay.
Visa: Required of all travelers.
Letter of Invitation: Required of all travelers.
Inoculations: Recommended up-to-date on DTaP (diphtheria, tetanus, and pertussis), Hepatitis A, Hepatitis B, MMR (measles, mumps, and rubella), polio booster, rabies, and typhoid.
Medical Insurance Requirement: Travelers to Belarus must have an insurance certificate from an approved insurance company, valid within Belarusian territory. Such a policy can be purchased at the Belarusian border.
Work Permit: Required of all those planning to work in Belarus.
International Driving Permit: Required of all those planning to drive in Belarus.

EMBASSIES AND CONSULATES. Foreign embassies to Belarus are in Minsk. Belarusian embassies abroad include: **Canada,** 130 Albert St., Ste. 600, Ottawa, ON K1P 5G4 (☎613-233-9994); **UK,** 6 Kensington Ct., London W8 5DL (☎20 79 37 32 88; www.belarus.embassyhomepage.com); and **US,** 1619 New Hampshire Ave., NW, Washington, D.C. 20009 (☎202-986-1604; www.belarusembassy.org).

VISA AND ENTRY INFORMATION. To visit Belarus, you must secure an invitation, a visa, and medical insurance—an expensive and head-spinning process. If an acquaintance or business in Belarus can provide you with an official invitation, you may obtain a transit visa (valid for 48hr.; 5-day service US$100, next-day US$180), tourist visa (valid for up to 30 days; 5-day service US$50, next-day US$90), business visa (valid for up to 90 days; 5-day service US$100, next-day US$180), or private visa (valid for any 90 days within a one-year period; 5-day service US$350, next-day US$620). Visas are single-, double-, or multiple-entry. **Belintourist** (www.belintourist.by), the country's official tourism office, offers visa support. Those without Belarusian contacts can obtain a letter of invitation from an official tourist organization, for which they must show proof of payment for tourist services (e.g. hotel reservations, visa support, tour booking). **Alatan Tour** (www.alatantour.com) and **SMOK Travel** (www.smoktravel.com) provide visa invitations and support services for a fee. Online visa services allow travelers to obtain a letter of invitation without paying in advance for tourist services; a relatively cheap option is **www.russia-visa.com** (letter for single-entry tourist visa US$50, double-entry US$70). Travelers should consult the Belarusian embassy in their country of origin to apply for visas; transit visas are also issued in the Minsk airport—but only if you have made arrangements with an official tourist agency.

Belarus requires all foreign nationals to either have documentation of **medical insurance** issued by an approved company or to purchase insurance at the port of entry (US$1 for a one-day stay, US$15 for 30 days, US$28 for 60 days, and up to US$85 for a year). While insurance can easily be obtained in airports, it is more difficult if you arrive by train. Some hotels sell insurance; it can also be purchased from **Belgosstrakh Insurance Company.** Check out www.belgosstrakh.by/en/branches for a list of offices in Belarus. To enter the country, you must fill out a migration card, which you are required to present to authorities when exiting the country. Travelers are also advised to avoid bringing any political materials, including books of a political nature, through customs. Those staying in Belarus for three or more business days (weekends and holidays not included) must **register** with the Belarusian foreign police. Hotels perform this service for a small fee. If not staying in a hotel, you must register with the tourist service from which you obtained your visa invitation or at the Passport and Visa Department in the city in which you are staying. Travelers who attempt to leave the country without a migration card, visa, and proof of registration typically face detention or stiff fines.

NO MORE STICKY FINGERS. While giving a *vzyat* (bribe) used to be a common and accepted practice, bribery is illegal in Belarus. The best way to prevent complications when passing through customs is to keep a low profile and avoid speaking Russian, which may provoke questioning from officials.

TOURIST SERVICES AND MONEY

Belinturist (Белитурист; www.belintourist.by) and the state-run **National Tourist Agency** are helpful and often the only resources. **Hotel Belarus** in Minsk has a private travel agency. The Belarusian unit of currency is the **рубель** (BR; ruble), plural рубли, which comes in denominations of 1BR, 5BR, 10BR, 20BR, 50BR, 100BR, 500BR, 1000BR, 5000BR, 10,000BR, 20,000BR, 50,000BR, and 100,000BR. It is divided into 100 **капеек** (kapeek), singular kapeyka. Currency is in the form of paper bills; there are no coins. After years of soaring inflation, prices are commonly quoted in US dollars, but transactions in foreign currencies remain illegal; always convert the given price into rubles before paying. In recent years, **inflation** has sharply decreased and now stands around 7%, though the currency remains somewhat volatile. Most **banks** and hotels exchange money, but currency other than Russian rubles, euro, or US dollars is difficult to exchange. Make sure that any currency you intend to exchange is unmarked and undamaged; exchange offices will only accept bills in the best condition. **Traveler's**

checks are never accepted by retailers but can be exchanged at banks in bigger cities. Only the largest hotels and restaurants will accept **credit cards:** Visa and MasterCard are the most common, while Discover and American Express are never accepted. **ATMs** typically offer the best exchange rates.

RUBLES (BR)		
	AUS$1 = 2140BR	BR1000 = AUS$0.59
	CDN$1 = 2016BR	BR1000 = CDN$0.50
	EUR€1 = 2886BR	BR1000= EUR€0.35
	NZ$1 = 1488BR	BR1000 = NZ$0.67
	UK£1 = 4240BR	BR1000 = UK£0.24
	US$1 = 2140BR	BR1000 = US$0.47

HEALTH AND SAFETY

EMERGENCY **Ambulance:** ☎03. **Fire:** ☎01. **Police:** ☎02.

Medical care in Belarus is inadequate. In a medical emergency, try to get to a more developed country; an evacuation to the US costs up to US$50,000. Belarus was affected by the 1986 **Chernobyl** accident more than any other region. Avoid cheap **dairy products,** which may come from contaminated areas, and **mushrooms** and **berries,** which collect radioactivity, particularly outside of Minsk. Drink **bottled water. Toilet paper** is available in most supermarkets, but not in most public toilets (marked by a triangle pointing down for men or a triangle pointing up for women). **Condoms, medications,** and **feminine hygiene** supplies from the West are becoming available, but bring your own. In an emergency, your embassy is a better bet than the police, who may seek to extort foreigners.

Tourists are often the targets of petty theft and mugging; be particularly careful in and near public transportation and around hotels frequented by foreigners. Criminals have been known to use force if resisted. Stay clear of dodgy nightclubs, which may be run by the **mafia.** It is advisable to pay close attention to one's surroundings in nightclubs and bars; some travelers have reported incidents of drugging and subsequent theft. Avoid street demonstrations, which are common in Minsk, as police have been known to arrest both participants and bystanders (even foreign nationals). **Women** traveling alone may face harassment by drunken men; it is advisable to avoid less-crowded areas at night. Belarus is ethnically homogenous, and people with dark skin may experience **discrimination,** although hate crimes are rare. **Homosexuality** is still looked down upon in Belarus; use discretion at all times, as displays of affection may incite violence.

TRANSPORTATION

Belavia (☎172 202 706; www.belavia.by), Belarus's national airline, flies into **Minsk-II (MSQ)** from many European capitals. **Lufthansa** has daily direct flights from Frankfurt, and **Czech Airlines** offers daily flights from Prague. A cheaper option is to fly into Vilnius, LAT and catch a train to Minsk. Local flights within Belarus are virtually non-existent. Taking a **train** into Belarus is typically cheaper and easier than flying, as border checkpoints tend to be less strict and time-consuming. Trains run to Minsk from most Central and Eastern European capitals, but if you are traveling from Poland, expect long delays, as officials must change the train's wheels to fit Belarusian track specifications at the border. Neither the **Eastpass** or **Eurail Pass** is accepted in Belarus. Though train travel is the best way to travel within the country—as road conditions are generally poor—**buses** do connect

Minsk with most European capitals. Local buses, however, are often poorly maintained and crowded. Purchase tickets at kiosks or from the driver and punch them on board. **Taxis** may be poorly maintained; rates vary widely and drivers may overcharge. If possible, call a well-known taxi company beforehand. Otherwise, guarantee that the driver uses the meter and agree on a price before getting in (usually base fare of 5000BR plus 1100BR per km). Never share a taxi with strangers. In order to **drive** in Belarus, all foreigners must have a **International Driving Permit.** When entering the country via car, make sure officials stamp the driver's visa; otherwise, he or she will not be able to leave the country with the car. Similarly, travelers with such a stamp on their visas will only be able to exit the country with that same car. Drivers of vehicles will be charged a **fee** depending on the length of stay. **Hitchhiking** is nonexistent in Belarus, and Let's Go does not recommend it.

KEEPING IN TOUCH

Country code: 375. **International dialing prefix:** 810. From outside Belarus, dial international dialing prefix (see inside back cover) + 375 + city code + local number. Within Belarus, simply dial the number for a local call or 8 + city code + local number for long-distance calls. To call a cell phone from a landline, dial 8 + 029 + the seven-digit number. To call a cell phone from a cell phone, dial 375 + city code + local number. To call a landline from a cell phone, simply dial # + number for local calls; for long distance calls, dial 375 + 029 or 025 + local number.

Avoid the **mail** system; it is extremely unreliable. **Local calls** require phone cards, available at the post office, kiosks, and some hotels. Make **international calls** at the telephone office and pay up front in cash. (Calls to the US and Western Europe US$1-3 per min.) International access numbers include: **AT&T Direct** (☎8 800 101); **MCI WorldPhone** (☎8 800 103); and **NZ Direct** (☎8 800 641). Dialing from the **Gomel** and **Mogilev** regions requires the insertion of 10 after the first 8. Only those with Belarusian passports can typically get a **cell phone** plan, but it is possible to rent a cell phone. **Email** is the easiest and cheapest way to communicate with the outside world. Internet cafes are becoming more common and are typically open 24hr.

ACCOMMODATIONS AND CAMPING

Hotels are generally expensive and run-down. Keep receipts from hotels; you might have to show them to the authorities to avoid fines when leaving Belarus. *Babushki* (old women; literally "grandmother") sometimes offer **private rooms** at train stations, but foreigners can legally stay only in hotels. Hostels and B&Bs are virtually non-existent in Belarus. Camping facilities are also extremely limited, though camping is permitted in the countryside.

FOOD AND DRINK

Eating **vegetarian** in Belarus is difficult and eating **Kosher** is virtually impossible. Traditional Belarusian dishes are often based on meat. Dinner typically begins with soup; try *borshch*, made from beetroot and accompanied by sour cream, or *mochanka*, a thick soup with lard served with pancakes. Avoid food sold on the street. **Beer** and **vodka** can be bought at almost any time of day from many kiosks. It is legal to drink beer, but not hard alcohol in public.

MOLDOVA

Once part of the Romanian province of Moldavia, Moldova gained independence in 1991 after enduring 45 years of Soviet rule. Today, as the poorest country in Europe, Moldova is struggling to overcome its poverty and instability, especially in the breakaway region of Transnistria.

FACTS AND FIGURES

Official Name: Republic of Moldova.
Capital: Chişinău.
Population: 4,321,000.
Land Area: 33,800 sq. km.
Arable Land: 54.5%.
Time Zone: GMT +2.
Language: Moldovan (closely related to Romanian).
Religion: Eastern Orthodox (98%).
GDP Per Capita: US$2000.

ESSENTIALS

DOCUMENTS AND FORMALITIES

ENTRANCE REQUIREMENTS.

Passport: Required for all travelers.
Visa: Required for citizens of Australia and New Zealand. Not required for citizens of Canada, the EU, Ireland, the UK, and the US for stays of up to 90 days.
Letter of Invitation: Required of citizens of Australia and New Zealand.
Inoculations: Recommended up-to-date on DTaP (diphtheria, tetanus, and pertussis), Hepatitis A, Hepatitis B, MMR (measles, mumps, and rubella), polio booster, and typhoid.
Work Permit: Required for all foreigners planning to work in Moldova.
International Driving Permit: Required of all foreigners planning to drive.

EMBASSIES AND CONSULATES. Foreign embassies to Moldova are in Chişinău. Embassies abroad include: **UK,** 5 Dolphin Square, Edensor Rd., Chiswick, London W4 2ST (☎020 89 95 68 18; www.moldovanembassy.org.uk); **US,** 2101 S Street, NW, Washington, D.C. 20008 (☎202-667-1130; moldova@dgs.dgsys.com. Also accredited to Canada).

VISA AND ENTRY INFORMATION. Citizens of Australia and New Zealand need both **visas** and **invitations** to travel in Moldova. As of 2007, citizens of Canada, the EU, and the US no longer need visas for stays of less than three months. Visas can be obtained at the border or at the airport. Single-entry, one-month visas cost US$40; multiple-entry travel visas US$50-120; single-entry transit visas US$20, double-entry US$40. There is also a US$5 **processing fee.** Passports must be valid two months after departure from Moldova. Regular service takes five business days; one-day **rush service** costs an additional 50% of the visa fee. Invitations can be obtained from acquaintances in Moldova or from a private organization such as **MoldovaTUR** (☎254 0301; www.moldovatur.com), which issues invitations after you book a hotel room. All foreigners in Moldova must **register** with the police within three days of arrival. Also **register your valuables** to avoid customs duties upon exit. Some international buses to and from Odessa pass through Moldova's unstable breakaway **Transnistrian Republic;** avoid the region if possible. If you do choose to enter Moldova through Transnistria, make sure to either get a visa in advance or to register with local authorities as soon as you arrive at your Moldovan destination, as visas are not available at the border.

TOURIST SERVICES AND MONEY

Though there are few resources for travelers, tourist office employees usually speak English, and Moldova's official tourist website, www.turism.md, provides a wealth of information on travel agencies, visa requirements, and accommodations. Do not confuse **Moldovan lei** (MDL), singular leu, which comes in denominations of 1, 5, 10, 20, 50, 100, 200, and 500, with the Romanian currency of the same name. 100 **bani** make up a single leu and come in denominations of 5, 10, 25, and 50. Current inflation is around 14%, and prices will likely continue to rise over the next year. **Bringing cash is necessary,** as few places outside Chişinău take traveler's checks or credit cards or give cash advances. Although **ATMs** are common in the capital, use only those machines that show no evidence of tampering and that are attached to or inside banks.

MOLDOVAN LEI (MDL)		
	AUS$1 = 9.48MDL	10MDL = AUS$1.06
	CDN$1 = 11.19MDL	10MDL = CDN$0.89
	EUR€1 = 16.02MDL	10MDL = EUR€0.62
	NZ$1 = 8.26MDL	10MDL = NZ$1.21
	UK£1 = 23.53MDL	10MDL = UK£0.42
	US$1 = 11.87MDL	10MDL = US$0.84

HEALTH AND SAFETY

EMERGENCY	**Ambulance:** ☎903. **Fire:** ☎ 901. **Police:** ☎902.

Medical facilities are far below Western standards. If possible, move to a more developed country, or, in an emergency, contact your embassy, which can provide info about local medical facilities. If you do decide to go to a hospital, you will be expected to pay with **cash.** Bring your own antibiotics, syringes, and bandages. **Pharmacies** are generally poorly stocked, lacking in English labels, and sometimes fraudulent. The **water** is not safe to drink. Boil water for 10min., or drink imported bottled water. Beware of food from street vendors. **Cholera, diphtheria, and tuberculosis** are still problematic in Moldova; talk with your doctor before going.

Streets are poorly lit after night; either take a taxi from a reputable company or walk with a local if you're out after dark, as theft, muggings, and petty crimes are rampant. Manhole covers have been scavenged for scrap metal, and random holes litter the streets; this makes biking and driving in cities unsafe. In rural areas, the prevalence of agricultural vehicles and livestock on unpaved roads makes driving difficult. Avoid fights in bars and clubs, as organized crime is widespread. **Do not travel through the Transnistria region;** the area is not under government control, and violence and illegal activity are widespread. Traveling to Ukraine through this area is a hassle, and foreign embassies can do little to help travelers in this region. **Women** should dress conservatively and should not stay out after dark. Moldovans harbor **prejudice** against **Roma** (gypsies) and others with dark skin. Individuals of foreign **ethnicities** may receive suspicious looks, and **anti-Semitic** attitudes are prevalent. **Homophobia** persists; discretion is strongly advised. Some travelers report that they have been detained for taking pictures of military facilities and government buildings. Before you leave for Moldova, make sure to check the **travel advisory information** released by your home department of state or consulate abroad.

TRANSPORTATION

BY PLANE. Air Moldova (☎252 5502, reservations 252 5002), the national airline, flies to a number of European destinations. Flying into **Chişinău International Airport**

(☎252 6060, flight info 252 5412), can cost US$1500 in the summer; flying into Odessa, Ukraine and taking a train to Moldova can be a bit cheaper.

BY TRAIN AND BUS. Moldovan **trains** are extremely inefficient. Generally, trains lack A/C and are prone to cancellation. If you do decide to take the train in Moldova, opt for first class. **Buses** are crowded and old but provide a much more cost-effective, comfortable, and reliable way of getting in, out, and around.

BY CAR AND TAXI. **Rental cars,** though they do exist, are rare, and are usually based out of the airport; try looking at www.e-sixt.com for price and availability info. A Moldovan driver's license is needed to drive, though an **International Driving Permit (IDP)** can be used for stays of less than 90 days. **Gas** stations and repair facilities are relatively uncommon; if you are driving in Moldova, stop for fuel whenever you see a gas station. **Taxis** in Moldova are generally overpriced, and drivers will often overcharge unsuspecting tourists. If you do take a taxi, be sure to ride only in officially marked cars and to agree on a price before getting in.

BY THUMB. Hitchhiking is particularly dangerous in Moldova; *Let's Go* strongly discourages this practice.

KEEPING IN TOUCH

PHONE CODES	**Country code:** 373. **International dialing prefix:** 00. From outside Moldova, dial the international dialing prefix (see inside back cover) + 373 + city code + local number. Within Moldova, simply dial the local number.

INTERNET. Internet access is cheap and widely available in Chişinău.

TELEPHONE. The city code for Chişinău is ☎22. There are no international access numbers in Moldova; collect calls also remain impossible. Most local phones use Moldtelecom cards, available at the post office and from kiosks. For an international operator, dial ☎819. For domestic calls, use ☎813. To call internationally, dial 8, wait for the tone, then dial 10, the country code, and the number. Travelers may have trouble finding public phones outside of Chişinău.

MAIL. Avoid the mail system, as postal services in Moldova are unreliable.

ACCOMMODATIONS

There are very few **hostels** in Moldova, though all are relatively inexpensive (under US$10) and concentrated in the capital. It is common to rent by the bed rather than by the room. **Homestays** are the cheapest option. You should have no problem finding quality **hotels** for under US$15. Reservations are only needed in summer.

FOOD

To a great extent, Moldovan cuisine is a result of its geography, making it something like a cross between Romanian and Ukrainian food. From Romania comes *Mămăligă*, a cornmeal mush better known as polenta, and *ţuică*, a strong Romanian plum brandy. From Ukraine comes a love of *borshch* and traditional meat jelly. And in the footsteps of other Central European countries blessed with the ability to grow grapes, Moldova makes excellent **wine.**

GATEWAY CITIES

EURO (€)		
	AUS$1 = EUR€0.59	1EUR€ = AUS$1.69
	CDN$1 = EUR€0.70	1EUR€ = CDN$1.43
	NZ$1 = EUR€0.52	1EUR€ = NZ€1.94
	UK£1 = EUR€1.46	1EUR€ = UK£0.68
	US$1 = EUR€0.74	1EUR€ = US$1.35

Getting to Eastern European cities like Warsaw, Kyiv, and Budapest has never been easier and cheaper; often, it involves traveling through more central cities first. With their world-class museums and monuments, nonstop cafe and club cultures, and irresistible budget options, Berlin, Munich, Vienna, and Venice are some of the best gateways to the east. Although they ease the west-east transition, however, these vibrant cities are hardly easy to leave.

GATEWAY CITIES	❶	❷	❸	❹	❺
ACCOMMODATIONS	under €15	€15-25	€26-35	€36-55	over €55
FOOD	under €5	€5-10	€11-18	€19-23	over €23

BERLIN

Berlin is larger than Paris, up later than New York, and wilder than Amsterdam. Dizzying and electric, this city of 3.4 million has an increasingly diverse population; as a result, it is difficult to keep track of which *Bezirk* (neighborhood) is currently the trendiest. Traces of the past century's Nazi and Communist regimes remain etched in residents' minds, and a psychological division between East and West Germany—the problem dubbed *Mauer im Kopf* ("wall in the head")—still exists nearly two decades after the Berlin Wall's destruction. Restless and contradictory, Germany's capital shows no signs of slowing down its self-reinvention, and the Berlin of next year may be radically different from the Berlin of today.

TRANSPORTATION

Flights: The city is now transitioning from 3 airports to 1 (Flughafen Schönefeld will become the Berlin-Brandenburg International Airport), but at least until 2011, **Flughafen Tegel (TXL)** will remain West Berlin's main international airport. For info on all 3 of Berlin's airports, call ☎01 80 50 00 186 or visit www.berlin-airport.de. Take express bus #X9 from Bahnhof Zoo, bus #109 from Jakob-Kaiser-Pl. on U7, bus #128 from Kurt-Schumacher-Pl. on U6, or bus TXL from Potsdamer Pl. or Bahnhof Zoo. **Flughafen Schönefeld (BER),** southeast of Berlin, is used for intercontinental flights, travel to developing countries, and Ryanair. Take S9 or 45 to Flughafen Berlin Schönefeld, or ride the Schönefeld Express train (2 per hr. through most major S-Bahn stations). **Flughafen Tempelhof (THF)** is slated to close October 31, 2008, but remains open until then for European flights. Take U6 to Pl. der Luftbrücke.

Trains: Berlin's massive new **Hauptbahnhof,** which opened in time for the 2006 World Cup, is the city's major transit hub, with some international and domestic trains continuing to **Ostbahnhof** in the East. Hauptbahnhof currently connects only to the S-Bahn, but a U55 line is scheduled to open in late 2007. **Bahnhof Zoologischer Garten** (a.k.a. **Bahnhof Zoo**), formerly the West's main station, now connects only to regional destinations. Many trains also connect to **Schönefeld** airport. A number of U- and S-Bahn lines stop at **Oranienburg, Potsdam,** and **Spandau.** Trains in the Brandenburg regional transit system tend to stop at all major stations, as well as Alexanderpl. and Friedrichstr.

Buses: ZOB (☎301 0380), the "central" bus station, is actually at the western edge of town, by the Funkturm near Kaiserdamm. U2: Kaiserdamm or S41/42: Messe Nord/ICC. Open M-F 6am-9pm, Sa-Su 6am-3pm. **Gullivers,** at ZOB (☎311 0211; www.gullivers.de), Hardenbergpl. 14 (☎08 00 48 55 48 37), and **Berlin Linien Bus** (☎03 08 51 93 31; www.berlinlinienbus.de) often have good deals on bus fares. Open in summer daily 8am-9:30pm; in winter reduced hours.

Public Transportation: The **BVG** (www.bvg.de) is one of the most efficient transportation systems in the world; the extensive **Bus, Straßenbahn** (streetcar or tram), **U-Bahn** (subway), and **S-Bahn** (surface rail) networks will get you to your destination quickly. The city is divided into 3 transit zones. **Zone A** encompasses central Berlin, including Flughafen Tempelhof. The rest of Berlin is in **Zone B; Zone C** consists of the outlying areas, including Potsdam and Oranienburg. An AB ticket is the best deal, as you can buy extension tickets for the outlying areas. A **one-way ticket** (Einzelfahrausweis) is good for 2hr. after validation. Zones AB €2.10, BC €2.30, ABC €2.60. Within the validation period, the ticket may be used on any S-Bahn, U-Bahn, bus, or tram.

Night Transport: U- and S-Bahn lines generally don't run M-F 1-4am. On F-Sa nights, all trains run (though less frequently), except for the U4, S45, and S85. An extensive system of approximately 70 **night buses** runs 2-3 per hr. and tends to follow major transit lines; pick up the free Nachtliniennetz map at a Fahrscheine und Mehr office. The letter N precedes night bus numbers. Trams continue to run at night.

Taxis: ☎08 00 26 30 000. Call at least 15min. ahead. Women can request female drivers. Trips within the city cost up to €21. Request a *Kurzstrecke* to travel up to 2km in any direction for a flat €3 fee.

Bike Rental: Fahrradstation, Dorotheenstr. 30 (☎20 45 45 00; www.fahrradstation.de), near the Friedrichstr. S-Bahn station. Turn in at the parking lot next to STA. €15 per day. Open in summer daily 8am-8pm; in winter M-F 8am-7pm, Sa 10am-3pm.

GATEWAY CITIES

ORIENTATION AND PRACTICAL INFORMATION

Berlin is rightly considered a collection of towns, not a homogeneous city; each neighborhood has a strong sense of its individual history. **Mitte** is currently its commercial heart. The neighboring eastern districts of **Friedrichshain** and **Prenzlauer Berg** are the city's liveliest and most youthful, while Kreuzberg is the outpost of counterculture in the west. **Charlottenburg** in the west has a more staid, upscale character, while **Schöneberg** is right in between **Kreuzberg** and Charlottenburg, both in geography and in spirit. Berlin's landmarks include the **Spree River,** which flows through the city from west to east, and the narrower **Landwehrkanal Canal** that dumps into the Spree from the south. The vast central park, **Tiergarten,** stretches between the waterways. Tree-lined **Straße des 17. Juni** runs east-west through the Tiergarten, ending at the **Brandenburger Tor,** the park's eastern border gate. The **Reichstag** (Parliament) is north of the gate; several blocks south, **Potsdamer Platz** lies beneath the glittering Sony Center. Heading east, Straße des 17. Juni becomes **Unter den Linden.**

PHONE CODES	**Country code:** ☎49. **Berlin city code:** ☎030 within Germany, 30 abroad. **International dialing code:** ☎00.

Tourist Office: Euraide (www.euraide.com), in the *Hauptbahnhof.* Sells phone cards, rail- and walking-tour tickets. Open June-Oct. daily 8am-noon and 1-6pm; Nov.-May M-F 8am-noon and 1-4:45pm.

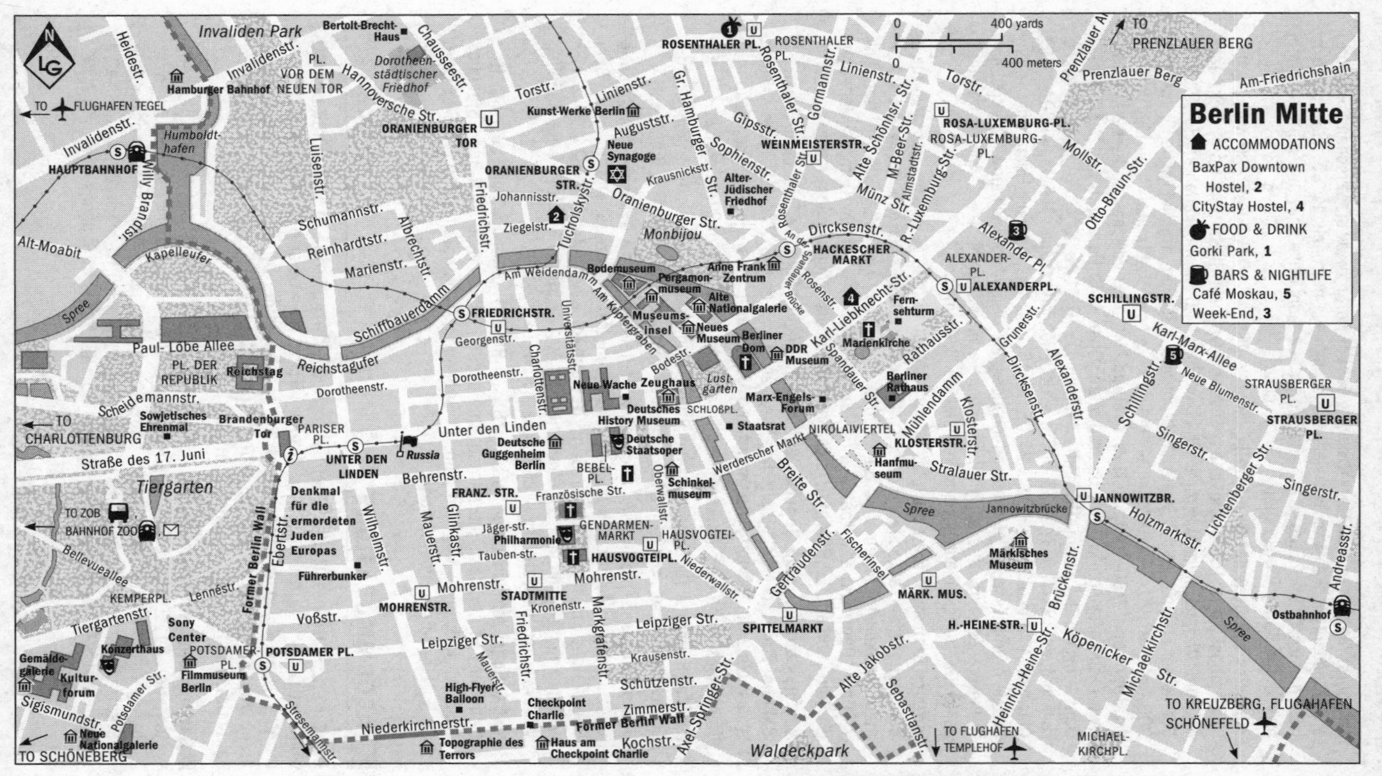

GATEWAY CITIES

City Tours: The guides at **Terry Brewer's Best of Berlin** (www.brewersberlintours.com) are legendary for their vast knowledge and engaging personalities. S5, 7, 9, or 75 or U6: Friedrichstr. 8hr. tours (€12) and shorter free tours leave daily at 10:30am from in front of the Bandy Brooks shop on Friedrichstr.

Embassies and Consulates: Australia, Mitte, Wallstr. 76-79 (☎880 0880; www.australian-embassy.de). U2: Märkisches Museum. Open M-Th 8:30am-5pm, F 8:30am-4:15pm. **Canada,** Mitte, Leipziger Pl. 17 (☎20 31 20; www.canada.de). S1, 2 or U2: Potsdamer Pl. Open M-F 8:30am-12:30pm and 1:30-5pm. **Ireland,** Mitte, Friedrichstr. 200 (☎22 07 20; www.botschaft-irland.de). U2 or 6: Stadtmitte. Open M-F 9:30am-12:30pm and 2:30-4:45pm. **New Zealand,** Mitte, Friedrichstr. 60 (☎20 62 10; www.nzembassy.com). U2 or 6: Stadtmitte. Open M-Th 9am-1pm and 2-5:30pm, F 9am-1pm and 2-4:30pm. **UK,** Mitte, Wilhelmstr. 70-71 (☎20 45 70; www.britischebotschaft.de). S1-3, 5, 7, 9, 25, or 75, or U6: Friedrichstr. Open M-F 9am-5:30pm. **US,** Clayallee 170 (☎832 9233; fax 83 05 12 15). U1: Oskar-Helene-Heim. After a long debate over the security of proposed locations, the US Embassy will move to a spot next to the Brandenburg Gate by 2008. Telephone advice available M-F 2-4pm; after hours, call ☎830 50 for emergency advice. Open M-F 8:30am-noon.

Currency Exchange: The best rates are usually found in large squares, at most major train stations, and at exchange offices with **Wechselstube** signs outside. **ReiseBank,** at the *Hauptbahnhof* (open M-Sa 8am-10pm), at Bahnhof Zoo (☎881 7117; open daily 7:30am-10pm) and at Ostbahnhof (☎296 4393; open M-F 7am-10pm, Sa 8am-8pm, Su 8am-noon and 12:30-4pm), is conveniently located, but has poor rates.

Luggage Storage: In **DB Gepack Center,** in the *Hauptbahnhof.* €3 for up to 3 bags. In **Bahnhof Zoo.** Lockers €3-5 per day. Max 72hr. Open daily 6:15am-10:30pm. Lockers, accessible 24hr., also at **Ostbahnhof** and **Alexanderpl.,** as well as the bus station.

Pharmacies: *Apotheken* (pharmacies) list a rotating schedule of 24hr. service.

Medical Services: The American and British embassies list English-speaking doctors. **Emergency doctor:** ☎31 00 31. **Emergency dentist:** ☎89 00 43 33. Both 24hr.

Internet Access: Free Internet access with admission to the **Deutsche Staatsbibliothek.** Cheap Internet cafes cluster on Oranienstr. in Kreuzberg and around U-Bahn Ebeswalder Str. in Prenzlauer Berg. **Netlounge,** Auguststr. 89 (☎24 34 25 97; www.netlounge-berlin.de). S1: Oranienburger Str. €2.50 per hr. Open noon-midnight. **WLAN** stickers indicate free or charge-based **Wi-Fi** access.

Post Offices: Joachimstaler Str. 7 (☎88 70 86 11), down Joachimstaler Str. from Bahnhof Zoo and near the Kantstr. intersection. Open M-Sa 9am-8pm. Branches: **Tegel Airport,** open M-F 8am-6pm, Sa 8am-noon; **Ostbahnhof,** open M-F 8am-8pm, Sa-Su 10am-6pm. **Postal Code:** 10706.

ACCOMMODATIONS

Longer stays are most conveniently arranged through one of Berlin's many **Mitwohnzentrale,** which can set up house-sitting gigs or sublets (from €250 per month). **Home Company Mitwohnzentrale,** Joachimstaler Str. 17, has a useful placement website. (☎194 45; www.homecompany.de. U9 or 15: Ku'damm. Open M-Th 9am-6pm, F 9am-5pm, Sa 11am-2pm. MC/V.)

BaxPax Downtown Hostel/Hotel, Ziegelstr. 28, Mitte (☎251 5202; www.baxpax-downtown.de). S1, 2, or 25: Oranienburger Str. or U6: Oranienburger Tor. A young, party-happy crowd and an unmatched array of hangout spaces. Wheelchair-accessible. Breakfast €4.50. Laundry €5-8. Internet €3 per hr.; Wi-Fi €1.50 per hr. K-Studio €13; dorms €16-21; singles €30-45; doubles €59-88; triples €66; quads €88. MC/V. ❸

CityStay Hostel, Rosenstr. 16, Mitte (☎23 62 40 31; www.citystay.de). S5, 7, 9, or 75 to Hackescher Markt or U2, 5, or 8: Alexanderpl. Central location, but it's still on a quiet side street. Individual showers and organic breakfast made to order. All-night bar serves dinner 6-10pm. Breakfast €4. Linens €2.50. Laundry €5. Internet €3 per hr.; free Wi-Fi. Dorms €17-21; singles €34-45; doubles €50-64; quads €84. Cash only. ❸

East Seven, Schwedter Str. 7, Prenzlauerberg (☎93 62 22 40; www.eastseven.de). U2: Senefelderpl. Hip, sophisticated hostel on a quiet street in trendy Prenzlauer Berg. Classy decor and a garden. Stag and hen party groups banned. Free tours. Kitchen. Linens €3. Laundry €4. Internet €0.50 per 20min.; free Wi-Fi. Dorms €15-17; singles €35; doubles €48; triples €63; quads €76. Low season reduced rates. MC/V. ❶

Bax Pax, Skalitzer Str. 104, Kreuzberg (☎69 51 83 22; www.baxpax.de). U1 or 15: Görlitzer Bahnhof. Pool table and balcony. Each room has a different country theme; the Germany room (#3) features a bed inside a VW Bug. Linens €3. Internet €3 per hr. Reception 24hr. Dorms €16; singles €30; doubles €46; triples €60. AmEx/MC/V. ❷

Globetrotter Hostel Odyssee, Grünberger Str. 23, Friedrichshein (☎29 00 00 81; www.globetrotterhostel.de). U1: Warschauer Str. or U5: Frankfurter Tor. Gothic statues and candlelit tables give the lobby a funky feel, while the tattooed staff keep everything spotless. Bar open until dawn. Breakfast €3. Linens deposit €3. Internet €0.50 per 10min.; free Wi-Fi. Reception 24hr. Check-in 4pm. Check-out noon. Reserve ahead. Dorms €14-22; singles €36-39; doubles €54-57; triples €66; quads €80. MC/V. ❷

Jugendhotel Berlincity, Crellestr. 22, Schöneberg (☎78 70 21 30; www.jugendhotel-berlin.de). U7: Kleistpark. Airy, stylish common rooms cause this small hotel to fill up fast. Breakfast included. Singles €35-40, with bath €45-55; doubles €55-65/60-79; triples €84/99; quads €108/118. Discounted rates for extended stays. MC/V. ❸

FOOD

Berlin's cuisine is quite diverse thanks to its Middle Eastern and Southeast Asian populations. Vendors of Currywurst or Bratwurst supply a quick bite; to satisfy a midnight craving, find a 24hr. Turkish *Imbiß* (snack food stand).

Cafe Bilderbuch, Akazienstr. 28, Schöneberg (☎78 70 60 57). U7: Eisenacher Str. Relax in the Venetian library or the airy courtyard of the "picturebook cafe." Known for daily breakfasts named after fairy tales (€7-8). Open M-Th 9am-1am, F-Sa 9am-2am, Su 10am-1am. Kitchen open M-Sa 9am-11pm, Su 10am-11pm. Cash only. ❸

Cafe Berio, Maaßenstr. 7, Schöneberg (☎216 1946; www.cafe-berio.de). U1, 2, 3, or 4: Nollendorfpl. Always packed with locals savoring late-afternoon breakfast, this subtly retro 2-floor Viennese-style cafe tempts passersby with its menu (€3.50-8.50) and perfect people-watching location. Open daily 8am-1am. Cash only. ❷

Café V, Lausitzer Pl. 12, Kreuzberg (☎612 4505). U1: Görlitzer Bahnhof. Vegan and fish entrees served in the romantic interior of Berlin's oldest vegetarian cafe. Top-of-the-line German and Middle Eastern entrees (€6-8). Open daily 10am-2am. Cash only. ❸

Gorki Park, Weinbergsweg 25, Mitte (☎448 7286; www.gorki-park.de). U8: Rosenthaler Pl. Nobody does borscht, *bliny,* or *pelmeni* like this feisty little Russian cafe. Outdoor seating. Entrees €4-10. Open M-Sa 9:30am-2am, Su 10am-2am. Cash only. ❷

Schwarzes Cafe, Kantstr. 148, Charlottenburg (☎313 8038). S3, 5, 7, 9, or 75 to Savignypl. Institution of bohemian Berlin is loud and romantic, with candlelit tables and a 24hr. breakfast menu (€4.90-8). Open M and W-Su 24hr., Tu 11am-3am. Cash only. ❸

Orchidee Sushi Restaurant, Stuttgarter Pl. 13, Charlottenburg (☎31 99 74 67). S to Charlottenburg. Though it touts its sushi, this pan-Asian cafe serves outstanding Vietnamese cuisine. Lunch special ½-price sushi or free appetizer with €5-11 entree. Open M-Sa 11am-midnight, Su 3pm-midnight. Cash only. ❸

I Due Forni, Schönhauser Allee 12, Prenzlauerberg (44 01 73 33). Locals swear by the stone-oven pizza at this hilltop pizzeria run by Italian rockers. Long summer waits are eased by lively graffiti on the walls. Pizzas €5.40-8.50; if you're feeling adventurous, try the one featuring *Pferdefleisch* (horse meat). Open daily noon-1am. Cash only. ❶

SIGHTS

Most of central Berlin's major sights lie along the route of **bus #100,** which runs every 5min. from Bahnhof Zoo to Prenzlauer Berg. It passes **Brandenburger Tor, Unter den Linden,** the **Berliner Dom,** and **Alexanderplatz.**

BRANDENBURGER TOR. Built as a tribute to 18th-century peace, this gate at the heart of Pariser Pl. came to symbolize the city's division: facing the Berlin Wall, it became a barricaded gateway to nowhere. After serving as the memorable backdrop for the fall of the Berlin Wall, the gate is now the most powerful emblem of reunited Germany. Visitors can reflect in the **Room of Silence** at the northern end.

THE REICHSTAG. Today home to the *Bundestag*, Germany's governing body, the Reichstag was central to one of the most critical moments in history. When it mysteriously burned down in 1933, Hitler declared a state of emergency and seized power. Today, a glass dome offers visitors 360° views of the city as they climb the spiral staircase inside. Go before 8am or after 8pm to avoid long lines. *(☎22 73 21 52; www.bundestag.de. Open daily 8am-midnight. Last entry 10pm. Free.)*

EAST SIDE GALLERY. The longest remaining portion of the Wall, this 1.3km stretch of cement slabs also serves as the world's largest open-air art gallery, unsupervised and open at all hours. The murals are from an international group of artists who gathered here in 1989 to celebrate the end of the city's division. It was expected that the wall would be destroyed soon after, but in 2000, with this portion still standing, many of the artists reconvened to repaint their work, covering others' scrawlings. Unfortunately, the new paintings are being rapidly eclipsed by graffiti. *(Along Mühlenstr. Take U1 or 15 or S3, 5-7, 9, or 75 to Warschauer Str., or S5, 7, 9, or 75 to Ostbahnhof and walk back toward the river. www.eastsidegallery.com.)*

DOKUMENTATIONSZENTRUM BERLINER MAUER. Nowhere else is the full structure of the Wall—two concrete barriers separated by the open **Todesstreife** (death strip)—preserved as it is here. The center assembles film clips, historic photos, and sound bites from the Wall's history in order to display it as authentically as possible. Ascend the spiral staircases for the full, desolate effect. *(Bernauer Str. 111. ☎464 1030; www.berliner-mauer-dokumentationszentrum.de. U8: Bernauer Str. Open Tu-Su Apr.-Oct. 10am-6pm; Nov.-Mar. 10am-5pm. Free.)*

HAUS AM CHECKPOINT CHARLIE. A strange mix of eastern sincerity and glossy western salesmanship, Checkpoint Charlie documents the history of the Berlin Wall and the dramatic escapes that once centered there. The museum showcases artwork, newspaper clippings, and photographs of the Wall, as well as a collection of contraptions used to get over, under, or through it. The surrounding area is given over to vendors hawking Cold War memorabilia. *(Friedrichstr. 43-45. U6: Kochstr. ☎253 7250; www.mauer-museum.de. Museum open daily 9am-10pm. German-language films with English subtitles every 2hr. €9.50, students €5.50. Audio tour €3.)*

BERLINER DOM. Berlin's most recognizable landmark, this multi-domed cathedral proves that Protestants can be as dramatic as Catholics. Enjoy the glorious view of Berlin from the tower or check out the nearly 100 Hohenzollern sarcophagi in the crypt. *(Open M-Sa 9am-8pm, Su noon-8pm, closed during services 6:30-7:30pm. Free organ recitals W-F 3pm. Frequent concerts in summer; buy tickets in the church or call ☎ 20 26 91 36. Combined admission to crypt, Dom, galleries, and tower €5, students €3.)*

MUSEUMS

Berlin is one of the world's great museum cities, with over 170 museums that include collections from every epoch in world history. The *Berlin Programm* (€1.60) lists them all.

SMB MUSEUMS

PERGAMONMUSEUM. One of the great ancient history museums, with almost an entire reconstructed ancient city. Named for the Turkish city from which the huge **Altar of Zeus** (180 BC) was taken, the museum's collection of artifacts from the ancient Near East includes the colossal blue **Ishtar Gate of Babylon** (575 BC) and the Roman **Market Gate of Miletus.** *(Bodestr. 1-3. ☎ 20 90 55 77. €10, students €5.)*

GEMÄLDEGALERIE. One of Germany's best-known museums, the Gemäldegalerie displays over 1000 masterpieces by Dutch, Flemish, German, and Italian masters from the 13th to 18th centuries, including works by Botticelli, Dürer, Raphael, Rembrandt, Titian, and Vermeer. *(Stauffenbergstr. 40. ☎ 266 2951. Open Tu-W and F-Su 10am-6pm, Th 10am-10pm. €8, students 4; Tu 6-10pm free.)*

HAMBURGER BAHNHOF/MUSEUM FÜR GEGENWART. Berlin's foremost contemporary art collection occupies 10,000 sq. m of this former train station. The museum hosts outrageous sculptures and attention-grabbing temporary exhibits. *(Invalidenstr. 50-51. S3, 5, 7, 9, or 75 to Hauptbahnhof, or U6 to Zinnowitzer Str. ☎ 39 78 34 11. Open Tu-F 10am-6pm, Sa 11am-8pm, Su 11am-6pm. €8, students €4; Th 2-6pm free.)*

INDEPENDENT MUSEUMS

JÜDISCHES MUSEUM BERLIN. Daniel Libeskind designed this museum so that no facing walls run parallel. Jagged hallways end in windows overlooking "the void." Wander through the labyrinthine **Garden of Exile** or shut yourself in the **Holocaust Tower,** a room nearly devoid of light and sound. End with the exhaustive exhibit on the last millennium of German Jewish history. *(Lindenstr. 9-14. U6: Kochstr., or U1, 6, or 15: Hallesches Tor. ☎ 308 785 681; www.jmberlin.de. Open M 10am-10pm, Tu-Su 10am-8pm. €5, students €2.50. Special exhibits €4.)*

FILMMUSEUM BERLIN. This interactive new museum chronicles German film's development, with a focus on older films and multimedia exhibits devoted to superstars including Leni Riefenstahl and Marlene Dietrich. *(Potsdamer Str. 2, 3rd and 4th fl. of the Sony Center. S1, 2, 25 or U2 to Potsdamer Pl. ☎ 300 9030; www.filmmuseum-berlin.de. Open Tu-W and F-Su 10am-6pm, Th 10am-8pm. €6, students €4, children €2.50.)*

ENTERTAINMENT

Berlin has one of the world's most vibrant cultural scenes. Most theaters and concert halls offer up to 50% off for students who buy at the *Abendkasse* (evening box office), which opens 1hr. before shows. Other ticket outlets charge 15-18% commissions and do not offer student discounts. Most theaters and operas close from mid-July to late August. The monthly pamphlets *Konzerte und Theater in Berlin und Brandenburg* (free) and *Berlin Programm* (€1.75) list concerts, film, and theater info, as do the biweekly *030*, *Kultur!news*, *Tip*, and *Zitty*.

Berliner Philharmoniker, Herbert Von Karajanstr. 1 (☎25 48 81 32; www.berlin-philharmonic.com). S1, 2, or 25 or U2: Potsdamer Pl. It may look bizarre, but this yellow building, designed by Scharoun in 1963, is acoustically perfect: every audience member hears the music exactly as it is meant to sound. The Berliner Philharmoniker is one of the world's finest orchestras. It is practically impossible to get a seat; check 1hr. before concert time or check their website. Open mid-Sept. to mid-June. Box office open M-F 3-6pm, Sa-Su 11am-2pm. Standing room from €7, seats from €13. AmEx/MC/V.

Deutsches Theater, Schumannstr. 13A (☎28 44 12 25; www.deutsches-theater.berlin.net). U6 or S1: Friedrichstr. Even former West Berliners admit it: the one-time East German state theater is Germany's best. Produces innovative takes on classics and works. The **Kammerspiel** (☎28 44 12 26) stages smaller, provocative productions. Box office for both open M-Sa 11am-6:30pm, Su 3-6:30pm. Tickets for Deutsches Theater €5-43, for Kammerspiel €12-30; students €8. AmEx/MC/V.

NIGHTLIFE

Berlin's nightlife is absolute madness. Bars typically open around 6pm and get going around midnight, just as clubs begin opening their doors. The bar scene winds down anywhere between 1 and 6am; meanwhile, clubs fill up and don't empty until well after dawn, when they pass the baton to after-parties and 24hr. cafes. Between 1 and 4am, take advantage of the night buses and U-Bahn 9 and 12, which run all night on Friday and Saturday. Info about bands and dance venues can be found in the pamphlets *Tip* (€2.50) and *Zitty* (€2.30), available at newsstands, or in *030* (free), distributed in bars, cafes, and hostels.

Weekend, Alexanderpl. 5, Mitte (www.week-end-berlin.de), on the 12th fl. of the building with the neon "Sharp" sign. A touch on the posh side, with a fashionable crowd, Weekend is a must-see for its panoramic rooftop terrace; watch the sun rise over the blockhousing of East Berlin. Cover €6-10. Open Th-Sa 11pm-late. Cash only.

Cafe Moskau, Karl-Marx-Allee 34, Mitte. U5: Schillingstr. The varied spaces tucked into this steel-and-glass GDR edifice play host to events from hip hop and electronic nights to fashion shows. Also home to the too-cool-for-a-name bar known by its address, **KMA 36.** Su gay night. Cover €7-13. Open Sa 11pm-6am, Su 10pm-5am. Cash only.

Club der Visionaere, Am Flutgraben 1, Kreuzberg (☎69 51 89 44; www.clubdervisionaere.de). U1: Schlesisches Tor or night bus #N65 to Heckmannufer. From the many languages drifting through the air to the people settled on ground-cushions, canal-side Club der Visionaere gives off a backpacker vibe. Drift on a raft attached to the terrace. DJ spins house inside. Beer €3. Open M-F 4pm-late, Sa-Su noon-late. Cash only.

Intersoup, Schliemannstr. 31, Prenzlauer Berg (☎23 27 30 45; www.intersoup.de). U2: Eberswalder Str. This bar eschews big-name drink brands and popular music in favor of worn 70s furniture, soup specials (€4.50-5), and retro floral wallpaper. Downstairs, the small club **Undersoup** has live music (most W and Sa), karaoke Th, films, and even puppet theater (M-Tu). DJs most nights. Club cover €3. Open daily 4pm-late. Cash only.

Rosi's, Revaler Str. 29, Friedrichshain (www.rosis-berlin.de). U or S: Warshauerstr. An unpretentious warren of bars, clubs, and outdoor lounges strung across a former industrial space. Art markets and exhibitions round out the roster of DJs and live bands. There's something for everyone, from pubbers to clubbers to people who just want to lie around on couches. Nightly music runs the gamut from indie to drum-and-bass to reggae. Open Th-Sa 8pm-late, Su 2pm-late. Occasional daytime events. Cash only.

Quasimodo, Kantstr. 12A, Charlottenberg (www.quasimodo.de). U2 or S5, 7, 9, or 75: Zoologischer Garten. Beneath a cafe, this cozy venue showcases mostly jazz with occasional R&B and soul. Concert tickets available from 5pm at the cafe upstairs or through the Kant-Kasse ticket service (☎313 4554). Concerts 11pm. Check website for schedules. Cover €8-20. Reserve ahead for cheaper tickets. Open daily noon-late. Cash only.

Slumberland, Goltzstr. 24, Schöneberg (☎216 5349). U1-4: Nollendorfpl. Quirky space with African art, palm trees, a sand floor and mixed drinks encourages jamming to the reggae music. Open M-F and Su 6pm-late, Sa 11am-late. Cash only.

GLBT NIGHTLIFE

Berlin is one of Europe's most gay-friendly cities. *Gay-yellowpages*, *Sergej*, and *Siegessäule* have GLBT entertainment listings.

Das Haus B, Warschauer Pl. 18 (☎296 0800; www.dashausb.de). U1 or S3, 5-7, 9, or 75 to Warschauer Str. East Berlin's most famous disco in the GDR era is still a color-saturated haven for dancers, spinning techno, Top 40, and German Schlager to a mixed crowd. Cover €2-6. Open W 10pm-5am, F-Sa 10pm-7am. Cash only.

Hafen, Motzstr. 19 (www.hafen-berlin.de). U1-4: Nollendorfpl. The owners of "Harbor" created its nautical decor. A fashionable—mostly gay male—crowd in summer. 1st M of each month English-language pub quiz 10pm. Open daily 8pm-late. Cash only.

Rose's, Oranienstr. 187 (☎615 6570). U1 or U8: Kottbusser Tor or U1: Görlitzer Bahnhof. Marked only by a "Bar" sign. A friendly, mixed clientele packs this claustrophobic party spot at all hours. The campy dark-red interior is filled with hearts, glowing lips, furry ceilings, feathers, and glitter. Vodka tonic €5 and absolutely "no fucking cocktails." Open daily 10pm-6am. Cash only.

GATEWAY CITIES

MUNICH (MÜNCHEN)

Bavaria's capital and cultural center, Munich (pop. 1.3 million) is a sprawling, liberal metropolis where world-class museums, handsome parks, colossal architecture, and a genial population create a thriving city. *Müncheners* party zealously during **Fasching** (Mardi Gras; Jan. 7-Feb. 5, 2008), shop with abandon during the **Christ Child Market** (Dec. 1-23), and chug unfathomable quantities of beer during the legendary **Oktoberfest** (Sept. 20-Oct. 5, 2008).

TRANSPORTATION

Flights: Flughafen München (MUC; ☎97 52 13 13). S1 and 8 run from the airport to the *Hauptbahnhof* and Marienpl. (40min., 3 per hr., €8 or 8 strips on the *Streifenkarte*). Buy a **Gesaskamtnetz** day pass that covers all zones (€10). The **Lufthansa** shuttle bus goes to the *Hauptbahnhof* (40min., 3 per hr., €10).

Trains: Munich's **Hauptbahnhof** (☎118 61) is the hub of southern Germany with connections to: **Berlin** (5¾-6½hr., 1-2 per hr., €105-119); **Frankfurt** (3-4½hr., 1-2 per hr., €64-81); **Budapest, HUN** (7½-9½hr., 8 per day, €98); **Prague, CZR** (6-8¼hr., 9 per day, €49-84); **Venice, ITA** (7-10hr., 6 per day, €92); **Vienna, AUT** (4¼-6hr., 1-2 per hr., €69-85). **EurAide,** in the station, sells tickets. **Reisezentrum** ticket counters at the station are open daily 7am-9:30pm.

Public Transportation: MVV (☎41 42 43 44; www.mvv-muenchen.de) operates buses, trains, the S-Bahn (underground trains), and the U-Bahn (subway). Most run M-Th 5am-12:30am, F-Sa 5am-2am. S-Bahn trains go until 2 or 3am daily. Night buses and trams serve Munich's dedicated clubbers ("N"). Eurail, Inter Rail, and German rail passes valid on the S-Bahn but not on buses, trams, or the U-Bahn.

Tickets: Buy tickets at the blue vending machines and validate them in the blue boxes before entering the platform or risk a €40 fine.

Prices: Single-ride tickets €2.20 (valid 2hr.). **Kurzstrecke** (short-trip) tickets €1.10 (1hr. or 2 stops on the U- or S-Bahn, 4 stops on a tramor bus). A **Streifenkarte** (10-strip ticket; €10) can be used by more than 1 person. Cancel 2 strips per person for a normal ride, or 1 strip for a short trip; for rides beyond the city center, cancel 2 strips per zone. A **Single-Tageskarte** (single day ticket; €5) for *Innenraum* (the city's central zone) is valid until 6am the next day; the **partner** day pass (€9) is valid for up to 5 people. **3-day** single pass €13; **5-person** pass €21. The **XXL Ticket** (single €6.70, partner €12) gives day-long transit in Munich's 2 innermost zones, white and green. Single **Gesamtnetz** (day ticket for all zones) €10; 5-person pass €18.

Taxis: Taxi-München-Zentrale (☎216 10 or 194 10).

Bike Rental: Mike's Bike Tours, Bräuhausstr. 10 (☎25 54 39 87). €12 per 1st day, €9 per day thereafter. 50% discount with tour (see below). After hours, call ☎0172 852 0660. Open daily mid.-Apr. to mid-Oct. 10am-8pm; Mar. to mid-Apr. and mid-Oct. to mid-Nov. 10:30am-1pm and 4:30-5:30pm.

ORIENTATION AND PRACTICAL INFORMATION

Downtown Munich is split into quadrants by thoroughfares running east-west and north-south. These intersect at Munich's central square, **Marienplatz,** and link the traffic rings at **Karlsplatz** (called Stachus by locals) in the west, **Isartorplatz** in the east, **Odeonsplatz** in the north, and **Sendlinger Tor** in the south. In the east beyond the Isartor, the Isar River flows north-south. The *Hauptbahnhof* is beyond Karlspl., to the west of the ring. To get to Marienpl. from the station, take any eastbound S-Bahn or use the main exit and make a right on Bahnhofpl., a left on Bayerstr. heading east through Karlspl., and continue straight. The **university** is to the north amid the **Schwabing** district's budget restaurants; to the east of Schwabing is the **English Garden** and to the west, **Olympiapark.** South of downtown is the **Glockenbachviertel,** filled with nightlife hot spots and gay bars. A seedy area with hotels and sex shops surrounds the *Hauptbahnhof.*

PHONE CODES	**Country code:** ☎49. **Munich city code:** ☎089 **International dialing prefix:** 00.

Tourist Offices: Main office (☎23 39 65 55), on the front side of the *Hauptbahnhof,* next to the SB-Markt on Bahnhofpl. Books rooms for free with a 10-15% deposit, and sells English-language city maps (€0.30). Open M-Sa 9:30am-6:30pm, Su 10am-6pm. **Branch office,** on Marienpl. at the entrance to the Neues Rathaus tower, books tickets for concerts and other events. Open M-F 10am-8pm, Sa 10am-4pm. MC/V. **EurAide** (☎59 38 89), room #2 along track 11 of the *Hauptbahnhof,* books train tickets for free and runs English-language city tours. Open June-Sept. M-Sa 7:45am-12:45pm and 2-6pm, Su 8am-noon; Oct.-May reduced hours.

Tours: **Mike's Bike Tours,** Bräuhausstr. 10 (☎25 54 39 87; www.mikesbiketours.com). If you only have 1 day in Munich, take this tour. Starting from the Altes Rathaus on Marienpl., the 4hr., 6.5km city tour includes a *Biergarten* break. Tours leave daily mid-Apr. to Aug. 11:30am and 4pm; Sept. to mid-Nov. and Mar. to mid-Apr. 12:30pm. €24. Look for €6 coupons at youth hostels.

Consulates: Canada, Tal 29 (☎219 9570). Open M-F 9am-noon; 2-4pm by appointment only. **Ireland,** Dennigerstr. 15 (☎20 80 59 90). Open M-F 9am-noon. **UK,** Möhlstr. 5 (☎21 10 90). Open M-Th 8:30am-noon and 1-5pm, F 8:30am-noon and 1-3:30pm. **US,** Königinstr. 5 (☎288 80). Open M-F 1-4pm.

Currency Exchange: ReiseBank (☎551 0813), at the front of the *Hauptbahnhof.* Slightly cheaper than other banks. Open daily 7am-10pm.

Medical Emergency: ☎192 22.

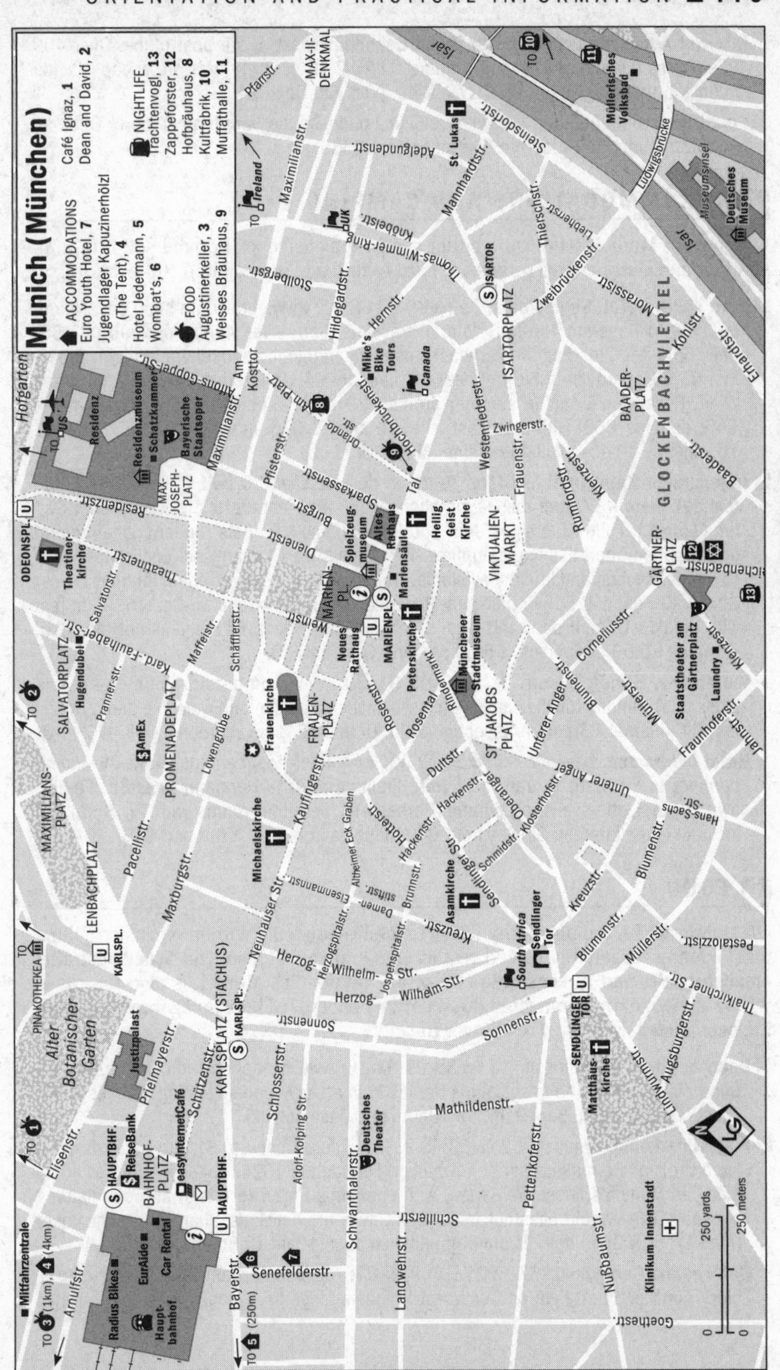

GATEWAY CITIES

Internet Access: easyInternetCafé, on Bahnhofpl. next to the post office. Over 400 PCs. Prices depend on demand (around €2.20-2.40 per hr.); rates are cheapest after midnight, dropping as low as €1.70. 24hr. pass €5. Open 24hr.

Post Office: Bahnhofpl. In the yellow building opposite the *Hauptbahnhof* exit. Open M-F 7:30am-8pm, Sa 9am-4pm. **Postal Code:** 80335.

ACCOMMODATIONS AND CAMPING

Lodgings in Munich tend to be either seedy, expensive, or booked solid. In midsummer and Oktoberfest, rooms are hard to find and prices jump 10% or more.

Euro Youth Hotel, Senefelderstr. 5 (☎59 90 88 11; www.euro-youth-hotel.de). *Hauptbahnhof* to Bayerstr. The fun, colorful travelers' bar serves *Augustinerbräu* (€2.80) daily 6pm-4am, lending the laid-back hostel an energetic atmosphere at night. Breakfast €3.90. Happy hour 6-9pm; beer €2. Laundry €4.10. Internet €1 per 30min.; free Wi-Fi. Reception 24hr. In summer dorms €20; 3- to 5-person dorms €24; singles €45; doubles €60, with breakfast, shower, and TV €75. In winter €10/13/45/60/75. Cheapest beds available online. MC/V. ❷

Jugendlager Kapuzinerhölzl (The Tent), In den Kirschen 30 (☎141 4300; www.thetent.de). Tram #17 from the *Hauptbahnhof* (dir.: Amalienburgstr.) to Botanischer Garten (15min.). Follow the signs. Join 250 international "campers" under a gigantic tent on a wooden floor. Evening campfires. W morning free German- and English-language city tours. Kitchen and laundry available. Free lockers; no lock provided. Internet €1 per 30min. Key deposit €25 or passport. Reception 24hr. Open June 15-Oct. 15. Giant tent with breakfast, foam pad, and wool blankets €7.50; beds €11, linens not included. Camping €5.50 per person, €5.50 per tent. Cash only. ❶

Wombat's, Senefelderstr. 1 (☎59 98 91 80; www.wombats.at/munich-hostel/index.php). Unique touches include a glass-enclosed garden and welcome drink. Breakfast €4. Internet €3 per hr. Reception 24hr. Dorms €24; private rooms €68. MC/V. ❷

Hotel Jedermann, Bayerstr. 95 (☎54 32 40; www.hotel-jedermann.de). Take the *Hauptbahnhof* to Bayerstr. or tram #19 (dir.: Freiham Süd) to Hermann-Lingg-Str. Family-owned hotel offers inviting common areas and beautiful rooms with TV. Breakfast included. Free Internet. Singles from €49; doubles from €67. Extra bed €15. MC/V. ❹

FOOD

Off **Ludwigstraße,** the university district supplies students with inexpensive, filling meals. Many reasonably priced restaurants and cafes cluster on **Schellingstraße, Amalienstraße,** and **Türkenstraße** (U3 or 6: Universität). Munich is also the place where someone first connected the separate concepts of beer and garden to create the **beer garden.** Now they're all over the city.

Dean & David, Schellingstr. 13 (☎33 09 83 18; www.deananddavid.com). U3 or U6: Universität. Curries and fresh salads (from €3) in an airy, modern setting. Entrees €5-7. Free Wi-Fi. Open M-F 8am-9pm, Sa 10am-7pm. Cash only. ❷

Augustinerkeller, Arnulfstr. 52 (☎59 43 93), at Zirkus-Krone-Str. S1-8 to Hackerbrücke. From the station, make a right on Arnulfstr. Founded in 1824, Augustiner is viewed by many as Munich's finest *Biergarten*, with enormous *Brez'n* (pretzels) and dim lighting beneath 100-year-old chestnut trees. Don't miss the delicious, sharp Augustiner beer (*Maß* €6.50). Open daily 10am-1am. Kitchen open 10am-10:30pm. AmEx/MC/V.

Café Ignaz, Georgenstr. 67 (☎271 6093). U2: Josephspl., then take Adelheidstr. 1 block north and turn right on Georgenstr. Dinners range from crepes to stir-fried dishes

(€5-9) at this eco-friendly vegetarian cafe. Breakfast buffet M and W-F 8-11:30am (€7); lunch buffet M-F noon-2pm (€6.50); brunch buffet Sa-Su 9am-1:30pm (€8). Open M and W-F 8am-10pm, Tu 11am-10pm, Sa-Su 9am-10pm. AmEx. ❷

Weisses Bräuhaus, Tal 7 (☎290 1380). This 500-year-old tavern provides traditional Bavarian fare. Adventurous eaters can pass on the roast pork dishes (€12-16), favoring *Münchener Voressen* (calf and pig lungs; €7.90). Entrees €10-20. Large daily specials menu. Open daily 8am-midnight. MC/V. ❹

SIGHTS AND MUSEUMS

RESIDENZ. Down the pedestrian zone from Odeonspl., the state rooms and apartments of the Residenz, home to the Wittelsbach dynasty from 1623 to 1918, reveal Neoclassical, Baroque, and Rococo influences. Highlights of the **Residenzmuseum** include the painting-packed **Antiquarium,** the royal **family portraits** in the ancestral gallery, and the **papal chambers.** The adjacent **Schatzkammer** (treasury) contains crowns, crucifixes, reliquaries, and swords. Out back, the manicured **Hofgarten** shelters the temple of Diana. *(Max-Joseph-Pl. 3. U3-6: Odeonspl. ☎29 06 71. Open daily Apr. to mid-Oct. 9am-6pm; mid-Oct. to Mar. 10am-4pm. Half of the Residenz is open in the morning until 1:30pm and the other half is open in the afternoon from 1:30. Each €6, students €5; both €9/8. Garden free. Free audio tour.)*

PINAKOTHEKEN. Designed by *Münchener* Stephan Braunfels, the beautiful **Pinakothek der Moderne** is four museums in one. Subgalleries display architecture, design, drawings, and paintings by artists ranging from Picasso to contemporary masters. *(Barerstr. 40. U2: Königspl or tram #27: Pinakotheken. ☎23 80 53 60. Open Tu-W and Sa-Su 10am-5pm, Th-F 10am-8pm. €9.50, students €6. Audio tour €2.)*

DEUTSCHES MUSEUM. Even if you don't know (or care) how engines power a Boeing 747, the Deutsches Museum's over 50 departments on science and technology will keep you entertained and educated. *(Museuminsel 1. S1-8 to Isartor or tram #18 to Deutsches Museum. ☎217 91; www.deutsches-museum.de. Open daily 9am-5pm. €9, students €3. English-language guidebook €4.)*

MARIENPLATZ. The **Mariensäule,** a 1683 monument to the Virgin Mary, commemorates Munich's survival of the Thirty Years' War. At the **Neues Rathaus,** the **Glockenspiel** chimes, pleasing tourists with jousting knights and dancing coopers. *(Daily in summer at 11am, noon, 3, 5pm; in winter 11am, noon, 3pm.)* At 9pm, a mechanical watchman marches out and the Guardian Angel escorts the *Münchner Kindl* (Munich Child) to bed.

PETERSKIRCHE AND FRAUENKIRCHE. Across from the Neues Rathaus, the 12th-century **Peterskirche** is the city's oldest parish church. Scale over 300 steps up the tower for a spectacular view. *(Open M-Tu and Th-Su 7:30am-7pm. Tower €1.50, students €1.)* From Marienpl., take Kaufingerstr. toward the *Hauptbahnhof* to the onion-domed towers of the 15th-century **Frauenkirche**—one of Munich's most notable landmarks and a city emblem. *(Frauenpl. 1. Open daily 7am-7pm. €3.50, students €1.50.)*

ENTERTAINMENT AND NIGHTLIFE

Monatsprogramm (€1.50) and *Munich Found* (free at the tourist office) list schedules for festivals, museums, and performances. In July, a magnificent **opera festival** arrives at the **Bayerische Staatsoper** (Bavarian National Opera), Max-Joseph-Pl. 2. (☎21 85 01; www.bayerische.staatsoper.de. U3-6: Odeonspl. or tram #19: Nationaltheater.)

Zappeforster, Corneliusstr. 16 (☎20 24 52 50). Students and 20-something hipsters huddle around the tables on Gärtner Platz or bop along to the alternative beats in the no-frills interior. During the day, *Müncheners* lounge around on cushions and blankets for coffee and conversation. Beer 0.3L €2.50. Open daily 9am-1am. Cash only.

Trachtenvogl, Reichenbachstr. 47 (☎201 5160; www.trachtenvogl.de). U1-2 or 7-8: Frauenhofer. Enjoy 1 of their 32 types of hot chocolate—some with alcohol, of course—in a cozy living room with chic lamps. F live bands. Su chocolate fondue; reservations required. Happy hour daily 6-7pm; Astra beer €1.60. Jäger hour daily 9-10pm; Jägermeister drinks ½-price. Open M-Th and Su 10am-1am, F-Sa 10am-3am. Cash only.

Muffathalle, Zellstr. 4 (☎45 87 50 10; www.muffathalle.de), in Haidhausen. Take S1-8 to Rosenheimerpl. and walk toward the river on Rosenheimer Str. for 2 blocks, or take tram #18 (dir.: St. Emmeram) to Deutsches Museum. This former power plant generates hip hop, jazz, spoken word, techno, and dance performances. Cover from €5. Open M-Th 5pm-late, F-Su noon-late. Buy tickets online or through München Ticket.

Kultfabrik, Grafingerstr. 6 (☎49 00 90 70; www.kultfabrik.info). Take U5 or S1-8: Ostbahnhof. With 23 clubs in 1 complex, Kultfabrik attracts dedicated partygoers for all-night revelry. The Russian-themed **Club Kalinka** is 1 of the more rowdy spots, popular with young locals and backpackers. Most doors open around 10pm and close late.

Hofbräuhaus, Platzl 9 (☎290 1360), 2 blocks from Marienpl. Come for the full beer hall experience: this is as jolly, as festive, and as loud as it gets. Go in the early afternoon to avoid tourists. *Maß* €6.20. *Weißwürste* €4.20. Open daily 9am-midnight. Cash only.

VIENNA (WIEN)

War, marriage, and Habsburg maneuvering transformed Vienna (pop. 1,800,000) from a Roman camp along the Danube into Europe's political lynchpin. Beethoven and Mozart made Vienna an everlasting arbiter of high culture. With dozens of coffee houses and museums, Vienna radiates artistic, intellectual energy. On any given afternoon, cafes turn the sidewalks into a sea of umbrellas while bars and clubs pulse with experimental techno and indie rock until dawn.

TRANSPORTATION

Flights: The **Wien-Schwechat Flughafen** (**VIE;** ☎700 70), 18km from the city center, is home to **Austrian Airlines** (☎517 89; www.aua.com). The cheapest way to reach the city, the S-Bahn (☎65 17 17) stops at **Wien Mitte** (30min., 2-3 per hr., €3). The Vienna Airport Lines **bus** (☎930 00 23 00) takes 20min. to reach Südbahnhof and 40min. to Westbahnhof (2 per hr.; €6, round-trip €11). The **City Airport Train** (**CAT;** ☎252 50; www.cityairporttrain.com) takes only 16min. to reach Wien Mitte (2 per hr. 6:05am-11:35pm; purchased online €8, round-trip €15; from a ticket machine €9, round-trip €16; on board €10; Eurail not valid.)

Trains: Vienna has 2 main train stations with international connections. Call ☎05 17 17 (24hr.) or check www.oebb.at for general train info. Ticket counters and machines generally take AmEx/MC/V.

Westbahnhof, XV, Mariahilferstr. 132. Info counter open daily 7:30am-9pm. Trains go to: **Berlin, GER** (9-11hr., every 2hr., €100-130); **Budapest, HUN** (3hr., 17 per day, €36); **Munich, GER** (5hr., 10 per day, €72).

Südbahnhof, X, Wiener Gürtel 1a. Info counter open daily 7am-8pm. Trains go south and east to: **Graz** (2½hr., 1 per hr., €30); **Kraków, POL** (7hr., 4 per day, €46); **Prague, CZR** (4-5hr., 8 per day, €44); **Venice, ITA** (7-11hr., 6 per day, €50-70).

Buses: Buses in Austria are rarely cheaper than trains; compare prices before buying a ticket. **Postbus** (☎517 17; www.postbus.at) provides regional bus service and

Eurolines (☎798 29 00; www.eurolines.at) connects to international destinations. Buses leave from the city stations at Erdberg, Floridsdorf, Heiligenstadt, Hütteldorf, Kagran, Reumannpl, and Wien Mitte/Landstr.

Public Transportation: Wiener Linien (general info ☎790 91 00; www.wienerlinien.at.) The **subway** (U-Bahn), **tram** (Straßenbahn), **elevated train** (S-Bahn), and **bus** lines operate on a 1-ticket system, so you can transfer between types of transportation without having to buy a new ticket. Purchase tickets at a counter, machine, on board, or at a tobacco shop. A **single fare** (€1.70 in advance, €2.20 on board) lets you travel to any destination in the city and switch from bus to U-Bahn to tram to S-Bahn in any order, provided your travel is uninterrupted. Other ticket options include a **1-day pass** (€5.70), **1-day "shopping" pass** (M-Sa 8am-8pm, €4.60), **3-day rover ticket** (€14), **7-day pass** (€14; valid M 9am to the next M 9am), and an **8-day pass** (€28; valid any 8 days, not necessarily consecutive; can be split between several people traveling together, but must be validated for each person). The **Vorteilscard** (Vienna Card; €19) allows for 72hr. of travel and discounts at museums and sights. **Night buses** run every 30min., 12:30-4:30am, along most routes; "N" signs designate night bus stops. A night bus schedule and discount passes are available from Wiener Linien information offices (open M-F 6:30am-6:30pm, Sa-Su 8:30am-4pm) in the Karlspl., Stephanspl., Westbahnhof, and some other U-Bahn stations, as well as at the tourist office.

Taxis: ☎313 00, 401 00, 601 60, or 814 00. Stands at Südbahnhof, Karlspl. in the city center, Westbahnhof, and by the Bermuda Dreieck. Accredited taxis have yellow-and-black signs on the roof. M-Sa base €2.80, €0.20 per 0.2km; Su base 11pm-6am €3; holidays slightly more expensive. €2 surcharge for calling a taxi.

Bike Rental: Citybike (www.citybikeien.at) has automated rental stations at 50 locations. €2 per day, €1 per 1st 2hr., €4 per hr. thereafter. MC/V.

ORIENTATION AND PRACTICAL INFORMATION

Vienna is divided into 23 **Bezirke** (districts). The first is **Innenstadt** (city center), defined by the **Ringstraße** (ring road) on three sides and the Danube Canal on the fourth. At the center of the Innenstadt lies **Stephansplatz** and much of the pedestrian district. Many of Vienna's major attractions are in District I and immediately around the Ringstr. Districts II-IX spread out from the city center following the clockwise traffic of the Ring. The remaining districts expand from yet another ring road, the **Gürtel** (Belt). Similar to the Ring, this major thoroughfare has numerous segments, including Margaretengürtel, Neubaugürtel, and Währinger Gürtel. Like Vienna's street signs, *Let's Go* indicates the district number in Roman or Arabic numerals before the street and number.

PHONE CODES	**Country code:** ☎43. **Vienna city code:** ☎01 within Austria, ☎011 43 1 abroad. **International dialing prefix:** 00

Main Tourist Office: I, Albertinapl. on the corner of Maysederg. (☎245 55; www.vienna.info). Follow Operng. up 1 block from the Opera House. Books rooms for a €2.90 fee. Open daily 9am-7pm.

Embassies and Consulates: Australia, IV, Mattiellistr. 2-4 (☎50 67 40). Open M-F 8:30am-4:30pm. **Canada,** I, Laurenzerberg 2 (☎531 38 30 00). M-F 8:30am-12:30pm and 1:30-3:30pm. **Ireland,** I, Rotenturmstr. 16-18, 5th fl. (☎715 42 46). Open M-F 9:30-11am and 1:30-4pm. **New Zealand,** III, Salesianerg. 15 (☎318 85 05). **UK,** III, Jaurèesg. 10 (☎716 13 53 33, after hours for UK nationals in emergencies only 0676 5694012). Open M-F 9:15am-12:30pm and 2-3:30pm. **US,** X, Boltzmanng. 16 (☎31 33 90). Open M-F 8-11:30am, 24hr. emergency services.

Currency Exchange and Banks: ATMs are your best bet. Nearly all accept Cirrus, MC, and V. **Banks** generally give the best available exchange rate. Most open M-W and F

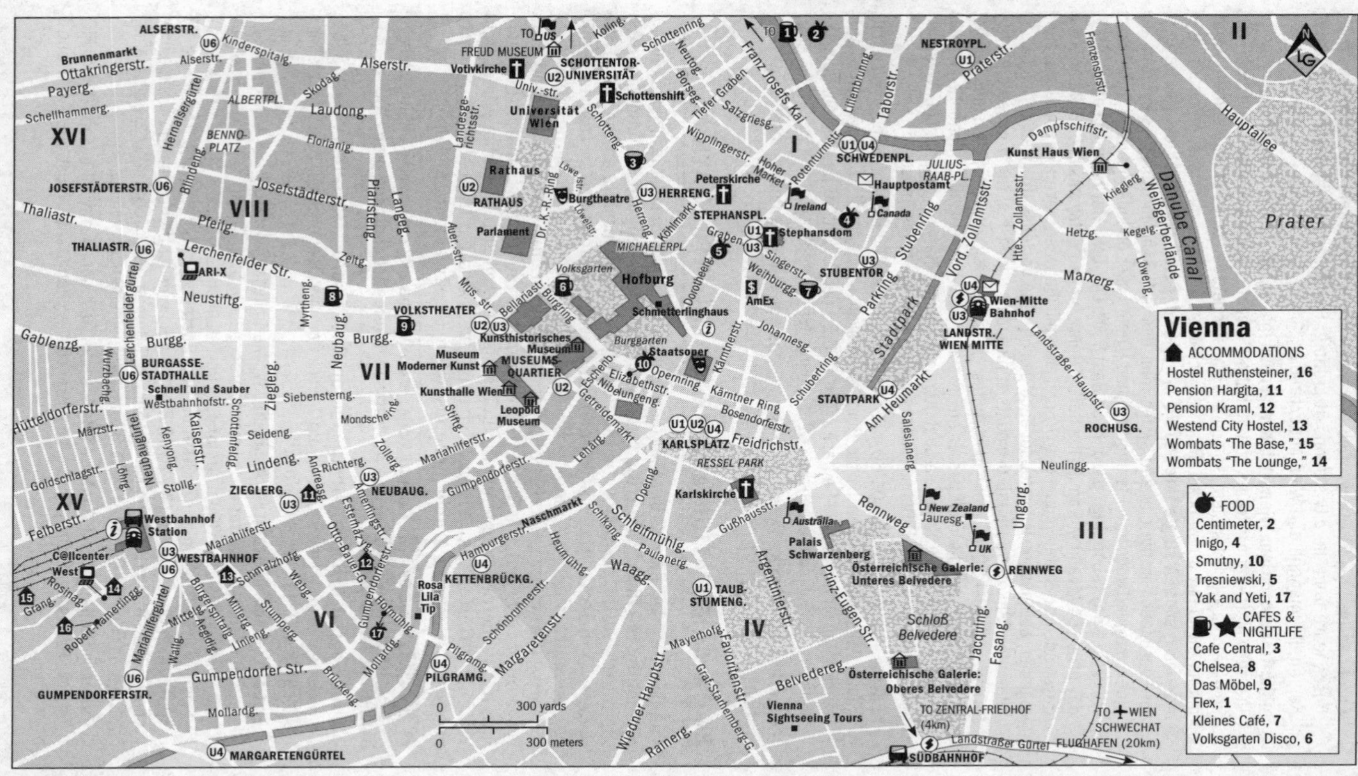
Vienna
ACCOMMODATIONS
Hostel Ruthensteiner, 16
Pension Hargita, 11
Pension Kraml, 12
Westend City Hostel, 13
Wombats "The Base," 15
Wombats "The Lounge," 14
FOOD
Centimeter, 2
Inigo, 4
Smutny, 10
Tresniewski, 5
Yak and Yeti, 17
CAFES & NIGHTLIFE
Cafe Central, 3
Chelsea, 8
Das Möbel, 9
Flex, 1
Kleines Café, 7
Volksgarten Disco, 6
Prater
Hauptallee
Danube Canal
Weißgerberlände
Franzensbrstr.
Kunst Haus Wien
Dampfschiffstr.
Praterstr.
NESTROYPL.
Taborstr.
Lilienbrunng.
SCHWEDENPL.
JULIUS-RAAB-PL.
Hauptpostamt
Canada
Stubenring
Vord. Zollamtsstr.
Wien-Mitte Bahnhof
LANDSTR./WIEN MITTE
Landstraßer Hauptstr.
ROCHUSG.
Stadtpark
Am Heumarkt
STADTPARK
STUBENTOR
Parkring
Stephansdom
Ireland
STEPHANSPL.
Singerstr.
Weihburgg.
AmEx
Franz Josefs Kai
Rotenturmstr.
Hoher Market
Peterskirche
HERRENG.
Graben
Kärntnerstr.
Hofburg
Schmetterlinghaus
Staatsoper
Opernring
Kärntner Ring
Schubertring
KARLSPLATZ
RESSEL PARK
Friedrichstr.
Karlskirche
Australia
Palais Schwarzenberg
Österreichische Galerie: Unteres Belvedere
Österreichische Galerie: Oberes Belvedere
Schloß Belvedere
Prinz-Eugen-Str.
Rennweg
RENNWEG
New Zealand
UK
Ungarg.
Fasang.
Jacquing.
SÜDBAHNHOF
TO ZENTRAL-FRIEDHOF (4km)
TO WIEN SCHWECHAT FLUGHAFEN (20km)
Argentinierstr.
TAUB-STUMENG.
Vienna Sightseeing Tours
Favoritenstr.
Wiedner Hauptstr.
Schleifmühlg.
Naschmarkt
Margaretenstr.
KETTENBRÜCKG.
PILGRAMG.
Rosa Lila Tip
SCHOTTENTOR-UNIVERSITÄT
Schottenshift
Universität Wien
Votivkirche
FREUD MUSEUM
US
Rathaus
RATHAUS
Parlament
Burgtheatre
Volksgarten
Burggarten
Kunsthistorisches Museum
MUSEUMS-QUARTIER
Leopold Museum
Museum Moderner Kunst
Kunsthalle Wien
VOLKSTHEATER
Mariahilferstr.
NEUBAUG.
ZIEGLERG.
Westbahnhof Station
WESTBAHNHOF
C@llcenter West
Gumpendorfer Str.
MARGARETENGÜRTEL
GUMPENDORFERSTR.
Mariahilfergürtel
Neubaugürtel
BURGGASSE-STADTHALLE
Schnell und Sauber
Lerchenfelder Str.
ARI-X
THALIASTR.
JOSEFSTÄDTERSTR.
ALSERSTR.
Josefstädterstr.
Alserstr.
Hernalsergürtel
Ottakringerstr.
Brunnenmarkt
I
II
III
IV
VI
VII
VIII
XV
XVI
0 300 yards
0 300 meters

8am-3pm, Th 8am-5:30pm. **Train station** exchanges have long hours (daily 7am-10pm at the Westbahnhof), but charge 1% with a €6 min. fee. Stay away from the 24hr. bill-exchange machines in Innenstadt, as they generally charge outrageous fees.

Luggage Storage: Lockers available at all trains stations. €2-3.50 per 24hr.

Emergency: ☎141.

24hr. Pharmacy: ☎15 50. Consulates have lists of English-speaking doctors.

Hospital: Allgemeines Krankenhaus, IX, Währinger Gürtel 18-20 (☎40 40 00).

Internet Access: C@llCenter West, XV, Mariahilferstr. 149. €1.40 per 30min., €2.50 per hr. Open daily 9am-midnight. **ARI-X,** VII (☎9911 151 612), corner of Kaiserstr. and Lerchenfelderstr. €1 per hr. Open M-Sa 9am-11pm, Su noon-11pm.

Post Office: Hauptpostamt, I, Fleischmarkt 19 (☎0577 677 10 10). Open daily 6am-10pm. Branches throughout the city and at the train stations; look for yellow signs with a trumpet logo. **Postal Codes:** A-1010 (1st district) through A-1230 (23rd district).

ACCOMMODATIONS

HOSTELS

Hostel Ruthensteiner, XV, Robert-Hamerlingg. 24 (☎893 4202; www.hostelruthensteiner.com). Exit Westbahnhof, turn right onto Mariahilferstr., then continue until Haidmannsg. Turn left before the Sato restaurant, then right on Robert-Hamerlingg. Knowledgeable staff, spotless rooms, kitchen, and a secluded courtyard. Breakfast €2.50. Linens €2. Internet €2 per 40min. Key deposit €10. Reception 24hr. 32-bed summer dorm €13; 8-bed dorms €15; singles €30; doubles €48, with bath €54; quads €68/76. AmEx/MC/V; €0.40-0.80 per day surcharge. ❶

Wombats City Hostel, (☎897 2336; www.wombats-hostels.com) offers 2 separate locations. **"The Lounge"** (XV, Mariahilferstr. 137). Exit Westbahnhof and turn right on Mariahilferstr. The bright walls and leather couches add a modern touch to the college dorm atmosphere. Popular and loud bar. **"The Base"** (XV, Grang. 6). Continue on Mariahilferstr., turn right on Rosinag., and left on Grang. Farther from the train station and a quieter street, this wildly colorful hostel compensates with an in-house pub, English-language movies nightly, and guided tours. Breakfast €3.50 daily 7:30-10am. Internet €2 per hr. Laundry €4.50. Dorms €21; doubles €50. MC/V. ❷

Westend City Hostel, VI, Fügerg. 3 (☎597 6729; www.westendhostel.at), near Westbahnhof. Exit on Äussere Mariahilferstr., cross the intersection, go right on Mullerg. and left on Fügerg. A rose-filled courtyard and plain dorms with bath. Breakfast included. Internet €2 per 20min. Reception 24hr. Check-out 10:30am. Lockout 10:30am-2pm. Open mid-Mar. to Nov. Dorms €18-21; singles €50-63; doubles €60-78. Cash only. ❷

PENSIONS

Pension Hargita, VII, Andreasg. 1 (☎526 19 28; www.hargita.at). U3: Zieglerg. Exit on Andreasg. Hungarian decorations in the halls and immaculately clean hardwood floors accompany blue-and-white furniture and bedding. Breakfast €5. Reception 8am-midnight. Singles €38, with shower €45, with shower and toilet €55; doubles €52/58/66; triples with shower €73, with shower and toilet €80. MC/V. ❹

Pension Kraml, VI, Brauerg. 5 (☎587 85 88; www.pensionkraml.at). U3: Zieglerg. Exit on Otto-Bauer-G., take 1st left onto Königsegg., then 1st right. Plush rooms in rich red and a lounge with cable TV. Breakfast included. Reception 24hr. Singles €30; doubles €50, with shower €60, with shower and toilet €70; triples €70/80. 3- to 5-person apartment with bath €95–125. Cash only. ❸

FOOD

The neighborhood north of the university, where Universitätsstr. and Währingerstr. meet (U2: Schottentor), is budget-friendly. Affordable cafes and restaurants also line **Burggasse** in District VII and in the area surrounding the Rechte and Linke Wienzeile near Naschmarkt (U4: Kettenbrückeng). The **Naschmarkt** itself hosts the city's biggest market for fresh (if pricey) produce, and its many eateries provide cheap and quick meals. (Produce stands open M-F 6am-6:30pm, Sa 6am-2pm.) The **Brunnenmarkt** (XVI, U6: Josefstädterstr.) has Turkish flair. The **kosher** supermarket is at II, Hollandstr. 10. (☎216 96 75. Open M-Th 8:30am-6:30pm, F 8am-2pm.)

Trzesniewski, I, Dorotheerg. 1 (☎512 32 91), from Stephansdom, 3 blocks down on the left side of the Graben. Once Kafka's favorite, this stand-up establishment has been serving open-faced mini-sandwiches (€0.90) for over 100 years. Open M-F 8:30am-7:30pm, Sa 9am-5pm. Cash only. ❶

Centimeter, IX, Liechtensteinstr. 42 (☎470 06 06; www.centimeter.at). Tram D to Bauernfeldpl. Huge portions of greasy Austrian fare (€6-7) and open-faced sandwiches (€0.15 per cm). Open M-F 10am-midnight, Sa-Su 11am-midnight. AmEx/MC/V. ❶

Yak and Yeti, VI, Hofmühlg. 21 (☎595 54 52; www.yakundyeti.at). U3: Zieglerg. This Himalayan restaurant serves ethnic specialties. *Momos* (Nepalese dumplings) €10-11. Lunch buffet €6.50. Entrees €7-13. Open May-Sept. M-Sa 11:30am-10:30pm; Oct.-Apr. M-F 11:30am-2:30pm and 6-10:30pm, Sa 11:30am-10:30pm. Cash only. ❸

Smutny, I, Elisabethstr. 8 (☎587 13 56; www.smutny.com), U6: Karlspl. A traditional Viennese restaurant serving *Wiener schnitzel* (€14) and *Fiakergulash* (goulash with beef, egg, potato, and sausage; €11). M-F lunch *Menü* €8 (soup and entree), Sa-Su €10, includes dessert. M-F daily special €5. Open daily 10am-midnight. AmEx/MC/V. ❷

Inigo, I, Bäckerstr. 18 (☎512 74 51; www.inigo.at). Founded by a Jesuit priest, Inigo aids the long-term unemployed by hiring them as cooks. Hearty entrees served with a complimentary salad. Soups €4. Salads €2-7. Vegetarian entrees €8-10. Open M-Sa 9:30am-midnight, Su 10am-4pm. AmEx/MC/V. ❷

COFFEE HOUSES

Kleines Café, I, Franziskanerpl. 3. Turn off Kärntnerstr. onto Weihburg. and follow it to the Franziskanerkirche. Escape from the busy pedestrian streets with a *mélange* (€3) and conversation on a leather couch in the relaxed interior, or by the fountain in the square. Sandwiches €3-5. Open daily 10am-2am. Cash only.

Café Central, I, Herreng. 14 (☎533 3763; www.palaisevents.at), at the corner of Strauchg. With green-gold arches and live music (M-Sa 3pm-9pm, Su 10am-6pm), this luxurious coffeehouse deserves its status as mecca of the cafe world. *Mélange* €3.50. Open M-Sa 7:30am-10pm, Su 10am-10pm. AmEx/MC/V.

SIGHTS

In District I, cafe tables spill into the streets lined by Romanesque arches and *Jugendstil* apartments. Some of Vienna's most famous modern architecture, however, is outside the Ring. This area is also home to a number of Baroque palaces and parks that were once beyond the city limits.

STEPHANSDOM AND GRABEN. In the heart of the city, the massive **Stephansdom** is one of Vienna's most treasured symbols. For a view of the Old City, take the elevator up the North Tower or climb the 343 steps of the South Tower. (☎515 5235

26. North Tower open daily Apr.-June and Sept.-Oct. 8:30am-5:30pm; Nov.-Mar. 8:30am-5pm; July-Aug. 9am-5pm. South Tower open daily 9am-5:30pm. North Tower €4. South Tower €3.) Downstairs, skeletons of plague victims fill the **catacombs.** The **Gruft** (vault) stores urns containing the Habsburgs' innards. *(Tours M-Sa 2 per hr. 10-11:30am and 1:30-4:30pm, Su and holidays 1:30-4:30pm. €4.)* From Stephanspl., follow Graben for Jugendstil architecture, including Otto Wagner's red-marble **Grabenhof** and the underground public toilet complex designed by **Adolf Loos.**

HOFBURG PALACE. A medieval castle expanded over 800 years, this imperial palace was the Habsburgs's home until 1918. It now contains the President's office and a few small museums. The palace is best admired from its **Michaelplatz** and **Heldenplatz** entrances. *(☎525 24, ext. 69 03; www.khm.at. U3: Herreng. Open Tu-W and F-Su 10am-6pm, Th 10am-9pm. €10, students €7.50.)*

SCHLOß SCHÖNBRUNN. Schönbrunn began as a humble hunting lodge, but Maria Theresa's ambition transformed it into a splendid palace. The **Imperial Tour** passes through the dazzling **Hall of Mirrors,** where six-year-old Mozart played. The longer **Grand Tour** also visits Maria Theresa's exquisite 18th-century rooms, including the ornate **Millions Room.** *(Schönbrunnerstr. 47. U4: Schönbrunn. ☎81 11 32 39; www.schoenbrunn.at. Open daily July-Aug. 8:30am-6pm; Apr.-June and Sept.-Oct. 8:30am-5pm; Nov.-Mar. 8:30am-4:30pm. Imperial Tour 22 rooms; 35min.; €9.50, students €8.50. Grand Tour 40 rooms; 50min.; €13/12. English-language audio tour included.)* As impressive as Schönbrunn itself, the **gardens** behind the palace contain a **labyrinth** and a profusion of manicured greenery, flowers, and statuettes. *(Park open daily 6am-dusk. Labyrinth open daily July-Aug. 9am-7pm; Apr.-June and Sept. 9am-6pm; Oct. 9am-5pm; Nov. 9am-3:30pm. Park free. Labyrinth €2.90, students €2.40.)*

ZENTRALFRIEDHOF. The Viennese describe the Central Cemetery as half the size of Geneva but twice as lively. **Tor II** (Gate 2) contains the tombs of Beethoven, Brahms, Schubert, Strauss, and an honorary monument to Mozart, whose true resting place is an unmarked pauper's grave in the **Cemetery of St. Marx,** III, Leberstr. 6-8. **Tor I** (Gate 1) holds the old **Jewish Cemetery,** where many headstones are cracked and neglected. To navigate through the 2.5 million graves, pick up a map at the info desk just inside Tor II. *(XI, Simmeringer Hauptstr. 234. Tram #71 from Schwarzenbergpl. or Simmering. ☎76 04 10. Open daily May-Aug. 7am-8pm; Apr. and Sept. 7am-7pm; Mar. and Oct. 7am-6pm; Nov.-Feb. 8am-5pm. Free.)*

MUSEUMS

For extended museum-hopping, invest in the **Vienna Card** (€19), which is available at the tourist office, large U-bahn stops, and most hostels. It entitles holders to museum and transit discounts for 72hr.

ÖSTERREICHISCHE GALERIE (AUSTRIAN GALLERY). The grounds of **Schloß Belvedere** house Österreichische Galerie's two museums. Home to *The Kiss* and other works by Klimt, the **Oberes Belvedere** supplements its magnificent collection of 19th- and 20th-century art with rotating exhibits. *(III, Prinz-Eugen-Str. 27. Walk up from the Südbahnhof or take tram D from Schwarzenbergpl. to Schloß Belvedere. €9.50, students €6.)* The **Unteres Belvedere** contains the Austrian Museum of Baroque Art and the Austrian Museum of Medieval Art. *(Unteres Belvedere, III, Rennweg 6. Tram #71 from Schwarzenbergpl. to Unteres Belvedere. €7.50, students €4.50. Both Belvederes ☎795 570. Open daily 10am-6pm. Combo ticket €13, students €8.50.)*

KUNST HAUS WIEN. Artist-environmentalist Friedenreich Hundertwasser built this museum without straight lines—even the floor bends. Arboreal "tree tenants" grow from the windowsills and the top floor. *(III, Untere Weißgerberstr. 13.*

U1 or 4 to Schwedenpl., then tram N to Radetzkypl. Take Löweng. to Kriegler-G. and then left on Untere Weißgerberstr. ☎712 0491; www.kunsthauswien.at. Open daily 10am-7pm. Each exhibit €9, both €12; students €7/9. M €4.50/6, except holidays.)

ÖSTERREICHISCHES MUSEUM FÜR ANGEWANDTE KUNST (MAK). This intimate and eclectic museum is dedicated to design, examining Thonet bentwood chairs' smooth curves, Venetian glass's intricacies, and modern architecture's steel heights. *(I, Stubenring 5. U3: Stubentor. ☎71 13 60; www.mak.at. Open Tu 10am-midnight, W-Su 10am-6pm. €7.90, students €5.50; Sa and holidays free.)*

KUNSTHISTORISCHES MUSEUM (MUSEUM OF FINE ARTS). One of the world's largest art collections features Italian paintings, Classical art, and an Egyptian burial chamber. The main building contains works by the Venetian and Flemish masters and across the street, in Neue Burg wing of the Hofburg Palace, the **Ephesos Museum** exhibits findings from excavations in Turkey. The **Sammlung alter Musikinstrumente** includes Beethoven's harpsichord and Mozart's piano. *(U2: Museumsquartier. Across from the Burgring and Heldenpl., to the right of Maria Theresienpl. ☎525 2441; www.khm.at. Main building open Tu-W and F-Su 10am-6pm, Th 10am-9pm; Ephesos and Sammlung open M and W-Su 10am-6pm. €10, students €7.50. English-language audio tour €3.)*

GATEWAY CITIES

MUSEUMSQUARTIER. Central Europe's largest collection of modern art, the **Museum Moderner Kunst (MUMOK),** highlights Classical Modernism, Pop Art, Photo Realism, Fluxus, and Viennese Actionism in a building made from basalt lava. *(Open M-W and F-Su 10am-6pm, Th 10am-9pm. €9, students €6.50.)* The **Leopold Museum** has the world's largest Schiele collection. *(Open M-W and F-Su 10am-6pm, Th 10am-9pm. €9, students €5.50.)* Themed exhibits of contemporary artists fill **Kunsthalle Wien.** *(U2: Museumsquartier. ☎52 57 00; www.mqw.at. Open M-W and F-Su 10am-7pm, Th 10am-10pm. Exhibition Hall 1 €7.50; students M €5, Tu-Su €6. Exhibition Hall 2 €6/3.50/4.50. Both €10.50/7/8.50. "Art" ticket admits visitors to all three museums; €22. "Duo" ticket admits to Leopold and MUMOK; €17, students €11.)*

ENTERTAINMENT AND NIGHTLIFE

Staatsoper, I, Opernring 2, Vienna's premier opera performs almost nightly September through June. (☎514 442 250; www.wiener-staatsoper.at. €2-254). The **Bundestheaterkasse,** I, Hanuschg. 3, sells tickets for the Staatsoper, the Volksoper, and the Burgtheater. (☎514 447 880. Open June to mid-Aug. M-F 10am-2pm; mid-Aug. to June M-F 8am-6pm, Sa-Su 9am-noon; Sa during Advent 9am-5pm.)

With one of the highest bar-to-cobblestone ratios in the world, Vienna is the place to party. Take U1 or 4 to Schwedenpl., which will drop you within blocks of the **Bermuda Dreieck** (Bermuda Triangle), an area packed with crowded clubs. Afterwards, head down **Rotenturmstraße** toward Stephansdom or walk around the areas bounded by the synagogue and Ruprechtskirche. Slightly outside the Ring, the streets off **Burggasse** and **Stiftgasse** in District VII and the **university quarter** in Districts XIII and IX have outdoor courtyards and hip bars. Viennese nightlife starts late, often after 11pm. For listings, pick up the indispensable *Falter* (€2.60).

Das Möbel, VII, Burgg. 10. U2 or 3: Volkstheater. (☎524 9497; www.das-moebel.at). An artsy crowd chats and reads amid metal couches and Swiss-army tables, all created by designers and available for sale. Don't leave without seeing the bathroom. Internet free for 1st 15min., €.90 per 15min. thereafter. Open daily 10am-1am. Cash only.

Chelsea, VIII, Lerchenfeldergürtel 29-31. U6: Thaliastr. or Josefstädterstr. (☎407 9309; www.chelsea.co.at), under the U-Bahn. International bands rock this underground club twice a week. Sa-Su DJs spin techno-pop. Beer €3.30 per 0.5L. Cover €6-12 for band performances. Happy hour 4-5pm. Open M-Sa 6pm-4am, Su 4pm-3am. Cash only.

Flex, I, Donaulände (☎533 7525; www.flex.at), near the Schottenring U-Bahn station (U2 or U4) down by the Danube. Dance, grab a beer or bring your own, and sit by the river with everyone else. DJs start spinning techno, reggae, house, ska, or electronic at 11pm. Beer €4. Cover €2-10, free after 3:30am. Open daily 8pm-4am. Cash only.

Volksgarten Disco, I, Burgring 1 (☎532 42 41; www.volksgarten.at). U2: Volkstheater. A fountain, palms, and a hot young crowd makes this one of Vienna's trendiest clubs. M tango, Th alternative and house, F hip hop, Sa house. Cover €5-10. Open June-Aug. M 8pm-2am, Th 8pm-4am, F 11pm-6am, Sa 9pm-6am; Sept.-May M 8pm-2am, Th 8pm-4am, F 11pm-6am, Sa 11pm-6am. MC/V; min. €70.

VENICE (VENEZIA)

There is a mystical, defeated quality to Venice's (pop. 274,000) decadence. Lavish palaces decorated with Renaissance masterworks stand proudly on a steadily sinking network of wood, treading in the clouded waters of age-old canals. The city that once earned the name *La Serenissima* (most serene) is now saturated with visitors, as Venice struggles to retain its authenticity in a climate where 70% of economic growth comes from tourism.

TRANSPORTATION

The **train station** is on the northwest edge of the city; be sure to get off at **Santa Lucia,** not at Mestre on the mainland. Buses and boats arrive at **Piazzale Roma,** just across the Canal Grande from the train station. To get from either station to **Piazza San Marco,** take *vaporetto* #82 or follow the signs for a 40min. walk.

Flights: Aeroporto Marco Polo (VCE; ☎260 9260; www.veniceairport.it), 10km north of the city. Take the **ATVO shuttlebus** (☎04 21 38 36 72) from the airport to Ple. Roma on the main island (30min., 1 per hr. 8am-midnight, €3).

Trains: Stazione Santa Lucia. Ticket windows open M-F 8:30am-7:30pm, Sa-Su 9am-1:30pm and 2-5:30pm. **Information office** (☎89 20 21) to the left as you exit the platforms. Open daily 7am-9pm. **Luggage storage** by track#14.

Buses: Local **ACTV** (☎24 24; www.hellovenezia.it), in Ple. Roma. Open daily 7:30am-8pm. **ACTV long-distance carrier** runs buses to **Padua** (1½hr., 2 per hr., €4).

Public Transportation: The **Canal Grande** can be crossed on foot only at the Scalzi, Rialto, and Accademia *ponti* (bridges). **Traghetti** (gondola ferry boats) traverse the canals at 7 locations, including Ferrovia, San Marculola, Cà d'Oro, and Rialto (€0.50). **Vaporetti** (V; water buses) provide 24hr. service around the city, with reduced service midnight-5am (single-ride €3.50, the Canal Grande €5; 24hr. *biglietto turistico* pass €12, 3-day €25). Buy tickets at *vaporetti* stops.

ISLAND HOPPING. *Vaporetto* ticket prices border on extortion. Buy the 24hr. *vaporetto* pass for €12, then leap from one island to the next.

ORIENTATION

Venice is composed of 118 islands in a lagoon, connected to the mainland by a thin causeway. To orient yourself, locate the following landmarks on a map: **Ponte di Rialto** (in the center), **Piazza San Marco** (central south), **Ponte Accademia** (southwest), **Ferrovia** (the train station, in the northwest), and **Piazzale Roma** (south of the station). The **Canal Grande** winds through the city, creating six *sestieri* (sections): **Cannaregio** is in the north and includes the train station, Jewish ghetto, and Cà

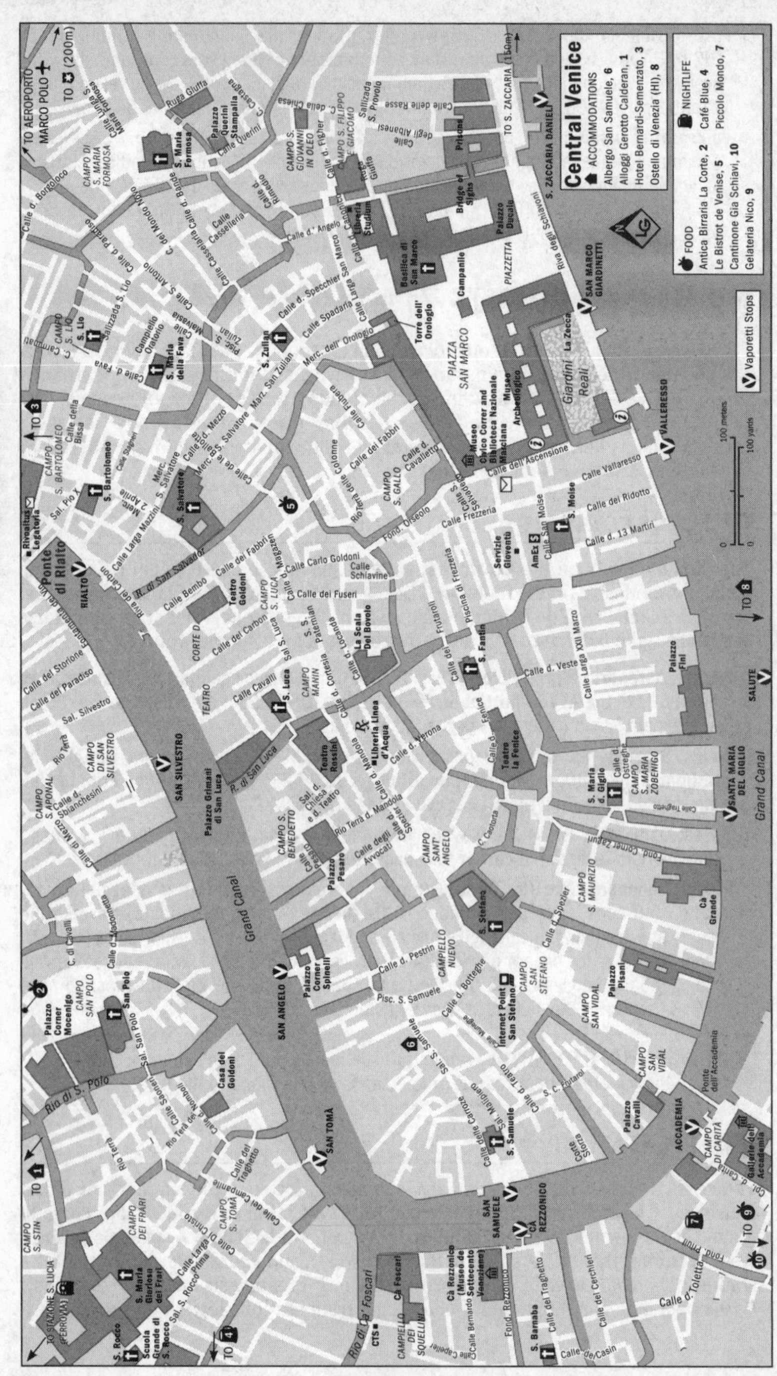
Central Venice
ACCOMMODATIONS
Albergo San Samuele, 6
Alloggi Gerotto Calderan, 1
Hotel Bernardi-Semenzato, 3
Ostello di Venezia (HI), 8
FOOD
Antica Birraria La Corte, 2
Le Bistrot de Venise, 5
Cantinone Gia Schiavi, 10
Gelateria Nico, 9
NIGHTLIFE
Café Blue, 4
Piccolo Mondo, 7
Vaporetti Stops
Grand Canal
PIAZZA SAN MARCO
Ponte di Rialto

d'Oro; **Castello** extends east toward the Arsenale; **Dorsoduro,** across the bridge from S. Marco, stretches the length of Canale della Giudecca and up to Campo S. Pantalon; **Santa Croce** lies west of S. Polo, across the Canal Grande from the train station; **San Marco** fills in the area between the Ponte di Rialto and Ponte Accademia; and **San Polo** runs north from Chiesa S. Maria dei Frari to the Ponte di Rialto.

PRACTICAL INFORMATION

PHONE CODES	**Country code:** ☎39. **Venice city code:** ☎041. The city code must always be dialed, even when calling from within the city. All 10-digit numbers below are mobile phones and do not require a city code. **International dialing prefix:** 00

Tourist Office: APT, Cal. della Ascensione, S. Marco 71/F (☎529 8740; www.doge.it), directly opposite the basilica. Open daily 9am-3:30pm. Avoid the mobbed branches at the train and bus stations. The **Rolling Venice Card** (€4) offers discounts on transportation and at over 200 restaurants, cafes, hotels, museums, and shops for ages 14-29. Cards are valid for 1 year from date of purchase, and can be purchased at APT, which provides a list of participating vendors, or at the **ACTV VeLa** office (☎274 7650) in Ple. Roma. Open daily 7am-8pm.

Budget Travel: CTS, F. Tagliapietra, Dorsoduro 3252 (☎520 5660; www.cts.it). From Campo S. Barnaba, cross the bridge and follow the road through the *piazza.* Turn left at the foot of the large bridge. Sells discounted student plane tickets and issues ISICs. English spoken. Open M-F 9:30am-1:30pm and 2:30-6pm. MC/V.

Pharmacy: Farmacia Italo-Inglese, Cal. della Mandola, S. Marco 3717 (☎522 4837). Follow Cal. Cortesia out of Campo Manin. Open Apr.-Nov. M-F 9am-1:30pm and 2:30-7:30pm, Sa 3:30-7:30pm; Dec.-Mar. M-F 9am-12:30pm and 3:45-7:30pm, Sa 3:30-7:30pm. MC/V. Pharmacies rotate staying open late-night and weekends; check the list posted in the window of any pharmacy.

Hospital: Ospedale Civile, Campo S. S. Giovanni e Paolo, Castello (☎529 4111).

Internet Access: ABColor, Lista di Spagna, Cannaregio 220 (☎524 4380). Look for the "@" symbol on yellow sign, left off the main street heading from the train station. €6 per hr., students €4. Printing €0.15 per page. Open M-Sa 10am-8pm.

Post Office: Poste Venezia Centrale, Salizzada Fontego dei Tedeschi, S. Marco 5554 (☎271 7111), off Campo S. Bartolomeo. Open M-Sa 8:30am-6:30pm. **Postal Codes:** 30121 (Cannaregio); 30122 (Castello); 30123 (Dorsoduro); 30135 (S. Croce); 30124 (S. Marco); 30125 (S. Polo).

ACCOMMODATIONS

Venice's budget accommodations fill quickly in the summer; reserve ahead.

Alloggi Gerotto Calderan, Campo S. Geremia 283 (☎71 55 62; www.casagerottocalderan.com). Half hostel, half hotel, all good. Location makes it the best deal in Venice. Check-in 2pm. Check-out 10am. Curfew 12:30am. Reserve at least 15 days ahead. Dorms €25; singles €40-50; doubles €50-90; triples €75-105. 10% Rolling Venice discount; reduced prices for extended stays. Cash only. ❷

Hotel Bernardi-Semenzato, Cal. dell'Oca, Cannaregio 4366 (☎522 7257; www.hotelbernardi.com). From V: Cà d'Oro, turn right on Str. Nuova, left on Cal. del Duca, and then right. Squeaky clean, elegantly furnished rooms, all with A/C and TV. Check-out 11am. Singles €30-40; doubles €70-75, with bath €60-90; triples €95; quads €120-130. 10% Rolling Venice discount on larger rooms. AmEx/MC/V. ❸

Ostello di Venezia (HI), F. Zitelle, Giudecca 87 (☎523 8211). From V: Zitelle, turn right along canal; the hostel is a 3min. walk to the left. This efficiently managed hostel has sparkling baths and sweeping views of the city. 250 beds on single-sex floors. Breakfast and linens included. Dinner €9.50. Reception 7-9:30am and 1:30pm-midnight. Lock-out 9:30am-1:30pm. Curfew 11:30pm. Reserve online at www.hostelbooking.com. Dorms €20. HI discount €3. MC/V. ❷

Albergo San Samuele, Salizzada S. Samuele, San Marco 3358 (☎522 8045; www.albergosansamuele.it). Follow Cal. delle Botteghe from Campo S. Stefano and turn left on Salizzada S. Samuele. Small but well-kept rooms, with welcoming staff and great location. Reserve 1-2 months ahead. Singles €55; doubles €75-90, with bath €100-120; triples €110-130. Cash only. ❹

FOOD

Beware the overpriced restaurants that line the canals around San Marco. With few exceptions, the best restaurants lie along less traveled alleyways. Venice's renowned Rialto **markets** spread between the Canal Grande and the San Polo foot of the Rialto every Monday through Saturday morning. A **BILLA supermarket,** Str. Nuova, Cannaregio 5660, is near Campo S. Fosca. (Open M-Sa 8:30am-8:30pm, Su 9am-8:30pm. AmEx/MC/V.)

Le Bistrot de Venise, Cal. dei Fabbri, San Marco 4685 (☎523 6651). From P. S. Marco, go through 2nd Sottoportego dei Dai under the awning. Follow road over a bridge and turn right. Delicious dishes, true to Medieval and Renaissance recipes. *Enoteca: cichetti* €3-4, meat and cheese plates €12-24. Restaurant: *primi* €12-22, *secondi* €29-32. Wine from €5 per glass. Service 12%. Open daily 10am-1am. MC/V. ❺

Cantinone Gia Schiavi, F. Meraviglie, Dorsoduro 992 (☎523 0034). From the Frari, follow signs for Ponte Accademia. Just before Ponte Meraviglie, turn right toward the church of S. Trovaso and cross the 1st bridge. Take your pick from hundreds of bottles (from €3.50), or enjoy a glass canal-side with some tasty *cichetti* (€1-4). Open M-Sa 8:30am-2:30pm and 3:15-8:30pm. Cash only. ❶

Gelateria Nico, F. Zattere, Dorsoduro 922 (☎522 5293). Near V: Zattere. Try the Venetian *gianduiotto de passeggio,* a brick of dense chocolate-hazelnut ice cream dropped into a cup of whipped cream (€2.50). Gelato €1, 2 scoops €1.70. Prices higher for sitdown. Open M-W and F-Su 6:45am-10pm. Cash only. ❶

Antica Birraria La Corte, Campo S. Polo, San Polo 2168 (☎275 0570). Large restaurant and bar with outside tables. Pizza €5-9. *Primi* €9-11. *Secondi* €11-19. Cover €2. Open mid-Aug. to mid-July daily 12:30-3pm and 7-10:30pm; mid-July to mid-Aug. M-F 12:30-3pm and 7-10:30pm, Sa-Su 12:30-3pm. AmEx/MC/V. ❸

SIGHTS

BASILICA DI SAN MARCO. The symmetrical arches and incomparable mosaics of Venice's crown jewel grace **Piazza San Marco.** The city's premier tourist attraction, the **Basilica di San Marco** also has the longest lines. Late afternoon visitors profit from the best natural light but experience the most crowding. Built to house the remains of St. Mark, 13th-century Byzantine and 16th-century Renaissance mosaics now make the interior sparkle. Behind the altar, the **Pala d'Oro** relief frames a parade of saints in gem-encrusted gold. Steep stairs in the atrium lead to the **Galleria della Basilica,** whose view is of tiny golden tiles in the basilica's vast ceiling mosaics and the original bronze **Cavalli di San Marco** (Horses of St. Mark). A balcony overlooks the *piazza. (Basilica open M-Sa 9:45am-5pm, Su 2-4pm. Modest dress required. Free. Pala d'Oro open M-Sa 9:45am-5:30pm, Su 2-4pm. €1.50. Treasury open M-Sa 9:45am-7pm, Su 2-4:30pm; €2. Galleria open M-F 9:45am-4:15pm, Sa-Su 9:45am-4:45pm. €3.)*

PALAZZO DUCALE (DOGE'S PALACE). Once the home of Venice's *doge* (mayor), the Palazzo Ducale is now a museum. Veronese's *Rape of Europa* is among its spectacular works of art. In the courtyard, Sansovino's enormous sculptures, *Mars* and *Neptune*, flank the **Scala dei Giganti** (Stairs of the Giants), upon which new *doges* were crowned. The Council of Ten, the *doge*'s administrators, would drop the names of suspected criminals into the **Bocca di Leone** (Lion's Mouth), on the balcony. Climb the **Scala d'Oro** (Golden Staircase) to the **Sala delle Quattro Porte** (Room of the Four Doors), whose ceiling depicts biblical judgements, and the **Sala dell'Anticollegio** (Antechamber of the Senate), whose decorations are myths about Venice. Courtrooms of the Council of Ten and the Council of Three lead to the **Sala del Maggior Consiglio** (Great Council Room), dominated by Tintoretto's *Paradise*, the largest oil painting in the world. Near the end, thick stone lattices line the **Ponte dei Sospiri** (Bridge of Sighs), named after the mournful groans of prisoners who walked it on their way to the prison's damp cells. *(Wheelchair-accessible. Open daily Apr.-Oct. 9am-7pm; Nov.-Mar. 9am-5pm. €12, students €6.50.)*

THE GRAND CANAL. The Grand Canal is Venice's "main street." Over 3km long and nearly 50m wide, it loops through the city and passes under three bridges: the **Ponte Scalzi, Rialto,** and **Accademia.** The *bricole*, candy-cane posts used for mooring boats on the canal, are painted with the colors of the family whose *palazzo* adjoins them. *(For great facade views, ride V. #1, 4 or 82 from the train station to P. S. Marco. The facades are lit at night and produce dazzling reflections.)*

COLLEZIONE PEGGY GUGGENHEIM. Guggenheim's Palazzo Venier dei Leoni displays works by Dalí, Duchamp, Ernst, Kandinsky, Klee, Magritte, Picasso, and Pollock. The Marini sculpture Angel in the City, in front of the palazzo, was designed with a detachable penis so that Ms. Guggenheim could avoid offending her more prudish guests. *(F. Venier dei Leoni, Dorsoduro 701. V: Accademia. Turn left and follow the yellow signs. Open M and W-Su 10am-6pm. €10; students and Rolling Venice €5.)*

ENTERTAINMENT AND NIGHTLIFE

Admire Venetian houses and *palazzi* via their original canal pathways, on **gondola** rides, most romantic about 50min. before sunset and most affordable if shared by six people. The most price-flexible gondoliers are those standing by themselves rather than those in groups at the "taxi-stands" throughout the city. The rate that a gondolier quotes is negotiable, but expect to pay €80-100 for a 40min. ride. The weekly *A Guest in Venice*, free at hotels, tourist offices, or online (www.unospitedivenezia.it), lists current festivals, concerts, and gallery exhibits.

Establishments come and go with some regularity, though student nightlife is consistently concentrated around **Campo Santa Margherita,** in Dorsoduro, while that of tourists centers around the **Lista di Spagna.**

Café Blue, Dorsoduro 3778 (☎71 02 27). From S. Maria Frari, take Cal. Scalater and turn right at the end. Grab a glass of wine (from €1.50) and a stool to watch the daytime coffee crowd turn into a chill, laid-back set as night falls. Free Wi-Fi and 1 computer for Internet. DJ W, live music in winter F. Open daily 8am-2am. MC/V.

Piccolo Mondo, Accademia, Dorsoduro 1056/A (☎520 0371). Facing toward the Accademia, turn right. Ring bell to enter. Disco, hip hop, and vodka with Red Bull (€10) keep a full house at this small, popular *discoteca,* which heats up late behind its heavy, locked doors. Drinks from €7. Open daily 11pm-4am. AmEx/MC/V.

GATEWAY CITIES

APPENDIX

LANGUAGE PHRASEBOOK

PHONETIC TRANSCRIPTION

	PRONOUNCED
a	Battle of Stalingrad
ai	Iron Curtain
ah	Prague
au	orange
aw	like saw, but shorter
ay	Romania (short)
b	Bosnia
ch	China
d	dictatorship
dz	comrades
e	lend
ee	Eastern Europe
eh	Estonia
ehr	aerial (rolled, with the tip of the tongue)
ey	vey!

	PRONOUNCED
f	Former USSR
g	glasnost (soft)
h	have
ih	betw. indie and evil
iy	ski
j	Joseph, edge
k	Kremlin
kh	fricative, Ger. Bach
l	Lenin
m	Macedonia
n	Non-Aggression Pact
oh	Croatia
oe	rounded, Fr. *sœur*
oo	Budapest
ow	wow (with rounded lips)

	PRONOUNCED
oy	Oy
p	Poland
r	revolution
rr	rascal (rolled, with the tip of the tongue)
t	tank
th	theft
s	Serbia
ts	Let's Go
sh	dictatorship
uh	Russia
v	Volga
w	workers of the world
y	Yalta
z	Communism
zh	mirage

CYRILLIC ALPHABET

Bulgaria and **Ukraine** use variations of the Russian Cyrillic alphabet.

CYRILLIC	ENGLISH	PRONOUNCED	CYRILLIC	ENGLISH	PRONOUNCED
А а	a	*ah* as in Prague	Р р	r	*r* as in revolution
Б б	b	*b* as in **B**osnia	С с	s	*s* as in **S**erbia
В в	v	*v* as in **V**olga	Т т	t	*t* as in **t**ank
Г г	g	*g* as in **G**lasnost	У у	u	*oo* as in B**u**dapest
Д д	d	*d* as in **d**ictatorship	Ф ф	f	*f* as in **f**ormer USSR
Е е	e	*yeh* as in **Ye**ltsin	Х х	kh	*kh* as in Ba**ch**
Ё ё	yo	*yo* as in **yo!**	Ц ц	ts	*ts* as in **ts**ar
Ж ж	zh	*zh* as in mira**g**e	Ч ч	ch	*ch* as in Gorba**ch**ev
З з	z	*z* as in communi**s**m	Ш ш	sh	*sh* as in Bol**sh**evik
И и	i	*ee* as in Gr**ee**k	Щ щ	shch	*shch* in Khru**shch**ev
Й й	y	*y* as in bo**y** or ke**y**	Ъ ъ	(hard sign)	(not pronounced)
К к	k	*k* as in **K**remlin	Ы ы	y	*y* as in s**i**lver
Л л	l	*l* as in **L**enin	Ь ь	(soft sign)	(not pronounced)
М м	m	*m* as in **M**oscow	Э э	e	*eh* as in **E**stonia
Н н	n	*n* as in **n**uclear	Ю ю	yu	*yoo* as in **U**kraine
О о	o	*o* as in Cr**o**atia	Я я	ya	*yah* as in **Ya**lta
П п	p	*p* as in **P**oland			

BULGARIAN (БЪЛГАРСКИ)

ENGLISH	BULGARIAN	PRONOUNCE
Hello	Добър ден	DOH-bir dehn
Yes/no	Да/Не	dah/neh
Please/you're welcome	Моля	MO-lyah
Thank you	Благодаря	blahg-oh-dahr-YAH
Goodbye	Довиждане	doh-VEEZH-dah-neh
Good morning	Добро утро	doh-BROH OO-troh
Good evening	Добър Вечер	DOH-buhr VEH-cher
Good night	Лека Нощ	LEH-kah nohsht
Sorry/excuse me	Извинете	iz-vi-NEH-teh
Help!	Помощ!	POH-mohsht
Where is...	Къде е...	kuh-DEH eh
...the bathroom?	...тоалетната?	toh-ah-LEHT-nah-tah
...the nearest phone booth?	...най-близкия телефон?	nai-bleez-kee-yah teh-leh-FOHN
...the center of town?	...центъра на града?	TSEHNT-ur-a nah grahd-AH
How much does this cost?	Колко Струва?	KOHL-koh STROO-vah
When?	Кога?	koh-GAH
Do you speak English?	Говорите ли Английски?	goh-VOH-ree-teh lee ahn-GLEEY-skee
I don't understand.	Не разбирам.	neh rahz-BEE-rahm
I don't speak Bulgarian.	Не говоря по-български.	neh gah-var-YA po-buhl-GAHR-skee
Please write it down.	Може ли да ми го запишете.	MOH-zhe LEE-dah mee goh za-pee-SHEE-teh
Do you have a vacancy?	Имате ли свободна стая?	ee-MAH-te lee svoh-BOHD-nah STAH-ya
I'd like a room.	Искам стая.	EES-kahm STAH-yah
I'd like to order...	Искам да поръчам...	EES-kahm dah por-RUH-cham
I don't eat...	Не ям...	neh yahm...
I'm allergic.	Имам алергия.	EE-mahm ah-LEHR-gee-yah
I'd like to pay.	Искам да платя.	EES-kahm dah plah-TYAH
I want a ticket to...	Искам билет да...	EES-kahm bee-LEHT dah
Go away.	Махнете се.	makh-NEH-teh seh
Cheers!	Наздраве!	nahz-DRAHV-eh
I love you.	Ас те обичам.	ahs tey OHB-ee-chahm

ENGLISH	BULGARIAN	PRONOUNCED
one	едно	ehd-NOH
two	две	dveh
three	три	tree
four	четири	CHEH-tee-ree

ENGLISH	BULGARIAN	PRONOUNCED
six	шест	shehst
seven	седем	SEH-dehm
eight	осем	O-sehm
nine	девет	DEH-veht

APPENDIX

ENGLISH	BULGARIAN	PRONOUNCED
five	пет	peht
single room	единична	ye-din-EECH-nah
double room	двойна	dvoy-NAH
reservation	резервация	re-zer-VAH-tsee-yah
departure	заминаващи	zaminavashti
arrival	пристигащи	pristigashti
airport	летище	LEHT-ee-shteh
train station	гара	gah-RAH
bus station	автогарата	AHV-toh-gah-rah-tah
luggage	багаж	bah-GAHZH
breakfast	закуска	za-KOO-ska
lunch	обяд	oh-BYAHD
dinner	вечеря	veh-cher-YAH
menu	меню	mehn-YOO
bread	хляб	hlyahb
vegetables	зеленчуци	ZEH-lehn-choot-see
left	ляво	LYAH-voh
right	дясно	DYAHS-noh
straight ahead	на право	nah PRAH-voh
doctor	лекарят	LEH-kahr-yaht
hospital	болницата	BOHL-neets-ah-ta

ENGLISH	BULGARIAN	PRONOUNCED
ten	десет	DEH-seht
one-way	отиване	o-TEE-vahn-eh
round-trip	отиване и Връщане	oh-TEE-vahn-eh ee VRUH-shtah-neh
ticket	билет	bee-LEHT
train	влак	vlahk
bus	автобус	ahv-toh-BOOS
bank	банка	BAHN-kah
police	полиция	poh-LEE-tsee-yah
exchange	обменно бюро	OHB-mehn-noh byoo-ROH
passport	паспорт	pahs-POHRT
market	пазар	pah-ZAHR
grocery	бакалия	bah-kah-LEE-yah
meat	месо	meh-SO
coffee	кафе	kah-FEH
milk	мляко	MLYAH-koh
beer	бира	BEE-rah
toilet	тоалетна	toh-ah-LEHT-nah
square	площад	PLOH-shtad
post office	поща	POH-shtah
stamp	марка	MAHR-kah
airmail	въздушна поща	vuhz-DOOSH-nah POH-shtah

CROATIAN (HRVATSKI)

ENGLISH	CROATIAN	PRONOUNCED
Hello/hi	Zdravo/bog	ZDRAH-vo/bohg
Yes/no	Da/ne	Dah/Neh
Please/you're welcome	Molim	MOH-leem
Thank you	Hvala lijepa/hvala	HVAH-la lee-ye-pah/hvah-lah
Goodbye	Bog	Bog
Good morning	Dobro jutro	DOH-broh YOO-tro
Good evening	Dobro večer	DOH-broh VEH-chehr
Good night	Laku noć	LAH-koo nohch
Sorry/excuse me	Oprostite	oh-PROH-stee-teh
Help!	U pomoć!	OO pohmohch
Where is...?	Gdje je...?	gdye yeh
...the bathroom?	...zahod?	ZAH-hod
...the nearest telephone booth?	...nalazi najbliža telefonska govornica?	NAH-lah-zee nai-BLEE-zhah teh-leh-FOHN-skah goh-vohr-NEE-tsah
...the center of town?	...centar grada?	TSEHN-tahr GRAH-dah
How much does this cost?	Koliko to košta?	KOH-lee-koh toh KOH-shtah

APPENDIX

ENGLISH	CROATIAN	PRONOUNCED
When?	Kada?	KAH-dah
Do you speak English?	Govorite li engleski?	GO-vohr-ee-teh lee ehn-GLEH-skee
I don't understand.	Ne razumijem.	neh rah-ZOO-mee-yehm
I don't speak Croatian.	Ne govorim hrvatski.	neh goh-VOH-reem KHER-va-tskee
Please write it down.	Molim, napišajte mi to.	MOH-leem, nah-PEE-shee-teh mee to
Do you have a vacancy?	Imate li slobodnih soba?	EE-mah-teh lee SLOH-boh-dneh SOH-bah
I'd like a room.	Želio bih sobu.	ZHEL-ee-oh beeh SOH-boo
I'd like some...	Želio bih ...	ZHEL-ee-oh beeh
I don't eat...	Ne jedem...	neh YEH-dem
I'm allergic.	Imam alergiju.	EE-mam ah-lehr-GEE-yoo
Do you have any vegetarian dishes?	Imate li vegetarijanska jela?	EE-mah-teh lee veh-geh-tah-ree-YAN-skah YEH-lah
Check, please.	Račun, molim.	ra-CHOON MOH-leem
I want a ticket to...	Htio bih kartu za...	HTEE-oh beeh KAHR-too zah...
Go away.	Bježi	BYEH-zhee
Cheers!	Živjeli!	ZHIV-yehl-ee
I love you.	Volim te.	VOH-leem teh.

ENGLISH	CROATIAN	PRONOUNCED
one	jedan	YEHD-ahn
two	dva	dvah
three	tri	tree
four	četiri	CHEH-tee-ree
five	pet	peht
single room	jedno-krevetnu sobu	yehd-noh-KREH-veht-noo SOH-boo
double room	dvokrevetnu sobu	dvoh-KREH-veht-noo SOH-boo
reservation	rezervacija	reh-zehr-VAH-tsee-yah
departure	odlazak	OHD-lahz-ahk
arrival	polazak	POH-lahz-ahk
Monday	ponedeljak	POH-neh-deh-lyahk
Tuesday	utorak	OO-toh-rahk
Wednesday	srijeda	SREE-yehdah
Thursday	četvrtak	CHEHT-vehr-tahk
Friday	petak	PEH-tahk
Saturday	subota	SOO-boh-tah
Sunday	nedjelja	NEH-dyehl-yah
today	danas	DAH-nahs
tomorrow	sutra	SOO-trah

ENGLISH	CROATIAN	PRONOUNCED
six	šest	shehst
seven	sedam	SEH-dahm
eight	osam	OH-sahm
nine	devet	DEH-veht
ten	deset	DEH-seht
one-way	u jednom smjeru	oo YEH-dnohm SMYEH-roo
round-trip	povratna karta	POHV-raht-nah KAHR-tah
ticket	kartu	KAHR-too
train	vlak	VLAHK
bus	autobus	OW-toh-bus
airport	zračna luka	ZRAH-chnah loo-kah
train (bus) station	(autobusni) kolodvor	(OW-toh-boos-nee) KOH-loh-dvohr
luggage	prtljaga	PEHRT-lyah-gah
bank	banka	BAHN-kah
police	policija	poh-LEE-tsee-yah
doctor	liječnik	lee-YECH-neek
hospital	bolnica	BOHL-neet-sa
exchange	mjenjačnica	myehn-YAHCH-nee-tsah
passport	putovnica	POO-toh-vnee-tsah

APPENDIX

ENGLISH	CROATIAN	PRONOUNCED
day	dan	dahn
week	tjedna	TYEHD-nah
morning	ujutro	oo-YOO-troh
afternoon	popodne	poh-POH-dneh
evening	večer	VEH-chehr
hot	vruće	VROO-cheh
cold	hladno	HLAHD-noh
left	lijevo	lee-YEH-voh
right	desno	DEHS-noh
straight ahead	pravo	PRA-vo
toilet	W.C.	vay-tsay
stamp	markica	MAHR-kee-tsah
square	trg	terg

ENGLISH	CROATIAN	PRONOUNCED
market/ grocery	trgovina	TER-goh-vee-nah
breakfast	doručak	doh-ROO-chahk
lunch	ručak	ROO-chahk
dinner	večera	VEH-cheh-rah
menu	karta	KAR-tah
bread	kruh	krooh
vegetables	povrće	POH-vehr-chay
meat	meso	meh-so
coffee	kava	KAH-vah
milk	mlijeko	mlee-YEH-koh
beer	pivo	PEE-voh
post office	pošta	POSH-tah
airmail	zrakoplovom	ZRAH-koh-ploh-vohm

CZECH (ČESKY)

ENGLISH	CZECH	PRONOUNCED
Hello	Dobrý den *(formal)*	DOH-bree dehn
Yes/no	Ano/ne	AH-noh/neh
Please/you're welcome	Prosím	PROH-seem
Thank you	Děkuji	DYEH-koo-yee
Goodbye	Nashledanou	NAS-kleh-dah-noh
Good morning	Dobré ráno	DOH-breh RAH-noh
Good evening	Dobrý večer	DOH-breh VEH-chehr
Good night	Dobrou noc	DOH-broh NOHTS
Sorry/excuse me	Promiňte	PROH-meen-teh
Help!	Pomoc!	POH-mots
Where is...?	Kde je...?	gdeh yeh
...the bathroom?	...koupelna?	KOH-pehl-nah
...the nearest telephone booth?	...nejbližší telefonní budka?	NEY-bleezh-shnee TEH-leh-foh-nee BOOT-kah
...the center of town?	...centrum města?	TSEN-troom MYEHST-steh
How much does this cost?	Kolik to stojí?	KOH-leek STOH-yee
When?	Kdy?	gdee
Do you speak English?	Mluvíte anglicky?	MLOO-veet-eh ahng-GLEET-skee
I don't understand.	Nerozumím.	NEH-rohz-oo-meem
I don't speak Czech.	Nemluvím Česky.	NEH-mloo-veem CHESS-kee
Please write it down.	Mohl byste to napsat?	MO-huhl BI-ste to NAP-sat
Do you have a vacancy?	Máte volný pokoj?	MAH-teh VOL-nee POH-koy
I'd like a room.	Prosím pokoj.	proh-SEEM PO-koy
I'd like to order...	Prosím...	proh-SEEM
I don't eat...	Nejím maso.	NEH-yeem MAH-soh
I'm allergic.	Jsem alergický.	ysehm AH-lehr-gits-kee
Check, please.	Paragon, prosím.	PAH-rah-gohn proh-SEEM

ENGLISH	CZECH	PRONOUNCED
I want a ticket to...	Chtěl bych jízdenku do...	khytel bikh YEEZ-den-koo DOH
How long does the trip take?	Jak dlouho ta cesta trva?	yahk DLOH-ho tah TSE-stah TER-vah
Go away.	Prosím odejděte.	pro-SEEM ODEY-dyeh-teh
Cheers!	Na zdraví!	nah ZDRAH-vee
I love you.	Miluji tě.	MEE-loo-yee tyeh

ENGLISH	CZECH	PRONOUNCED
one	jedna	YEHD-na
two	dvě	dvye
three	tři	trzhee
four	čtyři	CHTEER-zhee
five	pět	pyet
single room	jednolůžkový pokoj	YEHD-noh-loozh-koh-vee POH-koy
double room	dvoulůžkový pokoj	DVOH-loozh-ko-vee POH-koy
reservation	rezervace	REH-zehr-vah-tseh
departure	odjezd	OHD-yehzd
arrival	příjezd	PREE-yehzd
one-way	jedním směrem	YED-neem SMNYE-rem
round-trip	zpáteční	SPAH-tehch-nyee
Monday	pondělí	POHN-dyeh-lee
Tuesday	úterý	OO-teh-ree
Wednesday	středa	STRZHEH-dah
Thursday	čtvrtek	CHTVER-tehk
Friday	pátek	PAH-tehk
Saturday	sobota	SOH-boh-tah
Sunday	neděle	NEH-dyeh-leh
today	dnes	dnehs
tomorrow	zítra	ZEE-trah
day	den	dehn
week	týden	tee-dehn
morning	ráno	RAH-noh
afternoon	odpoledne	OHD-pohl-ehd-neh
evening	večer	VEH-chehr
hot	teplý	TEHP-leeh
cold	studený	STOO-deh-nee
left	vlevo	VLEH-voh
right	vpravo	VPRAH-voh
straight ahead	přímo	PRZHEE-moh
toilet	W.C.	VEE-TSEE
square	náměstí	NAH-myeh-stee

ENGLISH	CZECH	PRONOUNCED
six	šest	shest
seven	sedm	SEH-doom
eight	osm	OH-suhm
nine	devět	DE-vyet
ten	deset	DE-set
ticket	lístek	LEES-tehk
train	vlak	vlahk
bus	autobus	OW-toh-boos
airport	letiště	LEH-teesh-tyeh
station	nádraží	NAH-drah-zhee
bus station	autobusové nádražé	OW-toh-boo-sohv-eh NAH-drazh-eh
luggage	zavadla	ZAH-vahd-lah
bank	banka	BAHN-kah
police	policie	POH-leets-ee-yeh
doctor	doktor	DOHK-tohr
hospital	nemocnice	NEH-mo-tsnyi-tseh
exchange	směnárna	smyeh-NAHR-nah
passport	cestovní pas	TSEH-stohv-nee pahs
market	trh	terh
grocery	potraviny	POH-trah-vee-nee
breakfast	snídaně	SNEE-dahn-yeh
lunch	oběd	OHB-yehd
dinner	večeře	VEH-cher-zheh
menu	lístek/menu	LEES-tehk/meh-noo
bread	chléb	khlep
vegetables	zelenina	ZEH-leh-nee-nah
meat	maso	MAH-soh
coffee	káva	KAH-vah
milk	mléko	MLEH-koh
beer	pivo	PEE-voh
post office	pošta	POSH-tah
stamp	známka	ZNAHM-kah
airmail	letecky	LEH-tehts-kee

ESTONIAN (EESTI KEEL)

There are many dipthongs (double vowels) in Estonian. Note that the first vowel of the dipthong is always pronounced short.

ENGLISH	ESTONIAN	PRONOUNCED
Hello	Tere	TEH-reh
Yes/no	Jaa/ei	yah/ay
Please	Palun	PAH-loon
Thank you	Tänan	TAH-nahn
Goodbye	Head aega	heh-ahd AI-gah
Sorry/Excuse me	Vabandage	vah-bahn-DAHG-eh
Help!	Appi!	AHP-pee
ticket	pilet	PEE-leht
train/bus	rong/buss	rohng/boos
restroom	WC	vet-seh
doctor	arst	arzt

ENGLISH	ESTONIAN	PRONOUNCED
one	üks	ooks
two	kaks	kahks
three	kolm	kohlm
four	neli	NEH-lee
five	viis	vees
six	kuus	koos
seven	seitse	SAYT-seh
eight	kaheksa	KAH-hek-sah
nine	üheksa	OO-hek-sah
ten	kümme	KOO-me
hospital	haigla	hai-glah

ENGLISH	ESTONIAN	PRONOUNCED
Where is...?	Kus on...?	koos ohn
How much does this cost?	Kui palju?	kwee PAHL-yoo
Do you speak English?	Kas te räägite inglise keelt?	kahs teh RA-A-GEE-teh EEN-GLEE-seh kehlt
Go away!	Jätke mind rahule!	YAT-keh meend RA-hule
Cheers!	Proosit!	PROH-seet

HUNGARIAN (MAGYAR)

Stress falls on the first syllable of each word in Hungarian. After consonants, especially *g*, *l*, or *n*, the *y* is not pronounced but serves to soften the letter it follows.

ENGLISH	HUNGARIAN	PRONOUNCED
Hello	Szervusz (pol.)/Szia (inf.)/Hello	SAYHR-voose/See-ya/Hello
Yes/no	Igen/nem	EE-gehn/nehm
Please	Kérem	KAY-rehm
Thank you	Köszönöm	KUH-suh-nuhm
Goodbye	Viszontlátásra	VEE-sohnt-laht-ah-shrah
Good morning	Jó reggelt	YAW RAHg-gailt
Good evening	Jó estét	YAW EHSH-teht
Good night	Jó éjszakát	YAW AY-sah-kaht
Sorry/excuse me	Elnézést	EHL-nay-zaysht
Where is...?	Hol van...?	haul vahn
...the bathroom?	...a W.C.?	ah VAY-tsay
...the nearest telephone booth?	...a legközelebbi telefonfülke?	ah LEHG-kawz-ehl-ehb-ee teh-leh-FAWN-FOOHL-keh
...the center of town?	...a városközpont?	ah VAH-rosh-kohz-pohnt
How much does this cost?	Mennyibe kerül?	MEHN-yee-beh KEH-rool
When?	Mikor?	MEE-kohr
Do you speak English?	Beszél angolul?	BESS-ayl AHN-gawl-ool
I don't understand.	Nem értem.	nem AYR-tem
I don't speak Hungarian.	Nem tudok (jól) magyarul.	nehm TOO-dawk (yawl) MAW-jyah-rool

APPENDIX

ENGLISH	HUNGARIAN	PRONOUNCED
Please write it down.	Kérem, írja fel.	KAY-rem, EER-yuh fel
Do you have a vacancy?	Van üres szoba?	vahn oo-REHSH SAH-bah
I'd like a room.	Szeretnék egy szobát.	seh-reht-naik ehj SAW-baht
I'd like to order...	...kérek.	KAY-rehk
I don't eat...	Nem eszem...	nem eh-sem
I'm allergic.	Allergia's vagyok.	ah-lehr-ghee-ahsh vah-jawk
I'm a vegetarian.	Vegetarianus vagyok.	vej-et-ar-ee-an-ush vad-jawk
Check, please.	A számlát, kérem.	uh SAHM-lot KAY-rehm
I want a ticket.	Szeretnékegy jegyet.	sehr-eht-nayk-ehj yehj-at
Go away.	Távozzék.	TAH-vawz-zayk
Cheers!	Egészségedre!	ehg-eh-SHEHG-eh-dreh
I love you.	Szeretleu.	sehr-EHT-lyuh

ENGLISH	HUNGARIAN	PRONOUNCED
one	egy	ehj
two	kettő	KEHT-tuh
three	három	HAH-rohm
four	négy	naydj
five	öt	uht
single room	egyágyas	EHD-ahd-awsh
double room	kétágyas szoba	keht-AHGAHS soh-bah
reservation	helyfoglalás	HEY-fohg-lah-DASH
departure	indulás	IN-dool-ahsh
arrival	érkezés	ayr-keh-zaysh
Monday	hétfő	hayte-phuuh
Tuesday	kedd	kehd
Wednesday	szerda	SEHR-dah
Thursday	csütörtök	choo-ter-tek
Friday	péntek	payne-tek
Saturday	szombat	SAWM-baht
Sunday	vasárnap	VAHSH-ahr-nahp
today	ma	mah
tomorrow	holnap	HAWL-nahp
day	nap	nahp
week	hét	hayht
morning	reggel	REHG-gehl
afternoon	délután	deh-lu-taan
evening	este	EHS-te
hot	meleg	MEE-lehg
cold	hideg	HEE-dehg
left	bal	bohl
right	jobb	yawb

ENGLISH	HUNGARIAN	PRONOUNCED
six	hat	hawt
seven	hét	hayt
eight	nyolc	nyawltz
nine	kilenc	KEE-lehntz
ten	tíz	teehz
one-way	csak oda	chohk AW-doh
round-trip	oda-vissza	AW-doh-VEES-soh
ticket	jegyet	YEHD-eht
train	vonat	VAW-noht
bus	autóbusz	AU-OO-toh-boos
airport	repülőtér	rep-oo-loo-TAYR
train station	pályaudvar	pah-yoh-OOT-vahr
bus station	buszmegálló	boos-mehg-AH-loh
luggage	csomag	CHOH-mahg
bank	bank	bohnk
police	rendőrség	REHN-doer-shayg
doctor	kórház	KAWR-haaz
hospital	orvos	AWR-vahsh
exchange	pénzaváltó	pehn-zah-VAHL-toh
passport	az útlevelemet	ahz oot-leh-veh-leh-meht
market	piac	PEE-ohts
grocery	élelmiszerbolt	AY-lehl-meh-sehr-bawlt
breakfast	reggeli	REHG-gehl-ee
lunch	ebéd	EHB-ayd
dinner	vacsora	VAWCH-oh-rah
vegetables	zöldségek	ZUHLD-seh-gehk
meat	húst	hoosht
coffee	kávé	KAA-vay

ENGLISH	HUNGARIAN	PRONOUNCED
straight ahead	egyenesen	EHDJ-ehn-ehshen
toilet	W.C.	VAY-tsay
square	tér	tehr
post office	posta	PAWSH-tah

ENGLISH	HUNGARIAN	PRONOUNCED
milk	tej	tay
beer	sör	shurr
stamp	bélyeg	BAY-yeg
airmail	légiposta	LAY-ghee-PAWSH-tah

LATVIAN (LATIVSKA)

ENGLISH	LATVIAN	PRONOUNCED
Hello	Labdien	LAHB-deean
Yes/no	Jā/nē	yah/ney
Please/ you're welcome	Lūdzu	LOOD-zoo
Thank you	Paldies	PAHL-dee-ahs
Goodbye	Uz redzēšanos	ooz REH-dzeh-shan-nwas
doctor	ārsts	AHRsts
one	viens	vee-ahnss
two	divi	DIH-vih
three	trīs	treess
four	četri	CHEH-trih
five	pieci	PYET-sih

ENGLISH	LATVIAN	PRONOUNCED
Sorry/excuse me	Atvainojiet	AHT-vain-wa-eeat
Help!	Palīgā!	PAH-lee-gaah
ticket	biļete	BIH-leh-teh
train/bus	vilciens/auto-buss	VEEL-tsee-ehns/ AU-to-boos
toilet	tualete	TWA-leh-teh
hospital	slimnīca	SLIM-nee-tsah
six	seši	SEH-shee
seven	septini	SEHP-tih-nyih
eight	astoņi	AHS-toh-nyih
nine	devini	DEH-vih-nyih
ten	desmit	DES-miht

ENGLISH	LATVIAN	PRONOUNCED
Where is...?	Kur ir...?	koohr ihr
How much does this cost?	Cik maksā?	tsikh MAHK-sah
Do you speak English?	Vasi jūs runājat Angliski?	vai yoohss ROO-nai-yat AHN-glih-skih

LITHUANIAN (LIETUVIŠKAI)

ENGLISH	LITHUANIAN	PRONOUNCED
Hello	Labas	LAH-bahss
Yes/no	Taip/ne	tayp/neh
Please	Prašau	prah-SHAU
Thank you	Ačiū	AH-chyoo
doctor	gydytojas	GEE-dee-toh-yas
one	vienas	VYEH-nahss
two	du	doo
three	trys	treese
four	keturi	keh-tuh-RIH
five	penki	pehn-KIH

ENGLISH	LITHUANIAN	PRONOUNCED
Goodbye	Viso gero	VEE-soh GEH-roh
Sorry/excuse me	Atsiprašau	aht-sih-prah-SHAU
Help!	Gelbėkite!	GYEHL-behk-ite
ticket	bilietas	BEE-lee-tahs
hospital	ligoninė	LI-gon-een-eh
six	šeši	sheh-SHIH
seven	septyni	sehp-tee-NIH
eight	aštuoni	ahsh-too-oh-NIH
nine	devyni	deh-vee-NIH
ten	dešimt	DASH-imt

ENGLISH	LITHUANIAN	PRONOUNCED
Where is...?	Kur yra...?	Koor ee-RAH
How much does this cost?	Kiek kainuoja?	kee-yehk kai-NOO-OH-yah
Do you speak English?	Ar Jūs kalbate angliškai?	ahr yoos KAHL-bah-teh AHNG-leesh-kai

APPENDIX

POLISH (POLSKI)

ENGLISH	POLISH	PRONOUNCED
Hello	Cześć	cheshch
Yes/no	Tak/nie	tahk/nyeh
Please/you're welcome	Proszę	PROH-sheh
Thank you	Dziękuję	jehn-KOO-yeh
Goodbye	Do widzenia	doh veed-ZEHN-yah
Good evening	Dobry wieczór	doh-brih VYEH-choor
Good night	Dobranoc	doh-BRAH-nohts
Good morning	Dzień dobry	jehn DOH-brih
Sorry/excuse me	Przepraszam	psheh-PRAH-shahm
Help!	Pomocy!	poh-MOH-tsih
Where is...?	Gdzie jest...?	GJEH yehst
...the bathroom?	...łazienka?	wahzh-EHN-ka
...the nearest telephone booth?	...najbliższa budka telefonic-zna?	nai-BLEE-shah BOOT-kah teh-leh-foh-NEE-chnah
...the center of town?	...centrum miasta?	tsehn-troom MYAH-stah
How much does this cost?	Ile to kosztuje?	EE-leh toh kohsh-TOO-yeh
When?	Kiedy?	KYEH-dih
Do you (male/female) speak English?	Czy pan(i) mówi po angielsku?	chih pahn(-ee) MOO-vee poh ahn-GYEHL-skoo
I don't understand.	Nie rozumiem.	nyeh roh-ZOOM-yehm
I don't speak Polish.	Nie mowię po polsku.	nyeh MOO-vyeh poh POHL-skoo
Please write it down.	Proszę napisać.	PROH-sheh nah-PEE-sahch
Do you have a vacancy?	Czy są jakieś wolne pokoje?	chih SAWN yah-kyehsh VOHL-neh poh-KOY-eh
I (male/female) would like a room.	Chciał(a)bym pokój.	kh-CHOW-(ah)-bihm POH-kooy
I'd like to order...	Chciałbym zamówić...	kh-CHOW-bihm za-MOOV-eech
I don't eat...	Nie jadam...	nyeh JAH-dahm
I'm allergic.	Mam uczulenie.	MAHM oo-choo-LEHN-yeh
Check, please.	Proszę rachunek	PROH-sheh rah-HOON-ehk
I want a ticket to...	Poproszę bilet do...	poh-PROH-sheh BEE-leht do
Go away.	Spadaj.	SPAHD-ai
Cheers!	Sto lat/na zdrowie!	STOH laht/nah ZDROH-wyeh
I love you.	Kocham cię.	koh-HAHM cheh
Good morning	Dzień dobry	jehn DOH-brih

ENGLISH	POLISH	PRONOUNCED
one	jeden	YEH-den
two	dwa	dvah
three	trzy	tshih
four	cztery	ch-TEH-rih
five	pięć	pyainch
breakfast	śniadanie	shnyah-DAHN-yeh
lunch	obiad	OH-byahd
dinner	kolacja	koh-LAH-tsyah
bus	autobus	ow-TOH-booss
airport	lotnisko	loht-NEE-skoh

ENGLISH	POLISH	PRONOUNCED
six	sześć	sheshch
seven	siedem	SHEH-dehm
eight	osiem	OH-shehm
nine	dziewięć	JYEH-vyainch
ten	dziesięć	JYEH-shainch
menu	menu	MEH-noo
bread	chleb	khlehp
vegetables	jarzyny	yah-ZHIH-nih
meat	mięso	MYEN-soh
coffee	kawa	KAH-vah

ENGLISH	POLISH	PRONOUNCED
train station	dworzec	DVOH-zhehts
bus station	dworzec autobusowy	DVOH-zhehts ow-toh-boo-SOH-vih
luggage	bagaż	BAH-gahzh
bank	bank	bahnk
police	policja	poh-LEETS-yah
doctor	lekarz	LEH-kahsh
exchange	kantor	KAHN-tohr
passport	paszport	PAHSH-pohrt
market	rynek	RIH-nehk
grocery	sklep spożywczy	sklehp spoh-ZHIV-chih
Monday	poniedziałek	poh-nyeh-JOW-ehk
Tuesday	wtorek	FTOH-rehk
Wednesday	środa	SHROH-dah
Thursday	czwartek	CHVAHR-tehk
Friday	piątek	PYOHN-tehk
Saturday	sobota	soh-BOH-tah
Sunday	niedziela	nyeh-DZEH-lah
today	dzisiaj	JEE-shai
tomorrow	jutro	YOO-troh
day	dzień	JAYN
week	tydzień	TIH-jayn
morning	rano	RAH-noh
afternoon	popołudnie	poh-poh-WOOD-nyeh

ENGLISH	POLISH	PRONOUNCED
evening	wieczór	VYEH-choor
beer	piwo	PEE-voh
toilet	toaleta	toh-ah-LEH-tah
hospital	szpital	SHPEE-tahl
square	rynek	RIH-nehk
post office	poczta	POHCH-tah
stamps	znaczki	ZNAHCH-kee
airmail	lotniczą	loht-NEE-chawm
hot	gorący	goh-ROHN-tsih
cold	zimny	ZHIH-mnih
right	prawo	PRAH-voh
left	lewo	LEH-voh
straight ahead	prosto	PROH-stoh
single room	jednoosobowy	YEHD-noh-oh-soh-BOH-vih
double room	dwuosobowy	DVOO-oh-soh-BOH-vih
reservation	miejscówka	myay-STSOOF-ka
departure	odjazd	OHD-yahzd
arrival	przyjazd	PSHIH-yahzd
one-way	w jedną stronę	VYEHD-nowm STROH-neh
round-trip	tam i z powrotem	tahm ee spoh-VROH-tehm
ticket	bilet	BEE-leht
train	pociąg	POH-chaung
bus	autobus	au-TOH-boos

ROMANIAN (ROMÂNĂ)

ENGLISH	ROMANIAN	PRONOUNCED
Hello	Bună ziua	BOO-nuh ZEE wah
Yes/no	Da/nu	dah/noo
Please/you're welcome	Vă rog/cu plăcere	vuh rohg/koo pluh-CHEH-reh
Thank you	Mulţumesc	mool-tsoo-MEHSK
Goodbye	La revedere	lah reh-veh-DEH-reh
Good morning	Bună dimineaţa	BOO-nuh dee-mee-NYAH-tsah
Good evening	Bună seara	BOO-nuh seh-AH-rah
Good night	Noapte bună	NWAHP-teh BOO-nuh
Sorry/excuse me	Îmi pare rău/Scuzaţi-mă	uhm PAH-reh ruh-oo/skoo-ZAH-tsee muh
Help!	Ajutor!	ah-zhoo-TOHR
Where is...?	Unde e...?	OON-deh YEH
...the bathroom?	...toaleta?	twah-LEH-tah
...the nearest telephone booth?	...un telefon prin apropiere?	oon teh-leh-FOHN preen ah-proh-PYEH-reh

ENGLISH	ROMANIAN	PRONOUNCED
...the center of town?	...centrul oraşului?	CHEHN-trool oh-RAHSH-oo-loo-ee
How much does this cost?	Cât costă?	kuht KOH-stuh
When?	Cînd?	kuhnd
Do you speak English?	Vorbiţi englezeşte?	vohr-BEETS ehng-leh-ZEHSH-teh
I don't understand.	Nu înţeleg.	noo uhn-tzeh-LEHG
I don't speak Romanian.	Nu vorbesc Româneşte.	noo vohr-BEHSK roh-muh-NEHSH-teh
Please write it down.	Vă rog să scrieţi.	vuh rohg suh SKREE-ehts
Do you have a vacancy?	Aveţi camere libere?	a-VETS KAH-meh-reh LEE-beh-reh
I'd like a room.	Aş vrea o cameră.	ahsh vreh-AH oh KAH-meh-ruh
I'd like to order some...	Aş vrea nişte...	ahsh vreh-AH NEESH-teh
I have an allergy.	Eu am o alergie.	yau ahm oh ah-lehr-JEE-yeh
I don't eat...	Eu nu măńînc...	yau noo muh-NUHNK
Check, please.	Nota, vă rog.	noh-tah VUH rohg
I want a ticket to...	Vreau un bilet pentru...	vreh-ah-oo oon bee-LEHT PEHN-troo
Go away.	Du-te de aici.	doo-TEH deh ai-EECH
Cheers!/Bless you!/Good luck!	Noroc!	noh-ROHK
I love you.	Te iubesc.	TEH yoo-BEHSK

ENGLISH	ROMANIAN	PRONOUNCED
one	unu	OO-noo
two	doi	doy
three	trei	tray
four	patru	PAH-troo
five	cinci	CHEEN-ch
single room	o cameră cu un pat	oh KAH-meh-ruh koo oon paht
double room	o cameră dublă	oh KAH-meh-ruh DOO-bluh
reservation	rezervarea	reh-zehr-VAH-rah
departures	plecări	pleh-KUHR
arrivals	sosiri	soh-SEERH
Monday	luni	loonh
Tuesday	marţi	mahrts
Wednesday	miercuri	MEER-kuhr
Thursday	joi	zhoy
Friday	vineri	VEE-nehr
Saturday	sâmbătă	SUHM-buh-tuh
Sunday	duminică	doo-MEE-nee-kuh
today	azi	az
tomorrow	mâine	MOE-neh
day	zi	ZEE
week	săptămână	suhp-tuh-MUH-nuh
morning	dimineaţă	dee-mee-NYAH-tsuh

ENGLISH	ROMANIAN	PRONOUNCED
six	şase	SHAH-seh
seven	şapte	SHAHP-teh
eight	opt	ohpt
nine	nouă	NOH-uh
ten	zece	ZE-chuh
one-way	dus	doos
round-trip	dus-întors	doos-ihn-TOHRS
ticket	bilet	bee-LEHT
train	trenul	TREH-nuhl
bus	autobuz	au-toh-BOOZ
airport	aeroportul	ai-roh-POHR-tool
station	gară	GAH-ruh
luggage	bagajul	bah-GAHZH-ool
bus station	autogară	AU-toh-gah-ruh
bank	banca	BAHN-cah
police	poliţia	poh-lee-TSEE-ah
doctor	doctor	DOK-tohr
hospital	spital	spi-tahl
exchange	un birou de de schimb	oon bee-ROW deh skeemb
passport	paşaport	pah-shah-pohrt
grocery	alimentară	a-lee-men-TA-ra
breakfast	micul dejun	MEEK-ool deh-ZHOON

APPENDIX

ENGLISH	ROMANIAN	PRONOUNCED
afternoon	după-amiază	DOO-puh-MYAH-zuh
evening	seara	SYAH-rah
hot	cald	kahld
cold	rece	REH-cheh
left	stânga	STIHN-gah
right	dreapta	dryahp-TAH
straight ahead	drept înainte	drept uh-nah-een-teh
toilet	toaleta	twah-LEH-tah
square	piaţa	pee-ah-TSAH
post office	poşta	POH-shta
market	piaţa	pee-AH-tsah

ENGLISH	ROMANIAN	PRONOUNCED
lunch	prânz	proenz
dinner	cină	CHEE-nuh
menu	meniu	mehn-YOO
bread	pâine	POE-neh
vegetables	legume	leh-GOO-meh
meat	carne	CAHR-neh
coffee	cafea	kah-FEH-AH
milk	lapte	LAHP-teh
beer	bere	BEH-reh
stamp	timbru	TEEM-broo
airmail	avion	ah-vee-OHN

RUSSIAN (РУССКИЙ)

Voiced consonants are pronounced voiceless at the end of a word. *Ь* makes the previous consonant soft, adding a sound similar to the *y* in *yet*. *Ъ* may be used to indicate separations of syllables when pronouncing syllables on either side.

ENGLISH	RUSSIAN	PRONOUNCED
Hello	Здравствуйте	ZDRAHV-zvuht-yeh
Yes/no	Да/нет	dah/nyeht
Please/you're welcome	Пожалуйста	pah-ZHAHL-uy-stah
Thank you	Спасибо	spa-SEE-bah
Goodbye	До свидания	da svee-DAHN-yah
Good morning	Доброе утро	DOH-breh OO-trah
Good evening	Добрый вечер	DOH-bryy VEH-chehr
Good night	Спокойной ночи	spa-KOY-noy NOHCH-ee
Sorry/excuse me	Извините	ihz-vi-NEET-yeh
Help!	Помогите!	pah-mah-GEE-tyeh
Where is...?	Где...?	gdyeh
...the bathroom?	...туалет?	TOO-ah-lyet
...the nearest telephone booth?	...ближайший телефон-автомат?	blee-ZHAI-shiy teh-leh-FOHN-ahf-tah-MAHT
...the center of town?	...центр города?	TSEHN-tehr GOHR-rah-dah
How much does this cost?	Сколько это стоит?	SKOHL-kah EH-tah STOH-eet
When?	Когда?	kahg-DAH
Do you speak English?	Вы говорите по-английски?	vy gah-vah-REE-tyeh pah ahn-GLEE-skee
I don't understand.	Я не понимаю.	yah neh pah-nee-MAH-yoo
I don't speak Russian.	Я не говорю по-русски.	yah neh gah-vah-RYOO pah ROO-skee
Please write it down.	Напишите пожалуйста.	nah-pee-SHEET-yeh pah-ZHAHL-uy-stah
Do you have a vacancy?	У вас есть свободный номер?	oo vahs yehst svah-BOHD-neey NOH-myehr
I'd like a room.	Я бы хотел(а) номер.	yah bui khah-TYEHL(ah) NOH-myehr
I'd like to order...	Я хотел(а) бы...	ya khah-TYEHL(a) bih
I don't eat meat	Я не ем мясо	Yah nyeh yem MYAH-sah

ENGLISH	RUSSIAN	PRONOUNCED
I have an allergy	У меня алергия	oo mehn-YAH all-EHR-gee-yah
Check, please.	Счёт, пожалуйста.	SHYOHT pah-ZHAHL-oo-stah
I want a ticket to...	Один билет до...	ah-DEEN bee-LYEHT dah
Go away.	Уходите.	oo-khah-DEE-tyeh
Cheers!	Ваше здоровье!	vahsh-yeh zdah-ROH-vyeh
I love you.	Я люблю тебя.	yah lyoob-LYOO teh-BYAH

ENGLISH	RUSSIAN	PRONOUNCE
one	один	ah-DEEN
two	два	dvah
three	три	tree
four	четыре	chih-TIH-rih
five	пять	pyaht
single room	одноместны й номер	ahd-nah-MYEHS-nee NOH-myehr
double room	двухместный номер	dvookh-MYEHS-nee NOH-myehr
reservation	предварител ь- ный заказ	prehd-vah-REE-tyehl-nee zah-KAHZ
departure	отъезд	aht-YEHZD
arrival	приезд	pree-YEHZD
Monday	понедельник	pah-nyeh-DYEHL-neek
Tuesday	вторник	FTOHR-neek
Wednesday	среда	sryeh-DAH
Thursday	четверг	chyeht-VYEHRK
Friday	пятница	PYAHT-neet-sah
Saturday	суббота	soo-BOT-tah
Sunday	воскресенье	vahs-kryeh-SYEH-nye
today	сегодня	see-VOHD-nya
tomorrow	завтра	ZAHF-trah
day	день	dyehn
week	неделя	nyeh-DYEHL-yah
morning	утром	OO-trahm
afternoon	днём	dnyohm
evening	вечером	VYEH-chehr-ahm
hot	жаркий	ZHAHR-keey
cold	холодный	khah-LOHD-nee
left	налево	nah-LYEH-vah
right	направо	nah-PRAH-vah
straight ahead	прямо	PRYHA-moh
toilet	туалет	too-ah-LYET
square	площадь	PLOH-shahd'
post office	почта	POHCH-tah
airmail	авиа	AH-vee-ah

ENGLISH	RUSSIAN	PRONOUNCE
six	шесть	shest
seven	семь	syehm
eight	восемь	VOH-syehm
nine	девять	DYEHV-eet
ten	десять	DYEHS-eet
one-way	в один конец	v ah-DEEN kah-NYEHTS
round-trip	туда и обратно	too-DAH ee ah-BRAHT-nah
ticket	билет	beel-YEHT
train	поезд	POH-yehzd
bus	автобус	af-TOH-boos
airport	аэропорт	ah-eh-roh-POHRT
station	вокзал	vahk-ZAHL
luggage	багаж	bah-GAHZH
bus station	автовокзал	ahf-toh-vahk-ZAHL
bank	банк	bahnk
police	милиция	mee-LEE-tsee-yah
doctor	доктор	DOHK-tohr
hospital	больница	BOHL-nee-tsa
exchange	обмен валюты	ahb-MYEHN vahl-YOO-ty
passport	паспорт	PAHS-pahrt
market	рынок	RIYN-nahk
grocery	гастроном	gah-stra-NOHM
breakfast	завтрак	ZAHF-trahk
lunch	обед	ah-BYEHD
dinner	ужин	OO-zheen
menu	меню	mehn-YOO
bread	хлеб	khlyehp
vegetables	овощи	OH-vah-shee
meat	мясо	MYAH-sah
coffee	кофе	KOH-fyeh
milk	молоко	mah-lah-KOH
beer	пиво	PEE-vah
stamp	марка	MAHR-kah

SLOVAKIAN (SLOVENSKY)

ENGLISH	SLOVAKIAN	PRONOUNCED
Hello	Dobrý deò	dau-BREE deh-AU
Yes/no	Áno/Nie	AH-nau/ni-ye
Please.	Prosím Vás.	prau-SEEM vas
Thank you.	Ïakujem.	jah-KOO-yehm
You're welcome.	Nemáte zaè.	nem-AHT-eh tsa AY-au
Goodbye.	Dovidenia.	doh-veed-EHN-yah
Good morning.	Dobré ráno.	doh-breh RAH-no
Good day.	Dobrý den.	doh-bree den
Good evening.	Dobrý večer.	doh-bree veh-CHEHR
Good night.	Dobrú noc.	doh-broo naukh
Sorry/excuse me...	Prepáète...	pre-PAH-eh-te
Help!	Pomoc!	po-MAUTS
Go away!	Choď preč!	khauhd PRECH
When?	Kedy?	KEDH-ih
Where is...?	(Prosím Vás) kde je...?	(pro-SEEM vahs) kdeh yeh
...the bathroom?	...W.C.?	vay-TSAY
...the nearest telephone booth?	...najbližšia telefónna búdka?	nahy-blee-ZHEE-ah tel-eh-FOH-na BUHD-kah
...the center of town?	...centrum mesta do?	TSEN-truhm MEHS-ta dau
I would like a ticket to...	Prosím si lístok do...	pro-SEEM sih LEES-tauk dau
round-trip/one-way trip	spiatoèný/jednosmerný	spih-uh-toh-AY-NEE/yed-naus-mehr-NEE
How much does this cost?	Koľko to stojí?	kaull-kau tau STOH-yee
Do you speak English?	Hovoríte anglický?	hau-vau-REE-teh ahn-glihs-kee
I don't understand.	Nerozumiem.	neh-rau-ZOO-mee-ehm
I don't speak Slovak.	Neviem po slovensky.	neh-viee-ehm poh slo-VEN-skee
Please write it down.	Mohli by ste to napísať?	MOH-lih bih steh tau nap-EE-saht
Do you have a vacancy?	Máte voľnú izbu?	MAH-teh VOLL-noo ihz-boo
I'd like a single/double room.	Chcel(a) by som jednotku / dvojku.	kh-sehl (ah) bih sohm yed-NAUT-koo / DVOY-koo
I'd like to order...	Rád(a) by som si objednal...	RAHD (-ah) bih saum sih aub-YED-nal
Do you have any vegetarian options?	Mate vegetariánske jedlá?	MAH-teh vehg-eht-uhr-ih-AHN-skih YED-luh (note hard *g*)
Check, please.	Účet prosím.	uh-CHEHT pro-SEEM
Cheers!	Na zdravie!	nah ZDRAHV-ee
I love you.	Milujem Ta.	mih-LOO-yem TAH

SLOVENIAN (SLOVENSKO)

ENGLISH	SLOVENIAN	PRONOUNCED
Hello	Dober dan	DOH-behr dahn
Yes/no	Ja/ne	yah/nay
Please	Prosim	proh-SEEM
Thank you	Hvala	HVAHL-ah

ENGLISH	SLOVENIAN	PRONOUNCED
Sorry/excuse me	Oprostite	oh proh-STEE-teh
Help!	Na pomoč!	nah POH-mohch
ticket	karta	KAHR-tah
bus	avtobus	au-TOH-boos

APPENDIX

ENGLISH	SLOVENIAN	PRONOUNCED
Goodbye	Nasvidenje	nah-SVEE-dehn-yay
doctor	zdravnika	zdrav-NEE-kah
one	eden/eno	EH-dehn/EH-noh
two	dva	dvah
three	tri	tree
four	štiri	SHTIHR-ee
five	pet	peyt

ENGLISH	SLOVENIAN	PRONOUNCED
toilet	Toaleta	toh-ah-LEH-tah
hospital	bolnišnica	bohl-NIHSH-nihtsa
six	šest	sheyst
seven	sedem	SEH-dehm
eight	osem	OH-sehm
nine	devet	DEH-veht
ten	deset	DEH-seht

ENGLISH	SLOVENIAN	PRONOUNCED
Where is...?	Kje...?	kyay
How much does this cost?	Koliko to stane?	KOH-lee-koh toh STAH-nay
Do you speak English?	Ali govorite angleski?	AH-lee goh-VOHR-ee-tay AHNG-lehsh-kee
I don't eat meat.	Ne jem mesa.	neh yehm MEH-sa
Cheers!	Na zdravje!	nah zh-DRAHV-yay
I love you.	Ljubim te.	LYOO-bihm tay

UKRAINIAN (УКРАЇНСЬКА)

ENGLISH	UKRAINIAN	PRONOUNCED
Good day	добрий день	DOH-bree den
Good morning	доброго ранку	DOH-broh-hoh RAHN-koo
Good evening	добрий вечір	DO-bree VECH-eer
Goodbye	до побачення	DO po-BACH-ehn-yah
Yes/no	так/ні	tahk / nee
Please/you're welcome	прошу	PROH-shoo
Please/you're welcome (Kyiv and East)	будь ласка	bood-LAS-kah
Thank you	дякую	DYAH-koo-yoo
Sorry/excuse me	вибачте	Vih-bach-te
Help!	Допоможіть!	doh-poh-moh-ZHEET
Where is...?	Де...?	de
...the bathroom?	...ванна?	VAHN-nah
...a telephone?	...телефон?	te-le-fon
...the center of town?	...центр міста?	TSEN-trr MEES-tah
How much does this cost?	Скільки це коштує?	SKEEL-kih tseh KOHSH-too-ye
When?	Коли?	koh-LIH
Do you speak English?	Чи ви розмовляєте по-англійськи?	chih vih rohz-mohv-LYAI-eh-tuh poh-ahn-HLIYS-kih
I don't understand.	Я не розумію.	ya ne roh-zoo-MEE-yoo
I don't speak Ukrainian.	Я не розмовляю по-українськи.	ya ne rohz-mohv-LYAI-yoo poh-oo-krah-YEENS-kih
Speak slower, please.	Прошу, говоріть повільно.	PROH-shoo hoh-vohr-EET poh-VEEL-noh
Please write it down.	Прошу запишіть це.	PROH-shoo zah-PIH-sheet tse
I'd like a room.	Прошу, я хочу кімнату.	PROH-shoo yah KHO-choo keem-NAHT-oo

APPENDIX

ENGLISH	UKRAINIAN	PRONOUNCED
I want a ticket to...	Я хочу квиток до...	ya KHO-choo kvih-TOHK doh
Go away.	Іди геть.	Ih-dih het
Cheers!	за здоров'я!	zah zdohr-OH-vya
I love you.	Я кохаю тебе.	ya ko-KHAH-yoo TE-be

ENGLISH	UKRAINIAN	PRONOUNCED
one	один	OHD-ihn
two	два	dvah
three	три	trih
four	чотири	choh-TIHR-ee
five	п'ять	p'yat
single bed	односпальне ліжко	ohd-NOHS-pahl-ne LEEZH-koh
double room	двоспальне ліжко	dvos-PAHL-ne LEEZH-koh
reservation	попередне замовлення	poh-per-ED-neh zam-OV-len-nya
Monday	Понеділок	poh-ne-DEE-lohk
Tuesday	Вівторок	VEEV-tohr-ohk
Wednesday	Середа	ser-e-DAH
Thursday	Четвер	CHET-ver
Friday	П'ятниця	PYAT-nih-tsyah
Saturday	Субота	soo-BOHT-ah
Sunday	Неділя	ne-DEEHL-ya
today	сьогодні	soh-HOHD-nee
tomorrow	завтра	ZAHV-trah
day	день	den
week	тиждень	TIZH-den
morning	ранок	RAHN-ohk
afternoon	після полудня	PEES-lya poh-LOOD-nya
evening	вечір	VECH-eer
left	ліворуч	LIV-or-ooch
right	праворуч	PRAH-vohr-ooch
bus	автобус	AV-toh-boos
bus station	автобусний вокзал	av-toh-BOOS-niy vokh-ZAHL
airport	аеропорт	AY-RO-pohrt
luggage	багаж	ba-HAHZH
train station	вокзал	vog-ZAL

ENGLISH	UKRAINIAN	PRONOUNCED
six	шість	sheest
seven	сім	seem
eight	вісім	VEE-seem
nine	девять	DEV-yat
ten	десять	DES-yat
departure	відправлення	veed-PRAH-vlehn-yah
arrival	прибуття	pree-boot-YAH
round-trip	поїздка в обидва кінці	po-YEEZD-kah v ob-IHD-vah KEEN-tsee
ticket	квиток	KVY-tohk
train	поїзд	poh-YEEZD
bank	банк	bahnk
police	поліція	po-LEET-see-ya
passport	паспорт	PAS-pohrt
market	ринок	RIH-nohk
breakfast	сніданок	snee-DAH-nohk
lunch	обід	oh-BIHD
dinner	вечеря	vech-ER-ya
menu	меню	MEN-yoo
bread	хліб	khleeb
vegetables	овочі	OH-voh-chee
coffee	кава	KAH-vah
milk	молоко	moh-loh-KOH
beer	пиво	PIH-voh
toilet	туалет	too-ah-LET
post office	пошта	POHSH-tah
stamp	поштова марка	posh-TOHV-ah MAR-kah
airmail	авіапошта	ah-vee-ah-POSH-tah
doctor	лікар	LEE-kar
hospital	лікарня	li-KAR-nya

INDEX

INDEX

INDEX